A Guide to *Essentials of Psychology: Concepts and Applications*

6

Memory

Chapter Opening Features

1 **Chapter Opener** follows the Preview and provides an interesting vignette or overview that introduces the reader to the topics covered in the chapter.

2 **"Did You Know That . . ."** consists of a chapter-opening bulleted list of questions meant to stimulate student thinking and preview many of the issues to be discussed in the chapter modules. At the end of each question, a page reference is given to allow students to follow-up on areas of interest.

3 **Art Program** Both the text's illustrations and photos were carefully conceived, researched, and created with the goal of presenting a clear, concise, diverse, and pedagogically sound art program.

PREVIEW

MODULE 6.1 Remembering
MODULE 6.2 Forgetting
MODULE 6.3 The Biology of Memory
MODULE 6.4 Application: Powering Up Your Memory

2 DID YOU KNOW THAT . . .

- A man was able to memorize lists of hundreds of meaningless syllables and recite them again fifteen years later? (p. 193)
- Though most people can retain only about seven items in memory at any one time, you may be able to juggle sixteen, twenty, or more items in your mind by using a simple memory device? (p. 197)
- A good way to retain information you've just learned is to sleep on it? (p. 198)
- People can be misled into believing they saw a yield sign at an accident scene when they actually saw a stop sign? (p. 204)
- Fewer than half of the people tested in a research study could pick out the correct drawing of a penny? (p. 210)
- If your hippocampus were removed, each new experience would come and go without any permanent trace left in your brain that the event ever happened? (p. 214)

1

We are a nation that loves competitions. We watch or engage in competitions of all kinds, from sporting contests and tractor-pulls to the perennial game shows and award ceremonies on TV. But memory competitions? These are one of the newest entries in the competitive field. In the U.S. and world memory championships, experts compete in various challenges, such as recalling long lists of words or random numbers, or matching names to the faces of people they've seen in photographs. Some recent champions have demonstrated amazing feats of memory. The U.S. record holder in 1997 succeeded in memorizing in a mere 34.03 seconds each card (suit and number) in the order in which it appeared in a shuffled deck of fifty-two cards ("Instant Recall," 2000). But none of the feats of the recent champions can hold a candle to those of a Russian known only by his first initial, S. S. had perhaps the most prodigious memory ever studied. He could repeat seventy randomly selected numbers in the precise order in which he had just heard them (Luria, 1968). Even more amazingly, he could memorize lists of hundreds of meaningless syllables and recite them not only immediately after studying them but also when tested again some fifteen years later. He memorized long mathematical formulas that were utterly meaningless to him except as an enormously long string of numbers and symbols. After but a single reading, he could recite stanza after stanza of Dante's Divine Comedy in Italian, even though he could not speak the language (Rupp, 1998).

Imagine what it would be like to have such an extraordinary memory—to be able to remember everything you read word for word or to recall lists of facts you learned years ago. Yet if S.'s life story is any indication, it may be just as well you don't possess such a prodigious memory. S. didn't have an easy time of it. His mind was so crammed with meaningless details that he couldn't see the forest for the trees. He had difficulty distinguishing between the trivial and the significant (Turkington, 1996). He even had difficulty holding conversations, since individual words opened a floodgate of associations that distracted him from what the other person was saying. He was unable to shift gears when new information conflicted with fixed images he held in memory. For example, he had difficulty recognizing people who had changed small details of their appearance, such as getting a haircut or wearing a new suit. Unfortunately, S.'s life didn't end well. He spent the last years of his life confined to a mental hospital. Most of us will probably never possess the memory of someone like S., nor would we even want to. Yet learning how our memory works and what we can do to improve it can help us meet many of life's challenges, from performing better in school or on the job to remembering to water the plants before leaving the house.

Our study of memory begins with a discussion of the underlying processes that make memory possible. We then consider the loss of information that results from forgetting and the role of the brain in creating and storing memories. We end with some practical suggestions for improving your memory. ■

Module Features

4 Survey Questions introduce each module and help students test their recall of the major concepts in the module. These study questions also serve as the end-of-chapter summary structure to reinforce learning and aid the study process.

5 Key Concepts are numbered concepts extracted from the text and placed in the margins next to key discussions within the modules. These concepts are interspersed throughout the text to help students identify and recall the major concepts covered in each module.

6 Integrated Media Resources Descriptive icons throughout the chapter highlight media resources that support key concepts in the text including:

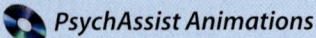 *PsychAssist Animations*

NetLabs and *Web Tutorials*.

7 Key Terms appear boldfaced within the text proper and in the margin alongside the introduction of each key term discussion. At the end of each chapter, a list of key terms is provided with page references for easy location by the reader.

8 "Try This Out" features "hands-on" activities or exercises in which students can apply their knowledge of psychological concepts discussed in the chapter.

9 "Think About It" features thought-provoking questions that help students sharpen their critical thinking skills and reflect on how the text material relates to their own experiences.

MODULE 2.4   Methods of Studying the Brain

- What recording and imaging techniques are used to study brain functioning?
- What experimental methods do scientists use to study brain functioning?

Scientists use various methods of studying brain structures and their functioning. One method is to observe the effects of diseases or injuries on the brain. As a result of this type of observation, scientists have known for nearly two centuries that damage to the left side of the brain is connected with loss of sensation or movement on the right side of the body, and vice versa.

Over the years, scientists have also used invasive experimental methods to study the brain at work, including surgical procedures. Today, thanks to advanced technology, they have other, less invasive recording and imaging methods at their disposal. Concept Chart 2.4 summarizes both types of methods.

CONCEPT 2.25
Modern technology provides ways of studying the structure and function of the brain without the need for invasive techniques.

Psych Assist: Methods of Studying the Living Brain

web, Netlab/Scanning the Brain

Recording and Imaging Techniques

Today, we have available a range of techniques that allow us literally to peer into the working brain and other parts of the body without surgery. These techniques are used to diagnose brain diseases and survey brain damage, as well as to help us learn more about brain functioning. Neuroscientists can probe the brain while the subject is awake and alert.

The **EEG (electroencephalograph)** is an instrument that records electrical activity in the brain (see Figure 2.11). Electrodes are attached to the scalp to measure the electrical currents, or *brain waves*, that are conducted between them. The EEG is used to study electrical activity in the brains of people with physical or psychological disorders and to explore brain wave patterns during stages of sleep.

The **CT (computed tomography) scan** (also called a *CAT* scan) is an imaging technique in which a computer measures the reflection of a narrow X-ray beam

Figure 2.11   The Electroencephalograph (EEG)
The EEG is a device that records electrical activity in the brain in the form of brain wave patterns. It is used to study the brains of people with physical or psychological disorders and to explore brain wave patterns during stages of sleep.

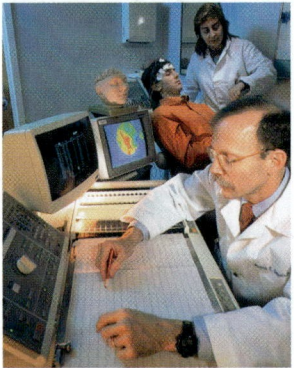

EEG (electroencephalograph)   A device that records electrical activity in the brain.

CT (computed tomography) scan   A computer-enhanced imaging technique in which an X-ray beam is passed through the body at different angles to generate a three-dimensional image of bodily structures (also called a CAT scan, short for *computerized axial tomography*).

PET (positron emission tomography) scan   An imaging technique in which a radioactive sugar tracer is injected into the bloodstream and used to measure levels of activity of various parts of the brain.

Figure 3.22*a* illustrates **proximity**, or nearness. Most observers would perceive the figure as consisting of three sets of parallel lines rather than six separate lines, although six lines are sensed. That is, we use the relative closeness of the lines as a perceptual cue for organizing them into a group.

How would you describe Figure 3.22*b*? Do you perceive nine separate geometric shapes or two columns of X's and one column of ●'s? If you describe it in terms of X's and ●'s, you are using the principle of **similarity**—that is, grouping figures that are similar to one another (in this case, geometric figures that resemble each other). If you see four bare-chested young men at a football game who've painted their bodies in the colors of the home team, you are likely to perceive them as a group distinct from other fans.

Figure 3.22*c* represents another way we group stimuli, **continuity**, which is the tendency to perceive a series of stimuli as a unified form when the stimuli appear to represent a continuous pattern. Here we perceive two intersecting continuous lines, one curved and one straight, rather than four separate lines.

TRY THIS OUT   **8**

Your Neighborhood Gestalt

Take a walk through your neighborhood or local area. Look around you. How many examples of the Gestalt laws of perceptual organization can you identify?

9

THINK
About It

Was It ESP?

Have you ever had any unusual experiences that you believe involved ESP? Think critically. What alternative explanations might account for these experiences?

Telepathy refers to the purported ability to project one's thoughts into other people's minds or to read what is in their minds—to perceive their thoughts or feelings without using the known senses. **Clairvoyance** is the perception of events that are not available to the senses. The clairvoyant may claim to know what someone across town is doing at that precise moment or to identify the contents of a sealed envelope. **Precognition** is the ability to foretell the future. **Psychokinesis** (formerly called *telekinesis*) is the ability to move objects without touching them. Strictly speaking, psychokinesis is not a form of ESP since it does not involve perception, but for the sake of convenience it is often classified as such.

Critical thinkers maintain an appropriate skepticism about claims of paranormal phenomena that seem to defy the laws of nature. Many claims of ESP have proven to be hoaxes, whereas others may be explained as random or chance occurrences. Despite many years of scientific study, we lack any reliable, replicable

CONCEPT CHART 5.3
Types of Cognitive Learning

Type of Learning	Description	Example
Insight learning	The process of mentally dissecting a problem until the pieces suddenly fit together to form a workable solution	A person arrives at a solution to a problem after thinking about it from a different angle.
Latent learning	Learning that occurs but remains "hidden" until there is a reward for performing the learned behavior	A person learns the words of a song playing on the radio but doesn't sing them until friends at a party begin singing.
Observational learning	Learning by observing and imitating the behavior of others	Through observation, a child learns to imitate the gestures and habits of older siblings.

MODULE 5.3 REVIEW

Cognitive Learning

CONCEPT CHECK

1. The type of learning that involves thinking, information processing, mental imaging, and problem solving is called _____.

2. The chimp named Sultan learned to reach bananas by attaching two sticks together. This type of learning is called
   a. insight learning.
   b. latent learning.
   c. observational learning.
   d. classical conditioning.

3. The type of learning that occurs without any apparent reinforcement and that is not displayed at the time it is acquired is called _____.

4. Observational learning
   a. is also known as latent learning.
   b. involves imitating the behavior of others.
   c. may lead to the acquisition of useful new skills but not to fear responses.
   d. is based on the principles of operant conditioning.

APPLICATION

MODULE 5.4   Putting Reinforcement into Practice

• What steps are involved in applying reinforcement principles?

When you smile at someone who compliments you or thank someone for doing you a favor, you are applying positive reinforcement, one of the principles of operant conditioning. Showing appreciation for desired behavior increases the likelihood that the behavior will be repeated.

To modify behavior through reinforcement, it is important to establish a clear *contingency*, or connection, between the desired behavior and the reinforcement. For example, making a child's weekly allowance of spending money contingent on certain behaviors (e.g., cleaning up after meals) will be far more effective than granting the allowance irrespective of behavior. *Contingency contracting*, which

Module and Chapter Review Features

10 **Concept Charts** summarize and review major concepts and visually make connections for students.

11 **Module Review Concept Checks** are short quizzes at the end of each module designed to help students test their knowledge of the material they just read. Answers are provided at the end of the chapter.

12 **Application Module** Each chapter ends with a short applied module aimed at helping students see how psychological principles are used to deal with real-world problems and issues and provides tips on how to apply this knowledge in their own lives.

13 **"Tying It Together"** appears at the end of each chapter, helping students see how the modules are integrated within the chapter structure as a whole.

14 **Summing Up: Q & A** provides an end-of-chapter summary in question-and-answer format, using the survey questions as a guide and bulleted summary points.

15 **"Thinking Critically About Psychology"** provides an end-of-chapter opportunity for students to sharpen their analytical skills by answering a critical thinking question or questions. Sample answers/solutions are provided in an appendix.

Thinking Critically About Psychology

Based on your reading of this chapter, answer the following questions. Then, to evaluate your progress in developing critical thinking skills, compare your answers to the sample answers found in Appendix A.

1. Two men observe an accident in which a car hits a pedestrian and speeds away without stopping. They both were alert enough to glance at the car's license plate before it disappeared around the corner. Later, when interviewed by the police, the first man says, "I only got a glimpse of it but tried to picture it in my mind. I think it began with the letters QW." The second man chimes in, "Yes, but the whole plate number was QW37XT." Why do you think the second man was able to remember more details of the license plate than the first man?

2. An English-speaking singer gives a concert in Italy and includes a popular Italian folk song in her repertoire. Her rendition is so moving that an Italian woman from the audience later comes backstage to congratulate the singer, telling her, "That song was one of my favorites as a little girl. I've never heard it sung so beautifully. But when did you learn to speak Italian so well?" The singer thanks her for the compliment but tells her she doesn't speak a word of Italian. Drawing on your knowledge of memory processes, explain how the woman was able to learn a song in a language she couldn't speak.

TYING IT TOGETHER

Without memory, experiences would leave no mark on our behavior. Memory permits us to retain and recall what we have learned through experience. Psychologists study the processes that make it possible for us to remember and that explain why we forget. We can conceptualize memory in terms of three underlying processes (encoding, storing, and retrieving information) occurring across three stages of memory (sensory memory, short-term memory, and long-term memory) (Module 6.1). Decay of memory traces, interference, retrieval failure, and motivated forgetting may each play a role in forgetting (Module 6.2). By exploring the biological bases of memory, we may come to a better understanding of how memories are formed and how they are lost (Module 6.3). Even as memory scientists continue to explore the foundations of memory, we can apply the knowledge we have acquired about how memory works to boost our memory power (Module 6.4).

SUMMING UP: Q & A

Remembering (Module 6.1)

What are the basic processes and stages of memory?

• The three basic memory processes are encoding (converting stimuli into a form that can be stored in memory), storage (retaining them in memory), and retrieval (accessing stored information).

What are flashbulb memories?

• Flashbulb memories are vivid, highly detailed, and long-lasting memories of emotionally charged personal or historical events.

What factors influence the accuracy of eyewitness testimony?

Essentials of Psychology
Concepts and Applications

Jeffrey S. Nevid
St. John's University

Houghton Mifflin Company   Boston   New York

Dedication

To my wife, Judy, and my children, Michael and Daniella, with love always.

Publisher: Charles Hartford
Sponsoring editor: Jane Potter
Senior development editor: Rita Lombard
Senior project editor: Carol Newman
Editorial assistant: Robert Woo
Senior designer: Henry Rachlin
Manufacturing coordinator: Chuck Dutton
Senior marketing manager: Jane Potter

Cover image: Lisa Henderling/© Images.com/CORBIS.
Text and photo credits begin on page A-61.

Printed in the U.S.A.

Library of Congress Catalog Card Number: 2003110187

ISBN: 0-618-43409-7

1 2 3 4 5 6 7 8 9-DOS-08-07 06 05 04

Brief Contents

CONTENTS

FEATURES

 ## Concept Charts

Features

Try This Out

Application Modules

PREFACE

Using Science to Advance the Art of Pedagogy

How can we help our students succeed in today's learning environment? As instructors, we face this challenge every day in the classroom. I approached the task of writing this introductory psychology text with this fundamental challenge in mind. I drew upon theory and research in psychology to develop a pedagogical approach designed to fit the learning needs of today's students and help them master complex material. I also undertook a research program to systematically examine two key features of this pedagogy, the **modular format** and **concept signaling**.[1] The results of these studies gave me confidence that combining a modular approach with concept signaling would help busy students better organize their study efforts and master key concepts. The pedagogy incorporated in this text was first developed in the research laboratory and then tested in classrooms throughout the country.

Why a Modular Approach?

The text is organized in a modular format that breaks down each chapter into smaller instructional units called modules. Each module is a cohesive study unit organized around a set of key concepts in a particular area of study.

Many students today juggle part-time jobs, families, and careers. Tight for time, they need to balance studying with other responsibilities. The modular approach helps busy students organize their study efforts by allowing them to focus on one module at a time rather than trying to tackle a whole chapter at once.

In our research with introductory psychology students, we found was that the majority of students preferred the modular format over the traditional format (57.3 percent versus 38.5 percent, with 4.2 percent expressing no preference) (Nevid & Carmony, 2002). In addition, we discovered that students who preferred the modular format performed significantly better when material was presented in the modular rather than the traditional format. It stands to reason that if students prefer a particular format, they will become more engaged in reading texts written in that format—an outcome that may translate into improved performance in classroom situations.

Targeting Learning: Effective Learning™ (EL): The Four E's

The text provides a broad perspective on psychology that covers the history, methods of research, major theories, and research findings of the discipline, as well as applications of the knowledge gained from contemporary research to the problems and challenges we face in today's world. But a text needs to be more than a compendium of information. It needs to be an effective learning tool.

The text is based on a comprehensive learning system derived from research on memory, learning, and textbook pedagogy. It incorporates four key elements of effective learning I call the "**Four E's**" (see Figure 1):

- Engaging Interest
- Encoding Information
- Elaborating Meaning
- Evaluating Progress

Engaging Interest

Learning begins with focused attention. A textbook can be an effective learning tool only if it succeeds in engaging and retaining the student's interest. Without focused attention, information is not likely to be encoded or retained.

Essentials of Psychology: Concepts and Applications is designed not only to generate interest but also to involve students directly in the material they read. Personal vignettes are used to draw the reader into the material and illustrate how the concepts discussed in the chapter relate to personal experiences. In addition, two distinctive pedagogical features are designed to further involve the student in the material:

[1]Nevid, J. S., & Carmony, T. M (2002). Traditional versus modular format in presenting textual material in introductory psychology. *Teaching of Psychology, 29*, 237–238.

Nevid, J. S., & Lampmann, J. L. (2001, April). *Do pedagogical aids in textbooks enhance learning?* Paper presented at the 15th Annual Conference on Undergraduate Teaching of Psychology, Ellenville, NY.

Nevid, J. S. (2003, September). *Helping students get the point: Concept signaling as a pedagogical aid.* Paper presented at the conference, Taking Off: Best Practices in Teaching Introductory Psychology, Atlanta, GA.

Nevid, J. S., & Lampmann, J. L. (2003). Effects on content acquisition of signaling key concepts in text material. *Teaching of Psychology, 30*, 227–229.

Nevid, J. S. (2004, January). *Graphing psychology: The effective use of graphs and figures in teaching introductory psychology.* Invited address presented at the 26th Annual National Institute on the Teaching of Psychology, St. Petersburg, FL.

Nevid, J. S. (2004, February). *Evidence-based pedagogy: Using research to find new ways to help students learn.* Invited address presented at the 11th Midwest Institute for Students and Teachers of Psychology (MISTOP), Glen Ellyn, IL.

Figure 1
The Four E's of Effective Learning™ (EL)

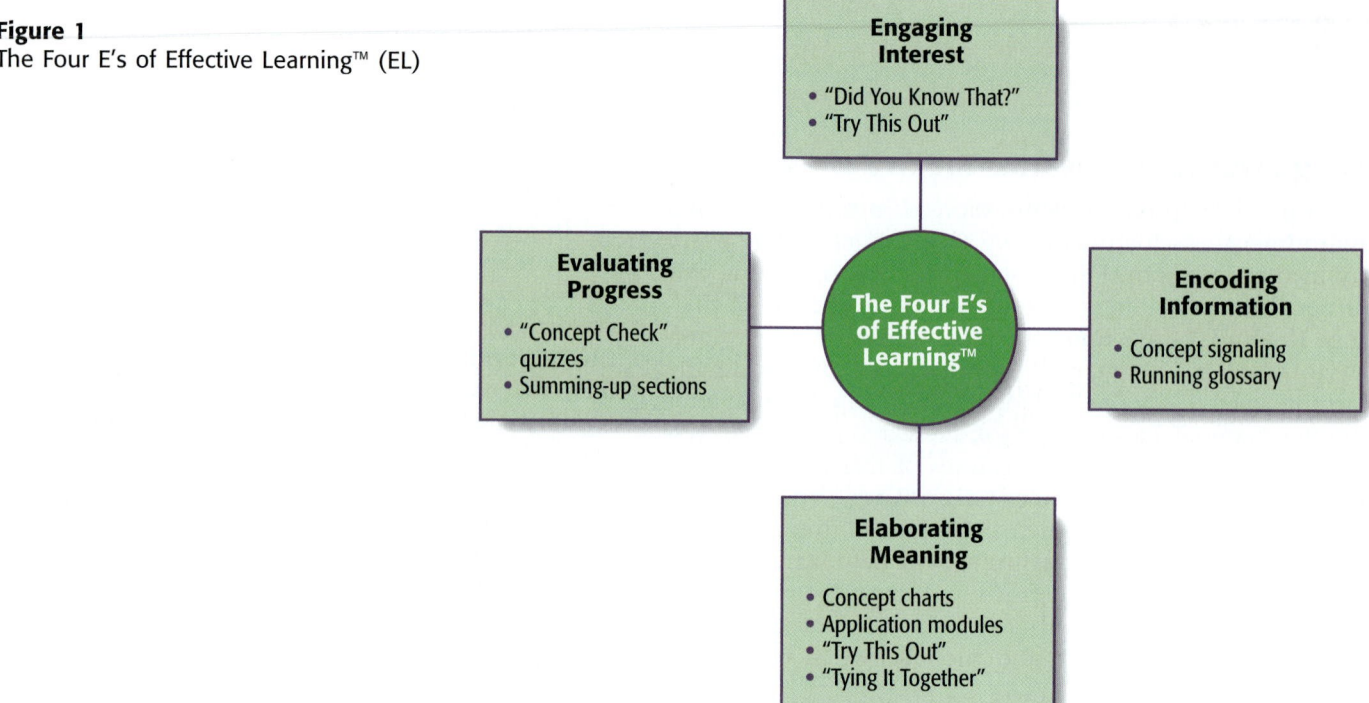

"Did You Know That..." These chapter-opening questions whet students' appetite for the material presented in the chapter and encourage them to read further. Some questions debunk common myths and misconceptions; others highlight interesting historical features or bring recent research developments into focus. Accompanying page numbers are provided for easy cross-referencing to the chapter sections in which the information is discussed. A small sample follows:

Did You Know That

- Our bodies produce natural painkillers that are chemically similar to morphine and other narcotic drugs? (p. 46)

- The mechanism that makes motion pictures possible lies in the viewer, not the projector? (p. 116)

- The "Big Five" is not the name of a new NCAA basketball conference but the label used to describe the leading trait theory of personality today? (p. 358)

- People who receive the label of psychopath are not psychotic? (p. 410)

"Try This Out" These "hands-on" exercises encourage students to apply psychological concepts to their own experiences. Whether the topic involves countering persuasive sales tactics or performing a personal experiment on lucid dreaming, students can work through problems, generate solutions, and test out concepts and principles. They can participate in *active learning* by applying the concepts in the text to real-life situations, rather than simply reading about them.

"Try This Out" activities also offer suggestions for service learning through participation in research and volunteer experiences, while the self-scoring questionnaires in this feature allow students to evaluate their behavior and attitudes about specific issues.

Encoding Information

What image appears on the back of a $10 bill? Though we may have handled countless numbers of $10 bills in our lifetime, many of us are stumped when it comes to identifying the image on the back. (The answer is the U.S. Treasury). The more important question is why this question leaves so many people stumped. As discussed in the text (Ch. 6) with the related example of the image on the back of a nickel, information must first be encoded in order to be retained. We tend to encode only enough information as we need to know. Since we don't need to know the images on the backs of coins or paper bills in order to use this currency, this information may never have been encoded in memory.

Learning and retaining key concepts in text material also requires that information is first encoded. The pedagogical technique of *signaling* or *cueing* can help people encode important information. Textbook authors have long used forms of signaling, such as headings and highlighted key terms. This text features two types of signaling, the *running glossary* and *concept signaling*.

Concept Signaling Key concepts in a field of study are the basic building blocks of knowledge. Some students can easily extract the major points and concepts from text material. Others struggle to "get the points" the author tries to convey.

As instructors, we may only find out at examination time which students are struggling to extract the key concepts we'd like them to learn.

I developed a unique pedagogical feature called *concept signaling* to help students encode and retain key concepts. Concept signaling extracts key concepts, highlights them in the margins of the text, and numbers them consecutively through each chapter. Think of it as a running glossary for key concepts. Here are some examples:

 CONCEPT 6.14
Research showing that false memories may seem as real as the actual events calls into question the credibility of recovered memories of childhood abuse.

CONCEPT 7.23
Intelligence tests are misused when children with low scores are labeled as innately incapable or inferior, when too much emphasis is placed on IQ scores, and when cultural biases in the tests put children at a disadvantage.

CONCEPT 9.5
Infants may seem to do little more than eat and sleep, but a closer look reveals they are both active learners and active perceivers of their environment.

Concept signaling directs the student's attention to material that is important to encode. Importantly, it also helps students gauge that they are "getting the points" as they read through the text.

In order to evaluate the learning benefits of concept signaling, we conducted a controlled study in which introductory psychology students read two different text passages—one that highlighted key concepts in the margins and one that did not. Our results showed that signaling key concepts significantly improved quiz performance overall as well as on the subset of quiz items that directly assessed knowledge of these key concepts (Nevid & Lampmann, 2003).

We also polled students in our study on which format they preferred—the one with signaled concepts or the one without. More than three-fourths of the students preferred the concept signaling format and found it easier to understand and more clearly presented than the nonsignaled format. (This was interesting in light of the fact that the content was exactly the same in both formats; the only difference was that the signaled format extracted and highlighted the key concepts from the text material.)

Not surprisingly, we found that signaling key concepts had no effects on learning surrounding material that was not signaled. This finding only reinforces what instructors have known for years—that students should not use pedagogical aids (whether they be summaries, interim quizzes, or cued concepts) as substitutes for reading the text in its entirety. Yet our results taught us that students are better able to learn key concepts when they are signaled or highlighted in the text.

Running Glossary Key terms are highlighted in the text and defined in the margins. Students need not interrupt their reading to thumb through a glossary at the end of the text whenever they encounter an unfamiliar term. (A full glossary is presented at the end of the text as well.)

Elaborating Meaning

Though information must first be encoded to be learned, new learning needs to be strengthened to help ensure long-term retention. Memory of newly acquired information can be strengthened through rote memorization involving rehearsal of particular words or phrases. But deeper processing and more enduring learning requires *elaborative rehearsal,* in which we reflect on the meaning of the material and relate it our life experiences. This text provides several pedagogical features designed to facilitate elaborative rehearsal:

Concept Charts Each module contains a Concept Chart that summarizes and reviews the key concepts in tabular form. Concept Charts reinforce knowledge of major concepts and help students make relational connections between concepts.

Application Modules The last module in each chapter is an application module. These modules illustrate how psychologists apply the knowledge they have gained from their research studies to real-life problems. Students will also see how they can apply the knowledge they gain from reading the chapter to their own lives. See the Features section on page xiv for a chapter-by-chapter listing of the application modules in the text. Examples of application modules include "Psychology and Pain Management" (Ch. 3), "Putting Reinforcement into Practice" (Ch. 5), "Becoming a Creative Problem Solver" (Ch. 7), and "Taking the Distress Out of Stress" (Ch. 13).

"Try This Out" These exercises not only engage student interest, but also encourage students to apply the concepts they learn in the text to their own experiences.

"Tying It Together" The "Tying it Together" sections appear at the end of each chapter to help students review how the modules are integrated within the chapter structure as a whole.

Strengthening Learning through Repeated Rehearsal
Concepts are repeated in several forms to reinforce learn-

ing—-through discussion in the text, in concept charts, in marginal inserts, and in schematic diagrams. The use of different contexts for presenting information strengthens new learning.

Evaluating Progress

The text contains a number of study aids to help students evaluate their progress:

Concept Checks At the end of each module is a short quiz designed to help students test their knowledge of the material they just read.

Summing-Up Sections At the end of each chapter is a "Summing Up" section organized in a question-and-answer (Q & A) format to encourage active learning. The questions correspond to the survey questions that introduce each module. This type of summary better fits the SQ3R model of encouraging recitation of answers to survey questions than does a traditional narrative summary. Students can recite their answers to the questions and compare them to the sample answers presented in the text.

Targeting Critical Thinking Skills

The text encourages students to challenge their preconceived assumptions about human behavior and to think critically about information they receive from the media and other sources in the light of scientific evidence. In the "Thinking Critically About Psychology" sections at the end of each chapter, students have the opportunity to sharpen their critical thinking skills. They can practice these skills by answering questions that require them to analyze problems and evaluate claims in relation to the information presented in the chapter. Students may then compare their answers to sample responses presented in the appendix.

Students can further reinforce their critical thinking skills by responding to the many thought-provoking "Think About It" questions that are interspersed throughout the text, and more generally, by applying in their daily lives the critical thinking skills discussed in Chapter 1.

Targeting Technology as a Tool for Learning

The learning environment of today is much different from the one I experienced when I sat in my first undergraduate class in psychology. One important change has been the increased availability of computerized resources—specifically, the Internet and CD-ROMs. The text is supported by two key media resources: the *text-specific web site* and the *Student CD-ROM with PsychAssist animations.*

This text contains a dynamic learning tool that allows instructors and students not only to keep abreast of rapidly changing developments in the field but also to further explore important and challenging concepts in an electronic environment. Icons embedded in the margins of the text indicate the availability of specific psychology-related destinations on the text-specific web site. Given the endless supply of Internet resources on psychology alone, the purpose of the integrated media icon strategy is to focus on three specific types of resources to support and expand the textual representation of key concepts and issues, as well as to provide clear identification of the corresponding category and topic of each resource. The three categories are as follows: (1) *PsychAssist animations—tutorials* that bring difficult concepts to life (available on CD-ROM and on the text-specific web site); (2) *NetLab interactive exercises, activities, and demonstrations;* and (4) *web tutorials* designed to enhance understanding of issues discussed in the modules.

Targeting Study Skills: The SQ3R+ Study Method

The *Survey, Question, Read, Recite, Review* (SQ3R) study method, a widely used technique for enhancing learning and encouraging students to adopt a more active role in the learning process is built directly into the text. The text expands upon the traditional SQ3R method by adding the "Think About It" feature, the "plus" in the SQ3R+ method that helps foster critical thinking skills.

- *Survey and Question* Survey methods are incorporated within both the chapter structure and the modular structure. Each chapter opens with a preview section showing the contents and organization of the chapter (including a numbered list of modules presented in the chapter). In addition, survey questions at the beginning of each module highlight important learning objectives and encourage students to use questions as advance organizers for studying.

- *Read* The writing style has been carefully developed for reading level, content, and style. Students are often addressed directly to engage them in the material and encourage them to examine how the information may relate to their own personal experiences.

- *Recite and Review* Each module ends with a study break consisting of a Concept Check quiz. These quizzes encourage students to review the material covered in the module and recite their knowledge by answering study questions (fill-ins, multiple choice, matching, and short answers). *Concept Charts* in each module provide further opportunities for students to review the knowledge they have acquired. And in the *Summing Up: Q & A* section at the end of each chapter, students can practice reciting answers to the study questions that introduced each module.

- *Think About It* The text goes beyond review and recitation by posing thought-provoking questions that encourage reflection, critical thought, and self-exploration. These questions foster critical thinking (e.g., Why is it incorrect to say that someone is right-brained or left-brained?) and encourage students to reflect on how the text material relates to their personal experiences (e.g., Have you ever taken an intelligence test? Did you think it was a fair appraisal of your intelligence?).

Additional Features of the Text

Keeping Pace with a Changing Field

The field of psychology stands still for no author! As you thumb through the pages of the text you'll find more than 1,000 references to research findings in psychology that have appeared just since the beginning of the twenty-first century. Psychology is a vibrant, dynamic discipline, and I have tried to approach the writing of this text with the same enthusiasm and vigor that psychologists bring to their research, teaching, and professional work every day.

Integrating Diversity

One primary objective of this text is to raise students' awareness of the importance of issues relating to diversity. Discussion of cultural and gender issues is therefore integrated within the main body of the text rather than relegated to boxed features. (A proliferation of boxes tends to break the flow of the text and to introduce unnecessary clutter that many students find distracting; it might even inadvertently convey the impression that material relating to diversity is less important than other material because it is boxed off.) For a reference guide to the integrated coverage of gender and sociocultural issues in the text, see the complete listings available in the *Instructor's Manual* to accompany *Essentials of Psychology: Concepts and Applications*.

Ancillaries

Even the most comprehensive text is incomplete without ancillaries. The ones accompanying *Essentials of Psychology: Concepts and Applications* help make it a complete teaching package.

Teacher Ancillaries

Instructor's Resource Manual The *Instructor's Resource Manual* (IRM) and *Media Integration Guide* contain a variety of resources to aid instructors in preparing and presenting text material in a manner that meets their personal preferences and course needs. The IRM begins with a comprehensive preface, which covers preparation, pitfalls, planning, execution, resources, and best practices for both new and seasoned instructors. Each chapter provides a preview and a goals and activity planner to help organize classes. In addition, each chapter of the IRM contains a detailed outline, lecture suggestions, topics for discussion, classroom and individual activities with handouts, and writing assignment ideas. Also, CD-ROM and other technology resources (web materials) are covered in our Media Integration Guide to allow for easier class preparation and use. The IRM is available online on the instructor web site as well as on the *HMClassPrep* CD-ROM.

Test Bank The *Test Bank* contains 2,400 items specifically developed for *Essentials of Psychology: Concepts and Applications*. Multiple-choice questions as well as essay questions with answers are written at both the chapter and the module level to provide flexibility to the instructor. These questions are labeled by type (factual, conceptual, applied), learning objective, module reference number, and page reference for easier use in creating exams. The test bank is available on the instructor's CD-ROM or *HMClassPrep* CD-ROM.

HMClassPrep CD-ROM with HMTesting This instructor CD-ROM collects in one place materials that instructors might want to have available electronically. It contains PowerPoint® slides of lecture outlines and art from the textbook, PDF files of all overhead transparencies, as well as the *Instructor's Resource Manual* and *Media Integration Guide* and *Test Bank* (in word and PDF format). Our *HMTesting* program offers delivery of test questions in an easy-to-use interface; compatible with both Mac OS® and Microsoft® Windows platforms.

HMClassPresent *HMClassPresent* includes 65 newly developed high-resolution PsychAssist animations that project effectively in a lecture hall. The CD also has an easy-to-navigate interface, with searchable files organized by topic. These animations can be easily inserted into PowerPoint® presentations or projected from the CD.

Transparency package Transparencies comprise 100 four-color images, charts, and tables taken directly from the main text.

Instructor's web site For maximum flexibility, much of the material from the *HMClassPrep* CD-ROM is also available on the web site including the complete *Instructor's Resource Manual* and *Media Integration Guide*, downloadable PDFs of the overhead transparencies, PowerPoint® lecture outlines and selected art from the textbook.

PowerPoint® Presentations The PowerPoint® presentations consist of an extensive set of slides providing lecture sequences that include tables, figures, and charts from the main text. The slides are available on the instructor web site as well as on the *HMClassPrep* CD-ROM.

Course Cartridges for WebCT and Blackboard These resources, available for *Essentials*, allow instructors to use text-specific material to create an online course on their own campus course management system. You can access a wealth of instructor resources including chapter outlines, PowerPoint® slides, and the computerized test bank. Additionally, you can directly link to other resources on the password protected web site including Ace Quizzes, Net Labs, and our new PsychAssist animations feature.

Eduspace® Eduspace® is a powerful course management system powered by Blackboard that makes preparing, presenting and managing courses easier. Using this distance-learning platform, you can not only easily manage large courses online, but can also access, customize, create and deliver course materials, and tests online. You can easily maintain student portfolios using the gradebook where grades for all assignments are automatically scored, averaged, and saved. The *Essentials* course includes suggested lesson plans, our new PsychAssist animations, comprehensive quizzing (including *HMTesting*) as well as Psych In Film® video clips with teaching tips and discussion questions, and high quality presentation tools such as PowerPoint® slides and art from the textbook. You can also enable access to password protected Houghton Mifflin student website resources direct from this course management solution to view interactive practice tests and other tools (Net Labs, Ace Quizzes, Flashcards) for your students.

Houghton Mifflin Psych in Film®   Houghton Mifflin *Psych in Film®* contains 35 clips from Universal Studios films illustrating key concepts in psychology. Clips from films like *Schindler's List, Snow Falling on Cedars,* and many others are combined with commentary and discussion questions to help bring psychology alive for students and demonstrate its relevance to contemporary life and culture. Teaching tips are correlated to specific text chapters and concepts on the instructor web site. Available on DVD and VHS. Please consult your Houghton Mifflin sales representative for other available video resources.

Online Teaching Tools   Useful and practical information on online teaching tools can be found on the Nevid *Essentials* web site including a link to *Research Online: A Practical Guide*. Houghton Mifflin also offers a useful print resource *Teaching Online: A Practical Guide* (0-618-00042-9).

Student Ancillaries

Study Guide   The study guide focuses on providing students with resources aimed at improving study skills and comprehension of the text material. For each chapter, this guide provides a one-page detailed outline, a list of objectives, chapter overview, key terms and concepts, and self-testing exercises and activities that highlight key concepts from the main text. In addition, students are provided an integrated set of media resources to further improve and expand their understanding of the main concepts of the course.

PsychAssist Animations   This newly developed material, available online and on CD-ROM contains interactive Psych-Assist animations—tutorials correlated to some of the more difficult concepts in the text. They are brought to life through creative game scenarios or simulated research and gives students several opportunities to test their understanding through a range of pre- and post-tests.

Student web site at http:psychology.college.hmco.com/ students   A student web site is also available to students using *Essentials of Psychology: Concepts and Applications*. Web icons placed in the chapter margins relate chapter topics to on-line resources. Identified by category and topic, these resources are easily accessed by logging on to the text's web site. Web categories include PsychAssist animations, quizzing, links, and NetLabs, each specifically related to the chapter content.

Acknowledgments

First, I am indebted to the thousands of psychologists and other scientists whose work has informed the writing of this text. Thanks to their efforts, the field of psychology has had an enormous impact in broadening our understanding of ourselves and enhancing the quality of our lives. On a more personal level, I owe a debt of gratitude to the many colleagues and publishing professionals who helped shape this manuscript into its present form. Let me begin by thanking the professional colleagues who reviewed the manuscript and helped me refine it through several stages of development including Camille Tessitore King, Stetson University; Kimberley J. Duff, Cerritos College; Lynn M. Wiljanen, Wor-Wic Community College; and Yozan Dirk Mosig, University of Nebraska-Kearney. My thanks also to the supplements team who helped produce wonderful teaching and study tools to accompany *Essentials*: Tami Eggleston, McKendree College and Gabie E. Smith, Elon University (*Instructor's Manual*); Patricia S. Laser, Bucks County Community College (*Study Guide*); Christine M. Vanchella (Test Bank), South Georgia College; David Strohmetz, Monmouth College (PowerPoint® slides of lecture outlines); and Travis Sola, Lake Land College (PsychAssist animations). And also special thanks to our panel of students who reviewed these newly-developed PsychAssist animations: Kristina Burton, Lake Land College, Matt Barcus, University of Illinois, Jennifer Rippy, Western Missouri State College, Derek Weaver, Lake Land College, and Allison Wolfe University of Illinois.

Second, I would like to thank the countless instructors and students who participated in our extensive market research conducted in the early stages of the text's development—including the instructors and students at Valencia Community College and the University of Central Florida, who provided us with great insight into their introductory psychology courses; the instructors who participated in the teleconference sessions and raised many important issues that impacted the day-to-day challenges of this course; and the 700-plus respondents who participated in our national survey on introductory psychology and this text. The overwhelming response we received from these professionals proved to be a rich resource throughout the development of the text.

Third, I am grateful to the people at Houghton Mifflin who made this book possible, especially Kerry Baruth, senior sponsoring editor, who brought this project it to Houghton Mifflin and has inspired and encouraged me and shepherded this text through many stages of development; Jane Potter, senior marketing manager and Erin Lane, marketing associate, for their continued enthusiasm and efforts on this project; Sarah Tasker, instructional technology sponsor, who shaped our integrated media package accompanying *Essentials*; Rita

Lombard, senior development editor, who helped keep my focus sharp and provided key insights in developing the unique pedagogical features of the book; senior project editor Carol Newman, who brought the project together and kept it on schedule; art editor, Charlotte Miller, for her creative art program; photo researcher, Ann Schroeder and Karen Lindsay, who found even the most difficult-to-find photographs; copyeditor, Christine Arden and proofreader, Talia Kingsbury for their talented and careful review of the text; senior designer Henry Rachlin, whose interior design enhanced the "student friendly" nature of *Essentials*; and editorial assistants Robert Woo and Liz Hogan for their help with both the text and supplements; and the many other talented and committed professionals at Houghton Mifflin. I thank you all.

Jeff Nevid

About the Author

Jeffrey S. Nevid is Professor of Psychology at St. John's University in New York. He earned his doctorate at the University at Albany of the State University of New York and was a Post-Doctoral Fellow at Northwestern University. He has conducted research and published in such areas of psychology as health psychology, clinical psychology, counseling psychology, social psychology, psychology of marketing, gender and human sexuality, adolescent development, and teaching of psychology. He also served as Consulting Editor for the journals *Health Psychology* and *Psychology and Marketing* and as Associate Editor of the *Journal of Consulting and Clinical Psychology*. Dr. Nevid has coauthored several college texts, including *Abnormal Psychology in a Changing World, Human Sexuality in a World of Diversity, Psychology and the Challenges of Life*, and *Health in the New Millennium*. He is also author of *Choices: Sex in the Age of STDs*. Dr. Nevid has been an invited speaker at a number of conferences on the teaching of psychology, including the National Institute on the Teaching of Psychology, the Annual Conference on Undergraduate Teaching of Psychology, and the Midwest Institute for Students and Teachers of Psychology. He lives in New York with his wife Judy and their two children, Michael and Daniella.

A Message to Students

How to Use This Textbook

You are about to embark on a journey through the field of psychology. As with any journey, it is helpful to have markers or road signs to help you navigate your course. This text provides a number of convenient markers to help you know where you've been and where you're headed. Take a moment to familiarize yourself with the terrain you're going to encounter in your journey. It centers on the unique organizational framework represented in this text—the concept-based modular format.

Why a concept-based modular approach? There are three key reasons:

1. *To help you organize your study activities.* The modular approach breaks down large chapters into smaller units of instruction. Rather than try to digest an entire chapter at once, you can chew on one module at a time.

2. *To help you master the material.* Each module is a self-contained unit of instruction. At the end of each module you'll find a Concept Check quiz to help you evaluate your knowledge before moving ahead.

3. *To help you learn key concepts that form the foundations of knowledge in each area of study.* As you make your way through each module, you will be learning a set of key concepts and how they relate to the theoretical and research foundations of the field of psychology. To help you master these concepts, they are listed in the margins of the text and identified with an accompanying lightbulb icon. Think about each concept before you read the corresponding text to ensure that you understand the major concepts as you read through the text.

How to Use the SQ3R+ Study Method

This text includes a built-in study system called the SQ3R+ study method, a system designed to help students develop more effective study habits that expands upon the SQ3R method developed by psychologist Francis P. Robinson. SQ3R is an acronym that stands for five key features: *survey, question, read, recite,* and *review.* This text adds an additional feature—*Think About It.* Here's how you can best use the method to master the material:

1. *Survey* Preview each chapter before reading it. Scan the outline and the introductory section to get a sense of how the chapter is organized and what general topics are covered. Familiarizing yourself with the contents of a chapter before reading it can activate related information that you already hold in memory, thereby assisting you in acquiring and retaining new information.

2. *Question* This text incorporates study questions at the start of each module that highlight key issues addressed in the module. Jot down these questions in a notebook or computer file so that you can answer them as you read along. You may also find it helpful to generate additional questions. Developing good questioning skills allows you to become a more active learner, which can enhance your ability to understand and retain information.

3. *Read* Read the material in the text in order to answer the study questions.

4. *Recite* Recite your answers to the study questions out loud. (Hearing yourself speak these answers will further enhance your retention and later retrieval of the information you have read.) For additional review as you get closer to exam time, jot down your answers in a notebook or computer file.

5. *Review* Establish a study schedule for reviewing the material on a regular basis. Test yourself each time you reread the material to further boost long-term retention. Use the *Concept Check* section that follows each module to gauge your knowledge of the material. Then reinforce your knowledge by comparing your answers to the study questions with the sample answers found in the *Summing Up* section at the end of the chapter.

6. *Think About It* This feature poses thought-provoking questions that encourage you to apply your critical thinking skills and to reflect on how the material may relate to your own experiences.

I hope you enjoy your journey through psychology. It began for me in my freshman year in college and has continued for me with a sense of wonder and joy ever since.

Please email your comments, questions, or suggestions to me at askauthor@aol.com.

Jeff Nevid
New York, NY

Essentials of Psychology
Concepts and Applications

Introduction to Psychology and Methods of Research

DID YOU KNOW THAT . . .

- One of the founders of modern psychology was such a poor student he was actually left back a grade in school? (p. 4)

- A movement that once dominated psychology believed that psychologists should turn away from the study of the mind? (p. 6)

- A major school of psychology was inspired by the view from a train? (p. 7)

- The school of psychology originated by Sigmund Freud holds that we are generally unaware of our underlying motives? (p. 8)

- A student successfully completed all Ph.D. requirements at Johns Hopkins University but was refused a doctorate because she was a woman? (p. 19)

- You can obtain listings and abstracts of articles from major psychology journals by using your home computer (and much of it is free of charge)? (p. 35)

Let me introduce you to the field of *psychology, the science of behavior and mental processes*. This is probably not your first exposure to many of the topics we will study. Your earliest encounter with the subject matter of psychology most likely began many years ago. Perhaps it came as you first wondered about why people do what they do or how their personalities differ. Perhaps you wondered why your third-grade classmate just couldn't seem to sit still and often disrupted the class. Or perhaps you wondered about the meaning of those nightly meanderings of the mind we call dreams. Or maybe you wondered mostly about yourself, about who you are and why you do the things you do. Perhaps one of the reasons you are taking this course is to learn more about yourself.

You may find answers to many questions you have about the behavior of humans and nonhuman animals in this introductory course in psychology. But you may not find all the answers you are seeking. There is still so much we do not understand, so much that remains to be explored. This text, like the field of psychology itself, is really about the process of exploration—the quest for knowledge about behavior and mental processes.

Psychology is a scientific discipline, but what makes it scientific? One answer is that being scientific means valuing evidence over opinion and tradition—even honored tradition or the opinions of respected scholars and thinkers. Psychologists don't dismiss opinion, tradition, or even folklore. Yet as scientists, they require that opinions, assumptions, beliefs, and theories be tested and scrutinized in the light of the available evidence. Psychologists seek answers to the questions they and others have posed about human nature by using scientific methods of study and investigation. Like other scientists, psychologists are professional skeptics. They have confidence only in those theories that can be tied to observable evidence. As in all branches of science, investigators within the field of psychology gather evidence to test their theories, beliefs, and assumptions.

Before we go further with our exploration of psychology, let us define what we mean by the term *psychology*. Though many definitions of psychology have been proposed, the one most widely used today defines psychology as the science of behavior and mental processes. But what do these terms mean—*behavior* and *mental processes*? Broadly speaking, anything an organism does is a form of behavior. Sitting in a chair is a form of behavior. Reading, studying, or watching TV are forms of behavior. Making yourself a sandwich and talking on the telephone are a forms of behavior. Smiling, dancing, or raising your arm are forms of behavior. Even thinking and dreaming are forms of behavior.

Mental processes are private experiences that comprise our inner life as individuals. These private experiences include thoughts, feelings, dreams and daydreams, sensations, perceptions, and beliefs that others cannot directly observe or experience. Among the challenges psychologists face is finding ways of making such inner experiences available to scientific study.

Before we begin exploring how psychologists study behavior and mental processes, let us take the story of psychology back to its origins to see how it developed as a scientific discipline and where it stands today. ■

MODULE 1.1 Foundations of Modern Psychology

- **What is psychology?**
- **What are the origins of psychology?**
- **What were the major early schools of psychology?**
- **What are the major contemporary perspectives in psychology?**

 **CONCEPT 1.1**
Psychology is the scientific discipline that studies behavior and mental processes.

 **CONCEPT 1.2**
Although psychology is a relatively young science, interest in understanding the nature of mind and behavior can be traced back to ancient times.

web Netlab/Is It Psychology of Common Sense?

Psychology: The Science of Behavior and Mental Processes Psychologists study what we do and what we think, feel, dream, sense, and perceive. They use scientific methods to guide their investigations of behavior and mental processes.

This first module in the text sets the stage for our study of psychology. It describes the development of psychology as a scientific discipline. How did psychology develop? What were the important influences that shaped its development as a scientific discipline? Here we address those questions by recounting a brief history of psychology. Let us begin by noting that although psychology is still a young science, its origins can be traced back to ancient times.

Origins of Psychology

The story of psychology has no clear beginning. We cannot mark its birth on any calendar. We can speculate that the story very likely began when early humans developed the capacity to reflect on human nature. Perhaps they were curious, as many of us are today, about what makes people tick. But what they may have thought or said about the nature of human beings remains unknown, as no record exists of their musings.

The word **psychology** is derived from two Greek roots: *psyche,* meaning "mind," and *logos,* meaning "study" or "knowledge." So it is not surprising that serious inquiries into psychology can be traced back to ancient Greece, when philosophers began to record their thoughts about the nature of mind and behavior. Psychology remained largely an interest of philosophers, theologians, and writers for several thousand years. It did not begin to emerge as a scientific discipline until the late nineteenth century.

The founding of psychology as an independent science is usually credited to a German scientist, Wilhelm Wundt (1832–1920). The credit is given to Wundt (pronounced *Voont*) because he established the first scientific laboratory dedicated to the study of psychology (E. Taylor, 2000). With the founding of Wundt's laboratory in Leipzig, Germany in 1879, psychology made the transition from philosophy to science (Benjamin, 2000).

Wundt was in some respects an unlikely candidate to found a new science. As a boy, he was a poor student and was even required to repeat a grade. The problem for young Wundt was that he tended to daydream in class. He would often be found sitting with an open book in his hand, staring off into space rather than reading his assigned text (a practice this author hopes you don't emulate too closely when you open your psychology text). But he persevered, eventually graduating from medical school and, from there, launching a successful research career as a physiologist. Later, he would apply his scientific training to his true passion, the understanding of conscious experience. In establishing the first psychology laboratory, the man who had once been left back in school because he was so absorbed in his own thoughts became the first scientist of the mind.

Like any scientific discipline, the field of psychology is an unfolding story of exploration and discovery. In this text, you will encounter many of the explorers and discoverers who have shaped the continuing story of psychology. The bridge from ancient thought to the pres-

1860	• Gustav Fechner publishes *Elements of Psychophysics*
1875	• William James gives first psychology lecture at Harvard
1878	• G. Stanley Hall receives first Ph.D. in psychology in the U.S.
1879	• Wilhelm Wundt establishes first psychology laboratory
1883	• First American psychology laboratory established at Johns Hopkins University by G. Stanley Hall
1887	• G. Stanley Hall initiates the *American Journal of Psychology*
1889	• James Mark Baldwin establishes first Canadian psychology laboratory at University of Toronto
1890	• James writes first psychology text, *Principles of Psychology*
1892	• American Psychological Association (APA) formed; G. Stanley Hall first president
1894	• Margaret Floy Washburn is first woman to receive a Ph.D. in psychology
1895	• Sigmund Freud publishes first work on psychology
1896	• Lightner Witmer establishes the first psychology clinic in the U.S.
1900	• Freud publishes *The Interpretation of Dreams*
1905	• Two Frenchmen, Alfred Binet and Théodore Simon, announce development of the first intelligence test, which they describe as "a measuring scale of intelligence" • Mary Whiton Calkins becomes first woman president of APA
1908	• Ivan Pavlov's work on conditioning first appears in an American scientific journal
1910	• Max Wertheimer and colleagues begin research on Gestalt psychology
1913	• Watson publishes the behaviorist manifesto, *Psychology as the Behaviorist Views It*
1920	• Francis Sumner is first African American to receive a Ph.D. in psychology in the U.S. • Henry Alston is first African American to publish his research findings in a major psychology journal in the U.S.

**Figure 1.1
Psychology, the Early Days:
A Timeline**

ent starts with Wundt; there we encounter his disciple Edward Titchener and structuralism, the school with which both men were associated. (See Figure 1.1 for a timeline of the early days of psychology.)

Wilhelm Wundt, Edward Titchener, and Structuralism

Wilhelm Wundt was interested in studying people's mental experiences. He used a method called **introspection**, or careful self-examination and reporting of one's conscious experience—what one is perceiving, feeling, thinking, or sensing at each particular moment in time. For example, he would expose people to a visual or auditory stimulus, a light or a sound, and ask them to report their conscious reactions to the stimulus (what it sounded like, how long it lasted, how it felt). In his laboratory, Wundt and his students conducted experiments to develop a model of conscious experience by breaking it down into its component parts— sensations, perceptions, and feelings—and then to determine how these elements are evoked by such stimuli as lights, sounds, and colors, and how they are related to each other.

Edward Titchener (1867–1927), an Englishman who was a disciple of Wundt, brought Wundt's teachings and methods of introspection to the United States and

Edward Titchener

psychology The science of behavior and mental processes.

introspection Inward focusing on mental experiences, such as sensations or feelings.

other English-speaking countries. The school of psychology identified with Wundt and Titchener became known as **structuralism**, an approach that attempted to define the structure of the mind by breaking down mental experiences into their component parts.

The first American to work in Wundt's experimental laboratory was the psychologist G. Stanley Hall (1844–1924) (Johnson, 2000). In 1892, Hall founded the American Psychological Association (APA), now the largest organization of psychologists in the United States, and he served as its first president (Pate, 2000). Nine years earlier, in 1883, he had established the first psychology laboratory in the United States, which was housed at Johns Hopkins University (Benjamin, 2000). Although Hall played a pivotal role in the early days of psychology in the United States, the psychologist generally recognized as the founder of American psychology is the Harvard psychologist William James.

William James and Functionalism

William James (1842–1910) was trained as a medical doctor but made important contributions to both psychology and philosophy (Pate, 2000). Although he used introspection, he shifted the focus to the *functions* of behavior. Unlike the structuralists, he did not believe that conscious experience could be parceled into discrete elements. Rather, he believed that mental experience is best understood in terms of the functions or purposes it serves.

James founded **functionalism**, the school of psychology that focused on how behavior helps individuals adapt to the demands placed upon them in the environment. Whereas structuralists were concerned with mental structures, functionalists were concerned with the functions of mental processes (Willingham, 2001). Functionalists examined the roles or functions that underlie our mental processes—*why* we do *what* we do. For example, James believed that we develop habits, such as the characteristic ways in which we use a fork or a spoon, because they enable us to perform more effectively in meeting the demands of daily life.

John Watson and Behaviorism

In the early 1900s, a new force in psychology gathered momentum. It was called **behaviorism**, and its credo was that psychology should limit itself to the study of overt behavior that observers could record and measure. The founder of behaviorism was the American psychologist John Broadus Watson (1878–1958). Watson reasoned that since you can never observe another person's mental processes, psychology would never advance as a science unless it eliminated mentalistic concepts like mind, consciousness, thinking, and feeling. He rejected introspection as a method of scientific inquiry and proposed that psychology should become a science of behavior, not of mental processes (Tweney & Budzynski, 2000; Willingham, 2001). In this respect, he shared with the ancient Greek philosopher Aristotle the belief that science should rely on observable events. Watson appealed to his fellow psychologists, as scientists, to focus on what we can observe—responses, reflexes, and other observable behaviors.

Watson believed that the environment molds the behavior of humans and other animals. He even boasted that if he were given control over the lives of infants, he could determine the kinds of adults they would become:

> *Give me a dozen healthy infants, well-formed, and my own specified world to bring them up in and I'll guarantee to take any one at random and train him to become any type of specialist I might suggest—doctor, lawyer, merchant-chief and, yes, even beggar-man and thief, regardless of his talents, penchants, tendencies, abilities, vocations, and the race of his ancestors.* (Watson, 1924, p. 82)

No one, of course, took up Watson's challenge, so we never will know how "a dozen healthy infants" would have fared under his direction. Psychologists today, however, believe that human development is much more complex than Watson thought. Few would believe that Watson could have succeeded in meeting the challenge he posed.

By the 1920s, behaviorism had become the main school of psychology in the United States, and it remained the dominant force in American psychology for several generations. Its popularity owed a great deal to the work of the Harvard University psychologist B. F. Skinner (1904–1990). Skinner studied how behavior is shaped by rewards and punishments, the environmental consequences that follow specific responses. Skinner showed that he could train animals to perform simple behaviors by rewarding particular responses. Thus, for example, a rat could learn to press a bar and a pigeon to peck a button if they were rewarded for these responses by receiving pellets of food. He also showed how more complex behaviors could be learned and maintained by manipulation of rewards, which he called *reinforcers*. In some of his more colorful demonstrations of the use of reinforcement, he trained a pigeon to play a tune on a toy piano and a pair of pigeons to play a type of Ping-Pong in which the birds rolled a ball back and forth between them. These methods could even be used to teach a raccoon to shoot a basketball, although the three-point shot is probably beyond its range.

Basketball-Playing Raccoon   By reinforcing particular behaviors, even a raccoon can be taught to shoot a basketball.

Although Skinner studied mainly pigeons and rats, he believed that the same principles of learning he observed in laboratory animals could be applied to humans as well. He argued that human behavior is as much a product of environmental consequences as the behavior of other animals. Everything we do, from saying "excuse me" when we sneeze, to attending class, to making a sandwich, represents responses learned through reinforcement, even though we cannot expect to recall the many reinforcement occasions involved in acquiring and maintaining these behaviors.

Max Wertheimer and Gestalt Psychology

In 1910, at about the time Watson was appealing to psychologists to abandon the study of the mind, another young psychologist, Max Wertheimer (1880–1943), was traveling by train through central Germany on his way to a vacation in the Rhineland (Hunt, 1993). What he saw from the train would lead him to found a new movement in psychology. Called **Gestalt psychology**, it is the school of psychology that studies the ways in which the brain organizes and structures our perceptions of the world.

What had captured Wertheimer from the train was the illusion that objects in the distance—telegraph poles, houses, and hilltops—appeared to be moving along with the train, even though they were obviously standing still. Countless other people had observed the same phenomenon of apparent movement but had paid little if any attention to it. Wertheimer was intrigued to find out why the phenomenon occurred. He had the idea that the illusion was not a trick of the eye but reflected higher-level processes in the brain that created the perception of movement. He promptly canceled his vacation and began experimental studies of the phenomenon. The experiments that he conducted with two assistants, Wolfgang Köhler (1887–1967) and Kurt Koffka (1886–1943), led to discoveries about the nature of perception—the processes by which we organize our sense impressions and form meaningful representations of the world around us.

The Gestalt psychologists rejected the structuralist belief that mental experience could be understood by breaking it down into its component parts. The German word **gestalt** can be roughly translated as "unitary form" or "pattern." The Gestaltists believed that the brain organizes how we see the world so that we perceive unified or organized wholes, not individual bits and pieces of sense

CONCEPT 1.6
Gestalt psychology was based on the principle that the human brain organizes our perceptions of the world, so that we perceive organized patterns or wholes, not individual bits and pieces of sense experiences added together.

 *web* **Netlab/Seeing Is Believing**

Gestalt psychology   The school of psychology that holds that the brain structures our perceptions of the world in terms of meaningful patterns or wholes.
gestalt   A German word meaning "unitary form" or "pattern."

About It

Early Schools of Psychology

Suppose you attempted to explain behavior in terms of how people's habits help them adapt to the environmental demands they face. What early school of psychology would you be adopting in your approach? Suppose you wanted to understand behavior in terms of underlying forces within the personality that influence behavior even though the person may not be aware of them? What early school of psychology would this approach represent?

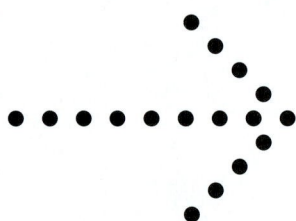

Figure 1.2   What Is This?

> **CONCEPT 1.7**
> According to Freud, much of our behavior is determined by unconscious forces and motives that lie beyond the reach of ordinary awareness.

unconscious   In Freudian theory, the part of the mind beyond conscious awareness that contains primitive drives or instincts.

psychodynamic perspective   The view that behavior is influenced by the struggle between unconscious sexual or aggressive impulses and opposing forces that try to keep this threatening material out of consciousness.

psychoanalysis   Freud's method of psychotherapy, which emphasizes the role of unconscious motives and conflicts in determining human behavior.

experiences added together. The well-known Gestalt maxim that the "whole is greater than the sum of the parts" expresses this core belief. You perceive the dots in Figure 1.2 not as a formless array of individual dots but as representing an arrow. When you see a large number of black objects flying overhead, you instantly recognize them as a flock of birds flying in formation. In other words, your brain interprets what your eyes see as organized patterns or wholes. Although Gestalt psychology extended into other areas of psychology, especially learning, it is best known for its contributions to perception, as we shall see in Chapter 3.

Sigmund Freud and Psychoanalysis

Around the time that behaviorism and Gestalt psychology were establishing a foothold in organized psychology, a very different model of psychology was emerging. It was based on the writings of an Austrian physician named Sigmund Freud (1856–1939). Freud's psychology focused not only on the mind, but on a region of the mind that lay beyond the reach of ordinary consciousness—a region he called the **unconscious**. Freud conceived of the unconscious as the repository of primitive sexual and aggressive drives or instincts, and of the wishes, impulses, and urges that arise from those drives or instincts. He believed that the motives underlying our behavior involve sexual and aggressive impulses that lie in the murky depths of the unconscious, hidden away from our ordinary awareness of ourselves. In other words, we may do or say things without understanding the true motives that prompted these behaviors.

Freud also believed that early childhood experiences play a determining role in shaping our personalities and behavior, including abnormal behaviors like excessive fears or phobias. He held that abnormal behavior patterns are rooted in unconscious conflicts originating in childhood. These conflicts involve a dynamic struggle within the unconscious mind between unacceptable sexual or aggressive impulses striving for expression and opposing mental forces seeking to keep this threatening material out of conscious awareness. Thus, Freud's view of psychology, and that of his followers, is often called the **psychodynamic perspective**.

Unlike Wundt, James, and Watson, Freud was a therapist, and his main aim was to help people overcome psychological problems. He developed a form of psychotherapy or "talk therapy" that he called **psychoanalysis** (discussed in Chapter 12). Psychoanalysis is a type of mental detective work. It incorporates methods, such as analysis of dreams and of "slips of the tongue," that Freud believed could be used to gain insight into the nature of the underlying motives and conflicts of which his patients were unaware. Freud maintained that once these unconscious conflicts were brought into the light of conscious awareness, they could be successfully resolved, or "worked through," during the course of therapy.

Contemporary Perspectives in Psychology

What do we find when we look over the landscape of psychology today? For one thing, we find a discipline that owes a great debt to its founders but is constantly reinventing itself to meet new challenges. Not all schools of thought have survived the test of time. Structuralism, for one, has essentially disappeared from the landscape; others maintain small groups of devoted followers who remain true to the original precepts. But by and large, the early schools of psychology—functionalism, behaviorism, Gestalt psychology, psychoanalysis—have continued to evolve or have been consolidated within broader perspectives. Today, the landscape of psychology can be divided into six major perspectives: the behavioral, psychodynamic, humanistic, physiological, cognitive, and sociocultural.

The Behavioral Perspective

The linchpin of the **behavioral perspective**, which focuses on observable behavior and the important role of learning in behavior, is, of course, behaviorism. However, many psychologists believe that traditional behaviorism is too simplistic or limited to explain complex human behavior. Though traditional behaviorism continues to influence modern psychology, it is no longer the dominant force it was during its heyday in the early to mid-1900s (Evans, 1999b).

Many psychologists today adopt a broader, learning-based perspective called **social-cognitive theory** (formerly called *social-learning theory*). This perspective originated in the 1960s with a group of learning theorists who broke away from traditional behaviorism (see Chapter 10). They believed that behavior is shaped not only by environmental factors, such as rewards and punishments, but also by *cognitive* factors, such as the value placed on different objects or goals (e.g., getting good grades) and expectancies about the outcomes of behavior ("If I do X, then Y will follow"). Social-cognitive theorists challenged their fellow psychologists to find ways to study these mental processes rather than casting them aside as unscientific, as traditional behaviorists would. Traditional behaviorists may not deny that thinking occurs, but they do believe that mental processes lie outside the range of scientific study.

The behavioral perspective led to the development of a major school of therapy, **behavior therapy**. Behavior therapy involves the systematic application of learning principles that are grounded in the behaviorist tradition of Watson and Skinner. Whereas the psychoanalyst is concerned with the workings of the unconscious mind, the behavior therapist helps people acquire more adaptive behaviors to overcome psychological problems like fears and social inhibitions. Today, many behavior therapists subscribe to a broader therapeutic approach, called *cognitive-behavioral therapy,* which incorporates techniques for changing maladaptive thoughts as well as overt behaviors (Dobson & Dozois, 2001) (see Chapter 12).

The Psychodynamic Perspective

The psychodynamic perspective remains a vibrant force in psychology. Like other contemporary perspectives in psychology, it continues to evolve. As we'll see in Chapter 10, "neo-Freudians" (psychodynamic theorists who have followed in the Freudian tradition) tend to place less emphasis on basic drives like sex and aggression than Freud did and more emphasis on processes of self-awareness, self-direction, and conscious choice.

The influence of psychodynamic theory extends well beyond the field of psychology. Its focus on our inner lives—our fantasies, wishes, dreams, and hidden motives—has had a profound impact on popular literature, art, and culture. Beliefs that psychological problems may be rooted in childhood and that people may not be consciously aware of their deeper motives and wishes continue to be widely endorsed, even by people not formally schooled in Freudian psychology.

CONCEPT 1.8
Although some early schools of psychology have essentially disappeared, contemporary perspectives in the field, including the behavioral, psychodynamic, humanistic, physiological, cognitive, and sociocultural perspectives, continue to evolve and to shape our understandings of behavior.

CONCEPT 1.9
Many psychologists today subscribe to a broad learning-based perspective, called social-cognitive theory, that emphasizes the roles of environmental and cognitive influences on behavior.

CONCEPT 1.10
The psychodynamic perspective focuses on the role of unconscious motivation (inner wishes and impulses of which we are unaware) and the importance of childhood experiences in shaping personality.

behavioral perspective   An approach to the study of psychology that focuses on the role of learning in explaining observable behavior.

social-cognitive theory   A contemporary learning-based model that emphasizes the roles played by both cognitive and environmental factors in determining behavior.

behavior therapy   A form of therapy that involves the systematic application of the principles of learning to bring about desired changes in emotional states and behavior.

THINK *About It*

What Brings Meaning to Your Life?

Humanistic psychologists emphasize the importance of finding a purpose or meaning in life. What are your purposes in life? How can you make your own life more meaningful?

CONCEPT 1.11

Humanistic psychology emphasizes personal freedom and responsibility for our actions and the value of self-awareness and acceptance of our true selves.

CONCEPT 1.12

The physiological perspective examines relationships between biological processes and behavior.

humanistic psychology The school of psychology that believes that free will and conscious choice are essential aspects of the human experience.

humanistic perspective An approach to the study of psychology that applies the principles of humanistic psychology.

physiological perspective An approach to the study of psychology that focuses on the relationships between biological processes and behavior.

evolutionary psychology A branch of psychology that focuses on the role of evolutionary processes in shaping behavior.

The Humanistic Perspective: A "Third Force" in Psychology

In the 1950s, another force began to achieve prominence in psychology. Known as **humanistic psychology**, it was a response to the two forces that dominated psychology at that time (i.e., behaviorism and Freudian psychology), and for that reason, it became known as a "third force" in psychology. Humanistic psychologists, including the Americans Abraham Maslow (1908–1970) and Carl Rogers (1902–1987), rejected the deterministic views of behaviorism and psychodynamic psychology—beliefs that human behavior is determined by the environment (in the case of behaviorism) or by the interplay of unconscious forces and motives lying outside the person's awareness (in the case of Freudian psychology). Humanistic psychologists believe that free will and conscious choice are essential aspects of the human experience.

Psychologists who adopt a **humanistic perspective** believe that psychology should focus on conscious experiences, even if those experiences are subjective and cannot be directly observed and scientifically measured. Humanistic psychologists view each of us as individuals who possess distinctive clusters of traits and abilities and unique frames of reference or perspectives on life. They emphasize the value of self-awareness and of becoming an authentic person by being true to oneself. They also stress the creative potentials of individuals and their ability to make choices that imbue their lives with meaning and purpose.

The Physiological Perspective

The **physiological perspective** examines relationships between biological processes and behavior. It is identified not with any one contributor but, rather, with many psychologists and neuroscientists who focus on the biological bases of behavior and mental processes.

Sitting atop your shoulders is a wondrous mass of tissue—your brain—that governs virtually everything you do. The brain is the center of an incredibly complex living computer, the nervous system, which allows you to sense the world around you, to think and feel, to move through space, to regulate heartbeat and other bodily functions, and to coordinate what you see and hear with what you do. Your nervous system also allows you to visualize the world you see and worlds that never were. As we'll find throughout this text, physiological psychology has illuminated our understanding of the biological bases of behavior and mental processes, including the roles of heredity, hormones, and the nervous system.

Evolutionary psychology is a movement within modern psychology that applies principles derived from Charles Darwin's theory of evolution to a wide range of behavior (Caporael, 2001; Gaulin & McBurney; 2001; Kenrick, Li, & Butner, 2003). Darwin (1809–1882) believed that all life forms, including humans, evolved from earlier life forms by adapting over time to the demands of their natural environments.

Evolutionary psychologists believe that behavioral *tendencies* or *predispositions,* such as aggressive tendencies, that might have helped ancestral humans survive could have been passed along genetically to successive generations, all the way down the genetic highway to us. They examine behaviors in different species that they believe may be influenced by evolutionary processes, including aggres-

***Might There Be an Evolutionary Basis to
Human Aggression?*** Evolutionary psychologists
believe behavioral tendencies that had survival
value to ancestral humans, such as aggressiveness, may have been passed down the genetic
highway to modern humans. Even our penchant
for aggressive sports might reflect these genetic
undercurrents.

sion, sexual behavior, and even altruism (i.e., self-sacrifice of the individual to
help perpetuate the group) (e.g., Thornhill & Palmer, 2000). But they recognize
that environmental factors, such as cultural learning and family influences, play
an important role in determining whether these behavioral tendencies or predispositions lead to actual behavior (e.g., whether a person acts aggressively or not).

The Cognitive Perspective

Like Wilhelm Wundt, cognitive psychologists study people's mental processes in
an effort to understand how people gain knowledge about themselves and the
world around them. The word cognitive comes from the Latin word cognitio,
meaning "knowledge." Psychologists who adopt the **cognitive perspective** study
the mental processes by which we acquire knowledge—how we learn, form concepts, solve problems, make decisions, and use language. Some cognitive psychologists apply principles of computer information processing (i.e., the methods by
which computers process information to solve problems) to explain how humans
process, store, retrieve, and manipulate information.

Cognitive psychologists make no apology for studying mental experience;
they believe the methods they use to study cognitions are well grounded in the
scientific tradition. After all, no one has ever observed subatomic particles like
protons and neutrons, but that hasn't prevented physicists from conducting scientific studies that attempt to investigate their properties. Chapter 7 examines the
intriguing research findings reported by cognitive psychologists.

The Sociocultural Perspective

Psychologists who adopt a **sociocultural perspective** examine how behavior and
attitudes are shaped by the social and cultural influences to which people are
exposed. More specifically, they focus on the influences of ethnicity, gender,
lifestyle, income level, and culture on behavior and mental processes. They have
brought issues relating to diversity to the forefront of psychological research and
thinking. Diversity in psychology is not limited to differences in ethnicity. It also
relates to differences in age, gender, sexual orientation, and disability status (see
Bingham et al., 2002; Garnets, 2002; Olkin, 2002; Reid, 2002). Nearly one in five
(19 percent) of adult Americans under the age of 65 have a disability (Farberman, 2003).

CONCEPT 1.13
Evolutionary psychology subscribes
to the view that our behavior reflects
inherited predispositions or tendencies
that increased the likelihood of survival
of our early ancestors.

CONCEPT 1.14
The cognitive perspective focuses
on understanding the mental processes
by which people gain knowledge about
themselves and the world around them.

CONCEPT 1.15
The sociocultural perspective places
behavior within a broad social context
by examining the influences of
ethnicity, gender, lifestyles,
socioeconomic status, and culture.

cognitive perspective An approach to
the study of psychology that focuses
on the processes by which we acquire
knowledge.

sociocultural perspective An approach
to the study of psychology that
emphasizes the role of social and cultural
influences on behavior.

THINK

About It

Examining Contemporary Perspectives

What are the major contemporary perspectives in psychology? How do they differ?

Consider some questions approached from the sociocultural perspective, to which we return later in the text: Does susceptibility to visual illusions vary across cultures? Are there gender differences in basic abilities in math or verbal skills? How does culture influence concepts of the self? Are there ethnic differences in drug-use patterns, and if so, how might we account for them? Are there racial differences in intelligence, and if so, what do we make of them? What role does acculturation play in the psychological adjustment of immigrant groups?

Psychologists recognize that research samples need to be broadly representative of the populations to which they wish to generalize their findings. Much of the past research in psychology focused almost exclusively on White, middle-class, male college students. We should not assume that findings based on narrowly defined groups of individuals necessarily generalize to other groups who have different life experiences.

Summary of Contemporary Perspectives

It's important to realize that no one perspective is necessarily right and the others wrong. Each major perspective in contemporary psychology focuses on different aspects of behavior or psychological functioning. Each has something unique to offer to our understanding of human behavior, and none offers a complete view. Given the complexity of human behavior and experience, it is not surprising that psychology has spawned multiple pathways for approaching its subject matter. It is also not surprising that many psychologists today identify with an *eclectic* approach to understanding human behavior—one that draws on theories and principles representing different perspectives. We should recognize, too, that contemporary psychology is not divided as neatly into different schools of thought as it seemed to be in its early days. There is considerable room for overlap among the different perspectives.

In addition to the six major perspectives that dot the landscape of contemporary psychology, a growing movement within psychology, called **positive psychology**, is directed toward the study of the positive aspects of human experience, such as love, happiness, and altruism (Kogan, 2001; Seligman, 2003; Seligman & Csikszentmihalyi, 2000, 2001). Much of psychology is directed to understanding human weaknesses and deficits, including troubling emotional states, the effects of traumatic stress, and problem behaviors such as violence and drug addiction. Founded by psychologist Martin Seligman, positive psychology balances the scales by focusing on our virtues and strengths, not our flaws. Throughout the text we will discuss many areas of interest in positive psychology, including love, helping behavior, optimism, successful aging, happiness, self-esteem, self-actualization, and creativity.

In Concept Chart 1.1, the first of many such charts in the text, you'll find examples of the kinds of general questions that psychologists from each of the major contemporary perspectives might ask, as well as the kinds of questions they might pose to learn more about specific topics. These topics are introduced here to help you distinguish among the various perspectives in contemporary psychology. They will be discussed further in later chapters.

positive psychology A contemporary movement within psychology that emphasizes the study of human virtues and assets, rather than weaknesses and deficits.

CONCEPT CHART 1.1
Contemporary Perspectives in Psychology: How They Differ

Perspective	General Questions	Questions About Specific Topics		
		Aggression	**Depression**	**Obesity**
Behavioral	How do early learning experiences shape our behavior as adults?	How is aggressive behavior learned? How is it rewarded or reinforced? Does exposure to violence in the media or among one's peers play a role?	How is depression related to changes in reinforcement patterns? What social skills are needed to establish and maintain social relationships that could serve as sources of reinforcement?	How might unhealthy eating habits lead to obesity? How might we change those habits?
Psychodynamic	How do unresolved conflicts from childhood affect adult behavior? How can people be helped to cope with these conflicts?	How is aggression related to unconscious impulses? Against whom are these impulses really directed?	How might depression be related to unresolved loss? Might it represent anger turned inward?	Might obesity relate to childhood conflicts revolving around unresolved needs for love and support? Might food have become a substitute for love?
Humanistic	How do people pursue goals that give their lives a sense of meaning and purpose?	Might violence be related to frustration arising when people are blocked from pursuing their goals? How might we turn this around to prevent violence?	Might depression be related to a lack of self-esteem or a threat to one's self-image? Might it stem from a sense of purposelessness or lack of meaning in life?	What sets the stage for obesity? Does food have a special meaning for obese people? How can we help them to find other sources of satisfaction?
Physiological	How do biological structures and processes make behavior possible? What roles do nature (heredity) and nurture (environment) play in such areas as intelligence, language development, and aggression?	What brain mechanisms control aggressive behavior? Might brain abnormalities explain violent behavior in some people?	How are changes in brain chemistry related to depression? What genetic links might there be?	Is obesity inherited? What genes may be involved? How would knowledge of a genetic basis lead to new approaches to treatment or prevention?
Cognitive	How do people solve problems, make decisions, and develop language?	What thoughts trigger aggressive responses? What beliefs do aggressive people hold that might increase their potential for violence?	What types of thinking patterns are related to depression? How might they be changed to help people overcome depression or prevent it from occurring?	How does obesity affect a person's self-concept? What thoughts lead to eating binges? How might they be changed?
Sociocultural	How do concepts of self differ across cultures? How do social and cultural influences shape behavior?	What social conditions give rise to drug use and aggressive behavior? Does our society condone or even reward certain forms of violence, such as sexual aggression against women or spousal abuse?	Is depression linked to social stresses, such as poverty or unemployment? Why is depression more common among certain groups of people, especially women? Does it have to do with their expected social roles?	Are some groups at greater risk of obesity than others? Do cultural differences in dietary patterns and customs play a role?

MODULE 1.1 REVIEW

Foundations of Modern Psychology

CONCEPT CHECK

1. The scientist generally credited with the founding of psychology as an independent science was _____.

2. The early school of psychology called structuralism
   a. rejected the use of introspection as a research method.
   b. focused on overt behavior.
   c. investigated the structure of the mind.
   d. was concerned with the functions of behavior.

3. The school of psychology that believes psychology should be limited to the study of observable behavior is _____.

4. Gestalt psychology focuses on
   a. the organization of the mind.
   b. the ways in which the brain organizes and structures our perceptions of the world.
   c. the functions of behavior.
   d. the role of self-actualization in motivating behavior.

6. Which psychological perspective originated with Sigmund Freud?

5. Humanistic psychologists rejected the notions that unconscious processes or environmental influences determine our behavior. Rather, they emphasized the importance of _____ in understanding behavior.
   a. conscious choice
   b. heredity and physiological processes
   c. classical and operant conditioning
   d. the underlying structures of the mind

MODULE 1.2 Psychologists: Who They Are and What They Do

- **What are the various specialties in psychology?**
- **What changes have occurred in the ethnic and gender characteristics of psychologists over time?**

When you think of a psychologist, do you form a mental image of someone working in a hospital or clinic who treats people with psychological problems? This image describes one particular type of psychologist—a clinical psychologist. But there are many other types. Psychology is a diverse profession because of the large number of areas in the field and because of the many different roles psychologists perform. Some psychologists teach and conduct research. Others provide psychological services to individuals or to organizations, such as schools or businesses. Psychologists are usually identified with one particular specialty or subfield within psychology—for example, experimental, clinical, developmental, educational, or social psychology.

Some psychologists conduct **basic research**—research that seeks to expand our understanding of psychological phenomena even if such knowledge does not lead directly to any practical benefits. These psychologists typically work for universities or government agencies. Some psychologists conduct **applied research**—research intended to find solutions to specific problems. For example, a psychologist might apply research on learning and memory to studying methods of enhancing the educational experiences of children with mental retardation. Still other psychologists work in applied areas of psychology in which they provide services to people or organizations. These include clinical, counseling, school, and industrial/organizational psychologists. Many of these applied psychologists also conduct research in the areas in which they practice. In this module, we take a closer look at the various types of psychologists.

CONCEPT 1.16

The field of psychology consists of an ever-growing number of specialty areas.

basic research Research focused on acquiring knowledge even if such knowledge has no direct practical application.

applied research Research that attempts to find solutions to specific problems.

Specialty Areas of Psychology

All psychologists study behavior and mental processes, but they pursue this knowledge in different ways, in different settings, and from different perspectives. The following sections provide a run-down of some of the major specialty areas within the field of psychology and some emerging ones.

 PsychAssist: Specialty Areas of Psychology

Most psychologists earn doctoral degrees in their area of specialization, such as experimental psychology, clinical psychology, or social psychology. The Ph.D. (Doctor of Philosophy) is the most common doctoral degree and is awarded after completion of required graduate coursework and a dissertation, which involves an original research project. Some psychologists seeking practice careers may earn a Doctor of Psychology degree (Psy.D.), a doctoral degree that is focused more on practitioner skills than on research skills. Others may pursue graduate programs in schools of education and be awarded a Doctorate in Education (Ed.D.). In some speciality areas, such as school psychology and industrial/organization (I/O) psychology, the Master's degree is recognized as the entry-level degree for professional work in the field.

Major Specialty Areas

Concept Chart 1.2 provides an overview of the major specialties in psychology discussed in this section. Figure 1.3 shows the percentages of psychologists working in major specialty areas, and Figure 1.4 summarizes where psychologists work.

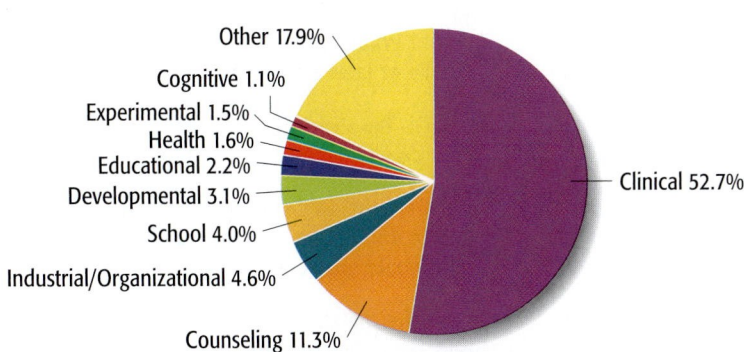

Figure 1.3   Psychologists' Areas of Specialization
Clinical psychologists make up the largest group of psychologists, followed by counseling psychologists and industrial/organizational psychologists.

Source: American Psychological Association, 2004.

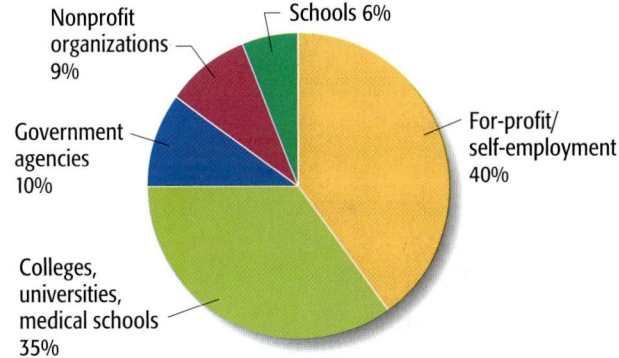

Figure 1.4   Where Psychologists Work
The largest group of psychologists work in settings providing psychological services. Many work at colleges and universities as teachers, researchers, administrators, or supervisors of psychologists in training. Some also work in schools or government agencies.

Source: American Psychological Association, 2003.

Experimental psychologists apply experimental methods to the study of behavior and mental processes. They study such processes as learning, sensation and perception, and cognition. Some experimental psychologists, called **comparative psychologists**, seek to understand animal behavior for its own sake and possibly for what it might teach us about human behavior (Dewsbury, 2000). Others, called **physiological psychologists** (also known as *biological psychologists*), study the biological bases of behavior.

Clinical psychologists evaluate and treat people with psychological disorders, such as depression and anxiety disorders. They may use psychotherapy to help people overcome psychological problems or cope better with the stresses they face in their lives. They may administer psychological tests to better understand people's problems or to evaluate their intellectual abilities or personalities.

experimental psychologists
Psychologists who apply experimental methods to the study of behavior.

comparative psychologists
Psychologists who study behavioral similarities and differences among animal species.

physiological psychologists
Psychologists who focus on the biological underpinnings of behavior.

clinical psychologists   Psychologists who use psychological techniques to evaluate and treat individuals with mental or psychological disorders.

CONCEPT CHART 1.2
Specialty Areas of Psychology

Types of Psychologists	Nature of Specialty	Typical Questions Studied
Experimental psychologists	Conduct research on learning, cognition, sensation and perception, biological bases of behavior, and animal behavior	How do various states of arousal affect learning? What brain centers are responsible for memory?
Clinical psychologists	Evaluate and treat people with psychological problems and disorders, such as depression and schizophrenia	How can we diagnose anxiety? Is depression treated more effectively with psychotherapy or drug therapy?
Counseling psychologists	Help people with adjustment problems	What kind of occupation would this student find fulfilling? Why does this person find it difficult to make friends?
School psychologists	Work in school systems to help children with academic problems or special needs	Would this child profit from special education, or would he or she be better off in a regular classroom?
Educational psychologists	Construct standardized psychological and educational tests (such as the SAT); improve course planning and instructional methods	Is this test a valid predictor of success in college? How can we teach algebra more efficiently?
Developmental psychologists	Study physical, cognitive, social, and personality development across the lifespan	At what age do children begin to walk or speak? What types of crises do people face in middle or later adulthood?
Personality psychologists	Study the psychological characteristics that make each of us unique	What is the structure of personality? How do we measure personality?
Social psychologists	Study the nature and causes of people's thoughts, feelings, and behavior in social situations	What are the origins of prejudice? Why do people do things as members of groups that they would not do as individuals?
Environmental psychologists	Study the ways in which people's behavior and mental processes influence, and are influenced by, their physical environments	What are the effects of city life on people? How does overcrowding affect people's health and behavior?
Industrial/Organizational psychologists	Study the relationships between people and their work environments	How can we find out who would perform well in this position? How can we make hiring and promotion fairer? How can we enhance employees' motivation?
Health psychologists	Study the relationships between psychological factors and the prevention and treatment of physical illness	How can we help people avoid risky sexual behaviors? How can we help people quit smoking and start to exercise?
Consumer psychologists	Study relationships between psychological factors and consumers' preferences and purchasing behavior	Why do people select particular brands? What types of people prefer a particular type of product?

Many conduct research in the field or train future psychologists. Others work in hospitals or clinics, while still others work in private practice or university settings. As Figure 1.4 shows, clinical psychologists represent the largest group of psychologists.

The professional roles of clinical psychologists in evaluating and treating psychological disorders often overlap with those of **psychiatrists**, medical doctors who complete residency training in the medical specialty of psychiatry. Unlike

THINK

About It

Specialties in Professional Psychology

If you were uncertain about what career to pursue and wanted help sorting through the vocational choices best suited to you, what type of psychologist would you consult?

Or suppose you read in a newspaper about a psychologist who was studying how people's behavior changes when they become part of an unorganized mob. What type of psychologist would this person likely be?

psychiatrists, however, psychologists cannot prescribe drugs. But even these lines may be blurring now that a small number of psychologists have been trained in a specialized program to prescribe drugs to treat psychological disorders (Foxhall, 2000b, 2000c).

Counseling psychologists help people who have adjustment problems that are usually not as severe as the kinds of problems treated by clinical psychologists. If you did not know what course of study to follow in college, or if you were having a difficult time adjusting to college, you might talk to a counseling psychologist about it. Counseling psychologists also help people make vocational decisions or resolve marital problems. Many work in college counseling centers or community-based counseling or mental health centers.

School psychologists work in school systems, where they help children with academic, emotional, and behavioral problems and evaluate students for placement in special-education programs (Quinn & McDougal, 1998). They are also team players who work collaboratively with teachers and other professionals in providing a broad range of services for children (DeAngelis, 2000).

Educational psychologists develop tests that measure intellectual ability or academic potential, help gear training approaches to students' learning styles, and create ways of helping students reach their maximum academic potential. Many also conduct research; among the issues they study are the nature of intelligence, how teachers can enhance the learning process, and why some children are more highly motivated than others to do well in school (Webster & Beveridge, 1997).

Developmental psychologists study people's physical, cognitive, social, and personality development throughout the life span. *Child psychologists* are developmental psychologists who limit their focus to child development.

Personality psychologists seek to understand the nature of personality—the cluster of psychological characteristics and behaviors that distinguishes us as unique individuals and leads us to act consistently over time. In particular, they study how personality is structured and how it develops and changes (Derlega, Winstead, & Jones, 1999).

Social psychologists study how group or social influences affect behavior and attitudes. Whereas personality psychologists look within the individual's psychological make-up to explain behavior, social psychologists focus on how groups affect individuals and, in some cases, how individuals affect groups.

Environmental psychologists study relationships between the physical environment and behavior. They are concerned with the ways in which people's behaviors and mental processes influence, and are influenced by, their physical environments. They examine such issues as the effects of outdoor temperature on aggression and the psychological impact of environmental factors like noise, air pollution, housing design, and overcrowding.

Industrial/organizational (I/O) psychologists study people at work. They are concerned with such issues as job satisfaction, personnel selection and training, leadership qualities, effects of organizational structure on productivity and work performance, and challenges posed by changes in the workplace. They may use psychological tests to determine the fit between applicants' abilities and interests

psychiatrists   Medical doctors who specialize in the diagnosis and treatment of mental or psychological disorders.

counseling psychologists   Psychologists who help people clarify their goals and make life decisions or find ways of overcoming problems in various areas of their lives.

school psychologists   Psychologists who evaluate and assist children with learning problems or other special needs.

educational psychologists Psychologists who study issues relating to the measurement of intelligence and the processes involved in educational or academic achievement.

developmental psychologists Psychologists who focus on processes involving physical, cognitive, social, and personality development.

personality psychologists   Psychologists who study the psychological characteristics and behaviors that distinguish us as individuals and lead us to act consistently over time.

social psychologists   Psychologists who study group or social influences on behavior and attitudes.

environmental psychologists Psychologists who study relationships between the physical environment and behavior.

industrial/organizational (I/O) psychologists   Psychologists who study people's behavior at work.

and the jobs available within an organization or corporation. Some I/O psychologists engage in *human factors research,* research that examines ways of making instrumentation and systems (e.g., airplane gauges and computer systems) more efficient and easier to use.

Health psychologists study how such psychological factors as stress, lifestyle, and attitude affect physical health. They apply this knowledge in developing disease prevention programs and interventions to improve the quality of life of patients with chronic diseases, such as heart disease, cancer, and HIV/AIDS (Schneiderman et al., 2001).

Consumer psychologists are interested in understanding consumer behavior—why people purchase particular products and particular brands. They examine consumers' attitudes toward different products and toward different ways of advertising or packaging products.

Emerging Specialty Areas

When G. Stanley Hall founded the American Psychological Association (APA) in 1892, it had 31 charter members (Benjamin, 1997); today, the membership exceeds 150,000. It's no wonder that psychology's interests and specialties cover so wide a range, including such emerging specialty areas as neuropsychology, geropsychology, forensic psychology, and sport psychology.

Neuropsychologists study relationships between the brain and behavior. While some neuropsychologists limit their activities to research, *clinical neuropsychologists* use specialized tests to evaluate the cognitive effects of brain injuries and strokes. These tests can help them pinpoint the particular areas of the brain affected by injury or disease. Clinical neuropsychologists may also work with rehabilitation specialists in designing programs to help people who have suffered various forms of brain damage regain as much of their functioning as possible.

Geropsychologists are interested in the psychological processes associated with aging. They may work with geriatric patients to help them cope with the stresses of later life, including retirement, loss of loved ones, and declining physical health.

Forensic psychologists work within the legal system (Otto & Heilbrun, 2002). They may perform psychological evaluations in child custody cases, testify about the competence of defendants to stand trial, develop psychological profiles of criminal types, give expert testimony in court on psychological issues, or assist attorneys in selecting potential jury members.

Sport psychologists apply psychology to sports and athletic competition (Singer, 2003). They help athletes develop relaxation and mental-focusing skills to overcome performance anxiety and improve performance. Some study personality traits associated with athletic performance, including the reasons that certain athletes "choke" in difficult situations. Others help athletes handle competitive pressures and balance travel, family, and life demands as well as team dynamics (Hacker, 2002). Still others counsel players who experience psychological difficulties adjusting to the rigors of competition (Anderson, Van Raalte, & Brewer, 2001; F. L. Gardner, 2001).

Professional Psychology: Becoming More Diverse

The early psychologists shared more than just a yearning to understand behavior: Almost all of them were White males of European background. The ranks of women in the early days of psychology were slim, and the ranks of racial and ethnic minorities even slimmer. Back then, women and minority members faced many barriers in pursuing careers in psychology, as they did in numerous other professions. The earliest woman pioneer in psychology was Christine Ladd-Franklin (1847–1930). She completed all the requirements for a Ph.D. at Johns

health psychologists Psychologists who focus on the relationship between psychological factors and physical health.

consumer psychologists Psychologists who study why people purchase particular products and brands.

neuropsychologists Psychologists who study relationships between the brain and behavior.

geropsychologists Psychologists who focus on psychological processes involved in aging.

forensic psychologists Psychologists involved in the application of psychology to the legal system.

sport psychologists Psychologists who apply psychology to understanding and improving athletic performance.

Hopkins University in 1882, but the university refused to award her the degree because at that time it did not issue doctoral degrees to women. Nonetheless, she went on to pursue a distinguished research career in psychology, during which she developed a new theory of color vision. She finally received her Ph.D. in 1926 (Furumoto, 1992).

Another woman pioneer was Mary Whiton Calkins (1863–1930). A brilliant student of William James, Calkins completed all her Ph.D. requirements at Harvard, but Harvard denied her a doctorate; like Johns Hopkins, it did not grant doctoral degrees to women. She was offered the doctorate through Radcliffe College, a women's academy affiliated with Harvard, but she refused it. Not easily deterred, she went on to a distinguished career in psychology—teaching and conducting important research on learning and short-term memory (Evans, 1999c). In 1905, she became the first female president of the APA.

Margaret Floy Washburn (1871–1939) encountered similar discrimination when she pursued studies in psychology at Columbia University. In 1894, having found a more receptive environment at Cornell University, she became the first woman in the United States to earn a Ph.D. in psychology (Evans, 1999c). She wrote an influential book, *The Animal Mind,* and in 1921 became the second female president of the APA.

In 1909, Gilbert Haven Jones (1883–1966), an African American, received a doctorate in psychology from a university in Germany. It wasn't until 1920, however, at Clark University in Worcester, Massachusetts, that Francis Sumner (1895–1954) became the first African American to receive a doctorate in psychology in the United States. Sumner went on to a distinguished career in teaching and research. He helped establish the psychology department at Howard University and served as its chairperson until his death in 1954 (Evans, 1999d).

In 1920, the same year Sumner earned his doctorate, J. Henry Alston became the first African American to publish his research findings (on the perception of warmth and cold) in a major U.S. psychology journal. It took another fifty years (until 1971) before the first—and, to this date, the only—African American psychologist, Kenneth Clark (b. 1914), was elected president of the APA. In 1999, Richard Suinn became the first Asian American psychologist to be elected president of the APA.

In recent years, as increasing numbers of ethnic minorities have entered the field of psychology, the professional ranks of psychologists have become more diverse. Figure 1.5 shows the ethnic make-up of persons holding doctorates in psychology. Despite the increased diversity, people of color are still underrepresented in the profession (Evans, 1999d). For example, there is but one Native American psychologist for every 30,000 Native Americans (Rabasca, 2000a).

CONCEPT 1.17
Women and minority members faced difficult obstacles in pursuing careers in psychology in the early days of the profession.

CONCEPT 1.18
Though the field of psychology has become more diverse, people of color are still underrepresented in professional psychology.

Mary Whiton Calkins

Margaret Floy Washburn

Gilbert Haven Jones

CONCEPT 1.19

The profession of psychology has undergone a major gender shift in recent years.

A different picture emerges when we examine gender shifts in professional psychology. Women comprise an ever-increasing proportion of degree recipients in psychology. They now account for about two-thirds of the undergraduate degrees and doctorates in the field (Kohout, 2001; Kyle, 2000) (see Figure 1.6). This gender shift mirrors the increased representation of women in occupations traditionally dominated by men, including medicine and law. However, the gender shift is occurring at a faster rate in psychology than in other professions.

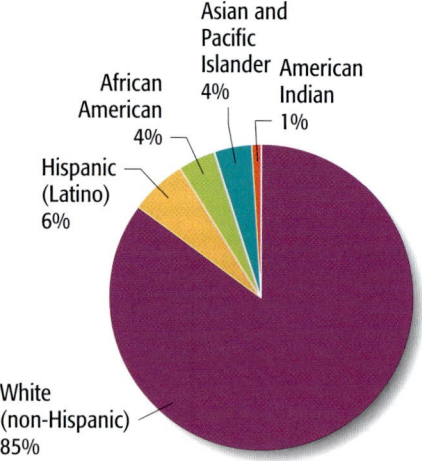

Figure 1.5 Ethnicities of Doctorate Recipients in Psychology
Though the percentages of minorities in the field of psychology have increased over the years, White Americans of European background still constitute the majority of new doctorate recipients in psychology.

Source: National Science Foundation, 2004.

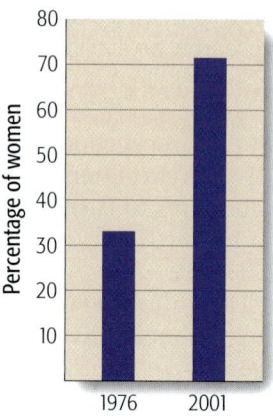

Figure 1.6 Women Ph.D. Recipients in Psychology
Women now represent about two-thirds of new Ph.D.s in psychology, as compared to one-third in 1976.

Source: American Psychological Association, 2003.

MODULE 1.2 REVIEW

Psychologists: Who They Are and What They Do

CONCEPT CHECK

1. _____ research focuses on expanding our understanding and knowledge, whereas _____ research focuses on finding answers or solutions to particular problems.

2. Match the following types of psychologists with the type of work they do: (a) counseling psychologists; (b) developmental psychologists; (c) environmental psychologists; (d) consumer psychologists.
   i. study changes in behaviors and attitudes throughout the life cycle
   ii. study effects of outdoor temperature on aggression
   iii. study psychological characteristics of people who buy particular products
   iv. help students adjust to college life

3. Neuropsychologists
   a. study relationships between the brain and particular behaviors and/or cognitive functions.
   b. investigate how stress and lifestyle choices can affect physical health.
   c. research social influences and personal adjustment problems.
   d. are psychologists who complete postdoctoral training in neurology.

4. The first African American to receive a doctorate in psychology in the United States was
   a. Mary Whiton Calkins.
   b. Francis Sumner.
   c. Gilbert Haven Jones.
   d. Kenneth Clark.

MODULE 1.3 Research Methods in Psychology

- **What is the scientific method, and what are its four general steps?**
- **What are the major research methods psychologists use?**
- **What ethical guidelines must psychologists follow in their research?**

Psychologists are trained to be skeptical of claims and arguments that are not grounded in evidence. They are especially skeptical of public opinion and folklore. What distinguishes psychology from other inquiries into human nature, including philosophy, theology, and poetry, is the use of scientific methods to gain knowledge. Psychologists adopt an **empirical approach**; that is, they base their beliefs on evidence gathered from experiments and careful observation.

The Scientific Method: How We Know What We Know

Like other scientific disciplines, psychology uses the scientific method in its pursuit of knowledge. The **scientific method** is a framework for acquiring knowledge based on careful observation and the use of experimental methods. It can be conceptualized in terms of four general steps that scientists use to test their ideas and to expand and refine their knowledge: (1) developing a research question, (2) framing the research question in the form of a hypothesis, (3) gathering evidence to test the hypothesis, and (4) drawing conclusions about the hypothesis. Figure 1.7 summarizes these steps.

1. *Developing a research question.* Psychologists generate research questions from many sources, including theory, careful observation, previous experience, and commonly held beliefs. For example, a researcher might be interested in the question "Does exposure to stress increase risk of the common cold?"

2. *Framing the research question in the form of a hypothesis.* An investigator reframes the research question in the form of a **hypothesis**—a precise prediction that can be tested through research. Hypotheses are often drawn from **theory**. For example, a researcher might theorize that stress weakens the immune system, the body's defense system against disease, leaving us more vulnerable to various kinds of illness, including the common cold. Based on this theoretical model, the investigator might frame the research question in the form of a testable hypothesis: "People who encounter high levels of stress in their lives will be more likely to develop a common cold after exposure to cold viruses than are people with lower levels of stress."

   Investigators may also develop hypotheses based on common beliefs or assumptions about behavior. Consider the commonly held belief that "opposites attract." An opposing belief is that people are attracted to those similar to themselves—that "birds of a feather flock together." A specific hypothesis drawn from the latter belief might be phrased as follows: "Most people choose romantic partners who are similar in educational level."

3. *Gathering evidence to test the hypothesis.* The investigator develops a research design or strategy for gathering evidence to provide a scientific test of the hypothesis. The type of research method used depends on the nature of the problem. In the stress and common cold example, the investigator might classify people into high-stress and low-stress groups and then expose them (with their permission, of course) to cold viruses to see if the high-stress group is more likely to develop a common cold. Researchers who have used this methodology (Cohen et al., 1998) found that people under high levels of

CONCEPT 1.20
The scientific method is a framework for acquiring knowledge through careful observation and experimentation.

CONCEPT 1.21
Scientists use the scientific method to test out predictions derived from theory, observation, experience, and commonly held beliefs.

CONCEPT 1.22
Psychologists frame their research questions in the form of hypotheses, or specific predictions about the outcomes they expect to find.

CONCEPT 1.23
Psychologists gather evidence to test out their hypotheses.

empirical approach A method of developing knowledge based on evaluating evidence gathered from experiments and careful observation.

scientific method A method of inquiry involving careful observation and use of experimental methods.

hypothesis A precise prediction about the outcomes of an experiment.

theory A formulation that accounts for relationships among observed events or experimental findings in ways that make them more understandable and predictable.

Developing a Research Question	**Forming a Hypothesis**	**Gathering Evidence**	**Drawing Conclusions**
Drawing on theory, observations, experiences, or common beliefs to formulate a researchable question	Reframing the question so that it becomes a specific prediction that can be tested through research	Testing the hypothesis	Using statistical methods of analysis to determine whether the data support the hypothesis

Figure 1.7 General Steps in the Scientific Method

CONCEPT 1.24

Psychologists evaluate the results of scientific studies by using statistical tests to determine if relationships between variables or differences between groups are unlikely to be due to chance.

chronic stress associated with prolonged unemployment or persistent family conflict were more likely to develop a cold after viral exposure than were people in the low-stress comparison group.

4. *Drawing conclusions about the hypothesis.* Investigators draw conclusions about their hypotheses based on the evidence their research has produced. To test their hypotheses, they turn to **statistics**, the branch of mathematics involving methods of tabulating and analyzing numerical data. Investigators use statistical methods to determine whether relationships between variables (e.g., stress and vulnerability to the common cold) or differences between groups (e.g., an experimental group that receives a treatment versus a control group that does not) are *statistically significant* (relatively unlikely to have been due to chance). A **variable** is a factor that varies in an experiment, such as the dosage level of an experimental drug or the scores that participants receive on a measure of interest.

When research findings do not support the study's hypotheses, scientists may adjust the theories from which the hypotheses were derived. Research findings may suggest new avenues of research or revision of the psychological theories themselves.

Another important factor in drawing conclusions is **replication**, the attempt to duplicate findings reported by others to determine whether they will occur again under the same experimental conditions. Scientists have more confidence in findings that can be reliably replicated by others.

Testing a Hypothesis Psychologists frame testable hypotheses that guide their research. For example, a psychologist might hypothesize that romantic partners with similar interests and attitudes are more likely to remain together than are couples with dissimilar interests and attitudes. Preferences for the same color in bathing suits may have no bearing on the longevity of the relationship, however.

statistics The branch of mathematics involving the tabulation, analysis, and interpretation of numerical data.

variable A factor or measure that varies within an experiment or among individuals.

replication The attempt to duplicate findings.

Research Methods:
How We Learn What We Know

The scientific method is a framework psychologists use to take their ideas for a test ride. Now let's consider the particular methods they employ to acquire knowledge about behavior and mental processes: the case study, survey, naturalistic observation, correlational, and experimental methods.

The Case Study Method

The **case study method** is a painstaking, in-depth study of one or more individuals. The psychologist draws information from interviews, observation, or written records. Sigmund Freud, for example, based much of his theory of personality and abnormal behavior on data from intensive observation and study of the patients he treated in his clinical practice. The Swiss scientist Jean Piaget (1896–1980) developed a theory of cognitive development by closely observing and interviewing a small number of children. Many of the early findings on brain function came from studies of brain-injured patients that matched the types of injuries they sustained with particular deficits in memory functioning and motor skills.

Problems with case studies can arise when investigators rely on people's memories of their past experiences, since memories can become distorted or filled with gaps. People may also withhold important information out of embarrassment or shame. To present a more favorable impression, some may even purposefully deceive the researcher. Interviewers themselves may hear only what they expect or want to hear, and observers may see only what they want or expect to see. In sum, though case studies can provide a treasure-trove of information and lead to testable hypotheses, they lack the rigorous controls of scientific experiments.

The Survey Method

The **survey method** gathers information from target groups of people through the use of structured interviews or questionnaires. A **structured interview** is a questioning technique that follows a preset series of questions in a particular order. A **questionnaire** is a written set of questions or statements to which people can reply by marking responses on an answer form.

Psychologists and other researchers conduct survey research to learn about the characteristics, beliefs, attitudes, and behaviors of certain populations. In survey research, a **population** represents the total group of people who are the subjects of interest. For example, a population might consist of all persons eighteen years of age or older in the United States, or perhaps all high school seniors. Generally speaking, it is impractical to study an entire population; an exception would be a very small population that could be studied in its entirety, such as the population of students living in a particular dormitory. In virtually all cases, however, surveys are conducted on **samples**, or segments, of populations.

To draw conclusions about a population based on the results of a sample, the sample must be representative of the target population. Representative samples allow researchers to *generalize,* or transfer, their results from a sample to the population it represents. To create representative samples, researchers use **random sampling**, a technique whereby individuals are selected at random from a given population for participation in a sample. This often entails the use of a computer program that randomly selects names of individuals or households within a given population. Political polls reported in the media typically use random samples of voters to predict outcomes of elections.

Like case studies, surveys may be limited by gaps in people's memories. Participants may also give answers that they believe are socially desirable rather than reflective of what they truly feel or believe. This response style results from what is

CONCEPT 1.25
Psychologists use a variety of research methods to learn about behavior and mental processes, including the case study, survey, naturalistic observation, correlational, and experimental methods.

CONCEPT 1.26
Case studies can provide a wealth of information and suggest testable hypotheses, but they lack the controls found in scientific experiments.

CONCEPT 1.27
Through survey research, psychologists can gather information about attitudes and behaviors of large numbers of people, but the information they obtain may be subject to memory gaps and biases.

case study method   An in-depth study of one or more individuals.

survey method   A research method that uses structured interviews or questionnaires to gather information about groups of people.

structured interview   An interview in which a set of specific questions is asked in a particular order.

questionnaire   A written set of questions or statements to which people reply by marking their responses on an answer form.

population   All the individuals or organisms that constitute particular groups.

samples   Subsets of a population.

random sampling   A method of sampling in which each individual in the population has an equal chance of being selected.

called **social desirability bias**. For example, many people exaggerate how frequently they attend church (Espenshade, 1993). Social desirability may be especially strong in situations where people have a considerable stake in what others think of them (McGovern & Nevid, 1986). Another form of bias in survey research is **volunteer bias**. This arises when people who volunteer to participate in surveys or other research studies are not representative of the population from which they are drawn.

The Naturalistic Observation Method

The **naturalistic observation method** takes the laboratory "into the field" to directly observe the behavior of humans or other animal species in their natural habitats or environments. The people or other animals serving as research participants may behave more "naturally" in their natural environments than they would in the artificial confines of the experimental laboratory. Psychologists have observed children at home with their parents to learn more about parent-child interactions and in schoolyards and classrooms to see how children relate to each other. Because people may act differently when they know they are being observed, the observers try to avoid interfering with the behaviors they are observing. To further minimize this potential bias, the observers may spend time allowing the subjects to get accustomed to them so that they begin acting more naturally before any actual measurement takes place. Observers may also position themselves so that the subjects can't see them.

Problems with this method may arise if observers introduce their own biases. For example, if observers have a preconceived idea about how a parent's interaction with a child affects the child's behavior, they may tend to see what they expect to see. To guard against this, pairs of observers may be used to check for consistency between observers. Experimenters may also make random spot-checks to see that observers are recording their measurements accurately.

Animals in laboratory or zoolike environments may act differently than they do in their natural habitats. To learn more about chimp behavior, naturalist Jane Goodall lived for many years among chimpanzees in their natural environment. Gradually she came to be accepted by the chimps. Her observations disputed the long-held belief that only humans use tools. For example, she watched as chimps used a stick as a tool, inserting it into a termite mound to remove termites, which they then ate. Not only did chimpanzees use tools, but they also showed other humanlike behavior, such as kissing when greeting one another.

Though the method of naturalistic observation may lack the controls available in controlled experiments, it can provide important insights into behavior as it occurs under natural conditions.

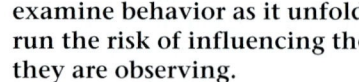

CONCEPT 1.28
With the naturalistic observation method, researchers in the field can examine behavior as it unfolds, but they run the risk of influencing the behavior they are observing.

Naturalistic Observation The famed naturalist Jane Goodall used naturalistic observation (also called a field study) to study the behavior of chimpanzees in Africa.

social desirability bias The tendency to respond to questions in a socially desirable manner.
volunteer bias The type of bias that arises when people who volunteer to participate in a survey or research study have characteristics that make them unrepresentative of the population from which they were drawn.
naturalistic observation method A method of research based on careful observation of behavior in natural settings.

The Correlational Method

Psychologists use the **correlational method** to examine relationships between variables. In Chapter 13, we will read about findings that show a *correlation,* or link, between optimism and outcomes following coronary bypass surgery. That is, patients who hold more optimistic attitudes tend to encounter fewer serious complications following this form of heart surgery than do less optimistic patients. In Chapter 9, we will find that maternal smoking during pregnancy is correlated with an increased risk of sudden infant death syndrome (SIDS) in babies.

A **correlation coefficient** is a statistical measure of association between two variables. Correlation coefficients can vary from -1.00 to +1.00. Coefficients with a positive sign reflect a positive correlation, in which higher values in one variable are associated with higher values in the other variable (e.g., the higher the level of stress, the greater the likelihood of depression). A negative correlation, which is denoted by a negative sign, means the reverse: Higher values in one variable are associated with lower values in the other. For example, level of education is negatively correlated with violent crime. The higher the correlation coefficient (the closer it is to -1.00 or +1.00), the stronger the relationship is.

Correlations are useful because they allow us to predict one variable on the basis of the other. A perfect correlation of +1.00 or -1.00 allows us to predict with certainty. Let's say we discovered a perfect correlation between certain genetic characteristics and the likelihood of developing a particular disease. Knowing that you possessed those genetic characteristics would allow us to know with certainty whether you will develop the disease. However, virtually all relationships, especially those of interest to psychologists, are less than perfect (varying between 0.00 and either +1.00 or –1.00). For example, while intelligence is correlated with academic achievement, not everyone with a high score on intelligence tests succeeds in school. A zero correlation means that there is no relationship between the two variables, that one variable is useless in predicting the other.

You may have heard the expression "correlation is not causation." *The fact that two variables are correlated, even highly correlated, doesn't mean that one causes the other.* For example, shoe size in children correlates strongly with vocabulary. While you may argue that some people seem to have more smarts in their little toes than others have in their whole brains, I don't think you'd argue that a growing foot causes vocabulary to expand. Rather, shoe size and vocabulary are correlated because older children tend to have larger feet and a larger vocabulary than younger children. Though the correlational method is limited in terms of specifying underlying causes, it has several benefits:

- *It offers clues to underlying causes.* Though correlational relationships cannot determine cause-and-effect relationships, they may point to possible causal factors that can be followed up in experimental research. For example, evidence of a correlation between smoking and lung cancer led to experimental studies with animals that showed that exposure to cigarette smoke induced the formation of cancerous lesions in the lungs.

- *It can identify groups of people at high risk for physical or behavioral problems.* Knowing that a relationship exists between the positive expectancies of adolescents toward alcohol use and the later development of problem drinking may

CONCEPT 1.29

With the correlational method, we can examine how variables are related to each other but cannot determine cause-and-effect relationships.

Are Your Brains in Your Feet? Though shoe size and vocabulary size are correlated in children, we should not infer that the size of a child's foot determines his or her vocabulary.

 *web.* **Netlab/Connect the Dots**

 *web.* **Web Tutorial/Correlations**

correlational method   A research method that examines relationships between variables.

correlation coefficient   A statistical measure of association between variables that can vary from –1.00 to +1.00.

THINK

About It

Correlation Is Not Causation

Can you think of examples in which two variables are correlated but not causally related?

CONCEPT 1.30

With the experimental method, researchers can explore cause-and-effect relationships by directly manipulating some variables and observing their effects on other variables under controlled conditions.

web Web Tutorial/Experiments

experimental method   A method of scientific investigation involving the manipulation of independent variables and observation or measurement of their effects on dependent variables under controlled conditions.

independent variables   Factors that are manipulated in an experiment.

dependent variables   The effects or outcomes of an experiment that are believed to be dependent on the values of the independent variables.

control groups   Groups of participants in a research experiment who do not receive the experimental treatment or intervention.

random assignment   A method of randomly assigning subjects to experimental or control groups.

placebo   An inert substance or experimental condition that resembles the active treatment.

placebo effects   Positive outcomes of an experiment resulting from the subjects' positive expectations rather than from the experimental treatment.

direct us toward developing alcoholism prevention efforts that focus on changing attitudes of youngsters before drinking problems arise.

- *It increases understanding of relationships between variables or events.* Such an understanding is one of the major objectives of science. From time to time in this text, we explore such relationships. For example, in Chapter 7 we look at the relationships between gender and mathematical and verbal abilities, and in Chapters 11 and 13 we explore whether stress is related not only to psychological disorders but also to physical illness.

The Experimental Method

With the **experimental method**, investigators directly explore cause-and-effect relationships by manipulating certain variables, called **independent variables**, and observing their effects on certain *measured* variables, called **dependent variables**. The dependent variables are so called because they are thought to depend on the independent, or manipulated, variable. Experimenters attempt to hold constant all other factors or conditions to ensure that the independent variable alone is the cause of the observed changes in the dependent variables.

Consider an experiment that examined whether the popularity of women's names affects judgments of their physical attractiveness. The experimenter paired women's photographs with either a currently popular name, such as Jessica, Jennifer, or Christine, or a traditional name that had fallen out of favor, such as Harriet, Gertrude, and Ethel (Garwood et al., 1980). You may not be surprised that the women who were assigned popular names were rated as more attractive than the women who were given out-of-fashion names. The experimenter controlled the *independent variable* (type of name) by assigning popular or old-fashioned names to women's photographs and measured the effects of the independent variable on the *dependent variable* (ratings of attractiveness).

Experimenters typically use **control groups** to ensure that the effects of an independent variable are not due to other factors, such as the passage of time. For example, in a study examining the effects of alcohol intake on aggressive behavior, the experimental group would receive a dose of alcohol but the control group would not. The investigator would then observe whether the group given alcohol showed more aggressive behavior in a laboratory task than the control group.

In well-designed studies, experimenters use **random assignment** to place participants randomly in experimental groups or control groups. Random assignment balances experimental and control groups in terms of the background and personality characteristics of the people who comprise the groups. This method of assignment gives us confidence that differences between groups in how they perform on dependent measures are due to the independent variable or variables and not to the characteristics of the people making up the groups (Ioannidis et al., 2001). However, random assignment is not always feasible or ethically responsible. For example, ethical experimenters would never randomly assign children to be exposed to abuse or neglect to see what effects these experiences might have on their development. They may rely on correlational methods to examine these relationships even though such methods do not necessarily determine cause and effect.

Experimenters may wish to keep research participants and themselves in the dark concerning which groups receive which treatments. In drug studies, subjects are typically assigned to receive either an active drug or a **placebo**—an inert pill, or "sugar pill," made to resemble the active drug (Charney et al., 2002; Kaptchuk, Eisenberg, & Komaroff, 2002). The purpose is to control for **placebo effects**—positive outcomes that reflect a person's hopeful expectancies rather than the chemical properties of the drug itself (Kirsch, 2004). If you took an antibiotic drug that would have no effect on your condition for twenty-four hours, but didn't know that and began feeling better an hour after taking it, you may have been experiencing a placebo effect. Placebos tend to have stronger effects on subjective feelings of distress or pain than on medical conditions that can be objectively measured, such as blood pressure (Bailar, 2001; Hrobjartsson & Gotzsche, 2001).

In drug studies, experimenters attempt to control for expectancy effects by preventing research participants from knowing whether they are receiving the active drug or a placebo. In **single-blind studies**, only the participants are kept in the dark. In **double-blind studies**, both the participants and the experimenters (prescribing physicians and other researchers) are "blinded" (kept uninformed) with respect to which participants are receiving the active drug. Keeping the experimenters "blind" helps prevent their own expectancies from affecting the results.

Unfortunately, the "blinds" in many double-blind studies are more like Venetian blinds with the slats slightly open; that is, participants and experimenters may be able to guess correctly whether they are receiving a placebo or an active drug (Kirsch et al., 2002; Mooney, White, & Hatsukami, 2004). Often, the active drugs have telltale side effects that give them away. Still, when conducted properly, double-blind, randomized studies are an important means of evaluating the effectiveness of new medications (Leber, 2000; Leon, 2000).

Anatomy of a Research Study: To Shoot or Not to Shoot?

Do you consider yourself prejudiced? Perhaps not, but the results of a recent study may lead you to consider whether your behavior, like those of the college students in the study, may be influenced by stereotypes you might consciously reject. Stereotypes are discussed further in Chapter 14, but here let us note that they are generalized beliefs that members of particular groups or categories, such as people of a particular gender or ethnicity, share certain common characteristics.

Social psychologists simulated the type of situation faced by police officers who must make split-second decisions about whether to use their weapons in ambiguous situations—situations in which someone facing them may be holding a gun or merely an object resembling a gun (Correll et al., 2002). The scenario modeled a real-life tragedy in 1999 in which New York City police officers searching for a rape suspect fired upon and killed an unarmed 22-year-old West African immigrant, Amadou Diallo. The police officers observed the man reaching into his pocket and believed he was reaching for a gun. The "gun" turned out to be his wallet.

In a series of experiments, investigators used a specialized videogame designed to simulate the situation in which a police officer is confronted with an ambiguous but potentially dangerous figure and must decide to shoot or not to shoot. The question was, Would the ethnicity or race of a target figure make a difference in the decision to shoot? Here we go under the hood and examine the workings of the first of these studies.

Study Hypothesis (What They Predicted Would Occur)

A hypothesis is a predicted outcome, but it is far from a wild guess. Hypotheses are informed by a careful review of theory and prior research. Based on current theories of stereotyping, the investigators hypothesized that race would be a determining factor in the decision to shoot or not shoot a target.

Procedure (What They Did and How They Did It)

Upon arriving at the laboratory, the participants were met by a male experimenter who briefly described the study as an investigation of perceptual vigilance, the ability to monitor and respond quickly to a variety of stimuli. Detailed instructions were then given for completing the experimental task, which involved

TRY THIS OUT

Getting Involved

You can learn about psychological research first-hand by volunteering as a research subject or a research assistant. Most psychology departments provide opportunities for students to participate in faculty research as subjects, research assistants, or both. Ask your instructor or department chairperson about how you can participate in the department's research activities. Serving as a research assistant will provide you with a front-row view of cutting-edge developments in the field and with opportunities to obtain valuable research experience, which you may need when applying for jobs or admission to graduate school.

single-blind studies   In drug research, studies in which subjects are kept uninformed about whether they are receiving the experimental drug or a placebo.

double-blind studies   In drug research, studies in which both participants and experimenters are kept uninformed about which participants are receiving the active drug and which are receiving the placebo.

playing a particular videogame. The participants were also informed that monetary prizes of $30, $20, and $10 would be given to the people receiving the highest score and the next two highest scores, respectively, and that five additional prizes would be distributed randomly to those scoring in the top 30 percent. The purpose of the prizes was to motivate participants to perform their best.

Participants were told that when an armed target appeared on a screen, they should act as though they were in imminent danger and to shoot the target as quickly as possible. But they were not to shoot at unarmed targets. To "shoot" a target, they needed to press a button labeled "shoot." They were to press another button labeled "don't shoot" if the target was unarmed. They had to make the decision to shoot or not shoot as quickly as possible once the target appeared. Targets were shown for a brief duration that varied randomly from 500 to 1,000 milliseconds. The targets were presented in a slide-show fashion against the different backgrounds. From the perspective of the participants, the target seemed to simply appear on the background.

Participants were instructed to use separate hands for each button and to rest their hands on a center console between trials. They received a designated number of points for correctly shooting an armed target and lost penalty points for incorrectly shooting an unarmed target or failing to shoot an armed target. Participants received 10 points for a "hit" (correctly shooting an armed target) and 5 points for a "nonshoot" (not shooting an unarmed target). The penalty points were structured to mimic the motivation of police officers on the street by assessing the highest penalty (loss of 40 points) for failing to protect themselves in a potential life-or-death situation by failing to shoot an armed target. Making the mistake of shooting an innocent suspect (unarmed target) was assessed 20 points. Failing to respond within the designated time interval resulted in a timed-out penalty of 10 points.

Results and Discussion
(What They Found and What It Means)

Statistical analyses were performed on two dependent measures, *reaction time* (time interval from presentation of stimulus target to response) and *error rate* (proportion of errors in relation to total number of trials). Errors were defined as failures to shoot an armed target and shooting an unarmed target.

The most important finding was that reaction times depended on a combination of object type (target armed vs. unarmed) and race of target (African American vs. White). Participants fired more quickly when an armed target was African American than when an armed target was White. Participants also responded more quickly in deciding *not to shoot* an unarmed target when the target was White than when the target was African American (see Figure 1.8). Pause over that finding and consider how you might explain these results.

The error rate was quite low, about 4 percent overall. The results on accuracy were not strong enough to lead to any firm conclusions. So the investigators conducted a second study to replicate and extend the results of the first study. They made the decision task more difficult by shortening the amount of time they gave the participants to respond. In the second experiment, the investigators found that participants were more likely to mistakenly shoot an unarmed African American figure than an unarmed White figure.

Taken together, these results support the existence of a "shooter bias"—that is, a tendency to respond more quickly to shoot an armed African American target than an armed White target and to err more often by shooting an unarmed African American than an unarmed White. These errors of omission (failing to shoot an armed assailant) and commission (shooting an innocent person) can have tragic results for a police officer in the first case and an innocent civilian in the second.

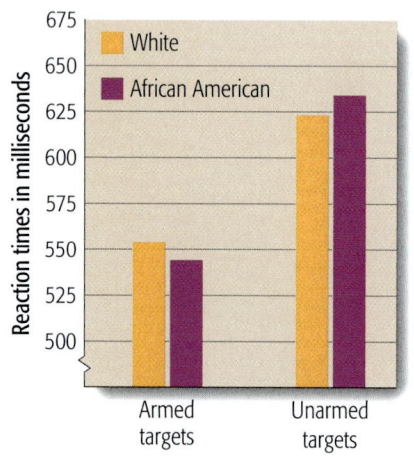

Figure 1.8   Reaction Times in Police Officer's Dilemma Study
Response times were shorter for armed targets when the target was African American than when the target was White. The reverse was the case when the target was unarmed. Do you think your responses would be affected by race?

Source: Adapted from Correll et al., 2002.

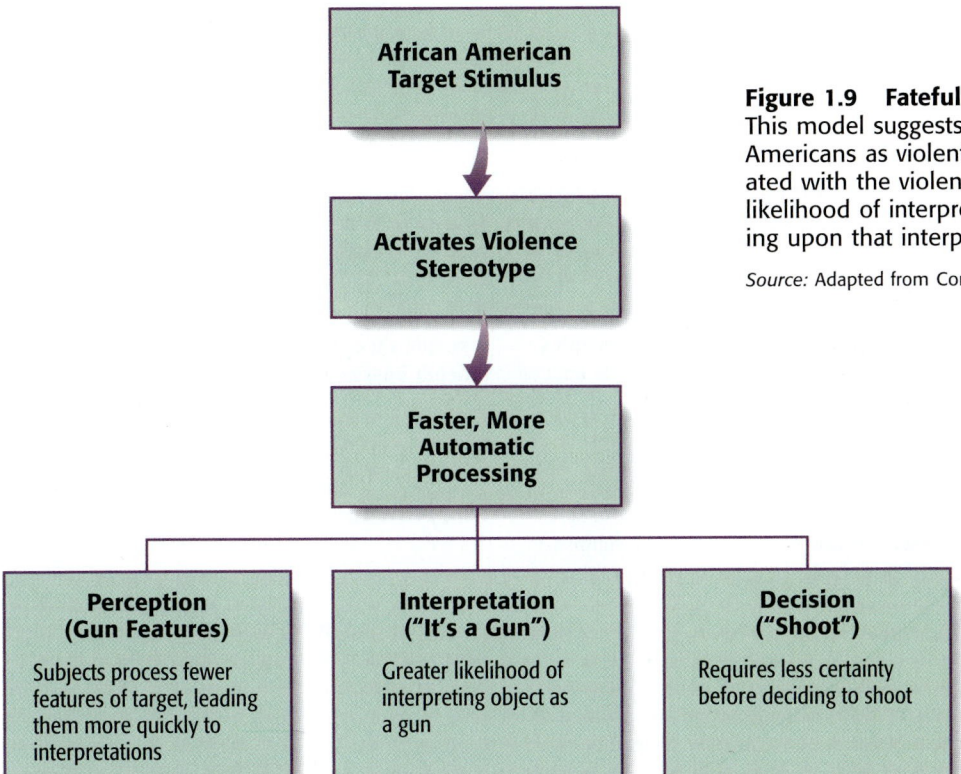

Figure 1.9   Fateful Decisions: The Role of Stereotyping
This model suggests that activating the stereotype of African Americans as violent leads to faster processing of stimuli associated with the violence stereotype. Consequently there is a greater likelihood of interpreting an ambiguous object as a gun and acting upon that interpretation by deciding to shoot.

Source: Adapted from Correll et al., 2002.

None of the participants in these first two studies were African American. But a "shooter bias" was also found in a diverse sample in a subsequent study that included African American participants. The investigators believe that the constant barrage of images in the popular media depicting African Americans in violent roles reinforces the cultural stereotype of African Americans as violent. Once the violence stereotype is activated, it leads to a greater likelihood of interpreting an object as a gun when it is in the hands of an African American (see Figure 1.9).

Does a "shooter bias" exist among trained police officers? We don't yet know, but future research may give us the answer. If a bias does exist, might specialized police training programs help reduce or eliminate it? Again, we must await future research. As the investigators concluded, social-psychological theory and research may prove invaluable in the effort to identify, understand, and eventually control processes that bias decisions to shoot (and possibly kill) a person as a function of his or her ethnicity (Correll et al., 2002).

Citing References

Psychologists use a particular style for citing references that was developed by the American Psychological Association. Here is the reference style for journal articles, using the Correll et al. study as an example:

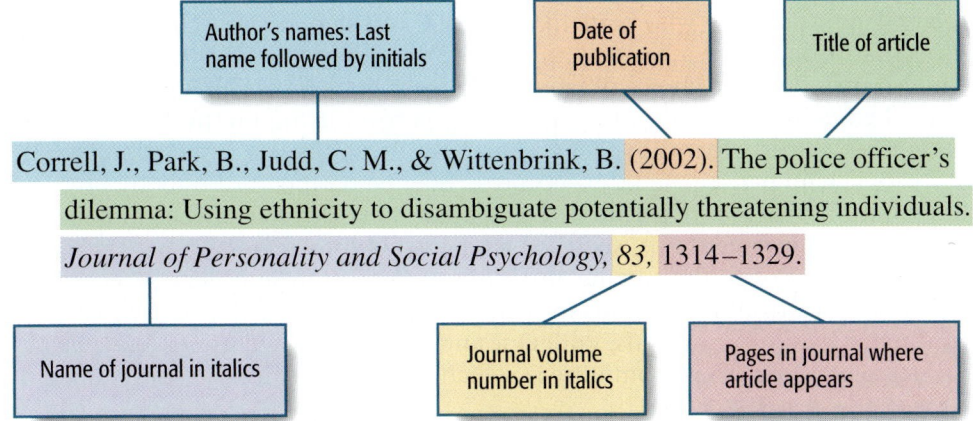

CONCEPT CHART 1.3
How Psychologists Do Research

What Researchers Do	Comments	Approaches to Research Questions About Love
In the **case study method**, the researcher interviews or observes an individual (or small group of individuals) or examines historical records of the lives of particular individuals.	The accuracy of case studies may be jeopardized by gaps or errors in people's memories or by their efforts to make a favorable impression on the researcher.	A psychologist interested in the reasons people choose their mates might conduct in-depth interviews with several married persons.
In the **survey method**, the researcher uses questionnaires or interviews to obtain information about a particular group of people.	Psychologists may use surveys to explore the attitudes of thousands of people about such topics as abortion, premarital sex, or leisure pursuits. Results of surveys may be compromised by volunteer bias and other problems.	Psychologists might survey thousands of individuals about the characteristics of the people they have chosen as mates.
In the **naturalistic observation method**, the researcher observes behavior in the field— that is, where it occurs naturally.	Psychologists attempt not to interfere with the behaviors they are observing. They may spend considerable time allowing their research participants to become accustomed to them before they begin their observations.	Psychologists might observe from a distance how lovers walk together and how they look at each other.
In the **correlational method**, the researcher uses statistical methods to reveal and describe positive and negative relationships (correlations) between variables.	This method may suggest the presence of cause and effect, but it does not demonstrate it. The degree to which variables are statistically associated is expressed as a correlation coefficient, which varies from −1.00 to +1.00.	Psychologists might study relationships between feelings of love, self-esteem, and sexual satisfaction.
In the **experimental method**, the psychologist manipulates one or more independent variables (makes changes in the participants' environments) and observes their effects on one or more dependent (measured) variables. Experiments are conducted to establish cause-and-effect relationships between independent and dependent variables.	Participants in experimental groups receive an experimental treatment; those in control groups do not. All other conditions are held constant to ensure that the independent variable alone is the cause of the observed effects. Random assignment to groups helps ensure that groups do not differ in characteristics that might affect the outcome.	Psychologists might expose dating partners to an experimental treatment in which they share an arousing experience, such as watching an emotionally powerful movie, and then measure the treatment's effects on the partners' feelings toward each other. (The control group would be exposed to a neutral movie.)

Concept Chart 1.3 summarizes the research methods we have discussed.

Ethical Principles in Psychological Research

CONCEPT 1.31
Psychologists engaged in research must follow ethical guidelines that are designed to protect the welfare of research participants.

Psychologists subscribe to a code of ethics that respects the dignity and welfare of their clients and those who participate in their research studies. This code recognizes that people have a basic right to make their own decisions and to exercise choices, including the choice of whether to participate in psychological research. Ethical guidelines also prohibit psychologists from using methods that would harm research participants or clients (American Psychological Association, 2002).

People who participate in experiments may be harmed not only by physical interventions, such as experimental drugs that have adverse effects, but also by psychological interventions, such as being goaded into aggressive behavior that leads to feelings of guilt or shame. Invasions of privacy are another concern.

Today, nearly all institutions in which biomedical and behavioral research is conducted, such as hospitals, colleges, and research foundations, have **ethics review committees**. These committees, which are usually composed of profession-

ethics review committees Committees that evaluate whether proposed studies meet ethical guidelines.

als and laypersons, must put their stamp of approval on all research proposals before the research can be carried out at their institutions. The committees review the proposals to see if they comply with ethical guidelines and advise the researchers concerning the potential harm of their proposed methods. In cases where individuals may experience harm or discomfort, the committees must weigh the potential benefits of the research against the potential harm. If the committees believe that the proposed research might be unacceptably harmful, they would withhold approval.

One of the foremost ethical requirements is that investigators obtain **informed consent** from research participants before they begin participating in the study. This means that participants must be given enough information about the study's methods and purposes to make an "informed" decision about whether they wish to participate. Participants must also be free to withdraw from the study at any time.

Many studies of historic importance in psychology, including the famous Milgram studies on obedience to authority (see Chapter 14), have required that subjects be deceived as to the true purposes of the study. The APA's *Ethical Principles of Psychologists and Code of Conduct* (American Psychological Association, 2002) specifies the conditions that psychologists must meet to use deceptive practices in research. These conditions include a determination that the research is justified by its scientific, educational, or practical value; that no nondeceptive alternative research strategy is possible;that research participants are not misled about any research that can reasonably be expected to result in physical harm or severe emotional distress; and that participants receive an explanation of the deception at the earliest time that it is feasible to do so.

Psychologists must also maintain the *confidentiality* of the records of research participants and of the clients they treat. That is, they must respect people's right to privacy. There are times, however, when societal laws require that psychologists disclose confidential information acquired through the course of research or clinical practice, as when a participant or a client in therapy threatens to do physical harm to someone else.

Ethical guidelines also extend to the use of animals in psychological research. The design of research projects often precludes the use of human participants, and in such cases the researchers use animals as subjects. For example, to determine which behaviors are instinctive and which are not, scientists have reared birds and fish in isolation from other members of their species; such research could not be conducted with humans because of the harmful effects of separating infants from their families. Scientists routinely test experimental drugs on animals to determine harmful effects before human trials are begun. And those who study the brain may destroy parts of the brains of laboratory animals, such as rats and monkeys, to learn how these parts of the brain are connected with behavior. (In Chapter 8, you will see how destruction of different parts of the brain cause laboratory animals to either overeat or stop eating completely.)

Issues concerning the ethical treatment of animals in research studies have risen to the fore in recent years. On one side of the debate are those who argue that significant advances in medicine and psychology could not have occurred without such research (Fowler, 1992). Yet recent polls find that most psychologists believe it is unethical to kill animals or expose them to pain, regardless of the potential benefits of the research to humans (Plous, 1996). According to APA ethical guidelines, animals may not be harm or subjected to stress unless there is no alternative way to conduct the research and the goals of the research are justified by their intended scientific, educational, or practical value (APA, 2002). Researchers must also obtain approval from their institutional review boards to ensure that ethical practices are followed.

informed consent Agreement to participate in a study following disclosure of information about the purposes and nature of the study and its potential risks and benefits.

MODULE 1.3 REVIEW

Research Methods in Psychology

CONCEPT CHECK

1. Which of the following is *not* one of the four general steps in the scientific method?
   a. developing a research question
   b. testing the hypothesis
   c. using the case study method as a starting point of investigation
   d. drawing conclusions

2. A distinct advantage of the naturalistic observation method, when used correctly, is that it
   a. allows us to establish cause-and-effect relationships.
   b. does not require experimenters to follow ethical guidelines governing other forms of research.
   c. allows us to generate hypotheses on the basis of intensive study of a person's life experiences.
   d. provides a view of behavior that occurs in natural settings.

3. Which research method is best suited to providing evidence of cause-and-effect relationships?

4. Ethical guidelines in psychological research
   a. provide a set of rules that govern research when obtaining approval from ethics review committees would cause critical delays in a project.
   b. are designed to protect research participants from physical or psychological harm.
   c. permit researchers to violate the principle of informed consent when experiments cannot be performed in accordance with that principle.
   d. are a set of standards that apply to human research but not animal research.

APPLICATION

MODULE 1.4 Becoming a Critical Thinker

- **What are the key features of critical thinking?**

💡 **CONCEPT 1.32**
Critical thinking involves adopting a skeptical, questioning attitude toward commonly held beliefs and assumptions and weighing arguments in terms of the available evidence.

Critical thinking involves adopting a questioning attitude, in which we weigh evidence carefully and apply thoughtful analysis in probing the claims and arguments of others. It is a way of evaluating information by maintaining a skeptical attitude toward what you hear and read, even what you read in the pages of this text.

Critical thinking requires a willingness to challenge conventional wisdom and common knowledge that many of us take for granted. When you think critically, you maintain an open mind and suspend belief until you can obtain and evaluate evidence that either supports or refutes a particular claim or statement. You find *reasons* to support your beliefs, rather than relying on impressions or "gut feelings." In this text, you'll be able to hone your critical thinking skills by answering the questions posed in the "Thinking Critically About Psychology" sections, which appear at the end of every chapter.

Features of Critical Thinking

Critical thinkers maintain a healthy skepticism. They question assumptions and claims made by others and demand to see the evidence upon which conclusions are based. Here are some suggestions for thinking critically about psychology (adapted from Nevid, Rathus, & Rubinstein, 1998):

1. *Question everything.* Critical thinkers do not blindly accept the validity of claims made by others, even claims made by authority figures, such as politi-

critical thinking The adoption of a skeptical, questioning attitude and careful scrutiny of claims or arguments.

cal or religious leaders, scientists, or even textbook authors. They keep an open mind and weigh the evidence upon which claims are made.

2. *Clarify what you mean.* Whether a claim is true or false may depend on how we define the terms we use. Consider the claim "Stress is bad for you." If we define stress only in terms of the pressures and hassles of daily life, then perhaps there is some truth to that claim. But if we define stress more broadly to include any events that impose a pressure on us to adjust, even positive events like the birth of a child or a promotion at work, then certain kinds of stress may actually be desirable (see Chapter 13). Perhaps we even need a certain amount of stress to be active and alert.

3. *Avoid oversimplifying.* Consider the claim "Alcoholism is inherited." In Chapter 4, we review evidence indicating that genetic factors may contribute to alcoholism. But the origins of alcoholism, as well as the origins of many other psychological and physical disorders, are more complex. Genetics alone does not tell the whole story. Many disorders involve the interplay of biological, psychological, and environmental factors, the nature of which we are only beginning to unravel.

4. *Avoid overgeneralizing.* People from China and Japan and other East Asian cultures tend to be more reserved about disclosing information about themselves to strangers than are Americans or Europeans (see Chapter 14). Yet this doesn't mean that every person from these East Asian cultures is more withholding or that every American or European is more disclosing.

5. *Don't confuse correlation with causation.* As you'll see in Chapter 9, girls who show earlier signs of puberty than their peers (e.g., early breast development) tend to have lower self-esteem, a more negative body image, and more emotional problems. But do physical changes associated with early puberty cause these negative psychological consequences, or might other factors be involved in explaining these links, such as how people react to these changes?

6. *Consider the assumptions upon which claims are based.* Consider the claim that homosexuality is a psychological disorder. The claim rests in part on underlying assumptions about the nature of psychological disorders. What is a psychological disorder? What criteria are used to determine whether someone has a psychological disorder? Do gays, lesbians, or people with a bisexual sexual orientation meet these criteria? Is there evidence to support these assertions? In Chapter 11, you will see that mental health professionals no longer classify homosexuality as a psychological disorder.

7. *Examine sources of claims.* In their publications, scientists cite the sources on which they base their claims. (See this book's reference list, which cites the sources used in its preparation.) When examining source citations, note such features as publication dates (to determine whether the sources are outdated or current) and the journals or other periodicals in which the sources may have appeared (to see whether they are well-respected scientific journals or questionable sources). Source citations allow readers to check the original sources for themselves to see if the information provided is accurate.

8. *Question the evidence upon which claims are based.* Are claims based on sound scientific evidence or on anecdotes and personal testimonials that cannot be independently verified? In Chapter 6, we consider the controversy over so-called recovered memories—memories of childhood sexual abuse that suddenly reappear during adulthood, usually during the course of psychotherapy or hypnosis. Are such memories accurate? Or might they be tales spun of imaginary thread?

9. *Consider alternative ways of explaining claims.* Do you believe in the existence of extrasensory perception (ESP)? Some people claim to have extrasensory skills that enable them, simply by using their minds, to read other people's minds, to transmit their thoughts to others, or to move objects or change their shapes. Are such claims believable? Or might more mundane explanations account for these strange phenomena, such as coincidence, deliberate fabrication, or sleight-of-hand? In Chapter 3, we consider the case of a psychic who claims to have relied on her extrasensory ability in finding a missing person. Was it ESP? Or might there be other explanations?

Thinking Critically About Online Information

One of the beauties of the Internet is that any user can post information that others can access. Yet this freedom carries with it the risk that the information posted may be inaccurate (Eysenbach et al., 2003). A recent study found that online health information was generally accurate, but it was often incomplete and difficult for many people to understand (Berland et al., 2001; Hilts, 2001). Yet the Internet may be an effective vehicle for disseminating information that may not be accessible through other sources, such as information young people can use to arm themselves with skills to prevent sexually transmitted diseases (Keller & Brown, 2002).

Critical thinkers don't suspend their skeptical attitude when they go online. They check out the credentials of the source by asking questions like these: Who is posting the material? Is the source a well-respected institution? Or is it an individual or group of individuals with no apparent credentials and perhaps with an axe to grind?

The most trustworthy online information comes from well-known scientific sources, such as leading scientific journals, government agencies like the National Institutes of Health, and major professional organizations like the American

Critical Thinking Adopt a skeptical attitude when using the Internet. Check out the credibility of the source of the material and be wary of information provided by companies or marketers seeking to promote or sell particular products or services.

Psychological Association and the American Psychological Society. One reason articles in scientific journals are so trustworthy is that they undergo a process of peer review in which independent scientists carefully scrutinize them before they are accepted for publication. Many leading scientific organizations provide links to abstracts (brief descriptions) of recent works. Much of this information is available without charge.

Sad to say, many people never question the information that comes to them on the printed page or on their computer screens. But as a critical thinker, you *can* evaluate assertions and claims for yourself. The critical thinking sections found at the end of each chapter will give you an opportunity to sharpen your critical thinking skills.

Another caution about Internet use is advised for students who are concerned about their grades. Recent evidence from a survey of college students showed that students who were heavier recreational users of the Internet were more likely than lighter users to report that their Internet use had hurt their academic performance (Kubey, Lavin, & Barrows, 2001). The link between heavy Internet use and poorer academic performance was much stronger for Internet use involving chat rooms and MUDs (a form of fantasy game playing called *Multiple User Dungeons*) than for email or newsgroups.

TYING IT TOGETHER

We began our study by focusing on the foundations of psychology as an organized field of study (Module 1.1). The early psychologists were all experimentalists, but as psychology matured as a profession it embraced a wider range of specialties. Today, it is a diverse discipline because of these many specialties and because of the diverse roles psychologists perform as researchers, teachers, and clinicians. Over time, it has also become more representative of the gender and ethnic diversity of the larger society (Module 1.2). At its core, psychology is a scientific discipline, and psychologists apply scientific methods in studying behavior and mental processes (Module 1.3). Psychologists are trained to be critical thinkers who are skeptical of claims and arguments not grounded in evidence. We, too, can learn to think critically by maintaining a skeptical, questioning attitude and examining claims in light of the evidence (Module 1.4).

SUMMING UP: Q & A

Foundations of Modern Psychology (Module 1.1)

What is psychology?

- Psychology is the science of behavior and mental processes.

What are the origins of psychology?

- Though systematic attempts to explain human behavior can be traced to philosophers in ancient times, psychology emerged as a scientific discipline in the nineteenth century with Wundt's founding of the first psychological laboratory in Leipzig, Germany in 1879.

What were the major early schools of psychology?

- Structuralism is the earliest school of psychology. It was identified with Wilhelm Wundt and Edward Titchener, and it attempted to break down mental experiences into their component parts—sensations, perceptions, and feelings.
- Functionalism is the school of psychology founded by William James. It attempts to explain our behavior in terms of the functions it serves in helping us adapt to the environment.
- Behaviorism is the school of psychology begun by James Watson. It holds that psychology should limit itself to observable phenomena—namely, behavior.
- Gestalt psychology is the school of psychology founded by Max Wertheimer. It is grounded in the belief that the brain structures our perceptions of the world in terms of organized patterns or wholes.
- Psychoanalysis, the school of thought originated by Sigmund Freud, emphasizes the role of unconscious motives and conflicts in determining human behavior.

What are the major contemporary perspectives in psychology?

- The behavioral perspective focuses on observable behavior and the influences of learning processes in behavior.
- The psychodynamic perspective represents the model of psychology developed by Freud and his followers. It holds that our behavior and personalities are shaped by unconscious motives and conflicts that lie outside the range of ordinary awareness.
- The humanistic perspective reflects the views of humanistic psychologists such as Carl Rogers and Abraham Maslow, who emphasized the importance of subjective conscious experience and personal freedom and responsibility.
- The physiological perspective examines the ways in which behavior and mental experience are influenced by biological processes such as heredity, hormones, and the workings of the brain and other parts of the nervous system.
- The cognitive perspective focuses on mental processes that allow us to gain knowledge about ourselves and the world.
- The sociocultural perspective examines how our behavior and attitudes are shaped by social and cultural influences.

Psychologists: Who They Are and What They Do (Module 1.2)

What are the various specialties in psychology?

- These include major subfields such as clinical and counseling psychology, school psychology, and experimental psychology, as well as emerging specialty areas such as geropsychology, forensic psychology, and sport psychology.

What changes have occurred in the ethnic and gender characteristics of psychologists over time?

- Though psychology is now a more diverse discipline, African Americans and other minority groups remain underrepresented in the professional ranks of psychologists.
- Unlike the early days of the profession when women were actively excluded from pursuing professional careers, they now comprise about two-thirds of the new Ph.D.s in psychology.

Research Methods in Psychology (Module 1.3)

What is the scientific method, and what are its four general steps?

- The scientific method is a set of guiding principles that directs the scientific process.
- The scientific method comprises four general steps that guide research: (1) developing a research question, (2) formulating a hypothesis, (3) gathering evidence, and (4) drawing conclusions.

What are the major research methods psychologists use?

- These include the case study method, the survey method, the naturalistic observation method, the correlational method, and the experimental method.

What ethical guidelines must psychologists follow in their research?

- Psychologists are committed to following ethical guidelines that promote the dignity of the individual, human welfare, and scientific integrity.
- Psychologists are precluded from using methods that harm research participants or clients and must receive approval of their research protocols from institutional review committees before undertaking research with humans or animals.

Application: Becoming a Critical Thinker (Module 1.4)

What are the key features of critical thinking?

- The key features of critical thinking include adoption of a questioning attitude, clarifying what you mean, avoiding oversimplification and overgeneralization, distinguishing correlation from causation, considering the assumptions or premises upon which arguments are based, examining sources, questioning evidence upon which claims are made, and considering alternative explanations of a given set of findings.

Key Terms

psychology *(p. 4)*
introspection *(p. 5)*
structuralism *(p. 6)*
functionalism *(p. 6)*
behaviorism *(p. 6)*
Gestalt psychology *(p. 7)*
gestalt *(p. 7)*
unconscious *(p. 8)*
psychodynamic perspective *(p. 8)*
psychoanalysis *(p. 8)*
behavioral perspective *(p. 9)*
social-cognitive theory *(p. 9)*
behavior therapy *(p. 9)*
humanistic psychology *(p. 10)*
humanistic perspective *(p. 10)*
physiological perspective *(p. 10)*
evolutionary psychology *(p. 10)*
cognitive perspective *(p. 11)*
sociocultural perspective *(p. 11)*
positive psychology *(p. 12)*
basic research *(p. 14)*
applied research *(p. 14)*
experimental psychologists *(p. 15)*
comparative psychologists *(p. 15)*
physiological psychologists *(p. 15)*

clinical psychologists *(p. 15)*
psychiatrists *(p. 16)*
counseling psychologists *(p. 17)*
school psychologists *(p. 17)*
educational psychologists *(p. 17)*
developmental psychologists *(p. 17)*
personality psychologists *(p. 17)*
social psychologists *(p. 17)*
environmental psychologists *(p. 17)*
industrial/organizational (I/O) psychologists *(p. 17)*
health psychologists *(p. 18)*
consumer psychologists *(p. 18)*
neuropsychologists *(p. 18)*
geropsychologists *(p. 18)*
forensic psychologists *(p. 18)*
sport psychologists *(p. 18)*
empirical approach *(p. 21)*
scientific method *(p. 21)*
hypothesis *(p. 21)*
theory *(p. 21)*
statistics *(p. 22)*
variable *(p. 22)*
replication *(p. 22)*
case study method *(p. 23)*

survey method *(p. 23)*
structured interview *(p. 23)*
questionnaire *(p. 23)*
population *(p. 23)*
samples *(p. 23)*
random sampling *(p. 23)*
social desirability bias *(p. 24)*
volunteer bias *(p. 24)*
naturalistic observation method *(p. 24)*
correlational method *(p. 25)*
correlation coefficient *(p. 25)*
experimental method *(p. 26)*
independent variables *(p. 26)*
dependent variables *(p. 26)*
control groups *(p. 26)*
random assignment *(p. 26)*
placebo *(p. 26)*
placebo effects *(p. 26)*
single-blind studies *(p. 27)*
double-blind studies *(p. 27)*
ethics review committees *(p. 30)*
informed consent *(p. 31)*
critical thinking *(p. 32)*

Thinking Critically About Psychology

Here is the first critical thinking exercise you will encounter in this text. Based on your reading of the chapter, answer the following questions. Then, to evaluate your progress in developing critical thinking skills, compare your answers with the sample answers in Appendix A.

An experimenter claims that listening to a professor's lectures while you sleep can help improve your grades. The experimenter based this conclusion on the following data:

The experimenter invited students in a large introductory psychology class to participate in a study in which they would be given audiotapes of the professor's lectures and asked to play them back while they slept. Each of the thirty-six students who agreed to participate received a specially equipped audiotape player. Secured in the machine with tamper-proof sealing tape were recordings of each lecture given in the two weeks before the final examination. The tape player automatically played the

tape two hours after the students went to bed. At other times, the play button was deactivated so that the students could not play the tape.

After the final examination, the experimenter compared the grades of the participating students with those of a group of students selected from the same class who had not participated in the study. The results showed that participating students achieved higher test grades.

1. Do you believe the experimenter's claims are justified? Why or why not?

2. What other factors might account for the observed differences in test scores between the two groups?

3. How might you design the study differently to strengthen the experimenter's conclusion?

Answers to Concept Check Questions

Module 1.1: 1. Wilhelm Wundt; 2. c; 3. behaviorism; 4. b; 5.a.
Module 1.2: 1. Basic, applied; 2. (a) iv, (b) i, (c) ii, (d) iii; 3. a; 4. b.   **Module 1.3:** 1. c; .2. d; 3. experimental method; 4. b.

2

Biological Foundations of Behavior

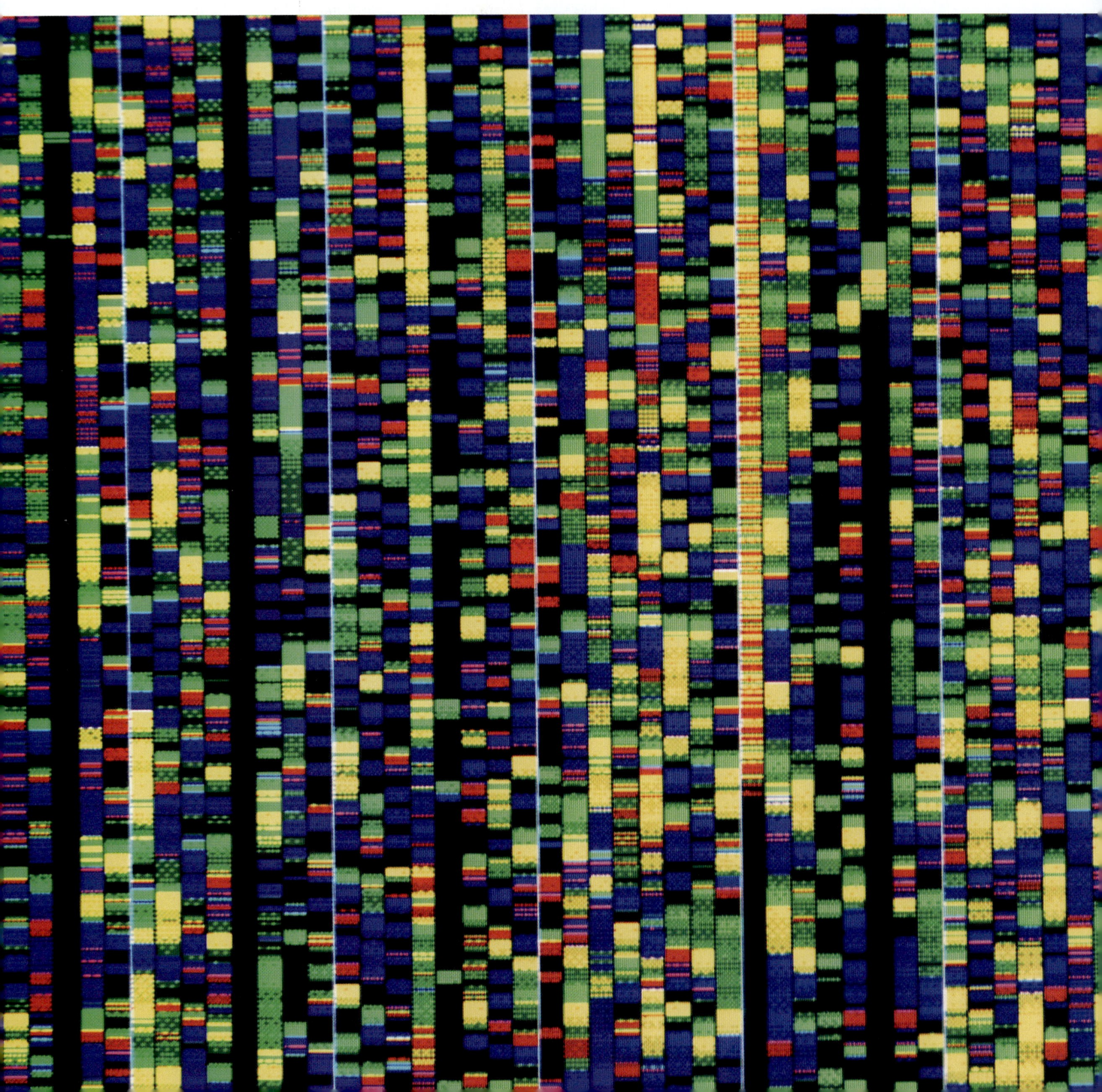

DID YOU KNOW THAT...

- Some cells in your nervous system are more than three feet long? (p. 40)

- Our bodies produce natural painkillers that are chemically similar to morphine and other narcotic drugs? (p. 46)

- Fetuses not only suck their thumbs in the womb, but 95 percent of them suck their right thumbs? (p. 64)

- Though a man survived an accident in which a thick metal rod was driven right through his skull, his personality changed so much that people thought he no longer was himself? (p. 66)

- Both men's and women's bodies produce the male sex hormone testosterone? (p. 70)

- Scientists have deciphered the entire human genetic code and posted it on the Internet? (p. 72)

- Raising the body temperature of a finger may relieve the pain of a migraine headache? (p. 77)

I n *The Man Who Mistook His Wife for a Hat,* neurologist Oliver Sacks (1985) recounts the case of Dr. P, a distinguished music teacher who had lost the ability to recognize objects by sight. Not only was he unable to recognize the faces of his students; he also sometimes perceived faces in objects when none existed. He would pat the fire hydrants and parking meters, believing them to be young children. As Dr. P was preparing to leave Sacks's office after a physical examination, he looked about for his hat, and then

> *reached out his hand, and took hold of his wife's head, tried to lift it off, to put it on. He had apparently mistaken his wife for a hat! His wife looked as if she was used to such things. (Sacks, 1985, p. 10)*

Dr. P's odd behavior may seem amusing in some respects, but his deficits in visual perception were caused by a large tumor in the part of the brain responsible for processing visual information. Perhaps the most remarkable aspect of Dr. P's case was his extraordinary ability to manage many tasks of daily life despite his nearly complete lack of visual perception. He was able to shower, dress himself, and eat meals by using music to coordinate his actions. He would sing various songs to himself to organize his efforts—eating songs and dressing songs, and so on. But when the music stopped, he would lose the ability to make sense of the world. If his dressing song was interrupted, for instance, he would lose his train of thought and be unable to recognize the clothes his wife had laid out for him or even to recognize his own body.

Dr. P's case reveals just how dependent we are on the brain. But it reveals something more—the remarkable capacity of the human brain to adapt to challenges imposed by physical illness or disability. The human brain can be regarded as the most remarkable feat of engineering ever achieved. Weighing a mere three pounds on the average, it is a living supercomputer of far more elegant design than any machine today's Silicon Valley wizards could hope to create. Yes, computers can crank out in a matter of milliseconds a stream of computations that would take teams of the most gifted humans years or even decades to accomplish. But even the most advanced computers lack the capacity for the basic insights and creativity that the human brain can achieve. What computer has written noteworthy music or a decent poem? What computer is aware of itself or aware that it even exists? Such wonders remain the stuff of science fiction.

To perform its many functions, the brain needs to communicate with the senses and other parts of the body. It does so through an information highway that took millions of years to construct. This complex network, of which the brain is a part, is called the *nervous system.*

In this chapter, we take an inward journey of discovery to explore the biological bases of our behavior, thinking processes, and moods. We begin the journey by studying the structure and workings of the fundamental unit of the nervous system—the nerve cell, or *neuron.* We then examine the workings of the two major divisions of the nervous system, the *central nervous system* and the *peripheral nervous system.* Finally, we consider how our behavior is influenced by the endocrine system and heredity. ■

Neurons: The Body's Wiring

- **What is a neuron?**
- **What are the parts of a neuron?**
- **What are the types of neurons and types of cells found in the nervous system?**
- **How is a neural impulse generated and transmitted from one neuron to another?**
- **What roles do neurotransmitters play in psychological functioning?**

Neurons do wondrous things, such as informing your **brain** when light strikes your eye and carrying messages from the brain that command your muscles to raise your arms and your heart to pump blood. They also enable you to think, plan, even to dream. They enable you to read this page and to wonder what will turn up in the next paragraph.

In this module, we first look at the structure of an individual neuron and then observe how neurons communicate with one another to transmit information within the nervous system.

The Structure of the Neuron

Neurons, the basic building blocks of the nervous system, are body cells that are specialized for transmitting information or messages in the form of electrical impulses. Each neuron is a single cell, consisting of a cell body (or *soma*), an axon, and dendrites. Figure 2.1 illustrates these structures; Concept Chart 2.1 summarizes their functions. The **soma** is the main body of the cell. It houses the cell nucleus, which contains the cell's genetic material, and carries out the *metabolic,* or life-sustaining, functions of the cell. Each neuron also has an **axon**, a long cable that projects trunklike from the soma and conducts outgoing messages to other neurons.

The axons of the neurons in your brain may be only a few thousandths of an inch long. Other axons, such as those that run from your spinal cord to your toes, are several feet long. Axons may branch off like the stems of plants, fanning out in different directions. At the ends of these branches are knoblike swellings called **terminal buttons**. It is here that chemicals called **neurotransmitters** are stored and released. These chemicals are synthesized in the soma and ferry outgoing messages to neighboring neurons across the **synapse**, a tiny gap that separates one neuron from another.

Dendrites are treelike structures that project from the soma. Dendrites have receptor sites, or docking stations, that enable them to receive neurotransmitters released by neighboring neurons (Häusser, Spruston, & Stuart, 2000). Through its dendrites, each neuron may receive messages from thousands of other neurons (Kennedy, 2000).

The nervous system has three types of neurons: sensory neurons, motor neurons, and interneurons. These different types play specialized roles in the nervous system.

Sensory neurons (also called *afferent neurons*) transmit information about the outside world to the spinal cord and brain. This information first registers on your sensory organs. So when someone touches your hand, sensory receptors within the skin transmit the message through sensory neurons to the spinal cord and brain, where the information is processed, resulting in the feeling of touch. Sensory neurons also carry information from your muscles and inner organs to your spinal cord and brain.

💡 **CONCEPT 2.1**

Neurons are the basic building blocks of the nervous system—the body's wiring through which messages are transmitted within the nervous system.

---

neurons   Nerve cells.

brain   The mass of nerve tissue encased in the skull that controls virtually everything we are and everything we do.

soma   The cell body of a neuron that contains the nucleus of the cell and carries out the cell's metabolic functions.

axon   The tubelike part of a neuron that carries messages away from the cell body toward other neurons.

terminal buttons   Swellings at the tips of axons from which neurotransmitters are dispatched into the synapse.

neurotransmitters   Chemical messengers that transport nerve impulses from one nerve cell to another.

synapse   The small fluid-filled gap between neurons through which neurotransmitters carry neural impulses.

dendrites   Rootlike structures at the end of axons that receive neural impulses from neighboring neurons.

Figure 2.1   The Neuron

A neuron, or nerve cell, consists of a cell body, or soma, which houses the cell nucleus; an axon, which carries the neural message; and dendrites, which receive messages from adjacent neurons. Terminal buttons are swellings at the end of the axon from which neurotransmitter molecules are released to ferry the message to other neurons. The axons of many neurons are covered with a type of insulating layer, called a myelin sheath, that speeds transmission of neural impulses.

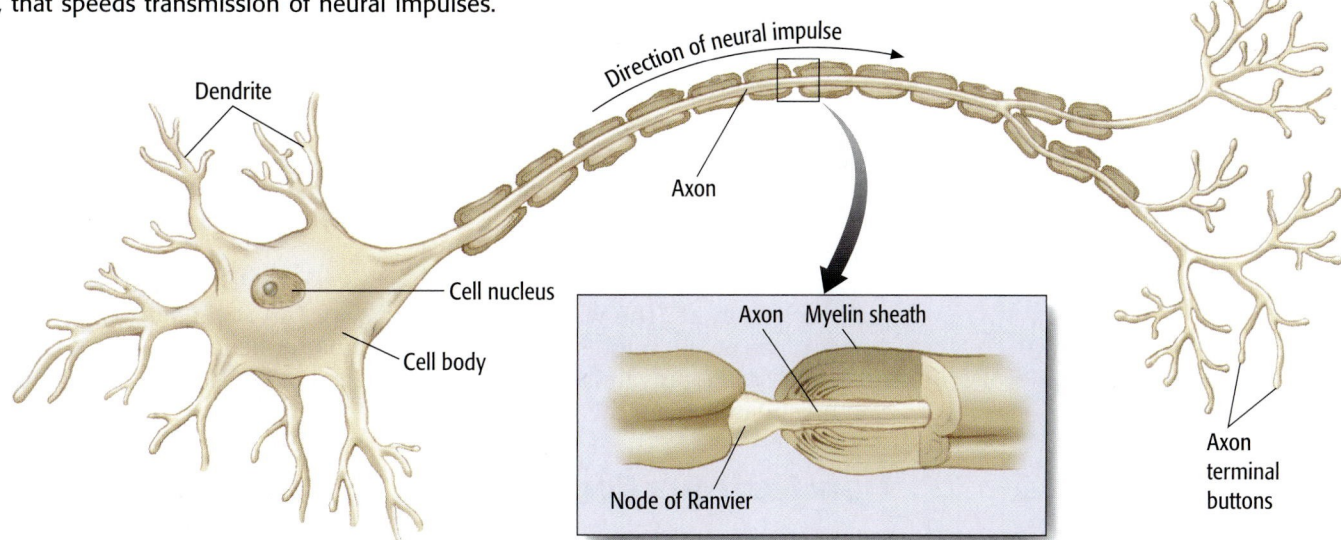

Direction of neural impulse

Dendrite

Axon

Cell nucleus

Cell body

Axon   Myelin sheath

Node of Ranvier

Axon terminal buttons

Motor neurons (also called *efferent neurons*) convey messages from the brain and spinal cord to the muscles that control the movements of your body. They also convey messages to your **glands**, causing them to release **hormones**, chemical substances that help regulate bodily processes.

Interneurons (also called *associative neurons*) are the most common type of neuron in the nervous system. They connect neurons to neurons. In the spinal cord, they connect sensory neurons to motor neurons. In the brain, they form complex assemblages of interconnected nerve cells that process information from sensory organs and control higher mental functions, such as planning and thinking.

A neuron is not the same thing as a nerve. A **nerve** is a bundle of axons from different neurons. An individual nerve—for example, the optic nerve, which transmits messages from the eyes to the brain—contains more than a million axons. Although individual axons are microscopic, a nerve may be visible to the

CONCEPT 2.2

The nervous system has three types of neurons: sensory neurons, motor neurons, and interneurons.

web Netlab/The Neuron Infrastructures of Behavior

CONCEPT CHART 2.1
Parts of the Neuron

Part	Description	Functions
Soma	Cell body containing the nucleus	Performs metabolic, or life-sustaining, functions of the cell
Axon	Long cable projecting from the soma	Carries neural impulses to the terminal buttons
Terminal buttons	Swellings at ends of axons	Release chemicals, called neurotransmitters, that carry neural messages to adjacent neurons
Dendrites	Fibers that project from the soma	Receive messages from neighboring neurons

sensory neurons   Neurons that transmit information from sensory organs, muscles, and inner organs to the spinal cord and brain.

motor neurons   Neurons that convey nerve impulses from the central nervous system to muscles and glands.

glands   Body organs or structures that produce secretions called hormones.

hormones   Secretions from endocrine glands that help regulate bodily processes.

interneurons   Nerve cells within the central nervous system that process information.

nerve   A bundle of axons from different neurons that transmit nerve impulses.

CONCEPT 2.3
The nervous system has two types of cells, neurons and glial cells.

CONCEPT 2.4
Many axons are covered with a protective coating, called a myelin sheath, which speeds the transmission of neural impulses.

web **Web tutorial/The Neuron**

CONCEPT 2.5
The nervous system is a massive communication network that connects billions of neurons throughout your body.

CONCEPT 2.6
A neuron fires when a stimulus triggers electrochemical changes along its cell membrane that lead to a chain reaction within the cell.

glial cells   Small but numerous cells in the nervous system that support neurons and that form the myelin sheath found on many axons.

myelin sheath   A layer of protective insulation that covers the axons of certain neurons and helps speed transmission of nerve impulses.

nodes of Ranvier   Gaps in the myelin sheath that create noninsulated areas along the axon.

ions   Electrically charged chemical particles.

resting potential   The electrical potential across the cell membrane of a neuron in its resting state.

naked eye. The cell bodies of the neurons that contain the axons are not part of the nerve itself.

Neurons are not the only cells found in the nervous system. Far more numerous are **glial cells**. Glial cells are smaller than neurons but account for about 90 percent of the cells in the adult human brain. The word *glial* is derived from the Greek word for "glue." Glial cells act as a kind of glue that helps hold neurons together. They also support the nervous system by nourishing neurons, removing their waste products, and assisting them in communicating with one another (Helmuth, 2001).

Glial cells serve yet another important function: They form the **myelin sheath**, a fatty layer of cells that—like the insulation that wraps around electrical wires—acts as a protective shield on many axons. The insulation provided by the myelin sheath helps speed transmission of neural impulses, which allows muscles to move more efficiently and smoothly.

As shown in Figure 2.1, myelinated axons resemble a string of sausages that are pinched in at "the waist" at various points, creating gaps called **nodes of Ranvier**. The neural impulse appears to jump from node to node as it speeds down the axon. Because myelin sheaths are white, parts of the nervous system that contain myelinated axons are referred to as "white matter."

How Neurons Communicate

The human brain is densely packed with more than one hundred billion neurons, perhaps as many as a trillion or more (Johnson, 1994). From the time we are born, as we begin learning about the world around us, our brains become an increasingly complex network of billions upon billions of interlaced neurons. These complex assemblages of cells form intricate circuits in the brain that allow us to interpret the world around us and respond to external stimuli, as well as to organize our behavior, think, feel, and use language.

Neurons accomplish these tasks by sending messages to one another. Let us break down the process into smaller steps to see how it works.

Both inside and outside the neuron are electrically charged atoms and molecules called **ions**. Like the poles of a battery, ions have either a positive (+) or negative (–) charge. The movements of ions across the cell wall, or *cell membrane,* cause electrochemical changes in the cell that generate an electrical signal to travel down the cell's axon in the form of a neural impulse. The most important ions in this process are two types of positively charged ions, *sodium* ions and *potassium* ions. The movement of ions through the cell membrane is controlled by a series of gates, or tiny doors, that open to allow ions to enter the cell and close to shut them out.

When a neuron is at rest (not being stimulated), the gates that control the passage of sodium ions are closed. A greater concentration of positively charged sodium ions remains outside the cell, causing the cell to have a slightly negative charge, called a **resting potential**, relative to the surrounding fluid. The resting potential of a neuron is about –70 millivolts (mV) (a millivolt is one-thousandth of a volt). Like a charged battery sitting on a shelf, a neuron in the resting state holds a store of potential energy that can be used to generate, or "fire," a neural impulse in response to stimulation. It awaits a source of stimulation that will temporarily reverse the electrical charges within the cell, causing it to fire.

THINK *About It*

A "Battery" That Charges Itself

Why is a neuron in a resting state like a battery sitting on a shelf?

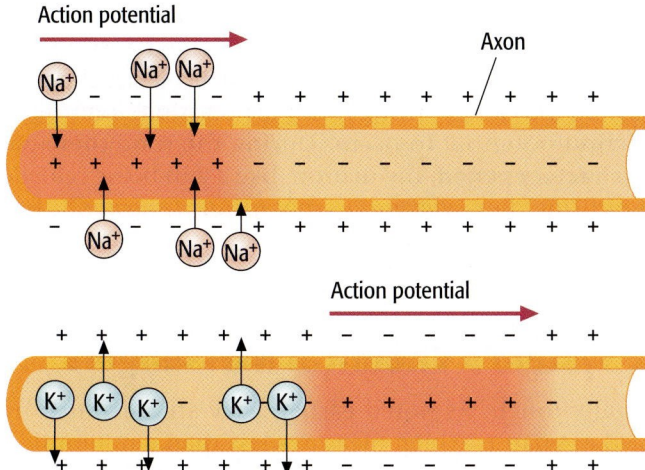

Figure 2.2   An Action Potential
When a neuron in a resting state is stimulated, sodium gates in the cell membrane open, allowing positively charged sodium ions to rush into the cell. When stimulation is sufficiently strong, the cell suddenly shifts from a negative to a positive charge. The sudden reversal of charge is an action potential, an electrical charge that shoots down the axon, momentarily reversing the charge as it goes along the cell membrane. Once the action potential passes, sodium gates close, preventing further inflows of positively charged sodium ions, and the cell pumps out positively charged ions, mostly potassium ions. This restores the cell's negatively charged resting state, allowing it to fire again in response to stimulation.

Generating a Charge

What is an action potential? How is it generated? What happens when it reaches the end of an axon?

When the cell is stimulated, usually by neurotransmitters released from adjoining neurons, sodium gates at the base of the axon open. Positively charged sodium ions from the surrounding fluid then rush in, which causes the area inside the cell membrane at the point of excitation to become less negatively charged. This process is called **depolarization**. When stimulation is sufficiently strong, as when enough of a neurotransmitter is present, depolarization quickly spreads along the axon. When this wave of depolarization reaches a critical threshold, the neuron abruptly shifts from a negative charge to a positive charge of about +40 mV. The sudden reversal of electrical charge is called an **action potential**, or *neural impulse*. The action potential shoots down the entire length of the axon as a wave of changing electrical charges. We refer to this action as a "firing" of the neuron, or as a *spike* (see Figure 2.2).

Once an action potential reaches the end of an axon, it causes the release of neurotransmitters from the terminal buttons that carry the neural message to the next neuron. Action potentials are generated according to the **all-or-none principle**. A neuron will fire completely (generate an action potential) if sufficient stimulation is available, or it will not fire; there is no halfway point. Different axons generate action potentials of different speeds depending on such characteristics as their thickness (generally the thicker the axon, the faster the speed) and whether or not they are covered with a myelin sheath (which speeds transmission). Speeds of action potentials range from between two miles an hour to a few hundred miles an hour. Even the most rapid neural impulses are much slower than a speeding bullet, which travels at the rate of several hundred miles a minute. Neural impulses reach their destinations in small fractions of seconds—fast enough to pull your hand in an instant from a burning surface, but perhaps not fast enough to avoid a burn.

For about one-thousandth of a second (one millisecond) after firing, a neuron busies itself preparing to fire again. Sodium gates along the cell membrane close, preventing further inflows of positively charged sodium ions into the cell. The

CONCEPT 2.7
An action potential is generated according to the all-or-none principle—it is produced only if the level of excitation is sufficient.

depolarization   A positive shift in the electrical charge in the neuron's resting potential, making it less negatively charged.

action potential   An abrupt change from a negative to a positive charge of a nerve cell, also called a neural impulse.

all-or-none principle   The principle by which neurons will fire only when a change in the level of excitation occurs that is sufficient to produce an action potential.

cell pumps out positively charged ions, mostly potassium ions, and as it rids itself of these positive ions, the neuron's negatively charged resting potential is restored. Then, in a slower process, the cell restores the electrochemical balance by pumping out sodium ions and drawing in some potassium ions, making it possible for another action potential to occur. During the time these changes are occurring, called a **refractory period**, the neuron, like a gun being reloaded, is temporarily incapable of firing. But *temporarily* truly means *temporarily,* for a neuron can "reload" hundreds of times per second.

Neurotransmitters: The Nervous System's Chemical Messengers

CONCEPT 2.8
When the neural impulse reaches the axon's terminal buttons, it triggers the release of chemicals that either increase or decrease the likelihood that neighboring cells will fire.

Neurons don't actually touch. As noted earlier, they are separated by the tiny fluid-filled gap called a synapse, which measures less than a millionth of an inch across. Neural impulses cannot jump even this tiniest of gaps. They must be transferred by neurotransmitters, the chemical agents or messengers that carry the message across the synapse. When a neuron fires, tiny vesicles (or sacs) in the axon's terminal buttons release molecules of neurotransmitters into the synaptic gap like a flotilla of ships casting off into the sea (see Figure 2.3). Neurotransmitters carry messages that control activities ranging from contraction of muscles that move our bodies, to stimulation of glands to release hormones, to the psychological states of thinking and emotion.

Each specific type of neurotransmitter has a particular chemical structure, or three-dimensional shape. It fits into only one kind of **receptor site**, like a key fitting into a lock. When neurotransmitters dock at receptor sites, they lock into

Figure 2.3   How Neurons Communicate
Neural impulses are carried by neurotransmitters released by the terminal buttons of the transmitting neuron. These chemical messengers travel across the tiny synapse and are taken up by receptor sites on the dendrites of the receiving neuron. Neurotransmitter molecules that do not dock at receptor sites are decomposed in the synaptic gap or are reabsorbed by the transmitting neuron.

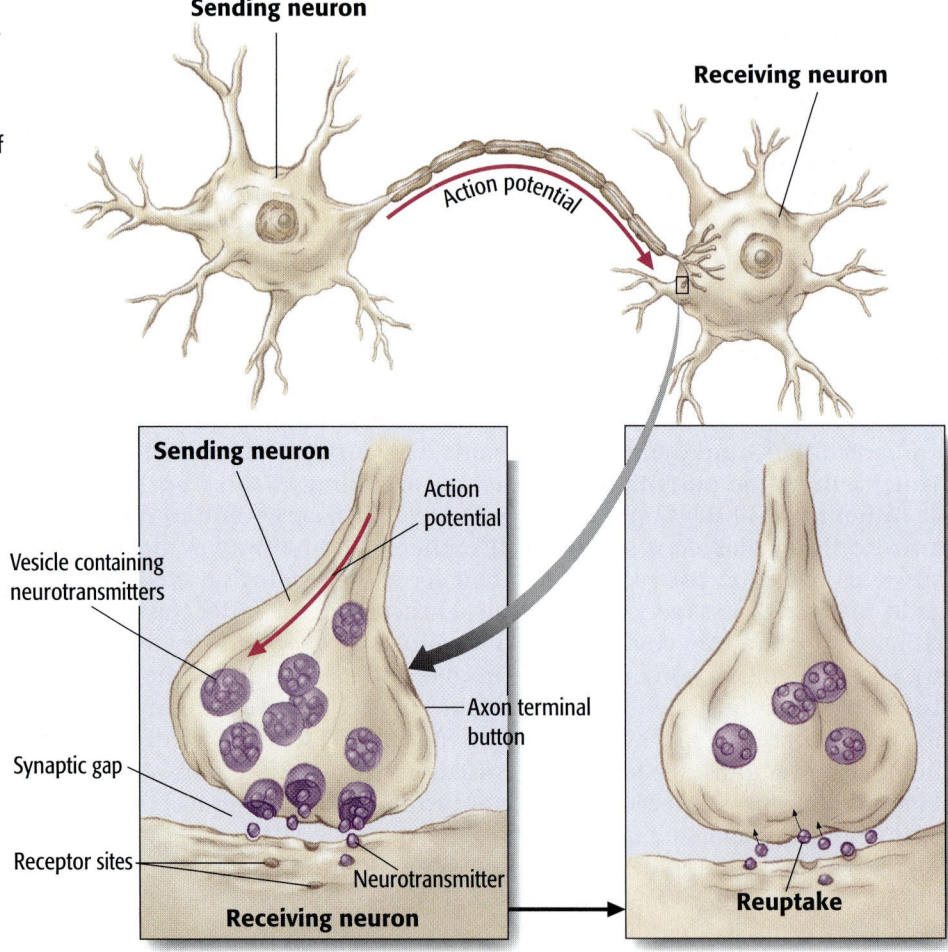

refractory period   A temporary state in which a neuron is unable to fire in response to continued stimulation.

receptor site   A site on the receiving neuron in which neurotransmitters dock.

place, causing chemical changes in the receiving (or *postsynaptic*) neuron. These changes have either an *excitatory effect* or an *inhibitory effect* (Kennedy, 2000). Excitatory effects make an action potential more likely to occur. Inhibitory effects put the brakes on an action potential, making it less likely to occur. Some neurotransmitters have excitatory effects; others, inhibitory effects; and still others, both excitatory and inhibitory effects. The nervous system depends on a balance between excitation and inhibition, or the turning on and turning off of neurons, in order to function smoothly and efficiently.

Several processes normally prevent excitatory neurotransmitters from continuing to stimulate a receiving cell. One process, called **reuptake**, is nature's own version of recycling. Through reuptake, neurotransmitters not taken up by the receiving cell are reabsorbed by their vesicles to be used again. In another process, **enzymes** in the synapse break down neurotransmitters, which are then eliminated from the body in the urine. In yet another process, terminal buttons release **neuromodulators**, chemicals that either increase or decrease the sensitivity of the receiving neuron to neurotransmitters.

Normal psychological functioning depends on the smooth transmission of messages among neurons in the brain. Your ability to think clearly, move your arms and legs at will, feel pain or emotions like joy, fear, or anger—everything you do, feel, or think—depends on neurotransmitters. When the body produces too little or too much of a neurotransmitter, problems may occur. Sometimes receptor sites allow too many neurotransmitter molecules to dock, or they do not accept neurotransmitters properly. Excesses or deficits of particular neurotransmitters in the brain, or irregularities in how they function, are associated with many disorders. For example, irregularities in neurotransmitter functioning are linked to eating disorders (see Chapter 8) and to depression and schizophrenia (see Chapter 11).

Drugs or chemicals that block the actions of neurotransmitters by occupying their receptor sites are called **antagonists**. By locking into these receptor sites, antagonists prevent transmission of the messages carried by the neurotransmitter. Consider *dopamine,* a neurotransmitter involved in controlling muscle contractions and in learning, memory, and emotional processing. It is of special interest to psychologists because irregularities in the utilization of dopamine in the brain may help explain the development of **schizophrenia**, a severe mental disorder affecting between 2 million and 3 million people in the United States (McGuire, 2000). People with schizophrenia may experience **hallucinations** (the phenomenon of "hearing voices" or seeing things that are not there) and **delusions** (fixed, false ideas, such as believing that aliens have taken over their bodies). *Antipsychotic drugs* are antagonists that block receptor sites for dopamine (Gründer, Carlsson, & Wong, 2003). They help control hallucinations and delusional thinking in many schizophrenia patients (see Chapter 12).

Parkinson's disease is a degenerative brain disease that leads to a progressive loss of motor function, or physical movement (Carroll, 2004). Parkinson's sufferers experience tremors (shakiness), muscle rigidity and stiffness, and difficulty walking and controlling the movements of their fingers and hands. These symptoms result from the loss of dopamine-producing cells in an area of the brain involved in regulating body movement. According to one expert, "Dopamine is

THINK *About It*

Blocking a Drug High

A scientist develops a drug that blocks the actions of cocaine by locking into the same receptor sites as cocaine. So long as a person is taking the drug, cocaine will no longer produce a high. Would this drug be an antagonist or an agonist to cocaine? Why?

CONCEPT 2.9

Irregularities in neurotransmitter functioning are implicated in many psychological disorders, including eating disorders, depression, and schizophrenia.

reuptake The process by which neurotransmitters are reabsorbed by the transmitting neuron.

enzymes Organic substances that produce certain chemical changes in other organic substances through a catalytic action.

neuromodulators Chemicals released in the nervous system that influence the sensitivity of the receiving neuron to neurotransmitters.

antagonists Drugs that block the actions of neurotransmitters by occupying the receptor sites in which the neurotransmitters dock.

schizophrenia A severe and chronic psychological disorder characterized by disturbances in thinking, perception, emotions, and behavior.

hallucinations Perceptions experienced in the absence of external stimuli.

delusions Fixed but patently false beliefs, such as believing that one is being hounded by demons.

Parkinson's disease A progressive brain disease involving destruction of dopamine-producing brain cells and characterized by muscle tremors, shakiness, rigidity, and difficulty in walking and controlling fine body movements.

Michael J. Fox Michael J. Fox quit his starring role in a hit TV show to focus his efforts on fighting Parkinson's disease, the degenerative brain disease from which he was suffering.

like the oil in the engine of a car. . . . If the oil is there, the car runs smoothly. If not, it seizes up" (cited in Carroll, 2004, p. F5).

Parkinson's affects an estimated 1.5 million Americans, including former heavyweight boxing champion Muhammad Ali and actor Michael J. Fox ("NSAID Use," 2003). Genetic factors play a key role in determining susceptibility to the disease (Bonifati et al., 2003; Nussbaum & Ellis, 2003; Pankratz et al., 2002).

In contrast to antagonists that compete with neurotransmitters at the same receptor sites, other drugs, called **agonists**, enhance the activity of neurotransmitters. Agonists work either by increasing the availability or effectiveness of neurotransmitters or by binding to their receptor sites and mimicking their actions. The mild **stimulant** caffeine, for example, increases the availability of a neurotransmitter called *glutamate*. Glutamate is an excitatory neurotransmitter that helps keep the central nervous system aroused (Goff & Coyle, 2001).

Stronger stimulants, such as **amphetamines** and cocaine, are agonists that increase the availability of dopamine in the brain by blocking its reuptake by the transmitting neuron. Dopamine is a key neurotransmitter in neural pathways that regulate states of pleasure, so the increased availability of dopamine in the brain may account for the pleasurable "high" these drugs produce (Friedman, 2002; Kauer et al., 2003; Leyton et al., 2002). (We'll return to this topic in Chapter 4).

Alcohol and antianxiety drugs like Valium act as agonists by increasing the sensitivity of receptor sites to the inhibitory neurotransmitter *gamma-aminobutyric acid (GABA)*. GABA regulates nervous activity by preventing neurons from overly exciting their neighbors. Thus, drugs that boost GABA's effects have a calming or relaxing effect. Reduced levels of GABA in the brain may play a role in emotional disorders in which anxiety is a core feature, such as panic disorder (Goddard et al., 2001).

Drugs that help relieve depression, called **antidepressants**, are agonists that increase the levels or activity of norepinephrine and serotonin in the brain. Norepinephrine (also called *noradrenaline*) is a chemical cousin of the hormone *epinephrine* (also called *adrenaline*). Norepinephrine does double duty as a neurotransmitter and a hormone (see Module 2.6). Serotonin functions mostly as an inhibitory neurotransmitter in regulating emotional responses, feelings of satiation after eating, and sleep. The widely used antidepressant *fluoxetine* (brand name Prozac) increases the availability of serotonin by interfering with the reuptake of the chemical by the transmitting neuron (discussed further in Chapter 12).

Did you know that the brain naturally produces neurotransmitters that are chemical cousins to narcotic drugs like morphine and heroin? These chemicals, called **endorphins** (short for *endogenous morphine*—morphine that "develops from

agonists Drugs that either increase the availability or effectiveness of neurotransmitters or mimic their actions.

stimulant A drug that activates the central nervous system, such as amphetamines and cocaine.

amphetamines A class of synthetically derived stimulant drugs, such as methamphetamine or "speed."

antidepressants Drugs that combat depression by affecting the levels or activity of neurotransmitters.

endorphins Natural chemicals released in the brain that have pain-killing and pleasure-inducing effects.

nervous system The body's system of communication by which messages are transmitted and processed through a complex network of neurons.

within") are inhibitory neurotransmitters. They lock into the same receptors in the brain as the drug morphine. (Narcotics and other psychoactive drugs are discussed further in Chapter 4.)

Endorphins are the body's natural painkillers (Aschwanden, 2000). They are similar in chemical structure to narcotic drugs. Like morphine, heroin, and other narcotics, they deaden pain by fitting into receptor sites for chemicals that carry pain messages to the brain, thereby locking out pain messages. They also produce feelings of well-being and pleasure and may contribute to the "runner's high" experienced by many long-distance runners (Grady, 1997). Morphine and heroin are agonists, since they mimic the effects of naturally occurring endorphins on the body.

MODULE 2.1 REVIEW

Neurons: The Body's Wiring

CONCEPT CHECK

1. As reported by neurologist Oliver Sacks, Dr. P, despite his deficits in visual perception, was able to function by
   a. employing mental roadmaps.
   b. using music to direct and organize his activities.
   c. taking drugs to expand the quantity of ions at neural junctions.
   d. undergoing surgery to reconnect both myelinated and unmyelinated fibers.

2. The part of the neuron that houses the cell nucleus is the _____.

3. What are the three types of neurons in the human body?

4. Which of the following is *not* correct?
   a. A myelin sheath helps speed transmission of neural impulses.
   b. The myelin sheath is formed by glial cells.
   c. Myelin sheaths are white.
   d. Myelin covers all parts of a neuron except the axon.

5. When a neuron is at rest,
   a. a greater concentration of sodium ions remains outside the nerve cell.
   b. the cell has a slightly positive charge (relative to surrounding fluid).
   c. the state is known as an action potential.
   d. it is in a state of depolarization.

6. Although nerve cells don't actually touch each other, they communicate by means of
   a. electrical impulses that travel from dendrites to receptor sites on adjacent neurons.
   b. neurotransmitters that carry the neural impulse across the synapse.
   c. interneurons that serve as relay stations between neurons.
   d. nerve cells that function independently and have no need to communicate with each other.

MODULE 2.2   The Nervous System: Your Body's Information Superhighway

- **How is the nervous system organized?**
- **What are spinal reflexes?**
- **What is the autonomic nervous system?**
- **What is the relationship between the sympathetic and parasympathetic divisions of the autonomic nervous system?**

Inside your body is an information superhighway that conducts information in the form of neural impulses. This superhighway—the **nervous system**—is an intricate network of neurons that are organized in a complex communication network. The nervous system is divided into two major parts, the *central nervous system,* consisting of the brain and spinal cord, and the *peripheral nervous system,* which connects the central nervous system to other parts of the body (see Figure 2.4). Concept Chart 2.2 shows the organization of the nervous system.

CONCEPT 2.10
The nervous system has two major parts: the central nervous system, which consists of the brain and spinal cord, and the peripheral nervous system, which consists of the nerves that connect the central nervous system to sensory organs, muscles, and glands.

Figure 2.4   Parts of the Nervous System
The nervous system has two major divisions, the central nervous system (brain and spinal cord) and the peripheral nervous system, which connects the central nervous system with sensory organs, muscles, and glands.

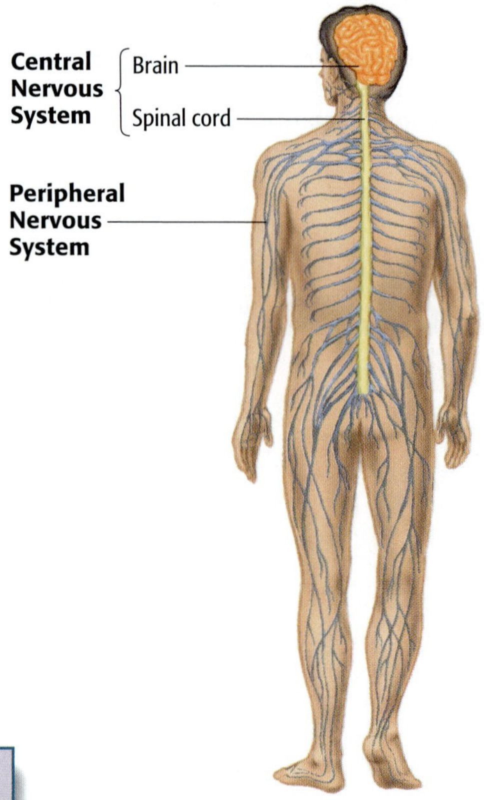

Central Nervous System
- Brain
- Spinal cord

Peripheral Nervous System

THINK About It

Running for the Bus

As you're running to catch a bus, your breathing quickens, and your heart starts pounding. Which part of your peripheral nervous system kicks into gear at such a time?

web Netlab/The Nervous System: The Big Picture

CONCEPT CHART 2.2
Organization of the Nervous System

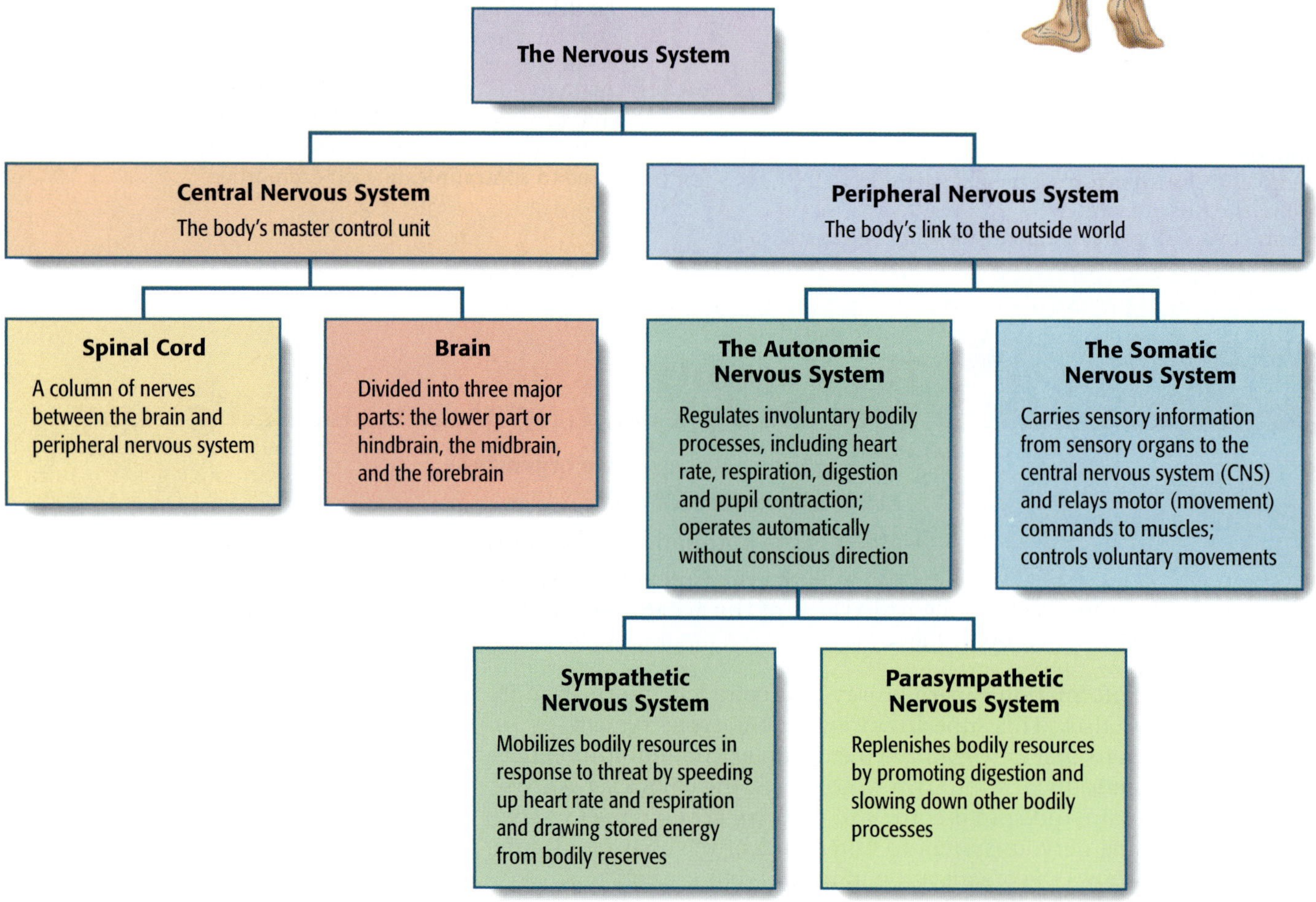

The Nervous System

Central Nervous System
The body's master control unit

Peripheral Nervous System
The body's link to the outside world

Spinal Cord
A column of nerves between the brain and peripheral nervous system

Brain
Divided into three major parts: the lower part or hindbrain, the midbrain, and the forebrain

The Autonomic Nervous System
Regulates involuntary bodily processes, including heart rate, respiration, digestion and pupil contraction; operates automatically without conscious direction

The Somatic Nervous System
Carries sensory information from sensory organs to the central nervous system (CNS) and relays motor (movement) commands to muscles; controls voluntary movements

Sympathetic Nervous System
Mobilizes bodily resources in response to threat by speeding up heart rate and respiration and drawing stored energy from bodily reserves

Parasympathetic Nervous System
Replenishes bodily resources by promoting digestion and slowing down other bodily processes

Central Nervous System: Your Body's Master Control Unit

You can compare the **central nervous system** to the central processing unit of a computer—the "brains" of the computer etched into a chip that controls the computer's central processing functions. The central nervous system is a master control system that regulates everything in your body, from the rate at which your heart beats, to the movements of your eyes as you scan these words, to your higher mental processes, such as thinking and reasoning. The central nervous system also enables you to sense the world around you and make sense of the sensations you experience (see Chapter 3).

The crowning glory of your central nervous system is your brain, that wondrous organ that regulates life processes and enables you to think, plan, and create. Fortunately, this tender mass of tissue is cushioned in a hard, bony shell called the skull.

As you'll see in Module 2.3, one way of studying the brain is by exploring its three major parts: the hindbrain, or lower brain—the brain's "basement;" the midbrain; and the forebrain, the highest region where thoughts and your sense of self "live." Here let us consider the other major part of the central nervous system, the spinal cord—the brain's link to the peripheral nervous system.

The Spinal Cord

The **spinal cord**—a column of nerves nearly as thick as your thumb—is literally an extension of the brain. The spinal cord begins at the base of your brain and runs down the center of your back, ending just below the waist. It is a neural pathway that transmits information between the brain and the peripheral nervous system. It receives incoming information from your sense organs and other peripheral body parts and carries outgoing commands from your brain to muscles, glands, and organs throughout your body.

The spinal cord is encased in a protective bony column called the **spine**. Despite this protection, the spinal cord can suffer injury. In severe spinal cord injuries, such as the one the actor Christopher Reeve sustained when he fell from a horse, signals cannot be transmitted between the brain and the peripheral organs, which may result in paralysis of the limbs and an inability to breathe on one's own. As a result of his injury, Reeve became quadriplegic (i.e., he lost control over both his arms and legs). Also, because he lost the ability to breathe, he required an artificial respirator. (At the time of this writing, he had regained some ability to breathe on his own.)

The spinal cord is not simply a conduit for neural transmission of signals between the brain and the peripheral nervous system. It also controls some *spinal reflexes* that let you respond as quickly as possible to particular types of stimuli. A **reflex** is an automatic, unlearned reaction to a stimulus; a **spinal reflex** is a reflex controlled at the level of the spinal cord—one that bypasses the brain. An example of a spinal reflex is the jerk your knee gives when a doctor who's examining you taps it lightly with a hammer. Some spinal reflexes, including the knee-jerk response, involve just two neurons—one sensory neuron and one motor neuron (see Figure 2.5). In other cases, such as the reflexive withdrawal of the hand upon touching a hot object, a third neuron in the spinal cord, an interneuron, transmits information from the incoming sensory neuron to the outgoing motor neuron.

Spinal reflexes allow us to respond almost instantly and with great efficiency to particular stimuli. The knee-jerk reflex takes a mere fifty milliseconds from the time the knee is tapped until the time the leg jerks forward (as compared with the hundreds of milliseconds it takes to voluntarily flex your leg). To appreciate the value of spinal reflexes, recall the times you've pulled your hand away from a hot stove or blinked when a gust of wind sent particles of debris hurtling toward your eyeballs. By saving the many milliseconds it would take to send a message to

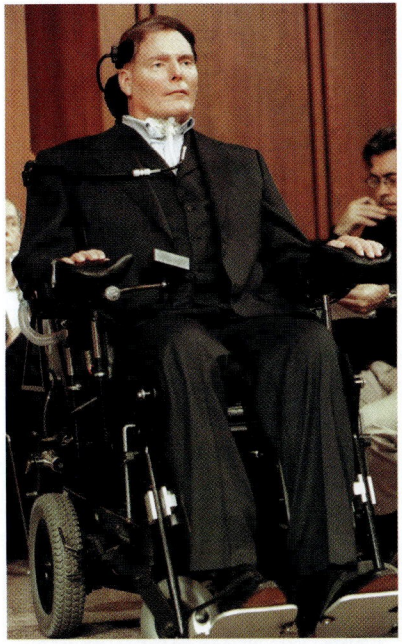

Christopher Reeve After a devastating fall from a horse severely injured his spinal cord and left him paralyzed, actor Christopher Reeve became a leading advocate for research on spinal cord injuries. Sadly, he died of heart failure in 2004 at age 52.

CONCEPT 2.11

The spinal cord is an information highway that conducts information between the brain and the peripheral nervous system.

CONCEPT 2.12

Spinal reflexes are innate, automatic responses controlled at the level of the spinal cord that allow you to respond quickly to particular stimuli.

central nervous system The part of the nervous system that consists of the brain and spinal cord.

spinal cord The column of nerves that transmits information between the brain and the peripheral nervous system.

spine The protective bony column that houses the spinal cord.

reflex An automatic, unlearned response to particular stimuli.

spinal reflex A reflex controlled at the level of the spinal cord that may involve as few as two neurons.

Figure 2.5   Anatomy of a Spinal Reflex
Tapping the knee *(a)* sends a signal through a sensory neuron to the spinal cord, where the information is transmitted directly to a motor neuron, which in turn signals muscles in the thigh to contract, causing the leg to kick forward. Touching a hot stove *(b)* sends a signal through a sensory neuron to the spinal cord, where it is relayed through an interneuron to a motor neuron, which signals muscles in the hand to contract, causing the hand to withdraw from the hot object.

(a) The Knee-Jerk Reflex

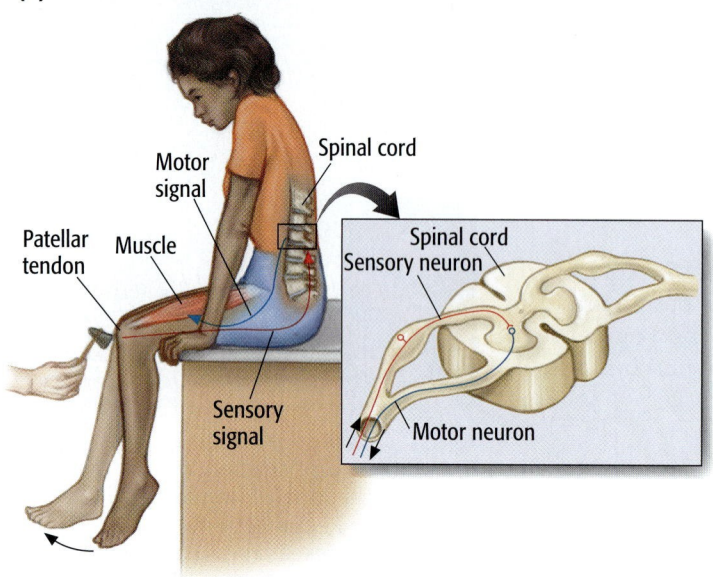

(b) The Withdrawal Reflex

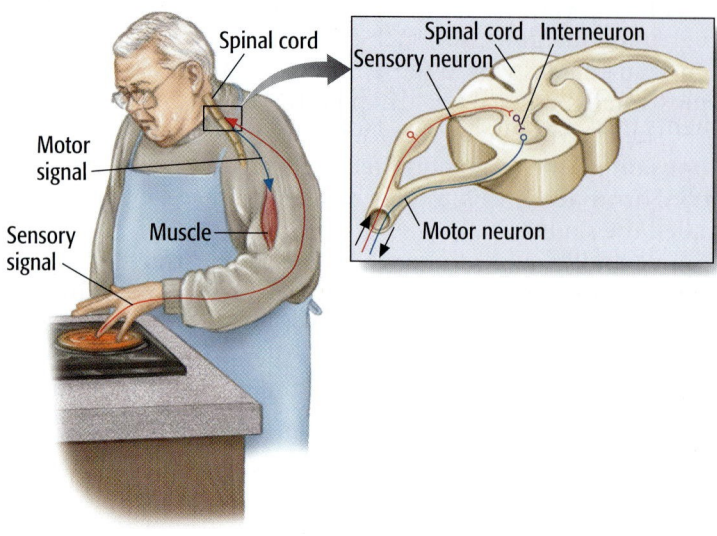

💡 **CONCEPT 2.13**
The somatic nervous system is the part of the peripheral nervous system that controls voluntary movements of muscles and relays information between the central nervous system and sensory organs.

peripheral nervous system   The part of the nervous system that connects the spinal cord and brain with the sensory organs, muscles, and glands.

somatic nervous system   The part of the peripheral nervous system that transmits information between the central nervous system and the sensory organs and muscles; also controls voluntary movements.

autonomic nervous system   The part of the peripheral nervous system that automatically regulates involuntary bodily processes, such as breathing, heart rate, and digestion.

sympathetic nervous system   The branch of the autonomic nervous system that accelerates bodily processes and releases stores of energy needed to meet increased physical demands.

parasympathetic nervous system   The branch of the autonomic nervous system that regulates bodily processes, such as digestion, that replenish stores of energy.

your brain, have it interpreted, and have a command sent back along the spinal highway to motor neurons, spinal reflexes can spell the difference between a minor injury and a serious one.

The Peripheral Nervous System: Your Body's Link to the Outside World

The central nervous system depends on a constant flow of information that it receives from your internal organs and sensory receptors, as well as on its ability to convey information to the muscles and glands that it regulates. These functions are performed by the **peripheral nervous system (PNS)**, the part of the nervous system that connects your central nervous system with other parts of your body.

Without the peripheral nervous system, your brain would be like a computer chip disconnected from the computer hardware—a marvelous feat of engineering but unable to function. Without information transmitted from your sensory organs—your eyes, ears, tongue, nose, and skin—you would be unable to perceive the world. Without commands sent to your muscles, you would be unable to act upon the world. The PNS is divided into two parts, the **somatic nervous system** and the **autonomic nervous system (ANS)**.

The Somatic Nervous System

The somatic nervous system transmits messages between your central nervous system and your sensory organs and muscles. It not only enables you to perceive the world, but it also ensures that your muscles will contract in response to an intentional command or a stimulus that triggers a reflex action. And, finally, it regulates subtle movements that maintain posture and balance.

The somatic nervous system is composed of sensory and motor neurons. As noted in Module 2.1, sensory neurons send messages from the sensory organs to the spinal cord and brain. In this way, information about stimuli that impinge upon our senses (light, sounds, odors, taste, pressure on our skin, and so on) is transmitted to the central nervous system. The brain then interprets these messages, allowing you to perceive a beautiful sunset or a threatening animal, distinguish a whisper from the rustling of the wind, determine whether you are sitting in a reclining or upright position, and experience sensations of warmth, cold, and pain.

The central nervous system processes the information it receives and sends messages back through motor neurons that control movements—such as walking and running, pulling your arm back reflexively upon touching a hot object, raising and lowering your arms at will—and the tiny, almost imperceptible, movements that regulate your balance and posture.

The Autonomic Nervous System

The autonomic nervous system (ANS) is the part of the peripheral nervous system that controls such internal bodily processes as heartbeat, respiration, digestion, and dilation of the pupils. The ANS does these tasks automatically, regulating these vital bodily processes without your having to think about them. (Autonomic means "automatic.") You can, however, exercise some voluntary control over some of these functions, as by intentionally breathing more rapidly or slowly.

The ANS is itself composed of two divisions, or branches, that have largely opposite effects, the *sympathetic nervous system* and the *parasympathetic nervous system*. The **sympathetic nervous system** speeds up bodily processes and draws energy from stored reserves. It serves as an alarm system that heightens arousal and mobilizes bodily resources in times of stress or physical exertion, or when defensive action might be needed to fend off a threat. It accelerates your heart rate and breathing rate and provides more fuel or energy for the body to use by releasing sugar (glucose) from the liver. Activation of the sympathetic nervous system is often accompanied by strong emotions, such as anxiety, fear, or anger. That is why we sense our hearts beating faster when we are anxious or angered.

The **parasympathetic nervous system** fosters bodily processes, such as digestion, that replenish stores of energy. Digestion provides the body with fuel by converting food into glucose (blood sugar), which cells use as a source of energy. The parasympathetic nervous system also helps conserve energy by slowing down other bodily processes. The sympathetic nervous system speeds up your heart; the parasympathetic slows it down. The sympathetic nervous system turns off (inhibits) digestive activity; the parasympathetic turns it on. The parasympathetic system is in command whenever you are relaxing or digesting a meal.

THINK About It

Reflex Actions

Can you think of any times in your life when a spinal reflex prevented serious injury?

CONCEPT 2.14
Like an automatic pilot, the autonomic nervous system, a division of the peripheral nervous system, automatically controls such involuntary bodily processes as heartbeat, respiration, and digestion.

CONCEPT 2.15
The autonomic nervous system is divided into two branches that have largely opposite effects: the sympathetic nervous system, the body's alarm system that heightens states of arousal, and the parasympathetic nervous system, which tones down bodily arousal and helps replenish bodily resources.

MODULE 2.2 REVIEW

The Nervous System: Your Body's Information Superhighway

CONCEPT CHECK

1. The two major divisions in the human nervous system are the _____ nervous system and the _____ nervous system.

2. The brain and spinal cord constitute the _____ nervous system.

3. Which part of the nervous system triggers changes that prepare the body to cope with stress?

4. The parasympathetic nervous system
   a. slows some bodily activity and allows for the replenishment of energy.
   b. is part of the central nervous system.
   c. is also known as the "fight-or-flight" mechanism.
   d. draws energy from bodily reserves to meet stressful demands on the body.

MODULE 2.3 — The Brain: Your Crowning Glory

- **How is the brain organized, and what are the functions of its various parts?**
- **How is the cerebral cortex organized?**
- **What are the major functions associated with the four lobes of the cerebral cortex?**

CONCEPT 2.16
The brain is divided into three major parts: the hindbrain, the midbrain, and the forebrain.

CONCEPT 2.17
The hindbrain, the lowest part of the brain, contains structures that control basic bodily functions, such as breathing and heart rate.

Let us take a tour of the brain, beginning with the lowest level, the *hindbrain*—the part of the brain where the spinal cord enters the skull and widens. We then work our way upward, first to the *midbrain*, which lies above the hindbrain, and then to the *forebrain*, which lies in the highest part of the brain. Concept Chart 2.3 shows these major brain structures.

The Hindbrain

The lowest part of the brain, the **hindbrain**, is also the oldest part in evolutionary terms. The hindbrain includes the *medulla, pons,* and *cerebellum.* These structures control such basic life-support functions as breathing and heart rate.

CONCEPT CHART 2.3
Major Structures of the Human Brain

web. Netlab/Know Your Brain

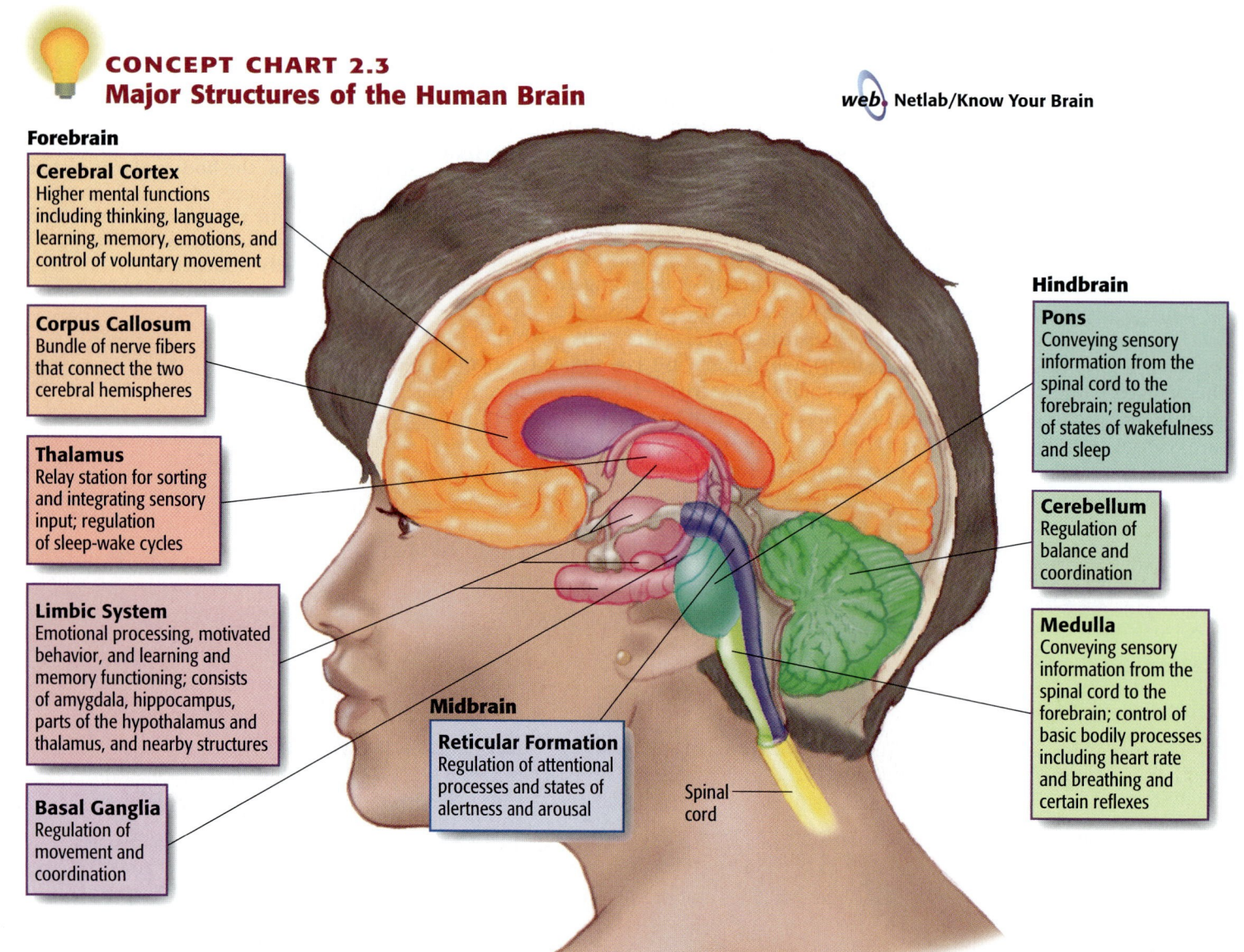

Forebrain

Cerebral Cortex
Higher mental functions including thinking, language, learning, memory, emotions, and control of voluntary movement

Corpus Callosum
Bundle of nerve fibers that connect the two cerebral hemispheres

Thalamus
Relay station for sorting and integrating sensory input; regulation of sleep-wake cycles

Limbic System
Emotional processing, motivated behavior, and learning and memory functioning; consists of amygdala, hippocampus, parts of the hypothalamus and thalamus, and nearby structures

Basal Ganglia
Regulation of movement and coordination

Midbrain

Reticular Formation
Regulation of attentional processes and states of alertness and arousal

Spinal cord

Hindbrain

Pons
Conveying sensory information from the spinal cord to the forebrain; regulation of states of wakefulness and sleep

Cerebellum
Regulation of balance and coordination

Medulla
Conveying sensory information from the spinal cord to the forebrain; control of basic bodily processes including heart rate and breathing and certain reflexes

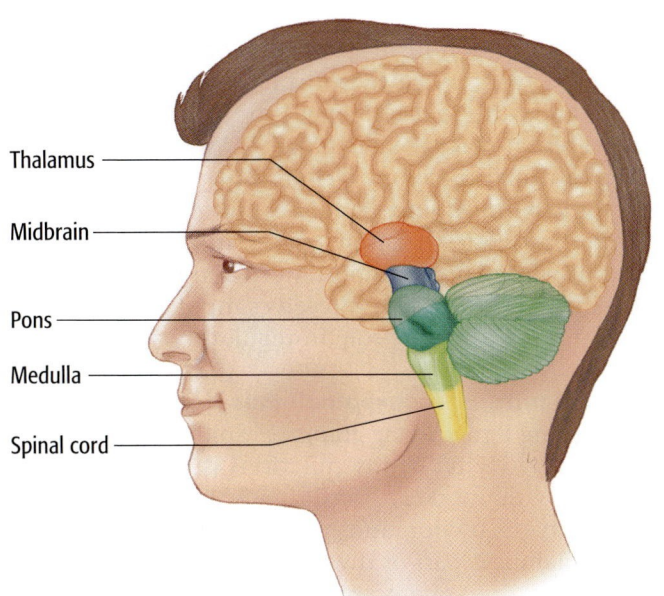

Thalamus

Midbrain

Pons

Medulla

Spinal cord

Figure 2.6   The Brainstem
The brainstem reaches from the top of the spinal cord up through the midbrain. It connects the spinal cord to the higher regions of the brain.

The **medulla** and **pons** contain sensory neurons that transmit information from the spinal cord to the forebrain. The medulla is the section of the hindbrain that lies closest to the spinal cord. It forms the marrow, or core, of the **brainstem**, the "stem" or "stalk" that connects the spinal cord to the higher regions of the brain (see Figure 2.6). (*Medulla* is a Latin word meaning "marrow.") The medulla controls such vital bodily processes as heart rate and breathing, and such reflexes as swallowing, coughing, and sneezing. The pons lies directly above the medulla. It contains nerve fibers that conduct information from the spinal cord and lower parts of the brain through the midbrain to the forebrain. It also helps regulate states of wakefulness and sleep.

Located behind the pons, the **cerebellum** is involved in controlling balance and coordination. Injury to the cerebellum can lead not only to problems with balance and coordination but also to difficulties in initiating voluntary movements, such as lifting an arm or a leg.

As we continue our brief tour of the brain, we come to the midrain, the part of the brain that serves as a major relay station for information passing between the lower brain and the forebrain.

The Midbrain

The **midbrain**, which lies above the hindbrain, contains nerve pathways that connect the hindbrain with the forebrain. Structures in the midbrain perform important roles, including control of automatic movements of the eye muscles, which allows you to keep your eyes focused on an object as your head changes position in relation to the object. Parts of the midbrain make up the brainstem.

The **reticular formation** (also called the *reticular activating system,* or *RAS*) is a weblike network of neurons that rises from the hindbrain and passes through the midbrain to the thalamus in the forebrain. The reticular formation plays a key role in regulating states of attention, alertness, and arousal. It screens visual and auditory information, filtering out irrelevant information while allowing important information to reach the higher processing centers of the brain, even when we are asleep.

The Forebrain

The **forebrain**, located toward the top and front of the brain, is the largest part of the brain. The major structures in the forebrain are the *thalamus,* the *hypothalamus,* the *limbic system,* and the *cerebral cortex.*

CONCEPT 2.18
The midbrain contains nerve pathways for relaying messages between the hindbrain and the forebrain, as well as structures that control some automatic movements.

hindbrain   The lowest and, in evolutionary terms, oldest part of the brain; includes the medulla, pons, and cerebellum.

medulla   A structure in the hindbrain involved in regulating basic life functions, such as heartbeat and respiration.

pons   A structure in the hindbrain involved in regulating states of wakefulness and sleep.

brainstem   The "stalk" in the lower part of the brain that connects the spinal cord to higher regions of the brain.

cerebellum   A structure in the hindbrain involved in controlling coordination and balance.

midbrain   The part of the brain that lies on top of the hindbrain and below the forebrain.

reticular formation   A weblike formation of neurons involved in regulating states of attention, alertness, and arousal.

forebrain   The largest and uppermost part of the brain; contains the thalamus, hypothalamus, limbic system, basal ganglia, and cerebral cortex.

CONCEPT 2.19

The largest part of the brain, the forebrain, controls higher mental functions, such as thinking, problem solving, use of language, planning, and memory.

CONCEPT 2.20

The limbic system plays an important role in the regulation of memory and emotions.

CONCEPT 2.21

The cerebrum is divided into two hemispheres and is covered by a thin, outer layer, the cerebral cortex, which is responsible for higher mental functions.

---

thalamus   A structure in the forebrain that serves as a relay station for sensory information and that plays a key role in regulating states of wakefulness and sleep.

basal ganglia   An assemblage of neurons lying in the forebrain that is important in controlling movement and coordination.

hypothalamus   A small, pea-sized structure in the forebrain that helps regulate many vital bodily functions, including body temperature and reproduction, as well as emotional states, aggression, and responses to stress.

limbic system   A formation of structures in the forebrain that includes the hippocampus, amygdala, and parts of the thalamus and hypothalamus.

amygdala   A set of almond-shaped structures in the limbic system believed to play an important role in aggression, rage, and fear.

hippocampus   A structure in the limbic system involved in memory formation.

cerebral cortex   The wrinkled, outer layer of gray matter that covers the cerebral hemispheres; controls higher mental functions, such as thought and language.

cerebrum   The largest mass of the forebrain, consisting of two cerebral hemispheres.

cerebral hemispheres   The right and left masses of the cerebrum, which are joined by the corpus callosum.

corpus callosum   The thick bundle of nerve fibers that connects the two cerebral hemispheres.

The **thalamus** is a relay station near the middle of the brain. It consists of a pair of egg-shaped structures that route information from sense receptors for touch, vision, hearing, and taste (but not smell) to the processing centers of the brain located in the cerebral cortex. The thalamus first sorts through sensory information, sending information about vision to one area, information about hearing to another, and so on. From these relay stations in the thalamus, the information is then transmitted to the appropriate parts of the cerebral cortex for processing. The thalamus also plays an important role in regulating states of sleep and wakefulness (Balkin et al., 2002), and it receives input from the **basal ganglia**, a cluster of nerve cells that plays a key role in regulating voluntary movement, such as walking.

Just beneath the thalamus is the **hypothalamus** (*hypo* meaning "under"), a pea-sized structure weighing a mere four grams. Despite its small size, the hypothalamus helps regulate many vital bodily functions, such as hunger and thirst, fluid concentrations, body temperature, and reproductive processes, as well as emotional states, aggressive behavior, and response to stress. As you will see in Module 2.6, the hypothalamus is part of the endocrine system, and it triggers the release of hormones throughout the body. Electrical stimulation of particular parts of the hypothalamus in other mammals, such as rats, can generate, or "switch on," stereotypical behavior patterns that range from eating to attacking rivals, courting, mounting attempts, and caring for the young.

The **limbic system** is a group of interconnected structures that includes the *amygdala, hippocampus,* parts of the *thalamus* and *hypothalamus,* and other nearby interconnected structures (see Concept Chart 2.3). The limbic system is much more evolved in mammals than in lower animals. It plays an important role in memory and emotional processing.

Referring again to Concept Chart 2.3, we find within the limbic system the **amygdala**, a set of two almond-shaped structures (*amygdala* is derived from the Greek root for "almond"). The amygdala helps regulate states of emotional arousal, especially states of aggression, rage, and fear that are evoked by unpleasant or aversive stimuli (see Chapter 8) (Hamann et al., 2003; LeDoux, 2000).

The **hippocampus** resembles a sea horse, from which it derives its name. Located just behind the amygdala, it plays an important role in the formation of memories (see Chapter 6).

Our journey through the brain now brings us to the uppermost part of the forebrain, the cerebral cortex. Because it is responsible for our ability to think, use language, calculate, organize, and create, we devote the entire next section to it.

The Cerebral Cortex: The Brain's Thinking, Calculating, Organizing, and Creative Center

The **cerebral cortex** forms the thin, outer layer of the largest part of the forebrain, which is called the **cerebrum**. The cerebrum consists of two large masses, the right and left **cerebral hemispheres**. The cerebral cortex covers the cerebrum like a cap and derives its name from the Latin words for brain ("cerebrum") and bark ("cortex"). A thick bundle of nerve fibers, called the **corpus callosum** (Latin for "thick body" or "hard body") connects the cerebral hemispheres and forms a pathway by which the hemispheres share information and communicate with each other. Structures in the brain that lie beneath the cerebral cortex are called *subcortical* structures (*sub* meaning "below" the cortex).

Though a mere one-eighth of an inch thick, no thicker than a napkin, the cerebral cortex accounts for more than 80 percent of the brain's total mass. The cortex owes its wrinkled or convoluted appearance to contours created by ridges and valleys. These contours enable its large surface area to be packed tightly within the confines of the skull (see Concept Chart 2.3). Its massive size in rela-

Figure 2.7   The Size of the Cerebral Cortex in Humans and Other Animals
The cerebral cortex accounts for a much greater portion of the brain in humans than in other animals.

| Frog | Rat | Cat | Chimpanzee | Human |

tion to the other parts of the brain reflects the amount of the brain devoted to higher mental functions, such as thinking, language use, and problem solving. Only in humans does the cortex account for so great a portion of the brain (see Figure 2.7). The cortex also controls voluntary movement, states of motivation and emotional arousal, and processing of sensory information.

Each hemisphere of the cerebral cortex is divided into four parts, or *lobes,* as shown in Figure 2.8. Thus, each lobe is represented in each hemisphere. The functions of the lobes are summarized in Table 2.1. Generally speaking, each of the cerebral hemispheres controls feeling and movement on the opposite side of the body.

The **occipital lobes**, located in the back of the head, process visual information. We experience vision when a source of light stimulates receptors in the eyes and causes neurons in the occipital lobes to fire (discussed further in Chapter 3). Even blows to the back of the head can produce visual experiences. Perhaps you have had the experience of "seeing stars" after being struck on this region of the head.

The **parietal lobes** are located on the sides of the brain, directly above and in front of the occipital lobes. At the front of the parietal lobes lies a strip of nerve cells called the **somatosensory cortex**, which processes sensory information received from receptors in the skin, giving rise to our experience of touch, pressure, temperature (hotness or coldness), and pain. Like your eyes and ears, your skin is a sensory organ that provides information about the world. The somatosensory cortex also receives information from receptors in your muscles and joints to keep you aware of the position of the parts of your body as you move about.

Figure 2.9 illustrates how specific parts of the somatosensory cortex correspond to sensory information (touch, pressure, pain, and temperature) received

CONCEPT 2.22
The corpus callosum is a bundle of nerve fibers that connect the two hemispheres of the brain, allowing them to share information.

CONCEPT 2.23
Each cerebral hemisphere has four main parts, or lobes: the occipital, parietal, frontal, and temporal lobes.

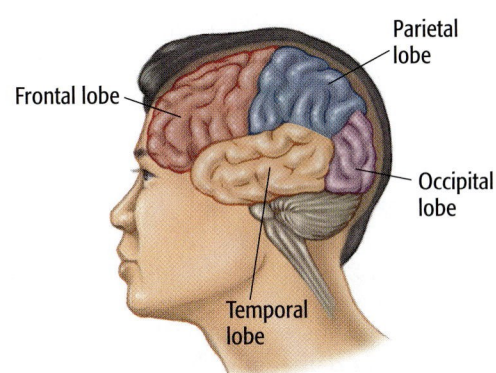

Figure 2.8   Lobes of the Cerebral Cortex
The cerebral cortex is divided into four parts, or lobes: the occipital, parietal, frontal, and temporal lobes.

TABLE 2.1	The Lobes of the Cerebral Cortex
Structure	**Functions**
Occipital lobes	Process visual information, giving rise to sensations of vision
Parietal lobes	Process information relating to sensations of touch, pressure, temperature (hot and cold), pain, and body movement
Frontal lobes	Control motor responses and higher mental functions, such as thinking, planning, problem solving, decision making, and accessing and acting on stored memories
Temporal lobes	Process auditory information, giving rise to sensations of sound

occipital lobes   The parts of the cerebral cortex, located at the back of both cerebral hemispheres, that process visual stimuli.

parietal lobes   The parts of the cerebral cortex, located on the side of each cerebral hemisphere, that process bodily sensations.

somatosensory cortex   The part of the parietal lobe that processes information about touch and pressure on the skin, as well as the position of the parts of our bodies as we move about.

Figure 2.9   Somatosensory Cortex and Motor Cortex
Here we see how various parts of the body are mapped in the somatosensory cortex and the motor cortex. The mapping structure of the two cortexes is nearly a mirror image. But notice how body parts are not mapped onto these cortexes in relation to where they actually lie in the body. The size of the projections of the parts of the body in each cortex corresponds to the degree of sensitivity or need for control of these parts.

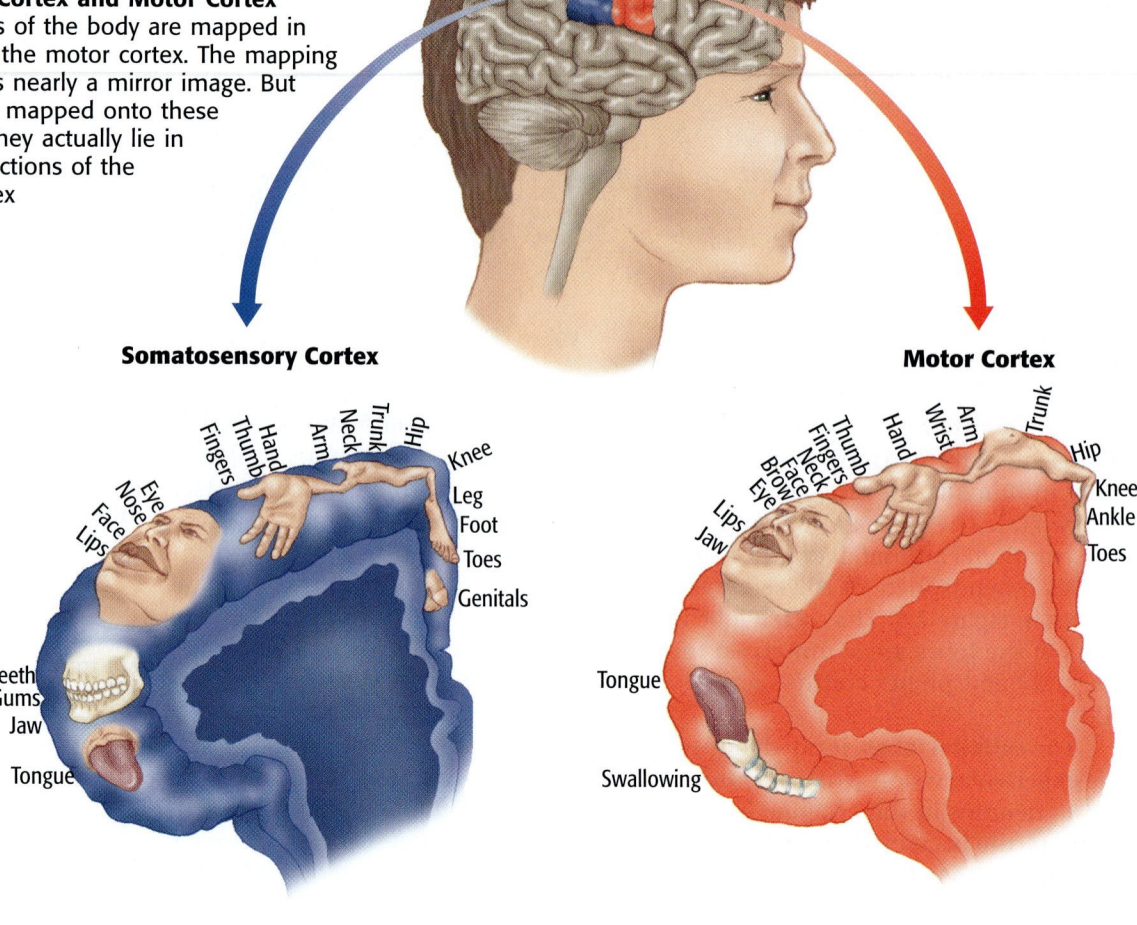

 **About It**

A Blow to the Head

A person suffers a serious fall and sustains severe damage to the back of the head. What sensory processes are most likely to be affected by the injury?

frontal lobes   The parts of the cerebral cortex, located at the front of the cerebral hemispheres, that are considered the "executive center" of the brain because of their role in higher mental functions.

motor cortex   A region of the frontal lobes involved in regulating body movement.

temporal lobes   The parts of the cerebral cortex lying beneath and somewhat behind the frontal lobes that are involved in processing auditory stimuli.

association areas   Areas of the cerebral cortex that piece together sensory information to form meaningful perceptions of the world and perform higher mental functions.

from specific parts of the body. Electrical stimulation of particular parts of the somatosensory cortex can make it seem as though your shoulder or your leg were experiencing touch or pressure, for example.

The strange-looking "figure" shown in Figure 2.10 is not a creature from the latest *Star Wars* installment. Sensory information from some parts of the body is transmitted to larger areas of the somatosensory cortex than is sensory information from other parts. This is because the brain devotes more of its capabilities to parts of the body that require greater sensitivity or control, such as the hands. Nor are the parts of the body represented in the somatosensory cortex in a way that directly corresponds to where they lie in the body. For example, sensory input from the genitals projects to an area that lies beneath the part receiving input from the toes, and the area that responds to stimulation of the tongue does not lie within the area that responds to stimulation of the lips. Why is this so? No one can say. But each of us knows the precise areas of our body that are touched. We know, for instance, when it is our lips that are touched and not our tongues, and vice versa.

The **frontal lobes** are located in the front part of the brain, just behind the forehead. Scientists call the frontal lobes the "executive center" of the brain, because they believe they contain your "you"—the part that accesses your memories, mulls things over, has self-awareness, and decides that the red plaid shirt is just "too retro." Like the central processing unit of a computer, parts of the frontal lobes retrieve memories from storage, place them in active memory, manipulate them, and make decisions based on them (Gazzaniga, 1999). For example, your frontal lobes pull sensory memories about visual cues, sounds, odors, even tastes from storage, so that the second time you see that oblong-shaped red pepper sitting innocently in your bowl of Kung Pao chicken, you'll remember not to bite into it. Your frontal lobes also allow you to solve problems, make decisions, plan actions, weigh evidence, and carry out coordinated actions.

Recent evidence further indicates that the frontal lobes are involved in processing emotional states, such as happiness and sadness (Davidson et al., 2000, 2002). In addition, they enable you to suppress tendencies to act on impulse, such as when you restrain yourself from telling your boss or professor what you really think of him or her.

The frontal lobes contain the **motor cortex**, which is located just across the border that separates them from the parietal lobes (see Figure 2.9). The motor cortex controls voluntary movements of specific parts of the body. For example, some neurons in the motor cortex control movements of the hands. When an electrode is used to stimulate a certain part of the motor cortex (a painless procedure sometimes used during brain surgery), muscles on the other side of the body contract. Depending on the electrode placement, the patient may lift a finger or tense a muscle in the leg. The representation of the body on the motor cortex is similar to that mapped out on the somatosensory cortex, as you can see in Figure 2.9.

The **temporal lobes** lie beneath and somewhat behind the frontal lobes, directly above the ears. The temporal lobes receive and process sensory information from the ears, producing the experience of hearing (discussed in Chapter 3).

The great majority of cortex consists of **association areas**. The association areas, which are found in each lobe, are more highly developed in humans than in other organisms. They are responsible for performing higher mental functions, such as piecing together sensory input to form meaningful perceptions of the world, thinking, learning, producing and understanding speech, solving math problems, planning activities, creating masterworks of architecture, and perhaps even composing the next hit song.

We cannot identify the precise locations where higher mental functions occur. Association areas are linked within intricate networks of neurons connecting many parts of the brain, the architecture of which we are only beginning to decipher.

Figure 2.10 **A Creature from *Star Wars*?** Actually, this is an artist's rendering of how we would appear if the size of our body parts were in proportion to the areas of the somatosensory cortex that process sensory information from these parts. Because much more cortex is devoted to the fingers and hands than to elbows or thighs, we can discern much finer differences in sensations of touch with our fingertips.

CONCEPT 2.24
Most of the cerebral cortex consists of association areas that are responsible for higher mental functions.

MODULE 2.3 REVIEW

The Brain: Your Crowning Glory

CONCEPT CHECK

1. In an evolutionary sense, the "oldest" part of the brain is
   a. the spinal cord.
   b. the midbrain.
   c. the forebrain.
   d. the hindbrain.

2. Match the following parts of the brain with the functions they control: (a) medulla; (b) cerebellum; (c) thalamus; (d) cerebral cortex.
   i. balance and coordination
   ii. thinking and organizing
   iii. relay of sensory information to the cerebral cortex
   iv. heart rate and breathing

3. Which of the following is *not* correct? The cerebral cortex
   a. is the part of the brain most directly responsible for reasoning, language, and problem solving.
   b. is divided into four lobes.
   c. forms the outer layer of the cerebral hemispheres.
   d. accounts for a much smaller percentage of brain mass in humans than in other animals.

4. Which part of the cerebral cortex processes auditory information?

MODULE 2.4

Methods of Studying the Brain

- **What recording and imaging techniques are used to study brain functioning?**
- **What experimental methods do scientists use to study brain functioning?**

Scientists use various methods of studying brain structures and their functioning. One method is to observe the effects of diseases or injuries on the brain. As a result of this type of observation, scientists have known for nearly two centuries that damage to the left side of the brain is connected with loss of sensation or movement on the right side of the body, and vice versa.

Over the years, scientists have also used invasive experimental methods to study the brain at work, including surgical procedures. Today, thanks to advanced technology, they have other, less invasive recording and imaging methods at their disposal. Concept Chart 2.4 summarizes both types of methods.

Recording and Imaging Techniques

Today, we have available a range of techniques that allow us literally to peer into the working brain and other parts of the body without surgery. These techniques are used to diagnose brain diseases and survey brain damage, as well as to help us learn more about brain functioning. Neuroscientists can probe the brain while the subject is awake and alert.

The **EEG (electroencephalograph)** is an instrument that records electrical activity in the brain (see Figure 2.11). Electrodes are attached to the scalp to measure the electrical currents, or *brain waves,* that are conducted between them. The EEG is used to study electrical activity in the brains of people with physical or psychological disorders and to explore brain wave patterns during stages of sleep.

The **CT (computed tomography) scan** (also called a *CAT* scan) is an imaging technique in which a computer measures the reflection of a narrow X-ray beam

CONCEPT 2.25
Modern technology provides ways of studying the structure and function of the brain without the need for invasive techniques.

Psych Assist: Methods of Studying the Living Brain

***web.* Netlab/Scanning the Brain**

Figure 2.11   The Electroencephalograph (EEG)
The EEG is a device that records electrical activity in the brain in the form of brain wave patterns. It is used to study the brains of people with physical or psychological disorders and to explore brain wave patterns during stages of sleep.

EEG (electroencephalograph)   A device that records electrical activity in the brain.

CT (computed tomography) scan   A computer-enhanced imaging technique in which an X-ray beam is passed through the body at different angles to generate a three-dimensional image of bodily structures (also called a CAT scan, short for *computerized axial tomography*).

PET (positron emission tomography) scan   An imaging technique in which a radioactive sugar tracer is injected into the bloodstream and used to measure levels of activity of various parts of the brain.

CONCEPT CHART 2.4
Methods of Studying the Brain

Recording and Imaging Techniques	Description
EEG (electroencephalograph)	A device that uses electrodes attached to the skull to record brain wave activity
CT (computed tomography) scan	A computer-enhanced X-ray technique that can provide images of the internal structures of the brain
PET (positron emission tomography) scan	A method that can provide a computer-generated image of the brain, formed by tracing the amounts of glucose used in different parts of the brain during different types of activity
MRI (magnetic resonance imaging)	A method of producing computerized images of the brain and other body parts by measuring the signals they emit when placed in a strong magnetic field
Experimental Techniques	**Description**
Lesioning	Destruction of brain tissue in order to observe the effects on behavior
Electrical recording	Placement of electrodes in brain tissue to record changes in electrical activity in response to particular stimuli
Electrical stimulation	The use of a mild electric current to observe the effects of stimulating various parts of the brain

from various angles as it passes through the brain or other bodily structures; it thus produces a three-dimensional image of the inside of the body (see Figure 2.12). The CT scan can reveal brain abnormalities associated with blood clots, tumors, and brain injuries (Haydel et al., 2000). It is also used to explore structural abnormalities that may be present in the brains of people with schizophrenia or other severe psychological disorders.

Whereas the CT scan reveals information about the shape and size of structures in the brain, the **PET (positron emission tomography) scan** provides a computerized image of the brain and other organs at work. The subject receives an injection of a radioactive isotope that acts as a tracer in the bloodstream. How the tracer is metabolized (converted by cells into energy) in the brain reveals the parts of the brain that are more active than others. More active areas metabolize more of the tracer than less active ones (see Figure 2.13). The PET scan can reveal which parts of the brain are most active when we are reading and writing, daydreaming, listening to music, or experiencing emotions ("Brain Scans," 2000; Damasio et al., 2000). From these patterns, we can determine which parts of the brain are involved in particular functions.

MRI (magnetic resonance imaging) provides a detailed image of the brain or other body parts. To produce a brain image, a technician places the person's head within a doughnut-shaped device that emits a strong magnetic field, aligning the atoms that spin in the brain. A burst of radio waves directed at the person disrupts the atoms, which release signals as they become realigned. A computer then integrates the signals into an image of the brain.

A new form of MRI, called *functional MRI (fMRI),* takes snapshots of the brain in action (see Figure 2.14). Whereas traditional MRI is limited to mapping brain structures, functional MRI is used to study both the function and the structure of the human brain (Thompson & Nelson, 2001).

Investigators use functional MRI to identify parts of the brain that become engaged when we perform particular tasks, such as seeing, hearing, remembering, using language, cooperating with others, and experiencing emotions, even

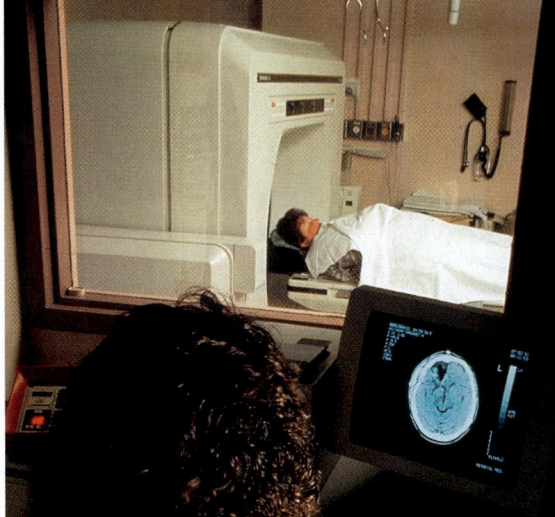

Figure 2.12   CT Scan
The CT scan provides a three-dimensional X-ray image of bodily structures. It can reveal structural abnormalities in the brain that may be associated with blood clots, tumors, brain injuries, or psychological disorders, such as schizophrenia.

MRI (magnetic resonance imaging)   A technique that uses a magnetic field to create a computerized image of internal bodily structures.

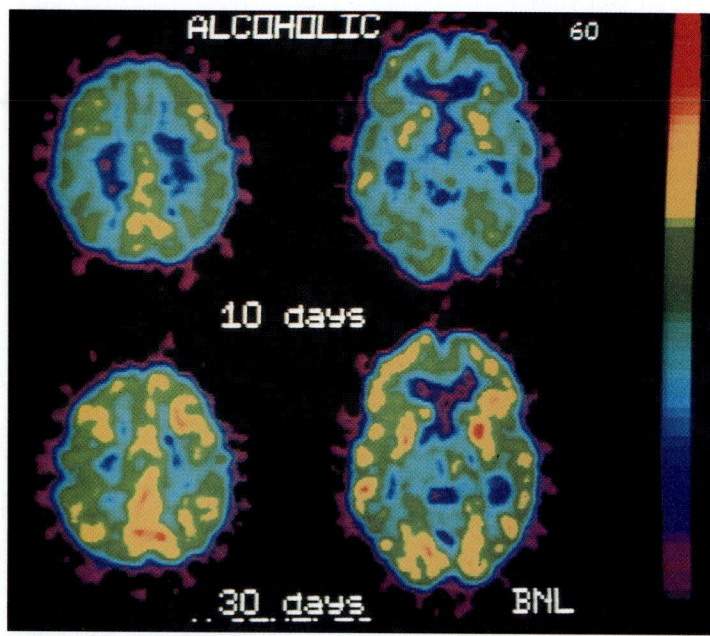

Figure 2.13   PET Scan
The PET scan measures the metabolic activity of the brain. More active regions are highlighted in yellow and red, whereas less active regions are shown in blues and greens. Here we see PET scan images of the brain of an alcoholic patient during withdrawal. By comparing relative levels of brain activity following 10 days (top row) and 30 days (bottom row) of withdrawal, we can observe that the brain becomes more active with greater length of time without alcohol.

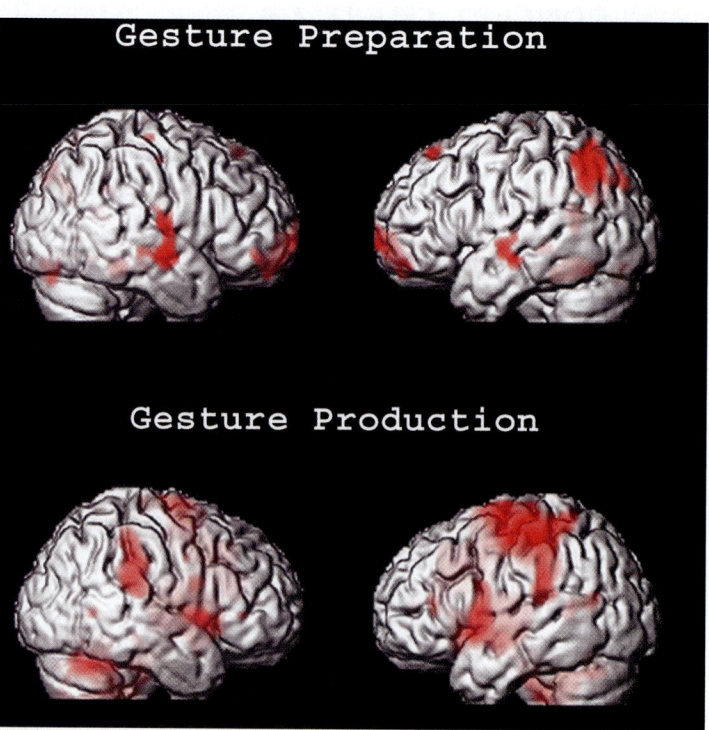

Figure 2.14   Functional Magnetic Resonance Imaging (fMRI)
Like the PET scan, the fMRI allows us to peer into the working brain. Here we see images of the brain when a person thinks about performing certain gestures (top), such as using a hammer or writing with a pen, and when actually performing these acts (bottom). The left hemisphere is depicted on the right side of the image, while the right hemispere is shown on the left. Areas in red are associated with greater levels of brain activity.

CONCEPT 2.26
Experimental methods used to study brain functioning include lesioning, electrical recording, and electrical stimulation.

lesioning   In studies of brain functioning, the intentional destruction of brain tissue in order to observe the effects on behavior.
electrical recording   As a method of investigating brain functioning, a process of recording the electrical changes that occur in a specific neuron or groups of neurons in the brain in relation to particular activities or behaviors.
electrical stimulation   As a method of investigating brain functioning, a process of electrically stimulating particular parts of the brain to observe the effects on behavior.

romantic feelings of love (Berthoz et al., 2002; Carpenter, 2000a; Ingram & Siegle, 2001; Rilling et al., 2002; Wheeler, Petersen, & Buckner, 2000). As noted, PET also maps functions of brain structures, but fMRI is less invasive in that it does not require injections of radioactive isotopes.

Functional MRI may well have helped clear up a long-standing scientific mystery—why it is impossible to tickle yourself (Begley, 2000b). Using this method, British researchers peered into the brains of people as they tickled themselves and as they were being tickled by a mechanical device. The part of the brain that processes sensations of touch, the somatosensory cortex, showed more activity when people were being tickled than when they tickled themselves. When we move our fingers to tickle ourselves, the brain center that coordinates these types of complex movements, the cerebellum, sends a signal that blocks some of the activity of the somatosensory cortex, which processes touch. But being tickled by an outside source comes as a surprise, so the cerebellum is unable to block sensory processing. Scientists believe this brain mechanism allows us to distinguish between stimuli we produce ourselves and outside stimuli that require further processing because they may pose a threat ("Scientists Answer Ticklish Question," 2000).

Experimental Methods

Scientists sometimes use invasive methods to investigate brain functioning. In one such method, called **lesioning**, the investigator destroys parts of the brain in experimental animals and then observes the effects. For example, destroying one part of a rhesus monkey's limbic system causes the animal to fly into a rage at the slightest provocation. But destroy another part of this system, and the monkey shows a placid response to all manner of provocation. Destroy one part of a rat's hypothalamus, and it gorges itself on food until it becomes extremely obese; destroy another part, and it stops eating. These experiments point to the parts of the brain engaged in these and other forms of behavior.

Other experimental techniques for studying brain function include *electrical recording* and *electrical stimulation*. In **electrical recording**, electrodes are implanted into particular neurons, groups of neurons, or nerves in specific parts of the brain. They provide a record of electrical changes in response to particular stimuli. Some experimental techniques are so refined that investigators can record electrical activity from a single brain cell. Using these methods, scientists discovered how individual neurons in the visual cortex respond to particular types of visual stimuli (see Chapter 3).

With the technique of **electrical stimulation**, investigators pass a mild electric current through particular parts of the brain and observe the effects. In this way, they can learn which parts of the brain are involved in controlling which behaviors. For example, we mentioned earlier how stimulation of parts of the hypothalamus in rats and other animals switches on stereotypical behavior patterns.

THINK

About It

Ethical Issues in Animal Research

Purposefully destroying parts of the brain to observe the results cannot be done ethically in humans, and it remains a controversial procedure even in animal research. Some animal rights advocates argue that animals should be accorded the same protections as human research participants. What is your opinion about using animals in experimental brain research? What safeguards do you think should be observed in this kind of research?

A Ticklish Question   Why is it that you can't tickle yourself? Researchers using a brain-imaging technique believe they have the answer.

MODULE 2.4 REVIEW

Methods of Studying the Brain

CONCEPT CHECK

1. Which of the following is a computer-enhanced imaging technique that uses X-ray beams to study structural abnormalities of the brain?
   a. fMRI
   b. PET scan
   c. CT scan
   d. MRI

2. Functional MRI (fMRI)
   a. is used to study both brain structure and brain functioning.
   b. involves an invasive technique known as lesioning.
   c. is a controversial procedure with ethical implications.
   d. is based on a sophisticated type of X-ray technique.

3. In the experimental technique for brain study called lesioning,
   a. parts of the brain of living organisms are destroyed.
   b. electrodes are surgically implanted in the brain.
   c. parts of the brain are electrically stimulated to observe the effects on behavior.
   d. connections between the brain and spinal cord are severed.

4. Scientists who use the experimental technique of electrical recording to study brain functioning
   a. also make use of a radioactive isotope that can be detected in the bloodstream.
   b. implant electrodes in particular neurons, groups of neurons, or nerves in particular parts of the brain.
   c. send a narrow X-ray beam through the head.
   d. are unable to get precise measurements from a single brain cell.

MODULE 2.5
The Divided Brain: Specialization of Function

- **What are the major differences between the left and right hemispheres?**
- **What determines handedness?**
- **What can we learn about brain lateralization from studies of "split-brain" patients?**

💡 **CONCEPT 2.27**
In most people, the left hemisphere is specialized for use of language and logical analysis, while the right hemisphere is specialized for spatial processing and other nonverbal tasks.

If you stub your left toe, cells in your right parietal lobe will "light up," producing sensations of pain. Conversely, a blow to your right toe will register in your left parietal lobe. This is because the sensory cortex in each hemisphere is connected to sensory receptors on the opposite sides of the body. Likewise, the motor cortex in your right frontal lobe controls the movements of the left side of your body, and vice versa. Thus, if we were to stimulate your left motor cortex in a certain spot, the fingers on your right hand would involuntarily contract. As we see next, evidence indicates that the right and left hemispheres are also specialized for certain types of functions.

The Brain at Work: Lateralization and Integration

The term **lateralization** refers to the division of functions between the right and left hemispheres (see Concept Chart 2.5). Generally speaking, the left hemisphere in most people appears to be dominant for language abilities—speaking, reading, and writing (Blakeslee, 1996; Gazzaniga, 1999). The left hemisphere also appears to be dominant for tasks requiring logical analysis, problem solving, and mathematical computations. The right hemisphere in most people appears to be dominant for nonverbal processing, such as understanding spatial relationships (e.g., piecing together puzzles, arranging blocks to match designs, reading maps), recognizing faces, interpreting people's gestures and facial expressions, perceiving and expressing emotion, and appreciating music and art.

Despite such differences, people are not "left-brained" or "right-brained" (Gazzaniga, 1995; Hellige, 1993). The functions of the hemispheres largely overlap, and messages rapidly zap back and forth across the corpus callosum, the bundle of nerve fibers that connects the hemispheres. In fact, though one hemisphere or the other may be dominant for a particular task, both hemispheres share the work in performing most tasks.

Language dominance is associated with handedness. For about 95 percent of right-handed people and even for about 70 percent of left-handed people, the left hemisphere is dominant for language functions (Damasio & Damasio, 1992; Pinker, 1994; Springer & Deutsch, 1993). For about 15 percent of left-handed people, the right hemisphere is dominant for language functions. The other 15 percent of left-handers show patterns of mixed dominance.

The French surgeon Paul Broca (1824–1880) was one of the pioneers in the discovery of the language areas of the brain. His most important discovery involved a male patient, fifty-one years old, who was admitted to the ward suffering from gangrene in his leg. The patient was also nearly unable to speak. He understood clearly what he heard, but his verbal utterances were limited primarily to one meaningless sound (*tan*).

The patient died a few days after being admitted. While conducting an autopsy, Broca found that an egg-shaped part of the left frontal lobe of the patient's brain had degenerated. The surgeon concluded that this area of the brain, now known as **Broca's area** in his honor, is essential to the production of speech (see Figure 2.15).

Lateralization of Brain Function The right hemisphere is dominant for spatial tasks, such as solving jigsaw puzzles, whereas the left hemisphere is dominant for verbal tasks, such as speaking, reading, and writing.

💭 **THINK**
About It

Is George a Left-Brainer?

Why is it incorrect to say that someone is either right-brained or left-brained?

lateralization The specialization of the right and left cerebral hemispheres for particular functions.

Broca's area An area of the left frontal lobe involved in speech.

CONCEPT CHART 2.5
Lateralization of Brain Functions

Areas of Left-Hemisphere Dominance	Areas of Right-Hemisphere Dominance
Verbal functions (for right-handers and most left-handers), including spoken and written use of language, as well as logical analysis, problem-solving, and mathematical computation	Nonverbal functions, including understanding spatial relationships (as presented, e.g., in jigsaw puzzles or maps), recognizing faces and interpreting gestures, perceiving and expressing emotion, and appreciating music and art

Figure 2.15   Broca's and Wernicke's Areas
Broca's area is an egg-shaped part of the frontal lobe that plays a key role in the production of speech. Wernicke's area, which is located in the temporal lobe, enables us to understand written or spoken language.

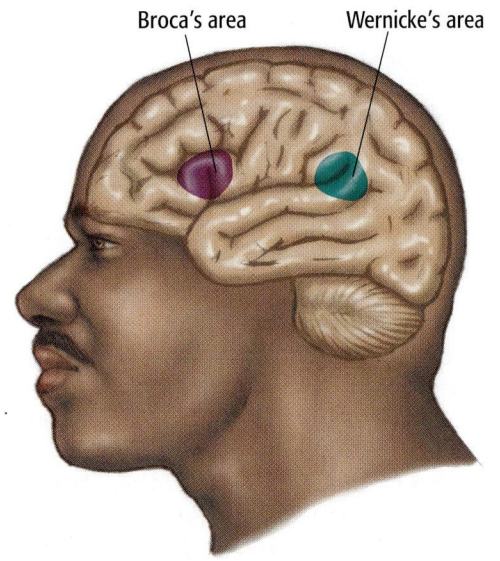

Broca's area   Wernicke's area

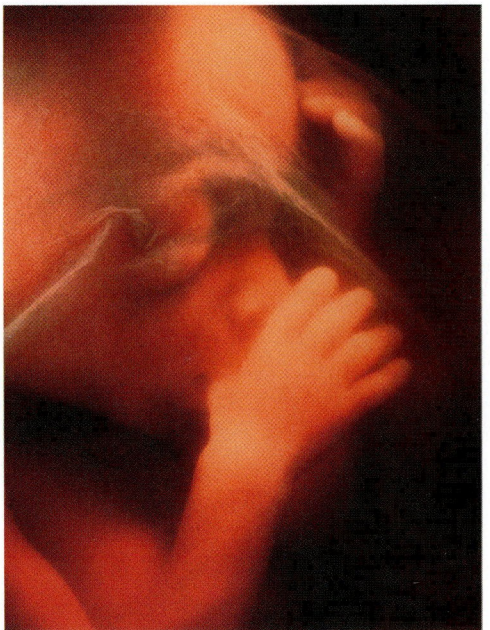

Broca's area is one of the brain's two vital language areas. The other, which is in the left temporal lobe, is **Wernicke's area** (see Figure 2.15). It is named after the German researcher Karl Wernicke (1848–1905). Wernicke's area is responsible for our ability to understand language in written or spoken form. Wernicke's and Broca's areas are connected by nerve fibers, so that there is an ongoing interaction between understanding language and being able to produce it or express it. Significant damage to Broca's area or Wernicke's area, or to the nerve connections between them, can lead to different forms of **aphasia**—the loss or impairment of the ability to understand or express language.

Already a Rightie?
The proportions of fetuses sucking their right or left thumbs parallel those of right-handed and left-handed people in the population, suggesting that handedness preferences may begin to develop before birth.

Handedness:
Why Are People Not More Even-Handed?

Though we may not be "right-brained" or "left-brained," most of us are primarily either right-handed or left-handed. Handedness runs in families (see Table 2.2), which points to the role of either heredity or family influences in its development. We don't yet know what causes handedness, but many scientists believe that genetic factors play an important role (Corballis, 2001; Jones & Martin, 2001). However, handedness differs in about one in five sets of identical twins (one twin may be right-handed, the other left-handed). Identical twins have identical genes, so if handedness were purely genetic in origin, we would not observe this difference. Thus, factors other than genetics must also contribute to handedness (Rosenbaum, 2000).

Social factors that may influence handedness include family pressures on children to use their right hand for writing. Prenatal hormones may also play a role, as evidence links left-handedness to high levels of male sex hormones during prenatal development (Coren, 1992). This may explain why twice as many males as

CONCEPT 2.28
Scientists suspect that handedness is strongly influenced by genetics.

Wernicke's area   An area of the left temporal lobe involved in processing written and spoken language.

aphasia   Loss or impairment of the ability to understand or express language.

TABLE 2.2
Parents' Handedness and Child's Odds of Being Left-Handed

Parents Who Are Left-Handed	Child's Odds
Neither parent	1 in 50
One parent	1 in 6
Both parents	1 in 2

Source: Springer and Deutsch, 1993.

CONCEPT 2.29

The results of split-brain operations show that under some conditions, the right hand literally doesn't know what the left hand is doing.

females turn out to be left-handed. Hormonal influences also depend on genetic factors, so the picture becomes yet more complex. Evidence does indicate that handedness preferences begin to develop before birth. In an ultrasound-based study of more than two hundred fetuses, researchers found that more than 95 percent of them sucked their right thumbs, while fewer than 5 percent sucked their left thumbs (Hepper, Shahidullah, & White, 1990). These percentages correspond closely to the distribution of right-handers and left-handers in the population.

Whatever the origins of handedness may be, forcibly imposing right-handedness on children may cause them to become secretive about using their left hands (e.g., by switching to the left hand when they are not being observed) and to develop emotional problems.

Split-Brain Research: Can the Hemispheres Go It Alone?

Epilepsy is a neurological disorder in which sudden, violent neural discharges of electrical activity in the brain cause seizures. In many cases, these discharges resemble a neural Ping-Pong match—the electrical discharges begin in one cerebral hemisphere and thunder into the other. As they bounce back and forth, they create a kind of wild electrical storm in the brain. Fortunately, most people with epilepsy are able to avoid or control seizures with medication.

When the disorder fails to respond to conventional forms of treatment, surgery may become an option. In the 1960s, neurosurgeons began to treat some severe cases of epilepsy by severing the corpus callosum. The intent of this type of surgery is to stop the neural storm by preventing the electrical activity in one hemisphere from crossing into the other. Severing the corpus callosum has become a more or less standard treatment for many cases of severe epilepsy (Engel, 1996). Those who have had the surgery are known as **split-brain patients**.

Split-brain patients retain their intellectual competence and distinctive personalities following surgery, which is all the more remarkable given that the surgery prevents communication between the cerebral hemispheres. Yet the two hemispheres now appear to be of two minds about some things (Gazzaniga, 1999). We might sometimes joke that it seems as if our left hand doesn't know what our right hand is doing. For split-brain patients, this strikes close to home, as illustrated in landmark research conducted by Nobel Prize winner Roger Sperry and his colleague Michael Gazzaniga.

In a typical experiment, these researchers placed a familiar object, such as a key, in the left hands of split-brain patients (Gazzaniga, 1992). When blindfolded, the patients could not name the object they were holding, although they were able to use the key to open a lock. The question is, *Why*?

Recall that the somatosensory cortex in the right hemisphere processes sensory information from the left side of the body (the touch of a key placed in the left hand, for instance). Since the right hemisphere shares this information with the left hemisphere, speech centers in the left hemisphere can respond by naming the object that was felt. Thus, people whose brains function normally have no trouble naming a familiar object placed in their left hands even if they can't see it.

But in split-brain patients, the right hemisphere cannot transmit information to the speech centers in the left hemisphere, making it impossible to name the object being held in the left hand. The right hemisphere literally cannot "say" what the left hand is holding (Gazzaniga, 1995). But despite this lack of ability to name the object, the right hemisphere recognizes the object by touch and can demonstrate through hand movements how it is used.

In perception studies with split-brain patients, researchers briefly flash pictures of objects on a screen and then ask the patients to identify them by naming them or by selecting them from among a group of objects hidden behind the screen (see Figure 2.16). The experimenters vary whether the stimuli are projected

epilepsy A neurological disorder characterized by seizures that involve sudden, violent discharges of electrical activity in the brain.

split-brain patients Persons whose corpus callosum has been surgically severed.

Figure 2.16   Split-Brain Study
The right part of this figure shows that information from the right half of the visual field is transmitted to the occipital cortex in the left hemisphere; conversely, information from the left half of the visual field goes to the right occipital cortex for processing. In split-brain patients, information received by one hemisphere cannot be transferred to the other.

In a typical study with split-brain patients, investigators present a visual stimulus to each hemisphere individually. When an object, such as a pencil, is flashed in the right visual field *(a)*, the visual information is transmitted to the patient's left hemisphere. Since the left hemisphere controls language, the patient can correctly name the object. But when visual information is presented to the nonverbal right hemisphere *(b)*, the patient is unable to name it. However, the patient is able to pick out the object by touch from a group of hidden objects when using the left hand *(c)*, since the tactile information from the left hand projects to the right hemisphere, which has already "seen" the object.

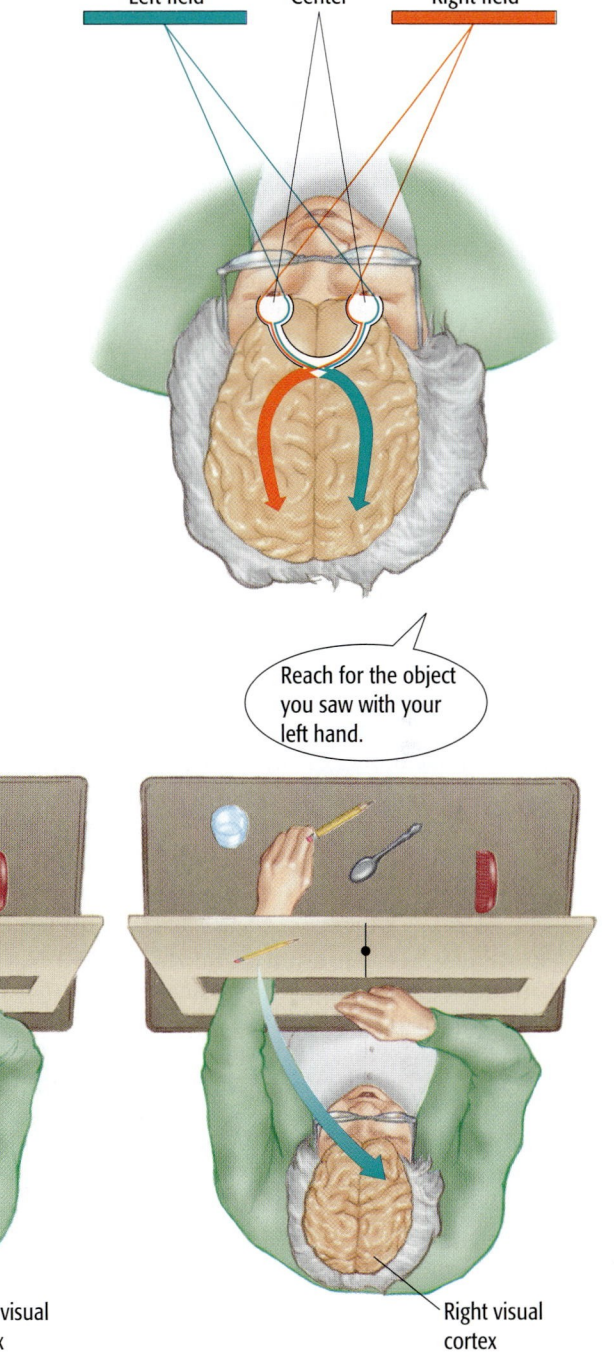

to the left or right visual cortex, which is located in the occipital lobes. If you look straight ahead and project a vertical line dividing your field of view into a right and left half, the area to the left of the line represents your left visual field. Information presented to the left visual field crosses over and is processed by the right visual cortex. Conversely, information presented to the right of your field of view (to the right visual field) is projected to the left visual cortex. In people whose corpus callosum is intact, information is quickly exchanged between the hemispheres, but in split-brain patients, one hemisphere does not communicate with the other.

When an image is flashed to the right visual field of a split-brain patient, the left hemisphere processes the information, and the patient is able to name the

CONCEPT 2.30

Brain damage can result in subtle or profound consequences in physical and psychological functioning.

prefrontal cortex The area of the frontal lobe that lies in front of the motor cortex and that is involved in higher mental functions, including thinking, planning, impulse control, and weighing the consequences of behavior.

plasticity The ability of the brain to adapt itself after trauma or surgical alteration.

object ("I saw a pencil"). This is not surprising when you consider that the left hemisphere in most people controls speech. But what happens when the picture of the object is flashed on the left side of the screen, which projects information to the right hemisphere, the one without language function? In this case, the patient cannot say what, if anything, is seen. The patient is likely to report, "I saw nothing." However, because the right hemisphere can recognize objects by touch, the patient is able to use the left hand to select the correct object from among those hidden behind the screen.

Findings from studies of split-brain patients provide additional evidence of the importance of the left hemisphere in speech and language production. Perhaps more revealing is the observation that split-brain patients appear to be quite normal in their outward behavior (Sperry, 1982). It seems as if their brains are able to adapt new strategies for processing information and solving problems that do not rely on communication between the hemispheres. As we will now see, this speaks to the remarkable ability of the human brain to adapt to new demands.

Brain Damage and Psychological Functioning

Many people have made remarkable recoveries from brain damage resulting from stroke or head trauma, perhaps none more remarkable than that of Phineas Gage, a nineteenth-century railroad worker whose case astounded the medical practitioners of his time. One day in 1848, Gage was packing blasting powder for a dynamite charge and accidentally set it off. The blast shot an inch-thick metal rod through his cheek and brain and out through the top of his head. Gage fell to the ground, but to the astonishment of his co-workers, he soon stood up, dusted himself off, and spoke to them. He was helped home, where his wounds were bandaged. Gage's wounds healed within two months, and he was able to function despite the massive head injury he had suffered. Then, however, changes in his personality began suggesting more subtle forms of brain damage. The formerly polite, conscientious worker became an irresponsible drifter (Jennings, 1999). He started brawling and drinking heavily. Those who knew him before the accident said, "Gage is no longer Gage."

Gage's skull is now on display at Harvard University. The trajectory of the metal rod is obvious (see Figure 2.17). With near-surgical precision, it apparently missed the parts of the brain controlling language and movement but damaged the **prefrontal cortex**, the area of the frontal lobe that lies in front of the motor cortex.

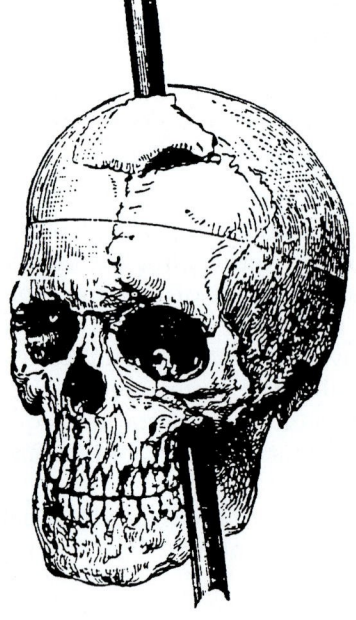

Figure 2.17   Yet He Survived
This illustration of the path of the metal rod through Phineas Gage's skull shows just how remarkable it was that he survived.

The prefrontal cortex is the part of the brain that weighs the consequences of our actions, makes plans for the future, solves problems, makes decisions, and constrains impulsive behavior. Scientists suspect that the seat of intelligence is located in the prefrontal cortex (Duncan et al., 2000). Contemporary research with patients who have suffered damage to the prefrontal cortex also points to the important role that this part of the brain plays in making moral judgments or decisions (S. W. Anderson et al., 1999; G. Johnson, 1999). Scientists now suspect there may be a kind of "morality circuit" in the prefrontal cortex, which if damaged can impair the person's ability to adhere to moral and social codes.

Brain Plasticity

In some cases of epilepsy and other neurological disorders, damage to one of the hemispheres is so severe that it must be surgically removed. Remarkably, most patients who undergo this radical procedure are able to function normally, at least when the operation is performed by the time the patient is about thirteen years old. Until that age, the functions of the left and right hemispheres appear to be quite flexible, or "plastic." When children under thirteen have the left (language-dominant) hemisphere removed, the right hemisphere is able to reorganize itself and adapt to new demands by developing language functions (Zuger, 1997). This is an amazing example of adaptability—perhaps even more amazing than the ability of a lizard to regenerate a lost limb.

The ability of the brain to adapt and reorganize itself following trauma or surgical alteration is called **plasticity**. When one part of the brain is damaged by injury or disease, another part of the brain may take over its functions to a certain extent (Bruer, 1999). As with patients who undergo surgical removal of one of their cerebral hemispheres, plasticity is greatest among young children whose brains are not fully lateralized. How the brain accomplishes these feats of reorganization—whether in building new circuitry or altering existing circuitry—remains uncertain. Yet, as in the case of many brain injuries, there are limits to how well the brain can compensate for damage to brain tissue.

CONCEPT 2.31
The brain is capable of reorganizing itself to a certain extent to adapt to new functions, even in some cases in which half of it is surgically removed.

MODULE 2.5 REVIEW

The Divided Brain: Specialization of Function

CONCEPT CHECK

1. One long-established fact about the brain is that
   a. it is completely lateralized with respect to functions.
   b. the left part of the brain controls language, but only in right-handed people.
   c. the right side of the brain controls functioning in the left part of the human body, and vice versa.
   d. the functions of the left and right cerebral hemispheres do not overlap.

2. Whereas for most people the _____ hemisphere appears to be dominant for language functions, the _____ hemisphere appears to be dominant for nonverbal functions.

3. The part of the brain directly involved in speech production is
   a. the corpus callosum.
   b. Wernicke's area.
   c. Broca's area.
   d. the anterior fissure.

4. The part of the brain directly involved in comprehending written or spoken language is
   a. the prefrontal cortex.
   b. Broca's area.
   c. the corpus callosum.
   d. Wernicke's area.

5. Which of the following is *not* true?
   a. Handedness runs in families.
   b. Handedness is determined entirely by genetic factors.
   c. Researchers have found that the great majority of fetuses suck their right thumbs.
   d. Imposing right-handedness on left-handed children can lead to emotional problems.

MODULE 2.6

The Endocrine System: The Body's Other Communication System

- **What are the major endocrine glands?**
- **What roles do hormones play in behavior?**

The nervous system is not the only means by which parts of the body communicate with each other. The *endocrine system* is also a communication system, although it is vastly slower than the nervous system. The messages it sends are conveyed through blood vessels rather than a network of nerves. The messengers it uses are hormones, which, as you may recall from Module 2.1, are chemical substances that help regulate bodily processes. Here we explore the endocrine system and the role that it plays in behavior.

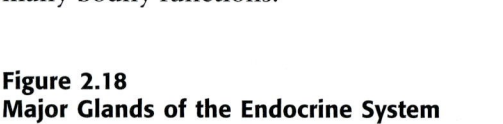

web Web Tutorial/The Endocrine System

Endocrine Glands: The Body's Pumping Stations

The **endocrine system** is a grouping of glands located in various parts of the body that release secretions, called hormones, directly into the bloodstream. Figure 2.18 shows the location of many of the major endocrine glands in the body. Concept Chart 2.6 summarizes the functions of the hormones they release.

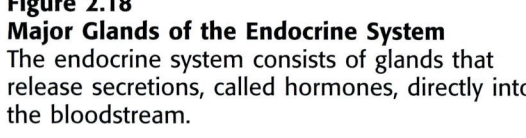

CONCEPT 2.32
Endocrine glands distributed throughout the body help coordinate many bodily functions.

Figure 2.18
Major Glands of the Endocrine System
The endocrine system consists of glands that release secretions, called hormones, directly into the bloodstream.

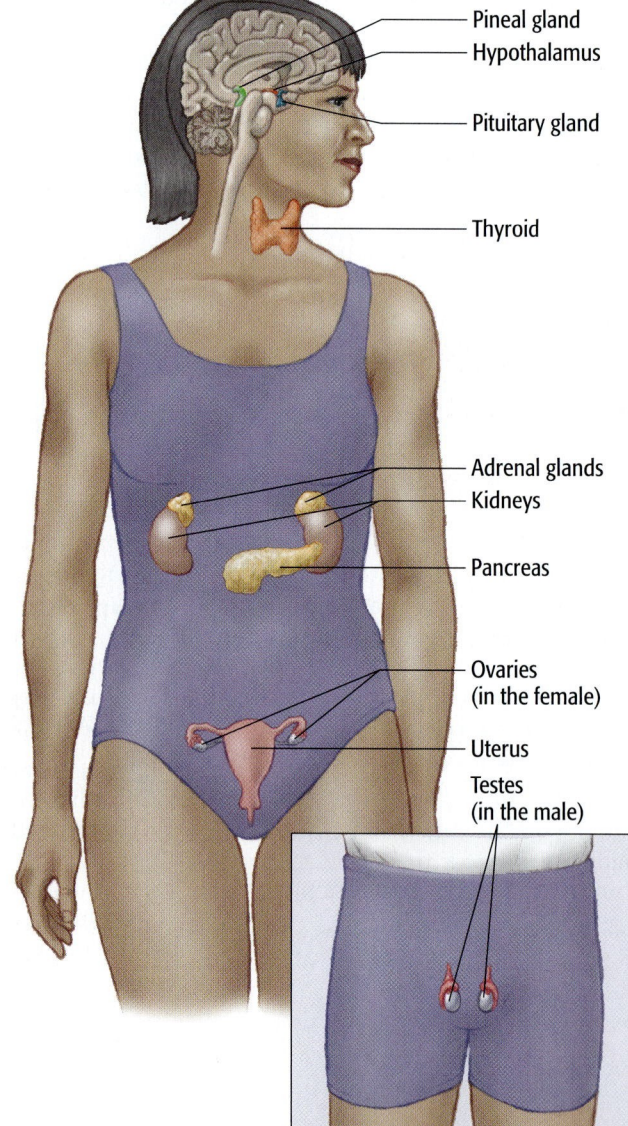

Pineal gland
Hypothalamus
Pituitary gland
Thyroid
Adrenal glands
Kidneys
Pancreas
Ovaries (in the female)
Uterus
Testes (in the male)

endocrine system The body's system of glands that release their secretions, called hormones, directly into the bloodstream.

pancreas An endocrine gland located near the stomach that produces the hormone insulin.

homeostasis The tendency of systems to maintain a steady, internally balanced state.

CONCEPT CHART 2.6
The Endocrine System

Gland/Hormone	Function
Pituitary gland	
Growth hormone (GH)	Stimulates growth, especially of bones
ACTH	Stimulates adrenal cortex to secrete cortical steroids
Oxytocin	Stimulates uterine contractions during childbirth and release of milk following childbirth
Hypothalamus	
Releasing factors	Stimulate the pituitary gland to release other hormones, including growth hormone
Pineal gland	
Melatonin	Helps regulate sleep-wake cycles
Pancreas	
Insulin	Facilitates entry of blood glucose (sugar) into cells; involved in regulation of blood sugar levels
Thyroid gland	
Thyroid hormones	Involved in regulating metabolic rate, growth, and maturation
Adrenal glands	
Cortical steroids	Help body cope with stress; promote muscle development; stimulate the liver to release stores of sugar
Epinephrine (adrenaline) and Norepinephrine (noradrenaline)	Speeds up bodily processes, such as heart rate and breathing rate
Ovaries	
Estrogen	Fosters female sexual maturation; helps regulate menstrual cycle
Progesterone	Helps maintain pregnancy; helps regulate menstrual cycle
Testes	
Testosterone	Promotes sperm production; fosters male sexual differentiation during prenatal development; stokes sexual maturation in pubertal males

The endocrine system regulates important bodily processes, such as growth, reproduction, and metabolism. To do so, it relies on hormones to communicate its messages to organs and other bodily tissues. (The word *hormone* is derived from Greek roots that mean "to stimulate" or "to excite.")

Like neurotransmitters, hormones lock into receptor sites on target cells to trigger changes in these cells. For example, *insulin,* a hormone produced by the **pancreas**, regulates the concentration of glucose (sugar) in the blood. Like a key fitting into a lock, insulin opens glucose receptors on cells, allowing sugar to pass from the bloodstream into the cells where it is used as fuel. Unlike neurotransmitters, which are found only in the nervous system, hormones travel through the bloodstream system to their destinations.

One of the important functions of the endocrine system is helping to maintain an internally balanced state, or **homeostasis**, in the body. When the level of sugar in the blood exceeds a certain threshold, or set point—as may happen when you eat a meal rich in carbohydrates (sugars and starches)—the pancreas releases more insulin into the bloodstream. Insulin stimulates cells throughout the body to draw more glucose from the blood, which decreases the level of glucose in the body. As this level declines to its set point, the pancreas reduces the amount of insulin it secretes.

CONCEPT 2.33
Hormones are released by endocrine glands directly into the bloodstream, and from there they travel to specific receptor sites on target organs and tissues.

CONCEPT 2.34
In concert with the nervous system, the endocrine system helps the body maintain a state of equilibrium, or homeostasis.

CONCEPT 2.35
The pituitary gland is often called the "master gland" because it helps regulate so many other endocrine glands.

THINK

About It

Hormones and Behavior

Do you believe your behavior is influenced by your hormones? Why or why not?

pituitary gland   An endocrine gland in the brain that produces various hormones involved in growth, regulation of the menstrual cycle, and childbirth.

pineal gland   A small endocrine gland in the brain that produces the hormone melatonin, which is involved in regulating sleep-wake cycles.

adrenal glands   A pair of endocrine glands located just above the kidneys that produce various stress-related hormones.

gonads   Sex glands (testes in men and ovaries in women) that produce sex hormones and germ cells (sperm in the male and egg cells in the female).

ovaries   The female gonads, which secrete the female sex hormones estrogen and progesterone and produce mature egg cells.

testes   The male gonads, which produce sperm and secrete the male sex hormone testosterone.

germ cells   Sperm and egg cells from which new life develops.

The two most important endocrine glands in the body, the hypothalamus and the **pituitary gland**, are located in the brain. The pituitary is often referred to as the "master gland" because it affects so many bodily processes. But even the so-called master gland operates under the control of another "master"—the hypothalamus.

The hypothalamus secretes hormones known as *releasing factors* that cause the nearby pituitary gland to release other hormones. For example, the hypothalamus releases *growth-hormone releasing factor (hGRF)*, which stimulates the pituitary to release *growth hormone (GH)*, which in turn promotes physical growth. Other pituitary hormones cause other glands, such as the testes in men and ovaries in women, to release their own hormones. The process is akin to a series of falling dominoes.

In addition to the hypothalamus and pituitary, the brain houses another endocrine gland, the **pineal gland**, which releases *melatonin,* a hormone that helps regulate sleep-wake cycles (see Chapter 4). The **adrenal glands** are a pair of glands that lie above the kidneys. They have an outer layer, called the *adrenal cortex,* and a core, called the *adrenal medulla.* The pituitary hormone *ACTH* stimulates the adrenal cortex to secrete hormones called *cortical steroids,* which promote muscle development and stimulate the liver to release stores of sugar in times of stress. More energy thus becomes available in response to stressful situations, such as emergencies in which the organism faces the imminent threat of a predator attack. Other stress hormones, *epinephrine* and *norepinephrine,* are released by the adrenal medulla. They help prepare the body to deal with stress by speeding up bodily processes, such as heart rate and respiration rate.

As noted earlier in the chapter, some chemicals, like norepinephrine, do double duty: They function both as neurotransmitters in the nervous system and as hormones in the bloodstream. In the brain, norepinephrine—and to a lesser degree, epinephrine—function as neurotransmitters. Norepinephrine plays an important role in the nervous system in regulating mood, alertness, and appetite.

The **gonads** are the sex glands—**ovaries** in women and **testes** in men. The gonads produce the **germ cells**—egg cells in women and sperm in men. The ovaries also produce the female sex hormones *estrogen* and *progesterone,* which help regulate the menstrual cycle. Progesterone also stimulates growth of the female reproductive organs and helps the uterus maintain pregnancy.

The testes produce the male sex hormone, *testosterone,* which leads to the development of male sex organs in male fetuses. Following puberty in males, release of testosterone by the testes fosters growth of the male genitals, development of a beard, and deepening of the voice.

Though the nervous system and endocrine system are separate systems, they are closely intertwined. The brain regulates the activity of the endocrine system so that the body responds not as separate systems but as an integrated whole. The brain controls endocrine functions through the autonomic nervous system. In times of stress, for example, the sympathetic nervous system transmits commands from the brain to the adrenal medulla, leading to the release of the stress hormones epinephrine and norepinephrine that help prepare the body to deal with stress (discussed further in Chapter 13).

Hormones and Behavior

Though human behavior is more strongly influenced by learning and experience than by hormones, hormones do play a role. For example, higher levels of the male sex hormone testosterone are linked to greater physical aggressiveness in both men and women (Pope et al., 2000; Rubinow & Schmidt, 1996; Sullivan, 2000). (Testosterone is produced in both men's and women's bodies, but in lesser amounts in women). Ingestion of anabolic steroids (synthetic testosterone), which some people use to build up muscle mass, is also linked to increased aggressive and belligerent behavior (Pope & Katz, 1990). We should recognize that testosterone is perhaps one of many factors interacting in complex ways that lead to aggressive behavior in humans. Deficiencies of testosterone can also lead to loss of sexual desire in both men and women.

Excesses and deficiencies in hormone levels are associated with many physical and psychological disorders. Thyroid hormones, produced by the **thyroid gland**, help regulate body metabolism, the rate at which the body turns food into energy. Excess thyroid hormones are associated with states of anxiety and irritability. Deficiencies of thyroid hormones can lead to sluggishness and weight gain, and retard intellectual development in children.

During the menstrual cycle, testosterone levels in women remain fairly stable, but levels of estrogen and progesterone shift dramatically. Most women, about three out of four, experience some form of **premenstrual syndrome (PMS)**—a constellation of physical and psychological symptoms in the days leading up to menstruation each month (Brody, 1996). These symptoms may include anxiety, depression, irritability, weight gain resulting from fluid retention, and abdominal discomfort. The cause or causes of PMS are unclear, but mounting evidence suggests that hormones play a role. We lack solid evidence to support the belief that hormonal imbalances—too much or too little circulating estrogen or progesterone—are causally responsible for PMS (Chrisler & Johnston-Robledo, 2002). It may turn out that differences in sensitivity to these hormones, and not to their levels per se, predispose some women to PMS (Rubinow & Schmidt, 1995). Other research links PMS to disturbances in the functioning of the neurotransmitter serotonin (Steiner et al., 1995). It is conceivable that estrogen affects mood by way of influencing serotonin activity (Rubinow, Schmidt, & Roca, 1998). Other factors—such as how women cope with menstrual symptoms, what their cultures teach them about menstruation, and their general mood states—may also influence the likelihood of a woman's experiencing PMS.

CONCEPT 2.36
Hormones are linked to a wide range of behaviors and mood states.

CONCEPT 2.37
Hormonal factors may be involved in explaining PMS, a syndrome affecting about three out of four women.

thyroid gland   An endocrine gland in the neck that secretes the hormone thyroxin, which is involved in regulating metabolic functions and physical growth.

premenstrual syndrome (PMS)   A cluster of physical and psychological symptoms occurring in the few days preceding the menstrual flow.

MODULE 2.6 REVIEW

The Endocrine System: The Body's Other Communication System

CONCEPT CHECK

1. Although it is vastly slower than the nervous system, the _____ system is another communication system in the human body.

2. Which of the following do glands secrete directly into the body's bloodstream?
   a. neurotransmitters
   b. hormones
   c. neuromodulators
   d. glial cells

3. What term is used to describe an internally balanced state in the body?

4. The gland known as the "master gland" because of its role in regulating the activity of many other glands is the _____ gland.

MODULE 2.7

Genes and Behavior: A Case of Nature and Nurture

- **What roles do genetic factors play in behavior?**
- **What are the methods used to study genetic influences on behavior?**

Within every living organism is a set of inherited instructions that determines whether it will have lungs or gills, a penis or a vagina, blue eyes or green. This set of instructions, called a **genotype**, constitutes a master plan for building and maintaining a living organism. The genetic instructions are encoded in the organism's **genes**, the basic units of heredity that are passed along from parent to offspring (G. Johnson, 2000).

Genes are composed of the complex, double-stranded spiraling molecule called **deoxyribonucleic acid (DNA)** (Gaulin & McBurney, 2001), and they are linked together on long strands called **chromosomes** that reside in the cell nucleus. Scientists believe there may some 30,000 genes in the human genome, the genetic blueprint that contains the precise chemical sequence that constitutes human DNA. They are not completely sure about this number, however; it may turn out to be higher or lower (Wade, 2003b). Each cell in the body contains the full complement of human genes, except for germ cells (egg cells and sperm cells). These carry half of the person's genetic code. Children inherit half of their chromosomes and the genes they carry from their mothers and half from their fathers. During conception, the twenty-three chromosomes in the mother's egg cell unite with the twenty-three chromosomes in the father's sperm cell, forming the normal human complement of forty-six chromosomes arranged in twenty-three pairs. With the exception of identical twins, no two people share the same genetic code.

Having recently succeeded in cracking the human genetic code or *genome*, scientists are now able to read the entire genetic script of a human being (Wade, 2003a). The code has even been placed on the Internet to enable scientists to study it (Baltimore, 2000).

In research involving the genetic code, scientists are focusing on understanding how genes work and tracking down the specific genes involved in physical and mental disorders (Bunney, 2003; Plomin, 2003; Plomin et al., 2003; Tecott, 2003). They hope the human genome will lead to new insights into the genetic origins of various diseases and spur development of gene-based therapies with the hope of blocking the actions of harmful genes and harnessing the actions of useful ones (Phillips et al., 2002; Plomin & Crabbe, 2001; Plomin & McGuffin, 2003; Sapolsky, 2003).

Genetic factors clearly determine physical characteristics like eye color and hair color, but what about their role in behavior? Is our behavior a product of our genes, our environment, or both?

Genetic Influences on Behavior

We have no doubt that genes influence many patterns of behavior (Cabib et al., 2000; Plomin et al., 2003). Some dogs are bold or placid in temperament; others are yappy. They all share enough genes to make them dogs and not cats, but they may differ greatly from one another in their behavior and physical traits. People have selectively bred animals to enhance specific behavior patterns as well as physical traits. But what about human behavior?

One of the oldest debates in psychology is the **nature-nurture problem**. Is our behavior governed by nature (genetics) or nurture (environment and culture)? Though the debate continues, most psychologists believe human behavior is influenced by a combination of genes and the environment (Cacioppo et al.,

genotype An organism's genetic code.

genes Basic units of heredity that contain the individual's genetic code.

deoxyribonucleic acid (DNA) The basic chemical material in chromosomes that carries the individual's genetic code.

chromosomes Rodlike structures in the cell nucleus that house the individual's genes.

nature-nurture problem The debate in psychology about the relative influences of genetics (nature) and environment (nurture) in determining behavior.

phenotype The observable physical and behavioral characteristics of an organism, representing the influences of the genotype and environment.

polygenic traits Traits that are influenced by multiple genes interacting in complex ways.

familial association studies Studies that examine the degree to which disorders or characteristics are shared among family members.

2000; Plomin et al., 2003). The contemporary version of the nature-nurture debate is more about the relative contributions of nature *and* nurture to particular behaviors than it is about nature *or* nurture.

Heredity influences not only many psychological characteristics, such as intelligence, shyness, aggressiveness, and sociability, but also special aptitudes in music and art as well as preferences for different types of occupations (Angier, 2003a; Ellis & Bonin, 2003; Plomin & Crabbe, 2000; Schwartz et al., 2003). Genes may even contribute to our tendency to have a happy or sad disposition (Lykken, 1999), and to our propensity to marry (Johnson et al., 2004). Heredity also plays a role in many psychological disorders, including anxiety disorders, substance abuse, mood disorders, and schizophrenia (Merikangas & Risch, 2003; Plomin & McGuffin, 2003).

The genotype, or genetic code, is a kind of recipe for determining the features or traits of an organism. But whether the genotype becomes expressed in the organism's observable traits, or **phenotype**, depends on a complex interaction of genes and the environment (Crabbe, 2002). Psychological traits, such as shyness, intelligence, or a predisposition to schizophrenia or alcoholism, appear to be **polygenic traits**, which means that they are influenced by multiple genes interacting with the environment in complex ways. In other words, no one gene accounts for complex psychological traits (Plomin & McGuffin, 2003; Uhl & Grow, 2004). Nor do genes dictate what our lives or personalities will become. Genetic factors create a *predisposition* or *likelihood* (not a certainty) that particular behaviors, abilities, personality traits, or psychological disorders will emerge (Frank & Kupfer, 2000; Sapolsky, 2000). Other factors, such as family relationships, stress, and learning experiences, play a large role in determining how, or even if, genetic factors become expressed in observable behaviors or psychological traits.

Landmark research by psychologist David Reiss and his colleagues showed that the degree to which genetic influences on the personality trait of shyness become expressed in the overt behavior of children depends on the interactions they have with their parents and other important people in their lives (Reiss et al., 2000). Parents who are overprotective of a shy child may accentuate an underlying genetic tendency toward shyness, whereas those who encourage more outgoing behavior may help the child overcome it.

But how can we separate the effects of environment from those of genetics? Let us consider several methods scientists use to untangle these effects.

Kinship Studies:
Untangling the Roles of Heredity and Environment

Scientists rely on several methods to examine genetic contributions to behavior, including familial association studies, twin studies, and adoptee studies. Concept Chart 2.7 provides a summary of these three basic types of kinship studies.

Familial Association Studies

The more closely related people are, the more genes they have in common. Each parent shares 50 percent of his or her genes with his or her children, as do siblings with each other. More distant relatives, such as uncles, aunts, and cousins, have fewer genes in common, but they still have a greater percentage of common genes than do unrelated people (see Figure 2.19). Therefore, if genes help determine a given trait or disorder, we would expect more closely related people to be more likely to share the trait or disorder in question (Gottesman & Gould, 2003).

Familial association studies have been used to study family linkages in schizophrenia (see Figure 2.20). Consistent with a role for genetics in the development of this disorder, we find a greater risk of the disorder among closer blood relatives

CONCEPT 2.38
The view held by most scientists today is that both heredity and environment interact in complex ways in shaping our personalities and intellectual abilities.

CONCEPT 2.39
Genetic factors create predispositions that increase the likelihood that certain behaviors, abilities, or personality traits will emerge, but whether they do emerge depends largely on environmental influences and individual experiences.

CONCEPT 2.40
Scientists use three basic types of kinship studies to examine genetic influences on behavior: familial association studies, twin studies, and adoptee studies.

 PsychAssist: Genetic Contributions to Behavior-Familial Association Study

CONCEPT CHART 2.7
Types of Kinship Studies

Type of Study	Method of Analysis	Evaluation
Familial association study	Analysis of shared traits or disorders among family members in relation to their degree of kinship	Provides supportive evidence of genetic contribution to behavior when concordance is greater among more closely related family members than among more distantly related ones; limited because the closer their blood relationship, the more likely people are to share similar environments
Twin study	Analysis of differences in the rates of overlap (concordance) for a given trait or disorder between identical and fraternal twins	Provides strong evidence of the role of genetic factors in behavior when concordance rates are greater among identical twins than among fraternal twins; may be biased by greater environmental similarity between identical twins than fraternal twins
Adoptee study	Analysis of similarity in traits or prevalences of psychological or physical disorders between adoptees and their biological and adoptive parents, or between identical twins reared apart and those reared together	The clearest way of separating the roles of heredity and environment, but may overlook common environmental factors in reared-apart twins early in life

of schizophrenia patients than among more distant relatives. The risk among blood relatives rises from 2 percent among first cousins and uncles and aunts to 48 percent among identical twins. However, we should note a major limitation of this kind of study. The closer their blood relationship, the more likely people are to share common environments. Thus, researchers look to other types of studies, such as twin studies and adoptee studies, to help disentangle the relative contributions of heredity and environment.

Figure 2.19   Genetic Overlap Among Family Members
As you can see in this family tree, the more closely related people are, the more genes they have in common. The fractions represent the proportion of genetic overlap. For example, siblings have one-half of their genes in common, while uncles or aunts share one-quarter of their genes with their nephews and nieces.

THINK
About It

Nature vs. Nurture

What methods do researchers use to disentangle the influences of heredity and environment on behavior? What are the limitations of these methods?

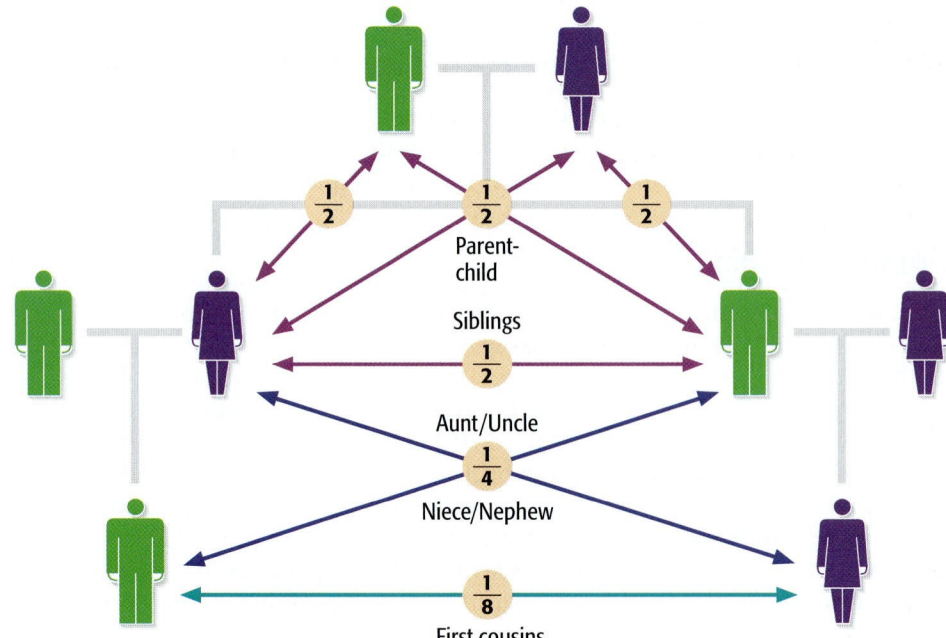

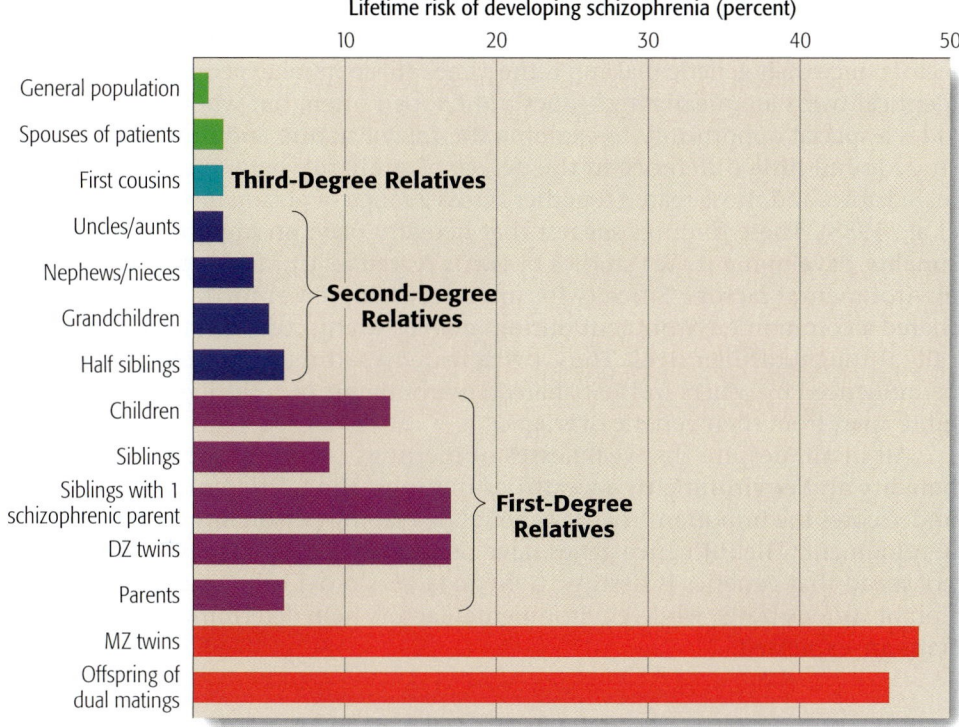

Lifetime risk of developing schizophrenia (percent)

Figure 2.20
Familial Risk in Schizophrenia
The risk of developing schizophrenia generally increases with the closeness of the family relationship with someone who has the disorder. We also need to look at other sources of evidence, such as data from twin studies and adoption studies, to help disentangle the effects of nature and nurture.

Source: Adapted from Gottesman et al., 1987.

Twin Studies

In the case of **identical twins** (also called *monozygotic,* or *MZ,* twins), a fertilized egg cell, or **zygote**, splits into two cells, and each one develops into a separate person. Because their genetic code had been carried in the single cell before it split in two, identical twins have the same genetic makeup. In the case of **fraternal twins** (also called *dizygotic,* or *DZ,* twins), the mother releases two egg cells in the same month. They are fertilized by different sperm cells, and each fertilized egg cell then develops into a separate person. Fraternal twins thus share only 50 percent of their genetic makeup, as do other brothers and sisters.

In **twin studies**, researchers compare **concordance rates**, or percentages of shared traits or disorders. A higher rate of concordance (percentage of time both twins have the same disorder or trait) among MZ twins than among DZ twins strongly suggests a genetic contribution to the disorder or trait. Researchers find that identical twins are more likely than fraternal twins to share some psychological traits, such as sociability and activity levels, as well as some psychological disorders, such as schizophrenia (Plomin et al., 1997).

Twin studies have a major limitation, however. The problem is that identical twins may be treated more alike than fraternal twins. Thus, environmental factors, not genes, may account for their higher rates of concordance. For example, identical twins may be encouraged to dress alike, take the same courses, even play the same musical instrument. Investigators believe that, despite this limitation, twin studies provide useful information on genetic contributions to personality and intellectual development (Winerman, 2004a).

Adoptee Studies

The clearest way to separate the roles of environment and heredity is to conduct **adoptee studies**, which compare adopted children with both their adoptive parents and their biological parents. If they tend to be more like their adoptive parents in their psychological traits or the disorders they develop, we can argue that environment plays the more dominant role. If they tend to be more like their biological parents, we may assume that heredity has a greater influence.

identical twins   Twins who developed from the same zygote and so have identical genes (also called *monozygotic,* or *MZ,* twins).

zygote   A fertilized egg cell.

fraternal twins   Twins who developed from separate zygotes and so have 50 percent of their genes in common (also called *dizygotic,* or *DZ,* twins).

twin studies   Studies that examine the degree to which concordance rates between twin pairs for particular disorders or characteristics vary in relation to whether the twins are identical or fraternal.

concordance rates   In twin studies, the percentages of cases in which both members of twin pairs share the same trait or disorder.

adoptee studies   Studies that examine whether adoptees are more similar to their biological or adoptive parents with respect to their psychological traits or to the disorders they develop.

When identical twins are separated at an early age and reared apart in separate adoptive families, we can attribute any differences between them to environmental factors since their genetic makeup is the same. This natural experiment—separating identical twins at an early age—does not happen often, but when it does, it provides a special opportunity to examine the role of nature and nurture. One such study found little difference in the degree of similarity between identical twins reared apart and those reared together across a range of personality traits (Tellegen et al., 1988). These findings suggest that heredity plays an important role in personality development. Yet studies of twins reared apart may overlook common environmental factors. Since twins are rarely adopted at birth, they may have shared a common environment during infancy. Many continue to meet periodically throughout their lives. Thus, twins reared apart may have opportunities to be influenced by others in their shared environments or to influence each other, quite apart from their genetic overlap.

All in all, despite the weaknesses of methods used to separate the roles of heredity and environment, a wealth of findings using different methodologies underscores the important role of genetics in shaping personality and intellectual development. The influence genes have on our psychological development does not mean that genetics is destiny. Genetic factors provide a *range* for the expression of various traits, while environmental factors help determine how *or if* these traits are expressed.

MODULE 2.7 REVIEW

Genes and Behavior: A Case of Nature and Nurture

CONCEPT CHECK

1. In the long-standing debate in psychology over the nature-nurture issue, the central question is,
   a. How much of our genetic code do we have in common with others?
   b. Which is a more influential factor in human behavior: the genotype or the phenotype?
   c. Does heredity or environment govern human behavior?
   d. To what extent do rearing influences affect our genotype?

2. Polygenic traits are
   a. traits that are influenced by multiple genes.
   b. traits that are influenced by polygenic genes.
   c. traits that are determined by genetic defects.
   d. traits that are fully determined by combinations of genes.

3. What are the basic types of studies used to examine the influence of genetics on behavior?

4. Dizygotic (fraternal) twins result when
   a. a zygote is formed and then splits into two cells.
   b. two egg cells are fertilized by different sperm.
   c. two different sperm fertilize the same egg cell, which then divides in half.
   d. two zygotes are formed from the fertilization of the same egg cell.

APPLICATION

MODULE 2.8   Biofeedback Training: Learning by Listening to the Body

- **What is biofeedback training?**

Normally, you're not aware of your internal bodily states, such as how fast your heart is beating, the electrical activity in your brain, the temperature in your extremities, or the degree of muscle tension in your forehead. Psychologists have found that providing people with feedback about their internal bodily functions ("biofeedback") can help them learn to control these functions, at least within certain limits.

In **biofeedback training (BFT)**, individuals are attached to monitoring equipment that provides them with a continual stream of information about their internal physiological functioning. A rising tone may indicate increasing heart rate or muscle tension, while a lower tone indicates changes in the opposite direction. With BFT, people have learned to modify their heart rates, blood pressure, muscle tension, body temperature, brain wave patterns, and other physiological processes (Gatchel, 2001; Schwartz, 1995; Weems, 1998). How do they do it? Basically, they use the feedback—the rising or lowering tone, for example—as a cue to help them identify behaviors they can control to bring about the desired effect. For example, they may find that slow, rhythmic breathing changes the tone in the desired direction.

One major application of BFT is symptom reduction. It turns out that reducing muscle tension in the forehead through the use of **electromyographic (EMG) biofeedback** can help relieve the pain of a tension headache. EMG biofeedback provides the user with feedback about changes in muscle tension in forehead muscles or other selected muscle groups. Similarly, the pain of a **migraine headache**—an intense headache brought on by changes in blood flow in the brain—can often be relieved by **thermal biofeedback**, which helps people learn to increase blood flow to their extremities (Blanchard & Diamond, 1996). In thermal biofeedback, a device that measures internal temperature is attached to the body, generally around a finger. As more blood flows into the finger and thus away from the head, the temperature in the finger rises, causing the device to beep more slowly. Raising the temperature in a finger may thus relieve the pain associated with migraine headaches.

We don't know whether people, or other animals, are capable of directly modifying autonomic nervous system activity without any involvement of their somatic (voluntary) nervous system. In other words, you may learn to lower your heart rate via your somatic nervous system by purposefully slowing your breathing rate. The biofeedback device doesn't directly teach you any new skills; it merely shows you whether desired changes in physiological processes have occurred. People use biofeedback signals as cues to help them learn strategies to produce desired changes in their physiological functioning. Some people, for example, can raise the temperature in their fingers simply by imagining a finger growing warmer.

Although initial enthusiasm for BFT led to some overblown and even outrageous claims, research findings continue to support its effectiveness in a wide range of applications. It has been used to reduce chronic low-back pain and other musculoskeletal pain (Newton et al., 1995), as well as headache pain (Gatchel, 2001); to teach self-relaxation skills to children with attention-deficit hyperactivity disorder (ADHD) (Robbins, 2000); to reduce blood pressure in people with mild hypertension (A. P. Shapiro, 2001); to increase muscular control in people with urinary and fecal incontinence (Burgio et al., 1998; Tries & Brubaker, 1996); and even to improve muscle control of the fingers to improve piano playing

CONCEPT 2.41
By providing information about changes in internal bodily processes, BFT helps people gain some degree of conscious control over their physiological functioning.

biofeedback training (BFT)   A method of learning to control certain bodily responses by using information transmitted by physiological monitoring equipment.

electromyographic (EMG) biofeedback   A form of BFT that involves feedback about changes in the level of muscle tension in the forehead or elsewhere in the body.

migraine headache   A prolonged, intense headache brought on by changes in blood flow in the brain's blood vessels.

thermal biofeedback   A form of BFT that involves feedback about changes in temperature and blood flow in selected parts of the body; used in the treatment of migraine headaches.

Biofeedback Training Through biofeedback training, people can learn to alter some internal bodily processes, such as heart rate, blood pressure, muscle tension, body temperature, and certain types of brain wave patterns.

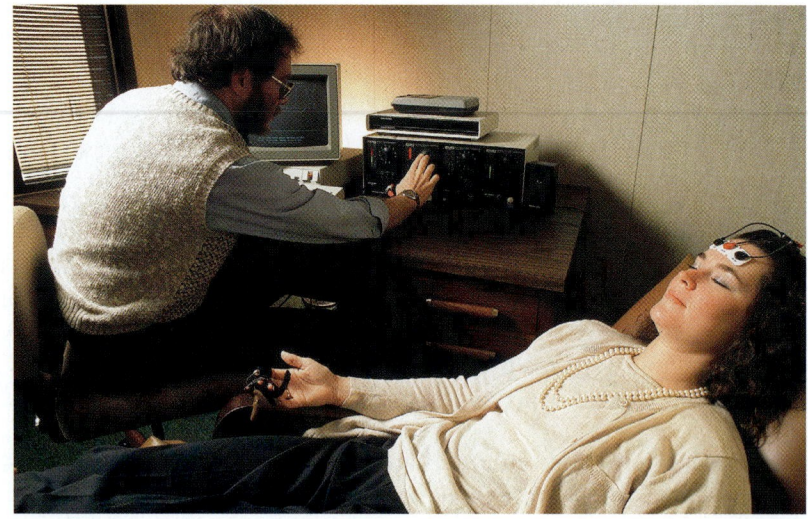

(Montes, Bedmar, & Martin, 1993). On the other hand, many of the benefits of BFT in treating such problems as headaches, mild hypertension, and chronic pain disorders may be achieved with simpler forms of relaxation training that don't require expensive equipment, such as muscle relaxation techniques and deep breathing exercises.

TYING IT TOGETHER

In this chapter, we explored the biological underpinnings of behavior. Our ability to sense and make sense of the world around us, to coordinate our movements, to think, learn, remember, and solve problems is dependent on the functioning of our nervous system. The basic units of the nervous system are neurons, nerve cells that transmit information and work together in complex assemblages in the brain to process information (Module 2.1). The nervous system consists of two major branches, the central nervous system, consisting of the brain and spinal cord, and the peripheral nervous system, which connects the central nervous system to other parts of the body (Module 2.2). The central nervous system is the body's master control unit; it receives and processes information from the peripheral nervous system, regulates bodily processes, and performs higher mental functions, such as thinking and memory (Module 2.3). Investigators explore the workings of the brain, the centerpiece of the central nervous system, by using brain-imaging techniques and experimental methods (Module 2.4). Based on studies of brain functioning, it appears that the left hemisphere of the brain is dominant for language and logical functions, whereas the right hemisphere of the brain appears to be dominant for nonverbal functions, such as understanding spatial relationships (Module 2.5).

The nervous system is not the only communication system in the body. The endocrine system consists of glands that release hormones that travel through the bloodstream to distant parts of the body. Hormones lock into receptor sites on specific target cells, triggering changes in these cells that are needed to regulate and coordinate important bodily processes. Hormones may also influence our behavior and moods (Module 2.6). Another biological influence on our behavior is heredity. Most psychologists believe that both genetic and environmental factors influence our behavior in varying degrees (Module 2.7).

Biofeedback training uses specialized equipment that allows people to listen to the internal workings of their bodies and respond in ways that alter their physiological functioning. Through BFT, people can gain some control over certain autonomic nervous system functions, such as heart rate and blood pressure (Module 2.8).

SUMMING UP: Q&A

Neurons: The Body's Wiring (Module 2.1)

What is a neuron?

- A neuron is a nerve cell, the basic building block of the nervous system through which information in the form of neural impulses is transmitted.

What are the parts of a neuron?

- Like other cells, neurons have a cell body, or soma, that houses the cell nucleus and carries out the metabolic work of the cell. Each neuron also has an axon, a long cable that conducts outgoing messages (neural impulses) to other neurons, as well as dendrites, which are fibers that receive neural messages from other neurons. Terminal buttons are swellings at the ends of the axon that release neurotransmitters, which are chemical messengers that carry the message to adjacent neurons.

What are the types of neurons and types of cells found in the nervous system?

- The nervous system has three types of neurons: sensory neurons, which carry information from sensory organs and internal bodily organs and tissues to the spinal cord and brain; motor neurons, which carry messages from the central nervous system to the muscles and inner organs; and interneurons, which connect neurons with each other.
- The nervous system has two types of cells: neurons, the nerve cells that conduct neural impulses, and glial cells, which support and nourish neurons. Glial cells also form the myelin sheath that covers some axons and that speeds transmission of neural impulses.

How is a neural impulse generated and transmitted from one neuron to another?

- Neural impulses are electrochemical events. When a neuron is stimulated beyond a threshold level, there is a rapid shift in its polarity from a negative to a positive charge. This reversal of charge, called an action potential or neural impulse, is generated along the length of the axon to the terminal buttons.
- When a neural impulse reaches the terminal buttons, it triggers the release of neurotransmitters, the chemical messengers that carry the message across the synapse to neighboring neurons. Neurotransmitters can have either excitatory or inhibitory effects on the neurons at which they dock.

What roles do neurotransmitters play in psychological functioning?

- Neurotransmitters are involved in such psychological processes as memory, learning, and emotional response. Irregularities in the functioning of particular neurotransmitters are implicated in various disorders, including schizophrenia and depression.

The Nervous System: Your Body's Information Superhighway (Module 2.2)

How is the nervous system organized?

- The major divisions of the nervous system are the central nervous system, which consists of the brain and spinal cord, and the peripheral nervous system, which connects the central nervous system to the rest of the body. The peripheral nervous system is divided into the somatic nervous system and autonomic nervous system.

What are spinal reflexes?

- Spinal reflexes are automatic, unlearned responses that are controlled at the level of the spinal cord. They may involve as few as two neurons.

What is the autonomic nervous system?

- The autonomic nervous system is the part of the peripheral nervous system that automatically regulates such internal bodily processes as heartbeat, respiration, digestion, and pupil dilation. It is divided into the sympathetic and parasympathetic branches.

What is the relationship between the sympathetic and parasympathetic divisions of the autonomic nervous system?

- These two divisions have largely opposite effects. The sympathetic nervous system speeds up bodily processes that expend energy, while the parasympathetic system slows down some bodily processes and fosters others, such as digestion, that replenish stores of energy.

The Brain: Your Crowning Glory (Module 2.3)

How is the brain organized, and what are the functions of its various parts?

- The brain has three major sections. The hindbrain, which houses the medulla, pons, and cerebellum, is involved in controlling basic bodily functions. The midbrain houses nerve bundles that relay messages between the hindbrain and the forebrain; it also houses structures that help regulate automatic movement. The forebrain is the largest part of the brain; its major structures are the thalamus, the hypothalamus, the limbic system, and the cerebral cortex.
- The thalamus relays sensory information to the cerebral cortex and helps regulate states of sleep and wakefulness.
- The hypothalamus plays a key role in controlling many vital bodily processes.
- The limbic system, which includes the amygdala, hippocampus, and parts of the thalamus and hypothalamus, is involved in memory and emotional processing.
- The cerebral cortex is responsible for processing sensory information, for higher mental functions such as thought, problem solving, and language, and for controlling voluntary movement, among other functions.

How is the cerebral cortex organized?

• Each hemisphere of the cerebral cortex has four lobes: the frontal, parietal, temporal, and occipital lobes. Each of the lobes is contained in each cerebral hemisphere. The corpus callosum is a nerve bundle that connects the two hemispheres.

What are the major functions associated with the four lobes of the cerebral cortex?

• The occipital lobes are primarily involved with vision; the parietal lobes, with somatosensory processing; the temporal lobes, with hearing; and the frontal lobes, with motor control and higher mental functions, including retrieving and acting upon stored memories, problem solving, decision making, and carrying out coordinated actions.

Methods of Studying the Brain (Module 2.4)

What recording and imaging techniques are used to study brain functioning?

• These techniques include the EEG, CT scan, PET scan, and MRI.

What experimental methods do scientists use to study brain functioning?

• Lesioning is a method that involves destroying certain parts of the brains of laboratory animals in order to observe the effects.
• Electrical recording involves implanting electrodes in the brain to record changes in brain activity associated with certain activities or behaviors.
• Electrical stimulation entails passing a mild electric current through the brain so that the effects on specific parts of the brain can be observed.

The Divided Brain: Specialization of Function (Module 2.5)

What are the major differences between the left and right hemispheres?

• In most people, the left hemisphere appears to play a larger role in verbal tasks, including the use of language and logic, while the right hemisphere is specialized for tasks involving nonverbal processing, such as understanding spatial relationships, recognizing faces, and appreciating music and art.

What determines handedness?

• Genetic factors appear to be a strong determinant of handedness, although hormonal factors and social and cultural influences may also play a role.

What can we learn about brain lateralization from studies of "split-brain" patients?

• Studies of split-brain patients, whose left and right cerebral hemispheres are surgically disconnected, can help us better understand the specialized functions of each cerebral hemisphere.

The Endocrine System: The Body's Other Communication System (Module 2.6)

What are the major endocrine glands?

• The major endocrine glands are the pituitary gland, hypothalamus, pineal gland, pancreas, adrenal glands, thyroid gland, and gonads (testes in males and ovaries in females).

What roles do hormones play in behavior?

• Excesses of thyroid hormones can cause anxiety and irritability, while too little can lead to sluggishness and weight gain and retard intellectual development in children.
• Testosterone has been linked to aggressiveness.
• Female sex hormones appear to play a role in PMS.

Genes and Behavior: A Case of Nature and Nurture (Module 2.7)

What roles do genetic factors play in behavior?

• Genetic factors are major influences on animal behavior and temperament.
• In humans, genetic factors interact in complex ways with environmental influences in determining personality and intellectual development.

What are the methods used to study genetic influences on behavior?

• Three types of kinship studies are used to study the role of genetics in human behavior: familial association studies, twin studies, and adoptee studies.

Application: Biofeedback Training: Learning by Listening to the Body (Module 2.8)

What is biofeedback training?

• Biofeedback training uses monitoring equipment that provides people with information about changes in their physiological functioning. Individuals use this feedback to learn to consciously control such physiological processes as brain wave patterns and internal body temperature.

Key Terms

neurons *(p. 40)*
brain *(p. 40)*
soma *(p. 40)*
axon *(p. 40)*
terminal buttons *(p. 40)*
neurotransmitters *(p. 40)*
synapse *(p. 40)*
dendrites *(p. 40)*
sensory neurons *(p. 40)*
motor neurons *(p. 41)*
glands *(p. 41)*
hormones *(p. 41)*
interneurons *(p. 41)*
nerve *(p. 41)*
glial cells *(p. 42)*
myelin sheath *(p. 42)*
nodes of Ranvier *(p. 42)*
ions *(p. 42)*
resting potential *(p. 42)*
depolarization *(p. 43)*
action potential *(p. 43)*
all-or-none principle *(p. 43)*
refractory period *(p. 44)*
receptor site *(p. 44)*
reuptake *(p. 45)*
enzymes *(p. 45)*
neuromodulators *(p. 45)*
antagonists *(p. 45)*
schizophrenia *(p. 45)*
hallucinations *(p. 45)*
delusions *(p. 45)*
Parkinson's disease *(p. 45)*
agonists *(p. 46)*
stimulant *(p. 46)*
amphetamines *(p. 46)*
antidepressants *(p. 46)*
endorphins *(p. 46)*
nervous system *(p. 47)*
central nervous system *(p. 49)*
spinal cord *(p. 49)*

spine *(p. 49)*
reflex *(p. 49)*
spinal reflex *(p. 49)*
peripheral nervous system *(p. 50)*
somatic nervous system *(p. 50)*
autonomic nervous system *(p. 50)*
sympathetic nervous system *(p. 51)*
parasympathetic nervous system *(p. 51)*
hindbrain *(p. 52)*
medulla *(p. 53)*
pons *(p. 53)*
brainstem *(p. 53)*
cerebellum *(p. 53)*
midbrain *(p. 53)*
reticular formation *(p. 53)*
forebrain *(p. 53)*
thalamus *(p. 54)*
basal ganglia *(p. 54)*
hypothalamus *(p. 54)*
limbic system *(p. 54)*
amygdala *(p. 54)*
hippocampus *(p. 54)*
cerebral cortex *(p. 54)*
cerebrum *(p. 54)*
cerebral hemispheres *(p. 54)*
corpus callosum *(p. 54)*
occipital lobes *(p. 55)*
parietal lobes *(p. 55)*
somatosensory cortex *(p. 55)*
frontal lobes *(p. 56)*
motor cortex *(p. 57)*
temporal lobes *(p. 57)*
association areas *(p. 57)*
EEG (electroencephalograph) *(p. 58)*
CT (computed tomography) scan *(p. 58)*
PET (positron emission tomography) scan *(p. 59)*
MRI (magnetic resonance imaging) *(p. 59)*
lesioning *(p. 60)*
electrical recording *(p. 61)*

electrical stimulation *(p. 61)*
lateralization *(p. 62)*
Broca's area *(p. 62)*
Wernicke's area *(p. 63)*
aphasia *(p. 63)*
epilepsy *(p. 64)*
split-brain patients *(p. 64)*
prefrontal cortex *(p. 66)*
plasticity *(p. 67)*
endocrine system *(p. 68)*
pancreas *(p. 69)*
homeostasis *(p. 69)*
pituitary gland *(p. 70)*
pineal gland *(p. 70)*
adrenal glands *(p. 70)*
gonads *(p. 70)*
ovaries *(p. 70)*
testes *(p. 70)*
germ cells *(p. 70)*
thyroid gland *(p. 71)*
premenstrual syndrome (PMS) *(p. 71)*
genotype *(p. 72)*
genes *(p. 72)*
deoxyribonucleic acid (DNA) *(p. 72)*
chromosomes *(p. 72)*
nature-nurture problem *(p. 72)*
phenotype *(p. 73)*
polygenic traits *(p. 73)*
familial association studies *(p. 73)*
identical twins *(p. 75)*
zygote *(p. 75)*
fraternal twins *(p. 75)*
twin studies *(p. 75)*
concordance rates *(p. 75)*
adoptee studies *(p. 75)*
biofeedback training (BFT) *(p. 77)*
electromyographic (EMG) biofeedback *(p. 77)*
migraine headache *(p. 77)*
thermal biofeedback *(p. 77)*

Thinking Critically About Psychology

Based on your reading of this chapter, answer the following questions. Then, to evaluate your progress in developing critical thinking skills, compare your answers to the sample answers found in Appendix A.

The case of Phineas Gage is one of the best-known case studies in the annals of psychology. In 1848, as you already know, Gage suffered an accident in which a metal rod pierced his cheek and brain and penetrated the top of his head. Yet not only did he survive this horrific accident, but he also managed to pick himself up and speak to workers who came to his aid. Though he

survived his injuries, his personality changed—so much so that people would remark, "Gage is no longer Gage."

1. Why do you think Gage's injury affected his personality but not the basic life functions that the brain controls, such as breathing and heart rate?

2. How might the nature of the injury that Gage sustained explain why this once polite and courteous man became aggressive and unruly?

Answers to Concept Check Questions

Module 2.1: 1. b; 2. soma; 3. sensory neurons, motor neurons, and interneurons; 4. d; 5. a; 6. b.   **Module 2.2:** 1. central, peripheral; 2. central; 3. sympathetic nervous system; 4. a.   **Module 2.3:** 1. d; 2. (a) iv, (b) i, (c) iii, (d) ii; 3. d; 4. temporal lobes.   **Module 2.4:** 1. c; 2. a; 3. a; 4. b.   **Module 2.5:** 1. c; 2. left, right; 3. c; 4. d; 5. b.   **Module 2.6:** 1. endocrine; 2. b; 3. homeostasis; 4. pituitary   **Module 2.7:** 1. c; 2. a; 3. familial association studies, twin studies, and adoptee studies; 4. b.

Sensation and Perception

DID YOU KNOW THAT . . .

- Our sense of smell may not be as keen as that of dogs, but humans can detect the presence of even one drop of perfume dispersed through a small house? (p. 84)

- Roy G. Biv is one of the most famous names learned by psychology students, but he is not a real person? (p. 87)

- Listening to music on a "Walkman" or similar device at too high a volume can permanently damage your hearing? (p. 97)

- Salmon use the sense of smell to sniff out the streams of their birth when they return to spawn? (p. 100)

- Some people are born with a distaste for broccoli? (p. 101)

- We have a sense that enables us to locate the parts of our body in the dark? (p. 104)

- Newborn babies prefer the sounds of their mothers' voices to the voices of other women? (p. 107)

- The mechanism that makes motion pictures possible lies in the viewer, not the projector? (p. 116)

One day, my infant daughter Daniella turned into a giant. Or so it seemed. I was making a video recording of her fledgling attempts to crawl. All was going well until she noticed the camera. She then started crawling toward this funny man holding the camera—me. As she approached, her image in the viewfinder grew larger and larger, eventually so large that she blotted out all other objects in my view. The image of my daughter that was cast upon my eyes was of a large and ever-growing giant! But I didn't panic. Despite the information my eyes were transmitting to my brain, I understood my daughter was not morphing into a giant. Fortunately, we tend to perceive objects to be of their actual size despite changes in the size of the image they project on our eyes as they grow nearer. Yet the sensation of seeing your infant grow to be a giant before your eyes can be an unsettling experience, especially when the "giant" then attempts to mouth the camera.

We are continually bombarded with stimuli from the outside world that impinge on our sensory organs. The world is a medley of lights and sounds that strike our eyes and ears, and of chemical substances that waft past our noses or land on our tongues as we consume food or drink liquids. In this chapter, you will see how your sense organs respond to external stimuli and transform these stimuli into sensory signals your brain uses to produce *sensations* of vision, hearing, touch, smell, and taste. You will learn how your brain assembles bits and pieces of sensory information into meaningful impressions of the world that are called *perceptions*. You will also learn how your brain senses changes in the position of your body, so you can move about without stumbling or losing your balance. Our sensory systems operate at blinding speeds, but the real marvel is how the brain processes all the information it receives from the body's sensory organs, making it possible for us not only to sense the world around us but also to make sense of it. As the example of my "giant" daughter illustrates, sensation and perception are different processes. What we perceive may not correspond to what our eyes observe.

The study of sensation and perception is critical to psychology because our investigation of behavior and mental processes begins with input from the world around us and the way the senses and brain interpret that information. Let us proceed, first, to explore how our sensory systems operate. Then we will explore how the brain assembles the sensory information it receives to form perceptions that help us make sense of the sensations that fill our lives with the colors and sounds that form the rich tapestry of sensory experience. ■

MODULE 3.1

Sensing Our World: Basic Concepts of Sensation

- **What is sensation?**
- **What is the difference between absolute thresholds and difference thresholds?**
- **What factors contribute to signal detection?**
- **What is sensory adaptation?**

CONCEPT 3.1

Sensation is the process by which physical stimuli that impinge on our sensory organs are converted into neural impulses that the brain uses to create our experiences of vision, touch, hearing, taste, smell, and so on.

CONCEPT 3.2

Sensory receptors convert sources of sensory stimuli, such as light and sound, into neural impulses the brain can use to create sensations.

CONCEPT 3.3

Psychophysics is the study of relationships between the features of physical stimuli, such as the intensity of lights and sounds, and the sensations we experience in response to these stimuli.

 PsychAssist: Basic Concepts of Sensation

CONCEPT 3.4

Our sensory systems vary in the amounts of stimulation needed to detect the presence of a stimulus and the differences among stimuli.

sensation The process by which we receive, transform, and process stimuli from the outside world to create sensory experiences of vision, touch, hearing, taste, smell, and so on.

sensory receptors Specialized cells that detect sensory stimuli and convert them into neural impulses.

psychophysics The study of the relationship between features of physical stimuli, such as the intensity of light and sound, and the sensation we experience in response to these stimuli.

absolute threshold The smallest amount of a given stimulus a person can sense.

difference threshold The minimal difference in the magnitude of energy needed for people to detect a difference between two stimuli.

Sensation is the process by which we receive, transform, and process stimuli that impinge on our sensory organs into neural impulses, or signals, that the brain uses to create experiences of vision, hearing, taste, smell, touch, and so on.

Each of our sense organs contains specialized cells, called **sensory receptors**, which detect stimuli from the outside world, such as light, sound, and odors. They are found throughout the body, in such organs as the eyes, ears, nose, and mouth, and in less obvious locations, such as the joints and muscles of the body and the entirety of the skin. In this module, we examine how sensory receptors respond to external stimuli and how they convert these stimuli into messages the brain uses to create sensations.

Our venture into sensation leads us back to **psychophysics**, the study of how physical sources of stimulation—light, sound, odors, and so on—relate to our experience of these stimuli in the form of sensations. Psychophysics began with the work of the nineteenth-century German scientist Gustav Theodor Fechner. Though Wilhelm Wundt is credited with establishing the first psychological laboratory in 1879, some historians believe that the publication of Fechner's *Elements of Psychophysics* in 1860 signaled the beginning of the scientific approach to psychology.

We begin our study of sensation by examining the common characteristics that relate to the functioning of our sensory systems: thresholds, signal detection, and sensory adaptation.

Absolute and Difference Thresholds: Is Something There? Is Something *Else* There?

Our sensory receptors are remarkably sensitive to certain types of stimuli. On a clear, dark night we can detect a flickering candle thirty miles away. We can also detect about one drop of perfume spread through a small house. The **absolute threshold** is the smallest amount of a stimulus that a person can reliably detect. Table 3.1 lists absolute thresholds for the senses of vision, hearing, taste, smell, and touch.

People differ in their absolute thresholds. Some are more sensitive than others to certain kinds of sensory stimulation—for example, sounds or odors. Fechner sought to determine the absolute thresholds for various senses by presenting people with stimuli of different magnitudes, such as brighter and duller lights, and then asking them whether they could see them. According to this method, the absolute threshold is defined as the minimal level of stimulus energy that people can detect 50 percent of the time. Stimuli detected less than 50 percent of the time are considered below the absolute threshold. Stimuli that can be detected more often are above the threshold.

The nineteenth-century German scientist Ernst Weber (1795–1878) (pronounced *Vay-ber*) studied the smallest differences between stimuli that people were able to perceive. The minimal difference between two stimuli that people can reliably detect is the **difference threshold**, or *just-noticeable difference (jnd)*. Just-noticeable differences apply to each of our senses.

TABLE 3.1   Absolute Thresholds for Various Senses

Sense	Stimulus	Receptors	Threshold
Vision	Light energy	Rods and cones in the eyes	The flame from a single candle flickering about thirty miles away on a dark, clear night
Hearing	Sound waves	Hair cells in the inner ear	The ticking of a watch placed about twenty feet away from a listener in a quiet room
Taste	Chemical substances that contact the tongue	Taste buds on the tongue	About one teaspoon of sugar dissolved in two gallons of water
Smell	Chemical substances that enter the nose	Receptor cells in the upper nostrils	About one drop of perfume dispersed in a small house
Touch	Movement of, or pressure on, the skin	Nerve endings in the skin	The wing of a bee falling on the cheek from about one centimeter away

Source: Adapted from Galanter, 1962.

How do difference thresholds apply to the range of stimuli we perceive with our senses? Weber summarized his findings in what is now known as **Weber's law**. According to this law, the amount you must change a stimulus to detect a difference is given by a constant fraction or proportion (called a *constant*) of the original stimulus. For example, Weber's constant for noticing a difference in weights is about 1/50 (or 2 percent). This means that if you were lifting a 50-pound weight, you would probably not notice a difference unless the weight were increased or reduced by about 2 percent (or 1 pound). But if you were lifting a 200-pound weight, the weight would have to be increased by about 4 pounds (2 percent) for you to notice the difference. Though the absolute weight needed to detect a difference is about quadruple as you increase the initial weight from 50 pounds to 200, the fraction remains the same (1/50).

Weber found that the difference threshold differed for each of the senses. People are noticeably more sensitive to changes in the pitch of a sound than to changes in volume. They will perceive the difference if you raise or lower the pitch of your voice by about one-third of 1 percent (1/333). Yet they will not perceive a difference in the loudness of a sound unless the sound is made louder or softer by about 10 percent. Table 3.2 lists Weber's constants for various senses.

Weber's constants for these stimuli have practical meanings. First, if you are going to sing, you had better be right on pitch (hit the note precisely), or people are going to groan. But you might be able to raise the volume on your stereo a little without the next-door neighbor noticing the difference. Then, too, your neighbor may not notice it if you lower the stereo by a notch.

Signal Detection: More Than a Matter of Energy

Scientists who study psychophysics describe sounds, flashes of light, and other stimuli as *signals*. According to **signal-detection theory**, the threshold for detecting a signal depends not only on the properties of the stimulus itself, such as its intensity—the loudness of a sound, for example—but also on the level of background stimulation, or noise, and, importantly, on the biological and psychological characteristics of the perceiver. The sensitivity or degree of sharpness of an individual's sensory systems (e.g., the acuity of your eyesight or hearing) partially determines whether a signal is detected. The organism's physical condition also plays a role. For instance, your sense of smell is duller when you have a cold and your nose is stuffed. Levels of fatigue or alertness also contribute to signal detection.

TABLE 3.2

Examples of Weber's Constants

Sensation	Weber's Constant (Approximate)
Saltiness of food	1/5
Pressure on skin	1/7
Loudness of sounds	1/10
Odor	1/20
Heaviness of weights	1/50
Brightness of lights	1/60
Pitch of sounds	1/333

CONCEPT 3.5

According to signal-detection theory, the ability to detect a stimulus depends not only on the properties of the stimulus, but also on the level of background stimulation and the biological and psychological characteristics of the perceiver.

Weber's law   The principle that the amount of change in a stimulus needed to detect a difference is given by a constant ratio or fraction, called a constant, of the original stimulus.

signal-detection theory   The belief that the detection of a stimulus depends on factors involving the intensity of the stimulus, the level of background stimulation, and the biological and psychological characteristics of the perceiver.

How Hot Is Your Bath?

You've probably noticed that when you draw a bath it seems hotter at first than it does a minute or two later. Based on your reading of the text, explain this phenomenon.

CONCEPT 3.6

Through the process of sensory adaptation, our sensory systems deal with repeated exposure to the same stimuli by becoming less sensitive to them.

Psychological factors, including attention levels and states of motivation like hunger, also play important roles in signal detection. As you are walking down a darkened street by yourself late at night, you may be especially attentive to even the slightest sounds because they may signal danger. You may fail to notice the same sounds as you walk along the same street in broad daylight. If you haven't eaten for a while, you may be more likely to notice aromas of food wafting from a nearby kitchen than if you had just consumed a hearty meal.

Sensory Adaptation: Turning the Volume Down

Through the process of **sensory adaptation**, sensory systems become *less* sensitive to constant or unchanging stimuli. When you are wearing a new wristwatch or ring, you may at first be aware of the sensation of pressure on your skin, but after a while you no longer notice it. We may be thankful for sensory adaptation when, after a few minutes of exposure, the water in a crisp mountain lake seems warmer and the odors in a locker room become less noticeable. However, sensory adaptation may not occur when we are repeatedly exposed to certain strong stimuli, such as the loud wail of a car alarm. In such cases, our sensory systems show no change in sensitivity to the stimulus.

Concept Chart 3.1 reviews the basic concepts in sensation.

CONCEPT CHART 3.1
Basic Concepts in Sensation

Sensation	The process of transforming stimuli that impinge on our sense organs into neural signals that the brain processes to create sensations of vision, touch, sound, taste, smell, and so on
Absolute threshold	The smallest amount of a stimulus that a person can reliably detect
Difference threshold	The minimal difference between two stimuli that people can reliably detect; also called *just-noticeable difference*
Weber's law	The amount of change in a stimulus needed to detect a difference, expressed as a constant ratio or fraction of the original stimulus
Signal-detection theory	The belief that the ability to detect a signal varies with the characteristics of the perceiver, the background, and the stimulus itself
Sensory adaptation	The process by which sensory systems adapt to constant stimuli by becoming less sensitive to them

sensory adaptation The process by which sensory receptors adapt to constant stimuli by becoming less sensitive to them.

MODULE 3.1 REVIEW

Sensing Our World: Basic Concepts of Sensation

CONCEPT CHECK

1. Specialized cells in the sense organs, which are geared to detect stimuli in the external environment, are called
   a. feature detectors.
   b. threshold detectors.
   c. sensory receptors.
   d. signal detectors.

2. The smallest amount of stimulation that a person can reliably detect is called a(n)
   a. minimal sensory field.
   b. absolute threshold.
   c. just-noticeable difference.
   d. vector of constants.

3. Jill notices the humming sound made by an air conditioner when she first enters the room, but within a few minutes she is no longer aware of the sound. What sensory process does this illustrate?

MODULE 3.2   Vision: Seeing the Light

- **How do the eyes process light?**
- **What are feature detectors, and what role do they play in visual processing?**
- **What are the two major theories of color vision?**
- **What are the two major forms of color blindness?**

Vision is the process by which light energy is converted into signals (neural impulses) that the brain interprets to produce the experience of sight. Our sense of vision allows us to receive visual information from a mere few inches away, as when we read from a book held close to our eyes, to many billions of miles away, as when we observe twinkling stars on a clear night. To understand vision, we first need to consider the source of physical energy that gives rise to vision: light.

CONCEPT 3.7
Vision is the process by which light energy is converted into neural impulses that the brain interprets to produce the experience of sight.

Light: The Energy of Vision

Light is physical energy in the form of electromagnetic radiation (electrically charged particles). X-rays, ultraviolet waves, and radio waves are other forms of electromagnetic energy. Visible light is the portion of the spectrum of electromagnetic radiation that gives rise to our sense of vision. As you can see in Figure 3.1, the visible spectrum occupies only a small portion of the full spectrum of electromagnetic radiation. It consists of the wavelengths from approximately 300 to 750 nanometers (a nanometer is 1-billionth of a meter).

Different wavelengths within the visible spectrum give rise to the experience of different colors (see Figure 3.2). Violet has the shortest wavelength (about 400-billionths of a meter long), and red has the longest (about 700-billionths of a meter). Psychology students are often told that they can remember the order of the colors of the spectrum by thinking of the name Roy G. Biv (standing for red, orange, yellow, green, blue, indigo, and violet).

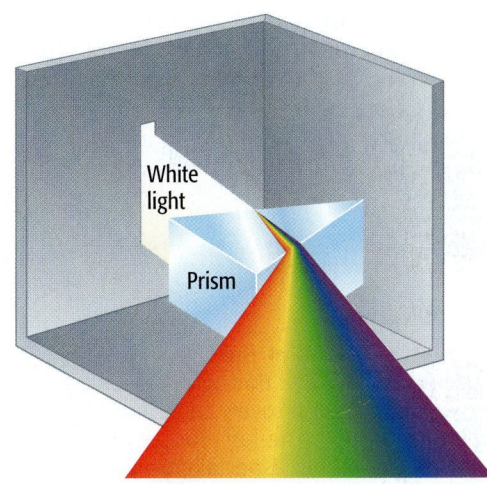

Figure 3.2   The Color Spectrum
A prism separates white light into the various hues that make up the part of the electromagnetic spectrum that is visible to humans.

Figure 3.1   The Electromagnetic Spectrum
Visible light occupies only a small portion of the range of electromagnetic radiation that is called the electromagnetic spectrum.

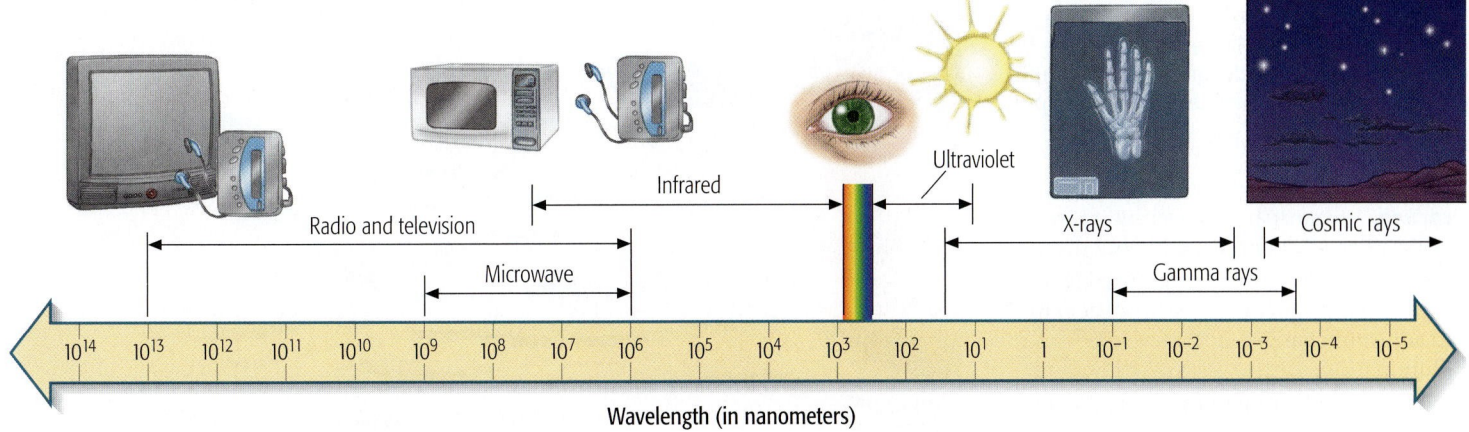

Wavelength (in nanometers)

The Eye: The Visionary Sensory Organ

The eye is the organ with receptor cells that respond to light. Light enters the eye through the **cornea**, a transparent covering on the eye's surface (see Figure 3.3). A muscle called the **iris** contracts or expands to determine the amount of light that enters. The iris is colored, most often brown or blue, and gives the eye its color. The **pupil** of the eye is the black opening inside the iris. The iris increases or decreases the size of the pupil reflexively to adjust to the amount of light entering the eye. The brighter the light, the smaller the iris makes the pupil. Under darkened conditions, the iris opens to allow more light to enter the pupil so that we can see more clearly. Because these are reflex actions, they happen automatically (you don't have to think about them).

The light enters the eye through the cornea and then passes through the pupil and **lens**. Through a process called **accommodation**, the lens changes its shape to adjust for the distance of the object, which helps focus the visual image on the inner surface of the eye called the **retina**. Like the film in a camera, the retina receives the image as light strikes it. But the retina is much more sophisticated than photographic film. It contains two kinds of **photoreceptors**, specialized receptor cells that are sensitive to light.

When light hits the retina, it comes into contact with these photoreceptors. Because of their shapes, they are called **rods** and **cones** (see Figure 3.4). The normal eye has about 120 million rods and 6 million cones. The rods and cones convert the physical energy of light into neural signals that the brain processes to create visual sensations.

CONCEPT 3.8
Light, a form of physical energy, is the stimulus to which receptors in the eyes respond, giving rise to our sense of vision.

CONCEPT 3.9
Light enters the eye through the cornea and then passes through the pupil and then through the lens, which focuses it on the retina, where it comes into contact with photoreceptor cells, the rods and cones, that convert light energy into neural signals that are transmitted to the brain.

CONCEPT 3.10
Rods, which are more sensitive to light than cones are, are responsible for peripheral vision and vision in dim light, whereas cones allow us to detect colors and to discern fine details of objects under bright illumination.

PsychAssist: Conversion of Light into Neural Impulses

Figure 3.3 Parts of the Eye
Light enters the eye through the cornea. The iris adjusts reflexively to control the size of the pupil. The lens focuses the light on the retina, especially on the fovea, the point of central focus that gives rise to clearest vision.

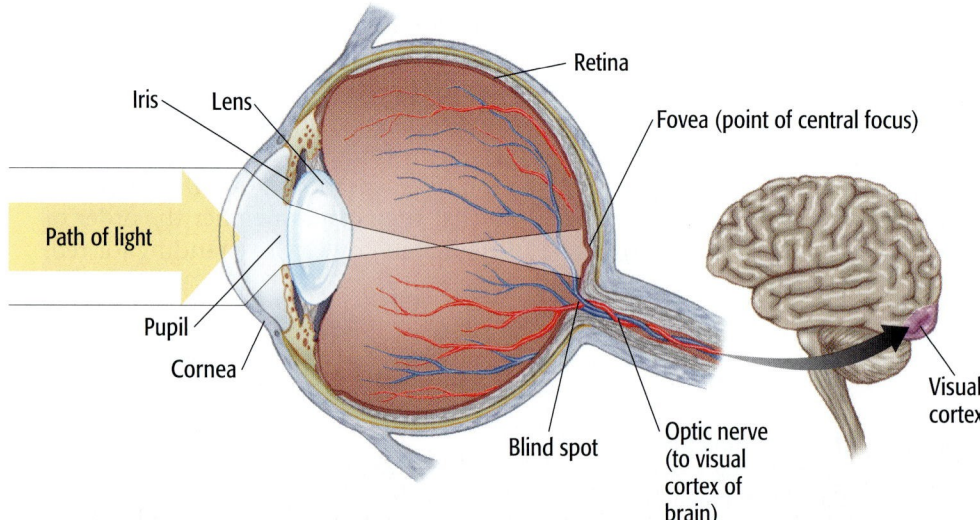

Figure 3.4 Rods and Cones
This close-up image of a portion of the retina shows cones (large reddish cone-like objects on the left side of the photograph) and rods (more numerous rod-like shaped objects).

cornea A transparent covering on the eye's surface through which light enters.

iris The pigmented, circular muscle in the eye that regulates the size of the pupil to adjust to changes in the level of illumination.

pupil The black opening inside the iris that allows light to enter the eye.

lens The structure in the eye that focuses light rays on the retina.

Figure 3.5
Conversion of Light into Neural Impulses
Light is converted into neural impulses that the brain uses to produce the sensation of vision.

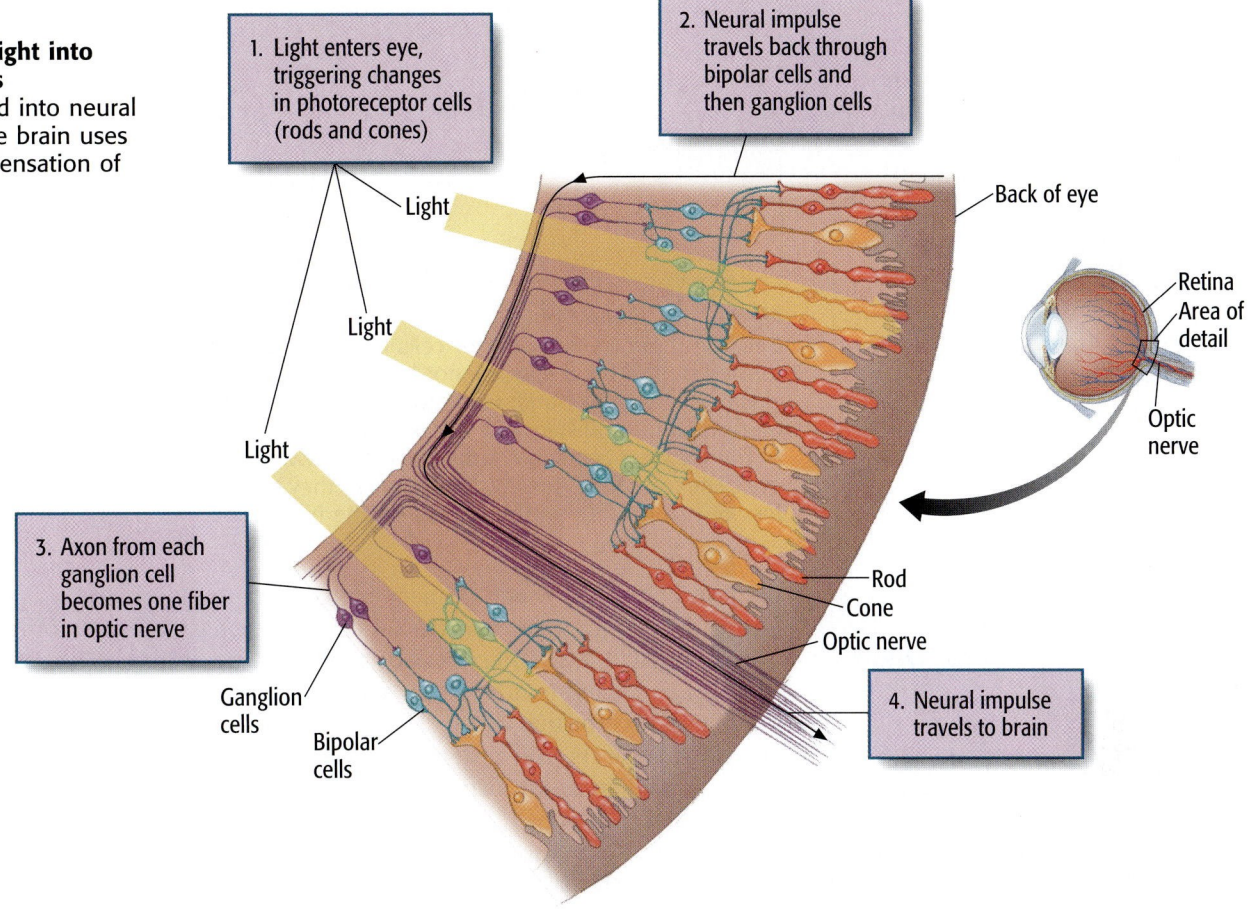

1. Light enters eye, triggering changes in photoreceptor cells (rods and cones)

2. Neural impulse travels back through bipolar cells and then ganglion cells

Light

Light

Light

Back of eye

Retina
Area of detail
Optic nerve

3. Axon from each ganglion cell becomes one fiber in optic nerve

Rod
Cone
Optic nerve

Ganglion cells

Bipolar cells

4. Neural impulse travels to brain

Have you ever noticed that when lighting is dim, you tend to make out the shapes of objects but not their colors? That's because cones are responsible for color vision but are less sensitive to light than rods are. Rods allow us to detect objects in low light. They are sensitive only to the intensity or brightness of light. They are also responsible for *peripheral vision*—the ability to detect objects, especially moving objects, at the edges (sides, as well as the top and bottom) of our visual field. Cones allow us to detect colors, as well as to discern fine details of objects in bright light (Hubel, 1988). Some animals, including certain birds, have only cones in their eyes (Gaulin & McBurney, 2001). They can see only during daylight hours when the cones are activated. Because they become totally blind at night, they must return to their roosts as evening approaches.

The neural signals produced by the rods and cones pass back through a layer of interconnecting cells called **bipolar cells** and then through a layer of neurons called **ganglion cells** (see Figure 3.5). The axon projecting from each ganglion cell makes up one nerve fiber in the **optic nerve**. The optic nerve, which consists of a million or so ganglion axons, transmits visual information to the brain. In the brain, this information is routed to the thalamus, a major relay station, and from there to the visual cortex. The visual cortex lies in the occipital lobes, the part of the cerebral cortex that processes visual information and produces the experience of vision.

The part of the retina where the optic nerve leaves the eye is known as the **blind spot** (see Figure 3.6). Because it contains no photoreceptors (rods or cones), we do not see images that form on the blind spot. By contrast, the **fovea** is the part of the retina that corresponds to the center of our gaze and that gives rise to our sharpest vision (see Figure 3.3). It contains only cones. Focusing our eyes on an object brings its image to bear directly on the fovea.

Farther away from the fovea, the proportion of cones decreases while the proportion of rods increases (Abramov & Gordon, 1994). Rods show the opposite

accommodation   The process by which the lens changes its shape to focus images more clearly on the retina.

retina   The light-sensitive layer of the inner surface of the eye that contains photoreceptor cells.

photoreceptors   Light-sensitive cells (rods and cones) in the eye upon which light registers.

rods   Photoreceptors that are sensitive only to the intensity of light (light and dark).

cones   Photoreceptors that are sensitive to color.

bipolar cells   A layer of interconnecting cells in the eye that connect photoreceptors to ganglion cells.

ganglion cells   Nerve cells in the back of the eye that transmit neural impulses in response to light stimulation, the axons of which make up the optic nerve.

optic nerve   The nerve that carries neural impulses generated by light stimulation from the eye to the brain.

blind spot   The area in the retina where the optic nerve leaves the eye and that contains no photoreceptor cells.

fovea   The area near the center of the retina that contains only cones and that is the center of focus for clearest vision.

CONCEPT 3.11
Objects are seen most clearly when their images are focused on the fovea, a part of the retina that contains only cones.

web Netlab/What's So Complicated About Seeing?

Figure 3.6 Blind Spot
Because there are no receptor cells in the blind spot—no rods or cones—images formed on the blind spot cannot be seen. You can demonstrate this for yourself by closing your left eye and, while focusing on the dot, slowly move the book farther away to about a distance of a foot. You'll notice there is a point at which the stack of money disappears. We are not typically aware of our blind spots because our eyes are constantly moving and because they work together to compensate for any loss of vision when an image falls on the blind spot.

TRY THIS OUT

Reading Sideways

Hold a book or magazine to the side and try reading it. Why do you suppose the words are blurry, if you can make them out at all?

CONCEPT 3.12
The brain's visual cortex contains cells so specialized that they fire only when they detect precise angles, lines, or points of light.

feature detectors Specialized neurons in the visual cortex that respond only to particular features of visual stimuli, such as horizontal or vertical lines.

trichromatic theory A theory of color vision that posits that the ability to see different colors depends on the relative activity of three types of color receptors in the eye (red, green, and blue-violet).

afterimage The visual image of a stimulus that remains after the stimulus is removed.

pattern. They are few and far between close to the fovea and more densely packed farther away from the fovea. The far ends of the retina contain only rods.

Visual acuity, or sharpness of vision, is the ability to discern visual details. Many of us have impaired visual acuity. People who need to be unusually close to objects to discern their details are *nearsighted.* People who need to be unusually far away from objects to see them clearly are *farsighted.* Nearsightedness and farsightedness result from abnormalities in the shape of the eye. Nearsightedness can occur when the eyeball is too long or the cornea is too curved. In either case, distant objects are focused in front of the retina. Farsightedness can occur when the eyeball is too short so that light from nearby objects is focused behind the retina. People with nearsightedness or farsightedness can correct their vision by wearing eyeglasses or contact lenses.

Feature Detectors: Getting Down to Basics

In 1981, David Hubel and Torsten Wiesel received a Nobel Prize for unraveling a small piece of the puzzle of how we transform sensory information into rich visual experiences of the world around us. They discovered that the visual cortex contains nerve cells that respond only when an animal (in their studies, a cat) is shown a line with a particular orientation—horizontal, vertical, or diagonal (Hubel, 1988; Hubel & Wiesel, 1979). Some of these nerve cells respond only to lines that form right angles; others, to dots of light that move from right to left across the visual field; and yet others, to dots of light that move from left to right. Hubel and Wiesel made their discoveries by implanting a tiny electrode in individual cells in the cat's visual cortex. They then flashed different visual stimuli on a screen within the cat's field of vision and observed which cells fired in response to which types of stimuli. Neurons that respond to specific features of the visual stimulus are called **feature detectors**.

Yet we do not see a world composed of scattered bits and pieces of sensory data, of lines, angles, and moving points of light. Somehow the visual cortex compiles information from various cells, combining them to form meaningful patterns. How do we go from recognizing specific features of a stimulus—its individual angles, lines, and edges—to discerning a meaningful pattern, such as letters, numbers, words, or the human face? Scientists believe that complex assemblages of neurons in the brain work together to analyze relationships among specific features of objects. Hubel and Wiesel opened a door to understanding the beginning steps in this process at the level of the individual feature detector. Yet we are still a long way from understanding how the brain transforms sensory stimulation into the rich visual world we experience.

Color Vision: Sensing a Colorful World

To be able to perceive different colors, color receptors in the retina of the eye must transmit different messages to the brain when visible lights having different wavelengths stimulate them. How are these messages transmitted? Two nineteenth-century German scientists, Hermann von Helmholtz (1821–1894) and Ewald Hering (1834–1918), proposed different answers to this question.

Helmholtz contributed to many fields of science, but he is perhaps best known to psychologists for his work on color vision. He was impressed by the earlier work on color vision of the English scientist Thomas Young (1773–1829) (Martindale, 2001). Young had reversed the process by which a prism breaks light down into component colors. He shone overlapping lights of red, green, and blue-violet onto a screen and found that he could create light of any color on the spectrum by varying the brightness of the lights (see Figure 3.7). Where all three lights overlapped, there was white light—the color of sunlight.

Building on Young's work, Helmholtz proposed what is now known as the Young-Helmholtz theory, or **trichromatic theory** (from Greek roots meaning "three" and "color"). Helmholtz believed that Young's experimental results showed that the eyes have three types of color receptors—red, green, and blue-violet. We now call these color receptors *cones*. These three types of cones have differing sensitivities to different wavelengths of light. Blue-violet cones are most sensitive to short wavelengths; green cones, to middle wavelengths; and red cones, to long wavelengths. According to the trichromatic theory, the response pattern of these three types of cones allows us to see different colors. So when green cones are most strongly activated, we see green. But when a combination of different types of cones is activated, we see other colors, just as mixing paint of different colors produces yet other colors. For example, when red and green receptors are stimulated at the same time, we see yellow.

Hering developed a different theory of color vision based on his work with *afterimages*. An **afterimage** is what you see if you gaze at a visual stimulus for a while and then look at a neutral surface, such as a sheet of white paper.

Pause for a demonstration. The flag in Figure 3.8 has all the shapes in the American flag, but the colors are off. Instead of being red, white, and blue, this flag is green, black, and yellow. Now, although you may not particularly wish to defend this oddly colored flag, gaze at it for a minute. (Time yourself; give yourself a full minute.) Then shift your gaze to a white sheet of paper. You are likely to see a more familiar flag; this is because red is the afterimage of green, white is the afterimage of black, and blue is the afterimage of yellow.

Figure 3.7   Primary Colors
The three primary colors of light—red, green, and blue-violet—combine to form white. Thomas Young showed that you could create any color of light by mixing these component colors and varying their brightnesses. For example, a combination of red and green light creates yellow.

Figure 3.8   Afterimages
The colors in the American flag shown here can be set right by performing a simple experiment. Stare at the dot in the center of the flag for about sixty seconds. Then quickly shift your gaze to a white wall or white sheet of paper. You will see the more familiar colors of the American flag as afterimages.

Hering's work with afterimages led him to develop the **opponent-process theory** of color vision. Opponent-process theory, like trichromatic theory, suggests that the eyes have three types of color receptors. According to this theory, however, each type of receptor consists of a pair of opposing receptors. Rather than there being separate receptors for red, green, and blue-violet, some receptors are sensitive to red or green; others, to blue or yellow; and others, to black or white. The black-white receptors detect brightness or shades of gray; the red-green and blue-yellow pairs detect differences in colors.

Hering believed that color vision arises from pairs of opposing processes. According to his theory, red-green receptors do not simultaneously transmit messages for red and green. Rather, they transmit messages for either one or the other. When the red cone is activated, the green one is blocked, or inhibited, and so we see red. Yet prolonged transmission of any one message, such as red or green, disturbs the balance of neural activity, making it more difficult to inhibit the opposing color receptor. Thus, according to Hering's theory, if you stare at the green, black, and yellow flag in Figure 3.8 for a minute or so, you will disturb the balance of neural activity, producing an *opponent process*. The afterimage of red, white, and blue you experience represents the eye's attempt to reestablish a balance between the two opposing receptors.

Which model of color vision has it right—the trichromatic model or the opponent-process model? Contemporary research shows that both theories are right to a certain extent (Hergenhahn, 1997; Hubel, 1988). The trichromatic theory is correct at the receptor level, since the photochemistry of cones responds in the way described by trichromatic theory—some are sensitive to red light; others, to green light; and still others, to blue-violet light. But Hering's opponent-process theory is correct in terms of the behavior of cells that lie between the cones and the occipital lobe of the cerebral cortex—including bipolar and ganglion cells. These cells operate in an opponent-process fashion. Some are turned on by red light but are prevented (inhibited) from firing by green light. Others are turned on by green light but are inhibited by red light. Most authorities today believe that color vision includes elements of both trichromatic and opponent-process theories.

Trichromats are people with normal color vision who can discern all the colors of the visible spectrum—red, green, and blue-violet—as well as colors formed by various combinations of these hues.

About one out of every forty thousand people is completely color-blind. Such people are referred to as **monochromats** because they see only in black and white, as in an old movie or TV show. Because of a genetic defect, they have only one type of cone, so their brains cannot discern differences in the wavelengths of light that normally give rise to color. They can detect only brightness, so the world appears in shades of gray. Much more common are **dichromats**—people who lack one of the three types of cones, making it difficult to distinguish between certain types of colors. The most common form is red-green color blindness, a genetic defect that makes it difficult to discriminate reds from greens. About 8 percent of men have red-green color blindness, as compared with fewer than 1 percent of women. Much

---

CONCEPT 3.13
The major theories of color, trichromatic theory and opponent-process theory, may each partially account for color vision.

CONCEPT 3.14
The most common form of color blindness is red-green color blindness, in which people cannot tell reds from greens.

---

opponent-process theory A theory of color vision that holds that the experience of color results from opposing processes involving two sets of color receptors, red-green receptors and blue-yellow receptors, and that another set of opposing receptors, black-white, is responsible for detecting differences in brightness.

trichromats People with normal color vision who can discern all the colors of the visual spectrum.

monochromats People who have no color vision and can see only in black and white.

dichromats People who can see some colors but not others.

THINK *About It*

What Color Is This?

Are you color blind? Do you know anyone who is? What type of color blindness do you (they) have? How has it affected your life, if at all? Have you (they) learned skills to compensate for color blindness?

CONCEPT CHART 3.2
Vision

Source of sensory information	Visible light
Receptor organs	The eyes. Light enters through the cornea and pupil and is focused on the retina.
Receptor cells	The retina has two kinds of photoreceptors. Rods are sensitive to the intensity of light, which is the basis of our sense of light and dark. Cones are sensitive to differences in the wavelengths of light, which is the basis of color vision. Visual information is transmitted to the brain by means of the optic nerve.
Color vision	Two major theories of color vision have been proposed, the trichromatic theory and the opponent-process theory. Each theory appears to account for some aspects of color vision.

Figure 3.9   Color Blindness
What do you see? People with normal color vision will see the triangle in this array of dots. People with red-green color blindness will not perceive it.

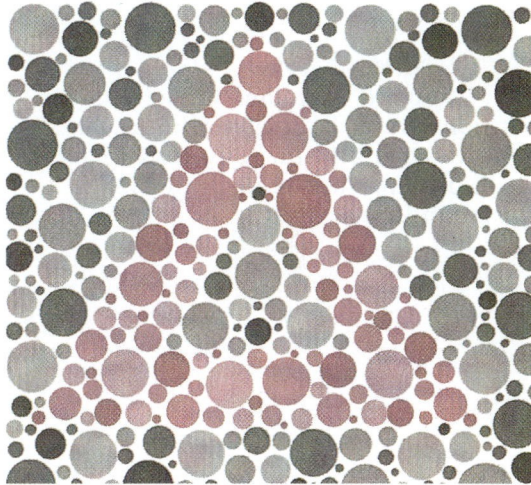

less common is blue-yellow color blindness, in which the person has difficulty distinguishing blues from yellows. Figure 3.9 shows a plate from a test used to assess color blindness.

People with red-green color blindness might put on one green sock and one red sock, as long as they were similar in brightness. But they would not confuse green with blue. Red-green color blindness appears to be a sex-linked genetic defect that is carried on the X sex chromosome (Neitz & Neitz, 1995). As noted, more males than females are affected by this condition. Because males have only one X chromosome, whereas females have two, a defect on one X chromosome is more likely to be expressed in males than in females.

Concept Chart 3.2 provides an overview of vision.

MODULE 3.2 REVIEW

Seeing the Light

CONCEPT CHECK

1. Which of the following is *not* correct? Visible light
   a. corresponds to wavelengths to which the human eye can respond.
   b. consists of wavelengths from approximately 300 to 750 nanometers.
   c. corresponds to the range of colors seen in a rainbow.
   d. is not in the form of electromagnetic radiation.

2. Which of the following statements is true? Rods
   a. are most heavily concentrated around the fovea.
   b. are primarily responsible for color vision.
   c. allow us to discern fine details of objects under high illumination.
   d. are more sensitive to light than cones.

3. The photoreceptors in the retina that are responsible for peripheral vision and vision in dim light are called _____; those responsible for color vision and for discerning fine details in bright light are called _____.

4. Match the following parts of the eye with their respective functions: (a) iris; (b) pupil; (c) lens; (d) retina; (e) fovea; (f) blind spot.
   i.   part of the eye that focuses the visual image on the retina
   ii. inner surface of the eye in which the photoreceptors are found
   iii. part of the retina from which the optic nerve leaves the eye
   iv. muscle controlling the size of the pupil
   v.   area on the retina responsible for clearest vision
   vi. opening through which light enters the eye

MODULE 3.3

Hearing: The Music of Sound

- **How does the ear enable us to hear sound?**
- **What determines our perception of pitch?**
- **What are the main types and causes of deafness?**

The chattering of birds, the voices of children playing in the yard, the stirring melodies of Tchaikovsky—we sense all these sounds by means of hearing, or **audition**. We hear by sensing sound waves, which result from changes in the pressure of air or water. When sound waves impinge upon the ear, they cause parts of the ear to vibrate. These vibrations are then converted into electrical signals that are sent to the brain.

Sound: Sensing Waves of Vibrations

Like visible light, sound is a form of energy that travels in waves. Yet while light can travel through the empty reaches of outer space, sound exists only in a medium, such as air, liquids, gases, or even solids (which is why you may hear your neighbor's stereo through a solid wall). A vibrating object causes molecules of air (or other substances, such as water) to vibrate. For example, your voice is produced when your vocal cords vibrate. The resulting vibrations spread outward from the source in the form of sound waves that are characterized by such physical properties as *amplitude* (the height of the wave, which is a measure of the amount of energy in the sound wave) and *frequency* (the number of complete waves, or cycles, per second) (see Figure 3.10).

The amplitude of sound waves determines their perceived loudness and is measured in *decibels* (dB). For each ten-decibel increase, loudness of the sound increases tenfold. Thus, a sound of twenty decibels is actually ten times, not two times, louder than a sound of ten decibels.

Light travels at 186,000 miles per second, which means that it takes about one and one-third seconds for a beam of light from the moon to reach the earth (a distance of about 240,000 miles). Sound is a slowpoke by comparison. Sound travels through air at only about 1,130 feet per second (or 770 miles per *hour*). Therefore, it may take about five seconds for the thunder from lightning a mile away to

CONCEPT 3.15

Sound vibrations are the stimuli transformed by receptors in the ears into signals the brain uses to let you experience the sounds of the world around you.

audition   The sense of hearing.

pitch   The highness or lowness of a sound that corresponds to the frequency of the sound wave.

eardrum   A sheet of connective tissue separating the outer ear from the middle ear that vibrates in response to auditory stimuli and transmits sound waves to the middle ear.

ossicles   Three tiny bones in the middle ear (the hammer, anvil, and stirrup) that vibrate in response to vibrations of the eardrum.

oval window   The membrane-covered opening that separates the middle ear from the inner ear.

cochlea   The snail-shaped organ in the inner ear that contains sensory receptors for hearing.

Figure 3.10   Sound Waves
Sound waves vary in such physical properties as amplitude, or height of the wave, and frequency, or number of complete cycles per second. Differences in amplitude give rise to perceptions of loudness, whereas differences in frequency lead to perceptions of pitch.

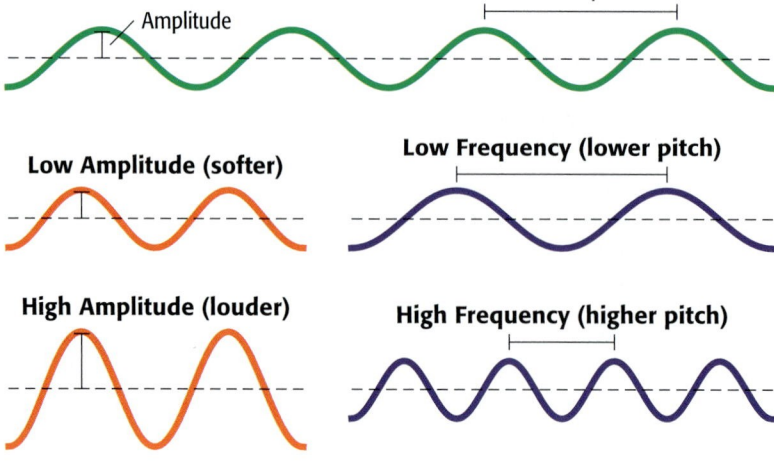

reach your ears. But most of the sounds that matter to us—the voice of a teacher or a lover, the screeches and whines of cars and buses, and the sounds of music—are so close that they seem to reach us in no time at all.

Although sound travels more slowly than light, the vibrations that give rise to sound still occur many times a second. The frequency with which they occur per second provides information that the brain uses to produce perceptions of **pitch**, or how high or low a sound seems. The human ear senses sound waves that vary in frequency from about 20 to perhaps 20,000 cycles per second. Sound waves that are higher in frequency are perceived as being higher in pitch. Women's voices are usually higher than men's because their vocal cords tend to be shorter and thus to vibrate more rapidly (at a greater frequency). The shorter strings on a harp (or in a piano) produce higher notes than the longer strings because they vibrate more rapidly.

The Ear: A Sound Machine

The ear is structured to capture sound waves, reverberate with them, and convert them into messages that are relayed to the brain in the form of neural impulses (see Figure 3.11). The outer ear funnels sound waves to the **eardrum**, a tight membrane that vibrates in response to them. The vibrations are then transmitted through three tiny bones in the middle ear called the **ossicles** (literally "little bones"). The first of these to vibrate, the "hammer" (*malleus*), is connected to the eardrum. It strikes the "anvil" (*incus*), which in turn strikes the "stirrup" (*stapes*), causing it to vibrate. The vibration is transmitted from the stirrup to the **oval window**, a membrane to which the stirrup is attached. The oval window connects the middle ear to a snail-shaped bony tube in the inner ear, called the **cochlea** (*cochlea* is the Greek word for "snail"). Vibrations of the oval window cause waves of motion

web. **Netlab/Build an Ear**

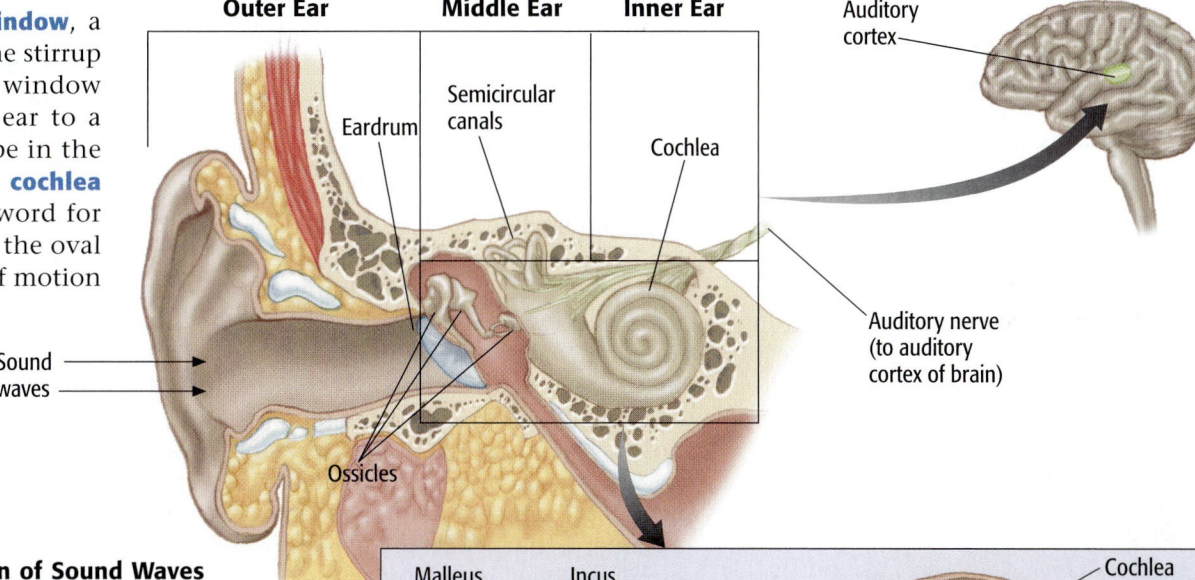

Figure 3.11 Conversion of Sound Waves into Neural Impulses
Sound waves are funneled by the outer ear to the eardrum, causing it to vibrate. These vibrations are transmitted through the ossicles, three tiny bones in the middle ear, and then to the oval window through which they are transmitted to the cochlea within the inner ear. Vibration of the oval window causes movement of fluid in the cochlea, which in turn causes the basilar membrane to vibrate. Hair-cell receptors in the organ of Corti bend in response to these vibrations, triggering neural impulses that travel through the auditory nerve to the brain.

CONCEPT 3.16
Sound waves cause parts of the ear to vibrate; this mechanical vibration in turn affects sensory receptors in the inner ear, called hair cells, triggering the transmission of auditory messages to the brain.

CONCEPT 3.17
Perception of pitch may best be explained by a combination of place theory (coding by the point on the basilar membrane of greatest vibration), frequency theory (coding by the frequency of neural firings), and the volley principle (coding by combining frequencies of alternating groups of neurons firing in rapid succession).

basilar membrane   The membrane in the cochlea that is attached to the organ of Corti.

organ of Corti   A gelatinous structure in the cochlea containing the hair cells that serve as auditory receptors.

hair cells   The auditory receptors that transform vibrations caused by sound waves into neural impulses that are then transmitted to the brain via the auditory nerve.

auditory nerve   The nerve that carries neural impulses from the ear to the brain, which gives rise to the experience of hearing.

place theory   The belief that pitch depends on the place along the basilar membrane that vibrates the most in response to a particular auditory stimulus.

frequency theory   The belief that pitch depends on the frequency of vibration of the basilar membrane and the volley of neural impulses transmitted to the brain via the auditory nerve.

volley principle   The principle that relates the experience of pitch to the alternating firing of groups of neurons along the basilar membrane.

in fluid within the cochlea. The motion of this fluid causes a structure within the cochlea, called the **basilar membrane**, to vibrate. The basilar membrane is attached to a gelatinous structure called the **organ of Corti**, which is lined with 15,000 or so **hair cells** that act as auditory receptors. These hair cells bend in response to movements of the basilar membrane, triggering the transmission of auditory messages to the brain by way of the **auditory nerve**. This auditory information travels to the auditory cortex, which is located in the temporal lobes of the cerebral cortex. The auditory cortex processes this information, producing the experience of sound.

Your brain determines where a sound is coming from by comparing the sounds you receive in your two ears. Unless sounds originate from sources equally distant from both ears—for example, exactly in front of or above you—they reach one ear before the other. Although you might not be able to say exactly how much sooner you hear a sound in one ear than in the other, your brain can detect a difference as small as 1/10,000th of a second. It uses such information to help locate the source of a sound. More distant sounds tend to be softer (just as more distant objects look smaller), which provides yet another cue for locating sounds.

Perception of Pitch: Perceiving the Highs and Lows

How do people distinguish whether one sound is higher or lower in pitch than another? As with perception of color, more than one theory is needed to help us understand how we perceive pitch. Two theories, *place theory* and *frequency theory,* help explain how we detect high and low pitches, and a combination of the two, called the *volley principle,* helps explain how we detect mid-range pitches.

Place theory, originally developed by Hermann von Helmholtz, suggests that people perceive a sound to have a certain pitch according to the place along the basilar membrane that vibrates the most when sound waves of particular frequencies strike the ear. It is as though neurons line up along the basilar membrane like so many keys on a piano, standing ready to respond by producing sounds of different pitch when they are "struck" (Azar, 1996a).

Georg von Békésy (1957) won a Nobel Prize for showing that high-frequency sounds cause the greatest vibration of hair cells close to the oval window, whereas those with lower frequencies cause the greatest vibration farther down the basilar membrane. Hair cells at the point of maximal vibration, like the crest of a wave, excite particular neurons that inform the brain about their location. The brain uses this information to code sounds for pitch. However, low-frequency sounds—those below about 4,000 cycles per second—cannot be coded for location because they do not cause the membrane to vibrate the most at any one spot. Yet we know that people can detect sounds with frequencies as low as 20 cycles per second.

Enter **frequency theory**, which may account for how we perceive the pitch of sounds of about 20 to 1,000 cycles per second. According to frequency theory, the basilar membrane vibrates at the same frequency as the sound wave itself. In other words, a sound wave with a frequency of 200 cycles per second would cause the basilar membrane to vibrate at that rate and generate a corresponding number of neural impulses to the brain. That is, there would be 200 neural impulses to the brain per second. But frequency theory also has its limitations. Most importantly, neurons cannot fire more frequently than about 1,000 times per second.

What, then, do we make of sounds with frequencies between 1,000 and 4,000 cycles per second? How do we bridge that gap? By means of the **volley principle**. In one of nature's many surprises, it seems that groups of neurons along the basilar membrane fire in volleys, or alternating succession. (Think of Revolutionary War or Civil War movies in which one group of soldiers stands and fires while an alternate group kneels and reloads.) By firing in rotation, groups of neurons combine their frequencies of firing to fill the gap.

In sum, frequency theory best explains pitch perception for low-frequency sounds, whereas place theory best explains pitch of high-frequency sounds. A combination of frequency and place theory, called the volley principle, suggests how we perceive the pitch of mid-range sounds.

Hearing Loss: Are You Protecting Your Hearing?

Nearly 30 million Americans have hearing problems, and as many as 2 million are deaf (Nadol, 1993). There are many causes of hearing loss and deafness, including birth defects, disease, advanced age, and injury—especially the kind of injury caused by exposure to loud noises. Prolonged exposure to noises of 85 decibels can cause hearing loss, as can brief exposure to sounds of 120 decibels or louder. Figure 3.12 shows the decibel levels of many familiar sounds. Note that the music levels at rock concerts typically exceed 100 decibels. (Many aging rock musicians and frequent concertgoers are now suffering from hearing loss.)

There are two main types of deafness: conduction deafness and nerve deafness. **Conduction deafness** is usually caused by damage to the middle ear. The eardrum may be punctured, or the three bones that amplify sound waves and conduct them to the inner ear may lose the ability to vibrate properly. People who experience conduction deafness may benefit from hearing aids that amplify sound waves.

Nerve deafness is usually caused by damage to the hair cells of the inner ear or to the auditory nerve. Exposure to loud sounds, disease, and aging can cause nerve deafness. The "ringing sensation" that can follow exposure to loud noises may indicate damage to hair cells. Cochlear implants, or "artificial ears," are sometimes successful in transmitting sounds past damaged hair cells to the auditory nerve. They work by converting sounds into electrical impulses. But these implants cannot correct for damage to the auditory nerve itself. If the auditory

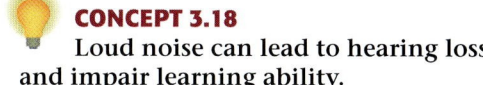

CONCEPT 3.18
Loud noise can lead to hearing loss and impair learning ability.

THINK *About It*

Preventing Hearing Loss

What steps are you taking to protect your hearing from the damaging effects of noise? Are you doing enough?

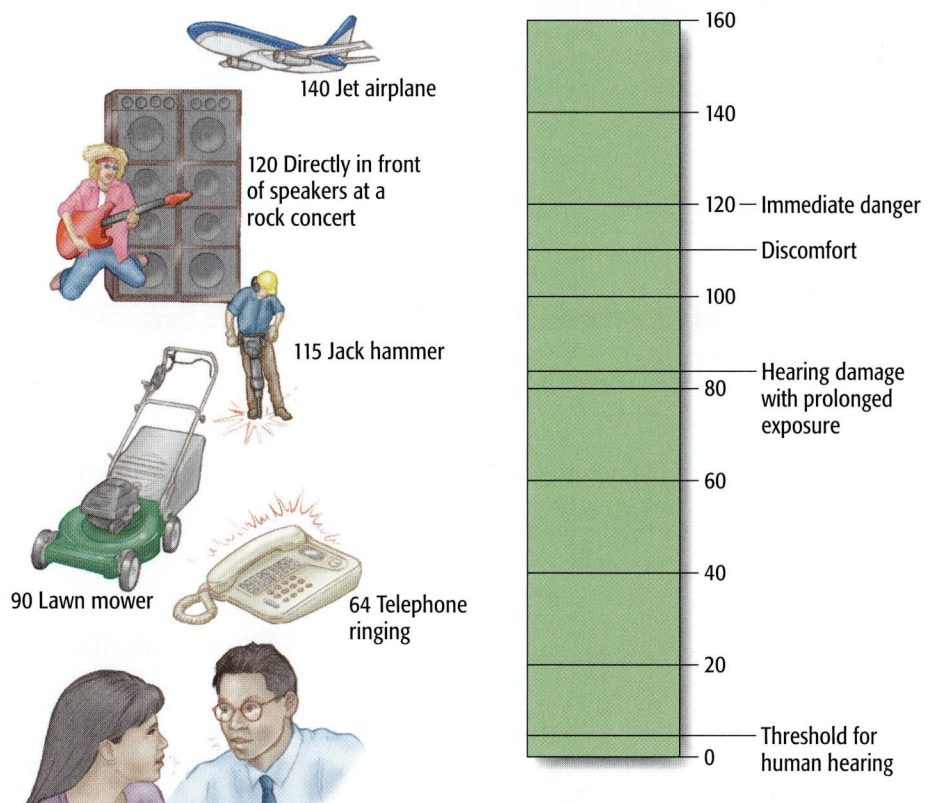

Figure 3.12   Sounds and Decibels
Permanent hearing loss may occur from prolonged exposure to sound over 85 decibels (dB). Exposure to 120 decibels or higher creates an immediate danger to hearing. Most people can detect faint sounds at a decibel level just above 0 dB.

140 Jet airplane

120 Directly in front of speakers at a rock concert

115 Jack hammer

90 Lawn mower

64 Telephone ringing

50 Normal conversation

160
140
120 — Immediate danger
— Discomfort
100
Hearing damage
80 with prolonged
exposure
60
40
20
Threshold for
0   human hearing

conduction deafness   A form of deafness, usually involving damage to the middle ear, in which there is a loss of conduction of sound vibrations through the ear.

nerve deafness   Deafness associated with nerve damage, usually involving damage to the hair cells or to the auditory nerve itself.

nerve does not function, even sounds that cause the hair cells on the basilar membrane to dance frantically will not be sensed in the auditory cortex of the brain.

Hearing loss in later life is not inevitable. It is largely due to years of abuse from loud music and noise. What can you do to avoid exposure to excessive noise and to help prevent noise-induced hearing loss later in life? Here are some suggestions:

- When you can't avoid excessive noise, as in worksites, wear hearing protectors or earplugs.

- Turn down the volume on your stereo, especially when using earphones, and avoid attending ear-splitting concerts.

- If you live in a particularly noisy area, organize your neighbors to pressure government officials to seek remedies.

Before moving on, you may wish to review the basic concepts in hearing that are outlined in Concept Chart 3.3.

CONCEPT CHART 3.3
Hearing

Source of sensory information	Sound waves
Receptor organs	The ears. The outer ear funnels sound waves through the eardrum to the middle ear, where they are amplified by three tiny bones and transmitted through the oval window to the inner ear.
Receptor cells	Hair cells on the basilar membrane within the cochlea of the inner ear
Pitch perception	Three theories contribute to our understanding of pitch perception. Frequency theory appears to account for pitch perception of low-frequency sounds of below 1,000 cycles per second. Place theory alone seems to account for pitch perception of high-frequency sounds above 4,000 cycles per second. The volley principle appears to explain pitch perception of moderate-frequency sounds in the range of approximately 1,000 to 4,000 cycles per second.

MODULE 3.3 REVIEW

Hearing: The Music of Sound

CONCEPT CHECK

1. Which characteristics of sound waves give rise to the perception of loudness and pitch?

2. According to the frequency theory of pitch perception, our ability to detect differences in pitch is due to the
   a. rate of vibration of the basilar membrane.
   b. location along the basilar membrane where the greatest vibration occurs.
   c. alternation between areas of greater and lesser vibration of the basilar membrane.
   d. rate of vibration of the oval window.

3. Match these parts of the ear with the descriptions that follow: (a) eardrum; (b) ossicles; (c) cochlea; (d) basilar membrane; (e) organ of Corti; (f) hair cells.
   i.   a membrane that separates the outer ear from the middle ear
   ii. sensory receptors for hearing
   iii. a gelatinous structure attached to the basilar membrane and lined with sensory receptors
   iv. the membrane in the cochlea that moves in response to sound vibration
   v.   three small bones in the middle ear that conduct sound vibrations
   vi. a snail-shaped bony tube in the inner ear in which fluid moves in response to the vibrations of the oval window

MODULE 3.4 | Our Other Senses: Chemical, Skin, and Body Senses

- **How do we sense odors and tastes?**
- **What are the skin senses?**
- **What are the kinesthetic and vestibular senses?**

We usually think of five senses—sight, hearing, smell, taste, and touch. Yet there are actually more. Here we take a look at the chemical, skin, and body senses. These are the sensory systems that allow us to smell, taste, and touch and that keep us informed about the position and movement of our bodies.

The nose and tongue are like human chemistry laboratories. Smell and taste are chemical senses because they are based on the chemical analysis of molecules of substances that waft past the nose or that land on the tongue. The chemical senses allow us to perform chemistry on the fly.

Olfaction: What Your Nose Knows

Many chemical substances found in the air, such as carbon monoxide, have no odor. Though they enter our noses as we breathe them in, they do not stimulate **olfaction**, our sense of smell. They are odorless because odor receptors in the nose do not detect their chemical structures. Stimulation of the sense of smell depends on the shape of the molecules of chemical substances.

We have about 5 million or so odor receptors in our nostrils that are capable of sensing about 10,000 different substances on the basis of the shape of their molecules (Axel, 1995). These molecules fit into particular odor receptors as keys fit into locks, triggering olfactory messages to be carried to the brain along the **olfactory nerve**. This olfactory information is then processed by the brain, giving rise to odors corresponding to these particular chemical stimuli (see Figure 3.13). The intensity of the odor appears to be a function of the number of olfactory receptors that are stimulated simultaneously.

Smell is the only sense in which sensory information does not go through the thalamus on its way to the cerebral cortex. Instead, olfactory information travels

CONCEPT 3.19
The sense of smell depends on receptors in the nose that detect thousands of chemical substances and transmit information about them to the brain.

TRY THIS OUT

The Smell of Taste

Ever notice that food tastes bland when your nose is stuffed? To demonstrate how olfaction affects gustation, try eating a meal while holding your nostrils closed. What effect does it have on your ability to taste your food? On your enjoyment of the meal?

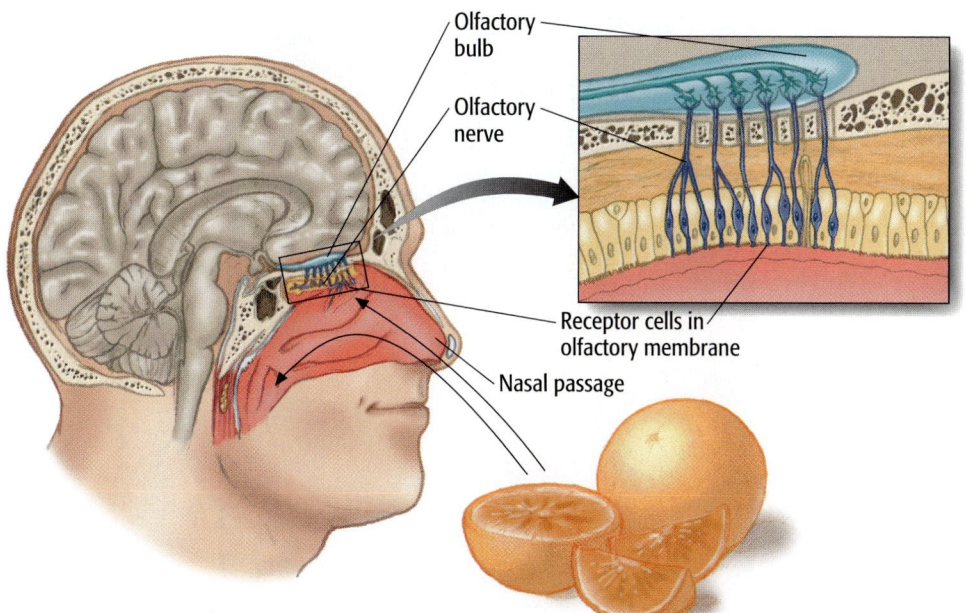

Olfactory bulb

Olfactory nerve

Receptor cells in olfactory membrane

Nasal passage

Figure 3.13   Olfaction
Receptor cells high in the nose respond to the molecular shapes of chemical substances, triggering nerve impulses that travel through the olfactory nerve to the olfactory bulb in the brain. This process gives rise to sensations of specific odors.

olfaction   The sense of smell.
olfactory nerve   The nerve that carries impulses from olfactory receptors in the nose to the brain.

THINK About It

By a Nose

Do you believe you are led around by your nose? How is your behavior affected by aromas?

💡 **CONCEPT 3.20**
Pheromones are chemical substances that play various roles in animal behavior, but their functions in human behavior remain unclear.

through the olfactory nerve directly to the **olfactory bulb**, a structure in the front of the brain above the nostrils. This information is then routed to the olfactory cortex in the temporal lobe and to several structures in the limbic system, which, as noted in Chapter 2, are a set of brain structures with important roles in emotion and memory. The connections between the olfactory system and the limbic system may account for the close relationship between odors and emotional memories. A whiff of chocolate pudding simmering on the stove or of someone's perfume may bring back strong feelings associated with childhood experiences or a particular person.

Olfaction is a key factor in the flavor of foods. Without the sense of smell, the flavor of a steak might not be all that different from that of cardboard. An apple might taste the same as a raw potato. A declining sense of smell in later life may be the major reason many older people complain that food doesn't taste as good as it once did.

Our sensory organs were shaped over the course of millions of years of adaptation to the environment. Olfaction, among our other senses, is critical to our survival. It helps us avoid rotten and potentially harmful foods long before we put our tongue to them. In various animal species, olfaction serves other functions as well. Fur seals and many other animal species recognize their own young from the pack on the basis of smell. Salmon roam the seven seas but sniff out the streams of their birth at spawning time on the basis of a few molecules of water emitted by those streams.

Many species emit chemical substances called **pheromones** that play important roles in numerous behaviors, including attracting mates, marking territory, establishing dominance hierarchies, controlling aggression, and organizing food-gathering efforts (Gaulin & McBurney, 2001; Rodriguez et al., 2000). Pheromones are found in bodily secretions, such as urine or vaginal secretions, and are detected by other members of the species through the sense of smell or taste.

We know that pheromones contribute to sexual attraction in various species of both animals and insects. But do they serve a similar purpose in humans? Most mammals have specialized organs in the nose that they use to detect pheromones, but claims that humans possess such an organ remain controversial (Doty, 2001). For now, there simply is not enough evidence to determine whether pheromones influence sexual attraction among humans. Suffice it to say that what the nose knows remains largely an open question.

A Sexy Scent? Scientists find that exposure to male sweat induces hormonal and mood changes in women. Whether bodily secretions or scents induce sexual attraction in people remains a question that scientists (as well as fragrance companies) continue to explore.

olfactory bulb   The area in the front of the brain above the nostrils that receives sensory input from olfactory receptors in the nose.

pheromones   Chemical substances that are emitted by many species and that have various functions, including sexual attraction.

taste cells   Nerve cells that are sensitive to tastes.

taste buds   Pores or openings on the tongue containing taste cells.

Yet intriguing evidence of a possible role of human pheromones emerged in 2003 when scientists discovered that male sweat relaxes women (Pilcher, 2003; Preti et al., 2003). Researchers applied male perspiration (thankfully disguised by fragrance) to the lips of women volunteers for a period of six hours. The women were led to believe they were testing other chemical compounds, such as fragrances and alcohol. Exposure to these dabs of male perspiration affected levels of a female reproductive hormone and induced feelings of relaxation, although none of the women reported feeling sexual aroused. Still, these findings suggest that bodily secretions can affect the brain even without our being aware of it.

Taste: The Flavorful Sense

Taste, like our other senses, plays an important role in adaptation and survival. We rely on both taste and smell to discriminate between healthy, nutritious food and spoiled or rotten food. (The sense organs are not perfect, however; some poisonous substances are undetectable by smell or taste.)

CONCEPT 3.21
Like the sense of smell, the sense of taste depends on receptors that detect chemical substances and transmit information about them to the brain.

There are thousands of different kinds of food and thousands of different flavors. Yet there are only four basic tastes: sweet, sour, salty, and bitter. The *flavor* of a food results from combinations of these taste qualities, the aroma of the food, its texture, and its temperature.

Tastes are sensed by receptors called **taste cells**. These are nerve cells located within pores or openings on the tongue called **taste buds**. Most taste buds are found near the edges and back of the tongue. Yet people without tongues can also sense taste because additional taste receptors are located on the roof of the mouth, inside the cheeks, and in the throat (Bartoshuk & Beauchamp, 1994). Some taste receptors are more sensitive to a specific taste quality. Others respond to several tastes. Despite these sensitivities, appropriate stimulation of virtually any part of the tongue that contains taste receptors can produce any of the primary tastes (Shiffman, 2000). Taste receptors differ from other neurons in that they regenerate very quickly—within a week to ten days. This is a good thing because people kill them off regularly by eating food that is overly hot.

Why do some people like their food spicy, while others like it plain? Differences in cultural background certainly play a part in food preferences. Babies may even be exposed to such cultural preferences in flavors when breastfeeding (Azar, 1998b). If a mother consumes garlic or vanilla, for example, the nursing baby will spend more time savoring these flavors by keeping the milk longer in its mouth.

Genetic factors also play a large role in determining taste sensitivities and preferences (Bartoshuk & Beauchamp, 1994; Goode, 2001a). Some people inherit a greater sensitivity to sweetness than others, and some inherit a sensitivity to bitter tastes (J. E. Brody, 2001b). Cats appear to be taste-blind to sweetness, but pigs can sense sweetness. (It might be accurate to say that while humans may eat like pigs, pigs may eat like humans.)

About one in four people (more women than men) are born with a very dense network of taste buds that makes them overly sensitive to certain tastes (Azar, 1998b; Goode, 2001a). These people are called "supertasters." Supertasters may recoil at the sharp or bitter tastes of many fruits and vegetables, including broccoli, or find sugary foods sickeningly sweet. Researchers find both gender and ethnic or racial differences in taste sensitivity. For example, Asian women are most likely to be supertasters, while White men are much less likely to belong to this group (Carpenter, 2000c). Recently, scientists discovered what we might term a tasty gene—a gene that allows one to taste a particular bitter-flavored chemical ("A Tasty Gene," 2003; Kim et al., 2003). The gene controls the shape of the specific receptor on the tongue that responds to this chemical.

These genetic traits help determine dietary chocies. For example, some people who douse their meat with salt may be nearly taste-blind to salt, another genetic trait. Others are extremely sensitive to salt, pepper, and other spices.

CONCEPT CHART 3.4
Chemical, Skin, and Body Senses

Chemical Senses	**Olfaction**	Source of sensory information	Molecules of the substance being sensed
		Receptor organ	The nose
		Receptor cells	Receptors in each nostril that can sense about 10,000 different substances on the basis of their molecular shapes
	Taste	Source of sensory information	Molecules of the substance being sensed
		Receptor organs	Mainly taste buds on the tongue, although there are additional receptors elsewhere in the mouth and throat
		Receptor cells	Taste receptors are sensitive to one or more of four basic tastes: sweet, sour, salty, and bitter
Skin Senses	**Skin Senses**	Source of sensory information	Touch, pressure, warmth, cold, and pain
		Receptor organ	The skin (pain can also originate in many other parts of the body)
		Receptor cells	Receptors that code for touch, pressure, warmth, cold, and pain
Body Senses	**Kinesthesis**	Source of sensory information	Movement and relative position of body parts
		Receptor cells	Receptors located mainly in joints, ligaments, and muscles
	Vestibular Sense	Source of sensory information	Motion of the body and orientation in space
		Receptor organs	Semicircular canals and vestibular sacs in the inner ear
		Receptor cells	Hair-cell receptors that respond to the movement of fluid in the semicircular canals and to shifts in position of crystals in vestibular sacs

Concept Chart 3.4 reviews the chemical senses—olfaction and taste.

The Skin Senses: Your Largest Sensory Organ

CONCEPT 3.22
Sensory receptors in the skin are sensitive to touch, pressure, temperature, and pain, and transmit information about these stimuli to your brain.

You may not think of your skin as a sensory organ. But it is actually the body's largest sensory organ. It contains receptors for the body's **skin senses** that code for sensations of touch, pressure, warmth, cold, and pain. Some skin receptors respond to just one type of stimulation, such as pressure or warmth. Others respond to more than one type of stimulation.

Nearly one-half million receptors for touch and pressure are distributed throughout the body. They transmit sensory information to the spinal cord, which relays it to the *somatosensory cortex,* the part of the cerebral cortex that processes information from our skin receptors and makes us aware of how and where we have been touched. Many touch receptors are located near the surface of the skin (see Figure 3.14). They fire when the skin is lightly touched—for example, caressed, stroked, or patted. Other receptors at deeper levels beneath the skin fire in response to pressure.

Receptors for temperature are also found just beneath the skin. Scientists generally agree that specific receptors exist for warmth and cold. In one of nature's more interesting surprises, sensations of hotness are produced by simultaneous stimulation of receptors for warmth and cold. If you were to clutch coiled pipes with warm and cold water circulating through them, you might feel as though your hand were being burned. Then, if the pipes were uncoiled, you would find that neither one by itself could give rise to sensations of hotness.

skin senses The senses of touch, pressure, warmth, cold, and pain that involve stimulation of sensory receptors in the skin.

gate-control theory of pain The belief that a neural gate in the spinal cord opens to allow pain messages to reach the brain and closes to shut them out.

acupuncture An ancient Chinese practice of inserting and rotating thin needles in various parts of the body in order to release natural healing energy.

Reflect for a moment about what it might mean if you did not experience pain. At first thought, not sensing pain might seem to be a good thing. After all, why go through life with headaches, toothaches, and backaches if you do not have to do so? Yet a life without pain could be a short one.

Pain is a sign that something is wrong. Without the experience of pain, you might not notice splinters, paper cuts, burns, and the many sources of injury, irritation, and infection that can ultimately threaten life if not attended to promptly. Pain is adaptive—that is, we use it to search for and do something about the source of the pain (Karoly & Ruehlman, 1996).

Pain receptors are located not just in the skin but also in other parts of the body, including muscles, joints, ligaments, and the pulp of the teeth—the source of tooth pain. We can feel pain in most parts of the body. Pain can be particularly acute where nerve endings are densely packed, as in the fingers and face.

People use many homespun remedies to control pain, such as rubbing or scratching a painful area or applying an ice pack. Why do these methods sometimes help? One possible answer lies in a theory developed by psychologist Ronald Melzack and biologist Patrick Wall (1965, 1983). According to their **gate-control theory of pain**, a gating mechanism in the spinal cord opens and closes to let pain messages through to the brain or to shut them out. The "gate" is not an actual physical structure in the spinal cord but, rather, a pattern of nervous system activity that results in either blocking pain signals or letting them through.

Creating a bottleneck at the "gate" may block out pain signals. Signals associated with dull or throbbing pain are conducted through the neural gate by nerve fibers that are thinner and slower than the nerve fibers that carry sensory signals for warmth, cold, and touch. The signals carried by the faster and thicker nerve fibers can cause a bottleneck at the neural gate, thus blocking the passage of other messages. Rubbing or scratching an area in pain sends signals to the spinal cord through fast nerve fibers. Those signals may successfully compete for space with pain messages carried by thin fibers, which closes the gate and temporarily blocks signals for dull and throbbing pain from reaching the brain. However, the first sharp pangs of pain you experience when you stub your toe or cut your finger are carried by large nerve pathways and apparently cannot be blocked out. This is a good thing, as it ensures that pain messages register quickly in the brain, alerting you instantly to the part of your body that has been injured.

An ice pack applied to the source of pain may help for several reasons. In addition to reducing inflammation and swelling—both of which contribute to the experience of pain—ice produces sensations of cold that help create a bottleneck at the gate in the spinal cord and thus, as in the earlier example, may temporarily block pain messages from reaching the brain.

The brain plays a critical role in controlling pain. In response to pain, the brain signals the release of *endorphins*. As you may recall from Chapter 2, endorphins are neurotransmitters that are similar in chemical composition to narcotic drugs, such as heroin. Like heroin, they have painkilling effects. They lock into receptor sites in the spinal cord that transmit pain messages, thereby closing the "pain gate" and preventing pain messages from reaching the brain.

The release of endorphins may explain the benefits of a traditional Chinese medical practice called **acupuncture**. The acupuncturist inserts thin needles at "acupuncture points" on the body and then rotates them. According to traditional Chinese beliefs, manipulation of the needles releases the body's natural healing energy. Though Western medicine has scoffed at this notion, there is evidence that acupuncture is often effective in providing short-term relief from pain (J. B. Murray, 1995; Podolsky, 1996). Some scientists, however, are not convinced that acupuncture works to relieve pain or that any pain relief it might produce is anything more than a placebo effect (I. M. Johnson, 1993).

For a summary of the skin senses, see Concept Chart 3.4.

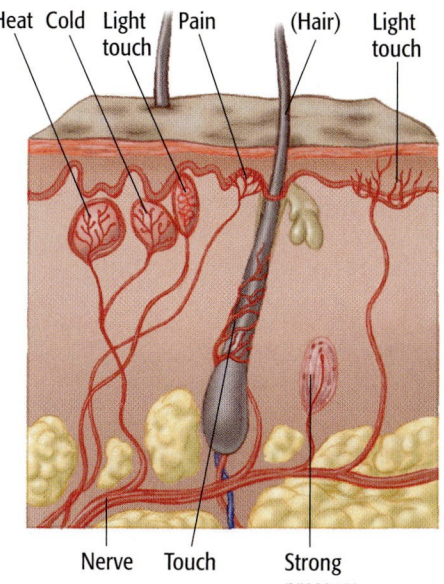

Figure 3.14   Your Largest Sensory Organ—Your Skin
The skin contains receptors that are sensitive to touch, pressure, warm and cold temperatures, and pain.

CONCEPT 3.23
The gate-control theory of pain proposes that the spinal cord contains a gating mechanism that controls the transmission of pain messages to the brain.

Blocking Pain   Applying an ice pack to an injured area may reduce pain. Based on your reading of the text, how would you explain this phenomenon?

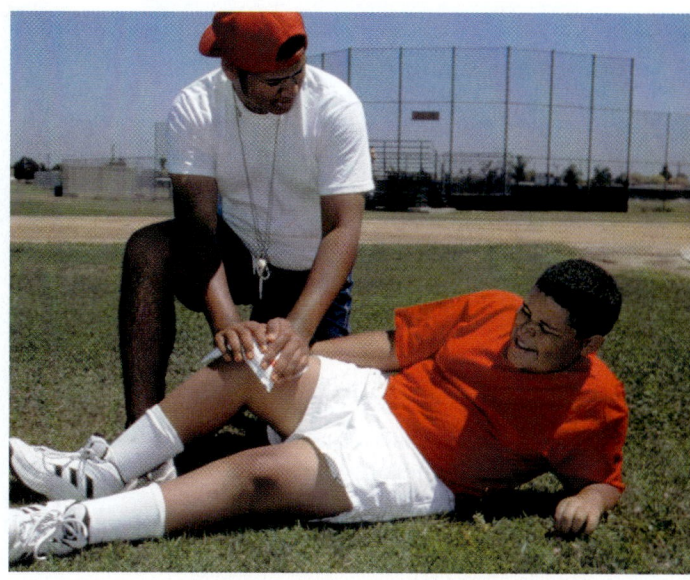

The Kinesthetic and Vestibular Senses: Of Grace and Balance

CONCEPT 3.24
Sensory receptors in your joints, ligaments, and muscles transmit information that the brain uses to keep you aware of the position and movement of parts of your body.

Kinesthesis is the body sense that keeps you informed about the movement of various parts of your body and their positions in relation to one another, even when your eyes are shut or you are in the dark. These sources of information are transmitted to the brain from receptors in the joints, ligaments, and muscles. It is kinesthesis that allows you to ride a bicycle without watching the movements of your legs. Kinesthesis also allows you to perfect the motions of swinging a bat, typing without looking at a keyboard, and washing the back of your neck. You may occasionally watch what you are doing, but most of the time your movements are based on feedback from your joints, ligaments, and muscles. All these tasks are accomplished automatically, without your thinking about them.

The **vestibular sense** is the sensory system that monitors the position of your body in space and helps you maintain your balance. It also allows you to know when the train or car in which you are riding is speeding up, slowing down, coming to a stop, or reversing direction. When the position of your head changes—rotates, tilts, or moves forward, backward, or sideways—movement of fluid within the **semicircular canals** in your inner ear, and shifts in the position of crystals in the **vestibular sacs** that connect the canals, stimulate hair-cell receptors (see Figure 3.15). These receptors then transmit messages to the brain that are interpreted as information about the position and movement of the head in relation to the external world (Anniko, Arnold, & Stigbrand, 1993; Probst, Katterbach, & Wist, 1995).

CONCEPT 3.25
Sensory organs within your inner ears respond to gravitational forces, which provide the brain with the sensory information it needs to maintain your balance and to know the position of your body in space.

If you spin around and around and come to an abrupt stop, you are likely to feel dizzy. The reason is that fluid in your ears' semicircular canals keeps swirling about for a while after you stop, making it seem as if the world is still spinning. We may experience *motion sickness* when our vestibular and visual senses receive conflicting information about movement, as when we are riding in a car headed in one direction while observing a moving train headed in the other direction.

For a summary of the kinesthetic and vestibular senses, see Concept Chart 3.4.

Kinesthesis Our kinesthetic sense allows us to fine-tune the movements of our body.

kinesthesis The sense that keeps us informed about movement of the parts of the body and their position in relation to each other.

vestibular sense The sense that keeps us informed about balance and the position of our body in space.

semicircular canals Three curved, tube-like canals in the inner ear that are involved in sensing changes in the direction and movement of the head.

vestibular sacs Organs in the inner ear that connect the semicircular canals.

Figure 3.15   The Vestibular Sense
Hair-cell receptors in the inner ear bend in relation to the position and movement of the head, providing information that the brain uses to allow us to maintain our balance and to sense changes in our movement through space.

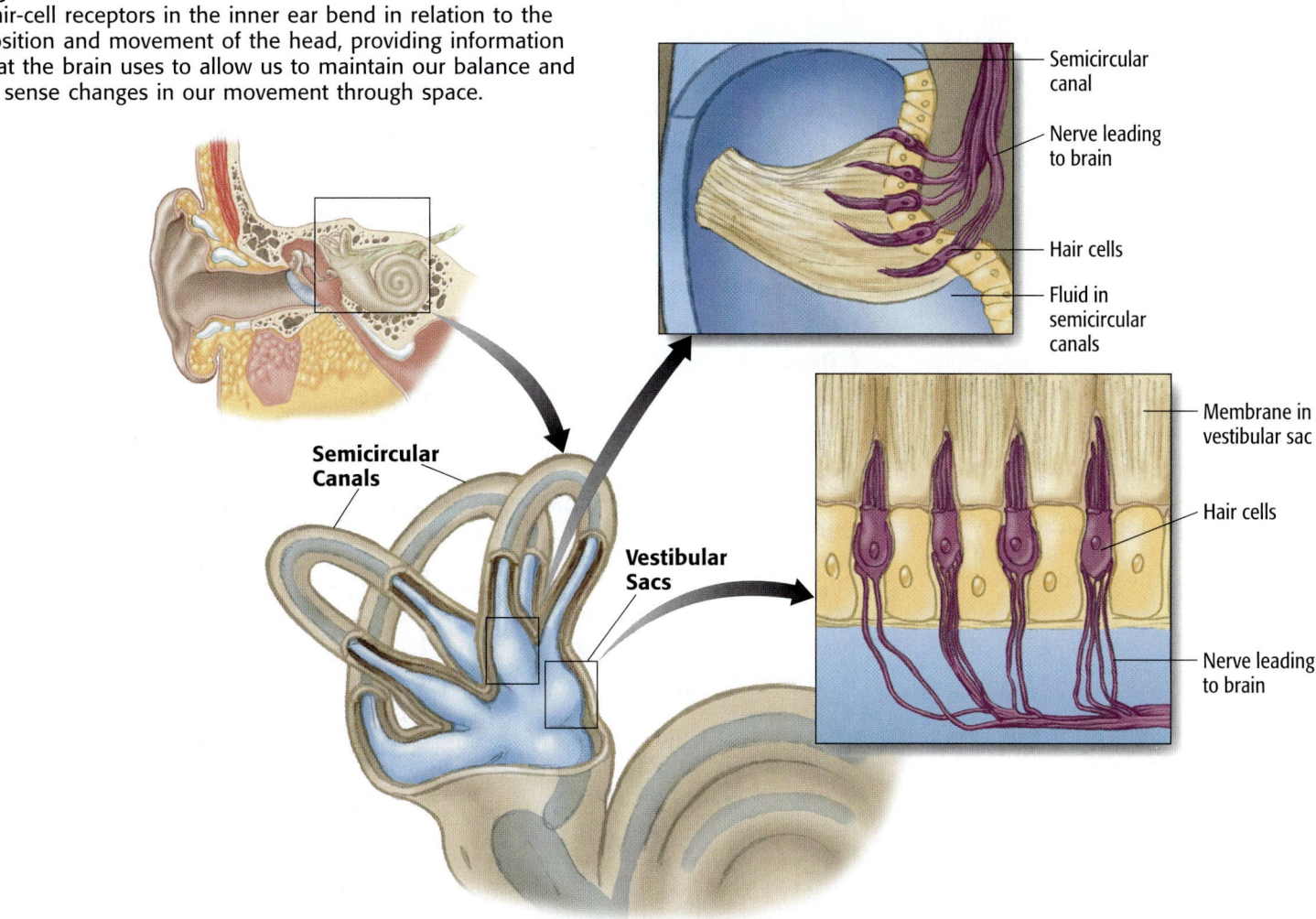

Semicircular canal

Nerve leading to brain

Hair cells

Fluid in semicircular canals

Semicircular Canals

Vestibular Sacs

Membrane in vestibular sac

Hair cells

Nerve leading to brain

MODULE 3.4 REVIEW

Our Other Senses: Chemical, Skin, and Body Senses

CONCEPT CHECK

1. Olfactory receptors in the nose recognize different chemical substances on the basis of their
   a. aromas.
   b. molecular shapes.
   c. density.
   d. vibrations.

2. Approximately how many different odors can our olfactory receptors sense?

3. Chemicals that function as sexual attractants are called _____.

4. What kinds of sensory receptors are found in the skin?

5. The receptors that provide sensory information that helps us maintain our balance are located in
   a. joints and ligaments.
   b. the back of the eye.
   c. muscles.
   d. the inner ear.

6. John is learning to swing a golf club. He relies on his _____ sense to know how far back he is swinging the club.

MODULE 3.5 — Perceiving Our World: Principles of Perception

- **What is perception?**
- **How is perception influenced by attention and perceptual set?**
- **What are the two general modes of processing visual stimuli?**
- **What are the Gestalt principles of perceptual organization?**
- **What is perceptual constancy, and what cues do we use to perceive depth and movement?**
- **What are visual illusions?**
- **Does subliminal perception exist?**
- **Does evidence support the existence of ESP?**

CONCEPT 3.26
Through the process of perception, the brain pieces together sensory information to form meaningful impressions of the world.

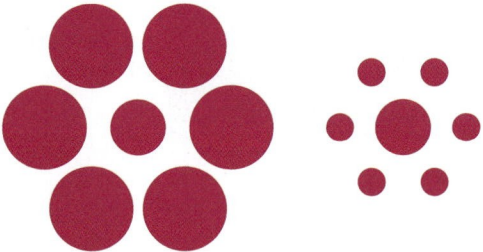

Figure 3.16 Perception vs. Reality? Which of the circles in the middle of these two groupings is larger?

Perception is the process by which the brain interprets sensory information, turning it into meaningful representations of the external world. Through perception, the brain attempts to make sense of the mass of sensory stimuli that impinge on our sensory organs. Were it not for perception, the world would seem like a continually changing hodgepodge of disconnected sensations—a buzzing confusion of lights, sounds, and other sensory impressions. The brain brings order to the mix of sensations we experience, organizing them into coherent pictures of the world around us. To paraphrase Shakespeare, sensation without perception would be "full of sound and fury but signifying nothing."

Consider what you see on this page. When the dots of black ink register on your retina, your brain transforms these images into meaningful symbols that you perceive as letters (D. D. Hoffman, 1999). Perception is an active process in which the brain pieces together bits and pieces of sensory information to form orderly impressions or pictures of the world.

Though perceptions help us make sense of the world, they may not accurately reflect external reality. Look at the central circles in the left and right configurations in Figure 3.16. Which of these two circles is larger? If you were to measure the diameter of each central circle with a ruler, you would find that they are exactly the same size. Yet you may perceive the central circle at the right to be larger than the one at the left. This is because the circle on the right is presented within an array of smaller circles, and your brain takes into account the context in which these shapes appear.

In this module, we explore basic concepts of perception, paying particular attention to visual perception—the area of perception that has captured the most research attention.

Attention: Did You Notice That?

Attention is the first step in perception. Through **selective attention**, you limit your attention to certain stimuli while filtering out other stimuli. Selective attention prevents you from being flooded with extraneous information. It explains why you may perceive certain stimuli but not others. It allows you to focus on the words you are reading but not perceive the sounds of a car passing outside the window or the feeling of your toes touching the inside of your shoes. We tend to pay selective attention to sensory signals that are most meaningful or important to us. For example, a parent in a deep sleep may perceive the faint cry of an infant in the next room but be undisturbed by the wail of a siren from an ambulance passing just outside the house.

Motivational states, such as hunger and thirst, play important roles in attention (R. R. Hoffman, Sherrick, & Warm, 1998). When we are hungry, we are more

perception The process by which the brain integrates, organizes, and interprets sensory impressions to create representations of the world.

selective attention The process by which we attend to meaningful stimuli and filter out irrelevant or extraneous stimuli.

habituation Reduction in the strength of a response to a repeated stimulus.

perceptual set The tendency for perceptions to be influenced by one's expectations or preconceptions.

likely than when we've just eaten to pay attention to odors wafting out of a restaurant. We also are more likely to notice billboards on the side of the road advertising nearby restaurants. I recall one professor who had the habit of dropping the words *"midterm exam"* into his lectures when he felt the class was nodding off. That seemed to motivate his students to pay closer attention.

Repeated exposure may increase attention to particular stimuli. Prenatal auditory exposure may explain why three-day-old infants prefer the sounds of their mother's voice—as measured by head turning—to the voices of other women (Freeman, Spence, & Oliphant, 1993).

On the other hand, exposure to a constant stimulus can lead us to become *habituated,* or accustomed, to it. When you first turn on an air conditioner or fan, you may notice the constant humming sound it makes. But after a time, you no longer perceive it, even though the sound continues to impinge on the sensory receptors in your ears. Your brain has adapted to the constant stimulus by tuning it out. **Habituation** makes sense from an evolutionary perspective, since constant stimuli are less likely than changing stimuli to require an adaptive response.

Perceptual Set: Seeing What You Expect to See

Perceptual set refers to the tendency for our perceptions to be influenced by our expectations or preconceptions. Do you see the number *13* or the letter *B* in Figure 3.17? In a classic study, Jerome Bruner and A. Leigh Minturn (1955) showed this figure to research participants after they had seen either a series of numbers or a series of letters. Among those who had viewed the number series, 83 percent said the stimulus was the number *13*. Of those who had seen the letter series, 93 percent said the stimulus was a *B*. When faced with ambiguous stimuli, people often base their perceptions on their expectations and preconceptions. We might speculate that devoted fans of science fiction would be more likely than others to perceive flickering lights in the night sky as a UFO. Figure 3.18 shows another example of a perceptual set.

Concept Chart 3.5 summarizes the principles of selective attention and perceptual set as well as other principles of perception discussed in the sections that follow in this module.

Modes of Visual Processing: Bottom-Up vs. Top-Down

As noted earlier, Hubel and Wiesel's (1979) work on feature detectors showed that specialized receptors in the visual cortex respond only to specific visual features, such as straight lines, angles, or moving points of light. Two general modes of visual processing, *bottom-up processing* and *top-down processing,* help account for how the brain transforms such bits and pieces of visual stimuli into meaningful patterns.

CONCEPT 3.27
Many factors affect our attention to particular stimuli, including motivation and repeated exposure.

CONCEPT 3.28
Our interpretations of stimuli depend in part on what we expect to happen in particular situations.

Figure 3.17   What Do You See Here, the Letter B or the Number 13?
Your answer may depend on your perceptual set.

CONCEPT 3.29
The brain forms meaningful visual patterns using two different modes of processing visual stimuli: bottom-up processing and top-down processing.

Figure 3.18   A Duck or a Rabbit?
The figure in *a* appears to be a duck when you see it after viewing the figure in *c.* But if you first observed the figure in *b,* then the figure in *a* appears to be a rabbit.

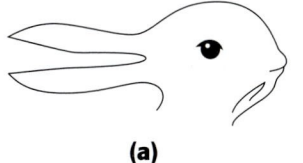

(a)

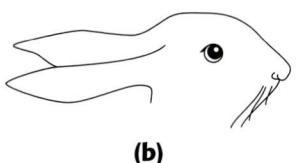

(b)

(c)

In **bottom-up processing**, the brain assembles specific features of shapes, such as angles and lines, to form patterns that we can compare with stored images we have seen before. For example, the brain combines individual lines and angles to form a pattern we recognize as the number *4*. Bottom-up processing may also be used to combine the individual elements of letters and words into recognizable

CONCEPT CHART 3.5
Overview of Perception

Selective Attention and Perceptual Set	**Selective attention**	We tend to pay attention to the types of sensory information that are important to us. Such factors as motivational states and repeated exposure influence whether we attend to particular stimuli.
	Perceptual set	Our expectations or preconceptions may influence our perceptions by creating a perceptual set for interpreting stimuli in ways that conform to those expectations or preconceptions.
Modes of Perceptual Processing	**Bottom-up**	The process by which the brain forms perceptions by piecing together bits and pieces of sensory data to form meaningful patterns
	Top-down	The process by which the brain forms perceptions by recognizing whole patterns without first piecing together their component parts
Gestalt Principles of Perceptual Organization	**Figure-ground**	The tendency to perceive the visual environment in terms of figures (objects) that stand out from the surrounding background, or ground
	Principles of Grouping — **Proximity**	The tendency to perceive objects as belonging together when they are close to one another
	Similarity	The tendency to group objects that have similar characteristics
	Continuity	The tendency to perceive a series of stimuli as a unified form when they appear to represent a continuous pattern
	Closure	The tendency to group disconnected pieces of information into a meaningful whole
	Connectedness	The tendency to perceive objects as belonging together when they are positioned together or are moving together
Cues for Depth Perception	*Binocular Cues* — **Retinal disparity**	The disparity in the images of objects projected onto the retina, which the brain uses as a cue to the distance of the objects. Nearby objects produce greater retinal disparity.
	Convergence	Turning the eyes inward to focus on a nearby object, which creates muscular tension that the brain uses as a cue for depth perception. The closer the object, the more the eyes must converge to maintain the single image.
	Monocular Cues — **Relative size**	An object that appears larger than another object believed to be of the same size is judged to be closer.
	Interposition	Objects that are obscured by other objects are perceived as being farther away.
	Relative clarity	Nearby objects are clearer than more distant objects.
	Texture gradient	The details of nearby objects appear to have a coarser texture than those of distant objects.
	Linear perspective	Objects and the spaces between them look smaller as they become more distant. Thus, parallel lines appear to converge as they recede into the distance.
	Shadowing	Shadows can create the appearance of curving surfaces or three dimensions, giving the impression of depth.
Controversies in Perception	**Subliminal perception**	Perception of stimuli presented below the threshold of conscious awareness
	Extrasensory perception (ESP)	Perception occurring without the benefit of the known senses

Figure 3.19   Do You Know These Men? At first glance, you may have thought you recognized George W. Bush and Dick Cheney. Actually, the photo of Cheney was doctored by combining the facial features of Bush with Cheney's hairline. We tend to recognize faces on the basis of their large-scale features rather than piecing together smaller details.

patterns. But how is it that we can read handwriting in which the same letter is never formed twice in exactly the same way? In this style of processing, called **top-down processing**, we recognize patterns as meaningful wholes without first piecing together their component parts. Top-down processing is based on acquired experience and knowledge with patterns, but it is not perfect. Perhaps you've had the experience of thinking you recognized someone approaching you from a distance, only to find out you were mistaken as you got a closer look at the person. You made the mistake because of the tendency to perceive faces on the basis of their whole patterns rather than building them up feature by feature (see Figure 3.19).

The two modes of perceptual processing are summarized in Concept Chart 3.5. Next, we focus on how we organize our visual perceptions.

Gestalt Principles of Perceptual Organization

You'll recall from Chapter 1 that Max Wertheimer, while aboard a moving train, observed the apparent movement of stationary objects in the distance and that this perception led him to establish the school of psychology known as Gestalt psychology.

Now let's return to Figure 3.16. Each of the central circles in the figure is perceived as part of a whole—in this case, as part of a grouping of seven circles. The central circle on the left clearly appears to be smaller than the surrounding circles. The central circle on the right clearly appears larger than the circles that surround it. Even though they are the same size, the context of the circles creates the perception that the central circle on the right is larger. But that is because we *perceive* the circles within their contexts, or wholes—not because we are able to *sense* a difference in size with our eyes.

Max Wertheimer and the other early Gestalt psychologists conducted studies in which they observed the ways in which people assemble bits of sensory stimulation into meaningful wholes. On this basis, they formulated **laws of perceptual organization**. Here we consider laws of figure-ground perception and laws of grouping.

Figure and Ground

Look around as you are walking down the street. What do you see? Are there people milling about? Are there clouds in the sky? Gestalt psychologists have shown that people, clouds, and other objects are perceived in terms of *figure*, and the background against which the figures are perceived (the street, for the people; the sky, for the clouds) serves as the *ground*. Figures have shapes, but ground does

CONCEPT 3.30
Gestalt psychologists described how the brain constructs meaning from sensations by organizing them into recognizable patterns.

bottom-up processing   A mode of perceptual processing by which the brain recognizes meaningful patterns by piecing together bits and pieces of sensory information.

top-down processing   A mode of perceptual processing by which the brain identifies patterns as meaningful wholes rather than as piecemeal constructions.

laws of perceptual organization   The principles identified by Gestalt psychologists that describe the ways in which the brain groups bits of sensory stimulation into meaningful wholes or patterns.

Figure 3.20   Reversible Figure
Whether you see two profiles facing each other in this picture or a vase depends on your perception of figure and ground. See if you can shift back and forth between perceiving the profiles and the vase by switching the parts you take to be figure and those you take to be ground.

Figure 3.21   Ambiguous Figure
Do you see an old woman or a young one? If you have trouble switching between the two, look at Figure 3.24, in which figure and ground are less ambiguous.

not (Baylis & Cale, 2001). We tend to perceive objects as figures when they have shapes or other characteristics, such as distinctive coloring, against the backdrop of the ground in which they appear.

Sometimes, however, when we perceive an outline, it may be unclear as to what constitutes the figure and what constitutes the ground. Does Figure 3.20 show a vase, or does it show two profiles? Which is the figure, and which is the ground? Outline alone does not tell the tale, because the same outline describes a vase and human profiles. What other cues do you use to decide which is the figure and which is the ground?

Let's now consider Figure 3.21, an ambiguous figure that can be perceived in different ways depending on how you organize your perceptions. What does the figure look like? Take a minute to focus on it before reading further.

Did you see an old woman or a young one? Are you able to switch back and forth? (Hints: The old woman is facing forward and downward, while the young woman is facing diagonally away. The old woman's nose is the young woman's chin, and her right eye is her counterpart's left ear.) Whether you see an old woman or a young woman depends on how you organize your perceptual experience—which parts you take to be the figure and which parts you take to be the ground. Figure 3.23 (page 112) provides an example in which figure and ground are less ambiguous.

Gestalt Laws of Grouping

People tend to perceive sensory stimuli in terms of their contexts, grouping bits and pieces of sensory information into unitary forms or wholes. Gestalt psychologists described several principles of grouping, including *proximity, similarity, continuity, closure,* and *connectedness.*

Figure 3.22   Gestalt Laws of Grouping
Gestalt psychologists recognized that people group objects according to certain organizational principles. Here we see examples of five such principles: proximity, similarity, continuity, closure, and connectedness.

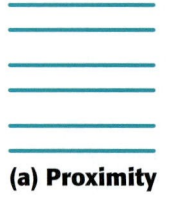

(a) Proximity

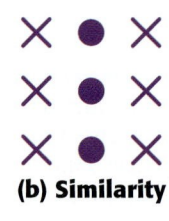

(b) Similarity

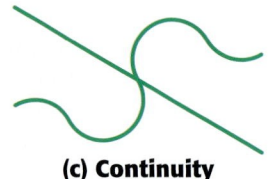

(c) Continuity

(d) Closure

(e) Connectedness

Figure 3.22*a* illustrates **proximity**, or nearness. Most observers would perceive the figure as consisting of three sets of parallel lines rather than six separate lines, although six lines are sensed. That is, we use the relative closeness of the lines as a perceptual cue for organizing them into a group.

How would you describe Figure 3.22*b*? Do you perceive nine separate geometric shapes or two columns of X's and one column of ●'s? If you describe it in terms of X's and ●'s, you are using the principle of **similarity**—that is, grouping figures that are similar to one another (in this case, geometric figures that resemble each other). If you see four bare-chested young men at a football game who've painted their bodies in the colors of the home team, you are likely to perceive them as a group distinct from other fans.

Figure 3.22*c* represents another way we group stimuli, **continuity**, which is the tendency to perceive a series of stimuli as a unified form when the stimuli appear to represent a continuous pattern. Here we perceive two intersecting continuous lines, one curved and one straight, rather than four separate lines.

Now, check Figure 3.22*d*. You sense a number of short lines, but do you perceive a meaningless array of lines or a broken triangle? If you perceive the triangle, your perception draws on the principle of **closure**—grouping disconnected pieces of information into a meaningful whole. You perceive a complete form even when there are gaps in the form. This illustrates the principle for which Gestalt psychologists are best known—that the whole is more than the sum of the parts.

Figure 3.22*e* gives an example of **connectedness**—the tendency to perceive objects as belonging together when they are positioned together or are moving together. Thus, you perceive three sets of connected triangles rather than six triangles with three interspersing lines. Perhaps you have noticed this tendency while watching two people walk down a street next to each other and being surprised when they suddenly walk off in different directions without saying goodbye. In such circumstances, we tend to perceive the people as belonging together because they are moving together (Sekuler & Bennett, 2001).

You'll find an overview of the Gestalt principles of perceptual organization in Concept Chart 3.5.

Perceptual Constancies

Here we focus on **perceptual constancy**—the tendency to perceive the size, shape, color, and brightness of an object as remaining the same even when the image it casts on the retina changes. We could not adjust to our world very well without perceptual constancy. The world is constantly shifting before our eyes as we look at objects from different distances and perspectives. Just turning our heads changes the geometry of an object projected on the retina. Yet we don't perceive objects as changing before our eyes. We perceive them as constant—a good thing, since they are indeed constant (Shebilske & Peters, 1995). For example, the ability to perceive that a tiger is a tiger and not a housecat regardless of the distance from which the animal is viewed could be a life-saving mechanism.

The tendency to perceive an object as being the same shape even when the object is viewed from different perspectives is **shape constancy**. If you observe a round bowl on a table from different angles, the image it casts on your retina changes shape. Nonetheless, you perceive the bowl as round. In other words, its shape remains constant despite the change in your angle of view. Similarly, you perceive a door as having an unchanging shape despite differences in the image it casts upon your retina depending on whether it is open or closed (see Figure 3.24). Moreover, as you approach the bowl at eye level, its size—in terms of the size of the retinal image—grows. As you move farther away from it, the size of its retinal image decreases. Yet you continue to perceive the bowl as being the same size, just as I knew my daughter did not suddenly become a giant as she approached the camera. The tendency to perceive an object as being the same size despite changes in the size of the retinal image it casts is **size constancy**.

TRY THIS OUT

Your Neighborhood Gestalt

Take a walk through your neighborhood or local area. Look around you. How many examples of the Gestalt laws of perceptual organization can you identify?

CONCEPT 3.31
We tend to perceive objects as having a constant size, shape, color, and brightness even when the image they cast on our retinas changes.

proximity The principle that objects that are near each other will be perceived as belonging to a common set.

similarity The principle that objects that are similar will be perceived as belonging to the same group.

continuity The principle that a series of stimuli will be perceived as representing a unified form.

closure The perceptual principle that people tend to piece together disconnected bits of information to perceive whole forms.

connectedness The principle that objects positioned together or moving together will be perceived as belonging to the same group.

perceptual constancy The tendency to perceive the size, shape, color, and brightness of an object as remaining the same even when the image it casts on the retina changes.

shape constancy The tendency to perceive an object as having the same shape despite differences in the images it casts on the retina as the viewer's perspective changes.

size constancy The tendency to perceive an object as having the same size despite changes in the images it casts on the retina as the viewing distance changes.

Figure 3.23 Old/Young Woman
The figure on the right shows the downward-looking "old woman" more clearly as figure than as ground, while the one on the left highlights the figural aspects of the "young woman" looking away from the perceiver. Now look back at Figure 3.22 and see if you can't switch back between the two impressions.

Experience teaches people about distance and perspective. We learn that an object seen at a distance will look smaller than when it is close and that an object seen from different perspectives will appear to have different shapes. If we are wrong, please send out an APB for a runaway giant infant.

People also perceive objects as retaining their color even when lighting conditions change. This tendency is called **color constancy** (Brainard, Wandell, & Chichilnisky, 1993). For example, if your car is red, you perceive it to be red even though it may look grayish as evening falls. The tendency for perceived brightness or lightness of an object to remain relatively constant despite changes in illumination is called **brightness constancy** or *lightness constancy* (Wilcox & Duke, 2003). For example, a piece of white chalk placed in the shade on a sunny day reflects less light than does a black hockey puck placed directly in sunlight. Yet we perceive the chalk to be brighter than the hockey puck.

Cues to Depth Perception

How do we know that some objects are closer than others? The answer is that we normally use both binocular and monocular cues for judging distance or depth.

Binocular Cues for Depth

For **binocular cues**, we depend on both eyes. Because our eyes are a few inches apart, each eye receives slightly different images of the world. The brain interprets the difference in the two retinal images—the **retinal disparity** between them—as cues to the relative distances of objects. The closer the object, the greater the retinal disparity.

> 💡 **CONCEPT 3.32**
> Our perception of depth depends on both monocular and binocular cues for judging distance.

Figure 3.24 Shape Constancy
Perception of an object's shape remains the same even when the image it casts on the retina changes with the angle of view. You perceive three rectangular doors, despite the fact that the image each projects on the retina is different.

You can readily see how retinal disparity works by holding a finger an inch in front of your nose. First close your left eye and look at the finger only with your right eye. The finger looks as if it is off to the left. Then close your right eye and look at the finger with your left eye. The finger seems off to the right. The finger appears to move from side to side as you open and close each eye. The distance between the two apparent fingers corresponds to the retinal disparity between the two images that form on your retina. Now hold a finger straight ahead at arm's length away from your eyes. Again close one eye and focus on the finger. Then close that eye and open the other. The finger may still seem to "move," but there will be less distance between the two "fingers" because retinal disparity is smaller at greater distances.

Now let's try an experiment to illustrate the binocular cue of **convergence**, which depends on the muscular tension produced by turning both eyes inward to form a single image. Hold a finger once more at arm's length. Keeping both eyes open, concentrate on the finger so that you perceive only one finger. Now bring it slowly closer to your eyes, maintaining the single image. As you do, you will feel tension in your eye muscles. This is because your eyes are *converging,* or looking inward, to maintain the single image, as shown in Figure 3.25. The closer the object—in this case, the finger—the greater the tension. Your brain uses the tension as a cue for depth perception.

Figure 3.25
Binocular Cues for Depth
When we rely on binocular cues for judging the depth of a nearby object, our eyes must converge on the object, which can give us that cross-eyed look.

Monocular Cues for Depth

Monocular cues depend on one eye only. When people drive, they use a combination of binocular and monocular cues to judge the distance of other cars and of the surrounding scenery. Although there are advantages to using binocular cues, most people can get by driving with monocular cues, which include relative size, interposition, relative clarity, texture gradient, linear perspective, and shadowing.

PsychAssist: Monocular Depth Cues

- *Relative Size.* When two objects are believed to be the same size, the one that appears larger is perceived to be closer (see Figure 3.26a).

- *Interposition.* When objects block or otherwise obscure our view of other objects, we perceive the obscured object as farther away. Notice that in Figure 3.26b we perceive the horses in front to be closer than the ones that are partially blocked.

- *Relative Clarity.* Smog, dust, smoke, and water droplets in the atmosphere create a "haze" that makes distant objects appear more blurry than nearer objects (see Figure 3.26c). You may have noticed how much closer far-away mountains appear on a really clear day.

- *Texture Gradient.* The relative coarseness or smoothness of an object is used as a cue for distance. Closer objects appear to have a coarser or more detailed texture than more distant objects. Thus, the texture of flowers that are farther away is smoother than the texture of those that are closer (Figure 3.26d).

- *Linear Perspective.* Linear perspective is the perception of parallel lines converging as they recede into the distance. As we look straight ahead, objects and the distances between them appear smaller the farther away they are from us. Thus, the road ahead of the driver, which consists of parallel lines, appears to grow narrower as it recedes into the distance (Figure 3.26e). It may even seem to end in a point.

- *Shadowing.* Patterns of light and dark, or shadowing, create the appearance of three-dimensional objects or curving surfaces. Shadowing can make an object appear to be concave or convex. Notice how the dents that appear in Figure 3.26f look like bumps when the image is turned upside down. We perceive objects that are lighter on top and darker on the bottom to be bumps, whereas the opposite is the case for dents (Gaulin & McBurney, 2001).

Concept Chart 3.5 summarizes the various cues we use to perceive depth.

color constancy   The tendency to perceive an object as having the same color despite changes in lighting conditions.

brightness constancy   The tendency to perceive objects as retaining their brightness even when they are viewed in dim light.

binocular cues   Cues for depth that involve both eyes, such as retinal disparity and convergence.

retinal disparity   A binocular cue for distance based on the slight differences in the visual impressions formed in both eyes.

convergence   A binocular cue for distance based on the degree of tension required to focus two eyes on the same object.

monocular cues   Cues for depth that can be perceived by each eye alone, such as relative size and interposition.

Figure 3.26 Monocular Cues for Depth
We use many different monocular cues to judge depth, including:

(a) Relative size

(b) Interposition

(c) Relative clarity

(d) Texture gradient

(e) Linear perspective

(f) Shadowing

Motion Perception

> **CONCEPT 3.33**
> We use two basic cues in perceiving movement: the path of the image as it crosses the retina and the changing size of the object.

We use various cues to perceive motion. One is the actual movement of an object across our field of vision as the image it projects moves from point to point on the retina. The brain interprets the swath that the image paints across the retina as a sign of movement (Derrington, 2004). Another cue is the changing size of an object. Objects appear larger when they are closer. When you are driving and you see the cars ahead suddenly looming much larger, you perceive that you are moving faster than they are—so fast you may need to slam on the brakes to avoid a collision. When cars ahead grow smaller, they appear to be moving faster than you are.

Visual Illusions: Do Your Eyes Deceive You?

> **CONCEPT 3.34**
> Visual illusions are misperceptions of visual stimuli in which it seems that our eyes are playing tricks on us.

Our eyes sometimes seem to play tricks on us in the form of **visual illusions**. Figure 3.27 shows two well-known visual illusions: the *Müller-Lyer illusion (a)* and the *Ponzo illusion (b)*. In both cases, what you think you see isn't exactly what you get when you pull out a ruler. Although the center lines in (a) are actually the same length, as are the center lines in (c) and (d), the line on the right in (a) seems longer, as does the center line in (d) as compared to the one in (c). The figure with the inward wings creates the impression of an outward corner of a room that appears to be closer *(c)*. In the Müller-Lyer illusion, the figure with the outward wings suggests the inner corner of a room *(d)*, which makes the center line seem farther away.

Although no one explanation may fully account for the Müller-Lyer illusion, a partial explanation may involve how the brain interprets size and distance cues.

> **visual illusions** Misperceptions of visual stimuli.

Figure 3.27   Müller-Lyer Illusion and Ponzo Illusion
Visual illusions involve misperceptions in which our eyes seem
to be playing tricks on us.

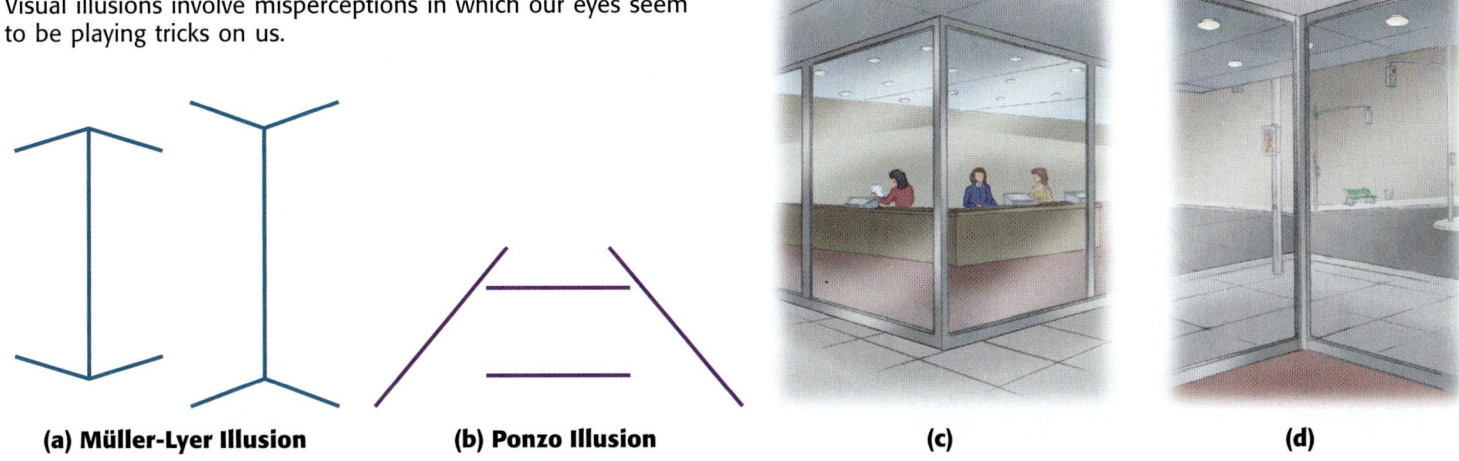

(a) Müller-Lyer Illusion   **(b) Ponzo Illusion**   **(c)**   **(d)**

As you'll recall from the discussion of size constancy, people tend to perceive an object as remaining the same size even as the image it projects on the retina changes in relation to distance from the observer. But when two objects of the same size appear to be at different distances from the observer, the one that is judged to be farther away is perceived to be larger. In the Müller-Lyer illusion, the figure with the outward wings suggests the inner corner of a room, which makes the center line seem farther away. The figure with the inward wings creates the impression of an outward corner of a room that appears to be closer to the observer. Since both center lines actually create the same-size image on the retina, the brain interprets the one that appears to be farther away as being longer.

Now consider the Ponzo illusion (also called the railroad illusion). Which of the two horizontal lines in Figure 3.27b looks longer? Why do you think people generally perceive the line at the top to be longer? Converging lines may create an impression of linear perspective, leading us to perceive the upper line as farther away. As with the Müller-Lyer illusion, since lines of equal length cast the same-size image on the retina, the one perceived as farther away is judged to be longer.

Another type of illusion involves *impossible figures,* such as the one in Figure 3.28. Impossible figures fool the brain into creating the impression of a whole figure when the figure is viewed from certain perspectives. An impossible figure appears to make sense when you look at parts of it, but not when you try to take into account the characteristics of the whole figure.

The well-known *moon illusion* has baffled people for ages (see Figure 3.29). When a full moon appears near the horizon, it may seem enormous compared with its "normal" size—that is, its apparent size when it is high in the evening sky. Actually, the image the moon casts on the retina is the same size whether it sits high in the sky or just over the horizon. We don't have an entirely satisfactory explanation of this illusion. One leading theory, the *relative-size hypothesis,* relates the phenomenon to the amount of space surrounding the perceived object (Baird, Wagner, & Fuld, 1990; Restle, 1970). When the moon is at the horizon, it appears larger by comparison with objects far off in the distance, such as tall trees and mountains. When the moon is high in the sky, there is nothing to compare it with except the vast featureless wastes of space, and this comparison makes it seem smaller.

You can test out the moon illusion for yourself by looking at the full moon on the horizon. Then, to remove any distance cues, look again at the moon through a rolled-up magazine. You'll find that the moon appears to shrink in size. One problem with the relative-size hypothesis is that it doesn't account for all cases in which the phenomenon is observed, including a planetarium in which the moon is depicted in the absence of intervening landscape cues (Suzuki, 1991).

Figure 3.28   Impossible Figure
Notice how the figure makes sense if you look at certain of its features, but not when you take all its features into account.

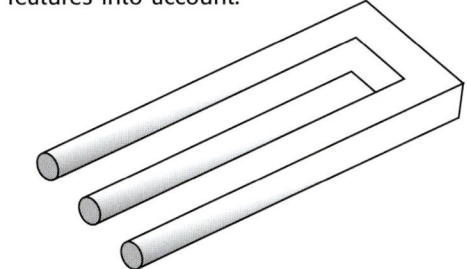

Figure 3.29 Moon Illusion
The moon illusion refers to the perception that the moon is larger when at the horizon than when it is high in the sky.

Figure 3.30 Stroboscopic Movement
The perception of movement in "moving pictures" is a feature of the viewer, not the projector.

We have discussed how we perceive actual movement, but there are also interesting examples of *apparent movement*, such as **stroboscopic movement** (see Figure 3.30). Stroboscopic movement puts the motion in motion pictures. We perceive the rapid progression of illuminated still images to be a seamless "motion picture." The film itself contains a series of still images projected at more than twenty pictures, or "frames," per second. Each frame differs somewhat from the one shown before. This is nothing but a quick slide show; the "movie" mechanism lies within us—the viewers.

Cultural Differences in Perceiving Visual Illusions

CONCEPT 3.35

The susceptibility to visual illusions is influenced by cultural factors, such as the types of structures to which people in a particular culture are accustomed.

Suppose you lived in a culture in which structures with corners and angles were uncommon. Would you be as likely to experience the Müller-Lyer illusion as someone raised in, say, Cleveland or Dallas? To find out, Darhl Pedersen and John Wheeler (1983) tested two groups of Navajo Indians on the Müller-Lyer illusion. One group lived in rectangular houses that provided daily exposure to angles and corners. Another group lived in traditional rounded huts with fewer of these cues. Those living in the rounded huts were less likely to be deceived by the Müller-Lyer illusion, suggesting that prior experience plays a role in determining susceptibility to the illusion. Other studies have produced similar results. For example, the illusion was observed less frequently among the Zulu people of southern Africa, who also live in rounded structures (Segall, 1994).

The **carpentered-world hypothesis** was put forth to account for cultural differences in susceptibility to the Müller-Lyer illusion (Segall, Campbell, & Herskovits, 1966). A carpentered world is one, like our own, that is dominated by structures (buildings, rooms, and furniture) in which straight lines meet at right angles. People living in noncarpentered worlds, which consist largely of rounded structures, are less prone to the illusion because of their limited experience with angu-

stroboscopic movement   A type of apparent movement based on the rapid succession of still images, as in motion pictures.

carpentered-world hypothesis   An attempt to explain the Müller-Lyer illusion in terms of the cultural experience of living in a carpentered, right-angled world like our own.

Carpentered-World Hypothesis
According to the carpentered-world hypothesis, people living in cultures in which right-angled structures are rare are less prone to the Müller-Lyer illusion.

lar structures. Cultural experience, rather than race, seems the determinant. Zulus who move to cities where they become accustomed to seeing angular structures are more likely to be fooled by the illusion (Segall, Campbell, & Herskovits, 1963).

Studies with the Ponzo (railroad) illusion also show cultural differences. The illusion is less prominent among the people of Guam, an island with a hilly terrain and no long, uninterrupted highways or railroads (Leibowitz, 1971).

The lesson here goes beyond cultural differences in visual illusions. Perception is influenced not only by our sensory systems but also by our experience of living in a particular culture. People from different cultures may perceive the physical world differently. Consider a classic example offered by the anthropologist Colin Turnbull (1961). Turnbull took Kenge, an African pygmy guide, on his first trip outside the dense forest into the open plain. When Kenge saw buffalo several miles away on the plain, he took them to be insects. When he got closer to the animals and recognized them as buffalo, he was aghast at how the animals had been able to grow so quickly. Why would Kenge mistake a buffalo for an insect? In Kenge's culture, people lived in remote villages in a dense forest. He had never before had an unobstructed view of objects at a great distance. He lacked the experience needed to acquire size constancy for distant objects—to learn that objects retain their size even as the image they project on our eyes grows smaller.

Next we focus on two controversies in perception that have sparked a continuing debate within both the scientific community and the society at large.

Controversies in Perception: Subliminal Perception and Extrasensory Perception

It created quite a stir in the U.S. presidential race in 2000 when a campaign commercial for candidate George W. Bush used what appeared to be a subliminal slur against opponent Al Gore ("Democrats Smell a Rat," 2000). The word *RATS* was flashed during an ad attacking Gore's health care plan. The producer of the ad claimed the message was not intended as a slur against Gore and simply represented a visual reminder of the word *bureaucrats* (*rats* being the last four letters of the word). Whether intended as a slur or not, it led people once again to wonder whether **subliminal perception** could affect attitudes and behavior.

An even more controversial topic is **extrasensory perception (ESP)**—perception that occurs without benefit of the known senses. Is it possible to read people's minds or to know the contents of a letter in a sealed envelope? Here we consider these long-standing controversies in light of the evidence that scientists have been able to gather.

subliminal perception   Perception of stimuli that are presented below the threshold of conscious awareness.

extrasensory perception (ESP)
Perception that occurs without benefit of the known senses.

CONCEPT 3.36
Though we sometimes perceive things we are not conscious of perceiving, there is no evidence that our attitudes or behavior are influenced by subliminal cues.

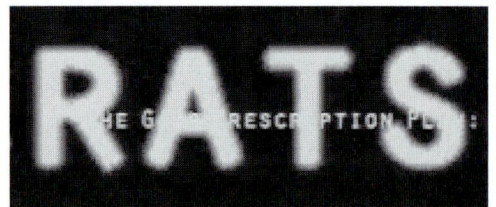

A Subliminal Slur? Did this campaign advertisement use subliminal perception in an attempt to sway voters?

CONCEPT 3.37
Claims of ESP remain just that—claims that have not met the rigorous tests of scientific inquiry.

Was It ESP?

Have you ever had any unusual experiences that you believe involved ESP? Think critically. What alternative explanations might account for these experiences?

parapsychology The study of paranormal phenomena.

telepathy Communication of thoughts from one mind to another that occurs without using the known senses.

clairvoyance The ability to perceive objects and events without using the known senses.

precognition The ability to foretell the future.

psychokinesis The ability to move objects by mental effort alone.

Subliminal Perception: Did You See Something Flash By?

A recent national poll found that two-thirds of Americans believe that subliminal perception does exist (Onion, 2000). But does scientific evidence support this belief? The answer, researchers report, is *yes*, but it is a qualified *yes*. The effects of subliminal perception appear to be subtle and to depend on very precise experimental conditions (Greenwald & Draine, 1997).

We know from laboratory studies that, under experimental conditions, people can detect stimuli presented below the threshold of awareness (Greenwald & Draine, 1997; Hull et al., 2002). Sheila Murphy and Robert Zajonc (1993) flashed either a smiling face or a frowning face to research participants at speeds too fast for them to perceive consciously. Yet those who were flashed the smiling face later reacted more favorably to a set of Chinese characters than those who had been flashed the frowning face. Apparently, some features of the subliminally presented stimulus had been perceived, even though participants could not report what they had seen. However, no convincing evidence exists that subliminal messages in ads or audiotapes can influence purchase decisions or help people become more successful in life (Bornstein, 1989; Druckman & Bjork, 1991; K. H. Smith & Rogers, 1994).

For a summary of subliminal perception, see Concept Chart 3.5.

Extrasensory Perception: Is It for Real?

A man claims to be able to bend spoons with his mind. A woman claims to be able to find the bodies of crime victims aided by nothing more than a piece of clothing worn by the victim. Another woman claims to be able to foretell future events. The study of such *paranormal phenomena*—events that cannot be explained by known physical, psychological, or biological mechanisms—is called **parapsychology**. The major focus of paranormal psychology is *extrasensory perception,* the so-called "sixth sense" by which people claim they can perceive objects or events without using the known senses. The forms of paranormal phenomena most commonly identified with ESP are *telepathy, clairvoyance, precognition* and *psychokinesis*.

Telepathy refers to the purported ability to project one's thoughts into other people's minds or to read what is in their minds—to perceive their thoughts or feelings without using the known senses. **Clairvoyance** is the perception of events that are not available to the senses. The clairvoyant may claim to know what someone across town is doing at that precise moment or to identify the contents of a sealed envelope. **Precognition** is the ability to foretell the future. **Psychokinesis** (formerly called *telekinesis*) is the ability to move objects without touching them. Strictly speaking, psychokinesis is not a form of ESP since it does not involve perception, but for the sake of convenience it is often classified as such.

Critical thinkers maintain an appropriate skepticism about claims of paranormal phenomena that seem to defy the laws of nature. Many claims of ESP have proven to be hoaxes, whereas others may be explained as random or chance occurrences. Despite many years of scientific study, we lack any reliable, replicable findings of ESP that have withstood scientific scrutiny. As critical thinkers, we need to maintain a skeptical attitude and insist that claims of extrasensory abilities be reliably demonstrated under tightly controlled conditions before we are willing to accept them.

A recent study showed that believers in the paranormal tended to view a demonstration of psychic abilities as an example of paranormal phenomena, even when they were informed beforehand that the effect was a magic trick (Hergovich, 2004). In any event, a study of college students at a mid-sized university in Arizona showed stronger beliefs in the paranormal among first-year college students than among seniors (Fitzpatrick & Shook, 1994). Perhaps greater exposure to college courses instills a more critical attitude toward these beliefs.

For a summary of extrasensory perception, see Concept Chart 3.5.

MODULE 3.5 REVIEW

Perceiving Our World: Principles of Perception

CONCEPT CHECK

1. The process by which the brain turns sensations into meaningful impressions of the external world is called _____.

2. The ability to focus on the words you are reading and to tune out irrelevant stimuli is called
   a. sensory inhibition.
   b. selective focusing.
   c. selective attention.
   d. the principle of maximal adherence.

3. The term used to describe the tendency for our expectations and preconceived notions to influence how we perceive events is _____.

4. What Gestalt principle describes the tendency to perceive objects as belonging together when they are positioned together or moving together?

5. The monocular cue by which we perceive objects to be closer to us when they obscure objects that are behind them is called _____.

6. Which of the following is *not* a monocular cue for depth?
   a. convergence
   b. relative clarity
   c. interposition
   d. shadowing

7. Subliminal perception involves
   a. acquiring knowledge or insight without using the known senses.
   b. perceiving information presented below the level of conscious awareness.
   c. perceiving stimuli in an underwater environment.
   d. sensory systems that can transmit all of a stimulus's features.

APPLICATION
MODULE 3.6   Psychology and Pain Management

• **What have psychologists learned about controlling pain?**

The brain is a marvel of engineering. By allowing us to experience the first pangs of pain, it alerts us to danger. Without such a warning, we might not pull our hand away from a hot object in time to prevent burns. Then, by releasing endorphins, the brain gradually shuts the gate on pain.

Yet pain is a constant and unwelcome companion for millions of people, and the management of it is a rapidly growing field. New technologies and approaches to pain management are being introduced to clinical practice each year. Although pain has a biological basis, researchers have found that psychological factors may influence the severity of pain and how well patients are able to cope with it. In this module, we focus on the role of psychological factors in pain management. However, before attempting to treat pain yourself, consult a health professional to determine the source of the pain and an appropriate course of treatment.

CONCEPT 3.38
People who suffer chronic pain may gain better control over their symptoms by using distraction, creating logjams at the "pain gate," changing their thoughts and attitudes, obtaining accurate information, and practicing meditation and biofeedback.

web. Netlab/Pain—Where Does It Come From?

Distraction

Distraction can be useful in directing attention away from pain. For example, children with cancer have reduced the unpleasant side effects of chemotherapy by playing video games (Kolko & Rickard-Figueroa, 1985; Redd, 1995). While receiving intravenous injections of nausea-inducing cancer drugs, the children focus on combating monsters on the video screen. Similarly, when faced with a painful medical or dental procedure, you can help keep your mind off your pain by focusing on a pleasing picture on the wall or some other stimulus or by letting your mind become absorbed in a pleasant fantasy. Chronic pain sufferers may find they are better able to cope with the pain if they distract themselves by exercising or by becoming immersed in a good book or video.

Creating a Bottleneck at the "Gate"

As noted earlier, the gate-control theory of pain holds that other sensory stimuli may temporarily block pain messages from passing through a neural gate in the spinal cord. You can attempt to create a traffic jam at the gate by lightly rubbing an irritated area. Interestingly, applying both heat and cold may help because each sends messages through the spinal cord that compete for attention. Cold packs have the additional advantage of reducing inflammation.

Changing Thoughts and Attitudes

What people say to themselves about their pain can affect how much pain they feel and how well they cope with it. Researchers find that pain patients who have pessimistic thoughts ("I can no longer do anything. . . . It isn't fair I have to live this way") report more severe pain and distress during flare-ups than those who maintain more positive thoughts (Gil et al., 1990). Negative thoughts can lead to perceptions of lack of control, which in turn can produce feelings of helplessness and hopelessness. Psychologists help pain sufferers examine their thoughts and replace negative or pessimistic self-evaluations with rational alternatives—thoughts like "Don't give in to hopelessness. Focus on what you need to do to cope with this pain." Changing thoughts and attitudes may not eliminate pain, but it can help people cope more effectively with their pain symptoms (Blanchard & Diamond, 1996; Mayou et al., 1997).

Obtaining Accurate Information

One of the most effective psychological methods for managing pain is obtaining factual and thorough information about the source of the pain and the available treatments. Many people try to avoid thinking about pain and its implications. Obtaining information helps people take an active role in controlling the challenges they face.

Meditation and Biofeedback

One study (Kabat-Zinn, 1993) showed that patients experienced a significant reduction in pain symptoms through a stress-reduction program that included regular practice in meditation. **Meditation** typically involves a process of focused attention that induces a relaxed, contemplative state. Though there are many forms of meditation, most of them narrow attention through some form of repetition—repeating a word, thought, or phrase—or through a steady focus on one object, such as a burning candle or the design on a vase.

As discussed in Chapter 2, *biofeedback training (BFT)* is also used to help relieve headache pain. In Chapter 4 we discuss another psychological technique that may be of help in controlling pain—hypnosis.

TYING IT TOGETHER

Sensation and perception are processes that enable us to sense and make sense of the world around us. The early psychologists laid out a number of basic concepts of sensation, including the absolute threshold, the difference threshold, and Weber's law (Module 3.1). Each of our sensory systems transforms sources of stimulation into information the brain can use to produce sensations. With vision, light energy is transformed into sensations of visual images (Module 3.2). With hearing, vibrations caused by sound waves impact on structures in the inner ear, where they are converted into auditory messages that the brain uses to create sensations of sound (Module 3.3). Through our other senses—the chemical, skin, and body senses—we are able to

meditation A process of focused attention that induces a relaxed, contemplative state.

experience sensations of odor, taste, touch, pressure, warmth and cold, pain, and body position and movement (Module 3.4).

Perception is the process by which we take sensory information and organize it in ways that allow us to form meaningful impressions of the world around us (Module 3.5). Some areas of perception remain steeped in controversy, especially claims about subliminal perception and extrasensory perception (Module 3.5). Psychologists and other professionals apply their knowledge of sensation and perception in helping people cope more effectively with chronic pain (Module 3.6).

SUMMING UP: Q&A

Sensing Our World: Basic Concepts of Sensation (Module 3.1)

What is sensation?

- Sensation is the process of taking information from the world, transforming it into neural impulses, and transmitting these signals to the brain where they are processed to produce experiences of vision, hearing, smell, taste, touch, and so on.

What is the difference between absolute thresholds and difference thresholds?

- An absolute threshold is the smallest amount of a stimulus that a person can sense. A difference threshold, or just-noticeable difference (jnd), is the minimal difference in magnitude of energy needed for people to detect a difference between two stimuli.

What factors contribute to signal detection?

- Factors affecting signal detection include the intensity of the stimulus; level of background stimulation, or noise; biological characteristics of the perceiver, such as the sharpness of the person's sensory system and levels of fatigue or alertness; and psychological factors, such as attention levels and states of motivation.

What is sensory adaptation?

- Sensory adaptation is the process by which sensory systems become less sensitive to unchanging stimuli.

Vision: Seeing the Light (Module 3.2)

How do the eyes process light?

- Light enters the eye through the cornea and passes through the pupil and then the lens, which focuses the image on the retina.
- The light then stimulates photoreceptor cells, rods or cones, which convert the light energy into neural impulses that are carried first through bipolar cells and then to ganglion cells that terminate in the optic nerve.

- When we focus on an object we bring its image to bear on the fovea, the cone-rich part of the retina in which we have our sharpest vision.
- Cones allow us to see colors but are less sensitive to light than rods are.
- Rods allow us to see objects in black and white in dim light; they are also responsible for peripheral vision.

What are feature detectors, and what role do they play in visual processing?

- Feature detectors are specialized cells in the visual cortex that respond only to specific features of visual stimuli, such as horizontal or vertical lines.

What are the two major theories of color vision?

- The trichromatic theory, or Young-Helmholtz theory, proposes that there are three kinds of color receptors (red, green, and blue-violet) and that all the colors in the spectrum can be generated by the simultaneous stimulation of a combination of these color receptors.
- The opponent-process theory developed by Ewald Hering proposes that there are three pairs of receptors (red-green, blue-yellow, black-white) and that opposing processes within each pair determine our experience of color.

What are the two major forms of color blindness?

- The two major forms of color blindness are complete color blindness (lack of any ability to discern colors) and partial color blindness (red-green or blue-yellow color blindness).

Hearing: The Music of Sound (Module 3.3)

How does the ear enable us to hear sound?

- Sound waves enter the outer ear and are funneled to the eardrum, causing it to vibrate. This mechanical energy is conveyed to tiny bones in the middle ear—the hammer, anvil, and stirrup—and then through the oval window to the cochlea in the inner ear.

- The organ of Corti in the cochlea is lined with hair cells that bend in response to the vibrations, triggering neural impulses that are fed through the auditory nerve to the auditory cortex in the temporal lobes of the brain, which leads to the experience of hearing.

What determines our perception of pitch?

- Perception of pitch is likely determined by a combination of the place on the basilar membrane of greatest vibration (place theory), the frequency of neural impulses (frequency theory), and the sequencing of firing of groups of neurons along the basilar membrane (volley principle).

What are the main types and causes of deafness?

- The main types of deafness are conduction deafness, usually caused by damage to the middle ear, and nerve deafness, usually caused by damage to the hair cells of the inner ear or to the auditory nerve.

Our Other Senses: Chemical, Skin, and Body Senses (Module 3.4)

How do we sense odors and tastes?

- Olfaction, or sense of smell, depends on receptors in the nostrils that are capable of sensing different chemical substances on the basis of their molecular shapes. This information is transmitted to the brain for processing, giving rise to the sensation of odor.
- The sense of taste involves stimulation of taste receptors located in taste buds, mostly on the tongue. Some taste receptors are sensitive to only one basic type of taste (sweet, sour, salty, bitter) while others respond to several tastes.

What are the skin senses?

- The skin senses enable us to detect touch, pressure, temperature, and pain. Different receptors in the skin respond to these stimuli and transmit the information to the brain for processing.
- The gate theory of pain holds that there is a gating mechanism in the spinal cord that opens to allow pain messages through to the brain to signal that something is wrong and closes to shut them off.

What are the kinesthetic and vestibular senses?

- The kinesthetic sense enables you to sense the movement of various parts of your body and their positions in relation to one another. Receptors in the joints, ligaments, and muscles transmit information about body movement and position to the brain for processing.
- The vestibular sense is the sensory system that enables you to detect your body's position and maintain your balance. As the position of your head changes, messages are transmitted to the brain, which interprets them as information about the position of your body in space.

Perceiving Our World: Principles of Perception (Module 3.5)

What is perception?

- Perception is the process by which sensory experiences are organized into meaningful representations or impressions of the world.

How is perception influenced by attention and perceptual set?

- Through the process of selective attention we focus on the most meaningful stimuli impinging upon us at any one time.
- Attention is influenced by such factors as motivational states and repeated exposure.
- The tendency for perceptions to be influenced by expectations and preconceptions is known as a perceptual set.

What are the two general modes of processing visual stimuli?

- These two general modes of visual processing are bottom-up processing, which involves piecing together specific features of visual stimuli to form meaningful patterns, and top-down processing, which involves recognizing patterns as meaningful wholes without first piecing together their component parts.

What are the Gestalt principles of perceptual organization?

- The Gestalt principles of perceptual organization include laws of figure-ground perception and laws of grouping (proximity, similarity, continuity, closure, and connectedness).

What is perceptual constancy, and what cues do we use to perceive depth and movement?

- Perceptual constancy is the tendency to perceive an object to be of the same shape, size, color, and brightness even when the images it casts on the retina change in response to changes in viewing perspective, distance, and lighting.
- Binocular cues include retinal disparity and convergence. Monocular cues include relative size, interposition, relative clarity, texture gradient, linear perspective, and shadowing.
- The movement of an object across our field of vision stimulates an array of points on the retina, which the brain interprets as movement. The changing size of the object is another cue for movement.

What are visual illusions?

- Visual illusions are misperceptions of visual stimuli in which our eyes seem to play tricks on us. Examples include the Müller-Lyer illusion, the Ponzo illusion, and the moon illusion.
- The brain may be fooled into perceiving apparent movement, as in the case of stroboscopic motion.

Does subliminal perception exist?

- Some limited forms of subliminal perception exist, but there is no evidence that exposure to subliminally presented messages in everyday life affects attitudes or behavior.

Does evidence support the existence of ESP?

- There is no hard evidence acceptable to a majority of scientists that proves the existence of such forms of ESP as telepathy, clairvoyance, precognition, and psychokinesis.

Application: Psychology and Pain Management (Module 3.6)

What have psychologists learned about controlling pain?

- Psychologists and other health professionals have learned that people may gain better control over pain by using distraction, creating logjams at the "pain gate," changing thoughts and attitudes, obtaining accurate information, and practicing meditation and biofeedback.

Key Terms

sensation *(p. 84)*
sensory receptors *(p. 84)*
psychophysics *(p. 84)*
absolute threshold *(p. 84)*
difference threshold *(p. 84)*
Weber's law *(p. 85)*
signal-detection theory *(p. 85)*
sensory adaptation *(p. 86)*
cornea *(p. 88)*
iris *(p. 88)*
pupil *(p. 88)*
lens *(p. 88)*
accommodation *(p. 88)*
retina *(p. 88)*
photoreceptors *(p. 88)*
rods *(p. 88)*
cones *(p. 88)*
bipolar cells *(p. 89)*
ganglion cells *(p. 89)*
optic nerve *(p. 89)*
blind spot *(p. 89)*
fovea *(p. 89)*
feature detectors *(p. 90)*
trichromatic theory *(p. 91)*
afterimage *(p. 91)*
opponent-process theory *(p. 92)*
trichromats *(p. 92)*
monochromats *(p. 92)*
dichromats *(p. 92)*
audition *(p. 94)*

pitch *(p. 95)*
eardrum *(p. 95)*
ossicles *(p. 95)*
oval window *(p. 95)*
cochlea *(p. 95)*
basilar membrane *(p. 96)*
organ of Corti *(p. 96)*
hair cells *(p. 96)*
auditory nerve *(p. 96)*
place theory *(p. 96)*
frequency theory *(p. 96)*
volley principle *(p. 96)*
conduction deafness *(p. 97)*
nerve deafness *(p. 97)*
olfaction *(p. 99)*
olfactory nerve *(p. 99)*
olfactory bulb *(p. 100)*
pheromones *(p. 100)*
taste cells *(p. 101)*
taste buds *(p. 101)*
skin senses *(p. 102)*
gate-control theory of pain *(p. 103)*
acupuncture *(p. 103)*
kinesthesis *(p. 104)*
vestibular sense *(p. 104)*
semicircular canals *(p. 104)*
vestibular sacs *(p. 104)*
perception *(p. 106)*
selective attention *(p. 106)*
habituation *(p. 107)*

perceptual set *(p. 107)*
bottom-up processing *(p. 108)*
top-down processing *(p. 109)*
laws of perceptual organization *(p. 109)*
proximity *(p. 111)*
similarity *(p. 111)*
continuity *(p. 111)*
closure *(p. 111)*
connectedness *(p. 111)*
perceptual constancy *(p. 111)*
shape constancy *(p. 111)*
size constancy *(p. 111)*
color constancy *(p. 112)*
brightness constancy *(p. 112)*
binocular cues *(p. 112)*
retinal disparity *(p. 112)*
convergence *(p. 113)*
monocular cues *(p. 113)*
visual illusions *(p. 114)*
stroboscopic movement *(p. 116)*
carpentered-world hypothesis *(p. 116)*
subliminal perception *(p. 117)*
extrasensory perception (ESP) *(p. 117)*
parapsychology *(p. 118)*
telepathy *(p. 118)*
clairvoyance *(p. 118)*
precognition *(p. 118)*
psychokinesis *(p. 118)*
meditation *(p. 120)*

Thinking Critically About Psychology

Based on your reading of this chapter, answer the following questions. Then, to evaluate your progress in developing critical thinking skills, compare your answers to the sample answers found in Appendix A.

A few years ago, a police department asked a woman who claimed to have psychic abilities to help them locate an elderly man who had disappeared in a wooded area outside of town. Despite an extended search of the area, the police had been unable to locate the man. Working only from a photograph of the man and a map of the area, the woman circled an area of the map where she felt the man might be found. The police were amazed to discover the man's body in the area she had indi-

cated. He had died of natural causes, and his body had been hidden by a dense thicket of bushes.

Critical thinkers adopt a skeptical attitude toward claims of ESP. They evaluate the evidence and consider more plausible alternative explanations. Consider these questions:

1. Do you believe this case demonstrates the existence of ESP? Why or why not?

2. What, if any, additional information would you need to help you evaluate the woman's claims or to generate alternative explanations?

Answers to Concept Check Questions

Module 3.1: 1. c; 2. b; 3. sensory adaptation.   **Module 3.2:** 1. d; 2. d; 3. rods, cones; 4. (a) iv; (b) vi; (c) i; (d) ii; (e) v; (f) iii. **Module 3.3:** 1. amplitude and frequency; 2. a; 3. (a) i; (b) v; (c) vi; (d) iv; (e) iii; (f) ii.   **Module 3.4:** 1. b; 2. 10,000; 3. pheromones; 4. touch, pressure, warmth, cold, and pain; 5. d; 6. kinesthetic.   **Module 3.5:** 1. perception; 2. c; 3. perceptual set; 4. connectedness; 5. interposition; 6. a; 7. b.

Consciousness

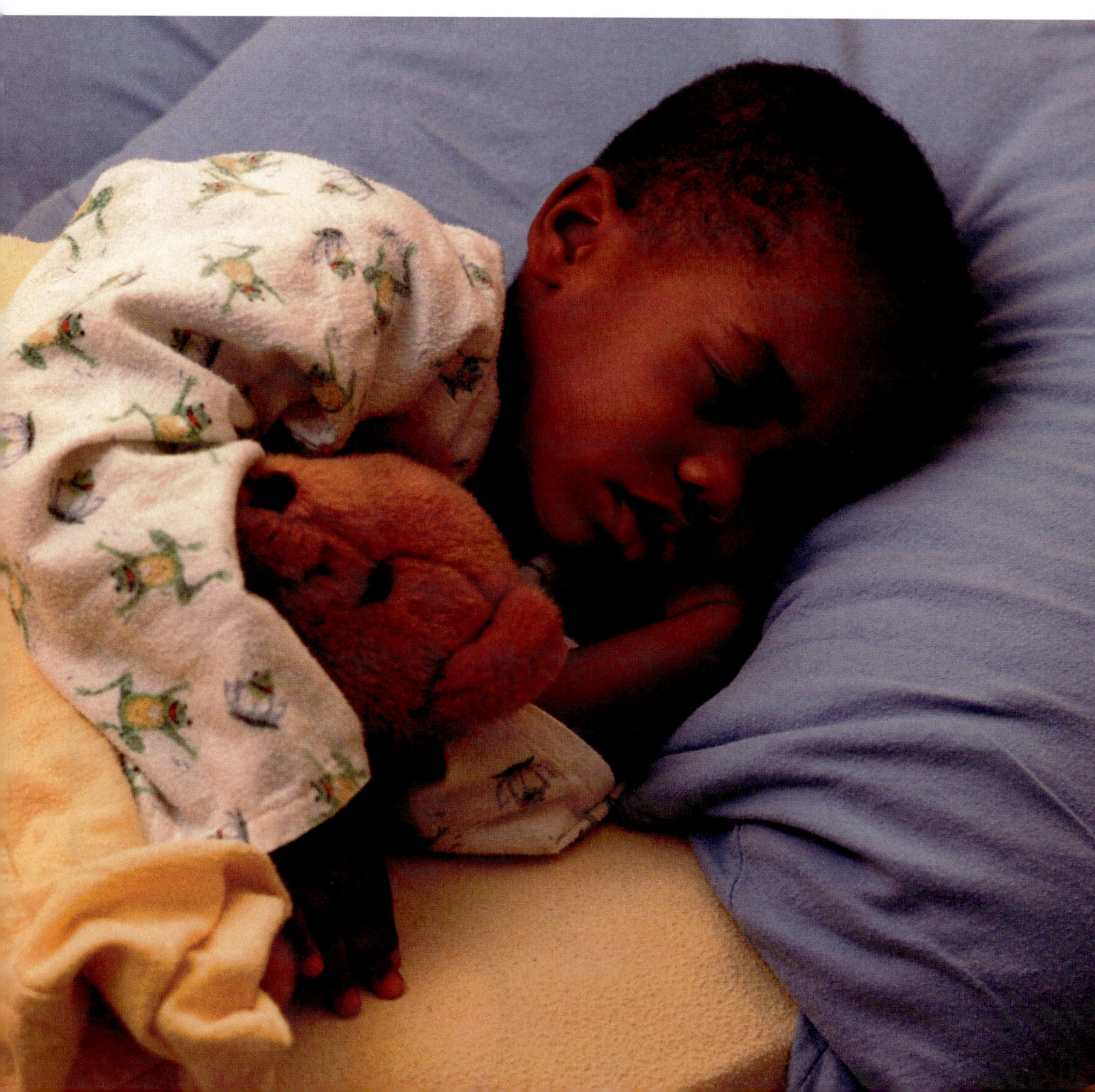

DID YOU KNOW THAT . . .

- Dividing your attention between driving and using a car phone is about as dangerous as driving with a blood alcohol level at the legal limit? (p. 127)

- Body temperature does not remain at a steady 98.6 degrees Fahrenheit throughout the day? (p. 129)

- People with narcolepsy may be holding a conversation one moment and collapse on the floor the next, fast asleep? (p. 136)

- It can be dangerous—indeed deadly—to let a person who blacks out from drinking too much to "sleep it off"? (p. 146)

- Coca-Cola once contained cocaine? (p. 148)

- You may be hooked on a drug you have with breakfast every morning? (p. 150)

Think about what you are doing right now. Is your attention fully absorbed by reading this page? Or is it divided between two or more tasks? As you are reading, are you also listening to music or perhaps musing about your plans for the weekend? We live in a multitasking world today in which we tend to keep one eye on one thing and another eye (or ear) on another. The word *multitasking* entered the popular vocabulary with the introduction of computer systems that allowed users to perform two or more tasks at the same time, such as word processing and emailing. But with advances in technology, multitasking has spilled into our daily lives. We make lists on our PDAs while attending lectures, talk on cell phones while shopping, and send emails or IM our buddies while listening to the latest hit song we just downloaded.

People today say they are multitasking more than ever before. For example, most of the people surveyed in a recent poll (54 percent) said that they read email while talking on the phone (Shellenbarger, 2003b).

Computers are becoming ever more sophisticated and capable of handling multiple tasks without a hitch, but what about the human brain? How well equipped are we to divide our attention between two or more tasks at once?

Though multitasking may be a time-saver, scientists are finding that it is often hard to do and may be dangerous under some circumstances, such as when talking on a car phone while driving (Logan, 2003). The effort needed to perform multiple tasks at the same time can overload our mental resources and make us less efficient (Rubinstein, Meyer, & Evans, 2001). The problem is that performing two mental tasks at the same time reduces the mental resources we need to perform either task (Shellenbarger, 2003a)—especially when the tasks are complex (e.g., balancing your checkbook while speaking on the phone) or when the tasks draw upon the same parts of the brain (e.g., carrying on a conversation while listening to the news on TV).

Still, the very fact that we are capable of multitasking means that we can divide our consciousness, or state of mental awareness, between different activities. We can focus part of our awareness on one task while engaging another part on something else.

In this chapter we set out on an inward exploration of human consciousness. We examine different states of consciousness and consider the various ways in which people have sought to alter their ordinary consciousness, such as through practicing meditation, undergoing hypnosis, or ingesting mind-altering drugs. We consider the psychological and physiological effects of these drugs and the risks they pose. ■

States of Consciousness

- **What are states of consciousness?**

CONCEPT 4.1
States of consciousness range from alert wakefulness to deep sleep.

William James is widely regarded as the father of American psychology. He was such an early figure in the field that the first psychology lecture he ever attended was the one he gave himself (Hothersall, 1995). At the time (1875) there were no psychology textbooks. It would be another fifteen years, in fact, before the first textbook on psychology would be written, a book James himself would write, which he entitled *Principles of Psychology* (James, 1890/1970).

James was interested in the nature of **consciousness**, which he described as a stream of thoughts. To James, consciousness was not a fixed state or a collection of "chopped bits" of disconnected thoughts and experiences. Rather, it was a continuous process of thinking in which one thought flows into another, like water flowing continuously down a river (James, 1890/1970). Today, we view consciousness in much the same way James envisioned it, as a *state of awareness of ourselves and of the world around us*. Your consciousness consists of whatever you happen to be aware of at a particular point in time—your thoughts, feelings, sensations, and perceptions of the outside world. Your consciousness shifts during the course of a day from states of alert wakefulness to drifting consciousness to unconsciousness during sleep. Psychologists refer to these changing levels of awareness as **states of consciousness**. In this module, we describe these states of consciousness, beginning with the levels of awareness you are likely to experience during the course of a day: focused awareness, drifting consciousness, and divided consciousness.

Focused Awareness

CONCEPT 4.2
The selectivity of consciousness allows us to direct our attention to meaningful stimuli, events, or experiences while filtering out other stimuli.

Consciousness is *selective*—we have the ability to direct our attention to certain objects, events, or experiences while filtering out extraneous stimuli. The selectivity of consciousness enables us to achieve a heightened state of alert wakefulness called **focused awareness**. In a state of focused awareness, we are wide awake, fully alert, and completely engrossed in the task at hand. We pay little if any heed to distracting external stimuli (traffic noises, rumbling air conditioners) or even disturbing internal stimuli (hunger pangs, nagging aches and pains). Focused awareness may be needed to perform tasks that require fixed attention, such as learning a new skill or studying for an exam.

Drifting Consciousness

CONCEPT 4.3
States of drifting consciousness are associated with mental meanderings called daydreams.

It is difficult to maintain a state of focused awareness for an extended period of time. Before long, your mind may start drifting from thought to thought. This state of **drifting consciousness** may lead to **daydreaming**, a form of consciousness during a waking state in which your mind wanders to dreamy thoughts or fantasies. You may be studying for an exam when before long you begin daydreaming about the upcoming school break or your weekend plans. We are particularly prone to daydreams when we are bored or engaged in unstructured activities, such as waiting for a bus. These mental wanderings may bring us to a realm of fantasy in which we take brief trips in our own imaginations. However, most daydreams involve mundane tasks of everyday life. Despite the popular belief, relatively few have sexual themes (Klinger, 1987).

Divided Consciousness

Learning a new skill typically requires focused awareness. When learning to drive, for example, you need to pay close attention to how far to turn the wheel when

consciousness A state of awareness of ourselves and of the world around us.

states of consciousness Levels of consciousness ranging from alert wakefulness to unconsciousness during deep sleep.

focused awareness A state of heightened alertness in which one is fully absorbed in the task at hand.

drifting consciousness A state of awareness characterized by drifting thoughts or mental imagery.

TRY THIS OUT

Savoring Your Food

How does mental focusing affect your experience of eating a meal? Try this out: Focus your attention completely on your next meal. Avoid talking, watching TV, or reading while eating. Notice the shape, color, and texture of the food. Take a deep whiff of the aroma of the food before chewing. Then slowly chew each morsel, savoring the distinctive flavor of each bite. Mix different foods together in your mouth to appreciate their distinctive flavors and how they blend together in a mélange of taste. What differences do you notice between this experience and your usual dining experience?

steering into a curve, how much pressure to apply to the brakes when stopping, and so on. But after a time, driving may become so routine that you experience a state of divided consciousness—dividing your attention between driving and other thoughts, such as trying to remember the words of a song or fantasizing about a vacation.

States of **divided consciousness** occur when we simultaneously perform two different activities, each of which demands some level of attention. Typically, one of these activities is a mechanical task, such as driving or doing the dishes. When we perform such tasks, part of our mind seems to be on "automatic pilot" while the other part is free to think about other things. Still, our consciousness can abruptly shift back to a state of focused awareness under certain circumstances. When driving in a blinding rainstorm, for example, you need to focus your awareness on road conditions and driving tasks.

With the introduction of car phones and cell phones, states of divided attention on the road have raised new safety concerns (McKinley, 2001; Strayer & Johnston, 2001). According to one study, drivers are four times more likely to have an automobile accident when they are talking on a car phone than when they are not (Redelmeier & Tibshirani, 1997). Driving while using a phone appears to be about as dangerous as driving with a blood alcohol level at the legal limit. The increased risk is associated with a loss of concentration, not from fiddling with the phone itself; whether the phone is hand-held or hands-free, driving performance is impaired (Benson, 2003d; "Cell Phones," 2001; Nagourney, 2003). The hazard of divided attention on the road is not limited to phone use. Fussing with a child in the back seat and putting on makeup are other dangerous distractions. Carrying on a complex conversation with a passenger can also be distracting, even dangerously so (Recarte & Nunes, 2003). "People may not realize how distracted they are," said Peter Kissinger, president of AAA's Foundation for Traffic Safety ("Driver Study," 2003). "Talking to a passenger seems quite safe, but even something that simple takes away from the road." Yet a study by the California Highway Patrol revealed that cell phone use was the most frequent cause of inattention accidents (second was fiddling with the car's stereo system) ("New Studies," 2003).

States of Unconsciousness

Sleeping and dreaming are states of **unconsciousness** in which we are relatively unaware of our external surroundings. Yet we may still be responsive to certain types of stimuli that are personally meaningful or relevant. As noted in Chapter 3, people may sleep soundly through the wail of a passing ambulance but be awakened instantly by their child's soft cry. The lowest levels of consciousness are

Divided Consciousness The ability to divide consciousness allows us to perform two tasks at once. But the combination of driving and using a car phone is associated with a fourfold increase in the risk of motor vehicle accidents.

CONCEPT 4.4
Our ability to divide consciousness allows us to perform more than one activity at a time.

daydreaming   A form of consciousness during a waking state in which one's mind wanders to dreamy thoughts or fantasies.

divided consciousness   A state of awareness characterized by divided attention to two or more tasks or activities performed at the same time.

unconsciousness   In ordinary use, a term referring to lack of awareness of one's surroundings or to loss of consciousness.

CONCEPT CHART 4.1
States of Consciousness

State of Consciousness	Level of Alertness/Attention	Examples or Features
Focused awareness	High; fully awake and alert	Learning a new skill; watching an engrossing movie
Drifting consciousness	Variable or shifting	Daydreaming, or letting one's thoughts wander
Divided consciousness	Medium; attention split between two activities	Thinking of other things while exercising or driving a car
Sleeping and dreaming	Low	States of unconsciousness in which the person is generally unaware of external surroundings but may respond to certain stimuli
Deep unconsciousness	Nil	Complete loss of consciousness with little or no awareness of the outside world; may be caused by a blow to the head, surgical anesthesia, or coma
Altered states of consciousness	Variable	Changes in consciousness associated with hypnosis, meditation, and drug use

CONCEPT 4.5
At the lower end of the continuum of awareness are states of sleeping and dreaming.

CONCEPT 4.6
Altered states of consciousness may be induced in different ways, such as by practicing meditation or undergoing hypnosis, or by using mind-altering drugs.

altered states of consciousness   States of awareness that differ from one's usual waking state.

states of deep unconsciousness resulting from head trauma, surgical anesthesia, or coma. A person in a coma may have no awareness of the outside world for months or even years.

In everyday speech, we use the term *unconscious* to refer to a lack of awareness. Freudian theorists, however, use the term to refer to a part of the mind that functions outside of conscious awareness. Freud's theory of the unconscious mind is discussed further in Chapter 10.

States of awareness that differ from one's usual waking state are called **altered states of consciousness**. Altered states of consciousness may occur during our waking states when we daydream, when we meditate or undergo hypnosis, or when we use mind-altering drugs like alcohol and marijuana. Repetitive physical activity, such as long-distance running or lap swimming, also may induce an altered state of consciousness—one in which the outside world seems to fade out of awareness. In some altered states, the person may experience changes in the sense of time (time may seem to stand still or speed up) and in sensory experiences (colors may seem more vibrant or, as in some drug-induced states, the person may hear voices or see visions). In Modules 4.2 to 4.4, we explore the range of human consciousness, from states of sleep and wakefulness to altered states of consciousness. Concept Chart 4.1 offers an overview of the states of consciousness.

MODULE 4.1 REVIEW

States of Consciousness

CONCEPT CHECK

1. The nineteenth-century psychologist William James likened consciousness to
   a. water flowing continuously down a river.
   b. a drifting cloud.
   c. a swirling ocean.
   d. a state of tranquility.

2. The _____ of consciousness allows us to focus on meaningful stimuli, events, and experiences.

3. The state of awareness in which we are completely alert and engrossed in a task is known as
   a. daydreaming.   c. altered consciousness.
   b. divided consciousness. d. focused awareness.

MODULE 4.2   Sleeping and Dreaming

- **How are our sleep-wake cycles regulated?**
- **What are the stages of sleep, and what functions does sleep serve?**
- **Why do we dream?**
- **What are sleep disorders?**

We spend about a third of our lives sleeping. During sleep, we enter our own private theater of the mind—a realm of dreams in which the mind weaves tales ranging from the mundane and ordinary to the fantastic and bizarre. The laws of the physical world don't apply when we dream. Objects change shape, one person may be transformed into another, and scenes move abruptly without regard to the physical limits of time and place. Though we've learned much about sleeping and dreaming, many mysteries remain. We lack a consensus about such basic questions as "Why do we sleep?" and "Why do we dream?" In this module, we venture into the mysterious domain of sleep and dreams. We begin by examining the bodily mechanisms responsible for our sleep-wake cycles.

Sleep and Wakefulness: A Circadian Rhythm

Many bodily processes—sleep-wake cycles, as well as body temperature, hormonal secretions, blood pressure, and heart rate—fluctuate daily in a pattern called a **circadian rhythm**. The word *circadian* is derived from the Latin roots *circa* ("about") and *dies* ("day"). Circadian (daily) rhythms are found in virtually all species, including organisms as varied as single-celled paramecia, humans, and even trees (American Association for the Advancement of Sciences, 1997). These rhythms are synchronized with the twenty-four-hour cycle of day and night. In humans, the sleep-wake cycle operates on a circadian rhythm that is close to twenty-four hours in length (Lavie, 2001). It may surprise you to learn that human body temperature is not maintained at a steady 98.6 degrees Fahrenheit throughout the day. It follows a circadian rhythm in which it falls a few degrees during the middle of the night, rises in early morning, and then peaks by mid-day.

A small area of the hypothalamus called the *suprachiasmatic nucleus* (SCN) regulates our sleep-wake cycles (Refinetti, 2000). This internal body clock responds to light impinging on the retina. When light enters the eye, its energy is transformed into neural impulses that travel to the SCN (Barinaga, 2002; Berson, Dunn, & Takao, 2002). The SCN in turn regulates the pineal gland, which, as noted in Chapter 2, is a gland in the brain that releases the hormone melatonin. Melatonin helps synchronize the body's sleep-wake cycle by making us feel sleepy. Exposure to darkness during evening hours increases the production of melatonin. During exposure to bright light, melatonin production falls off, which helps us maintain wakefulness during daylight hours. (This might also explain why we often feel sleepy on cloudy days.)

Frequent time shifts can play havoc with the body's circadian rhythms (Scott, 1994; R. Sullivan, 1998). If you've ever traveled by plane across several time zones, you've probably experienced jet lag. **Jet lag** occurs when a change in local time conflicts with your internal body clock, making it difficult to fall asleep earlier than usual or to stay awake later than usual, depending on whether you've lost time by traveling east or gained time by traveling west. Jet lag is associated not only with disruption of sleep-wake cycles but also with irritability, fatigue, and difficulty in concentrating.

For occasional travelers, jet lag may be only a mild annoyance. But shift workers who pull duty at night, when their body temperatures are normally low, must

 CONCEPT 4.7
A clocklike mechanism in the hypothalamus is responsible for regulating our sleep-wake cycles.

CONCEPT 4.8
Your internal body clock does not adjust easily to time shifts associated with changes in time zones or shift work.

circadian rhythm   The pattern of fluctuations in bodily processes that occur regularly each day.

jet lag   A disruption of sleep-wake cycles caused by the shifts in time zones that accompany long-distance air travel.

THINK About It

Preventing Jet Lag

Have you experienced jet lag? How did it affect you? What might you do differently in the future to cope with it? One suggestion is to gradually alter your body clock by adjusting the time you go to bed by an hour a day for several days before your trip. If you will be away for only a brief time, you might be better off to follow your body clock as much as possible during the trip.

CONCEPT 4.9

During sleep, your body cycles through four stages, followed by a period of REM sleep, in which most dreaming occurs.

often fight to stay awake (R. Sullivan, 1998). Night-shift workers in sensitive positions, such as air traffic controllers, firefighters, and nuclear power workers, tend to be less alert, sleepier, more fatigued, and less able to perform their jobs than day-shift workers in similar positions (G. Costa, 1996; Luna, French, & Mindtcha, 1997; L. Smith, Totterdell, & Folkard, 1995). Exposure to bright light for a few minutes at the start of a night shift may help reset circadian rhythms. Light exposure has been associated with better job performance and improved sleep patterns in shift workers (Kamei et al., 1994).

The Stages of Sleep

The electroencephalograph (EEG) is one of several devices researchers use to determine how our bodies respond when we sleep. The EEG tracks brain waves, which vary in intensity or amplitude (height of the wave) and speed or frequency (wave cycles per second). When you are awake and alert, your brain wave pattern is dominated by fast, low-amplitude *beta waves*. As you close your eyes and relax in bed, you enter a state of relaxed wakefulness. In this state, your brain wave pattern is dominated by slower, rhythmic cycles called *alpha waves*. When you slip into sleep, the EEG shows that you progress through several distinct stages of sleep characterized by different brain wave patterns (see Figure 4.1).

Stages 1 to 4: From Light to Deep Sleep

When you enter Stage 1 sleep, brain waves become small and irregular with varying frequencies. You can be easily awakened during this stage and may not even realize that you had been sleeping. Stage 2 sleep begins about two minutes after

Figure 4.1 Brain Wave Patterns During Wakefulness and Sleep
Here we see the characteristic brain wave patterns associated with each stage of sleep. *(a)* Ordinary wakefulness: fast, low-amplitude beta waves; *(b)* relaxed wakefulness: rhythmic alpha waves; *(c)* Stage 1 sleep: small, irregular brain waves with varying frequencies; *(d)* Stage 2 sleep: sleep spindles; *(e)* Stage 3 and Stage 4 sleep: large, slow, delta waves; *(f)* REM sleep: rapid, active pattern similar to that in ordinary wakefulness.

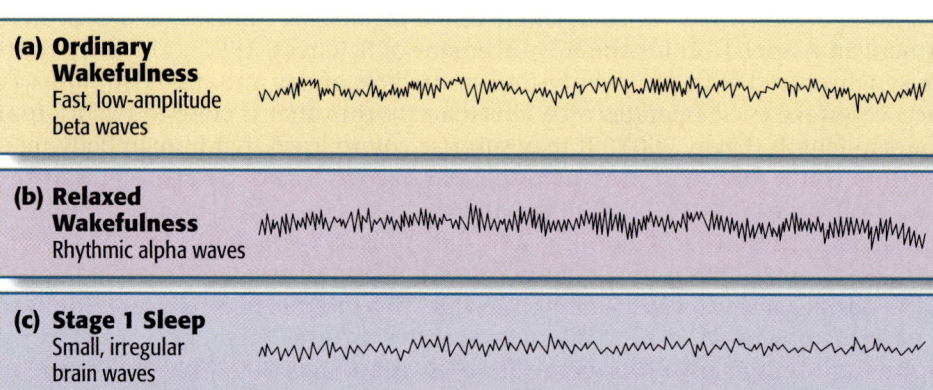

(a) Ordinary Wakefulness
Fast, low-amplitude beta waves

(b) Relaxed Wakefulness
Rhythmic alpha waves

(c) Stage 1 Sleep
Small, irregular brain waves

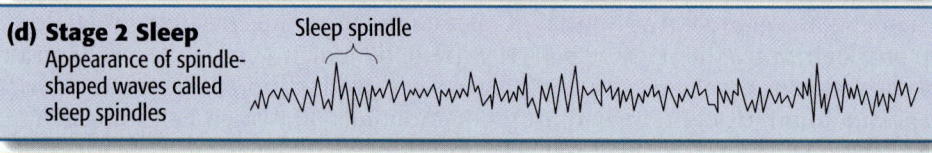

(d) Stage 2 Sleep
Appearance of spindle-shaped waves called sleep spindles

Sleep spindle

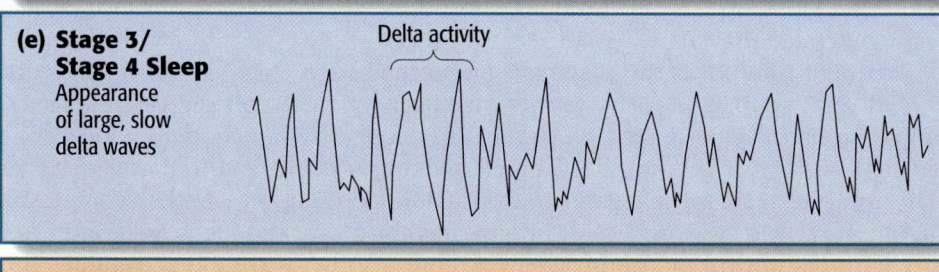

(e) Stage 3/ Stage 4 Sleep
Appearance of large, slow delta waves

Delta activity

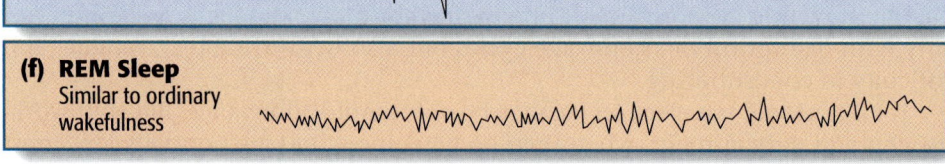

(f) REM Sleep
Similar to ordinary wakefulness

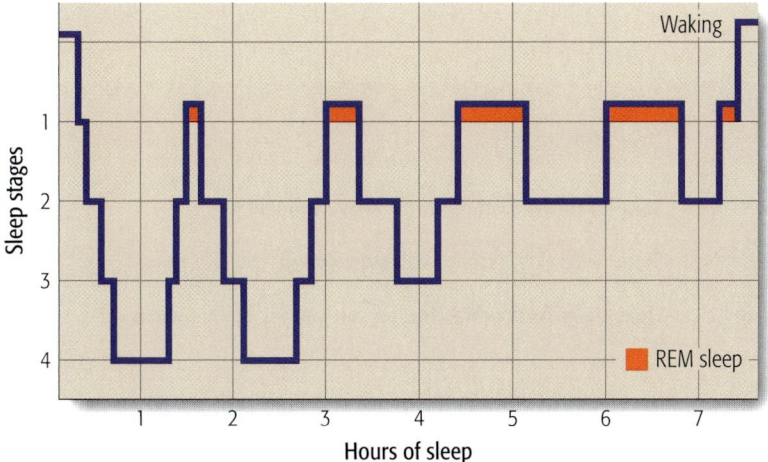

Figure 4.2   REM Sleep Through the Night
Notice how periods of REM sleep become longer as sleep progresses through the night.

Stage 1 sleep and is characterized by bursts of brain wave activity that are represented by spindle-shaped waves called *sleep spindles*. You spend more than half your sleep time in Stage 2 sleep. This is a deeper stage of sleep, but you can still be readily awakened. Stages 3 and 4 of sleep, called *delta sleep* or *slow-wave sleep (SWS)*, are characterized by the appearance of large, slow brain waves called *delta waves*. This is the period of deep sleep in which it is difficult to arouse you. The distinction between Stage 3 and Stage 4 is based on the proportion of delta waves. In Stage 3, delta waves constitute 50 percent or fewer of the brain wave patterns; in Stage 4, they constitute more than 50 percent.

REM Sleep: The Stuff of Which Dreams Are Made

Rapid-eye-movement (REM) sleep is the stage of sleep in which one's eyes dart about under closed eyelids. After Stage 4 sleep, the sleeper briefly recycles through Stages 3 and 2 and from there enters REM sleep. REM is the stage of sleep most closely associated with dreaming. Dreams also occur during Stages 1 to 4—which are collectively called non-REM (NREM) sleep—but they are generally briefer, less frequent, and more thoughtlike than those experienced during REM sleep.

The brain becomes more active during REM sleep, which is why it is sometimes called *active* sleep. Brain wave patterns during REM sleep are similar to those during states of alert wakefulness. REM sleep is also called *paradoxical sleep*. What makes it paradoxical is that despite a high level of brain activity, muscle activity is blocked to the point that the person is practically paralyzed. This is indeed fortunate, as it prevents injuries that might occur if the dreamer were suddenly to bolt from bed and try to enact a dream.

Sleep cycles generally repeat about every ninety minutes. The average person has about four or five sleep cycles during a night's sleep. It may take about an hour to reach Stage 4 sleep in the first cycle and then another thirty or forty minutes to reach REM. As the night goes on, the amount of time spent in REM sleep increases (see Figure 4.2). Moreover, Stage 4 sleep disappears during the course of the night, which means that we progress faster to REM sleep as the night wears on.

Concept Chart 4.2 summarizes the different states of wakefulness and stages of sleep.

Why Do We Sleep?

Humans and nearly all other animals sleep, although the average length of sleep varies across species. The near universality of sleep suggests that it may help a species survive. One function of sleep may be protective—keeping the individual out of harm's way. The sleeping animal may be less conspicuous to predators that

CONCEPT 4.10
Three major functions of sleep have been proposed: a protective function, an energy-conservation function, and a restorative function.

rapid-eye-movement (REM) sleep
The stage of sleep that involves rapid eye movements and that is most closely associated with periods of dreaming.

CONCEPT CHART 4.2
Wakefulness and Sleep

State of Wakefulness/ Stage of Sleep	Characteristic Brain Wave Pattern	Key Features
Alert wakefulness	Fast, low-amplitude beta waves	State of focused attention or active thought
Relaxed wakefulness	Slower, rhythmic alpha waves	State of resting quietly with eyes closed
Stage 1 sleep	Small, irregular brain waves with varying frequencies	Light sleep from which the person can be easily awakened
Stage 2 sleep	Sleep spindles	Deeper sleep, but the sleeper is still readily awakened
Stage 3 sleep	Large, slow delta waves	Deep sleep (called delta sleep or slow-wave sleep) from which it is difficult to arouse the sleeper
Stage 4 sleep	Dominance of delta waves	Deepest level of sleep
REM sleep	Rapid, active pattern, similar to that in alert wakefulness	Sleep in which the brain becomes more active but muscle activity is blocked (also called active sleep or paradoxical sleep); stage associated with dreaming

roam about at night and less likely to suffer dangerous falls or accidents that could arise from moving about in the dark (Gaulin & McBurney, 2001).

Sleep may also help organisms conserve energy. The lowering of body temperature during sleep may give warm-blooded animals, such as humans and other mammals, more energy to maintain a higher body temperature during the waking state (Berger & Phillips, 1995). But perhaps the major function of sleep is to restore bodily processes by helping replenish necessary proteins used by the body during the waking state and by helping the brain recover from daily wear-and-tear (Cai, 1995).

The view that sleep is restorative is consistent with the subjective experience of feeling rested and mentally alert after a good night's sleep. It is also consistent with evidence that sleep deprivation makes it more difficult to consolidate newly learned information and to perform decision-making tasks (Bowman, 2000; Carpenter, 2001c; Harrison & Horne, 2000). (Watch those all-nighters.) Research evidence also suggests that sleep may bolster the body's ability to defend itself against disease-causing agents (Collinge, 1999). Not surprisingly, you may find yourself more susceptible to the common cold and other ailments when you've gone without your necessary quota of sleep. In short, sleep appears to serve multiple purposes.

Dreams and Dreaming

CONCEPT 4.11
Though we all dream while asleep, the question of why we dream remains unanswered.

Why do we dream? The short answer is that no one really knows. Some evidence suggests that dreaming may help us consolidate memories and new learning that occurred during the day (Maquet, 2001; Stickgold et al., 2001). Though about half the dreams people report relate to events that occurred during the day (Botman & Crovitz, 1989–1990), research support for the memory-consolidating function of dreams remains weak and inconsistent (Siegel, 2001).

activation-synthesis hypothesis
The proposition that dreams represent the brain's attempt to make sense of the random discharges of electrical activity that occur during REM sleep.

Dreams may have other functions as well. Ernest Hartmann, a leading dream investigator, believes that dreams help us sort through possible solutions to everyday problems and concerns (cited in Talan, 1998). Another prominent view of dreaming, called the **activation-synthesis hypothesis** (Hobson, 1988; Hobson & McCarley, 1977), holds that dreams represent an attempt by the cere-

Figure 4.3   Activation-Synthesis Hypothesis
According to the activation-synthesis hypothesis, dreams arise when the cerebral cortex attempts to make sense of random electrical discharges emanating from the brainstem during REM sleep.

Example: Electrical signals generated from neurons in the brainstem that control balance and posture are synthesized by the cortex in a dream of the person riding on a roller-coaster

2. Cerebral cortex creates meaning from these random signals, weaving dream stories that integrate personal memories and stored information

1. Neurons in the brainstem spontaneously generate random discharges of electrical activity

PsychAssist: The Activation-Synthesis Hypothesis

bral cortex to make sense of the random discharges of electrical activity that occur during REM sleep. The electrical activity arises from the brainstem, the part of the brain responsible for such basic functions as breathing and heart rate (see Figure 4.3). According to this hypothesis, the cerebral cortex creates a story line based on the individual's store of knowledge and memories to explain these random signals and the emotions and sensory experiences they generate.

We know from brain-imaging studies that areas in the brainstem are activated during REM sleep, as are other brain regions involved in emotions, memory, and visual processing (Goode, 1999b; Kalb, 1999). Interestingly, areas of the brain that show decreased activity during REM sleep include parts of the cerebral cortex involved in logical thought. This pattern of neural activity suggests why dreams may lack the orderliness or logic of ordinary conscious thought—why they may form from bits and pieces of emotionally charged memories and vivid imagery that unfold in a chaotic sequence of events.

Even if dreams emanate from a hodgepodge of electrical discharges from the deep recesses of the brain, they may be filled with personal meaning since they are based on individual memories and associations. But what, if anything, do they mean?

Sigmund Freud (1900) had an answer to this question that continues to fascinate and challenge us. He believed that dreams represent a form of *wish fulfill-ment*. According to Freud, dreams contain symbols that represent the sleeper's underlying wishes, usually of a sexual or aggressive nature. He called dreams the

Why Do We Dream? Although speculations about dreams abound, their meaning remains a mystery.

"royal road" to the unconscious, but he believed you needed a kind of psychological road map to interpret them because the dream symbols mask their true meanings. Freud distinguished between two types of dream content:

1. *Manifest content.* The manifest content refers to events that occur in the dream. You might dream, for example, of driving fast and getting a speeding ticket from a police officer.

2. *Latent content.* This is the true, underlying meaning of the dream, disguised in the form of dream symbols. The disguise conceals the dream's real meaning, thereby helping preserve sleep by preventing emotionally threatening material from waking you up. Driving fast might symbolize an unacceptable sexual wish. The police officer, a symbol of male authority, might represent your father punishing you for having the sexual wish.

In Freud's view, phallic objects like trees, skyscrapers, snakes, and guns are symbols of male genitalia, and enclosed objects like boxes, closets, and ovens symbolize female genitalia. But Freud believed we shouldn't rush to judgment when interpreting dream symbols—that sometimes "a cigar is just a cigar." Freud also recognized that the same dream events might have different meanings for different people, so individual analysis is necessary to ferret out their meanings (Lear, 2000).

Dream interpretation makes for an interesting exercise, but how do we know that our interpretations are accurate? Unfortunately, although the meaning of dreams has been studied and debated for more than a century since Freud's initial work, we still lack any objective means of verifying the accuracy of dream interpretations. Nor is there evidence that dreams serve the function of preserving sleep, as Freud alleged (Fisher & Greenberg, 1978). At the very least, we should credit Freud with raising our awareness that dreams may have a psychological meaning and may express emotional issues (Squier & Domhoff, 1998).

Whatever the underlying meaning of dreams may be, investigators find that some people report **lucid dreams**—dreams in which the person is aware of dreaming (LaBerge & Gackenbach, 2000). Some lucid dreamers claim they can determine beforehand what they will dream about or can consciously direct the action of a dream as it unfolds. But we have little evidence to support such claims (Squier & Domhoff, 1998). Moreover, relatively few people report experiencing lucid dreams regularly.

CONCEPT 4.12
Though people vary in how much sleep they need, most people require seven to nine hours of sleep to feel refreshed and to perform at their best.

TRY THIS OUT

Dream a Little Dream for Me

Can you determine what you dream about? To find out, try this experiment:

1. Before retiring for the night, select a topic to dream about—for example, meeting a famous person or playing your favorite sport—and put a pen and pad within handy reach of your bed.

2. For ten or fifteen minutes before retiring, mentally rehearse the dream by fantasizing about the topic.

3. Upon retiring, say to yourself, "I think I'll dream some more about this."

4. As you grow sleepier, return to the fantasy, but don't resist letting your mind wander off.

5. When you awake, whether in the middle of the night or the next morning, lie still while you recollect what you dreamed about and then immediately reach for your pen and pad and write down the dream content.

6. Evaluate your results. Were you able to program your dream in advance?

Sleep Deprivation: Getting By on Less

People vary in their need for sleep. Most require between 7 and 9 hours of sleep to feel fully refreshed and to function at their best (Kelley, 1997). Others seem to need only 5 or 6 hours of sleep, but some of these "short-sleepers" may be sleep-deprived and not realize it. College students report averaging only 6 to 6.9 hours sleep a night, which may help explain the grogginess that many students experience during the day (Markel, 2003). Only about 15 percent of high school students report sleeping the recommended 8.5 hours they need (Kantrowitz & Springen, 2003).

Sleep patterns change during the life cycle. Newborn infants sleep for about two-thirds of the day. Infants spend about one-half of their sleep time in REM sleep, while adults spend about one-fifth. Children spend more time in REM sleep than adults, but as they mature, the proportion of REM sleep declines, while periods of NREM sleep and wakefulness increase. During adulthood, amounts of REM sleep, deep sleep, and total sleep decline (Blackman, 2000; Van Cauter, Leproult, & Plat, 2000). By the time we reach our sixties or seventies, we may require only six hours of sleep per night.

If you miss a few hours of sleep, you may feel a little groggy the next day but will probably be able to muddle through. However, sleep deprivation slows reaction times; impairs concentration, memory, and problem-solving ability; makes it more difficult to retain newly acquired information; and impairs academic performance, such as performance on math tasks (Bowman, 2000; Harrison & Horne, 2000; Stickgold, LaTanya, & Hobson, 2000).

Not surprisingly, sleep deprivation is among the most common causes of motor vehicle accidents. Such accidents are most likely to occur in the early morning hours when drivers are typically at their sleepiest (see Figure 4.4).

Chronic sleep deprivation is a major stress faced by medical residents and a cause of concern for patients treated by doctors who may be nearly asleep on their feet (Lingenfelser et al., 1994). Fortunately, temporary periods of sleep deprivation are not known to produce lasting ill effects (Anch et al., 1988). We shouldn't become alarmed if we miss a few hours of sleep; rather, we should attempt to restore our normal sleep pattern the following night.

It's not just the total amount of sleep that affects our functioning, but also the type of sleep. From laboratory studies in which volunteers have been deprived of REM sleep, we know that loss of REM sleep impairs learning ability and memory (T. Adler, 1993). After REM deprivation, people experience a "rebound effect"—they make up for the loss by spending more of their next sleep period in REM sleep.

Rating Your Sleep Habits

How would you rate your sleep habits? What specific changes can you make to improve them? (For some suggestions on developing healthier sleep habits, see Module 4.5.)

web, Netlab/How Are You Sleeping?

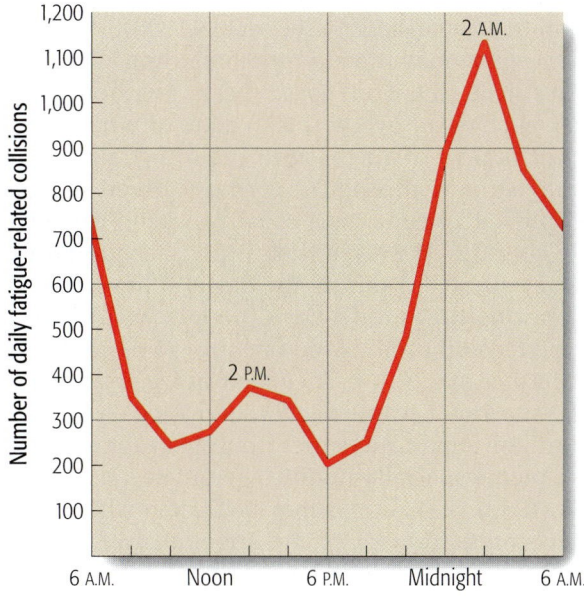

Figure 4.4   Motor Vehicle Accidents in Relation to Time of Day
The greatest risk of motor vehicle accidents occurs in the early morning hours when drivers are typically at their sleepiest.

Source: Adapted from *Wake Up*, AAA Foundation for Traffic Safety, 1996.

lucid dreams   Dreams in which the dreamer is aware that he or she is dreaming.

web Netlab/Identifying Sleep Disorders

CONCEPT 4.13
When people are deprived of REM sleep, they tend to make up for it in the next sleep period by spending more of their sleep time in REM sleep.

CONCEPT 4.14
Sleep disorders are disturbances of sleep that prevent a person from getting a good night's sleep and remaining awake or alert during the day.

Sleep Deprived   Sleep deprivation does not just leave you feeling groggy; it also slows your reaction times and impairs your concentration, memory, and problem-solving ability.

insomnia   Difficulty falling asleep, remaining asleep, or returning to sleep after nighttime awakenings.

narcolepsy   A disorder characterized by sudden unexplained "sleep attacks" during the day.

sleep apnea   Temporary cessation of breathing during sleep.

nightmare disorder   A sleep disorder involving a pattern of frequent, disturbing nightmares.

sleep terror disorder   A sleep disorder involving repeated episodes of intense fear during sleep, causing the person to awake abruptly in a terrified state.

sleepwalking disorder   A sleep disorder characterized by repeated episodes of sleepwalking.

Sleep Disorders: When Normal Sleep Eludes Us

Sleep disorders—disturbances of sleep that interfere with getting a good night's sleep and remaining alert during the day—affect about 70 million people in the United States (R. Sullivan, 1998).

An estimated 15 percent of the adult population suffers from persistent **insomnia**, the most common sleep disorder (Morin & Wooten, 1996). People with insomnia have difficulty falling asleep, remaining asleep, or returning to sleep after nighttime awakenings (Pallesen et al., 2001). Insomnia prevents people from achieving restorative sleep, the type of sleep that leaves them feeling refreshed and alert in the morning.

Insomnia is caused by many factors, including substance abuse, physical illness, and psychological disorders like depression (Kryger, Roth, & Dement, 2000; Lamberg, 2000; Morin, 2000). If the underlying problem is resolved, chances are that sleep patterns will return to normal. Problem sleep habits, such as bringing daily worries and concerns to bed, may also lead to insomnia. Worrying is accompanied by increased bodily arousal, which can prevent normal sleep. People who have trouble falling asleep may also begin worrying about not getting enough sleep, which can bump up their arousal level even more. They may find that the harder they try to fall asleep, the more difficult it becomes. The lesson here is that sleep is a natural function that cannot be forced. Ruminating about your concerns while trying to fall asleep also contributes to poorer quality of sleep (Thomsen et al., 2003).

Narcolepsy, a sleep disorder afflicting some 150,000 Americans, is characterized by sudden, unexplained "sleep attacks" occurring during daytime hours (Bazell, 2000b; Siegel, 2004). People with narcolepsy may be engaged in conversation one moment and collapse on the floor the next, fast asleep. In contrast to the normal sleep pattern in which REM sleep occurs after several stages of non-REM sleep, REM sleep usually begins almost immediately after the onset of a narcoleptic attack. The sleep episode lasts usually for about fifteen minutes. In some cases, the sleep attack is preceded by frightening hallucinations that may involve several senses—visual, auditory, tactile, or kinesthetic (body movement).

Sleep attacks can be very dangerous. Household accidents due to falls are common. Even more disturbing are reports that more than 65 percent of people with narcolepsy have episodes in which they suddenly fall asleep while driving (Aldrich, 1992; Cohen, Ferrans, & Eshler, 1992). Narcolepsy may be caused by a loss of brain cells in an area of the hypothalamus responsible for producing a sleep-regulating chemical (Bazell, 2000b; Mignot & Thorsby, 2001). Currently available treatments include daytime naps and use of stimulant drugs (amphetamines) to help maintain wakefulness (Parkes et al., 1995).

People with **sleep apnea** may literally stop breathing as many as five hundred times during a night's sleep (the word *apnea* means "without breath"). The cause is a structural defect, such as an overly thick palate or enlarged tonsils, that partially or fully blocks the flow of air through the upper airways. With complete blockage, people may stop breathing for perhaps fifteen seconds or as long as ninety seconds. People with sleep apnea usually awaken the next morning with no memory of these episodes. However, their fitful sleep patterns deprive them of solid sleep so that they are sleepy during the day and have difficulty functioning at their best. For reasons that aren't clear, people with sleep apnea have an increased risk of hypertension (high blood pressure), a major risk factor in cardiovascular disease (Nieto et al., 2000). They also snore very loudly (described as "industrial strength" snoring) because of their narrowed airways. Experts estimate that as many as 18 million Americans suffer from sleep apnea (D. Smith, 2001a). It is more common in men, especially middle-aged men, and among obese people (Partinen & Telakivi, 1992). Sleep apnea may be treated with appliances, such as a nose mask that exerts pressure to keep the upper airway passages open during sleep, or with surgery that opens narrowed airways.

People with **nightmare disorder** have frequent, disturbing nightmares. Children are especially prone to nightmare disorder. Nightmares are storylike dreams that contain threats to the dreamer's life or safety. The action of the nightmare may be vivid and intense—falling through space or fleeing from attackers or giant insects. Nightmares typically take place during REM sleep. People are usually more susceptible to nightmares when they are under emotional stress, have high fevers, or are suffering from sleep deprivation.

People with **sleep terror disorder** have frequent "night terrors," which are more intense than ordinary nightmares. Unlike nightmares, which occur mainly during REM sleep, night terrors occur during deep sleep. The disorder primarily affects children, and it affects boys more often than girls. Night terrors begin with a loud panicky scream (American Psychiatric Association, 2000). The child may sit up in bed, appear dazed and frightened, and be able to remember only fragmentary dream images, rather than the detailed dream stories that typically are remembered after nightmares. Most children outgrow the problem by adolescence.

Sleepwalking disorder is another sleep disorder that occurs more often in children than in adults (American Psychiatric Association, 2000). Occasional sleepwalking episodes in children are normal, but persistent sleepwalking is indicative of a sleep disorder. As many as 5 percent of children have a sleepwalking disorder. In a sleepwalking episode, the person remains soundly asleep while walking about with eyes open and perhaps an expressionless look on his or her face. Though sleepwalkers generally avoid knocking into things, accidents do occur. The following morning, the sleepwalker usually remembers nothing of the nighttime wanderings. Sleepwalking typically occurs during deep, dreamless sleep. Despite the belief to the contrary, there is no harm in awakening a sleepwalker.

Sleep disorders are often treated with sleep medications that help induce sleep. However, these drugs can lead to physiological dependence and should be used for only a brief period of time, a few weeks at most (Pollack, 2004b). Psychologists have obtained good results in treating insomnia using cognitive-behavioral approaches that help people develop more adaptive sleep habits, including techniques such as those described in Module 4.5 of this chapter (Espie, 2002; Pollack, 2004a; Rybarczyk et al., 2002). Sleep experts believe that cognitive-behavioral techniques are just as effective as sleep medication in treating insomnia in the short term and more effective over the long term (D. Smith, 2001a).

MODULE 4.2 REVIEW

Sleeping and Dreaming

CONCEPT CHECK

1. Many bodily processes, including body temperature, heart rate, and sleep-wake cycles, fluctuate daily in a pattern called a
   a. circadian rhythm.
   b. melatonin cycle.
   c. hypothalamus shift.
   d. shifting state of consciousness.

2. Deep sleep, which is characterized by delta brain wave patterns, occurs during
   a. Stages 1 and 2 of sleep.   c. Stages 3 and 4 of sleep.
   b. Stages 2 and 3 of sleep.   d. REM sleep.

3. Sleep may help the body replenish resources expended during wakefulness. What is this function of sleep called?

4. Match each of the sleep disorders listed on the left with the appropriate description on the right:
   i. narcolepsy   a. frequent, frightening dreams that usually occur during REM sleep
   ii. sleep terror disorder b. intense nightmares that occur during deep sleep and primarily affect children
   iii. sleep apnea   c. sudden, unexplained "sleep attacks" during the day
   iv. nightmare disorder   d. temporary cessation of breathing during sleep

MODULE 4.3 Altering Consciousness Through Meditation and Hypnosis

- **What is meditation?**
- **What is hypnosis?**
- **What are the major theories of hypnosis?**

We venture now from considering states of ordinary wakefulness and sleep to considering states of altered consciousness. People use many methods to alter their states of conscious awareness. Some turn to drugs; others turn to such practices as meditation and hypnosis. You might not think of meditation and hypnosis as having much in common, but both involve rituals that focus on the narrowing of attention or concentration to achieve an altered state of consciousness.

Meditation: Achieving a Peaceful State by Focusing Your Attention

CONCEPT 4.15
Meditation involves practices that induce an altered state of consciousness through techniques of focused attention.

People from many different cultures practice meditation, which, as you may recall from Chapter 3, is a process of focused attention that induces a relaxed, contemplative state. To remove all other thoughts from consciousness, practitioners of meditation narrow their attention to a single object or thought. The particular meditative technique used varies among cultures. In ancient Egypt, practitioners stared at an oil-burning lamp, a custom that inspired the tale of Aladdin's lamp. Yogis focus on the design of a vase or other graphic symbol. Other practitioners focus on a burning candle.

In **transcendental meditation (TM)** practitioners focus their attention by repeating a phrase or sound (such as *ommm*), which is known as a **mantra**. In **mindfulness meditation**, they learn to focus on their unfolding experience on a moment-to-moment basis without bringing judgment to bear on their experience (Kabat-Zinn, 2003). Mindfulness meditation is receiving a great deal of attention among psychologists as a promising technique for treating many problems, including physical health problems such as chronic pain and mental health problems such as anxiety (Baer, 2003; Logsdon-Conradsen, 2002; Roemer & Orsillo, 2003).

People who practice meditation describe it as a relaxed but alert state, and evidence based on physiological measurement of their responses backs up their claims (Jevning, Wallace, & Beidebach, 1992). Though people may be able to achieve similar responses through other forms of relaxation, even by resting quietly with eyes closed, some researchers argue that meditation is more effective than other relaxation methods in reducing physiological arousal (Alexander et al., 1995).

Some people who practice meditation believe it does more than just relax the body and mind—that it can expand consciousness to help them achieve a state of pure awareness or inner peace. Perhaps meditation achieves these effects by helping people tune out the outside world, thus allowing them more opportunity for inward focus. Yet many people practice meditation not to expand consciousness but to find relief from the stress of everyday life. Evidence shows that regular practice of meditation does help relieve the effects of stress on the body (McLean et al., 1997). Meditation also has therapeutic benefits in the treatment of many psychological and physical disorders, including alcohol and substance abuse (Alexander, Robinson, & Rainforth, 1995); anxiety disorders (Miller, Fletcher, & Kabat, 1995); stress-related disorders (L. R. Murphy, 1996); and chronic pain, including the pain of tension headaches (*Mind Over Matter*, 2000).

Meditation Meditation can induce a relaxed but alert state.

transcendental meditation (TM) A form of meditation in which practitioners focus their attention by repeating a particular mantra.

mantra A sound or phrase chanted repeatedly during transcendental meditation.

mindfulness meditation A form of meditation in which one adopts a state of nonjudgmental attention to the unfolding of experience on a moment-to-moment basis.

Hypnosis: "You Are Now Getting Sleepier"

Hypnosis is derived from the Greek word *hypnos,* meaning "sleep." People who undergo hypnosis may feel sleepier, but they are not asleep. Though you may find many different definitions of the word, **hypnosis** is most commonly defined as an altered state of consciousness characterized by focused attention, deep relaxation, and heightened susceptibility to suggestion. Techniques for inducing hypnosis vary, but they usually include a narrowing of attention to the hypnotist's voice. During a hypnotic induction, the hypnotist may ask the person to focus on an object, such as a swinging watch, and listen only to the sound of his or her voice. The hypnotist may also suggest that the person's eyelids are getting heavier and heavier and that the person is becoming sleepy.

Once the person becomes deeply relaxed, the hypnotist begins giving the person hypnotic suggestions that may lead to unusual experiences. These experiences include **hypnotic age regression** (reliving past events, usually from childhood) and **hypnotic analgesia** (loss of feeling or responsiveness to pain in certain parts of the body). Other hypnotic experiences include distortions of reality—seeing, hearing, or feeling something that is not present in reality (a *positive* hallucination), or not perceiving something, such as a pen or a chair, that truly does exist (a *negative* hallucination). Another kind of hypnotic experience in response to hypnotic suggestions is **posthypnotic amnesia**, an inability to recall what happened during hypnosis. About one in four college students exhibit posthypnotic amnesia in response to suggestions (J. F. Kirsch et al., 1995; J. F. Kirsch & Lynn, 1998). Yet another type of hypnotic experience is **posthypnotic suggestion**, in which the hypnotist plants the idea that, after coming out of the hypnotic state, people will respond in particular ways (such as touching their ears or scratching their heads) when they hear a cue word—for example, *elephant.* A person may respond in the suggested way but deny any awareness of having performed the behavior.

Theories of Hypnosis

Despite more than one hundred years of scientific study, there is still no consensus among leading experts about what hypnosis is or even how it should be defined (Lynn & Rhue, 1991). One view of hypnosis is that it is a trance state—an altered state of awareness characterized by heightened *suggestibility.* Suggestibility is the readiness with which one complies with suggestions offered by others, including a hypnotist. Some psychologists reject the view that hypnosis is a trance state, or even that it constitutes an altered state of consciousness. An alternative view proposes that hypnosis is best understood in terms of the social demands of the hypnotic situation (I. Kirsch, 1994). This view, generally called the *role-playing model,* proposes that hypnosis is a social interaction that exists between a hypnotist and a person assuming the role of a "good" hypnotic subject— one who faithfully follows the hypnotist's directions. This doesn't mean that hypnotic subjects are necessarily faking their responses, any more than you are faking when you perform the role of a good student, as when you raise your hand before speaking in class.

Some research supports the role-playing model. For example, investigators find that people who supposedly are hypnotically regressed to childhood do not accurately display childlike behavior; instead, they act like adults playing the role of children (McGreal & Evans, 1994; Nash, 1987). Moreover, when subjects are given a role-playing explanation of hypnosis before a hypnotic induction takes place, their later responses to hypnotic suggestions are either reduced or eliminated (Wagstaff & Frost, 1996). On the other hand, a recent brain-imaging study showed that patterns of brain activity in subjects who were hypnotized differed from those in subjects who were *acting* as if they were hypnotized (Kosslyn et al., 2000). More research in this area is needed, but there appears to be something more to hypnosis than just role playing (Bryant & Mallard, 2002).

CONCEPT 4.16
Hypnosis is not sleep but, rather, a relaxed state of focused attention in which a person may become more responsive to suggestions.

THINK **About It**

Were You Ever Hypnotized?

If you have been hypnotized, what was the experience like? Whether or not you've experienced hypnosis, has reading this module changed any of your views about hypnosis? If so, how?

web Netlab/Hypnosis Myths

CONCEPT 4.17
Two theoretical models that have guided recent research on hypnosis are the role-playing model and neodissociation theory.

hypnosis   An altered state of consciousness characterized by focused attention, deep relaxation, and heightened susceptibility to suggestion.
hypnotic age regression   A hypnotically induced experience that involves reexperiencing past events in one's life.
hypnotic analgesia   A loss of feeling or responsiveness to pain in certain parts of the body occurring during hypnosis.
posthypnotic amnesia   An inability to recall what happened during hypnosis.
posthypnotic suggestion   A hypnotist's suggestion that the subject will respond in a particular way following hypnosis.

CONCEPT CHART 4.3
Altering Consciousness Through Meditation and Hypnosis

Technique	Method of Induction	Key Points
Meditation	Narrowing attention to a single object, word, or thought or performing a repetitive ritual	Meditation relaxes the body and mind, helps combat stress, and can help people cope with pain. Some people believe it leads to a state of inner peace or spiritual enlightenment, but others practice it for its stress- and pain-relieving effects.
Hypnosis	Narrowing attention to the hypnotist's voice or repetitive stimulus	Debate about the nature of hypnosis continues. Role-playing theory and neodissociation theory have emerged as the major contemporary theories of hypnosis. All forms of hypnosis may actually involve self-hypnosis.

CONCEPT 4.18

The effectiveness of hypnosis may have more to do with the psychological characteristics of the hypnotized subject than with the skills of the hypnotist.

One leading theorist who believed that hypnosis is a special state of consciousness was psychologist Ernest Hilgard. According to Hilgard's (1977, 1994) **neodissociation theory**, hypnosis involves a splitting off or dissociation of a part of consciousness. It is this dissociated part that follows the hypnotist's suggestions. Another part, called the **hidden observer**, remains detached from the hypnotic experience but continues to monitor everything that happens. In hypnotic pain relief, for example, subjects may be able to split off, or dissociate, the part of consciousness that is aware of the pain (the hidden observer) from another part that is not.

The belief that hypnotists have special powers that give them control over the hypnotized subject may be part of the mystique of hypnosis, but it is not consistent with contemporary views. It is a widely held myth that hypnosis can cause people to commit murder or other immoral and illegal acts they wouldn't otherwise perform. On the contrary, hypnosis depends on the willingness of subjects to go along with imagining the alternate realities suggested by the hypnotist. In hypnotic age regression, for instance, people do not actually relive childhood incidents or experiences; they merely imagine that they are again children (T. X. Barber, 1999). In general, responsiveness to hypnotic suggestions may have more to do with the efforts and skills of the people who are hypnotized than with those of the hypnotist (I. Kirsch & Lynn, 1995).

Though most people can be hypnotized to some extent, some are more hypnotizable, or susceptible to suggestions, than others. Typical characteristics of highly hypnotizable people include a well-developed fantasy life, a vivid sense of imagination, a tendency to be forgetful, and a positive attitude toward hypnosis (T. X. Barber, 1999; Barrett, 1996). These traits help them think along with the hypnotist—to imagine whatever the hypnotist suggests, perhaps so vividly that it seems real to them.

Hypnosis has a legitimate therapeutic role in treating a wide range of problems. For example, hypnotic suggestions may be helpful when combined with other forms of treatment, such as behavior therapy, in assisting people who want to quit smoking or lose weight (I. Kirsch, 1996; Kirsch, Montgomery, & Sapirstein, 1995). Hypnosis may even boost the body's immune system to function better during times of stress (Kiecolt-Glaser et al., 2001; Patterson & Jensen, 2003). It can also help alleviate pain and may allow physicians to use lesser amounts of sedation or anesthesia during invasive procedures (Kessler & Dane, 1996). Though hypnosis may have therapeutic benefits, it should be used only as an adjunctive treatment, not as a substitute for traditional treatments.

For a summary of altering consciousness through meditation and hypnosis, see Concept Chart 4.3.

neodissociation theory A theory of hypnosis based on the belief that hypnosis represents a state of dissociated (divided) consciousness.

hidden observer Hilgard's term for a part of consciousness that remains detached from the hypnotic experience but aware of everything that happens during it.

MODULE 4.3 REVIEW

Altering Consciousness Through Meditation and Hypnosis

CONCEPT CHECK

1. The type of meditation in which practitioners focus their attention by repeating a mantra is called _____.

2. The loss of feeling or responsiveness to pain as a result of hypnotic suggestion is called _____.

3. The concept of a "hidden observer" is a central feature of which theory of hypnosis?

MODULE 4.4   Altering Consciousness Through Drugs

- **When does drug use cross the line from use to abuse and dependence?**
- **What are the different types of psychoactive drugs, and what effects do they have?**
- **What factors contribute to alcohol and drug-abuse problems?**
- **What treatment alternatives are available to help people with drug problems?**

Most people who want to change their states of waking consciousness don't turn to meditation or hypnosis. They are more likely to pop a pill, drink an alcoholic beverage, or smoke a joint.

Psychoactive drugs are chemical substances that act on the brain to affect emotional or mental states. They affect mood, thought processes, perceptions, and behavior. People use psychoactive drugs for many reasons: to change their level of alertness (stimulants to perk them up; depressants to relax them and make them drowsy so they can fall asleep), to alter their mental states by getting "high" or induce feelings of intense pleasure (a euphoric "rush"), to blunt awareness of the stresses and strains of daily life, or to seek some type of inner truth.

Some psychoactive drugs, including heroin, cocaine, and marijuana, are illegal or *illicit*. Others, such as alcohol and nicotine (found in tobacco), are legally available, but restrictions are placed on their use or sale. Another legal psychoactive drug, caffeine, is so widely used that many people don't realize they are ingesting a psychoactive drug when they drink a caffeinated beverage or eat a chocolate bar (yes, chocolate contains caffeine).

According to a 2003 survey, nearly one in four students in grades six through twelve report using illicit drugs, with marijuana being the most used of these drugs ("Teen Drug Use," 2003). More than half of today's high school seniors also report having used illicit drugs at some point in their lives—and, again, marijuana is the illegal substance most commonly cited (Miller, 2000). Although only about one in fifty high school seniors have used heroin, about one in ten have used cocaine. But the use of illicit drugs is dwarfed by the use of two legally available substances, alcohol and tobacco (see Figure 4.5). Alcoholic beverages contain the depressant drug alcohol, whereas tobacco products, such as cigarettes, contain the stimulant drug nicotine.

In this module, we examine drugs that alter consciousness or levels of alertness. We consider their effects, the risks they pose to health, the factors that may lead people to use and abuse them, and ways of helping people with substance abuse problems. We begin by defining the terms that professionals use to characterize problems associated with the misuse of drugs.

 CONCEPT 4.19

Psychoactive substances—depressants, stimulants, and hallucinogens—are drugs that alter the user's mental state.

psychoactive drugs Chemical substances that affect a person's mental or emotional state.

Figure 4.5 Rates of Drug Use in the United States
Though more than one third of U.S. adults have used an illicit drug at some point in their lives, relatively few Americans report that they are current users—that is, that they have used an illicit drug in the past month. Two psychoactive substances that adults may use legally—alcohol and nicotine (cigarettes)—are far and away the most commonly used drugs in the United States.

Source: USDHHS, 2001.

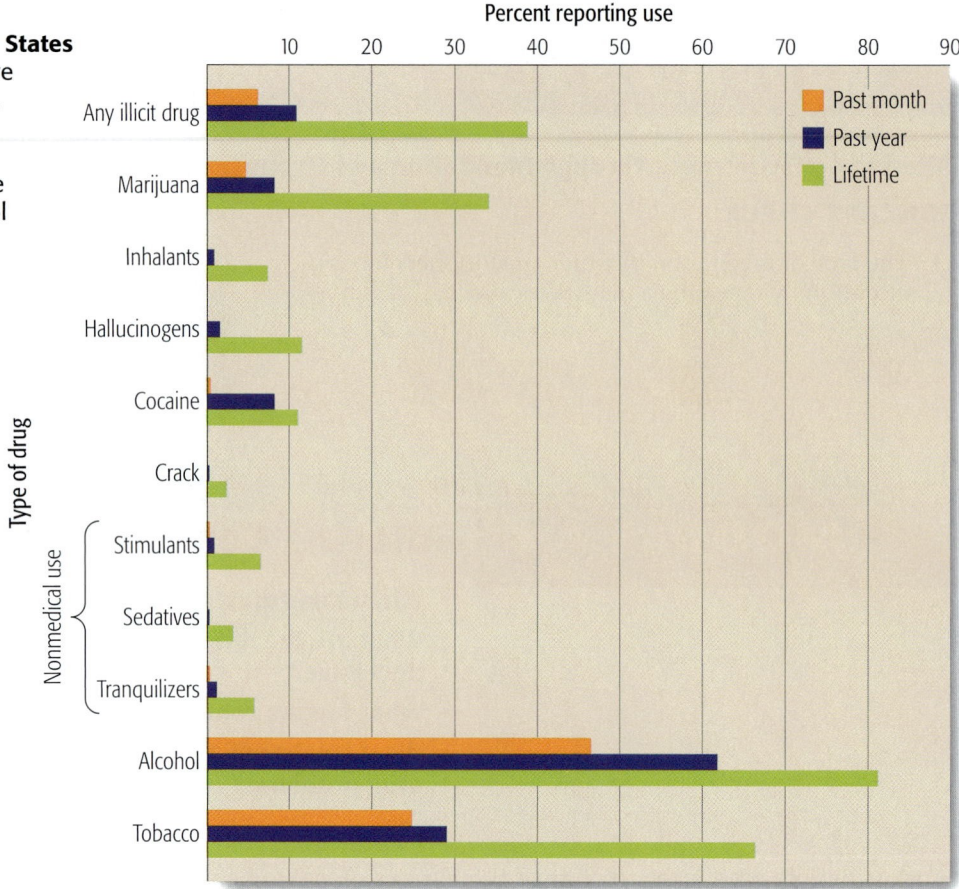

CONCEPT 4.20
Drug use becomes abuse when it becomes maladaptive and either causes or contributes to personal, occupational, or health-related problems.

CONCEPT 4.21
People who are psychologically dependent on drugs use them habitually or compulsively to cope with stress or to relieve negative feelings.

drug abuse   Maladaptive or dangerous use of a chemical substance.

polyabusers   People who abuse more than one drug at a time.

drug dependence   A severe drug-related problem characterized by impaired control over the use of the drug.

physiological dependence   A state of physical dependence on a drug caused by repeated usage that changes body chemistry.

withdrawal syndrome   A cluster of symptoms associated with abrupt withdrawal from a drug.

tolerance   A form of physical habituation to a drug in which increased amounts are needed to achieve the same effect.

Drug Abuse: When Drug Use Causes Harm

Drug use becomes *drug abuse* when repeated use causes or aggravates personal, occupational, or health-related problems (American Psychiatric Association, 2000). **Drug abuse** is maladaptive or dangerous use of a chemical substance. If drug use impairs a person's health or ability to function at home, in school, or on the job, or if it becomes associated with dangerous behavior such as drinking and driving, the person has crossed the line from use to abuse. If you repeatedly miss school or work because you are drunk or "sleeping it off," you are abusing alcohol. You may not admit you have a drug problem, but you do. People who abuse more than one drug at a time are called **polyabusers**.

Drug Dependence: When the Drug Takes Control

Drug abuse often leads to **drug dependence**, a severe drug-related problem characterized by impaired control over the use of a drug. People who become dependent on a drug feel compelled to use the drug or powerless to stop using it, even when they know the drug use is ruining their lives.

Drug dependence is usually, but not always, associated with *physiological dependence* (also called *chemical dependence*). In **physiological dependence**, a person's body chemistry changes as the result of repeated use of a drug so that the body comes to depend on having a steady supply of the drug. When physiologically dependent people abruptly stop their drug use, they may experience a cluster of unpleasant and sometimes dangerous symptoms called a **withdrawal syndrome** (also called an *abstinence syndrome*). Another frequent sign of physiological dependence is **tolerance**, the need to increase the amount of a drug so that it has the same effect.

When Does Use Become Abuse? Many people use alcohol socially, but when does use cross over into abuse? According to mental health professionals, drug use becomes drug abuse when it leads to damaging or dangerous consequences.

Professionals use the terms *drug abuse* and *drug dependence* to describe the different types of substance-use disorders. Laypeople more often use the term *drug addiction,* but it has different meanings to different people. Here, let us define **drug addiction** (also called *chemical addiction*) as a pattern of drug dependence accompanied by physiological dependence. By this definition, we consider people to be addicted when they feel powerless to control their use of the drug *and* have developed signs of physiological dependence—typically a withdrawal syndrome.

Bear in mind that people may become *psychologically* dependent on a drug without becoming physiologically dependent on it. **Psychological dependence** is a pattern of compulsive or habitual use of a drug that serves a psychological need, such as lessening anxiety or escaping from stress. People who are psychologically dependent on a drug come to rely on it to counter unpleasant feelings or to cope with personal problems or conflicts with others. Some drugs, like nicotine, alcohol, and heroin, can lead to both psychological and physiological dependence. Others, such as marijuana, can produce psychological dependence but are not known to produce physiological dependence.

Now let us turn to the major classes of psychoactive drugs: depressants, stimulants, and hallucinogens.

Depressants

Depressants are drugs that reduce central nervous system activity, which in turn depresses (slows down) such bodily processes as heart rate and respiration rate. The major types of depressants are alcohol, barbiturates and tranquilizers, and opioids. Psychologically, depressants induce feelings of relaxation and provide relief from states of anxiety and tension. Some depressants also produce a "rush" of pleasure. In high doses, depressants can kill by arresting vital bodily functions, such as breathing. Depressants are highly addictive and can be dangerous, even lethal, in overdose or when mixed with other drugs. The deaths of famed entertainers Marilyn Monroe and Judy Garland were blamed on the deadly mix of barbiturates and alcohol.

Alcohol: The Most Widely Used and Abused Depressant

Alcohol is an **intoxicant**—a chemical substance that produces a state of drunkenness. The more a person drinks, the stronger the intoxicating effects become. Table 4.1 summarizes how increasing blood alcohol levels (BALs) affect behavior.

web **Netlab/Test Your Alcohol Knowledge**

💡 **CONCEPT 4.22**
Depressants are addictive drugs that can be deadly when used in high doses or when mixed with other drugs.

drug addiction Drug dependence accompanied by signs of physiological dependence, such as the development of a withdrawal syndrome.

psychological dependence A pattern of compulsive or habitual use of a drug to satisfy a psychological need.

depressants Drugs, such as alcohol and barbiturates, that dampen central nervous system activity.

intoxicant A chemical substance that induces a state of drunkenness.

TABLE 4.1 **Behavioral Effects of Blood Alcohol Levels**

Blood Alcohol Level (%)	Behavioral Effects
.05	Lowered alertness; usually a "high" feeling; release of inhibitions; impaired judgment
.10	Slowed reaction times; impaired motor function; less caution
.15	Large, consistent decreases in reaction time
.20	Marked depression in sensory and motor capability; decidedly intoxicated
.25	Severe motor disturbance; staggering; sensory perceptions greatly impaired
.30	Stuporous but conscious; no comprehension of the external world
.35	Condition equivalent to surgical anesthesia; minimal level at which death occurs
.40	Death in about 50 percent of cases

Source: Ray & Ksir, 1990.

CONCEPT 4.23

Alcohol is the most widely used and abused depressant.

A Tragic Ending The movie star Marilyn Monroe died at the age of thirty-six, apparently as the result of mixing barbiturates and alcohol.

CONCEPT 4.24

Alcohol has various psychological effects, including clouding judgment; impairing attention, concentration, and the ability to weigh the consequences of behavior; and reducing inhibitions, which may lead to aggressive or impulsive behavior.

Impairment of driving skills begins with even the first drink. In heavier doses, the depressant effects of the drug on the central nervous system can induce a state of stupor, unconsciousness, and even death.

Women typically become intoxicated at lower doses of alcohol than men do. One reason is that women usually weigh less than men, and the less people weigh, the less alcohol it usually takes to produce intoxication. But another reason is that women have less of an enzyme that breaks down alcohol in the stomach than men do and thus more pure alcohol reaches their bloodstreams. Women become about as intoxicated from one drink as men do from two. Yet women's greater sensitivity to alcohol can work in their favor in that it may serve as a biological constraint on excessive drinking.

Alcohol directly affects the brain, clouding judgment and impairing concentration and attention, as well as the ability to weigh the consequences of behavior (MacDonald et al., 2000). Thus, people may do or say things when they are drinking that they might not otherwise. They may take unnecessary risks without considering the consequences of their actions, which can have tragic results. The slogan from a recent public health campaign bears repeating: "First you get drunk. Then you get stupid. Then you get AIDS."

Alcohol has a *disinhibiting* (inhibition-releasing) effect, which may lead to aggressive or impulsive behavior (Curtin et al., 2001). Not everyone who drinks becomes aggressive or acts foolishly or recklessly, of course. Individual differences play a large role. Yet alcohol use is associated with many forms of aggression, from rape and spousal abuse to other violent crimes, such as robbery, assault, and homicide. We examine the relationship between alcohol and violent behavior in Chapter 14.

Alcohol accounts for more than 100,000 deaths per year in the United States. Most of these deaths are the result of alcohol-related diseases and accidents, particularly motor vehicle accidents (Kalb, 2001a; O'Donnell, 2003). Alcohol-related accidents are the leading causes of death of young people in the 17-to-24-year age range (Ham & Hope, 2003). Alcohol is also linked to more than 25 percent of suicides and more than 45 percent of homicides (see Figure 4.6).

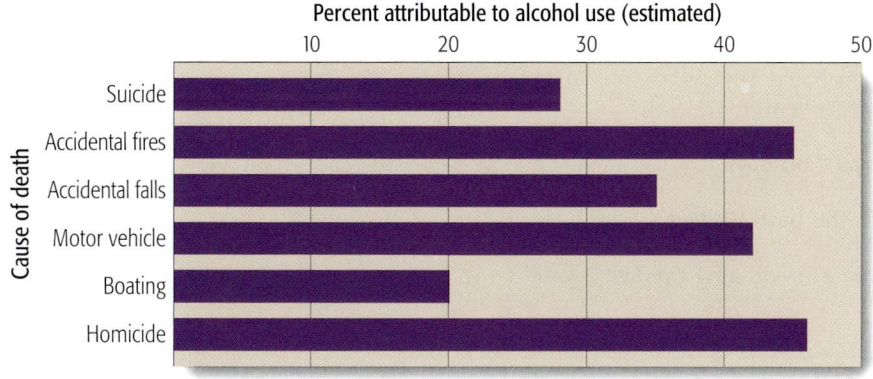

Percent attributable to alcohol use (estimated)

Figure 4.6 Alcohol Use and Causes of Death
Alcohol use is involved in a large percentage of homicides, suicides, and deaths due to motor vehicle accidents and other types of mishaps.

Source: National Institute on Alcohol Abuse and Alcoholism (1996); *Epidemiologic Data Reference Manuals, 1979–92.*

Alcohol and Women Women absorb more pure alcohol into their bloodstreams than men do. They become about as intoxicated from one drink as men become from two.

Alcoholism

Most people who drink alcohol do so in moderation. However, about one in ten adult Americans—approximately 14 million people—suffer from **alcoholism** (alcohol dependence), a form of chemical dependence in which people become physically dependent on alcohol and unable to control their use of the drug (Leary, 1996; Miller & Brown, 1997). Relatively few people who suffer from alcoholism, perhaps only 5 percent, fit the stereotype of the "skid-row bum." Most have families and work for a living. They are the kinds of people you're likely to meet in your daily life—neighbors, co-workers, friends, and even family members. Yet alcoholism is an equal-opportunity destroyer, leading to devastating health problems, motor vehicle accidents, and ruined careers and marriages. Alcoholism typically develops in early adulthood, usually between the ages of 20 and 40, although it may develop in teenagers and even in younger children (Langenbucher & Chung, 1995).

Alcohol abuse involving regular, heavy consumption of alcohol can damage nearly every major organ and body system. Heavy drinking often has its most damaging effects on the liver, the organ that primarily metabolizes (breaks down) alcohol. *Cirrhosis of the liver,* an irreversible scarring of liver tissue typically caused by alcohol abuse, accounts for some 26,000 deaths annually in the United States.

Ironically, despite the health risks associated with heavy drinking, recent research links moderate use of alcohol (one to two drinks per day) to a lower risk of heart attacks and strokes, and to a lower death rate overall (e.g., Carmichael, 2003a; Mukamal et al., 2003). This research is correlational, so we cannot yet draw conclusions about the beneficial effects of alcohol on our health. But scientists suspect that moderate use of alcohol may increase high-density lipoproteins (HDL), the "good" cholesterol that helps remove blockages from arteries (I. J. Goldberg et al., 2001; Wood, Vinson, & Sher, 2001).

Binge Drinking: A Dangerous College Pastime

Three out of four college students drink alcohol at least once monthly, although most of them are under the legal drinking age (see Table 4.2). Drinking has become so ingrained in college life that it is virtually as much a part of the college experience as attending a dance or basketball game.

Binge drinking on campus is a top concern among parents and school officials, and for good reason ("College Binge Drinking Tops Parents' Fears," 2001). Overall,

CONCEPT 4.25
Only a small percentage of people with alcoholism fit the stereotype of the "skid-row" bum.

CONCEPT 4.26
Binge drinking is linked to increased risks of alcohol dependence, alcohol overdoses, unsafe or unplanned sex, and driving while impaired, among other problems.

alcoholism A chemical addiction characterized by impaired control over the use of alcohol and physiological dependence on it.

TABLE 4.2	**Alcohol Use Among College Students**
86.6	Percentage who have used alcohol in their lifetime 86.6
83.2	Percentage who have used alcohol within the past year
67.4	Percentage who have used alcohol within the past 30 days
3.6	Percentage who have used alcohol daily within the past 30 days
39.3	Percentage who have had five or more drinks in a row during the last 2 weeks

Source: Johnston, O'Malley, & Bachman, 2001.

TABLE 4.3
Signs of Alcohol Overdose

Failure to respond when talked to or shouted at

Failure to respond to being pinched, shaken, or poked

Inability to stand unaided

Failure to wake up

Purplish or clammy skin

Rapid pulse rate, irregular heart rhythm, low blood pressure, or difficulty breathing

CONCEPT 4.27

Barbiturates and tranquilizers are depressants that help calm the nervous system, but they are addictive and potentially dangerous in high doses, especially when mixed with other drugs, such as alcohol.

about two out of five college students engage in binge drinking (Lam & Hope, 2003). *Binge drinking* is usually defined as having five or more drinks (for men) or four or more drinks (for women) on one occasion ("Binge Drinking," 2000).

Patterns of early drinking and binge drinking are strong predictors of later alcoholism (Chassin, Pitts, & Prost, 2002; K. G. Hill et al., 2000). Those who start drinking before the age of fifteen are five times more likely than their peers to develop alcohol dependence (Kluger, 2001). Binge drinkers face additional risks. For example, college students who binge drink are three times more likely than their peers to engage in unsafe or unplanned sexual activities, which increases their risks of both unwanted pregnancies and sexually transmitted diseases (Cooper, 1992; Kruger & Jerrells, 1992). A recent study showed adult binge drinkers were fourteen times more likely than other adults to drive while impaired (Naimi et al., 2003).

Binge drinking and related drinking games (beer-chugging) are a serious concern primarily because they can place people at risk of death from alcohol overdose. Blackouts and seizures may also occur with consumption of large amounts of alcohol. Choking on one's own vomit is a frequent cause of alcohol-induced deaths. Heavy drinking can cause people to vomit reflexively, but the drug's depressant effects on the central nervous system interfere with the normal vomiting response. As a result, vomit accumulates in the air passages, which can lead to asphyxiation and death.

Prompt medical attention is needed if a person overdoses on alcohol. But how can you tell if a person has drunk too much? Table 4.3 lists some signs of alcohol overdose. A person who is unresponsive or unconscious should not be left alone. Don't simply assume that he or she will "sleep it off." Stay with the person until you or someone else can obtain medical attention. Most important, call a physician or local emergency number immediately and ask for advice.

It may seem easier to walk away from the situation and let the person "sleep it off." You may think you have no right to interfere. You may have doubts about whether the person is truly in danger. But ask yourself, if you were in the place of a person who showed signs of overdosing on alcohol, wouldn't you want someone to intervene to save your life?

Barbiturates and Tranquilizers

Barbiturates are calming or sedating drugs that have several legitimate medical uses. They are used to regulate high blood pressure, to block pain during surgery, and to control epileptic seizures. Yet they are also highly addictive and used illicitly as street drugs to induce states of euphoria and relaxation. Among the more widely used barbiturates are amobarbital, pentobarbital, phenobarbital, and secobarbital. Methaqualone (brand names, Quaalude and Sopor; street names, "ludes" and "sopors") is a sedating drug with effects similar to those of barbiturates, and with similar risks.

Barbiturates can induce drowsiness and slurred speech and impair motor skills and judgment. Overdoses can lead to convulsions, coma, and death. The mixture of barbiturates or methaqualone with alcohol can be especially dangerous and potentially lethal. People who are physiologically dependent on barbiturates or methaqualone should withdraw under careful medical supervision, since abrupt withdrawal can cause convulsions and even death.

Tranquilizers are a class of depressants widely used to treat anxiety and insomnia. Though they are less toxic than barbiturates, they can be dangerous in high doses, especially if combined with alcohol or other drugs. They also carry a risk of addiction, so they should not be used for extended periods of time. The most widely used tranquilizers include Valium, Xanax, and Halcion, which are members of the *benzodiazepine* family of drugs. Benzodiazepines act by boosting the availability of the neurotransmitter GABA in the brain (see Chapter 2). GABA, an inhibitory neurotransmitter, reduces excess nervous system activity.

Opioids

Opioids (also called *opiates*) are **narcotics**—addictive drugs that have pain-relieving and sleep-inducing properties. They include morphine, heroin, and codeine, naturally occurring drugs derived from the poppy plant. Synthetic opioids, including Demerol, Percodan, and Darvon, are manufactured in a laboratory to have effects similar to those of the natural opioids. Opioids produce a "rush" of pleasurable excitement and dampen awareness of personal problems, which are two main reasons for their popularity as illicit street drugs.

Opioids have legitimate medical uses as painkillers. They are routinely used to deaden postsurgical pain and for some other pain conditions. Because of their high potential for addiction, their medical use is strictly regulated. However, they are sometimes obtained and used illegally, as in the case of *OxyContin,* a prescription painkiller widely used as a street drug (Adler, 2003; Belluck, 2003).

Opioids are similar in chemical structure to endorphins and lock into the same receptor sites in the brain. You'll recall from Chapter 2 that endorphins are neurotransmitters that regulate states of pleasure. Opioids mimic the actions of endorphins, our own "natural opioids," thereby stimulating brain centers that produce pleasurable sensations (Van-Ree, 1996).

Heroin, the most widely abused opioid, induces a euphoric rush, lasting perhaps five to fifteen minutes. The rush is so intense and pleasurable that users liken it to the pleasure of orgasm. After the rush fades, a second phase sets in that is characterized by a relaxed, drowsy state. Worries and concerns seem to evaporate, which is why heroin often appeals to people seeking a psychological escape from their problems. This mellow state soon fades, too, leading the habitual user to seek another "fix" to return to the drugged state. Tolerance develops, and users begin needing higher doses, which can lead to dangerous overdoses. The life of the heroin addict is usually organized around efforts to obtain and use the drug. Many turn to crime or prostitution to support their habit. Users who become addicted to heroin undergo a severe withdrawal syndrome.

Stimulants

Stimulants are drugs that heighten the activity of the central nervous system. They include amphetamines, cocaine, MDMA ("Ecstasy"), nicotine, and caffeine. Stimulants can produce both physiological and psychological dependence. Some, like amphetamines and cocaine, can induce a pleasurable "high."

Amphetamines

Like the synthetic opioids, *amphetamines* are not found in nature; they are chemicals manufactured in a laboratory. They activate the sympathetic branch of the

CONCEPT 4.28
Opioids, such as morphine and heroin, are depressants that induce a euphoric high.

CONCEPT 4.29
Stimulants increase activity in the central nervous system, heightening states of alertness and in some cases producing a pleasurable "high" feeling.

narcotics   Addictive drugs that have pain-relieving and sleep-inducing properties.

stimulants   Drugs that activate the central nervous system.

autonomic nervous system, causing heart rate, breathing rate, and blood pressure to rise. At low doses, they boost mental alertness and concentration, reduce fatigue, and lessen the need for sleep. At high doses, they can induce an intense, pleasurable rush.

Amphetamines act on the brain by boosting levels of the neurotransmitters norepinephrine and dopamine (Leyton et al., 2002). The increased supply of these chemicals induces neurons to keep firing, which helps maintain high levels of arousal and alertness. Amphetamines produce pleasurable feelings by directly stimulating the reward pathways in the brain.

The most widely used amphetamines are amphetamine sulfate (brand name, Benzedrine; street name, "bennies"), methamphetamine (Methedrine, or "speed"), and dextroamphetamine (Dexedrine, or "dexies"). They can be used in pill form, smoked in a relatively pure form of methamphetamine called "ice" or "crystal meth," or injected in the form of liquid methamphetamine.

More than a million Americans use amphetamines in one form or another, nearly three times as many as use heroin (Bonné, 2001). Overdoses, which often occur as users develop tolerance to the drug and keep increasing the amount they consume, can have dangerous, even fatal, consequences. In high doses, amphetamines can cause extreme restlessness, loss of appetite, tremors, and cardiovascular irregularities that may result in coma or death. High doses can also induce *amphetamine psychosis,* a psychotic reaction characterized by hallucinations and delusions that resembles acute episodes of schizophrenia. Brain-imaging studies show that methamphetamine abuse can damage the brain, causing deficits in learning, memory, and other functions (Toomey et al., 2003; Volkow et al., 2001).

Cocaine

CONCEPT 4.30
Cocaine is a highly addictive stimulant that induces a euphoric high by directly stimulating reward pathways in the brain.

Cocaine is a natural stimulant derived from the leaves of the coca plant. Cocaine can be administered in several ways. It can be sniffed in powder form, smoked in a hardened form called *crack,* injected in liquid form, or ingested as a tea brewed from coca leaves. You may be surprised to learn that when Coca-Cola was introduced in 1886, it contained cocaine and was soon being marketed as "the ideal brain tonic." (Cocaine was removed from Coca-Cola in the early twentieth century, but the beverage is still flavored with a nonpsychoactive extract from the coca plant.)

Like amphetamines, cocaine increases brain levels of the neurotransmitters norepinephrine and dopamine. This helps maintain high levels of bodily arousal and mental alertness. Also like amphetamines, cocaine directly stimulates reward pathways in the brain, inducing feelings of extreme pleasure or euphoria. Though amphetamines and cocaine have similar effects, the high induced by cocaine is typically shorter-lived, especially in the form of crack. Smoking crack delivers the drug almost instantaneously to the brain, producing an immediate, intense high. But the high fades within five or ten minutes, leaving the user craving more. Though patterns of cocaine abuse vary, many abusers go on binges lasting perhaps twelve to thirty-six hours. They will then abstain for several days until cravings for the drug increase to a level that prompts another binge (Gawin et al., 1988).

Regular use of cocaine can damage the heart and circulatory system and other body organs. High doses can have life-threatening or fatal consequences, including irregular heart rhythms, heart stoppage, strokes caused by spasms of blood vessels in the brain, and respiratory arrest (cessation of breathing) (A. Goldstein, 1994).

Prolonged use may also lead to psychological problems, such as anxiety, irritability, and depression. At high doses, cocaine can induce a type of psychosis, called *cocaine psychosis,* that is characterized by hallucinations and delusions of persecution (unfounded beliefs that one is being pursued by others or by mysterious forces).

Cocaine is highly addictive and can lead to a withdrawal syndrome involving intense cravings for the drug, feelings of depression, and an inability to experience pleasure in the activities of everyday life. People addicted to cocaine will often return to using the drug to gain relief from these unpleasant withdrawal symptoms. Tolerance also develops quickly, yet another sign of the physically addicting properties of cocaine. Users may also become psychologically dependent on the drug, using it compulsively to deal with life stress.

MDMA (Ecstasy)

MDMA (3,4-methylenedioxymethamphetamine), better known as *Ecstasy,* is an amphetamine-like drug synthesized in underground laboratories. MDMA produces mild euphoric and hallucinogenic effects (Kuhn & Wilson, 2001). It is especially popular among high school and college students and is widely available in many late-night dance clubs in U.S. cities (Butterfield, 2001; Strote, Lee, & Wechsler, 2002). Users may experience undesirable psychological effects, such as depression, anxiety, insomnia, and even states of paranoia and psychosis. Use of the drug may also interfere with learning ability and attention and may have long-lasting effects on memory functioning (Gouzoulis-Mayfrank et al., 2000; Reneman et al., 2001). The drug has physical effects as well, such as increased heart rate and blood pressure, a tense or chattering jaw, and feelings of body warmth and/or chills (S. Braun, 2001). High doses of MDMA can be lethal (Kuhn & Wilson, 2001). Perceptions do not always square with reality, however, as many teens see no risk in experimenting with MDMA ("Teens See Little Risk," 2003).

Nicotine

Nicotine is a mild stimulant that is highly addictive (Kessler et al., 1997). It is found naturally in tobacco, and users typically administer the drug by smoking, snorting, or chewing tobacco. Physiological dependence can begin within the first few weeks of cigarette smoking. Nicotine use can also lead to psychological dependence, as we see in people who smoke habitually as a means of coping with the stress of everyday life.

As a stimulant, nicotine speeds up the heart rate, dampens appetite, and produces a mild rush or psychological kick. It increases states of arousal, alertness, and concentration. But it may also have "paradoxical" effects, such as inducing feelings of relaxation or mental calmness. In fact, since nicotine causes the release of endorphins in the brain, it can produce states of pleasure and reduce pain.

CONCEPT 4.31
Nicotine, a stimulant, is an addictive substance found in tobacco.

"Ecstasy" The drug Ecstasy has become increasingly popular among young people, especially among those who frequent late-night dance clubs. Use of the drug can impair learning ability and memory functioning, and high doses can be lethal.

You certainly are aware by now that smoking is dangerous. But just how dangerous? It is the leading cause of premature death in the United States and elsewhere in the world, accounting annually for more than 400,000 deaths in this country and about 4 million deaths worldwide. In the United States, cigarette smoking is responsible for nearly one in three cancer deaths, most of them due to lung cancer, the leading cancer killer of both men and women. Smoking is also a major contributor to cardiovascular disease (heart and artery disease), the biggest killer of all, and to other physical problems, including emphysema and even cataracts.

Smoking is more prevalent among men than women, among younger adults, and among less-educated people (see Droomers, Schrijvers, & Mackenbach, 2002). Slightly more than 25 percent of adult Americans smoke, a rate that hardly budged during the 1990s. Smoking rates began to climb sharply among teenagers in the 1990s, reversing an earlier steady decline. By the beginning of the twenty-first century, about 33 percent of college and high school students were smoking cigarettes, as were nearly 10 percent of students in grades six through eight (Centers for Disease Control, 2000b).

Tobacco use often begins in adolescence and is difficult to eliminate once a pattern of regular use is established. Estimates are that 3,000 young people take up smoking each day and that one in three of them will eventually die of smoking-related diseases.

Caffeine

CONCEPT 4.32

Caffeine, a mild stimulant found in coffee, tea, cola drinks, chocolate, and other substances, is the most widely used psychoactive drug.

Caffeine, a mild stimulant found in coffee, tea, cola drinks, chocolate, and other substances, is our most widely used psychoactive drug. Americans consume perhaps 500 million or more cups of coffee a day, or more than two cups for every adult. Regular use of caffeine leads to physiological dependence. If your daily routine includes one or more cups of coffee or caffeinated tea and you feel on edge or have headaches when you go without your daily supply of caffeine, chances are you're physiologically dependent, or "hooked," on caffeine. Drinking just a cup or two of coffee or tea or even a few cans of caffeinated soft drinks each day can lead to dependence. The good news is that most caffeine users are able to maintain control over their use of the drug despite being physiologically dependent on it. In other words, they may limit themselves to one or two cups of coffee a day without feeling uncontrollable urges to increase their usage. Fortunately, too, caffeine is not known to be associated with health risks (other than during pregnancy) when used in moderation. Caffeine has some desirable effects in terms of enhancing wakefulness and mental alertness (A. Goldstein, 1994), although negative effects, such as jitteriness or nervousness, are reported at higher dosages (from 200 to 600 milligrams).

Our Most Widely Used Drug Caffeine is the most widely used psychoactive drug. Most regular users can control their use of the drug despite being physiologically dependent on it.

Hallucinogens

Hallucinogens are drugs that alter sensory perceptions, producing distortions or hallucinations in visual, auditory, or other sensory forms. They are also called *psychedelics,* a word that literally means "mind-revealing." Hallucinogens may induce feelings of relaxation and calmness in some users but cause feelings of paranoia or panic in others. Though they are not known to produce physiological dependence, they can lead to psychological dependence when users come to depend on them for help in coping with problems or stressful life experiences. Hallucinogens include LSD, mescaline, psilocybin, PCP, and marijuana. Of these, the two most widely used are LSD and marijuana.

LSD

LSD (lysergic acid diethylamide; street name, "acid") produces vivid hallucinations and other sensory distortions. The experience of using the drug is called a "trip," and it may last as long as twelve hours. About one in thirteen Americans (7 percent) report having used LSD at least once (National Institute on Drug Abuse, 1995).

LSD has various effects on the body, including pupil dilation and increases in heart rate, blood pressure, and body temperature. It may also produce sweating, tremors, loss of appetite, and sleeplessness. The psychological effects on the user are variable and unpredictable. Users often report distortions of time and space. Higher doses are likely to produce more vivid displays of colors and outright hallucinations. The psychological effects depend not only on the amount used but also on the user's personality, expectancies about the drug, and the context in which it used (USDHHS, 1992c). Some users experience "bad trips," in which they suffer intense anxiety or panic or have psychotic reactions, such as delusions of persecution. Others have flashbacks, which involve a sudden reexperiencing of some of the perceptual distortions of an LSD trip.

Mescaline, Psilocybin, and PCP

For centuries, Native Americans have used the hallucinogens *mescaline* (derived from the cactus plant) and *psilocybin* (derived from certain mushrooms) for religious purposes. *PCP* (phencyclidine), or "angel dust," is a synthetic drug that produces **delirium**, a state of mental confusion characterized by excitement, disorientation, and difficulty in focusing attention. PCP can produce distortions in the sense of time and space, feelings of unreality, and vivid, sometimes frightening, hallucinations. It may lead to feelings of paranoia and blind rage and prompt bizarre or violent behavior. High doses can lead to coma and death.

Marijuana

Marijuana ("pot," "weed," "grass," "reefer," "dope") is derived from the cannabis plant. The psychoactive chemical in marijuana is THC (delta-9-tetrahydrocannabinol). The leaves of the plant are ground up and may be smoked in a pipe or rolled into "joints." The most potent form of the drug, called hashish ("hash"), is derived from the resin of the plant, which contains the highest concentration of THC. Though marijuana and hashish are usually smoked, some users ingest the drug by eating parts of the plant or foods into which the cannabis leaves have been baked.

Marijuana is generally classified as a hallucinogen because it alters perceptions and can produce hallucinations, especially in high doses or when used by susceptible individuals. At lower doses, users may feel relaxed and mildly euphoric. It may seem as if time is passing more slowly. Bodily sensations may seem more pronounced, which can create anxiety or even panicky feelings in

CONCEPT 4.33
Hallucinogens alter or distort sensory perceptions and produce feelings of relaxation in some people but paranoid or panicky feelings in others.

LSD Trip The hallucinogen LSD can produce vivid perceptual distortions and outright hallucinations. Some users experience "bad trips," which are characterized by panicky feelings and even psychotic states.

hallucinogens Drugs that alter sensory experiences and produce hallucinations.
delirium A mental state characterized by confusion, disorientation, difficulty in focusing attention, and excitable behavior.

some users (e.g., a pronounced sense of the heartbeat may cause some users to fear they are having a heart attack). High doses can cause nausea and vomiting, feelings of disorientation, panic attacks, and paranoia.

Marijuana is the most widely used illicit drug in the United States and throughout the Western world. About 33 percent of the U.S. population aged twelve to fifty report having used marijuana at least once in their lives (Iversen, 2000). Yet only about 5 percent of adult Americans are current users (USDHHS, 1993).

CONCEPT 4.34
Marijuana induces feelings of relaxation and mild euphoria at low doses, but it can produce hallucinations in high doses or when used by susceptible individuals.

Although marijuana is not known to lead to physiological dependence, it can create strong psychological dependence as people may come to rely on it to deal with stress or personal difficulties. We have also learned that marijuana use is linked to later use of harder drugs such as heroin and cocaine (Kandel, 2003; "Marijuana Leads," 2002). Whether marijuana use plays a causal role in leading to harder drug use remains an open question. In any event, programs that aim at preventing or stopping marijuana use appear to prevent progression to use of harder drugs (Kandel, 2002).

Let us note some other concerns. Marijuana use increases heart rate and possibly blood pressure, which can put people with cardiovascular problems at risk (A. Goldstein, 1994). It can impair motor performance and coordination, which, together with causing perceptual distortions, makes marijuana and driving an especially dangerous combination. Because THC also affects parts of the brain involved in learning and memory, long-term use may lead to problems in these areas (Verhovek, 2000). In addition, use of marijuana and hashish introduces cancer-causing agents into the body, increasing the risk of cancer (Iversen, 2000; "Marijuana Linked," 2000). Though marijuana use is also associated with greater risk of developing psychological problems, such as depression and anxiety, researchers can't yet say whether marijuana use plays a causal role in these problems (Patton et al., 2002; Rey & Tennant, 2002).

In Concept Chart 4.4, you'll find a listing of the major types of psychoactive drugs in terms of their potential for psychological and physiological dependence, major psychological effects, and major risks.

Understanding Drug Abuse

CONCEPT 4.35
Drug abuse and dependence are complex problems arising from an interplay of social, biological, and psychological factors.

To understand drug use and abuse, we need to consider the roles of the social environment and the effects that drugs have on the body (Kahler et al., 2003; Leshner, 1999). Pleasurable effects of drugs, peer pressure, and exposure to family members who smoke or use alcohol or other drugs are important influences in leading young people to begin experimenting with these substances (Hestick et al., 2001; Read et al., 2003; Simons-Morton et al., 2001). Some young people who feel alienated from mainstream culture come to identify with subcultures in which drug use is sanctioned or encouraged, such as the gang subculture. While initiation into drug use may be motivated by the desire to "fit in" or appear "cool" in the eyes of peers, people generally continue using drugs because of the pleasurable effects of the drugs themselves. With prolonged use of a drug, the body comes to depend on a steady supply of it, leading to physiological dependence. As people become chemically dependent, they may continue using drugs primarily to avoid unpleasant withdrawal symptoms and cravings that occur when they stop using them.

Unemployment is another social factor linked to drug abuse. Young adults who are out of work are more than twice as likely as their employed peers to turn to drugs (USDHHS, 1991b). The relationship appears to be two-sided: Drug abuse may increase the likelihood of unemployment, while unemployment may increase the likelihood of drug abuse.

Use of alcohol and other drugs is strongly affected by cultural norms. Cultural beliefs and customs may either encourage or discourage drinking. Some ethnic groups—Jews, Greeks, Italians, and Asians, for example—have low rates of alco-

CONCEPT CHART 4.4
Major Types of Psychoactive Drugs

	Drug	Potential for Psychological/ Physiological Dependence	Major Psychological Effects	Major Risks
Depressants	Alcohol	Yes/Yes	Induces relaxation, mild euphoria, and intoxication; relieves anxiety; reduces mental alertness and inhibitions; impairs concentration, judgment, coordination, and balance	With heavy use, can cause liver disorders and other physical problems; in overdose, can cause coma or death
	Barbiturates and tranquilizers	Yes/Yes	Reduces mental alertness; induces relaxation and calm; may produce pleasurable rush (barbiturates)	High addictive potential; dangerous in overdose and when mixed with alcohol and other drugs
	Opioids	Yes/Yes	Induces relaxation and a euphoric rush; may temporarily blot out awareness of personal problems	High addictive potential; in overdose, may cause sudden death
Stimulants	Amphetamines	Yes/Yes	Boosts mental alertness; reduces need for sleep; induces pleasurable rush; causes loss of appetite	In high doses, can induce psychotic symptoms and cardiovascular irregularities that may lead to coma or death
	Cocaine	Yes/Yes	Effects similar to those of amphetamines but shorter-lived	High addictive potential; risk of sudden death from overdose; in high doses, can have psychotic effects; risk of nasal defects from "snorting"
	MDMA ("Ecstasy")	Yes/Yes	Mild euphoria and hallucinogenic effects	High doses can be lethal; may lead to depression or other psychological effects; may impair learning, attention, and memory
	Nicotine	Yes/Yes	Increases mental alertness; produces mild rush but paradoxically may have relaxing and calming effects	Strong addictive potential; implicated in various cancers, cardiovascular disease, and other physical disorders
	Caffeine	Yes/Yes	Increases mental alertness and wakefulness	In high doses, can cause jitteriness and sleeplessness; may increase risk of miscarriage during pregnancy
Hallucinogens	LSD	Yes/No	Produces hallucinations and other sensory distortions	Intense anxiety, panic, or psychotic reactions associated with "bad trips"; flashbacks
	Marijuana	Yes/No	Induces relaxation and mild euphoria; can produce hallucinations	In high doses, can cause nausea, vomiting, disorientation, panic, and paranoia; possible health risks from regular use

holism, largely because of tight social controls imposed on excessive and underage drinking. In traditional Islamic cultures, alcohol is prohibited altogether.

Ethnic and racial groups also differ in reported use of illicit drugs. Figure 4.7 shows the reported rates of cocaine and marijuana use by African Americans and (non-Hispanic) White Americans. The data are drawn from an ongoing survey of American households. Later in the chapter we will ask you to think critically about these data. Do they in fact demonstrate that race or ethnicity is responsible for these differences?

Acculturation also plays a role in drug abuse. Traditional Hispanic cultures place severe restrictions on women's use of alcohol, especially on heavy drinking.

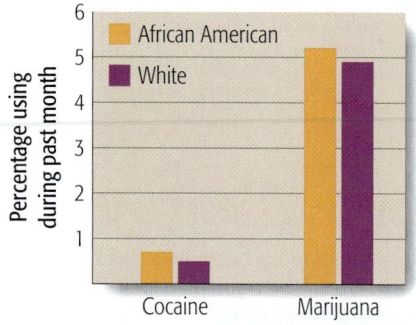

Figure 4.7 Ethnicity and Drug Use
This figure shows the percentages of people in two ethnic groups who reported using illicit drugs during the past month. The data are from an ongoing federally sponsored study of drug-use patterns in the United States. But can we infer from these data that drug use—especially cocaine use—is a problem associated with minority group status?

Source: USDHHS, 2001.

Self-Medication? Many problem drinkers use alcohol in an attempt to wash away their problems or troubling emotions.

Not surprisingly, highly acculturated Hispanic American women who have been exposed to the loose constraints on female drinking in mainstream U.S. society are much more likely to drink heavily than are relatively unacculturated Hispanic American women (Caetano, 1987).

Research findings provide strong evidence of genetic factors at work in drug dependence, including alcoholism (Crabbe, 2002; Nurnberger et al., 2001; Slutske et al., 2002; Wall et al., 2001; Wall, Carr, & Ehlers, 2003). We know, for instance, that identical twins are much more likely to have alcoholism in common than are fraternal twins (Wood, Vinson, & Sher, 2001). Researchers do not think that one gene alone is responsible for alcoholism or other forms of substance abuse. Rather, they suspect that multiple genes act together with environmental factors to increase the potential for these problems (Dick et al., 2001; Kendler et al., 2003). Evidence indicates that some people may have a genetic tendency that makes the effects of certain drugs especially rewarding or stimulating (Azar, 1995; Haney et al., 1994).

Another genetic factor, at least for alcoholism, may be inheritance of a greater tolerance for the drug's negative effects (the nausea and so on), which may make it more difficult to learn when to say *no more*. People who inherit a greater sensitivity to the negative effects of alcohol—those whose bodies more readily "put the brakes" on excess drinking—may be less likely to develop problems with alcohol abuse or dependence (Pihl, Peterson, & Finn, 1990; Pollock, 1992). Thus, ironically, having a greater ability to hold one's liquor may put one at greater risk of developing problems with alcohol.

We also need to consider the role of neurotransmitters in drug abuse. Drugs such as cocaine, alcohol, heroin, amphetamines, and marijuana produce pleasurable or euphoric effects by increasing the concentration of the neurotransmitter dopamine, a chemical that activates the brain's reward or pleasure circuits (Adler, 2003; "Drugs All Stimulate Brain," 2003; Kauer, 2003; Saal et al., 2003). Chronic use of drugs alters the delicate biochemistry of the brain's natural dopamine system, making it more difficult for the person to reap pleasure from the normal activities of everyday life, such as enjoying a good meal or attending a concert (Begley, 2001e; "Cocaine Impairs," 2003). The chronic drug user comes to depend on drugs to produce feelings of pleasure or to erase negative feelings, such as anxiety or depression. Without drugs, life may no longer seem worth living.

Endorphins are affected by drug abuse, too. Opioids lock into the same receptor sites as endorphins. When the brain becomes accustomed to having opioids available, it suppresses production of endorphins. The person dependent on opioids comes to rely on them to perform the pain-relieving and pleasure-inducing functions normally served by endorphins.

Psychological factors, such as feelings of hopelessness, the need to seek sensation, and the desire to escape troubling emotions, are major contributors to the development of drug use and dependence. Young people from troubled backgrounds may turn to drugs out of a sense of futility and despair. People with a high need for sensation—those who become easily bored with the ordinary activities that fill most people's days—may come to rely on drugs to provide the stimulation they seek. Other people use alcohol or other drugs as a form of self-medication to relieve anxiety or emotional pain, or to temporarily escape from their problems or conflicts with others (Delfino, Jamner, & Whalen, 2001; Mohr et al., 2001; Ozegovic, Bikos, & Szymanski, 2001; Swendsen et al., 2000).

Cognitive factors, such as positive attitudes and expectancies toward drugs, also play important roles in drug use and abuse (Goldberg et al., 2002; Wiers & Kummeling, 2004). One study found that the strongest determinant of which adolescents would begin drinking was the expectancy that alcohol makes one more socially relaxed and outgoing (G. T. Smith et al., 1995). Times are a-changing, though. Adolescents who were studied recently in a Midwestern community had more negative attitudes toward smoking than did adolescents in the same community a generation ago (Chassin et al., 2003).

Drug Treatment

The most effective drug-treatment programs use a variety of approaches in dealing with the wide range of problems faced by people with drug-abuse problems (Litt et al., 2003; McLellan et al., 2000). People with chemical dependencies may first need to undergo **detoxification**, a process in which their bodies are cleared of addictive drugs. To ensure that medical monitoring is available, detoxification usually requires a hospital stay. Follow-up services, including professional counseling, can assist people in remaining free of drugs by helping them confront the psychological problems that may underlie their drug abuse, such as depression and low self-esteem (Brems & Johnson, 1997).

Therapeutic drugs may be used in combination with psychological counseling to fight drug addiction. Some of these drugs prevent opioids and alcohol from producing a high (Kalb, 2001c; Kiefer et al., 2003; Markel, 2002). Methadone, a synthetic opioid, is one such drug; when used in normal doses, it does not produce the rush or stuporous state associated with heroin, but it does curb withdrawal symptoms from heroin (Belluck, 2003; R. E. Johnson et al., 2000). It can help heroin abusers gain employment and get their lives back on track (Goode, 2001d; P. G. O'Connor, 2000). In addition, self-help programs, such as the twelve-step program of Alcoholics Anonymous (AA), may motivate individuals to maintain abstinence and rebuild their lives free of drugs, especially those who commit themselves to abstinence goals (McKellar, Stewart, & Humphreys, 2003; Moos & Moos, 2004; Morgenstern et al., 2002).

CONCEPT 4.36
Effective drug treatment requires a multifaceted approach to helping people free themselves of chemical dependence and develop more adaptive ways of coping with their problems.

detoxification A process of clearing drugs or toxins from the body.

MODULE 4.4 REVIEW

Altering Consciousness Through Drugs

CONCEPT CHECK

1. Chemical substances that alter mental states are called _____ drugs.

2. When repeated use of a drug alters a person's body chemistry so that the body comes to rely on having a steady supply of the drug, the condition is called
   a. drug abuse.
   b. drug misuse.
   c. psychological dependence.
   d. physiological dependence.

3. Alcohol and heroin belong to which class of drugs?

4. The most widely used and abused type of depressant is
   a. nicotine.   c. heroin.
   b. alcohol.   d. caffeine.

5. _____ are drugs that are widely used in treating anxiety and insomnia but that can become addictive when used for extended periods of time.

6. Hallucinogens are drugs that alter sensory perceptions and produce hallucinations. Which of the following is *not* a hallucinogen?
   a. cocaine   c. LSD
   b. marijuana   d. psilocybin

APPLICATION

MODULE 4.5

Getting Your Zs

• **What steps can you take to combat insomnia?**

CONCEPT 4.37
Developing healthy sleep habits can help people overcome insomnia not caused by underlying physical or psychological problems.

Many people have difficulty falling asleep or getting enough sleep to feel refreshed upon awakening. Since insomnia may result from an underlying medical or psychological disorder, it is best to have the condition evaluated by a health professional. In many cases, however, insomnia reflects unhealthy sleep habits. Fortunately, people can change such habits by becoming better aware of behavioral patterns and making adaptive changes in behavior (Edinger et al., 2001; Quesnel et al., 2003). Here are some suggestions for developing healthier sleep habits (Nevid, Rathus, & Rubenstein, 1998):

• *Adopt a regular sleep schedule.* Help get your internal body clock in sync by retiring and awakening at about the same times every day. You may cut yourself some slack on weekends, but be aware that sleeping late in the morning can throw off your body clock.

• *Don't try to force sleep.* Sleep is a natural process that cannot be forced. If you are wide-eyed and full of energy, allow your body and mind to wind down before going to bed.

• *Establish a regular bedtime routine.* Adopt a regular routine before going to bed. You may find that reading, watching TV, or practicing a relaxation or meditation technique helps prepare you for sleep.

• *Establish the proper cues for sleeping.* Make your bed a cue for sleeping by limiting as much as possible other activities in bed, such as eating, reading, watching TV, or talking on the telephone.

• *Avoid tossing and turning.* If you can't fall asleep within twenty minutes, don't continue tossing and turning. Get out of bed, move to another room, and achieve a state of relaxation by reading, listening to calming music, or meditating. When you are feeling relaxed, return to bed. Repeat this process as necessary until you are able to fall asleep.

Making Your Bed a Cue for Sleeping
If you have a problem with insomnia, you might find it helpful to make your bed a stronger cue for sleep by limiting other activities in bed, such as eating, reading, watching TV, or talking on the phone.

- *Avoid daytime naps if you miss sleep.* Many people try to make up for nighttime sleeplessness by napping during the day. Napping can throw off your natural body clock, making it more difficult to fall asleep the following night.

- *Don't take your problems to bed.* Retiring to bed should be conducive to sleeping, not to mulling over your problems or organizing your daily schedule. Tell yourself you'll think about tomorrow, tomorrow. Or, before you go to bed, write reminder notes to yourself about the things you need to do the following day.

- *Use mental imagery.* Picturing relaxing scenes in your mind—for example, imagining yourself basking in the sun on a tropical beach or walking through a pristine forest—can help you slip from ordinary consciousness into the realm of sleep.

- *Adopt a regular exercise program.* Vigorous exercise can help relieve the stresses of daily life and prepare the body for restful sleep. But avoid exercising for several hours before sleep, since exercise increases states of bodily arousal.

- *Limit your intake of caffeine, especially in the afternoon.* The caffeine in coffee, tea, and other substances can increase states of bodily arousal for up to ten hours. Also avoid smoking, not only because of its harmful effects on your health but also because tobacco contains nicotine, a mild stimulant.

- *Practice rational "self-talk."* Disturbing thoughts you silently mumble to yourself under your breath can lead to anxiety and worry that may keep you up well into the night. Replace such anxious "self-talk" with coping thoughts. For example, instead of thinking "I must get to sleep or I'll be a wreck tomorrow," substitute a thought like "I might not feel as sharp as usual but I'm not going to fall apart. I've gotten by with little sleep before and can do so again." Don't fall into the trap of blowing things out of proportion.

TYING IT TOGETHER

Our state of consciousness, or level of awareness, shifts during the course of a day from periods of focused awareness through states of drifting and divided unconsciousness to states of unconsciousness experienced during sleeping and dreaming (Module 4.1). When we sleep, we experience a state of unconsciousness in which we are generally unaware of our external surroundings but can respond to certain kinds of stimuli (Module 4.2). Some people seek to achieve altered states of consciousness through meditation or hypnosis (Module 4.3) or by using mind-altering drugs (Module 4.4). By applying our knowledge of sleep-wake cycles and adopting healthy sleep habits to keep our body clocks in sync, we can help ensure that we receive the restful sleep we need (Module 4.5).

SUMMING UP: Q & A

States of Consciousness (Module 4.1)

What are states of consciousness?

- States of consciousness are different levels of awareness that may range during the course of the day from alert wakefulness to deep sleep.
- States of deep unconsciousness are caused by head trauma, surgical anesthesia, or coma.
- Altered states of consciousness are states of awareness that differ from one's usual waking state.

Sleeping and Dreaming (Module 4.2)

How are our sleep-wake cycles regulated?

- The suprachiasmatic nucleus (SCN), a clocklike mechanism in the hypothalamus, regulates our sleep-wake cycles according to a circadian rhythm that approximates the twenty-four-hour day.

What are the stages of sleep, and what functions does sleep serve?

- In addition to REM sleep, there are four non-REM stages of sleep (Stages 1 through 4); in these stages, sleep becomes increasingly deeper. The brain is relatively active during REM sleep, which is when most dreaming occurs.
- Though no one knows for sure, sleep experts suspect that sleep may serve several functions, including a protective function, an energy-conservation function, and a restorative function.

Why do we dream?

- Again, no one can say for sure, but theories include the belief that dreams are needed to consolidate memories and experiences that occur during the day, Hartmann's view that dreams help people work out their everyday problems, the activation-synthesis hypothesis, and Freud's view that dreaming helps preserve sleep by disguising potentially threatening wishes or impulses in the form of dream symbols.

What are sleep disorders?

- Sleep disorders are disturbances in the amount or quality of sleep. They include insomnia, narcolepsy, sleep apnea, nightmare disorder, sleep terror disorder, and sleepwalking. The most common sleep disorder is insomnia.

Altering Consciousness Through Meditation and Hypnosis (Module 4.3)

What is meditation?

- Meditation is an altered state of consciousness induced by narrowing attention to a single object, word, or thought or performing a repetitive ritual.
- Meditation produces a relaxed state that may have therapeutic benefits in relieving stress and pain.

What is hypnosis?

- Although there is no consensus about the nature of hypnosis, it has traditionally been defined as an altered state of consciousness characterized by focused attention, deep relaxation, and heightened susceptibility to suggestion. Hypnosis is increasingly being used within mainstream psychology and medicine.

What are the major theories of hypnosis?

- The two major contemporary views of hypnosis are the role-playing model, which proposes that hypnosis is a form of social role playing, and neodissociation theory, which holds that hypnosis is a state of divided consciousness.

Altering Consciousness Through Drugs (Module 4.4)

When does drug use cross the line from use to abuse and dependence?

- Drug use becomes drug abuse when it involves the maladaptive or dangerous use of a drug (use that causes or aggravates personal, occupational, or physical problems).
- Drug dependence is a state of impaired control over the use of a drug. It is often accompanied by signs of physiological dependence. Drug abuse frequently leads to drug dependence.
- Physiological dependence means that the person's body has come to depend on having a steady supply of the drug. When psychologically dependent, people rely on a drug as a way of coping with anxiety, stress, and other negative feelings.

What are the different types of psychoactive drugs, and what effects do they have?

- Depressants, such as alcohol, barbiturates, tranquilizers, and opioids, are addictive drugs that reduce the activity of the central nervous system. They have a range of effects, including reducing states of bodily arousal, relieving anxiety and tension, and, in the case of barbiturates and opioids, producing a pleasurable or euphoric rush.
- Stimulants, which include amphetamines, cocaine, MDMA ("Ecstasy"), nicotine, and caffeine, heighten the activity of the nervous system. Stimulants may induce feelings of euphoria, but they also can lead to physiological dependence. Cocaine directly stimulates reward pathways in the brain, producing states of euphoria, but it is a highly addictive and dangerous drug. MDMA is a chemical knockoff of amphetamines that can have serious psychological and physical consequences. Nicotine, a mild stimulant, is the addictive substance found in tobacco. Though regular use of caffeine may lead to psychological dependence, most users can maintain control over their consumption of it.
- Hallucinogens are drugs that alter sensory perceptions and produce hallucinations. They include LSD, mescaline, psilocybin, PCP, and marijuana. PCP ("angel dust") is a synthetic drug that produces delirium—a state of confusion and disorientation that may be accompanied by hallucinations and violent behavior. Marijuana, the most widely used illicit drug, has a range of effects depending on dosage level.

What factors contribute to alcohol and drug-abuse problems?

- In addition to the reinforcing effects of the drugs themselves, social, biological, and psychological factors contribute to drug abuse. Among the contributing social factors are peer pressure and exposure to family members and friends who use drugs. Biological factors include high tolerance for negative drug effects. Psychological factors include feelings of hopelessness and the desire to escape troubling emotions.

What treatment alternatives are available to help people with drug problems?

- Approaches to treating people with drug problems include detoxification programs, professional counseling, the use of therapeutic drugs, and self-help programs such as Alcoholics Anonymous.

Application: Getting Your Zs (Module 4.5)

What steps can you take to combat insomnia?

- You can take such steps as establishing a regular sleep schedule, recognizing that sleep cannot be forced, developing a regular bedtime routine, making the bed a cue for sleeping, getting up if you are unable to sleep, avoiding daytime naps, not taking your problems to bed, using mental imagery to let your mind drift off, exercising regularly, limiting caffeinated beverages, and practicing coping thoughts.

Key Terms

consciousness (p. 126)
states of consciousness (p. 126)
focused awareness (p. 126)
drifting consciousness (p. 126)
daydreaming (p. 126)
divided consciousness (p. 127)
unconsciousness (p. 127)
altered states of consciousness (p. 128)
circadian rhythm (p. 129)
jet lag (p. 129)
rapid-eye-movement (REM) sleep (p. 131)
activation-synthesis hypothesis (p. 132)
lucid dreams (p. 134)
insomnia (p. 136)
narcolepsy (p. 136)
sleep apnea (p. 136)

nightmare disorder (p. 137)
sleep terror disorder (p. 137)
sleepwalking disorder (p. 137)
transcendental meditation (TM) (p. 138)
mantra (p. 138)
mindfulness meditation (p. 138)
hypnosis (p. 139)
hypnotic age regression (p. 139)
hypnotic analgesia (p. 139)
posthypnotic amnesia (p. 139)
posthypnotic suggestion (p. 139)
neodissociation theory (p. 140)
hidden observer (p. 140)
psychoactive drugs (p. 141)
drug abuse (p. 142)

polyabusers (p. 142)
drug dependence (p. 142)
physiological dependence (p. 142)
withdrawal syndrome (p. 142)
tolerance (p. 142)
drug addiction (p. 143)
psychological dependence (p. 143)
depressants (p. 143)
intoxicant (p. 143)
alcoholism (p. 145)
narcotics (p. 147)
stimulants (p. 147)
hallucinogens (p. 151)
delirium (p. 151)
detoxification (p. 155)

Thinking Critically About Psychology

Based on your reading of this chapter, answer the following questions. Then, to evaluate your progress in developing critical thinking skills, compare your answers to the sample answers found in Appendix A.

Do statistics lie? While statistics may not actually lie, they can certainly mislead if we don't apply critical thinking skills when interpreting them. Recall Figure 4.7 from p. 154, which showed racial/ethnic differences in reported use of cocaine and marijuana. These survey results showed that African Americans were more likely to report using these drugs within the past month than were (non-Hispanic) White Americans (USDHHS, 2001). Now apply your critical thinking skills to answer the following questions:

1. Does this evidence demonstrate that ethnicity accounts for differences in rates of drug use? Why or why not?

2. What other explanations might account for these findings?

Answers to Concept Check Questions

Module 4.1: 1. a; 2. selectivity; 3. d. **Module 4.2:** 1. a; 2. c; 3. restorative; 4. i. c, ii. b, iii. d, iv. a. **Module 4.3:** 1. transcendental meditation; 2. hypnotic analgesia; 3. neodissociation theory. **Module 4.4:** 1. psychoactive; 2. d; 3. depressants; 4. b; 5. Tranquilizers; 6. a.

5

Learning

DID YOU **KNOW** THAT . . .

- Déjà-vu may be a learned response? (p. 164)

- In an early study, a young boy learned to fear a white rat after experimenters repeatedly made loud noises by banging steel bars behind his head while the rat was present? (p. 167)

- Phobias may be acquired through the same principles of learning that Pavlov discovered, based on his studies of digestion in dogs? (p. 167)

- Salivating to the sound of a tone may not be harmful, but salivating at the sight of a Scotch bottle may well be dangerous to people battling alcoholism? (p. 168)

- Scheduling tests on specific days may inadvertently reinforce students to cram just before exams and to slack off afterwards? (p. 178)

- Many people develop fears of various creatures even though they have had no direct negative experiences with them? (p. 186)

I hate eggs. It's not just the taste of eggs I can't stand. The smell, the feel, the very sight of eggs is enough to make me sick. Watching other people eat eggs can make me nauseous. It's not that I'm allergic to eggs. I like all kinds of baked goods that are made with eggs. I'm fine with eggs as long as they are cooked into other foods so they are no longer recognizable as, well, eggs. But eggs themselves, especially runny eggs, fill me with disgust.

I wasn't born with a disgust for eggs. Nor did I always dislike eggs. My parents tell me I was actually quite fond of eggs as a young child. But somewhere along the line, I acquired an aversion to eggs. Chances are I had an unpleasant experience with eggs. No, I don't think I was chased around a barn by a clutch of crazed chickens. Most likely, I had an experience in which eggs made me sick. Or perhaps I was forced to eat eggs when I wasn't feeling well. In any event, I have no memory of it. All I know is that I hate eggs and have hated them for as long as I can recall.

I have described my aversion to eggs to introduce you to the topic of learning. Some responses, such as pulling your hand away from a hot stove, are reflexive. We don't learn reflexes; we are biologically equipped to perform them automatically. Other behaviors develop naturally as the result of maturation. As a child's muscles mature, the child becomes capable of lifting heavier weights or throwing a ball a longer distance. But other responses, such as my aversion to eggs, are acquired through *experience*. Psychologists generally define *learning* as a relatively permanent change in behavior that results from experience. It is through experience that we learn about the world and develop new skills, such as riding a bicycle or cooking a soufflé. Acquired taste preferences or aversions, including my aversion to eggs, are also learned behaviors. Note the use of the term *relatively permanent* in the definition of learning. Psychologists believe that for learning to occur, changes in behavior must be enduring. But change need not be permanent. It is possible to unlearn behavior. For example, you would need to unlearn the behavior of driving on the right side of the road if you wanted to drive in a country where people drive on the left side of the road.

Psychologists recognize that learning is adaptive; it enables organisms to adapt their behavior to the demands of the environment. Through learning, organisms acquire behaviors that increase their chances of survival. Even taste aversions can be adaptive. They prevent animals, including humans, from eating foods that have sickened or poisoned them in the past. But not all learned responses are adaptive. My own aversion to eggs limits the range of foods I might enjoy. By and large, however, learning helps prepare organisms to meet the demands that their environments impose on them.

Psychologists study many forms of learning, including three major types that are the focus of this chapter: classical conditioning, operant conditioning, and cognitive learning. ■

MODULE 5.1 Classical Conditioning: Learning Through Association

- **What is learning?**
- **What is classical conditioning?**
- **What roles do extinction, spontaneous recovery, and stimulus generalization and discrimination play in classical conditioning?**
- **What stimulus characteristics strengthen conditioned responses?**
- **What is the cognitive perspective on classical conditioning?**
- **What are some examples of classical conditioning in daily life?**

CONCEPT 5.1
Pavlov's discovery that dogs would salivate to particular sounds in his laboratory led him to identify a process of learning called classical conditioning.

learning A relatively permanent change in behavior acquired through experience.

classical conditioning The process of learning by which a previously neutral stimulus comes to elicit a response identical or similar to one that was originally elicited by another stimulus as the result of the pairing or association of the two stimuli.

unconditioned response (UR) An unlearned response to a stimulus.

unconditioned stimulus (US) A stimulus that elicits an unlearned response.

neutral stimulus (NS) A stimulus that before conditioning does not produce a particular response.

conditioned response (CR) An acquired or learned response to a conditioned stimulus.

conditioned stimulus (CS) A previously neutral stimulus that comes to elicit a conditioned response after it has been paired with an unconditioned stimulus.

extinction The gradual weakening and eventual disappearance of a conditioned response.

spontaneous recovery The spontaneous return of a conditioned response following extinction.

reconditioning The process of relearning a conditioned response following extinction.

Do your muscles tighten at the sound of a dentist's drill? Do you suddenly begin to salivate when passing your favorite bakery? You weren't born with these responses—you learned them. But how does **learning** occur?

To understand how responses are learned, we need to consider the work of the Russian physiologist Ivan Pavlov (1849–1936). Pavlov discovered the form of learning we call **classical conditioning**. Pavlov, who at the time was studying digestive processes in dogs, made this discovery when he observed that dogs would salivate to sounds in his laboratory that had become associated with food, such as the sound of metal food carts being wheeled into his laboratory.

You might think of classical conditioning as *learning by association*. If you associate the sound of a dentist's drill with pain because of past experiences, the stimulus of that sound will probably cause you to respond with the muscle tension that is a natural reflex to pain. If you associate a certain bakery with a particularly tasty treat, you may find yourself salivating as you walk by that bakery. Responses are learned by experiences in which one stimulus is paired with another that elicits such natural reactions. Although classical conditioning is a relatively simple form of learning, it plays an important role in our lives—as you will see in this module.

Principles of Classical Conditioning

Pavlov performed many experiments in classical conditioning. In a typical experiment, he harnessed dogs in an apparatus similar to the one shown in Figure 5.1. When food is placed on a dog's tongue, the dog naturally salivates. This reflexive behavior is called an **unconditioned response (UR)** (*unconditioned* means "unlearned"). A stimulus that elicits an unconditioned response—in this case, the dog's food—is called an **unconditioned stimulus (US)**.

Figure 5.2 outlines the steps involved in a Pavlovian experiment. As you can see in Figure 5.2b, the introduction of a **neutral stimulus (NS)**, such as a tone or buzzer, does not initially elicit a response of salivation. It may produce other responses, however. A dog's ears may turn up in response to a sound, but the dog doesn't naturally salivate when it hears a tone or buzzer. However, through repeated pairings of the neutral stimulus and the unconditioned stimulus (Figure 5.2c), the dog acquires a *learned* response: salivation in response to the tone or buzzer alone (Figure 5.2d). Salivation to the sound of a tone or buzzer alone is an example of a **conditioned response (CR)**. A previously neutral stimulus becomes a **conditioned stimulus (CS)** when it is repeatedly paired with an unconditioned stimulus and begins to elicit the conditioned response. In addition to showing that salivation (CR) could be made to occur in response to a stimulus that did not naturally elicit the response, Pavlov observed that the strength of the conditioned response (the amount of salivation) increased with the number of pairings of the CS and US.

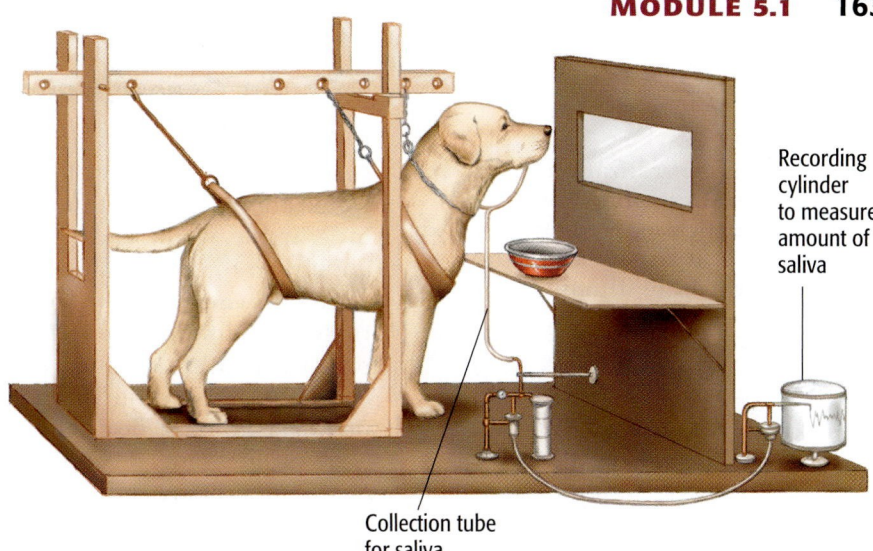

Figure 5.1   Apparatus Similar to One Used in Pavlov's Experiments on Conditioning
In Pavlov's studies, a research assistant positioned behind a mirror sounded a tone as food was placed on the dog's tongue. After several pairings of the tone and food, the dog acquired a conditioned response of salivation. The amount of saliva dripping through a tube to a collection vial was taken as the measure of the strength of the conditioned response.

Recording cylinder to measure amount of saliva

Collection tube for saliva

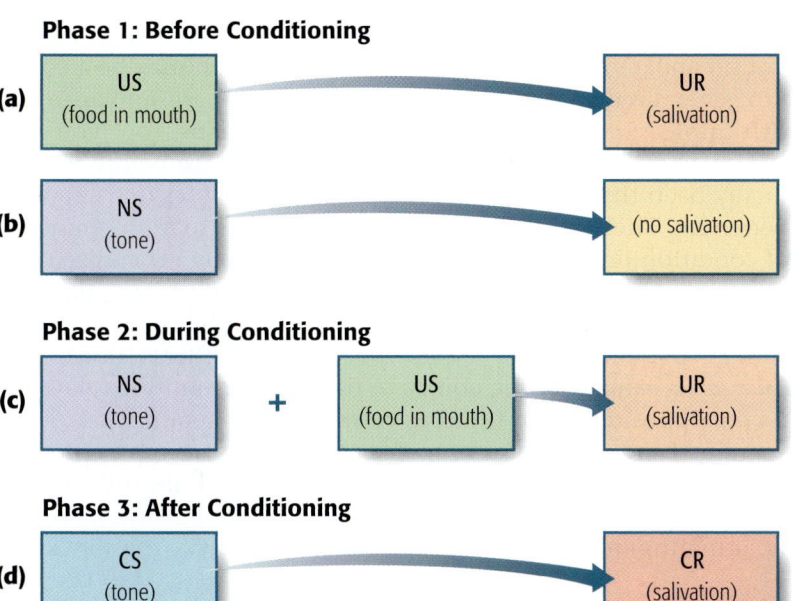

Phase 1: Before Conditioning

(a) US (food in mouth) → UR (salivation)

(b) NS (tone) → (no salivation)

Phase 2: During Conditioning

(c) NS (tone) + US (food in mouth) → UR (salivation)

Phase 3: After Conditioning

(d) CS (tone) → CR (salivation)

Figure 5.2
Diagramming Classical Conditioning
In classical conditioning, a neutral stimulus (the tone) is paired with an unconditioned stimulus (food) that normally elicits an unconditioned response (salivation). With repeated pairings, the neutral stimulus becomes a conditioned stimulus that elicits the conditioned response of salivation.

We next examine other characteristics of classical conditioning: extinction and spontaneous recovery, stimulus generalization and discrimination, and stimulus characteristics that strengthen conditioned responses.

Extinction and Spontaneous Recovery

Pavlov noticed that the conditioned response of salivation to the sound of a tone would gradually weaken and eventually disappear when he repeatedly presented the tone in the absence of the US (food). This process is called **extinction**. The extinguished response is not forgotten or lost to memory. It may return spontaneously at a later time when the animal is again exposed to the conditioned stimulus. This phenomenon is called **spontaneous recovery**. The recovered response will once again extinguish if the CS occurs in the absence of the US.

Pavlov discovered that when the CS and US are paired again after extinction has occurred, the response is likely to be learned more quickly than in the original conditioning. In many cases, the animal needs only one or two pairings. The process of relearning a conditioned response after extinction is called **reconditioning**.

CONCEPT 5.2
Through a process of extinction, conditioned responses gradually weaken and eventually disappear as the result of the repeated presentation of the conditioned stimulus in the absence of the unconditioned stimulus.

CONCEPT 5.3
Extinguished responses are not forgotten but may return spontaneously in the future if the conditioned stimulus is presented again.

Stimulus Generalization and Stimulus Discrimination

Pavlov found that once animals were trained to salivate to a particular stimulus, such as a tone, they would also salivate, but less strongly, to related stimuli that varied along some continuum, such as pitch. A tone with a higher or lower pitch, for example, would elicit some degree of salivation. The tendency of stimuli that are similar to the conditioned stimulus to elicit a conditioned response is called **stimulus generalization**. Generally speaking, the greater the difference between the original stimulus and the related stimulus, the weaker the conditioned response is. Were it not for stimulus generalization, the animal would need to be conditioned to respond to each stimulus no matter how slightly it varied from the original conditioned stimulus.

Stimulus generalization has survival value. It allows us to respond to a range of stimuli that are similar to an original threatening stimulus. Perhaps you were menaced or bitten by a large dog when you were young. Because of stimulus generalization, you may find yourself tensing up whenever you see a large dog approaching. Not all large dogs are dangerous, of course, but stimulus generalization helps prepare us just in case.

Have you ever walked into a room and suddenly felt uncomfortable or anxious for no apparent reason? Your emotional reaction may be a conditioned response to generalized stimuli in the environment that are similar to cues associated with unpleasant experiences in the past. Perhaps, too, you may have experienced déjà-vu—a feeling of having been in a place before when you've never actually been there. Stimulus generalization provides one explanation of such experiences. The feeling of familiarity in novel situations may involve a process of conditioning in which responses are evoked by generalized stimuli in these new environments that resemble conditioned stimuli encountered before. A fleeting odor, the way light bounces off a ceiling, even the color of walls—all are cues that may evoke conditioned responses acquired in other settings.

Stimulus discrimination, the ability to differentiate among related stimuli, represents the opposite side of the coin to stimulus generalization. This ability allows us to fine-tune our responses to the environment. Suppose, for example, that an animal in a laboratory study receives a mild shock shortly after it hears a tone. After a few pairings of the tone and shock, the animal shows signs of fear (cowering, urinating) to the tone alone. The tone is the CS, the shock is the US,

stimulus generalization The tendency for stimuli that are similar to the conditioned stimulus to elicit a conditioned response.

stimulus discrimination The tendency to differentiate among stimuli so that stimuli that are related to the original conditioned stimulus, but not identical to it, fail to elicit a conditioned response.

Figure 5.3 Stimulus Generalization and Discrimination
In stimulus generalization, a conditioned response generalizes to stimuli that are similar to the original conditioned stimulus. In stimulus discrimination, the organism differentiates between related stimuli.

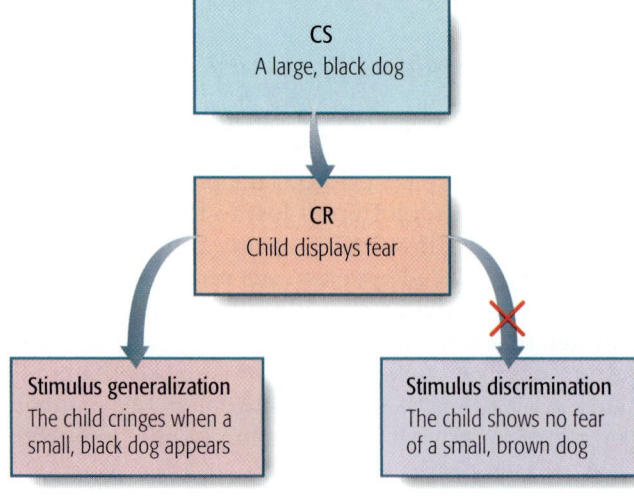

CONCEPT CHART 5.1
Key Concepts in Classical Conditioning

Concept	Description	Example: Fear of Dentistry
Classical conditioning	A form of learning in which a response identical or similar to one originally elicited by an unconditioned stimulus (US) is made in response to a conditioned stimulus (CS) based on the pairing of the two stimuli	The pairing of pain during dental procedures with environmental stimuli in the dentist's office leads to the development of a fear response to the environmental cues alone.
Extinction	Gradual weakening and eventual disappearance of the conditioned response (CR) when the CS is repeatedly presented without the US	The use of anesthetics and painless dental techniques leads to the gradual reduction and elimination of fear of dentistry.
Spontaneous recovery	Spontaneous return of the CR some time after extinction occurs	Fear of dentistry returns spontaneously a few months or a few years after extinction.
Stimulus generalization	CR evoked by stimuli that are similar to the original CS	Person shows a fear response when visiting the office of a new dentist.
Stimulus discrimination	CR not evoked by stimuli that are related but not identical to the CS	Person shows a fear response to the sight of a dentist's drill but not to equipment used for cleaning teeth.

and the pairing of the two leads to the acquisition of a CR of fear to the tone alone. Now, let's say the pairings of the tone and the shock continue but are interspersed with a tone of a higher pitch that is not accompanied by a shock. What happens next is that the animal learns to discriminate between the two stimuli, responding with fear to the original tone but remaining calm when the higher-pitched tone is sounded.

Stimulus discrimination in daily life allows us to differentiate between threatening and nonthreatening stimuli. For example, through repeated noneventful encounters with certain breeds of dogs, we may learn to respond with fear to a large dog of an unfamiliar breed but not to the friendly Labrador that lives next door.

Figure 5.3 illustrates the processes of stimulus generalization and stimulus discrimination.

Concept Chart 5.1 presents an overview of the major concepts in classical conditioning.

web Netlab/Understanding Classical Conditioning

Stimulus Characteristics
That Strengthen Conditioned Responses

Psychologists have identified several key factors relating to the timing and intensity of stimuli that serve to strengthen conditioned responses:

1. *Frequency of pairings.* Generally, the more often the CS is paired with the US, the stronger and more reliable the conditioned response will be. In some cases, however, even a single pairing can produce a strong conditioned response. An airline passenger who experiences a sudden free-fall during a flight may develop an immediate and enduring fear of flying.

2. *Timing.* The strongest conditioned responses occur when the CS is presented first and remains present throughout the administration of the US. Weaker conditioned responses develop when the CS is presented first but is with-

CONCEPT 5.6
The strength of a classically conditioned response depends on the frequency of pairings and the timing of the stimuli, as well as the intensity of the US.

drawn before the US is introduced. Other timing sequences, such as the simultaneous presentation of the CS and US, produce even weaker conditioned responses, if any at all.

3. *Intensity of US.* A stronger US will typically lead to faster conditioning than a weaker one. For example, a puff of air (US) may be delivered shortly after a conditioned stimulus (e.g., a tone or light) is presented. The air puff produces a reflexive eye-blinking response (UR). After a few pairings, a conditioned eye-blink (CR) occurs in response to the CS (tone or light) alone. A stronger air puff will lead to faster conditioning than a weaker one.

A Cognitive Perspective on Classical Conditioning

Psychologist Robert Rescorla (1967, 1988) challenged the conventional behaviorist view that classical conditioning is explained simply by the repeated pairings of a previously neutral stimulus and an unconditioned stimulus. He argued that conditioning depends on the informational value that the conditioned stimulus acquires in *predicting* the occurrence of the unconditioned stimulus. Consider a study in which Rescorla exposed laboratory rats to a series of electric shocks (US) that were preceded by a tone (CS) either on *all* occasions or on *most,* but not all, occasions. The rats whose shocks were always preceded by the tone learned a conditioned response of fear to the tone alone, whereas the rats whose shocks were usually, but not always, preceded by the tone did not. Rescorla argued that classical conditioning depends on more than the simple pairing of stimuli; it requires that the CS come to reliably predict the occurrence of the US.

Rescorla's perspective on classical conditioning is a cognitive one. In his view, humans and other animals actively seek information that helps them make predictions about important events in their environment. Conditioned stimuli are cues that organisms use to make these predictions. Rescorla's model, which has been supported by other research (Miller, Barnet, & Grahame, 1995), has important survival implications. Dogs and other animals may be more likely to survive if they learn to respond with salivation to cues that food is present, since salivation helps them prepare to swallow food. Animals are also more likely to survive if they learn a fear response (heightened bodily arousal) to cues that signal the presence of threatening stimuli. Consider an animal that hears a sound or gets a whiff of an odor (a CS) previously associated with the presence of a particular predator (a US). By responding quickly with heightened arousal to such a stimulus, the animal is better prepared to take defensive action if the predator appears. Thus, classical conditioning serves as a kind of built-in early warning system.

Rescorla's model also explains why you are likely to develop a fear of dentistry more quickly if you experience pain during each dental visit than if you have pain only every now and then. In other words, the more reliably the CS (dental cues) signals the occurrence of the US (pain), the stronger the conditioned response is likely to be.

Examples of Classical Conditioning

Pavlov's studies might merit only a footnote in the history of psychology if classical conditioning were limited to the salivary responses of dogs. However, Pavlovian conditioning played an important role in psychology, especially in the development of behaviorism. John B. Watson, the founder of behaviorism, believed that Pavlov's principles of conditioning could explain emotional responses in humans. In 1919, Watson set out with Rosalie Rayner, a student who was later to become his wife, to prove that a fear response could be acquired through classical conditioning. After taking a look at Watson and Rayner's experiment, we consider other examples of conditioning in humans.

CONCEPT 5.7

In Rescorla's view, classical conditioning involves a cognitive process by which organisms learn to anticipate events based on cues or signals that reliably predict the events.

Classical Conditioning of Fear Responses

As their subject, Watson and Rayner selected an eleven-month-old boy whom they called Albert B., but who is better known in the annals of psychology as "Little Albert" (Watson & Rayner, 1920). Albert had previously shown no fear of a white rat that was placed near him and had even reached out to stroke the animal (see Figure 5.4). In the experimental procedure, the rat was placed close to Albert, and as he reached for it, the experimenters banged a steel bar with a hammer just behind his head, creating a loud sound. Watson believed that loud sounds naturally make infants cringe and shudder with fear. Sure enough, Albert showed signs of fear when the bar was struck—crying and burying his face in the mattress. Watson and Rayner then repeatedly paired the rat and the loud sound, which resulted in Albert's developing a fear response to the sight of the rat alone. Such an acquired fear response is called a **conditioned emotional reaction (CER)**. Later experiments showed that Albert's fear response had generalized to other furry stimuli, including a dog, a rabbit, and even a Santa Claus mask that Watson had worn.

Let us examine the Watson and Rayner study by applying what we know about classical conditioning. Before conditioning, Albert showed no fear of the white rat; it was a neutral stimulus. The unconditioned stimulus (US) was the loud banging sound, a stimulus that naturally elicits a fear response (UR) in young children. Through repeated pairings of the white rat and the banging sound (US), the white rat alone (CS) came to elicit a fear response (CR).

Though the Little Albert experiment is among the most famous studies in psychology, it would not pass muster with the stricter ethical standards in place today. Exposing a child to intense fear, even with the parents' permission, fails to adhere to the responsibility that investigators have to safeguard the welfare of their research subjects. In addition, Watson and Rayner made no attempt to undo or extinguish Albert's fear of white rats, as present ethical codes would require, although they did discuss techniques they might use to do so.

Many **phobias**, or excessive fears, such as Albert's fear of white rats or the fear of dentistry, may be acquired through classical conditioning. In one example, a thirty-four-year-old woman had been terrified of riding on elevators ever since a childhood incident in which she and her grandmother were trapped on an elevator for hours. For her, the single pairing of previously neutral stimuli (cues associated with riding on elevators) and a traumatic experience was sufficient to produce an enduring phobia (fear of elevators). In some cases, the original conditioning experiences may be lost to memory, or they may have occurred even before language developed (as in Albert's case).

Early work on the conditioning of fear responses set the stage for the development of a model of therapy called **behavior therapy**, which is the systematic application of the principles of learning to help people overcome phobias and other problem behaviors, including addictive behaviors, sexual dysfunctions, and childhood behavior problems. We discuss specific applications of behavior therapy in Chapter 12.

CONCEPT 5.8
Classical conditioning helps explain the development of conditioned emotional reactions, such as conditioned fear responses.

THINK
About It

What Do You Fear?

Have you developed any fears you find troubling or that interfere with your daily life? Based on your reading of the chapter, what do you think might be the origin of these fears? How are you coping with them? Have you talked to anyone about them? Is there anyone you might contact to help you overcome them, such as a college health official or a health care provider or clinic in your area?

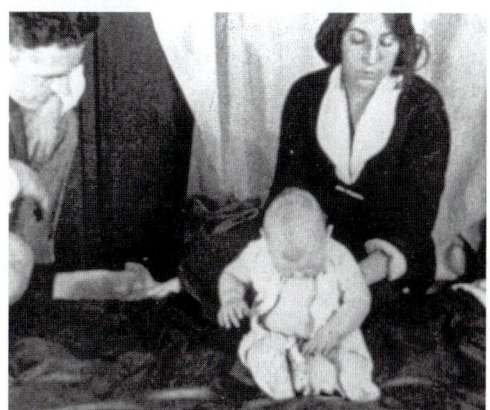

John Watson and Rosalie Rayner with Little Albert

Figure 5.4
The Conditioning of "Little Albert"

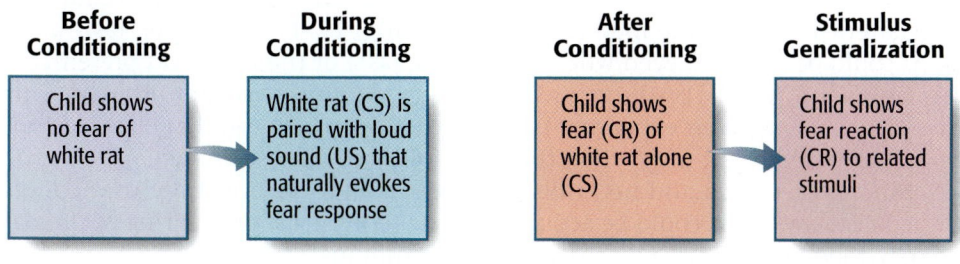

Before Conditioning	During Conditioning	After Conditioning	Stimulus Generalization
Child shows no fear of white rat	White rat (CS) is paired with loud sound (US) that naturally evokes fear response	Child shows fear (CR) of white rat alone (CS)	Child shows fear reaction (CR) to related stimuli

conditioned emotional reaction (CER) An emotional response to a particular stimulus acquired through classical conditioning.

phobias   Excessive fears of particular objects or situations.

behavior therapy   A form of therapy that involves the systematic application of the principles of learning.

Classical Conditioning of Positive Emotions

It's not just negative emotions like fear that can be classically conditioned. Perhaps you've had the experience of suddenly smiling or feeling cheerful, or experiencing a tinge of sexual arousal, when you hear a certain song on the radio. Chances are the song evoked past experiences associated with pleasant emotions or sexual arousal. Similarly, feelings of nostalgia may represent classically conditioned responses elicited by stimuli associated with pleasant experiences in the past—a whiff of perfume or perhaps even the mist in the air on a spring day.

Classical Conditioning of Drug Cravings

People with chemical dependencies frequently encounter drug cravings, especially when they undergo drug withdrawal or go "cold turkey." Though cravings may have a physiological basis (they constitute part of the withdrawal syndrome for addictive drugs), classical conditioning can also contribute to these strong desires. Cravings may be elicited by cues in the environment that were associated with previous drug use (O'Brien et al., 1992; Weiss & Mirin, 1987). A person battling alcoholism who goes "on the wagon" may experience strong cravings for a drink whenever he or she passes a familiar "watering hole" or socializes with former "drinking buddies." Cravings may represent conditioned responses that continue to be elicited long after the physiological signs of withdrawal have passed.

Drug Cravings as Conditioned Responses Drug cravings may be conditioned responses elicited by exposure to cues (conditioned stimuli) associated with drug-using behavior.

The conditioning model of drug cravings is supported by research showing that people with alcoholism salivate more at the sight and odor of alcohol than do nonalcoholic subjects (Monti et al., 1987). Salivating to the sound of a tone may be harmless enough, but salivating when looking at a picture of a Scotch bottle in a magazine can be dangerous to a person struggling with alcoholism. Not surprisingly, drug counselors encourage recovering drug and alcohol abusers to avoid cues associated with their former drug-use patterns.

Classical Conditioning of Taste Aversions

The principles of classical conditioning can also be used to explain **conditioned taste aversions**, such as my disgust for eggs (Limebeer & Parker, 2000). Psychologist John Garcia was the first to demonstrate experimentally the role of classical conditioning in the acquisition of taste aversions. Garcia and his colleague Bob Koelling noticed something unusual in the behavior of rats that had been exposed to nausea-inducing radiation. The rats developed an aversion or "conditioned nausea" to flavored water sweetened with saccharine when the water was paired with the nausea-producing radiation (Garcia & Koelling, 1966). In classical conditioning terms, the radiation is the US; the nausea it produces is the UR; the flavored water is the CS; and the aversion (nausea) the CS elicits on its own is the CR.

In related work, Garcia was able to demonstrate that an aversion to a particular food could also be classically conditioned by administering a nausea-inducing drug after the rats ate the food (Garcia & Koelling, 1971). Moreover, taste aversions could be acquired even when the CS (the taste of the food) was presented a few hours before the US (the nausea-inducing stimulus) was administered. This discovery shocked their experimental colleagues, who believed that classical conditioning could occur only when the CS is followed almost immediately by the US. Moreover, Garcia and his colleagues were able to demonstrate that conditioned taste aversions could be acquired on the basis of a single pairing of the flavor of a food or drink with a nausea-inducing stimulus.

Conditioned Taste Aversion in Coyotes Experimenters left sheep carcasses on the range after injecting them with a nausea-producing chemical. Shortly after eating the meat from one of these carcasses, a coyote would fall to the ground with extreme nausea.

Like other forms of classical conditioning, conditioned taste aversions have clear survival benefits. Our ancestors lived without the benefit of refrigeration or preservatives. Acquiring an aversion to foods whose rancid smells and tastes sickened them would have helped them avoid such foods in the future. In a classic study that literally applied the principles of classical conditioning on the range, John Garcia and his colleagues came up with an ingenious way to help sheep ranchers protect their sheep from coyotes (Gustavson & Garcia, 1974; Gustavson et al., 1974). At the time of the study, free-ranging coyotes were killing thousands of sheep, and ranchers seeking to protect their flocks were killing so many coyotes that their survival as a species was endangered. It was therefore important to find a way of stopping the coyotes' destructive behavior without killing them. As an experiment, the researchers injected sheep carcasses with a poison that would sicken but not kill the coyotes and scattered the carcasses over the range. Not only did sheep killings drop, but some coyotes developed such an aversion to the taste of the sheep meat that they ran away just at the sight or smell of sheep.

John Garcia

 **PsychAssist: Classical Conditioning in the Development of Taste Aversions**

Conditioning the Immune System

In a landmark study, Robert Ader and Nicholas Cohen (1982) showed that classical conditioning extends even to the workings of the **immune system**. The immune system is the body system that protects us from disease-causing organisms. These researchers simultaneously gave rats saccharin-sweetened water (CS) and a drug (US) that suppresses immune-system responses (UR). After several pairings, immune suppression (CR) occurred in response to drinking the sweetened water alone. Other investigators have found that conditioned immune suppression occurs with different conditioned stimuli, such as odors and sounds, as well as in different species, including guinea pigs, mice, and even humans (Kusnecov, 2001).

The ability to learn an immune-suppressant response through classical conditioning may have important health implications for humans. In people who receive organ transplants, the immune system attacks the transplanted organs as foreign objects. Perhaps classical conditioning can be used to suppress the tendency of the body to reject transplanted organs, lessening the need for immune-suppressant drugs. This hope was bolstered by findings that classical conditioning of immune suppression increased the survival rate of mice that had undergone heart-tissue transplants (Grochowicz et al., 1991). Whether similar procedures can be used successfully with humans who undergo organ transplants remains to be

CONCEPT 5.11
Investigators have found that even immune-system responses can be classically conditioned.

conditioned taste aversions   Aversions to particular tastes acquired through classical conditioning.

immune system   The body's system of defense against disease.

seen. We may also be able to use classical conditioning to give the immune system a boost in its fight against disease, perhaps even strengthening the body's ability to defend itself against cancer (Hollis, 1997). One intriguing possibility involves pairing odors and other conditioned stimuli with drugs that enhance the functioning of the immune system. These stimuli might be used to trigger an immune-system response on their own, lessening the need for drugs that may have adverse side effects.

MODULE 5.1 REVIEW

Classical Conditioning: Learning Through Association

CONCEPT CHECK

1. The process by which conditioned responses occur in response to stimuli that are similar to conditioned stimuli is called _____.

2. Which of the following does *not* affect the strength of conditioned responses?
   a. frequency of pairings of the CS with the US
   b. timing of the presentation of the CS and US
   c. intensity of the US
   d. alternation of a US-CS presentation with a CR-UR presentation

3. In John Garcia's study of conditioned taste aversions, rats refused to drink from the plastic water bottles in the chambers in which they were given radiation because they associated the plastic-tasting water with the nausea from the radiation. In classical conditioning terms, the radiation in Garcia's research on taste aversion is the _____.
   a. UR   b. CS   c. US   d. CR

4. Robert Rescorla's study, in which a group of rats was often, but not always, given a shock after hearing a tone, suggests that
   a. under such conditions, rats will always learn to respond to the CS.
   b. there is a cognitive component in classical conditioning.
   c. whether the CS reliably predicts the US does not seem to be a factor in conditioning.
   d. rats respond to a shock but not to a tone.

5. In Watson and Rayner's study of "Little Albert," the child became frightened of a white rat and similar stimuli because
   a. children are naturally afraid of white rats.
   b. a loud noise occurred whenever the rat was in Albert's presence.
   c. the rat was repeatedly paired with a neutral stimulus.
   d. Albert had a traumatic experience with a rat.

MODULE 5.2 Operant Conditioning: Learning Through Consequences

- **What is Thorndike's Law of Effect?**
- **What is operant conditioning?**
- **What are the different types of reinforcers?**
- **What are schedules of reinforcement, and how do they differ?**
- **How are schedules of reinforcement related to learning?**
- **Why are psychologists concerned about the use of punishment?**
- **What are some applications of operant conditioning?**

Classical conditioning can explain how we learn relatively simple, reflexive responses, such as salivation and eye-blinks, as well as emotional responses associated with fear and disgust. But classical conditioning cannot explain how we learn the more complex behaviors that are part and parcel of our daily experiences. You get up in the morning, dress, go to work or school, prepare meals, take care of household chores, run errands, socialize with friends, and perhaps have an hour or two to relax at the end of the day. To account for such behaviors, we need to consider a form of learning called *operant conditioning*. With classical conditioning, we examined learning that results from the association between stimuli before a response occurs. With operant conditioning, we explore learning that results from the association of a response with its consequences. As you will see, in this form of learning, responses are acquired and strengthened by the effects they have in the environment.

We focus on the contributions of two American psychologists: Edward Thorndike, whose Law of Effect was the first systematic attempt to describe how behavior is affected by its consequences, and B. F. Skinner, whose experimental work laid out many of the principles of operant conditioning.

Thorndike and the Law of Effect

Edward Thorndike (1874–1947) used animals in his studies of learning because he found them easier to work with than people (Hunt, 1993). He constructed a device called a "puzzle box"—a cage in which the animal (usually a cat) had to perform a simple act (such as pulling a looped string or pushing a pedal) in order to make its escape and reach a dish of food placed within its view just outside the cage (see Figure 5.5). The animal would first engage in seemingly random behaviors until it accidentally performed the response that released the door. Thorndike argued that the animals did not employ reasoning, insight, or any other form of higher intelligence to find their way to the exit. Rather, it was through a random process of *trial and error* that they gradually eliminated useless responses and eventually chanced upon the successful behavior. Successful responses were then "stamped in" by the pleasure they produced and became more likely to be repeated in the future.

Based on his observations, Thorndike (1905) proposed a principle that he called the **Law of Effect**, which holds that the tendency for a response to occur depends on the effects it has on the environment. More specifically, Thorndike's Law of Effect states that responses that have satisfying effects are strengthened and become more likely to occur again in a given situation, while responses that lead to discomfort are weakened and become less likely to recur. Modern psychologists call the first part of the Law of Effect *reinforcement* and the second part *punishment* (L. T. Benjamin, 1988).

Thorndike went on to study how the principles of animal learning that he formulated could be applied to human behavior and especially to education. He believed that while human behavior is certainly more complex than animal behavior, it, too, can be explained on the basis of trial-and-error learning in which accidental successes become "stamped in" by positive consequences.

CONCEPT 5.12
According to Thorndike's Law of Effect, we are more likely to repeat responses that have satisfying effects and are less likely to repeat those that lead to discomfort.

Figure 5.5
Thorndike's Puzzle Box
Cats placed in Thorndike's puzzle box learned to make their escape through a random process of trial and error.

Law of Effect   Thorndike's principle that responses that have satisfying effects are more likely to recur, while those that have unpleasant effects are less likely to recur.

B. F. Skinner and Operant Conditioning

Thorndike laid the groundwork for an explanation of learning based on the association between responses and their consequences. It would fall to another American psychologist, B. F. Skinner (1904–1990), to develop a more formal model of this type of learning, which he called *operant conditioning.*

Skinner was arguably not only the most famous psychologist of his time but also the most controversial. What made him famous was his ability to bring behaviorist principles into the public eye through his books, articles in popular magazines, and public appearances. What made him controversial was his belief in **radical behaviorism**, which holds that behavior, whether animal or human, is completely determined by environmental and genetic influences. Free will, according to Skinner, is but an illusion or a myth. Though the staunch behaviorism he espoused was controversial in his own time and remains so today, there is no doubt that his concept of operant conditioning alone merits him a place among the pioneers of modern psychology.

Like Watson, Skinner was a strict behaviorist who believed that psychologists should limit themselves to the study of observable behavior. Because "private events," such as thoughts and feelings, cannot be observed, he believed they have no place in a scientific account of behavior. For Skinner, the mind was a "black box" whose contents cannot be illuminated by science.

Skinner allowed that some responses occur reflexively, as Pavlov had demonstrated. But classical conditioning is limited to explaining how new stimuli can elicit existing behaviors, such as salivation. It cannot account for new behaviors, such as the behavior of the experimental animals in Thorndike's puzzle box. Skinner found in Thorndike's work a guiding principle that behavior is shaped by its consequences. However, he rejected Thorndike's mentalistic concept that consequences influence behavior because they produce "satisfying effects." Skinner held that organisms learn responses that *operate* on the environment to produce consequences; he therefore called this learning process *operant conditioning.*

Skinner studied animal learning using a device we now call a **Skinner box**. The Skinner box is a cage that contains a food-release mechanism the animal activates when it responds in a certain way—for example, by pressing a lever or pushing a button.

Through **operant conditioning**, organisms learn responses, such as pressing a bar, that produce changes in the environment (release of food). In this form of learning, the consequences of a response determine the likelihood that the response will occur again. The response itself is called an **operant response** or, more simply, an "operant." Behaviors that produce rewarding effects are strengthened—that is, they become more likely to occur again. In effect, a well-trained operant response becomes a habit (Staddon & Cerutti, 2003). For example, if your teacher responds to a question only if you first raise your hand, you will become more likely to develop the habit of raising your hand before asking a question.

Operant conditioning is also called *instrumental learning* since the behavior is instrumental in bringing about rewarding consequences. The term **reinforcer** refers to a stimulus or event that increases the likelihood that the behavior it follows will be repeated. For example, the act of answering questions when students raise their hands is a reinforcer.

Skinner observed that the longer reinforcement is delayed, the weaker its effects will be. An animal in the Skinner box or a child in the classroom will learn the correct responses faster when reinforcement follows the response as quickly as possible. In general, learning progresses more slowly as the delay between response and reinforcement increases.

Skinner also showed how operant conditioning could explain some forms of **superstitious behavior**. Consider a baseball player who hits a home run after a long slump and then wears the same pair of socks he had on at the time for good luck in every remaining game of the season. The superstitious behavior could be

---

CONCEPT 5.13
B. F. Skinner believed that human behavior is completely determined by environmental and genetic influences and that the concept of free will is but an illusion or myth.

---

radical behaviorism   The philosophical position that free will is an illusion or myth and that human and animal behavior is completely determined by environmental and genetic influences.

Skinner box   An experimental apparatus developed by B. F. Skinner for studying relationships between reinforcement and behavior.

operant conditioning   The process of learning in which the consequences of a response determine the probability that the response will be repeated.

operant response   A response that operates on the environment to produce certain consequences.

reinforcer   A stimulus or event that increases the probability that the response it follows will be repeated.

superstitious behavior   In Skinner's view, behavior acquired through coincidental association of a response and a reinforcement.

discriminative stimulus   A cue that signals that reinforcement is available if the subject makes a particular response.

positive reinforcement   The strengthening of a response through the introduction of a stimulus after the response occurs.

negative reinforcement   The strengthening of a response through the removal of a stimulus after the response occurs.

understood in terms of mistaking a mere coincidence between a response (wearing a particular pair of socks) and a reinforcement (home run) for a connection between the two.

Many commonly held superstitions, from not stepping on cracks in the sidewalk to throwing salt over one's shoulder for good luck, are part of our cultural heritage, handed down from generation to generation. Perhaps there was a time when these behaviors were accidentally reinforced, but they have become so much a part of our cultural tradition that people no longer recall their origins.

In the next sections, we review the basic principles of operant conditioning.

Principles of Operant Conditioning

Experimental work by Skinner and other psychologists established the basic principles of operant conditioning, including those we consider here: discriminative stimuli, positive and negative reinforcement, primary and secondary reinforcers, shaping, and extinction.

Discriminative Stimuli

Put a rat in a Skinner box and reinforce it with food when it presses a bar, but only if it makes that response when a light is turned on. When the light is off, it receives no reinforcement no matter how many times it presses the bar. How do you think the rat will respond? Clearly, the rate of response will be much higher when the light is on than when it is off. The light is an example of a **discriminative stimulus**, a cue that signals that reinforcement is available if the subject makes a particular response.

Our physical and social environment is teeming with discriminative stimuli. When is the better time to ask someone for a favor: when the person appears to be down in the dumps or is smiling and appears cheerful? You know the answer. The reason you know is that you have learned that a person's facial cues serve as discriminative stimuli that signal times when requests for help are more likely to be positively received. You also know that your professors are more likely to respond to your raising your hand if they are facing you than if their backs are turned. A green traffic light is another type of discriminative stimulus—one that signals driving a car through an intersection is likely to be reinforced by a safe passage through the intersection.

Positive and Negative Reinforcement

Skinner distinguished between two types of reinforcement, *positive reinforcement* and *negative reinforcement*. In **positive reinforcement**, a response is strengthened by the introduction of a stimulus after the response occurs. This type of stimulus is called a *positive reinforcer* or *reward*. Examples of positive reinforcers include food, money, and social approval. You are more likely to continue working at your job if you receive a steady paycheck (a positive reinforcer) than if the checks stop coming. You are more likely to study hard for exams if your efforts are rewarded with good grades (another positive reinforcer) than if you consistently fail (see Figure 5.6).

In **negative reinforcement**, a response is strengthened when it leads to the removal of an "aversive" (unpleasant or painful) stimulus. Negative reinforcers are aversive stimuli such as loud noise, cold, pain, nagging, or a child's crying. We are more likely to repeat behaviors that lead to their removal. A parent's behavior in picking up a crying baby to comfort it is negatively reinforced when the baby stops crying; in this case, the aversive stimulus of crying has been removed.

Note that both forms of reinforcement strengthen responses. The difference is that in positive reinforcement, behaviors are strengthened when they are followed by the *introduction* of a stimulus, whereas in negative reinforcement, behaviors are strengthened when they lead to the *removal* of a stimulus.

CONCEPT 5.14
Skinner showed how superstitious behavior can be learned through the coincidental pairing of responses and reinforcement.

PsychAssist: Reinforcement Versus Punishment in Operant Conditioning

CONCEPT 5.15
Discriminative stimuli set the stage for reinforcement—a useful thing to know if you want to ask someone for a favor.

Red Light, Green Light A green light is a discriminative stimulus signaling that driving a car through an intersection is likely to be reinforced by a safe passage through the intersection.

CONCEPT 5.16
In positive reinforcement, the introduction of a reward (positive reinforcer) after a response occurs strengthens the response. In negative reinforcement, the removal of an aversive stimulus (negative reinforcer) after a response occurs strengthens the response.

Figure 5.6 Types of Reinforcers
The introduction of a positive reinforcer after a behavior occurs strengthens the behavior. The removal of a negative reinforcer after a behavior occurs strengthens the behavior. Can you think of examples of positive and negative reinforcers that have influenced your behavior?

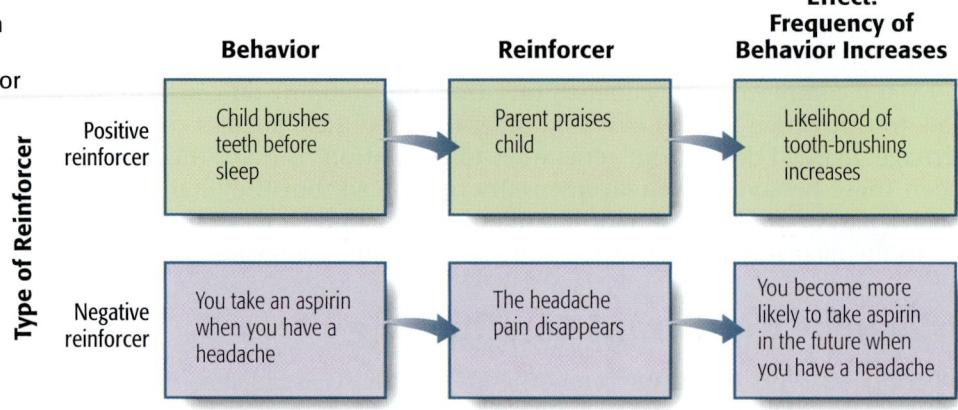

Type of Reinforcer	Behavior	Reinforcer	Effect: Frequency of Behavior Increases
Positive reinforcer	Child brushes teeth before sleep	Parent praises child	Likelihood of tooth-brushing increases
Negative reinforcer	You take an aspirin when you have a headache	The headache pain disappears	You become more likely to take aspirin in the future when you have a headache

Negative reinforcement can be a "two-way street." Crying is the only means infants have of letting us know when they are hungry or wet or have other needs. It is also an aversive stimulus to anyone within earshot. It is a negative reinforcer because parents will repeat behaviors that succeed in stopping the infant's crying. The baby's crying is positively reinforced by the parents' responses. (Like Skinner's pigeons, parents may need to do some "pecking around" to find out what Junior wants: "Let's see, he's not wet, so he must be hungry.")

Negative reinforcement may have undesirable effects in some situations. Consider a child who throws a tantrum in a toy store when the parent refuses the child's request for a particular toy. The child may have learned from past experience that tantrums get results. In operant learning terms, when a tantrum does get results, the child is positively reinforced for throwing the tantrum (because the parent "gives in"), while the parent is negatively reinforced for complying with the child's demands because the tantrum stops. Unfortunately, this pattern of reinforcement only makes the recurrence of tantrums more likely.

Who Is Reinforcing Whom?   Reinforcement is not a one-way street. Children and parents continually reinforce each other. By stopping a tantrum when she gets her way, the child negatively reinforces the parent. Unwittingly, perhaps, the parent positively reinforces tantrum-throwing behavior by giving in. How would you suggest the parent change these reinforcement patterns?

Primary and Secondary Reinforcers

At sixteen months of age, my daughter Daniella became intrigued with the contents of my wallet. It wasn't those greenbacks with the pictures of Washington and Lincoln that caught her eye. No, she ignored the paper money but was fascinated with the holograms on the plastic credit cards. The point here is that some stimuli, called **primary reinforcers**, are intrinsically rewarding because they satisfy basic biological needs or drives. Their reward or reinforcement value does not depend on learning. Primary reinforcers include food, water, sleep, relief from pain or loud noise, oxygen, sexual stimulation, and novel visual stimuli, such as holograms.

Other reinforcers, called **secondary reinforcers**, acquire their reinforcement value through a learning process by which they become associated with primary reinforcers. Money is a secondary reinforcer (also called a *conditioned reinforcer*). It acquires reinforcement value because we learn it can be exchanged for more basic reinforcers, such as food or clothing. Other types of secondary reinforcers include good grades, awards, and praise. Much of our daily behavior is influenced by secondary reinforcers in the form of expressions of approval from others.

CONCEPT 5.17
Some reinforcers are rewarding because they satisfy basic biological needs; other reinforcers acquire reward value as the result of experience.

Shaping

Rats don't naturally press levers or bars. If you place a rat in a Skinner box, it may eventually happen upon the correct response through trial and error. The experimenter can help the animal learn the correct response more quickly through a process called **shaping**. Shaping is an application of the **method of successive approximations**. In this method, the experimenter reinforces a series of responses that represent ever-closer approximations of the correct response. The experimenter may at first reinforce the rat when it moves to the part of the cage that contains the bar. Once this behavior is established, reinforcement occurs only if the animal moves closer to the bar, then closer still, then touches the bar with its paw, and then actually presses the bar. If you have ever observed animal trainers at work, you will recognize how shaping is used to train animals to perform a complex sequence of behaviors.

We put the method of successive approximations into practice in our daily lives when we attempt to teach someone a new skill, especially one involving a complex set of behaviors. When teaching a child to swim, the instructor may deliver verbal reinforcement (telling the child he or she is doing "great") each time the child successfully performs a new step in the series of steps needed to develop proper form.

CONCEPT 5.18
Organisms can learn complex behaviors through a process of shaping, or reinforcement of successive approximations to the desired behaviors.

THINK About It

Changing Reinforcement Patterns

The parents of a thirteen-year-old boy would like him to help out more around the house, including doing his share of the dishes. After a meal at which it is his turn to do the dishes, he first refuses, pleading that he has other things to do that are more important. Frustrated with his refusal, his parents start yelling at him and continue until he complies with their request. But as he washes the dishes, his mother notices that he is doing a very poor job, so she relieves him of his duty and finishes the job herself.

What type of reinforcement did the parents use to gain the boy's compliance? What behaviors of the parents did the boy reinforce by complying with their request? What behavior did the mother inadvertently strengthen by relieving the boy of his chores? Based on your reading of the text, how would you suggest this family change these reinforcement patterns?

primary reinforcers   Reinforcers, such as food or sexual stimulation, that are naturally rewarding because they satisfy basic biological needs or drives.

secondary reinforcers   Learned reinforcers, such as money, that develop their reinforcing properties because of their association with primary reinforcers.

shaping   A process of learning that involves the reinforcement of increasingly closer approximations of the desired response.

method of successive approximations   The method used to shape behavior by reinforcing ever-closer approximations of the desired response.

CONCEPT 5.19

In operant conditioning, extinction is the weakening and eventual elimination of a response that occurs when the response is no longer reinforced.

Extinction

You'll recall from Module 5.1 that extinction of classically conditioned responses occurs when the conditioned stimulus is repeatedly presented in the absence of the unconditioned stimulus. Similarly, in operant conditioning, extinction is the process by which responses are weakened and eventually eliminated when the response is repeatedly performed but is no longer reinforced. Thus, the bar-pressing response of a rat in the Skinner box will eventually be extinguished if reinforcement (food) is withheld. If you repeatedly raise your hand in class but aren't called upon, you will probably in time stop raising your hand.

Schedules of Reinforcement

In the Skinner box, an animal can be reinforced for each peck or bar press, or for some portion of pecks or bar presses. One of Skinner's major contributions was to show how these different **schedules of reinforcement**—predetermined plans for timing the delivery of reinforcement—influence learning.

CONCEPT 5.20

The schedule by which reinforcements are dispensed influences the rate of learning and resistance to extinction.

web. Netlab/Schedules of Reinforcement

In a **schedule of continuous reinforcement**, reinforcement follows each instance of the operant response. The rat in the Skinner box receives a food pellet every time it presses the lever. Similarly, if a light comes on every time you flick a light switch, you will quickly learn to flick the switch each time you enter a darkened room. Operant responses are learned most rapidly under a schedule of continuous reinforcement. However, continuous reinforcement also leads to rapid extinction when reinforcement is withheld. How long will it take before you stop flicking the light switch if the light fails to come on because the bulb needs replacing? Just one or two flicks of the switch without results may be sufficient to extinguish the response. But extinction does not mean the response is forgotten or lost to memory (Baeyens, Eelen, & Crombez, 1995). It is likely to return quickly once reinforcement is reinstated—that is, once you install a new bulb.

Responses are more resistant to extinction under a **schedule of partial reinforcement** than under a schedule of continuous reinforcement (Rescorla, 1999). In a schedule of partial reinforcement, only a portion of responses is reinforced. Because this makes it more unlikely that an absence of reinforcement will be noticed, it takes a longer time for the response to fade out.

Schedules of partial reinforcement are much more common than schedules of continuous reinforcement in daily life. Think what it would mean to be reinforced on a continuous basis. You would receive a reinforcer (reward) each time you came to class, cracked open a textbook, or arrived at work on time. However desirable this rate of reinforcement might seem, it is no doubt impossible to achieve in daily life. Fortunately, partial-reinforcement schedules produce overall high response rates and have the added advantage of greater resistance to extinction.

CONCEPT 5.21

There are four types of partial-reinforcement schedules: fixed-ratio, variable-ratio, fixed-interval, and variable-interval schedules.

Partial reinforcement is administered under two general kinds of schedules: *ratio schedules* and *interval schedules*. In ratio schedules, reinforcement is based on the *number* of responses. In interval schedules, reinforcement is based on the *timing* of responses. Within each type, reinforcement can be administered on either a *fixed* or *variable* basis.

Figure 5.7 shows typical rates of response under different schedules of partial reinforcement. Notice how much faster response rates are in ratio schedules than in interval schedules. To account for this difference, remember that in ratio schedules, reinforcement depends on the number of responses and not on the length of time elapsed since the last reinforcement, as is the case with interval schedules.

schedules of reinforcement
Predetermined plans for timing the delivery of reinforcement.

schedule of continuous reinforcement
A system of dispensing a reinforcement each time an operant response is produced.

schedule of partial reinforcement   A system of reinforcement in which only a portion of responses is reinforced.

Fixed-Ratio (FR) Schedule

In a fixed-ratio (FR) schedule, reinforcement is given after a specified number of correct responses. For example, in an "FR-6" schedule, reinforcement is given after each sixth response. The classic example of fixed-ratio schedules is piecework, in

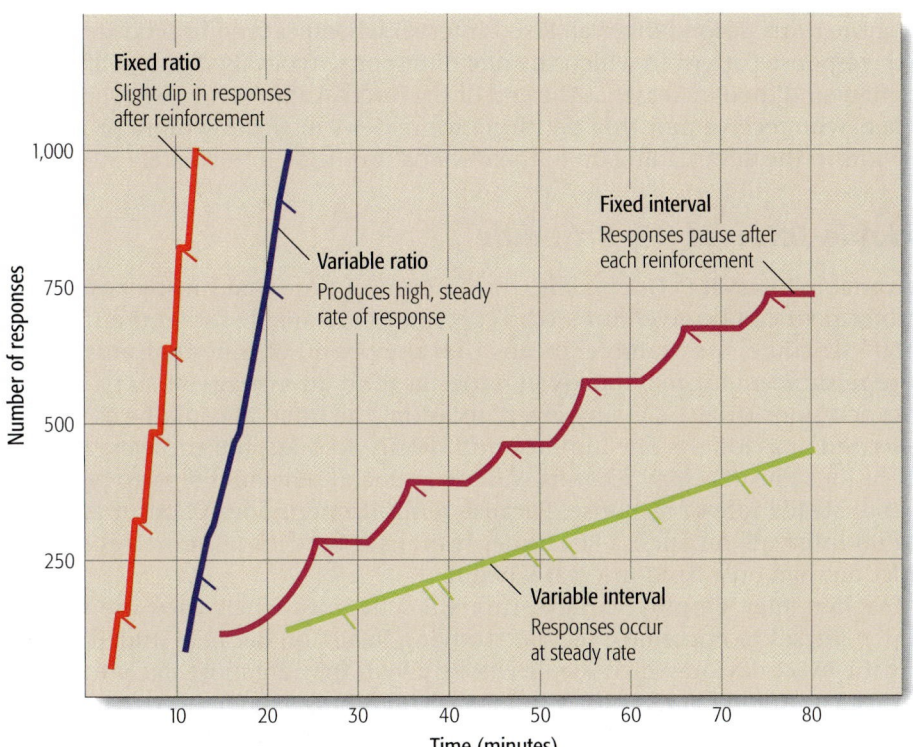

Figure 5.7   Rates of Response Under Different Schedules of Partial Reinforcement Here we see rates of response we typically find under different schedules of partial reinforcement. The diagonal lines that intersect with these response curves show the times at which reinforcement is given. Notice how ratio schedules produce much faster response rates than the interval schedules. However, there is usually a short pause following each reinforced set of responses under fixed-ratio schedules. Fixed-interval schedules produce a "scalloped" effect with long pauses following each reinforcement, while variable-interval schedules typically produce a slow but steady rate of response.

Source: Adapted from Skinner, 1961.

which workers are paid according to the number of items they produce. Fixed-ratio schedules produce a constant, high level of response, with a slight dip in responses occurring after each reinforcement (see Figure 5.7). On fixed-ratio schedules, the faster people work, the more items they produce and the more money they earn. However, quality may suffer if quantity alone determines how reinforcements are dispensed.

Variable-Ratio (VR) Schedule

In a variable-ratio (VR) schedule, the number of correct responses needed before reinforcement is given varies around some average number. For example, a "VR-20" schedule means that reinforcement is administered after an average of every twenty responses. In some instances, reinforcement may be delivered after only two, five, or ten responses; at other times, thirty or forty responses may be required. Gambling is an example of behavior that is reinforced on a variable-ratio schedule. With a slot machine, for instance, a win (reinforcement) may occur after perhaps one, two, ten, or fifty or more tries. (No wonder it's called a one-armed bandit.)

Variable-ratio schedules typically produce high, steady rates of response (see Figure 5.7). They are also more resistant to extinction than fixed-ratio schedules since one cannot reliably predict whether a given number of responses will be rewarded. Perhaps this explains why many people routinely buy state lottery tickets even though they may win only piddling amounts every now and then. As an advertisement for one state lottery puts it, "Hey, you never know."

Fixed-Interval (FI) Schedule

In a fixed-interval (FI) schedule, reinforcement is given only for a correct response made after a fixed amount of time has elapsed since the last reinforcement. On an "FI-30" schedule, for example, an animal in a Skinner box receives a food pellet if it makes the required response after an interval of thirty seconds has elapsed since the last food pellet was delivered, regardless of the number of responses it made during the thirty-second interval. Fixed-interval schedules tend to produce a "scalloped" response pattern in which the rate of response typically dips just after reinforcement and then increases as the end of the interval approaches (see Figure 5.7). Workers who receive monthly performance reviews may show more productive behaviors in the days leading up to their evaluations than immediately afterward.

Variable-Interval (VI) Schedule

In a variable-interval (VI) schedule, the amount of time that must elapse before reinforcement can be given for a correct response is variable rather than fixed. A "VI-60" schedule, for example, means that the period of time that must elapse before reinforcement may be given varies around an average of sixty seconds across occasions (trials). On any given occasion, the interval could be as short as one second or as long as one hundred and twenty seconds, but the average across all occasions must be sixty seconds. Variable-interval schedules tend to produce a slow but steady rate of response. Because reinforcement doesn't occur after predictable intervals on such a schedule, responses tend to be more resistant to extinction than on a fixed-interval schedule.

Teachers may employ variable-interval schedules when they use surprise ("pop") quizzes to encourage regular studying behavior. Because students never know the exact day on which a quiz will be given, they are more likely to receive reinforcement (good grades) if they study regularly from day to day. With scheduled tests, reinforcement is based on a fixed-interval schedule; that is, rewards for studying become available only at the regular times the tests are given. In this case, we would expect to find the scalloped rate of response that is typical of fixed-interval reinforcement—an increased rate of studying, or perhaps even cramming, just before the test and a decline afterward.

Escape Learning and Avoidance Learning

In **escape learning**, an organism learns to *escape* an aversive stimulus by performing an operant response. The escape behavior is negatively reinforced by the removal of the aversive stimulus. A rat may be taught to press a bar to turn off an electric shock. We may learn to escape from the heat of a summer day by turning on a fan or air conditioner.

In **avoidance learning**, the organism learns to perform a response that *avoids* an aversive stimulus. The rat in a Skinner box may receive a signal (e.g., a tone) that a shock is about to be delivered. The animal learns to avoid the shock by performing the correct response, such as pressing a bar. You open an umbrella before stepping out in the rain to avoid the unpleasant experience of being drenched.

Like other forms of learning, escape learning and avoidance learning may be adaptive in some circumstances but not in others. We learn to apply sunscreen to avoid sunburn, which is adaptive. But skipping regular dental visits to avoid unpleasant or painful dental procedures is not, as it can lead to more serious dental problems or even to tooth loss. People may turn to alcohol or other drugs to escape from their problems or troubling emotions. But the escape is short-lived, and problems resulting from drug or alcohol abuse can quickly compound the person's initial difficulties.

You may at this point wish to review the key concepts in operant conditioning outlined in Concept Chart 5.2.

Punishment

Skinner observed that behaviors that are not reinforced or that are punished are less likely to be repeated. **Punishment** is the flip side of reinforcement. It involves the introduction of an aversive stimulus (e.g., physical pain or harsh criticism) or the removal of a reinforcing stimulus (e.g., turning off the TV) after a response,

CONCEPT 5.22

In escape learning, organisms learn responses that allow them to escape aversive stimuli, whereas in avoidance learning, they learn responses that allow them to avoid aversive stimuli.

escape learning The learning of behaviors that allow an organism to escape from an aversive stimulus.

avoidance learning The learning of behaviors that allow an organism to avoid an aversive stimulus.

punishment The introduction of an aversive stimulus or the removal of a reinforcing stimulus after a response occurs, which leads to the weakening or suppression of the response.

CONCEPT CHART 5.2
Key Concepts in Operant Conditioning

Concept	Description	Example
Nature of operant conditioning	A form of learning in which responses are strengthened by the effects they have in the environment	If students receive answers to their questions only when they raise their hands before asking them, hand-raising behavior is strengthened.
Discriminative stimulus	A stimulus that indicates that reinforcement will be available if the correct response is made	A child learns to answer the phone when it rings and to wait for a dial tone before dialing.
Positive reinforcer	A stimulus or event that makes the response it follows more likely to occur again	Praising children for picking up their clothes increases the likelihood that they will repeat the behavior.
Negative reinforcer	An aversive stimulus whose removal strengthens the preceding behavior and increases the probability that the behavior will be repeated	The annoying sound of a buzzer on an alarm clock increases the likelihood that we will get out of bed to turn it off.
Primary reinforcer	A stimulus that is innately reinforcing because it satisfies basic biological needs or drives	Food, water, and sexual stimulation are primary reinforcers.
Secondary reinforcer	A stimulus whose reinforcement value derives from its association with primary reinforcers	Money, which can be exchanged for food and clothing, is a secondary reinforcer.
Shaping	A process of learning that involves the reinforcement of increasingly closer approximations to the desired response	A boy learns to dress himself when the parent reinforces him for accomplishing each small step in the process.
Extinction	The gradual weakening and elimination of an operant response when it is not reinforced	A girl stops calling out in class without first raising her hand when the teacher fails to respond to her.
Schedule of continuous reinforcement	A schedule for delivering reinforcement every time a correct response is produced	A girl receives praise each time she puts her clothes away.
Schedule of partial reinforcement (fixed-ratio, variable-ratio, fixed-interval, or variable-interval schedule)	A schedule of delivering reinforcement in which only a portion of responses is reinforced	A boy receives praise for putting his clothes away every third time he does it (fixed-ratio schedule).
Escape learning	Learning responses that result in escape from an aversive stimulus	A motorist learns detours that provide an escape from congested traffic.
Avoidance learning	Learning responses that result in avoidance of an aversive stimulus	A person leaves for work an hour early to avoid heavy traffic.

which leads to the weakening or suppression of the response (see Figure 5.8). In physical punishment—spanking, for example—an aversive stimulus (pain) is applied following an undesirable behavior. Other forms of punishment include imposing monetary penalties (e.g., parking or traffic tickets), taking away privileges (e.g., grounding teenagers), or removing a misbehaving child from a reinforcing environment ("time-out").

Figure 5.8 Types of Punishment
Punishment involves the introduction of an aversive stimulus or the removal of a reinforcing stimulus to weaken or suppress a behavior.

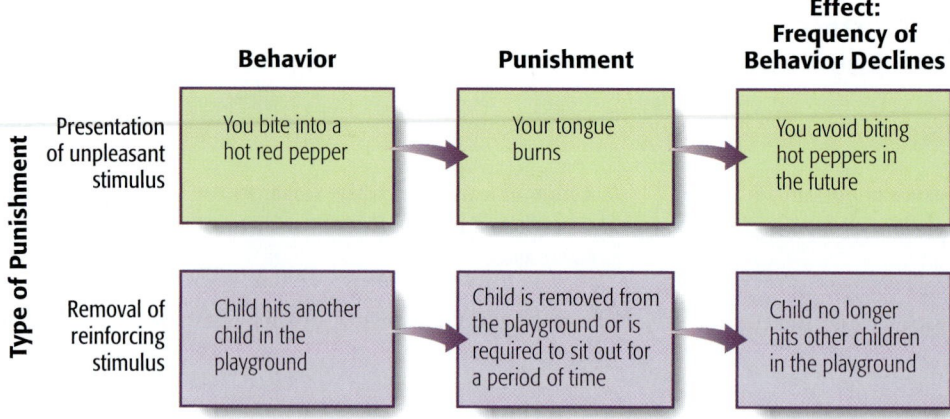

Punishment is often confused with negative reinforcement, since both rely on aversive stimuli. But here's the difference: With punishment, the *introduction* of an aversive stimulus or negative consequence (e.g., a time-out) after a behavior occurs *weakens* or *suppresses* the behavior (hitting other children in the playground). With negative reinforcement, the *removal* of an aversive stimulus (a baby's crying) after a behavior occurs *strengthens* the behavior (picking up the baby).

Psychologists and pediatricians encourage parents not to rely on punishment as a means of disciplining their children; instead, they recommend reinforcing desirable behaviors (American Academy of Pediatrics, 1998; Gershoff, 2002a, 2002b). Punishment, especially physical punishment, has many drawbacks, including the following:

CONCEPT 5.23

Though punishment may suppress or weaken behavior, psychologists generally advise parents not to rely on punishment as a means of disciplining their children.

- *Punishment may suppress undesirable behavior, but it doesn't eliminate it.* The punished behavior often returns when the punishing stimulus is withdrawn. For example, the child who is punished for misbehavior may perform the undesirable behavior when the parents aren't looking.

- *Punishment does not teach new behaviors.* Punishment may suppress an undesirable behavior, but it does not help the child acquire a more appropriate behavior in its place.

- *Punishment can have undesirable consequences.* Punishment, especially physical punishment, can lead to strong negative emotions in children, such as anger, hostility, and fear directed toward the parent or other punishing agent. Fear may also generalize. Children repeatedly punished for poor performance in school may lose confidence in themselves or develop a fear of failure that handicaps their academic performance. They may begin cutting classes, withdraw from challenging courses, or even drop out of school.

- *Punishment may become abusive.* Stopping a child's undesirable behavior, at least temporarily, may reinforce the parents for using spankings or other forms of physical punishment. This may lead to more frequent physical punishment that crosses the line between discipline and abuse (Gershoff, 2002a, 2002b). Another type of abusive situation occurs when parents turn to ever-harsher forms of punishment when milder punishments fail. Abused children may harbor intense rage or resentment toward the punisher, which they may vent by responding aggressively against that person or other less physically imposing targets, such as peers or siblings.

- *Punishment may represent a form of inappropriate modeling.* When children observe their parents resorting to physical punishment to enforce compliance with their demands, the lesson they learn is that using force is an acceptable way of resolving interpersonal problems.

TABLE 5.1 Comparing Reinforcement and Punishment

	What Happens?	When Does This Occur?	Example	Consequence on Behavior
Positive reinforcement	A positive event or stimulus is introduced	After a response	Your instructor smiles at you (a positive stimulus) when you answer a question correctly.	You become more likely to answer questions in class.
Negative reinforcement	An aversive stimulus is removed	After a response	Buckling the seat belt turns off the annoying buzzer.	You become more likely to buckle your seat belt before starting the engine.
Punishment (application of aversive stimulus)	An aversive stimulus is applied	After a response	A parent scolds a child for slamming a door.	The child becomes less likely to slam doors.
Punishment (removal of a reinforcing stimulus)	A reinforcing stimulus is removed	After a response	A child loses TV privileges for hitting a sibling.	The child becomes less likely to engage in hitting.

Do the drawbacks of punishment mean that it should never be used? There may be some occasions when punishment is appropriate. Parents may need to use punishment to stop children from harming themselves or others (e.g., by running into the street or hitting other children in the playground). But parents should avoid using harsh physical punishment (Foote, 2000). Examples of milder punishments include (1) *verbal reprimand* ("No, Johnny, don't do that. You can get hurt that way"); (2) *removal of a reinforcer,* such as grounding teenagers or taking away a certain number of points or tokens that children receive each week that are exchangeable for tangible reinforcers (toys, special activities); and (3) *time-out,* or temporary removal of a child from a reinforcing environment following misbehavior.

Parents who use punishment should help the child understand why he or she is being punished. Children may think they are being punished because they are "bad." They may think negatively of themselves or fear that Mommy and Daddy no longer love them. Parents need to make clear exactly what behavior is being punished and what the child can do differently in the future. In this way, parents can help children learn more desirable behaviors. Punishment is also more effective when it is combined with positive reinforcement for desirable alternative behaviors. Before going further, you may wish to review Table 5.1, which compares reinforcement and punishment.

Applications of Operant Conditioning

In many ways, the world is like a huge Skinner box. From the time we are small children, reinforcements and punishments mold our behavior. We quickly learn which behaviors earn approval and which incur disapproval. How many thousands upon thousands of reinforcements have shaped your behavior over the years? Would you be taking college courses today were it not for the positive reinforcement you received from an early age for paying attention in class, doing your homework, studying for exams, and getting good grades? Who were the major reinforcing agents in your life? Your mother or father? A favorite uncle or aunt? Your teachers or coaches? Yourself?

Psychologists have developed a number of applications of operant conditioning, including biofeedback training, behavior modification, and programmed instruction.

CONCEPT 5.24
Principles of operant conditioning are used in biofeedback training, behavior modification, and programmed instruction.

Biofeedback Training: Using Your Body's Signals as Reinforcers

Chapter 2 introduced the topic of biofeedback training, a technique for learning to change certain bodily responses, including brain wave patterns and heart rate. Biofeedback training relies on operant conditioning principles. Physiological monitoring devices record changes in bodily responses and transmit the information to the user, typically in the form of auditory signals that provide feedback regarding desirable changes in these responses. The feedback reinforces behaviors (e.g., thinking calming thoughts) that bring about these desirable changes.

Behavior Modification: Putting Learning Principles into Practice

Behavior modification (B-mod) is the systematic application of learning principles to strengthen adaptive behavior and weaken maladaptive behavior. Various learning-based methods are used, especially operant conditioning techniques.

Skinner and his colleagues applied operant conditioning principles in a real-world setting by establishing the first **token economy program** in a mental hospital. In a token economy program, patients receive tokens, such as plastic chips, for performing desired behaviors, such as dressing and grooming themselves, making their beds, or socializing with others. The tokens are exchangeable for positive reinforcers, such as extra privileges. Token economy programs continue to be used in mental hospitals, where they have been successful in improving social functioning and reducing aberrant behavior (Mueser & Liberman, 1995).

Behavior modification programs are also applied in the classroom, where they have produced measurable benefits in academic performance and social interactions and reductions in aggressive and disruptive behaviors and truancy (e.g., Brondolo et al., 1994; Lewis, 1995). Teachers may use tokens or gold stars to reward students for appropriate classroom behavior and academic achievement. Children can use the tokens or gold stars at a later time to "purchase" small prizes or special privileges, such as more recess time.

Parent training programs have helped bring behavior modification into the home (Kazdin, 1997). After training in using B-mod techniques, parents implement them with their children, rewarding appropriate behaviors and punishing, when necessary, noncompliant and aggressive behaviors through the use of "time-outs" and loss of privileges or rewards.

Programmed Instruction

Skinner applied operant conditioning to education in the form of **programmed instruction**. In programmed instruction, the learning of complex material is broken down into a series of small steps. The learner proceeds to master each step at his or her own pace. Skinner even designed a "teaching machine" that guided students through a series of questions of increasing difficulty. After the student responded to each question, the correct response would immediately appear. This provided immediate reinforcement for correct responses and allowed students to correct any mistakes they had made. Since questions were designed to build upon each other in small steps, students would generally produce a high rate of correct responses and thus receive a steady stream of reinforcement. Teaching machines have since given way to computerized forms of programmed instruction, called **computer-assisted instruction**, in which the computer guides the student through an inventory of increasingly more challenging questions.

behavior modification (B-mod) The systematic application of learning principles to strengthen adaptive behavior and weaken maladaptive behavior.

token economy program A form of behavior modification in which tokens earned for performing desired behaviors can be exchanged for positive reinforcers.

programmed instruction A learning method in which complex material is broken down into a series of small steps that learners master at their own pace.

computer-assisted instruction A form of programmed instruction in which a computer is used to guide a student through a series of increasingly difficult questions.

MODULE 5.2 REVIEW

Operant Conditioning: Learning Through Consequences

CONCEPT CHECK

1. In operant conditioning, learning results from the association of a behavior with
   a. its consequences.
   b. conditioned stimuli.
   c. cognitions.
   d. unconditioned stimuli.

2. B. F. Skinner's belief that all behavior is determined by environmental and genetic influences and that free will is an illusion or myth is called _____.

3. Skinner demonstrated that superstitious behavior can be acquired through the coincidental pairing of a(n) _____ with a(n) _____.

4. In negative reinforcement, a behavior is strengthened by the
   a. introduction of a negative reinforcer.
   b. extinction of a positive stimulus.
   c. introduction of a positive reinforcer.
   d. removal of an aversive stimulus.

5. Operant responses are learned most rapidly under a schedule of _____ reinforcement; responses are most resistant to extinction under a schedule of _____ reinforcement.
   a. continuous; continuous
   b. partial; partial
   c. continuous; partial
   d. partial; continuous

MODULE 5.3   Cognitive Learning

- **What is cognitive learning?**
- **What is insight learning?**
- **What is latent learning?**
- **What is observational learning?**

Let's say you wanted to learn the way to drive to your friend's new house. You could stumble around like Thorndike's laboratory animals until you happened upon the correct route by chance. Then again, you could ask for directions and form a mental image of the route ("Let's see, you make a left at the blue house on the corner, then a right turn at the stop sign, and then . . ."). Forming a mental roadmap allows you to perform new behaviors (e.g., driving to your friend's house) even before you have had the opportunity to be reinforced for it. Many psychologists believe that we need to go beyond classical and operant conditioning to explain this type of learning, which is called **cognitive learning**. Cognitive learning involves mental processes that cannot be directly observed—processes like thinking, information processing, problem solving, and mental imaging. Psychologists who study cognitive learning maintain that humans and other animals are, at least to a certain extent, capable of new behaviors without actually having had the chance to perform them or being reinforced for them.

In Chapter 7, we elaborate on cognitive processes involved in information processing, problem solving, and creativity. Here we focus on three types of cognitive learning: insight learning, latent learning, and observational learning.

Insight Learning

In an early experiment with a chimp named Sultan, German psychologist Wolfgang Köhler (1927) placed a bunch of bananas outside the animal's cage beyond its reach. Sultan, who was obviously hungry, needed to use a nearby

cognitive learning   Learning that occurs without the opportunity of first performing the learned response or being reinforced for it.

object, a stick, as a tool to obtain the fruit. Before long, the chimp succeeded in using the stick to pull in the bananas. Köhler then moved the bananas farther away from Sultan, beyond the reach of the stick, but made a longer stick available to him. Sultan looked at the two sticks and held them in his hands. He tried reaching the bananas with one of the sticks and then the other, but to no avail. The bananas were too far away. He again held the two sticks, tinkered with them a bit, then attached one to the other to form a longer stick (the sticks were attachable), and *voilà*—the problem was solved. Sultan used the longer stick to pull the bananas into the cage. Unlike the animals in Thorndike's or Skinner's operant conditioning studies, Sultan did not gradually happen upon the reinforced response through an overt process of trial and error. Köhler believed Sultan had solved the problem on the basis of *insight,* the sudden flash of inspiration that reveals the solution to a problem.

Insight learning is the process of mentally working through a problem until the sudden realization of a solution occurs (the "Aha!" phenomenon) (Jones, 2003). But insight learning does not depend on waiting for a flash of inspiration to arise "out of the blue." To work through a problem mentally, you restructure or reorganize the problem in your mind until you see how its various parts fit together to form a solution.

Some critics, especially behaviorists, remain unconvinced by demonstrations of insight learning. They argue that "insight" is neither sudden nor free of prior reinforcement (Windholz & Lamal, 1985). They suggest that what you don't see is the history of reinforced behavior leading to an apparently sudden flash of "insight." In the behaviorist's view, insight learning is nothing more than the chaining of previously reinforced responses (Epstein et al., 1984). Perhaps there is room for compromise between these positions. Insight learning may arise from a *mental* process of trial and error—the working out in your mind of possible solutions to a problem based on responses that were reinforced in the past.

Latent Learning

In an early study of the role of cognitive processes in learning, Edward Tolman and C. H. Honzik (1930) trained rats to run a maze. Some rats were rewarded with food placed in goal boxes at the end of the maze; others went unrewarded for their efforts. Each day for ten days, the rats were put in the maze and the experimenters counted the number of wrong turns they made. The rewarded rats quickly learned the maze, but the unrewarded rats did not. They seemed to wander aimlessly through the maze, making many wrong turns.

On the eleventh day, food was placed in the goal boxes of some of the previously unrewarded rats. The next day, these rats ran the maze with even fewer errors than the rats that had been rewarded during the previous ten days (see Figure 5.9). The investigators argued that a single reinforced trial could not account for this dramatic improvement in performance. These rats must have learned the maze earlier, without reinforcement, but only demonstrated what they had learned when they were reinforced for doing so. This type of learning is called **latent learning**—a kind of "hidden" learning that occurs without apparent reinforcement and that is not revealed in performance at the time it occurs. The learned behavior is displayed only when it is reinforced. But what had the rats learned? The lead investigator, psychologist Edward Tolman (1886–1959), believed he had an answer. He argued that the rats had developed a **cognitive map**—a mental representation of the maze that allowed them to find their way to the goal box. Tolman's research laid a foundation for the view that humans and other animals create mental representations of the world around them. In Chapter 7, we explore the mental representations that people use to gain knowledge about the world.

CONCEPT 5.25
By reworking a problem in your mind, you may come to see how the various parts fit together to form a solution.

CONCEPT 5.26
Latent learning occurs without apparent reinforcement and is not displayed until reinforcement is provided.

Figure 5.9   Tolman and Honzik's Study of Latent Learning
Notice the sharp reduction in errors that occurred among the rats that had not previously received reinforcement when on the eleventh day they were reinforced for reaching the goal. Tolman argued that learning had occurred in these rats during the previous trials but that it had remained hidden until rewarded.

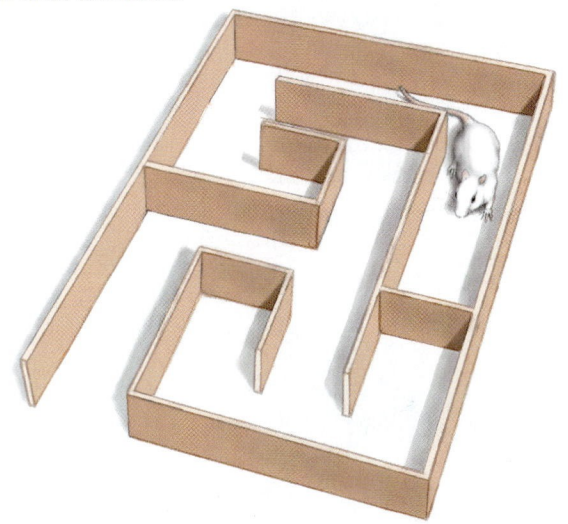

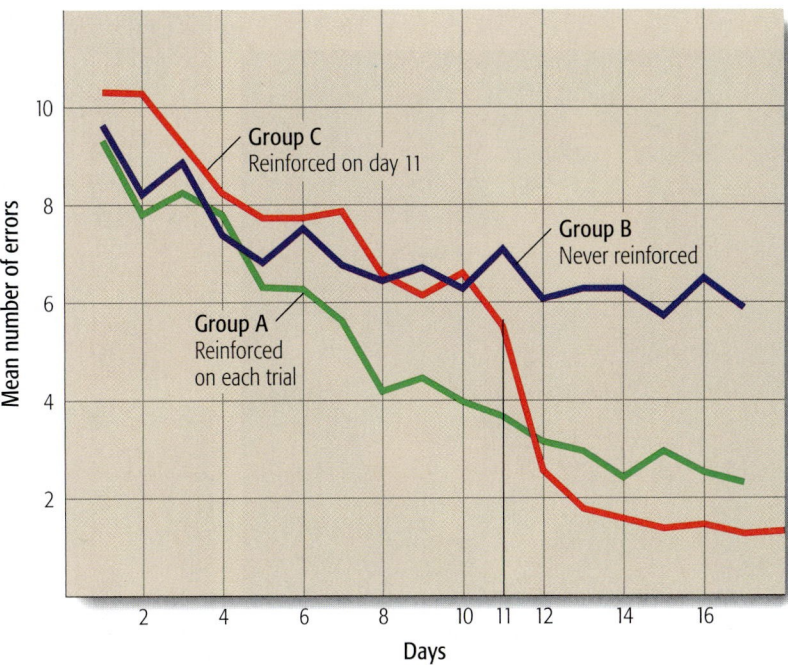

Observational Learning

In preschool, Jenny sees that the teacher praises Tina for picking up the blocks after playing with them. Tina's behavior provides Jenny with a cue that she can use to guide her own behavior. In **observational learning** (also called *vicarious learning* or *modeling*), we acquire new behaviors by imitating behaviors we observe in others. The person whose behavior is observed is called a *model*.

Through observational learning, we become capable of behaviors even before we have had the chance to perform them ourselves. I have never fired a gun, but I expect I can do so because of having observed countless gun battles on television and in the movies. I expect I could even learn the basics of making a soufflé by watching a chef demonstrate each step in the process. Whether you'd want to eat it is another matter, which only goes to underscore a limitation of learning by observation—practice and aptitude also count in developing and refining skilled behavior.

Social-cognitive theorists such as psychologist Albert Bandura (1973, 1986) believe that children learn to imitate aggressive behavior they observe in the home, in the schoolyard, and on television. Bandura and his colleagues showed that children imitated aggressive behavior of characters they observed on television, even cartoon characters (Bandura, Ross, & Ross, 1963). Figure 5.10 illustrates children imitating an adult model who was shown striking a toy (the "Bobo doll"). Other studies point to the same general conclusion: Exposure to violence on TV or in other mass media contributes to aggressive and violent behavior in children and adolescents (Clay, 2003; Huesmann et al., 2003). Childhood exposure to media violence is also linked to greater aggressive behavior in adulthood ("Adult Aggression," 2003; Huesmann et al., 2003).

The influence of modeling is generally stronger when the model is similar to the learner and positive reinforcement for performing the behavior is evident. In other words, we are more likely to imitate models with whom we can identify and who receive rewards for performing the observed behavior. Modeling influences a wide range of behavior, from learning what outfit to wear at a social occasion to how to change a tire. People also develop styles of dealing with conflicts in intimate relationships based on their observations during childhood of how their

 **CONCEPT 5.27**
In observational learning, behaviors are acquired by observing and imitating the behaviors of others.

insight learning   The process of mentally working through a problem until the sudden realization of a solution occurs.

latent learning   Learning that occurs without apparent reinforcement and that is not displayed until reinforcement is provided.

cognitive map   A mental representation of an area that helps an organism navigate its way from one point to another.

observational learning   Learning by observing and imitating the behavior of others (also called *vicarious learning* or *modeling*).

Figure 9.10   Imitation of Aggressive Models
Research by psychologist Albert Bandura and his colleagues shows that children will display aggressive behavior after exposure to aggressive models. Here we see a boy and girl striking a toy "Bobo doll" after observing an adult model strike the doll.

mothers and fathers dealt with marital disagreements (Reese-Weber & Marchand, 2002). For example, young people may learn to imitate an attack style for handling disputes that they had observed in the relationship between their parents or between their parents and themselves (Reese-Weber, 2000).

Does the idea of holding a rat make you squirm? Does the sight of a crab on the beach make you want to run in the other direction? How about touching an insect? Many of us have fears of various creatures even though we have never had any negative experience with them. These fears may be acquired by modeling—that is, by observing other people squirm or show fright when confronted with them (Merckelbach et al., 1996). In a study of forty-two people with a phobia about spiders, modeling experiences were found to be a greater contributor to the acquisition of the phobia than were direct conditioning experiences (Merckelbach, Arntz, & de Jong, 1991).

Concept Chart 5.3 provides an overview of the three types of cognitive learning.

TRY THIS OUT

The Fine Art of Observing Others

How might you use modeling to expand your social skills? Here's an example. If you're at a loss to know what to say to someone you meet at a party, observe how others interact with each other, especially people you believe are socially skillful. What do you notice about their body language, facial expressions, and topics of conversation that could be helpful to you? Begin practicing these behaviors yourself. Note how other people respond to you. Fine-tune your skills to produce a more favorable response. With some practice and fine-tuning, the behaviors are likely to become part of your regular behavioral repertoire.

CONCEPT CHART 5.3
Types of Cognitive Learning

Type of Learning	Description	Example
Insight learning	The process of mentally dissecting a problem until the pieces suddenly fit together to form a workable solution	A person arrives at a solution to a problem after thinking about it from a different angle.
Latent learning	Learning that occurs but remains "hidden" until there is a reward for performing the learned behavior	A person learns the words of a song playing on the radio but doesn't sing them until friends at a party begin singing.
Observational learning	Learning by observing and imitating the behavior of others	Through observation, a child learns to imitate the gestures and habits of older siblings.

MODULE 5.3 REVIEW

Cognitive Learning

CONCEPT CHECK

1. The type of learning that involves thinking, information processing, mental imaging, and problem solving is called _____.

2. The chimp named Sultan learned to reach bananas by attaching two sticks together. This type of learning is called
   a. insight learning.
   b. latent learning.
   c. observational learning.
   d. classical conditioning.

3. The type of learning that occurs without any apparent reinforcement and that is not displayed at the time it is acquired is called _____.

4. Observational learning
   a. is also known as latent learning.
   b. involves imitating the behavior of others.
   c. may lead to the acquisition of useful new skills but not to fear responses.
   d. is based on the principles of operant conditioning.

APPLICATION

MODULE 5.4 Putting Reinforcement into Practice

• **What steps are involved in applying reinforcement principles?**

When you smile at someone who compliments you or thank someone for doing you a favor, you are applying positive reinforcement, one of the principles of operant conditioning. Showing appreciation for desired behavior increases the likelihood that the behavior will be repeated.

To modify behavior through reinforcement, it is important to establish a clear *contingency*, or connection, between the desired behavior and the reinforcement. For example, making a child's weekly allowance of spending money contingent on certain behaviors (e.g., cleaning up after meals) will be far more effective than granting the allowance irrespective of behavior. *Contingency contracting*, which

CONCEPT 5.28
To modify behavior through reinforcement, it is important to establish a clear connection, or contingency, between the desired behavior and the reinforcement.

involves an exchange of desirable reinforcers, is a more formal way of establishing a contingency. In contingency contracting, two people in a relationship list the behaviors of the other that they would like changed. They then agree to reinforce each other for carrying out the desired behavioral changes by making a quid pro quo contract, as in this example between two college roommates:

Carmen: I agree to keep the stereo off after 8:00 p.m. every weekday evening if you agree to forbid your friends to smoke in the apartment.

Lukisha: I agree to replace the toilet paper when we run out if you, in return, clean your hair out of the bathroom sink.

Applying Reinforcement

As noted in our earlier discussion of behavior modification programs, teachers and parents apply reinforcement to help children develop more appropriate behaviors. Here are some guidelines for enhancing the effectiveness of reinforcement (adapted from Eberlein, 1997; Samalin & Whitney, 1997):

1. *Be specific.* Identify the specific behavior you want to increase, such as having five-year-old Johnny put the blocks back on the shelf after playing with them.

2. *Use specific language.* Rather than saying "Johnny, I'd like you to clean your room when you finish playing," say "Johnny, when you finish with the blocks, you need to put them back on the shelf."

3. *Select a reinforcer.* Identify a reinforcer that the child values, such as access to TV or gold stars the child can accumulate and later redeem for small gifts. The reinforcer should be one that is readily available and that can be used repeatedly.

4. *Explain the contingency.* "Johnny, when you put back all of the blocks on the shelf, you'll get a gold star."

5. *Apply the reinforcer.* Reinforce the child immediately after each occurrence of the desired behavior. If the child cannot achieve the desired standard of behavior (e.g., a few blocks are left on the floor), demonstrate how to do so and give the child the opportunity to perform the behavior satisfactorily. Pair the reinforcer with praise: "Johnny, you did a great job putting those blocks away."

6. *Track the frequency of the desired behavior.* Keep a running record of the behavior in terms of how often it occurs each day.

7. *Wean the child from the reinforcer.* After the desired response is well established, gradually eliminate the reinforcer but continue using social reinforcement (praise) to maintain the behavior: "Johnny, I think you did a good job in putting the blocks where they belong."

Giving Praise

Praise can be a highly effective reinforcer in its own right. Here are some guidelines for using praise to strengthen desirable behavior in children:

- Make eye contact with the child and smile when giving praise.

- *Use hugs.* Combine physical contact with verbal praise.

- *Be specific.* Connect praise with the desired behavior (Belluck, 2000). Rather than offering vague praise—"You're a great older brother"—connect it with the noteworthy effort or accomplishment. Say, for example, "Thanks for watching your little brother while I was on the phone. It was a big help."

- *Avoid empty flattery.* Children can see through empty flattery. Empty flattery may prompt them to think, why do people need to make up stuff about me? What is so wrong with me that people feel they need to cover up? (Henderlong

Hugs as Reinforcers Hugs are a form of positive reinforcement when they follow desirable behavior.

& Lepper, 2002). Indiscriminant praise can also have the unfortunate effect of leading to an inflated sense of self-importance (Baumeister et al., 2003).

- *Reward the effort, not the outcome.* Instead of saying "I'm so proud of you for getting an A in class," say "I'm so proud of you for how well you prepared for the test." Praising the accomplishment, not the effort, may convey the message that the child will be prized only if he or she continues to get A's.

- *Avoid repeating yourself.* Avoid using the same words each time you praise the child. If you tell Timmy he's terrific each time you praise him, the praise will soon lose its appeal.

- *Don't end on a sour note.* Don't say "I'm proud of how you cleaned your room by yourself, but next time I think you can do it faster."

TYING IT TOGETHER

Our capacity to learn, or change our behavior as the result of experience, helps us adapt to the demands of the environment. Whether we are learning to garner rewards and avert punishments or simply to dress warmly in cold weather, we are continually modifying and adjusting our behavior in light of environmental demands. The modules in this chapter focus on three major types of learning. Classical conditioning, or learning by association, is a form of learning in which the repeated pairing of two stimuli leads to a response to one stimulus that was previously elicited by the other stimulus (Module 5.1). Whereas classical conditioning explains the development of relatively simple, reflexive responses, operant conditioning, or learning by consequences, focuses on the development of more complex behaviors (Module 5.2). The third major form of learning is cognitive learning, which involves mental processes that cannot be directly observed (Module 5.3). Teachers and parents apply reinforcement, a principle of operant conditioning, to help children develop more appropriate behaviors (Module 5.4).

SUMMING UP: Q & A

Classical Conditioning:
Learning Through Association (Module 5.1)

What is learning?

- Psychologists generally define learning as a relatively permanent change in behavior that results from experience.

What is classical conditioning?

- Classical conditioning is a process of learning in which the pairing of two stimuli leads to a response to one stimulus that is the same as or similar to the response previously elicited by the other stimulus.

What roles do extinction, spontaneous recovery, and stimulus generalization and discrimination play in classical conditioning?

- Extinction is the process by which learned responses gradually weaken and eventually disappear when the conditioned stimulus (CS) is presented repeatedly in the absence of the unconditioned stimulus (US).
- Spontaneous recovery is the return of the conditioned response some time after extinction.

- Stimulus generalization refers to the tendency of stimuli that are similar to the conditioned stimulus to elicit a conditioned response.
- Through stimulus discrimination, organisms learn to differentiate among stimuli so that stimuli that are related to the conditioned stimulus, but not identical to it, fail to elicit a conditioned response.

What stimulus characteristics strengthen conditioned responses?

- Factors related to the strength of conditioned responses include the frequency of the pairings of the conditioned stimulus and unconditioned stimulus, the timing of the presentation of the two stimuli, and the intensity of the unconditioned stimulus.

What is the cognitive perspective on classical conditioning?

- Developed by Robert Rescorla, the cognitive perspective on classical conditioning holds that conditioning depends on the informational value that the conditioned stimulus acquires in predicting the occurrence of the unconditioned stimulus. According to this model, humans and other animals actively seek information that helps them make pre-dictions about important events in their environment; condi-tioned stimuli are cues that they use to make these predictions.

What are some examples of classical conditioning in daily life?

• Examples of classical conditioning in daily life include the acquisition of fear responses and taste aversions. Classical conditioning also plays a role in positive emotions and drug cravings.

Operant Conditioning: Learning Through Consequences (Module 5.2)

What is Thorndike's Law of Effect?

• Edward Thorndike's Law of Effect holds that responses that have satisfying effects will be strengthened while those that lead to discomfort will be weakened.

What is operant conditioning?

• Operant conditioning is a form of learning in which the con-sequences of behavior influence the strength or likelihood of occurrence of the behavior.

What are the different types of reinforcers?

• Positive reinforcers are stimuli or events whose introduction following a response strengthens the response.
• Negative reinforcers are aversive stimuli whose removal fol-lowing a response strengthens the response.
• Primary reinforcers, such as food and water, are stimuli that are naturally reinforcing because they satisfy basic biological needs.
• Secondary reinforcers, such as money and social approval, acquire reinforcing value because of their association with primary reinforcers.

What are schedules of reinforcement, and how do they differ?

• Schedules of reinforcement are predetermined plans for tim-ing the delivery of reinforcement. In a schedule of continuous reinforcement, reinforcement is given after every correct response. In a partial-reinforcement schedule, only a portion of correct responses is reinforced.
• Partial reinforcement is administered under ratio or interval schedules.
• In a fixed-ratio schedule, reinforcement follows a specified number of correct responses.
• In a variable-ratio schedule, the number of correct responses needed before reinforcement is given varies around some average number.
• In a fixed-interval schedule, a specified period of time must pass before a correct response can be reinforced.
• In a variable-interval schedule, the period of time that must elapse before a response can be reinforced varies around some average interval.

How are schedules of reinforcement related to learning?

• A schedule of continuous reinforcement produces the most rapid learning but also the most rapid extinction of a response when reinforcement is withheld.
• Response rates in partial-reinforcement schedules vary, as does the resistance of responses to extinction.

Why are psychologists concerned about the use of punishment?

• The reasons psychologists recommend that parents not rely on punishment to discipline their children include the fol-lowing: Punishment may only suppress behavior, not elimi-nate it; it doesn't teach new and more appropriate behaviors; it can have undesirable emotional and behavioral conse-quences; it may cross the line into abuse; and it can model inappropriate ways of resolving conflicts.

What are some applications of operant conditioning?

• Principles of operant conditioning are used in biofeedback training, behavior modification, and programmed instruction.

Cognitive Learning (Module 5.3)

What is cognitive learning?

• In cognitive learning, an organism learns a behavior before it can perform the behavior or be reinforced for it. Cognitive learning depends on mental processes such as thinking, prob-lem solving, and mental imaging.

What is insight learning?

• Insight learning is a mental process in which the restructur-ing of a problem into its component parts leads to the sudden realization of a solution to the problem.

What is latent learning?

• Latent learning is a kind of "hidden" learning that occurs without apparent reinforcement and is not displayed until reinforcement is provided.

What is observational learning?

• In observational learning, behaviors are acquired by observ-ing and imitating the behaviors of others.

Application: Putting Reinforcement into Practice (Module 5.4)

What steps are involved in applying reinforcement principles?

• Establishing a clear contingency between the desired behav-ior and the reinforcement is an important step in applying reinforcement. Other steps include specifying the behavior to be changed, selecting a reinforcer, explaining the contin-gency, applying the reinforcer, tracking the rate of occurrence of the desired behavior, and phasing out the reinforcer once the desired behavior is well established.

Key Terms

learning *(p. 162)*
classical conditioning *(p. 162)*
unconditioned response (UR) *(p. 162)*
unconditioned stimulus (US) *(p. 162)*
neutral stimulus (NS) *(p. 162)*
conditioned response (CR) *(p. 162)*
conditioned stimulus (CS) *(p. 162)*
extinction *(p. 163)*
spontaneous recovery *(p. 163)*
reconditioning *(p. 163)*
stimulus generalization *(p. 164)*
stimulus discrimination *(p. 164)*
conditioned emotional reaction (CER) *(p. 167)*
phobias *(p. 167)*
behavior therapy *(p. 167)*
conditioned taste aversions *(p. 168)*

immune system *(p. 169)*
Law of Effect *(p. 171)*
radical behaviorism *(p. 172)*
Skinner box *(p. 172)*
operant conditioning *(p. 172)*
operant response *(p. 172)*
reinforcer *(p. 172)*
superstitious behavior *(p. 172)*
discriminative stimulus *(p. 173)*
positive reinforcement *(p. 173)*
negative reinforcement *(p. 173)*
primary reinforcers *(p. 175)*
secondary reinforcers *(p. 175)*
shaping *(p. 175)*
method of successive approximations *(p. 175)*
schedules of reinforcement *(p. 176)*

schedule of continuous reinforcement *(p. 176)*
schedule of partial reinforcement *(p. 176)*
escape learning *(p. 178)*
avoidance learning *(p. 178)*
punishment *(p. 178)*
behavior modification (B-mod) *(p. 182)*
token economy program *(p. 182)*
programmed instruction *(p. 182)*
computer-assisted instruction *(p. 182)*
cognitive learning *(p. 183)*
insight learning *(p. 184)*
latent learning *(p. 184)*
cognitive map *(p. 184)*
observational learning *(p. 185)*

Thinking Critically About Psychology

Based on your reading of this chapter, answer the following questions. Then, to evaluate your progress in developing critical thinking skills, compare your answers to the sample answers found in Appendix A.

Recall the experiment described on page 169 in which psychologist John Garcia and his colleagues left sheep carcasses on the open range that were laced with a poison that sickened coyotes when they ate the tainted meat. Apply your critical thinking skills in breaking down this study in classical conditioning terms.

1. What was the unconditioned stimulus in this example?

2. What was the conditioned stimulus?

3. What was the unconditioned response?

4. What was the conditioned response?

Answers to Concept Check Questions

Module 5.1: 1. stimulus generalization; 2. d; 3. c; 4. b; 5. b.
Module 5.2: 1. a; 2. radical behaviorism; 3. response, reinforcement; 4. d; 5. c.   **Module 5.3:** 1. cognitive learning; 2. a; 3. latent learning; 4. b.

Memory

DID YOU KNOW THAT . . .

- A man was able to memorize lists of hundreds of meaningless syllables and recite them again fifteen years later? (p. 193)

- Though most people can retain only about seven items in memory at any one time, you may be able to juggle sixteen, twenty, or more items in your mind by using a simple memory device? (p. 197)

- A good way to retain information you've just learned is to sleep on it? (p. 198)

- People can be misled into believing they saw a yield sign at an accident scene when they actually saw a stop sign? (p. 204)

- Fewer than half of the people tested in a research study could pick out the correct drawing of a penny? (p. 210)

- If your hippocampus were removed, each new experience would come and go without any permanent trace left in your brain that the event ever happened? (p. 214)

We are a nation that loves competitions. We watch or engage in competitions of all kinds, from sporting contests and tractor-pulls to the perennial game shows and award ceremonies on TV. But memory competitions? These are one of the newest entries in the competitive field. In the U.S. and world memory championships, experts compete in various challenges, such as recalling long lists of words or random numbers, or matching names to the faces of people they've seen in photographs. Some recent champions have demonstrated amazing feats of memory. The U.S. record holder in 1997 succeeded in memorizing in a mere 34.03 seconds each card (suit and number) in the order in which it appeared in a shuffled deck of fifty-two cards ("Instant Recall," 2000). But none of the feats of the recent champions can hold a candle to those of a Russian known only by his first initial, S. S. had perhaps the most prodigious memory ever studied. He could repeat seventy randomly selected numbers in the precise order in which he had just heard them (Luria, 1968). Even more amazingly, he could memorize lists of hundreds of meaningless syllables and recite them not only immediately after studying them but also when tested again some fifteen years later. He memorized long mathematical formulas that were utterly meaningless to him except as an enormously long string of numbers and symbols. After but a single reading, he could recite stanza after stanza of Dante's Divine Comedy in Italian, even though he could not speak the language (Rupp, 1998).

Imagine what it would be like to have such an extraordinary memory—to be able to remember everything you read word for word or to recall lists of facts you learned years ago. Yet if S.'s life story is any indication, it may be just as well you don't possess such a prodigious memory. S. didn't have an easy time of it. His mind was so crammed with meaningless details that he couldn't see the forest for the trees. He had difficulty distinguishing between the trivial and the significant (Turkington, 1996). He even had difficulty holding conversations, since individual words opened a floodgate of associations that distracted him from what the other person was saying. He was unable to shift gears when new information conflicted with fixed images he held in memory. For example, he had difficulty recognizing people who had changed small details of their appearance, such as getting a haircut or wearing a new suit. Unfortunately, S.'s life didn't end well. He spent the last years of his life confined to a mental hospital. Most of us will probably never possess the memory of someone like S., nor would we even want to. Yet learning how our memory works and what we can do to improve it can help us meet many of life's challenges, from performing better in school or on the job to remembering to water the plants before leaving the house.

Our study of memory begins with a discussion of the underlying processes that make memory possible. We then consider the loss of information that results from forgetting and the role of the brain in creating and storing memories. We end with some practical suggestions for improving your memory. ∎

MODULE 6.1 Remembering

- **What are the basic processes and stages of memory?**
- **What is the constructionist theory of memory?**
- **What are flashbulb memories?**
- **What factors influence the accuracy of eyewitness testimony?**
- **Are recovered memories of childhood sexual abuse credible?**

In Chapter 5, we defined learning as a relatively permanent change in behavior that occurs as the result of experience. But learning could not occur without memory. **Memory** is the system by which we retain information and bring it to mind. Without memory, experience would leave no mark on our behavior; we would be unable to retain the information and skills we acquire through experience. In this module, we focus on the factors that make memory possible.

Human Memory as an Information Processing System

CONCEPT 6.1
The three basic processes that make memory possible are encoding, storage, and retrieval.

Many psychologists conceptualize human memory as a type of information processing system that has three basic processes: *encoding, storage,* and *retrieval.* These processes allow us to take information from the world, encode it in a form that can be stored in memory, and later retrieve it when it is needed (see Figure 6.1). As we shall see, these underlying processes work through a sequence of stages leading to the formation of enduring memories.

Figure 6.1 Three Basic Processes of Memory
Human memory can be represented as an information processing system consisting of three basic processes: encoding, storage, and retrieval of information.

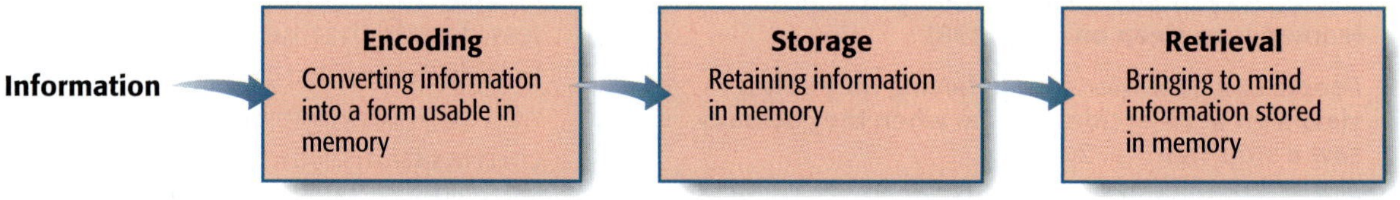

Information →

Encoding	Storage	Retrieval
Converting information into a form usable in memory	Retaining information in memory	Bringing to mind information stored in memory

Memory Encoding: Taking in Information

Information about the outside world comes to us through our senses. But for this information to enter memory, it must undergo a process of **memory encoding**, or conversion into a form we can store in memory. We encode information in different ways, including *acoustically* (coded by sound), *visually* (coded by forming a mental picture), and *semantically* (coded by meaning). We encode information acoustically by converting auditory signals into strings of recognizable sounds. For example, you use acoustic coding when trying to keep a phone number in mind by repeating it to yourself. Or you might encode this information visually by picturing a mental image of the digits of the telephone number. But visual coding tends to fade more quickly than auditory coding, so it is generally less efficient for remembering strings of numbers. We encode information semantically when we transform sounds or visual images into recognizable words.

Encoding information semantically—by meaning—helps preserve information in memory. You're more likely to remember material when you make a conscious effort to understand what the material means than when you rely on rote

memory The system that allows us to retain information and bring it to mind.

memory encoding The process of converting information into a form that can be stored in memory.

memorization (just repeating the words). We tend to use visual coding when forming memories of people's faces. We use acoustic codes to retain melodies and familiar rhymes or catch phrases, such as "Hmmm good." Advertisers introduce such catch phrases because their meter or rhyme is easily remembered.

Memory Storage: Retaining Information in Memory

Memory storage is the process of retaining information in memory. Some memories—your first kiss or your wedding, for example—may last a lifetime. But not all information becomes an enduring or long-term memory. As we shall see when we discuss the stages of memory, some information is retained for only a fraction of a second.

Memory Retrieval: Accessing Stored Information

Memory retrieval is the process of accessing stored information to make it available to consciousness. Retrieving long-held information is one of the marvels of the human brain. At one moment, we can summon to mind the names of the first three presidents of the United States and, at the next moment, recall our Uncle Roger's birthday. But memory retrieval is far from perfect ("Now, when is Uncle Roger's birthday anyway?"). Though some memories seem to be retrieved effortlessly, others depend on the availability of **retrieval cues**, cues associated with the original learning, to jog them into awareness.

Memory Stages

Some memories are fleeting; others are more enduring. The **three-stage model** of memory proposes three distinct stages of memory that vary with the length of time information is stored: *sensory memory, short-term memory,* and *long-term memory* (Atkinson & Shiffrin, 1971).

Sensory Memory: Getting to Know What's Out There

Sensory memory is a storage system that holds sensory information in memory for a very short time. Visual, auditory, and other sensory stimuli constantly strike your sensory receptors, forming impressions you briefly hold in sensory memory in a kind of temporary storage device called a **sensory register**. This information lasts in memory for perhaps a fraction of a second to as long as three or four seconds. The sensory impression then disappears and is replaced by the next one.

Visual stimuli encoded in the form of mental images enter a sensory register called **iconic memory**. Iconic memory is a type of photographic memory that allows us to hold an image of a visual stimulus in sensory memory for a fraction of a second. A visual image held in iconic memory is so clear and accurate that people can report exact details of the image.

Some people can recall a visual image they had previously seen in such vivid detail it is as if they are still looking at it. This form of visual memory is called **eidetic imagery**, or *photographic memory*. (The term *eidetic* is derived from the Greek word *eidos,* meaning "image".) Eidetic images may be quite vivid, but they are not perceived as clearly as actual photographs (Jahnke & Nowaczyk, 1998). Eidetic imagery is rare in adults, but it occurs in about 5 percent of young children (Haber, 1979). It typically disappears before the age of ten.

Auditory stimuli encoded as mental representations of sounds are held in a sensory register called **echoic memory**. The memory traces of auditory stimuli create the impression of hearing a sound "echo" in your mind for a few seconds after you hear it. Although sounds held in echoic memory fade quickly, they last about two or three seconds longer than visual images.

CONCEPT 6.2
The three-stage model of memory proposes three stages of memory organized around the length of time that information is held in memory: sensory memory, short-term memory, and long-term memory.

memory storage   The process of retaining information in memory.

memory retrieval   The process of accessing and bringing into consciousness information stored in memory.

retrieval cues   Cues associated with the original learning that facilitate the retrieval of memories.

three-stage model   A model of memory that posits three distinct stages of memory: sensory memory, short-term memory, and long-term memory.

sensory memory   The storage system that holds memory of sensory impressions for a very short time.

sensory register   A temporary storage device for holding sensory memories.

iconic memory   A sensory store for holding a mental representation of a visual image for a fraction of a second.

eidetic imagery   A lingering mental representation of a visual image (commonly called *photographic memory*).

echoic memory   A sensory store for holding a mental representation of a sound for a few seconds after it registers in the ears.

web Netlab/How's Your Short-Term Memory?

Short-Term, or Working, Memory: The Mind's Blackboard

Many sensory impressions don't just fade away into oblivion. They are transferred into **short-term memory (STM)** for further processing. Short-term memory is a storage system that permits you to retain and process sensory information for a maximum of about thirty seconds. It relies on both visual and acoustic coding, but mostly on acoustic coding. For example, you attempt to keep a phone number in mind long enough to dial it by repeating it to yourself.

Most psychologists refer to short-term memory as *working memory,* since information held in short-term memory is actively "worked on," or processed, by the brain (Baddeley, 2001; Barch et al., 2002). Working memory is a kind of mental workspace or blackboard for holding information long enough in mind to process it and act on it (MacAndrew et al., 2002). For example, we engage working memory when we form an image of a person's face and hold it in memory for the second or two it takes the brain to determine whether it is the face of someone we know. We also employ working memory whenever we perform arithmetical operations in our heads or engage in conversation. During a conversation, our working memory allows us to retain memory of sounds long enough to convert them into recognizable words.

In the 1950s, psychologist George Miller performed a series of landmark studies in which he sought to determine the storage capacity of short-term memory. Just how much information can most people retain in short-term memory? The answer, Professor Miller determined, was about seven items, plus or minus two (Kareev, 2000). Miller referred to the limit of seven as the "Magic 7."

The magic number seven appears in many forms in human experience, including the "seven ages of man" in Shakespeare's *As You Like It,* the Seven Wonders of the World, the Seven Deadly Sins, and even the seven dwarfs of Disney fame (Logie, 1996). People can normally repeat a maximum of six or seven single-syllable words they have just heard. Think about the "Magic 7" in the context of your daily experiences. Telephone numbers are seven-digit numbers, which means you can probably retain a telephone number in short-term memory just long enough to

CONCEPT 6.3
People can normally retain a maximum of about seven items in short-term memory at any one time.

TRY THIS OUT

Breaking Through the "Magic 7" Barrier

At right are seven rows containing series of numbers. Read aloud the series in the first row. Then look away and repeat the numbers out loud in the order in which they appeared. Check whether your answer was correct or incorrect, and record it in the appropriate "yes" or "no" column. Repeat this procedure for each of the remaining rows.

How well did you do? Chances are you had little trouble with the first four series consisting of four to seven numbers. But you probably stumbled as you bumped up against the "Magic 7" barrier in the next two series, which have eight and ten digits. You may have had more success with the last series, which consists of sixteen digits. But why should you perform better with sixteen digits than with eight or ten? The text offers an explanation.

		Get It Right?	
Row 1:	6293	____Yes	____No
Row 2:	73932	____Yes	____No
Row 3:	835405	____Yes	____No
Row 4:	3820961	____Yes	____No
Row 5:	18294624	____Yes	____No
Row 6:	9284619384	____Yes	____No
Row 7:	1992199319941995	____Yes	____No

dial it. Before proceeding further, you can test your short-term memory by taking the challenge posed in the Try This Out feature.

If you answered the challenge in the *Try This Out* feature, you probably found it easier to remember the numbers in Row 7 than those in Rows 5 and 6. Why? The answer is **chunking**, the process of breaking a large amount of information into smaller chunks to make it easier to recall. The sixteen-digit number in Row 7 consists of four chunks of consecutive years (1992, 1993, 1994, 1995). Instead of remembering sixteen separate bits of information, we need only remember four, a quantity that falls within the short-term memory capacity of most people. Similarly, children learn the alphabet by chunking series of letters. That's why they often say the letters *lmnop* as if they were one word (Rupp, 1998).

Most information that passes through short-term memory fades away after a few seconds or is transferred to long-term memory. You can extend short-term memory beyond thirty seconds by engaging in **maintenance rehearsal**, the conscious rehearsal of information by repeating it over and over again in your mind. You practice maintenance rehearsal whenever you try to remember a person's name by rehearsing it again and again in your mind. But when your rehearsal is interrupted, even for just a few seconds, the contents of short-term memory quickly fade away. This is why it is difficult to keep a particular thought in mind and at the same time follow what someone is saying in conversation.

Memory theorists have developed a number of models to explain how working memory functions. The leading model, called the *three-component model,* was formulated by Alan Baddeley and Graham Hitch (1974; Baddeley, 1996). They proposed that working memory consists of three components (sometimes called *subsystems*): the *phonological loop,* the *visuospatial sketchpad,* and the *central executive* (see Figure 6.2).

1. The **phonological loop** is the speech-based, or verbal, part of working memory. It is a storage device or buffer that holds numbers and words we rehearse or repeat in our minds at any given moment, such as telephone numbers, people's names, or plans for dinner.

2. The **visuospatial sketchpad** is a storage buffer for visual and spatial material. Think of it as a kind of drawing pad in the brain (Logie, 1996). You engage your visuospatial sketchpad whenever you picture in your mind an object, pattern, or image—the face of your beloved, the map of your home state, or the arrangement of the furniture in your living room.

CONCEPT 6.4
The major contemporary model of working memory holds that it consists of three components, or subsystems: the phonological loop, the visuospatial sketchpad, and the central executive.

Figure 6.2   Three-Component Model of Working Memory
According to the three-component model, working memory consists of three subsystems: (1) a phonological loop for storing speech-based, or verbal, material; (2) a visuospatial sketchpad for storing visual and spatial material; and (3) a central executive for coordinating the other two subsystems, receiving and processing information retrieved from long-term memory, and filtering out distracting thoughts.

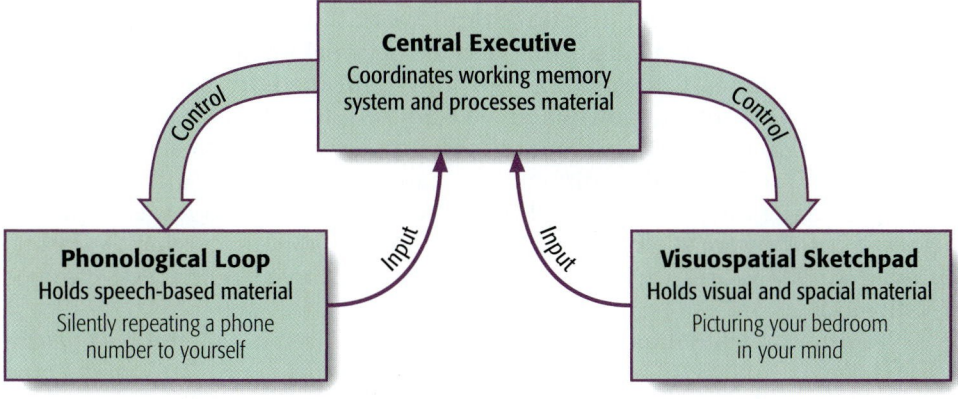

short-term memory (STM)   The memory subsystem that allows for retention and processing of newly acquired information for a maximum of about thirty seconds (also called *working memory*).

chunking   The process of enhancing retention of a large amount of information by breaking it down into smaller, more easily recalled chunks.

maintenance rehearsal   The process of extending retention of information held in short-term memory by consciously repeating the information.

phonological loop   The speech-based part of working memory that allows for the verbal rehearsal of sounds or words.

visuospatial sketchpad   The storage buffer for visual-spatial material held in short-term memory.

3. The **central executive** is the control unit of working memory. It doesn't store information. Rather, it receives input from the other two components and coordinates the working memory system. It also receives and processes information from long-term memory and filters out distracting thoughts so we can focus our attention on information we hold in mind at any given moment. The other components—the phonological loop and the visuospatial sketchpad—are called "slaves" because they do the bidding of the central executive (Willingham, 2001).

Since the two "slaves" work independently, they can operate at the same time without interfering with one another. When you drive an automobile, visual images of the road are temporarily stored in the visuospatial sketchpad. At the same time, your phonological loop allows you to carry on a conversation with a passenger or sing along with a song on the radio. However, as we noted in Chapter 4, it can be dangerous to engage in a complex conversation while you are driving.

As we also noted in Chapter 4, conflicts can arise when two or more simultaneous demands are placed on either component. It is difficult, as well as dangerous, to drive and read a roadmap at the same time. It is also difficult to hold two conversations at the same time.

Long-Term Memory: Preserving the Past

Long-term memory (LTM) is a storage system that allows you to retain information for periods of time beyond the capacity of short-term memory. Though some information may remain in long-term memory for only days or weeks, other information may remain for a lifetime. Whereas the storage capacity of short-term memory is limited, long-term memory is virtually limitless in what it can hold. We may never reach a point at which we can't squeeze yet one more experience or fact into long-term memory.

Consolidation is the process by which the brain converts unstable, fresh memories into stable, long-term memories (Dudai, 2004). The first twenty-four hours after information is acquired are critical for consolidation to occur. As noted in Chapter 4, REM sleep appears to play an important role in consolidating daily experiences into long-term memories (Wixted, 2004). This means that if you are studying for a test you have the next day and want to increase your chances of retaining the information you've just learned, make sure you get a good night's sleep.

Whereas short-term memory relies largely on acoustic coding, long-term memory depends more on semantic coding, or coding by meaning. One way of transferring information from short-term to long-term memory is maintenance rehearsal, which, as we've noted, is the repeated rehearsal of words or sounds. But a better way is **elaborative rehearsal**, a method of rehearsal in which you focus on the *meaning* of the material. A friend of mine has a telephone number that ends with the digits 1991, a year I remember well because it was the year my son Michael was born. I have no trouble remembering my friend's number because I associate it with something meaningful (my son's birth year). But I need to look up other friends' numbers that end in digits that have no personal significance for me.

How do we manage to organize our long-term memory banks so we can retrieve what we want to know when we want to know it? Imagine being in a museum where bones, artifacts, and other holdings were strewn about without any organization. It would be difficult, perhaps impossible, to find the exhibit you were looking for. Now imagine how difficult it would be to retrieve specific memories if they were all scattered about in LTM without any rhyme or reason. Fortunately, LTM is organized in ways that provide relatively quick access to specific memories.

A leading conceptual model of how LTM is organized is called the **semantic network model** (Collins & Quillian, 1969; Collins & Loftus, 1975). This model pro-

central executive The component of working memory responsible for coordinating the other subsystems, receiving and processing stored information, and filtering out distracting thoughts.

long-term memory (LTM) The memory subsystem responsible for long-term storage of information.

consolidation The process of converting short-term memories into long-term memories.

elaborative rehearsal The process of transferring information from short-term to long-term memory by consciously focusing on the meaning of the information.

semantic network model A representation of the organizational structure of long-term memory in terms of a network of associated concepts.

levels-of-processing theory The belief that how well or how long information is remembered depends on the depth of encoding or processing.

declarative memory Memory of facts and personal information that requires a conscious effort to bring to mind (also called *explicit memory*).

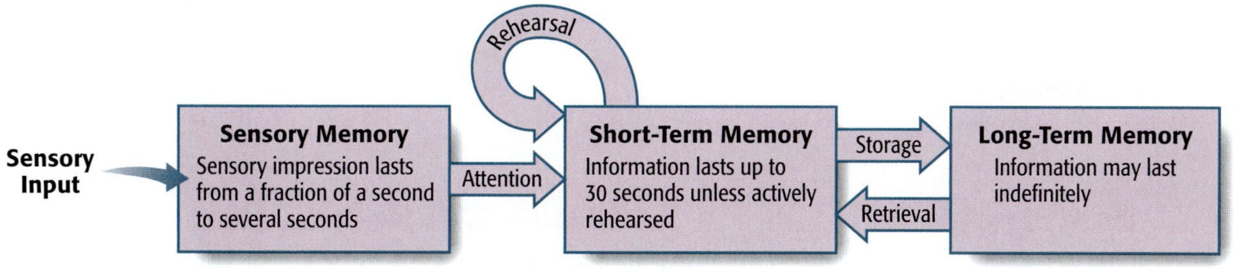

Figure 6.3   Three-Stage Model of Memory
Although human memory is more complex than the three-stage model would suggest, it does provide a useful framework for understanding relationships among the three memory storage systems. *Sensory input* (visual images, sounds, etc.) creates impressions that are held briefly in temporary storage buffers called sensory registers. If we attend to this information, it may enter *short-term memory*. We can use active rehearsal strategies (maintenance rehearsal and elaborative rehearsal) to transfer information from short-term memory into *long-term memory*. Once information is stored in long-term memory, it must be retrieved and enter short-term memory again before it can be used.

poses that information is held in networks of interlinking concepts. We understand the meaning of something by linking it to related things. For example, the concept of "animal" might be linked to concepts of "fish" and "bird," which in turn might be linked to associated concepts such as "salmon" and "robin," respectively. The act of thinking of a particular concept causes a ripple effect throughout the semantic network. This rippling effect, called *spreading activation,* triggers recall of related concepts (Nelson, McEvoy, & Pointer, 2003). In other words, you think of "fish" and suddenly related concepts begin springing to mind, such as "salmon" or "cod," which in turn trigger other associations such as "is pink," "tastes fishy," and so on.

Why should elaborative rehearsal (rehearsal by meaning) result in better transfer of information from short-term to long-term memory than maintenance rehearsal (rehearsal by repetition)? One explanation, called the **levels-of-processing theory**, holds that the level at which information is encoded or processed determines how well or how long information is stored in memory (Craik & Lockhart, 1972). In this view, information is better retained when it is processed more "deeply," which means when it is encoded on the basis of its meaning. By contrast, shallow processing is encoding by superficial characteristics, such as the rhyming of words or the upper- or lower-casing of words (Willingham, 2001).

We began our discussion of how memory works by recognizing that memory depends on underlying processes (encoding, storage, retrieval) that proceed through a series of stages (sensory memory, short-term memory, long-term memory). Concept Chart 6.1 summarizes these processes and stages; Figure 6.3 shows the three stages in schematic form. Through them, we come to form long-term memories that we can recall at will or with some help (retrieval cues). Next we focus on the contents of long-term memory—the kinds of memories that enrich our lives.

What We Remember:
The Contents of Long-Term Memory

What types of memories are stored in long-term memory? At the broadest level, we can distinguish between two types of long-term memory: *declarative memory,* or "knowing that," and *procedural memory,* or "knowing how" (see Figure 6.4) (Eichenbaum, 1997; Rupp, 1998; E. R. Smith, 1998).

Declarative Memory: "Knowing That"

Declarative memory (also called *explicit memory*) is memory of facts and personal information that requires a conscious effort to bring to mind. Declarative memory

CONCEPT 6.5
According to the semantic network model, when you think of a particular concept, it causes a ripple effect to occur within the network of interlinking concepts, triggering memory of related concepts.

CONCEPT 6.6
According to the levels-of-processing theory, information is better retained in memory when it is encoded or processed at a "deeper" level.

CONCEPT 6.7
The two major types of long-term memory are declarative memory ("knowing that") and procedural memory ("knowing how").

CONCEPT CHART 6.1
Stages and Processes of Memory

Memory Stage	Memory Process		
	Encoding	**Storage**	**Retrieval**
Sensory memory	Iconic and echoic	Very brief, from a fraction of a second to three or four seconds	No retrieval. Information is either lost or transferred to short-term memory.
Short-term memory	Acoustic and visual, but primarily acoustic	A maximum of about thirty seconds, but maintenance rehearsal or elaborative rehearsal can maintain the memory longer or convert it into long-term memory	No retrieval. Information is either lost or transferred to long-term memory.
Long-term memory	Acoustic, visual, and semantic, but primarily semantic	Long-term, possibly lifelong	Retrieval is assisted by retrieval cues and activation of semantic networks.

Figure 6.4 Types of Long-Term Memory
This organizational chart shows how long-term memory can be divided into two general types, declarative memory and procedural memory.

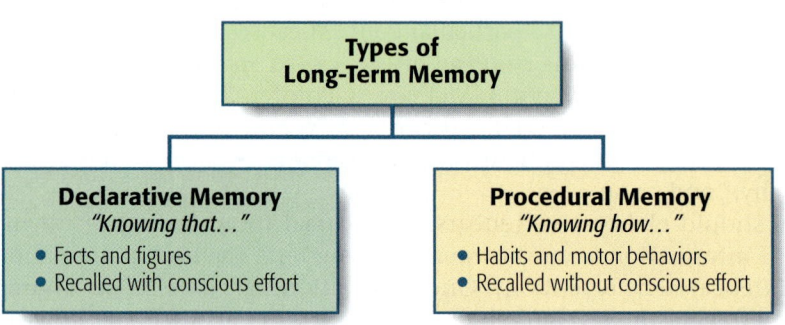

CONCEPT 6.8

Declarative memory consists of semantic memory (memory of facts) and episodic, or autobiographical, memory (memory of life events and experiences).

semantic memory Memory of facts.
episodic memory Memory of personal experiences.
retrospective memory Memory of past experiences or events and previously acquired information.
prospective memory Memory of things one plans to do in the future.
procedural memory Memory of how to do things that require motor or performance skills.

allows us to know "what" and "that." We know that there are fifty states in the United States, that we live on such-and-such a street, and that water and oil don't mix. We know what elements are found in water and what colors are in the American and Canadian flags. We can group declarative memories into two general categories organized according to (1) type of memory (*semantic* or *episodic memory*) and (2) time frame (*retrospective* or *prospective memory*) (see Figure 6.5).

Semantic memory is memory of facts. We can compare semantic memory to a mental encyclopedia or storehouse of information we carry around in our heads. It allows us to remember who wrote *The Grapes of Wrath*, which film won the Academy Award for best picture last year, how to spell the word *encyclopedia*, and what day Japan attacked Pearl Harbor. Semantic memories are not indelibly imprinted in our brains, which is why you may no longer remember last year's Oscar winner or the author of *The Grapes of Wrath* (John Steinbeck). Semantic memories are better remembered when they are retrieved and rehearsed from time to time. So if you stumbled when it came to remembering the name of the author of *The Grapes of Wrath*, reminding you of it today will probably help you remember it tomorrow.

Episodic memory (also called *autobiographical memory*) is memory of personal experiences that constitute the story of your life—everything from memories of what you had for dinner last night to the time you fell from a tree when you were ten years old and needed fifteen stitches. Episodic memory is like a personal diary of one's life experiences, whereas semantic memory is like an encyclopedia of general facts and information (Baddeley, Conway, & Aggleton, 2002; Tulving, 2002).

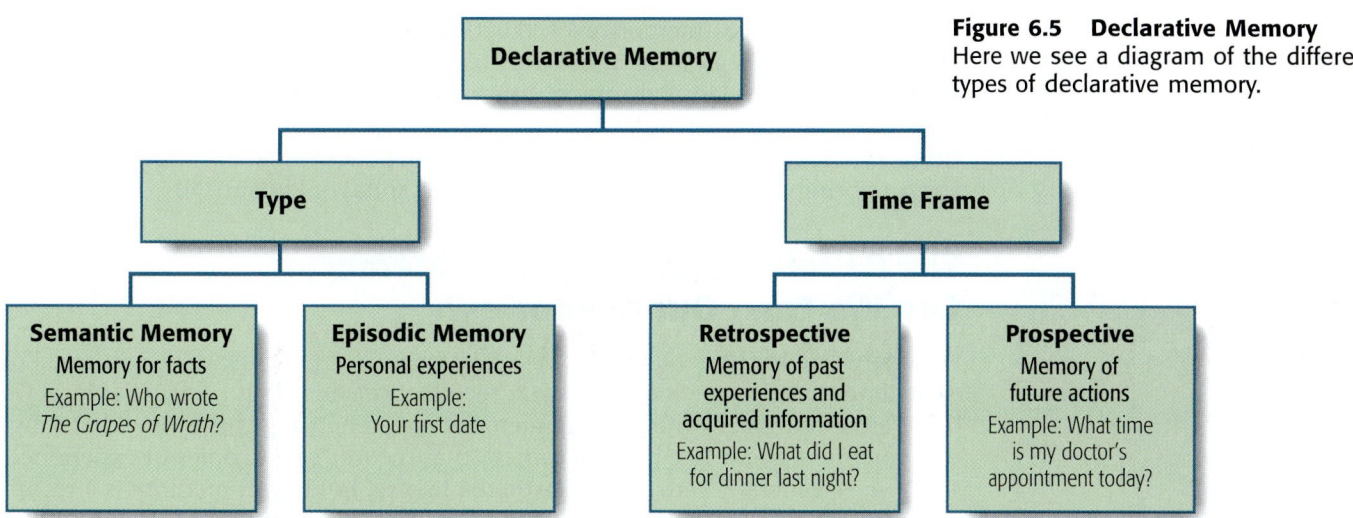

Figure 6.5   Declarative Memory
Here we see a diagram of the different types of declarative memory.

Another difference between semantic and episodic memory is the context in which the event or experience occurred. Knowing that the United States was attacked by terrorists on September 11, 2001, is a semantic memory. Knowing where you were at the time you heard the news of the tragedy is an episodic memory.

Retrospective memory is memory of past experiences or events and previously acquired information. **Prospective memory** is memory of things you need to do in the future (Chasteen, Park, & Schwarz, 2001; Marsh, Hicks, & Watson, 2002). You rely on prospective memory when remembering to take your medication, to pay your phone bill on time, or to call your mother on her birthday. It is remembering to remember. Some of our most embarrassing lapses of memory involve forgetting to do things ("Sorry, I forgot to call the restaurant for reservations. It just slipped my mind").

CONCEPT 6.9
Prospective memory, or remembering to remember, has important applications in daily life, involving everything from remembering appointments to remembering to call people on their birthdays.

Procedural Memory: "Knowing How"

Procedural memory is memory of how to do things, such as how to ride a bicycle, climb stairs, tie shoelaces, perform mathematical operations, or play a musical instrument. Whereas declarative memory is brought to mind by conscious effort, procedural memory is engaged without any conscious effort. Another difference between these two types of memory is that declarative memory involves information that can be verbalized, whereas procedural memory involves motor or performance skills that cannot be explained in words, at least not easily. Try, for example, to describe how you move your muscles when riding a bicycle. Touch typing is a skill requiring procedural memory of how keys are arranged on a keyboard, even though you may not be able to name the keys in each row of the keyboard from memory.

"Muscle Memory"   New York Yankees' manager Joe Torre once referred to the ability to throw a baseball accurately as "muscle memory." We rely on muscle memory, or procedural memory, whenever we perform complex motor skills, such as riding a bike, dancing, typing, climbing stairs, or hitting or throwing a baseball.

We can distinguish between two types of memory, implicit and explicit memory, that differ in terms of whether we make a conscious effort to bring information to mind.

CONCEPT 6.11
The constructionist theory holds that memory is a process of reconstructing past events and experiences, not of replaying them exactly as they occurred.

PsychAssist: Constructionist Theory of Memory

Implicit memory—memory evoked without any deliberate effort to remember—is closely related to procedural memory and is perhaps even a form of procedural memory. Hearing a familiar song on the radio may evoke pleasant feelings associated with past experiences even though you made no conscious attempt to recall these experiences. In contrast, **explicit memory** requires a conscious or *explicit* effort to bring it to mind ("Hmm, what is the capital of Finland?").

The Reliability of Long-Term Memory: Can We Trust Our Memories?

We might like to think our memories accurately reflect events we've witnessed or experienced. But evidence shows that recollections may not be as reliable as we believe them to be. Contemporary memory researchers reject the view that long-term memory works like a video camera that records exact copies of experience. Their view, generally called **constructionist theory**, holds that memory is a reconstructive process. What we recall from memory is not a replica of the past but a representation, or *reconstruction,* of the past. We stitch together bits and pieces of information stored in long-term memory to form a coherent explanation or account of past experiences and events. Reconstruction, however, can lead to distorted memories of events and experiences.

According to constructionist theory, memories are not carbon copies of reality. From this vantage point, it is not surprising that people who witness the same event or read the same material may have very different memories of the event or of the passage they read. Nor would it be surprising if recollections of your childhood are not verbatim records of what actually occurred but, rather, reconstructions based on pieces of information from many sources—from old photographs, from what your mother told you about the time you fell from the tree when you were ten, and so on.

Constructionist theory leads us to expect that memories may be distorted. These distortions can range from simplifications, to omissions of details, to outright fabrications (Koriat & Goldsmith, 1996). Even so, we shouldn't presume that all memories are distorted. Some may be more or less accurate reflections of events. Others, perhaps most, can be likened more to impressionist paintings than to mental snapshots of experiences.

The constructionist account of memory provides an interesting perspective on how *negative stereotyping*—ascribing negative traits to people of certain groups—can influence perceptions and attitudes of people subjected to stereotyping. Given the long history of exclusion, prejudice, and discrimination on the basis of skin color, it is not surprising that members of the dominant culture often perceive African Americans with darker skin tones more negatively—as less intelligent, less attractive, and less successful—than African Americans with lighter skin tones. Since African Americans are raised in the same culture, we should not be surprised if they, too, hold these negative stereotypes, at least to a certain degree.

Cara Averhart and Rebecca Bigler (1997) examined the influence of racial stereotypes on memory in African-American children of elementary school age. They used a memory test in which children recalled information embedded in stories in which light- and dark-complexioned African American characters were associated with either positive ("nice") or negative ("mean") attributes. The results showed that children had better memory for stories in which more favorable attributes were associated with light-complexioned characters and more negative characteristics were associated with dark-complexioned characters. The memory bias was even greater among children who rated themselves as having light skin tones. The results support a constructionist view that people are better able to recall information that is consistent with their existing concepts or *schemas,* even when these schemas are grounded in prejudice. A schema is an organized knowledge structure, such as a set of beliefs, that reflects one's past

implicit memory Memory accessed without conscious effort.

explicit memory Memory accessed through conscious effort.

constructionist theory A theory that holds that memory is not a replica of the past but a representation, or *reconstruction,* of the past.

flashbulb memories Enduring memories of emotionally charged events that seem permanently seared into the brain.

TRY THIS OUT

What's in the Photograph?

Look briefly at the photograph of a professor's office that appears in Figure 6.6. Then continue with your reading of the chapter. After a few minutes, return here and, without looking at the photo again, list all the objects you saw in the office.

_____

_____

_____

_____

Now look again at the photo. Did you list any objects not actually present in the office but that may have fit your concept, or schema, of what a professor's office looks like, like filing cabinets and bookshelves? Investigators who used this photograph in a similar experiment found that many subjects remembered seeing such objects, demonstrating that their memories were affected by their existing schemas (W. F. Brewer & Treyens, 1981).

Figure 6.6   Professor's Office

experiences, expectancies, and knowledge about the world. You can test out for yourself whether your memory schemas lead to distorted memories by completing the exercise in the nearby _Try This Out_ feature, "What's in the Photograph?"

In the next sections, we take a look at two controversial issues that call into question the credibility of long-term memory: eyewitness testimony and recovery of repressed memories. These issues place memory research squarely in the public eye. First, however, we examine another type of long-term memory: flashbulb memories, which, regardless of their accuracy, seem indelibly etched in the brain.

> **CONCEPT 6.12**
> **Emotionally arousing events may leave vivid, lasting impressions in memory, called flashbulb memories, which seem permanently etched into our brains.**

Flashbulb Memories: What Were You Doing When . . . ?

Extremely stressful or emotionally arousing personal or historical events may leave vivid, lasting, and highly detailed memories called **flashbulb memories** (Tekcan & Peynircioglu, 2002). They are called flashbulb memories because they seem to have been permanently seared into the brain by the pop of the flashbulb on an old-fashioned camera. Many of us share a flashbulb memory of the World Trade Center disaster. We remember where we were and what we were doing at the time we heard of the attack, just as though it had happened yesterday. Many baby-boomers share the flashbulb memory of the assassination of President John Kennedy in 1963.

Despite the vividness of flashbulb memories, they may be as inaccurate and prone to distortion as other forms of long-term memory (Hertel, 1996). A recent study of flashbulb memories of the terrorist attacks of September 11, 2001, showed that they were not any more accurate than ordinary memories (Talarico & Rubin, 2003).

Frozen in Memory?   Emotionally charged experiences can create "flashbulb memories" that seem indelibly etched in our brains. Yet such memories may not be as accurate as we think they are.

Eyewitness Testimony:
"What Did You See on the Day in Question?"

Elizabeth Loftus

In reaching a verdict, juries give considerable weight to eyewitness testimony. Yet memory researchers find that eyewitness testimony can be as flawed and strewn with error as other forms of memory (Loftus, 1993b). Psychologist Elizabeth Loftus (1993b), a leading expert on eyewitness testimony, points out that a shockingly high number of people are wrongly convicted of crimes each year because of faulty eyewitness testimony.

Loftus describes how a **misinformation effect** may lead to distortions in eyewitness testimony. The distortions are caused by events that occur in the interval between the witnessed event and recall of that event. In one study, Loftus and her colleagues had subjects view a film of a car accident that occurred at an intersection with a stop sign (Loftus, Miller, & Burns, 1978). Some subjects were then given misleading information telling them that the traffic sign was a yield sign. When subjects were later asked what traffic sign they saw at the intersection, those given the false information tended to report seeing the yield sign (see Figure 6.7). Subjects who were not given the false information were much more likely to recall the correct traffic sign. This research calls into question the credibility of eyewitness testimony, especially when witnesses are subjected to leading or suggestive questioning that might "plant" ideas in their heads (Begley, 2001d).

False memories of events that never took place can also be induced experimentally (Gleaves et al., 2004; Kihlstrom, 2004; Loftus, 2003). Imagination, too, can play tricks on your memory. Simply imagining a past experience can induce a false memory that the event actually occurred (Mazzoni & Memom, 2003).

Since eyewitness testimony may often be flawed, should we eliminate it from court proceedings? Loftus (1993a) argues that if we dispensed with eyewitness testimony, many criminals would go free. As an alternative, we can attempt to increase the accuracy of eyewitness testimony. One way of boosting accuracy is to find corroborating evidence or independent witnesses who can back up each other's testimony. The accuracy of eyewitness testimony also involves the following factors:

1. *Ease of recall.* People who take longer to answer questions in giving testimony are less likely to be accurate in their recall than those who respond without hesitation (Robinson, Johnson, & Herndon, 1997). Similarly, eyewitnesses

Figure 6.7 Misinformation Effect
Subjects saw a film of a car accident at an intersection marked by a stop sign. Some were then given the false information that they had seen a yield sign at the intersection. If you were one of these subjects, would your memory be based on what you had seen or on what you were told afterward?

misinformation effect A form of memory distortion that affects eyewitness testimony and that is caused by misinformation provided during the retention interval.

who are quicker in making identifications of a perpetrator from a lineup tend to be more accurate than those who take longer (Dunning & Perretta, 2002; Wells & Olson, 2003).

2. *Degree of confidence.* Confidence in memory is only modestly associated with better accuracy (Fruzzetti et al., 1992). People who say with solid certainty "That's the person who did it" are not necessarily more accurate than those who admit they could be mistaken. However, many juries are swayed by eyewitnesses who express confidence in their memories.

3. *General knowledge about a subject.* People who are knowledgeable about a subject are more likely than those who know less about the subject to be reliable witnesses. For example, when asked by a police officer to identify a motor vehicle involved in a crime, a person familiar with the various makes and models of automobiles will be better equipped to give a reliable answer than one who knows little or nothing of the subject (Davies et al., 1996).

4. *Racial identification.* People are generally better able to recognize faces of people of their own race than the faces of people of other races (Ellis & Shepherd, 1992). Thus, eyewitnesses are more likely to make mistakes when identifying members of another race (Egeth, 1993).

5. *Types of questions.* Leading or suggestive questions by investigators can result in the misidentification of perpetrators (Loftus, 1997), whereas open-ended questions—for example, "What did you see?"—tend to increase the accuracy of eyewitness testimony (Fruzzetti et al., 1992). On the other hand, open-ended questions tend to elicit fewer details from witnesses.

6. *Facial characteristics.* Faces with distinctive features are much more likely to be accurately recognized than nondistinctive faces (Wells & Olson, 2003). Also, highly attractive or highly unattractive faces are more likely to be accurately identified than are those of average attractiveness.

Recovery of Repressed Memories

Controversy has swirled around the issue of whether long-repressed memories of childhood experiences that suddenly surface in adulthood are credible. In most cases, such memories come to light during hypnosis or psychotherapy. On the basis of recovered memories of sexual trauma in childhood, authorities have brought charges of sexual abuse against hundreds of people. A number of these cases have resulted in convictions and long jail sentences, even in the absence of corroborating evidence. But should recovered memories be taken at face value?

A total lack of memory of traumatic childhood events is rare, although it is possible that such memories may be lost in some cases (Bradley & Follingstad, 2001; Goodman et al., 2003). We also know that false memories of childhood experiences can be experimentally induced in many subjects (Clancy et al., 2002; Zoellner et al., 2000). Entire events that never happened can enter a subject's memory and seem just as real and accurate as memories of events that really did occur. However, evidence of false-memory creation in experimental studies does not prove that recovered memories in actual cases are, in fact, false.

In sum, many investigators believe that while some recovered memories may be genuine, others are undoubtedly false (e.g., Gleaves et al., 2004; L. J. Rubin, 1996). The problem is that we simply lack the tools to differentiate between true memories and false ones (Cloitre, 2004; McNally, 2003). From a constructionist standpoint, we should not be surprised that memories may be distorted, even when the person believes them to be true. The use of hypnosis or of suggestive interviewing or therapeutic techniques can heighten susceptibility to false memories.

CONCEPT 6.14
Research showing that false memories may seem as real as actual events calls into question the credibility of recovered memories of childhood abuse.

CONCEPT 6.15
Though some recovered memories of childhood abuse may be genuine, we lack the tools to determine which are true.

MODULE 6.1 REVIEW

Remembering

CONCEPT CHECK

1. Memory is
   a. a relatively permanent change in behavior that occurs as the result of experience.
   b. the system by which we retain information and bring it to mind.
   c. a mental process that occurs independent of learning.
   d. all of the above.

2. The type of memory that corresponds to "knowing how" is called _____.

3. Which of the following is *not* correct? Constructionist theory suggests that
   a. memory recall may not be accurate.
   b. information is best recalled when it is consistent with a person's memory schemas.
   c. eyewitness testimony may be influenced by misinformation.
   d. flashbulb memories are immune to distortion.

4. Match the concepts on the left with their descriptions on the right:

   i. sensory memory   a. process by which short-term memory is converted to long-term memory

   ii. short-term memory   b. also known as "working" memory

   iii. consolidation   c. process that uses semantic coding to transfer short-term memory to long-term memory

   iv. elaborative rehearsal   d. storage system for fleeting iconic and echoic memories

MODULE 6.2   Forgetting

- **What are the major theories of forgetting?**
- **How is recall related to the methods used to measure it?**
- **What is amnesia, and what causes it?**

Everyone is forgetful. Some of us are more forgetful than others. But why do we forget? Is it simply a matter of memories fading over time? Or are there other factors that account for forgetfulness? Degenerative brain diseases, such as Alzheimer's disease, are one cause of forgetfulness; another is amnesia, a memory disorder we discuss at the end of this module. Our main focus here, however, is on normal processes of forgetting. We recount several leading theories of forgetting and highlight the role of factors that make it easier or harder to remember information. We begin with decay theory.

Decay Theory: Fading Impressions

The belief that memories consist of traces laid down in the brain that gradually deteriorate and fade away over time dates back to the writings of the Greek philosopher Plato some 2,500 years ago (Morris & Gruneberg, 1996; Willingham, 2001). This theory of forgetting, now known as **decay theory** (also called *trace theory*), was bolstered by early experimental studies conducted by one of the founders of experimental psychology, Hermann Ebbinghaus (1850–1909).

An interesting aspect of Ebbinghaus's experimental work on forgetting is that the only subject in his early studies was himself. To study the processes of memory and forgetting, Ebbinghaus knew he had to eliminate any earlier associations to the material to be remembered. He devised a method for testing memory that

CONCEPT 6.16

The oldest theory of forgetting, decay theory, may explain memory loss that occurs due to the passage of time, but it fails to account for why some memories endure better through time than others.

used nonsense syllables (combinations of letters that don't spell out anything), such as *nuz* and *lef* (Ebbinghaus, 1885). He presented these lists of syllables to himself and determined the number of trials it took for him to recall them perfectly. He then tested himself again at different intervals to see how much he would forget over time. The results showed a decline in memory that has since become known as the *Ebbinghaus forgetting curve* (see Figure 6.8). Forgetting occurred rapidly in the first few hours after learning but then gradually declined. It seemed as though memories simply faded over time. By the end of the first day, 66 percent of the information had been lost, and after a month, nearly 80 percent was gone (Rupp, 1998).

Ebbinghaus also employed a **savings method** to test his memory retention . He first counted the number of times needed to rehearse a list of nonsense syllables in order to commit it to memory. Then he counted the number of times it took to relearn the list after a period of time had elapsed. If it took ten repetitions to learn the list the first time and five the second, the savings would be 50 percent.

Memory researchers recognize that when people attempt to memorize information, they generally retain more information when they space their study sessions than when they cram them together (Payne & Wenger, 1996). One reason for this effect, called the **massed vs. spaced practice effect**, is that massed, or crammed, practice causes mental fatigue that interferes with learning and retention. A practical implication of this effect should be obvious: When studying for exams, don't cram; space out your study sessions.

One major weakness of the decay theory of forgetting is that it fails to account for the unevenness with which memory decays over time. Some memories remain well preserved over time, whereas others quickly fade. Decay theory may account for memory loss due to the passage of time, but other factors, including the meaningfulness of the material, influence forgetting. Ebbinghaus had studied retention of meaningless syllables. But if we examine the retention of more meaningful information, such as poetry or prose, we find a more gradual loss of memory over time. For other meaningful information, such as important historic events, specific job-related knowledge, and personal data like birth dates and schools attended, little if any forgetting occurs over time. Another factor to help explain forgetting is interference.

Interference Theory: When Learning More Leads to Remembering Less

Chances are you have forgotten what you ate for dinner a week ago Wednesday. The reason for your forgetfulness, according to **interference theory**, is interference from memories of dinners that preceded and followed that particular dinner. On the other hand, you are unlikely to forget your wedding day because it is so unlike any other day in your life (except for those, perhaps, who have taken many walks down the aisle). Interference theory helps explain why some events may be easily forgotten while others remain vivid for a lifetime. The greater the similarity between events, the greater the risk of interference. There are two general kinds of interference, *retroactive interference* and *proactive interference*.

Interference occurring after material is learned but before it is recalled is called **retroactive interference**. Perhaps you have found that material you learned in your 9:00 A.M. class, which seemed so clear when you left the classroom, quickly began to fade once you started soaking in information in the next class. In effect, new memories retroactively interfere with unstable earlier memories that are still undergoing the process of memory consolidation (Wixted, 2004).

Proactive interference is caused by the influence of previously learned material. Because of proactive interference, you may have difficulty remembering a new area code (you keep dialing the old one by mistake). Or you may forget to advance the year when writing checks early in a new year. Figure 6.9 illustrates retroactive and proactive interference.

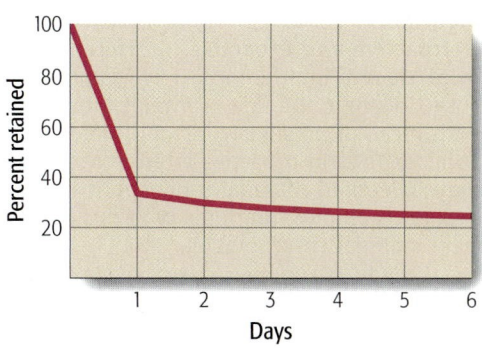

Figure 6.8   Ebbinghaus Forgetting Curve
As Ebbinghaus showed, forgetting occurs most rapidly shortly after learning and then gradually declines over time.

CONCEPT 6.17
Interference theory posits that memories held in short-term or long-term memory may be pushed aside by other memories.

decay theory   A theory of forgetting that posits that memories consist of traces laid down in the brain that gradually deteriorate and fade away over time (also called *trace theory*).

savings method   A method of testing memory retention by comparing the numbers of trials needed to learn material with the number of trials needed to relearn the material at a later time.

massed vs. spaced practice effect   The tendency for retention of learned material to be greater with spaced practice than with massed practice.

interference theory   The belief that forgetting is the result of the interference of memories with each other.

retroactive interference   A form of interference in which newly acquired information interferes with retention of material learned earlier.

proactive interference   A form of interference in which material learned earlier interferes with retention of newly acquired information.

Figure 6.9
Retroactive and Proactive Interference
In retroactive interference, new learning (psychology in the first example) interferes with recall of previously learned material (philosophy). In proactive interference, previously learned material (philosophy in the second example) interferes with recall of new material (psychology).

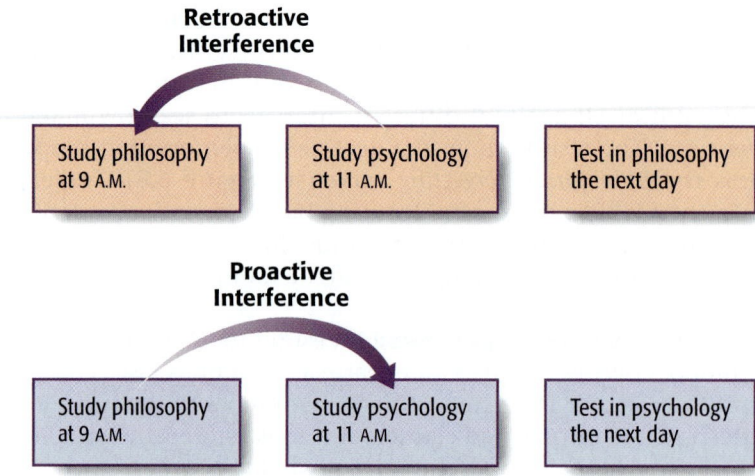

PsychAssist: Interference Theory of Forgetting

web Netlab/Memories Are Made of This: Primacy and Recency Effect

CONCEPT 6.18
The serial position effect explains why we are more likely to forget the middle items in a list than those at the beginning or end.

overlearning Practice repeated beyond the point necessary to reproduce material without error.

serial position effect The tendency to recall items at the start or end of a list better than items in the middle of a list.

primacy effect The tendency to recall items better when they are learned first.

recency effect The tendency to recall items better when they are learned last.

retrieval theory The belief that forgetting is the result of a failure to access stored memories.

tip-of-the-tongue (TOT) phenomenon An experience in which people are sure they know something but can't seem to bring it to mind.

Though some interference is unavoidable, we can take steps to minimize its disruptive effects:

- *Sleep on it.* Sleeping is an activity that is minimally disruptive of newly learned material. In fact, as noted in Module 6.1, REM sleep may help consolidate new memories into lasting ones. Studying material directly before sleep may help you retain what you learn.

- *Rehearse fresh memories.* New long-term memories are fragile. Practicing or rehearsing fresh memories aloud or silently can strengthen them, making them more resistant to the effects of interference. Repeated practice beyond the point necessary to reproduce material without error is called **overlearning**. Apply the principle of overlearning to help ensure retention by rehearsing newly learned material at least two times beyond the point of minimal competence.

- *Give yourself a break.* Try not to schedule one class directly after another. Give your recent memories time to consolidate in your brain.

- *Avoid sequential study of similar material.* Try not to study material that is similar in content in back-to-back fashion—for example, avoid scheduling a French class right after a Spanish one.

Interference may help explain the **serial position effect**, the tendency to recall the first and last items in a list, such as a shopping list, better than those in the middle of the list. The unfortunate items in the middle are often forgotten. Researchers find that when people are asked to name the last seven U.S. presidents in order, they are more likely to make mistakes in the middle of the list than at either the beginning or the end (Storandt, Kaskie, & Von Dras, 1998). Serial position effects influence both short-term and long-term memory.

Interference is the likely culprit in serial position effects. Items compete with one another in memory, and interference is greatest in the middle of a list than at either end of the list. For example, in a list of seven items, the fourth item may interfere with the item that it follows and the item that it precedes. But interference is least for the first and last items in the list—the first, because no other item precedes it; the last, because no other item follows it. The tendency to recall items better when they are learned first is called the **primacy effect**. The tendency to recall items better when they are learned last is called the **recency effect**. As the delay between a study period and a test period increases, primacy effects become stronger whereas recency effects become weaker (Knoedler, Hellwig, & Neath, 1999). This recency-primacy shift means that as time passes after you committed a list to memory, it becomes easier to remember the early items but harder to remember those that appeared later in the list.

In sum, evidence shows that both the passage of time and interference contribute to forgetting. But neither decay theory nor interference theory can determine whether forgotten material becomes lost to memory or just more difficult to retrieve. Some forgotten material can be recovered if subjects are given retrieval cues to jog their memory, such as exposure to stimuli associated with the original situations in which the memories were formed. This brings us to a third model of forgetting, retrieval theory.

Retrieval Theory: Forgetting as a Breakdown in Retrieval

According to **retrieval theory**, forgetting is the result of a failure to access stored memories (Koriat, 1993; Rovee-Collier, 1996). Let us consider two principal ways in which the retrieval process can break down, *encoding failure* and *lack of retrieval cues*.

Encoding Failure: What Image Is on the Back Side of a Nickel?

Memories cannot be retrieved if they were never encoded in the first place. The failure to encode information may explain why people often cannot recall details about common objects they use every day. For example, do you know what image appears on the back of a nickel? Before you rummage through your pockets, let me tell you it is an image of Monticello, the home of Thomas Jefferson, whose image is on the front of the coin. You may have glanced at this image of Monticello countless times but never brought it into memory because you failed to encode it. We tend to encode only as much information as we need to know (Rupp, 1998). Since we don't need to encode more specific details of a coin to recognize one or use it correctly, such information may not be encoded and thus cannot be retrieved.

Events that stand out tend to be better remembered. You are more likely to remember your first date than your twenty-third one. You are also more likely to remember events that occur irregularly (e.g., visits to a doctor because of an injury) than regularly occurring events (e.g., visits to an allergist) (Means & Loftus, 1991). Events that are similar are generally encoded in terms of their common features rather than their distinctive characteristics (Conrad & Brown, 1996). Because similar events tend to be encoded in similar ways, it becomes more difficult to retrieve memories of the specific events.

Lack of Retrieval Cues: What's His Name?

Information may be encoded in memory but remain inaccessible because of a lack of appropriate retrieval cues. A common and often embarrassing difficulty with memory retrieval is recalling proper names. Proper names have no built-in associations, no convenient retrieval cues or "handles" that can be used to distinguish among the many Jennifers, Susans, Davids, and Johns of the world.

A lack of retrieval cues may account for a common experience called the **tip-of-the-tongue (TOT) phenomenon**, in which the information seems to be at the tip of one's tongue but just outside reach. If you've ever felt frustrated trying to recall something you're certain you know but just can't seem to bring to mind, you've experienced the TOT phenomenon. People who experience TOTs (and that includes most of us) may have partial recall of the information they are trying to retrieve, which is why they feel so certain the information is stored somewhere in memory (Carpenter, 2000b; Schwartz & Smith, 1997). They may recall the first few letters or sounds of the word or name ("I know it starts with a *B*"), or perhaps a similar-sounding word comes to mind. TOTs may result not only from a lack of

But I Remembered the Broccoli!   This man remembered the broccoli his wife asked him to pick up at the store, but not the tuna fish. Based on your knowledge of the serial position effect, why do you suppose he remembered the broccoli and not the tuna fish?

CONCEPT 6.19
Memory retrieval may be impaired by a failure to encode information and by a lack of retrieval cues to access stored memories.

CONCEPT 6.20
A common problem with memory retrieval involves the tip-of-the-tongue phenomenon, the experience of sensing you know something but just can't seem to bring it to mind.

TRY THIS OUT

What Does a Penny Look Like?

How well do you remember the features of a penny, the most commonplace of coins? Researchers Raymond Nickerson and Marilyn Jager Adams (1979) decided to find out. They showed subjects an array of drawings of a penny, only one of which was correct. Fewer than half of their subjects were able to pick out the correct one. Without looking at the coins in your pocket, can you tell which drawing of a penny in Figure 6.10 is the correct one? The answer appears on page 221.

Figure 6.10   What Image Appears on the Front of a Penny?

THINK About It

I Know I Know It, but I Just Can't Think of It

Have you had any tip-of-the-tongue experiences? Were you eventually able to retrieve the memory you were searching for? If so, how were you able to retrieve it?

CONCEPT 6.21
Sigmund Freud theorized that the psychological defense mechanism of repression, or motivated forgetting, banishes threatening material from consciousness.

available retrieval cues but also from more general difficulties with word retrieval. They tend to increase in later life, when word retrieval typically becomes more difficult (Burke & Shafto, 2004).

Motivated Forgetting: Memories Hidden from Awareness

Sigmund Freud believed that certain memories are not forgotten but are kept hidden from awareness by **repression**, or motivated forgetting. In Freud's view, repression is a psychological defense mechanism that protects the self from awareness of threatening material, such as traumatic sexual experiences, aggressive impulses, and unacceptable sexual desires (e.g., incestuous wishes). Were it not for repression, Freud believed, we would be flooded with overwhelming anxiety whenever threatening material enters consciousness. Repression, or motivated forgetting, is not simple forgetting; the repressed contents do not disappear but remain in the unconscious mind, hidden from awareness.

Freud's concept of repression does not account for ordinary forgetting—the kind that occurs when you try to retain information you read in your psychology textbook, to use a convenient example. Another problem with this concept is that people who are traumatized by rape, combat, or natural disasters, such as earthquakes or floods, tend to retain vivid if somewhat fragmented memories of these experiences. They often find it difficult to put such anxiety-evoking events out of their minds, which is the opposite of what we might expect from Freud's concept of repression. Moreover, since repression operates unconsciously, we may lack direct means of testing it scientifically. Nonetheless, many memory researchers, including a panel of experts appointed by the American Psychological Association, believe that repression can occur (Alpert, Brown, & Courtois, 1998; Willingham, 2001).

Measuring Memory: How It Is Measured May Determine How Much Is Recalled

Students who are given the choice generally prefer multiple-choice questions to questions that require a written essay. Why? The answer has to do with the different ways in which memory is measured.

The methods used to measure memory can have an important bearing on how well you are able to retrieve information stored in memory. In a *recall task*, such as an essay question, you are asked to reproduce information you have committed to memory. There are three basic types of recall task. In **free recall**, you are asked to recall as much information as you can in any order you wish (e.g., randomly naming starting players on your college's basketball team). In a *serial recall* task, you are asked to recall a series of items or numbers in a particular order (e.g., reciting a telephone number). In *paired-associates recall* you are first asked to memorize pairs of items, such as pairs of unrelated words like *shoe-crayon* and *cat-phone*. You are then presented with one item in each pair, such as the word *shoe,* and asked to recall the item with which it was paired (*crayon*). If you've ever taken a foreign language exam in which you were presented with a word in English and asked to produce the foreign word for it, you know what a paired-associates recall task is.

In a **recognition task**, you are asked to pick out the correct answer from among a range of alternative answers. Tests of recognition memory, such as multiple-choice tests, generally produce much better retrieval than those of recall memory, largely because recognition tests provide retrieval cues. You're more likely to remember the name of the author of *Moby Dick* if you see the author's name among a group of multiple-choice responses than if you are asked to complete a recall task, such as a fill-in-the-blank item in which you are required to insert the author's name (Herman Melville, in case you're stumped).

Amnesia: Of Memories Lost or Never Gained

A medical student is brought by ambulance to the hospital after falling from his motorcycle and suffering a blow to his head. His parents rush to his side, keeping a vigil until he regains consciousness. Fortunately, he is not unconscious for long. As his parents are explaining what has happened to him, his wife suddenly bursts into the hospital room, throwing her arms around him and expressing her great relief that he wasn't seriously injured or killed. When his wife, whom he had married only a few weeks earlier, leaves the room, the medical student turns to his mother and asks, "Who is she?" (cited in Freemon, 1981, p. 96).

How can we explain this severe loss of memory? The medical student suffered from a type of **amnesia**, or memory loss. The term *amnesia* is derived from the Greek roots *a* ("not") and *mnasthai* ("to remember").

Types of Amnesia

The medical student suffered from **retrograde amnesia**, or loss of memory of past events (Riccio, Millin, & Gisquet-Verrier, 2003). A football player knocked unconscious by a blow to the head during a game may remember nothing beyond suiting up in the locker room. A boxer knocked cold in the ring may not remember the fight. A blow to the head can interfere with *memory consolidation*—which, as we noted in Module 6.1, is the process of converting unstable, short-term memories into stable and enduring ones. When this process is disrupted, memories of events occurring around the time of the disruption may be lost permanently. Some cases go beyond problems with memory consolidation. The medical student's memory loss extended beyond the time of his head injury to before he had met his wife. In such cases, whole chunks of memory are lost. Nonetheless, recent

💡 **CONCEPT 6.22**
The methods used to measure memory, such as recall tasks and recognition tasks, affect how much we are able to recall.

Amnesia Amnesia is often caused by a traumatic injury to the brain, such as a blow to the head. This football player was knocked unconscious and may not remember anything about the play in which he was injured or other events preceding the play.

💡 **CONCEPT 6.23**
There are two general types of amnesia, retrograde amnesia (loss of memory of past events) and anterograde amnesia (loss or impairment of the ability to form or store new memories).

free recall   A type of recall task in which individuals are asked to recall as many stored items as possible in any order.

recognition task   A method of measuring memory retention that assesses the ability to select the correct answer from among a range of alternative answers.

amnesia   Loss of memory.

retrograde amnesia   Loss of memory of past events.

CONCEPT CHART 6.2
Forgetting: Key Concepts

	Concept	Description	Example
Theories of Forgetting	Decay theory	Gradual fading of memory traces as a function of time	Facts you learned in school gradually fade out of memory over time.
	Interference theory	Disruption of memory caused by interference of previously learned material or newly learned material	After sitting through your biology lecture, you forget what you learned in chemistry class the hour before.
	Retrieval theory	Failure to access material stored in memory because of encoding failure or lack of retrieval cues	You have difficulty remembering something you know is stored in memory.
	Motivated forgetting	Repression of anxiety-provoking material	You cannot remember a traumatic childhood experience.
Measuring Methods	Recall tasks	Test of the ability to reproduce information held in memory	You recite a phone number or the capital cities of the United States or provinces of Canada.
	Recognition tasks	Test of the ability to recognize material held in memory	You recognize the correct answer in a multiple-choice question.
Types of Amnesia	Retrograde amnesia	Loss of memory of past events	After suffering a blow to the head in a car accident, you are unable to remember details of the accident itself.
	Anterograde amnesia	Loss or impairment of the ability to form or store new memories	Due to a brain disorder, you find it difficult to retain new information.

memories are generally more susceptible to retrograde amnesia than remote events (James & MacKay, 2001). In another form of amnesia, **anterograde amnesia**, people cannot form or store new memories or have difficulty doing so.

Causes of Amnesia

The causes of amnesia may be physical or psychological. Physical causes include blows to the head, degenerative brain diseases (such as Alzheimer's disease; see Chapter 9), blockage of blood vessels to the brain, infectious diseases, and chronic alcoholism. Early detection and treatment of the underlying physical condition are critical. Perhaps as many as 30 percent of physically induced amnesias can be corrected with proper treatment (D. Cohen, 1986).

Amnesia resulting from psychological causes is called **dissociative amnesia** (Maldonado, Butler, & Speigel, 1998). *Dissociation* means "splitting off." Memories of a traumatic experience may become "dissociated" (split off) from consciousness, producing a form of amnesia for events occurring during a specific time (see Chapter 11). These events may be too emotionally troubling—provoking too much anxiety or guilt—to be consciously experienced. A soldier may have at best a dim memory of the horror he experienced on the battlefield and remember nothing of his buddy's being killed; yet his memory of other past events remains intact. Rarely is dissociative amnesia of the type that has fueled many a daytime soap opera, the type in which people forget their entire lives—who they are, where they live, and so on.

Concept Chart 6.2 provides an overview of the key concepts of forgetting.

anterograde amnesia Loss or impairment of the ability to form or store new memories.

dissociative amnesia A psychologically based form of amnesia involving the "splitting off" from memory of traumatic or troubling experiences.

MODULE 6.2 REVIEW

Forgetting

CONCEPT CHECK

1. According to the decay theory of memory,
   a. similar kinds of experiences block memories of a given event.
   b. memories are repressed or kept hidden from conscious awareness.
   c. memory traces in the brain fade or disappear over time.
   d. distinctive memory cues are not encoded or are unavailable.

3. Which of the following is *not* a helpful way to reduce the effects of interference on memory?
   a. Avoid overlearning.
   b. Study material just before going to bed.
   c. Rehearse or practice material repeatedly.
   d. Avoid studying similar content simultaneously.

2. The type of interference that accounts for why you may forget to advance the year when writing checks early in a new year is called _____.

4. The tip-of-the-tongue phenomenon may result from a lack of _____ cues.

5. Memory loss in which earlier life events are forgotten is known as
   a. dissociative amnesia.
   b. retrograde amnesia.
   c. retroactive amnesia.
   d. anterograde amnesia.

MODULE 6.3   The Biology of Memory

- **Where are memories stored in the brain?**
- **What is LTP, and what role do scientists believe it plays in memory formation?**
- **What is the role of the hippocampus in memory?**
- **What have scientists learned about the genetic basis of memory?**

How are memories formed in the brain? Where are they stored? Breakthrough research is beginning to answer these and other questions that probe the biological underpinnings of memory. In this module, we examine what is presently known about those underpinnings.

Brain Structures in Memory: Where Do Memories Reside?

Psychologist Karl Lashley (1890–1958) spent much of his career attempting to track down the elusive **engram**, the term he used to describe a physical trace or etching in the brain where he believed a memory is stored. A rat that learns to run a maze, for example, should have an engram somewhere in its brain containing a memory trace of the correct route leading to the exit or goal box.

Lashley spent years training rats to run mazes, then surgically removing parts of their cerebral cortexes, and testing them again to see if their memories for mazes remained intact. He reasoned that if removal of a part of the cortex wiped away a given memory, that part must be where the particular memory was stored. Despite years of painstaking research, he found that rats continued to run mazes they had learned previously regardless of the parts of the cortex he removed. The rats simply did not forget. He concluded that memories are not housed in any specific brain structure but must be scattered about the brain.

engram   Lashley's term for the physical trace or etching of a memory in the brain.

Neuronal Networks: The Circuitry of Memory

CONCEPT 6.24
Memories are stored in complex networks of interconnected brain cells called neuronal networks.

Researchers today believe that memories are not etched into particular brain cells but, instead, are stored in the intricate circuitry of constellations of neurons in the brain, called **neuronal networks** (also called *neural networks*), especially in the cerebral cortex (S. S. Hall, 1998; Matsumoto, Suzuki, & Tanaka, 2003; Rupp, 1998). Though the biochemical bases of memory are surely complex, we can think of memory in the simplest biological terms as the form in which information is encoded within the circuitry of neuronal networks in the brain.

The Hippocampus: A Storage Bin for Memory

Scientists suspect that the hippocampus, a structure in the brain's limbic system, plays an important role in converting short-term memory into long-term declarative memory—that is, into memory of facts (semantic memory) and life experiences (episodic memory) (Eichenbaum & Fortin, 2003; Jacobs & Schenk, 2003; Yasuno et al., 2003). But the hippocampus doesn't appear to play a role in procedural memory, the kind of memory we utilize when riding a bicycle or using tools. Nor does it appear that the hippocampus is the final destination for new declarative memories. Rather, it may be a temporary storage bin for holding new memories, perhaps for weeks or even months, before they are transferred to the cerebral cortex and other parts of the brain for long-term storage.

CONCEPT 6.25
Damage to the hippocampus could prevent you from forming new memories, such that you might be unable to remember someone you've just met.

If you suffered extensive damage to your hippocampus, you might develop anterograde amnesia and be unable to form new memories (Wixted, 2004). Depending on the extent of the damage, you might retain earlier memories but each new experience would fail to leave any mark in your memory. It would seem as if the event had never happened.

Memory also depends on other brain structures, including the thalamus and the amygdala. We know, for example, that damage to the thalamus can result in amnesia. And the amygdala plays an important part in encoding emotional experiences, such as fear and anger. Scientists believe that the amygdala and hippocampus become especially active during emotionally charged experiences, helping to strengthen and preserve memories of these meaningful events (Adelson, 2004; Hassert et al., 2004). All told, no one part of the brain is entirely responsible for memory formation (see Figure 6.11).

Figure 6.11 Brain Structures in Memory
There is no single memory center in the brain. Among the structures that work in coordination with the cerebral cortex in memory processes are the hippocampus, amygdala, and thalamus.

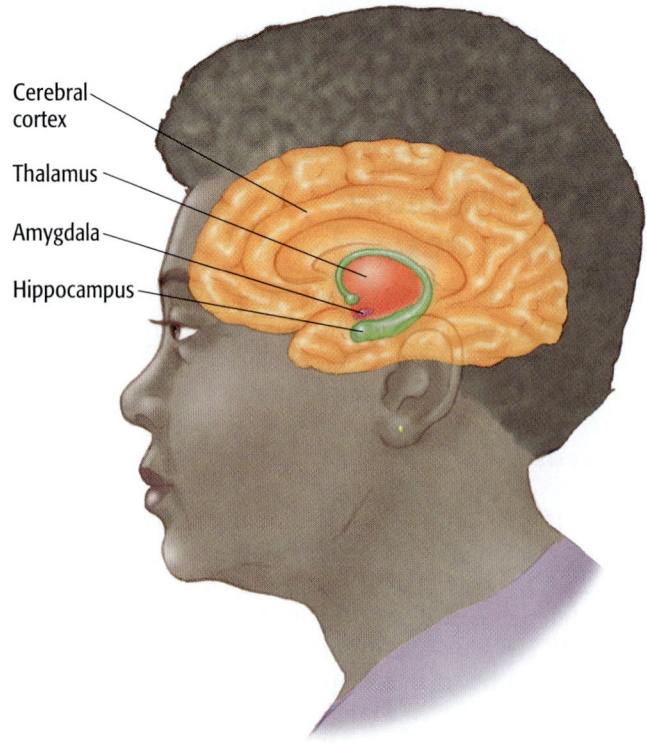

Cerebral cortex

Thalamus

Amygdala

Hippocampus

Strengthening Connections Between Neurons: The Key to Forming Memories

Locating neuronal networks corresponding to particular memories makes finding the proverbial needle in the haystack seem like child's play. The human brain contains billions of neurons and trillions of synapses among them. Any individual neuron in the brain may have some ten thousand synaptic connections with other neurons (S. S. Hall, 1998). In the hope of tracking down specific networks of cells where memories are formed, researchers have turned to a relatively simple animal, a large sea snail (*Aplysia*) that possesses a mere twenty thousand neurons.

The landmark research that Erik Kandel, a molecular biologist and Nobel Prize winner, performed on *Aplysia* represented a major step forward in unraveling the biological bases of memory (Kandel, 1995; Kandel & Hawkins, 1993). Since learning results in the formation of new memories, Kandel needed to demonstrate that these animals were capable of learning new responses. To accomplish this, he and his colleagues first desensitized the snails to receiving a mild squirt of water. After a number of trials, the animals became habituated to the water squirt so that it no longer caused them to budge. In the second phase of the experiment, the researchers paired the squirt with a mild electric shock. The animals showed they could learn a simple conditioned response—reflexively withdrawing their gills (their breathing apparatus) when squirted with water alone. This self-defensive maneuver is the equivalent of the snails' battening down the hatches in anticipation of impending shock (Rupp, 1998).

Kandel observed that the amount of neurotransmitter released into synapses between the nerve cells that control the withdrawal reflex increased as the animals learned the conditioned response. The added neurotransmitter kicked the reflex into overdrive, making it more likely to fire. In effect, these synapses became stronger—that is, more capable of transmitting neural messages. Kandel had shown that memory formation involves biochemical changes occurring at the synaptic level.

Synaptic connections can also be strengthened by repeated electrical stimulation of brain cells. This long-lasting increase in the strength of synaptic connections is called **long-term potentiation (LTP)**. Potentiation means "strengthening." A potentiated (stronger) synaptic connection means that neural messages can be transmitted more readily from nerve cell to nerve cell.

Many memory scientists today believe that the conversion of short-term memory into long-term memory depends on production of LTP, or long-term strengthening of synaptic connections within neuronal networks in the brain (Chen, Sweatt, & Klann, 1997; Hoelscher, 2001). LTP may result from the repeated stimulation of nerve cells within these neuronal networks as the result of learning and rehearsal of information.

CONCEPT 6.26
The key to forming memories may lie in strengthening the interconnections between the neurons that form neuronal networks in the brain.

The Biology of Memory   Nobel Prize winner Erik Kandel holding an *Aplysia*, the sea snail he used to study the biological bases of memory.

CONCEPT 6.27
Scientists suspect that long-term potentiation (LTP) may be needed for long-term memory to occur.

 **About It**

Did You Take Your Memory Pill Today?

Suppose memory boosters are found that would allow you to preserve perfect memories of everything you read and experience. Though memory pills might help you around exam time, would you really want to retain crystal-clear memories of every personal experience, including disappointments, personal tragedies, and traumatic experiences? Life is bumpy. Perhaps it is best that some memories fade with time. What do you think?

neuronal networks   Memory circuits in the brain that consist of complicated networks of nerve cells.

long-term potentiation (LTP)   The long-term strengthening of neural connections as the result of repeated stimulation.

CONCEPT CHART 6.3
Biology of Memory: Key Concepts

Concept	Description
Lashley's engram	Despite years of research, Karl Lashley failed to find evidence of an engram, his term for a physical trace or etching in the brain where he believed a memory is stored.
Neuronal networks	Memory scientists believe that memories may "reside" in complex networks of neurons distributed across different parts of the brain.
Biological underpinnings of memory	The hippocampus is a key brain structure in converting short-term memory into long-term memory. A leading contemporary view of the conversion of short-term to long-term memory holds that it depends on long-term potentiation, the strengthening of synaptic connections between neurons.
Genetic factors in memory	Conversion of short-term memory to long-term memory depends on brain proteins whose production is regulated by certain genes. Advances in genetic engineering show that it is possible to enhance learning and memory ability in nonhuman organisms by genetic manipulation.

Genetic Bases of Memory

Promising research with genetic engineering is offering new insights into how memory works. The transformation of short-term memory into long-term memory depends on the production of certain proteins. The production of these proteins is regulated by certain genes. Scientists have found that manipulation of a particular gene in fruit flies can enhance learning and memory ability, producing a kind of "smart fly" (S. S. Hall, 1998). Perhaps a similar gene might one day be found in humans.

Scientists hope that knowledge gained about the role of brain proteins in memory and the genes that help regulate their production may eventually lead to the development of drugs to treat or even cure Alzheimer's disease and other memory disorders (S. S. Hall, 1998). Perhaps we'll even have drugs that boost the memory functioning of normal individuals (Goode, 2000a). In the meantime, think critically if you encounter claims about so-called memory-enhancing drugs. We have no scientific evidence that any drug or supplement available today can enhance memory in normal individuals (e.g., Solomon et al., 2002).

Concept Chart 6.3 summarizes some of the key concepts relating to the biology of memory.

CONCEPT 6.28

Scientists have begun to unravel the genetic bases of memory, which may lead to the development of safe drugs that can help preserve or restore memory functioning.

MODULE 6.3 REVIEW

The Biology of Memory

CONCEPT CHECK

1. Researchers today believe memories are stored in constellations of brain cells known as _____.

2. Which of the following does *not* seem to be a function of the hippocampus?
   a. converting short-term memories into long-term declarative memories
   b. forming procedural memories
   c. creating long-term memories of facts (semantic memory) and life experiences (episodic memory)
   d. serving as a temporary storage area for new memories

3. The strengthening of synaptic connections that may underlie the conversion of short-term memory into long-term memory is called _____.

4. Researchers are finding genetic influences in memory. How do genes appear to influence memory functioning?
   a. Genes regulate the production of certain proteins that are critical to long-term memory.
   b. A memory gene leads to the production of specialized neurotransmitters involved in learning and memory.
   c. Genes regulate the production of a memory molecule that allows new memories to form.
   d. Memories are directly encoded in genes, which are then passed from one generation to the next.

APPLICATION

MODULE 6.4   Powering Up Your Memory

- **What can you do to power up your memory?**

Even if you never compete in a memory championship, you can learn to boost your memory power. Techniques specifically aimed at enhancing memory are called *mnemonics,* some of which have been practiced since the time of the ancient Greeks. Yet perhaps the most important ways to power up your memory are to take care of your health and to adopt more effective methods of studying, such as the SQ3R+ system (see "To the Student" in the preface of the text).

CONCEPT 6.29
You can boost your memory power in many ways, including using mnemonics, focusing your attention, practicing repeatedly, taking care of your health, and adopting effective study habits.

Using Mnemonics to Improve Memory

A **mnemonic** is a device for improving memory. The word *mnemonic* is derived from the name of the Greek goddess of memory, Mnemosyne, and is pronounced neh-MAHN-ik (the first *m* is silent). Here are some of the most widely used mnemonic devices. .

Acronyms and Acrostics

The method of acronyms (also called the *first-letter system*) is among the easiest and most widely used mnemonic devices. An **acronym** is a word composed of the first letters of a series of words. The acronym HOMES can help you remember the names of the Great Lakes (Huron, Ontario, Michigan, Erie, and Superior). In Chapter 3, you learned the acronym Roy G. Biv, which spells out the first letters of the colors of the spectrum. You might try devising some acronyms to help you retain information you learned in class.

An **acrostic** is a verse or saying in which a letter of each word, typically the first letter, stands for something else. Generations of musicians have learned the lines of the treble clef staff (E, G, B, D, and F) by committing to memory the acrostic "*Every Good Boy Does Fine.*"

Popular Sayings and Rhymes

Popular sayings and poems help us remember a variety of things, including when to turn the clock forward or back ("Fall back, spring forward"). Rhymes can be used as a mnemonic for remembering specific information. A common example is the rhyme for remembering the number of days in each month: "Thirty days hath September, April, June, and November. . . ."

Visual Cues and Visual Imagery

Visual cues can help us remember to remember. When you need to remember to do something, pin a reminder note where you will be most likely to notice it, such as on your shoes, the front door, or the steering wheel of your car.

Visual imagery can help us remember new words, names, and word combinations. For example, to remember the word *hippocampus,* think of an associated image, such as the image of a hippopotamus. To remember the name Bill Smith, picture a blacksmith who has a mouth shaped like a duck's bill (Turkington, 1996). The well-known memory expert Harry Lorayne (2002) recommended linking imagery to tasks that need to be remembered. For example, if you want to remember to mail a letter, picture the letter on the handle of the front door. Seeing the front door handle may cue you to take the letter to the mailbox.

mnemonic A device for improving memory.

acronym A word composed of the first letters of a series of words.

acrostic A verse or saying in which the first or last letter of each word stands for something else.

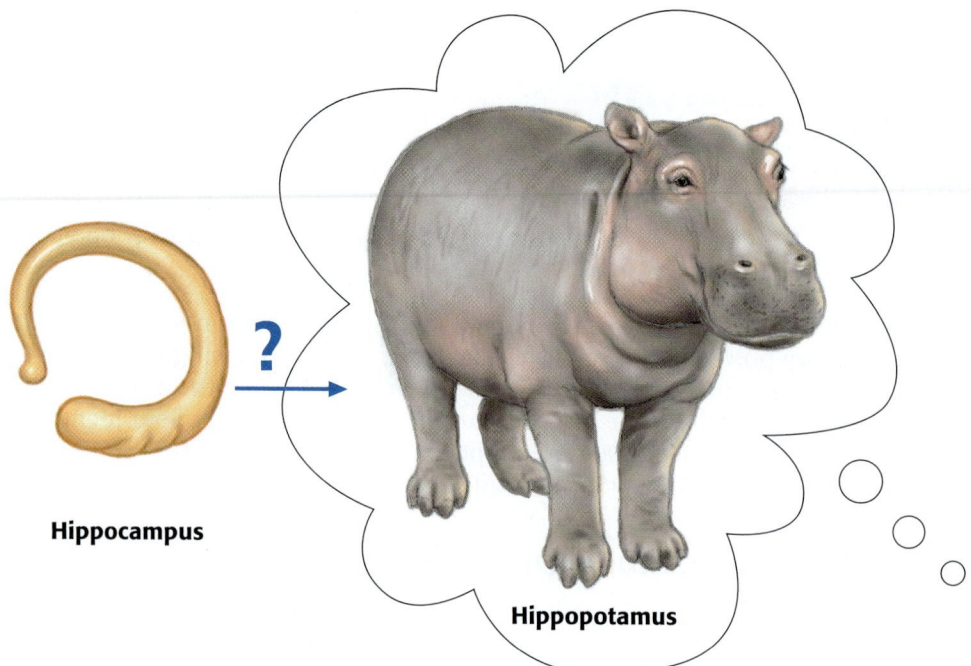

Hippocampus

Hippopotamus

Funny, It Doesn't Look Like a Hippopotamus
You may be better able to remember the word *hippocampus* if you link it to a visual image of a hippopotamus.

Chunking

Chunking, which we discussed in Module 6.1, is one of the easiest ways to remember a series of numbers. To use it, break down a number series into more easily remembered bits. For example, the number 7362928739 may be difficult to remember as one long series. The task becomes easier when the digits are chunked like a telephone number into three bits: 736-292-8739. Learning the zip code 10024 becomes easier when it is chunked into 100-24.

General Suggestions for Improving Memory

Though mnemonic devices can help you remember bits and pieces of information, they are of little use when it comes to remembering more complex material, such as the content of your college courses. But following the guidelines offered below and adopting good study habits will help you keep your learning and memory processes as sharp as possible (Herrmann & Palmisano, 1992; Turkington, 1996).

Pay Attention

One of the best ways to boost your learning or memory ability is to pay close attention. Paying attention not only means focusing more closely on the material at hand; it also means placing yourself in a quiet area that is conducive to studying and free of distractions (no TV, radio, phone, etc.).

Practice, Practice, Practice

You may have heard the old saw that the way to get to Carnegie Hall is to practice. Well, a good way to retain information is to rehearse it, and then rehearse it some more. Repeating information out loud or silently can help convert it from a short-term memory into a more enduring long-term memory. Make it a practice to "overlearn" material by repeating it two or more times beyond the point necessary for minimal proficiency.

You can also use "elaborative rehearsal" to strengthen retention of material you want to remember. One way of doing this is to relate the material to your personal experiences. For example, find examples in your own life of the concepts discussed in this chapter, such as declarative memory, procedural memory, implicit memory, and the tip-of-the-tongue phenomenon.

Spaced practice is more effective than massed practice at boosting retention. Spacing study sessions throughout the semester is a better strategy for preparing for exams than cramming at the end. Moreover, don't try to retain all the material in a chapter at one time. Break it down by sections or parts and rehearse your knowledge of each part. Then rehearse how the parts relate to each other as a whole.

Use External Memory Aids

Our daily lives are so packed with bits and pieces of information to be remembered that it makes sense to use whatever resources we can. Yes, you could use a mnemonic device to remember to tell your roommate that her mother called. But writing a reminder note to yourself will allow you to expend your mental efforts more profitably on something else. Other types of notes, such as class notes, are tools that you can use to retain more information. External memory aids, such as electronic organizers and computerized to-do lists, may also be helpful. You might even try putting objects, such as your key ring, in conspicuous places (thereby reducing occurrences of the common cry, "Now, where did I leave those keys?").

Link Time-Based Tasks to External Cues

Linking time-based tasks to external cues or activities can help boost prospective memory. For example, if you need to take medication at 6:00 P.M., link it with having dinner (Einstein & McDaniel, 1996). Setting an alarm to go off at a certain time may prompt you to take your medicine or to make an important phone call. Even the time-honored tradition of tying a string around your finger may be helpful.

Mentally Rehearse What You Intend to Do

Rehearsing what you plan to do may increase the likelihood of performing the intended action (Chasteen, Park, & Schwarz, 2001). Before leaving the house in the morning, practice saying to yourself the intended action, as for example, "I intend to pick up my clothes from the dry cleaners today." Or form a mental image of yourself performing the intended action.

Control Stress

Though we may need some level of stress to remain active and alert, prolonged or intense stress can interfere with the transfer of new learning into long-term memory (LeDoux, 1996). The stress management techniques discussed in Chapter 13 can help you keep stress within manageable levels.

Adopt Healthy Habits

Adopting a healthy diet and a regular exercise program can enhance memory performance (Herrmann & Palmisano, 1992). You should also avoid eating a large meal before cracking open your textbook, since consumption of large amounts of food puts your body in a restful mood that facilitates digestion, not mental alertness. On the other hand, avoid studying on an empty stomach, as hunger pangs make it more difficult to concentrate and retain new information. Remember, too, that using alcohol and other drugs does not mix with the mental alertness needed to learn and retain information. Finally, make sure to get enough sleep. Skipping sleep to cram for exams may make it more difficult to retain the information you've learned.

TYING IT TOGETHER

Without memory, experiences would leave no mark on our behavior. Memory permits us to retain and recall what we have learned through experience. Psychologists study the processes that make it possible for us to remember and that explain why we forget. We can conceptualize memory in terms of three underlying processes (encoding, storing, and retrieving information) occurring across three stages of memory (sensory memory, short-term memory, and long-term memory) (Module 6.1). Decay of memory traces, interference, retrieval failure, and motivated forgetting may each play a role in forgetting (Module 6.2). By exploring the biological bases of memory, we may come to a better understanding of how memories are formed and how they are lost (Module 6.3). Even as memory scientists continue to explore the foundations of memory, we can apply the knowledge we have acquired about how memory works to boost our memory power (Module 6.4).

SUMMING UP: Q & A

Remembering (Module 6.1)

What are the basic processes and stages of memory?

- The three basic memory processes are encoding (converting stimuli into a form that can be stored in memory), storage (retaining them in memory), and retrieval (accessing stored information).
- We encode information by means of acoustic codes (coding by sounds), visual codes (coding by mental imaging), and semantic codes (coding by meaning). Though we often encode auditory information acoustically, semantic coding typically leads to more enduring memories.
- The three stages of memory are sensory memory (momentary storage of sensory impressions), short-term memory (working memory of information held in awareness for up to about thirty seconds), and long-term memory (long-term or permanent storage of information).
- The three-component model holds that working memory consists of three subsystems: (1) the speech-based phonological loop; (2) the visuospatial sketchpad for holding visual or spatial information; and (3) the central executive, which coordinates the other subsystems, processes material held in working memory, and filters out distracting thoughts.
- The semantic network model posits that information is held in long-term memory in networks of interlinking concepts. Through a process of spreading activation, thinking of one concept brings related concepts within that semantic network to mind.
- The two major types of long-term memory are declarative memory ("knowing what or that") and procedural memory ("knowing how").
- Declarative memory is brought to mind by conscious effort, whereas procedural memory is engaged without any conscious effort.

What is the constructionist theory of memory?

- Constructionist theory holds that memory is a representation, or reconstruction, of past events or experiences.

What are flashbulb memories?

- Flashbulb memories are vivid, highly detailed, and long-lasting memories of emotionally charged personal or historical events.

What factors influence the accuracy of eyewitness testimony?

- Factors affecting the accuracy of eyewitness testimony include ease of recall, confidence in memory, general knowledge about the subject, same-race identification, and occurrence of leading or suggestive questioning.

Are recovered memories of childhood sexual abuse credible?

- Some recovered memories may be credible, but others are not. We presently lack the tools to determine which are accurate and which are not.

Forgetting (Module 6.2)

What are the major theories of forgetting?

- Decay theory holds that forgetting results from the gradual deterioration of memory traces in the brain.
- Interference theory is the belief that forgetting results from the interference of memories with each other. In retroactive interference, newly acquired information interferes with retention of material learned earlier. In proactive interference, material learned earlier interferes with retention of newly acquired information.
- Retrieval theory holds that forgetting is the result of a failure to access stored memories.
- Motivated forgetting, or repression, is the Freudian belief that people banish emotionally troubling events, impulses, and wishes from conscious awareness.

How is recall related to the methods used to measure it?

- Recognition tasks (such as multiple-choice questions) generally produce better memory retrieval than recall tests (free recall, serial recall, or paired-associates recall) because they provide more retrieval cues that help jog memory.

What is amnesia, and what causes it?

- Amnesia, or memory loss, may be caused by psychological factors or by physical factors such as degenerative brain diseases and brain trauma. There are two general types of amnesia: retrograde amnesia and anterograde amnesia.

The Biology of Memory (Module 6.3)

Where are memories stored in the brain?

- Memories are stored within the circuitry of constellations of nerve cells in the brain called neuronal networks.

What is LTP, and what role do scientists believe it plays in memory formation?

- LTP (long-term potentiation) is the biochemical process by which repeated stimulation strengthens the synaptic connections between nerve cells.
- Scientists suspect that the conversion of short-term memory into long-term memory may depend on the production of LTP.

What is the role of the hippocampus in memory?

- The hippocampus appears to play a key role in the formation and temporary storage of declarative memory, such as memory of events and daily experiences.

What have scientists learned about the genetic basis of memory?

- Scientists have identified genes that appear to play important roles in biochemical processes needed for long-term memory.

Application: Powering Up Your Memory (Module 6.4)

What can you do to power up your memory?

- To boost your memory, you can use mnemonics, such as acronyms and acrostics; pay close attention; practice repeatedly; use external memory aids; link time-based tasks to external cues; mentally rehearse what you intend to do; control stress; and adopt healthy habits.

Key Terms

memory (p. 194)
memory encoding (p. 194)
memory storage (p. 195)
memory retrieval (195)
retrieval cues (p. 195)
three-stage model (p. 195)
sensory memory (p. 195)
sensory register (p. 195)
iconic memory (p. 195)
eidetic imagery (p. 195)
echoic memory (p. 195)
short-term memory (STM) (p. 196)
chunking (p. 197)
maintenance rehearsal (p. 197)
phonological loop (p. 197)
visuospatial sketchpad (p. 197)

central executive (p. 198)
long-term memory (LTM) (p. 198)
consolidation (p. 198)
elaborative rehearsal (p. 198)
semantic network model (p. 198)
levels-of-processing theory (p. 199)
declarative memory (p. 199)
semantic memory (p. 200)
episodic memory (p. 200)
retrospective memory (p. 201)
prospective memory (p. 201)
procedural memory (p. 201)
implicit memory (p. 202)
explicit memory (p. 202)

constructionist theory (p. 202)
flashbulb memories (p. 203)
misinformation effect (p. 204)
decay theory (p. 206)
savings method (p. 207)
massed vs. spaced practice effect (p. 207)
interference theory (p. 207)
retroactive interference (p. 207)
proactive interference (p. 207)
overlearning (p. 208)
serial position effect (p. 208)
primacy effect (p. 208)
recency effect (p. 208)
retrieval theory (p. 209)

tip-of-the-tongue (TOT) phenomenon (p. 209)
repression (p. 210)
free recall (p. 211)
recognition task (p. 211)
amnesia (p. 211)
retrograde amnesia (p. 211)
anterograde amnesia (p. 212)
dissociative amnesia (p. 212)
engram (p. 213)
neuronal networks (p. 214)
long-term potentiation (LTP) (p. 215)
mnemonic (p. 217)
acronym (p. 217)
acrostic (p. 217)

Thinking Critically About Psychology

Based on your reading of this chapter, answer the following questions. Then, to evaluate your progress in developing critical thinking skills, compare your answers to the sample answers found in Appendix A.

1. Two men observe an accident in which a car hits a pedestrian and speeds away without stopping. They both were alert enough to glance at the car's license plate before it disappeared around the corner. Later, when interviewed by the police, the first man says, "I only got a glimpse of it but tried to picture it in my mind. I think it began with the letters QW." The second man chimes in, "Yes, but the whole plate number was QW37XT." Why do you think the second man was able to remember more details of the license plate than the first man?

2. An English-speaking singer gives a concert in Italy and includes a popular Italian folk song in her repertoire. Her rendition is so moving that an Italian woman from the audience later comes backstage to congratulate the singer, telling her, "That song was one of my favorites as a little girl. I've never heard it sung so beautifully. But when did you learn to speak Italian so well?" The singer thanks her for the compliment but tells her she doesn't speak a word of Italian. Drawing on your knowledge of memory processes, explain how the woman was able to learn a song in a language she couldn't speak.

Answers to Concept Check Questions

Module 6.1: 1. b; 2. procedural memory; 3. d, 4. i-d, ii-b, iii-a, iv-c.
Module 6.2: 1. c; 2. proactive interference; 3. a; 4. retrieval; 5. b.
Module 6.3: 1. neuronal networks; 2. b; 3. long-term potentiation (LTP); 4. a.

Answer to *Try This Out* (page 210)

Drawing (h) shows the correct image of a penny in Figure 6.10.

7

Thinking, Language, and Intelligence

DID YOU KNOW THAT . . .

- Albert Einstein used visual imagery in developing his theory of relativity? (p. 225)

- People generally have a hazy idea about what makes a fruit a fruit. (p. 226)

- A commonly used rule of thumb could lead you to make a bad decision about which movie to attend? (p. 229)

- Alexander Graham Bell used an analogy based on the human ear in developing the design for the first telephone? (p. 231)

- A psychological test can be reliable but not valid? (p. 241)

- A leading psychological theory of intelligence proposes not one but many different intelligences? (p. 245)

- The closer the genetic relationship between two people, the closer their IQ scores are likely to be? (p. 249)

While working on adhesives, Arthur Fry, a chemist for the 3M Company, came upon an unusual compound: an adhesive that could be used to stick paper to other objects. It was not nearly as strong as other adhesives then available, such as the adhesive in Scotch Tape (Bellis, 2001), and the 3M Company did not at first see any commercial use for it. Nothing more might have been made of the new compound had Fry not had a recurring problem finding his place in his church hymnal. The slips of paper he used as bookmarks often fell to the floor, leaving him scrambling to find his place. Then it dawned on him that the unusual compound he had developed in the lab might be of help in keeping bookmarks in place. What product that many people now use in their daily lives is based on Fry's adhesive?

Here's another story about a sticky invention (Bellis, 2001). In 1948, a man in Switzerland took his dog out for a nature walk. Both returned covered with burrs, the plant seed sacs that stick to clothing and animal fur. The man decided to inspect the burrs under a microscope to determine what made them so sticky. It turned out that they contained tiny hooks that grabbed hold of small loops in the fabric of his clothing. The man, George de Mestral, looked up from the microscope and a smile crossed his face. He knew in a flash what he must do. What do you think de Mestral did with his discovery of how burrs stick to fabrics? What widely used product resulted from this discovery?

You may never have heard of Arthur Fry and George de Mestral. But chances are you make use of their discoveries in your daily life. Arthur Fry's sticky compound is the adhesive in the stick-it pads that people use to post reminder notes. George de Mestral's discovery led him to develop the fastening fabric we now call Velcro®.

The insights of Fry and de Mestral are examples of the creative mind at work. Creativity is a form of thinking in which we combine information in new ways that provide useful solutions to problems. Creative thought is not limited to a few creative geniuses. It is a basic mental capability available to nearly all of us. This chapter focuses on creativity and other aspects of thinking, including concept formation, problem solving, and decision making.

We start out by looking at various forms of thinking, including ways we represent information in our minds. Then we examine language development and how language affects our thinking. We also venture into the controversy about whether humans are the only species to use language. Next, we explore the nature and measurement of intelligence—the mental ability or abilities allowing us to solve problems, learn from our experiences, and adapt to the demands of the environment. We end by focusing specifically on skills you can use to become a more creative problem solver. ■

<table>
<tr><td>MODULE 7.1</td><td></td></tr>
</table>

MODULE 7.1 Thinking

- **What is cognitive psychology?**
- **What is thinking?**
- **What are the major types of concepts people use, and how are they applied?**
- **What can we do to solve problems more efficiently?**
- **How do cognitive biases influence decision making?**
- **What cognitive processes underlie creative thinking?**

A Sticky Invention Thanks to the creative insight of George de Mestral, an ordinary nature walk led to the development of a fastening device used by millions of people today.

CONCEPT 7.1
When we think, we represent information in our minds in the form of images, words, and concepts, and manipulate that information to solve problems, make decisions, and engage in creative pursuits.

CONCEPT 7.2
Mental images help us perform cognitive functions, such as remembering directions and finding creative solutions to problems.

Thinking, or *cognition,* is a major focus of study in **cognitive psychology**, the branch of psychology that explores how we acquire knowledge about the world. Cognitive psychologists investigate how we think, process information, use language, and solve problems.

Psychologists generally define **thinking** as the mental representation and manipulation of information. We represent information in our minds in the form of images, words, and concepts (such as truth and beauty). We manipulate information in our minds when we solve problems, make decisions, and engage in creative pursuits. Let us first examine the ways in which we mentally represent and act upon information.

Mental Images: In Your Mind's Eye

When we think, we represent information in our minds in the form of images, words, or concepts. Some information is better represented by words and concepts than by images. Abstractions like justice, honor, liberty, and respect fall into this category. After all, we may be able to describe in words what we mean by the term *justice,* but what sort of mental image would represent what justice looks like? On the other hand, nonabstract objects in the "real world" are generally better represented by mental pictures. If, for example, you were asked whether a rhino has one horn or two, you would most likely try to picture a rhino in your mind. You may more readily bring to mind an image of a flower than a memory of one (Tracy, Fricano, & Greco, 2001).

A **mental image** is a mental picture or representation of an object or event. People form mental images of many different objects—faces of familiar people, the layout of the furniture in their homes, the letters of the alphabet, a graduation or religious ceremony. A mental image is not an actual or photographic representation of an object. Rather, it is a reconstruction of the object or event from memory.

Researchers find that the parts of the visual cortex we use when we form mental images are very similar to the parts we use when we actually observe the objects themselves (Kosslyn, 1994) Yet there is a difference between an image imagined and an image seen: The former can be manipulated, but the latter cannot. For example, we can manipulate imagined images in our minds by rotating them or perusing them from different angles. Figure 7.1 provides an opportunity to test your ability to manipulate mental images.

The ability to hold and manipulate mental images helps us perform many cognitive tasks, including remembering directions. You could use verbal representations ("Let's see, that was two lefts and a right, right?"). But forming a mental image—for example, by picturing the church where you make a left turn and the gas station where you make a right—may work better.

Mental imaging can also lead to creative solutions to puzzling problems. For example, when the famed physicist Albert Einstein was developing his breakthrough theory of relativity, he found it helpful to visualize himself traveling

Figure 7.1   Mental Rotation
Are the objects in each pair the same or different? Answering this question depends on your ability to rotate objects in your mind's eye.*

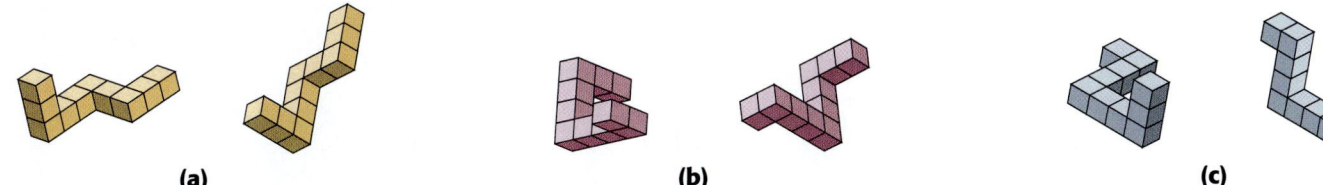

(a)   (b)   (c)

*Answer: The objects in pair *a* and *b* are the same; those in pair *c* are different.

along a beam of light (Finke, Ward, & Smith, 1992). In writing to a friend, Einstein commented that words did not play any role in his creative thought. They came only after he was able to reproduce mental images of the new ideas he had formulated.

Investigators find gender differences in mental imagery. In one study, women reported more vivid images of past experiences and greater use of imagery to remember past experiences than men did, but men more often reported using imagery to solve problems (Harshman & Paivio, 1987). Women also tend to out-perform men in forming still images of objects. Perhaps that's why husbands seem so often to ask their wives where they have put their keys or their glasses. Women may be better at recalling where things are placed because of their greater skill in visually scanning an image of a particular location in their minds.

Mental imagery is not limited to visual images. Most people can experience mental images of other sensory experiences, such as "hearing" in their minds the rousing first chords of Beethoven's Fifth Symphony or recalling the taste of a fresh strawberry or the feel of cotton brushing lightly against the cheek. Yet people generally have an easier time forming visual images than images of other sensory experiences.

Concepts: What Makes a Bird a Bird?

Not only do we form representations of objects in our mind's eye; we also represent objects in terms of the mental categories in which we place them. You see objects moving along a road and think of them as "trucks" or "cars." Trucks and cars are examples of **concepts**, the mental categories we use to group objects, events, and ideas according to their common features. Forming concepts helps bring a sense of order to the world. It also makes us better able to anticipate or predict future events. For example, classifying a slithering creature in the woods as a snake prompts us to keep a respectful distance, a response that could be a life-saver. Think how differently you'd react to an approaching animal if you classified it as a skunk rather than a rabbit. Imagine, too, what it would be like if you were unable to form any concepts. Each time you encountered a four-legged furry creature that went "woof" you would have no idea whether to pet it or to run from it. Nor would you know whether a spherical object placed before you is one to be eaten (a meatball) or played with (a ball).

Concepts also help us respond more quickly to events by reducing the need for new learning each time we encounter a familiar object or event. Having acquired the concept *ambulance,* we immediately know how to respond when we see one pulling up behind us on the road.

Concepts can be classified as *logical concepts* or *natural concepts* (Jahnke & Nowaczyk, 1998). **Logical concepts** are those that have clearly defined rules for determining membership. Schoolchildren learn that the concept of a triangle applies to any three-sided form or figure. If a figure has three sides, it must be a

 CONCEPT 7.3
Forming concepts or mental categories for grouping objects, events, and ideas helps bring a sense of order and predictability to the world.

 PsychAssist: Cogitive Psychologists and the Hierarchy of Concepts

cognitive psychology   The branch of psychology that focuses on such mental processes as thinking, problem solving, decision making, and use of language.

thinking   The process of mentally representing and manipulating information.

mental image   A mental picture or representation of an object or event.

concepts   Mental categories for classifying events, objects, and ideas on the basis of their common features or properties.

logical concepts   Concepts with clearly defined rules for membership.

Is a Penguin a Bird? Although a penguin doesn't fly, it is classified as a bird. Yet people may not recognize it as a bird if it does not closely resemble the model of a bird they have in mind, such as a robin.

CONCEPT 7.4
Cognitive psychologists classify concepts in two general categories, logical concepts and natural concepts.

CONCEPT 7.5
People form their judgments of whether objects belong to particular categories by comparing them with models or examples of category members.

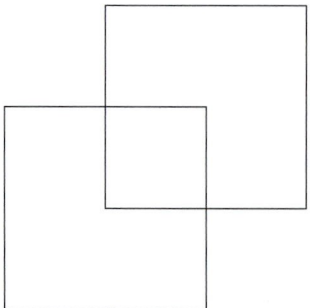

Figure 7.2
Two Interlocking Squares?

Source: Adapted from de Bono, 1970.

triangle. However, most of the concepts we use in everyday life are **natural concepts**, in which the rules for determining how they are applied are poorly defined or fuzzy.

Natural concepts include various *objects,* such as furniture, mammals, and fruit; *activities,* such as games, work, and sports; and *abstractions,* such as justice, honor, and freedom (Jahnke & Nowaczyk, 1998). A botanist may use a logical concept (one having fixed rules) for classifying objects as fruits or as vegetables, but most people use natural concepts for classifying these and other objects, even if they are hazy about the rules they use in applying their concepts. For example, most people have an imprecise idea about what makes a fruit a "fruit." They might readily agree that an apple is a fruit, but they may not be sure about an avocado, a pumpkin, or an olive.

How do people apply natural concepts? How do they determine whether a particular animal—say, an ostrich or a penguin—is a bird? Cognitive psychologists believe we base these judgments on the *probability* that objects are members of particular categories (Willingham, 2001). In other words, we decide whether an object is more or less likely to belong to a particular category by comparing its characteristics with a mental representation of a model or example of a category member (Minda & Smith, 2001). For instance, if we pictured a robin as a model or "best example" of a bird, we would more readily classify a sparrow as a bird than we would an ostrich or a penguin because the sparrow has more robinlike features (sparrows fly; ostriches and penguins don't).

We now turn to considering ways in which we act upon the information we represent in our minds, beginning with problem solving. Before going any further, try answering the following questions, which are intended to probe the way you think through problems. The answers are provided in various places throughout the chapter.

1. Do you perceive two interlocking squares in Figure 7.2? Or might this figure represent something else?

2. Jane and Sue played six games of chess, and each of them won four. There were no ties. How was that possible? (Adapted from Willingham, 2001)

3. An airliner from France crashes just off the coast of New Jersey within the territorial waters of the United States. Although all of the passengers and crew were French citizens, none of the survivors was returned to France for burial. Why not?

4. A man used a key that allowed him to enter but could not be used to open any locks. What kind of key was it?

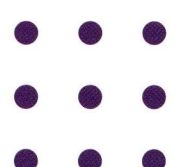

5. Figure 7.3 shows a classic problem called the nine-dot problem. Your task is to draw no more than four lines that connect all the dots without lifting your pen or pencil from the paper.

Figure 7.3
The Nine-Dot Problem

Problem Solving: Applying Mental Strategies to Solving Problems

Problem solving is a cognitive process in which we employ mental strategies to solve problems. As you may recall from Chapter 5, psychologist Edward Thorndike observed that animals placed in his puzzle box used trial and error to solve the problem of escaping from the enclosed compartment. The animals would try one response after another until they stumbled upon the action that activated the escape mechanism. Solving a problem by trial and error is a "hit-or-miss" approach in which one tries one solution after another until the correct one is found.

Some people arrive at solutions to problems by trial and error, while others report "Eureka-type" experiences in which solutions seem just suddenly to "pop" into their minds. You'll recall from Chapter 5 that the Gestalt psychologist Wolfgang Köhler referred to this sudden awareness of a solution to a problem as *insight.* Cognitive psychologists believe that insight results from restructuring a problem so that its elements suddenly fit together to render a solution. Restructuring may occur when the person sees the problem from a different perspective, notices new information, or recognizes connections between elements of the problem that were previously overlooked. Recall the question of how Jane and Sue could each win four games of chess if they played six games and there were no ties. The answer is that Jane and Sue did not play against each other. The solution comes from restructuring the problem so that it does not depend on their playing each other. Figure 7.4 shows another type of insight problem.

Though we sometimes arrive at correct solutions through trial and error or insight, these approaches to problem solving have certain drawbacks. Trial and error is tedious. You must try one solution after another until you happen upon the right one. And mulling over a problem while waiting for a sudden flash of insight to occur may require quite a long wait. How might we approach problem solving more efficiently? Here we consider two problem-solving strategies that may prove helpful, *algorithms* and *heuristics.* We also explore common pitfalls that can impede our problem-solving efforts.

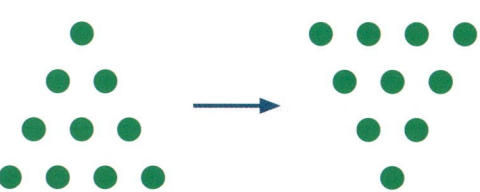

Figure 7.4   An Insight Problem
Your task here is to move only three of the dots to make a downward-facing triangle. You can try it using a stack of poker chips. If you get stuck, see Figure 7.5 on page 228 for the answer.

Source: Metcalfe, 1986.

Algorithms

An **algorithm** is a step-by-step set of rules for solving a problem. You probably first became acquainted with algorithms when you learned the basic rules (algorithms) of arithmetic, such as carrying the number to the next column when adding columns of numbers. The major drawback to algorithms is that none may precisely apply to a particular problem. Lacking a precise algorithm, you might still boost your chances of solving a problem by following an imprecise algorithm, or general set of guidelines. For example, a general set of guidelines for achieving a good grade in introductory psychology would be to set aside a certain number of hours to study the text and other readings each week, attend class regularly, and participate in a study group. Will this guarantee success? Perhaps not. But the odds are in your favor.

CONCEPT 7.6
Algorithms and heuristics are problem-solving strategies that can help you solve problems more efficiently.

natural concepts   Concepts with poorly defined or fuzzy rules for membership.

problem solving   A form of thinking focused on finding a solution to a particular problem.

algorithm   A step-by-step set of rules that will always lead to a correct solution to a problem.

heuristic   A rule of thumb for solving problems or making judgments or decisions.

Heuristics

A rule of thumb used as an aid in solving problems or making judgments or decisions is called a **heuristic**. Heuristics do not guarantee a solution, but they may help you arrive at one more quickly. In using a *backward-working* heuristic, we

Problem
Move only three of these dots to make a downward-facing triangle

Solution

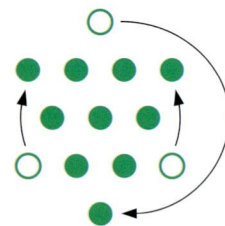

Figure 7.5 Solution to the Insight Problem in Figure 7.4
Assuming you solved the problem, did you rely on the trial-and-error method—moving the dots (or chips) around until you chanced upon the correct solution? Or did you mull the problem over in your mind until a moment of illumination, or insight, arrived? If so, what do you think accounted for this sudden awareness?

CONCEPT 7.7
Mental set and functional fixedness are examples of cognitive tendencies that can impede problem solving.

mental set The tendency to rely on strategies that worked in similar situations in the past but that may not be appropriate to the present situation.

functional fixedness The tendency to perceive objects as limited to the customary functions they serve.

decision making A form of problem solving in which we must select a course of action from among the available alternatives.

start with a possible solution and then work backward to see if the data support the solution. A psychologist seeking the causes of schizophrenia might approach the problem by proposing a model (schizophrenia as a genetic disease) and then examine whether the available data fit the model. Using the *means-end heuristic,* we evaluate our current situation and compare it to the end result we want to achieve. Then we develop a step-by-step procedure to reduce the distance between the two. Another heuristic, *creating subgoals,* involves breaking the problem down into smaller, more manageable problems. Scientists use this strategy when they assign different teams to work on different parts of a problem. In AIDS research, for example, one team might work on how HIV penetrates the cell, another on how it reproduces, and so on. Solving the riddle of HIV may depend on knowledge gained from achieving each of the subgoals.

Mental Roadblocks to Problem Solving

Chris is sitting in the front passenger seat of a car waiting for the driver to return when the car suddenly begins to roll backward down a hill. In panic, he tries to climb over the gearshift lever, clumsily reaching with his foot for the brake pedal in order to stop the car. Unfortunately, he can't reach the brake pedal in time to prevent the car from slamming into a pole. What could he have done differently in this situation? Why do you think he responded the way he did? (adapted from M. Levine, 1994).

Perhaps Chris should have realized that a much simpler solution was available: pulling the emergency brake. Yet Chris was locked into a preconceived way of solving the problem: depressing the brake pedal. This solution works well if you're sitting in the driver's seat but may not be effective if you need to climb over from the passenger side. The tendency to rely on strategies that worked well in similar situations in the past is called a **mental set**.

In some instances, as when a new problem is similar to an old one, a mental set may help you reach an appropriate solution more quickly. But a mental set can be an impediment to problem solving if a new problem requires a solution different from an old one, as the example of Chris illustrates.

Another impediment to problem solving is **functional fixedness**, the inability to see how familiar objects can be used in new ways. Suppose you're working at your desk and a sudden wind blows in from an open window, scattering your papers about (M. Levine, 1994). Would functional fixedness prevent you from recognizing new uses for familiar objects? Or would you reach for objects that don't ordinarily serve as paperweights, such as your eyeglasses or wallet, and use them to hold down your papers long enough for you to get up and close the window? The box-candle problem and the two-string problem are classic examples of functional fixedness (see Figures 7.6 and 7.7).

Yet another impediment to problem solving is the tendency to allow irrelevant information to distract one's attention from the relevant information needed to solve the problem. Recall the problem on page 226, which stated that none of the survivors of the crash of the French airliner were buried in France. Did the geographical details distract you so that you overlooked the statement that no *survivors* were returned for burial?

Mental Roadblocks in Decision Making

We constantly face the need to make decisions, ranging from everyday ones ("What should I wear?" "What should I have for dinner?") to important life decisions ("What should I major in?" "Should I get married?" "Should I take this job or stay in college?"). **Decision making** is a form of problem solving in which we must select a course of action from among the available alternatives.

We may think we approach decision making logically, but researchers find that underlying biases in thinking often hamper our ability to make rational choices (Kahneman, 1991; Kahneman & Tversky, 1973). One example is the **confirmation bias**—the tendency to stick to an initial hypothesis even in the face of strong evidence that is inconsistent with it. The confirmation bias leads us to place greater weight on information confirming our prior beliefs and expectations than on contradictory evidence. Consider a juror who decides whether a defendant is guilty based on the preliminary evidence and then fails to reconsider that decision even when strong contradictory evidence presents itself.

Though heuristics may help us solve problems, they can sometimes lead to bad decisions. For instance, the **representativeness heuristic** may lead us to make more of something than we should. In using this heuristic, we assume that a given sample is representative of a larger population (Kahneman & Tversky, 1973). Using the representativeness heuristic, we might base our decision about whether to see a movie on the opinion of someone we just happened to overhear talking about it; thus, we might end up attending a bad movie or passing up a good one. The representativeness heuristic also underlies the tendency to judge people by first impressions. We might reject a potential romantic partner on the basis of a two-minute conversation or even how the person dressed on a particular occasion. We infer that the sample of behavior we observe is representative of the person's behavior in general, which may not be the case. The *Try This Out* feature offers an example of how the representativeness heuristic may bias your thinking.

The **availability heuristic** is the tendency to base decisions on information that readily comes to mind (Kahneman & Tversky, 1973). Consider the many uncertainties we face in life. Driving to work, flying on an airplane, eating a fat-filled dessert—all entail some degree of risk. Even getting out of bed in the morning is somewhat risky (you could fall). The availability heuristic may lead us to make errors in assessing relative risk. For instance, vivid images of a plane crash on a television news program may stick in our minds, leading us to overestimate the risk we face in flying on a commercial airliner.

CONCEPT 7.8
We may think we approach decision making in a logical way, but underlying biases in our thinking often hamper our ability to make rational decisions.

CONCEPT 7.9
The confirmation bias, the representativeness heuristic, and the availability heuristic are examples of biases in thinking that can lead us to make bad decisions.

Figure 7.6   The Box-Candle Problem
Using only the material you see on the table, figure out a way to mount a candle on the wall so that it doesn't drip wax on the floor when it burns. The answer is shown in Figure 7.9 on page 230.

Source: Adapted from Duncker, 1945.

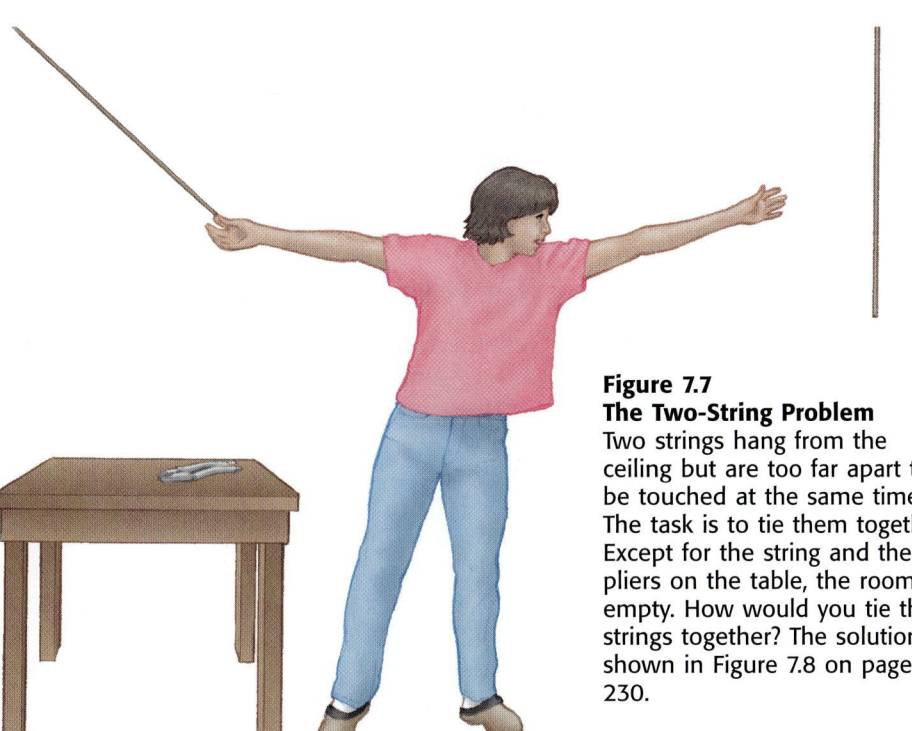

Figure 7.7
The Two-String Problem
Two strings hang from the ceiling but are too far apart to be touched at the same time. The task is to tie them together. Except for the string and the pliers on the table, the room is empty. How would you tie the strings together? The solution is shown in Figure 7.8 on page 230.

confirmation bias   The tendency to maintain allegiance to an initial hypothesis despite strong evidence to the contrary.
representativeness heuristic   A rule of thumb for making a judgment that assumes a given sample is representative of the larger population from which it is drawn.
availability heuristic   The tendency to judge events as more likely to occur when information pertaining to them comes readily to mind.

Figure 7.8   Solution to the Two-String Problem
The solution? Think of an alternate use for the pliers. By attaching them as a weight to the end of one of the strings, you can swing the string as a pendulum. Then move to the other string and wait for the swinging string to come close enough to catch it so that you can tie the two strings together.

Source: Adapted from Maier, 1931.

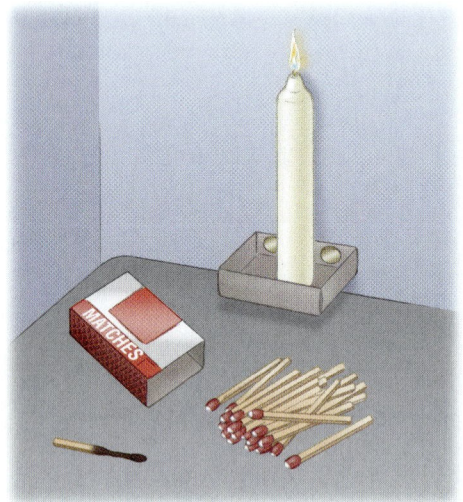

Figure 7.9   Solution to the Box-Candle Problem

TRY THIS OUT

The Coin Toss

A quarter is tossed six times. It lands heads up three times and tails up three times. Which of the sequences at the right was most likely to have occurred?

Did you select the last sequence? Many people do. Yet each of these sequences is equally likely to have occurred. The representativeness heuristic leads people to judge the irregular sequence in the last item to be more representative of a random order than the others.

1. HHHTTT

2. HTHTHT

3. TTTHHH

4. HTTHHT

Creativity: Not Just for the Few

Creativity involves thinking in ways that lead to original, practical, and meaningful solutions to problems or that generate new ideas or forms of artistic expression. The creation of a new product, for example, may solve a problem in a novel and useful way.

Creativity is not limited to a few creative geniuses in the arts or sciences. Psychologists recognize that virtually all of us have the ability to be creative and to apply creativity to many aspects of our daily life (Runco, 2004; Simonton, 2000). For example, a parent who invents a new activity for a four-year-old, a chef who combines ingredients in innovative ways, a worker who improves on a production method—all demonstrate creativity.

Though most of us have the potential to be creative, some people are clearly more creative than others. More creative people typically have at least an average to high-average IQ. However, there doesn't seem to be any relationship between creativity and IQs in the high range (above 120) (Csikszentmihalyi, 1996). As psy-

CONCEPT 7.10
Creativity is a cognitive ability found in varying degrees in most people.

creativity   Originality of thought associated with the development of new, workable products or solutions to problems.

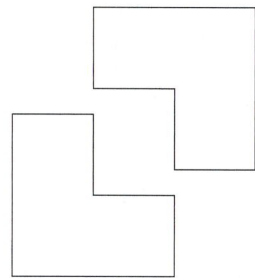

chologist Robert Sternberg (2001) notes, products developed by highly intelligent people may be of high quality, but they are not necessarily novel. Creativity goes beyond general intelligence.

Creativity is measured in different ways but most commonly through tests that tap *divergent thinking*. **Divergent thinking** is the wellspring of invention; it is the ability to conceive of new ways of viewing situations and new uses for familiar objects. By contrast, **convergent thinking** is the attempt to find the one correct answer to a problem. Refer back to problem 1 on page 226. The answer (two interlocking squares) seems so obvious we may not think of any alternatives. Yet by thinking divergently we can find other answers: three squares (note the one in the area of intersection), two L-shaped pieces separated by a square (see Figure 7.10), and a rectangle divided into two pieces that have been pushed askew.

Psychologist J. P. Guilford and his colleagues were the originators of tests that tap divergent thinking. One widely used measure, the Alternate Uses Test, has subjects list possible uses for a common object, such as a newspaper (Guilford et al., 1978). The person's score is based on the number of acceptable responses the person is able to generate.

When we think creatively, we use cognitive processes to manipulate or act upon stored knowledge. Investigators identify a number of cognitive processes that underlie creative thinking, including the use of *metaphor* and *analogy, conceptual combination,* and *conceptual expansion* (Ward, Smith, & Vaid, 1997):

1. *Metaphor and analogy.* Metaphor and analogy are creative products in their own right; they are also devices we use to generate creative solutions to puzzling problems. A *metaphor* is a figure of speech for likening one object or concept to another. In using metaphor, we speak of one thing as if it were another. For example, we might describe love as a candle burning bright.

   An *analogy* is a comparison between two things based on their similar features or properties—for example, likening the actions of the heart to those of a pump. Alexander Graham Bell showed a creative use of analogy when he invented the telephone. In studying the human ear, Bell had noticed how sounds were transmitted when the membrane known as the eardrum vibrated. He applied this idea of a membrane that vibrates in response to sounds in his design of the telephone (M. Levine, 1994).

2. *Conceptual combination.* Combining two or more concepts into one can result in novel ideas or applications that reflect more than the sum of the parts (Costello & Keane, 2001). Examples of **conceptual combinations** include "cell phones," "veggie burgers," and "home page." Can you think of other ways in which concepts can be creatively combined?

3. *Conceptual expansion.* One way of developing novel ideas is to expand familiar concepts. Examples of **conceptual expansion** include an architect's adaptation of an existing building to a new use, a writer's creation of new scenes using familiar characters, and a chef's variation on a traditional dish that results in a new culinary sensation (Ward et al., 1997).

Figure 7.10 Divergent Thinking
Compare Figure 7.2 on page 226 with the cutout shown here. Now imagine these two L-shaped figures pushed together so that they are separated by a square.

CONCEPT 7.11
Creativity involves using cognitive processes to manipulate or act upon stored knowledge.

About It

Alternate Uses Test

The Alternate Uses Test is widely used to measure creativity. Before reading the next paragraph, write down all the uses you can think of for the following objects: brick, newspaper, coffee mug, hanger. Most people start off with conventional uses, such as using bricks to build a house, a barbecue, or a patio. How many of your uses fall within a traditional category? How many represent innovative uses, such as using a brick as a doorstop, a paperweight, or a tool in weight-lifting exercises?

Source: Adapted from M. Levine, 1994.

divergent thinking The ability to conceive of new ways of viewing situations and new uses for familiar objects.

convergent thinking The attempt to narrow down a range of alternatives to converge on the one correct answer to a problem.

conceptual combinations
Combinations of two or more concepts into one concept, resulting in the creation of a novel idea or application.

conceptual expansion The expansion of familiar concepts into new uses.

CONCEPT 7.12
When people approach creative tasks, they tend to expand on what is familiar to them.

Creativity typically springs from the expansion or modification of familiar categories or concepts. The ability to take what we know and modify and expand upon it is one of the basic processes of creative thinking.

Before going further, you may wish to review the cognitive processes involved in thinking, which are outlined in Concept Chart 7.1.

CONCEPT CHART 7.1
Cognitive Processes in Thinking

Cognitive Process	Definition	Description
Mental imaging	Forming mental representations of objects or events	Images can be formed based on various sensory experiences, including vision, hearing, taste, and touch. Mental images can be manipulated to help us solve certain kinds of problems.
Concept formation	Grouping objects, events, and ideas on the basis of their common features	Most concepts are natural concepts, which have fuzzy or imprecise rules for membership. Logical concepts are those that have strict rules for membership.
Problem solving	The process of arriving at a solution to a given problem	Strategies include algorithms and heuristics. Pitfalls include mental set and functional fixedness.
Decision making	The process of deciding which of two or more courses of action to take	Decision making is often influenced by errors in thinking associated with the confirmation bias, the representativeness heuristic and the availability heuristic.
Creativity	The generation of novel, workable products or ideas	Creativity applies cognitive processes that act upon or manipulate stored knowledge. These processes include the use of metaphor and analogy, conceptual combination, and conceptual expansion.

MODULE 7.1 REVIEW

Thinking

CONCEPT CHECK

1. Psychologists generally define thinking as _____.

2. A category with clearly defined rules for membership is called a _____, whereas a category with poorly defined rules for membership is a _____.

3. One mental roadblock to problem solving is the inability to see how a familiar object can be used in new ways. This impediment is known as
   a. mental set.
   b. functional fixedness.
   c. incubation period.
   d. confirmation bias.

4. Match the terms on the left with their descriptions on the right:
   i. problem solving   a. process of using mental strategies to find solutions to problems
   ii. algorithm   b. a comparison between two things based on their similar features or properties
   iii. heuristic   c. set of step-by-step rules for solving problems
   iv. analogy   d. rule of thumb for solving problems or making decisions

5. Merging two or more concepts to produce novel ideas or applications is called
   a. conceptual expansion.
   b. creative combination.
   c. divergent thinking.
   d. conceptual combination.

MODULE 7.2   Language

- **What are the major components of language?**
- **How does language develop?**
- **What is the linguistic relativity hypothesis?**
- **Can nonhuman animals use language?**

Language is a system of communication composed of symbols—words or hand signs (as in the case of American Sign Language)—that are arranged according to a **grammar**, a set of rules governing the proper use of words, phrases, and sentences to express meaning. Language is so tightly woven into the human experience, says prominent linguist Steven Pinker (1994, p. 17), that "it is scarcely possible to imagine life without it. Chances are that if you find two or more people together anywhere on earth they will soon be exchanging words. When there is no one to talk with, people talk to themselves, to their dogs, even to their plants."

In this module, we examine the remarkable capacity of humans to communicate through language. We consider the basic components of language, developmental milestones in language acquisition, and leading theories of language acquisition. We also consider the question of whether language is a uniquely human characteristic.

Components of Language

The basic units of sound in a spoken language are called **phonemes**. English has about forty phonemes to sound out the 500,000 or so words found in modern unabridged English dictionaries. The word *dog* consists of three phonemes: "d," "au," and "g." From this example, you can see that phonemes in English correspond both to individual letters and to letter combinations, including the "au" in *dog* and the sounds "th" and "sh." The same letter can make different sounds in different words. The "o" in the word *two* is a different phoneme from the one in the word *one*. Changing one phoneme in a word can change the meaning of the word. Changing the "r" sound in *reach* to the "t" sound makes it *teach*. Different languages have different phonemes. In some African languages, various clicking sounds are phonemes. Hebrew has a guttural "chhh" phoneme, as in the expression *l'chaim* ("to life").

Phonemes are combined to form **morphemes**, the smallest units of meaning in a language. Simple words such as *car, ball,* and *time* are morphemes, but so are other linguistic units that convey meaning, such as prefixes and suffixes. The prefix "un," for example, means "not," and the suffix "ed" following a verb means that the action expressed by the verb occurred in the past. More complex words are composed of several morphemes. The word *pretested* consists of three morphemes: "pre," "test," and "ed."

Language requires more than phonemes and morphemes. It also requires **syntax**, the rules of grammar that determine how words are ordered within sentences and phrases to form meaningful expressions, and **semantics**, the set of rules governing the meaning of words. The sentence "buy milk I" sounds odd to us because it violates a basic rule of English syntax—that the subject ("I") must precede the verb ("buy"). We follow rules of syntax in everyday speech even if we are not aware of them or cannot verbalize them. But even when our speech follows proper syntax, it may still lack meaning. The famed linguist Noam Chomsky, to whose work we will return shortly, illustrated this point with the example "Colorless green ideas sleep furiously." The sentence may sound correct to our ears since it follows the rules of English syntax, but it doesn't convey any mean-

💡 **CONCEPT 7.13**
Language consists of four basic components: phonemes, morphemes, syntax, and semantics.

language   A system of communication composed of symbols (words, hand signs, etc.) that are arranged according to a set of rules (grammar) to form meaningful expressions.

grammar   The set of rules governing how symbols in a given language are used to form meaningful expressions.

phonemes   The basic units of sound in a language.

morphemes   The smallest units of meaning in a language.

syntax   The rules of grammar that determine how words are ordered within sentences or phrases to form meaningful expressions.

semantics   The set of rules governing the meaning of words.

ing. The same word may convey very different meanings depending on the context in which it is used. "Don't *trip* going down the stairs" means something very different from "Have a good *trip*."

Language Development

CONCEPT 7.14

Young children pass through a series of milestones of language acquisition, from crying and cooing to babbling, to one- and two-word phrases, and then to more complex speech.

Children the world over develop language in basically the same stages, which unfold at basically the same ages. Until about six months of age, infants are limited to nonlinguistic forms of communication—crying and cooing. At around that time, the first sounds resembling human speech appear in the form of babbling. The child then progresses through stages of one- and two-word phrases, and between the ages of two and three begins developing more complex speech patterns (see Concept Chart 7.2).

The similar course of language development across cultures and the ease with which children naturally acquire language suggest that language depends on an innate mechanism that may be "prewired" in the human brain. Noam Chomsky (1965) called this mechanism the **language acquisition device**. We acquire the ability to speak, much as we do the ability to walk and jump, because we have an inborn propensity to develop it. As Steven Pinker (1994) has put it, "We don't teach our children to sit, stand, and walk, and they do it anyway." Children learn to use the rules of grammar without any formal instruction. In English-speaking cultures, they begin placing the subject before the verb long before they learn what the terms *subject* and *verb* mean. According to Chomsky and Pinker, children are able to learn grammatical structures as rapidly and easily as they do because the human brain contains the basic blueprints or neural circuitry for using grammar.

Noam Chomsky

Critics point out that Chomsky's language acquisition device is not an actual physical structure in the brain but a hypothesis—an abstract concept of how language centers in the brain work—and that it does not explain the mechanisms by which language is produced. In fairness to Chomsky, we should point out that brain mechanisms responsible for language are extremely complex, consisting of complicated circuits in many areas of the brain that link together to produce language in ways we don't yet understand (Lieberman, 1998). Yet the pieces of the puzzle may be starting to fall into place. In 2001, scientists discovered the first gene linked to the development of brain mechanisms responsible for speech and language (Balter, 2001; Lai et al., 2001).

CONCEPT CHART 7.2
Milestones in Language Acquisition

Age (Approximate)	Vocal Activity	Description
Birth	Crying	Crying expresses distress.
Two months	Cooing	Infant begins making cooing sounds (e.g., "aah" and "oooh").
Six to twelve months	Babbling	Phonemes, the basic units of sound, appear.
Twelve months	One-word phrases	Baby imitates sounds and can understand some words; begins to say single words.
Eighteen to twenty-four months	Two-word phrases or sentences	Vocabulary grows to about fifty words, and baby emits two-word phrases or sentences.
Twenty-four to thirty-six months	Complex speech	Sentences become longer and more complex and include plurals and past tense; speech shows elements of proper syntax.

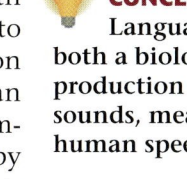

Regardless of the exact mechanisms involved in language production, both nature and nurture are clearly necessary for language to develop. Our ability to use language depends not only on a biological capacity for language production but also on experience with the sounds, meanings, and structures of human speech. Children may have a natural capacity for language, but they learn grammar by listening to the speech of others, and they enlarge their vocabularies by imitating the words others use to refer to particular objects (Pinker, 1994). Parents can help children develop language skills by talking and reading to them frequently. They can also use principles of operant conditioning and observational learning (discussed in Chapter 5) by modeling proper language use and rewarding children for imitating it.

However language develops, it is clear that language and thinking are closely intertwined. As discussed in the next section, some theorists even propose that language determines how we think.

Culture and Language: Does the Language We Use Determine How We Think?

Does the language we speak affect how we think? Might French Canadians, Chinese, and Africans see the world differently because of the vocabulary and syntax of their native languages? According to the **linguistic relativity hypothesis**, the answer is yes. This hypothesis—also called the *Whorfian hypothesis* after Benjamin Whorf, the amateur linguist who developed it—holds that the language we use determines how we think and how we perceive reality. Whorf (1956) pointed out that some cultures have many different words for colors, whereas others have only a few. English has eleven words for basic colors: black, white, red, green, yellow, blue, brown, purple, pink, orange, and gray. At the other end of the spectrum is the Navajo language, which has no separate words for blue and green.

Does the lack of color vocabulary determine how people perceive colors? Apparently not, according to landmark research by Eleanor Rosch (Heider, Rosch, & Olivier, 1972; Rosch, 1975). Rosch and her colleagues showed that members of a preliterate tribe in New Guinea, whose language contained but two color names, were just as capable as English-speaking subjects in recognizing different colors. This finding suggests that people have the capacity to recognize colors, regardless of differences in the words they use to describe them.

CONCEPT 7.15
Language development depends on both a biological capacity for language production and experience with the sounds, meanings, and structures of human speech.

CONCEPT 7.16
The belief that the language we speak determines how we think and perceive the world is a controversial viewpoint that has not been supported by research evidence.

The Whorfian Hypothesis Eleanor Rosch's research findings ran contrary to the Whorfian hypothesis. Members of a New Guinea tribe, even though they used only two words to distinguish among different colors, were just as able as English-speaking subjects to identify different colors.

language acquisition device
Chomsky's concept of an innate, prewired mechanism in the brain that allows children to acquire language naturally.
linguistic relativity hypothesis The proposition that the language we use determines how we think and how we perceive the world (also called the *Whorfian hypothesis*).

CONCEPT 7.17
Though research findings have not supported the original form of the linguistic relativity hypothesis, a weaker version that holds that culture and language influence thinking may have merit.

Overall, research evidence does not support the original version of the Whorfian hypothesis, which holds that language determines how we think and perceive the world (Pinker, 2003; Siegal, Varley, & Want, 2001). But a weaker version of the theory does have merit, a version that proposes that the culture in which we are raised and the language we use influences how we think and even how we perceive the world (e.g., Özgen & Davies, 2002). For example, whereas English speakers perceive blue- and green-colored objects as different from each other, speakers of African languages that use a single term to describe the colors blue and green tend to perceive these objects as belonging to the same category (Özgen, 2004).

Consider another way in which language can influence thinking. Take this sentence: "A person should always be respectful of *his* parents." If the very concept of personhood embodies maleness, where does that leave females? As *nonpersons*? Not surprisingly, investigators find that women feel excluded when they read texts that use the generic *he* to represent a person (Romaine, 1994). If Sally sees that *he* is almost always used when referring to professionals like doctors, engineers, or scientists, might she get the idea that such careers are not as available to her as they are to her brother?

Is Language Unique to Humans?

Can other animals, such as apes, communicate through language? A small number of apes have been taught American Sign Language (ASL), the language used by hearing-impaired people, or artificial languages constructed by experimenters. Apes lack the vocal apparatus needed to form human sounds, so researchers have turned to these nonverbal means of expression to try to communicate with them. Beatrice and Allen Gardner trained a chimpanzee named Washoe to use about one hundred and sixty signs, including signs for "apple," "tickle," "flower," and "more" (Gardner & Gardner, 1969, 1978). Washoe learned to combine signs into simple phrases, such as "more fruit" and "gimme flower." She even displayed a basic grammar by changing the position of the subject and object in her signing to reflect a change in meaning. For example, when she wanted her trainer to tickle her, she would sign, "You tickle Washoe." But when she wanted to do the tickling, she would sign, "Washoe tickle you" (Gardner & Gardner, 1978).

David Premack developed an artificial language in which plastic chips of different sizes, colors, and shapes symbolize different words (see Figure 7.11). Using shaping and reinforcement techniques, he trained a chimp named Sarah to communicate by placing the chips on a magnetic board. Sarah learned to form simple sentences. For example, she would request food by putting together a sequence of chips that signaled "Mary give apple Sarah" (Premack, 1971).

Policeman or Police Officer? Language influences thinking in many ways. Traditional gender constructions of occupational titles that embody maleness, such as *policeman* and *fireman*, may lead young women to think that such careers are not available to them.

Figure 7.11 Examples of Materials Used in Premack's Study

Mary

Sarah

Apple

Banana

Not

Give

Perhaps the most remarkable demonstration of simian communication involved Kanzi, a male pygmy chimpanzee (Savage-Rumbaugh et al., 1993). Kanzi's mother had been trained to communicate by pushing geometric symbols into a keyboard, but Kanzi had received no special training himself. However, he was present at his mother's training sessions and apparently learned the keyboard system by observation and imitation. At age two and a half, Kanzi stunned his trainers when he suddenly began manipulating symbols on the keyboard to ask for a specific fruit. By age six, he was using some two hundred symbols to communicate (Gibbons, 1991). Kanzi was able to put the symbols in the appropriate order to reflect changes in actions—for example, switching symbols representing "person chase Kanzi" to "Kanzi chase person" (Begley, 1998a; Savage-Rumbaugh et al., 1986).

Kanzi with Trainer Questions remain about whether an ape's ability to manipulate symbols on a keyboard, as Kanzi is demonstrating here, is tantamount to human language.

Are we to conclude that apes can acquire and use language? Critics claim that Washoe, Sarah, and others merely learned to imitate gestures and other responses for which they were reinforced, rather than learning the complex syntax and morphemes of a true human language like ASL (Pinker, 1994; Terrace, 1980). Herbert Terrace based his claims in part on his own work with a chimp called Nim Chimpsky (named after the linguist Noam Chomsky). A chimp signing "me cookie" is no different, these critics say, than a pigeon learning to perform a series of responses to obtain a food pellet. Perhaps the question of whether apes can use language depends on how broadly we define language. If our definition includes communicating through the use of symbols, then apes as well as other nonhuman species may indeed be able to use language. But if our definition hinges on the use of complex syntax and grammatical structures, then the ability to use language may be unique to humans. The language abilities of Kanzi and other chimps may represent a kind of primitive grammar that is similar to that used by human infants or toddlers (Seyfarth & Cheney, 2003).

CONCEPT 7.18
Whether humans are unique in possessing the ability to communicate through language remains a controversial question.

MODULE 7.2 REVIEW

Language

CONCEPT CHECK

1. The set of rules governing the proper use of words, phrases, and sentences is called
   a. language.
   b. grammar.
   c. cultural determinism.
   d. syntax.

2. The basic units of sounds in a language are called
   a. phonemes.
   b. morphemes.
   c. semantics.
   d. syntax.

3. The belief that language determines how we think and perceive reality is called the linguistic _____ hypothesis.

4. Apes have been taught American Sign Language (ASL) because
   a. researchers have agreed to use this universal language.
   b. sign language is easier to acquire than spoken language.
   c. they lack the vocal apparatus needed to form human sounds.
   d. sign language is more effective than spoken language in communicating basic needs.

MODULE 7.3 Intelligence

- **What is intelligence, and how is it measured?**
- **What constitutes a good intelligence test?**
- **What are some examples of the misuse of intelligence tests?**
- **What are some of the major theories of intelligence?**
- **Is intelligence determined by heredity or environment?**

Perhaps no subject in psychology has sparked as much controversy as intelligence. Psychologists have long argued about how to define it, how to measure it, what factors govern it, whether different racial and ethnic groups have more or less of it, and, if so, what accounts for these differences. These debates are still very much at the forefront of contemporary psychology.

What Is Intelligence?

Just what is **intelligence**? Is it the ability to acquire knowledge from books or formal schooling? Or might it be "street smarts"—practical intelligence of the kind we see in people who survive by their wits rather than by knowledge acquired in school? Is it the ability to solve problems? Or is it the ability to adapt to the demands of the environment? Psychologists believe intelligence may be all these things and more. Though definitions of intelligence vary, a central belief of each is that intelligence is the ability to adapt to the environment. Perhaps the most widely used definition of intelligence is the one offered by psychologist David Wechsler (1975): "Intelligence is the global capacity of the individual to act purposefully, to think rationally, and to deal effectively with the environment."

Some theorists believe there are many different forms of intelligence, perhaps even multiple intelligences. Before we explore theories of intelligence, let us consider the history and nature of intelligence testing in modern times as well as extremes of intelligence.

How Is Intelligence Measured?

The type of intelligence test used today originated with the work of a Frenchman, Alfred Binet (1857–1911). In 1904, school officials in Paris commissioned Binet to develop methods of identifying children who were unable to cope with the demands of regular classroom instruction and who required special classes to meet their needs. Today, we might describe such children as having learning disabilities or mild mental retardation.

To measure mental abilities, Binet and a colleague, Theodore Simon, developed an intelligence test consisting of memory tasks and other short tasks representing the kinds of everyday problems children might encounter, such as counting coins. By 1908, Binet and Simon had decided to scale the tasks according to the age at which a child should be able to perform them successfully. A child began the testing with tasks scaled at the lowest age and then progressed to more difficult tasks, stopping at the point at which he or she could no longer perform them. The age at which the child's performance topped off was considered the child's **mental age**.

Binet and Simon calculated intelligence by subtracting the child's mental age from his or her chronological (actual) age. Children whose mental ages sufficiently lagged behind their chronological ages were considered in need of special education. In 1912, a German psychologist, William Stern, suggested a different way of computing intelligence, which Binet and Simon adopted. Stern divided mental age by chronological age, yielding a "mental quotient." It soon was labeled the **intelligence quotient (IQ)**. IQ is given by the following formula, in which MA is mental age and CA is chronological age:

$$IQ = \frac{MA}{CA} \times 100$$

Thus, if a child has a mental age of 10 and a chronological age of 8, the child's IQ would be 125 (10 ÷ 8 = 1.25 × 100 = 125). A child with a mental age of 10 who is 12 years of age would have an IQ of 83 (10 ÷ 12 = .8333 × 100 = 83).

Researchers following in Binet's footsteps developed intelligence tests that could be used with groups other than French schoolchildren. Henry Goddard (1865–1957), a research director at a school for children with mental retardation, brought the Binet-Simon test to the United States and translated it into English for use with American children. The U.S. Army developed group-administered intelligence tests to screen millions of recruits during World War I.

Stanford University psychologist Lewis Terman (1877–1956) adapted the Binet-Simon test for American use, adding many items of his own and establishing criteria, or **norms**, for comparing an individual's scores with those of the general population. The revised test, known as the Stanford-Binet Intelligence Scale (SBIS), was first published in 1916.

The Stanford-Binet Intelligence Scale is still commonly used to measure intelligence in children and young adults. However, tests developed by David Wechsler (1896–1981) are today the most widely used intelligence tests in the United States and Canada. Wechsler, a psychologist at Bellevue Hospital in New York, developed tests of intelligence for preschool children (Wechsler Preschool and Primary Scales of Intelligence—Revised, or WPPSI-R), for school-age children (Wechsler Intelligence Scale for Children, now in a third edition called WISC-III), and for adults (Wechsler Adult Intelligence Scale, now in a third edition called WAIS-III). The Wechsler scales introduced the concept of the *deviation IQ*—an IQ score based on the deviation, or difference, of a person's test score from the norms for the person's age group, rather than on the ratio of mental age to chronological age. The Wechsler scales are standardized in such a way that an average score is set at 100. The contemporary version of the Stanford-Binet Intelligence Scale also uses the deviation method to compute IQ scores.

Wechsler believed that intelligence consists of various mental abilities, and he designed his tests to measure these abilities. The WAIS-III contains various subtests, which are organized in two groupings. "Verbal subtests" focus on comprehension, vocabulary, and the like, whereas "performance subtests" assess one's skill at block design, picture arrangement, object assembly, and similar tasks (see Figure 7.12). The person who completes the test receives an IQ score on overall performance, an IQ score on the verbal subtests, and an IQ score on the performance subtests. By examining how well the person does overall and on each of the subtests, the test administrator can assess the person's general level of intelligence and the areas in which the person is relatively strong or weak.

What Are the Characteristics of a Good Test of Intelligence?

Like all psychological tests, tests of intelligence must be standardized, reliable, and valid. If they do not meet these criteria, we cannot be confident of the results.

Standardization

Standardization is the process of establishing norms for a test by administering it to large numbers of people. These large numbers make up the *standardization sample*. The standardization sample must be representative of the population for

CONCEPT 7.21
The Stanford-Binet Intelligence Scale and the Wechsler scales of intelligence are the major tests of intelligence in use today.

CONCEPT 7.22
Like all psychological tests, intelligence tests must be standardized, reliable, and valid if we are to be confident of the results.

Figure 7.12 Examples of Items Similar to Those on the WAIS-III

Verbal Subtests

Comprehension

Why do people need to obey traffic laws? What does the saying, "The early bird catches the worm," mean?

Vocabulary

What does *capricious* mean?

Arithmetic

John wanted to buy a shirt that cost $31.50, but only had 17 dollars. How much more money would he need to buy the shirt?

Similarities

How are a stapler and a paper clip alike?

Digit Span

Listen to this series of numbers and repeat them back to me in the same order:
6 4 5 2 7 3

Listen to this series of numbers and then repeat them backward:
9 4 2 5 8 7

Letter-Number Sequencing

Listen to this series of numbers and letters and repeat them back, first saying the numbers from least to most, and then saying the letters in alphabetical order:
S-2-C-1

Performance Subtests

Digit Symbol

Fill in as many boxes as you can with the correct symbol in the time allowed.

Picture Completion

What's missing from this picture?

Block Design

Using these blocks, match the design shown.

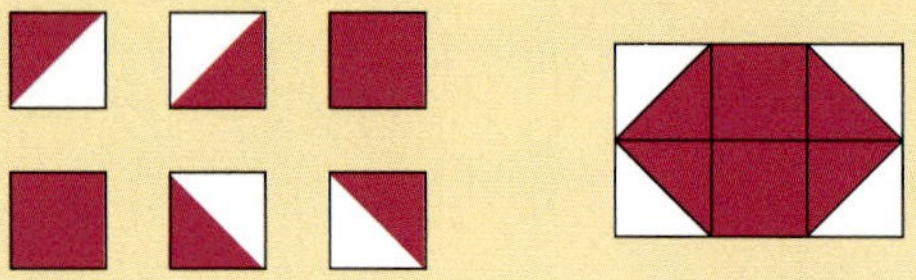

Picture Arrangement

Arrange the pictures in the correct order to tell a story.

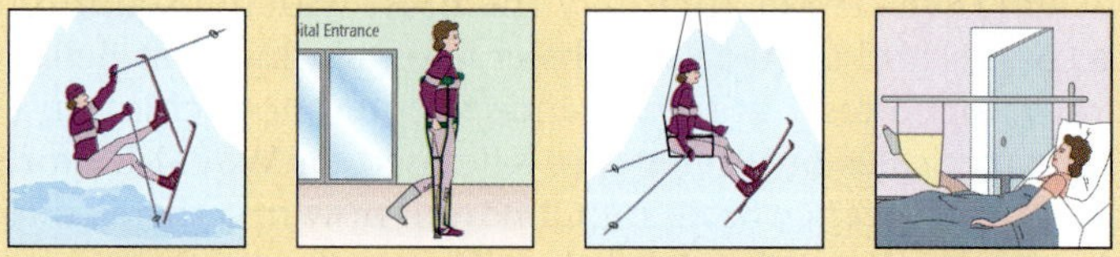

Object Assembly

Arrange the pieces of the puzzle so that they form a meaningful object.

Completed form

whom the test is intended. As noted earlier, norms are the criteria, or standards, used to compare a person's performance with the performance of others. You can determine how well you do on an intelligence test by comparing your scores with the norms for people in your age group in the standardization sample.

As noted above, IQ scores are based on the deviation of a person's score from norms for others of the same age, and the mean (average) score is set at 100. IQ scores are distributed around the mean in such a way that two-thirds of the scores in the general population fall within an "average" range of 85 to 115. Figure 7.13 shows that the distribution of IQ scores follows a bell-shaped curve. As you can see from the figure, relatively few people score at either the very high or very low end of the curve.

Standardization has another meaning in test administration. It also refers to uniform procedures that must be followed to ensure that the test is used correctly.

reliability The stability of test scores over time.

validity The degree to which a test measures what it purports to measure.

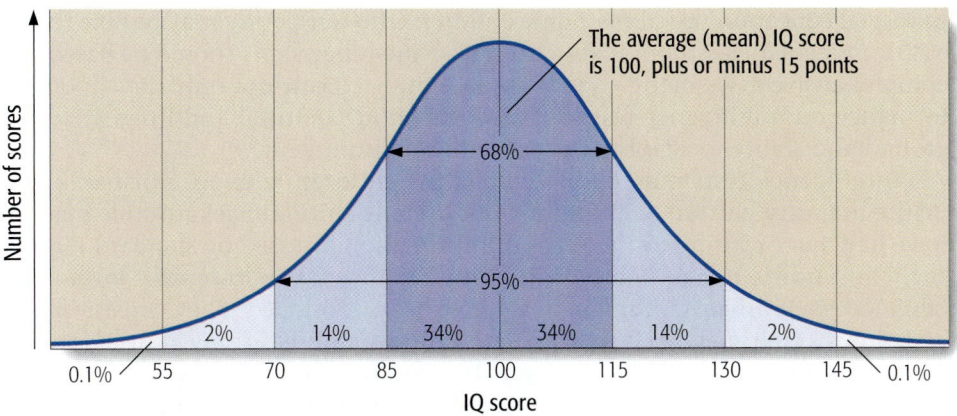

Figure 7.13   Normal Distribution of IQ Scores
The average (mean) IQ score is 100, plus or minus 15 points. The percentages shown are rounded off.

Reliability

Reliability refers to the consistency of test scores over time. You wouldn't trust a bathroom scale that gave you different readings each time you used it. Nor would you trust an IQ test that gave you a score of 135 one day, 75 the next, and 105 the day after that. A reliable test is one that produces similar results over time. One way of assessing reliability is the *test-retest method.* With this method, the subject takes the same test again after a short interval. Because familiarity with the test questions can result in consistent performance, psychologists sometimes use the *alternate-forms method.* When this method is used, subjects are given a parallel form of the test.

Validity

Validity is the degree to which a test measures what it purports to measure. A test may be reliable—producing consistent scores over time—but not valid. For example, a test that measures head size may be reliable, yielding consistent results over time, but invalid as a measure of intelligence.

There are several types of validity. One type is *predictive validity,* the degree to which test scores accurately predict future behavior or performance. IQ tests are good predictors of academic achievement and performance on general aptitude tests, such as the Scholastic Aptitude Test (SAT) and the Graduate Record Examination (GRE) (Neisser et al., 1996; Wadsworth et al., 1995). But that's not all. It turns out that IQ also predicts long-term health and longevity, perhaps because people who tend to do well on IQ tests have the kinds of learning and problem-solving skills needed to acquire and practice healthier behaviors (Gottfredson & Deary, 2004).

Misuses of Intelligence Tests

Even Binet, the father of the modern IQ test, was concerned that intelligence tests may be misused if teachers or parents lose interest or hope in children with low IQ scores and set low expectations for them. Low expectations can in turn become self-fulfilling prophecies, as children who are labeled as "dumb" may give up on themselves and become underachievers.

Misuse also occurs when too much emphasis is placed on IQ scores. Though intelligence tests do predict future academic performance, they are far from perfect predictors, and they should not be used as the only basis for placing children

web Netlab/Test Your Mental Rotation Ability

CONCEPT 7.23
Intelligence tests are misused when children with low scores are labeled as innately incapable or inferior, when too much emphasis is placed on IQ scores, and when cultural biases in the tests put children at a disadvantage.

Taking the Test

Have you ever taken an intelligence test? Did you think it was a fair appraisal of your intelligence? How were the results used? Do you feel you benefited from the experience? If so, how? What would you do differently if you were called upon to develop a new intelligence test?

CONCEPT 7.24

Researchers find that, on average, girls outperform boys on some verbal skills whereas boys typically do better on some visual-spatial tasks.

culture-fair tests Tests designed to eliminate cultural biases.

dyslexia A learning disorder characterized by impaired ability to read.

in special education programs. Some children who test poorly may be able to benefit from regular classroom instruction. Placement decisions should be based on a comprehensive assessment—one that takes into account not only the child's performance on intelligence tests but also the child's cultural and linguistic background and ability to adapt to the academic environment.

Intelligence tests may be biased against children who are not part of the White majority culture. Children from different cultural backgrounds may not have had any exposure to the types of information assessed by standard IQ tests, such as knowledge of famous individuals. Several **culture-fair tests**—tests designed to eliminate cultural biases—have been developed. They consist of nonverbal tasks that measure visual-spatial abilities and reasoning skills. However, these tests are not widely used, largely because they don't predict academic performance as well as standard tests. This is not surprising, since academic success in the United States and other Western countries depends heavily on the types of linguistic and knowledge-acquisition skills reflected in standard IQ tests. It may be impossible to develop a purely culture-free IQ test because the skills that define intelligence depend on the values of the culture in which the test is developed (Benson, 2003c).

Gender Differences in Cognitive Abilities

Generally speaking, the differences between males and females in cognitive ability are overshadowed by the similarities. Males and females overall do not differ in either general intelligence (IQ), ability to learn, or problem-solving ability (Hyde & Linn, 1988). However, girls do hold an edge in such verbal skills as reading, writing, and spelling (Applebome, 1997; Hedges & Nowell, 1995). Boys are also more likely to have problems in reading that range from reading below grade level to more severe disabilities such as **dyslexia** (American Psychiatric Association, 2000).

Boys, on the other hand, typically show better performance in math skills (Beller & Gafni, 2000; Halpern & LaMay, 2000). However, this gender gap has narrowed considerably in recent years. Today the average scores of boys and girls on standardized math tests are quite close. Still, a greater proportion of boys is found at both the high end and the low end of the spectrum of math ability (Hedges & Nowell, 1995; Murray, 1995).

Males, on average, continue to outperform females in some visual-spatial skills, such as map reading and ability to mentally rotate three-dimensional figures, like the ones you saw in Figure 7.1 (see Figure 7.14 for examples of gender-based differences) (Halpern & LaMay, 2000; Liben et al., 2002). The ability to perceive relationships among three-dimensional objects may explain why boys and men tend to excel in certain skills, such as playing chess, solving geometry problems, and finding embedded shapes within geometric figures.

Women, again on average, are better skilled at remembering where objects are located, which may explain why women tend to have keener ability in finding lost keys (Azar, 1996b). But notice the qualifying term *on average*. Many individuals exhibit abilities in which the opposite gender tends to excel: Many women excel in math and science, and many men shine in writing and verbal skills. In fact, greater variations in cognitive abilities exist within genders than between genders. Thus it is important to avoid using traditional stereotypes to limit the interests and vocations that boys and girls may pursue.

What accounts for gender differences in cognitive ability? Some researchers believe that the brains of boys and men may be more highly specialized for certain kinds of visual-spatial skills. Male fetuses are exposed to higher levels of testosterone, which scientists suspect may facilitate the development of neural connections in the brain responsible for performing certain spatial tasks (McGuffin & Scourfield, 1997).

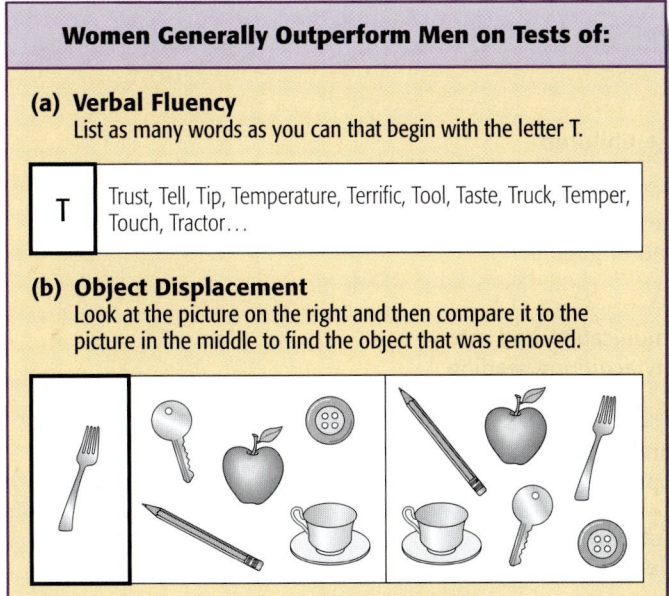

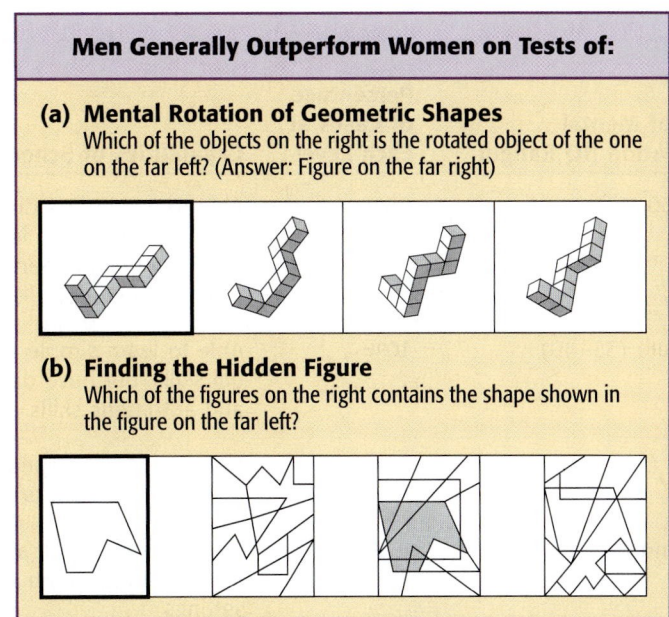

Figure 7.14 Gender Differences in Abilities

Source: Kimura, 1992.

Other researchers believe that psychosocial factors may account for differences in cognitive skills. Parents who hold the stereotypical view that "girls are not good at math and science" may not encourage their daughters to develop math skills or take science courses. Negative expectancies may then become a self-fulfilling prophecy, as they may lead girls to doubt their abilities in math or science and discourage them from developing interests in these areas. It's as though our culture trains women to perform a simple deduction based on a faulty premise that math is "masculine": Math = Male, Me = Female, Therefore Math ≠ Me (Nosek, Banaji, & Greenwald, 2003). The narrowing of gender differences in math and science in recent years lends further credence to the influence of social or cultural factors. In all likelihood, a combination of biological and psychosocial factors account for gender differences in cognitive abilities.

Extremes of Intelligence: Mental Retardation and Giftedness

Low IQ scores alone are not sufficient to determine **mental retardation**, a psychological disorder in which there is a general delay in the development of intellectual and social skills. In addition to having an IQ score of approximately 70 or below, the person must have difficulty coping with the tasks appropriate to his or her age and life situation (Robinson, Zigler, & Gallaher, 2001). The kinds of educational and support services needed by children with mental retardation depend to a large extent on the severity of the retardation.

Table 7.1 shows the capabilities of school-age children according to levels of mental retardation. Most individuals with mental retardation fall in a mild range of severity and are capable of meeting basic educational challenges, such as reading and solving arithmetic problems. Many children with mild retardation are placed in regular classrooms, a practice called **mainstreaming**. Those with severe intellectual deficits require more supportive programs, which may include institutional placement, at least until the person can function in less restrictive settings in the community.

The causes of mental retardation can be biological, environmental, or both. Biological factors include genetic or chromosomal disorders, brain damage, and

CONCEPT 7.25
Most people with mental retardation are able to acquire basic reading and arithmetic skills and can learn to function relatively independently and perform productive work.

mental retardation A generalized deficit or impairment in intellectual and social skills.

mainstreaming The practice of placing children with special needs in a regular classroom environment.

TABLE 7.1   Levels of Mental Retardation and Capabilities of School-Age Children

Level of Mental Retardation (IQ Range)	Percentage of Cases at Each Level	Capabilities of School-Age Children
Mild (50–70)	85%	Able to acquire reading and arithmetic skills to about a sixth-grade level and can later function relatively independently and engage in productive work
Moderate (35–49)	10%	Able to learn simple communication and manual skills, but have difficulty acquiring reading and arithmetic skills
Severe (20–34)	3–4%	Capable of basic speech and may be able to learn repetitive tasks in supervised settings
Profound (below 20)	1–2%	Severe delays in all areas of development, but some may learn simple tasks in supervised settings

Source: Adapted from American Psychiatric Association, 2000.

exposure to lead (Canfield et al., 2003). Environmental factors include a deprived family environment, one that is lacking in verbal interactions between the child and parents or in intellectually stimulating play activities (Thapar et al., 1994).

People at the upper end of the IQ spectrum (typically about 130 or higher) are generally classified as intellectually gifted (Winner, 2000). As children, they may benefit from enriched educational programs that allow them to progress at a faster pace than standard programs. Today, the concept of giftedness includes not only children with high IQ scores but also those with special talents, such as musical or artistic ability—skills not typically assessed by standard IQ tests. Gifted children may play musical instruments as well as highly trained adults or solve algebra problems at an age when their peers have not yet learned to carry numbers in addition.

Theories of Intelligence

CONCEPT 7.26

Psychologists have been debating the nature of intelligence ever since intelligence tests were first introduced.

Does intelligence consist of one general ability or a cluster of different abilities? Might there be different forms of intelligence or even different intelligences? Throughout the history of modern psychology, theorists have been attempting to explain intelligence. There are perhaps as many theories about it as there are theoreticians. Here we consider several major theories.

Spearman's "g": In Search of General Cognitive Ability

primary mental abilities   Seven basic mental abilities that Thurstone believed constitute intelligence.

multiple intelligences   Gardner's term for the distinct types of intelligence that characterize different forms of intelligent behavior.

The British psychologist Charles Spearman (1863–1945) observed that people who scored well on one test of mental ability tended to score well on other tests (Spearman, 1927). He reasoned that there must be an underlying general factor of intelligence that allows people to do well on mental tests, a factor he labeled "g" for general intelligence. However, he also believed that intelligence includes specific abilities that, along with "g," contribute to performance on individual tests (R. M. Thorndike, 1997). For example, a person's performance on an arithmetic test might be determined by both general intelligence and specific mathematical ability. Intelligence tests, such as the SBIS and the Wechsler scales, were developed to measure Spearman's concept of general intelligence, or "g," which is expressed as an IQ score.

Thurstone's Primary Mental Abilities: Not Two Factors, But Seven

Psychologist Louis L. Thurstone (1887–1955) did not believe that any one large, dominating factor like "g" could account for intelligence. Rather, his studies pointed to a set of seven **primary mental abilities**: verbal comprehension, numerical ability, memory, inductive reasoning, perceptual speed, verbal fluency, and spatial relations (Thurstone & Thurstone, 1941). Though Thurstone did not deny the existence of "g," he argued that a single IQ score does not hold much value in assessing intelligence. He and his wife, Thelma Thurstone, developed a test called the *Primary Mental Abilities Test* to measure the seven primary abilities they believed constitute intelligence.

CONCEPT 7.27

Though IQ tests were developed to measure Spearman's concept of general intelligence, or "g," theorists like Thurstone believed that intelligence consists of a range of mental abilities that cannot be measured by one general IQ score.

Gardner's Model of Multiple Intelligences

Psychologist Howard Gardner (b. 1943) rejects the view that there is a single entity called "intelligence" (Gardner & Traub, 1999). Rather, he believes there exist different types of intelligence, called **multiple intelligences**, that vary from person to person. Gardner identifies eight different intelligences: linguistic, logical-mathematical, musical, spatial, bodily-kinesthetic, interpersonal, intrapersonal, and naturalist (H. Gardner, 1993, 1998) (see Figure 7.15 and Table 7.2). These separate intelligences are believed to be independent of one another. Thus, a person could be high in some intelligences but low in others (Gardner & Traub, 1999). For example, you might have a high level of linguistic, or verbal, intelligence but a lower level of intelligence in mathematics, music, or spatial relationships. Some people have good "people skills" (interpersonal intelligence) but may not be highly skilled at mathematical and logical tasks.

Gardner's model has had enormous influence, especially in educational settings. It has prompted schools to enrich their programs by cultivating specific

CONCEPT 7.28

According to Gardner's model of multiple intelligences, we possess separate intelligences that we rely on to perform different types of tasks.

Musical Intelligence

Linguistic Intelligence

Bodily-kinesthetic Intelligence

Interpersonal Intelligence

Figure 7.15   Gardner's Model of Multiple Intelligences
Gardner conceptualizes intelligence in terms of distinct intelligences that vary from person to person. Some people may be strong in musical intelligence, while others may be gifted in bodily-kinesthetic or linguistic intelligence. What types of intelligence best represent your strengths or abilities?

TABLE 7.2 Gardner's Multiple Intelligences

Type of Intelligence	Description	Groups with High Levels of the Intelligence
Linguistic	Ability to understand and use words	Writers, poets, effective public speakers
Logical-mathematical	Ability to perform mathematical, computational, or logical operations	Scientists, engineers, computer programmers
Musical	Ability to analyze, compose, or perform music	Musicians, singers, composers
Spatial	Ability to perceive spatial relationships and arrange objects in space	Painters, architects, sculptors
Bodily-kinesthetic	Ability to control bodily movements and manipulate objects effectively	Dancers, athletes, race-car drivers, mechanics
Interpersonal	Ability to relate effectively to others and to understand others' moods and motives	Industrial and political leaders, effective supervisors
Intrapersonal	Ability to understand one's own feelings and behavior (self-perception)	Psychologically well-adjusted people
Naturalist	Ability to recognize objects and patterns in nature, such as flora and fauna	Botanists, biologists, naturalists

intelligences in children rather than focusing just on verbal and mathematical abilities (P. D. Klein, 1997; Wallach & Callahan, 1994). Yet critics of his model point out that it fails to account for how multiple intelligences interact with one another (Guenther, 1998). Most cognitive activities involve an interaction of multiple abilities, not just one type of intelligence. For example, the ability to relate effectively to others (interpersonal intelligence) depends in part on the linguistic skills needed to express oneself clearly (linguistic intelligence). Other critics claim that Gardner's theory provides no firm evidence supporting the existence of multiple intelligences (Gustafsson & Undheim, 1996).

An even broader concern is where to draw the line in determining how many intelligences are needed to account for the full range of mental abilities. Why eight intelligences (Gardner now believes there may be nine) and not ten, fifteen, or twenty or more? (H. Gardner & Traub, 1999). Why musical intelligence but not, say, culinary intelligence or practical intelligence (common sense, or "street-smarts")? (Guenther, 1998).

Sternberg's Triarchic Theory of Intelligence

Whereas Gardner focuses on different types of intelligence, psychologist Robert Sternberg (b. 1949) emphasizes how we bring together different aspects of our intelligence to meet the demands we face in our daily lives. Sternberg (1997) proposes a **triarchic theory of intelligence**, which holds that intelligence has three aspects: analytic, creative, and practical (see Figure 7.16).

Sternberg believes that people with high levels of intelligence are better able to integrate or organize these three aspects of intelligence in their daily lives. *Analytic intelligence* is the kind of intelligence measured by traditional intelligence tests. It comes into play when you analyze and evaluate familiar problems, break them down into their component parts, and develop strategies to solve them. *Creative intelligence* allows us to invent new ways of solving unfamiliar problems. *Practical intelligence* is the ability to apply what we know to everyday life—the

CONCEPT 7.29

Sternberg's triarchic theory of intelligence focuses on how we bring together the analytic, creative, and practical aspects of our intelligence to solve the range of problems we face in everyday situations.

triarchic theory of intelligence
Sternberg's theory of intelligence that posits three aspects of intelligence: analytic, creative, and practical.

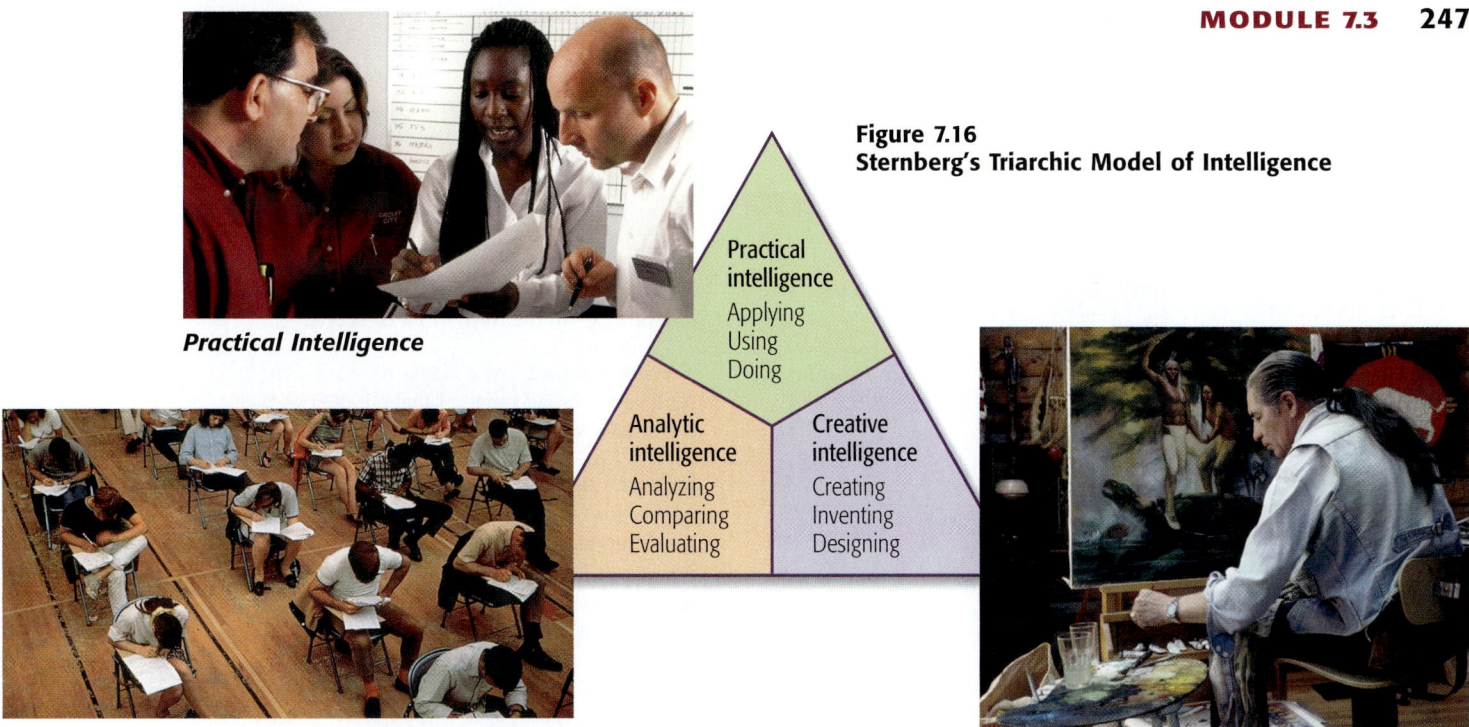

Practical Intelligence

Figure 7.16
Sternberg's Triarchic Model of Intelligence

Practical intelligence
Applying
Using
Doing

Analytic intelligence
Analyzing
Comparing
Evaluating

Creative intelligence
Creating
Inventing
Designing

Analytic Intelligence

Creative Intelligence

common sense, or "street smarts," that traditional intelligence tests fail to measure. Sternberg argues that we need all three types of intelligence to succeed in life. He also believes we need to supplement standard intelligence tests with measures of creative intelligence and practical intelligence.

Overview of Theories of Intelligence

Conventional views of intelligence, as represented by Spearman's and Thurstone's theories, focus on the structure of intelligence and ways of measuring the amount of intelligence a person possesses. Recent evidence supports the importance of a general factor of intelligence, or "g," in predicting not only school performance but job performance as well (Greer, 2004; Kuncel, Hezlett, & Ones, 2004). Yet scientists continue to debate how much importance to place on "g" in explaining cognitive ability (see Flynn, 2003; Gottfredson, 2004; Grigorenko, 2002; Jensen, 2002).

Gardner's and Sternberg's models of intelligence take us in a different direction. They raise our awareness that traditional intelligence tests fail to capture important dimensions of intelligence, such as how people use their intelligence to meet the challenges and demands they face in everyday contexts. But critics contend that we lack sufficient evidence to support the existence of separate types of intelligence, such as Gardner's multiple intelligences or Sternberg's practical intelligence (Goode, 2001c). Though Gardner's and Sternberg's theories are prompting renewed interest in the nature of intelligence, they have yet to be thoroughly evaluated through scientific tests (Gottfredson, 2003a, 2003b).

What can we conclude about these various theories of intelligence? First, it is clear that human intelligence consists of multiple abilities, perhaps even multiple intelligences (Horn & Noll, 1997). Second, we need to take into account the cultural contexts in which intelligent behavior occurs. The abilities a society values determines how it defines and measures intelligence. Our society places a high value on verbal, mathematical, and spatial skills, so it is not surprising that conventional IQ tests measure these abilities and little else. Perhaps, as Sternberg argues, we need to think about measuring intelligence more broadly to assess the wider range of abilities that may constitute human intelligence. Concept Chart 7.3 offers an overview of the major theories of intelligence.

CONCEPT CHART 7.3
Theories of Intelligence

Theorist	Major Concepts	Comments
Spearman	Intelligence involves general cognitive ability, or "g."	Traditional intelligence tests are designed to measure "g" in the form of an IQ score.
Thurstone	Intelligence consists of seven primary mental abilities.	Thurstone argued that a single IQ score cannot capture the broad range of mental abilities that constitutes intelligence.
Gardner	Multiple intelligences are needed to account for the range of mental abilities.	Gardner's theory has popular appeal but does not account for the interrelationships among the different intelligences. It also does not draw the line in determining how many separate intelligences are needed to account for the full range of mental abilities.
Sternberg	Sternberg's triarchic theory proposes three aspects of intelligence: analytic, creative, and practical.	The triarchic theory is important because it provides a much-needed focus on how people use their intelligence in everyday life.

Intelligence and the Nature-Nurture Question

Scientists have long sought to answer the question of whether intelligence is primarily the result of nature (genetics) or nurture (environment). A heated focus of the nature-nurture debate is whether genetic factors or environmental ones are responsible for racial differences in IQ scores.

Separating the Effects of Nature and Nurture

The closer the genetic relationship between two people, the closer their IQ scores tend to be (Horn & Noll, 1997). Consider Figure 7.17, which is based on over one hundred kinship studies of more than 100,000 pairs of relatives (Plomin & Petrill, 1997). Notice that the statistical association (correlation) between IQs of twins raised together is greater among monozygotic (MZ), or identical, twins than among dizygotic (DZ), or fraternal, twins. Since MZ twins share 100 percent of their genes and DZ twins, like other siblings, have only a 50 percent genetic overlap, this finding suggests that heredity does indeed contribute to intelligence. Another compelling piece of evidence supporting the role of genetics, also shown in Figure 7.17, is that the IQ scores of MZ twins who are raised in separate households are more similar than the IQ scores of DZ twins who are raised together.

Adoptee studies provide yet more evidence of the role of genetics in determining IQ. Studies have consistently shown that the IQ scores of adopted children are closer to those of their biological parents than to those of their adoptive parents (Bishop et al., 2003; Fulker, DeFries, & Plomin, 1988).

Yet heredity doesn't tell the whole story. Refer again to Figure 7.17. Notice that the correlation for the IQ scores of MZ twins raised together is greater than the correlation for the IQ scores of MZ twins raised apart. Since MZ twins share the same genes, the difference in these correlations is evidence that the environment also plays a role in determining IQ. Most experts believe that environmental influences are important factors in intellectual development. A home environment that emphasizes verbal interaction, reading, and exploration can foster children's intellectual development.

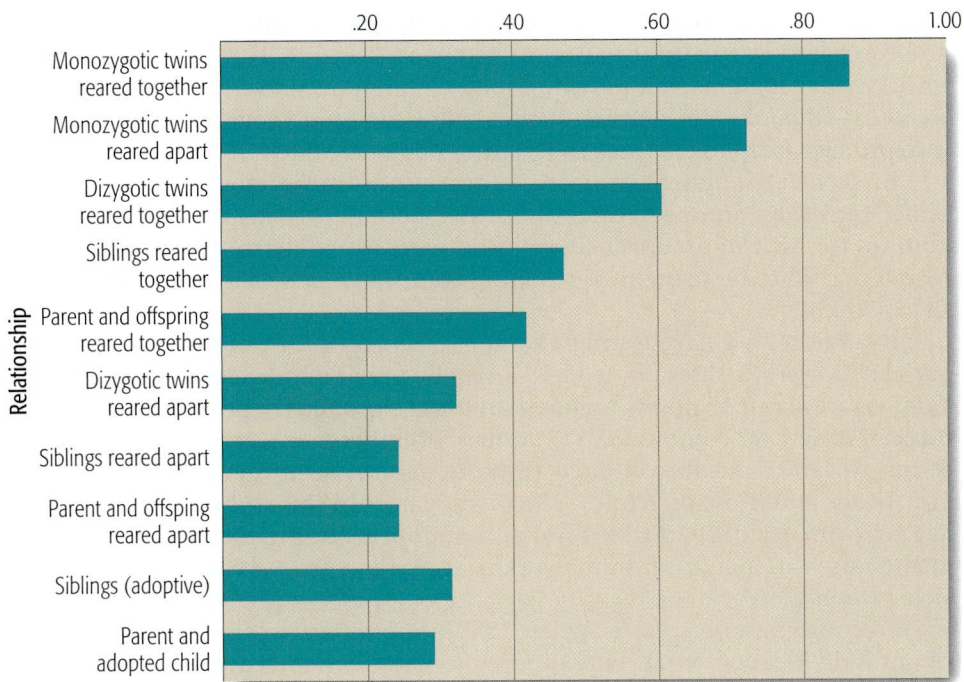

Figure 7.17   Similarity and Intelligence
Here we see the average correlations of IQ scores of people in different family relationships. The closer the genetic and enviromental similarity between family members, the closer their IQ scores tend to be.

Source: Adapted from Plomin & Petrill, 1997.

Taken together, the evidence makes a compelling case that both genetic and environmental factors interact in complex ways in determining intelligence (Dickens & Flynn, 2001). Heredity shapes intelligence throughout the life span, not just during early development (e.g., McGue & Christensen, 2001). Studies of twins in their eighties show similarities in intelligence that are virtually identical to those among pairs of adolescent twins (McClearn et al., 1997).

But just how much of intelligence is explained by genetics and how much by the environment? The **heritability** of a trait is the degree to which genetic factors explain the variability among people on the trait (Merikangas & Risch, 2003). A heritability estimate of 50 percent for intelligence—at least intelligence as measured by IQ tests—would mean that genetics accounts for 50 percent of the differences (variability) among people in IQ scores; the environment or other unspecified factors would account for the rest. Heritability estimates of intelligence vary, typically ranging from about 50 to 75 percent (Begley, 2001a; Gottesman, 1997). Note, however, that although genetics may account for 50–75 percent of the variability of IQ scores in the population, we cannot conclude that 50–75 percent of a given person's IQ results from genetic factors and the rest from environmental or other influences. Heritability estimates apply to the population in general, not to any given individual in the population.

Racial Differences in IQ

Non-Hispanic White Americans of European descent (Euro-Americans) tend to score higher on IQ tests than African Americans—about 15 points higher, on average (Fagan & Holland, 2002). This racial gap in IQ scores exists even when differences in income levels are taken into account.

Are racial differences in IQ genetic or environmental in origin? Converging lines of evidence point to environmental factors in explaining racial differences in IQ. For one thing, racial differences in IQ scores have narrowed in recent years, possibly owing to increased educational spending benefiting historically disadvantaged groups (Ceci, Rosenblum, & Kumpf, 1998; W. M. Williams, 1998). Moreover, investigators have found that racial differences in knowledge of word meanings

CONCEPT 7.30
Evidence indicates that genetic and environmental factors interact in complex ways in shaping intelligence.

heritability   The degree to which heredity accounts for variations on a given trait within a population.

can be eliminated when African Americans students are given equal opportunities to be exposed to the information to be tested (Fagan & Holland, 2002). Formal enrichment programs that provide young children from low-income families with exposure to books and puzzles, such as the Head Start program for preschoolers, also produce measurable gains in IQ scores (Zigler & Styfco, 1994).

In fact, IQ scores have been rising slightly more rapidly among African Americans than among White Americans, perhaps because educational opportunities for African Americans have been increasing (Flynn, 1999). IQ scores are also observed to be rising in developing countries, such as in rural Kenya (Daley et al., 2003).

In addition, we have learned that the IQ scores of African American and interracial children who are adopted and raised by upper middle-class White American families are about 15 points higher than those expected of the average child in the African American community (Waldman, Weinberg, & Scarr, 1994) This finding seems to cancel out the oft-cited 15-point gap between the IQ scores of African Americans and those of Whites. The investigators in this study attributed the better performance of the African American adoptees to the sociocultural effects of being raised in a cultural framework that places a strong value on educational achievement.

Of course, we need to recognize that group differences in IQ tell us nothing about individual potential. Any group, no matter what its average IQ scores may be, can produce its share of intellectually gifted people.

At the same time, however, we need take into account cultural factors that can negatively affect how members of particular groups perform on structured tests. For example, children from some cultures may interpret the lack of feedback from a test administrator as a cue that they are doing well and thus fail to modify their test-taking approach when they encounter difficulties (Miller-Jones, 1989). Or they may misunderstand the instructions or fail to take them seriously. Because African Americans and members of some other cultural groups place a value on creative expression, children from these groups may not give the obvious answers to questions on IQ tests. Psychologist Janet Helms (1992) suggests that test administrators talk to subjects who give incorrect answers to determine whether a "wrong" answer is the result of cultural differences. She notes that if people use reasoning strategies that differ from those that members of the majority group use to solve a problem, their doing so does not necessarily mean they are any less intelligent.

💡 **CONCEPT 7.31**

Most investigators attribute racial differences in IQ scores to environmental factors.

In sum, despite some dissenting voices, most investigators today believe that the environment, rather than genetics, is the factor that determines racial differences in IQ scores (e.g., Neisser et al., 1996; Waldman, Weinberg, & Scarr, 1994).

Emphasizing Education   Parental emphasis on education can have an important bearing on a child's intellectual development.

MODULE 7.3 REVIEW

Intelligence

CONCEPT CHECK

1. Match the terms on the left with the definitions on the right:

   i. standardization   a. a test's ability to measure what it is designed to measure

   ii. validity   b. the practice of placing children with mild mental retardation in regular classrooms

   iii. mainstreaming   c. an underlying general factor of intelligence

   iv. Spearman's "g"   d. the generation of test norms based on representative samples of the population

2. Problems with intelligence tests include
   a. excessive emphasis on test scores.
   b. low expectations for children with low scores.
   c. cultural biases in how test content is presented.
   d. all of the above.

3. The theory of intelligence that emphasizes how we integrate various aspects of intelligence in meeting the challenges and demands of everyday life is called
   a. Sternberg's triarchic theory of intelligence.
   b. Gardner's model of multiple intelligences.
   c. Thurstone's theory of primary mental abilities.
   d. Spearman's theory of "g."

4. Similarities in IQ scores are greatest among which of the following?
   a. fraternal twins raised together
   b. fraternal twins raised apart
   c. identical twins raised together
   d. identical twins raised apart

APPLICATION

MODULE 7.4   Becoming a Creative Problem Solver

- **What are the keys to becoming a creative problem solver?**

The range of problems we face in our personal lives is virtually limitless. Consider some common examples: getting to school or work on time; helping a friend with a personal problem; resolving disputes; juggling school, work, and family responsibilities. Creative problem solvers challenge preconceptions and consider as many alternative solutions to a problem as possible. Were you stumped by the problem on page 226 about the key that opened no locks but allowed the man to enter? Perhaps it was because you approached the problem from only one vantage point—that the key was a door key. Solving the problem requires that you consider an alternative that may not have seemed obvious at first—that the key was an enter key on a keyboard. Speaking of keys, here are some key steps toward becoming a creative problem solver.

CONCEPT 7.32
Creative problem solvers challenge preconceptions and consider as many alternative solutions to a problem as possible.

Adopt a Questioning Attitude

Finding creative solutions to problems begins with adopting a questioning attitude. The creative problem solver asks, "What alternatives are available? What has worked in the past? What hasn't worked? What can I do differently?"

Gather Information

Creative problem solvers acquire the information and resources they need to explore possible solutions. People today have access to a wider range of information resources than ever before, including newspapers and magazines, college courses, and, of course, the Internet. Want to know more about combating a common problem like insomnia? Why not search the Internet to see what information is available? However, think critically about the information you find.

Avoid Getting Stuck in Mental Sets

Here's a question for you: "If there were three apples and you took two away, how many would you have?" If you answered one, chances are you had a mental set to respond to this type of problem as a subtraction problem. But the question did not ask how many apples were left. The answer is that you would have two apples—the two you took away.

To avoid slipping into a mental set that impairs problem-solving efforts, think through each question carefully. Ask yourself:

- What am I required to do?

- What type of problem is this?

- What problem-solving strategy would work best for this type of problem?

Put these skills into practice by responding to a few brainteasers (the answers are given on page 255) (*Brainteaser Quizzes*, 2001):

1. How many two-cent stamps are there in a dozen?

2. You are holding two U.S. coins that total 55 cents. One of the coins is not a nickel. What are the coins you are holding?

3. A farmer has 18 cows and all but 11 of them died. How many were left?

Generate Alternatives

Creative problem solvers generate as many alternative solutions to a problem as possible. They may then decide to return to their original solution. Or they may decide that one of the alternatives works best. Sifting through alternatives can help us rearrange our thinking so that a more workable solution becomes obvious. Here are a few suggestions for generating alternatives:

1. *Personal brainstorming.* Alex Osborne (1963) introduced the concept of brainstorming to help business executives and engineers solve problems more creatively. The basic idea is to encourage divergent thinking. **Brainstorming** encourages people to propose as many solutions to a problem as possible without fear of being judged negatively by others, no matter how far-fetched their proposals may seem. There are three general rules for brainstorming:

    Rule 1: *Write down as many solutions to the problem as you can think of.* Quantity counts more than quality.

    Rule 2: *Suspend judgment.* Don't evaluate any of the possible solutions or strike them off your list.

    Rule 3: *Seek unusual, remote, or even weird ideas.* Today's strange or oddball idea may turn into tomorrow's brilliant solution.

2. *After generating your list, put it aside for a few days.* When you return to it, ask yourself which solutions are worth pursuing. Take into account the resources or additional information you will need to put these solutions into practice.

3. *Find analogies.* Finding a situation analogous to the present problem can lead to a creative solution. Ask yourself how the present problem is similar to problems you've encountered before. What strategies worked in the past? How can they be modified to fit the present problem? This is constructive use of mental sets—using past solutions as a guide, not an impediment, to problem solving.

brainstorming A method of promoting divergent thinking by encouraging people to propose as many solutions to a problem as possible without fear of being judged negatively by others, no matter how far-fetched their proposals may be.

4. *Think outside the box.* Recall the nine-dot problem in Figure 7.3 (p. 227). People have difficulty with this problem because of a tendency to limit the ways they think about it. If you didn't solve the nine-dot problem, you're in good company. In a laboratory test, none of the research participants who were given several minutes to solve the problem were able to do so (MacGregor et al., 2001). The problem is solvable only if you think "outside the box"—literally, as shown below. Creative problem solvers make an effort to conceptualize problems from different perspectives, steering their problem-solving efforts toward finding new solutions (Ormerod, MacGregor, & Chronicle, 2002).

Two Solutions to the Nine-Dot Problem in Figure 7.3

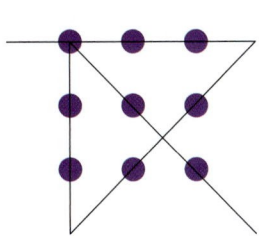
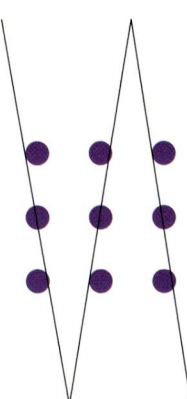

Sleep On It

In cases where people are faced with difficult problems, evidence supports the age-old wisdom of "sleeping on it." Investigators have found that sleep enhances the insight and creative thinking of research subjects challenged with solving difficult math problems (Wagner et al., 2004). Indeed, the cognitive benefits of getting a good night's sleep may account for the experiences of many famous scientists and artists whose inspired ideas occurred shortly upon awakening (Komaroff, 2004).

Test It Out

Try out possible solutions to see how they work. Gather information that will help you evaluate what you need to do differently to achieve a better solution. If you get stuck, take time away from the problem. Allow the problem to "incubate" in your mind. When you return to it, you may have a fresh perspective that will help you discover a workable solution.

TYING IT TOGETHER

Cognitive psychology focuses on how we acquire knowledge about the world, communicate with others, and solve problems we face in daily life. Through the cognitive process of thinking, we acquire knowledge of the world by mentally representing and manipulating information in our minds (Module 7.1). But to share information with others requires that we use a shared system of communication called language (Module 7.2). Understanding how people acquire knowledge, solve problems, and adapt to their environments leads us to consider individual differences in intelligence (Module 7.3). Psychologists are interested in studying the nature of intelligence and ways of measuring it. We can apply knowledge gained from studies of problem solving to become more creative problem solvers, such as by challenging preconceptions and generating as many possible solutions to a problem as possible (Module 7.4).

SUMMING UP: Q&A

Thinking (Module 7.1)

What is cognitive psychology?

- Cognitive psychology is the study of thinking and other mental processes, including problem solving, language use, and information processing.

What is thinking?

- Thinking is the creation of mental representations of the external world and the manipulation of these representations.

What are the major types of concepts people use, and how are they applied?

- The major types of concepts are logical concepts, which have clearly defined rules for membership, and natural concepts, in which the rules for determining how they are applied are poorly defined.
- People apply natural concepts probabilistically by judging whether something is likely to belong to a certain category.

What can we do to solve problems more efficiently?

- Rather than relying on trial and error or a sudden insight, we can use such problem-solving strategies as algorithms and heuristics.
- We can also remove impediments to problem solving, such as mental sets and functional fixedness.

How do cognitive biases influence decision making?

- The confirmation bias leads people to discount evidence that contradicts their prior beliefs and expectations.
- The representativeness heuristic leads people to make more of a given sample of data than they should.
- The availability heuristic leads people to make snap decisions based on whatever information comes most readily to mind.

What cognitive processes underlie creative thinking?

- Cognitive processes involved in creative thinking include the use of metaphor and analogy, conceptual combination, and conceptual expansion.

Language (Module 7.2)

What are the major components of language?

- The major components of language are phonemes (basic units of sounds), morphemes (basic units of meaning), syntax (the rules of grammar that determine how words are ordered in sentences and phrases to express meaning), and semantics (the set of rules governing the meaning of words).

How does language develop?

- According to Noam Chomsky, language development depends on an innate mechanism that is "prewired" in the human brain.
- Language development also depends on exposure to the speech of others. Thus, both nature and nurture are necessary.

What is the linguistic relativity hypothesis?

- In its original form, this hypothesis (also called the Whorfian hypothesis) holds that language determines how we think and how we perceive the world. Research findings fail to support this version of the hypothesis, but a weaker version, which maintains that culture and language influence thinking, has some merit.

Can nonhuman animals use language?

- Scholars continue to debate the question of whether animals other than humans can use language. The answer may hinge on how we define language.
- Research with chimps and gorillas has shown that these primates are capable of learning elementary forms of communication—for example, manipulating symbols to request food—but questions remain about whether these communication skills are equivalent to human language.

Intelligence (Module 7.3)

What is intelligence, and how is it measured?

- Though theorists define intelligence in different ways, one widely used definition holds that intelligence is the capacity to act purposefully, think rationally, and deal effectively with the environment.
- Standardized intelligence tests, such as the Stanford-Binet Intelligence Scale and the Wechsler scales of intelligence, are generally used to measure intelligence.
- The IQ, or intelligent quotient, is a measure of general intelligence. The Stanford-Binet Intelligence Scale and the Wechsler scales compute IQ on the basis of the deviation of a person's test score from the norms for the person's age group.

What constitutes a good intelligence test?

- The basic requirements of a good intelligence test are standardization (generation of norms based on samples representative of the population), reliability (stability of test scores over time), and validity (the test's ability to measure what it purports to measure).

What are some examples of the misuse of intelligence tests?

- Intelligence tests are misused when children with low scores are labeled as innately incapable or inferior, when too much emphasis is placed on IQ scores, and when cultural biases in the tests put children from diverse cultural backgrounds at a disadvantage.
- Mental retardation is assessed on the basis of IQ score—typically 70 or below—as well as delayed or impaired social skills. Giftedness is usually associated with IQ scores of about 130 or above or with evidence of special talents.

What are some of the major theories of intelligence?

- Major theories of intelligence include Spearman's concept of general intelligence, or "g," Thurstone's theory of primary mental abilities, Gardner's model of multiple intelligences, and Sternberg's triarchic theory. Some theorists favor the view that intelligence consists of a general cognitive ability, while others favor a model based on multiple abilities or even multiple intelligences.

Is intelligence determined by heredity or environment?

• Most authorities believe that intelligence is based on a complex interaction of nature (genetic influences) and nurture (environmental influences).

Application: Becoming a Creative Problem Solver (Module 7.4)

What are the keys to becoming a creative problem solver?

• The keys to creative problem solving include adopting a questioning attitude, gathering information, avoiding getting stuck in mental sets, generating alternatives, getting adequate sleep, and testing out potential solutions.

Key Terms

cognitive psychology *(p. 224)*
thinking *(p. 224)*
mental image *(p. 224)*
concepts *(p. 225)*
logical concepts *(p. 225)*
natural concepts *(p. 226)*
problem solving *(p. 227)*
algorithm *(p. 227)*
heuristic *(p. 227)*
mental set *(p. 228)*
functional fixedness *(p. 228)*
decision making *(p. 228)*
confirmation bias *(p. 229)*
representativeness heuristic *(p. 229)*
availability heuristic *(p. 229)*

creativity *(p. 230)*
divergent thinking *(p. 231)*
convergent thinking *(p. 231)*
conceptual combinations *(p. 231)*
conceptual expansion *(p. 231)*
language *(p. 233)*
grammar *(p. 233)*
phonemes *(p. 233)*
morphemes *(p. 233)*
syntax *(p. 233)*
semantics *(p. 233)*
language acquisition device *(p. 234)*
linguistic relativity hypothesis *(p. 235)*
intelligence *(p. 238)*
mental age *(p. 238)*

intelligence quotient (IQ) *(p. 239)*
norms *(p. 239)*
standardization *(p. 239)*
reliability *(p. 241)*
validity *(p. 241)*
culture-fair tests *(p. 242)*
dyslexia *(p. 242)*
mental retardation *(p. 243)*
mainstreaming *(p. 243)*
primary mental abilities *(p. 245)*
multiple intelligences *(p. 245)*
triarchic theory of intelligence *(p. 245)*
heritability *(p. 249)*
brainstorming *(p. 252)*

Thinking Critically About Psychology

Based on your reading of this chapter, answer the following questions. Then, to evaluate your progress in developing critical thinking skills, compare your answers to the sample answers found in Appendix A.

1. An ambulance is heading toward the hospital on a country road, carrying an injured man who needs emergency surgery. When the ambulance comes around a bend, the driver notices a large flock of sheep blocking the road. The driver starts pounding on the horn and sounding the siren to part the sheep, but to no effect. A medical technician jumps out of the ambulance and tries to shove the rearmost sheep out of the way, hoping the others will follow. The driver starts screaming at the shepherd, imploring him to clear the road. The shepherd also starts screaming, but the sheep just keep on bleating. Suddenly, the shepherd raises his hand to signal the ambulance to stop. He then succeeds in clearing a path ahead for the ambulance but not by parting the sheep or by guiding the ambulance past them. (Adapted from M. Levine, 1994.)

a. How did the shepherd clear the road for the ambulance?

b. What impediment to problem solving does the behavior of the medical technician represent?

2. John receives an inheritance, which he decides to invest in the stock market. Like many other investors today, he decides to open an online trading account. At first, he does well. Then he begins to trade more actively, buying and selling stocks almost daily. His losses soon begin to mount. Concerned, he consults a financial adviser who asks him about his trading strategy. John recounts that he buys stocks in companies he hears positive things about and sells stocks in companies whenever he notices negative news items.

a. What cognitive error(s) in decision making might explain John's losses in the stock market?

b. How would you advise him to avoid such errors in the future?

Answers to Concept Check Questions

Module 7.1: 1. the mental representation and manipulation of information; 2. logical, natural; 3. b; 4. i-a, ii-c, iii-d, iv-b; 5. d.
Module 7.2: 1. b; 2. a; 3. relativity; 4. c.   **Module 7.3:** 1. i-d; ii-a; iii-b; iv-c; 2. d; 3. a; 4. c.

Answers to Brainteasers *(page 252)*

1. There are 12 two-cent stamps, since a dozen of anything is 12.

2. You are holding a fifty-cent piece and a nickel. One of the two coins (the fifty-cent piece) is not a nickel.

3. There are 11 cows left. All but 11 died.

Motivation and Emotion

DID YOU KNOW THAT . . .

- **The founding father of American psychology believed there is a human instinct for cleanliness? (p. 258)**

- **Obese people typically have more fat cells than people of normal weight have? (p. 267)**

- **The male sex hormone testosterone energizes sexual drives in women as well as men? (p. 276)**

- **Winning the lottery has only a short-term effect on boosting happiness? (p. 281)**

- **Practicing smiling can lift your mood? (p. 282)**

- **There is no emotion center in the brain? (p. 283)**

- **Responding without thinking can be a lifesaver in some situations? (p. 285)**

Imagine you came into a windfall of an enormous amount of money—let's say $10 million. How would you spend your days? Would you continue with your college studies, or would you just lounge about in luxury? Maybe you'd relax on a tropical beach for a few weeks, or even a few months. Sooner or later, however, you'd probably want to do something more meaningful. Perhaps you'd devote your time and energy to philanthropy. Or perhaps you'd start a new business in the hope of accumulating even more wealth. Or perhaps you'd pursue a career that you would enjoy for reasons other than its financial rewards. In any event, you wouldn't simply crawl into a ball and remain motionless for the rest of your life. You would be motivated to do something and get on with your life.

Although few people ever attain great wealth, we might learn something about human motivation from someone who became so wealthy that the sheer size of his fortune boggles the imagination. Bill Gates—co-founder of Microsoft, the world's leading software company—remains the world's richest person, with a whopping net worth of $46.6 billion dollars according to a recent estimate (Kroll & Goldman, 2004). Yet Gates is still plugging away, though perhaps not at the frenetic pace of his youth.

What motivates someone like Bill Gates? After all, he has more money than he or anyone else could spend in a dozen lifetimes, short of buying half a dozen small countries. Evidently, his motivation has to do with sources of gratification that cannot be deposited in a bank account. As he told an interviewer, life for him is a continuous process of challenge and achievement (Playboy Enterprises Inc., 1994). For Gates and others like him, there are always more mountains to climb, more challenges to test one's mettle. Such people prize wealth not for what it can buy but for what it represents—winning.

What about you? What drives your behavior? Is it the desire to satisfy your biological needs—to have sufficient food, water, sexual gratification, and protection from the elements? Or are you, like Bill Gates, driven by a need to achieve, succeed, and prove something about yourself to the world? What is it that starts your engine and keeps it going?

In this chapter, we explore the factors that energize and direct human behavior—not just motivation but also emotion. Both words—*motivation* and *emotion*—are derived from the Latin *movere,* meaning "to move." Like motivation, emotion moves us to act. The emotion of fear, for instance, can motivate us to act defensively to escape a threatening situation. The emotion of anger can motivate us to act aggressively to rectify an injustice. The emotion of happiness inspires us to repeat the behavior that creates it. Throughout the ages, love has been considered a prime motivator, the emotion that "makes the world go round."

We begin by considering the sources of motivation that prompt behavior and keep it going. We then focus on one of the most basic motives, hunger, and examine in depth the problems of obesity and eating disorders. Finally, we explore the complex phenomenon of emotion. ∎

MODULE 8.1 Motivation: The "Whys" of Behavior

- **What is motivation?**
- **What is instinct theory?**
- **What is drive theory?**
- **How does arousal theory account for differences in motivational states?**
- **How does incentive theory differ from drive theory?**
- **What are psychosocial needs?**
- **What is Maslow's hierarchy of needs?**

Motivation refers to factors that *activate, direct,* and *sustain* goal-directed behavior. If, after a few hours of not eating, you get up from your chair and go to the kitchen to fix yourself a snack, we might infer that the *motive* for your behavior is hunger. The hunger motive activates your behavior (causing you to stand), directs it (moving you toward the kitchen), and sustains it (as you make yourself a snack and consume it) until you've achieved your goal (satisfying your hunger).

Motives are the "whys" of behavior—the needs or wants that drive behavior and explain why we do what we do. We don't actually observe a motive; rather, we infer that one exists based on the behavior we observe.

In this module, we focus on the biological and psychological sources of motivation and the various theories psychologists have constructed to explain motivated behavior. None of these theories offers a complete explanation of motivated behavior, but each contributes something to our understanding of the "whys" of behavior.

Biological Sources of Motivation

We need oxygen to breathe, food for energy, water to drink, and protection from the elements. These basic biological needs motivate much of our behavior. Biological needs are inborn. We don't learn to breathe or to become hungry or thirsty. Nonetheless, learning and experience influence how we satisfy our biological needs, especially our need for food. Eating tamales or mutton stew might satisfy our hunger, but our cultural backgrounds and learning experiences influence our choice of food and the ways in which we prepare and consume it.

Instincts: Behavior Programmed by Nature

Birds build nests, and salmon return upstream to their birthplaces to spawn. They do not acquire these behaviors through experience or by attending nest-building or spawning schools. These are **instinctive behaviors**—fixed, inborn patterns of response that are specific to members of a particular species. **Instinct theory** holds that behavior is motivated by instincts.

Though we can find examples of instinctive behaviors in other species, do instincts motivate human behavior? One theorist who thought so was Sigmund Freud, who believed that human behavior is motivated primarily by sexual and aggressive instincts (see Chapters 1 and 10). Another was William James (1890/1970), the father of American psychology, who compiled a list of thirty-seven instincts that he believed could explain much of human behavior. His list included physical instincts, such as sucking, and mental instincts, such as curiosity, jealousy, and even cleanliness. (Yes, cleanliness.) Other early psychologists, notably William McDougall (1908), expanded on James's list. The list kept growing and growing, so much so that by the 1920s, it had ballooned to some ten thousand instincts covering a wide range of human behavior (Bernard, 1924).

CONCEPT 8.1
Motivation refers to the "whys" of behavior—factors that activate, direct, and sustain goal-directed behavior.

Bill Gates What makes Bill run? What drives your behavior?

CONCEPT 8.2
Instinct theorists believe that humans and other animals are motivated by instincts—fixed, inborn patterns of response that are specific to members of a particular species.

The instinct theory of human motivation has long been out of favor. One reason for its decline is that the list of instincts simply grew too large to be useful. Another is that explaining behavior on the basis of instincts is merely a way of describing it, not explaining it (Gaulin & McBurney, 2001). For example, saying a person is lazy because of a laziness instinct or stingy because of a stinginess instinct doesn't really explain the person's behavior. It merely attaches a label to it. Perhaps most important, psychologists recognized that human behavior is much more variable and flexible than would be the case if it were determined by instinct. Moreover, instinct theory fails to account for the important roles of culture and learning in determining human behavior. Though instincts may account for some stereotypical behavior in other animals, most psychologists reject the view that instincts motivate complex human behavior.

Needs and Drives: Maintaining a Steady Internal State

By the early 1950s, **drive theory** had replaced instinct theory as the major model of human motivation. Its foremost proponent, psychologist Clark Hull (1943, 1952), believed we have biological needs that demand satisfaction, such as the needs for food, water, and sleep. A **need** is a state of deprivation or deficiency. A **drive** is a state of bodily tension, such as hunger or thirst that arises from an unmet need. The satisfaction of a drive is called **drive reduction**.

Drive theory is based on *homeostasis,* the tendency of the body to maintain a steady internal state (see Chapter 2). Homeostatic mechanisms in the body monitor temperature, oxygen, and blood sugar, and maintain them at a steady level. According to drive theory, whenever homeostasis is disturbed, drives activate the behavior needed to restore a steady balance. For example, when our blood sugar level drops because we haven't eaten in a while, we become hungry. Hunger is the drive that motivates us to seek nourishment, which restores homeostasis. Although drive theory focuses on biological needs, some needs, such as the needs for comfort and safety, have a psychological basis.

Though needs and drives are related, they are distinct from each other. We may have a bodily need for a certain vitamin but not become aware of it until we develop a vitamin deficiency disorder. In other words, the need may exist in the absence of a corresponding drive. Moreover, the strength of a need and the drive to satisfy it may differ. People who fast for religious or other reasons may find they are less hungry on the second or third day of a fast than on the first, even though their need for food is even greater.

Unlike instinct theory, drive theory posits an important role for learning, especially operant conditioning (discussed in Chapter 5). We learn responses (like ordering a pizza when we're hungry) that are reinforced by drive reduction. A behavior that results in drive reduction is more likely to be repeated the next time the need arises. Drives may also be acquired through experience. Biological drives, such as hunger, thirst, and sexual desire, are called **primary drives** because they are considered inborn; drives that are the result of experience are called **secondary drives**. For example, a drive to achieve monetary wealth is not something we are born with; we acquire it as a secondary drive because we learn that money can be used to satisfy many primary and other secondary drives.

Optimal Level of Arousal: What's Optimal for You?

Drive theory focuses on drives that satisfy survival needs, such as needs for food and water. But classic experiments by psychologist Harry Harlow and his colleagues challenged the notion that all drives satisfy basic survival needs. When they placed a mechanical puzzle in a monkey's cage, they found that the monkey began manipulating it and taking it apart, even though the animal didn't receive any food or other obvious reinforcement for its efforts (Harlow, Harlow, & Meyer,

---

💡 **CONCEPT 8.3**
Drive theorists maintain that we are motivated by drives that arise from biological needs that demand satisfaction.

motivation   Factors that activate, direct, and sustain goal-directed behavior.

motives   Needs or wants that drive goal-directed behavior.

instinctive behaviors   Genetically programmed, innate patterns of response that are specific to members of a particular species.

instinct theory   The belief that behavior is motivated by instinct.

drive theory   The belief that behavior is motivated by drives that arise from biological needs that demand satisfaction.

need   A state of deprivation or deficiency.

drive   A state of bodily tension, such as hunger or thirst, that arises from an unmet need.

drive reduction   Satisfaction of a drive.

primary drives   Innate drives, such as hunger, thirst, and sexual desire, that arise from basic biological needs.

secondary drives   Drives that are learned or acquired through experience, such as the drive to achieve monetary wealth.

1950). Human babies, too, manipulate objects placed before them. They shake rattles, turn knobs, push buttons on activity toys, and mouth new objects, even though none of these behaviors is connected with satisfaction of their basic survival needs.

The work of Harlow and others suggests that humans and many other animals may have innate, biologically based needs for exploration and activity. These needs, which prod organisms to explore their environments and manipulate objects—especially unusual or novel objects—are called **stimulus motives**. Stimulus motives don't disappear as we get older. Adults seek to touch and manipulate interesting objects, as attested to by the many grown-ups who try their hand at the latest gizmos displayed at stores like The Sharper Image.

Drive theory would lead us to expect that organisms are motivated to reduce *states of arousal*—that is, states of general alertness and nervous-system activation. For example, when we are hungry, we experience a state of heightened arousal until we eat; after eating, we may feel tranquil or even sleepy. But with stimulus motives, we observe motivated behavior that leads to increased arousal—not decreased arousal, as drive theory would suggest. In other words, even when our basic needs for food and water are met, we seek out stimulation that heightens our level of arousal.

Some theorists believe stimulus motives represent a biologically based need to maintain an *optimal* level of arousal (Hebb, 1955; Zuckerman, 1980). This theory, called **arousal theory**, holds that whenever the level of stimulation dips below an organism's optimal level, the organism seeks ways of increasing it. When stimulation exceeds an optimal level, the organism seeks ways of toning it down.

The optimal level of arousal varies from person to person. Some people require a steady diet of highly stimulating activities, such as mountain climbing, snowboarding, bungee jumping, or parasailing. Others are satisfied to spend quiet evenings at home, curled up with a good book or relaxing by watching TV.

People with a high need for arousal see life as an adventure. To maintain their optimal level of stimulation, they seek exciting experiences and thrills. Psychologist Marvin Zuckerman (1996, 2004) calls such people *sensation-seekers*. Sensation-seekers tend to get bored easily and may have difficulty restraining their impulses. Some get into trouble because their desire for stimulation leads them to take undue risks; some may experiment with illicit drugs or engage in other illegal activities (Roberti, 2004). Yet many sensation-seekers limit their sensation-seeking to sanctioned, reasonably safe activities. Not surprisingly, surfers tend to score higher on sensation-seeking than do golfers (Diehm & Armatas, 2004). Sensation-seeking appears to have a strong genetic component—the taste for thrills may be something we are born with.

CONCEPT 8.4
Stimulus motives prod organisms to explore their environments and manipulate objects.

CONCEPT 8.5
Arousal theory postulates a biologically based need to maintain stimulation at an optimal level.

A High Need for Sensation? Actor Jason Priestly's interests in thrill-seeking activities include motorcycles, racing boats, race car driving, and bungee jumping. He nearly died when the race car he was driving at 186 mph slammed into a wall at the track. Jason reported that he had suffered fourteen concussions in his life.

stimulus motives Internal states that prompt inquisitive, stimulation-seeking, and exploratory behavior.

arousal theory The belief that whenever the level of stimulation dips below an organism's optimal level, the organism seeks ways of increasing it.

TRY THIS OUT

Are You a Sensation-Seeker?

Do you pursue thrills and adventure? Or do you prefer quiet evenings at home? To evaluate whether you fit the profile of a sensation-seeker, circle the number on each line that best describes you.

Interpreting your responses. Responses above five indicate a high level of sensation-seeking; those five or below indicate a low level. On which side of the continuum do your responses lie? Draw a line connecting your responses. The further to the right the line falls, the stronger your personality fits the profile of a sensation-seeker.

Prefer a job in one location	1 2 3 4 5 6 7 8 9 10	Prefer a job with lots of travel
Prefer staying out of the cold	1 2 3 4 5 6 7 8 9 10	Enjoy a brisk walk on a cold day
Prefer being with familiar people	1 2 3 4 5 6 7 8 9 10	Prefer meeting new people
Like to play it safe	1 2 3 4 5 6 7 8 9 10	Like living "on the edge"
Would prefer not to try hypnosis	1 2 3 4 5 6 7 8 9 10	Would like to try hypnosis
Would prefer not to try parachute jumping	1 2 3 4 5 6 7 8 9 10	Would like to try parachute jumping
Prefer quiet evenings at home	1 2 3 4 5 6 7 8 9 10	Prefer going out dancing at night
Prefer a safe and secure life	1 2 3 4 5 6 7 8 9 10	Prefer experiencing as much as possible
Prefer calm and controlled people	1 2 3 4 5 6 7 8 9 10	Prefer people who are a bit wild
Like to sleep in a comfortable room with a good bed	1 2 3 4 5 6 7 8 9 10	Enjoy camping out
Prefer avoiding risky activities	1 2 3 4 5 6 7 8 9 10	Like to do things that are a little dangerous

Source: Adapted from Zuckerman, 1980.

Psychological Sources of Motivation

If motivation were simply a matter of maintaining homeostasis in our bodies, we would rest quietly until prompted again by hunger, thirst, or some other biological drive. But we don't sit idly by when our bellies are full and our other biological needs are met. We are also motivated by psychological needs, such as the need for friendship or achievement. We perceive certain goals as desirable or rewarding even though attaining them will not satisfy any biological needs. Clearly, such motivated behaviors are best addressed by considering the role of psychological factors in motivation. These factors include incentives and psychosocial needs.

Incentives: The "Pull" Side of Motivation

According to **incentive theory**, our attraction to particular goals or objects motivates much of our behavior. **Incentives** are rewards or other stimuli that motivate us to act. The attraction, or "pull," exerted by an incentive stems from our perception that it can satisfy a need or is in itself desirable.

In contrast to drive theory, which explains how unmet biological needs push us in the direction of satisfying them, incentive theory holds that incentives motivate us by pulling us toward them. Incentive theory thus focuses on the lure, or "pull," of incentives in motivating behavior, rather than the "push" of internal need states or drives. You may crave a scrumptious-looking dessert even though you've just eaten a full meal and no longer feel "pushed" by the drive of hunger. You may feel drawn to buy the latest fashions or technological gizmos even though obtaining these objects will not satisfy any biological need.

CONCEPT 8.6
Incentives motivate us by exerting a pull on our behavior; their strength varies in relation to the value we place on them.

incentive theory   The belief that our attraction to particular goals or objects motivates much of our behavior.
incentives   Rewards or other stimuli that motivate us to act.

The strength of the "pull" that a goal or reward exerts on our behavior is its **incentive value**. Incentive values are influenced by many factors, including an individual's learning experiences and expectancies. We place more value on a goal if we have learned from past experience to associate it with pleasure and if we expect it will be rewarding when we obtain it. Many employers spur productivity in their employees by offering them incentives in the form of bonuses. Marketers manipulate the incentive value of the products they want us to buy. They try to persuade us that to be cool, healthy, sexy, or successful, we need to use their products.

Cultural influences play a large part in determining incentive values. Some cultures place great value on individual achievement and accumulation of wealth. Others place a premium on meeting obligations to one's family, religious group, employer, or community. What incentives motivate your behavior—a college diploma, wealth, the man or woman of your dreams, status, or the respect of your family or community? Which of these incentives has the strongest "pull" on your behavior?

Psychosocial Needs

Although fulfilling biological needs is necessary for survival, human beings seek more out of life than mere survival. We are social creatures who are motivated to satisfy **psychosocial needs** (also called *interpersonal needs*), such as the need for social relationships (also called the *need for affiliation*) and the need to achieve. Here we focus on the most widely studied of these needs—the need to excel at what we do, which is known as the **need for achievement**.

Some people strive relentlessly to get ahead, to earn vast sums of money, to invent, to create—in short, to achieve. People with a high need for achievement are found in many walks of life, from business and professional sports to academia and the arts. Like Bill Gates, they have a strong desire to excel at what they do. They are hard-driving and ambitious and take pride in accomplishing their goals.

Harvard psychologist David McClelland found that the goals that people with a high need for achievement set for themselves are challenging but realistic (McClelland, 1958, 1985). Goals that are too easily achieved are of no interest to them, nor are goals that are patently unobtainable. Such people may not always succeed, but they take failure in stride and keep pushing ahead. By contrast, people with a low need for achievement are motivated by a desire to avoid failure. They set goals either so low that anyone can achieve them or so unrealistically high that no one can achieve them. If the bar is set too high, who can blame them if they fail? When they meet with failure, they are more likely to quit than to persevere.

People with a high need for achievement typically receive higher grades and earn more promotions and money than people with similar abilities and opportunities but a lower need for achievement. They generally seek positions that offer moderate levels of risk, opportunities for decision making, and a chance at becoming highly successful (McClelland, 1965). They often pursue careers as entrepreneurs or in business management or sales.

The need for achievement is driven by *extrinsic motivation, intrinsic motivation,* or both (Harackiewicz & Elliot, 1993; Ryan & Deci, 2000). **Extrinsic motivation** reflects a desire for external rewards, such as money or the respect of one's peers or family. **Intrinsic motivation** reflects a desire for internal gratification, such as the self-satisfaction or pleasure derived from accomplishing a particular goal or performing a certain task. In other words, extrinsic motivation is a "means to an end," whereas intrinsic motivation is an "end in itself" (Pittman, 1998).

In achievement situations, we may be pulled in opposite directions by two kinds of motives: **achievement motivation** (the desire to achieve success) and **avoidance motivation** (the desire to avoid failure). Achievement motivation leads us to undertake challenges that run the risk of failure but that may also lead to success. Avoidance motivation leads us to avoid taking chances that could result in failure; it prompts us to stick with the sure and safe path. Although avoidance

---

CONCEPT 8.7
Many psychologists believe we are motivated by drives that arise from biological needs that demand satisfaction.

web Netlab/How Do You Motivate Others?

---

incentive value The strength of the "pull" of a goal or reward.

psychosocial needs Needs that reflect interpersonal aspects of motivation, such as the need for friendship or achievement.

need for achievement The need to excel in one's endeavors.

extrinsic motivation Motivation reflecting a desire for external rewards, such as wealth or the respect of others.

intrinsic motivation Motivation reflecting a desire for internal gratification, such as the self-satisfaction derived from accomplishing a particular goal.

achievement motivation The motive or desire to achieve success.

avoidance motivation The motive or desire to avoid failure.

Need for Achievement How strong is your need for achievement—your need not just to succeed, but to excel?

motivation may reduce the chance of failure, it also reduces the likelihood of success. A recent study found that students with a lower level of avoidance motivation did better in their courses and showed higher levels of emotional well-being than those with a higher level of avoidance motivation (Elliot & Sheldon, 1997).

Achievement motivation develops early in life and is strongly influenced by parents. Parents of children with a high need for achievement typically encourage them to be independent and to attempt difficult tasks. They reward them for their persistence at difficult tasks with praise and other reinforcements and encourage them to attempt even more challenging tasks (Dweck, 1997; McClelland, 1985).

The Hierarchy of Needs: Ordering Needs from the Basement to the Attic of Human Experience

We have seen that both biological and psychological needs play important roles in human motivation. But how do these needs relate to each other? We now consider a model that bridges both sources of motivation—the **hierarchy of needs** developed by humanistic psychologist Abraham Maslow (1970).

As Figure 8.1 shows, Maslow's hierarchy has five levels: (1) *physiological needs,* such as hunger and thirst; (2) *safety needs,* such as the need for secure housing; (3) *love and belongingness needs,* such as the need for intimate relationships; (4) *esteem needs,* such as the need for the respect of one's peers; and (5) *the need for self-actualization,* which is the need that motivates individuals to fulfill their unique potentials and become all they are capable of being. In Maslow's view, our needs are ordered in such a way that we are motivated to meet basic needs before moving upward in the hierarchy. In other words, once we fill our bellies, we strive to meet higher-order needs, such as our needs for security, love, achievement, and **self-actualization**. Maslow believed that achieving a full measure of psychological integration and well-being depends on meeting all five levels of need.

Since no two people are perfectly alike, the drive for self-actualization leads people in different directions. For some, self-actualization may involve creating works of art, but for others it may mean striving on the playing field, in the classroom, or in a corporate office. Not all of us climb to the top of the hierarchy; we don't all achieve self-actualization.

Maslow's hierarchical model of needs has an intuitive appeal. We generally seek satisfaction of our basic needs for food, drink, and shelter before concerning ourselves with psychologically based needs like belongingness. But critics point out that our needs may not be ordered in as fixed a manner as Maslow's hierarchy suggests. An artist might go for days with little if any nourishment in order to

CONCEPT 8.8
According to Maslow, human needs are organized in a hierarchy that ranges from biological needs at the base to the need for self-actualization at the top.

hierarchy of needs Maslow's concept that there is an order to human needs, which starts with basic biological needs and progresses to self-actualization.

self-actualization The motive that drives individuals to express their unique capabilities and fulfill their potentials.

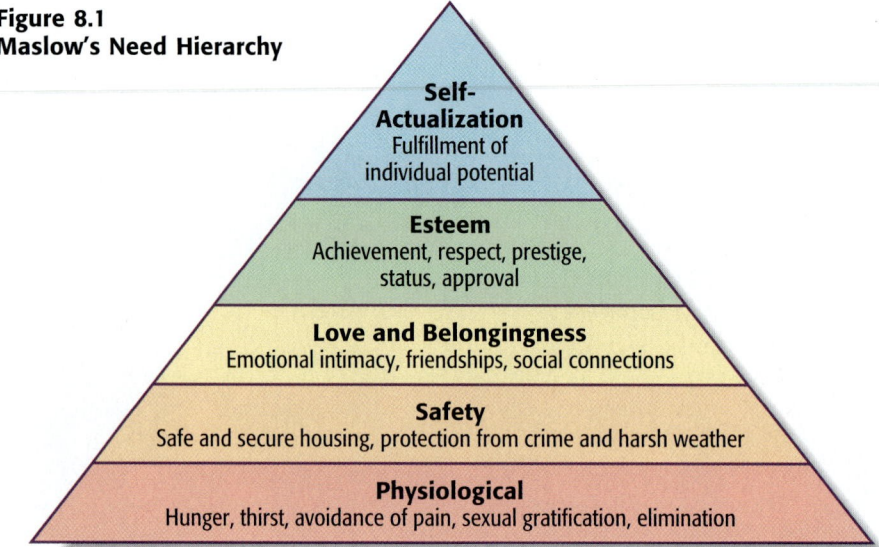

Figure 8.1
Maslow's Need Hierarchy

complete a new work. People may forgo seeking satisfaction of their need for intimate relationships to focus their energies on career aspirations. Maslow might counter that eventually the emptiness of their emotional lives would motivate them to fill the gap.

Another problem with Maslow's model is that the same behavior may reflect multiple needs. Perhaps you are attending college to satisfy physiological and safety needs (to prepare for a career so that you can earn money to live comfortably and securely), love and belongingness needs (to form friendships and social ties), esteem needs (to achieve status or approval), and self-actualization needs (to fulfill your intellectual or creative potential). Despite its limitations, Maslow's model leads us to recognize that human behavior is motivated by higher pursuits as well as satisfaction of basic needs.

Before going forward, you may wish to review the sources of motivation outlined in Concept Chart 8.1.

CONCEPT CHART 8.1
Sources of Motivation

	Source	Description
Biological Sources	Instincts	Instincts are fixed, inborn response patterns that are specific to members of a particular species.
	Needs and drives	Unmet needs create internal drive states, which motivate behavior that leads to drive reduction.
	Stimulus motives and optimal level of arousal	Stimulus motives arise from biologically based needs to be curious and active and to explore the environment. Arousal theory holds that we are motivated to maintain a level of stimulation that is optimal for us.
Psychological Sources	Incentives	The value we place on goals or objects creates a lure, or "pull," to obtain them.
	Psychosocial needs	These reflect psychosocial (interpersonal) needs, such as the needs for achievement and social relationships.

Note: According to Maslow, human needs are organized within a hierarchy that ranges from basic biological needs at the base to the need for self-actualization at the pinnacle.

MODULE 8.1 REVIEW

Motivation: The "Whys" of Behavior

CONCEPT CHECK

1. Factors that activate, direct, and sustain goal-directed behavior are referred to as _____.

2. Fixed, inborn patterns of response that are specific to members of a particular species are called
   a. reinforcers.
   b. instincts.
   c. drives.
   d. self-actualization.

3. Match the terms on the left with the definitions on the right:
   i.   primary drive   a. a drive acquired through experience
   ii. secondary drive b. the tendency to maintain a steady internal state
   iii. need   c. a state of deprivation or deficiency
   iv. homeostasis   d. an innate biological drive

4. Sources of motivation that prompt us to explore our environment and manipulate objects, especially novel or unusual objects, are called _____.

5. The strength of the "pull" that a goal or reward exerts on our behavior is called its _____.

6. At the top of Maslow's hierarchy of needs is the need that motivates people to fulfill their unique potentials and become all they are capable of being. This is known as the need for
   a. esteem.
   b. love and belongingness.
   c. achievement.
   d. self-actualization.

MODULE 8.2   Hunger and Eating

- **How are hunger and appetite regulated?**
- **What causes obesity?**
- **What is anorexia nervosa?**
- **What is bulimia nervosa?**
- **What are the causes of eating disorders?**

Hunger is one of the most basic drives—and one of the most difficult to ignore. If your stomach is growling at this moment, you are unlikely to pay close attention to what you are reading. But is hunger a product of a grumbling stomach? Or does it arise in the brain?

What Makes Us Hungry?

It may seem that pangs of hunger arise from the grumblings of an empty stomach, but it is the brain, not the stomach, that controls hunger. Here's how it works: When we haven't eaten for a while, our blood sugar levels drop. When this happens, fat is released from *fat cells*—body cells that store fat—to provide fuel that cells use until we are able to eat again. The *hypothalamus,* a small structure in the forebrain that helps regulate hunger and many other bodily processes (discussed in Chapter 2), detects these changes and triggers a cascading series of events, leading to the feelings of hunger that motivate us to eat (Campfield et al., 1995). Eating restores an internally balanced state, or homeostasis, by bringing blood sugar levels back into balance and replenishing fat cells.

Different parts of the hypothalamus play different roles in regulating hunger and eating (see Figure 8.2). Stimulating the **lateral hypothalamus** causes a laboratory animal to start eating even if it has just consumed a full meal. If the lateral hypothalamus is surgically destroyed, the animal will stop eating and eventually starve to death. Thus, we know that the lateral hypothalamus is involved in initiating, or "turning on," eating.

CONCEPT 8.9
The hypothalamus detects decreases in blood sugar levels and depletion of fat from fat cells, which leads to the feelings of hunger that motivate eating.

lateral hypothalamus   A part of the hypothalamus involved in initiating, or "turning on," eating.

Figure 8.2 Parts of the Hypothalamus Involved in Hunger and Eating
The parts of the hypothalamus involved in regulating hunger and eating include the lateral hypothalamus and the ventromedial hypothalamus. What roles do these structures play?

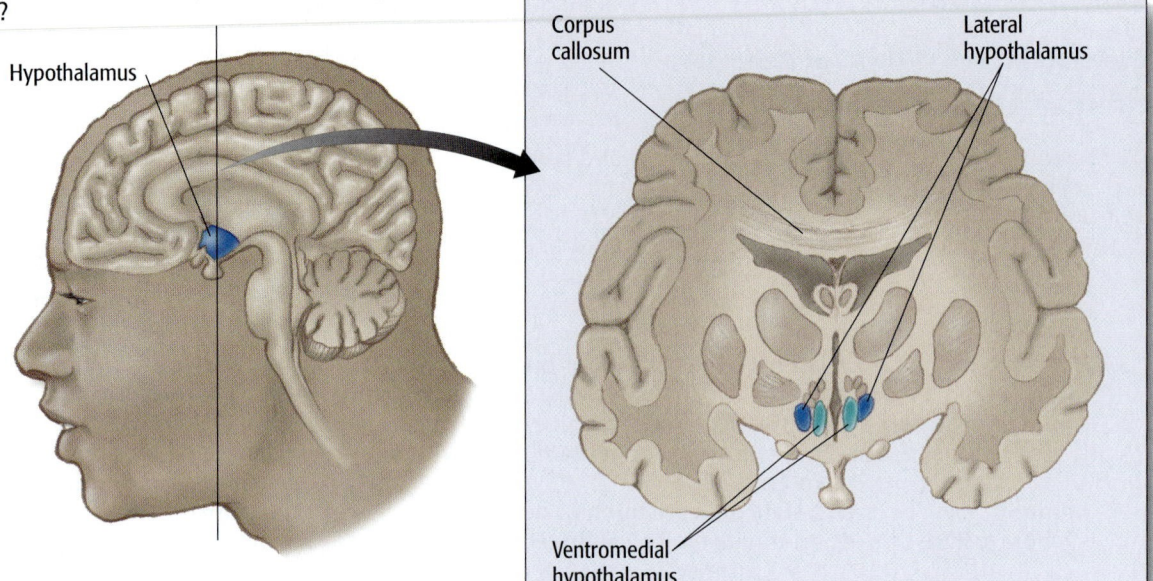

Location of the Hypothalamus

Cross-section Showing Parts
of the Hypothalamus

PsychAssist: Parts of the Brain Involved in Hunger and Eating

CONCEPT 8.10
Neurotransmitters and hormones also play important roles in regulating both appetite and feelings of satiety.

Obese Rat Destroying the ventromedial hypothalamus of laboratory rats induces insatiable eating, which leads to severe obesity.

Another part of the hypothalamus, the **ventromedial hypothalamus**, acts as an off-switch that signals when it is time to stop eating. When this area is destroyed, animals will overeat and eventually become severely obese.

A mixture of chemicals in our bodies, including neurotransmitters and hormones, play important roles in regulating hunger (Bouret, Draper, & Simerly, 2004; Cummings et al., 2002). One of these chemicals, the neurotransmitter *neuropeptide Y*, works on the hypothalamus to stimulate appetite and eating. When we haven't eaten in a while, the brain releases additional amounts of neuropeptide Y (Siegel, 2004). Other brain chemicals work to curb appetite and eating when we've had enough to eat (Korner & Leibel, 2003).

Obesity: A National Epidemic

Obesity, a state of excess body fat, is a national epidemic. We Americans are fatter than ever before. About two of three U.S. adults are overweight, as compared to fewer than one in four in the early 1960s (Manson & Bassuk, 2003). Nearly one in three Americans are obese (Vastag, 2004). The prevalence of overweight among U.S. children is also rising sharply, having doubled during the past twenty-five years (Dietz, 2004).

Why should it matter if we weigh too much? It matters because obesity is a major health risk. Obese people stand an increased risk of many serious health problems, including heart disease, hypertension, respiratory disorders, stroke, diabetes, gall bladder disease, gout, and certain types of cancer (e.g., Carmichael, 2003b; Hirosumi et al., 2002; Mokdad et al., 2003).

Obesity-related diseases account for an estimated 300,000 deaths in the United States each year, including 90,000 cancer deaths (Mitka, 2003). Not surprisingly, obesity cuts life expectancy markedly, by about six to seven years on the average (Fontaine et al., 2003).

Why is overweight and obesity on the rise? Health experts cite two main factors: too many calories consumed and too little exercise (Pollan, 2003). On the average, Americans consume 530 more calories per day today than they did thirty years ago (Gorman, 2003). Many of us have become "couch potatoes" or "cyber-slugs" who exercise too little and who eat too much in the way of high-fat, high-calorie foods. Portion sizes in restaurants are also up—way up (Smith, 2003). Meanwhile, we have become increasingly dependent on the automobile rather than on foot power to get from place to place, especially those of us living in the increasingly sprawling suburban areas (Ewing et al., 2003; McKee, 2003).

Causes of Obesity

Maintaining a healthy weight is a matter of striking a balance between energy-in (calories consumed) and energy-out (calories expended through bodily processes and physical activity) (Pi-Sunyer, 2003). Excess calories are converted into body fat, adding both weight and girth to the body.

Research points to the large role that genetics plays in obesity (Farooqi et al., 2003). Obese people may have a genetic predisposition to gain weight more readily than lean people. Body weight is influenced by one's *basal metabolic rate* (also called *basal metabolism*), the rate at which the body burns calories while at rest. The slower the body's metabolic rate, the more likely the person is to gain weight easily. Heredity may explain why some people have slower metabolic rates than others.

According to **set point theory**, the brain regulates body weight around a genet-ically predetermined level or "set point" (Keesey & Powley, 1986). This theory proposes that when weight gain or loss occurs, the brain adjusts the basal meta-bolic rate to keep body weight around its set point (Pinel, Assanand, & Lehman, 2000). When people lose weight, the brain slows the body's metabolic rate, and as this rate slows, the body conserves stores of fat. This perhaps explains why dieters often find it hard to continue losing weight or even to maintain their weight loss. The body's ability to adjust its metabolic rate downward when caloric intake falls off is a bane to many dieters today, but it may have helped ancestral humans sur-vive times of famine (Grady, 2002).

The number of fat cells in one's body may also contribute to obesity. Obese people typically have more fat cells than do people of normal weight. Severely obese people may have 200 billion or more fat cells, as compared with the 25 bil-lion or 30 billion fat cells in people of normal weight. As noted earlier, depletion of fat cells is a factor in triggering hunger. Since obese people typically have more fat cells than normal-weight individuals, they may feel hungry sooner after eating than do people with fewer fat cells. The human body may be designed as a kind of fat-storage machine that retains its fat cells to provide reserves of energy (stored

CONCEPT 8.11
Obesity is a complex health problem in which behavioral patterns, genetics, and environmental and emotional factors may all play a role.

All in the Family?   We've learned from studies of twins and adoptees that genetics plays an important role in obesity.

ventromedial hypothalamus   A part of the hypothalamus involved in regulating feelings of satiety.

set point theory   The belief that brain mechanisms regulate body weight around a genetically predetermined "set point."

fat) through lean times. Although genetics plays a role in determining the numbers of fat cells we have, early dietary patterns, such as excessive eating in childhood, may also play a role.

Whatever roles behavioral patterns and genetics play in obesity, they don't tell the whole story. Environmental factors play a significant part as well (Hill et al., 2003). We are constantly bombarded with food cues—TV commercials showing displays of tempting foods, aromas permeating the air as we walk by the bakery in the supermarket, and on and on. Consider that, among children, Ronald McDonald is the second most widely recognized figure, after Santa Claus (Parloff, 2003). Ads for fast-food restaurants typically feature burgers, shakes, and other high-calorie, high-fat items; more nutritious items, such as salads, are notably missing.

Emotional states, such as anger, fear, and depression, can prompt excessive eating. Many of us overeat in anger, or when we're feeling lonely, bored, or depressed. Have you ever tried to quell anxiety over an upcoming examination by finishing off a carton of ice cream? We may find we can soothe our negative feelings, at least temporarily, by treating ourselves to food.

What's the bottom line (or curve) on the causes of obesity? Behavioral patterns, genetics, environmental factors, and emotional cues all play a role. Yet even people whose genes predispose them to weight problems can achieve and maintain a healthy body weight by eating sensibly and exercising regularly. Regular physical activity not only burns calories; it also increases the metabolic rate because it builds muscles, and muscle tissue burns more calories than fatty tissue. Thus, regular exercise combined with gradual weight reduction can help offset the reduction in the body's metabolic rate that may occur when we begin losing weight. Though people can expect to gain a modest amount of weight as they age, obesity is neither a natural nor an inevitable consequence of aging.

Health experts recognize that "quickie" diets are not the answer to long-term weight management. More than 90 percent of people regain the weight they lose on a diet (Kolata, 2000a). Diet drugs and antiobesity drugs offer at best only a temporary benefit and may carry serious side effects. Experts doubt that we will find a safe and effective antiobesity drug any time soon (Grady, 2003). Long-term success in losing excess weight and keeping it off requires a lifelong commitment to a sensible, low-calorie, low-fat diet combined with regular exercise (Irwin et al., 2002; Manson et al., 2004). People also need to become more calorie conscious. For example, they need to recognize that "low fat" does not necessarily mean "low calorie." (Check the nutritional labels.) Even if obesity is not a current concern in your life, adopting healthy eating and exercise habits can help you avoid weight problems in the future. Table 8.1 offers suggestions for maintaining a healthy weight.

Eating Disorders

Karen, the twenty-two-year-old daughter of a famed English professor, felt her weight was "just about right" (Boskind-White & White, 1983). But at seventy-eight pounds on a five-foot frame, she looked more like a prepubescent eleven-year-old than a young adult. Her parents tried to persuade her to seek help with her eating behavior, but she continually denied she had a problem. Ultimately, however, after she lost yet another pound, her parents were able to convince her to enter a residential treatment program where her eating could be closely monitored.

Nicole, nineteen, wakes up each morning hoping this will be the day she begins living normally—that today she'll avoid gorging herself and inducing herself to vomit. But she doesn't feel confident that her eating behavior and purging are under her control (Boskind-White & White, 1983). The disordered eating behavior of Karen and Nicole are characteristic of the two major types of eating disorders: *anorexia nervosa* and *bulimia nervosa*.

CONCEPT 8.12

Effective weight management requires a lifelong commitment to healthy eating and exercise habits that balance caloric intake with energy output.

CONCEPT 8.13

Eating disorders, such as anorexia nervosa and bulimia nervosa, disproportionately affect young women, in large part because of a cultural obsession to achieve unrealistic standards of thinness.

TABLE 8.1	Suggestions for Maintaining a Healthy Weight
Limit fat intake.	The number of calories you need to maintain a healthy weight depends on many factors, including your body size, metabolic rate, and activity level. Health officials recommend limiting total intake of fat to less than 30 percent of daily calories and keeping intake of saturated fat at less than 10 percent (USDA, 1991). If 2,000 calories per day are needed to maintain one's weight, this means consuming no more than 66 grams of fat and limiting saturated fat to 22 grams. (Note that 1 gram of fat contains 9 calories.)
Control portion size.	The major factor in controlling weight is striking a balance between calories consumed and calories expended. Controlling portion size can help you maintain this caloric balance.
Slow down the pace pace of eating.	It takes about fifteen minutes for your brain to register that your stomach feels full. Give it a chance to catch up with your stomach.
Beware of hidden calories.	Some fruit drinks and other beverages are loaded with calories, so be sure to check product labels for calorie contents. Try diluting fruit drinks with water, or substitute the actual fruit itself. Also be aware that many processed foods, especially baked goods, contain a lot of sugar and fat.
Make physical activity a part of your lifestyle.	Health experts recommend thirty minutes a day of moderate physical activity—activity equivalent in strenuousness to walking three to four miles per hour (Fogelholm et al., 2000; R. R. Pate et al., 1995). This doesn't mean you must work out in a gym or jog around a park every day. Taking a brisk walk from your car to your office or school, climbing stairs, or doing vigorous work around the house can help you meet your daily exercise needs. But additional aerobic exercise—like running, swimming, or using equipment specially designed for aerobic exercise—may help even more. Before starting any exercise program, discuss your health needs and concerns with a health care provider.

Source: Adapted from Nevid, Rathus, & Rubenstein, 1998.

Anorexia Nervosa

Anorexia nervosa is a form of self-starvation that results in an unhealthy and potentially dangerously low body weight. It is characterized by both an intense fear of becoming fat and a distorted body image. More than 95 percent of cases are found among women, typically adolescents or young adults. The young woman with anorexia is convinced she is too fat, even though others see her as little more than "skin and bones."

Anorexia is a dangerous medical condition and poses serious risks, including cardiovascular problems, such as irregular heartbeat and low blood pressure; gastrointestinal problems, such as chronic constipation and abdominal pain; loss of menstruation; and even deaths due to suicide or to medical complications associated with severe weight loss.

In a typical case, the young woman begins to notice some weight gain in adolescence. She becomes overly concerned about getting fat. She resorts to extreme dieting and perhaps excessive exercise to reduce her weight to a prepubescent level. She denies that she is too thin or losing too much weight, despite the concerns of others. In her mind's eye, she is heavier than she actually is.

Bulimia Nervosa

Bulimia nervosa is a disorder in which episodes of binge eating are followed by purging. The purging is accomplished through self-induced vomiting or other means, such as excessive use of laxatives. Some bulimic individuals purge regularly after meals, not just after binges. Some engage in excessive, even compulsive, exercise regimens to try to control their weight. Like those with anorexia, people with bulimia are obsessed with their weight and unhappy with their bodies. But unlike those with anorexia, they typically maintain a relatively normal weight.

Do You See What I See?
Young women with anorexia have a distorted body image. They perceive themselves as fat even though others see them as just "skin and bones."

Bulimia usually begins in late adolescence following a period of rigid dieting to lose weight. Bingeing may alternate with strict dieting. The binge itself usually occurs in secret. During the binge, the person consumes enormous amounts of foods that are sweet and high in fat. Bulimia can lead to many medical complications, including potentially dangerous potassium deficiencies and decay of tooth enamel from frequent vomiting, and severe constipation from overuse of laxatives.

Causes of Eating Disorders

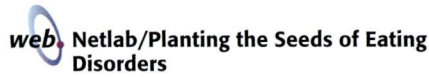 **Netlab/Planting the Seeds of Eating Disorders**

The preoccupation with thinness in our society and social pressures to conform to an ultrathin ideal contribute to the development of eating disorders in young women (The McKnight Investigators, 2003). As many as 50 to 75 percent of adolescent girls are unhappy with their weight and body image (Rubinstein & Caballero, 2000). Young women are continually bombarded with images of slender, often emaciated-looking female models and actresses who personify the contemporary ideal of the ultrathin feminine form.

Pressure on women to achieve and maintain thinness is so prevalent in our culture that dieting has become a normative eating pattern among American women. Concerns about weight become expressed in different ways, such as in feelings of guilt or shame associated with eating treats or even purchasing them. A recent survey showed that about one in seven college women said they would be embarrassed to buy a chocolate bar in a store (Rozin, Bauer, & Catanese, 2003).

Social pressure to achieve and maintain a slender figure falls most heavily on women in our society, especially young women. In reality, however, the gender gap in obesity is quite small. Overall, 27 percent of women are obese, as compared with 24 percent of men. Moreover, gender differences in obesity tend not to develop until midlife.

Anorexia is believed to affect about 0.5 percent of young women in our society (about one in two hundred), whereas bulimia is thought to affect approximately 1 to 3 percent of young women (American Psychological Association, 2000). Though these eating disorders disproportionately affect young women, clinicians have noted an increasing number of young men with anorexia. Many of these young men participate in sports, such as wrestling, in which they face pressures to maintain a lower weight.

Eating disorders are far less common, even rare, in non-Western countries that lack our cultural emphasis on thinness. They are also less common among African American women and women from other minority groups for whom body image is not as closely tied to body weight as it is among non-Hispanic White women (Angier, 2000c; Striegel-Moore et al., 2003). However, evidence shows a higher rate of disordered eating behaviors among African American women who tend to identify with the White majority culture (Abrams, Allen, & Gray, 1993).

Factors other than societal expectations of thinness also play a part in eating disorders. Many young women with eating disorders have issues relating to perfectionism and control. They may place unreasonable pressures on themselves to achieve a "perfect body" or feel that the only part of their lives they can control is their dieting (Cockell et al., 2002). Eating disorders also frequently develop in young women with histories of childhood sexual or physical abuse or whose families are wracked by conflict (Jacobi et al., 2004). Some theorists speculate that anorexia may arise from an unconscious wish in female adolescents to remain little girls.

Biological factors, such as genetics and disturbances in brain mechanisms that control hunger and satiety, are also believed to contribute to eating disorders (Lamberg, 2003; Strober et al., 2000). Irregularities in the activity of serotonin, a neurotransmitter involved in regulating feelings of satiety, may prompt bulimic binges. Antidepressant drugs that boost the availability of serotonin in the brain can help reduce binges (Walsh, Wheat, & Freund, 2000).

Although promising results in treating eating disorders with psychological and drug therapies have been reported (e.g., Walsh et al., 2004; Wilson et al., 2002), recovery is typically a long-term process and relapses and continuing symptoms are common (e.g., Fairburn et al., 2003; Halmi et al., 2003).

Concept Chart 8.2 presents an overview of our discussion of hunger, obesity, and eating disorders.

CONCEPT CHART 8.2
Hunger, Obesity, and Eating Disorders

Hunger and Appetite	Obesity	Eating Disorders

The hypothalamus detects low blood sugar levels and depletion of fat in fat cells, leading to feelings of hunger that motivate eating. Hormones and neurotransmitters also play important roles in regulating hunger and appetite.	Causes of obesity are genetic, psychological, and environmental. They include metabolic rate, number of fat cells in the body, behavioral patterns (such as an unhealthy diet and lack of exercise), and emotional and environmental cues that prompt eating.	Cultural pressure to achieve unrealistic standards of thinness is a major factor in fostering anorexia (self-starvation) and bulimia (binge eating followed by purging).
		
		    Psychological causes of eating disorders may include issues of control and perfectionism, sexual or physical abuse during childhood, family conflicts, and, for anorexia, underlying fears of adulthood and sexual maturity.
		
		    Biological factors that may be implicated in eating disorders include abnormalities in brain mechanism controlling feelings of hunger and satiation, genetics, and irregularities in serotonin activity.

MODULE 8.2 REVIEW

Hunger and Eating

CONCEPT CHECK

1. Which of the following does *not* describe what happens physiologically after a person has not eaten for a while?
   a. Blood sugar level drops.
   b. Fat is released from fat cells.
   c. The ventromedial hypothalamus signals that it is time to start eating.
   d. The brain releases more neuropeptide Y.

2. If the lateral hypothalamus in a laboratory animal is stimulated, the animal
   a. stops eating.
   b. starves to death.
   c. begins to eat even if it has just consumed a full meal.
   d. becomes obese.

3. Match the terms on the left with the definitions on the right:

   i.   lateral hypothalamus a. the rate at which the body at rest burns calories

   ii. ventromedial hypothalamus b. works like an on-switch for eating

   iii. basal metabolic rate c. a genetically predetermined range for weight

   iv. set point d. works likes an off-switch for signaling when it is time to stop eating

4. Which of the following factors is *not* linked to the development of eating disorders?
   a. relatively high levels of serotonin in the brain
   b. unrealistic cultural standards of thinness
   c. issues of control and perfectionism
   d. childhood abuse

MODULE 8.3 Sexual Motivation

- **What are the phases of the sexual response cycle?**
- **How do researchers conceptualize sexual orientation?**
- **What are the causes of sexual dysfunctions, and how are they treated?**

CONCEPT 8.14

Each society defines masculinity and femininity by imposing a set of gender-based expectations, called gender roles, that designate the behaviors and roles deemed appropriate for men and women.

Our sexuality is another important source of motivation, but it also has an important bearing on our personality—the qualities that make us unique. For example, our **gender identity** (sense of maleness or femaleness) and **sexual orientation** (direction of erotic attraction) are essential parts of our self-identity. Each society not only imposes rules for governing sexual conduct, but it also establishes a set of expectations, or **gender roles**, that designate the behaviors and roles it deems appropriate for men and women to perform. Gender roles stipulate how men and women should behave, how they should dress, what work they should do, and how they should interact with each other.

There is great variety in human sexual expression, including such sexual practices as oral sex, anal sex, and masturbation. Our bodies can respond to many forms of sexual stimulation, but our sexual behavior is more strongly determined by such factors as cultural learning, personal values, and individual experiences than by biological drives or capacities for sexual response.

The range of sexual behavior can be seen in the results of a large-scale, national survey of sexual practices (Laumann et al., 1994). About one in four men (27 percent) but fewer than one in ten women (7.6 percent) reported masturbating at least once a week (Laumann et al., 1994). (Many more probably did so but failed to report it.) Among married couples, 80 percent of the men and 71 percent of the women reported performing oral sex on their partners; 80 percent of the men and 74 percent of the women reported receiving oral sex. Much lower percentages of the people surveyed—26 percent of the men and 20 percent of the women—reported engaging in anal intercourse at some point in their lives. Results from another study show that, on the average, married couples report having intercourse at a frequency of slightly more than once a week (Deveny, 2003), but here again there is considerable diversity (see Figure 8.3).

In this module we focus on how our bodies respond to sexual stimulation. We then examine sexual orientation, or the direction of our erotic attractions and interests. Finally, we consider the different types of sexual dysfunctions and how helping professionals treat these problems. In Chapter 13, we shall consider the important relationships between sexual behavior and risks of sexually transmitted diseases.

gender identity The psychological sense of maleness or femaleness.

sexual orientation The directionality of one's erotic interests.

gender roles The cultural expectations imposed on men and women to behave in ways deemed appropriate for their gender.

sexual response cycle The term used by Masters and Johnson to refer to the characteristic stages of physiological response to sexual stimulation.

vasocongestion Swelling of tissues with blood, a process that accounts for penile erection and vaginal lubrication during sexual arousal.

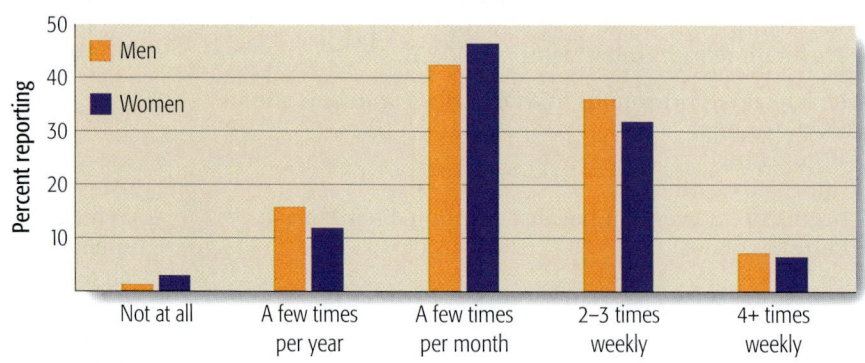

Figure 8.3
Frequency of Marital Sexual Relations During the Past Year

Source: Adapted from Laumann et al., 1994.

The Sexual Response Cycle: How Your Body Gets Turned On

Much of what we've learned about the physical response of the body to sexual stimulation comes from the pioneering research of William Masters and Virginia Johnson. They demonstrated that the body responds to sexual stimulation with a characteristic pattern of changes, which they called the **sexual response cycle**. They divided the sexual response cycle into four phases: *excitement, plateau, orgasm,* and *resolution* (Masters & Johnson, 1966). Figures 8.4(a) and 8.4(b) show the levels of sexual arousal during the phases of the sexual response cycle in men and women, respectively. These changes are summarized in Table 8.2.

There are obvious gender differences in how our bodies respond to sexual stimulation. The penis in males becomes erect; the vagina in women becomes moist through a process called *vaginal lubrication*. Yet both of these markers of sexual excitement (arousal) reflect the same underlying biological process, **vasocongestion**, or pooling of blood in bodily tissues. Overall, the similarities in the sexual responses of men and women listed in Table 8.2 may surprise you. Yet there is one important difference. Unlike women, men enter a *refractory period* following orgasm. This is the period of time in which men are physiologically incapable of achieving another orgasm or ejaculation. Women do not experience a refractory period. With continued stimulation they are capable of becoming quickly rearoused to the point of repeated (multiple) orgasms.

Now that we've considered how the body responds to sexual stimulation, let us consider the variations that exist in the direction of our sexual interests.

Sexual Orientation

Sexual orientation refers to the direction of one's erotic attraction and romantic interests—whether one is attracted toward members of one's sex, the opposite sex, or both sexes. Heterosexuals are sexually attracted to members of the opposite sex. Gay males and lesbians are attracted to members of their own sex, and bisexuals are attracted to members of both sexes. Yet the boundaries between these different sexual orientations may not be as clearly drawn as you might think. Today, many investigators conceptualize sexual orientation as a continuum with many

CONCEPT 8.15
Landmark research by Masters and Johnson showed that the body's response to sexual stimulation can be characterized in terms of a sexual response cycle consisting of four phases: excitement, plateau, orgasm, and resolution.

CONCEPT 8.16
Sexual orientation is generally conceptualized as a continuum ranging from exclusive homosexuality on one end to exclusive heterosexuality on the other end.

Figure 8.4   The Sexual Response Cycle
Here we see the level of sexual arousal across the four phases of the cycle. Men enter a refractory period after orgasm in which they become unresponsive to sexual stimulation. But as indicated by the broken line, men may become rearoused to the point of orgasm once the refractory period is past. Women do not enter a refractory period. Pattern A shows a woman's cycle with multiple orgasms, as indicated by the dotted line. Pattern B shows a response cycle in which the woman reaches the plateau stage but does not achieve orgasm. Pattern C shows a pattern leading to orgasm in which the woman quickly passes through the plateau phase.

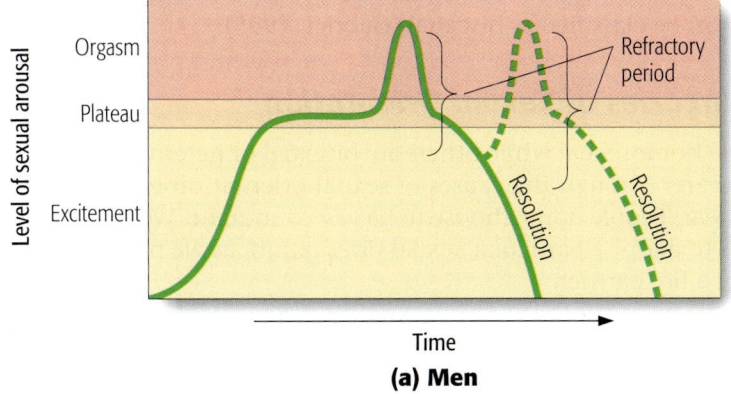

(a) Men

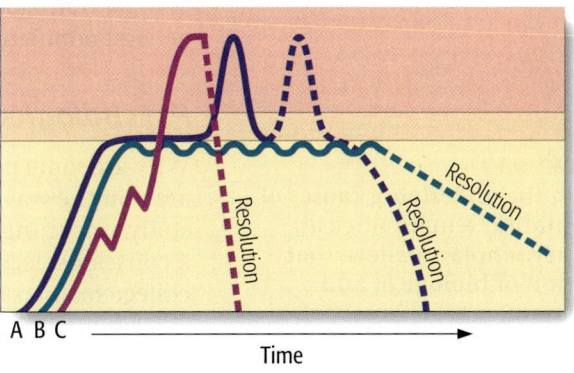

(b) Women

TABLE 8.2 Sexual Response Cycle: How Our Bodies Respond to Sexual Stimulation

Phase of Sexual Response	In Males	In Females	In Both Genders
Excitement Phase	Vasocongestion results in erection. The testes begin to elevate. Skin on the scrotum tenses and thickens.	Vasocongestion swells the vaginal tissue, the clitoris, and the area surrounding the opening of the vagina. Vaginal lubrication appears. The inner two-thirds of the vagina expand, and the vaginal walls thicken and turn a deeper color.	Vasocongestion of the genital tissues occurs. Heart rate, muscle tension (*myotonia*), and blood pressure increase. Nipples may become erect.
Plateau Phase	The tip of the penis turns a deep reddish-purple. The testes become completely elevated. Droplets of semen may be released from the penile opening before ejaculation.	The inner two-thirds of the vagina expand fully. The outer third of the vagina thickens. The clitoris retracts behind its hood, and the uterus elevates and increases in size.	Vasocongestion increases. Myotonia, heart rate, and blood pressure continue to increase.
Orgasm Phase	Sensations of impending ejaculation lasting 2 to 3 seconds precede the ejaculatory reflex. Orgasmic contractions propel semen through the penis and out of the body.	Contractions of the pelvic muscles surrounding the vagina occur.	Orgasmic release of sexual tension occurs, producing intense feelings of pleasure. Muscle spasms occur throughout the body; blood pressure, heart rate, and breathing rate reach a peak.
Resolution Phase	Men become physiologically incapable of achieving another orgasm or ejaculation for a period of time called the refractory period.	Multiple orgasms may occur if the woman desires it and sexual stimulation continues.	Lacking continued sexual stimulation, myotonia and vasocongestion lessen and the body gradually returns to its prearoused state.

gradations ranging from exclusive homosexuality on one end to exclusive heterosexuality on the other (DeAngelis, 2001).

Surveys in the United States and Europe find that about 1 to 3 percent of men, and about 1 to 2 percent of women, identify themselves as exclusively gay (Billy et al., 1993; Laumann et al., 1994). Higher percentages (about 20 to 25 percent of men and about 17 percent of women) report having had some same-sex sexual contact during adolescence or adulthood. In addition, some 1 to 4 percent of the general population can be classified as bisexual (Gabriel, 1995).

Psychological Theories of Sexual Orientation

CONCEPT 8.17
Though the underlying causes of sexual orientation remain unclear, contemporary scholars believe that a combination of biological and environmental factors is involved.

Why are some people homosexual while others are bisexual or heterosexual? Why are you the way you are? Though the causes of sexual orientation remain under study, one thing is clear: People don't choose to be gay or straight. We don't make a conscious decision to adopt a particular sexual orientation, as we might select a college major, say, or a life partner.

Freud (1922/1959) believed that heterosexuality develops from a "normal" process of identification with the parent of the same sex. In contrast, he believed that homosexuality results from an *overidentification* with the parent of the opposite sex—boys with their mothers, girls with their fathers. Freud's views have been provocative, but are they supported by evidence? Investigators find such great variation among families of gay males, lesbians, and heterosexuals that no one pattern applies in all cases (Isay, 1990). Many gay males had close relationships with their fathers, while many heterosexual males had close relationships with their mothers.

Compared with their heterosexual counterparts, gay males and lesbians typically recall more cross-gender behavior in childhood, such as preferring clothes and playing games and with toys typically associated with the opposite sex—a finding that squares with Freud's expectations (Bailey & Zucker, 1995; Rahman & Wilson, 2002). But does such evidence confirm Freud's views? Not necessarily. Recent evidence suggests that genetics may play a role in determining gender nonconformity in childhood for both genders (Bailey, Dunne, & Martin, 2000). We should also note some limitations to these findings. Many gay males and lesbians had interest patterns in childhood that were typical of their own gender. Recognize, too, that gay males are found among the ranks of the most "macho" football and hockey players.

Many gay males report childhood recollections of feeling and acting "different" than their peers at a very young age—often as early as three or four (Isay, 1990). Gay men are more likely than heterosexual comparison groups to recall being more sensitive than other boys and having fewer male buddies (Bailey & Zucker, 1995). Perhaps, as these boys mature, feelings of differentness become transformed into erotic attractions. As psychologist Darryl Bem (1996) put it, what was exotic now becomes erotic. A similar process may occur in girls who develop a lesbian sexual orientation.

PsychAssist: Myths and Facts About Homosexuality

Biological Theories of Sexual Orientation

Identical (MZ) twins are more likely to share their sexual orientation in common than fraternal (DZ) twins, a finding that supports a genetic contribution (Bailey, Dunne, & Martin, 2000; Rahman & Wilson, 2002). This pattern is found even among twins who were separated shortly after birth and raised in different families. But the fact that one identical twin is gay or heterosexual doesn't necessarily mean that the other will follow suit. Life experiences and environmental influences also contribute to the development of sexual orientation (Kendler et al., 2000a). Moreover, genetic factors appear to play a larger role in determining homosexuality in men as compared to women (LeVay, 2003).

What about the role of sex hormones? Most studies fail to find any differences in circulating sex hormones in adult gay males and lesbians in comparison with their heterosexual counterparts (LeVay, 2003). However, scientists speculate that the male sex hormone testosterone may play a role in shaping the developing brain during prenatal development in ways that later affect sexual orientation (Williams et al., 2000; LeVay, 2003).

In sum, research on the origins of sexual orientation remains inconclusive (Gooren & Kruijver, 2002). Most experts believe that sexual orientation is explained not by any single factor but, rather, by a combination of genes, hormones, and the environment interacting throughout the life span (Bailey, Dunne, & Martin, 2000; Jones & Yarhouse, 2001). As it is possible to arrive at the same destination via different routes, we should allow for the possibility that multiple pathways are involved in explaining how people develop their sexual orientations (Garnets, 2002).

THINK *About It*

Coming to Terms with Your Sexual Orientation

Are you struggling with issues concerning your sexual orientation? Do you know someone who is? Are there resources on your campus or in your community that provide counseling services to people with these types of questions? How can you find out more about these services?

Sexual Dysfunctions

Occasional problems with sexual interest or response are quite common and may affect virtually everyone at one time or another. Men may occasionally have difficulty achieving erections or may ejaculate sooner than they desire. Women may

CONCEPT 8.18

Though occasional problems with sexual interest, arousal, or response are common, persistent problems that are the cause of personal distress are classified as sexual dysfunctions.

occasionally have problems becoming sexually aroused or reaching orgasm. When such problems become persistent and cause distress, they are classified as **sexual dysfunctions**.

Sexual dysfunctions involve problems relating to lack of sexual desire or interest, or difficulties becoming sexually aroused or achieving orgasm. Women are more likely than men to experience lack of sexual interest or desire and difficulty reaching orgasm (Bancroft et al., 2003; Laumann et al., 1994). Men may also lack sexual desire or be troubled by *erectile dysfunction* (difficulty or inability achieving or maintaining erections) or *premature ejaculation* (rapid ejaculation with minimum stimulation). The causes of sexual dysfunctions involve biological as well as psychosocial factors.

Biological Causes

Neurological or circulatory conditions or diseases can interfere with sexual interest, arousal, or response. These include diabetes, multiple sclerosis, spinal-cord injuries, epilepsy, complications from surgery (such as prostate surgery in men), side-effects of certain medications, and hormonal problems. Psychoactive drugs, such as cocaine, alcohol, and narcotics, may dampen sexual interest or impair sexual responsiveness. Most cases of erectile disorder can be traced to biological factors, with circulatory problems topping the list (Bivalacqua et al., 2000; Kleinplatz, 2003)

Testosterone energizes sexual drives in both sexes, and deficiencies of the hormone can dampen sexual desire (Bachmann et al., 2002; Shifren et al., 2000). In fact, though it is a male sex hormone produced in the male testes, testosterone is also produced in smaller amounts in women's ovaries and in the adrenal glands of both men and women. That being said, most men and women with sexual dysfunctions have normal sex hormone levels.

Psychosocial Causes

Children who are reared in homes in which negative attitudes toward sexuality prevail may encounter anxiety, guilt, or shame when they become sexually active, rather than sexual arousal and pleasure. This is especially true of young women exposed to sexually repressive cultural attitudes. Such socialization pressures may discourage women from learning about their sexual responsiveness or inhibit them from asserting their sexual needs with their partners.

Some couples fall into a sexual routine, perhaps even a rut. Couples who fail to communicate their sexual preferences or to regularly invigorate their lovemaking routines may find themselves losing interest. Relationship problems can also impair a couple's sexual responsiveness, as conflicts between them and long-simmering resentments may be carried into bed.

Survivors of rape and other sexual traumas often develop deep feelings of disgust or revulsion toward sex (Bean, 2002). Not surprisingly, they often have difficultly responding sexually, even with loving partners. Other emotional factors, especially anxiety, depression, and anger, can also lessen sexual interest or responsiveness.

CONCEPT 8.19

The underlying causes of sexual dysfunctions include biological factors, such as neurological or circulatory problems, and psychosocial factors, such as performance anxiety.

Anxiety, especially **performance anxiety**, may make it impossible for a man to achieve or sustain an erection or for a woman to become adequately lubricated or achieve orgasm. Failure to perform then fuels further self-doubts and fears of repeated failure, which in turn heighten anxiety on subsequent occasions, leading to yet more failure experiences and so on in a vicious cycle.

Premature ejaculation may arise from a failure to keep the level of stimulation below the man's ejaculatory threshold, or "point of no return." Though ejaculation is a reflex, men need to learn (usually through a trial-and-error procedure) to gauge their level of stimulation so that it does not exceed their ejaculatory thresh-

sexual dysfunctions   Persistent or recurrent problems with sexual interest, arousal, or response.

performance anxiety   Anxiety experienced in performance situations stemming from a fear of negative evaluation of one's ability to perform.

old. They need to signal their partners to stop stimulation before this point so that their sensations can subside before resuming again.

Treatment of Sexual Dysfunctions

The good news is that most cases of sexual dysfunctions can be treated successfully through either biological or psychological approaches, or a combination approach. Sex therapy, a relatively brief form of psychological treatment, was pioneered by William Masters and Virginia Johnson (Masters & Johnson, 1970). In sex therapy, individuals, but most usually couples, meet with a therapist or a pair of male and female therapists, and specific, behavioral techniques are used to help them overcome their sexual difficulties.

Biological therapies are also available to help people with sexual dysfunctions. Testosterone therapy may be helpful in treating problems of low sexual interest or desire (Goldstat et al., 2003). Viagra and other similar drugs are effective in producing erections in the majority of men suffering from erectile disorder (Naughton, 2004; Walker, 2004). They work by relaxing blood vessels in the penis, allowing them to expand and carry more blood to the penis. We still lack safe and effective pharmacological treatments for female sexual dysfunction, though testing of Viagra and other drugs is ongoing (Berman et al., 2003; Kleinplatz, 2003).

Some drugs commonly used to treat depression, such as the antidepressant Zoloft (generic name sertraline), have been used successfully in treating premature ejaculation as well (Segraves & Althof, 1998). Delayed ejaculation appears to a common side effect of these drugs, which may be a benefit to men suffering from premature ejaculation.

Before moving ahead, you may wish to review the major concepts relating to sexual motivation outlined in Concept Chart 8.3.

Communication Problems and Sexual Dysfunctions
Sexually dysfunctional couples often have difficulty communicating their sexual needs and interests.

CONCEPT CHART 8.3
Sexual Response and Behavior

Concept	Description	Additional Comments
Sexual response cycle	The characteristic pattern of bodily responses to sexual stimulation	According to Masters and Johnson, the sexual response cycle consists of four phases: excitement, plateau, orgasm, and resolution.
Sexual orientation	The direction of sexual attraction to one's own gender, to the opposite gender, or to both genders	The roots of sexual orientation remain obscure, but most investigators hold the view that genetic, hormonal, and environmental factors interact in the development of sexual orientation.
Sexual behavior	Includes masturbation, sexual intercourse, oral sex, and anal sex	Though the human body can respond to many forms of sexual stimulation, sexual behavior is strongly influenced by cultural learning, personal values, and individual experiences, not simply by biological drives or capacities for sexual response.
Sexual dysfunctions	Persistent problems with sexual interest, arousal, or response	The causes of sexual dysfunctions include biological factors (hormonal or medical problems) and psychosocial factors (guilt or anxiety, relationship issues, history of sexual trauma). Psychological and biological treatments are available to help people overcome sexual dysfunctions.

MODULE 8.3 REVIEW

Sexual Motivation

CONCEPT CHECK

1. Our sense of maleness or femaleness describes
   a. our sexual orientation.
   b. the gender roles we perform.
   c. our gender identity.
   d. our androgyny.

2. Regarding the human sexual response cycle, match the following terms with the ones listed below: (a) sexual release, intense pleasure; (b) body returns to prearoused state; (c) increased muscle tension and further increases in vasocongestion; (d) initial response to sexual stimulation.
   i. excitement phase
   ii. plateau phase
   iii. orgasmic phase
   iv. resolution phase

3. Which of the following statements best describes how the drug Viagra works?
   a. It increases sex drive.
   b. It relaxes blood vessels in the penis.
   c. It lowers blood pressure.
   d. It stimulates the muscles of the penis.

4. The failure to keep the level of stimulation below the man's ejaculatory threshold can lead to _____.

MODULE 8.4   Emotions

- **What are the three components of emotions?**
- **Are facial expressions of emotion universal?**
- **Does money buy happiness?**
- **What role do brain structures play in emotions?**
- **What are the major theories of emotions?**
- **What is emotional intelligence?**
- **What is the polygraph?**

From the joy we feel at graduating from college or landing a desirable job, to the sadness we feel at the loss of a loved one, to the ups and downs we experience in everyday life, our lives are filled with emotions. **Emotions** infuse our lives with color. We commonly say we are "red" with anger, "green" with envy, and "blue" with sadness. Imagine how colorless life would be without emotions. But what are emotions? How do we recognize emotions in others? Are emotional expressions recognized universally or only by members of the same culture? What is the physiological basis of emotions?

What Are Emotions?

CONCEPT 8.20

To psychologists, emotions are more than just feelings; they have physiological, cognitive, and behavioral components.

Most people think of emotions simply as feelings, such as feelings of joy or anger. But psychologists view emotions as more complex feeling states that have three basic components: *bodily arousal* (nervous system activation), *cognition* (subjective, or conscious, experience of the feeling, as well as the thoughts or judgments we have about people or situations that evoke the feeling), and *expressed behavior* (outward expression of the emotion, such as approaching a love object or avoiding a feared one).

When you experience fear, your body is in a heightened state of arousal (e.g., your heart races, your palms sweat). The cognitive component of fear includes the subjective experience of feeling afraid, as well as the judgment that the situation

emotions Feeling states that psychologists view as having physiological, cognitive, and behavioral components.

is threatening. (If someone tosses a rubber snake at your feet, it may startle you, but it will not evoke fear when you appraise it as a fake.) The cognitive component of anger includes the judgment (cognitive appraisal) that events or the actions of others are unjust.

The behavioral expression of emotions generally takes two forms. We tend to approach objects or situations associated with pleasant emotions, such as joy or love, and to avoid those associated with fear, loathing, or disgust. When afraid, we approach the feared object in the hope of fighting it off, or we try to flee from it. Similarly, when angry, we tend to attack (approach) the object of our anger or to withdraw from it (i.e., keep it at a distance). The behavioral component of emotions also encompasses ways in which we express emotions through facial features and other outward behaviors, such as gestures, tone of voice, and bodily posture.

Emotional Expression: Read Any Good Faces Lately?

Charles Darwin (1872) believed that emotions evolved because they have an adaptive purpose in helping species survive and flourish. Fear mobilizes animals to take defensive action in the face of a threatening predator; anger can be adaptive in provoking aggression that helps secure territory, resources, or mating partners. Darwin also recognized that the expression of emotions has communication value. For example, an animal displaying fear through its bodily posture or facial expression may signal others of its kind that danger lurks nearby. Darwin was the first to link specific facial expressions to particular emotions.

We can see the evolutionary roots of emotional expression in the similarity of the facial expressions of humans and nonhuman primates, such as gorillas. You don't need instructions to interpret the emotion expressed by the bared teeth of the ape and human shown in Figure 8.5. This cross-species similarity in facial expression supports Darwin's view that human modes of emotional expression evolved from nonhuman primate ancestors (Chevalier-Skolnikoff, 1973).

Facial Expressions of Emotion: Are They Universal?

Cross-cultural studies show that people in many different cultures can accurately identify six basic emotions from facial expressions: anger, fear, disgust, sadness, happiness, and surprise (Ekman, 2003; Matsumoto, 2004). In one intriguing study, researchers had American students watch Japanese soap operas. Although the students didn't speak a word of Japanese, they recognized the emotions displayed by the characters simply by observing the facial expressions of the actors (Krauss, Curran, & Ferleger, 1983).

The evidence thus supports the view that six basic emotional expressions are universally recognized. Yet some emotions may be more widely recognized than others (Russell, Bachorowski, & Fernández-Dol, 2003). For example, most people recognize a smile as a sign of happiness, but agreement between people falls off when they are asked to decipher other facial expressions.

Cultural and Gender Differences in Emotions

Though people the world over may recognize the same basic facial expressions of emotions, subtle differences exist across cultures in the appearance of these expressions (Marsh, Elfenbein, & Ambady, 2003). Such cultural differences in facial expressions may be likened to nonverbal accents.

Research has also uncovered cultural differences in how accurately emotions are recognized and how they are experienced and displayed. For example, people are generally more accurate when recognizing facial expressions of emotions in people of their own national, ethnic, and regional groups (Elfenbein & Ambady,

CONCEPT 8.21
Though we may say that people wear their hearts on their sleeves, it is more accurate to say that they wear their emotions on their faces.

Figure 8.5   Cross-Species Similarity in Facial Expression
The bared teeth of both ape and man signal readiness to defend or to attack.

CONCEPT 8.22
Evidence supports the view that facial expressions of at least six basic emotions are recognized universally.

2002a, 2002b). In addition, certain emotions are more common in some cultures than in others, or perhaps even unique to a particular culture. For example, Japanese people commonly report such emotions as *fureai* (feeling closely linked to others) and *oime* (an unpleasant feeling of indebtedness to others, similar to our feeling of being "beholden") (Ellsworth, 1994; Markus & Kitayama, 1991). These emotions are not unknown in the United States, but they are not as central to our lives as they are in Japan, where there is a greater cultural emphasis on communal values and mutual obligations.

Cultures also differ in how, or even whether, emotions are displayed. For example, Asian cultures tend to frown on public displays of emotion (Bond, 1993; Zane & Sue, 1991). In these cultures, people are expected to suppress their feelings in public; a failure to keep their feelings to themselves reflects poorly on their upbringing (Huang, 1994). Psychologist Paul Ekman (1980) uses the term **display rules** to describe the cultural customs and norms that regulate the display of emotion. Display rules are learned as part of the socialization process and become so ingrained that they occur automatically among members of the same culture (LeDoux, 1996).

Cultures also have rules for governing the appropriate display of emotions by men and women. In many cultures, women are given greater latitude than men in expressing certain emotions, such as joy, love, fear, and sadness, whereas men are permitted more direct displays of anger (Dittman, 2003). Cross-cultural evidence shows that women report experiencing emotional states such as affection, joy, fear, and sadness more frequently than men (Brebner, 2003; Fischer et al., 2004).

Women overall are also better able than men to express emotions in both words and facial expressions and to recognize and recall feelings in others (DePaulo & Friedman, 1998). Women's brains may be wired differently than men's, allowing them to better perceive and recall emotional cues (Canli et al., 2002).

CONCEPT 8.23

Each culture has display rules that determine how emotions are expressed and how much emotion it is appropriate to express.

TRY THIS OUT

Reading Emotions in Facial Expressions

The same emotional expressions found in the streets of Chicago are found in the distant corners of the world. The photographs accompanying this exercise show a man from a remote area of New Guinea. You'll probably have little difficulty recognizing the emotions he is portraying. Before reading further, match the following emotions to the numbers on the photos: (a) disgust, (b) sadness, (c) happiness, and (d) anger.

The man was asked to make faces as he was told stories involving the following: "Your friend has come and you are happy"; "Your child has died"; "You are angry and about to fight"; and "You see a dead pig that has been lying there a long time." So the correct answers are 1 (c), 2 (b), 3 (d), and 4 (a).

 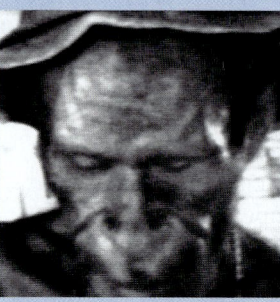  

1. _____ 2. _____ 3. _____ 4. _____

Source: Ekman, 1980.

In Western cultures, men aren't supposed to cry or show their emotions, or even to smile very much. Not surprisingly, evidence shows that women tend to smile more than men (LaFrance, Hecht, & Paluck, 2003). However, the ideal of the stoic unemotional male epitomized by Hollywood action heroes may be giving way to a new ideal: the "sensitive" male character.

Happiness: What Makes You Happy?

Happiness may be a primary human emotion, but it has long been neglected by psychologists who have focused mostly on understanding negative emotions, such as fear, anger, and sadness. However, promoting human happiness is a key goal of *positive psychology,* a growing movement within psychology (see Chapter 1). The architects of the positive psychology movement believe that psychology should focus more of its efforts on promoting human happiness and building human strengths and assets.

What makes people happy? It's not money, researchers tell us. Factors such as health, wealth, and marital status make but a small contribution to explaining variations among people in levels of happiness or life satisfaction (Diener, Oishi, & Lucas, 2003). Multinational surveys shows that people in some poor countries, such as Colombia and Costa Rica, are happier on average than those in such wealthier countries as Japan, Canada, and the United States (Altman, 2004). Moreover, though lottery winners may get an emotional boost shortly after their windfalls, within a year their happiness levels tend to return to their earlier levels (Corliss, 2003). It seems that people have a "set point" for happiness—a general disposition that remains fairly constant during the course of life, despite the ups and downs of daily existence.

We don't yet understand how individual set points are determined, but evidence suggests that genetics plays an important role (Diener & Lucas, 1999; Rowe, 2001). A leading researcher in the field, David Lykken, believes that genetic factors account for about half of the differences among people in levels of happiness (Lykken & Csikszentmihalyi, 2001). Even so, genes alone do not determine happiness or well-being (Inglehart & Klingemann, 2000). There's much we can do to enrich our lives and increase our personal happiness.

Martin Seligman (2003) argues that psychologists should become guides to help people lead the good life—the happy and meaningful life. He speaks of three kinds of human happiness: (1) *pleasure* of doing things, (2) *gratification* (being absorbed and engaged in life activities), and (3) *meaning* (finding personal fulfillment in life activities). Drawing upon his research, Seligman offers a number of suggestions people can use in their daily lives to increase personal happiness. Here are a few of these suggestions (adapted from Seligman, 2003):

- *Gratitude visit.* Seligman believes that expressing gratitude is a key component of personal happiness. Close your eyes and visualize someone who has had a huge positive effect on your life—someone you never really thanked. Spend time during the next week writing a testimony of thanks to this person. Then schedule a visit to the person. When you arrive, read the testimonial and discuss with that person what he or she has meant to you. Gratitude visits can be infectious in a positive way. The recipients of the visit begin to think about the people *they* haven't thanked. They then make their own pilgrimage of thanks, which in turn leads to a kind of daisy chain of gratitude and contentment (Pink, 2003).

- *Three blessings.* Every night, before going to bed, think of three things that went well during the day. Write them down and reflect upon them.

- *One door closes, another opens.* Think about the times in your life that a door closed because of a death or a loss. Then think of a later experience in which a door opened. Come to appreciate the ebbs and flows of your experience.

- *Savorings.* Plan a perfect day. But be sure to share it with another person.

CONCEPT 8.24
People seem to have a particular "set point" for happiness, a level that remains fairly constant during the course of life, despite the ups and downs of life.

display rules Cultural customs and norms that govern the display of emotional expressions.

Figure 8.6 In Which Photo Is Paul Really Smiling?
As you probably guessed, the photo on the right shows a genuine smile; the smile in the photo on the left is simulated. One way to tell the difference is to look for crow's feet around the eyes, a characteristic associated with genuine smiles.

All in all, happiness is not so much a function of what you've got as what you make of it. Happiness is most likely to be found in meaningful work, investment in family and community life, and development of strong spiritual or personal values.

The Facial-Feedback Hypothesis: Putting on a Happy Face

Can practicing smiling lift your mood? According to the **facial-feedback hypothesis**, mimicking the facial movements associated with an emotion will induce the corresponding emotional state (Izard, 1990a). Consistent with this hypothesis, researchers have found that practicing smiling can induce more positive feelings (e.g., Soussignan, 2002). Practicing smiling several times a day may lift your spirits, at least temporarily, perhaps because it prompts you to recall pleasant experiences.

Despite these findings, the facial-feedback hypothesis has its limitations. A "put-on" smile is not the equivalent of a real one. Putting on a smile may induce more positive feelings, but it is not accompanied by the feeling of enjoyment that produces a genuine smile. In addition, the two types of smiles flex different facial muscles. A genuine smile is called a **Duchenne smile**, named after Guillaume Duchenne de Boulogne (1806–1875), the French physician who discovered the facial muscles used to produce a genuine smile. You can see the difference between a genuine smile and a phony one in the photographs of researcher Paul Ekman in Figure 8.6.

Brain Structures in Emotions: Where Do Emotions Reside?

There is a certain truth to the belief that we feel with our hearts. Strong emotions, such as fear and anger, are accompanied by activation of the sympathetic branch of the autonomic nervous system (ANS). As we noted in Chapter 2, activation of the sympathetic nervous system prompts the adrenal glands to release epinephrine and norepinephrine—the stress hormones that speed up bodily processes, such as heart rate and breathing rate. By increasing the flow of oxygen and nutrient-rich blood to our muscles and internal organs, these bodily events enable us to respond more quickly to the situation at hand and, if necessary, either to fight or flee from a threat. (This bodily response to a threat—the *"fight-or-flight"* mechanism—is discussed further in Chapter 13.) An opposing series of bodily changes, orchestrated by the parasympathetic branch of the ANS, returns the body to a calm, relaxed state when the threat has passed.

You may recall from Chapter 2 that the limbic system, which includes the amygdala and hippocampus, plays an important role in the brain's control of emotions. The almond-shaped amygdala can be likened to an "emotional com-

CONCEPT 8.25
Evidence supports the view that practicing or mimicking facial movements associated with particular emotions can produce corresponding emotional states.

facial-feedback hypothesis The belief that mimicking facial movements associated with a particular emotion will produce the corresponding emotional state.

Duchenne smile A genuine smile that involves contraction of a particular set of facial muscles.

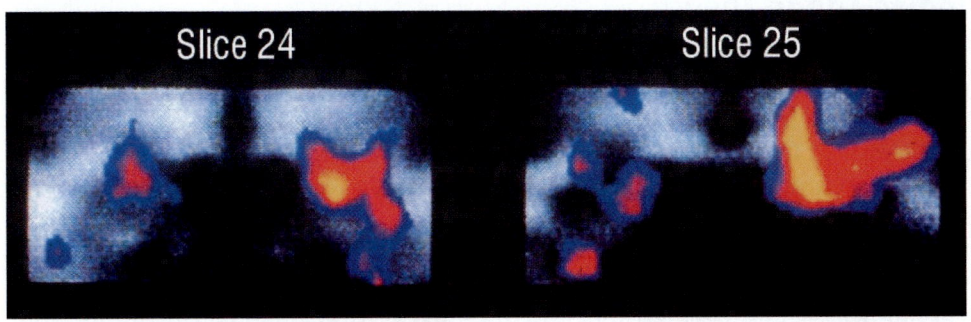

Slice 24   Slice 25

Figure 8.7 Activation of Amygdala in Response to a Fearful Face
Here we see functional MRI images of the amygdala in response to viewing a fearful face. More intense colors show greater activation in relation to a visual fixation point (control). Slice 24 shows the forward part of the amygdala, whereas Slice 25 shows the back part. The image is viewed as though the person were looking out from the page.

Sources: NIMH, 2001

puter" for processing fearful stimuli and evaluating whether stimuli represent a threat (LeDoux, 2000; Öhman & Mineka, 2001). The amygdala becomes active in response to threatening or fearful stimuli. In Figure 8.7 we see activation of the amygdala in response to viewing a fearful face (NIMH, 2001). The hippocampus processes information relating to the context in which fear responses are acquired. For example, it helps you remember the circumstances associated with a fearful event, such as the bend in the road where you lost control of your car.

What of the cerebral cortex itself, the "thinking center" of the brain? It is connected to the limbic system and plays several roles in the processing of emotions. For one thing, it evaluates the meaning of emotionally arousing stimuli, and it plans and directs how to respond to them. It determines whether we should approach stimuli (as in the case of a love interest or a pleasurable event) or avoid them (as in the case of a threat). It is also responsible for processing the subjective, or felt, experience of emotions, and it controls the facial expression of emotion.

Scientists suspect there is a difference in how the right and left cerebral hemispheres process emotions. Evidence shows that positive emotions, such as happiness, are associated with increased activity in the prefrontal cortex of the left cerebral hemisphere, whereas negative emotions, such as disgust, are associated with increased activity in the right prefrontal cortex (Davidson et al., 2000, 2002; Harmon-Jones & Sigelman, 2001). (As noted in Chapter 2, the prefrontal cortex is the part of the frontal lobe that lies in front of the motor cortex.)

Where, then, do emotions reside in the brain? Suffice it to say that no one center in the brain is solely responsible for emotions. Structures in the limbic system play important roles, as do higher brain regions in the cerebral cortex to which they connect (Fischer et al., 2002). The role of brain structures in emotion helps set the stage for our discussion of the major theories of emotion.

CONCEPT 8.26
Although the cerebral cortex and the brain structures that make up the limbic system play key roles in regulating emotional responses, there is no one seat of emotions in the brain.

Theories of Emotion: Which Comes First—the Thought or the Feeling?

One night while I was driving home, my car hit an icy patch in the road and went out of control. The car spun completely around twice and wound up facing oncoming traffic. At that instant, I felt the way a deer must feel when it is caught in the headlights of a car bearing down on it—terrified and helpless. Fortunately, the cars coming toward me stopped in time, and I was able to regain control of my car. I arrived home safely but still shaking in fear. At the time, I didn't stop to consider the question pondered by many psychologists: Did my awareness of my fear precede or follow my bodily response (shaking, sweating, heart pounding)? The *common sense* view of emotion is that we first perceive a stimulus (the car spinning out of control), then feel the emotion (fear), then become physiologically aroused (heart pounding), and then take action (grip the steering wheel). Yet one of the more enduring debates in psychology concerns which comes first—the subjective experience of the emotion or the physiological or behavioral response?

CONCEPT 8.27
The James-Lange theory proposes that emotions follow bodily reactions to triggering stimuli.

James-Lange Theory

William James (1890/1970) argued that bodily reactions or sensations precede emotions. Because Carl Georg Lange, a Danish physiologist, postulated similar ideas independently, this view is called the **James-Lange theory**. James used the now-classic example of confronting a bear in the woods. James asked the question, "Do we run from the bear because we are afraid, or do we become afraid because we run?" He answered this question by proposing that the response of running comes first. We see the bear. We run. Then we become afraid. We become afraid because we sense the particular pattern of bodily arousal associated with running, such as a pounding heart, rapid breathing, and muscular contractions. Thus, emotions *follow* bodily reactions. In this view, we experience fear because we tremble; we experience the emotion of sadness because we cry. If this theory is correct, then my body would have reacted first when my car spun out of control. Only when I sensed my body's reaction would I have become consciously aware of fear.

James argued that distinct bodily changes are associated with each emotion. This is why fear feels different from other emotions, such as anger or love.

CONCEPT 8.28
The Cannon-Bard theory proposes that the subjective experience of an emotion and the bodily reactions associated with it occur virtually simultaneously.

Cannon-Bard Theory

In the 1920s, physiologist Walter Cannon (1927) proposed a second major theory of emotions. He based his theory on research conducted by his laboratory assistant, Philip Bard. This theory, called the **Cannon-Bard theory**, challenged the James-Lange theory. It holds that the same bodily changes that result from the activation of the sympathetic nervous system accompany different emotions. Sympathetic activation makes our hearts race, the pace of our breathing quicken, and our muscles contract whether we are experiencing anger, fear, or sexual arousal. How could these common responses in the body evoke different emotions, as the James-Lange theory suggests? The Cannon-Bard theory proposes that the subjective experience of an emotion and the bodily reactions associated with it occur virtually simultaneously. In other words, our emotions accompany our bodily responses but are not caused by them. In simplest terms, the Cannon-Bard theory postulates that we see the bear, we experience fear and a pounding heart, and then we run.

CONCEPT 8.29
The two-factor model proposes that the combination of physiological arousal and cognitive appraisal (labeling) of the source of the arousal produces the specific emotional state.

Two-Factor Model

Let us turn to the **two-factor model** which holds that emotions depend on two factors: (1) a state of general arousal and (2) a cognitive interpretation, or *labeling* (Schachter, 1971; Schachter & Singer, 1962). According to this model, when we experience states of bodily arousal, we look for cues in the environment to

James-Lange theory The belief that emotions occur after people become aware of their physiological responses to the triggering stimuli.

Cannon-Bard theory The belief that emotional and physiological reactions to triggering stimuli occur almost simultaneously.

two-factor model The theory that emotions involve two factors: a state of general arousal and a cognitive interpretation (or labeling) of the causes of the arousal.

THINK *About It*

Tracking Your Emotions

Keep track of your emotions for a day or two by using a notebook to record situations in which you experience emotion. Include brief descriptions of your emotional state (joy, fear, anger, etc.), your bodily reactions (e.g., rapid heartbeat, rapid breathing, sweating, tingling sensation, jumpiness, shakiness), and the thoughts that passed through your mind at the time. Afterward, examine the relationships among your emotions, your bodily reactions, and your thought patterns. Compare your bodily reactions in different emotional states. Also compare the thoughts you had while in different emotional states. What does this exercise teach you about the connections between your emotional states and your bodily reactions and thought patterns?

explain why we feel aroused or excited. Your heart may race when you see a monster in the latest sci-fi thriller jump onto the movie screen; it may also race when your car spins out of control. Your arousal in the safe confines of the movie theater is likely to be labeled and experienced as "pleasurable excitement." But the same pattern of arousal experienced in the spinning car will probably be labeled and experienced as "sheer terror."

The two-factor model continues to generate interest, but it fails to account for the distinctive physiological features associated with different emotions. Anger may feel different from fear not merely because of how we label our arousal but also because it is associated with different bodily responses.

Experimental evidence also casts doubt on whether we must label the state of arousal in order to experience an emotion. Psychologist Robert Zajonc (1980, 1984) exposed subjects to brief presentations of Japanese ideographs (written symbols). Later, he found that subjects preferred particular characters they had seen, even if they had no recall of ever having seen these stimuli. Zajonc believes that some emotional responses, such as liking and disliking, may not involve any cognitive appraisal—that they may occur through mere exposure to a stimulus.

Dual-Pathway Model of Fear

According to the **dual-pathway model of fear** formulated by psychologist Joseph LeDoux (1994, 2000), the brain uses two pathways to process fear messages. Stimulus information from the environment ("seeing a car barreling down on you") is first processed by the thalamus. From there the information branches off, with one pathway (the "high road") leading to the cerebral cortex, where it can be processed more carefully. Another pathway (the "low road") leads directly to the amygdala, where the information can be acted upon more quickly than if it had first passed through the cortex (see Figure 8.8). The "low road" thus allows a faster response to danger cues.

Suppose you are walking in the woods and see a curved object in the bush. This visual image is first processed by the thalamus, which makes a rough appraisal of the object as potentially dangerous (possibly a snake). The thalamus transmits this information directly to the amygdala via the "low road," which prompts an immediate bodily response. Heart rate and blood pressure jump, and muscles throughout the body contract as the body prepares to respond quickly to a possible threat. The cortex, slower to respond, processes the information further ("No, that's not a snake. It's just a stick."). From the standpoint of survival, it is better to act quickly on the assumption that the suspicious object is a snake and to ask questions later. Responding without thinking can be a lifesaver. As LeDoux puts it, "The time saved by the amygdala in acting on the thalamic information, rather than waiting for the cortical input, may be the difference between life and death. It is better to have treated a stick as a snake than not to have responded to a possible snake" (1994, p. 270). Depending on whether the cortex interprets the object as a "snake" or a "stick" determines whether a fear response continues or is quickly quelled. It is in the cortex that the subjective experience of fear arises.

What Does All This Mean?

Where do these various theories of emotions, as represented in Figure 8.9, leave us? The James-Lange theory implies that distinctive bodily responses are associated with each emotion, whereas the Cannon-Bard theory postulates that a similar pattern of bodily responses accompanies different emotions. Both views may be at least partially correct. There certainly are common physiological responses associated with such emotions as fear, anger, and love, as the Cannon-Bard theory proposes. We feel our hearts beating faster when we are in the presence of a new love and when we are faced with an intruder in the night. Yet, as the James-Lange

CONCEPT 8.30
The dual-pathway model suggests two pathways for processing fear stimuli in the brain: a "high road" leading to the cerebral cortex and a "low road" leading to the amygdala.

dual-pathway model of fear   LeDoux's theory that the brain uses two pathways (a "high road" and a "low road") to process fear messages.

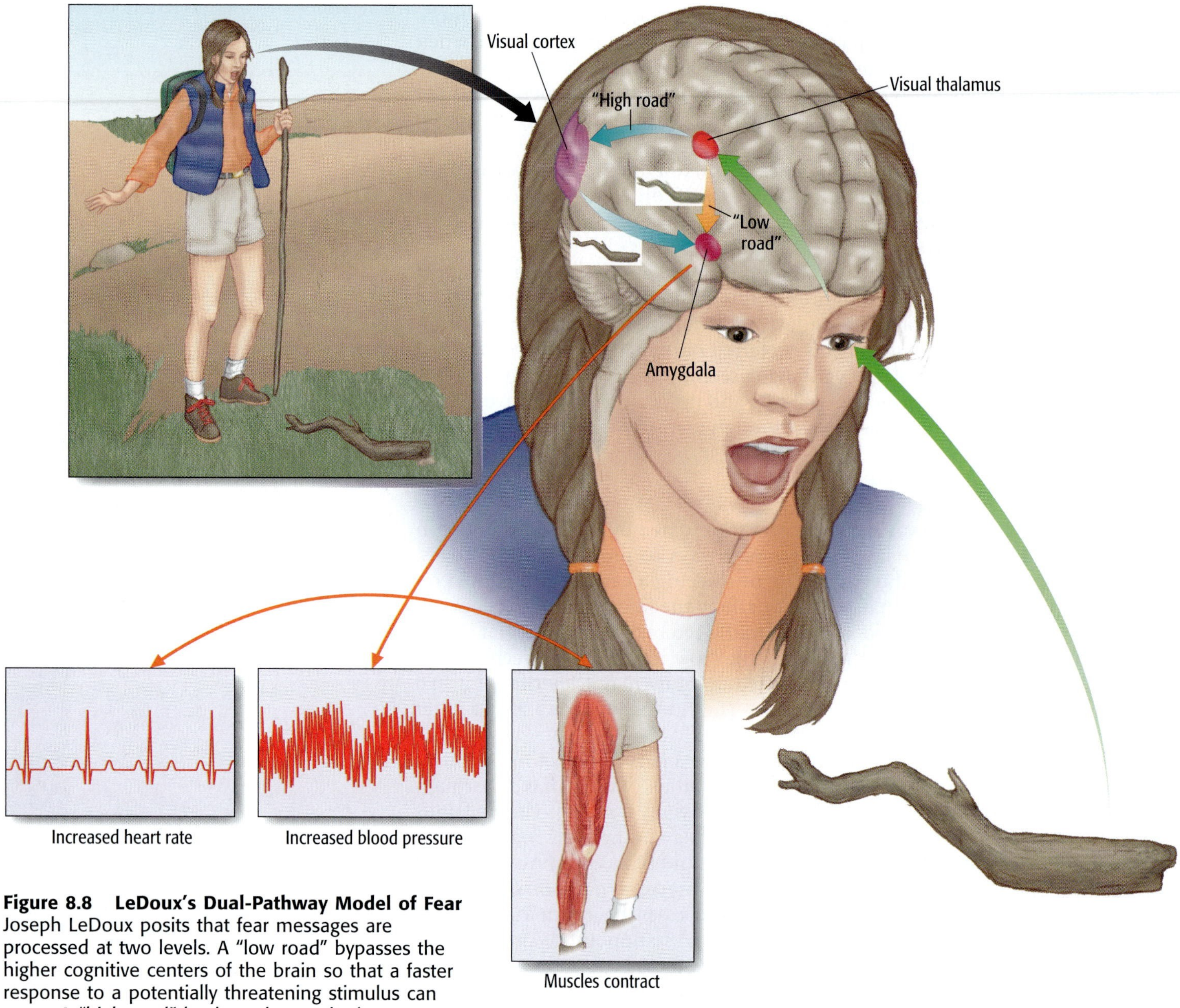

Visual cortex

Visual thalamus

"High road"

"Low road"

Amygdala

Increased heart rate

Increased blood pressure

Muscles contract

Figure 8.8 LeDoux's Dual-Pathway Model of Fear
Joseph LeDoux posits that fear messages are
processed at two levels. A "low road" bypasses the
higher cognitive centers of the brain so that a faster
response to a potentially threatening stimulus can
occur. A "high road" leads to the cerebral cortex,
where the message is interpreted more carefully.

Source: Adapted from LeDoux, 1996.

**PsychAssist: LeDoux's Dual-Pathway
Model of Fear**

theory proposes, there are also distinctive bodily reactions associated with different emotions. Less blood flows to our extremities during states of fear than of anger, which is why we may experience a sensation of "cold feet" when we are afraid but not when we are angry (Levenson, 1994). Anger is accompanied by a dramatic rise in skin temperature, which may explain why people who are angry are often described as "hot under the collar."

Different emotions are also connected with different facial expressions. Blushing, for instance, is a primary characteristic of embarrassment. James considered facial expressions to be among the bodily responses that distinguish one emotion from another. Evidence favoring the facial-feedback hypothesis lends at least partial support to James-Lange theory, because it shows that our response to muscular cues associated with certain emotions can influence our feeling states (Izard, 1990b).

Emotions may precede cognitions under some conditions, as suggested by Zajonc's studies and by the dual-pathway model proposed by LeDoux. That emo-

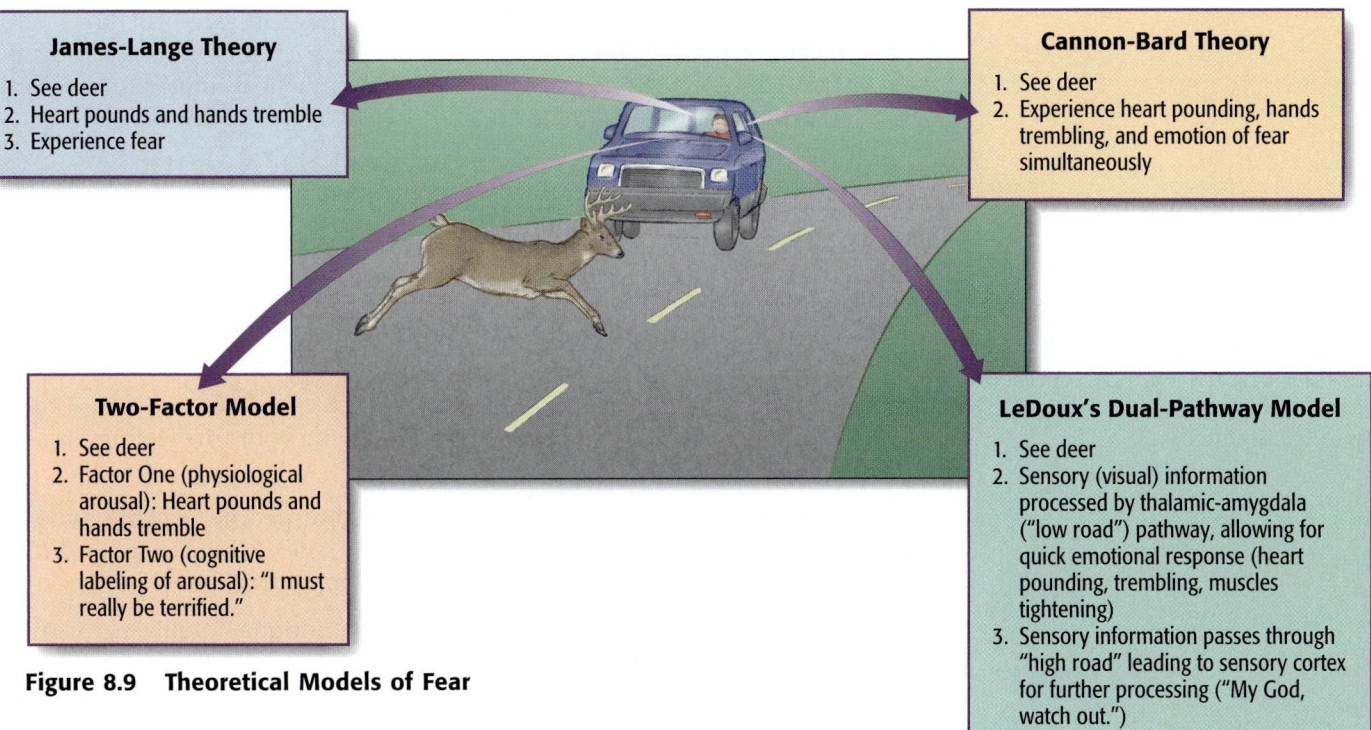

James-Lange Theory

1. See deer
2. Heart pounds and hands tremble
3. Experience fear

Cannon-Bard Theory

1. See deer
2. Experience heart pounding, hands trembling, and emotion of fear simultaneously

Two-Factor Model

1. See deer
2. Factor One (physiological arousal): Heart pounds and hands tremble
3. Factor Two (cognitive labeling of arousal): "I must really be terrified."

LeDoux's Dual-Pathway Model

1. See deer
2. Sensory (visual) information processed by thalamic-amygdala ("low road") pathway, allowing for quick emotional response (heart pounding, trembling, muscles tightening)
3. Sensory information passes through "high road" leading to sensory cortex for further processing ("My God, watch out.")

Figure 8.9   Theoretical Models of Fear

tions may occur before cognitions does not dismiss the important role that cognitions play in emotions. Whether you are angered when an instructor springs an unexpected assignment on you or frightened when a doctor points to a spot on your X-ray depends on the appraisal of the situation made in the cerebral cortex, not on automatic processing of stimuli by lower brain structures.

How we appraise events also depends on what the events mean to us personally (Lazarus, 1995). The same event, such as a pregnancy or a change of jobs, can lead to feelings of joy, fear, or even anger depending on the meaning the event has for the individual and its perceived importance.

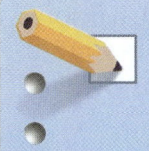

TRY THIS OUT

Can You Produce an Emotion Without Thought?

One way to appreciate the connection between thoughts and feelings is to perform a thought experiment. See if you can make yourself feel angry for the next minute or so while keeping your mind blank. After you read this sentence, put the book down and just try to feel angry, really angry, without thinking any thoughts at all.

Were you able to do it? Were you able to produce a feeling of anger for more than a passing moment? Perhaps you tried to keep your mind blank while clenching your fists the way you might if you were really angry. Or perhaps you tried to capture the feeling by furrowing your brow and gritting your teeth. Did you really feel angry, or did it seem as if you were just going through the motions? No doubt you felt that something was missing.

What was missing are the thoughts that are the bridges to emotions. You have to have something to be angry about to feel anger. Anger stems from angering thoughts, such as thinking that you have been treated unfairly.

Trying to make yourself feel angry may be an interesting thought experiment, but the more common problem people face is the just the opposite—turning off their anger. Anger can have serious negative consequences (the application module at the end of the chapter describes how to manage anger to avoid them).

The final chapter in the debate about how emotions are processed in the brain is still to be written. Yet the belief that distinctive bodily changes are associated with different emotions has had at least one practical implication. It is the basis of a method of lie detection, which is discussed later in this module.

Emotional Intelligence: How Well Do You Manage Your Emotions?

CONCEPT 8.31
The ability to recognize emotions in yourself and others and to regulate your emotions effectively may represent a form of intelligent behavior called emotional intelligence.

Some theorists believe that a person's ability to manage emotions represents a form of intelligent behavior, called **emotional intelligence**, or EI (Goleman, 1995c). Emotional intelligence is difficult to define precisely, but it can be generally described in terms of five main characteristics:

1. *Knowing your emotions.* Self-awareness, or knowing your true feelings, is a core feature of emotional intelligence.

2. *Managing your emotions.* Emotionally intelligent people are able to handle their emotions in appropriate ways. They can soothe themselves in difficult times, and they bounce back quickly from disappointments and setbacks.

3. *Motivating yourself.* People with a high level of emotional intelligence can marshal their emotions to pursue their goals. They approach challenges with enthusiasm, zeal, and confidence, which makes them better equipped to attain high levels of achievement and productivity. They also are able to delay gratification and constrain their impulses as they pursue long-term goals.

4. *Recognizing emotions in others.* Empathy, the ability to perceive emotions in others, is an important "people skill." It not only helps build strong relationships but also contributes to success in teaching, sales, management, and the helping professions.

5. *Helping others handle their emotions.* The ability to help others deal with their feelings is an important factor in maintaining meaningful relationships.

Emotional intelligence may contribute more to success in life than IQ (Goleman, 1995c). Perhaps you know people who are intellectually brilliant but have no clue about their own or other people's emotions. Some evidence links EI to success in life, including success in intimate relationships such as marriage (Ciarrochi et al., 2001; Fitness, 2001). However, more research is needed before we can determine whether EI improves prediction of success in life beyond that which we can predict using measures of general intelligence and personality.

The Polygraph: How Credible Is It?

Is This Woman Lying? The polygraph is widely used to detect lying, but scientific evidence demonstrating its reliability is lacking.

CONCEPT 8.32
Polygraphs are widely used, even though scientists remain skeptical of their ability to detect lying.

emotional intelligence The ability to recognize emotions in yourself and others and to manage your own emotions effectively.

Let us end this module by commenting on the use of the polygraph, a device used to detect whether people are lying based on their responses to control (neutral) and test questions about the crime in question. It is based on the assumption that there are distinctive patterns of physiological activity, including electrical reactivity of the skin and respiration and heart rates, that can be used to distinguish whether a person is lying or telling the truth. The polygraph measures patterns of bodily arousal, not lying per se. Critics contend that the polygraph is often inaccurate and cannot distinguish between lying and feelings of anxiety or guilt (e.g., Iacono & Lykken, 1997). Many innocent people react strongly to test questions, perhaps out of fear that they could be accused of the crime in question. Critics also point out that some (perhaps many) people—especially those who are seasoned liars—can lie without any telltale physiological reactions. Unfortunately, the false findings of polygraphs have damaged the lives of many innocent people.

Though the polygraph may occasionally catch a person in a lie, it is not reliable enough to pass scientific muster. More sophisticated methods of detecting lying are currently under study.

Concept Chart 8.4 provides an overview of the major concepts of emotion discussed in this module.

CONCEPT CHART 8.4
Major Concepts of Emotion

Concept	Description
Facial expressions of emotion	Evidence from cross-cultural studies supports universal recognition of the facial expressions of six basic emotions: anger, fear, disgust, sadness, happiness, and surprise.
Facial-feedback hypothesis	According to this hypothesis, mimicking facial movements associated with an emotion can produce the corresponding emotional state.
Physiological bases of emotions	Emotions are accompanied by activation of the sympathetic branch of the autonomic nervous system. Emotions are processed by the structures of the limbic system (the amygdala, hippocampus, and parts of the hypothalamus) and by the cerebral cortex.
James-Lange theory of emotions	Emotions follow our bodily reactions to triggering stimuli—we become afraid because we run; we feel sad because we cry.
Cannon-Bard theory of emotions	Emotions accompany bodily responses to triggering stimuli but are not caused by them.
Two-factor model of emotions	The combination of physiological arousal and cognitive appraisal (labeling) of the source of the arousal produces the emotional state.
LeDoux's dual-pathway model of fear	A pathway leads from the thalamus to the amygdala, which produces the initial fear response (bodily arousal), while a second pathway leads to the cortex, which further processes the fear stimulus and produces the conscious awareness of fear.
Emotional intelligence	According to this concept, the ability to manage emotions effectively is a form of intelligent behavior.
Polygraph	A device used to detect lying based on analysis of differences in physiological responses to control questions and relevant questions.

MODULE 8.4 REVIEW

Emotions

CONCEPT CHECK

1. All of the following are basic components of emotion *except*
   a. bodily arousal.
   b. production of neuropeptide Y.
   c. cognition.
   d. expressed behavior.

2. Facial expressions of six basic emotions are recognized universally. What are these six emotions?

3. The belief that the subjective experience of an emotion and the bodily response that accompanies it occur at virtually the same time is the
   a. James-Lange theory.
   b. Cannon-Bard theory.
   c. two-factor model.
   d. dual-pathway model of fear.

4. Which of the following statements is *not* correct?
   a. Women are generally better able than men to express emotions in words
   b. Women are generally better able than men to express emotions through facial expressions.
   c. In many cultures, men are given greater latitude in displaying anger.
   d. Evidence shows that men tend to smile more often than women.

MODULE 8.5   Managing Anger

- **What can you do to control your anger?**

CONCEPT 8.33
By identifying and correcting anger-inducing thoughts, people can gain better control over their anger and develop more effective ways of handling conflicts.

Do you know people who have problems controlling their temper? Do you yourself do things in anger that you later regret? Anger can be a catalyst for physical or verbal aggression. But even if you never express your anger through aggression, frequent episodes of anger can take a toll on your health, putting you at increased risk of cardiovascular disorders, such as hypertension and heart disease (see Chapter 13). Anger floods the body with stress hormones that may eventually damage the cardiovascular system.

Cognitive theorists recognize that anger is prompted by a person's reactions to frustrating or provocative situations, not by the situations themselves. Though people often blame the "other guy" for making them angry, people make themselves angry by thinking angering thoughts or making anger-inducing statements to themselves. To gain better control over their anger, people need to identify and correct such thoughts and statements. By doing so, they can learn to avoid hostile confrontations and perhaps save wear and tear on their cardiovascular systems. Here are some suggestions psychologists offer for identifying and controlling anger:

- *Become aware of your emotional reactions in anger-provoking situations.* When you notice yourself getting "hot under the collar," take this as a cue to calm yourself down and think through the situation. Learn to replace anger-arousing thoughts with calming alternatives.

- *Review the evidence.* Might you be overreacting to the situation by taking it too personally? Might you be jumping to the conclusion that the other person means you ill? Are there other ways of viewing the person's behavior?

- *Practice more adaptive thinking.* For example, say to yourself, "I can handle this situation without getting upset. I'll just calm down and think through what I want to say."

- *Engage in competing responses.* You can disrupt an angry response by conjuring up soothing mental images, by taking a walk, or by practicing self-relaxation. The time-honored practice of counting to ten when you begin to feel angry may also help defuse an emotional response. If it doesn't, you can follow Mark Twain's advice and count to a hundred instead. While counting, try to think calming thoughts.

- *Don't get steamed.* Others may do dumb or hurtful things, but you make yourself angry by dwelling on them. Take charge of your emotional responses by not allowing yourself to get steamed.

- *Oppose anger with empathy.* Try to understand what the other person is feeling. Rather than saying to yourself "He's a miserable so-and-so who deserves to be punished," say "He must really have difficulties at home to act like this. But that's his problem. I won't take it personally."

- *Congratulate yourself for responding assertively rather than aggressively.* Give yourself a mental pat on the back when you handle stressful situations with equanimity rather than with anger.

- *Scale back your expectations of others.* Perceptions of unfairness may result from the expectation that others "should" or "must" fulfill your needs or expectations. By scaling back your expectations, you're less likely to get angry with others when they disappoint you.

TABLE 8.3   Anger Management: Replacing Anger-Inducing Thoughts with Calming Alternatives

Situation	Anger-Inducing Thoughts	Calming Alternatives
A provocateur says, "So what are you going to do about it?"	"That jerk. Who does he think he is? I'll teach him a lesson he won't forget!"	"He must really have a problem to act the way he does. But that's his problem. I don't have to respond at his level."
You get caught in a monster traffic jam.	"Why does this always happen to me? I can't stand this."	"This may be inconvenient, but it's not the end of the world. Don't blow it out of proportion. Everyone gets caught in traffic every now and then. Just relax and listen to some music."
You're in a checkout line at the supermarket, and the woman in front of you is cashing a check. It seems as if it's taking hours.	"She has some nerve holding up the line. It's so unfair for someone to make other people wait. I'd like to tell her off!"	"It will take only a few minutes. People have a right to cash their checks in the market. Just relax and read a magazine while you wait."
You're looking for a parking spot when suddenly another car cuts you off and seizes a vacant space.	"No one should be allowed to treat me like this. I'd like to punch him out."	"Don't expect people always to be considerate of your interests. Stop personalizing things." Or "Relax, there's no sense going to war over this."
Your spouse or partner comes home several hours later than expected, without calling to let you know he or she would be late.	"It's so unfair. I can't let him (her) treat me like this."	Explain how you feel without putting your spouse or partner down.
You're watching a movie in a theater, and the people sitting next to you are talking and making a lot of noise.	"Don't they have any regard for others? I'm so angry with these people I could tear their heads off."	"Even if they're inconsiderate, it doesn't mean I have to get angry about it or ruin my enjoyment of the movie. If they don't quiet down when I ask them, I'll just change my seat or call the manager."

Source: Adapted from Nevid, Rathus, & Greene, 2003.

- *Modulate verbal responses.* Avoid raising your voice or cursing. Stay cool, even when others do not.
- *Learn to express positive feelings.* Expressing positive feelings can help diffuse negative emotions. Tell others you love them and care about them. They are likely to reciprocate in kind.

Think about situations in which you have felt angry or have acted in anger. How might you handle these situations differently in the future? What coping responses can you use to help you keep your cool? Table 8.3 offers some calming alternatives to thoughts that trigger anger.

TYING IT TOGETHER

Motivation and emotion are processes that move us to action. Motives are the "whys" of behavior—the factors that drive goal-directed behavior and explain why we do what we do (Module 8.1). Hunger is a major source of motivation—a drive that motivates us to seek nourishment to satisfy a basic biological need for food (Module 8.2). The desire for sexual gratification is another biologically based drive (Module 8.3). But our sexual behavior is governed more by our learning experiences, culture, and personal values than by biological demands. Emotions are complex feeling states, but, like motives, they also have a behavioral component—tendencies to approach or avoid particular objects or situations (Module 8.4). Anger is a negative emotion that can cause serious health problems. People can gain better control over their anger by identifying and correcting anger-inducing thoughts (Module 8.5).

SUMMING UP: Q & A

Motivation: The "Whys" of Behavior (Module 8.1)

What is motivation?

- Motivation consists of the factors or internal processes that activate, direct, and sustain behavior toward the satisfaction of a need or the attainment of a goal.

What is instinct theory?

- Instinct theory proposes that behavior is motivated by genetically programmed, species-specific, fixed patterns of responses called instincts. While this model may have value in explaining some forms of animal behavior, human behavior is too complex to be explained by instincts.

What is drive theory?

- Drive theory asserts that animals are driven to satisfy unmet biological needs, such as hunger and thirst. The theory is limited, in part because it fails to account for motives involving the desire to increase states of arousal.

How does arousal theory account for differences in motivational states?

- According to arousal theory, the optimal level of arousal varies from person to person. To maintain arousal at an optimal level, some people seek exciting, even potentially dangerous, activities, while others seek more tranquil ones.

How does incentive theory differ from drive theory?

- Incentive theory focuses on the "pull," or lure, of goals or objects that we perceive as attractive, whereas drive theory focuses on the "push" of unmet biological needs.

What are psychosocial needs?

- Psychosocial needs are distinctly human needs that are based on psychological rather than biological factors. They include the need for social relationships and the need for achievement.
- People with a high need for achievement are hard-driving and ambitious. They set challenging but realistic goals for themselves. They accomplish more than people with similar abilities and opportunities but a lower need for achievement.

What is Maslow's hierarchy of needs?

- Maslow believed we are motivated to meet basic biological needs, such as hunger and thirst, before fulfilling our psychological needs. His hierarchy has five levels, ranging from physiological needs at the base to self-actualization at the top.

Hunger and Eating (Module 8.2)

How are hunger and appetite regulated?

- Homeostatic processes in the brain regulate hunger and appetite. The hypothalamus plays a pivotal role. It senses changes in blood sugar levels and depletion of fat from fat cells, which leads to the feelings of hunger that motivate eating. Neurotransmitters and hormones also play important roles in regulating hunger and appetite.

What causes obesity?

- Obesity is a complex problem that has multiple causes, including behavioral patterns, genetics, metabolic factors, and environmental and emotional factors. Genetics may affect basal metabolic rate and the number of fat cells in the body.

What is anorexia nervosa?

- Anorexia nervosa is an eating disorder in which people starve themselves because of exaggerated concerns about weight gain.

What is bulimia nervosa?

- Bulimia nervosa is an eating disorder characterized by episodes of binge eating followed by purging. Purging is accomplished through self-induced vomiting or other means, such as excessive use of laxatives.

What are the causes of eating disorders?

- Many factors are implicated in eating disorders. They include cultural pressure on young women to achieve unrealistic standards of thinness, issues of control and perfectionism, childhood abuse, family conflicts, and possible disturbances in brain mechanisms that control hunger and satiety.

Sexual Motivation (Module 8.3)

What are the phases of the sexual response cycle?

- The excitement phase is characterized by erection in the male and vaginal lubrication in the female.
- The plateau phase is an advanced state of arousal that precedes orgasm.
- The orgasm phase is characterized by orgasmic contractions of the pelvic musculature.
- During the resolution phase, the body returns to its pre-aroused state.

How do researchers conceptualize sexual orientation?

- Most researchers conceptualize sexual orientation as a continuum with many gradations ranging from exclusive homosexuality on one end to exclusive heterosexuality on the other.

What are the causes of sexual dysfunctions, and how are they treated?

- Sexual dysfunctions can have biological causes, such as declining hormone levels and health problems, and psychosocial causes, such as sex-negative attitudes, communication problems, sexually traumatic experiences, and performance anxiety. They may be treated by a form of psychological treatment called sex therapy, by the use of therapeutic drugs, or by a combination of techniques.

Emotions (Module 8.4)

What are the three components of emotions?

- Psychologists conceptualize emotions as having a physiological component (heightened bodily arousal), a cognitive component (a feeling state, as well as thoughts and judgments about experiences linked to the feeling state), and a behavioral component (approach or avoidance behaviors).

Are facial expressions of emotion universal?

- Evidence from cross-cultural studies supports the view that facial expressions of six basic emotions—anger, fear, disgust, sadness, happiness, and surprise—are universal.
- Cultural differences, as well as some similarities, exist in how emotions are experienced. Each culture has rules, called display rules, that determine how emotions are expressed and how much emotion is appropriate to express. Gender differences in emotional expression may reflect cultural expectations.

Does money buy happiness?

- Apparently not, as there is but a modest relationship between wealth and personal happiness or life satisfaction. Happiness may vary around a genetically-influenced set point. Still, there is much we can do to make our lives happier and more fulfilling.

What role do brain structures play in emotions?

- Parts of the limbic system, including the amygdala and the hippocampus, play key roles in emotional processing.
- The cerebral cortex interprets stimuli and plans strategies for either approaching or avoiding stimuli, depending on whether they are perceived as "friend" or "foe." The cortex also controls facial expression of emotions and is responsible for processing the felt experience of emotions.

What are the major theories of emotions?

- The major theories of emotions are the James-Lange theory (emotions occur after people become aware of their physiological responses to the triggering stimuli), the Cannon-Bard theory (emotional and physiological reactions to triggering stimuli occur almost simultaneously), the two-factor model (emotions depend on an arousal state and a labeling of the causes of the arousal), and LeDoux's dual-pathway model of fear (the amygdala responds to fear stimuli before the cerebral cortex gets involved).

What is emotional intelligence?

- Emotional intelligence refers to the ability to recognize emotions in oneself and others and to manage emotions effectively. Emotional intelligence may have an important bearing on our success in life and ability to maintain successful intimate relationships.

What is the polygraph?

- The polygraph is a device used to detect physiological response patterns believed to indicate when a person is lying. However, scientific evidence supporting the utility of the polygraph in detecting lying is lacking.

Application: Managing Anger (Module 8.5)

What can you do to control your anger?

- You can learn to apply anger-management skills, which include paying attention to your angry feelings, replacing angry thoughts with more adaptive ones, practicing coping responses, changing your response to annoying people, and countering anger with empathy.

Key Terms

motivation (p. 258)
motives (p. 258)
instinctive behaviors (p. 258)
instinct theory (p. 258)
drive theory (p. 259)
need (p. 259)
drive (p. 259)
drive reduction (p. 259)
primary drives (p. 259)
secondary drives (p. 259)
stimulus motives (p. 260)
arousal theory (p. 260)
incentive theory (p. 261)
incentives (p. 261)
incentive value (p. 262)

psychosocial needs (p. 262)
need for achievement (p. 262)
extrinsic motivation (p. 262)
intrinsic motivation (p. 262)
achievement motivation (p. 262)
avoidance motivation (p. 262)
hierarchy of needs (p. 263)
self-actualization (p. 263)
lateral hypothalamus (p. 265)
ventromedial hypothalamus (p. 266)
set point theory (p. 267)
gender identity (p. 272)
sexual orientation (p. 272)
gender roles (p. 272)
sexual response cycle (p. 273)

vasocongestion (p. 273)
sexual dysfunctions (p. 276)
performance anxiety (p. 276)
emotions (p. 278)
display rules (p. 280)
facial-feedback hypothesis (p. 282)
Duchenne smile (p. 282)
James-Lange theory (p. 284)
Cannon-Bard theory (p. 284)
two-factor model (p. 284)
dual-pathway model of fear (p. 285)
emotional intelligence (p. 288)

Thinking Critically About Psychology

Based on your reading of this chapter, answer the following questions. Then, to evaluate your progress in developing critical thinking skills, compare your answers to the sample answers found in Appendix A.

People often think of thinking and feeling as opposite mental states. Is it correct to think of them as opposites? Why or why not?

Answers to Concept Check Questions

Module 8.1: 1. motivation; 2. b; 3. i-d, ii-a, iii-c, iv-b; 4. stimulus motives; 5. incentive value; 6. d. **Module 8.2:** 1. c; 2. c; 3. i-b, ii-d, iii-a, iv-c; 4. a. **Module 8.3:** 1. c; 2. (a) iii, (b) iv, (c) ii, (d)i; 3. b; 4. premature ejaculation **Module 8.4:** 1. b; 2. anger, fear, disgust, sadness, happiness, and surprise; 3. b; 4. d.

Human Development

DID YOU KNOW THAT . . .

- A fertilized egg cell is not yet attached to the mother's body during the first week or so after conception? (p. 297)

- Pregnant women cannot assume it is safe to have even one or two alcoholic beverages a day? (p. 300)

- By one year of age, infants have already mastered the most difficult balancing problems they will ever face in life? (p. 303)

- Baby geese followed a famous scientist around as if he was their mother? (p. 307)

- It is normal for a 4-year-old to believe the moon has feelings? (p. 316)

- An identity crisis is considered a normal part of adolescent development? (p. 326)

- Dementia or senility is not a normal consequence of aging? (p. 334)

- Older people usually lead better lives when they do more rather than less? (p. 335)

Annette and Rafael are ready. After three years of marriage, they feel the time is right to bring a baby into their lives. They have planned the changes they must make. Annette, a graduate student in finance, will take off a semester after the baby is born. Rafael, a high school science teacher, will quit his after-school job to help out at home. They will set up the spare room Rafael uses for an office as a nursery and begin gathering opinions about the local pediatricians. Privately, though, both wonder if they will make good parents.

When they make love that night, Rafael will ejaculate hundreds of millions of *sperm*, the male germ cell, into Annette's vagina. From there the sperm will begin a journey through Annette's cervix and uterus to their eventual destination, a Fallopian tube through which the slow-moving *ovum*, or egg cell, travels once it is released from an ovary following ovulation. Of the hundreds of millions of sperm released in the vagina, only a few hundred may succeed in reaching the ovum. Later that night, as Annette sleeps soundly, one surviving sperm will penetrate the ovum's thick covering, resulting in *fertilization* (also called conception), the union of a single sperm and ovum. From this single fertilized cell, called a *zygote*, a new life will begin to form.

A few weeks later, Annette notices her period is overdue. Excitedly, she tests her urine with a home pregnancy testing kit. The test reveals the news that will change her and Rafael's lives forever: She is pregnant! Over breakfast, she proudly shows Rafael the test stick revealing that a new life is forming within her.

Annette recognizes that good prenatal care is important and so visits her obstetrician/gynecologist (OB-GYN) regularly. Like many women today, Annette delayed starting a family to pursue her career. Because of her age (36), her physician recommends an *amniocentesis* during her fourth month of pregnancy. The "amnio" tests for abnormalities such as *Down syndrome*, a chromosomal disorder in which three chromosomes are present on the twenty-first pair instead of the normal two. This disorder results in mental retardation and physical abnormalities. Down syndrome occurs more frequently in children born to women in their late thirties and early forties.

Annette and Rafael are relieved to learn the test results are negative. The test also reveals the baby's gender, but the couple prefers not to be told. "It's better to be surprised," Rafael explains. "Besides, we're kind of old-fashioned that way." The obstetrician is careful not to mention the baby's gender as she records the information in Annette's medical records. As for Annette and Rafael, they will spend the next few months selecting both boys' and girls' names.

In this chapter we trace the remarkable journey that is human development. We begin before the baby takes its first breath and conclude by considering the steps we can take to improve our chances of leading longer and healthier lives. ■

MODULE 9.1   Prenatal Development: A Case of Nature and Nurture

- **What are the major stages of prenatal development?**
- **What are some major threats to prenatal development?**

We can think of development progressing chronologically in terms of the stages shown in Table 9.1. The branch of psychology that studies the systematic changes that occur during the life span is called **developmental psychology**. We begin our story of human development by considering the important events that occur well before a child takes its first breath.

Prenatal development brings into focus the long-debated issue of how much of our development is due to nature (genes) and how much to nurture (the environment). Most psychologists today recognize that heredity and environment are closely intertwined. Though some physical traits, such as hair color, are determined by a single gene, scientists today believe that complex behavioral traits are influenced by multiple genes interacting with environmental factors (Li, 2003; Plomin & McGuffin, 2003).

Maturation, the biological unfolding of an organism according to its underlying genetic blueprint, largely determines how organisms, including ourselves, grow and develop physically. It explains why children of tall parents tend to be tall themselves. Yet development also depends on environmental factors, such as nutrition. The influences of nature and nurture begin to shape development even in the womb.

Stages of Prenatal Development

Scientists believe that sexual reproduction began some 240 to 320 million years ago, long before humans ever strode upon the Earth (Lahn & Page, 1999). They believe it began with a single chromosome that mutated to form the X and Y sex chromosomes that determine sex in mammals, including humans. The male of the species carries a combination of X and Y sex chromosomes, while the female carries two X chromosomes. Each reproductive cell or germ cell—the sperm in males and the ovum (egg cell) in females—contains only one copy of the two sex chromosomes. All other body cells have two sex chromosomes. Thus, a sperm cell carries either one X or one Y sex chromosome, whereas an ovum carries only one X. When an ovum is fertilized, the resulting combination (XX or XY) determines the baby's sex.

developmental psychology The branch of psychology that explores physical, emotional, cognitive, and social aspects of development.

maturation The biological unfolding of the organism according to the underlying genetic code.

zygote A fertilized egg cell.

germinal stage The stage of prenatal development that spans the period from fertilization through implantation.

fertilization The union of sperm and ovum.

uterus The female reproductive organ in which the fertilized ovum becomes implanted and develops to term.

embryonic stage The stage of prenatal development from implantation through about the eighth week of pregnancy during which the major organ systems begin to form.

embryo The developing organism at an early stage of prenatal development.

neural tube The area in the embryo from which the nervous system develops.

amniotic sac The uterine sac that contains the fetus.

TABLE 9.1	Stages of Development Through the Life Span
Stage	**Approximate Ages**
Prenatal period	Conception to birth
Infancy period	Birth to 1 year
Toddler period	2 to 3 years
Preschool period	3 to 6 years
Middle childhood	6 to 12 years
Adolescence	12 to 18 years
Young adulthood	18 to 40 years
Middle adulthood	40 to 65 years
Late adulthood	65 years and older

The single cell, called a **zygote**, that forms from the uniting of sperm and ovum soon undergoes cell division. First, it divides into two cells; then each of these two cells divides, forming four cells; each of these four cells divides, resulting in eight cells; and so on. In the months that follow, organ systems form as the developing organism increasingly takes on the form and structure of a human being.

A typical nine-month pregnancy is commonly divided into three trimesters, or three-month periods. From the standpoint of prenatal development, we can also identify three major prenatal stages or periods: the germinal stage, which roughly corresponds to the first two weeks after conception; the embryonic stage, which spans the period of about two weeks to about eight weeks after conception; and the fetal stage, which continues until birth (see Figure 9.1).

The **germinal stage** spans the time from **fertilization** to implantation in the wall of the **uterus**. For the first three or four days following conception, the mass of dividing cells moves about the uterus before implantation. The process of implantation is not completed for perhaps another week or so.

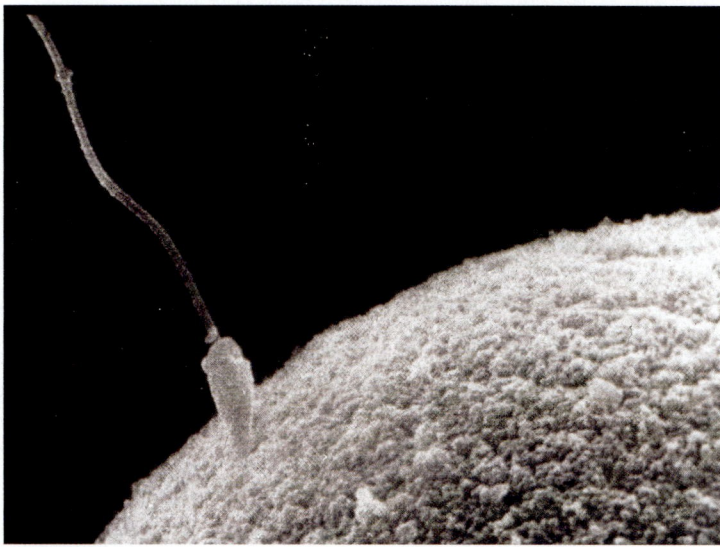

Dance of Life In this remarkable photograph, a single sperm is attempting to penetrate the egg covering. If it succeeds, the genetic material from both parents will combine into a single cell that marks the beginning of a new life.

The **embryonic stage** spans the period from implantation to about the eighth week of pregnancy. The major organ systems begin to take shape in the developing organism, which we now call the **embryo**. About three weeks into pregnancy, two ridges fold together to form the **neural tube**, from which the nervous system will develop. The head and blood vessels also begin to form at this time. By the fourth week, a primitive heart takes shape and begins beating. It will normally (and hopefully) continue beating without a break for at least the next eighty or ninety years.

The embryo is suspended in a protective environment within the mother's uterus called the **amniotic sac** (see Figure 9.2). Surrounding the embryo is amniotic fluid, which acts as a kind of shock absorber to cushion the embryo and later the fetus from damage that could result from the mother's movements. Nutrients

(a)

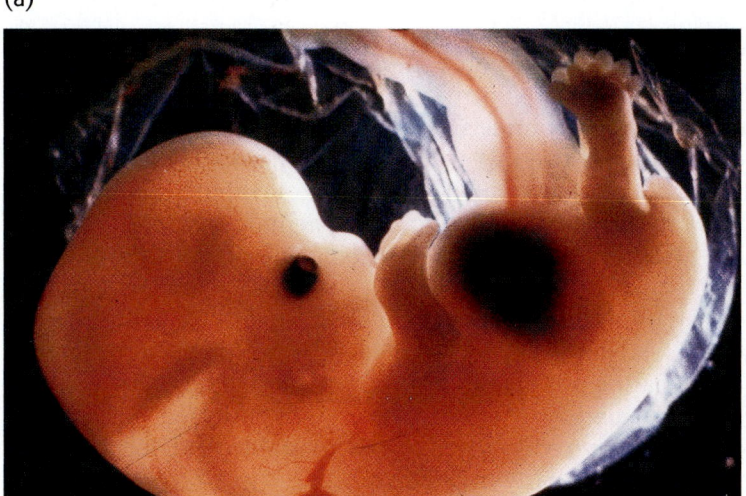

(b)

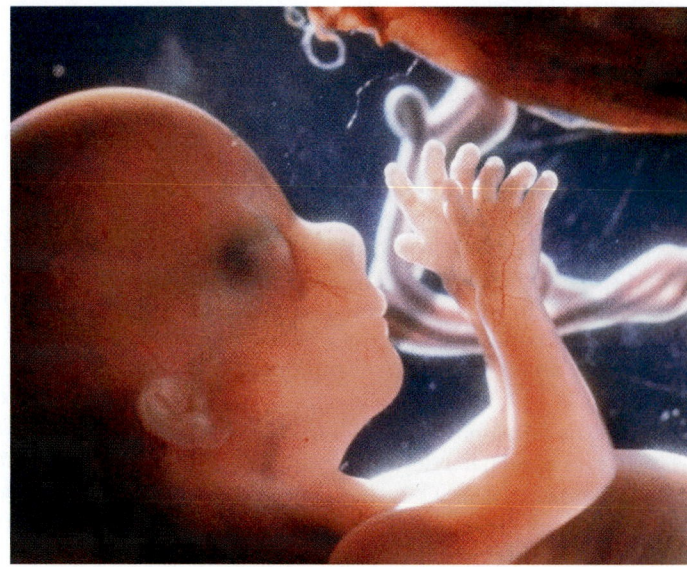

Figure 9.1 Prenatal Development
Dramatic changes in shape and form occur during prenatal development. Compare the embryo (a) at about six to seven weeks of development with the fetus (b) at approximately sixteen weeks. The fetus has already taken on a clearly recognizable human form.

Figure 9.2 Structures in the Womb
During prenatal development, the embryo lies in a protective enclosure within the uterus called the amniotic sac. Nutrients and waste materials are exchanged between mother and embryo/fetus through the placenta. The umbilical cord connects the embryo and fetus to the placenta.

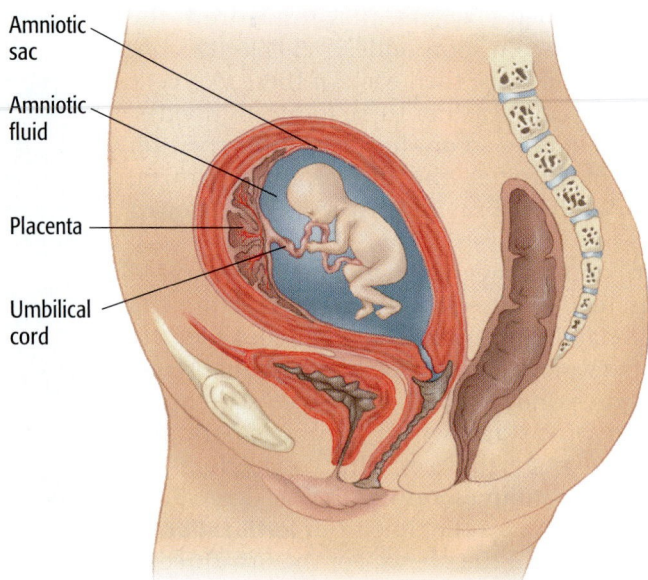

Amniotic sac

Amniotic fluid

Placenta

Umbilical cord

and waste materials are exchanged between the mother and the embryo (and fetus) through the **placenta**. The embryo and fetus are connected to the placenta by the umbilical cord. The placenta allows nutrients and oxygen to pass from mother to fetus. Their blood streams do not mix.

The **fetal stage**, or stage of the **fetus**, begins around the ninth week of pregnancy and continues until the birth of the child. All of the major organ systems, as well as the fingers and toes, are formed by about the twelfth week of prenatal development, which roughly corresponds to the end of the first trimester. They continue to develop through the course of the pregnancy. The fetus increases more than thirtyfold in weight during the second trimester of pregnancy, from about one ounce to about two pounds. It grows from about four inches in length to about fourteen inches. Typically the mother will feel the first fetal movements around the middle of the fourth month. By the end of the second trimester, the fetus approaches the *age of viability*, the point at which it becomes capable of sustaining life on its own. However, fewer than half of infants born at the end of the second trimester weighing less than two pounds will survive on their own, even with the most intense medical treatment.

Threats to Prenatal Development

A pregnant woman requires adequate nutrition for the health of the fetus as well as for her own. Maternal malnutrition is associated with a greater risk of premature birth (birth prior to thirty-seven weeks of gestation) and low birth weight (less than 5 pounds, or about 2,500 grams). Preterm and low-birth-weight babies face a higher risk of infant mortality and later developmental problems, including cognitive deficits and attention difficulties (e.g., Lemons et al., 2001; Marcus et al., 2001).

Women may receive prescriptions from their obstetricians for multivitamin pills to promote optimal fetal development. The federal government recommends that all women of childbearing age take four hundred micrograms daily of the B vitamin *folic acid* and that pregnant women take eight hundred micrograms (Mills, 2000). Folic acid greatly reduces the risk of neural tube defects such as **spina bifida**, but only if it is taken early in pregnancy.

The word **teratogen** is derived from the Greek root *teras,* meaning "monster." Teratogens include certain drugs taken by the mother, X-rays, environmental contaminants such as lead and mercury, and infectious organisms capable of passing through the placenta to the embryo or fetus. The risks posed by teratogens are greatest during certain critical periods of development. For example, teratogens

CONCEPT 9.1
The developing fetus faces many risks, including maternal malnutrition and teratogens.

placenta The organ that provides for the exchange of nutrients and waste materials between mother and fetus.

fetal stage The stage of prenatal development in which the fetus develops, beginning around the ninth week of pregnancy and lasting until the birth of the child.

fetus The developing organism in the later stages of prenatal development.

spina bifida A neural tube defect in which the child is born with a hole in the tube surrounding the spinal cord.

teratogen An environmental influence or agent that may harm the developing embryo or fetus.

CONCEPT CHART 9.1
Critical Periods in Prenatal Development

Germinal stage	Embryonic stage					Fetal stage				Full term
Weeks 1, 2	3	4	5	6	7	8	12	16	20 – 36	38

Period of dividing zygote and implantation

Labels indicate common sites of action of teratogen

Central nervous system — Eye — Heart — Eye — Heart — Teeth — Ear — Palette — Ear — Brain

Heart — Leg — Arm — Leg — Arm — Palette — External genitalia — External genitalia

Implantation of embryo

Dividing zygote

- Central nervous system
- Heart
- Ears
- Arms
- Eyes
- Legs
- ▇ Risk of major structural abnormalities
- ▇ Risk of minor structural abnormalities
- Teeth
- Palate
- External genitalia

Source: Adapted from Berger & Thompson, 1995.

that may damage the arms and legs are most likely to have an effect during the fourth through eighth weeks of development (see Concept Chart 9.1).

Let us now consider several of the most dangerous teratogens.

Infectious Diseases

Rubella (also called *German measles*) is a common childhood disease that can lead to serious birth defects, including heart disease, deafness, and mental retardation, if contracted during pregnancy. Women exposed to rubella in childhood acquire immunity to the disease. Those who lack immunity may be vaccinated before becoming pregnant to protect their future offspring.

Some sexually transmitted infections, such as HIV/AIDS and syphilis, may be transmitted from mother to child during pregnancy. Fortunately, aggressive treatment of HIV-infected mothers with the antiviral drug AZT greatly reduces the risk of maternal transmission of the virus to the fetus. Children born with congenital syphilis may suffer liver damage, impaired hearing and vision, and deformities in their teeth and bones. The risk of transmission can be reduced if the infected mother is treated effectively with antibiotics prior to the fourth month of pregnancy.

Smoking

Maternal smoking can lead to miscarriage (spontaneous abortion), premature birth, low birth weight, and increased risk of infant mortality (Ebrahim et al.,

CONCEPT 9.2
Certain environmental influences or agents, called teratogens, may harm the developing embryo or fetus.

rubella A common childhood disease that can lead to serious birth defects if contracted by the mother during pregnancy (also called *German measles*).

2000; Floyd et al., 1993). The more the mother smokes, the greater the risks. Maternal smoking during pregnancy is also linked to increased risks of **sudden infant death syndrome (SIDS)** and childhood asthma, as well as to developmental problems such as reduced attention span, lower IQ, and hyperactivity.

Alcohol and Drugs

Fetal alcohol syndrome (FAS), which results from maternal alcohol use during pregnancy, is a leading cause of mental retardation and is also associated with facial deformities such as a flattened nose, an underdeveloped upper jaw, and widely spaced eyes (Wood, Vinson, & Sher, 2001). Though FAS is more likely to occur with heavy maternal drinking, there is actually no established safe limit for alcohol use in pregnancy. FAS may occur in babies whose mothers drink as little as two ounces of alcohol a day during the first trimester. Any drug used during pregnancy, whether legal or illegal (illicit), or any medication, whether prescribed or bought over the counter, is potentially harmful to the fetus.

sudden infant death syndrome (SIDS) The sudden and unexplained death of infants that usually occurs when they are asleep in their cribs.

fetal alcohol syndrome (FAS) A syndrome caused by maternal use of alcohol during pregnancy in which the child shows developmental delays and facial deformities.

MODULE 9.1 REVIEW

Prenatal Development: A Case of Nature and Nurture

CONCEPT CHECK

1. When a sperm successfully penetrates an egg, a process known as *fertilization*, the result is a single cell called a(n)
   a. zygote.
   b. blastocyst.
   c. embryo.
   d. fetus.
2. Name two major risks to the developing embryo or fetus.

3. Match the following terms to their descriptions: (a) the first stage of pregnancy; (b) a protective environment; (c) the organ in which nutrients and wastes are exchanged within the uterus; (d) a structure in the developing organism from which the nervous system develops.
   i.   neural tube
   ii. amniotic sac
   iii. placenta
   iv. germinal stage

MODULE 9.2 — Infant Development

- **What reflexes do newborn babies show?**
- **What abilities do infants possess with respect to sensory functioning, perception, and learning?**
- **How do the infant's motor abilities develop during the first year?**

It may seem as though newborns do little more than sleep and eat, but, in fact, they come into the world with a wider range of responses than you might think. Even more remarkable are the changes that take place during development in the first two years of life. Let us enter the world of the infant and examine these remarkable changes.

Reflexes

CONCEPT 9.3
Infants enter the world with some motor reflexes that may have had survival value among ancestral humans.

A reflex is an unlearned, automatic response to a particular stimulus. Babies are born with a number of basic reflexes (see Figure 9.3). For example, if you lightly touch a newborn's cheek, the baby will reflexively turn its head in the direction of

(a) Palmar grasp reflex

(c) Moro reflex

(b) Rooting reflex

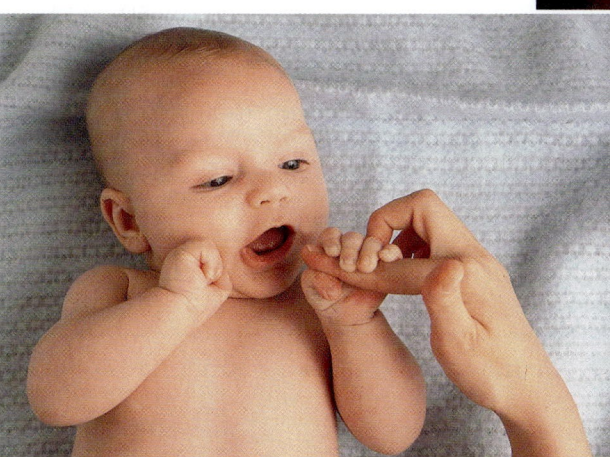

Figure 9.3   Infant Reflexes
The palmar grasp reflex (a) is so strong that the infant can literally be lifted by its hands. In the rooting reflex (b), the infant turns its head in the direction of a touch to its cheek. In the Moro reflex (c), when the infant is exposed to a noise or loss of support, it arches its back, extends its arms outward, and then brings the arms toward each other. What survival functions might these reflexes serve?

the tactile (touch) stimulation. This is the **rooting reflex**, which, like many basic reflexes, has important survival value. It helps the baby obtain nourishment by orienting its head toward the breast or bottle. Another reflex that has survival value is the **eyeblink reflex**, the reflexive blinking of the eyes that protects the baby from bright light or foreign objects. Another is the **sucking reflex**, the rhythmic sucking action that enables the infant to obtain nourishment from breast or bottle. It is prompted whenever an object like a nipple or a finger is placed in the mouth.

Some reflexes appear to be remnants of our evolutionary heritage that may no longer serve any adaptive function. For example, if the infant is exposed to a loud noise, or if its head falls backward, the **Moro reflex** is elicited: The infant extends its arms, arches its back, and then brings its arms toward each other as if attempting to grab hold of someone. The **palmar grasp reflex**, or curling of the fingers around an object that touches the palm, is so strong that the infant can literally be lifted by its hands. In ancestral times, these reflexes may have had survival value by preventing infants from falling as their mothers carried them around all day. The **Babinski reflex** involves fanning out and curling of the toes and inward twisting of the foot when the sole of the foot is stroked.

Most newborn reflexes disappear within the first six months of life. The presence and later disappearance of particular reflexes at expected periods of time are taken as signs of normal neurological development.

During the first year of life, infants on average triple their birth weight from about seven pounds to about twenty-one or twenty-two pounds. They also grow

rooting reflex   The reflexive turning of the newborn's head in the direction of a touch on its cheek.

eyeblink reflex   The reflexive blinking of the eyes that protects the newborn from bright light and foreign objects.

sucking reflex   Rhythmic sucking in response to stimulation of the tongue or mouth.

Moro reflex   An inborn reflex, elicited by a sudden noise or loss of support, in which the infant extends its arms, arches its back, and brings its arms toward each other as though attempting to grab hold of someone.

palmar grasp reflex   The reflexive curling of the infant's fingers around an object that touches its palm.

Babinski reflex   The reflexive fanning out and curling of the infant's toes and inward twisting of its foot upon stroking the sole of the foot.

in height from about twenty inches to around thirty inches. Between birth and adulthood, the brain quadruples in volume (Johnson, 1997). But perhaps most remarkable is the rapid development of the infant's abilities to sense, perceive, learn, and direct its movements.

Sensory, Perceptual, and Learning Abilities in Infancy

Infants are capable of sensing a wide range of sensory stimuli and of learning simple responses and retaining them in memory.

Sensory and Perceptual Ability

CONCEPT 9.4
Shortly after birth, the infant is able to discern many different stimuli, including the mother's odor, face, and voice, as well as different tastes.

Vision is the slowest of the senses to develop (Raymond, 2000b). Infants have about 20/400 vision at birth, which corrects to about 20/20 by age five (see Figure 9.4). The infant's visual world may be blurry, but it is not a complete blur. Hours after birth, infants show preferences for looking at facelike patterns over nonface-like patterns (Turati, 2004). They can even recognize their own mother's face and show a preference for looking at her face over other faces (Raymond, 2000a).

One-month-old infants can visually track a moving object (Von Hofsten & Rosander, 1996). Basic color vision develops by about 8 weeks (Kellman & Banks, 1997). Depth perception develops by around 6 months (Raymond, 2000b). Using a *visual cliff apparatus* consisting of a glass panel that covers an apparent sudden drop-off, Eleanor Gibson and Richard Walk (1960) showed that most infants about 6 months or older will hesitate and then refuse to crawl across to the deep side, indicating that they have developed depth perception (see Figure 9.5).

Newborns can hear many different types of sounds. They are particularly sensitive to sounds falling within the frequency of the human voice. In fact, they can discern their mother's voice from other voices. Even fetuses respond more strongly (show greater heart rate responses) to their mother's voice than to the voices of female strangers (Kisilevsky, 2003). By several months of age, infants can differentiate among various speech sounds, such as distinguishing "ba" from "ma." The ability to discriminate among speech sounds helps prepare them for the development of language.

Figure 9.4   Newborn Vision and Face Recognition
To a newborn, mother's face may appear as blurry as the photograph on the left. But a newborn can still recognize its mother's face and shows a preference for her face over other faces.

web, PsychAssist: Developmental Psychologists and Depth Perception

Figure 9.5   The Visual Cliff
The visual cliff apparatus consists of a glass panel covering what appears to be a sudden drop-off. An infant who has developed depth perception will crawl toward a parent on the opposite end but will hesitate and refuse to venture into the "deep" end even if coaxed by the parent.

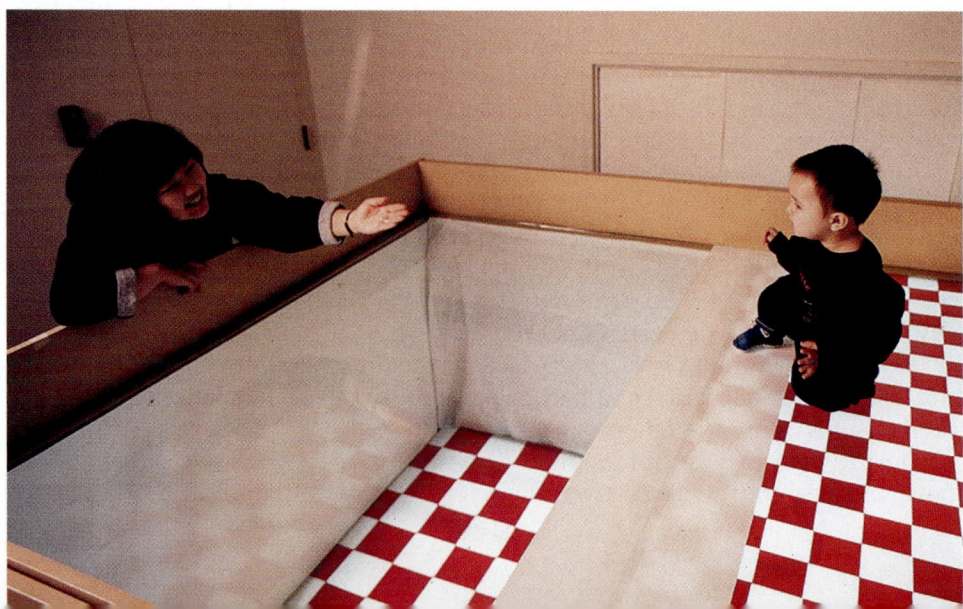

At 5 to 6 days of age, infants can detect their mother's odor. They react with a frown to the smell of rotten eggs but show a smile when they get a whiff of chocolate or bananas. Newborns can also discriminate among different tastes and show preferences for sweetness (no surprise!) (Raymond, 2000b). They will suck faster and longer if given sweetened liquids than if given bitter, salty, or plain-water solutions.

The perceptual world of the infant is not a blooming, buzzing confusion of meaningless stimuli, as people once believed. Rather, infants begin making meaningful discriminations among stimuli shortly after birth. For example, newborns are extremely sensitive to a soothing voice and to the way in which they are held.

By the age of 4 to 6 months, babies can discriminate among happy, angry, and neutral facial expressions (Pascalis, de Haan, & Nelson, 2002; Saxe, Carey, & Kanwisher, 2004). What we don't know is what, if anything, different facial expressions mean to infants. We might think "Mom looks mad," but what infants make of different facial expressions remains unclear.

Learning Ability

Infants are capable of learning simple responses and retaining memories of these learned behaviors for days or even weeks. For example, infants as young as 2 to 6 months can learn and remember a kicking response that activates a crib mobile (Rovee-Collier & Fagen, 1981). They can remember this response for several days at 2 months of age and for as long as several weeks at 6 months (Hartshorn & Rovee-Collier, 1997). Infants as young as 6 or 7 months can also retain memories for faces (Pascalis et al., 1998) and for the sounds of particular words one day after hearing them (Houston & Jusczyk, 2003). Learning even occurs prenatally, as shown by newborns' preference for their mother's voice and for sounds reflecting their native language (Moon, Cooper, & Fifer, 1993).

CONCEPT 9.5
Infants may seem to do little more than eat and sleep, but a closer look reveals they are both active learners and active perceivers of their environment.

Motor Development

Newborns' motor skills are not limited to simple reflexes. They can engage in some goal-directed behaviors, such as bringing their hands to their mouths to suck their thumbs, an ability that first appears prenatally during the third trimester. Minutes after birth, newborns can imitate their parents' facial expressions (Gopnik, 2000). Imitative behavior may be the basis for shared communication between the infant and others. The infant and caregiver begin imitating each other's facial expressions in a kind of nonmusical duet (Trevarthen, 1995).

During the first three months, infants slowly begin replacing reflexive movements with voluntary, purposive movements (Raymond, 2000a). By the second or third month, they begin bringing objects to their mouths. By 4 or 5 months of age, infants seem to prefer bringing objects into their fields of view—to have a first look at them—before bringing them to their mouths (Rochat, 1993). By about 6 months, they can reliably grasp stationary objects and begin catching moving objects.

By 2 months of age, infants can lift their chins; by 5 months, they can roll over; and by 9 months, they can sit without support. By the end of the first year, infants will master the most difficult balancing problem they'll ever face in life: standing without support. Why is standing alone so difficult? Because of its smaller size, a 1-year-old will sway about 40 percent more while standing than will an adult and consequently will have less time to respond to balance disturbances to maintain itself in an upright position. To appreciate the challenge the 1-year-old faces in attempting to stand, imagine trying to keep your balance while standing on a bridge that is constantly swaying. The development of motor skills, as outlined in Concept Chart 9.2, occurs in the same sequence among nearly all infants at about the same ages and in all cultures.

CONCEPT 9.6
Motor development in infancy progresses rapidly through a series of steps from near immobility to coordinated running by around eighteen months of age.

CONCEPT CHART 9.2
Milestones in Infant Development

Approximate Ages	Sensory Skills and Learning Abilities	Motor Skills
Birth to 1 month	• Has 20/600 vision • Can visually track a moving object • Sensitive to sounds within range of human voice • Shows preference for mother's voice and native language sounds (develops prenatally) • Can detect mother's odor • Can discern certain pleasant or unpleasant basic odors • Shows taste preference for sweetness • Responds to a soothing voice • Can discern differences in how they are held • Shows preferences for face-like stimuli and responds to certain facial features	• Basic reflexes • Thumb sucking • Mimicking facial acts
2–3 months	• Can discriminate direction of a moving object • Has developed basic color vision • Can discern differences in the tempo (beat) of a pattern of sounds • Can discriminate among faces of different people • Can learn simple responses and remember them for several days (at 2 months) to several weeks (at 6 months)	• Lifts chin • Brings objects to mouth
4–6 months	• Depth perception develops • Can discern differences among certain facial expressions • Can retain memory for certain faces	• Grasps stationary objects • Catches moving objects • Brings objects into field of view • Able to roll over
7–9 months	Further development of depth perception and visual acuity	• Sits without support • Stands holding on
10–12 months	Has developed near 20/20 vision	• Walks holding on • Stands without support

 **web.** Netlab/Milestones of Motor Development

MODULE 9.2 REVIEW

Infant Development

CONCEPT CHECK

1. Match the following reflexes to the appropriate description:
   (a) rooting reflex; (b) eyeblink reflex; (c) sucking reflex;
   (d) Moro reflex.
   i. a rhythmic action that enables an infant to take in nourishment
   ii. a reflex action protecting one from bright lights and foreign objects
   iii. a grabbing movement, often in response to a loud noise
   iv. turning in response to a touch on the cheek; helps the baby find breast or bottle.

2. Babies seem to learn even while still in the womb. What evidence (based on the sense of hearing) do we have to support this notion?

3. Motor abilities develop extremely rapidly in infants. Which of the following is *not* a motor ability of a baby during the first year of life?
   a. imitation of parents' facial expressions
   b. development of voluntary, goal-directed movement
   c. balancing itself while sitting, without support
   d. speaking in complete sentences

MODULE 9.3 Years of Discovery: Emotional, Social, and Cognitive Development in Childhood

- What are the three basic types of infant temperament identified in the New York Longitudinal Study, and what are the major differences among them?
- What are the three types of attachment styles identified by Ainsworth?
- What roles do peer relationships play in children's emotional and social development?
- What are the three major styles of parenting in Baumrind's model, and how do they differ?
- What are the stages of psychosocial development during childhood, according to Erikson?
- What are the major features associated with Piaget's stages of cognitive development?
- What is the basic theme in Vygotsky's theory of cognitive development?

Childhood is a period of wonderment, discovery, and, most of all, change. Here we examine the world of the growing child from the standpoint of emotional, social, and cognitive development, beginning with differences in temperament among infants. We then focus on two major stage theories of development, Erikson's stages of psychosocial development and Piaget's stages of cognitive development.

Stage theorists such as Erikson and Piaget believe that development occurs as sudden transformations or abrupt leaps rather than in smaller steps. (Kohlberg, another stage theorist, is discussed in the next module.) Stage theorists believe that development remains relatively stable within each stage, but then abruptly jumps to the next stage. Though they recognize that many skills, such as vocabulary and arithmetical abilities, develop gradually through practice and experience, stage theorists argue that the child must reach a stage of developmental readiness for such training and experience to matter.

Temperament: The "How" of Behavior

Janet was talking about her two daughters, Tabitha (age 7) and Alicia (age 2½). "They're like day and night. Tabitha is the sensitive type. She's very tentative about taking chances or joining in with the other children. She can play by herself for hours. Just give her a book to read and she's in heaven. What can I say about Alicia? Where Tabitha would sit at the top of the slide and have to be coaxed to come down, Alicia goes down head first. Most kids her age stay in the part of the playground for the toddlers, but Alicia is off running to the big climbing equipment. She even thinks she's one of the older kids and tries to join them in their games. Can you picture that? Alicia is running after a baseball with the 6- and 7-year-olds." Ask parents who have two or more children and you're likely to hear a similar refrain: "They're just different. I don't know why they're different, but they just are."

We may attempt to explain these differences in terms of the construct of **temperament**. A temperament is a characteristic style of behavior, or disposition. Some theorists refer to temperament as the "how" of behavior—the characteristic way in which behavior is performed (Chess & Thomas, 1996). One child may display a cheerful temperament in approaching new situations, whereas another may exhibit a fearful or apprehensive temperament.

CONCEPT 9.7
Many psychologists believe that children differ in their basic temperaments and that these differences are at least partially determined by genetic factors.

temperament A characteristic style of behavior or disposition.

The most widely used classification of temperaments is based on a study of middle-class and upper-middle-class infants from the New York City area—the New York Longitudinal Study (NYLS) (Chess & Thomas, 1996). The investigators identified three general types of temperament that could be used to classify about two out of three of the children in the study group:

1. *Easy children.* These children are playful and respond positively to new stimuli. They adapt easily to changes; display a happy, engaging mood; and are quick to develop regular sleeping and feeding schedules. About 40 percent of the NYLS children were classified in this category.

2. *Difficult children.* These children react negatively to new situations or people, have irritable dispositions, and have difficulty establishing regular sleeping and feeding schedules. About 10 percent of the group fell into this category.

3. *Slow-to-warm-up children.* These children (called "inhibited children" by others) have low activity levels; avoid novel stimuli; require more time to adjust to new situations than most children; and typically react to unfamiliar situations by becoming withdrawn, subdued, or mildly distressed. This category described about 15 percent of the group.

The remaining 35 percent of the children studied represented a mixed group who could not be easily classified.

Subsequent research has found that the three distinct types of temperament observed in infancy predict later differences in adjustment (Rothbart & Bates, 1997). The easy infant is generally better adjusted as an adult than infants with other temperaments. The slow-to-warm-up infant is more likely to experience anxiety or depression in childhood than other infants. The difficult infant is at higher risk for developing acting-out or other problem behaviors in childhood. Of the three temperament groups, the difficult infants are most likely to develop psychiatric problems in later childhood (Kagan, 1997). However, they may also have positive qualities, such as being highly spirited and not becoming a "pushover."

Developmental psychologists believe temperament is shaped by both nature and nurture—that is, by genetics as well as by environmental influences (Kagan, 2003; Rothbart, Ahadi, & Evans, 2000). But the question of whether it is possible to change basic temperament remains unanswered. Even if basic temperament can't be changed, however, children are better able to adapt successfully to their environment when parents, teachers, and other caregivers take their underlying temperaments into account. For example, the difficult or slow-to-warm-up child may need more time and gentle encouragement when adjusting to new situations such as beginning school, making friends, or joining in play activities with other children. Kagan (1997) found that mothers whose infants show signs of inhibited temperament but who relate to them in nurturing but not overly protective ways can help them overcome fearfulness of new experiences.

Attachment Attachment behaviors are the ties that bind infants to their caregivers.

Attachment: Binding Ties

In human development, **attachment** is the enduring emotional bond that infants and older children form with their caregivers. Do not confuse attachment with *bonding,* which is the parent's tie to the infant that may form in the hours following birth. Rather, attachment develops over time during infancy. Infants may crawl to be near their caregivers, pull or grab at them to maintain contact, and cry and show other signs of emotional distress when separated from them, even if only momentarily.

Attachment Behaviors in Other Animal Species

Many species exhibit attachment behaviors. Baby chimpanzees, tigers, and lions will cling for dear life to their mothers' fur. The famed scientist Konrad Lorenz

attachment The enduring emotional bond that infants and older children form with their caregivers.

Father Goose Goslings that had imprinted on scientist Konrad Lorenz followed him everywhere.

Contact Comfort Harry Harlow showed that baby monkeys preferred contact with a "cloth mother," even though a "wire mother" fed them.

studied the process of imprinting in geese and other species. **Imprinting** is the formation of a strong bond of attachment to the first moving object seen after birth. A gosling (baby goose) will instinctively follow its mother wherever she goes. But goslings hatched in incubators will imprint on objects that happen to be present at their birth, including humans (Lorenz was one) and even mechanical toys. The goslings that imprinted on Lorenz followed him everywhere, even to the point of ignoring adult female geese.

In landmark research, psychologists Harry and Marguerite Harlow showed that baby monkeys developed attachment behaviors to inanimate objects placed in their cages (Harlow & Harlow, 1966). Newborn rhesus monkeys were separated from their mothers within hours of birth and raised in experimental cages in which various objects served as surrogate (substitute) mothers. In one study, infant monkeys were raised in cages containing two types of surrogate mothers: a wire cylinder or a soft, terry-cloth-covered cylinder (Harlow & Zimmermann, 1959). The infant monkeys showed clear preferences for the cloth mother, even when they were fed by an apparatus containing a bottle attached to the wire mother. Contact comfort apparently was a stronger determinant of attachment than food.

Attachment in Human Infants

Psychologist Mary Ainsworth developed a laboratory-based method, called the *strange situation,* to observe how infants react to separations and reunions with caregivers, typically their mothers (Ainsworth, 1979; Ainsworth et al., 1978). Based on these observations, Ainsworth noted three basic attachment styles in infants, one characterized by secure attachments and the other two by insecure attachments:

1. *Secure type (Type B).* These infants used their mothers as a secure base for exploring the environment, periodically looking around to check on her whereabouts and limiting exploration when she was absent. They sometimes

CONCEPT 9.8
Attachment behaviors are found in a wide range of species, from ducks to humans.

web **Netlab/Baby's First Love Affair**

CONCEPT 9.9
Using a laboratory method for measuring attachment behavior in infants, investigators can classify infants according to their basic attachment style.

imprinting The formation of a strong bond of the newborn animal to the first moving object seen after birth.

cried when the mother left but warmly greeted her and were easily soothed by her when she returned. Soon they began exploring again. About 65 to 70 percent of middle-class samples of infants were classified as having secure attachments (Seifert & Hoffnung, 2000; Thompson, 1997). Cross-cultural studies indicate that most infants show a secure pattern of attachment (Main, 1996).

2. *Insecure-avoidant type (Type A).* These infants paid little attention to the mother when she was in the room and separated easily from her to explore the environment. They showed little distress when the mother departed and ignored her when she returned. About 20 percent of the infants in the typical sample fit this type (Thompson, 1997).

3. *Insecure-resistant type (Type C).* These infants clung to the mother and were reluctant to explore the environment despite the presence of desirable toys. They showed a high level of distress when the mother departed and continued to experience some distress despite her attempts to comfort them when she returned. They also showed ambivalence or resistance toward the mother, reaching out to her to be picked up one moment and rebuffing her the next by pushing her away or twisting their bodies to get free of her. About 10 percent of the infants showed this attachment pattern.

In later studies, researchers identified a fourth type of attachment style, labeled *Type D* for *disorganized/disoriented* attachment (Cassidy, 2003; Main & Solomon, 1990). These infants appeared to lack a consistent or organized strategy for responding to separations and reunions. They seemed confused and were unable to approach the mother directly for support even when they were very distressed.

The Ainsworth method may not be appropriate for assessing attachment behaviors in children from cultures with different child-rearing practices (Sroufe, Cooper, & DeHart, 1992). For example, Japanese cultural practices emphasize mother-infant closeness and interdependence, which may make it more difficult for these infants to manage brief separations from their mothers (Takahashi, 1990). More broadly, we need to recognize that substantial variations exist in attachment behavior across cultures (Rothbaum et al., 2000). For example, Americans place a greater emphasis on exploration and independence in young children than do the Japanese.

Attachment styles forged in early infancy may have lasting consequences for later development. A more securely attached infant is likely to be better adjusted in childhood and adolescence than a less securely attached infant (Belsky & Cassidy, 1994; Main, 1996; Scarr & Eisenberg, 1993). For example, the more securely attached infant is likelier to have higher self-esteem, to show greater cooperativeness and independence, to have fewer problem behaviors (such as aggressiveness or withdrawal), to have better relationships with peers, and to exhibit better overall emotional health (Main, 1996; Schneider, Atkinson, & Tardif, 2001).

Effects of Day Care on Attachment

CONCEPT 9.10

Evidence shows that placing infants in day care does not prevent the development of secure attachments to their mothers.

Today more mothers of preschool children are in the labor force than remain at home (Lewin, 2001). Children under five are more likely to be enrolled in organized day-care centers than to be cared for at home or in relatives' homes (Greenberg & Springen, 2000). Despite earlier concerns raised by some researchers that full-time day care may interfere with the infant's attachment to its mother, recent studies have found no effects of day-care placement on the security of infant-mother attachments (NICHD, 1997; Sandlin-Sniffen, 2000). To the contrary, high-quality center-based day care has positive effects on children's cognitive and emotional development, such as fostering independence and cooperative play (Loeb et al., 2004; McNamar, 2004). That said, a recent study showed that kindergartners who had spent long hours in day care were more aggressive, on the

CONCEPT CHART 9.3
Differences in Temperaments and Attachment Styles

	Source	Major Types	General Characteristics
Temperaments	New York Longitudinal Study	Easy child	Playful; shows interest in new situations or novel stimuli; quickly develops regular sleeping and eating patterns
		Difficult child	Irritable; has difficulty adjusting to new situations or people and establishing regular sleeping and feeding schedules
		Slow-to-warm-up child	Shows low activity levels; becomes inhibited, withdrawn, or fretful when exposed to new situations
Attachment styles	Ainsworth's research using the *strange situation*	Secure type (Type B)	Uses mother as a secure base to explore the environment while frequently checking on her whereabouts; may cry when mother leaves, but quickly settles down and warms up to her when she returns and then begins exploring again
		Insecure-avoidant type (Type A)	Pays little attention to mother when she is present and shows little distress when she leaves
		Insecure-resistant type (Type C)	Clings to mother, avoiding venturing into unfamiliar situations; becomes very upset when mother leaves and fails to be comforted completely when she returns; shows some ambivalence or resistance toward mother

average, than their peers (Stolberg, 2001a). The causes for the link remain under study, investigators suspect that a lack of high-quality day care may be to blame (Love, 2003, as cited in Gilbert, 2003).

Before we move on, you may want to review the differences that researchers have observed in infant temperaments and attachment styles shown in Concept Chart 9.3.

Child-Rearing Influences

Many factors influence a child's intellectual, emotional, and social development, including genetics, peer group influences, and the quality of parenting (Brazelton & Greenspan, 2000; Parke & Buriel, 1997; McCrae et al., 2000). Peer relationships provide the child with opportunities to develop socially competent behaviors in relating to others outside the family and as a member of a group. The acceptance and approval of peer group members help shape the child's developing self-esteem and sense of competence. Peer relationships can also have negative consequences. Children and adolescents have a strong need for peer acceptance and may be influenced by peers to engage in deviant activities they might never attempt on their own.

Good parenting encompasses many qualities, including spending time with children (plenty of time!), modeling appropriate behaviors, helping children acquire skills to develop healthy peer relationships, stating rules clearly, setting limits, being consistent in correcting inappropriate behavior and praising good behavior, and providing a warm, secure environment. Explaining to children how their behavior affects others can also help them develop more appropriate social behaviors (Kaplan, 2000). Children whose parents use discipline inconsistently, rely on harsh punishment, and are highly critical are more likely than others to develop problem behaviors at home and school and less likely to develop healthy peer relationships (Kilgore, Snyder, & Lentz, 2000).

CONCEPT 9.11
Peer relationships provide opportunities for children to develop social competencies and establish feelings of closeness and loyalty that can serve as the basis for later relationships.

CONCEPT 9.12
The quality of parenting is an important influence on children's intellectual, emotional, and social development.

Father's Influence

Though many studies of parent-child relationships focus on children and their mothers, we shouldn't lose sight of the importance of fathers in child development. Children whose fathers share meals with them, spend leisure time with them, and assist them with schoolwork tend to perform better academically than those with less engaged fathers (Cooksey & Fondell, 1996). Researchers have also found that children in two-parent, mother-father households tend to fare better academically and socially than those in mother-partner or single-mother households, even after accounting for differences in income levels (Thomson, Hanson, & McLanahan, 1994).

Mothers and fathers tend to differ in their parenting behavior. Compared to mothers, fathers typically provide less basic care (changing, feeding, bathing, etc.) but engage in more physically active play with their children (Parke & Buriel, 1997). For example, a father might zoom the baby in the air ("play airplane"), whereas a mother might engage in more physically restrained games like peek-a-boo and patty-cake, and talk and sing soothingly to the infant (Berger, 1998). However, greater physical play with fathers is not characteristic of all cultures. In Chinese, Malaysian, and Indian cultures, for example, fathers and mothers rarely engage in physical play with their children (Parke & Buriel, 1997).

Cultural Differences in Parenting

Cultural learning has a strong bearing on child rearing, leading to variations across cultures in the ways that children are raised. African American families, for example, tend to have strong kinship bonds and to distribute childcare responsibilities among different family members (Nevid, Rathus, & Greene, 2003). The grandmother in such families often assumes direct parenting responsibilities and is often referred to as "mother." In traditional Hispanic families, the father is expected to be the provider and protector of the female, whereas the mother assumes full responsibility for childcare (De La Cancela & Guzman, 1991). These traditional gender roles are changing, however, as more Hispanic women are entering the work force and pursuing advanced educational opportunities. Hispanic families also tend to adopt strict disciplinary standards and to place a high value on children's development of a proper demeanor and respect toward adults (Kaplan, 2000). Likewise, Asian cultures emphasize respect for parental authority, especially the father's, and warm maternal relationships (Berk, 2000; Nevid & Sta. Maria, 1999). All cultures help children move from a state of complete dependency in infancy toward assuming more responsibility for their own behavior. However, they vary in the degree to which they promote early independence in children and expect them to assume responsible roles within the family and community.

Taking Responsibility In some cultures, children are expected to perform responsible roles needed to ensure the survival of the family and community.

CONCEPT 9.13
Diana Baumrind identified three different parenting styles: authoritative, authoritarian, and permissive.

Parenting Styles

An important avenue of investigation into parenting influences on children's development focuses on differences in parenting styles. Diana Baumrind, a leading researcher in this area, identified three basic parenting styles: authoritative, authoritarian, and permissive (Baumrind, 1971, 1991):

1. *Authoritative style.* Authoritative parents set reasonable limits for their children but are not overcontrolling. The parent is the authority figure, firm but understanding, willing to give advice, but also willing to listen to children's concerns. Parents explain the reasons for their decisions rather than just "laying down the law." To Baumrind, authoritative parenting is the most successful parenting style. Evidence shows that children of authoritative parents tend to achieve the most positive outcomes in childhood and adolescence (Baumrind, 1971, 1991). They tend to have high self-esteem and to be popu-

TABLE 9.2   Keys to Becoming an Authoritative Parent

Authoritative parents set firm limits but take the time to explain their decisions and to listen to their children's point of view. They also help children develop a sense of competence by setting reasonable demands for mature behavior. Here are suggestions for becoming an authoritative parent:

Rely on reason, not force.	Explain the rules, but keep explanations brief. When the child throws food against the wall, you can say, "We don't do that. That makes a mess, and I'll have to clean it up."
Show warmth.	Children's self-esteem is molded by how others, especially their parents, relate to them. Express your feelings verbally by using praise and physically by means of hugs, kisses, and holding hands when walking together. Praise the child for accomplishing tasks, even small ones.
Listen to your children's opinions.	Encourage the child to express his or her opinions and feelings, but explain why it is important to follow the rules.
Set mature but reasonable expectations.	Encourage children to adopt more mature behaviors in line with their developmental level. If a child requires assistance, demonstrate how to perform the expected behavior, and give the child encouragement and feedback when he or she attempts it independently.

lar with peers, self-reliant, and competent (Parke & Buriel, 1997). The flexible but firm child-rearing approach of authoritative parents encourages children to be independent and assertive but also respectful of the needs of others. Table 9.2 outlines some key steps in becoming an authoritative parent.

2. *Authoritarian style.* Authoritarian parents are rigid and overcontrolling. They expect and demand unquestioned obedience from their children. If children dare to ask why they are being told to do something, the answer is likely to be "Because I say so." Authoritarian parents are unresponsive to their children's needs and rely on harsh forms of discipline while allowing their children little control over their lives. Children of authoritarian parents tend to be inhibited, moody, withdrawn, fearful, and distrustful of others. The most negative outcomes in adolescence are found in boys with authoritarian parents. They typically perform poorly in school; lack initiative and self-confidence; and tend to be conflicted, unhappy, and unfriendly toward peers (Baumrind, 1991; Parke & Buriel, 1997).

3. *Permissive style.* Permissive parents have an "anything goes" attitude toward raising their children. They may respond affectionately to children but are extremely lax in setting limits and imposing discipline. Children with permissive parents tend to be impulsive and lacking in self-control. They lack the experience of conforming to other people's demands that is important in developing effective interpersonal skills (Parke & Buriel, 1997).

Table 9.3 summarizes these three parenting styles. We need to take sociocultural realities into account when applying Baumrind's parenting styles. Some cultures emphasize authoritarian styles of parenting more than others do. It may be

THINK
About It

Better Parenting

Based on your reading of Baumrind's work on parent-child relationships, what do you think you need to do to become a better parent now or in the future?

TABLE 9.3   Baumrind's Styles of Parenting

	Authoritative Style	Authoritarian Style	Permissive Style
Limit setting	High	High	Low
Style of discipline	Reasoning	Forceful	Lax
Maturity expectations	High	High	Low
Communications with children	High	Low	Moderate
Warmth and support	High	Low	High

unfair or misleading to apply the same categories in classifying parenting styles in other cultures that have different child-rearing traditions. Within our own society, authoritarian styles in lower socioeconomic status (SES) families may represent a type of adaptation to stresses that families in poorer neighborhoods might face, such as heightened risks of violence and drug abuse. Parents in lower-SES families may believe they need to enforce stricter limits on their children to protect them from these outside threats (Parke, 2004).

Erikson's Stages of Psychosocial Development

Erik Erikson (1902–1994), a prominent psychodynamic theorist, emphasized the importance of social relationships in human development (Erikson, 1963). In his view, psychosocial development progresses through a series of stages that begin in early childhood and continue through adulthood. He believed our personalities are shaped by how we deal with a series of psychosocial crises or challenges during these stages. In this section, we focus on the four stages of psychosocial development that occur during childhood.

CONCEPT 9.14

Erik Erikson described four stages of psychosocial development in childhood, each characterized by a particular life crisis or challenge: trust versus mistrust, autonomy versus shame and doubt, initiative versus guilt, and industry versus inferiority.

Trust Versus Mistrust

The first psychosocial challenge the infant faces is the development of a sense of trust toward its social environment. When parents treat the infant warmly and are responsive to its needs, a sense of trust develops. But if the parents are seldom there when the infant needs them, or if they are detached or respond coldly, the infant develops a basic mistrust of others. The world may seem a cold and threatening place.

Autonomy Versus Shame and Doubt

Erikson believed the central psychosocial challenge faced during the second and third years of life concerns autonomy. The child is now becoming mobile within the home and is "getting into everything." Parents may warmly encourage the child toward greater independence and nurture this newly developed sense of autonomy. However, if they demand too much too soon or make excessive demands that the child cannot meet (such as in the area of toilet training), the child may become riddled with feelings of self-doubt and shame that come to pervade later development, even into adulthood.

Initiative Versus Guilt

This stage, corresponding to the preschool years of three to six, is a time of climbing gyms and play dates, a time at which the child is challenged to initiate actions and carry them out. Children who largely succeed in their efforts and are praised for their accomplishments will come to develop a sense of initiative and competence. In contrast, children who frequently fail to accomplish tasks and can't seem to "get things right" may develop feelings of guilt and powerlessness, especially if they are ridiculed or harshly criticized for their awkwardness or missteps.

Industry Versus Inferiority

At this stage, which corresponds to the elementary school period of six to twelve years, the child faces the central challenge of developing industriousness and self-confidence. If children believe they perform competently in the classroom and on the playing field in relation to their peers they will likely become industrious by taking an active role in school and extracurricular activities. But if the pendulum swings too far in the other direction and failure outweighs success, feelings of inadequacy or inferiority may develop, causing the child to become withdrawn and unmotivated.

TABLE 9.4   Erik Erikson's Stages of Psychosocial Development in Childhood

Approximate Ages	Life Crisis	Major Challenge in Psychosocial Development
Infancy (birth to 1 year)	Trust versus mistrust	Developing a basic sense of trust in the caregiver and the environment
Toddlerhood (1 to 3 years)	Autonomy versus shame and doubt	Building a sense of independence and self-control
Preschool period (3 to 6 years)	Initiative versus guilt	Learning to initiate actions and carry them out
Elementary school period (6 to 12 years)	Industry versus inferiority	Becoming productive and involved

Source: Adapted from Erikson, 1963.

Table 9.4 provides an overview of Erikson's stages of psychosocial development in childhood. Though Erikson believed childhood experiences can have lasting effects on the individual's psychological development, he emphasized that later experiences in life may counter these earlier influences and lead eventually to more successful resolutions of these life challenges.

Cognitive Development

Seven-year-old Jason is upset with his younger brother Scott, age 3. Scott just can't seem to get the basic idea of hide-and-go-seek. Every time Scott goes off to hide, he curls up in the corner of the room in plain sight of Jason. "You're supposed to hide where I can't see you," Jason complains. So Scott goes off and hides in the same spot, but now he covers his eyes. "Now you can't see me," he calls back to Jason. Though they live in the same home and share many family outings together, the world of a 3-year-old like Scott is very different from that of a 7-year-old like Jason. Let's consider how different by examining the changes in the way children think and reason as they progress through childhood. We begin with the work of the most influential theorist on cognitive development, Jean Piaget.

Piaget's Theory of Cognitive Development

Jean Piaget (1896–1980) is arguably the most important developmental theorist of all time—a "giant with a giant theory," to borrow a phrase from the social historian Morton Hunt (1993). Piaget believed the best way to understand how children think is to observe them closely as they interact with objects and solve problems. Much of his work was based on his observations of his own three children. He was less concerned with whether children answered questions correctly than with how they arrived at their answers.

To understand Piaget's theory of cognitive development, we must look at what he means by the term *schema*. To Piaget, a **schema** is an organized system of actions or a mental representation that people use to understand the world and interact with it (Piaget, 1952). The child is born with simple schemas comprising basic reflexes such as sucking. This schema obviously has adaptive value, since the infant needs to obtain nourishment from its mother's breast or the bottle by sucking.

Eventually the infant discovers that the schema works more effectively for some objects than for others. For my daughter Daniella, the sucking schema crashed the day we introduced her to an infant cup. Her dad demonstrated how to tip the cup at an angle to draw the liquid into the mouth. Daniella was unimpressed and continued to hold the cup upright and suck on its lip, which unhappily failed to produce the desired result.

CONCEPT 9.15
To Piaget, a schema is an action strategy or a mental representation that helps people understand and interact with the world.

CONCEPT 9.16
In Piaget's view, adaptation to the environment consists of two complementary processes, assimilation and accommodation.

schema   To Piaget, a mental framework for understanding or acting on the environment.

Eventually schemas change as the child adapts to new challenges and demands. According to Piaget, **adaptation** is a process by which people adapt or change to function more effectively to meet challenges they face in the environment. Through adaptation, we adjust our schemas to meet the changing demands the environment imposes on us. Adaptation, in turn, consists of two complementary processes: *assimilation* and *accommodation.*

Assimilation is the process of incorporating new objects or situations into existing schemas. For example, newborns will reflexively suck any object placed in their mouths, such as a finger or even a piece of cloth. Daniella applied her sucking schema to an infant cup by attempting to suck on its lip. Older children develop classification schemas, which consist of mental representations of particular classes of objects. When Daniella was a toddler, she applied her "dog schema" to any nonhuman animal, including cats, horses, sheep, and even fish. To her, all were "bow-wows."

Assimilation is adaptive when new objects fit existing schemas, as when the infant sucks on the nipple of a baby bottle for the first time rather than the mother's breast. But horses and fish are not dogs, and infant cups cannot be sucked to draw liquid into the mouth. **Accommodation** is the process of altering existing schemas or creating new ones to deal with objects or experiences that don't fit readily into existing schemas. Eventually Daniella developed a new "tipping schema" for using an infant cup: tipping it in her mouth so the contents would drip in.

Stages of Cognitive Development

CONCEPT 9.17

Piaget proposed that children progress at about the same ages through a series of four stages of cognitive development: the sensorimotor, preoperational, concrete operational, and formal operational stages.

PsychAssist: Piaget's Stages of Cognitive Development

In Piaget's view, the processes of assimilation and accommodation are ongoing throughout life. However, he held that the child's cognitive development progresses through a series of stages that occur in an ordered sequence at about the same ages in all children. Children at the different stages of cognitive development differ in how they view and interact with the world. Here we take a closer look at Piaget's four stages of cognitive development: the sensorimotor, preoperational, concrete operational, and formal operational stages.

Sensorimotor Stage: Birth to Two Years The sensorimotor stage spans a period of momentous growth in the infant's cognitive development. During this stage, which actually consists of six substages, the child becomes increasingly capable of performing more complex behaviors and skills. Piaget used the term *sensorimotor* because the infant explores its world by using its senses and applying its developing motor skills (body movement and hand control). The infant's intelligence is expressed through action and purposeful manipulation of objects.

At birth through 1 month, the infant's behaviors are limited to inborn reflexes, such as grasping and sucking. From months 1 through 8, the infant gains increasing voluntary control over some of its movements, such as acquiring the ability to grasp objects placed above its crib. The infant is now beginning to act on the world and to repeat actions that have interesting effects, such as repeatedly squeezing a rubber duck to produce a squealing sound. By 8 to 12 months, the infant's actions are intended to reach a particular goal. The child will perform purposeful actions such as crawling to the other side of the room to open the bottom drawers of cabinets where toys are kept.

Early in the sensorimotor stage, infants are aware of an object's existence only if it is physically present. Out of sight is, quite literally, out of mind. If you block a 4-month-old's view of an object that he or she has been looking at, the child will immediately lose interest and begin looking at other objects. By about 8 months, the child will begin looking for a hidden object. Now, if you place a pillow over a teddy bear, she or he will push the pillow out of the way to get the toy. By this age, the child has begun to develop a concept of **object permanence**, the recognition that objects continue to exist even if they have disappeared from sight.

adaptation To Piaget, the process of adjustment that enables people to function more effectively in meeting the demands they face in the environment.

assimilation To Piaget, the process of incorporating new objects or situations into existing schemas.

accommodation To Piaget, the process of creating new schemas or modifying existing ones to account for new objects or experiences.

object permanence The recognition that objects continue to exist even if they have disappeared from sight.

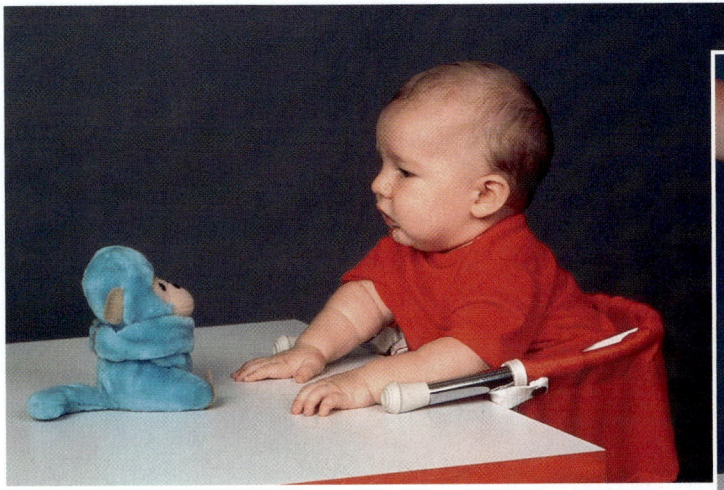

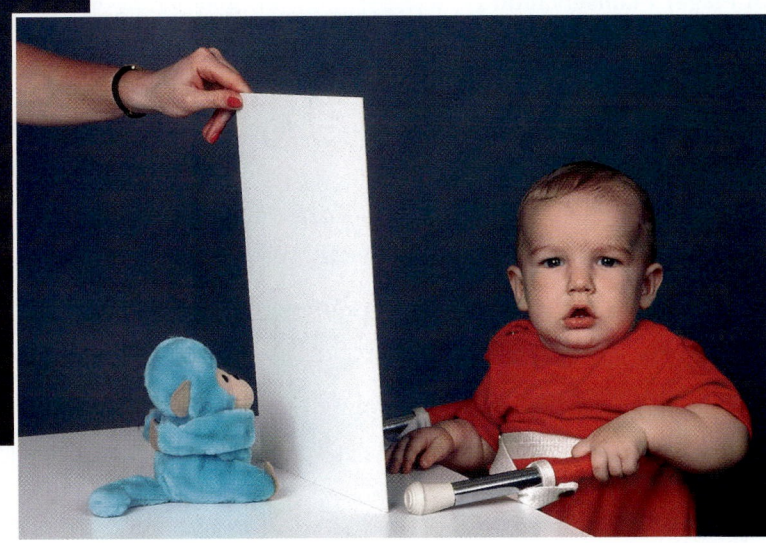

Object Permanence   Infants who have not yet developed object permanence act as though objects that have disappeared from sight no longer exist.

Piaget believed that object permanence is not yet complete at this point. It reaches a mature level toward the end of the sensorimotor stage when the child begins to acquire the ability to form a mental representation of an object that is not visibly present. One sign that 22-month-old Daniella had acquired object permanence was that she began asking for her brother Michael upon awakening. She apparently was able to retain a mental representation of Michael. Her parents tried not to take it personally that she always asked for Michael first!

Preoperational Stage: Two to Seven Years   Piaget used the term *preoperational* to describe the cognitive abilities of children roughly ages 2 to 7 years because they lacked the ability to perform basic logical operations—to apply basic principles of logic to their experiences. During this period, however, extraordinary growth occurs in the ability to form mental or **symbolic representations** of the world, especially with the use of language. Specifically, a child forms symbolic representations of objects and experiences by naming or describing them in words. Language makes the child's thinking processes far more expansive and efficient than was possible in the sensorimotor stage.

Another form of representational thinking is make-believe or pretend play. In pretend play, children form mental representations that allow them to enact scenes with characters that are not physically present. Pretend play becomes increasingly complex as children progress through the preoperational stage. By age 5 or 6, children are creating scenes with imagined characters or reenacting scenes they have seen on TV or in movies.

Though cognitive abilities expand dramatically during the preoperational stage, Piaget noted that the child's thinking processes are still quite limited. For example, the preoperational child demonstrates **egocentrism**, the tendency to view the world only from one's own point of view. Egocentric thinking doesn't mean the child is selfish or unconcerned about others; rather, the child at this stage lacks the cognitive ability to take another person's point of view or perspective. In the child's mind, he or she is the center of the universe. For example, 5-year-old Michelle wants to play with Mommy but doesn't understand that Mommy is tired and needs to rest. When Michelle feels like playing, she thinks Mommy should feel like playing too. In our earlier example, 3-year-old Scott is unable to take his brother's perspective when playing hide-and-go-seek. He doesn't realize that his hiding place is in plain view of his brother. He also assumes that since he can't see his brother when he covers his own eyes, his brother can't see him.

symbolic representations   A term referring to the use of words to represent (name) objects and describe experiences.

egocentrism   To Piaget, the tendency to see the world only from one's own perspective.

Figure 9.6   Examples of Piaget's Conservation Tasks

Source: Adapted from Berger & Thompson, 1995.

Type of Conservation	Initial Presentation	Transformation	Question	Preoperational Child's Answer
Liquids	Two equal glasses of liquid	Pour one into a taller, narrower glass	Which glass contains more?	The taller one
Number	Two equal lines of checkers	Increase spacing of checkers in one line	Which line has more checkers?	The longer one
Mass	Two equal balls of clay	Squeeze one ball into a long, thin shape	Which piece has more clay?	The long one
Length	Two sticks of equal length	Move one stick	Which stick is longer?	The one that is farther to the right

Which Beaker Holds More Juice?
Preoperational children fail to recognize that the quantity of an object remains the same when placed in a different-size container.

animistic thinking   To Piaget, the child's belief that inanimate objects have living qualities.

irreversibility   To Piaget, the inability to reverse the direction of a sequence of events to their starting point.

centration   To Piaget, the tendency to focus on only one aspect of a situation at a time.

conservation   In Piaget's theory, the ability to recognize that the quantity or amount of an object remains constant despite superficial changes in its outward appearance.

Egocentrism leads to another type of thinking typical of the preoperational child: **animistic thinking**. The child believes that inanimate objects like the moon, the sun, and the clouds have living qualities such as wishes, thoughts, and feelings just as she or he does. A 4-year-old, for instance, may think the moon is his friend and follows him as he walks home with his parents at night.

Two other limitations of the preoperational child's thinking are irreversibility and centration. **Irreversibility** is the inability to reverse the direction of a sequence of events to their starting point. **Centration** is the tendency to focus on only one aspect of a situation at a time to the exclusion of all other aspects.

Piaget illustrated these principles through his famous **conservation** tasks (see Figure 9.6). (Conservation, the hallmark of the concrete operational stage, is discussed in the next section.) In a volume conservation task, the child is shown two identical glasses of water. Once the child agrees that the glasses contain the same amounts of water, the water in one glass is poured into a shorter, wider glass, which causes the water to come to rest at a lower level in the shorter glass than in the taller one. The preoperational child now insists that the taller, narrower glass contains more water. Because of centration, the child focuses on only one thing: the height of the column of water. Because of irreversibility, the child fails to recognize that the process can be reversed to its starting point—that pouring the water back into its original container would restore it to its original state.

Concrete Operational Stage: Seven to Eleven Years   The stage of concrete operations is marked by the development of conservation. To Piaget, conservation is the ability to recognize that the amount or quantity of a substance does not change if its outward appearance is changed, so long as nothing is either added to it or subtracted from it. The kinds of conservation tasks that stymied the 6-year-old become mere "child's play" to the average 7-or-8-year-old. The child at the concrete operational stage is able to mentally reverse the process in the conservation task and recognize that the amount of water doesn't change when poured into a container of a different shape. The child also becomes capable of decentered thinking, the ability to take into account more than one aspect of a situation at a time. The child now recognizes that a rise in the water level in the narrower container is offset by a change in the width of the column of water.

The child's thinking at this stage also becomes much less egocentric. The child recognizes that other people's thoughts and feelings may differ from his or her own. The child can also perform simple logical operations, but only when they are tied to concrete examples. Seven-year-old Timmy can understand that if he has more baseball cards than Sally and Sally has more than Sam, then he also has more than Sam. But Timmy would have great difficulty understanding the question if it were posed abstractly, such as "If A is greater than B and B is greater than C, is A greater than C?"

Formal Operational Stage The stage of **formal operations** is the final one in Piaget's theory—the stage of full cognitive maturity. In Western societies, formal operational thought tends to begin around puberty, at about age 11 or 12. However, not all children enter this stage at this time, and some never do even as adults. Formal operations are characterized by the ability to think logically about abstract ideas, generate hypotheses, and think deductively. The person with formal operations can think through hypothetical situations, including the "A is greater than B" example earlier. He or she can follow arguments from their premises to their conclusions and back again. We will return to this stage of cognitive development when we consider the thinking processes of the adolescent.

Piaget's Shadow: Evaluating His Legacy Piaget is a luminous figure in the annals of psychology who left a rich legacy that continues to guide an enormous amount of scholarly activity. Concepts such as schemas, assimilation and accommodation, egocentricity, conservation, and irreversibility, among many others, provide researchers with a strong basis for understanding cognitive processes in children and how they change during development. Piaget was correct in recognizing the dramatic shifts in cognitive structures and abilities that occur during infancy and childhood. He encouraged us to view children not as passive responders to stimuli but as natural scientists who seek to understand the world and to operate on it. Although Piaget's theory of cognitive development offers many insights into the mental abilities of children, a number of criticisms of his theory have emerged, as we see next.

Some theorists challenge Piaget's basic premise that cognitive development unfolds in stages. They believe a child's cognitive abilities develop through a more continuous process of gradual change over time (e.g., Bjorklund, 1995). Critics also contend that Piaget underestimated the abilities of young children (Haith & Benson, 1997; Meltzoff & Gopnik, 1997). We noted earlier, for example, that even newborns can imitate facial expressions. Piaget believed this ability doesn't develop until late in the first year. Evidence also suggests that children may begin to develop object permanence and the ability to view events from other people's perspectives at earlier ages than Piaget's model would suppose (Aguiara & Baillargeon, 2002; Flavell, 1992; Munakata et al., 1997).

Another frequent criticism of Piaget is that he failed to account for cultural differences in the timing by which these stages unfold. In some respects, Piaget was right: Evidence from cross-cultural studies shows that children do progress through the stages of cognitive development in the order Piaget described (Dasen, 1994). But cross-cultural evidence also shows that the ages at which children pass through these stages depend greatly on cultural factors.

Despite these challenges, Piaget's observations and teachings about how children develop have provided a guiding framework for generations of researchers to study and explore, and they will likely continue to do so for future generations.

Vygotsky's Sociocultural Theory of Cognitive Development

Whereas Piaget focused on children's understanding of their physical environment—the world of objects and things—the Russian psychologist Lev Vygotsky (1978, 1986) was concerned primarily with how children come to understand their social world. He believed that cultural learning is acquired through a gradual process of social interactions between children and parents, teachers, and other

---

TRY THIS OUT

Learning Through Observation

You may be able to acquire more direct knowledge of children's cognitive development by serving as a volunteer in a nursery or preschool setting. To what extent does the cognitive development of preschoolers correspond to Piaget's concepts of egocentrism, animistic thought, centration, and irreversibility?

CONCEPT 9.18
Though Piaget continues to have an enormous impact on the field of developmental psychology, a number of challenges to his theory have surfaced.

CONCEPT 9.19
Vygotsky's theory of cognitive development emphasizes the role of social and cultural factors.

formal operations The level of full cognitive maturity in Piaget's theory, characterized by the ability to think in abstract terms.

CONCEPT CHART 9.4
Theories of Cognitive Development

Theory	Overview	
Piaget's theory of cognitive development	Piaget emphasized the role of adaptation in cognitive development, which he believed consists of two complementary processes: assimilation (incorporation of unfamiliar objects or situations into existing schemas) and accommodation (modification of existing schemas or creation of new ones to take into account new objects and situations).	
Piaget's stages of cognitive development	The child progresses through a fixed sequence of stages involving qualitative leaps in ability and ways of understanding and interacting with the world.	
	Sensorimotor stage (birth to 2 years)	During the sensorimotor stage (birth to 2 years), the child uses its senses and developing motor skills to explore and act upon the world. The child begins to develop a concept of object permanence, which is the recognition that objects continue to exist even if they are not presently in sight.
	Preoperational stage (2 to 7 years)	By this stage, which lasts from about age 2 through about age 7, the child acquires the ability to use language to symbolize objects and actions in words. Yet the child's thinking is limited by egocentrism, animistic thought, centration, and irreversibility.
	Concrete operational stage (7 to 11 years)	By the stage of concrete operations, beginning around age 7, the child becomes capable of performing simple logical operations as long as they're tied to concrete problems. A key feature of this stage is the acquisition of the principle of conservation, or ability to recognize that the amount of a substance does not change if its shape or size is rearranged.
	Formal operational stage (begins around puberty)	The child becomes capable of abstract thinking during the stage of formal operations, which typically begins around the time of puberty (about age 11 or 12). Yet not all children, nor all adults, progress to this stage.
Critique of Piaget's theory	Piaget's observations and teachings remain a guiding framework for understanding cognitive development, but his theory has been challenged on some grounds, including the ages at which he believed children acquire certain abilities and his lack of attention to cultural factors in development.	
Vygotsky's sociocultural theory	Vygotsky emphasizes the social interaction between children and adults as the basis for the child's acquisition of skills, values, and behaviors needed to meet the demands imposed by the particular culture.	

members of the culture. These interactions provide the basis for acquiring knowledge that children need to solve everyday challenges and to meet the demands the culture imposes on them. In Vygotsky's view, the adult is the expert and the child is the novice, and the relationship between them is one of tutor and student.

To Vygotsky, children are born as cultural blank slates (Zukow-Goldring, 1997). They must learn the skills, values, and behaviors valued by the given culture. In American culture, this social knowledge includes such everyday behaviors as using the proper eating utensils, brushing teeth before bed, saying "excuse me" after sneezing, and waiting in line patiently.

Vygotsky emphasized that social learning occurs within a **zone of proximal development (ZPD)**, also called the *zone of potential development*. The ZPD refers to the range between the skills children can currently perform and those they could perform if they received proper guidance and instruction. Working in the "zone" means that people with greater expertise are providing less experienced individuals, or novices, with the instruction the novices need to surpass or "stretch" what they would otherwise be able to accomplish on their own (Zukow-Goldring, 1997).

Concept Chart 9.4 provides an overview of the two theories of cognitive development reviewed in this module.

zone of proximal development (ZPD)
In Vygotsky's theory, the range between children's present level of knowledge and their potential knowledge state if they receive proper guidance and instruction.

MODULE 9.3 REVIEW

Years of Discovery: Emotional, Social, and Cognitive Development in Childhood

CONCEPT CHECK

1. Unlike the developmental concept of bonding, attachment
   a. occurs in the hours of contact immediately after birth.
   b. takes time to develop, at least over the course of infancy.
   c. does not seem to be as crucial to a young child's well-being.
   d. refers to the parent's ties to the infant.

2. Match the following types of attachment identified by Ainsworth and other researchers to the appropriate descriptions below: (a) secure; (b) insecure-avoidant; (c) insecure-resistant; (d) disorganized/disoriented.
   i.   child clings to mother, yet shows signs of ambivalence or negativity
   ii. mother is an important "base" for exploration; child is happy in mother's presence
   iii. child appears confused; seems unable to utilize mother for any support
   iv. child ignores mother when she is present and is unaffected by her departure or return

3. Parenting style is an important influence on children's development. Which of the following terms describes a parent who is warm, supportive, and consistent; understands the child's point of view; and communicates well?
   a. permissive   c. authoritative
   b. authoritarian   d. laissez-faire

4. In which of the following stages in Erikson's theory of psychosocial development do children compare their abilities to those of their friends and classmates?
   a. Stage 1: trust versus mistrust
   b. Stage 2: autonomy versus shame and doubt
   c. Stage 3: initiative versus guilt
   d. Stage 4: industry versus inferiority

5. In which stage does Piaget suggest a child learns by interacting with the environment through using his or her senses and developing motor skills?
   a. sensorimotor   c. concrete operational
   b. preoperational   d. formal operational

MODULE 9.4 Adolescence

- **What is puberty?**
- **What changes in cognitive development occur during adolescence?**
- **What are Kohlberg's levels of moral reasoning?**
- **Why did Gilligan criticize Kohlberg's theory?**
- **What did Erikson believe is the major developmental challenge of adolescence?**

During **adolescence**, the young person's body may seem to be sprouting in all directions at once. Adolescents may wonder what they will look like next year or even next month—who and what they will be. Intellectually they may feel they are suddenly grown-ups, or expected to act as though they are, as they tackle more demanding subjects in middle school and high school and are expected to begin thinking seriously about what lies ahead for them when they leave high school. Yet their parents and teachers may continue to treat them as children—children masquerading in adult bodies who often must be restrained for their own good. Adolescents may find themselves in constant conflict with their parents over issues such as dating, using the family car, spending money, and_____ (you fill in the blank). At a time when young people are stretching their wings and preparing to fly on their own, they remain financially, and often emotionally, dependent on their parents. No wonder the early psychologist and founder of the American Psychological Association, G. Stanley Hall, characterized adolescence as a time of *sturm und drang,* or "storm and stress." Contemporary research bears out

adolescence The period of life beginning at puberty and ending with early adulthood.

TABLE 9.5 A Snapshot of Today's Teens
A snapshot of today's teens at the turn of the new millennium:
70% say they face more stress than their parents did as teens
48% say they use a computer almost every day at home
21% say they have looked at something on the Internet that they wouldn't want their parents to know about
59% worry about violence in society
56% worry about sexually transmitted diseases
54% worry about the cost of a college education
43% worry about their future job opportunities
69% say they would rather accomplish something outstanding than fit in with their friends
24% say they spend too little time with their parents, 15% say they spend too much time, while 61% say they spend enough time

Source: Newsweek, May 8, 2000, p. 56.

THINK

About It

Sturm und Drang

Was your adolescence a period of *sturm und drang* (storm and stress), or was it relatively peaceful? Why do you suppose some teenagers move through adolescence with relative ease, whereas others find it a difficult period? What made adolescence easy or difficult for you?

CONCEPT 9.20

The major event in physical development in adolescence is puberty, the period of physical growth and sexual maturation during which we attain full sexual maturity.

puberty The stage of development at which individuals become physiologically capable of reproducing.

secondary sex characteristics Physical characteristics that differentiate males and females but are not directly involved in reproduction.

primary sex characteristics Physical characteristics, such as the gonads, that differentiate males and females and play a direct role in reproduction.

menarche The first menstruation.

the belief that many, though certainly not all, young people experience adolescence as a turbulent, pressure-ridden period. Table 9.5 offers a snapshot of today's teenagers.

Let us now consider the physical, cognitive, social, and emotional changes that occur during the years when many young people feel they are betwixt and between—no longer children but not quite adults.

Physical Development

After the rapid growth that takes place during infancy, children typically gain two to three inches and four to six pounds a year until the growth spurt of adolescence. The spurt lasts for two to three years, during which time adolescents may shoot up eight inches to one foot or more. Girls experience their growth spurt earlier than boys, so they may be taller than their male agemates for a while. But boys, on the average, eventually surpass girls in height and body weight. Boys also develop greater upper-body musculature.

The major landmark of physical development during adolescence is **puberty**, the period in which young people reach full sexual maturity (see Figure 9.7). Puberty begins with the appearance of **secondary sex characteristics**, physical characteristics that differentiate men and women but are not directly involved in reproduction, such as pubic hair, breast development, and deepening of the voice. **Primary sex characteristics** also emerge; these are changes in sex organs directly involved in reproduction, such as enlargement of the testes and penis in boys and of the uterus in girls. Puberty lasts about three to four years, by the end of which time adolescents become physically capable of reproduction.

Girls typically experience **menarche**, the beginning of menstruation, between ages ten and eighteen, or at an average age of twelve to thirteen (Kolata, 2001a; Ravert & Martin, 1997). Girls today enter puberty and experience menarche at much earlier ages than did girls in previous generations. The average European American girl today shows breast development and other signs of puberty by age ten, compared to age fifteen at the beginning of the twentieth century (Brody, 1999; Kantrowitz & Wingert, 1999). The average African American girl today begins showing signs of puberty and experiences menarche at a somewhat earlier age (Anderson et al., 2003; Belkin, 2000).

The timing of puberty may have different consequences for boys and girls. For earlier-maturing boys, their greater size and strength give them an advantage in

Figure 9.7 Physical Changes Occurring During Puberty
This graph illustrates a number of changes occurring during puberty in boys and girls. Note how the growth spurt begins sooner in girls than boys. Note too that the graph represents the average ages at which these changes occur and that growth patterns in individuals often vary from these averages.

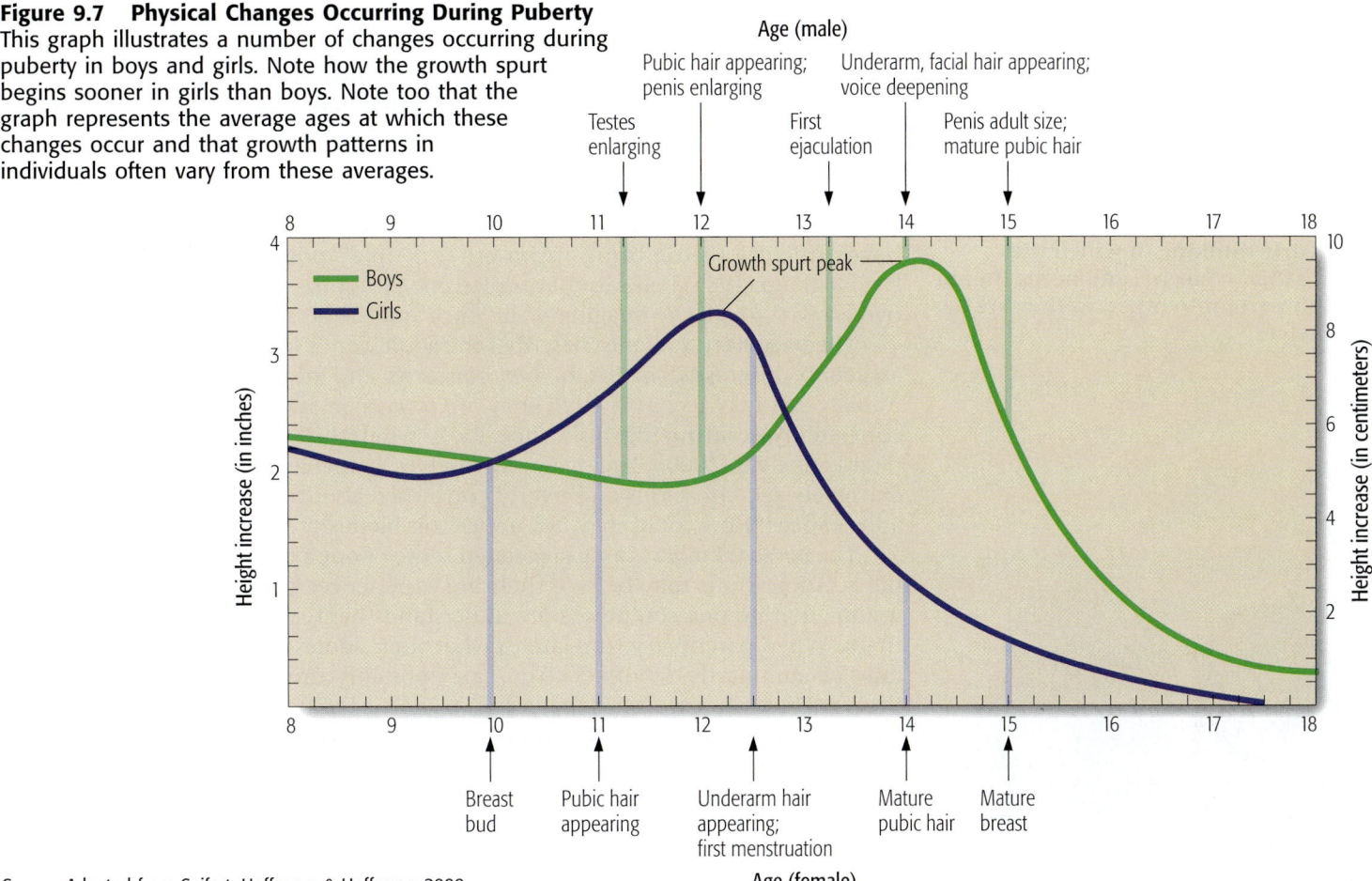

Source: Adapted from Seifert, Hoffnung, & Hoffnung, 2000.

athletics and contribute to a more positive self-image. Later-maturing boys tend to be less popular than earlier-maturing boys and may be subject to ridicule or become socially ostracized (Berger, 2001). Early-maturing boys are also more likely to engage in deviant social behavior such as drinking, smoking, or breaking the law (Duncan et al., 1985). But overall, earlier maturation in boys is associated with more positive outcomes.

For girls, the most obvious physical sign of maturation is the development of breasts. Earlier-maturing girls may encounter unwelcome sexual attention and believe they no longer "fit in" with their peers. They tend to have lower self-esteem, a more negative body image, and more symptoms of depression than later-maturing girls (Caspi & Moffitt, 1991; Ge et al., 2003; Stattin & Magnusson, 1990). Research suggests that the ways in which people react to the physical changes associated with maturation, rather than the changes themselves, are what account for the social and emotional effects of pubertal timing.

The physical changes of adolescence may be the most obvious signs of adolescent development. However, major changes in cognitive abilities and social behavior also occur during adolescence. We consider these developments next.

Cognitive Development

Piaget noted that not all adolescents, or even adults, reach the stage of formal operations in which they are capable of abstract thinking. People who develop formal operational thought become capable of creating hypothetical situations

CONCEPT 9.21
Adolescents who develop formal operational thinking become capable of solving abstract problems.

and scenarios and playing them through in their minds. They can mount an argument in favor of something that runs counter to their own views (Flavell, Miller, & Miller, 20023). They are also able to use deductive reasoning in which one derives conclusions about specific cases or individuals based on a set of premises. For example, they may deduce "who-done-it" from the facts of a crime long before the guilty party in the television drama is revealed.

The ability to think abstractly doesn't mean adolescents are free from egocentric thinking. As Piaget noted, preschoolers are egocentric in the sense that they have difficulty seeing things from other people's points of view. Psychologist David Elkind (1985) believes that adolescent egocentrism basically reveals itself in two ways: through the imaginary audience and the personal fable.

The **imaginary audience** describes the adolescent's belief that other people are as keenly interested in his or her concerns and needs as the adolescent is. Adolescents may feel as though they are always on stage, as though all eyes are continually scrutinizing how they look, what they wear, and how they act (Frankenberger, 2000). They view themselves as the center of attention and feel extremely self-conscious and overly concerned about the slightest flaw in their appearance ("How could they not notice this blemish? Everybody will notice!").

The **personal fable** is an exaggerated sense of one's uniqueness and invulnerability. Adolescents may believe their life experiences or personal feelings are so unique that no one could possibly understand them, let alone have experienced them. When parents try to relate to what their adolescent is experiencing, they may be summarily rebuffed: "You can't possibly understand what I'm going through!" Another aspect of the personal fable is the belief that "Bad things can't happen to me." This sense of personal invulnerability may underlie risky behavior patterns such as reckless driving, unsafe sex, and getting drunk (Arnett, 1992; Cohn et al., 1995). Indeed, teenagers tend to underestimate the dangers posed by such behaviors (Cohn et al., 1995), leading them to engage in riskier behaviors than they might otherwise had they judged risks more accurately. Factors such as poor school performance, having close friends who engage in risky behavior, impulsivity, and strained family relationships are also linked to riskier health behaviors, including drinking, smoking, engaging in sexual intercourse, and suicide attempts (Blum et al., 2000; Carpenter, 2001a; Cooper et al., 2003). (Adolescent suicide is discussed further in Chapter 11.)

The developing cognitive abilities of adolescents change the way they see the world, including themselves, family and friends, and broad social and moral issues. These changes influence the ways people form judgments about questions of right and wrong, as we will see next.

💡 CONCEPT 9.22
Adolescents often show a form of egocentric thinking in which they believe their concerns and needs should be as important to others as they are to themselves.

How Could They Not Notice?
Adolescents may constantly scrutinize their appearance and become overly concerned about the slightest flaw.

Kohlberg's Stages of Moral Reasoning

Psychologist Lawrence Kohlberg (1927–1987) studied how individuals make moral judgments about conflict-laden issues. He was interested in the process by which people arrive at moral choices—what makes something right or wrong—rather than in the particular choices they make. He developed a methodology in which he presented subjects with hypothetical situations involving conflicting moral values, or moral dilemmas. Let's look at his most famous example:

> In Europe, a woman lies near death from a certain type of cancer. Only one drug that might save her is available, from a druggist in the same town who is charging ten times what it costs him to make it. Lacking this sum, the woman's husband, Heinz, attempts to borrow money from everyone he knows but can raise only about half the amount. Heinz tells the druggist his wife is dying and pleads with him to sell it for less so he can buy it now or allow him to pay for it later. The druggist refuses. Desperate, Heinz breaks into the druggist's store and steals the drug to give to his wife. (Adapted from Kohlberg, 1969)

Now Kohlberg poses the questions: "Should Heinz have stolen the drug? Why or why not?" Here we have the making of a moral dilemma, a situation that pits

imaginary audience The common belief among adolescents that they are the center of other people's attention.

personal fable The common belief among adolescents that their feelings and experiences cannot possibly be understood by others and that they are personally invulnerable to harm.

two opposing moral values against each other—in this case, the moral injunction against stealing versus the human value of attempting to save the life of a loved one. Kohlberg believed that one's level of moral development is reflected in the way one reasons about the moral dilemma, not in whether one believes the behavior in question was right or wrong.

Based on his studies of responses to these types of hypothetical situations, Kohlberg determined that moral development progresses through a sequence of six stages organized into three levels of moral reasoning: the preconventional level, the conventional level, and the postconventional level.

Preconventional Level Children at the *preconventional level* base their moral judgments on the perceived consequences of behavior. Kohlberg divided preconventional moral reasoning into two stages. Stage 1 is characterized by an *obedience and punishment orientation:* Good behavior is defined simply as behavior that avoids punishment by an external authority. In our example, we might reason that Heinz should take the drug because if he does not, he may be blamed for his wife's death; or he shouldn't take the drug because he could get caught and sent to jail. Stage 2 represents an *instrumental purpose orientation:* A behavior is judged good when it serves the person's needs or interests. Thus, we might reason that Heinz should have taken the drug because, by saving his wife, he would ensure that she'd be available to meet his needs for companionship, love, and support; or Heinz shouldn't have taken the drug because if he were caught and sent to jail, he would have done neither himself nor his wife any good.

Conventional Level At the *conventional level,* moral reasoning is based on conformity with conventional rules of right and wrong. Individuals at this level recognize that the purpose of social rules is to preserve the social order and ensure harmonious relationships among people.

Stage 3 is characterized by a *"good boy–good girl" orientation:* Individuals believe that conformity with rules and regulations is important because of the need to be perceived by others as a "good boy" or a "good girl." They value the need to do the "right thing" in the eyes of others. Thus, Heinz should steal the drug because others would be displeased with him for failing to help save his wife's life; or Heinz should not steal the drug because if he is caught, he will bring dishonor on himself and his family.

Stage 4 has an *authority* or *law-and-order orientation.* Moral reasoning now goes beyond the need to gain approval from others: Rules must be obeyed and applied evenhandedly because they are needed for the orderly functioning of society. Each of us has a duty to uphold the law, simply because it is the law. Heinz should steal the drug because it is a husband's duty to protect his wife's life, but he must repay the druggist as soon as he is able and accept responsibility and punishment for breaking the law. Or Heinz should not steal the drug because although we may sympathize with his wish to save his wife's life, people cannot be permitted to break the law even when they face such dire circumstances.

Postconventional Level Individuals generally reach the *postconventional level* of moral reasoning during adolescence, if they reach it at all. Postconventional reasoners apply their own moral standards or principles rather than relying on those of authority figures or blindly adhering to social rules or conventions. The postconventional thinker believes that when laws are unjust, a moral person is bound to disobey them. In Kohlberg's (1969) studies, only about one in four people had reached the postconventional level by age sixteen. Even in adulthood, most people remain at the level of conventional moral reasoning.

Kohlberg identified two stages of postconventional moral reasoning. Stage 5, the *social contract orientation,* involves the belief that laws are based on mutual agreement among members of a society, but are not infallible. They should be open to question rather than followed blindly out of respect for authority. Stage 5 reasoners weigh the rights of the individual against the rights of society. They might argue that although laws should be obeyed, protection of a life is a more important value than protection of property, and so an exception should be made

CONCEPT 9.23
Psychologist Lawrence Kohlberg explored how individuals make moral judgments; his theory of moral development consists of a sequence of six stages organized in terms of three levels of moral reasoning.

in Heinz's case. Or they might reason that individuals must obey the law because the common good takes precedence over the individual good and that the ends, no matter how noble they may be, do not justify the means.

Stage 6 thinking involves adoption of *universal ethical principles,* an underlying set of self-chosen, abstract ethical principles that serve as a guiding framework for moral judgments. Beliefs in the sanctity of human life or in the "Golden Rule" exemplify such universal ethical principles. People at this stage are guided by their own internal moral compass, regardless of the dictates of society's laws or the opinions of others. They may believe that if laws devalue the sanctity of human life, it becomes *immoral* to obey them. Hence it would be immoral for Heinz to obey laws that would ultimately devalue the sanctity of his wife's life. Kohlberg believed that very few people, even those within the postconventional level, reach Stage 6. Concept Chart 9.5 summarizes the six stages of moral reasoning in Kohlberg's model.

Kohlberg's model of moral development continues to foster understanding of how people develop a sense of morality. But does moral reasoning dictate moral behavior? Do people who achieve higher levels of moral reasoning in Kohlberg's system actually practice what they preach? The answer seems to be that although there is some overlap between moral reasoning and moral behavior, situational factors are more likely to determine how people act when confronted by ethical or moral dilemmas (Bandura, 1986).

CONCEPT CHART 9.5
Kohlberg's Levels and Stages of Moral Development

	Stage of Moral Reasoning	Arguments Favoring Heinz Stealing the Drug	Arguments Against Heinz Stealing the Drug
LEVEL I Preconventional Level	**Stage 1:** Obedience and punishment orientation; behavior is judged good if it serves to avoid punishment	Heinz should steal the drug to avoid being blamed if his wife dies.	Heinz shouldn't steal the drug because he would be punished for stealing it if he were caught and would be sent to jail.
	Stage 2: Instrumental purpose orientation; behavior is judged good when it serves personal needs or interests	Heinz should steal the drug because he needs his wife and she might die without it.	Heinz would likely be sent to prison and his wife would probably die before he gets out, so it wouldn't do her or himself any good to steal the drug.
LEVEL II Conventional Level	**Stage 3:** "Good boy–good girl" orientation; conforming with rules to impress others	People would lose respect for Heinz if he didn't at least try to save his wife by stealing the drug.	Heinz shouldn't take the drug because others will see him as a criminal, and that would bring shame and dishonor to his family.
	Stage 4: Authority or law-and-order orientation; obeying rules and laws because they are needed to maintain social order	Heinz must steal the drug because he has a duty to protect his wife. People need to do their duty even if they might get punished for it.	People should not be permitted to break the law under any circumstances. The law must be respected.
LEVEL III Postconventional Level	**Stage 5:** Social contract orientation; viewing rules and laws as based on mutual agreement in the service of the common good.	While laws should be obeyed to maintain order in society, an exception should be made in Heinz's case because a law should not take precedence over protecting a human life.	Though Heinz faces a difficult choice, he reasons that respect for the law outweighs individual needs no matter what the circumstances.
	Stage 6: Universal ethical principle orientation; adopting an internal moral code based on universal values that takes precedence over social rules and laws.	Heinz would be morally wrong not to steal the drug because it would violate his belief in the absolute value of a human life.	Sometimes doing what we believe is right requires personal sacrifice. If Heinz truly feels that stealing is worse than letting his wife die, he must not steal the drug.

Source: Adapted from Kohlberg, 1981.

Cross-Cultural and Gender-Based Research on Kohlberg's Model

Evidence supports the view that children and adolescents progress through the stages Kohlberg suggested, even if they may not reach the level of postconventional reasoning (Flavell, Miller, & Miller, 1993; Walker, 1989). Moreover, Kohlberg's own studies of people in other countries led him to believe in the universality of his first four stages, a belief that was later supported by a review of forty-four studies conducted in twenty-seven countries (Snarey, 1985). Nevertheless, critics have challenged Kohlberg's model for both cultural and gender biases.

Critics contend that Kohlberg's model may be culturally biased because it emphasizes ideals found primarily in Western cultures, such as individual rights and social justice (Shweder, 1994). Cross-cultural evidence based on a study comparing moral reasoning in Americans and Indians showed cultural differences in the priorities placed on justice and interpersonal considerations (Miller & Bersoff, 1992). Americans placed greater value than did Indians on a justice orientation in determining morally correct choices—believing that what is just or fair governs what is right. Indians placed a greater weight on interpersonal responsibilities, such as upholding one's obligations to others and being responsive to other people's needs.

Harvard psychologist Carol Gilligan addressed the issue of gender bias in Kohlberg's work. Earlier research applying Kohlberg's model suggested that men attained higher levels of moral reasoning than women did. Gilligan did not believe women are less capable of developing moral reasoning; rather, she argued that Kohlberg's model was gender-biased because it had been derived entirely from studies of male subjects. The voices of girls and women had not been heard.

Gilligan began listening to women's views and soon discovered that women applied a different moral standard than men (Gilligan, 1982). She found that females adopted a *care orientation,* whereas males applied a *justice orientation.* Young men appealed to abstract principles of justice, fairness, and rights in making moral judgments of right and wrong. They would argue, for example, that Heinz should steal the drug because the value of life supercedes that of property. Young women sought solutions that responded both to the druggist's needs to protect his property and to Heinz's need to save his wife—solutions that expressed a caring attitude and the need to preserve the relationship between them. However, because young women are less willing to apply abstract moral principles when facing ethical situations like that of Heinz, they may be classified at lower levels in Kohlberg's system. Gilligan argued that the moral standards of men and women represent two different ways of thinking about moral behavior, with neither way standing on higher moral ground than the other.

Researchers find partial support for Gilligan's belief in gender differences in moral reasoning (e.g., Jaffee & Hyde, 2000; Walker, 1997). Females do place somewhat more emphasis on the care orientation, whereas males place somewhat greater stress on the justice orientation. However, there is little support for the view that men adopt primarily a justice orientation in making moral judgments or that women adopt primarily a care orientation (Jaffee & Hyde, 2000). Nor is there much evidence of systematic biases against females in how they are classified according to Kohlberg's model. On the whole, Gilligan's work remains influential, partly because it encourages investigators to listen to female voices and partly because it encourages young women to find and develop their own voices.

CONCEPT 9.24
Though evidence generally supports Kohlberg's stage model of moral reasoning, critics contend that his model may contain cultural and gender biases.

Psychosocial Development

In this section we examine the psychosocial development of adolescents as they negotiate the transition from childhood to young adulthood. Throughout we focus on their relationships with parents and peers and the challenges they face in establishing a clear psychological identity of their own. We also consider an aspect of psychosocial development that often takes center stage during adolescence: sexuality.

Adolescent-Parent Relationships

Adolescent yearnings for independence often lead to some degree of withdrawal from family members and to arguments with parents over issues of autonomy and decision making. Such distancing may be healthy during adolescence, as young people need to form meaningful relationships outside the family and develop a sense of independence and social competence. Yet research indicates that adolescents and their parents typically express love and respect for each other and agreement on many of the principal issues in life (Arnett, 2004). Though disagreements with parents are common, serious conflict is neither normal nor helpful for adolescents. Parents also influence their adolescents in more subtle ways, and not always for the better. For example, adolescents tend to mimic their parents' health-related behaviors, which may include negative behaviors such as smoking (Kodl & Mermelstein, 2004).

By psychologically separating from their parents, adolescents may begin to grapple with the major psychosocial challenge they face: developing a clear sense of themselves and of their future direction in life. As we will see next, the theorist Erik Erikson believed that the process of coming to terms with the question "Who am I?" represents the major life challenge of adolescence.

Identity Versus Role Diffusion: Who Am I?

Earlier we saw that Erik Erikson believed children progress through a series of four stages of psychosocial development. Erikson's fifth stage of psychosocial development occurs during adolescence: the stage of *identity versus role diffusion*.

Ego identity is the attainment of a firm sense of self—who one is, where one is headed in life, and what one believes in. People who achieve ego identity clearly understand their personal needs, values, and life goals. Erikson coined the term **identity crisis** to describe the stressful period of soul-searching and serious self-examination that many adolescents experience when struggling to develop a set of personal values and direction in life. Although Erikson believed that an identity crisis is a normal part of the development of the healthy personality, some contemporary scholars use the term *exploration* rather than *crisis* to avoid implying that the process of examining one's different possibilities in life is inherently fraught with anguish and struggle (Arnett, 2004).

Conflicts with Parents Though conflicts between adolescents and parents are common, most adolescents say they have good relationships with their parents.

Adolescents who successfully weather an identity crisis emerge as their own persons, as people who have achieved a state of ego identity. Ego identity, however, continues to develop throughout life. Our occupational goals and our political, moral, and religious beliefs often change over time. Therefore, we may weather many identity crises in life.

Many adolescents or adults never grapple with an identity crisis. No, it's not the stressful period of life they avoid; it's the identity crisis. They may develop a firm sense of ego identity by modeling themselves after others, especially parents, without undergoing any type of identity crisis. Others may fail to develop a clear sense of ego identity. They stay at sea, aimlessly taking each day as it comes without any clear values or goals. They remain in a state of **role diffusion**, a confused and drifting state in which they lack direction in life. They may be especially vulnerable to negative peer influences such as illicit drug use.

Peer Relationships

As adolescents experiment with greater independence, peer relationships become increasingly important influences in their psychosocial development. "Fitting in" or belonging comes to play an even greater role in determining their self-esteem and emotional adjustment.

Parents are often concerned that their teenagers may "run with the wrong crowd." They tend to perceive their teens as being subject to a greater amount of peer pressure to engage in negative behaviors such as stealing or alcohol or drug use than do the teens themselves (see Table 9.6). Evidence bears out at least some parental concerns, as studies show that peer pressure is a major determinant of adolescent tobacco, alcohol, and marijuana use and sexual intercourse (Curran, Stice, & Chassin, 1997; Thompson, 1995; Wills & Cleary, 1999). However, studies with Hispanic and African American teens show that family support can reduce the negative influence of drug-using peers on the teens' use of tobacco and other drugs (Farrell & White, 1998; Frauenglass et al., 1997). Parent-adolescent connectedness has protective effects not only against substance abuse but also against emotional distress, suicidal thoughts and behavior, and violent behavior (Resnick et al., 1997).

Why do some teens become sexually active whereas others abstain? For one thing, peer pressure, whether real or imagined, can promote or restrain sexual activity. Moral reasons, on the other hand, are often a basis for restraint. Teens who abstain may also be concerned about getting caught, becoming pregnant, or contracting a sexually transmitted disease. Other factors linked to teens' sexual

CONCEPT 9.27
Peer pressure is an important influence in the social and emotional development of adolescents.

 **Netlab/Peers and Psychological Development**

TABLE 9.6   Teens and Peer Pressure

"How much peer pressure from friends do you feel (does your teen feel) today to do the following?"

Those Responding "a lot"	Teens	Parents
Have sex	10%	20%
Grow up too fast	16	34
Steal or shoplift	4	18
Use drugs or abuse alcohol	10	10
Defy parents or teachers	9	16
Be mean to kids who are different	11	14

Source: Newsweek poll, based on a national sample of teens 13 to 19 years of age and 509 parents of these teens. Results reported in *Newsweek*, May 8, 2000, p. 56.

role diffusion In Erikson's model, a lack of direction or aimlessness with respect to one's role in life or public identity.

restraint include the following (Carvajal et al., 1999; Hardy & Raffaelli, 2003; Keith et al., 1991; McBride, Paikoff, & Holmbeck, 2003):

- Living in an intact family
- Having a family with low levels of conflict
- Having at least one parent who graduated from college
- Placing importance on religion and attending religious services frequently

Many gay adolescents face the challenge of coming to terms with their sexuality against the backdrop of social condemnation and discrimination against gays in the broader culture (Meyer, 2003). Their struggle for self-acceptance often requires stripping away layers of denial about their sexuality. Some gay men and lesbians fail to achieve a "coming out" to themselves—that is, a personal acceptance of their sexual orientation—until young or middle adulthood. The process of achieving self-acceptance can be so difficult that many gay adolescents consider or even attempt suicide (Bagley & D'Augelli, 2000).

Before we leave our discussion of adolescence, it's important to note that most adolescents are generally happy and optimistic about their futures (Arnett, 2004). Though adolescents may have wider and more frequent changes in moods than adults, most of their mood swings fall within a mild range. However, adolescents who undergo more intense negative events, such as peer rejection, school problems, a failed romantic relationship, or serious conflicts with parents, are more likely than others to experience significant psychological distress, especially depression (Buchanan et al., 1992; Monroe et al., 1999).

MODULE 9.4 REVIEW

Adolescence

CONCEPT CHECK

1. The physical growth period during which young people mature sexually and reach their full reproductive capacity is known as _____.
   a. adolescence
   b. menarche
   c. formal operations
   d. puberty

2. The beginning of menstruation is called _____.

3. What are two ways in which egocentric thinking becomes expressed during adolescence?

4. Lawrence Kohlberg posed moral dilemmas to children and then classified their responses. Children whose responses indicated that they based their moral judgments on the perceived consequences of actions were classified at the _____ level of moral reasoning.
   a. preconventional   c. concrete operational
   b. conventional   d. postconventional

5. Cite two types of biases for which Kohlberg's theory has been criticized.

6. According to Erikson, what is the major psychosocial challenge facing adolescents?
   a. trust versus mistrust   c. identity versus role diffusion
   b. initiative versus guilt   d. intimacy versus inferiority

MODULE 9.5   Early and Middle Adulthood

- What cognitive and physical changes take place as people age?
- How do theorists conceptualize social and personality development during early and middle adulthood?

Development doesn't stop with the end of puberty. Physical and psychological development is a continuing process that lasts a lifetime. Early adulthood encompasses the twenties and thirties. Middle adulthood spans the period from about ages forty to sixty or sixty-five (Lachman, 2004). In this module, we continue our journey through human development by examining the changes in our physical and psychological development that occur as we progress from early adulthood through middle age.

Physical and Cognitive Development

In many respects, physical and cognitive development reach a peak in early adulthood. During their twenties, most people are at their height in terms of memory functioning, ability to learn new skills, sensory acuteness, muscle strength, reaction time, and cardiovascular condition.

By and large, people also perform best on standardized intelligence tests during early adulthood (Baltes, 1997). Some decline in mental functioning is expected as people age during middle and late adulthood. The greatest declines occur in **fluid intelligence**, or mental flexibility—the type of intelligence needed to solve problems quickly, perceive relationships among patterns, remember newly acquired information, form and recognize concepts, and reason abstractly and rapidly (Lachman, 2004). Another form of intelligence, **crystallized intelligence**, represents the person's accumulated knowledge, vocabulary, numerical ability, and ability to apply acquired knowledge. It shows little decline with age and may even improve in certain respects, such as increased vocabulary size (Mayr & Kliegl, 2000; Verhaeghen, 2003) (see Figure 9.8).

Fluid Intelligence

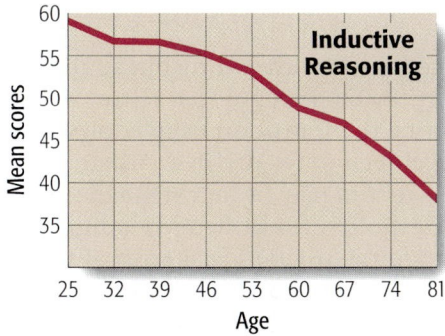

Crystallized Intelligence

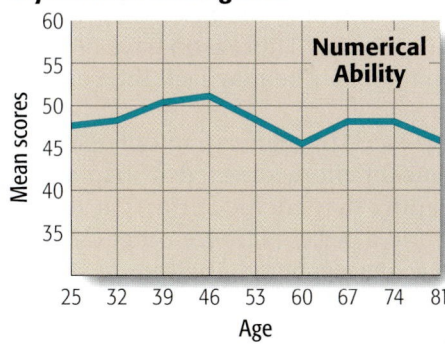
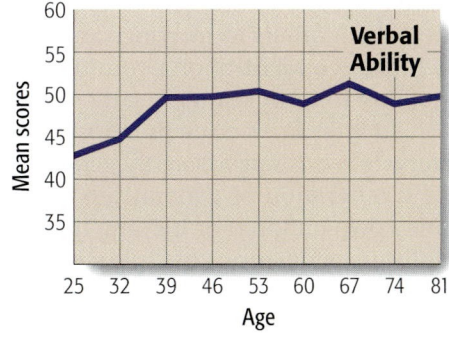

Figure 9.8   Age-Related Changes in Intellectual Ability
Crystallized intelligence, which includes abilities such as verbal meaning (vocabulary comprehension) and numerical skills, remains relatively stable or may even improve as we age. The sharpest declines occur with fluid intelligence, the kind of intelligence needed for abstract reasoning skills, such as inductive reasoning, and spatial orientation.

Source: Schaie, 1996.

fluid intelligence   A form of intelligence associated with the ability to think abstractly and flexibly in solving problems.

crystallized intelligence   A form of intelligence associated with the ability to use accumulated knowledge.

CONCEPT 9.28
Though many cognitive abilities reach a peak in early adulthood, declines in memory functioning that normally occur with age may not interfere with occupational or social functioning.

CONCEPT 9.29
Menopause is a major life event for most women and may symbolize other issues they may face in middle adulthood, including changes in appearance, health, and sexuality.

CONCEPT 9.30
Men experience a gradual decline in production of the male sex hormone testosterone as they age, but unlike women they may maintain reproductive capability well into late adulthood.

CONCEPT 9.31
Psychosocial development in early adulthood often centers on establishing intimate relationships and finding a place in the world.

menopause   The time of life when menstruation ends.

emerging adulthood   The period of psychosocial development, roughly spanning ages eighteen to twenty-five, during which the person makes the transition from adolescence to adulthood.

As people age, they typically experience some decline in memory functioning, especially working memory, memory for recent experiences, lists of words, names just heard, or text just read (Lachman, 2004; Nyberg et al., 2003). Apart from the occasional social embarrassment of fumbling over people's names, cognitive declines in midlife usually occur gradually and may not be noticeable or interfere with social or occupational functioning (Willis & Schaie, 1999). These declines may also be offset by increased knowledge and experience (Miller & Lachman, 2000).

Beginning in the late twenties, people start losing lean body tissue, especially muscle. With each passing decade, they tend to lose about seven pounds of lean body mass as more and more lean tissue turns to fat (Evans & Rosenberg, 1991). From ages 20 to 70, people are likely to lose as much as 30 percent of their muscle cells.

With the loss of muscle tissue comes a gradual loss of muscle strength. A person can help offset this loss, however, by following a regular weight-bearing exercise program. Regular exercise, in combination with a proper diet, can also help prevent significant gains in weight. Major weight gains are neither a normal nor an inevitable consequence of aging.

The most dramatic physical change during middle age is the cessation of menstruation and reproductive capability in women. This biological event, called **menopause**, typically occurs in a woman's late forties or early fifties. With menopause, the ovaries no longer ripen egg cells or produce the sex hormones estrogen and progesterone.

A persistent stereotype about menopause is that it signals the end of the woman's sexual appetite or drive. In fact, a woman's sex drive is fueled by the small amounts of male sex hormones (androgens) produced by her adrenal glands, not by estrogen. Still, the meaning that menopause holds for the individual woman can have a strong bearing on her adjustment. Women who have been raised to believe menopause is connected with a loss of femininity may lose sexual interest or feel less sexually desirable. Others may actually feel liberated by the cutting of ties between sex and reproduction.

Unlike women, men can maintain fertility well into later adulthood. Men do experience a gradual decline in testosterone as they age, in contrast to the sharp decline in estrogen production that occurs in women during menopause.

Psychosocial Development

The challenges of young adulthood have largely to do with sorting out adult roles and relationships (Zucker, Ostrove, & Stewart, 2002). Psychologist Jeffrey Arnett coined the term **emerging adulthood** to describe the transition from adolescence to adulthood that occurs roughly from ages eighteen to twenty-five (Arnett, 2000, 2004). Yet for many young adults today, the twenties may be an extended adolescence, with age thirty becoming the threshold of full-fledged adulthood (Grigoriadis, 2003). Erikson (1963) characterized the psychosocial crisis of young adulthood as one of *intimacy versus isolation*, of forming intimate relationships on the one hand versus remaining lonely and isolated on the other. Young adults who had forged a strong sense of ego identity during adolescence may be prepared in early adulthood to form intimate attachments—to "fuse" their identities—with others in marriage and in lasting friendships. Those who have failed to achieve ego identity or a commitment to a stable life role may lack the personal stability to form lasting, secure relationships.

To Erikson, the key psychosocial challenge faced by adults in midlife pits *generativity versus stagnation*. By generativity, he meant efforts directed at shaping the new generation or generations to come. Shaping may include efforts at raising one's own children or helping to make the world a better place for other children or future generations of children. A failure to achieve generativity leads to stagnation, a kind of self-absorption in which people indulge themselves as though they themselves were "their one and only child" (Erikson, 1980). Research evidence supports Erikson's view that generativity is primarily a task of midlife (Zucker, Ostrove, & Stewart, 2002).

To Erikson, each stage of adult life presents unique challenges that can either strengthen and enrich us or weaken and diminish us. Other investigators and social observers focus less on stages of adult development and more on how people cope with the transitions they face during the course of their lives. For example, psychologist Daniel Levinson and his colleagues (1978) suggested that a midlife transition begins at about age forty. To Levinson, this age is a time of reckoning when we assess our lives in terms of whether or not we have reached the dreams we held in our youth. We may feel life is starting to slip away and realize we are now a full generation older than the youngest of the young adults. We may start to wonder whether we have more to look back on than forward to. Many middle-age adults compare their accomplishments to their earlier dreams and may despair if they find they have fallen short.

This midlife transition may trigger a **midlife crisis**: a sense of entrapment from the closing down of future options, of feeling that life is open-ended no more, of a loss of purpose or a sense of failure from not having fulfilled one's youthful ambitions or aspirations. Yet a midlife crisis is not inevitable and may in fact be more the exception than the rule (Goode, 1999a: Lachman, 2004). Many people in middle adulthood today are focusing on what they believe will be another three to four decades of promise rather than decline.

Concept Chart 9.6 provides an overview of development during young and middle adulthood.

CONCEPT 9.32
Erikson characterized the challenge faced by people in midlife as one of generativity versus stagnation.

CONCEPT 9.33
Although some people experience a midlife crisis, most appear to weather the changes in their middle years without a period of personal upheaval or state of crisis.

CONCEPT CHART 9.6
Development in Young and Middle Adulthood

Physical development	People tend to reach their physical and mental peaks in early adulthood. Declines in lean body tissue and muscle mass begin in the twenties. In middle age, women experience menopause, the cessation of menstruation which is accompanied by a sharp drop in estrogen production. Men encounter a more gradual reduction in testosterone as they age.
Cognitive development	While fluid intelligence tends to decline during middle and late adulthood, crystallized intelligence shows little, if any, decline and may actually improve in some respects. Memory skills, such as the ability to memorize lists of words or names, may show the greatest age-related declines but typically do not have a significant impact on the person's social and occupational functioning.
Psychosocial development	Erikson proposed two stages of psychosocial development in young and middle adulthood, respectively: *intimacy* vs. *isolation* and *generativity* vs. *stagnation*. Levinson focused on the important transitions that occur during adulthood.

midlife crisis   A state of psychological crisis, often occurring during middle adulthood, in which people grapple with the loss of their youth.

MODULE 9.5 REVIEW

Early and Middle Adulthood

CONCEPT CHECK

1. In general, people perform best on standardized tests of intelligence
   a. in middle childhood.
   c. in early adulthood.
   b. in adolescence.
   d. at any time during their lives.

2. Which of the following statements about menopause is *not* true?
   a. Menopause is a normal physiological process.
   b. Menopause involves the cessation of menstruation.
   c. Loss of estrogen results in diminished sex drive.
   d. With menopause, the ovaries no longer produce ripened egg cells.

3. The major psychosocial challenge of early adulthood, according to Erikson, is that of
   a. role identity versus confusion.
   b. intimacy versus isolation.
   c. generativity versus stagnation.
   d. ego integrity versus despair.

4. Psychologist Daniel Levinson believes that at about the age of forty, people experience a time of reckoning or _____.

MODULE 9.6 Late Adulthood

- **What physical and cognitive changes occur in late adulthood?**
- **What is Alzheimer's disease?**
- **How do theorists characterize the psychosocial challenges of late adulthood?**
- **What qualities are associated with successful aging?**
- **What are the stages of dying as identified by Kübler-Ross?**

CONCEPT 9.34
Americans are living longer than ever, on the average.

If you are fortunate enough, you may one day join the ranks of the fastest-growing segment of the population: people ages sixty-five and older. We are in the midst of a "graying of America," an aging of the population that has already begun to have profound effects on our society. Life expectancy has been rising and is expected to keep climbing through at least the middle of the twenty-first century (*Americans Living Longer,* 2002) (see Figure 9.9). So many people are living longer today that the overall age of the population has risen sharply. By the year

Figure 9.9 Increasing Life Expectancy
Life expectancy in the United States increased sharply in the early to mid twentieth century and is expected to increase slightly more through the first half of the twenty-first century.

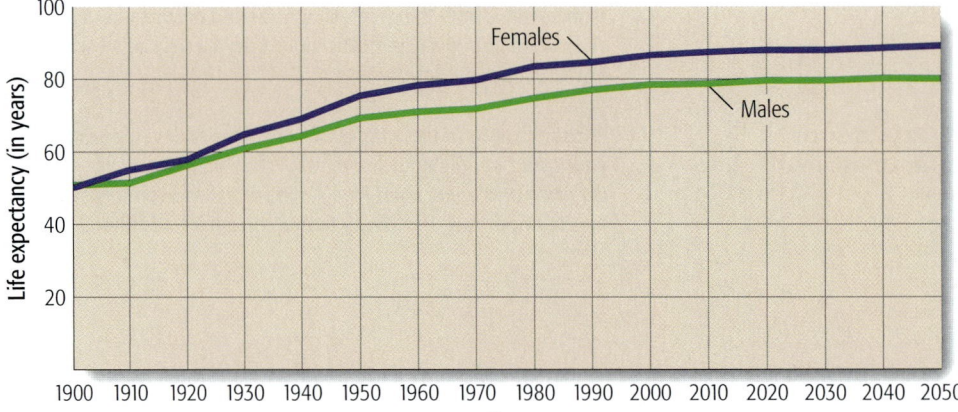

2050, more than one in five Americans—approximately 74 million people—will be in the 65-plus age group (*American Dream,* 2001; Clements, 2003) (see Figure 9.10). The percentage of Americans over age 75 is expected to nearly double by the year 2050, to 11.4 percent, from 5.9 percent in 2000 (Kawas & Brookmeyer, 2001).

A major determinant of psychological adjustment in later life is physical health status. For older adults in good health, reaching age sixty-five is experienced more as an extension of middle age than as entry into old age, particularly if they continue to work.

Physical and Cognitive Development

As people age, they experience a general decline in sensory and motor abilities. They continue to lose bone density as well as muscle mass, and their senses become less acute. The skin loses elasticity, and wrinkles and folds appear. Night vision fades and joints stiffen. Since older people take longer to respond to stimuli, older drivers may require more time to respond to other cars and traffic signals. Declines in the functioning of the immune system, the body's system of defense against disease-causing agents, makes older people more susceptible to illness, including life-threatening illnesses such as cancer.

We noted in Module 9.5 that performance on tasks requiring fluid intelligence also tends to decline as people age. Older people typically require more time to solve problems and have greater difficulties with tasks involving pattern recognition, such as piecing together jigsaw puzzles (Jenkins et al., 2000). In addition, they may encounter more difficulties with memory for new information, such as remembering people's names, and with working memory—keeping information briefly in mind while mulling it over (MacPherson, Phillips, & Della Sala, 2002; Rypma et al., 2001). Nevertheless, declines in memory functioning generally do not significantly impair daily functioning (Burke, 1992; Hertzog & Dunlosky, 1996). Some decline in mental processing speed can also be expected as people age. On the other hand, performance on tasks involving crystallized intelligence, such as vocabulary skills, remains relatively intact as people age. Our fund of information and knowledge actually increases across much of the life span and only begins to decline around the advanced age of ninety (Park et al., 2002; Singer et al., 2003).

All told, most people retain the bulk of their mental abilities throughout their lives. A long-term longitudinal study of cognitive ability shows that preserved

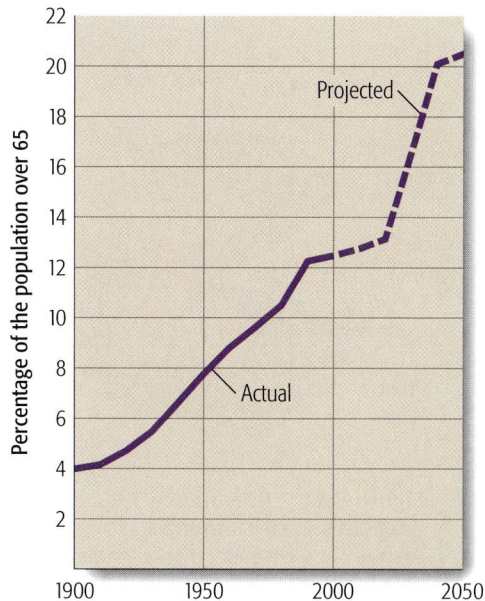

Figure 9.10   The Aging of America The "graying of America" is in full stride. The percentage of the population over age sixty-five is projected to continue to increase through the first half of the twenty-first century.

Source: Data from U.S. Bureau of the Census, 1995.

CONCEPT 9.35
In older adults, declines in problem-solving ability and memory functioning are typically not significant enough to impair daily functioning.

CONCEPT 9.36
A major longitudinal study on aging revealed that factors such as engagement in stimulating activities and openness to new experiences are associated with retention of intellectual functioning in later life.

Keeping the Mind Sharp   Remaining open to new experiences and challenges can help keep the mind sharp in later life.

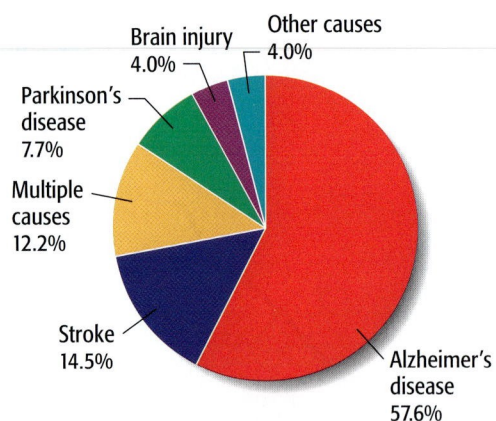

Figure 9.11   Prevalence and Causes of Dementia
Alzheimer's disease is the leading cause of dementia, accounting for more than half of the cases.

Source: Tune, 1998.

Do You Know My Name?
The man shown here can sometimes recall the names of his loved ones when he is prompted by viewing old photographs.

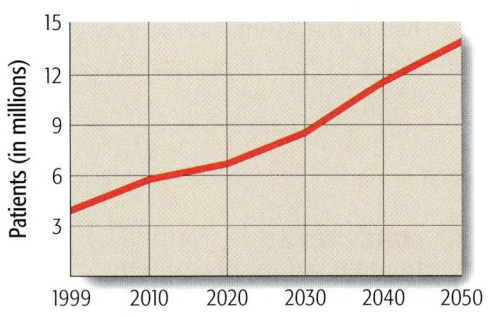

Figure 9.12   Projections of Numbers of Alzheimer's Patients Through 2050
The number of Alzheimer's patients is expected to soar through at least the first half of the twenty-first century.

Source: Cowley, 2000c, p. 35.

CONCEPT 9.37
Alzheimer's disease is a degenerative brain disease and is not a consequence of normal aging.

dementia   A condition involving a major deterioration or loss of mental abilities involved in memory, reasoning, judgment, and ability to carry out purposeful behavior.

Alzheimer's disease   An irreversible brain disease with a progressive course toward inevitable deterioration of mental functioning.

intellectual ability in later life is associated with such factors as general physical health, engagement in stimulating activities, and openness to new experiences (Schaie, 1996).

In contrast, some people develop **dementia** in late adulthood. Dementia is characterized by a sharp decline in mental abilities, especially memory and reasoning ability. Dementia is *not* a normal consequence of aging. It is a disease that damages or destroys brain tissue involved in higher mental functions, resulting in more severe memory loss than ordinary forgetfulness and difficulty performing routine activities. Dementia has many causes, including brain infections, tumors, Parkinson's disease, brain injuries, strokes, and chronic alcoholism. But the most common cause of dementia is Alzheimer's disease (Coyle, 2003) (see Figure 9.11).

Alzheimer's disease, or AD, is an irreversible brain disease with a gradual onset and a slow but progressive course toward inevitable deterioration of mental functioning. As the disease progresses, people require help selecting clothes, driving, recalling names and addresses, and maintaining personal hygiene. They may start wandering and no longer be able to recognize family and friends or speak coherently.

Alzheimer's disease affects about four million Americans and is among the leading causes of death in older adults in the United States (Blakey, 2002; Brookmeyer et al., 2002). One in ten people over age 65 suffer from Alzheimer's, a proportion that rises to about one in two by age 85 (Cowley, 2000c; Lemonick & Park, 2001). As the U.S. population continues to age, cases of AD are expected to nearly quadruple by the middle of the twenty-first century to about fourteen million (Kawas & Brookmeyer, 2001) (see Figure 9.12). The disease can also affect younger people, but it is rare in those under 65.

Alzheimer's disease is associated with progressive death of brain cells in many parts of the brain (Näslund et al., 2000; Thompson et al., 2003). The causes of AD remain unknown, but scientists believe that genetic factors play important roles (Mattson, 2003; Plomin & McGuffin, 2003). Although there is no cure for AD, some drugs are available that produce modest benefits in boosting memory functioning in AD patients (Reisberg et al., 2003; Trinh et al., 2003). Hopes lie with the development of an effective vaccine (Check, 2003).

Psychosocial Development

Erik Erikson characterized the central challenge of psychosocial development in late adulthood as one of *ego integrity versus despair.* He believed that the basic psychological challenge of later adulthood is the struggle to maintain a sense of meaning and satisfaction in life rather than drifting into a state of despair and bitterness. People who achieve a state of ego integrity are able to come to terms with their lives: to accept the joys and sorrows, and the successes and failures, that make up the totality of their life experiences. Erikson, who himself lived and worked productively into his nineties, was basically an optimist, believing we can remain fulfilled and maintain a sense of purpose at any stage of life and avoid falling into despair. Table 9.7 offers an overview of Erikson's stages of psychosocial development from adolescence through late adulthood.

Other theorists, such as Daniel Levinson, also recognize that late adulthood is characterized by increasing awareness of the psychological and physical changes that accompany aging and the need to come to terms with death. He points out that one of the important life tasks older adults face is the need to rediscover the self—to understand who one is and find meaningful activities that continue to fill life with meaning and purpose—as well as to maintain connections to families and friends. Lacking connections to others and engagement in meaningful activities that imbue life with purpose can set the stage for depression, the most common emotional problem faced by older adults (Beekman et al., 2002; Bruce et al., 2004; Charney et al., 2003).

Despite the challenges faced by older adults, most people in their seventies say they are generally satisfied with their lives (Margoshes, 1995). Factors such as income level and social contacts (quality more than quantity) figure prominently in predicting a sense of well-being in late adulthood (Pinquart & Sörensen, 2000). There is much we can do to preserve our mental health as we age, such as coping with the loss of a spouse or other loved one by increasing our contacts with existing friends and seeking out new friends. Studies suggest that happiness may even increase with age, along with perceptions of having greater control over such areas of life as work, finances, and marriage (Goode, 1998; Lachman & Weaver, 1998). Developmental psychologists highlight the importance of several key characteristics associated with more successful aging:

1. *Selective optimization and compensation.* Successful aging is associated with the ability to optimize one's time and use available resources to compensate for shortcomings in physical energy, memory, or fluid intelligence (Baltes, 1997;

CONCEPT 9.38
Erikson believed the major psychosocial challenge of late adulthood involves maintaining a sense of ego integrity or meaningfulness even as one approaches the end of life.

Depression in Late Adulthood
Depression is a common emotional problem in late adulthood. What factors contribute to depression among older adults?

TABLE 9.7   **Erikson's Stages of Psychosocial Development During Adolescence and Adulthood**

Life Period	Life Crisis	Major Challenge in Psychosocial Development
Adolescence	Identity versus role diffusion	To develop a sense of who one is and what one stands for; committing oneself to an occupational choice and adoption of a set of firmly held personal beliefs
Early adulthood	Intimacy versus isolation	To develop close, abiding relationships and friendships with others, including intimate relationships
Middle adulthood	Generativity versus stagnation	To contribute to the development and well-being of young people and future generations
Late adulthood	Integrity versus despair	To maintain one's sense of dignity and psychological integrity as one approaches the final years of life

Source: Adapted from Erikson, 1963.

CONCEPT CHART 9.7
Development in Late Adulthood

Physical development	With aging, sensory acuity declines; muscles and bones lose mass; skin loses elasticity, causing wrinkles; reaction times increase; immune functioning declines.
Cognitive development	Declines are noted in learning and memory, especially recall of word lists or names, and in fluid intelligence. Crystallized intelligence—general verbal ability and accumulated knowledge—tends to remain stable or even improve in certain respects as we age. Dementias such as Alzheimer's disease are not normal aspects of aging but result from brain diseases or abnormalities.
Psychosocial development	Erikson postulated that adults in later life face a psychosocial crisis of ego integrity vs. despair. Levinson focused on the tasks that accompany advancing age, such as maintaining meaningful connections to families and activities that continue to imbue life with meaning. Depression is a major emotional concern faced by many older adults.

CONCEPT 9.39
Developmental psychologists have identified certain behavior patterns associated with successful aging, including selective optimization and compensation, optimism, and self-challenge.

THINK About It

Aging Successfully

What key features of successful aging are highlighted in the text? How might you put this information to use in your own life?

Freund & Baltes, 1999). Rather than compete on the athletic field or in the business arena where younger people may have the advantage, older people may optimize their time by focusing on things that are more meaningful and important, such as visiting with family and friends more often—activities that allow them to pursue emotional goals that afford satisfaction. They may compensate for declining functioning by writing notes to jog their memories; giving themselves more time to learn; and using mechanical devices, such as hearing aids or canes, to compensate for loss of sensory or motor ability (Greenberg & Springen, 2001).

2. *Optimism.* Maintaining an optimistic frame of mind is linked to higher levels of life satisfaction and lower levels of depressive symptoms in later life (Chang & Sanna, 2001). Moreover, people who hold more positive views about aging tend to live longer—an average 7.6 years longer—than those with more negative perceptions (Levy et al., 2002).

3. *Self-challenge.* Seeking new challenges is a primary feature of successful adjustment at any age. The key for most older people, as for younger people, is not to do less but to do more of the things that matter. Maintaining an engaged lifestyle is also associated with better-preserved verbal intellectual ability (Pushkar et al., 1999).

Concept Chart 9.7 summarizes developmental changes in late adulthood.

The Last Chapter: On Death and Dying

Now let us turn to a topic many of us would rather not think about: life's final transition, the one leading to death. When young, we may feel immortal. Our bodies may be strong and flexible, and our senses and minds sharp. We parcel thoughts about death and dying into a mental file cabinet to be opened much later in life, along with items like retirement, social security, and varicose veins. But death can occur at any age—by accident, violence, or illness. Death can also affect us deeply at any stage of life through the loss of loved ones. The issue of death raises questions well worth thinking about at any age, questions such as: Should I be an organ donor? How can I best leave my assets to those I care about? Shall I be buried or cremated? Shall I donate my body to science? Should I prepare a living will so that doctors will not need to use heroic measures to prolong my life when things are beyond hope?

Psychiatrist Elisabeth Kübler-Ross (1969) focused on how people cope with impending death. Based on her interviews with terminally ill people, she observed some common themes and identified five stages of dying through which many people pass:

1. *Denial.* At first, the person thinks, "It can't be me. I'm not really dying. The doctors made a mistake."

2. *Anger.* Once the reality of impending death is recognized, feelings of anger and resentment take center stage. Anger may be directed at younger or healthier people or toward the physicians who cannot save the person.

3. *Bargaining.* By the next stage, the person attempts to make a deal with God, such as promising to do good deeds in exchange for a few more months or years.

4. *Depression.* Depression reflects the growing sense of loss over leaving behind loved ones and losing life itself. A sense of utter hopelessness may ensue.

5. *Final acceptance.* As the person works through the earlier stages, he or she eventually achieves some degree of inner peace and acceptance. The person may still fear death, but comes to accept it with a kind of quiet dignity.

Kübler-Ross believed family members and health professionals can help dying people by understanding the stages through which they are passing and helping them attain a state of final acceptance. Many dying people have experiences similar to those Kübler-Ross observed, but not necessarily all of them and not always in the order she proposed (Schneidman, 1983). Some dying people do not deny the inevitable but arrive at a rapid though painful acceptance of death. Some become hopelessly depressed, others experience mainly fear, and still others have rapidly shifting feelings.

CONCEPT 9.40
Elisabeth Kübler-Ross described the psychological experience of dying in terms of five identifiable stages.

MODULE 9.6 REVIEW

Late Adulthood

CONCEPT CHECK

1. Which of the following cognitive skills is *not* likely to show a substantial decline as people age?
   a. rapid problem solving
   b. memory for new information
   c. speed at pattern recognition
   d. ability to apply acquired knowledge

2. List several factors that may help preserve intellectual functioning in later life.

3. What is closest in meaning to Erikson's term *ego integrity*?
   a. focusing attention on oneself
   b. achieving a sense of meaningfulness and satisfaction with one's life
   c. the development of generativity, or the ability to give of oneself to the next generation
   d. living an honest life

4. List three characteristics associated with successful aging.

MODULE 9.7   Living Longer, Healthier Lives

- **What are some ways people can increase the likelihood of a longer and healthier life?**

CONCEPT 9.41

Longevity is partly determined by genetic inheritance and partly by factors people can directly control, such as a healthy diet, regular exercise, avoidance of harmful substances, and an active, involved lifestyle.

Longevity is partly determined by genes, a factor that for now lies beyond our control (Hasty et al., 2003). But factors other than genetics enter the longevity equation. How people live—the behaviors and habits they acquire—may be even more important determinants of longevity. These lifestyle factors, such as exercise and dietary habits, contribute not only to longevity but also to the quality of life as people age. Young people who believe aging is a concern only for older people should note that the earlier they establish healthier habits, the greater their chances of living a longer and healthier life. In this section, we look at some guidelines for acquiring healthier behaviors (after Nevid, Rathus, & Rubenstein, 1998).

Developing Healthy Exercise and Nutrition Habits

Ponce de León, the Spanish explorer who searched for the mythical "Fountain of Youth," might have been more successful had he just stayed home and built a gym. Exercise at any age is healthful, but especially as we age (Adler & Raymond, 2001; O'Neil, 2003). Mounting evidence points to the role of physical exercise in slowing the effects of aging such as loss of lean body mass, bone, and muscle strength. Regular exercise is also associated with a lower risk of certain cancers, such as cancer of the colon, and with other major killers such as heart disease, stroke, and diabetes, as well as the potentially disabling bone disorder **osteoporosis** (NIH Consensus Development Panel, 2001). Weight-bearing exercise that requires working against gravity helps build bone density and keeps bones and muscles strong (Adler & Raymond, 2001).

Not surprisingly, regular exercise is associated with increased life expectancy (Gregg et al., 2003). Exercise also helps preserve mental sharpness in later life,

Exercise: Not Just for the Young   Regular exercise in late adulthood can enhance longevity and physical health, and maintain mental sharpness.

osteoporosis   A bone disease characterized by a loss of bone density in which the bones become porous, brittle, and more prone to fracture.

including memory functioning, and helps combat depression (Colcombe & Kramer, 2003; Underwood & Watson, 2001).

Following a nutritious, balanced diet is another key factor in promoting health and longevity. Adopting a low-fat diet rich in fruits, vegetables, and whole grains can help reduce the risks of potentially life-shortening diseases, such as coronary heart disease.

Staying Involved

Staying actively involved in meaningful activities and personal projects can contribute not only to preserving mental sharpness but also to emotional well-being (Lawton et al., 2002). Older adults who remain productive and participate in active leisure activities and in social or volunteer organizations are less likely than their less involved counterparts to encounter depression (Herzog et al., 1998; LaGory & Fitzpatrick, 1992). Staying actively involved in different activities is also linked to increased longevity (Pollak, 1999). Even helping others may wind up helping oneself to live a longer life. We now have evidence based on a study of older married adults that giving support may be more beneficial to extending longevity than receiving it (Brown et al., 2003).

Avoiding Harmful Substances

Tobacco use, illicit drug use, and excessive use of alcohol can lead to physical health problems that can cut life expectancy significantly. Moreover, many lives, both young and old, have been lost to drug overdoses.

Maintaining a Healthy Weight

In Chapter 8 we noted that obesity is a major risk factor for several life-threatening and life-shortening diseases, such as coronary heart disease, diabetes, and some forms of cancer. Since metabolism tends to slow down with age, maintaining a healthy weight in middle and late adulthood requires compensating accordingly by curtailing calorie intake and exercising regularly to burn off excess calories.

Managing Stress

In Chapter 13, you will learn how stress affects physical health and emotional well-being. Prolonged or intense stress can impair the immune system, the body's line of defense against disease-causing organisms and damaged cells. In turn, a weakened immune system makes people more likely to develop infectious diseases and less able to protect themselves from chronic diseases associated with aging such as hypertension, cancer, and heart disease. The stress management techniques described in Chapter 13 can help take the distress out of stress and hopefully reduce the risk of developing stress-related disorders.

Exercising the Mind

Researchers have found that intellectually stimulating activities and participation in memory training programs can help preserve cognitive functioning in later life, including memory ability (Ball et al., 2002; Kramer & Willis, 2002). Intellectual activities that help preserve mental sharpness include mentally challenging games (such as chess), crossword or jigsaw puzzles, reading, writing, painting, and sculpting, to name but a few. High levels of cognitive activity are also linked to a reduced risk of developing Alzheimer's disease (R. S. Wilson et al., 2002; Wilson & Bennett, 2003).

Do Healthy Habits Pay Off?

People who adopt healthier habits (avoiding smoking, remaining physically and socially active, following a healthy diet, controlling excess body weight, and avoiding excessive drinking) and who maintain favorable levels of blood cholesterol and blood pressure are more likely to live longer, healthier lives than those with unhealthier habits (Hu et al., 2000; Stamler et al., 1999).

Critical thinkers recognize that we cannot draw a cause-and-effect relationship between healthy habits and longevity based simply on a statistical relationship. Since longevity researchers may not be able to control whether people adopt healthier habits, they are generally limited to studying differences in outcomes between those who do and those who do not. Still, correlations can point to possible causal relationships, and it stands to reason that the adoption of healthier habits may help extend life.

All in all, it is wise to take stock of your health habits sooner rather than later. It is like salting away money for your later years: Developing healthy habits now and maintaining them throughout life are likely to boost your chances of living a longer and healthier life.

TYING IT TOGETHER

The study of development begins with understanding the changes that occur during prenatal development (Module 9.1), and it continues with exploration of the rapid, dramatic changes that occur in the infant's sensory, motor, and learning ability during the first two years of life (Module 9.2). Though healthy infants develop sensory and motor skills in about the same sequence and at about the same ages, infants and young children vary widely in their behaviors, ways of relating to others, and emerging personalities and ways of understanding the world (Module 9.3). We also consider influences that affect children's development, including parenting influences and peer relationships. Adolescence, a time of significant physical, cognitive, social, and emotional changes, covers the period of development spanning the end of childhood and the beginning of adulthood (Module 9.4). As adolescence passes and people progress through early and middle adulthood, they face major life challenges in establishing independent identities, assuming an occupational role, and forming intimate relationships (Module 9.5). The major life challenges that people face as they progress through late adulthood typically revolve around keeping active and involved and coping with age-related physical and mental changes (Module 9.6). We may increase our chances of living longer and healthier lives by developing healthier habits early in life and maintaining those habits as we age (Module 9.7).

SUMMING UP: Q & A

Prenatal Development: A Case of Nature and Nurture (Module 9.1)

What are the major stages of prenatal development?

- The germinal stage is the period from conception to implantation.
- The embryonic stage begins with implantation and extends to about the eighth week of development; it is characterized by differentiation of the major organ systems.

- The fetal stage begins around the ninth week and continues until birth; it is characterized by continued maturation of the fetus's organ systems and dramatic increases in size.

What are some major threats to prenatal development?

- Threats include maternal diet, maternal diseases and disorders, and use of certain medications and drugs.
- Exposure to particular teratogens causes the greatest harm during critical periods of vulnerability.

Infant Development (Module 9.2)

What reflexes do newborn babies show?

- Reflexes include the rooting, eyeblink, sucking, Moro, palmar grasp, and Babinski reflexes.

What abilities do infants possess with respect to sensory functioning, perception, and learning?

- The newborn can detect objects visually (though not with perfect acuity) and can discriminate among different sounds, odors, and tastes.
- The abilities to respond to depth cues and discern facial expressions develop within the first six months.
- Infants are also capable of learning simple responses and retaining memories of those responses.

How do the infant's motor abilities develop during the first year?

- During the first year, the infant acquires the ability to move its body, sit without support, turn over, crawl, and begin to stand and walk on its own.

Years of Discovery: Emotional, Social, and Cognitive Development in Childhood (Module 9.3)

What are the three basic types of infant temperament identified in the New York Longitudinal Study, and what are the major differences among them?

- The three types are the easy child, the difficult child, and the slow-to-warm-up child.
- Easy children have generally positive moods, react well to changes, and quickly develop regular feeding and sleep schedules.
- Difficult children have largely negative moods and have difficulty reacting to new situations and people and developing regular feeding and sleep schedules.
- Slow-to-warm-up children tend to become withdrawn when facing new situations and experience mild levels of distress.

What are the three types of attachment styles identified by Ainsworth?

- The secure type of infant attaches to the mother and uses her as a secure base to explore the environment.
- The insecure-avoidant type freely explores the environment but tends to ignore the mother.
- The insecure-resistant type clings excessively to the mother but shows ambivalence or resistance toward her.
- Securely attached infants tend to show better social and emotional adjustment in later development than insecurely attached infants.

What roles do peer relationships play in children's emotional and social development?

- Peers are important influences on children's psychosocial adjustment, especially on self-esteem and development of social competencies.
- Peer relationships may also set the stage for deviant behavior.

What are the three major styles of parenting in Baumrind's model, and how do they differ?

- Authoritative parenting involves a combination of maturity expectations, use of reasoning, and firm limit setting.
- Authoritarian parenting involves firm limit setting but is overly controlling and relies on harsh styles of discipline.
- Permissive parenting involves an "anything goes" style characterized by a lax approach to limit setting.
- Authoritative parenting is generally associated with better emotional and social adjustment in children than the other parenting styles.

What are the stages of psychosocial development during childhood, according to Erikson?

- Erikson's stages are the (1) stage of trust versus mistrust (birth to 1 year), (2) stage of autonomy versus shame and doubt (ages 1 to 3), (3) stage of initiative versus guilt (ages 3 to 6), and (4) stage of industry versus inferiority (ages 6 to 12).

What are the major features associated with Piaget's stages of cognitive development?

- During the sensorimotor stage, from birth to about 2 years, children explore their world through their senses, motor responses, and purposeful manipulation of objects.
- During the preoperational stage, from about 2 to 7 years of age, the child's thinking is more representational but is limited by centration, egocentricity, animistic thinking, and irreversibility.
- The concrete operational stage, beginning around age 7 in Western cultures, is characterized by development of the principles of conservation and reversibility and the ability to draw logical relationships among concrete objects or events.
- The formal operational stage, the most advanced stage of cognitive development according to Piaget, is characterized by the ability to engage in deductive thinking, generate hypotheses, and engage in abstract thought.

What is the basic theme in Vygotsky's theory of cognitive development?

- Vygotsky focused on how children acquire knowledge of their social world. He believed this knowledge is achieved through the interaction of the child (novice) with the parent (expert) within a zone of proximal development that takes into account the child's present and potentially realizable knowledge structures.

Adolescence (Module 9.4)

What is puberty?

- Puberty spans the period of physical development that begins with the appearance of secondary sex characteristics and ends with the attainment of full sexual maturity.

What changes in cognitive development occur during adolescence?

- Adolescents may progress to the stage of formal operations, which, according to Piaget, is denoted by the ability to engage in abstract thinking and reasoning.
- According to Elkind, egocentricity in adolescence involves concepts of the imaginary audience (believing everyone else is as concerned about us as we are ourselves) and the personal fable (an exaggerated sense of uniqueness and perceptions of personal invulnerability).

What are Kohlberg's levels of moral reasoning?

- At the preconventional level, moral judgments are based on the perceived consequences of behavior. Behaviors that avoid punishment are good; those that incur punishment from an external authority are bad.
- At the conventional level, conformity with conventional rules of right and wrong are valued because of the need to do what others expect or because one has an obligation to obey the law.
- At the postconventional level, moral judgments are based on the value systems the individual develops through personal reflection, such as valuing the importance of human life and the concept of justice above that of the law. Postconventional thinking does not develop until adolescence, if ever.

Why did Gilligan criticize Kohlberg's theory?

- Gilligan pointed out that Kohlberg's model was based only on the responses of males and did not take female voices into account.
- Through her own research, Gilligan concluded that females tend to adopt a care orientation, whereas males tend to adopt a justice orientation. Other researchers have found that differences in moral reasoning between men and women are less clear-cut, although women have a greater tendency to adopt a care orientation.

What did Erikson believe is the major developmental challenge of adolescence?

- Erikson believed the achievement of a sense of who one is and what one stands for (ego identity) is the major developmental challenge of adolescence.
- Erikson coined the term *identity crisis* to describe a period of serious soul-searching in which adolescents attempt to come to terms with their underlying beliefs and future direction in life.

Early and Middle Adulthood (Module 9.5)

What cognitive and physical changes take place as people age?

- Beginning in their twenties, people start to experience a gradual decline in lean body mass and muscle tissue.
- Fluid intelligence—including rapid problem-solving ability and memory for lists of words, names, or text—tends to decline with increasing age during middle and late adulthood.
- Crystallized intelligence remains relatively intact and may actually improve in some respects.
- Menopause, the cessation of menstruation, is the major physical marker of middle adulthood in women. Menopause is associated with a dramatic decline in estrogen production.
- Testosterone production in men also declines with age, but more gradually.

How do theorists conceptualize social and personality development during early and middle adulthood?

- Erikson focuses on the stages of psychosocial development: intimacy versus isolation (forming intimate, stable relationships versus remaining emotionally detached) during early adulthood and generativity versus stagnation (making meaningful contributions to the future generation or generations versus becoming stagnant and self-absorbed) during middle adulthood.
- Theorist Daniel Levinson focuses on the transitions through which people may need to navigate as they age.

Late Adulthood (Module 9.6)

What physical and cognitive changes occur in late adulthood?

- In late adulthood, the skin wrinkles, hair grays, and the senses become less acute. Reaction time increases, and lean body mass, bone density, and strength decline. Other physical processes, including immune system functioning, decline.
- People generally experience a decline in some aspects of learning and memory, especially ability to learn or recall lists of words or names, and in fluid intelligence.
- Crystallized intelligence remains relatively stable and may even increase in some respects with age.

What is Alzheimer's disease?

- Alzheimer's disease (AD) is a form of dementia (loss of mental abilities) that is progressive and irreversible. Though no one knows what causes AD, genetic factors appear to be involved.

How do theorists characterize the psychosocial challenges of late adulthood?

- To Erikson, late adulthood is characterized by the psychosocial crisis of ego integrity versus despair (remaining meaningfully engaged in life while coming to terms with one's life versus despairing over the approaching finality of life).
- Other theorists, such as Levinson, focus on the transitions and challenges that older adults are likely to face.

What qualities are associated with successful aging?

- Successful aging is associated with the ability to concentrate on what is important and meaningful, to maintain a positive outlook, and to continue to challenge oneself.

What are the stages of dying as identified by Kübler-Ross?

- The stages of dying identified by Kübler-Ross are denial, anger, bargaining, depression, and final acceptance.

Application: Living Longer, Healthier Lives (Module 9.7)

What are some ways people can increase the likelihood of a longer and healthier life?

- The likelihood of enjoying a longer, healthier life can be enhanced through engaging in regular exercise and proper nutrition; maintaining an active, involved lifestyle; maintaining a healthy weight; avoiding unhealthy habits; managing stress; and exercising the mind as well as the body.

Key Terms

developmental psychology (p. 296)
maturation (p. 296)
zygote (p. 297)
germinal stage (p. 297)
fertilization (p. 297)
uterus (p. 297)
embryonic stage (p. 297)
embryo (p. 297)
neural tube (p. 297)
amniotic sac (p. 297)
placenta (p. 298)
fetal stage (p. 298)
fetus (p. 298)
spina bifida (p. 298)
teratogen (p. 298)
rubella (p. 299)

sudden infant death syndrome (SIDS) (p. 300)
fetal alcohol syndrome (FAS) (p. 300)
rooting reflex (p. 301)
eyeblink reflex (p. 301)
sucking reflex (p. 301)
Moro reflex (p. 301)
palmar grasp reflex (p. 301)
Babinski reflex (p. 301)
temperament (p. 305)
attachment (p. 306)
imprinting (p. 307)
schema (p. 313)
adaptation (p. 314)
assimilation (p. 314)
accommodation (p. 314)

object permanence (p. 314)
symbolic representations (p. 315)
egocentrism (p. 315)
animistic thinking (p. 316)
irreversibility (p. 316)
centration (p. 316)
conservation (p. 316)
formal operations (p. 317)
zone of proximal development (ZPD) (p. 318)
adolescence (p .319)
puberty (p. 320)
secondary sex characteristics (p. 320)
primary sex characteristics (p. 320)

menarche (p. 320)
imaginary audience (p. 322)
personal fable (p. 322)
ego identity (p. 326)
identity crisis (p. 326)
role diffusion (p. 327)
fluid intelligence (p. 329)
crystallized intelligence (p. 329)
menopause (p. 330)
emerging adulthood (p. 330)
midlife crisis (p. 331)
dementia (p. 334)
Alzheimer's disease (p. 334)
osteoporosis (p. 338)

Thinking Critically About Psychology

Based on your reading of this chapter, answer the following questions. Then, to evaluate your progress in developing critical thinking skills, compare your answers to the sample answers found in Appendix A.

1. One evening after the sun sets, Nick asks his three-year-old son Trevor, "Where did the sun go?" Trevor responds, "It went to sleep." Nick then asks, "Why did it go to sleep?" Trevor answers, "Because it was sleepy."

   Based on your understanding of Piaget's theory of cognitive development, explain why Trevor believes that the sun went to sleep because it was sleepy.

2. This critical thinking exercise asks you to apply Erikson's model of psychosocial development to yourself. To Erikson, *ego identity* is the achievement of a firm set of beliefs about who we are, what we believe, and where we are headed in life. Many college-age students are in the process of creating their ego identities. But creation takes time, and the process need not be completed by graduation. Psychologist James Marcia (Marcia, 1966, 1980; Marcia et al., 1993) identified four identity statuses that describe where people stand in their ego identities at any given time:

   Identity achievement describes people who have emerged from an identity crisis (a period of serious self-reflection) with a commitment to a relatively stable set of personal beliefs and to a course of action in pursuing a particular career. An example of a career commitment would be pursuing a major course of study leading to a future career.

Foreclosure describes people who have adopted a set of beliefs or a course of action, though with no period of serious self-exploration or self-examination. They did not go through an identity crisis to arrive at their beliefs and occupational choices. Most base their commitments on what others, especially their parents, instilled in them.

Moratorium is a state of identity crisis concerning one's beliefs or career choices. People in moratorium are currently working through their personal beliefs or struggling to determine which career course to pursue.

Identity diffusion is the status describing people who are not yet committed to a set of personal beliefs or career choices and show no real interest in developing these commitments. Issues of ego identity have not yet taken center stage in their lives.

Now think critically about yourself in relation to these categories:

a. How would you determine your identity status in areas such as occupational choice and personal (political and moral) beliefs? What evidence would you need to make this determination? Bear in mind that you may have a different identity status in each area.

b. Apply these criteria to yourself. Based on this self-appraisal, which identity status best describes your ego identity at this point in time in the areas of career choice and personal beliefs?

Answers to Concept Check Questions

Module 9.1: 1. a; 2. maternal malnutrition, teratogens; 3. (a) iv, (b) ii, (c) iii, (d) i. **Module 9.2:** 1. (a) iv, (b) ii, (c) i, (d) iii; 2. Newborns show preferences for their mothers' voices; 3. d. **Module 9.3:** 1. b; 2. (a) ii, (b) iv, (c) i, (d) iii; 3. c; 4. d; 5. a. **Module 9.4:** 1. d; 2. menarche; 3. imaginary audience and personal fable; 4. a; 5. gender and cultural biases; 6. c. **Module 9.5:** 1. c; 2. c; 3. b; 4. midlife transition. **Module 9.6:** 1. d; 2. general physical health, involvement in stimulating activities, openness to new experiences; 3. b; 4. selective optimization and compensation, optimism, and self-challenge.

Personality

DID YOU KNOW THAT . . .

- **According to the originator of psychodynamic theory, Sigmund Freud, slips of the tongue may reveal hidden motives and wishes of which we are unaware? (p. 348)**

- **According to Carl Gustav Jung, another psychodynamic theorist, we inherit a shared unconscious mind containing images that can be traced to ancestral times? (p. 352)**

- **According to a leading personality theorist, extraverted people may require more stimulating activities than introverted people to maintain an optimal level of arousal? (p. 356)**

- **The "Big Five" is not the name of a new NCAA basketball conference but the label used to describe the leading trait theory of personality today? (p. 358)**

- **A leading humanistic theorist, Carl Rogers, believed that children should receive love and approval unconditionally from their parents regardless of their behavior at any particular point in time? (p. 365)**

- **According to a widely held view in the nineteenth century, you can learn about a person's character and mental abilities by examining the pattern of bumps on the person's head? (p. 369)**

Know thyself.
—Socrates

Who is that person who stares back at you in the bathroom mirror? Do you know the person well, or is she or he still something of a mystery? How would you describe the person you see? What is special or unique about the person? How is the person similar to other people you know? How is the person different? Do you like the person you see? What would you like to change about the person you see?

This chapter is about the person in the mirror—you. It is also about every other human. Specifically, we are interested in *personality,* the relatively stable set of psychological characteristics and behavior patterns that make individuals unique and account for the consistency of their actions over time. Personality is a composite of the ways in which individuals relate to others and adapt to the demands placed on them by the environment.

The study of personality involves the attempt to describe and explain the characteristics that make each of us unique as individuals. Psychologists seek to understand these characteristics by drawing upon knowledge from the many other areas of psychology discussed elsewhere in the text. They consider how learning experiences, biological factors, social and cultural influences, and cognitive and developmental processes shape the persons we become.

In this chapter we consider the views of several leading personality theorists. Each brings a different perspective to bear on the study of personality (Funder, 2001). Some, including Sigmund Freud, the originator of psychodynamic theory, emphasize unconscious influences on personality. They believe that our personalities are shaped by a struggle between opposing forces within the mind that occurs outside the range of ordinary consciousness.

Other theorists, called trait theorists, view personality as composed of a set of underlying traits that account for the consistencies in behavior from one situation to another. Social-cognitive theorists view personality in terms of the individual's learning history and ways of thinking. To humanistic psychologists, such as Carl Rogers and Abraham Maslow, our personalities are expressed through our efforts to actualize our unique potential as human beings. We explore these different perspectives and examine what each has to say about personality, beginning with the psychodynamic model of personality espoused by Freud and his followers. ■

MODULE 10.1

The Psychodynamic Perspective

- **What is personality?**
- **What three levels of consciousness did Freud believe comprise the human mind?**
- **What are the structures of personality in Freud's theory?**
- **What are psychological defense mechanisms?**
- **What are the five stages of psychosexual development in Freud's theory?**
- **What are some of the major contributions of other psychodynamic theorists?**

CONCEPT 10.1
Your personality is the sum total of the psychological characteristics and behavior patterns that define you as a unique individual and characterize the ways in which you relate to the world and adapt to demands placed upon you.

Sigmund Freud

CONCEPT 10.2
Freud developed the first psychodynamic theory of personality, the belief that personality is shaped by underlying conflicts between opposing forces within the mind.

CONCEPT 10.3
Freud believed that the mind consists of three levels of consciousness: the conscious, the preconscious, and the unconscious.

personality The relatively stable constellation of psychological characteristics and behavioral patterns that account for our individuality and consistency over time.

psychoanalytic theory Freud's theory of personality that holds that personality and behavior are shaped by unconscious forces and conflicts.

Sigmund Freud was the architect of the first major theory of **personality**, called **psychoanalytic theory**. The central idea underlying his theory of personality is the belief that a *dynamic* struggle takes place within the human *psyche* (mind) between unconscious forces. For this reason, Freud's views and those of his followers are often called *psychodynamic theory*. In this module, we first discuss Freud's ideas and then describe the contributions of other theorists in the psychodynamic tradition who followed in Freud's footsteps.

Sigmund Freud: Psychoanalytic Theory

In the tradition of Darwin, Freud recognized that we share with nonhuman animals certain common processes that have *survival* as their aim. We need to breathe, feed, and eliminate bodily wastes. And to survive as a species, we need to reproduce. Freud believed we are endowed with a sexual instinct that has as its purpose the preservation of the species. He later would add an aggressive instinct to explain human aggression. Yet Freud believed that giving free rein to these instincts might tear apart the very fabric of society and of the family unit itself. To live in an ordered society, Freud maintained, humans need to control their primitive sexual and aggressive impulses. In other words, humans need to channel their sexual and aggressive instincts in socially appropriate ways so as to live harmoniously with one another. We need to learn that aggression or sexually touching is unacceptable, except in socially acceptable contexts such as the football field in the case of expressing aggressive impulses and the marital bed in the case of satisfying sexual impulses.

Freud developed psychoanalytic theory to account for how the human mind accomplishes the task of balancing these conflicting demands of instinct and social acceptability. Freud's theory of personality is complex, but it can be represented in terms of four major concepts: levels of consciousness, structure of personality, defense mechanisms, and stages of psychosexual development.

Levels of Consciousness: The Conscious, the Preconscious, and the Unconscious

Freud compared the human mind to a giant iceberg. Like an iceberg, which has much of its mass hidden below the surface of the water, most of the human mind lies below the surface of conscious awareness (see Figure 10.1). Freud represented the human mind as consisting of three levels of consciousness: the **conscious**, the **preconscious**, and the **unconscious**. The conscious is the tip of the iceberg. It is the level of consciousness that corresponds to our present awareness—what we are thinking or feeling at any given moment in time. The preconscious holds information we've stored from past experience or learning. This information can be

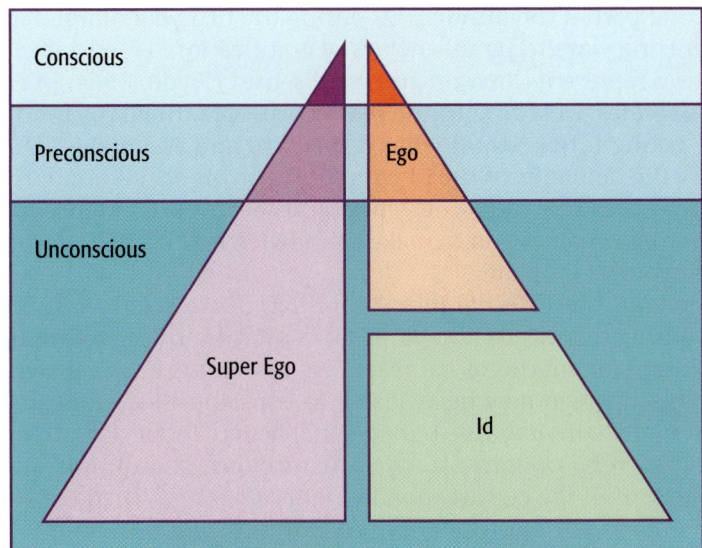

Figure 10.1   Levels of Consciousness in Freud's Theory
The human mind in Freudian theory can be likened to an iceberg in which only the tip rises above the level of conscious awareness. While information held in the preconscious can be brought into the conscious mind at any time, much of the contents of the mind—including many of our deepest wishes, ideas, and urges—remain mired in the dark recesses of the unconscious.

Source: Adapted from Nevid et al., 2003.

retrieved from memory and brought into awareness at any time. Your telephone number, for example, is information stored in the preconscious that you can bring into awareness when needed.

The unconscious is like the large mass of the iceberg lying under the surface of the water. It contains primitive sexual and aggressive impulses as well as memories of troubling emotional experiences (e.g., traumatizing events) and unacceptable sexual or aggressive wishes or ideas. The contents of the unconscious cannot be brought directly into consciousness simply by focusing on them; they are brought into consciousness only with great difficulty, if at all. With so much of the contents of the mind mired in the unconscious, we remain unaware of our deepest wishes, ideas, and urges.

The Structure of Personality: Id, Ego, and Superego

Freud proposed that personality consists of three mental entities called **id**, **ego**, and **superego**. The balance and interactions of these three parts of the personality largely determine our behavior and our ability to function effectively in meeting the life challenges we face. Freud did not consider these mental entities to be actual structures we could locate in the brain. Rather, he conceived of them as hypothetical concepts that represent the opposing forces within the personality.

As Figure 10.1 shows, the id (literally, "it") operates only in the unconscious. The id contains our baser animal drives and instinctual impulses, including hunger, thirst, elimination, sex, and aggression. The id stirs us to action to ensure that our basic biological needs are met. It is the only psychic structure present at birth and follows what Freud called the **pleasure principle**, the demand for instant gratification without regard to social rules or customs. In essence, the id wants what it wants when it wants it. Think of the infant. When a need arises, such as hunger or elimination, the infant demands immediate satisfaction of that need. It doesn't wait patiently until an appropriate time comes to feed or to move its bowels. However, according to Freud, when the desired object (mother's nipple, for example) is not available, the id is able to achieve some partial gratification by forming a mental image of the desired object.

The infant soon finds that not every demand is instantly gratified. It also learns that conjuring a mental image of the desired object is a poor substitute for the real thing. It finds it must cope with frustration and learn to delay gratifica-

CONCEPT 10.4
Freud believed that personality consists of three mental entities: the id, the ego, and the superego.

conscious   To Freud, the part of the mind corresponding to the state of present awareness.

preconscious   To Freud, the part of the mind whose contents can be brought into awareness through focused attention.

unconscious   To Freud, the part of the mind that lies outside the range of ordinary awareness and that holds troubling or unacceptable urges, impulses, memories, and ideas.

id   Freud's term for the psychic structure existing in the unconscious that contains our baser animal drives and instinctual impulses.

ego   Freud's term for the psychic structure that attempts to balance the instinctual demands of the id with social realities and expectations.

superego   Freud's term for the psychic structure that corresponds to an internal moral guardian or conscience.

pleasure principle   In Freudian theory, a governing principle of the id that is based on demand for instant gratification without regard to social rules or customs.

tion. So a second part of the mind forms during the first year of life that is responsible for organizing ways to handle delays of gratification. Freud called this entity the ego. The ego represents "reason and good sense" (Freud, 1964, p. 76).

The ego operates according to the **reality principle**, the basis for operating in the world by taking into account what is practical and acceptable. The ego seeks ways to satisfy the demands of the id without incurring social disapproval. The id may motivate you to rise from your chair and seek nourishment when you are hungry. But the ego enables you to make a sandwich and keeps you from grabbing food from someone else's plate.

The superego is our internal moral guardian or conscience. By three to five years of age, during middle childhood, it splits off from the ego, forming through a process of internalizing the moral teachings of parents or other significant figures. Part of the superego may be available to consciousness, the part that corresponds to our moral convictions—our personal beliefs about right and wrong. But much of the superego operates in the unconscious, standing in judgment of whether the actions of the ego are morally right or wrong. When they are not, the superego can impose self-punishment in the form of guilt or shame.

The ego is the great compromiser. It stands between the superego and the id. It seeks to satisfy the demands of the id without offending the moral standards of the superego. Our behavior is a product of the dynamic struggles among the id, the ego, and the superego. These conflicts take place outside of conscious awareness, on the stage of the unconscious mind. Part of the ego rises to the level of consciousness, such as when we consciously seek to fix ourselves a sandwich in response to hunger pangs. But much of the ego operates below the surface of consciousness, where it employs strategies called *defense mechanisms* to prevent awareness of unacceptable sexual or aggressive impulses or wishes.

Defense Mechanisms

In Freud's view, the ego uses **defense mechanisms** to prevent the anxiety that would result if troubling desires and memories residing in the unconscious were fully realized in conscious awareness (Murray, Kilgour, & Wasylkiw, 2000). The major defense mechanism—**repression**, or motivated forgetting—involves the ejection of threatening desires, impulses, and emotionally troubling memories from awareness into the depths of the unconscious.

Repression permits people to remain outwardly calm and controlled even though they harbor hateful or lustful urges under the surface of awareness. Yet repressed desires or memories may become revealed in disguised forms, such as in dream symbols and in slips of the tongue (so-called *Freudian slips*) (Freud, 1938). To Freud, slips of the tongue may reveal underlying motives and wishes kept hidden by repression. If a friend intended to say "I know what you're saying" but it comes out as "I hate what you're saying," perhaps the friend is expressing a repressed feeling (Nevid, Rathus, & Greene, 2003). Other defense mechanisms identified by Freud include **denial**, **reaction formation**, **rationalization**, **projection**, **sublimation**, **regression**, and **displacement** (see Table 10.1).

Though defense mechanisms may be a normal process of adjusting to the unreasonable demands of the id, they can give rise to abnormal behavior. For example, a man who sexually assaults a woman may rationalize to himself that "she had it coming" rather than directly confronting his aggressive urges. A person who regresses to a dependent infantile-like state during times of extreme stress may be shielded from the anxiety of facing the stressful situation but be unable to function effectively.

Stages of Personality Development

In Freud's view, personality develops through five psychosexual stages of development. These stages are considered psychosexual in nature because they are charac-

---

web **Netlab/Defensive Strategies**

CONCEPT 10.5
Freud believed that the ego uses defense mechanisms as a means of preventing anxiety that would result from conscious awareness of disturbing impulses, wishes, or ideas arising from the id.

reality principle In Freudian theory, the governing principle of the ego that takes into account what is practical and acceptable in satisfying basic needs.

defense mechanisms In Freudian theory, the reality-distorting strategies of the ego to prevent awareness of anxiety-evoking or troubling ideas or impulses.

repression In Freudian theory, a defense mechanism involving motivated forgetting of anxiety-evoking material.

denial In Freudian theory, a defense mechanism involving the failure to recognize a threatening impulse or urge.

reaction formation In Freudian theory, a defense mechanism involving behavior that stands in opposition to one's true motives and desires so as to prevent conscious awareness of them.

rationalization In Freudian theory, a defense mechanism involving the use of self-justification to explain away unacceptable behavior, impulses, or ideas.

projection In Freudian theory, a defense mechanism involving the projection of one's own unacceptable impulses, wishes, or urges onto another person.

sublimation In Freudian theory, a defense mechanism involving the channeling of unacceptable impulses into socially sanctioned behaviors or interests.

TABLE 10.1   Major Defense Mechanisms in Psychodynamic Theory

Type of Defense Mechanism	Description	Example
Repression	Expulsion from awareness of unacceptable ideas or motives	A person remains unaware of harboring hateful or destructive impulses toward others.
Regression	The return of behavior that is typical of earlier stages of development	Under stress, a college student starts biting his nails or becomes totally dependent on others.
Displacement	The transfer of unacceptable impulses away from their original objects onto safer or less threatening objects	A worker slams a door after his boss chews him out.
Denial	Refusal to recognize a threatening impulse or desire	A person who nearly chokes someone to death acts afterward like it was "no big deal."
Reaction formation	Behaving in a way that is the opposite of one's true wishes or desires in order to keep these repressed	A sexually frustrated person goes on a personal crusade to stamp out pornography.
Rationalization	The use of self-justifications to explain away unacceptable behavior	When asked why she continues to smoke, a woman says, "Cancer doesn't run in my family."
Projection	Imposing one's own impulses or wishes onto another person	A sexually inhibited person misinterprets other people's friendly approaches as sexual advances.
Sublimation	The channeling of unacceptable impulses into socially constructive pursuits	A person channels aggressive impulses into competitive sports.

terized by changes in how the child seeks physical pleasure from sexually sensitive parts of the body, called **erogenous zones**. He further believed that physical activities connected to basic life functions, such as feeding, elimination, and reproduction, are basically "sexual" because they are inherently pleasurable. So the infant sucking at the mother's breast or eliminating bodily wastes is performing acts that are sexual in Freud's view. And why are these activities pleasurable? The answer, Freud believed, is clear: They are essential to survival. The infant needs to suck to obtain nourishment. If sucking weren't pleasurable, the infant wouldn't do it and would likely die. As the child progresses through the stages of psychosexual development, the primary erogenous zone shifts from one part of the body to another.

Psychological conflicts may emerge during each psychosexual stage of development. These conflicts, which often arise from receiving too much or too little gratification, can lead to the development of **fixations**—personality traits or behavior patterns characteristic of the particular stage. It's as though one's personality gets "stuck" at an early level of development. Let us briefly consider these five stages and the conflicts that may emerge during each one.

Oral Stage   The **oral stage** spans the period of birth through about twelve to eighteen months of age. During this stage the primary erogenous zone is the mouth. The infant seeks sexual pleasure through sucking at its mother's breast and mouthing (taking into the mouth) or, later, biting objects that happen to be nearby, including nibbling at the parents' fingers. Whatever fits into the mouth goes into the mouth. Too much gratification in the oral stage may lead to oral fixations in adulthood such as smoking, nail biting, alcohol abuse, and overeating. Too little gratification, perhaps from early weaning, may lead to the development of traits, such as passivity, clinging dependence, and a pessimistic outlook, that suggest a failure to have met needs for nurturance and care during infancy.

CONCEPT 10.6
Freud believed that personality develops through five stages of psychosexual development: the oral, anal, phallic, latency, and genital stages.

regression   In Freudian theory, a defense mechanism in which an individual, usually under high levels of stress, reverts to a behavior characteristic of an earlier stage of development.

displacement   In Freudian theory, a defense mechanism in which an unacceptable sexual or aggressive impulse is transferred to an object or person that is safer or less threatening than the original object of the impulse.

erogenous zones   Parts of the body that are especially sensitive to sexual or pleasurable stimulation.

fixations   Constellations of personality traits characteristic of a particular stage of psychosexual development, resulting from either excessive or inadequate gratification at that stage.

oral stage   In Freudian theory, the first stage of psychosexual development during which the infant seeks sexual gratification through oral stimulation (sucking, mouthing, and biting).

An Oral Fixation? Freud believed that insufficient or excessive gratification in the oral stage can lead to the development of an oral fixation that becomes a feature of the individual's personality.

anal stage   In Freudian theory, the second stage of psychosexual development, during which sexual gratification is centered on processes of elimination (retention and release of bowel contents).

anal-retentive personality   In Freudian theory, a personality type characterized by perfectionism and excessive needs for self-control as expressed through extreme neatness and punctuality.

anal-expulsive personality   In Freudian theory, a personality type characterized by messiness, lack of self-discipline, and carelessness.

phallic stage   In Freudian theory, the third stage of psychosexual development, marked by erotic attention on the phallic region (penis in boys, clitoris in girls) and the development of the Oedipus complex.

Oedipus complex   In Freudian theory, the psychological complex in which the young boy or girl develops incestuous feelings toward the parent of the opposite gender and perceives the parent of the same gender as a rival.

Electra complex   The term given by some psychodynamic theorists to the form of the Oedipus complex in young girls.

castration anxiety   In Freudian theory, unconscious fear of removal of the penis as punishment for having unacceptable sexual impulses.

penis envy   In Freudian theory, jealousy of boys for having a penis.

Anal Stage   By about the age of eighteen months, the child has entered the **anal stage**. The anal cavity becomes the primary erogenous zone as the child develops the ability to control elimination by contracting and releasing the sphincter muscles at will. Yet this stage, which lasts until about age three, is set for conflict between the parents and the child around the issue of toilet training. To earn the parents' approval and avoid their disapproval, the child must learn to "go potty" at the appropriate time and to delay immediate gratification of the need to eliminate whenever the urge is felt.

In Freud's view, anal fixations reflect either too harsh or too lenient toilet training. Training that is too harsh may lead to traits associated with the so-called **anal-retentive personality**, such as perfectionism and extreme needs for self-control, orderliness, cleanliness, and neatness. Extremely lax training may lead to an opposite array of traits associated with the **anal-expulsive personality**, such as messiness, lack of self-discipline, and carelessness.

Phallic Stage   During the phallic stage, which roughly spans the ages of three to six, the erogenous zone shifts to the phallic region—the penis in males and the clitoris in females. Conflicts with parents over masturbation (self-stimulation of the phallic area) may emerge at this time. But the core conflict of the **phallic stage** is the **Oedipus complex**, which involves the development of incestuous desires for the parent of the opposite sex leading to rivalry with the parent of the same sex. Freud named the Oedipus complex after the ancient Greek myth of Oedipus the King—the tragic story of Oedipus who unwittingly slew his father and married his mother. He believed that this ancient tale revealed a fundamental human truth about psychosexual development. Some of Freud's followers dubbed the female version of the Oedipus complex the **Electra complex**, after another figure in ancient Greek tragedy, Electra, who avenged her father's death by killing his murderers—her own mother and her mother's lover.

In Freud's view, boys normally resolve the conflict by forsaking their incestuous wishes for their mother and identifying with their rival—their father. Girls normally surrender their incestuous desires for their father and identify with their mother. Identification with the parent of the same sex leads to the development of gender-based behaviors. Boys develop aggressive and independent traits associated with masculinity, and girls develop nurturant and demure traits associated with femininity. Another by-product of the Oedipus complex is the development of the superego—the internalization of parental values in the form of a moral conscience.

Freud believed that the failure to successfully resolve Oedipal conflicts may cause boys to become resentful of strong masculine figures, especially authority figures. For either boys or girls, failure to identify with the parent of the opposite gender may lead to the development of traits associated with the opposite gender and perhaps homosexuality.

Freud also believed that young boys develop **castration anxiety**, the fear that their father will punish them for their sexual desires for their mother by castrating them. An unconscious fear of castration motivates boys to forsake their incestuous desires for their mother and to identify with their father. In Freud's view, girls experience **penis envy**, or jealousy of boys for having a penis. Penis envy makes girls feel inferior or inadequate in relation to boys and to unconsciously blame their mother for bringing them into the world so "ill-equipped." But fears of losing their mother's love and protection over their incestuous desires for their fathers prompts girls to forsake these incestuous desires and to identify with their mother. As the girl becomes sexually mature, she forsakes her wish to have a penis of her own (to "be a man") for a desire to have a baby—that is, as a kind of penis substitute for her missing penis. Bear in mind that Freud believed the Oedipus complex, with its incestuous desires, rivalries, and castration anxiety and penis envy, largely occurs at an unconscious level. On the surface, all may seem quiet, masking the turmoil occurring within.

TABLE 10.2   Freud's Psychosexual Stages of Development

Psychosexual Stage	Approximate Age	Erogenous Zone	Source of Sexual Pleasure	Source of Conflict	Adult Characteristics Associated with Conflicts at This Stage
Oral	Birth to 12 to 18 months	Oral cavity	Sucking, biting, and mouthing	Weaning	Oral behaviors such as smoking, alcohol use, nail-biting; dependency; passivity; pessimism
Anal	18 months to 3 years	Anal region	Retention and release of feces	Toilet training	Anal-retentive vs. anal-expulsive traits
Phallic	3 to 6 years	Penis in boys; clitoris in girls	Masturbation	Masturbation; Oedipus complex	Homosexuality; resentment of authority figures in men; unresolved penis envy in women
Latency	6 years to puberty	None	None (focus on play and school activities)	None	None
Genital	Puberty to adulthood	Genitals (penis in men; vagina in women)	Return of sexual interests expressed in mature sexual relationships	None	None

Latency Stage The turbulent psychic crisis of the phallic period gives way to a period of relative tranquility—the **latency stage**, spanning the years between about six and twelve. The latency stage is so named because of the belief that sexual impulses remain latent (dormant) during this time.

Genital Stage The child enters the **genital stage** at about the time of puberty. The forsaken incestuous desires for the parent of the opposite sex give rise to yearnings for more appropriate sexual partners of the opposite gender. Girls may be attracted to boys who resemble "dear old Dad" while boys may seek "the kind of girl who married dear old Dad." Sexual energies seek expression through mature (genital) sexuality in the form of sexual intercourse in marriage and the bearing of children.

See Table 10.2 for a summary of Freud's psychosexual stages of development.

Other Psychodynamic Approaches

Freud attracted a host of followers, many of whom are recognized as important personality theorists in their own right. These followers held views that differed from Freud's in some key respects, but they retained certain central tenets of psychodynamic theory, especially the belief that behavior is influenced by unconscious conflicts within the personality. Yet, as a group, the theorists who followed in Freud's footsteps (often called *neo-Freudians*) placed a lesser emphasis on sexual and aggressive motivations and a greater emphasis on social relationships and the workings of the ego, especially the development of a concept of the self. Here we discuss the major ideas of several of the leading neo-Freudians: Carl Jung, Alfred Adler, and Karen Horney. The contributions of another neo-Freudian, Erik Erikson, were discussed in Chapter 9.

Carl Jung: Analytical Psychology

Carl Gustav Jung (1875–1961) was once part of Freud's inner circle, but he broke with Freud as he developed his own distinctive views of personality. Jung shared with Freud the beliefs that unconscious conflicts influence human behavior and

CONCEPT 10.7
As a group, neo-Freudians placed a lesser emphasis on sexuality than did Freud and a greater emphasis on the roles of conscious choice, self-direction, creativity, and ways of relating to others.

latency stage In Freudian theory, the fourth stage of psychosexual development, during which sexual impulses remain latent or dormant.

genital stage In Freudian theory, the fifth and final stage of psychosexual development, which begins around puberty and corresponds to the development of mature sexuality and emphasis on procreation.

defense mechanisms distort or disguise people's underlying motives. However, he placed greater emphasis on the present than on infantile or childhood experience as well as greater emphasis on conscious processes, such as self-awareness and pursuit of self-directed goals (Boynton, 2004; Kirsch, 1996).

Jung believed that people possess both a **personal unconscious**, which consists of repressed memories and impulses, and a **collective unconscious**, or repository of accumulated ideas and images in the unconscious mind that is shared among all humans and passed down genetically through the generations (Neher, 1996). The collective unconscious contains primitive images called **archetypes** that reflect the ancestral or universal experiences of humans, including images such as an omniscient and all-powerful God, the young hero, and the fertile and nurturant mother figure. Jung believed that while these images remain unconscious, they influence our dreams and waking thoughts and emotions. It is the collective unconscious, Jung maintained, that explains similarities among cultures in dream images, religious symbols, and artistic expressions (such as movie heroes and heroines).

Alfred Adler: Individual Psychology

Alfred Adler (1870–1937) was another member of Freud's inner circle who broke away to develop his own theory of personality. Adler called his theory **individual psychology** because of its emphasis on the unique potential of each individual. He believed that conscious experience plays a greater role in our personalities than Freud had believed. The **creative self** is what he called the part of the personality that is aware of itself and organizes goal-seeking behavior. As such, our creative self strives toward overcoming obstacles that lie in the path of pursuing our potentials, of becoming all that we seek to become.

Adler is perhaps best known for his concept of the **inferiority complex**. He believed that because of their small size and limited abilities, all children harbor feelings of inferiority to some degree. How they compensate for these feelings influences their emerging personalities. Feelings of inferiority lead to a desire to compensate, which Adler called the **drive for superiority** or *will-to-power*. The drive for superiority may motivate us to try harder and achieve worthwhile goals, such as professional accomplishments and positions of prominence. Or it may lead us to be domineering or callous toward others, to perhaps step on or over people as we make our way up the professional or social ladder.

Karen Horney: An Early Voice in Feminine Psychology

One of the staunchest critics of Freud's views on female development was one of his own followers, Karen Horney (1885–1952) (pronounced *HORN-eye*), a German physician and early psychoanalyst who became a prominent theorist in her own right. Horney accepted Freud's belief that unconscious conflicts shape personality, but she focused less on sexual and aggressive drives and more on the roles of social and cultural forces. She also emphasized the importance of parent-child relationships. When parents are harsh or uncaring, children may develop a deep-seated form of anxiety she called **basic anxiety**, which is associated with the feeling of "being isolated and helpless in a potentially hostile world" (cited in Quinn, 1987, p. 41). Children may also develop a deep form of resentment toward their parents, which she labeled **basic hostility**. Horney believed, as did Freud, that children repress their hostility toward their parents out of fear of losing them or suffering their reprisals. Yet repressed hostility generates more anxiety and insecurity.

Horney accepted the general concept of penis envy in girls, but she believed that the development of young women must be understood within a social con-

Karen Horney

text as well. For example, she rejected Freud's belief that a female's sense of inferiority derives from penis envy. She argued that if women feel inferior, it is because they envy men their social power and authority, not their penises (Stewart & McDermott, 2004). Horney even raised the possibility that men may experience "womb envy" over the obvious "physiological superiority" of women with respect to their biological capacity for creating and bringing life into the world.

Evaluating the Psychodynamic Perspective

Psychodynamic theory remains the most detailed and comprehensive theory of personality yet developed. Many of the terms Freud introduced—such as ego, superego, repression, fixation, and defense mechanisms—are used today in everyday language, although perhaps not precisely in the ways that Freud defined them.

Perhaps the major contribution of Freud and later psychodynamic thinkers was to increase our awareness that unconscious drives and impulses may motivate our behavior. To know oneself, Freud believed, means to plumb the depths of our unconscious mind. As we shall see in Chapter 12, Freud developed a method of psychotherapy, called *psychoanalysis,* that focuses on helping people gain insight into the unconscious motives and conflicts that he believed were at the root of their problems.

Psychodynamic theory has had its critics, however. Many, including some of Freud's own followers, believe Freud placed too much importance on sexual and aggressive drives and too little emphasis on the role of social relationships in the development of personality. Other psychodynamic thinkers, including Horney, did place greater emphasis on social influences in personality development. Another challenge to Freud is the lack of evidence to support many of the principles on which his theory is based, including his beliefs in castration anxiety and penis envy and the universality of the Oedipus complex. Some critics even question whether the Oedipus complex exists at all (see Kupfersmid, 1995).

Other critics challenged the progression and timing of Freud's psychosexual stages of development. Still others challenged psychodynamic theory itself as resting almost entirely on evidence gathered from a relatively few case studies. Case studies may be open to varied interpretations. Moreover, the experiences of the few individuals who are the subjects of case studies may not be representative of people in general. Yet perhaps the greatest limitation of the psychodynamic approach is the difficulty of putting many of its concepts, especially unconscious phenomena, to more formal scientific tests. The scientific method requires that theories lend themselves to testable hypotheses. But by their nature, unconscious processes are not open to direct observation or scientific measurement, which makes them difficult—some would say impossible—to study scientifically. Still, we find today a number of investigators attempting to objectively test certain aspects of psychodynamic theory, including Freud's beliefs about repression. A growing body of evidence from different areas of research in psychology supports the existence of psychological functioning outside of awareness, including defense mechanisms (Cramer, 2000; Westen & Gabbard, 2002).

Concept Chart 10.1 provides an overview of the psychodynamic perspective on personality. In subsequent modules, we will consider other leading perspectives on personality—namely, the trait, social-cognitive, and humanistic approaches.

CONCEPT 10.8
Although the psychodynamic perspective has had a major impact on psychology and beyond, critics contend that it lacks support from rigorous scientific studies for many of its key concepts.

personal unconscious Jung's term for an unconscious region of mind comprising a reservoir of the individual's repressed memories and impulses.

collective unconscious In Jung's theory, a part of the mind containing ideas and archetypal images shared among humankind that have been transmitted genetically from ancestral humans.

archetypes Jung's term for the primitive images contained in the collective unconscious that reflect ancestral or universal experiences of human beings.

individual psychology Adler's theory of personality, which emphasizes the unique potential of each individual.

creative self In Adler's theory, the self-aware part of personality that organizes goal-seeking efforts.

inferiority complex In Adler's theory, a concept involving the influence that feelings of inadequacy or inferiority in young children have on their developing personalities and desires to compensate.

drive for superiority Adler's term for the motivation to compensate for feelings of inferiority. Also called the *will-to-power.*

basic anxiety In Horney's theory, a deep-seated form of anxiety in children that is associated with feelings of being isolated and helpless in a world perceived as potentially threatening and hostile.

basic hostility In Horney's theory, deep feelings of resentment that children may harbor toward their parents.

CONCEPT CHART 10.1
Major Concepts in Psychodynamic Theory

	Concept	Description	Summary
Freud's Psychoanalytic Theory	Levels of consciousness	The mind consists of three levels of consciousness: the conscious, the preconscious, and the unconscious.	Only a small part of the mind is fully conscious. The unconscious mind, the largest part of the mind, contains our baser drives and impulses.
	Structure of personality	Id, ego, and superego	The id, which exists only in the unconscious, represents a repository of instinctual impulses and wishes that demand instant gratification. The ego seeks to satisfy the demands of the id through socially acceptable channels without offending the superego, the moral guardian of the personality.
	Governing principles	Pleasure principle and reality principle	The id follows the pleasure principle, the demand for instant gratification regardless of social necessities. The ego follows the reality principle by which gratification of impulses must be weighed in terms of social acceptability and practicality.
	Defense mechanisms	The ego uses defense mechanisms to conceal or distort unacceptable impulses, thus preventing them from rising into consciousness.	The major defense mechanisms include repression, regression, projection, rationalization, denial, reaction formation, sublimation, and displacement.
	Stages of psychosexual development	Sexual motivation is expressed through stimulation of different body parts or erogenous zones as the child matures.	The five stages of psychosexual development are oral, anal, phallic, latency, and genital. Overgratification or undergratification at any stage can lead to personality features or fixations characteristic of that stage.
Other Theories	Key points	Greater emphasis on the ego and social relationships than was the case with Freud, and lesser emphasis on sexual and aggressive motivation	Carl Jung's analytical psychology introduced such concepts as the personal unconscious, archetypes, and the collective unconscious. Alfred Adler's individual psychology emphasized self-awareness, goal-striving, and ways in which people compensate for underlying feelings of inadequacy or inferiority. Karen Horney focused on ways in which people relate to each other and the importance of parent-child relationships.

MODULE 10.1 REVIEW

The Psychodynamic Perspective

CONCEPT CHECK

1. Psychoanalytic theory attempts to explain how humans balance
   a. sexual instincts and social standards.
   b. demands for productivity with demands for leisure.
   c. desire for wealth with desires for sexual reproduction.
   d. basic biological needs with self-actualization needs.

2. To Freud, the part of the mind that organizes efforts to satisfy basic impulses in ways that avoid social condemnation is the
   a. id.   b. superego.   c. ego.   d. preconscious.

3. To Freud, the psychosexual developmental stage during which a young boy experiences the Oedipus complex is the
   a. oral stage.   c. phallic stage.
   b. anal stage.   d. genital stage.

4. Match the following terms with their descriptions:
   (a) defense mechanisms; (b) repression; (c) Freudian slip; (d) projection.
   i.   motivated forgetting
   ii. accidentally revealing underlying thought
   iii. protect the self from anxiety
   iv. imposing one's own impulses or desires on others

5. Which of the following psychodynamic theorists supported the view that humans share a collective unconscious?
   a. Carl Jung   c. Erik Erikson
   b. Karen Horney   d. Alfred Adler

The Trait Perspective

- **What are the three types of traits in Allport's trait model?**
- **What was Cattell's view on the organization of traits?**
- **What three traits are represented in Eysenck's model of personality?**
- **What is the "Big Five" trait model of personality?**
- **What role do genes play in personality?**

Like psychodynamic theorists, trait theorists look within the personality to explain behavior. But the structures of personality they bring into focus are not opposing mental states or entities. Rather, they believe that personality consists of a distinctive set of relatively stable or enduring characteristics or dispositions called **traits**. They use personality traits to predict how people are likely to behave in different situations. For example, they may describe Rosa as having personality traits such as cheerfulness and outgoingness. Based on these traits, they might predict that she is likely to be involved in many social activities and to be the kind of person people describe as always having a smile on her face. We might describe Derek, however, as having traits such as suspiciousness and introversion. Based on these traits, they might expect Derek to shun social interactions and to feel that people are always taking advantage of him.

Trait theorists are interested in learning how people differ in their underlying traits. They are also interested in measuring traits and understanding how traits are organized or structured within the personality. Some trait theorists believe that traits are largely innate or inborn; others argue that traits are largely acquired through experience. In this module, we focus on the contributions of several prominent trait theorists, beginning with an early contributor to the trait perspective, Gordon Allport.

Gordon Allport: A Hierarchy of Traits

To Gordon Allport (1897–1967), personality traits are inherited but are influenced by experience. He claimed that traits could be ranked within a hierarchy in relation the degree to which they influence behavior (Allport, 1961). **Cardinal traits** are at the highest level. They are pervasive characteristics that influence a person's behavior in most situations. For example, we might describe the cardinal trait in Martin Luther King's personality as the commitment to social justice. Yet Allport believed that relatively few people possess such dominant traits. More common but less wide-reaching traits are **central traits**, the basic building blocks of personality that influence behavior in many situations. Examples of central traits are characteristics such as competitiveness, generosity, independence, arrogance, and fearfulness—the kinds of traits you would generally use when describing the general characteristics of other people's behavior. At a more superficial level are **secondary traits**, such as preferences for particular styles of clothing or types of music, which affect behavior in fewer situations.

Raymond Cattell: Mapping the Personality

Trait theorist Raymond Cattell (1905–1998) believed that there are two basic levels of traits (Cattell, 1950, 1965). **Surface traits** lie on the "surface" of personality. They are characteristics of personality that can be inferred from observations of behavior. Surface traits are associated with adjectives commonly used to describe personality, such as friendliness, stubbornness, emotionality, and carelessness. Cattell observed that surface traits often occur together. A person whom people

CONCEPT 10.9
Allport believed that personality traits are ordered in a hierarchy of importance from cardinal traits at the highest level through central traits and secondary traits at the lower levels.

traits   Relatively enduring personal characteristics.

cardinal traits   Allport's term for the more pervasive dimensions that define an individual's general personality.

central traits   Allport's term for personality characteristics that have a widespread influence on the individual's behavior across situations.

secondary traits   Allport's term for specific traits that influence behavior in relatively few situations.

surface traits   Cattell's term for personality traits at the surface level that can be gleaned from observations of behavior.

TRY THIS OUT

Sizing Up Your Personality

You can use the personality traits found in Cattell's 16PF to compare your personality with those of the occupational groups shown in Figure 10.2. Place a mark at the point on each dimension that you feel best describes your personality. Connect the points using a black pen. Then examine your responses in relation to those of the other groups. Which of these groups most closely matches your perceptions of your own personality? Were you surprised by the results? Did you learn anything about yourself by completing this exercise?

CONCEPT 10.10

Raymond Cattell believed that the structure of personality consists of two levels of traits: surface traits that correspond to ordinary descriptions of personality, and a deeper level of more general traits, called source traits, that give rise to these surface traits.

CONCEPT 10.11

Eysenck believed that the combinations of three general traits of introversion-extraversion, neuroticism, and psychoticism could be used to classify basic personality types.

source traits   Cattell's term for traits at a deep level of personality that are not apparent in observed behavior but must be inferred based on underlying relationships among surface traits.

introversion-extraversion   One of the three underlying dimensions of personality in Eysenck's model, referring to tendencies toward being solitary and reserved on the one end or outgoing and sociable on the other end.

neuroticism   One of the three underlying dimensions of personality in Eysenck's model, referring to tendencies toward emotional instability, anxiety, and worry.

psychoticism   One of the three underlying dimensions of personality in Eysenck's model, referring to tendencies to be perceived as cold and antisocial.

perceive as stubborn also tends to be perceived as rigid and foul-tempered. These linkages suggested that there is a deeper level of personality consisting of more general, underlying traits that give rise to surface traits. To explore this deeper level, Cattell used statistical techniques to map the structure of personality by analyzing the relationships among surface traits (Horn, 2001). Through this work, he derived a set of more general factors of personality, which he called **source traits**. Cattell went on to construct a paper-and-pencil personality scale to measure sixteen source traits, which he called the Sixteen Personality Factor Questionnaire, or 16PF. Each trait on the 16PF is represented on a continuum, such as "reserved vs. outgoing." Figure 10.2 compares the scores of groups of writers, airline pilots, and creative artists on the 16PF.

Hans Eysenck: A Simpler Trait Model

In contrast to Cattell's model, which organized personality traits into a complex hierarchy, Hans Eysenck (1916–1997) constructed a simpler model of personality. This model describes personality using three major traits (Eysenck, 1981):

1. **Introversion-Extraversion** People who are introverted are solitary, reserved, and unsociable, whereas those who are extraverted are outgoing, friendly, and people-oriented.

2. **Neuroticism** People who are high on neuroticism, or emotional instability, tend to be tense, anxious, worrisome, restless, and moody. Those who are low on neuroticism tend to be relaxed, calm, stable, and even-tempered.

3. **Psychoticism** People who are high on psychoticism are perceived as cold, antisocial, hostile, and insensitive. Those who are low on psychoticism are described as warm, sensitive, and concerned about others.

Eysenck classified people according to four basic personality types based on the combinations of these traits: extraverted-neurotic, extraverted-stable, introverted-stable, and introverted-neurotic (Eysenck, 1982). Figure 10.3 shows these four types, as represented by the four quadrants of the chart, along with the observed characteristics identified with each type.

Eysenck believed that biological differences are responsible for variations in personality traits from person to person. He argued that introverts inherit a nervous system that operates at a higher level of arousal than does that of extraverts. Consequently, introverts require less stimulation to maintain an optimal level of arousal. An introvert would be most comfortable enjoying quiet activities.

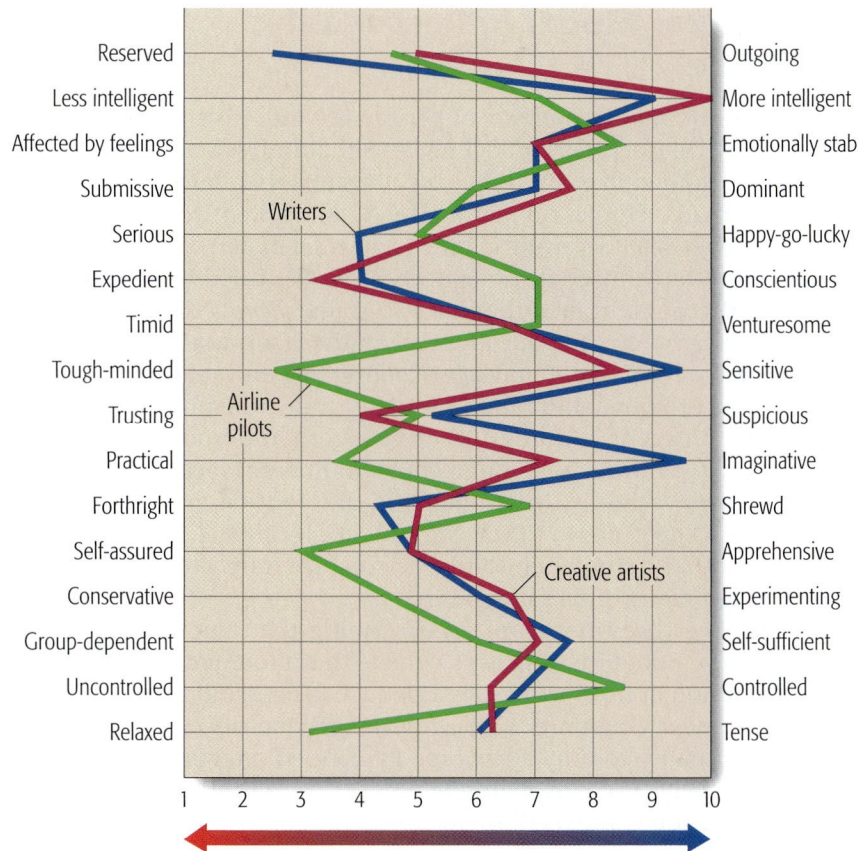

Reserved — Outgoing
Less intelligent — More intelligent
Affected by feelings — Emotionally stable
Submissive — Dominant
Serious — Happy-go-lucky
Expedient — Conscientious
Timid — Venturesome
Tough-minded — Sensitive
Trusting — Suspicious
Practical — Imaginative
Forthright — Shrewd
Self-assured — Apprehensive
Conservative — Experimenting
Group-dependent — Self-sufficient
Uncontrolled — Controlled
Relaxed — Tense

Writers
Airline pilots
Creative artists

1 2 3 4 5 6 7 8 9 10

Figure 10.2   Cattell's 16PF
The 16PF is a personality test that compares individuals on sixteen source traits or key dimensions of personality, each of which is represented on a continuum ranging from one polar extreme to the other. Here we see the average scores of samples composed of three occupational groups: creative artists, airline pilots, and writers. Notice the differences in the personalities in these groups. For example, compared to the other groups, airline pilots tend to be more controlled, self-assured, and relaxed—traits that should help put airline passengers at ease.

Source: Adapted from Cattell, Eber, & Tatsuoka, 1970.

Extraverts may require more stimulation to raise their arousal to optimal levels, which could explain why they are drawn to more exciting activities. It would come as no surprise to Eysenck that a group of mountain climbers who were attempting to scale Mt. Everest, the world's tallest peak, scored high on extraversion (Egan & Stelmack, 2003). They were also low on neuroticism (emotional instability), which is a good thing if you happen to be climbing the face of a mountain.

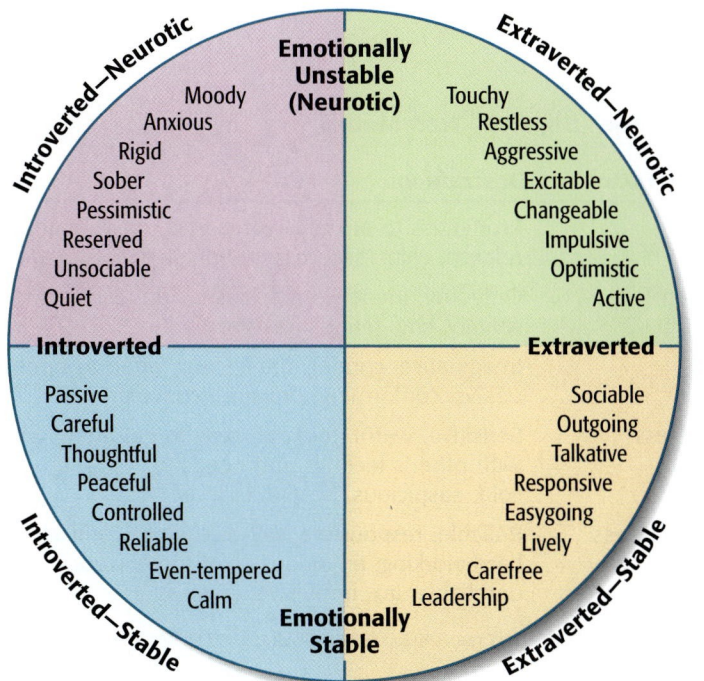

Figure 10.3   Eysenck's Personality Types
Combining the dimensions of introversion-extraversion and emotional instability in Eysenck's model of personality yields four basic personality types as represented by these four quadrants: extraverted-neurotic, extraverted-stable, introverted-stable, and introverted-neurotic. Personality traits associated with these personality types are shown within each quadrant.

Source: Adapted from Eysenck, 1982.

The Five-Factor Model of Personality: The "Big Five"

The most widely adopted trait model of personality today is the **five-factor model (FFM)**, or "Big Five" model. This model suggests that individual differences in personality can be classified in terms of five broad factors that have most consistently been found in research studies on personality (Gosling, Rentfrow, & Swann, 2003; McCrae, 2004). The "Big Five" isn't so much a new set of personality traits as it is a consolidation and integration of traits previously identified by Cattell, Eysenck, and other trait theorists. In fact, the first two traits, *neuroticism* and *extraversion*, parallel those in Eysenck's model. The three other factors making up the "Big Five" are *openness, agreeableness,* and *conscientiousness* (see Table 10.3).

Cross-cultural studies show that personality traits resembling the "Big Five" emerge in many different cultures, in both Western and non-Western cultures, among men as well as women, among people of different races, and when measured in different ways and by instruments in different languages and different language groups (Egger et al., 2003; McCrae et al., 2004a, 2004b; Paunonen, 2003). It appears that a similar cluster of personality traits corresponding to the "Big Five" exists in many different cultures.

Is the "Big Five" the final word on describing the structure of personality traits? Perhaps not. Some investigators believe that more factors may provide a better approximation of how people describe each other's and their own personalities in terms of underlying traits. Other researchers question whether any model that reduces personality to only a few broadly defined categories can capture the richness and uniqueness of personality or account for an individual's behavior in specific environmental contexts (Epstein, 1996; Paunonen, 1998).

The Genetic Basis of Traits: Moving Beyond the Nature-Nurture Debate

Increasing evidence points to the important role that heredity plays in shaping our personalities. For example, scientists recently linked a particular gene to the trait of neuroticism. This gene appears to account for half of the variability (differences among people) on this trait, with the other half accounted for by environmental factors such as early learning experiences (Plomin, Owen, & McGuffin,

⌕ **CONCEPT 10.12**
The five-factor model of personality—the "Big Five"—identifies the five most common personality factors derived from research on personality.

One of the "Big Five" Conscientiousness is one of the five major traits that make up the "Big Five" model of personality. People who are conscientious are reliable, hard-working, and self-disciplined. Where do you think you stand on each of the "Big Five" traits?

five-factor model (FFM) The dominant contemporary trait model of personality, consisting of five broad personality factors: neuroticism, extraversion, openness, agreeableness, and conscientiousness.

TABLE 10.3	The "Big Five" Trait Model
Personality Factor	**Description**
Neuroticism	Proneness to anxiety, worry, guilt, emotional instability vs. relaxed, calm, secure, emotionally stable
Extraversion	Outgoing, friendly, enthusiastic, fun-loving vs. solitary, shy, serious, reserved
Openness	Imaginative, curious, intellectual, open to nontraditional values vs. conforming, practical, conventional
Agreeableness	Sensitive, warm, tolerant, easy to get along with, concerned with other's feelings and needs vs. cold, suspicious, hostile, callous
Conscientiousness	Reliable, responsible, self-disciplined, ethical, hard-working, ambitious vs. disorganized, unreliable, lax, impulsive, careless

Sources: Adapted from Costa & McCrae, 1992a, 1992b; Goldberg, 1993; McCrae & Costa, 1986, 1996.

1994). Genetics also appears to play a role in many other personality traits, including shyness, aggressiveness, and novelty-seeking (Arbelle et al., 2003; Benjamin et al., 2002; Sen et al., 2003).

Researchers today are moving beyond the old nature-nurture debate. They are increasingly concerned with understanding the interactions of biology and environment. They believe that early life experiences can affect the developing brain, which in turn can affect personality development. How this research will play out in determining relationships among biology, environment, and personality remains to be seen. In the meantime, refer to Concept Chart 10.2 for a review of the major trait models of personality.

Evaluating the Trait Perspective

Let us note on the positive side of the ledger that the trait perspective has an intuitive appeal. People commonly use trait terms when describing their own and other people's personalities. We might describe Samantha as cold or callous, while we might think of Li Ming as kind and compassionate. Thus, trait theories are useful to the extent that they provide convenient categories or groupings of traits that people commonly use. Trait theories also led to the development of personality tests, including Cattell's 16PF and the Eysenck Personality Inventory, which psychologists use to compare how people score on different traits. Childhood personality traits do tend to be associated with adult personality traits, as reported by a recent study that showed similar traits, such as negative emotionality, in children 8 to 12 years of age and then again ten years later at ages 17 to 23 (Shiner, Masten, & Tellegen, 2002).

But trait theories have their drawbacks. Perhaps the major challenge is that they simply attach a label to behavior rather than explaining it. Consider the following example:

1. You can always count on Mary. She's very reliable.
2. Why is Mary reliable? Because she is a conscientious person.
3. How do you know she is a conscientious person? Because she's reliable.

CONCEPT 10.13
Psychologists are moving beyond the nature-nurture debate to examine how heredity and environment interact in the development of personality.

THINK *About It*

Can You Change Your Personality?

Do you believe that your personality traits are fixed or unchangeable? Or might your personality be open to adjustment here and there? What would you like to change about yourself and how you relate to others? Are you willing to see whether or not you're a leopard who can change its spots?

CONCEPT 10.14
Though trait theories provide convenient ways of describing personality features, they have been criticized on grounds of circular reasoning and failure to account for specificity of behavior across situations.

CONCEPT CHART 10.2
Trait Models of Personality

Trait Theorist/Model	Traits	Summary
Gordon Allport	Cardinal traits, central traits, and secondary traits	Allport believed that traits were physical entities that influenced behavior. Relatively few people possess cardinal traits, the more encompassing traits that determine behavior across most situations.
Raymond Cattell	Surface traits and source traits	Cattell used factor analysis to group traits. Traits corresponding to clusters of observed behaviors are surface traits. More general traits, called source traits, account for relationships among surface traits.
Hans Eysenck	Three major traits: introversion-extraversion, neuroticism, and psychoticism	Eysenck believed that differences in introversion-extraversion result from biological differences in the nervous system.
Five-Factor Model (FFM): The "Big Five"	Neuroticism, extraversion, openness, agreeableness, and conscientiousness	The most widely accepted trait model today, the FFM is based on five trait factors that have most consistently emerged in research on personality. Yet critics contend that such broad factors cannot explain the richness or uniqueness of personality.

Notice the *circular reasoning* here—explaining Mary's behavior in terms of a trait ("conscientiousness") whose existence is based on observing the very same behavior. Traits may be nothing more than shorthand descriptions of the apparent behaviors of people, with little to offer in terms of explaining the underlying causes of the behaviors. Even as descriptions, trait theories are based on broadly defined traits, such as the "Big Five," that may fail to capture the unique characteristics of individuals (Epstein, 1996; McAdams, 1992).

Another argument against trait theories is that behavior may not be as stable across time and situations as trait theorists suppose. How you act with your boss, for example, may be different from how you act around the house. How you relate to people today may be very different from how you related to people in the past. Learning theorists argue that we need to take into account environmental or situational factors, such as stimulus cues and reinforcements, in order to more accurately predict behavior.

Some personality theorists, such as Walter Mischel, whose own contributions will be discussed in the next module, argue that behavior depends more on situational factors than trait theorists would suppose. Mischel argues that people act consistently when the situations they face, and the meanings these situations hold for them, are similar (Mischel & Shoda, 1999). But Mischel recognizes that individual differences in underlying traits do exist. As he says, ". . . on the whole, some people are more sociable than others, some are more open-minded, some are more punctual, and so on" (Mischel, 2004). A developing consensus in the field seems to be emerging around the concept of *interactionism*—the belief that behavior involves an interaction between traits and situational factors. This view holds that people tend to show enduring styles of behavior associated with personality traits, but their behavior in given situations is also influenced by the demands they face in particular situations (Malloy et al., 1997; Tett & Burnett, 2003; Wu & Clark, 2003).

MODULE 10.2 REVIEW

The Trait Perspective

CONCEPT CHECK

1. In the field of personality, "relatively stable or enduring characteristics or dispositions" are referred to as
   a. instinctual impulses.
   b. traits.
   c. desires.
   d. objectives.

2. In Gordon Allport's view, the most common characteristics that form the basic building blocks of personality are
   a. cardinal traits.
   b. central traits.
   c. secondary traits.
   d. universal traits.

3. The 16PF Questionnaire, developed by Raymond Cattell, is designed to measure
   a. source traits.
   b. surface traits.
   c. introversion-extraversion.
   d. psychoticism traits.

4. Among the personality psychologists discussed in this module, who described personality on the basis of three major traits?

5. The personality dimensions of neuroticism, extraversion, openness, agreeableness, and conscientiousness together comprise
   a. the Eysenck Personality Inventory.
   b. the 16PF.
   c. the Big Five model of personality.
   d. the MMPI.

6. Name some of the personality characteristics for which a genetic link has been supported.

MODULE 10.3   The Social-Cognitive Perspective

- What are expectancies and subjective values?
- What is reciprocal determinism?
- What are situation and person variables?

Some psychologists developed models of personality that were quite different from Freud's and from the trait theorists. Behaviorists such as John Watson and B. F. Skinner believed that personality is shaped by environmental influences (rewards and punishments), not by unconscious influences, as in Freud's theory, or by underlying traits, as the trait theorists believed. The behaviorists believed that personality consists of the sum total of an individual's learned behavior. Consider your own personality as a behaviorist might view it. Others may see you as friendly and outgoing; but to a behaviorist, terms like *friendly* and *outgoing* are merely labels describing a set of behaviors, such as showing an interest in others and participating in a wide range of social activities.

Behaviorists believe that behavior is learned on the basis of classical and operant conditioning. Rather than probe the depths of your unconscious to understand the roots of your behavior, behaviorists might explore how you were reinforced in the past for displaying friendly and outgoing behaviors. People with different histories of rewards and punishments develop different patterns of behavior. If Maisha is respectful and conscientious in her work habits, it is because she has been rewarded for this kind of behavior in the past. If Tyler spends more time socializing than studying, it is likely he has been reinforced more for social interactions than for academic performance.

Many learning theorists today adopt a broader view of learning than did the traditional behaviorists, such as Watson and Skinner. This contemporary model, called **social-cognitive theory**, maintains that to explain behavior we need to take into account cognitive and social aspects of behavior, not just the rewards and punishments to which we are exposed in the environment. These social and cognitive variables include expectancies we hold about the outcomes of our behavior, the values we place on rewards, and the learning that occurs when we imitate the behavior of others we observe interacting in social situations. To social-cognitive theorists, personality comprises not only learned behavior but also the ways that individuals think about themselves and the world. They believe that humans act upon the environment in pursuing their goals, not just react to it (Bandura, 2001). The three primary contributors to social-cognitive theory are the psychologists Julian Rotter, Albert Bandura, and Walter Mischel.

Julian Rotter: The Locus of Control

To Julian Rotter (1990), explaining and predicting behavior involves knowing an individual's reinforcement history as well as the person's expectancies and subjective values. **Expectancies** are your personal predictions of the outcomes of your behavior. For example, students who hold a positive expectancy about school-work believe that studying will improve their chances of getting good grades. **Subjective value** is the worth you place on desired outcomes. A dedicated student will place a high subjective value on getting good grades. In this instance, a student with high positive expectancy and high subjective value would be more likely to study for a forthcoming exam than someone who does not link studying with grades or who does not care about grades.

Rotter also believed that people acquire general expectancies about their ability to obtain reinforcements in their lives. Some, for example, have an internal **locus of control** (*locus* is the Latin word for "place"). They believe they can obtain

CONCEPT 10.15
To behaviorists, the concept of personality refers to the sum total of an individual's learned behavior.

CONCEPT 10.16
Social-cognitive theorists expanded traditional learning theory by focusing on the cognitive and social learning aspects of behavior.

CONCEPT 10.17
Social-cognitive theorists believe that personality consists of individuals' repertoires of behavior and ways of thinking about themselves and the world.

social-cognitive theory   A learning-based model of personality that emphasizes both cognitive factors and environmental influences in determining behavior.

expectancies   In social-cognitive theory, personal predictions about the outcomes of behavior.

subjective value   In social-cognitive theory, the importance that individuals place on desired outcomes.

locus of control   In Rotter's theory, one's general expectancies about whether one's efforts can bring about desired outcomes or reinforcements.

CONCEPT 10.18
Rotter believed that our ability to explain and predict behavior depends on knowing an individual's reinforcement history as well as the person's expectancies and subjective values.

reinforcements through work and effort. Others feel that reinforcements are largely controlled by external forces beyond their control, such as luck or fate. They have an external locus of control. Locus of control is linked to various outcomes. For example, "internals" are more likely than "externals" to succeed in school (Hackett et al., 1992; Kalechstein & Nowicki, 1997), to cope with pain (Melding, 1995), and, among overweight individuals, to make changes in diet and exercise patterns (Holt, Clark, & Kreuter, 2001).

Albert Bandura: Reciprocal Determinism and the Role of Expectancies

CONCEPT 10.19
Bandura's model of reciprocal determinism holds that cognitions, behaviors, and environmental factors mutually influence each other.

Albert Bandura's (1986) model of **reciprocal determinism** holds that cognitions, behaviors, and environmental factors influence each other (see Figure 10.4). Bandura focuses on the interaction between what we do (our behavior) and what we think (our cognitions). For example, suppose a motorist is cut off by another motorist on the road. The first motorist may think angering thoughts, such as "I'm going to teach that guy a lesson." These thoughts or cognitions increase the likelihood of aggressive behavior (e.g., cutting in front of the other motorist). The aggressive behavior, in turn, affects the social environment (the other motorist responds aggressively). The other motorist's actions then lead the first to have even more angering thoughts ("I can't let him get away with that!"), which, in turn, lead to more aggressive behavior. This vicious cycle of escalating aggressive behavior and angering thoughts may result in an incident of *road rage,* which can have tragic consequences.

Bandura (1989, 1997) emphasized the role of *observational learning,* or learning by observing and imitating the behavior of others in social contexts. He also distinguished between two types of expectancies: outcome expectations and efficacy expectations. **Outcome expectations** are predictions of the outcomes of behavior. You are more likely to drink alcohol in a social situation if you believe it

Figure 10.4 Bandura's Model of Reciprocal Determinism Bandura's model holds that cognitions, behaviors, and environmental factors mutually influence each other.

Source: Adapted from Bandura, 1986.

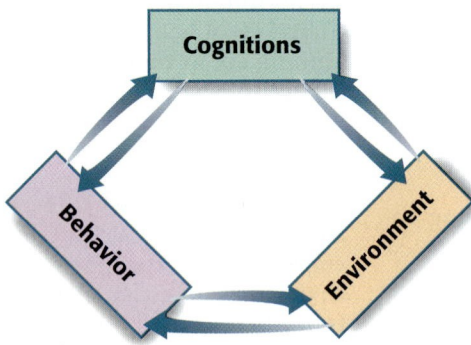

"I Can Do This" Bandura's social-cognitive model of personality emphasizes the importance of cognitive factors such as self-efficacy—the belief in our ability to accomplish tasks we set out to do.

reciprocal determinism Bandura's model in which cognitions, behaviors, and environmental factors both influence and are influenced by each other.

outcome expectations Bandura's term for our personal predictions about the outcomes of our behavior.

will be a pleasant experience and perhaps increase your self-confidence than if you thought it would make you sick or act silly. **Efficacy expectations** are predictions about your personal ability to perform the behaviors you set out to accomplish. People with high *self-efficacy,* or beliefs in their personal effectiveness, are generally more likely to undertake challenges, such as academic and social challenges, and persevere to see them through.

Self-efficacy is associated with better health outcomes in which adherence to medical directives is important, such as with diabetic patients (Johnston-Brooks, Lewis, & Garg, 2002; Senécal, Nouwen, & White, 2000). People with higher levels of self-efficacy are more likely to persevere and accomplish tasks they undertake. For example, investigators link self-efficacy to a lower likelihood of relapse following smoking cessation (Shiffman et al., 2000) and to maintenance of greater physical activity in young women (Motl et al., 2002). Yet success also boosts efficacy expectations. This is one reason that success experiences are so important to children and adults alike.

Walter Mischel: Situation Versus Person Variables

Walter Mischel's (1973) theoretical model overlaps to a large extent with Rotter's and Bandura's. Mischel argues that behavior is influenced by both **situation variables**, which are environmental factors such as rewards and punishments, and **person variables**, or internal personal factors. Two of these person variables, *expectancies* and *subjective values,* have the same meaning as in Rotter's model. But Mischel adds other person variables, including (1) *competencies,* or the knowledge and skills we possess, such as the ability to play an instrument or to speak a foreign language; (2) *encoding strategies,* or personal perceptions of events, such as whether we see a sudden gift of a basket of flowers as a gesture of love or as a way of making amends; and (3) *self-regulatory systems and plans,* or the ability to plan courses of action to achieve our goals and to reward ourselves for accomplishing them. In Mischel's view, as in Bandura's, environmental and personal factors interact to produce behavior. In predicting a specific person's behavior, we need to take into account what we know about the person as well as the situation at hand.

In his more recent work, Mischel focuses on the interactions of emotions (affects) and person variables. One example he considers is how negative feeling states such as depression cast a dim outlook on the ways that people encode experiences and form expectancies about future outcomes (Mischel & Shoda, 1995). But Mischel also recognizes that our emotional reactions, in turn, depend on how we interpret and label experiences, a point to which we shall return when we consider cognitive theories of depression in Chapter 11.

Evaluating the Social-Cognitive Perspective

Learning theorists have increased our understanding of how behavior is influenced by environmental factors, such as a history of rewards and punishments. Reinforcement principles are now applied in a wide range of programs, including those designed to help parents learn better parenting skills and to help children learn more effectively in the classroom. Learning theory has also given rise to a major contemporary model of psychotherapy, *behavior therapy,* in which learning principles are applied to help people deal with emotional and behavioral problems (see Chapter 12).

Social-cognitive theorists broadened the scope of learning theory to include cognitive influences on learning and the recognition that much of what we learn occurs by observing others in social contexts. Today, many behavior therapists subscribe to a broader treatment model, called *cognitive-behavioral therapy,* or *CBT* (see Chapter 12), which incorporates cognitive as well as behavioral approaches to

CONCEPT 10.20
Mischel proposed that behavior is influenced both by environmental factors, called situation variables, and by internal personal factors, called person variables.

efficacy expectations   Bandura's term for the expectancies we have regarding our ability to perform behaviors we set out to accomplish.

situation variables   Mischel's term for environmental influences on behavior, such as rewards and punishments.

person variables   Mischel's term for internal personal factors that influence behavior, including competencies, expectancies, and subjective values.

CONCEPT CHART 10.3
Behavioral and Social-Cognitive Perspectives on Personality

Traditional Behaviorism	Social-Cognitive Theory
Behaviorists believe that personality is the sum total of an individual's learned behavior and that distinctive patterns of behavior are determined by differences between people in their learning experiences.	To social-cognitive theorists, personality consists of both learned behaviors and ways of thinking. They believe that we need to attend to the role of cognitions and observational learning in explaining and predicting behavior, not just to the role of environmental influences such as rewards and punishments.

therapy and mirrors the teachings of the social-cognitive theorists. But perhaps the most important influence of the social-cognitive theorists is that they have presented us with a view of people as active seekers and interpreters of information, not just responders to environmental influences. Indeed, many psychologists have come to believe that behavior is best explained by the reciprocal interactions between the person and the environment.

CONCEPT 10.21

Though social-cognitive theories broadened traditional learning theory, critics claim that it doesn't account for unconscious processes and genetic factors in personality.

To some of its critics, social-cognitive theory presents a limited view of personality because it fails to account for the roles of unconscious influences and heredity. To others, specifically trait theorists, social-cognitive theorists fail to take personality traits into account when attempting to explain underlying consistencies in behavior across situations. Social-cognitive theorists would counter that traits don't explain behavior but merely attach labels to behavior—and, moreover, that behavior is not as consistent across situations as trait theorists may suppose. Finally, social-cognitive theory is criticized by those who believe that it focuses too little on subjective experience, such as self-awareness and the flow of consciousness. Social-cognitive theorists may believe that the emphasis they place on cognitive factors, such as expectancies and subjective values, addresses these concerns. As you'll see next, subjective experience takes center stage in another perspective on personality, the humanistic approach. But first you may want to review Concept Chart 10.3, which summarizes the major concepts associated with the behavioral and social-cognitive perspectives on personality.

MODULE 10.3 REVIEW

The Social-Cognitive Perspective

CONCEPT CHECK

1. Unlike Freudian and trait theorists, behaviorists believe that personality is due to
   a. deep, underlying unconscious conflicts.
   b. the sum total of a person's history of reinforcements and punishments.
   c. ways we think about ourselves and the world.
   d. ways we think about others in the world.

2. According to Julian Rotter, the individual who expects a good outcome due to hard work and effort has a(n) _____ locus of control.
   a. internal   c. positive
   b. external   d. negative

3. Describe Albert Bandura's concept of *reciprocal determinism*.

4. Match the following terms with the appropriate descriptions: (a) self-efficacy; (b) situation variables; (c) competencies; (d) encoding strategies.
   i.   personal perceptions of events
   ii. belief in personal effectiveness
   iii. personal knowledge and skills
   iv. environmental influences

MODULE 10.4 The Humanistic Perspective

- **What is self-theory?**
- **How do collectivistic and individualistic cultures view the concept of self?**

Humanistic psychology departed from the psychodynamic and behaviorist schools in proposing that conscious choice and personal freedom are central features of what it means to be a human being (Bargh & Chartrand, 1999). To humanistic psychologists, we are not puppets whose movements are controlled by strings pulled by the unconscious mind or the environment; rather, we are endowed with the ability to make free choices that give meaning and personal direction to our lives. Two of the major contributors to humanistic thought were the American psychologists Carl Rogers (1902–1987) and Abraham Maslow (1908–1970).

Carl Rogers: The Importance of Self

Rogers (1961, 1980) believed that each of us possesses an inner drive that leads us to strive toward *self-actualization*—toward realizing our own unique potentials. The roadway toward self-actualization is an unfolding process of self-discovery and self-awareness, of tapping into one's true feelings and needs, accepting them as our own, and acting in ways that genuinely reflect them. To Rogers and other humanists, personality is expressed through the conscious experience of directing ourselves toward fulfilling our unique potentials as human beings.

Rogers believed that the self is the center of the human experience. Thus it is no surprise that he referred to his theory of personality as **self-theory**. To Rogers, the self is the executive part of your personality that organizes how you relate to the world. It is the sense of being "I" or "me"—the person who looks back at you in the mirror, the sense of being a distinct individual with your own likes, dislikes, needs, and values. The self also includes the impressions you have of yourself, impressions that comprise your *self-concept*. The theory of personality Rogers developed reflects the importance of coming to know yourself and being true to yourself, regardless of what others might think or say.

One of the primary functions of the self, as Rogers viewed it, is the development of self-esteem, or degree of liking we have for ourselves. Rogers noted that self-esteem at first mirrors how other people value us, or fail to value us. For this reason, he believed it is crucial for parents to bestow on their children **unconditional positive regard**, or acceptance of a person's basic worth regardless of whether their behavior pleases or suits us. In other words, Rogers believed that parents should prize their children regardless of their behavior at any particular moment in time. In this way, children learn to value themselves as having intrinsic worth, rather than judging themselves as either good or bad depending on whether they measure up to other people's expectations or demands. Rogers didn't mean that parents should turn a blind eye toward undesirable behavior. Parents do not need to accept all of their children's behavior; they can correct their children's poor behavior without damaging their self-esteem. However, parents need to clarify that it is the *behavior* that is undesirable, not the child.

Unfortunately, many parents show **conditional positive regard** toward their children. They bestow approval only when the children behave "properly." Children given conditional positive regard may learn to think of themselves as being worthwhile only when they are behaving in socially approved ways. Their self-esteem may become shaky, as it comes to depend on what other people think of them at a particular moment in time. To maintain self-esteem, they may need

The Makings of Unconditional Positive Regard? Rogers emphasized the importance of unconditional positive regard in the development of self-esteem.

> **CONCEPT 10.22**
> Rogers's theory of personality emphasizes the importance of the self, the sense of the "I" or "me" that organizes how you relate to the world.

self-theory Rogers's model of personality, which focuses on the importance of the self.

unconditional positive regard Valuing another person as having intrinsic worth, regardless of the person's behavior at the particular time.

conditional positive regard Valuing a person only when the person's behavior meets certain expectations or standards.

to deny their genuine feelings, interests, and desires. They learn to wear masks or to don social facades in order to please others. Their sense of themselves, or self-concept, may become so distorted that they feel like strangers to themselves. They may come to question who they really are.

Our self-esteem is ultimately a function of how close we come to meeting our **self-ideals**—our idealized sense of who or what we should be. When these ideals are shaped by what others expect of us, we may have a hard time measuring up to them. Our self-esteem may plummet. The model of therapy Rogers developed, called *client-centered therapy* (discussed in Chapter 12), helps people get in touch with their true feelings and come to value and prize themselves.

Rogers was an optimist who believed in the essential worth and goodness of human nature. He believed that people become hurtful toward each other only when their own pathways toward self-actualization are blocked or stymied by obstacles. Parents can help their children in this personal voyage of discovery by bestowing on them unconditional approval, even if the children's developing interests and values differ from their own.

As you reflect on the importance of self-esteem, consider the results of a classic 1939 study by Kenneth and Mamie Clark on the self-esteem of African American preschool children. They discovered that the children preferred playing with a white doll over a black one and attributed more positive characteristics to the white doll—a result they believed reflected the negative effects of segregation on self-esteem. In the intervening years, many other researchers have examined self-esteem in African American children using a number of different methods. The findings? Overall, African American children, adolescents, and young adults actually show higher levels of self-esteem, on average, than their White counterparts (Gray-Little & Hafdahl, 2000; Hafdahl & Gray-Little, 2002). One explanation of the self-esteem advantage among young African Americans is that they tend to have a stronger sense of ethnic identity than young Whites. Ethnic identity is a strong predictor of self-esteem among African Americans and Hispanic Americans (Gray-Little & Hafdahl, 2000; Umaña-Taylor, 2004).

The application module at the end of the chapter focuses on ways of enhancing self-esteem.

Abraham Maslow: Scaling the Heights of Self-Actualization

CONCEPT 10.23
Whereas Freud was primarily concerned with our baser instincts, Maslow focused on the highest reaches of human endeavor, the process of realizing our unique potentials.

Like Rogers, Maslow believed in an innate human drive toward self-actualization—toward becoming all that we are capable of being (Maslow, 1970, 1971). To Maslow, this drive toward self-actualization shapes our personality by motivating us to develop our unique potentials as human beings. He believed that if people were given the opportunity, they would strive toward achieving self-actualization. Yet he recognized that few of us become fully self-actualized. In the humanistic view, personality is perhaps best thought of as a continuing process of personal growth and realization—more a road to be followed than a final destination.

Humanistic psychologists, following the principles established by Maslow and Rogers, note that each of us has unique feelings, desires, and needs. Therefore, we cannot completely abide by the wishes of others and still be true to ourselves. The path to psychological health is paved with awareness and acceptance of *all* parts of ourselves, warts and otherwise.

Culture and Self-Identity

self-ideals Rogers's term for the idealized sense of how or what we should be.

collectivistic culture A culture that emphasizes people's social roles and obligations.

How you define yourself may depend on the culture in which you were raised. If you were raised in a **collectivistic culture**, you might define yourself in terms of the social roles you assume or the groups to which you belong (Markus & Kitayama,

1991; Triandis & Suh, 2002). You might say, "I am a Korean American" or "I am Jonathan's father." By contrast, if you were raised in an **individualistic culture**, you are likely to define yourself in terms of your unique individuality (the characteristics that distinguish you from others) and your personal accomplishments. You might say, "I am a systems analyst" or "I am a caring person." (Of course, these descriptions represent general cultural trends; differences certainly exist among individuals within cultures as well as between cultures themselves.)

Many cultures in Asia, Africa, and Central and South America are considered collectivistic, whereas those of the United States, Canada, and many Western European countries are characterized as individualistic. Collectivistic cultures value the group's goals over the individual's. They emphasize communal values such as harmony, respect for authority and for one's elders, conformity, cooperation, interdependence, and avoiding conflicts with others. For example, traditional Filipino culture emphasizes deference to elders at any cost (Nevid & Sta. Maria, 1999). Filipino children are taught to never disrespect their older siblings, no matter how small the age difference and, in many cases, regardless of who is "right."

Individualistic cultures, by contrast, emphasize values relating to independence and self-sufficiency. They idealize rugged individualism as personified in tales of the nineteenth-century American West. Despite differences between individualistic and collectivistic cultures, the human mind possesses the ability to think both individualistically and collectivistically depending on the circumstances (Oyserman, Coon, & Kemmelmeier, 2002).

Extremes of either individualism or collectivism can have undesirable outcomes. Excessive collectivism may stifle creativity, innovation, and personal initiative, whereas excessive individualism may lead to unmitigated greed and exploitation.

Evaluating the Humanistic Perspective

The humanistic perspective provided much of the impetus for the broad social movement of the 1960s and 1970s in which many people searched inward to find direction and meaning in their lives. It renewed the age-old debate about free will and determinism and focused attention on the need to understand the subjective or conscious experiences of individuals. Rogers's method of therapy, *client-centered therapy,* remains highly influential. And perhaps most important of all, humanistic theorists helped restore to psychology the concept of self—that center of our conscious experience of being in the world.

Yet the very strength of the humanistic viewpoint, its focus on conscious experience, is also its greatest weakness when approached as a scientific endeavor. Ultimately your conscious experience is known or knowable only to an audience of one—you. As scientists, how can humanistic psychologists ever be certain that they are measuring with any precision the private, subjective experience of another person? Humanistic psychologists might answer that we should do our best to study conscious experience scientifically, for to do less is to ignore the very subject matter—human experience—we endeavor to know. Indeed, they have been joined by cognitive psychologists in developing methods to study conscious experience, including rating scales and thought diaries that allow people to make public their private experiences—to report their thoughts, feelings, and attitudes in systematic ways that can be measured reliably.

Critics also contend that the humanistic approach's emphasis on self-fulfillment may lead some people to become self-indulgent and so absorbed with themselves that they develop a lack of concern for others. Even the concept of self-actualization poses challenges. For one thing, humanistic psychologists consider self-actualization to be a drive that motivates behavior toward higher purposes. Yet how do we know that this drive exists? If self-actualization means different things to different people—one person may become self-actualized by pursuing an interest in

CONCEPT 10.24
Whether we define ourselves in terms of our individuality or social roles that we perform is influenced by the values of the culture in which we are raised.

CONCEPT 10.25
The humanistic perspective focuses attention on the need to understand conscious experience and one's sense of self, but difficulties exist in studying private, subjective experiences and in measuring such core concepts as self-actualization.

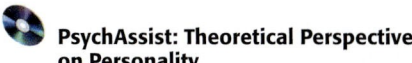
PsychAssist: Theoretical Perspectives on Personality

individualistic culture   A culture that emphasizes individual identity and personal accomplishments.

botany, another by becoming a skilled artisan—how can we ever measure self-actualization in a standardized way? To this, humanistic psychologists might respond that because people are unique, we should not expect to apply the same standard to different people.

Concept Chart 10.4 provides a summary of the major concepts in the humanistic perspective on personality.

CONCEPT CHART 10.4
The Humanistic Perspective: Key Points

Concept	Summary	Key Principle
Rogers's self theory	The self is the executive or organizing center of the personality—the "I" that determines how we relate to the world and pursue our goals.	People who are not encouraged in their upbringing to develop their individuality and uniqueness—but instead are valued only when they meet other people's expectations—tend to develop distorted self-concepts.
Maslow's concept of self-actualization	Self-actualization is a key element of personality and human motivation.	If given the chance, people will strive toward achieving self-actualization, a goal that is better thought of as a continuing journey rather than as a final destination.
Culture and self-identity	Self-identity may be influenced by collectivistic or individualistic cultural values.	Collectivistic cultures foster the development of communal or interdependent concepts of the self, whereas individualistic cultures encourage definitions of the self that embody individuality and uniqueness.

MODULE 10.4 REVIEW

The Humanistic Perspective

CONCEPT CHECK

1. Which statement best describes the humanistic belief about our freedom to make personal choices in our lives?
   a. The ability to make conscious choices is true only of people who were raised in cultures that encouraged them to think freely.
   b. Free will is but an illusion.
   c. The choices we make are largely determined by the social influences we encounter.
   d. Our free will is a basic feature of our humanity

2. Self-actualization involves
   a. self-awareness and self-discovery.
   b. tapping into one's true feelings and needs.
   c. acknowledging and acting upon one's individual characteristics.
   d. all of the above.

3. What did Rogers believe was the center of our experience of being human?

4. Defining oneself in terms of the roles one plays within the group or society is most likely to occur in
   a. a collectivist culture.
   b. an individualistic culture.
   c. Western European cultures.
   d. the traditional U.S. culture.

MODULE 10.5   Personality Tests

- **What are self-report personality inventories?**
- **What are projective tests of personality?**

Let us now move from attempts to describe or explain personality to ways of measuring it. Attempts to measure personality actually have a long history. In the eighteenth and nineteenth centuries, many well-respected scientists believed one could make reasonable judgments about a person's character and mental abilities by examining the bumps on the person's head, or even the shape of the person's nose. According to **phrenology**, a popular view at the time, you could judge people's character and mental abilities based on the pattern of bumps on their heads. Such views have long been debunked. We no longer believe you can assess people's personality traits by their superficial biological characteristics.

The methods used by psychologists today to assess personality include case studies, interviews, observational techniques, and experimental studies (see Chapter 1). But the most widely used method for learning about personality is based on the use of formal **personality tests**. The two major types of personality tests are self-report personality inventories and projective tests.

Self-Report Personality Inventories

Self-report personality inventories are structured psychological tests in which individuals are given a set of questions to answer about themselves in the form of "yes-no" or "true-false" or "agree-disagree" types of response formats. Self-report personality inventories are also called **objective tests**. They are not objective in the same sense that your bathroom scale is an objective measure of your weight. Unlike scales of weight, they rely on people's opinions or judgments as to whether they agree or disagree with particular statements. The tests are objective in the sense that they can be scored objectively because the responses they require are limited to a few choices, such as true or false. They are also considered objective because they were constructed from evidence gathered from research studies. Some self-report personality tests measure single dimensions of personality, such as assertiveness or hostility. Others attempt to capture multiple dimensions of personality. A leading example of a multidimensional personality test is the Minnesota Multiphasic Personality Inventory (MMPI), the most widely used self-report personality inventory in the world (Camara, Nathan, & Puente, 2000).

Minnesota Multiphasic Personality Inventory (MMPI)

Do you like fashion magazines? Are you frequently troubled by feelings of anxiety or nervousness? Do you feel that others "have it in for you"? What might your answers to questions such as these tell us about your underlying personality or mental health?

These questions model the items found in the MMPI, now in a revised edition called the MMPI-2 (Butcher, 2000). The MMPI-2 consists of 567 true-false items that yield scores on ten clinical scales (see Table 10.4) and additional scales measuring other personality dimensions and response tendencies.

The MMPI was constructed to help clinicians diagnose mental disorders. Items are grouped on particular scales if they tended to be answered differently by particular diagnostic groups than by normal reference groups. For example, an item such as "I feel moody at times" would be placed on the depression scale if it tended to be endorsed more often by people in a depressed group than by normal controls. The more items a person endorses in the same direction as the diagnostic group, the higher the score the person receives on the scale.

CONCEPT 10.26
Self-report personality inventories are widely used measures of personality in which a person's response options are limited, so as to make scoring them objective.

phrenology   The now-discredited view that one can judge a person's character and mental abilities by measuring the bumps on his or her head.

personality tests   Structured psychological tests that use formal methods of assessing personality.

self-report personality inventories   Structured psychological tests in which individuals are given a limited range of response options to answer a set of questions about themselves.

objective tests   Tests of personality that can be scored objectively and that are based on a research foundation.

TABLE 10.4 **Clinical Scales of the MMPI**

Scale Number and Label	Items Similar to Those Found on MMPI Scale	Sample Traits of High Scorers
1 Hypochondriasis	I am frequently bothered by an upset stomach. At times, my body seems to ache all over.	Many physical complaints, cynical defeatist attitudes, often perceived as whiny, demanding
2 Depression	Nothing seems to interest me anymore. My sleep is often disturbed by worrisome thoughts.	Depressed mood; pessimistic, worrisome, despondent, lethargic
3 Hysteria	I sometimes become flushed for no apparent reason. I tend to take people at their word when they're trying to be nice to me.	Naive, egocentric, little insight into problems, immature; develops physical complaints in response to stress
4 Psychopathic deviate	My parents often disliked my friends. My behavior sometimes got me into trouble at school.	Difficulties incorporating values of society, rebellious, impulsive, antisocial tendencies; strained family relationships; poor work and school history
5 Masculinity-femininity*	I like reading about electronics. (M) I would like to work in the theater. (F)	Males endorsing feminine attributes: have cultural and artistic interests, effeminate, sensitive, passive. Females endorsing male interests: aggressive, masculine, self-confident, active, assertive, vigorous
6 Paranoia	I would have been more successful in life but people didn't give me a fair break. It's not safe to trust anyone these days.	Suspicious, guarded, blames others, resentful, aloof, may have paranoid delusions
7 Psychasthenia	I'm one of those people who have to have something to worry about. I seem to have more fears than most people I know.	Anxious, fearful, tense, worried, insecure, difficulties concentrating, obsessional, self-doubting
8 Schizophrenia	Things seem unreal to me at times. I sometimes hear things that other people can't hear.	Confused and illogical thinking, feels alienated and misunderstood, socially isolated or withdrawn, may have blatant psychotic symptoms such as hallucinations or delusional beliefs, or may lead a detached lifestyle
9 Hypomania	I sometimes take on more tasks than I can possibly get done. People have noticed that my speech is sometimes pressured or rushed.	Energetic, possibly manic, impulsive, optimistic, sociable, active, flighty, irritable, may have overly inflated or grandiose self-image or unrealistic plans
10 Social introversion*	I don't like loud parties. I was not very active in school activities.	Shy, inhibited, withdrawn, introverted, lacks self-confidence, reserved, anxious in social situations

*The construction of these scales was based on nonclinical comparison groups.
Source: Nevid, Rathus, & Greene, 2000, p. 73.

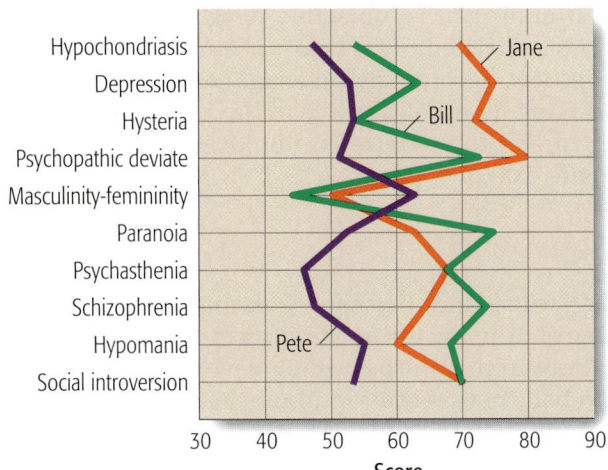

Figure 10.5 Sample MMPI-2 Profiles
(a) Jane is a twenty-one-year-old woman who was admitted to a psychiatric facility following a suicide attempt; (b) Bill is a thirty-four-year-old schizophrenia patient; and (c) Pete is a well-adjusted, twenty-five-year-old editor.

Note: Scores of 50 are average. Scores on masculinity-femininity are keyed here in the masculine direction for females and in the feminine direction for males.

When scoring the MMPI, one converts raw scores (number of items scored in the same direction as the diagnostic group) into **standard scores**, which are then plotted on a graph similar to the one shown in Figure 10.5. Scores of 65 or higher on the clinical scales are considered clinically elevated or abnormally high. Examiners take into account the elevations on individual scales and the pattern of relationships among the scale scores to form impressions of individuals' personality characteristics and possible psychological problems they may have.

Evaluation of Self-Report Personality Tests

A large body of evidence supports the validity of the MMPI and other self-report personality inventories (e.g., Graham, 2000; McGrath, Pogge, & Stokes, 2002). The MMPI provides a wealth of information about a person's interests, areas of concern, needs, and ways of relating to others, and it assists clinicians in making diagnoses of psychological or mental disorders. However, it should not be used by itself to make a diagnosis. A high score on the depression scale does not necessarily mean that a person has a depressive disorder, for example. Yet the person may share certain personality traits or complaints in common with people who do.

Self-report personality inventories have several strengths. They are relatively inexpensive to administer and score—in fact, many can be machine-scored and interpreted by computer. People may also be more willing to disclose personal information on paper-and-pencil tests than when facing an interviewer. Most important, the results of these tests may be used to predict a wide range of behaviors, including ability to relate effectively to others and to achieve positions of leadership or dominance.

Reliance on self-report data in personality tests such as the MMPI can introduce potential biases, however. Some responses may be outright lies. Others may be prone to more subtle distortions, such as tendencies to respond in a socially desirable direction—in other words, to put one's best foot forward. The more sophisticated self-report scales, including the MMPI, have validity scales that help to identify response biases. Yet even these scales may not be able to eliminate all sources of bias (McGovern & Nevid, 1986; Nicholson et al., 1997).

Projective Tests

In **projective tests**, people are presented with a set of unstructured or ambiguous stimuli, such as inkblots, that can be interpreted in various ways. Projective tests are based on the belief in psychodynamic theory that people transfer, or "project," their unconscious needs, drives, and motives onto their responses to

TRY THIS OUT

What Should I Become?

Many college counseling centers use personality tests to help students make more informed career decisions. These instruments allow people to compare their own personality profiles and interest patterns to those of people in different occupational groups. If you think you might benefit from a vocational evaluation, why not check out whether your college counseling center offers such services?

CONCEPT 10.27
Projective tests are based on the belief that the ways in which people respond to ambiguous stimuli are determined by their underlying needs and personalities.

standard scores Scores that represent an individual's relative deviation from the mean of the standardization sample.

projective tests Personality tests in which ambiguous or vague test materials are used to elicit responses that are believed to reveal a person's unconscious needs, drives, and motives.

unstructured or vague stimuli. Unlike objective tests, projective tests have a response format that is not restricted to "yes-no" or multiple-choice answers or other limited response options. Accordingly, an examiner must interpret the subject's responses, thus bringing more subjectivity to the procedure. Here we focus on the two most widely used projective tests, the Rorschach test and the TAT (Camara, Nathan, & Puente, 2000).

Rorschach Test

As a child growing up in Switzerland, Hermann Rorschach (1884–1922) amused himself by playing a game of dripping ink and folding the paper to make symmetrical inkblot figures. He noticed that people would perceive the same blots in different ways and came to believe that their responses revealed something about their personalities. His fascination with inkblots earned him the nickname *Klex*, which means "inkblot" in German ("Time Capsule," 2000). Rorschach, who went on to became a psychiatrist, turned his childhood pastime into the psychological test that bears his name. Unfortunately, Rorschach did not live to see how popular and influential his inkblot test would become. He died at the age of thirty-seven from complications following a ruptured appendix, only months after the publication of his test (Exner, 2002).

The Rorschach test consists of ten cards, similar to the one appearing in Figure 10.6. Five have splashes of color and the others are in black and white and shades of gray. Subjects are asked what each blot looks like. After the responses to each card are obtained, the examiner conducts a follow-up inquiry to probe more deeply into the person's responses.

Scoring Rorschach responses is a complex task. The scoring is based on such features as content (what the blot looked like—a "bat," for example) and form level (consistency of the response with the actual shape of the blot). Poor form level may indicate problems with perceiving reality clearly or perhaps an overly fertile imagination. Those who see formless figures dominated by color—who see reddened areas as "blood," for instance—may have difficulties controlling their emotions. The content of the response may indicate underlying conflicts with others. For example, someone who sees only animal figures and no human forms may have difficulties relating to other people.

Thematic Apperception Test (TAT)

Harvard psychologist Henry Murray developed the Thematic Apperception Test (TAT) in the 1930s (Murray, 1938). The test consists of a set of pictures depicting ambiguous scenes that may be interpreted differently. The subject is asked to tell a story about the scene, what led up to these events, and what the eventual outcome will be. Murray believed that the stories people tell reveal aspects of their own personalities, or projections of their own psychological needs and conflicts into the events they describe. For example, people whose stories consistently touch upon themes of parental rejection may be saying something about their own underlying psychological issues.

Evaluation of Projective Tests

One drawback of projective tests is that the scoring of test responses is largely based on the examiner's subjective impressions. Two examiners may disagree on the scoring of the form level of a particular Rorschach response, for example. Psychologist John Exner (1993) advanced efforts at standardizing the scoring of the Rorschach by introducing a comprehensive scoring system. Yet concerns about reliability, including those directed at Exner's scoring system, persist (e.g., Wood et al., 2001). Even if projective tests can be scored reliably, are they valid? Do they measure what they purport to measure?

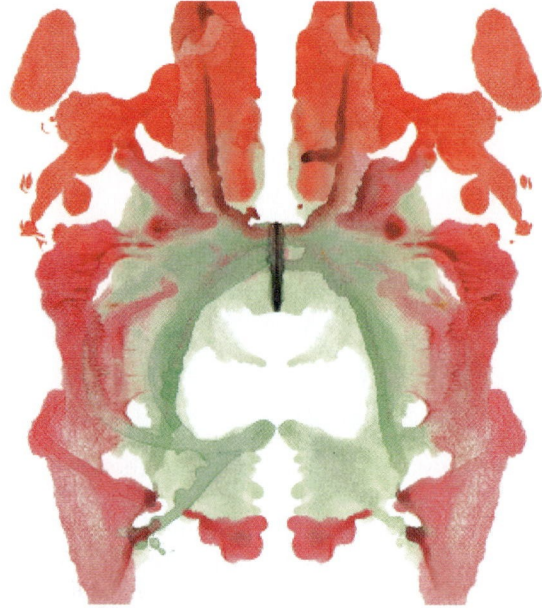

Figure 10.6 Inkblot Similar to Rorschach Inkblot
What do you think this looks like? The Rorschach test is based on the assumption that people project aspects of their own personalities onto their responses to ambiguous figures.

CONCEPT 10.28
Though projective tests are widely used by psychologists, controversy over their validity and clinical utility persists.

One problem with projective tests is *stimulus pull.* Despite efforts to make stimuli ambiguous, they often contain cues, such as sad-looking faces in the TAT, that may elicit (pull for) certain types of responses. In such cases, responses may involve reactions to the stimulus properties of the test materials themselves rather than projections of one's underlying personality (Murstein & Mathes, 1996).

 **web** Netlab/Personality Testing in the Workplace

Although the validity of the Rorschach continues to be debated, recent evidence supports the validity of at least some types of Rorschach interpretations (Ganellen, 2001; Lilienfeld, Wood, & Garb, 2000; Meyer et al., 2001). For example, investigators find that Rorschach responses can be used to predict success in psychotherapy (Meyer, 2000), distinguish between different types of mental disorders (Kubiszyn et al., 2000), predict aggressive behavior (Baity & Hilsenroth, 2002), and detect underlying needs for psychological dependency (Bornstein, 1999). Yet critics claim that we lack compelling evidence to support the overall validity and utility of the Rorschach (Lilienfeld, Wood, & Garb, 2000; Hunsley & Bailey, 2001). However, proponents of projective testing argue that in skilled hands, these tests can yield valuable information about personality that cannot be gleaned from self-report tests or interviews (Stricker & Gold, 1999).

Concept Chart 10.5 compares the methods of assessment and forms of therapy associated with each of the major perspectives on personality covered in this chapter.

CONCEPT CHART 10.5
Overview of Theoretical Perspectives on Personality

Theoretical Model	Key Theorists	Major Concepts	Assessment Techniques	Associated Therapy
Psychoanalytic	Freud	Personality is influenced by an unconscious dynamic struggle among the id, the ego, and the superego.	Interviews, projective techniques	Psychoanalysis (discussed in Chapter 12)
Psychodynamic (neo-Freudians)	Adler, Jung, Horney, Erikson	Social factors and development of self are more important influences on personality than sexual motivation.	Interviews, projective techniques	Psychodynamic therapy (discussed in Chapter 12)
Trait	Allport, Cattell, Eysenck	Personality consists of a set of underlying traits that account for the characteristic ways people act in different situations.	Self-report personality inventories, such as Cattell's 16PF and the Eysenck Personality Inventory (EPI)	None
Behaviorism	Watson, Skinner	Personality consists of learned behavior acquired through classical and operant conditioning.	Behavioral observation	Behavior therapy (discussed in Chapter 12)
Social-cognitive	Rotter, Bandura, Mischel	Personality consists of the individual's repertoire of behavior and ways of thinking about the world.	Behavioral observation, interviewing, self-report measures, thought checklists	Cognitive-behavioral therapy (discussed in Chapter 12)
Humanistic	Rogers, Maslow	Personality consists of the subjective experience of being in the world, organized around a concept of the self.	Interviews, self-concept measures	Rogers's client-centered therapy (discussed in Chapter 12)

MODULE 10.5 REVIEW

Personality Tests

CONCEPT CHECK

1. What are two major types of personality tests?

2. Which of the following is *not* correct with regard to the Minnesota Multiphasic Personality Inventory?
   a. It was originally designed to detect mental disorders.
   b. Scales are composed of items that differentiate responses of people from particular diagnostic groups from those of people in a normal reference group.
   c. It is the most widely used self-report personality inventory in the world.
   d. Test responses to self-report personality inventories are free of response biases.

3. Which of the following statements about projective tests is *true*?
   a. Projective tests rely upon limited response options, such as "yes-no" type questions.
   b. Projective tests are based on the Freudian defense mechanism of regression.
   c. Projective tests are most closely associated with the behaviorist perspective.
   d. Projective tests were developed to help reveal unconscious desires and motives.

4. The greatest concern about projective tests is that
   a. pictures in the TAT resemble known historical figures.
   b. the validity of interpreting subjective responses is still being debated.
   c. they were developed from a psychodynamic perspective.
   d. people may reveal their inner needs and desires in their responses.

APPLICATION

MODULE 10.6 | Building Self-Esteem

• **What are some ways of building self-esteem?**

CONCEPT 10.29

Self-esteem, rather than being a fixed quality, can be enhanced by developing competencies and adopting more realistic goals and expectations.

The humanistic psychologists Carl Rogers and Abraham Maslow recognized the importance of self-esteem in developing a healthy personality. When our self-esteem is low, it is usually because we see ourselves as falling short of some ideal. Yet our self-esteem is not a fixed quality; it goes through ups and downs throughout the course of life (Robins et al., 2002). We can build self-esteem by developing competencies—skills and abilities that allow us to achieve our goals and thus enhance our sense of self-worth. But to build self-esteem, we must also challenge perfectionistic expectations and learn to accept ourselves when we inevitably fall short of our ideals (adapted from Nevid, Rathus, & Rubenstein, 1998).

Acquire Competencies: Become Good at Something

Social-cognitive theorists recognize that our self-esteem is related to the skills or competencies we can marshal to meet the challenges we face. Competencies include academic skills such as reading, writing, and math; artistic skills such as drawing and playing the piano; athletic skills such as walking a balance beam and throwing a football; social skills such as knowing how to start conversations; and job or occupational skills. The more competencies we possess, especially in areas that matter most to us, the better we feel about ourselves.

Competencies can be acquired through training and practice. You may not be able to throw a baseball at ninety miles per hour unless you have certain genetic advantages in arm strength and coordination. However, most skills can be developed within a normal range of genetic variation. Most people can learn to play the piano well, although only a few can become concert pianists. Indeed, a majority of the skills valued in our society are achievable by most people.

Set Realistic, Achievable Goals

Part of boosting self-esteem is setting realistic goals. This does not mean that you should not strive to be the best that you can be. It does mean that you may find it helpful to evaluate your goals in light of your true needs and capabilities.

Enhance Self-Efficacy Expectations

Success breeds success. You can enhance your self-efficacy expectations by choosing tasks that are consistent with your interests and abilities and working at them. Start with smaller, clearly achievable goals. Meeting these challenges will boost your self-confidence and encourage you to move toward more challenging goals. Regard the disappointments that life inevitably has in store as opportunities to learn from your mistakes, not as signs of ultimate failure.

Create a Sense of Meaningfulness in Your Life

To psychologically healthy individuals, life is not just a matter of muddling through each day. Rather, each day provides opportunities to pursue higher purposes. There are many different kinds of meaning in life, many different purposes. Some people find meaning in connecting themselves spiritually to something larger—whether it be a specific religion or the cosmos. Other people find meaning in community, among those who share a common ethnic identity and cultural heritage. Still others find meaning in love and family. Their spouses and their children provide them with a sense of fulfillment. People may also find meaning in their work.

Challenge Perfectionistic Expectations

Many of us withdraw from life challenges because of unreasonable demands we impose on ourselves to be perfect in everything we attempt. If you place perfectionistic demands on yourself, consider an attitude shift. Try lightening up on yourself and adopting more realistic expectations based on a fair-minded appraisal of your strengths and weaknesses. You may not measure up to an idealized image of perfection, but chances are you already have some abilities and talents you can cultivate, thus bolstering your self-esteem.

Challenge the Need for Constant Approval

The psychologist Albert Ellis believed that an excessive need for social approval is a sure-fire recipe for low self-esteem (Ellis, 1977; Ellis & Dryden, 1987). Inevitably we will all encounter the disapproval of people who are important to us. But Ellis asks us to consider whether encountering disapproval is truly as awful as we might imagine. Replacing irrational needs for approval with more rational expectations can help bolster our self-esteem, especially when we run into people who fail to appreciate our finer points.

TYING IT TOGETHER

In this chapter we have explored different models of personality and ways of measuring it. The psychodynamic perspective focuses on how conflicts between opposing forces or mental states shape our personalities and behaviors (Module 10.1). The trait perspective also looks inward, but not to sources of inner conflict. Rather, trait theorists conceptualize personality in terms of a set of traits that predispose people to act in characteristic ways (Module 10.2). The social-cognitive perspective looks both inward and outward by focusing, respectively, on the roles of cognitive variables and the environment in shaping behavior (Module 10.3). The humanistic perspective rejects the deterministic viewpoints of both the psychodynamic and behaviorist perspectives by arguing that conscious choice and personal freedom are core features of what it means to be human (Module 10.4). Psychologists are concerned not only with understanding personality but also with measuring it. They have developed various means of assessing personality, including observation and interviewing techniques as well as formal personality tests (Module 10.5). Self-esteem is an important part of our personalities, and one that we can bolster by developing competencies and learning to accept ourselves (Module 10.6).

SUMMING UP: Q&A

The Psychodynamic Perspective (Module 10.1)

What is personality?

- Psychologists generally speak of personality in terms of the relatively stable constellation of traits, thoughts, feelings, and behaviors that make individuals unique and that account for the ways in which they relate to others and adapt to the environment.

What three levels of consciousness did Freud believe comprise the human mind?

- According to Freud, the three levels of consciousness are the conscious, the preconscious, and the unconscious.
- The conscious represents your present awareness, the preconscious represents the region of mind that contains information you can readily retrieve from memory, and the unconscious represents a darkened region of mind that contains primitive urges, wishes, and troubling memories that cannot be directly summoned to consciousness.

What are the structures of personality in Freud's theory?

- Freud represented personality as composed of three mental structures: the id, the ego, and the superego.
- The ego attempts to satisfy the sexual and aggressive urges of the id in ways that avoid social disapproval or condemnation from the superego, the internal moral guardian or conscience.

What are psychological defense mechanisms?

- Psychological defense mechanisms are strategies used by the ego, such as repression, displacement, and projection, to prevent awareness of troubling desires and memories.

What are the five stages of psychosexual development in Freud's theory?

- Freud believed that psychological development is influenced by changes in the sexually sensitive areas of the body, or erogenous zones, during early childhood.
- The stages of psychosexual development parallel these changes in erogenous zones and are ordered as follows: oral, anal, phallic, latency, and genital.

What are some of the major contributions of other psychodynamic theorists?

- Jung believed in both a personal unconscious and a shared unconscious he called the collective unconscious.
- Adler developed the concept of the "inferiority complex," the tendency to compensate for feelings of inferiority by developing a drive to excel ("drive for superiority").
- Horney challenged Freud's ideas about female psychology and focused on the emotional effects in children of impaired relationships with their parents.

The Trait Perspective (Module 10.2)

What are the three types of traits in Allport's trait model?

- The three types of traits are cardinal traits (pervasive characteristics that govern behavior), central traits (more commonly found general characteristics around which behavior is organized), and secondary traits (interests or dispositions that influence behavior in specific situations).

What was Cattell's view on the organization of traits?

- Cattell believed that traits are organized in terms of surface traits (consistencies in a person's observed behavior) and source traits (general, underlying traits that account for relationships among surface traits).

What three traits are represented in Eysenck's model of personality?

- Eysenck believed that variations in personality could generally be explained in terms of three major traits: introversion-extraversion, neuroticism, and psychoticism.

What is the "Big Five" trait model of personality?

- The "Big Five" (neuroticism, extraversion, openness, agreeableness, conscientiousness) are five broad dimensions or traits that have consistently emerged in personality research.

What role do genes play in personality?

- Genetic influences are implicated in many personality traits, including neuroticism, shyness, aggressiveness, and novelty-seeking. Scientists today are exploring how genes interact with environmental influences in the development of personality.

The Social-Cognitive Perspective (Module 10.3)

What are expectancies and subjective values?

- Rotter believed that to explain and predict behavior we need to take into account a person's expectancies (personal predictions about the outcomes of events) and subjective values (worth placed on particular goals).

What is reciprocal determinism?

- Reciprocal determinism refers to Bandura's belief that cognitions, behaviors, and environmental factors mutually influence each other.

What are situation and person variables?

- Mischel proposed that both situation variables (environmental influences such as rewards and punishments) and person variables (factors relating to the person such as competencies, expectancies, encoding strategies, subjective values, and self-regulatory systems and plans) are needed to explain and predict behavior.

The Humanistic Perspective (Module 10.4)

What is self-theory?

- In Rogers' view, the self is the organized center of our experience. The self naturally moves toward self-actualization, or development of its unique potential.
- Movement toward self-actualization is assisted when the person receives unconditional positive regard (noncontingent approval) from others. By contrast, when approval is contingent on "proper" behavior, the person may develop a distorted self-concept and become detached from his or her genuine feelings and needs.

How do collectivistic and individualistic cultures view the concept of self?

- Collectivistic cultures view the self in terms of the role or place of the individual within the larger group or society.
- Individualistic cultures emphasize the uniqueness or individuality of the self.

Personality Tests (Module 10.5)

What are self-report personality inventories?

- Self-report personality tests are psychological tests that consist of sets of questions that people answer about themselves by using limited response options. They are classified as objective tests because they use objective methods of scoring and are based on a research foundation.

What are projective tests of personality?

- Projective tests are based on the use of ambiguous test materials that are answered in ways believed to reflect projections of the person's unconscious needs, drives, and motives.

Application: Building Self-Esteem (Module 10.6)

What are some ways of building self-esteem?

- Suggestions include acquiring competencies; setting realistic, achievable goals; enhancing self-efficacy expectations; creating a sense of meaningfulness in life; challenging perfectionistic expectations; and challenging the need for constant approval.

Key Terms

personality *(p. 346)*
psychoanalytic theory *(p. 346)*
conscious *(p. 346)*
preconscious *(p. 346)*
unconscious *(p. 346)*
id *(p. 347)*
ego *(p. 347)*
superego *(p. 347)*
pleasure principle *(p. 347)*
reality principle *(p. 348)*
defense mechanisms *(p. 348)*
repression *(p. 348)*
denial *(p. 348)*
reaction formation *(p. 348)*
rationalization *(p. 348)*
projection *(p. 348)*
sublimation *(p. 348)*
regression *(p. 348)*
displacement *(p. 348)*
erogenous zones *(p. 349)*
fixations *(p. 349)*
oral stage *(p. 349)*
anal stage *(p. 350)*
anal-retentive personality *(p. 350)*

anal-expulsive personality *(p. 350)*
phallic stage *(p. 350)*
Oedipus complex *(p. 350)*
Electra complex *(p. 350)*
castration anxiety *(p. 350)*
penis envy *(p. 350)*
latency stage *(p. 351)*
genital stage *(p. 351)*
personal unconscious *(p. 352)*
collective unconscious *(p. 352)*
archetypes *(p. 352)*
individual psychology *(p. 352)*
creative self *(p. 352)*
inferiority complex *(p. 352)*
drive for superiority *(p. 352)*
basic anxiety *(p. 352)*
basic hostility *(p. 352)*
traits *(p. 355)*
cardinal traits *(p. 355)*
central traits *(p. 355)*
secondary traits *(p. 355)*
surface traits *(p. 355)*
source traits *(p. 356)*
introversion-extraversion *(p. 356)*

neuroticism *(p. 356)*
psychoticism *(p. 356)*
five-factor model (FFM) *(p. 358)*
social-cognitive theory *(p. 361)*
expectancies *(p. 361)*
subjective value *(p. 361)*
locus of control *(p. 361)*
reciprocal determinism *(p. 362)*
outcome expectations *(p. 362)*
efficacy expectations *(p. 363)*
situation variables *(p. 363)*
person variables *(p. 363)*
self-theory *(p. 365)*
unconditional positive regard *(p. 365)*
conditional positive regard *(p. 365)*
self-ideals *(p. 366)*
collectivistic culture *(p. 366)*
individualistic culture *(p. 367)*
phrenology *(p. 369)*
personality tests *(p. 369)*
self-report personality inventories *(p. 369)*
objective tests *(p. 369)*
standard scores *(p. 371)*
projective tests *(p. 371)*

Thinking Critically About Psychology

Based on your reading of this chapter, answer the following questions. Then, to evaluate your progress in developing critical thinking skills, compare your answers to the sample answers found in Appendix A.

Personality and Astrology: Is Your Personality All in the Stars? What's in store for you? Let's see what the stars say about "Geminis" and "Scorpios":

Gemini (May 21–June 20): It is now time to focus on meeting your personal needs. Your energy level is high, and you can make the best use of your personal resources. There are many creative opportunities available to you, but you will need to apply yourself to take full advantage of them. You are the type of person who can go beyond what others expect of you. You are facing an important financial decision that can have a great impact on your future. But allow others to counsel you in reaching the best decision. All in all, now is the time to fully enjoy the many blessings in your life.

Scorpio (October 23–November 21): Your best-laid plans may need to be altered because of an unforeseen development. This can cause stress with others, but you will be able to use your sense of humor to ease the situation. You are a caring person whose concern for others shines through. Even though the next month or two may be unsettled, it is best to stay calm. Pursue what it is that is important to you and take advantage of the romantic

opportunities you may find or discover. Above all, maintain that sense of humor through trying times and don't accept more responsibilities than you can handle.

Believers in astrology hold that our personalities and destinies are fixed at the time of our birth by the positions of the sun, the moon, and the planets in the zodiac. Do you believe your personality was determined by the alignment of the heavens at the time of your birth? Do you read the astrology charts in your local newspaper? Do you believe them?

Astrology can be traced back thousands of years and still attracts many adherents, even among people with advanced education. More than 30 percent of college students polled in a recent survey expressed beliefs in astrology (Duncan, Donnelly, & Nicholson, 1992).

A recent study examined scores on the Eysenck Personality Inventory (EPI) in relation to the birth positions of the sun and moon. The results failed to confirm beliefs that such personality factors as extraversion and neuroticism conform to astrological predictions (Clarke, Gabriels, & Barnes, 1996). Other research points to the same conclusion—namely, that there is no scientific basis for astrology (Crowe, 1990; Dean, Mather, & Kelly, 1996). Given the absence of scientific evidence supporting astrology, why does it remain so popular?

One reason may be the *Barnum effect*—the tendency to believe overgeneralized descriptions of personality as accurate descriptions of oneself. The "Barnum" after whom the effect is named was the famous nineteenth-century circus showman P. T. Barnum, who once said, "There's a sucker born every minute."

The next time you glance at an astrology forecast in your local paper, notice how often the statements are phrased in general terms that can apply to just about anyone (e.g., "Now is the time to focus on your personal needs . .," "Even though the next month or two may be unsettled . . ."). Look again at the astrological readings for "Geminis" and "Scorpios" given above. Chances are that you will identify with characteristics found in both descriptions, regardless of your particular date of birth.

The Barnum effect may also explain the continued popularity of other pseudosciences, such as psychic reading and fortune-telling. The special "insights" into our futures that psychics and fortune-tellers claim they have are based on general characteristics that fit just about everyone ("You are likely to encounter some financial difficulty . . ."). In addition, they tend to be good observers who notice subtle cues in their clients' attire, gestures, or responses to leading questions that they can use to personalize their predictions.

Another contributor to beliefs in astrology and other pseudosciences is the tendency for people to filter information about themselves in terms of how it reflects upon them. For instance, we tend to give greater credence to information that confirms a positive image of ourselves than to information that casts us in a negative light. Notice that the astrology readings shown above contained many positive attributes (e.g., "caring person," "sense of humor"). The tendency to place greater emphasis on information that bolsters a positive self-image is called the *self-serving bias*—a bias that also accounts for the tendency of people to take credit for their successes and to explain away their failures or disappointments (see Chapter 14).

Now it's your turn to try a little critical thinking. Explain how another type of cognitive bias, the *confirmation bias* (see Chapter 7), contributes to beliefs in astrology.

Answers to Concept Check Questions

Module 10.1: 1. a; 2. c; 3. c; 4. (a) iii, (b) i, (c) ii, (d) iv; 5. a. **Module 10.2:** 1. b; 2. b; 3. a; 4. Hans Eysenck; 5. c; 6. shyness, neuroticism, aggressiveness, novelty-seeking. **Module 10.3:** 1. b; 2. a; 3. Thoughts, behaviors, and environmental factors mutually influence each other; 4. (a) ii, (b) iv, (c) iii, (d) i. **Module 10.4:** 1. d; 2. d; 3. the self; 4. a. **Module 10.5:** 1. self-report personality inventories and projective tests; 2. d; 3. d; 4. b.

Psychological Disorders

DID YOU KNOW THAT . . .

- Behavior considered abnormal in one culture may be deemed perfectly normal in another? (p. 383)

- Psychological disorders affect nearly everyone in one way or another? (p. 387)

- Some people have such fear of leaving the house that they literally are unable to go out to buy a quart of milk? (p. 390)

- Some people have lost all feeling in an arm or leg but remain unconcerned about their ailments? (p. 396)

- Some people with schizophrenia sit motionless for hours as though they were statues? (p. 407)

- People who receive the label of psychopath are not psychotic? (p. 410)

- Despite popular beliefs to the contrary, people who threaten suicide are quite likely to be serious about taking their lives? (p. 413)

It was about 2 A.M. when the police brought Claire to the emergency room. She seemed to be about forty-five; her hair was matted, her clothing disheveled, and her face was fixed in a blank stare. She clutched a clove of garlic in her right hand. She did not respond to the interviewer's questions: "Do you know where you are? Can you tell me your name? Can you tell me if anything is bothering you?" (cited in Nevid, Rathus, & Greene, 1997).

The police officers filled in the details. Claire had been found meandering along the painted line that divided the main street through town, apparently oblivious to the cars swerving around her. She was waving the clove of garlic in front of her. She said nothing to the officers when they arrived on the scene, but she offered no resistance.

Claire was admitted to the hospital and taken to the psychiatric ward. The next morning, she was brought before the day staff, still clutching the clove of garlic, and interviewed by the chief psychiatrist. She said little but her intentions could be pieced together from mumbled fragments. Claire said something about "devils" who were trying to "rob" her mind. The garlic was meant to protect her. She had decided that the only way to rid the town of the "devils" that hounded her was to walk down the main street, waving the garlic in front of her. Claire would become well known to the hospital. This was but one of a series of such episodes.

Phil was forty-two, a police photographer. It was his job to take pictures at crime scenes. "Pretty grisly stuff," he admitted, "corpses and all." Phil was married and had two teenage sons. He sought a psychological consultation because he was bothered by fears of being confined in enclosed spaces. Many situations evoked his fears. He was terrified of becoming trapped in an elevator and took the stairs whenever possible. He felt uncomfortable sitting in the back seat of a car. He had lately become fearful of flying, although in the past he had worked as a news cameraperson and would often fly to scenes of news events at a moment's notice—usually by helicopter.

"I guess I was younger then and more daring," he related. "Sometimes I would hang out of the helicopter to shoot pictures with no fear at all. But now, just thinking about flying makes my heart race. It's not that I'm afraid the plane will crash. I just start trembling when I think of them closing that door, trapping us inside. I can't tell you why."

In this chapter we examine the behavior of people like Claire and Phil—behavior that psychologists would consider abnormal. Let us begin by examining the criteria that psychologists use to determine when behavior crosses the line between normal and abnormal. Later we will explore different kinds of abnormal behavior patterns that psychologists and other professionals classify as psychological or mental disorders.

The descriptions in this chapter may raise your awareness about psychological problems of people you know, or perhaps even problems you've faced yourself. But it is not intended to make you a diagnostician. If the problems discussed in the chapter hit close to home, it makes sense to discuss your concerns with a qualified professional. ■

<table>
<tr><td>

MODULE 11.1

</td><td>

What Is Abnormal Behavior?

- **What criteria are used to determine whether behavior is abnormal?**
- **What are the major models of abnormal behavior?**
- **What are psychological disorders?**

</td></tr>
</table>

CONCEPT 11.1

Psychologists use several criteria in determining whether behavior is abnormal, including unusualness, social deviance, emotional distress, maladaptive behavior, dangerousness, and faulty perceptions of reality.

Determining whether behavior is abnormal is a more complex problem than it may seem at first blush. Most of us get anxious or depressed from time to time, but our behavior is not abnormal. The same behavior may be deemed normal under some circumstances but abnormal in others. For example, anxiety during a job interview is normal, but anxiety experienced whenever you board an elevator is not. Deep feelings of sadness are appropriate when you lose a loved one, but not when things are going well or following a mildly upsetting event that others take in stride.

Charting the Boundaries Between Normal and Abnormal Behavior

Where, then, might we draw the line between normal and abnormal behavior? Psychologists typically identify abnormal behavior based on a combination of the following criteria (Nevid, Rathus, & Greene, 2003):

1. *Unusualness.* Behavior that is unusual, or experienced by only a few, may be abnormal—but not in all cases or situations. Surely it is unusual for people to report "hearing voices" or, like Claire, to walk through town warding off demons. Yet uncommonness, by itself, is not sufficient to be deemed abnormal. Exceptional behavior, such as the ability to hit a three-point jump shot with some regularity or to become a valedictorian, is also unusual; but it is not abnormal.

2. *Social deviance.* All societies establish standards or social norms that define socially acceptable behaviors. Deviation from these norms is often used as a criterion for labeling behavior as abnormal. The same behavior might be considered abnormal in some contexts but perfectly acceptable in others. For example, we might consider it abnormal to shout vulgarities at strangers in the street. Yet shouting vulgarities at an umpire or referee who misses an important call in a ballgame may fall within the range of acceptable social norms, however offensive it might be.

Is This Man Abnormal? Abnormality must be judged in relation to cultural standards. The behavior and style of dress of this football fan may be in bad taste but would probably not be considered abnormal in a contemporary context.

3. *Emotional distress.* States of emotional distress, such as anxiety or depression, are considered abnormal when inappropriate, excessive, or prolonged relative to the person's situation.

4. *Maladaptive behavior.* Behavior is maladaptive when it causes personal distress, is self-defeating, or is associated with significant health, social, or occupational problems. For example, abuse of alcohol or other drugs may threaten an individual's health and ability to function in meeting life's responsibilities.

5. *Dangerousness.* Violent or dangerous behavior is another criterion for which we need to examine the social context. For example, engaging in behavior that is dangerous to oneself or others may be an act of bravery in times of war, but not in peacetime. Hockey players and football players regularly engage in physically aggressive behavior that may be dangerous to themselves or their opponents, but their (controlled) violent behavior is often rewarded with lucrative contracts and endorsement deals. Outside the sanctioned contexts of warfare and sports, however, violent behavior is likely to be considered abnormal.

6. *Faulty perceptions or interpretations of reality.* **Hallucinations** ("hearing voices" or seeing things that are not there) involve distorted perceptions of reality. Similarly, fixed but unfounded beliefs, called **delusions**, such as believing that FBI agents are listening in on your phone conversations, represent faulty interpretations of reality (unless of course the FBI really is tapping your phone).

As we shall see next, the cultural context in which behavior occurs must also be evaluated when making judgments about whether behavior is abnormal.

Cultural Bases of Abnormal Behavior

Psychologists take into account the cultural context when making judgments about abnormal behavior (Arrindell, 2003).They realize that the same behavior can be normal in one culture but abnormal in another. For example, in the majority American culture, "hearing voices" is deemed abnormal. Yet among some Native American peoples, it is considered normal for individuals to hear voices of their recently deceased relatives. They believe that the voices of the departed call out as their spirit ascends to the afterworld (Kleinman, 1987). Such behavior, because it falls within the normal spectrum of the culture in which it occurs, is not deemed abnormal—even if it may seem so to people from other cultures.

Abnormal behavior patterns may be expressed differently in different cultures. For example, people in Western cultures may experience anxiety in the form of excessive worries about financial, health, or job-related concerns. Among some native African peoples and Australian aboriginal peoples, anxiety may be expressed in the form of fears of witchcraft or sorcery (Kleinman, 1987). Among the Chinese, depression is characterized more strongly by physical symptoms, such as headaches, fatigue, and weakness, than by feelings of sadness or guilt (Draguns & Tanaka-Matsumi, 2003; Parker, Gladstone, & Chee, 2001).

Alternatively, the same behavior may be judged abnormal at some points in time but not at others. For example, although the American Psychiatric Association once classified homosexuality as a type of mental disorder, it no longer does so. Many professionals today consider homosexuality a variation of sexual behavior rather than an abnormal behavior pattern.

Applying the Criteria

Reconsider the examples of Claire and Phil described at the start of this chapter. Is their behavior abnormal? Claire's behavior certainly met several of the criteria of abnormal behavior. It was clearly unusual as well as socially deviant, and it

CONCEPT 11.2
Behavior that is deemed to be normal in some cultures may be considered abnormal in others.

THINK
About It

Normal vs. Abnormal?

What criteria do you use to distinguish between normal and abnormal behavior? How do the criteria you use stack up against those described in the text?

hallucinations   Perceptions ("hearing voices" or seeing things) that are experienced in the absence of external stimuli.

delusions   Fixed but patently false beliefs, such as believing that one is being hounded by demons.

represented what most people would take to be a delusion—believing you are protecting the community from demons. It was also clearly maladaptive and dangerous, as it put at risk not only Claire herself but also the drivers who were forced to swerve out of the way to avoid hitting her.

Phil, on the other hand, had good contact with reality. He understood that his fears exceeded the dangers he faced. Yet his phobia was a source of considerable emotional distress and was maladaptive because it impaired his ability to carry out his occupational and family responsibilities. We might also employ a criterion of unusualness here. Relatively few people have such fears of confinement that they avoid flying or taking elevators. Yet, as we have noted, unusualness alone is not a sufficient criterion for abnormality.

The behavior of these individuals could be considered abnormal, although they invoke different criteria. Overall, professionals apply multiple criteria when making judgments about abnormality.

Models of Abnormal Behavior

Abnormal behavior has existed in all societies, even though the view of what is or is not abnormal varies from culture to culture and has changed over time. In some cases, these explanations have led to humane treatment of people with abnormal behavior, but more frequently, people deemed to be "mad" or mentally ill were treated cruelly or harshly.

Early Beliefs

Exorcism Exorcism was used in medieval times to expel evil spirits from people believed to be possessed.

💡 **CONCEPT 11.3**
Throughout much of Western history, the prevailing view of abnormal behavior was based on a concept of demonic possession.

Throughout much of Western history, from ancient times through the Middle Ages, people thought that those displaying abnormal behavior were controlled by supernatural forces or possessed by demonic spirits. Beliefs in supernatural causes of abnormal behavior, especially the doctrine of demonic possession, held sway until the rise of scientific thinking in the seventeenth and eighteenth centuries. The treatment of choice for demonic possession—*exorcism*—was used to ferret out satanic forces or the Devil himself from the afflicted person's body. If that didn't work, there were even more forceful "remedies," such as the torture rack. Not surprisingly, many recipients of these "cures" attempted to the best of their ability to modify their behavior to meet social expectations.

The Medical Model

💡 **CONCEPT 11.4**
With the rise of scientific thought, attention began to shift from religious dogma to scientific or naturalistic explanations of human behavior.

The eighteenth and nineteenth centuries were times of rapid advances in medical science. Among the more notable advances were the development of a vaccine against the ancient scourge of smallpox, the discovery of the bacterial causes of diseases such as anthrax and leprosy, and the introduction of antiseptics in surgery to prevent infections. It was against this backdrop of medical discovery and shifts from religious dogma to scientific or naturalistic explanations of human behavior that the first modern model of abnormal behavior was developed, the **medical model**. The medical model is based on the belief that abnormal behavior patterns represent *mental illnesses* that have a biological, not demonic, basis and can be classified by their particular characteristics, or symptoms.

Psychological Models

Even as the medical model was taking shape, theorists were actively developing psychological models of abnormal behavior. The first major psychological model of abnormal behavior was the psychodynamic model developed by Sigmund Freud. Freud believed that abnormal behavior arises from unconscious conflicts during childhood that remain unresolved in the personality. These conflicts result from the need to control primitive sexual and aggressive impulses or to channel

medical model A framework for understanding abnormal behavior patterns as symptoms of underlying physical disorders or diseases.

them into socially acceptable outlets. Psychological symptoms (a phobia, for example) are merely the outward expressions of inner turmoil. The person may be aware of the symptom (the phobia) but not of the unconscious conflicts that gave rise to it. Contemporary psychodynamic theorists differ from Freud in some respects, but they retain the central belief that unconscious conflicts are at the root of abnormal behavior patterns.

At about the time that Freud was plumbing the depths of the unconscious, behaviorists were exploring the role of learning in the development of abnormal behavior. Pavlov's discovery of the conditioned response gave the early behaviorist movement a model for studying how maladaptive behaviors, such as phobias, could be learned or acquired through experience. The behavioral model is based on the belief that most forms of abnormal behavior are learned in the same ways that normal behavior is learned. Among the early demonstrations of the role of learning in the development of abnormal behavior was the experiment with "Little Albert" (discussed in Chapter 5). In this experiment, John B. Watson and his colleague Rosalie Rayner (1920) induced a fear of white rats in a young boy by presenting a noxious stimulus (loud banging sound) whenever a rat was brought close to the child. The repeated pairing of the conditioned stimulus (rat) and unconditioned stimulus (loud banging) instilled a conditioned response (fear evoked by the rat itself).

The humanistic model offers another psychological perspective on abnormal behavior. Humanistic theorists such as Carl Rogers and Abraham Maslow rejected the belief that human behavior is the product of either unconscious processes or simple conditioning. Human beings, they argued, possess an intrinsic ability to make conscious choices and to strive toward self-actualization. Abnormal behavior develops when people encounter roadblocks on the path toward personal growth or self-actualization. To satisfy the demands of others to think, feel, and act in certain ways, people may become detached from their true selves and develop a distorted self-image that can lead to emotional problems such as anxiety and depression. Humanistic theorists believe that people with psychological problems need to become more aware of their true feelings and come to accept themselves for who they truly are.

Cognitive theorists, such as Albert Ellis and Aaron Beck, believe that irrational or distorted thinking leads to emotional problems and maladaptive behavior. Examples of faulty styles of thinking include magnifying or exaggerating the consequences of negative events ("making mountains out of molehills") and interpreting events in an overly negative way, as though one were seeing things through blue-colored glasses.

The Sociocultural Model

The sociocultural model views the causes of abnormal behavior within the broader social and cultural contexts in which the behavior develops. Theorists in this tradition believe that abnormal behavior may have more to do with social ills or failures of society than with problems within the individual. Accordingly, they examine a range of social and cultural influences on behavior, including social class, poverty, ethnic and cultural background, and racial and gender discrimination. Sociocultural theorists believe that the stress of coping with poverty and social disadvantage can eventually take its toll on mental health. This view receives support from a study showing that severe forms of abnormal behavior, such as schizophrenia and depression, occur proportionately more often among poor and socially disadvantaged groups (Ostler et al., 2001).

Sociocultural theorists also focus on the effects of labeling people as mentally ill. They recognize that because of social prejudices, people who are labeled mentally ill are often denied job or housing opportunities and become stigmatized or marginalized in society. These theorists join with other professionals in arguing for greater understanding and support for people with mental health problems.

CONCEPT 11.5
Psychodynamic, behavioral, humanistic, and cognitive models focus on the psychological roots of abnormal behavior.

CONCEPT 11.6
The sociocultural model views abnormal behavior in terms of the social and cultural contexts in which it occurs.

The Biopsychosocial Model

Today we have many different models to explain abnormal behavior. Indeed, because there are different ways of looking at a given phenomenon, we can't conclude that one particular model is necessarily right and all the others wrong. Each of these models—medical, psychological, and sociocultural—has something unique to offer our understanding of abnormal behavior. None offers a complete view.

Abnormal behavior presents us with many puzzles as we attempt to unravel its causes. How is mental functioning affected by biology—by genes, brain structures, and neurotransmitter systems? What psychological factors are involved, such as underlying motives or conflicts, personality traits, cognitions, and learned behaviors? And how is our behavior affected by society and culture? Many psychologists today subscribe to the view that most forms of abnormal behavior are not simply products of biology or environment alone; rather, they result from complex interactions of biological, psychological, and sociocultural factors. The view that multiple factors representing these different domains interact in the development of abnormal behavior is called the **biopsychosocial model** (Kiesler, 1999). We are only beginning to put together the pieces of what has turned out to be a very complicated puzzle—the subtle and often complex patterns of underlying factors that give rise to abnormal behavior patterns.

A prominent example of the biopsychosocial model is the **diathesis-stress model**. According to this model, certain people have a vulnerability or predisposition, called a **diathesis**, that increases their risks of developing a particular disorder. Though usually genetic in nature, the diathesis may include psychological factors such as maladaptive personality traits or dysfunctional thinking patterns (Just, Abramson, & Alloy, 2001; Lewinsohn, Joiner, & Rohde, 2001; Ormel, Oldehinkel, & Brilman, 2001). Whether the person possessing a diathesis develops the particular disorder depends on the level of stress he or she experiences. Stressors may include family conflict, prolonged unemployment, loss of loved ones, physical or sexual abuse, brain trauma, or infectious illness. If the person encounters a low level of stress, or has effective skills for handling stress, the disorder may never emerge even if a diathesis is present. But the stronger the diathesis, the less stress is typically needed to produce the disorder (see Figure 11.1). In some cases, the diathesis may be so strong that the disorder develops even under the most benign life circumstances.

What Are Psychological Disorders?

Distinctive patterns of abnormal behavior are classified as **psychological disorders**—also known as *mental disorders* or *mental illnesses* within the medical model. Psychological disorders involve disturbances of mood, behavior, thought processes,

Figure 11.1   The Diathesis-Stress Model
The diathesis-stress model posits that the development of particular disorders involves an interaction of a predisposition (diathesis), usually genetic in nature, and exposure to life stress.

Source: Nevid, Rathus, & Greene, 2003.

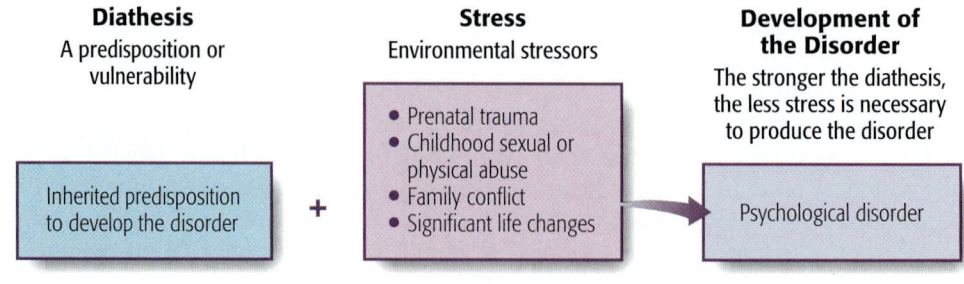

Diathesis	**Stress**	**Development of the Disorder**
A predisposition or vulnerability	Environmental stressors	The stronger the diathesis, the less stress is necessary to produce the disorder
Inherited predisposition to develop the disorder	• Prenatal trauma • Childhood sexual or physical abuse • Family conflict • Significant life changes	Psychological disorder

or perception that result in significant personal distress or impaired functioning. Examples of psychological disorders include schizophrenia, anxiety disorders such as phobias and panic disorder, and mood disorders such as major depression.

How Many Are Affected?

Psychological disorders are far more common than many people think. Chances are that either you or someone you know will be affected by a psychological disorder at one time or another. Investigators find that about one in two adult Americans develops a diagnosable psychological disorder at some point in her or his life (Kessler, 1994). If we also take into account the economic costs of diagnosing and treating these disorders, and the lost productivity and wages that result from them, it is fair to say that virtually everyone is affected by psychological disorders (Druss et al., 2000).

How Are Psychological Disorders Classified?

One reference book found on the shelves of virtually all mental health professionals and probably dog-eared from repeated use is the *Diagnostic and Statistical Manual of Mental Disorders,* or DSM—currently in a fourth, text-revised edition, the DSM-IV-TR (American Psychiatric Association, 2000). The manual contains descriptions and diagnostic criteria for every recognized psychological disorder, which in the manual are called *mental disorders.*

The DSM classifies mental disorders on the basis of their distinctive features or symptoms. But the DSM goes beyond merely classifying various disorders. It represents a multiaxial system consisting of multiple axes or dimensions that help the examiner conduct a comprehensive evaluation of a person's mental health (see Table 11.1). Axis I and Axis II comprise the diagnostic classifications. The DSM classifies mental disorders into several major groupings, including *anxiety disorders, mood disorders, eating disorders,* and *personality disorders.*

CONCEPT 11.9
The DSM, the diagnostic system used most widely for classifying psychological or mental disorders, consists of five dimensions or axes of evaluation.

TABLE 11.1   The Multiaxial DSM System

Axis	Type of Information	Brief Description
Axis I	Clinical disorders	Mental disorders that impair functioning or cause distress, including anxiety disorders, mood disorders, dissociative and somatoform disorders, schizophrenia, eating disorders, sleep disorders, and disorders usually first diagnosed in infancy, childhood, or adolescence
	Other conditions that may be a focus of clinical attention	Problems that may warrant attention, but do not represent diagnosable mental disorders, such as academic, vocational, or social problems affecting daily functioning
Axis II	Personality disorders	A class of mental disorders characterized by excessively rigid, enduring, and maladaptive ways of relating to others and adjusting to external demands
	Mental retardation	A generalized delay or impairment in the development of intellectual and adaptive skills or abilities
Axis III	General medical conditions	Illnesses and other medical conditions that may be important to the understanding or treatment of the person's psychological disorder
Axis IV	Psychosocial and environmental problems	Problems in the person's social or physical environment that may affect the diagnosis, treatment, and outcome of mental disorders
Axis V	Global assessment of functioning	Overall judgment of the person's level of functioning in meeting the responsibilities of daily life

Source: Adapted from the DSM-IV-TR (American Psychiatric Association, 2000).

Axis III lists general medical conditions and diseases, such as cancer and AIDS, that may affect a person's mental health, whereas Axis IV allows the examiner to note any psychosocial and environmental problems that impair the person's ability to function, such as stressful life events, homelessness, and lack of social support. Finally, Axis V allows the examiner to make a global assessment of the person's overall level of functioning in meeting life responsibilities.

Though the DSM is the most widely used diagnostic system, it is not without its critics. Questions remain about the reliability and validity of certain diagnostic classifications (e.g., Kendell & Jablensky, 2003; Widiger & Clark, 2000). Some mental health professionals challenge the system as based too heavily on the medical model in which abnormal behaviors are assumed to be symptoms of underlying disorders or mental illnesses. Yet many clinicians find the system useful in providing designated criteria to help them formulate diagnostic impressions. Perhaps it is best to think of the DSM as a work in progress rather than as a finished product.

CONCEPT CHART 11.1
Contemporary Models of Abnormal Behavior

	Model	Focus	Key Questions
Medical Model	**Medical model**	**Biological underpinnings of abnormal behavior**	**What role is played by neurotransmitters in abnormal behavior? By genetics? By brain abnormalities?**
Psychological Models	**Psychodynamic model**	**Unconscious conflicts and motives underlying abnormal behavior**	**How do particular symptoms represent or symbolize unconscious conflicts?** **What are the childhood roots of a person's problem?**
	Behavioral model	**Learning experiences that shape the development of abnormal behavior**	**How are abnormal patterns of behavior learned?** **What role does the environment play in explaining abnormal behavior?**
	Humanistic model	**Roadblocks that block self-awareness and self-acceptance**	**How does a person's emotional problems reflect a distorted self-image?** **What roadblocks did the person encounter in the path toward self-acceptance and self-realization?**
	Cognitive model	**Faulty thinking underlying abnormal behavior**	**What styles of thinking characterize people with particular types of psychological disorders?** **What role do personal beliefs, thoughts, and ways of interpreting events play in the development of abnormal behavior patterns?**
	Sociocultural model	**Social ills contributing to the development of abnormal behavior, such as poverty, racism, and prolonged unemployment; relationships between abnormal behavior and ethnicity, gender, culture, and socioeconomic level**	**What relationships exist between social-class status and risks of psychological disorders?** **Are there gender or ethnic group differences in various disorders? How are these explained?** **What are the effects of stigmatization of people who are labeled mentally ill?**
	Biopsychosocial model	**Interactions of biological, psychological, and sociocultural factors in the development of abnormal behavior**	**How might genetic or other factors predispose individuals to psychological disorders in the face of life stress?** **How do biological, psychological, and sociocultural factors interact in the development of complex patterns of abnormal behavior?**

Let us next consider several of the major classes of psychological disorders. The following modules describe the prominent symptoms of specific disorders within each class, the rates of occurrence of these disorders, and theories about their underlying causes.

See Concept Chart 11.1 for a listing of the major contemporary models of abnormal behavior.

MODULE 11.1 REVIEW

What Is Abnormal Behavior?

CONCEPT CHECK

1. List the six criteria for defining abnormal behavior discussed in the text.

2. _____ are distorted perceptions of reality; _____ are fixed but unfounded beliefs.
   a. Delusions; hallucinations
   b. Dreams; fantasies
   c. Fantasies; dreams
   d. Hallucinations; delusions

3. The explanation for abnormal behavior during much of the history of Western civilization was
   a. brain malfunction or chemical disorder.
   b. harsh and cruel treatment by close family members.
   c. possession by demons or supernatural forces.
   d. falsehoods or other retaliation spread by a sufferer's enemies.

4. Match the following psychological models for abnormal behavior with the appropriate descriptions: (a) psychodynamic; (b) behavioral; (c) humanistic; (d) cognitive.
   i. distorted self-image, loss of sense of true self
   ii. faulty styles of thinking, exaggeration of negative aspects of events
   iii. learned patterns of behavior
   iv. unresolved unconscious conflicts dating from childhood

5. Why is it important to consider the cultural context when determining abnormal behavior?

MODULE 11.2   Anxiety Disorders

- **What are anxiety disorders?**
- **What causal factors are implicated in anxiety disorders?**

There is much we might be anxious about—our health, our jobs, our families, the hole in the ozone layer, the state of the nation and the world. Indeed, anxiety can be an adaptive response in some situations. It can motivate us to study before an exam and to seek regular medical checkups, for example. But when anxiety is excessive in a given situation or interferes with the ability to function, it can become abnormal. *Fear* is the term we use to describe anxiety experienced in specific situations, as when boarding an airplane or taking a final exam.

Types of Anxiety Disorders

Anxiety disorders are among the most commonly experienced psychological disorders among adults. Called *neuroses* in earlier diagnostic manuals, these disorders are characterized by excessive or inappropriate anxiety reactions. The major types of anxiety disorders are phobias, panic disorder, generalized anxiety disorder, and obsessive-compulsive disorder. A fifth major type, posttraumatic stress disorder, is discussed in Chapter 13.

 CONCEPT 11.10
An anxiety disorder is a psychological disorder characterized by excessive or inappropriate anxiety reactions.

💡 **CONCEPT 11.11**

The major types of anxiety disorders are phobias, panic disorder, generalized anxiety disorder, obsessive-compulsive disorder, and posttraumatic stress disorder.

Phobias

A **phobia** is an irrational or excessive fear of some object or situation. The DSM classifies three types of phobic disorders: *social phobia, specific phobia,* and *agoraphobia.* People with **social phobia** have intense fears of social interactions, such as meeting others, dating, or giving a speech or presentation in class. People with **specific phobia** have excessive fears of specific situations or objects, such as animals, insects, heights (**acrophobia**), or enclosed spaces (**claustrophobia**). People with **agoraphobia** fear venturing into open places or going out in public.

People with claustrophobia may refuse to use elevators despite the inconvenience of climbing many flights of stairs several times a day. Those with agoraphobia may become literally housebound, unable even to go to the local store to buy a quart of milk. And those with social phobia may have difficulty maintaining a normal social life. People with phobias usually recognize that their fears are irrational or excessive, but they still avoid the objects or situations they fear.

Panic Disorder

People with **panic disorder** experience sudden episodes of sheer terror called *panic attacks.* Panic attacks are characterized by intense physical symptoms: profuse sweating, nausea, numbness or tingling, flushes or chills, trembling, chest pain, shortness of breath, and pounding of the heart (Glass, 2000). These symptoms may lead people to think they are having a heart attack, or "going crazy," or losing control. A specific attack can last anywhere from a few minutes to more than an hour. One person recounted the experience by saying, "All of a sudden, I felt a tremendous wave of fear for no reason at all. My heart was pounding, my chest hurt, and it was getting harder to breathe. I thought I was going to die."

Panic attacks initially seem to come "out of the blue." Yet they can later become connected with the situations in which they occur, such as shopping in a crowded department store or riding on a train. Agoraphobia, too, sometimes develops in people with panic disorder when they begin avoiding public places out of fear of having panic attacks while away from the security of their homes.

Panic Attack The symptoms associated with a panic attack, such as shortness of breath and a pounding heart, may lead people to think they are having a heart attack and are about to die.

phobia An irrational or excessive fear of an object or situation.

social phobia A type of anxiety disorder involving excessive fear of social situations.

specific phobia Phobic reactions involving specific situations or objects.

acrophobia Excessive fear of heights.

claustrophobia Excessive fear of enclosed spaces.

agoraphobia Excessive, irrational fear of being in public places.

panic disorder A type of anxiety disorder involving repeated episodes of sheer terror called panic attacks.

Generalized Anxiety Disorder

People with **generalized anxiety disorder (GAD)** experience persistent anxiety that is not tied to any particular object or situation. In such cases the anxiety has a "free-floating" quality, as it seems to travel with the person from place to place. The key feature of GAD is excessive worry (Ruscio, Borkovec, & Ruscio, 2001). People with the disorder tend to worry over just about everything. They are seldom if ever free of worry. Other characteristics of GAD include shakiness, inability to relax, fidgeting, and feelings of dread and foreboding.

Obsessive-Compulsive Disorder

Have you ever had a thought you couldn't shake off? Have you ever felt compelled to repeat the same behavior again and again? People with **obsessive-compulsive disorder (OCD)** experience persistent obsessions and/or compulsions. Obsessions are nagging, intrusive thoughts the person feels unable to control. Compulsions are repetitive behaviors or rituals the person feels compelled to perform again and again. Some people with this disorder are obsessed with the thought that germs contaminate their skin, spending hours each day compulsively washing their hands or showering. Others repeatedly perform checking rituals upon leaving the house to ensure that the doors and windows are securely locked and the gas jets on the stove are turned off.

Causes of Anxiety Disorders

Nearly everyone experiences anxiety from time to time, but only some people develop anxiety disorders. Although we don't know precisely why these disorders develop, we can identify biological and psychological factors that contribute to them, and surmise that an interaction of these factors affects their development.

Biological Factors

Evidence from studies of twins and adoptees supports a role for heredity in the development of many anxiety disorders, including panic disorder, generalized anxiety disorder, obsessive-compulsive disorder, and phobic disorders (Gorman et al., 2000; Kendler et al., 2000, 2001).

Other biological causes have also been implicated. Regarding panic disorder, for example, one possibility is that biochemical changes in the brain trigger a kind of internal alarm system that induces feelings of panic in susceptible people (Glass, 2000; Klein, 1993). And in cases of OCD, obsessional thinking appears to be associated with heightened activity in parts of the brain that respond to cues of danger (Rosenberg et al., 1997). The brains of people with this disorder may be continually sending messages that something is terribly wrong and requires immediate attention—a situation that then leads to obsessional, worrisome thoughts. The compulsive aspect of OCD may result from a disturbance in other brain circuits that normally curtail repetitive behaviors.

Psychological Factors

Some phobias may be learned through classical conditioning in which a previously neutral or benign stimulus becomes paired with an aversive stimulus. A person bitten by a dog during childhood may come to develop a fear of dogs or other small animals; a person trapped in an elevator for hours may acquire a fear of elevators or of confinement in other enclosed spaces. The previously neutral stimulus is the conditioned stimulus (CS), the aversive stimulus is the unconditioned stimulus (US), and the acquired fear response is the conditioned response (CR).

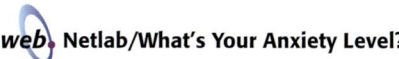
web Netlab/What's Your Anxiety Level?

web Netlab/The Case of the Confused Clerk

CONCEPT 11.12
Both biological factors, such as disturbed neurotransmitter functioning, and psychological factors, such as learning experiences, are implicated as causal influences in anxiety disorders.

generalized anxiety disorder (GAD) A type of anxiety disorder involving persistent and generalized anxiety and worry.

obsessive-compulsive disorder (OCD) A type of anxiety disorder involving the repeated occurrence of obsessions and/or compulsions.

Operant conditioning may help account for avoidance behavior. Avoidance of the phobic object or situation (as when a person with an elevator phobia takes the stairs instead of the elevator) is negatively reinforced by relief from anxiety. However, though avoiding a fearful situation may offer short-term relief from anxiety, it doesn't help people overcome their fears. (The principle of negative reinforcement is discussed in Chapter 5.)

Negative reinforcement (relief from anxiety) may also contribute to obsessive-compulsive disorder. People with OCD often become trapped in a repetitive cycle of obsessive thinking and compulsive behavior. Obsessive thoughts ("my hands are covered with germs") trigger anxiety, which, in turn, is partially relieved through performance of a compulsive ritual (repetitive hand-washing). In effect, the solution to obsessive thinking (performing the compulsive ritual) becomes the problem (Salkovskis et al., 2003). However, since relief from the obsessive thoughts is at best incomplete or fleeting, the thoughts soon return, prompting yet more compulsive behavior—and so on in a continuing cycle.

A cognitive model of panic disorder focuses on the interrelationship between biological and psychological factors. Specifically, it holds that people with panic attacks misinterpret minor changes in bodily sensations (e.g., sudden light-headedness or dizziness) as signs of an imminent catastrophe, such as an impending heart attack or loss of control (Clark, 1986; Zoellner, Craske, & Rapee, 1996). These misinterpretations generate symptoms of anxiety (sweating, racing heart), which, like falling dominoes, lead to more catastrophic thinking, then to more anxiety symptoms, and so on in a cycle that may quickly spiral into a full-blown panic attack (see Figure 11.2). Internal cues (dizziness, heart palpitations) and external cues (boarding a crowded elevator) that were connected with panic attacks in the past may also become conditioned stimuli (CS) that elicit anxiety or panicky symptoms when the person encounters them (Bouton, Mineka, & Barlow, 2001).

Cognitive factors come into play in other anxiety disorders as well. Social phobias, for example, can arise from excessive concerns about social embarrassment or being judged negatively by others.

In sum, anxiety disorders involve a complex interplay of biological and psychological factors. Before going further, you may wish to review the summary of anxiety disorders presented in Concept Chart 11.2.

Figure 11.2 Cognitive Model of Panic
Cognitive theorists conceptualize panic disorder in terms of a panic cycle that involves an interaction of physiological and cognitive factors. A triggering stimulus, such as sudden light-headedness or boarding a crowded train, sets the cycle in motion. The stimulus is perceived as threatening, leading to feelings of apprehension (anxiety and worry), which in turn lead to bodily sensations associated with anxiety, such as a tightening feeling in the chest. These sensations are misconstrued as signs of an impending catastrophe—a heart attack, for example. Perceptions of threat are increased, further raising the level of anxiety, and so on in a vicious cycle that can quickly spiral into a full-fledged panic attack.

Source: Adapted from Clark, 1986.

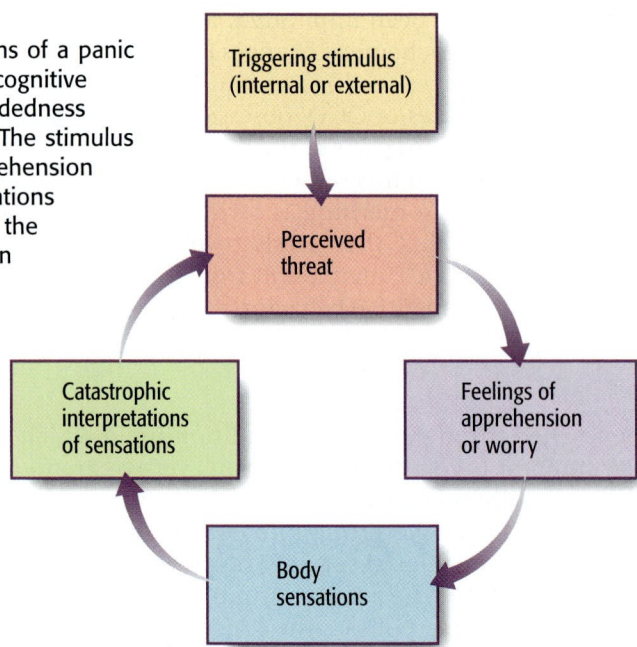

CONCEPT CHART 11.2
Anxiety Disorders

Type of Disorder	Lifetime Prevalence in Population (%)	Symptoms	Associated Features
Agoraphobia	6 to 7	Fear and avoidance of public places	Agoraphobia often develops secondarily to panic disorder, as the person attempts to avoid situations in which attacks have occurred or in which help might be unavailable in the event of an attack.
Panic disorder	1 to 4	Repeated panic attacks accompanied by persistent concern about future attacks	Panic attacks have strong physiological symptoms; beginning attacks occur without warning.
Generalized anxiety disorder	Approximately 5	Persistent, excessive levels of anxiety and worry	Anxiety has a free-floating quality in that it is not tied to particular objects or situations.
Specific phobia	7 to 11	Fear and avoidance of specific objects or situations	Avoidance of the phobic object or situation is negatively reinforced by relief from anxiety.
Social phobia	3 to 13.3	Fear and avoidance of social situations or performance situations	Social phobia is characterized by an underlying fear of rejection, humiliation, or embarrassment in social situations.
Obsessive-compulsive disorder	2 to 3	Recurrent obsessions and/or compulsions	A repetitive cycle may ensue in which obsessive thoughts engender anxiety that, in turn, is partially relieved (negatively reinforced) by performing the compulsive ritual.

Note: Another type of anxiety disorder, posttraumatic stress disorder, is discussed in Chapter 15.
Sources: American Psychiatric Association, 2000; Magee et al., 1996; USDHHS, 1999.

MODULE 11.2 REVIEW

Anxiety Disorders

CONCEPT CHECK

1. The earlier diagnostic term for anxiety disorders was
   a. frenzy.
   b. phobias.
   c. neuroses.
   d. psychoses.

2. Acrophobia and claustrophobia are two examples of
   _____ phobia.

3. Match the following anxiety disorders with the appropriate descriptions: (a) phobic disorder; (b) panic disorder; (c) generalized anxiety disorder; (d) obsessive-compulsive disorder.
   i.   sudden onset; intense fear and dread
   ii. excessive, persistent worry
   iii. irrational, extreme fear of a particular object or situation
   iv. repeated, uncontrollable thoughts or behaviors

MODULE 11.3 Dissociative and Somatoform Disorders

- **What are dissociative disorders and somatoform disorders?**
- **What causal factors are implicated in dissociative and somatoform disorders?**

Among the most puzzling psychological disorders are the **dissociative disorders** and **somatoform disorders**. People with dissociative disorders may show multiple personalities, have amnesia that cannot be explained by a physical cause, or even assume a completely new self-identity. The dissociative disorders are fodder for countless television melodramas and soap operas. In real life they are relatively uncommon, even rare. Indeed, there is controversy among professionals as to whether multiple personality (now called *dissociative identity disorder*) even exists.

Although they have different symptoms or characteristics, dissociative disorders and somatoform disorders are often grouped together because of the classic view that they involve psychological defenses against anxiety. Here we examine several of these mystifying disorders, beginning with dissociative disorders.

Dissociative Disorders

Dissociative disorders involve problems with memory or changes in consciousness or self-identity that fracture the continuity or wholeness of an individual's personality. Normally we know who we are and where we've been. We may forget how we spent last weekend, but we don't suddenly lose the capacity to remember whole chunks of our lives or abruptly shift back and forth between very different personalities. Dissociative disorders, however, affect the ability to maintain a cohesive sense of self or unity of consciousness, resulting in unusual, even bizarre behavior. Here we consider two major types of dissociative disorders: dissociative identity disorder and dissociative amnesia.

Dissociative Identity Disorder

Consider the following case history:

> [Margaret explained that] she often "heard a voice telling her to say things and do things." It was, she said, "a terrible voice" that sometimes threatened to "take over completely." When it was finally suggested to [Margaret] that she let the voice "take over," she closed her eyes, clenched her fists, and grimaced for a few moments during which she was out of contact with those around her. Suddenly she opened her eyes and one was in the presence of another person. Her name, she said, was "Harriet." Whereas Margaret had been paralyzed, and complained of fatigue, headache and backache, Harriet felt well, and she at once proceeded to walk unaided around the interviewing room. She spoke scornfully of Margaret's religiousness, her invalidism, and her puritanical life, professing that she herself liked to drink and "go partying" but that Margaret was always going to church and reading the Bible. "But," she said impishly and proudly, "I make her miserable—I make her say and do things she doesn't want to." At length, at the interviewer's suggestion, Harriet reluctantly agreed to "bring Margaret back," and after more grimacing and fist clenching, Margaret reappeared, paralyzed, complaining of her headache and backache, and completely amnesiac for the brief period of Harriet's release from prison. (Adapted from Nemiah, 1978, pp. 179–180)

In **dissociative identity disorder (DID)**, commonly called *multiple personality* or *split personality*, two or more distinct personalities exist within the same individ-

dissociative disorders A class of psychological disorders involving changes in consciousness, memory, or self-identity.

somatoform disorders A class of psychological disorders involving physical ailments or complaints that cannot be explained by organic causes.

dissociative identity disorder (DID) A type of dissociative disorder characterized by the appearance of multiple personalities in the same individual.

ual. Each of the personalities has its own distinctive traits, manner of speech, and memories—even, in some cases, its own eyeglass prescription (Miller et al., 1991). The different personalities may also exhibit varying allergic reactions and responses to medication (Braun, 1986). In some cases, there is a core personality that is generally known to the outside world and hidden *alternate personalities* that reveal themselves at certain times or in certain situations. Sometimes alternate personalities compete for control. The alternate personalities may represent different genders, ages, sexual orientations, or—as in the case of Margaret—conflicting sexual urges. One personality may be morally upright, another licentious; one heterosexual, another homosexual. The dominant personality may be unaware of the existence of these alternates, though it may vaguely recognize that something is wrong. Women with the disorder tend to have fifteen or more identities, whereas men average about eight (American Psychiatric Association, 2000).

Dissociative Amnesia

People with *dissociative amnesia* (first discussed in Chapter 6) experience a loss of memory for information about themselves or their life experiences. The absence of any physical cause for their amnesia (a blow to the head, a neurological condition, drug or alcohol abuse) suggests that the disorder is psychological in nature. The information lost to memory is usually a traumatic or stressful experience that the person may be motivated to forget. A soldier returning from the battlefield or a survivor of a serious accident may have no memory of the battle or the accident. These memories sometimes return, perhaps gradually in bits and pieces, or suddenly all at once. Much less common, except in the imaginations of soap opera writers, is *generalized amnesia* in which people forget their entire lives. They forget who they are, what they do for a living, and whom they are married or related to. More typically, the amnesia is limited to memories associated with traumatic events that generated strong negative emotions.

Causes of Dissociative Disorders

Dissociative amnesia may represent an attempt to disconnect or dissociate one's conscious state from awareness of traumatic experiences or other sources of psychological pain or conflict (Dorahy, 2001). Dissociative symptoms may protect the self from anxiety that might occur if these memories and experiences became fully conscious. Similarly, individuals with dissociative identity disorder may split off parts of themselves from consciousness. Severe, repetitive physical or sexual abuse in childhood, usually beginning before the age of five, figures prominently in case histories of people with dissociative identity disorder (DID) (Burton & Lane, 2001).

We also know that many people with DID were highly imaginative as children, often creating games of make-believe. In these early years, they may have used their fertile imaginations to split off parts of themselves to distance themselves psychologically from the abusive situations they faced. Over time, these parts may have become consolidated as distinct personalities. And in adulthood, they may continue to use their alternate personalities to block out memories of childhood trauma and of the conflicting emotions that these experiences evoked. The alternate personalities themselves may represent a psychological means of expressing the deep-seated hatred and anger they are unable to integrate within their primary personalities.

Some psychologists believe that DID is a rare but genuine disorder that arises in a few individuals as a way of coping with terrible physical and sexual abuse dating back to childhood (Gleaves, 1996). But there are dissenting voices. Among these are authorities who doubt the existence of DID, ascribing the behavior to a

CONCEPT 11.13
In dissociative identity disorder, the personality is split into two or more distinct alternate personalities residing within the same individual.

CONCEPT 11.14
In dissociative amnesia, people experience a loss of memory for personal information that cannot be explained by a blow to the head or some other physical cause.

CONCEPT 11.15
The formation of alternate personalities in dissociative identity disorder may represent a psychological defense against trauma or unbearable abuse.

form of attention-seeking role playing (Lilienfeld et al., 1999; Spanos, 1994). Perhaps troubled individuals with a history of abuse might inadvertently be cued by their therapists to enact alternate personalities that help them make sense of the confusing and conflicting emotions they experience, eventually identifying so closely with the role they are performing that it becomes a reality to them. This description is not meant to suggest that people with DID are faking their alternate selves, any more than we would suggest that you are faking your behavior whenever you adopt the role of a student, spouse, or worker. Whatever the underlying process in DID may be, authorities agree that people with the disorder need help dealing with the underlying traumas they have experienced and working through the often-conflicting emotions and impulses these brutal experiences evoked.

Somatoform Disorders

People with somatoform disorders have physical ailments or complaints that cannot be explained medically. Or they may hold the belief that they are gravely ill, despite reassurances from their doctors to the contrary. One type of somatoform disorder, **conversion disorder**, figured prominently in the history of psychology. It was conversion disorder—called *hysteria* or *hysterical neurosis* at the time—that attracted a young physician named Sigmund Freud to study the psychological bases of abnormal behavior.

Conversion Disorder

In conversion disorder, a person suffers a loss of physical function, such as loss of movement in a limb (hysterical paralysis), loss of vision (hysterical blindness), or loss of feeling in a hand or arm (anesthesia). Yet there is no physical cause that can account for these symptoms. Conversion disorder or hysteria appears to have been much more common in Freud's day but is relatively rare today. In Freud's time, hysteria was considered a female problem; however, experience with male soldiers in combat who experience a loss of function (blindness or paralysis) that cannot be explained medically has taught us that the disorder can affect both men and women.

If you suddenly lost feeling in your hand, you would probably be quite upset. But curiously, some people with conversion symptoms appear indifferent to their situations—a phenomenon called *la belle indifférence* ("beautiful indifference"). This lack of concern suggests that the symptoms may be of psychological value to the individual, perhaps representing a way of avoiding anxiety associated with painful or stressful conflicts or situations.

Let us note that many cases, perhaps as many as four out of five, that initially appear to be conversion disorders turn out upon further testing to be unrecognized medical conditions (Fishbain & Goldberg, 1991). In other cases, the causes remain obscure and are believed to be psychological in nature.

Hypochondriasis

People with **hypochondriasis** are preoccupied with the idea that there is something terribly wrong with their health. They attribute their physical complaints or symptoms to a serious underlying disease, perhaps cancer or heart disease (Barsky & Ahem, 2004). Though they may receive assurances from their doctors that their concerns are groundless, they believe the doctors are wrong or may have missed something. They may not realize how their anxiety about their symptoms contributes to their physical complaints—for example, by leading to sweating, dizziness, rapid heartbeat, and other signs of sympathetic nervous system arousal. Not surprisingly, they have more health worries and more psychological problems than do other people.

Causes of Somatoform Disorders

To Freud, the hysterical symptom (loss of movement in a limb) is the outward sign of an unconscious dynamic struggle between opposing motives. On the one side are the sexual or aggressive impulses of the id seeking expression. On the other side are the forces of restraint, marshaled by the ego. The ego seeks to protect the self from the flood of anxiety that would occur if these unacceptable impulses were to become fully conscious. It employs defense mechanisms, especially repression, to keep these impulses buried in the unconscious. The leftover energy from these impulses becomes "strangulated," or cut off from its source, and is then converted into physical symptoms like paralysis or blindness. One problem with Freud's view, however, is that it doesn't explain how conversion occurs—that is, how leftover sexual or aggressive energy becomes channeled into particular physical symptoms (Miller, 1987).

Freud also believed that the symptom itself both symbolizes the underlying struggle and serves an underlying purpose. For instance, hysterical paralysis of the arm serves the purpose of preventing the person from using the arm to act out an unacceptable sexual (e.g., masturbatory) or aggressive (e.g., murderous) impulse. The symptom has yet another function, called **secondary gain**. It can prevent the individual from having to confront stressful or conflict-laden situations. If Freud was correct in his belief that conversion symptoms serve hidden purposes, it may explain why many people with conversion appear strangely unconcerned or untroubled about their symptoms.

Learning theorists, too, recognize that conversion symptoms may serve a secondary role of helping the individual avoid painful or anxiety-evoking situations. (The bomber pilot who develops hysterical night blindness may avoid the danger of night missions, for example.) People with conversion disorders may also be reinforced by others for adopting a "sick role," drawing sympathy and support from them and being relieved of ordinary work or household responsibilities. This is not to suggest that such individuals are consciously faking their symptoms. Perhaps they are deceiving themselves, but they do not appear to be deliberately faking.

Cognitive theorists focus on cognitive biases associated with somatoform disorders (e.g., Cororve & Gleaves, 2001; Salkovskis & Clark, 1993). People with hypochondriasis, for example, may "make mountains out of molehills" by misinterpreting bodily sensations as signs of underlying catastrophic causes (cancer, heart disease, etc.). In this respect they may resemble people with panic disorder, who tend to misinterpret their bodily sensations as signs of an impending catastrophe.

Dissociative and somatoform disorders are summarized in Concept Chart 11.3.

CONCEPT 11.18
Though Freudian and learning theory explanations of somatoform disorders differ, they both focus on the anxiety-reducing role of somatoform symptoms.

CONCEPT CHART 11.3
Dissociative and Somatoform Disorders

	Type of Disorder	Lifetime Prevalence	Features	Comments
Dissociative Disorders	Dissociative identity disorder	Rare	Development of multiple personalities within the same individual	May represent a type of psychological defense against trauma or unbearable abuse from childhood
	Dissociative amnesia	Rare	Loss of memory that cannot be explained as the result of head trauma or other physical cause	Typically involves loss of memories associated with specific traumatic events
Somatoform Disorders	Conversion disorder	Rare	A loss or change of physical function that cannot be explained by a medical condition	Appears to have been much more common in Freud's day than our own
	Hypochondriasis	Unknown	Preoccupation with fear of having a serious illness	May have features similar to those of obsessive-compulsive disorder

MODULE 11.3 REVIEW

Dissociative and Somatoform Disorders

CONCEPT CHECK

1. Another term often used to describe dissociative identity disorder is
   a. intermittent neurotic disorder.
   b. multiple personality.
   c. obsessive-compulsive personality.
   d. amnesiac identity disorder.

2. Dissociative amnesia
   a. involves a clear physical underlying cause.
   b. does not seem to be related to a particular traumatic event.
   c. involves extensive and permanent memory loss.
   d. has no apparent neurological cause.

3. What are some common characteristics of individuals with dissociative identity disorder?
   a. Their early childhood experiences included severe and prolonged abuse.
   b. They tended to be highly imaginative as youngsters.
   c. Their alternate personalities have very different and distinctive traits.
   d. All of the above are correct.

4. Which of the following is *not* correct? Conversion disorder
   a. is classified as one of the somatoform disorders.
   b. was known as hysteria in earlier times.
   c. involves loss of a physical function.
   d. is caused by underlying physical problems.

MODULE 11.4 — Mood Disorders

- **What are mood disorders?**
- **What causal factors are implicated in mood disorders?**
- **Who is at risk for suicide?**
- **Why do people commit suicide?**

CONCEPT 11.19
Two of the major types of mood disorders are major depression and bipolar disorder.

CONCEPT 11.20
In major depression, there is a dampening of mood to the point that the person may become unmotivated, lose interest in pleasurable activities, develop feelings of worthlessness, or attempt suicide.

mood disorders A class of psychological disorders involving disturbances in mood states, such as major depression and bipolar disorder.

major depression The most common type of depressive disorder, characterized by periods of downcast mood, feelings of worthlessness, and loss of interest in pleasurable activities.

Most people have occasional ups and downs, but those with **mood disorders** have more severe or persistent disturbances of mood. These mood disturbances limit their ability to function and may even sap their will to live. It is normal to feel sad when unfortunate events occur and to be uplifted when fortune shines on us. But people with mood disorders often feel down when things are going right. Or they remain down following a disappointing experience long after others would have snapped back. Some people with mood disorders have exaggerated mood swings. Their moods may alternate between dizzying heights and abysmal depths.

Types of Mood Disorders

Here we focus on two major forms of mood disorder: major depression and bipolar disorder.

Major Depression

In **major depression** (also called *major depressive disorder*) people typically feel sad or "down in the dumps" and may experience feelings of worthlessness, changes in sleep or appetite, lethargy, and loss of interest in pleasurable activities. When left untreated, episodes of major depression can last months, even a year or more (USDHHS, 1999).

People with major depression may feel they cannot get out of bed to face the day. They may be unable to make decisions, even about small things, such as what to have for dinner. They may be unable to concentrate. They may feel helpless or say that they don't "care" anymore. They may have recurrent thoughts of suicide or attempt suicide.

About 16 percent of the U.S. adult population develop major depression at some point in their lives (Duenweld, 2003; Kessler et al., 2003). Women are twice as likely as men to develop the disorder—5 to 12 percent of men versus 10 to 25 percent of women (American Psychiatric Association, 2000). Although underlying hormonal or other biological differences between men and women may help explain the greater prevalence of depression in women (Cyranowski et al., 2000), we also need to consider the greater levels of stress experienced by many women today. Women are more likely to encounter such stressors as physical and sexual abuse, poverty, single parenthood, and sexism. Even when both spouses work, women typically shoulder the bulk of household and childcare chores. Women also are more likely than men to provide support for aging family members or those coping with disabling medical conditions. These additional caregiving burdens add to the stress that women endure (Shumaker & Hill, 1991).

Differences in how men and women cope with depression may also come into play. Researchers find that men are more likely to distract themselves when they are feeling depressed, whereas women are more likely to ruminate about their problems, which may only worsen their depression (Nolen-Hoeksema, Morrow, & Fredrickson, 1993). Ruminating or dwelling on one's problems may only worsen depression, whereas distraction may blunt the emotional effects of disappointments and setbacks (Gilbert, 2004).

Gender Differences in Depression Many psychologists believe that the stressors faced by many women today contribute to their increased risk of depression.

TRY THIS OUT

Self-Screening for Depression

Many people suffer depression in silence out of ignorance or shame. They believe that depression is not a real problem because it doesn't show up on an X-ray or CT scan. They think it's just all in their heads. Or they may feel that asking for help is an admission of weakness and that they should bear it on their own.

The following test, developed by the organizers of the National Depression Screening Day, is widely used to help people become more aware of the warning signs of depression. The test is not meant to provide a diagnosis of a depressive disorder; rather, its purpose is to raise awareness of problems that should be evaluated further by a mental health professional.

YES	NO	
☐	☐	1. I feel downhearted, blue, and sad.
☐	☐	2. I don't enjoy the things that I used to.
☐	☐	3. I feel that others would be better off if I were dead.
☐	☐	4. I feel that I am not useful or needed.
☐	☐	5. I notice that I am losing weight.
☐	☐	6. I have trouble sleeping through the night.
☐	☐	7. I am restless and can't keep still.
☐	☐	8. My mind isn't as clear as it used to be.
☐	☐	9. I get tired for no reason.
☐	☐	10. I feel hopeless about the future.

Scoring key: If you answered "yes" to at least five of the statements, including either the first or second one, and if these complaints have persisted for at least two weeks, then professional help is strongly recommended. If you answered "yes" to the third statement, we suggest that you immediately consult a health professional. Contact your college or university counseling or health center. Or talk to your instructor.

Source: Adapted from Brody, 1992.

Bipolar Disorder

People with **bipolar disorder** (formerly called *manic-depression*) experience mood swings that shift between periods of euphoric or elevated mood, or **manic episodes** (mania), and periods of depression. They may have intervening periods of normal moods. During a manic episode, people may feel unusually euphoric or become extremely restless, excited, talkative, and argumentative. They may spend lavishly, drive recklessly, destroy property, or become involved in sexual escapades that appear out of character with their usual personalities. Even those who care about such individuals may find them abrasive. Other symptoms are *pressured speech* (talking too rapidly), *flight of ideas* (jumping from topic to topic), and an inflated sense of self-worth (grandiosity). During manic episodes, people may become delusional—believing, for example, that they have a special relationship with God. They may undertake tasks beyond their abilities, such as writing a symphony, or show poor judgment, such as giving away their life savings. They may have boundless energy and little need for sleep. Then, when their moods sink into depression, they may feel hopelessness and despair. Some people with bipolar disorder commit suicide on the way down, apparently wanting to avoid the depths of depression they have learned to expect. About 1 percent of the adult U.S. population suffers from some sort of bipolar disorder (USDHHS, 1999).

Causes of Mood Disorders

Like anxiety disorders, mood disorders are believed to have both psychological and biological causes.

Psychological Factors

CONCEPT 11.22
Psychological causes implicated in mood disorders include changes in reinforcement levels, distorted ways of thinking, depressive attributional style, and stress.

Several psychological models of depression have been proposed. The classic psychodynamic theory espoused by Freud (1917/1957) and his followers (e.g., Abraham, 1916/1948) held that depression involves anger turned inward against the self. By contrast, the behavioral model attempts to account for depression in terms of changes in reinforcement levels (Lewinsohn, 1974). In order to maintain motivation, one needs a balance between output and input, between the effort one expends and the reinforcement one receives. A shortfall in reinforcement, especially social reinforcement, may occur for many reasons: The loss of a loved one removes that person as a potential reinforcing agent; attending college away from home may limit opportunities for reinforcement from friends at home; a disabling injury may cut us off from our usual sources of reinforcement. In addition, we may find it difficult to make new friends or develop new social networks that provide opportunities for reinforcement. According to this model, loss of reinforcement saps motivation and induces depression. The more depressed we become, the less motivated we feel to make the effort to find new sources of reinforcement. In the manner of a vicious cycle, the less reinforcement we receive, the more we withdraw, and so on. In some cases, reinforcement opportunities abound but the individual needs to develop more effective social skills to establish and maintain relationships that can lead to a continuing flow of reinforcements.

Cognitive theorists believe that the way in which people interpret events contributes to emotional disorders such as depression. One of the most influential cognitive theorists is the psychiatrist Aaron Beck, the developer of cognitive therapy (discussed in Chapter 12). Beck and his colleagues (Beck, 1976; Beck et al., 1979; Beck & Young, 1985) believe that people who adopt a negatively biased or distorted way of thinking become prone to depression when they encounter disappointing or unfortunate life events. Negative thinking becomes a kind of mental filter that puts a slant on how people interpret their life experiences, especially disappointments such as getting a bad grade or losing a job. A minor disappointment is blown out of proportion—experienced more as a crushing blow than as a

bipolar disorder A type of mood disorder characterized by mood swings from extreme elation (mania) to severe depression.

manic episodes Periods of mania, or unusually elevated mood and extreme restlessness.

TABLE 11.2   Cognitive Distortions Linked to Depression

Type of Cognitive Distortion	Description	Example
All-or-nothing thinking	Viewing events in black or white terms, as either all good or all bad	Do you view a relationship that ended as a total failure, or are you able to see some benefits in the relationship? Do you consider any less-than-perfect performance as a total failure?
Misplaced blame	Tendency to blame or criticize yourself for disappointments or setbacks while ignoring external circumstances	Do you automatically assume when things don't go as planned that it's your fault?
Misfortune telling	Tendency to think that one disappointment will inevitably lead to another	If you get a rejection letter from a job you applied for, do you assume that all the other applications you sent will meet the same fate?
Negative focusing	Focusing your attention only on the negative aspects of your experiences	When you get a job evaluation, do you overlook the praise and focus only on the criticism?
Dismissing the positives	Snatching defeat from the jaws of victory by trivializing or denying your accomplishments; minimizing your strengths or assets	When someone compliments you, do you find some way of dismissing it by saying something like "It's no big deal" or "Anyone could have done it"?
Jumping to conclusions	Drawing a conclusion that is not supported by the facts at hand	Do you usually or always expect the worst to happen?
Catastrophizing	Exaggerating the importance of negative events or personal flaws (making mountains out of molehills)	Do you react to a disappointing grade on a particular examination as though your whole life is ruined?
Emotion-based reasoning	Reasoning based on your emotions rather than on a clear-headed evaluation of the available evidence	Do you think that things are really hopeless because it feels that way?
Shouldisms	Placing unrealistic demands on yourself that you *should* or *must* accomplish certain tasks or reach certain goals	Do you feel that you *should* be further along in your life than you are now? Do you feel you *must* ace this course *or* else? (Not that it wouldn't be desirable to ace the course, but is it really the case that you *must*?)
Name calling	Attaching negative labels to yourself or others as a way of explaining your own or others' behavior	Do you label yourself *lazy* or *stupid* when you fall short of reaching your goals?
Mistaken responsibility	Assuming that you are the cause of other people's problems	Do you automatically assume that your partner is depressed or upset because of something you said or did (or didn't say or do)?

Source: Adapted from Burns, 1980; Nevid, Rathus, & Rubenstein, 1998.

mild setback. Beck and his colleagues have identified a number of faulty thinking patterns, called *cognitive distortions,* that they believe increases vulnerability to depression following negative life events. The more these distorted thinking patterns dominate a person's thinking, the greater the vulnerability to depression. Table 11.2 lists the cognitive distortions most closely associated with depression.

Another psychological model of depression, the **learned helplessness model**, suggests that people become depressed when they come to believe that they are helpless to control the reinforcements in their lives. This concept, developed by psychologist Martin Seligman (1973, 1975), is based on experiments showing that laboratory animals who were exposed to inescapable shocks failed to learn to

 PsychAssist: Cognitive Distortions Linked to Depression

learned helplessness model   The view that depression results from the perception of a lack of control over the reinforcements in one's life that may result from exposure to uncontrollable negative events.

"Why Do I Always Screw Up?" Cognitive theorists believe that the way in which we interpret negative events has an important bearing on our proneness to depression in the face of disappointing life experiences.

About It

"It's All My Fault"

Which, if any, of the errors in thinking and negative attributions described in the text describe how you typically explain disappointing events in your life? How do your thinking patterns affect your moods? Your motivation? Your feelings about yourself? How might you change your ways of thinking about negative experiences in the future?

avoid the shocks when the conditions changed in such a way as to make escape possible. The animals seemed to give up trying, becoming lethargic and unmotivated—behaviors that resembled depression in people. Seligman proposed that exposure to uncontrollable situations may induce a learned helplessness effect in humans, leading to depression. In essence, when repeated efforts prove futile, the person may eventually give up trying and sink into a state of depression.

Seligman and his colleagues later revised the helplessness model to include cognitive factors (Abramson et al., 1978). In particular, they borrowed from social psychology the concept of **attributional style**, which refers to the characteristic ways in which individuals explain the causes of events that happen to them. The reformulated helplessness model proposes that attributions vary along three dimensions: *internal vs. external, global vs. specific,* and *stable vs. unstable.*

Consider a negative event, such as receiving a poor grade on a math test. An internal attribution fixes blame on oneself ("I screwed up"), while an external attribution places responsibility on external factors ("The exam was too hard"). A global attribution treats the cause as reflecting generally on one's underlying personality or abilities ("I'm really not very good at math"), while a specific attribution knocks it down to size ("I tripped up on the equations"). A stable attribution treats the cause as more or less permanent ("I'll never be able to learn this stuff"), while an unstable attribution views it as changeable ("Next time I'll be better prepared"). Seligman and his colleagues posit that a **depressive attributional style** consisting of *internal, global,* and *stable* attributions for disappointments and failure experiences predisposes individuals to become depressed following exposure to negative or disappointing life events.

Evidence links negative, distorted thinking and depression, just as Beck's model would suppose (Clark, Cook, & Snow, 1998; McDermut, Haaga, & Bilek, 1997). Similarly, people who attribute their failures and disappointments to internal, stable, and global factors are at greater risk of developing major depression, just as the reformulated helplessness theory would predict (Alloy et al., 2000). Yet questions remain about whether distorted thinking or attributional styles are causes or effects of depression. Perhaps depression leads people to develop negative, distorted thoughts and to adopt a depressive attributional style, rather than the other way around. Or perhaps the causal linkages work both ways, such that thinking styles affect moods and moods affect thinking styles.

Stress also contributes to depression. Studies indicate that vulnerability to depression is increased by stressful life events such as the loss of a loved one, prolonged unemployment, serious physical illness, marital problems, pressures at work, and financial hardship (Kendler, Kuhn, & Prescott, 2004; Whooley et al., 2002).

attributional style A person's characteristic way of explaining outcomes of events in his or her life.

depressive attributional style A characteristic way of explaining negative events in terms of internal, stable, and global causes.

CONCEPT CHART 11.4
Mood Disorders

	Type of Disorder	Lifetime Prevalence (%)	Symptoms	Associated Features
Depressive Disorders	Major depression	10 to 25 in women; 5 to 12 in men	Downcast mood, feelings of hopelessness and worthlessness, changes in sleep patterns or appetite, loss of motivation, loss of pleasure in pleasant activities	Following a depressive episode, the person may return to his or her usual state of functioning, but recurrences are common.
Bipolar Disorders	Bipolar disorder	0.4 to 1.6 (4 to 16 people in 1,000)	Periods of shifting moods between mania and depression, perhaps with intervening periods of normal mood	Manic episodes are characterized by pressured speech, flight of ideas, poor judgment, hyperactivity, and inflated mood and sense of self.

Sources: American Psychiatric Association, 2000; USDHHS, 1999.

Biological Factors

Depression is linked to biochemical imbalances in the brain involving the levels or activity of neurotransmitters (Bremner et al., 2003). Drugs that help relieve depression, called *antidepressants,* increase the levels of certain neurotransmitters, especially *norepinephrine* and *serotonin.* For example, *Prozac,* a widely used antidepressant, boosts levels of serotonin by interfering with the reabsorption (reuptake) of this mood-regulating chemical by the transmitting neuron (Gupta, 2003).

Depression does not appear to be caused simply by a lack of these neurotransmitters. Rather, investigators suspect that depression involves irregularities in the number or sensitivity of receptors where neurotransmitters dock (Duman, Heninger, & Nestler, 1997). Other investigators report finding abnormalities in the pathways that regulate mood in the brains of people with mood disorders (e.g., Blumberg et al., 2003; Davidson et al., 2003).

Results from twin studies point to the role of heredity in mood disorders, especially bipolar disorder (McGuffin et al., 2003; Sullivan, Neale, & Kendler, 2000). Researchers are now zeroing in on several chromosomes they believe may carry genes that increase susceptibility to mood disorders (e.g., Caspi et al., 2003; Konradi et al., 2004). However, biological causes of mood disorders do not entirely account for their development. Psychological factors also play a role. All told, mood disorders are complex phenomena in which a number of factors interact in complex ways (see Concept Chart 11.4).

Suicide

Nearly one-half million Americans each year make suicide attempts that are serious enough to require medical treatment (Duryea, 2000). About 30,000 people in the United States, and about 1 million people worldwide, commit suicide each year (Lemonick, 2003b; Olson, 2001). Suicide is the third leading cause of death among people fifteen to twenty-four years of age and the second leading cause of death among college students. A recent national survey showed that about 10 percent of college students had seriously thought of killing themselves during the preceding year (Brener, Hassan, & Barrios, 1999). A representative U.S. sample of fifteen- to fifty-four-year-olds showed that nearly one in twenty adult Americans (4.6 percent) reported making a prior suicidal attempt (Kessler, Borges, & Walters, 1999).

CONCEPT 11.23
Biological causes implicated in mood disorders include disturbances in neurotransmitter functioning in the brain and genetic influences.

Suicide Hotline Suicide hotlines are available in many communities to provide immediate support to people experiencing suicidal thoughts and to assist them in getting help.

web, Netlab/How Much Do You Know About Suicide?

Who Is Most at Risk?

Suicide cuts across every stratum of our society. Yet certain factors are related to an increased risk:

- *Age.* Though much attention is focused on adolescent suicides, suicide rates are greater among older adults, especially White males aged seventy-five and above (Pearson & Brown, 2000; Szanto et al., 2003) (see Figure 11.3).

- *Gender.* More women attempt suicide, but about four times as many men complete the act (Cochran & Rabinowitz, 2003; Stein et al., 2002; Westman et al., 2003) (see Figure 11.4). Why do more women attempt suicide but more men succeed? The primary reason is that men typically use more lethal means, especially firearms. Women are more apt to use pills, poison, or other methods that may be less lethal.

- *Race/Ethnicity.* European (non-Hispanic) Americans and Native Americans are more likely to take their own lives than African Americans and Hispanic Americans (Gone, 2004). Young Native Americans living on reservations are at especially high risk. The widespread sense of hopelessness among Native Americans arising from lack of opportunities and segregation from the dominant culture helps set the stage for alcohol and drug abuse, which are often preludes to depression and suicide. Figure 11.4 shows differences in the overall suicide rates between African Americans and White (non-Hispanic) Americans.

Figure 11.3   Suicide Rates in Relation to Age
As you can see, the risk of suicide is greatest among older adults.

Source: Statistical Abstracts of the United States, U.S. Bureau of the Census, 2000.

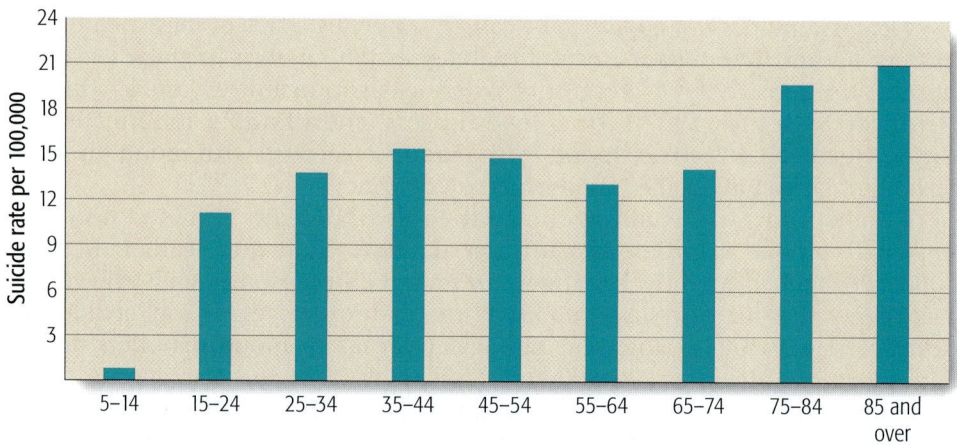

Figure 11.4   Suicide Rates in Relation to Gender and Ethnicity
Rates of completed suicide are highest among males in general and White males in particular. Though more women attempt suicide, they tend to use less lethal means.

Source: Statistical Abstracts of the United States, U.S. Bureau of the Census, 2000.

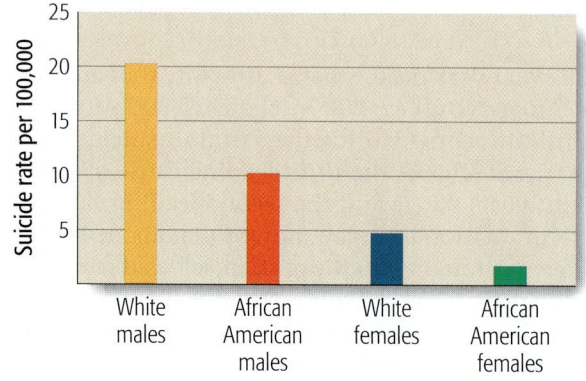

TABLE 11.3	Myths About Suicide
Myth	**Fact**
People who threaten suicide are only seeking attention.	Not so. Researchers report that most people who kill themselves gave clear clues concerning their intentions prior to the act, such as disposing of all their possessions or securing a burial plot (Cordes, 1985; Gelman, 1994).
A person must be insane to attempt suicide.	Most people who attempt suicide may feel hopeless, but they are not insane (i.e., out of touch with reality).
Talking about suicide with a depressed person may prompt the person to attempt it.	An open discussion of suicide with a depressed person does not prompt the person to attempt it. In fact, extracting a promise that the person will not attempt suicide before calling or visiting a mental health worker may well *prevent* a suicide.
People who attempt suicide and fail aren't serious about killing themselves.	Most people who commit suicide have made previous unsuccessful attempts.
If someone threatens suicide, it is best to ignore it so as not to encourage repeated threats.	Though some people do manipulate others by making idle threats, it is prudent to treat every suicidal threat as genuine and to take appropriate action.

Factors in Suicide

Suicide is closely linked to mood disorders, especially major depression and bipolar disorder, and to the deep feelings of hopelessness and helplessness that often accompany depression (Kaslow et al., 2002). The belief that things are hopeless and that one is helpless to change them can lead to overwhelming feelings of distress that many suicidal individuals experience. Like depression, suicide may also be linked to biochemical factors, such as reduced utilization of serotonin in the brain (Dwivedi et al., 2003; Lemonde et al., 2003). Serotonin helps curb or inhibit excess nervous system activity. A lack of serotonin may lead to a **disinhibition effect**—the removal of inhibitions that might otherwise constrain impulsive behavior, including impulses to commit suicide.

Drug and alcohol dependence is an important risk factor in suicide, as is alcohol intoxication itself (Preuss et al., 2003). Use of alcohol may lead people to act impulsively, with the result that suicidal thoughts are carried over into action. Posttraumatic stress disorder or other anxiety disorders, prolonged unemployment, and serious medical illness also figure in many suicides (e.g., Ben-Ya'acov & Amir, 2004; Oquendo et al., 2003; Qin et al., 2003; Roy, 2003).

Suicide expert Edwin Shneidman (1987) also points to a lack of coping responses among people who attempt or commit suicide. Suicidal people may see no other way of resolving their problems or ending their unendurable psychological or physical pain. In addition, suicide is linked to *exit events,* or losses of supportive persons through death, divorce or separation, or family separations. Exit events leave vulnerable people feeling stripped of crucial sources of social support.

Teenagers have been known to commit copycat suicides in the wake of widely publicized suicides in their communities. The sensationalism that attends a teenage suicide may make it seem a romantic or courageous statement to impressionable young people with problems of their own. Researchers find that adolescents who have a friend who attempted suicide are more likely than their peers to attempt suicide themselves (Blum et al., 2000).

It is clear that many suicides could be prevented if people received effective treatment for the disorders that give rise to suicidal behavior, especially depression and alcohol and substance abuse. It is also clear that myths about suicide abound (see Table 11.3).

 **CONCEPT 11.24**
Most suicides are linked to depression and, especially, to feelings of utter hopelessness.

disinhibition effect The removal of normal restraints or inhibitions that serve to keep impulsive behavior in check.

MODULE 11.4 REVIEW

Mood Disorders

CONCEPT CHECK

1. The two major types of mood disorders are _____ and _____ .
   a. dysthymic disorder; seasonal affective disorder
   b. minor affective states; major affective states
   c. major depression; bipolar disorder
   d. hysteria; narcissism

2. Which of the following terms was previously used to refer to bipolar disorder?
   a. manic-depression
   b. mood-swing disorder
   c. obsessive-compulsive disorder
   d. cyclothymic disorder

3. Which factors may help explain the greater prevalence of depression in women than in men? (Identify at least one factor.)

4. In Seligman's research on learned helplessness,
   a. young children gave up when reading did not come easily to them.
   b. prisoners became depressed when faced with situations they could not control.
   c. animals who were earlier exposed to inescapable shock failed to try to escape shock when it became possible to do so.
   d. battlefield experiences left soldiers feeling incapable and ineffective.

MODULE 11.5 Schizophrenia

- **What is schizophrenia?**
- **What are the three specific types of schizophrenia?**
- **What causal factors are implicated in schizophrenia?**
- **What is the diathesis-stress model of schizophrenia?**

CONCEPT 11.25
Schizophrenia is a puzzling and disabling disorder that fills the mind with distorted perceptions, false ideas, and loosely connected thoughts.

 **Web Tutorial/Schizophrenia**

schizophrenia   A severe and chronic psychological disorder characterized by disturbances in thinking, perception, emotions, and behavior.

Schizophrenia is the disorder that most closely corresponds to popular concepts of insanity, madness, or lunacy. The word *schizophrenia* comes from Greek roots meaning "split brain." In cases of schizophrenia, the mind is stripped of the intimate connections among thoughts, perceptions, and feelings. Individuals with this disorder may giggle in the face of disaster, hear or see things that aren't physically present, or maintain beliefs that are firmly held but patently false.

Schizophrenia affects about one adult in a hundred (Freedman, 2003). The disorder is characterized by bizarre, irrational behavior; recall the case of Claire, who was convinced she was protecting the populace from demons. In the United States, an estimated 2.5 million people are diagnosed with schizophrenia, and about a third of these individuals require hospitalization (McGuire, 2000). Treatment of schizophrenia accounts for 75 percent of the nation's mental health expenditures.

Schizophrenia is somewhat more common in men than in women (Aleman, Kahn, & Selten, 2003). Men also tend to develop the disorder somewhat earlier than women and to experience a more severe course of the disorder. Schizophrenia follows a lifelong course and typically develops in late adolescence or early adulthood, at about the time that people are beginning to make their way in the world (Cowan & Kandel, 2001; Harrop & Trower, 2001). It affects about 24 million people worldwide and occurs about as frequently in other cultures as in our own, although the particular symptoms may vary from culture to culture (Jablensky et al., 1992; Olson, 2001).

Symptoms of Schizophrenia

Schizophrenia is a **psychotic disorder**—that is, a disorder in which an individual confuses reality with fantasy, seeing or hearing things that aren't there (hallucinations) or holding fixed but patently false beliefs (delusions). *Hallucinations* are perceptions that occur in the absence of external stimuli. They may affect different senses. Auditory hallucinations ("hearing voices") are most common. Visual hallucinations (seeing things that are not there) and other sensory hallucinations (sensing odors or having taste sensations without any physical stimulus) are much less common. *Delusions* may represent many different themes, but the most common are themes of persecution, such as the belief that demons or "the Devil" are trying to harm the person.

People with schizophrenia may exhibit bizarre behavior, incoherent speech, and illogical thinking. They may not know the time of day, or what day or year it is. Or where they are. Or *who* they are. Note that not all of these symptoms must be present for a diagnosis of schizophrenia to be given.

Many people with schizophrenia exhibit a **thought disorder**, a breakdown in the logical structure of thinking and speech characterized by *loose associations* between expressed ideas (Docherty et al., 2003). Normally, our thoughts are tightly connected or associated; one thought follows another in a logical sequence. But in schizophrenia, there may be an absence of logical connections between thoughts. The ideas expressed are strung loosely together or jumbled in such a way that the listener is unable to follow the person's train of thought. In severe cases, speech becomes completely incoherent or incomprehensible. The person may begin to form meaningless words or mindless rhymes.

The more flagrant signs of schizophrenia, such as hallucinations, delusions, bizarre behavior, and thought disorder, are behavioral excesses classified as **positive symptoms**. Yet people with schizophrenia may also have behavioral deficits or **negative symptoms**, such as extreme withdrawal or social isolation, apathy, and absent or blunted emotions (Roth et al., 2004). Positive symptoms may fade after acute episodes, but negative symptoms are typically more enduring, making it difficult for the person to meet the demands of daily life.

Types of Schizophrenia

Several types of schizophrenia have been identified on the basis of their distinctive symptoms or characteristics. Here we discuss the three major subtypes.

Disorganized Type

The **disorganized type** of schizophrenia is characterized by confused behavior, incoherent speech, vivid and frequent hallucinations, inappropriate emotions or lack of emotional expression, and disorganized delusions that often have religious or sexual themes. People with this form of schizophrenia may giggle inappropriately, act silly, or talk nonsensically. They tend to neglect their personal hygiene, may have difficulty controlling their bladders or bowels, and have significant problems relating to others.

Catatonic Type

People with the **catatonic type** of schizophrenia show bizarre movements, postures, or grimaces. Some persist in a motionless or stuporous state for hours and then abruptly switch into a highly agitated state. Others display highly unusual body movements or positions, such as holding a fixed posture for hours. They may be mute or uncommunicative during these episodes, showing no evidence of responding to the environment. Later, however, they may report that they heard

CONCEPT 11.26
There are three distinct types of schizophrenia: the disorganized, catatonic, and paranoid types.

psychotic disorder A psychological disorder, such as schizophrenia, characterized by a "break" with reality.

thought disorder A breakdown in the logical structure of thought and speech, revealed in the form of a loosening of associations.

positive symptoms Symptoms of schizophrenia involving behavioral excesses, such as hallucinations and delusions.

negative symptoms Behavioral deficits associated with schizophrenia, such as withdrawal and apathy.

disorganized type A subtype of schizophrenia characterized by confused behavior and disorganized delusions, among other features.

catatonic type A subtype of schizophrenia characterized by bizarre movements, postures, or grimaces.

Catatonic Type The body position of some persons with catatonic schizophrenia can be molded by others into unusual postures that they then hold for hours at a time.

CONCEPT 11.27

Though the causes of schizophrenia remain a mystery, scientists suspect that a combination of biological factors, including heredity, biochemical imbalances, and structural abnormalities in the brain, together with stressful life experiences contribute to its development.

waxy flexibility A feature of catatonic schizophrenia in which people rigidly maintain the body position or posture in which they were placed by others.

paranoid type The most common subtype of schizophrenia, characterized by the appearance of delusional thinking accompanied by frequent auditory hallucinations.

what others were saying at the time. Less commonly they may show **waxy flexibility**, a behavior pattern in which their body position can be molded by others (like wax) into unusual, even uncomfortable positions that they then hold for hours at a time. The catatonic type is a rare form of schizophrenia.

Paranoid Type

The most common form of schizophrenia, the **paranoid type**, is characterized by delusions that are accompanied by frequent auditory hallucinations. The delusions often have themes of grandeur (e.g., believing that one is Jesus or has superhuman abilities), persecution (e.g., believing that one is being persecuted by demons or by the Mafia), or jealousy (e.g., believing that one's spouse or lover is unfaithful despite an absence of evidence).

Causes of Schizophrenia

Schizophrenia remains a puzzling—indeed, mystifying—disorder. Though we have not solved the puzzle, researchers have made substantial progress in putting many of the pieces into place (Walker et al., 2004).

Genetic Factors

One thing we know is that heredity plays an important role in schizophrenia (Gottesman, 2001; Thaker, 2002; Tienari et al., 2003). The closer the genetic relationship a person shares with someone who has schizophrenia, the greater the likelihood the person will also have or develop schizophrenia. Consistent with a genetic contribution, twin studies show a higher concordance rate among monozygotic twins (about 45 to 50 percent) than among dizygotic twins (about 17 percent) (see Figure 2.20 on page 75).

Adoptee studies add further evidence of a genetic predisposition (Tienari et al., 2003). A classic study that investigated adopted children whose biological parents had schizophrenia showed that these children were more likely to develop schizophrenia than were adopted-away children of parents who were free of schizophrenia (Rosenthal et al., 1968, 1975). Investigators believe that multiple genes are responsible for creating a genetic predisposition to this disorder (Plomin & McGuffin, 2003; Waterworth, Bassett, & Brzustowicz, 2002).

Though heredity clearly plays an important role in schizophrenia, genes do not tell the whole story. Consider that only about 13 percent of people who have a parent with schizophrenia develop the disorder themselves. Consider, too, that if one identical twin has schizophrenia, the other twin, though genetically identical, has no more than a 50 percent chance of having the disorder as well. If only genetics were involved, we would expect 100 percent concordance among monozygotic twins. In short, genetic vulnerability is not genetic inevitability (Sapolsky, 2000). Whether a person develops schizophrenia depends on a combination of factors, not on genes alone. Some of these other factors may have a biological basis, such as early brain trauma. Others may be environmental or psychological in origin, such as child abuse, family conflict, or life stress.

Biochemical Imbalances

Researchers suspect that biochemical imbalances in nerve pathways in the brain that utilize the neurotransmitter dopamine contribute to the development of schizophrenia (McGowan et al., 2004). Dopamine is suspected largely because *antipsychotic drugs* that help quell hallucinations and delusions, such as Thorazine and Mellaril, work on the brain to reduce dopamine activity by blocking dopamine receptors (Gründer, Carlsson, & Wong, 2002). Yet the brains of schizophrenia patients do not appear to produce too much dopamine. Rather, they may have an excess number of dopamine receptors (Walker et al., 2004). Or perhaps their dopamine receptors are overly sensitive to the chemical. Hopefully, future research will clarify these underlying mechanisms.

Brain Abnormalities

Brain imaging techniques such as magnetic resonance imaging (MRI) and computed tomography (CT) show evidence of abnormal brain development in many schizophrenia patients (e.g., Bagary et al., 2003; Callicott et al., 2003; Kasai et al., 2003). Brain abnormalities may develop during critical prenatal periods when brain structures are first forming or during early childhood when they are developing further (Walker et al., 2004).

The areas of the brain that seem to be most affected in schizophrenia are the *prefrontal cortex* and the *limbic system* (e.g., Barch, 2003; Gaser et al., 2004; Winterer et al., 2004). The prefrontal cortex is the part of the brain responsible for the ability to keep information in mind (working memory), to organize our thoughts and behavior, and to allow us to formulate and carry out goals and plans—the very functions that are often disrupted in schizophrenia. The limbic system plays key roles in memory formation and processing of emotional experiences.

Psychosocial Influences

Psychosocial influences may also be part of the matrix of causes of schizophrenia. For example, life stress may interact with genetic vulnerability in leading to schizophrenia (Byrne et al., 2003). The belief that schizophrenia results from the interaction of a genetic predisposition (diathesis) and stressful life experiences is expressed in the form of a diathesis-stress model (Zubin & Spring, 1977) (again, see Figure 11.1). The sources of stress are varied and may include biological influences, such as prenatal or early brain trauma; psychosocial influences, such as being raised in an abusive family environment or experiencing disturbed patterns of communication in the family; and negative life events, such as the loss of a loved one or failure in school. Though we lack a precise understanding of how these factors fit together, one possibility is that genetic and stressful influences combine to produce abnormalities in the brain that interfere with thinking, memory, and perceptual processes, leading eventually to the welter of confusing thoughts and perceptions that we see in people with schizophrenia.

The symptoms and suspected causes of schizophrenia are summarized in Concept Chart 11.5.

Paranoid Type Paranoid schizophrenia, the most common subtype, is characterized by delusional thinking and auditory hallucinations. John Nash, played by Russell Crowe in the movie *A Beautiful Mind,* is a brilliant mathematician who was diagnosed with paranoid schizophrenia.

CONCEPT 11.28
The diathesis-stress model holds that schizophrenia results from the interaction of a genetic predisposition and stressful life events or trauma.

CONCEPT CHART 11.5
Schizophrenia

What It Is	Symptoms	Probable Causes
A chronic psychotic disorder affecting about 1 percent of the population	Delusions, hallucinations, bizarre behavior, incoherent or loosely connected speech, inappropriate emotions or lack of emotional expression, social withdrawal, and apathy	An interaction of a genetic predisposition and life stress; underlying brain abnormalities

MODULE 11.5 REVIEW

Schizophrenia

CONCEPT CHECK

1. Regarding schizophrenia, which of the following is *not* true?
   a. Schizophrenia is classified as a psychotic disorder, whereby affected individuals cannot distinguish between reality and fantasy.
   b. Schizophrenia is much more prevalent in our own culture than in other cultures throughout the world.
   c. Slightly more males than females are affected by the disorder.
   d. The onset of schizophrenia most frequently occurs during late adolescence or early adulthood.

2. About how many people will develop schizophrenia if they have an identical (MZ) twin with this disorder?
   a. 10 to 15 percent
   b. 20 to 25 percent
   c. 45 to 50 percent
   d. more than 50 percent

3. Scientists believe that abnormalities involving the neurotransmitter _____ are closely linked to the development of schizophrenia.
   a. serotonin
   b. dopamine
   c. epinephrine
   d. acetylcholine

4. Match the following terms with the appropriate descriptions: (a) catatonic schizophrenia; (b) paranoid schizophrenia; (c) disorganized schizophrenia; (d) hallucinations.
   i. the most common type of schizophrenia
   ii. perceiving things that are not really there
   iii. confused behavior, incoherent speech, neglect of personal hygiene
   iv. holding a fixed posture for hours

MODULE 11.6 Personality Disorders

- **What are personality disorders?**
- **What characteristics are associated with antisocial personality disorder?**
- **What causal factors are implicated in antisocial personality disorder?**

CONCEPT 11.29
People with personality disorders exhibit excessively rigid patterns of behavior that ultimately make it difficult for them to relate to others or meet the demands that are placed upon them.

CONCEPT 11.30
Antisocial personality disorder is characterized by a blatant disregard for social rules and regulations, antisocial behavior, impulsivity, irresponsibility, lack of remorse for wrongdoing, and a tendency to take advantage of others.

personality disorders   A class of psychological disorders characterized by rigid personality traits that impair people's ability to adjust to the demands they face in the environment and that interfere with their relationships with others.

narcissistic personality disorder   A type of personality disorder characterized by a grandiose sense of self.

paranoid personality disorder   A type of personality disorder characterized by extreme suspiciousness or mistrust of others.

Personality disorders are a cluster of psychological disorders characterized by excessively rigid patterns of behavior. These behavioral patterns become self-defeating because they make it difficult for people to adjust to external demands and interfere with their relationships with others. People with personality disorders have maladaptive personality traits that become so deeply ingrained that they are highly resistant to change. In many cases, such people believe that others should change to accommodate them, not the reverse.

People with **narcissistic personality disorder** have an inflated or grandiose sense of self. Those with **paranoid personality disorder** show an extreme degree of suspiciousness or mistrust of others. Those with **schizoid personality disorder** have little if any interest in social relationships, display a limited range of emotional expression, and are perceived as distant and aloof. And those with **borderline personality disorder** tend to have stormy relationships with others, dramatic mood swings, and an unstable self-image. In all, the DSM identifies ten personality disorders (see Concept Chart 11.6). The most widely studied of these is **antisocial personality disorder (APD)**, which is the focus of our attention here.

Symptoms of Antisocial Personality Disorder

People with antisocial personalities (sometimes called *psychopaths* or *sociopaths*) show a flagrant disregard for the rules of society and a lack of concern for the welfare of others. They are not psychotic; they maintain contact with reality. But they tend to act on impulse—doing what they want, when they want. They are typically irresponsible and take advantage of other people for their own needs or personal gain. They lack remorse for their misdeeds or mistreatment of others and appear to be untroubled by anxiety or undeterred by the threat of punishment or by punishment itself.

CONCEPT CHART 11.6
Personality Disorders

Type of Disorder	Major Features or Symptoms
Paranoid personality disorder	High levels of suspiciousness of the motives and intentions of others but without the outright paranoid delusions associated with paranoid schizophrenia
Schizoid personality disorder	Aloof and distant from others, with shallow or blunted emotions
Schizotypal personality disorder	Persistent difficulties establishing close social relationships; holding beliefs or showing behaviors that are odd or peculiar but not clearly psychotic
Antisocial personality disorder	A pattern of antisocial and irresponsible behavior, callous treatment of others, and lack of remorse for wrongdoing
Borderline personality disorder	A failure to develop a stable self-image, together with a pattern of tumultuous moods and stormy relationships with others and lack of impulse control
Histrionic personality disorder	Dramatic and emotional behavior; excessive demands to be the center of attention; excessive needs for reassurance, praise, and approval
Narcissistic personality disorder	Grandiose self-image and excessive needs for admiration
Avoidant personality disorder	Pattern of avoiding social relationships out of fear of rejection
Dependent personality disorder	Pattern of excessive dependence on others and difficulty making independent decisions
Obsessive-compulsive personality disorder	Excessive needs for orderliness and attention to detail, perfectionism, and rigid ways of relating to others

Some people with antisocial personalities engage in criminal behavior, but most are law-abiding. They may display a high level of intelligence and a superficial charm that attracts others. APD is found more often among men than women, with estimates of lifetime rates of 3 to 6 percent in men and 1 percent in women (American Psychiatric Association, 2000; Cale & Lilienfeld, 2002; Kessler et al., 1994).

Causes of Antisocial Personality Disorder

Men with APD may have brain abnormalities that make it difficult for them to restrain their impulses and aggressive behavior (Damasio, 2000). Evidence from brain imaging studies shows that many men with APD have lower levels of activity in the frontal lobes of the cerebral cortex, the area of the brain responsible for inhibiting impulsive behavior (Deckel, Hesselbrock, & Bauer, 1996). Other research reveals greater evidence of structural damage in the frontal lobes of APD patients than in control subjects (Raine et al., 2000).

Still other research points to a genetic contribution to the development of antisocial behavior (Caspi et al., 2002; Rhee & Waldman, 2002). We also have evidence showing that many people with antisocial personalities have exaggerated cravings for stimulation (Arnett, Smith, & Newman, 1997). They may need higher-than-normal levels of stimulation to maintain an optimum state of arousal. These findings may explain why such individuals seem to become quickly bored with routine activities and turn to more dangerous activities that provide immediate thrills, such as alcohol and drug use, racing cars or motorcycles, high-stakes gambling, or risky sexual encounters.

What role does the environment play? Research shows that many people with APD were raised in families characterized by lack of parental warmth, neglect, rejection, and use of harsh punishment (Luntz & Widom, 1994). A history of

CONCEPT 11.31
Evidence points to an interaction of environmental and biological factors in the development of antisocial personality disorder.

schizoid personality disorder A type of personality disorder characterized by social aloofness and limited range of emotional expression.

borderline personality disorder A type of personality disorder characterized by unstable emotions and self-image.

antisocial personality disorder (APD) A type of personality disorder characterized by callous attitudes toward others and by antisocial and irresponsible behavior.

emotional or physical abuse in childhood may lead to a failure to develop a sense of empathy or concern for the welfare of others. It may also lead to a failure to develop a moral compass or sense of conscience. This lack of empathy and moral values may explain why people with APD act in a callous way toward others. In all likelihood, then, both genetic and environmental factors contribute to the development of APD, as is the case with many forms of abnormal behavior.

MODULE 11.6 REVIEW

Personality Disorders

CONCEPT CHECK

1. What are some of the characteristics of individuals with personality disorders?

2. Investigators find that people with antisocial personality disorder are more likely than others to have damage in which part of the brain?

3. Match the following types of personality disorder with the appropriate descriptions: (a) paranoid personality disorder; (b) schizoid personality disorder; (c) narcissistic personality disorder; (d) borderline personality disorder.
   i.   stormy interpersonal relationships, unstable self-image
   ii. distant, aloof, limited emotional and social interaction
   iii. inflated, grandiose sense of self
   iv. extreme suspiciousness and distrust of others

APPLICATION

MODULE 11.7   Suicide Prevention

- **What steps can you take to help someone who is threatening suicide?**

"I don't believe it. I saw him just last week and he looked fine."

"She sat here just the other day, laughing with the rest of us. How were we to know what was going on inside her?"

"I knew he was depressed, but I never thought he'd do something like this. I didn't have a clue."

"Why didn't she just call me?" (Nevid, Rathus, & Greene, 2003)

CONCEPT 11.32

A suicide threat should be taken seriously and the immediacy of the threat should be assessed; but above all, professional help should be sought at the first opportunity.

We may respond to the news of a suicide of a friend or family member with shock or with guilt that we failed to pick up any warning signs. Yet even professionals have difficulty predicting whether someone is likely to commit suicide (Rudd et al., 1999). But when signs are present, the time to take action is now. Encourage the person, calmly but firmly, to seek professional assistance. Offer to accompany the person to a helping professional—or make the first contact yourself.

Facing the Threat

Suppose a friend confides in you that he or she is contemplating suicide. You know your friend has been going through a difficult time and has been depressed. You didn't think it would come to this, however. You want to help but are unsure about what to do. It's normal to feel frightened, even flustered. Here are some suggestions to consider if you ever face this situation. They are offered as general guidelines, not as direct instructions since the situation at hand may call for specific responses:

1. *Recognize the seriousness of the situation.* Don't fall for the myth of thinking that people who talk about suicide are not truly serious. Treat any talk of suicide as a clear warning sign.

2. *Take implied threats seriously.* Some suicidal people don't come right out and say they are planning to kill themselves. They might say something like "I just don't feel I can go on anymore."

3. *Express understanding.* Engage the person in conversation to allow his or her feelings to be expressed. Show that you understand how troubled the person is. Don't dismiss his or her concerns by saying something like "Everyone feels like this from time to time. It'll pass."

4. *Focus on alternatives.* Tell the person that other ways of dealing with his or her problems may be found, even if they are not apparent at the moment.

5. *Assess the immediate danger.* Ask the person whether he or she has made a specific plan to commit suicide. If the person plans to use guns or drugs kept at home, prevent the person from returning home alone.

6. *Enlist the person's agreement to seek help.* Insist that the person accompany you to a health professional or nearby hospital emergency room. If that's not immediately possible, have the person accompany you to a telephone and call a health professional or suicide prevention hotline. Help is available by calling 1-800-SUICIDE or a local crisis center or health center.

7. *Accompany the person to seek help.* Above all, don't leave the person alone. If you do get separated for any reason, or if the person refuses help and leaves, call a mental health professional, suicide hotline service, or the police for assistance.

TYING IT TOGETHER

Psychologists apply multiple criteria in determining when behavior crosses the line between normal and abnormal (Module 11.1). Mental or psychological disorders are patterns of abnormal behavior associated with significant personal distress or impaired functioning. This chapter reviews several examples of psychological disorders, including anxiety disorders (Module 11.2), dissociative and somatoform disorders (Module 11.3), mood disorders (Module 11.4), schizophrenia (Module 11.5), and personality disorders (Module 11.6). It ends with a discussion of suicide and steps we can take to help someone who may be contemplating suicide (Module 11.7).

SUMMING UP: Q&A

What Is Abnormal Behavior? (Module 11.1)

What criteria are used to determine whether behavior is abnormal?

- There are several criteria used, including unusualness, social deviance, emotional distress, maladaptive behavior, dangerousness, and faulty perceptions or interpretations of reality.

What are the major models of abnormal behavior?

- The major contemporary models are the medical model, the psychological model, the sociocultural model, and the biopsychosocial model.

What are psychological disorders?

- Varying in symptoms and severity, psychological disorders (also called *mental disorders*) are disturbances in behavior,

thought processes, or emotions that are associated with significant personal distress or impaired functioning. About one person in two in the United States develops a diagnosable psychological disorder at some point in life.

- The DSM (*Diagnostic and Statistical Manual of Mental Disorders*) is the American Psychiatric Association's diagnostic manual for classifying mental disorders.

Anxiety Disorders (Module 11.2)

What are anxiety disorders?

- Anxiety disorders are characterized by excessive or inappropriate anxiety reactions.
- Anxiety disorders include phobias, panic disorder, generalized anxiety disorder, obsessive-compulsive disorder, and posttraumatic stress disorder.

What causal factors are implicated in anxiety disorders?

- These include psychological factors, such as prior learning experiences and thinking patterns, and biological factors, such as genetic influences, imbalances of neurotransmitters in the brain, and underlying brain abnormalities.

Dissociative and Somatoform Disorders (Module 11.3)

What are dissociative disorders and somatoform disorders?

- Dissociative disorders involve disturbances in memory, consciousness, or identity that affect the ability to maintain an integrated sense of self. These disorders include dissociative identity disorder and dissociative amnesia.
- People with somatoform disorders either exaggerate the meaning of physical complaints or have physical complaints that cannot be accounted for by organic causes. Two major somatoform disorders are conversion disorder and hypochondriasis.

What causal factors are implicated in dissociative and somatoform disorders?

- Exposure to childhood abuse figures prominently in the backgrounds of people with dissociative identity disorder, leading theorists to believe the disorder may represent a psychological defense that protects the self from troubling memories or feelings. Avoidance of painful or troubling memories is also implicated in dissociative amnesia.
- Freud believed that conversion disorder represents the transformation of inner psychological conflicts into physical symptoms. Learning theorists focus on the anxiety-reducing roles of somatoform symptoms, while cognitive theorists focus on underlying cognitive biases.

Mood Disorders (Module 11.4)

What are mood disorders?

- Mood disorders are disturbances in mood that are unusually severe or prolonged. Two of the major types of mood disorder are major depression and bipolar disorder.

What causal factors are implicated in mood disorders?

- Suspected causes include genetic factors, heredity, biochemical imbalances in neurotransmitter activity in the brain, self-directed anger, changes in reinforcement patterns, and dysfunctional thinking.

Who is at risk for suicide?

- Groups at highest risk for suicide include older White men and Native Americans. Men are more likely than women to "succeed" at suicide attempts because they tend to use more lethal means.

Why do people commit suicide?

- Most suicides result from deep feelings of hopelessness and despair. Teenagers have been known to commit copycat suicides.

Schizophrenia (Module 11.5)

What is schizophrenia?

- Schizophrenia is a psychotic disorder, meaning that it is characterized by a break with reality. Gross confusion, delusions, and hallucinations may be present in individuals with this disorder.

What are three specific types of schizophrenia?

- Three specific types of schizophrenia are the disorganized type, the catatonic type, and the paranoid type. The paranoid type is the most common.

What causal factors are implicated in schizophrenia?

- Precise causes are unknown, but suspected causes include biological factors such as a genetic predisposition, disturbed neurotransmitter activity in the brain, brain abnormalities, and stress.

What is the diathesis-stress model of schizophrenia?

- The diathesis-stress model refers to the belief that schizophrenia arises from an interaction of a genetic predisposition and stressful life experiences.

Personality Disorders (Module 11.6)

What are personality disorders?

- Personality disorders are deeply ingrained patterns of behavior that become maladaptive because they either cause personal distress or impair the person's ability to relate to others.
- Personality disorders include narcissistic personality disorder, paranoid personality disorder, schizoid personality disorder, borderline personality disorder, and antisocial personality disorder.

What characteristics are associated with antisocial personality disorder?

- The characteristics associated with antisocial personality disorder include impulsivity, irresponsibility, a callous disregard for the rights and feelings of others, and antisocial behavior.

What causal factors are implicated in antisocial personality disorder?

- A number of causal factors are implicated, including environmental factors, such as a family environment characterized by a lack of parental warmth, neglect, rejection, and use of harsh punishment, and biological factors, such as a genetic predisposition, abnormalities in higher brain centers that control impulsive behavior, and a greater need for arousing stimulation.

Application: Suicide Prevention (Module 11.7)

What steps can you take to help someone who is threatening suicide?

- Above all, take any threats of suicide seriously. Engage the person in conversation and convey understanding of the person's problems and feelings. Assess the immediacy of any danger, and insist that the person accompany you to contact a health professional.

Key Terms

hallucinations *(p. 383)*
delusions *(p. 383)*
medical model *(p. 384)*
biopsychosocial model *(p. 386)*
diathesis-stress model *(p. 386)*
diathesis *(p. 386)*
psychological disorders *(p. 386)*
phobia *(p. 390)*
social phobia *(p. 390)*
specific phobia *(p. 390)*
acrophobia *(p. 390)*
claustrophobia *(p. 390)*
agoraphobia *(p. 390)*
panic disorder *(p. 390)*
generalized anxiety disorder (GAD) *(p. 391)*
obsessive-compulsive disorder (OCD)
  (p. 391)

dissociative disorders *(p. 394)*
somatoform disorders *(p. 394)*
dissociative identity disorder (DID)
  (p. 394)
conversion disorder *(p. 396)*
hypochondriasis *(p. 396)*
secondary gain *(p. 397)*
mood disorders *(p. 398)*
major depression *(p. 398)*
bipolar disorder *(p. 400)*
manic episodes *(p. 400)*
learned helplessness model *(p. 401)*
attributional style *(p. 402)*
depressive attributional style *(p. 402)*
disinhibition effect *(p. 405)*
schizophrenia *(p. 406)*
psychotic disorder *(p. 407)*

thought disorder *(p. 407)*
positive symptoms *(p. 407)*
negative symptoms *(p. 407)*
disorganized type *(p. 407)*
catatonic type *(p. 407)*
waxy flexibility *(p. 408)*
paranoid type *(p. 408)*
personality disorders *(p. 410)*
narcissistic personality disorder *(p. 410)*
paranoid personality disorder *(p. 410)*
schizoid personality disorder *(p. 410)*
borderline personality disorder *(p. 410)*
antisocial personality disorder (APD) *(p. 410)*

Thinking Critically About Psychology

Based on your reading of this chapter, answer the following questions. Then, to evaluate your progress in developing critical thinking skills, compare your answers to the sample answers found in Appendix A.

1. Ron, a twenty-two-year-old stock clerk in an auto parts store, sought a consultation with a psychologist because he was feeling "down in the dumps." He explained that he was involved in a three-year-long relationship with Katie. The relationship followed a seesawing pattern of numerous breakups and brief reconciliations. Most of the breakups occurred after incidents in which Ron became angry when he felt Katie was becoming distant from him. On one occasion, he accused her of sitting too far away from him in the car. If she was in a bad mood, he assumed it was because she didn't really want to be with him. The relationship meant everything to him, he told the psychologist, saying further that "I don't know what I'd do if she left me, you know, for good. I've got to figure out how to make this relationship work" (adapted from Nevid, Rathus & Greene, 2003).

   Review the characteristic errors in thinking associated with depression listed in Table 11.2. Give some examples of these cognitive errors in Ron's thinking.

2. Lonnie, a thirty-eight-year-old chemical engineer for a large pharmaceutical company, sought a consultation at the urging of his wife, Maria. He told the psychologist that Maria

had grown exasperated over "his little behavioral quirks." It seems that Lonnie was a compulsive checker. Whenever the two of them would leave their apartment, he would insist on returning to check and recheck that the gas jets were turned off, the windows were shut, the door was securely locked, and the refrigerator door was tightly shut. Sometimes he'd get as far as the garage before the compulsion to return to the apartment would strike. He would apologize to Maria and leave her fuming. When retiring to bed at night, he performed an elaborate ritual of checking and rechecking to see that everything was secure. But even then, he would often bolt out of bed to check everything again, which would disturb Maria's sleep. Leaving for vacation was especially troublesome, as it required checking rituals that consumed the better part of the morning. Yet he would still be bothered by nagging doubts that would plague him throughout his trip. Lonnie recognized that his compulsive behavior was wrecking his marriage and causing him emotional distress. However, he feared that giving it up would leave him defenseless against the anxieties it helps to ease (adapted from Nevid, Rathus, & Greene, 2003).

Review the six criteria used to define abnormal behavior. Which of these criteria do you think would apply to Lonnie's case? Which wouldn't apply?

Answers to Concept Check Questions

Module 11.1: 1. unusualness, social deviance, emotional distress, maladaptive behavior, dangerousness, faulty perceptions or interpretations of reality; 2. d; 3. c; 4. (a) iv, (b) iii, (c) i, (d) ii; 5. Because behaviors may be acceptable in one culture and considered aberrant in another.   **Module 11.2:** 1. c; 2. specific; 3. (a) iii, (b) i, (c) ii, (d) iv.   **Module 11.3:** 1. b; 2. d; 3. d; 4. d.

Module 11.4: 1. c; 2. a; 3. Women appear to be exposed to greater stress and are more likely to ruminate or dwell on their problems; 4. c.   **Module 11.5:** 1. b; 2. c; 3. b; 4. (a) iv, (b) i, (c) iii, (d) ii.   **Module 11.6:** 1. excessively rigid patterns of behavior, difficulty adjusting to external demands and relating to other people; 2. frontal lobes; 3. (a) iv, (b) ii, (c) iii, (d) i.

Methods of Therapy

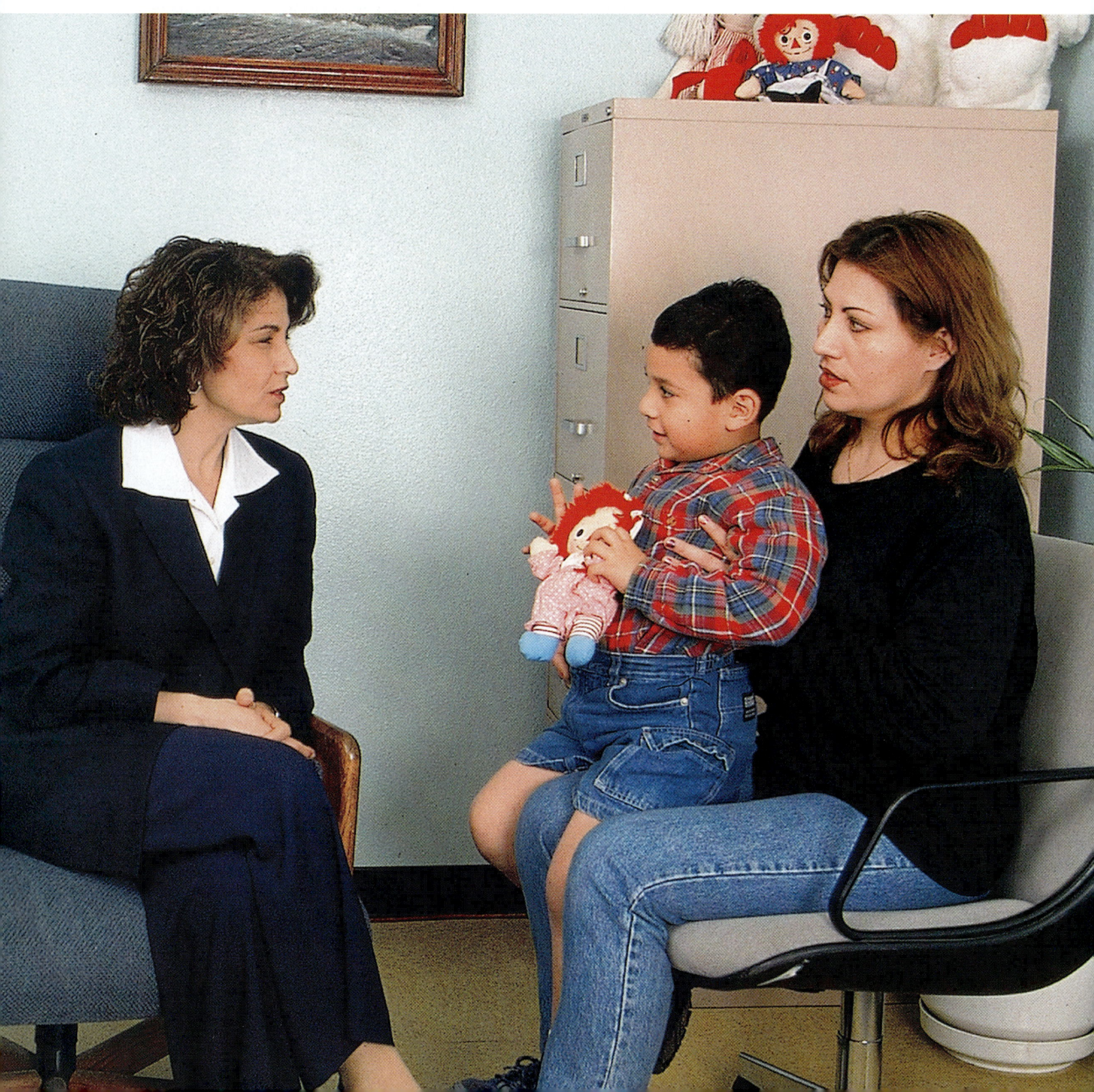

DID YOU KNOW THAT . . .

- Sigmund Freud believed that clients bring into the therapeutic relationship the conflicts they have had with important persons in their lives? (p. 420)

- Gestalt therapists have their clients talk to an empty chair? (p. 423)

- Behavior therapists have used virtual reality to help people overcome fear of heights? (p. 425)

- Cognitive therapists believe that emotional problems, such as anxiety and depression, are caused not directly by troubling events we experience but by the ways in which we interpret these events? (p. 426)

- Antidepressant drugs have been used to treat not only depression but other disorders as well, such as panic disorder and even bulimia? (p. 432)

- Stimulant drugs are widely used to improve attention spans and reduce disruptive behavior of hyperactive children and adolescents? (p. 438)

- Sending jolts of electricity through a person's head can help relieve severe depression? (p. 439)

- In many states, anyone can practice psychotherapy? (p. 444)

They're talking about us in the hall," Amanda explained. "Who?" I asked. She replied: "Well, you know, the voices. They're saying you think I'm cute or something." "What else are the voices telling you, Amanda?" "The usual stuff, you know. That F.B.I. agents are hiding in the bushes outside my house. But I'm too smart for them. I always enter through the back of the house." Amanda went on: "Yesterday on TV, this reporter was sending me secret messages. My mother couldn't hear them. Nobody could hear them except me. He was telling me to watch out for my next-door neighbor, that he's doing something with the wiring in my house."

Amanda, twenty-three, was diagnosed with schizophrenia. She was first hospitalized at age twenty, shortly after she began hearing voices and wouldn't leave her college dorm out of fear that something terrible would happen to her. This interview occurred during Amanda's third hospitalization in the past year.

In this chapter, we discuss ways of helping people like Amanda who suffer from psychological disorders. As we shall see in Modules 12.1 and 12.2, help takes many forms, including psychotherapy and such biomedical therapies as drug therapy and electroconvulsive therapy (ECT). We will then review the information that informed consumers need to know—and the questions they need to ask—when seeking the assistance of mental health professionals. ■

MODULE 12.1 — Types of Psychotherapy

- **What is psychotherapy?**
- **What are the major types of mental health professionals?**
- **What are the major forms of psychotherapy?**
- **Is psychotherapy effective?**
- **What cultural factors do therapists need to consider when working with members of diverse groups?**

CONCEPT 12.1
Psychotherapy consists of one or more verbal interactions between a therapist and a client and is used to help people understand and resolve their psychological problems.

CONCEPT 12.2
Mental health services are offered by different types of professionals who vary in their training backgrounds and areas of competence.

CONCEPT 12.3
Psychodynamic therapy is based on the belief that insight into unresolved psychological conflicts originating in childhood can help people overcome psychological problems.

Psychotherapy is a psychologically based form of treatment used to help people better understand their emotional or behavioral problems and resolve them. It consists of a series of verbal interactions between a therapist and a client, which is why it is often referred to as "talk therapy." In some forms of psychotherapy, there is an ongoing back-and-forth dialogue between the therapist and client, whereas in others, especially in classical psychoanalysis, the client does most or virtually all of the talking. There are many different types of psychotherapy, literally hundreds of types, but the most widely used ones have been derived from the major psychological models of abnormal behavior introduced in Chapter 11: the psychodynamic, behavioral, humanistic, and cognitive models. Although most forms of psychotherapy focus on the individual, some therapists extend their model of treatment to couples, families, and groups of unrelated individuals. Let us consider the major forms of psychotherapy used today. Before we do so, you may wish to review the training backgrounds and areas of expertise of the types of mental health professionals who provide psychotherapy and other mental health services, as shown in Table 12.1.

Psychodynamic Therapy

What comes to mind when you think of psychotherapy? If you picture a person lying on a couch and talking about the past, especially early childhood, you are probably thinking of **psychoanalysis**, the first form of *psychodynamic therapy* to be developed. Psychodynamic therapies share in common the belief that psychological problems are rooted in unconscious psychological conflicts dating from childhood. They also assume that gaining insight into these conflicts and working them through in the light of the individual's adult personality are the key steps toward restoring psychological health.

Traditional Psychoanalysis: Where Id Was, Ego Shall Be

Psychoanalysis, the form of psychotherapy developed by Sigmund Freud, is based on the belief that unconscious conflicts originating in childhood give rise to psychological problems. Practitioners of psychoanalysis are called **psychoanalysts**, or *analysts* for short. Recall from Chapter 10 that Freud believed that conflicts over primitive sexual or aggressive impulses cause the ego to employ *defense mechanisms*, especially *repression,* to keep these impulses out of conscious awareness. In some instances, these unconscious impulses threaten to leak into consciousness, resulting in feelings of anxiety. The person may report feeling anxious or experience a sense of dread or foreboding but have no idea about its cause. In other instances, the energy attached to the impulse is channeled or converted into a physical symptom, as in cases of hysterical blindness or paralysis. The symptom itself, such as inability to move an arm, serves a hidden purpose: It prevents the person from acting upon the underlying impulse. Thus, for example, the person with hysterical paralysis becomes unable to use the arm to engage in unacceptable

psychotherapy A verbal form of therapy derived from a psychological framework that consists of one or more treatment sessions with a therapist.

psychoanalysis The method of psychotherapy developed by Freud that focuses on uncovering and working through the unconscious conflicts that he believed were at the root of psychological problems.

psychoanalysts Practitioners of psychoanalysis who are schooled in the Freudian tradition.

TABLE 12.1   Major Types of Mental Health Professionals

Clinical psychologists

Clinical psychologists have earned a doctoral degree in psychology (either a Ph.D., Doctor of Philosophy; a Psy.D., Doctor of Psychology; or an Ed.D., Doctor of Education) from an accredited college or university and have passed a licensing examination. Clinical psychologists specialize in administering psychological tests, diagnosing mental disorders, and practicing psychotherapy. Until recently, they were not permitted to prescribe psychiatric drugs. By 2004, however, two states (New Mexico and Louisiana) had enacted laws to grant prescription privileges to psychologists who complete specialized training programs (Dittman, 2003; Holloway, 2004). Whether other states will follow suit remains to be seen. Moreover, the granting of prescription privileges to psychologists remains a hotly contested issue between psychologists and psychiatrists and within the field of psychology itself (e.g., McGrath et al., 2004; Welsh, 2003; Willis, 2003).

Counseling psychologists

Counseling psychologists hold doctoral degrees in psychology and have passed a licensing examination. They typically provide counseling to people with psychological problems falling within a milder range of severity than those treated by clinical psychologists, such as difficulties adjusting to college or uncertainties regarding career choices. Many counseling psychologists in college settings are also involved in providing appropriate services to students covered by the Americans with Disabilities Act (ADA).

Psychiatrists

Psychiatrists have earned a medical degree (M.D.) and completed residency training programs in psychiatry, which usually are three years in length. They are physicians who specialize in the diagnosis and treatment of psychological disorders. As licensed physicians, they can prescribe psychiatric drugs and may employ other medical techniques, such as electroconvulsive therapy (ECT). Many also practice psychotherapy based on training they receive during their residency programs or in specialized training institutes.

Clinical or psychiatric social workers

Clinical or psychiatric social workers have earned a master's degree in social work (M.S.W.) and use their knowledge of community agencies and organizations to help people with severe mental disorders receive the services they need. Many clinical social workers practice psychotherapy or specific forms of therapy, such as marital or family therapy.

Psychoanalysts

Psychoanalysts are typically either psychiatrists or psychologists who have completed extensive additional training in psychoanalysis. They are required to undergo psychoanalysis themselves as part of their training.

Counselors

Counselors have typically earned a master's degree and work in settings such as public schools, college testing and counseling centers, and hospitals and health clinics. Many specialize in vocational evaluation, marital or family counseling, or substance abuse counseling. Counselors may focus on providing psychological assistance to people with milder forms of disturbed behavior or those struggling with a chronic or debilitating illness or recovering from a traumatic experience.

Psychiatric nurses

Psychiatric nurses are typically R.N.'s who have completed a master's program in psychiatric nursing. They may work in a psychiatric facility or in a group medical practice where they treat people suffering from severe psychological disorders.

---

sexual acts such as masturbation. Similarly, the person with a fear of heights may harbor unconscious self-destructive impulses that are kept in check by avoiding height situations in which the person might lose control over the impulse to jump. The task of therapy, Freud believed, was to help people gain insight into their unconscious conflicts and work them through—to allow the conscious light of the ego to shine on the darkest reaches of the id. With self-insight, the ego would no longer need to maintain defensive behaviors or psychological symptoms that shield the self from the inner turmoil lying within. The ego would then be free to focus its efforts on pursuing more constructive interests, such as work and love relationships.

Freud used psychoanalysis to probe the unconscious mind for these inner conflicts, a lengthy process that typically would take years. He believed that unconscious conflicts are not easily brought into consciousness, so he devised several techniques to help clients gain awareness of them, including free association, dream analysis, and interpretation.

Free Association   In **free association**, the client is instructed to say anything that crosses his or her mind, no matter how trivial or irrelevant it may seem. Freud believed these free associations would eventually work their way toward

CONCEPT 12.4
Freud devised a number of techniques, including free association, dream analysis, and interpretation, to help clients gain awareness of their unconscious conflicts.

free association   A technique in psychoanalysis in which the client is encouraged to say anything that comes to mind.

uncovering deep-seated wishes and desires that reflect underlying conflicts. In classical psychoanalysis, the client lies on a couch with the analyst sitting off to the side, out of the client's direct view, saying little. By remaining detached, the analyst hopes to create an atmosphere that encourages the client to focus inwardly on his or her own thoughts.

Dream Analysis In **dream analysis**, the analyst helps the client gain insight into the symbolic or *latent* content of dreams, as opposed to the overt or *manifest* content (see Chapter 4). Freud called dreams the "royal road to the unconscious." He encouraged clients to freely associate to the manifest content of their dreams, hoping that doing so would lead to a better understanding of the dreams' hidden meanings.

Interpretation **Interpretation** is an explanation of the connections between the client's behavior and verbal expressions—how the client acts and what the client says—and the client's unconscious motives and conflicts. By offering interpretations, the analyst helps the client gain **insight** into the unconscious origins of the problem.

Interpretation of the client's **resistance** plays an important role in psychoanalysis. Resistance is the blocking that occurs when the therapy evokes anxiety-related thoughts and feelings. The client may suddenly draw a blank when free associations touch upon sensitive areas, or suddenly "forget" to show up for an appointment when deeper issues are being discussed. Psychoanalysts see resistance as a tactic used by the ego to prevent awareness of unconscious material, interpreting signs of resistance as clues to important underlying issues that need to be addressed in therapy.

The most important use of interpretation, in Freud's view, is analysis of the **transference relationship**. Freud believed that clients reenact troubled, conflicted relationships with others in the context of the relationship they develop with the analyst. A female client may respond to the analyst as a "father figure," perhaps transferring her ambivalent feelings of love and hate toward her own father onto the therapist. A young man may view the analyst as a competitor or rival, reenacting an unresolved Oedipal conflict from his childhood. By interpreting the transference relationship, the analyst raises the client's awareness about how earlier conflicted relationships intrude upon the client's present relationships. Freud believed that the client's ability to come to an understanding of the transference relationship is an essential ingredient in a successful analysis.

Transference is a two-way street. Freud himself recognized that he sometimes responded to clients in ways that carried over from his relationships with others. He called this process **countertransference** and believed that it damaged the therapeutic relationship. A male therapist, for example, may react to a male client as a competitor or rival or to a female client as a rejecting love interest.

Modern Psychodynamic Approaches: More Ego, Less Id

Traditional psychoanalysis is a lengthy, intensive process. It may require three to five sessions a week for many years. Some contemporary psychoanalysts continue

THINK

About It

Getting Help

If you or someone you know needed mental health services, where would you turn? How might you find out what types of mental health services are available in your college and your community?

💡 **CONCEPT 12.5**
Freud believed that the ability to understand the transference relationship is essential to the client's success in psychoanalysis.

dream analysis A technique in psychoanalysis in which the therapist attempts to analyze the underlying or symbolic meaning of the client's dreams.

interpretation In psychoanalysis, the attempt by the therapist to explain the connections between the material the client discloses in therapy and his or her unconscious conflicts.

insight In Freud's theory, the awareness of underlying, unconscious wishes and conflicts.

resistance In psychoanalysis, the blocking that occurs when therapy touches upon anxiety-evoking thoughts or feelings.

transference relationship In therapy, the tendency of clients to reenact earlier conflicted relationships in the relationship they develop with their therapists.

countertransference The tendency for therapists to relate to clients in ways that mirror their relationships with important figures in their own lives.

to practice in much the same way as Freud did. However, many psychodynamic therapists today focus less on sexual issues than on the adaptive functioning of the ego. They may also focus more on the client's present relationships than on the remote past. Moreover, because many modern analysts adopt a briefer therapy format, they tend to take a more direct approach to exploring how clients' defenses and transference relationships cause difficulties in their relationships with others (Messer, 2001). One obvious difference is that many analysts today prefer to have their clients sit facing them, rather than lying on a couch. There is also more dialogue between analyst and client, and clients typically come to only one or two sessions a week (Grossman, 2003).

Here we see an example of the give-and-take between a contemporary psychoanalyst and a young adult patient. The analyst focuses on the client's competitiveness with him. In an analytic framework, this competitiveness represents a transference of the client's unresolved Oedipal rivalry with his own father:

Contemporary Psychoanalysis Many modern psychoanalysts have replaced the traditional couch with more direct, face-to-face verbal interactions with clients.

> *Client:* . . . I continue to have success, but I have been feeling weak and tired. I saw my doctor yesterday and he said there's nothing organically wrong.
>
> *Analyst:* Does anything come to mind in relation to weak and tired feelings?
>
> *Client:* I'm thinking of the way you looked last year after you came out of the hospital. (The patient was referring to a hospitalization that, in fact, I had the previous year during which time our treatment sessions were suspended.)
>
> *Analyst:* Do you recall how you felt when you saw me looking that way?
>
> *Client:* It made me upset, even guilty.
>
> *Analyst:* But why guilty?
>
> *Client:* I'm not sure why I said that. There was nothing to feel guilty about.
>
> *Analyst:* Perhaps you had some other feelings.
>
> *Client:* Well, it's true that at one point I felt faintly pleased that I was young and vigorous and you seemed to be going downhill. . . .
>
> *Analyst:* . . . Clearly you're not very comfortable when you contrast your state with mine—to your advantage.
>
> *Client:* Well, you know, I've never felt comfortable when thinking of myself outdoing you in any way. . . .
>
> *Analyst:* . . . Perhaps your weak and tired feelings represent an identification with me brought on by your feeling guilty about your successes, since that implies that you are outdoing me. . . . Your discomfort with feeling that in certain respects you're surpassing me is posing a problem for you.

Source: Silverman, 1984, pp. 226–227.

CONCEPT 12.6
Compared to traditional psychoanalysis, modern forms of psychodynamic therapy are briefer, allow for more interaction between therapist and client, and focus more on the ego.

Humanistic Therapy

Humanistic therapists believe that human beings possess free will and can make conscious choices that enrich their lives. The methods of therapy developed within the humanistic tradition emphasize the client's subjective, conscious experiences. Humanistic therapists focus on what the individual is experiencing at the particular moment in time, rather than on the distant past. It's not that they view the past as unimportant; they believe that past experiences do affect present behavior and feelings. But they emphasize that change must occur in the present, in the *here-and-now.* The two major forms of humanistic therapy are *client-centered therapy,* developed by Carl Rogers, and *gestalt therapy,* developed by Fritz Perls.

CONCEPT 12.7
Humanistic therapies emphasize subjective, conscious experience and development of one's unique potential.

Client-Centered Therapy

Rogers (1951) believed that when children are valued only when they behave in ways that please others, they may become psychologically detached from parts of themselves that meet with disapproval or criticism. They may become so good at playing the "good boy" or "good girl" role that they develop a distorted self-concept—a view of themselves that does not reflect who they really are and what they truly feel. Well-adjusted people make choices that are consistent with their own unique selves, needs, and values. But people with a distorted self-concept remain largely strangers to themselves.

As the name *client-centered* therapy implies, Rogerian therapy focuses on the person. Client-centered therapists strive to achieve a warm and accepting therapeutic atmosphere in which clients feel safe to explore their innermost feelings and become accepting of their true selves. Client-centered therapists take a *nondirective* approach to therapy by allowing the client to take the lead and set the tone. The therapist's role is to *reflect back* the client's feelings so as to encourage self-exploration and self-acceptance (Hill & Nakayama, 2000). Here, Rogers illustrates how a client-centered counselor uses reflection to help a client clarify and further explore her feelings:

> *Client:* Now—one of the things that . . . had worried me was . . . living at the dorm, it's hard—not to just sort of fall in with a group of people . . . that aren't interesting, but just around. . . . So, now I find that I'm . . . getting away from that group a little bit . . . and being with a group of people . . . I really find I have more interests in common with.
>
> *Counselor:* That is, you've really chosen to draw away from the group you're just thrown in with by chance, and you pick people whom you want more to associate with. Is that it?
>
> *Client:* That's the idea. . . . They [my roommates] . . . had sort of pulled me in with a group of their friends that I wouldn't have picked myself, especially. And . . . so that I found that all my time was being taken up with these people, and now I'm beginning to seek out people that I prefer myself . . . rather than being drawn in with the bunch.
>
> *Counselor:* You find it a little more possible, I gather, to express your real attitudes in a social situation . . . [to] make your own choice of friends. . . .
>
> *Client:* . . . I tried to see if I was just withdrawing from this bunch of kids I'd been spending my time with. . . . It's not a withdrawal, but it's more of an assertion of my real interest.
>
> *Counselor:* M-hm. In other words, you've tried to be self-critical in order to see if you're just running away from the situation, but you feel really, it's an expression of your positive attitudes.
>
> *Client:* I—I think it is.
>
> *Source:* Rogers, 1951, pp. 154–155.

CONCEPT 12.8

Carl Rogers believed that for therapists to be effective, they must demonstrate empathy and unconditional positive regard for their clients as well as genuineness in their expression of feelings.

Rogers believed that effective therapists display three qualities that are necessary to create an atmosphere of emotional support needed for clients to benefit from therapy:

1. *Unconditional positive regard.* The therapist is unconditionally accepting of the client as a person, even though he or she may not approve of all of the client's choices or behaviors.

2. *Empathy.* The therapist demonstrates *empathy,* the ability to accurately mirror or reflect back the client's experiences and feelings—to see the world through the client's eyes or frames of reference. By entering the client's subjective world, the therapist encourages the client to do likewise—to get in touch with deeper feelings of which he or she may be only dimly aware.

3. *Genuineness.* The therapist is able to express genuine feelings and demonstrates that one's feelings and actions can be congruent or consistent. Even when the therapist is feeling bored or down, it is best to express these feelings, so as to encourage the client to do the same, rather than distorting true feelings or concealing them.

Gestalt Therapy

Fritz Perls (1893–1970), the originator of gestalt therapy, was trained as a psychoanalyst but became dissatisfied with the lack of emphasis on the client's subjective experiences in the present. Perls was influenced by Gestalt psychology and believed that it was important to help clients blend the conflicting parts of their personalities into an integrated whole or "gestalt." Unlike client-centered therapists, who attempt to create a warm and accepting atmosphere, gestalt therapists take a direct and even confrontational approach in helping clients get in touch with their underlying feelings. They repeatedly challenge clients to express how they are feeling at each moment in time—in the here-and-now. They don't let them off the hook by allowing them to slide into discussing events from their past or to ramble in general, abstract terms about their feelings or experiences.

Gestalt therapists use role-playing exercises to help clients integrate their inner feelings into their conscious experience. In the *empty chair* technique, therapists place an empty chair in front of the clients (Greenberg & Malcolm, 2002). The clients are told to imagine that someone with whom they have had a troubled relationship (mother, father, spouse, boss) is sitting in the chair and to express their feelings toward that person. In this way, clients feel they can safely express their innermost feelings and unmet needs without fear of criticism from the other person.

Perls also had clients role-play different parts of their own personalities. One part might bark a command, like "Take chances. Get involved. . . ." A more restrained part might bark back, "Play it safe. Don't risk it." By helping the individual become more aware of these opposing parts, gestalt therapists hope to bring about an integration of the client's personality that may take the form of a compromise between opposing parts.

Behavior Therapy

In **behavior therapy** (also called *behavior modification*), therapists systematically apply principles of learning to help individuals make adaptive changes in their behavior. Behavior therapists believe that psychological problems are largely learned and thus can be unlearned. Like humanistic and cognitive therapies, behavior therapy addresses the client's present situation, not the distant past. But behavior therapy focuses directly on changing problem behaviors, rather than on exploring the client's feelings. Behavior therapy is relatively brief, usually lasting weeks or months rather than years.

Methods of Fear Reduction

Behavior therapists use several techniques to treat phobias, including systematic desensitization, gradual exposure, and modeling. In **systematic desensitization**, the client is first taught skills of deep muscle relaxation, typically using a relaxation technique that consists of tensing and relaxing selected muscle groups in the body. An ordered series of fear-inducing stimuli, called a **fear hierarchy**, is then constructed, scaled from the least to the most fearful stimulus. The therapist then guides the client in practicing deep relaxation. Once a state of deep relaxation is achieved, the client is instructed to imagine confronting the first stimulus in the fear hierarchy (or perhaps views the stimulus, as through a series of slides). If anxiety occurs, the client stops imagining the feared stimulus and restores deep

CONCEPT 12.9
Fritz Perls, who developed gestalt therapy, believed that therapists should help clients blend the conflicting parts of their personalities into an integrated whole or "gestalt."

web. Netlab/What's My Specialty?

CONCEPT 12.10
Behavior therapy involves the systematic application of learning principles to weaken undesirable behaviors and strengthen adaptive behaviors.

CONCEPT 12.11
To help people overcome phobic responses, behavior therapists use learning-based techniques such as systematic desensitization, gradual exposure, and modeling.

behavior therapy   A form of therapy that involves the systematic application of the principles of learning to bring about desired changes in emotional states and behavior.

systematic desensitization   A behavior therapy technique for treating phobias through the pairing of exposure in imagination to fear-inducing stimuli and states of deep relaxation.

fear hierarchy   An ordered series of increasingly fearful objects or situations.

Gradual Exposure Through gradual exposure, the client confronts increasingly fearful stimuli or situations, sometimes assisted by the therapist or supportive others.

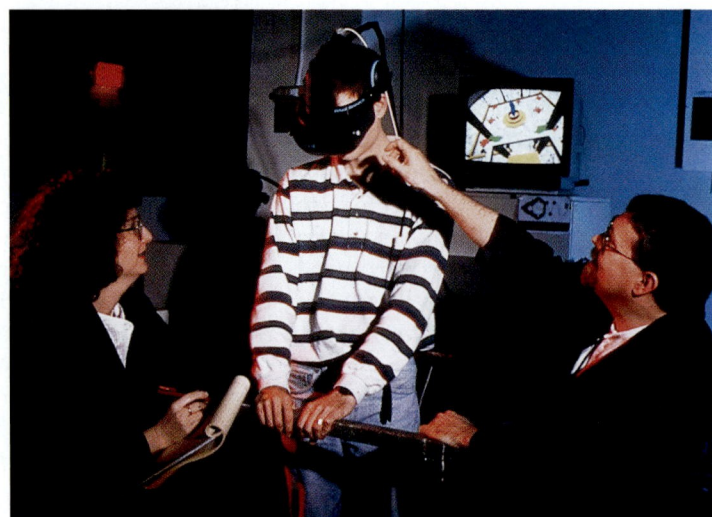

Virtual Therapy Virtual therapy has been used to help people overcome a fear of heights by guiding them through a series of encounters with height situations in virtual reality.

relaxation before trying the exercise again. When the client can remain relaxed during the imagined exposure to the first stimulus on several trials, he or she then moves to the next stimulus in the hierarchy. This procedure is repeated for each step in the hierarchy. The objective is to use relaxation as an incompatible response to fear in order to weaken the bonds between frightening stimuli and the fear they evoke.

Behavior therapists also use **gradual exposure** (alternately called *in-vivo exposure,* meaning exposure in "real life") to help people overcome phobias. In this technique, people gradually expose themselves to a hierarchy of increasingly fearful stimuli. By progressing at their own pace through the hierarchy, they learn to tolerate these fearful situations or stimuli. Clients may first be taught self-relaxation skills that they can use during their exposure trials. They are also trained to use calming coping statements to help them through these encounters—statements they can repeat to themselves under their breath, like "I can do this. Just take a few deep breaths and the fear will pass."

A sample hierarchy for a person with an elevator phobia might include the following steps:

1. Standing outside the elevator.
2. Standing in the elevator with the door open.
3. Standing in the elevator with the door closed.
4. Taking the elevator down one floor.
5. Taking the elevator up one floor.
6. Taking the elevator down two floors.
7. Taking the elevator up two floors.
8. Taking the elevator down two floors and then up two floors.
9. Taking the elevator down to the basement.
10. Taking the elevator up to the highest floor.
11. Taking the elevator all the way down and then all the way up.

gradual exposure A behavior therapy technique for treating phobias based on direct exposure to a series of increasingly fearful stimuli. Also called *in-vivo ("real-life") exposure.*

Gradual exposure is used to help people overcome not only specific types of fears, such as a fear of riding on trains or elevators, but also social phobias, such as a fear of meeting new people or of speaking in public (Hoffman, 2000a, 2000b). For example, people with a social phobia might be instructed to create a hierarchy of fearful social situations. They would then be trained in relaxation skills and would begin a series of exposure encounters starting with the least socially stressful situation and working their way up to the most stressful.

A form of observational learning known as **modeling** is often used to help people overcome fears and acquire more adaptive behaviors (Braswell & Kendall, 2001). Specifically, individuals acquire desirable behaviors by observing and imitating others whom they observe performing the behaviors. Psychologist Albert Bandura (Bandura, Blanchard, & Ritter, 1969) pioneered the use of modeling as a therapeutic technique to help people overcome phobias, such as fears of snakes, dogs, and other small animals.

Behavior therapists have also adapted the technology of virtual reality to create simulated environments in which phobic individuals can gradually expose themselves to increasingly fearful "virtual" stimuli. For example, using a specialized helmet and gloves connected to a computer, a phobic person with a fear of heights can simulate a ride in a glass-enclosed virtual elevator or peer out over a virtual balcony on the thirty-third floor. With this form of exposure therapy, called **virtual therapy**, therapists can simulate real-life environments, including some that would be difficult to arrange in reality (e.g., simulated airplane take-offs). Virtual therapy has been shown to be effective in treating a wide range of phobias, including fear of heights, fear of flying, and fear of spiders (Kamphuis, Emmelkamp, & Krijn, 2002; Rothbaum et al., 2002).

Aversive Conditioning

In **aversive conditioning**, a form of classical conditioning, stimuli associated with an undesirable response are paired with aversive stimuli, such as an electric shock or a nausea-inducing drug. The idea is to make these stimuli elicit a negative response (fear or nausea) that would discourage the person from performing the undesirable behavior. For example, adults who are sexually attracted to children might receive a mild but painful electric shock when they view sexually provocative pictures of children. Or in alcoholism treatment, a nausea-inducing drug could be paired with sniffing or sipping an alcoholic beverage. In conditioning terms, the nausea-inducing drug is the unconditioned stimulus (US) and nausea is the unconditioned response (UR). The alcoholic beverage becomes a conditioned stimulus (CS) that elicits nausea (CR) when it is paired repeatedly with the US. Unfortunately, the effects of aversive conditioning are often temporary; outside the treatment setting, the aversive stimulus no longer accompanies the undesirable behavior. Partly for this reason, aversive conditioning is not in widespread use, although it may be useful as a component of a broader treatment program.

Operant Conditioning Methods

Behavior therapists apply operant principles of reinforcement and punishment to help strengthen desirable behavior and weaken undesirable behavior. For example, therapists may train parents to reward children for appropriate behavior and to withdraw attention (a social reinforcer) following problem behavior in order to weaken or eliminate it. Or they may train parents to use mild forms of punishment, such as a *time-out* procedure in which children are removed from a rewarding environment when they misbehave and "sit out" for a prescribed period of time before resuming other activities.

In Chapter 5 you were introduced to another operant conditioning technique, the *token economy,* a behavior modification program used in mental hospitals and other settings such as schools. For example, residents of mental hospitals

CONCEPT 12.12
Aversive conditioning is used to create an unpleasant response to stimuli associated with undesirable behaviors.

PsychAssist: Classical and Aversive Conditioning

CONCEPT 12.13
Behavior therapists apply operant conditioning principles to strengthen desirable behavior and weaken or eliminate undesirable behavior.

modeling   A behavior therapy technique for overcoming phobias and acquiring more adaptive behaviors, based on observing and imitating models.

virtual therapy   A form of exposure therapy in which virtual reality is used to simulate real-world environments.

aversive conditioning   A form of behavior therapy in which stimuli associated with undesirable behavior are paired with aversive stimuli to create a negative response to these stimuli.

may receive tokens, or plastic chips, as positive reinforcers for performing certain desirable behaviors such as self-grooming, tidying their rooms, and socializing appropriately with others. Tokens can then be exchanged for tangible reinforcers such as extra privileges or candy. Token economy programs have been used successfully in mental hospitals, institutions and group homes for people with mental retardation, and residential treatment facilities for delinquents.

Cognitive-Behavioral Therapy

Cognitive-behavioral therapy (CBT) combines behavioral techniques, such as gradual exposure, with cognitive techniques that focus on challenging and correcting faulty patterns of thinking (Dobson & Dozois, 2001; McGinn & Sanderson, 2001). Cognitive-behavioral therapists draw upon the principles and techniques of cognitive models of therapy, such as those pioneered by psychologist Albert Ellis and psychiatrist Aaron Beck, whose work we consider in the next section.

Cognitive Therapies

Cognitive therapists focus on helping people change how they think. Their techniques are based on the view that distorted or faulty ways of thinking underlie emotional problems (e.g., anxiety disorders and depression) as well as self-defeating or maladaptive behavior. In short, they argue that emotional problems are caused not by external events or life experiences but, rather, by the ways people interpret them.

Cognitive therapies are relatively brief forms of treatment (involving months rather than years). Like the humanistic approach, they focus more on what is happening in the present than on what happened in the distant past. Clients are given homework assignments to help them not only identify and challenge distorted thoughts as they occur but also adopt more adaptive behaviors and rational ways of thinking. The two major cognitive therapies are *rational-emotive behavior therapy,* which was developed by Ellis, and *cognitive therapy,* which was developed by Beck.

Rational-Emotive Behavior Therapy: The Importance of Thinking Rationally

Albert Ellis (b. 1913) developed **rational-emotive behavior therapy (REBT)** based on his view that irrational or illogical thinking is at the root of emotional problems (Dryden & Ellis, 2001; Ellis, 1997, 2001). To overcome these problems, the therapist must teach the client to recognize these irrational beliefs and replace them with logical, self-enhancing beliefs. Ellis viewed this process as a kind of "pounding-away" at the client's irrational beliefs until the client is persuaded to change these beliefs and adopt more logical ways of thinking in their place.

Ellis contends that irrational beliefs often take the form of *shoulds* and *musts,* such as the belief that one must always have the approval of the important people in one's life. Ellis notes that while the desire for approval is understandable, it is irrational to believe that one will always receive approval or that one couldn't possibly survive without it. REBT encourages clients to replace irrational beliefs (such as those listed in Table 12.2) with rational alternatives, and to face their problems rationally.

To Ellis, negative emotional reactions, such as anxiety and depression, are not produced directly by life experiences. Rather, they stem from the irrational beliefs that we hold about life experiences. Irrational beliefs are illogical because they are based on a distorted, exaggerated appraisal of the situation, not on the facts at hand. Ellis uses an "ABC" approach to explain the causes of emotional distress. This model can be diagrammed as follows:

Activating event ⟶ *Beliefs* ⟶ *Consequences*

CONCEPT 12.14
Many behavior therapists subscribe to a broader concept of behavior therapy called cognitive-behavioral therapy, which focuses on changing maladaptive thoughts and beliefs as well as problem behaviors.

CONCEPT 12.15
Cognitive therapists help clients challenge maladaptive thoughts and beliefs and replace them with more adaptive ways of thinking.

CONCEPT 12.16
Rational-emotive behavior therapy is based on the view that irrational beliefs cause people to suffer emotional distress in the face of disappointing life experiences.

cognitive-behavioral therapy (CBT) A form of therapy that combines behavioral and cognitive treatment techniques.

rational-emotive behavior therapy (REBT) Developed by Albert Ellis, a form of therapy based on identifying and correcting irrational beliefs that are believed to underlie emotional and behavioral difficulties.

TABLE 12.2   Examples of Irrational Beliefs According to Ellis

- You absolutely must have love and approval from virtually all the people who are important to you.
- You must be completely competent in all your activities in order to feel worthwhile.
- It is awful and catastrophic when life does not go the way you want it to go. Things are awful when you don't get your first choices.
- People must treat each other fairly, and it is horrible when they don't.
- It's awful and terrible when there is no clear or quick solution to life's problems.
- Your past must continue to affect you and determine your behavior.

Source: Adapted from Ellis, 1991.

Consider a person who feels worthless and depressed after getting a poor grade on a college exam (see Figure 12.1). The poor grade is the *activating event* (A). The *consequences* (C), or outcomes, are feelings of depression. But the activating event (A) does not lead directly to the emotional consequences (C). Rather, the event is filtered through the person's *beliefs* (B) ("I'm just a complete jerk. I'll never succeed"). People often have difficulty identifying their beliefs (B)—in part, because they are generally more aware of what they are feeling than of what they are thinking in response to the activating event (A) and, in part, because the event (A) and the emotional consequences (C) occur so closely together that the event seems to be the cause of the emotion. They may have difficulty stopping themselves in the middle of a situation and asking, "What am I saying to myself that is causing this distress?"

Ellis recognizes that disappointment is a perfectly understandable reaction in the face of upsetting or frustrating events. But when people exaggerate the consequences of negative events, they convert disappointment into depression and despair.

Consider the case of Jane, a shy and socially inhibited twenty-seven-year-old woman (Ellis & Dryden, 1987, p. 69). Jane's therapist first helped her identify her underlying irrational beliefs, such as the belief that if she became anxious and tongue-tied when speaking to people at a social gathering, it would mean she was a stupid, inadequate person. Her therapist helped her replace this irrational belief with a rational alternative: "If people do reject me for showing them how anxious I am, that will be most unfortunate, but I can stand it." Jane also rehearsed more rational beliefs several times a day, as in these examples:

"I would like to speak well, but I never have to."

"When people I favor reject me, it often reveals more about them and their tastes than about me."

REBT has a strong behavioral component as well. Therapists help clients develop more effective interpersonal behaviors to replace self-defeating or maladaptive behavior. They give clients specific tasks or homework assignments, like

Figure 12.1   The Ellis "ABC" Model

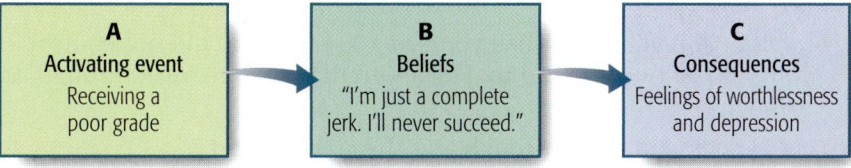

| A
Activating event
Receiving a poor grade | → | B
Beliefs
"I'm just a complete jerk. I'll never succeed." | → | C
Consequences
Feelings of worthlessness and depression |

disagreeing with an overbearing relative or asking someone for a date. They also help them practice or rehearse more adaptive behaviors.

Cognitive Therapy: Correcting Errors in Thinking

As a psychiatrist, Albert Beck (b. 1921) found that his work with depressed clients mirrored personal experiences of his own in which he found that his emotional reactions to events were rooted in distorted thinking. The form of therapy he developed, **cognitive therapy**, helps clients identify and correct errors in thinking and to replace them with rational alternatives (Beck et al., 1979; DeRubeis, Tang, & Beck, 2001).

Beck used cognitive techniques on himself long before he developed cognitive therapy. He suffered from childhood phobias that continued to plague him as an adult, including a fear of tunnels (Hunt, 1993). He attributed this phobia to a fear of suffocation he had developed as a child following a severe case of whooping cough. He succeeded in overcoming this phobia by repeatedly pointing out to himself that his expectations of danger had no basis in reality.

Beck refers to errors in thinking as "cognitive distortions." For example, Beck believes that depressed people tend to magnify or exaggerate the consequences of negative events and to blame themselves for disappointments in life while ignoring the role of external circumstances.

Cognitive therapists also give clients homework assignments in which they are to record the distorted thoughts that accompany their negative emotional responses and practice substituting rational alternative thoughts.

Another type of homework assignment is *reality testing*, in which clients are encouraged to test out their negative beliefs to determine if they are valid. For example, a depressed client who feels unwanted by everyone might be asked to call two or three friends on the phone to gather data about how the friends react to the calls. The therapist might then ask the client to report on the assignment: "Did they immediately hang up the phone? Or did they seem pleased that you called? Did they express any interest at all in talking to you again or getting together sometime? Does the evidence support the conclusion that *no one* has any interest in you?"

In the following case example, Beck and his colleagues illustrate how a cognitive therapist challenges the distortions in a client's thinking—in this instance, all-or-nothing thinking that leads the client to judge herself as completely lacking in self-control:

> *Client:* I don't have any self-control at all.
>
> *Therapist:* On what basis do you say that?
>
> *Client:* Somebody offered me candy and I couldn't refuse it.
>
> *Therapist:* Were you eating candy every day?
>
> *Client:* No, I just ate it this once.
>
> *Therapist:* Did you do anything constructive during the past week to adhere to your diet?
>
> *Client:* Well, I didn't give in to the temptation to buy candy every time I saw it at the store. . . . Also, I did not eat any candy except that one time when it was offered to me and I felt I couldn't refuse it.
>
> *Therapist:* If you counted up the number of times you controlled yourself versus the number of times you gave in, what ratio would you get?
>
> *Client:* About 100 to 1.
>
> *Therapist:* So if you controlled yourself 100 times and did not control yourself just once, would that be a sign that you are weak through and through?
>
> *Client:* I guess not—not through and through [smiles].

Source: Adapted from Beck et al., 1979, p. 68.

CONCEPT 12.17

Cognitive therapy focuses on helping clients identify and correct distorted thoughts and beliefs that have no basis in reality.

cognitive therapy Developed by Aaron Beck, a form of therapy based on a collaborative effort between clients and therapists that helps clients recognize and correct distorted patterns of thinking believed to underlie their emotional problems.

TRY THIS OUT

Replacing Distorted Thoughts with Rational Alternatives

For each of the automatic thoughts listed below, fill in a rational alternative response. If necessary, refer again to Table 11.2 (p. 401) for a listing of the common types of cognitive distortions. Sample rational alternatives can be found in the key at the end of the chapter.

Automatic Thought	Type of Cognitive Distortion	Rational Alternative
1. This relationship is a disaster, a complete disaster.	All-or-nothing thinking	_____
2. I'm falling apart. I can't handle this.	Catastrophizing	_____
3. Things must really be awful for me to feel this way.	Emotion-based reasoning	_____
4. I know I'm going to flunk this course.	Jumping to conclusions	_____
5. _____'s problems are really my fault.	Mistaken responsibility	_____
6. I'm just a loser.	Name calling	_____
7. Someone my age should be further along than I am.	Shouldism	_____
8. It would be awful if I don't get this job.	Catastrophizing	_____
9. I know that if _____ got to know me, he/she would not like me.	Jumping to conclusions	_____
10. All I can think about are the negatives.	Negative focusing	_____

REBT and cognitive therapy are similar in many respects. Both focus primarily on helping people replace dysfunctional thoughts and beliefs with more adaptive, rational ones. The major difference may be one of therapeutic style: The REBT therapist typically adopts a more direct and sometimes confrontational approach in disputing the client's irrational beliefs, whereas the cognitive therapist usually takes a more gentle, collaborative approach to help clients identify and correct the distortions in their thinking.

The differences between specific psychotherapies are not as clear-cut as they may seem. On the one hand, there is a blurring of lines between cognitive and behavioral therapies in the sense that we can classify the cognitive therapies of Ellis and Beck as forms of cognitive-behavioral therapy. Both rely on behavioral and cognitive techniques to help people develop more adaptive behaviors and to change dysfunctional thinking patterns. On the other hand, many therapists identify themselves with an even broader eclectic approach, as we see next.

Eclectic Therapy

Therapists who practice **eclectic therapy** look beyond the theoretical barriers that divide one school of psychotherapy from another. They seek common ground among the different schools and integrate principles and techniques representing these different approaches (Beutler, Harwood, & Caldwell, 2001; Stricker & Gold, 2001). In a particular case, an eclectic therapist might use behavior therapy to help the client change problem behaviors and psychodynamic approaches to help the client develop insight into underlying conflicts.

Eclecticism is the most widely endorsed theoretical orientation among clinical and counseling psychologists today (Bechtoldt et al., 2001; see Figure 12.2). Eclectic therapists tend to be older and more experienced than other therapists

CONCEPT 12.18
Many therapists identify with an eclectic orientation in which they adopt principles and techniques from different schools of therapy.

eclectic therapy A therapeutic approach that draws upon principles and techniques representing different schools of therapy.

Figure 12.2 Clinical and Counseling Psychologists Identifying with Each Theoretical Orientation
According to a recent survey, a greater proportion of clinical and counseling psychologists endorse an eclectic or integrative orientation than any other therapeutic orientation.

Source: Adapted from Bechtoldt et al., 2001.

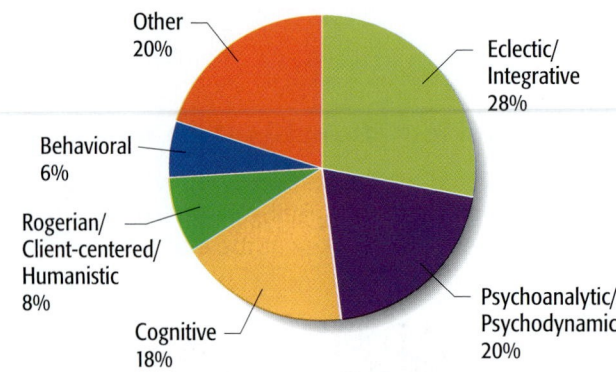

(Beitman, 1989). Perhaps they have learned through experience about the value of drawing upon diverse points of view.

Not all therapists subscribe to an eclectic approach. Many believe that the differences between schools of therapy are so compelling that therapeutic integration is neither desirable nor achievable. Trying to combine them, they argue, leads to a veritable hodgepodge of techniques that lack a cohesive conceptual framework. Nevertheless, the movement toward eclecticism continues to grow within the therapeutic community.

Group, Family, and Couple Therapy

Group therapy brings people together in small groups to help them explore and resolve their problems. Compared to individual therapy, it offers several advantages. For one thing, because the therapist treats several people at a time, group therapy is generally less costly than individual therapy. For another, it may be particularly helpful for people experiencing interpersonal problems such as loneliness, shyness, and low self-esteem. These individuals often benefit from interacting with supportive others in a group treatment program. The give-and-take within the group may help improve a member's social skills. And clients in group therapy can learn how others in the group have coped with similar problems in their lives.

Group therapy may not be for everyone. Some clients prefer the individual attention of a therapist. They may feel that one-on-one therapy provides an opportunity for a deeper exploration of their emotions and experiences. They may also be reluctant to disclose their personal problems to other members of a group. Or they may feel too inhibited to relate comfortably to others in a group, even if they themselves are perhaps the ones for whom group interaction is most beneficial.

Group therapists can offset some of these drawbacks by creating an atmosphere that promotes trust and self-exploration. In particular, they require that information disclosed by group members is kept in strict confidence, ensure that group members relate to each other in a supportive and nondestructive fashion, and prevent any single member from monopolizing their attention or dominating the group. In short, effective group therapists attempt to provide each member with the attention he or she needs.

Family therapy helps troubled families learn to communicate better and resolve their differences. The family, not the individual, is the unit of treatment. Most family therapists view the family unit as a complex social system in which individuals play certain roles. In many cases there is one family member whom the family brands as the source of the family's problems. Effective family therapists demonstrate how the problems of this individual are symptomatic of larger problems in the family involving a breakdown in the family system, not in the individual per se. They help dysfunctional families change how family members interact and relate to one another so that members can become more accepting and supportive of each other's needs and differences.

CONCEPT 12.19
Therapists often treat individuals in group settings, where the "group" may be a collection of unrelated persons, a family, or a couple.

group therapy A form of therapy in which clients are treated within a group format.

family therapy Therapy for troubled families that focuses on changing disruptive patterns of communication and improving the ways in which family members relate to each other.

Group Therapy Group therapy brings together small groups of people to help them explore and work through their psychological problems.

About It

Which Type of Therapy Would You Prefer?

Which approach to therapy would you prefer if you were seeking help for a psychological problem? Why would you prefer this approach?

In **couple therapy** (often called *marital therapy* when applied to married couples), the couple is the unit of the treatment. Couple therapy builds healthier relationships by helping couples acquire more effective communication and problem-solving skills (Christensen et al., 2004). Couple therapists identify power struggles and lack of communication as among the typical problems faced by troubled couples seeking help. Their aim is to help open channels of communication between partners and encourage them to share personal feelings and needs in ways that do not put each other down.

 **PsychAssist: Types of Psychotherapy**

Is Psychotherapy Effective?

Yes, psychotherapy works. A wealth of scientific findings supports the effectiveness of psychotherapy. Yet questions remain about whether some forms of therapy are more effective than others.

Measuring Effectiveness

The strongest body of evidence supporting the effectiveness of psychotherapy comes from controlled studies in which people who received psychotherapy are compared with those who received control treatments or were placed in waiting-list control groups. Investigators commonly use a statistical technique called **meta-analysis** to average the results across a large number of such studies.

An early but influential meta-analysis was conducted by Mary Lee Smith, Gene Glass, and Thomas Miller (1980). Based on an analysis of more than 400 controlled studies comparing particular types of therapy (psychodynamic, behavioral, humanistic, etc.) against control groups, they reported that the average person receiving psychotherapy achieved better results on outcome measures than did 80 percent of the people placed in waiting-list control groups (see Figure 12.3). More recent meta-analyses also point to better outcomes for people treated with psychotherapy than for those placed in control groups (e.g., Shadish et al., 2000; Weisz et al., 1995). Meta-analysis supports the overall effectiveness of marital, family, and group therapy techniques as well (McDermut, Miller, & Brown, 2001; Shadish et al., 1993).

The greatest gains in therapy are typically achieved during the first few months of treatment. Fifty percent of people who participate in psychotherapy show significant improvement within the first twenty-one sessions (Anderson &

CONCEPT 12.20
A wealth of scientific findings supports the effectiveness of psychotherapy, but questions remain about whether some forms of therapy are more effective than others.

couple therapy Therapy that focuses on helping distressed couples resolve their conflicts and develop more effective communication skills.

meta-analysis A statistical technique for averaging results across a large number of studies.

Figure 12.3 Effectiveness of Psychotherapy
A meta-analysis of more than 400 outcome studies showed that the average therapy client achieved greater improvement than 80 percent of untreated controls.

Source: Adapted from Smith, Glass, & Miller, 1980.

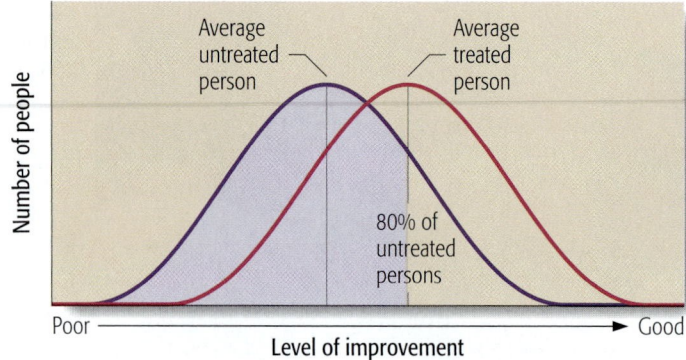

 **Netlab/Name That Therapy!**

CONCEPT 12.21
Evidence points to both specific and nonspecific factors in accounting for the benefits of psychotherapy.

Lambert, 2001; Lambert, Hansen, & Finch, 2001). Many other patients respond with additional treatment. But not everyone benefits from therapy, and some people even deteriorate. Then too, individuals receiving other forms of treatment, such as drug therapy, sometimes have negative outcomes.

Which Therapy Is Best?

To say that therapy overall is effective does not mean that all therapies are equally effective, or that one form of therapy is as good as any other for a particular problem. Studies using meta-analysis show little difference in the magnitude of the outcomes achieved when comparing different forms of therapy against control groups or even against each other (Luborsky et al., 2002; Nathan, Stuart, & Dolan, 2000; Wampold et al., 1997).

Does this mean that different therapies are about equally effective? Not necessarily. Therapies often differ with respect to the types of problems they treat and the ways in which they measure outcomes. In other words, we need to know which therapy works best for which particular type of problem when outcomes are measured in the same way.

For example, behavior therapy and cognitive-behavioral therapies have produced impressive results in treating a range of disorders including anxiety disorders such as panic disorder, generalized anxiety disorder, social phobia, posttraumatic stress disorder (PTSD, which is discussed in Chapter 13), agoraphobia, and obsessive-compulsive disorder, as well as other disorders such as bulimia, depression, and personality disorders (e.g., Bryant et al., 2003; Clark, 2004; Dugas et al., 2003; Furmark et al., 2002; Heimberg, Turk, & Mennin, 2004; Leichsenring & Leibing, 2003).

Other behavioral approaches, such as the token economy, help improve social functioning of patients in institutional settings. Evidence also supports a role for cognitive-behavioral therapy in the treatment of schizophrenia (Rector & Beck, 2001; Wiersma et al., 2001).

Some forms of psychodynamic therapy show good results in treating disorders such as depression, borderline personality disorder, and bulimia (see Bateman & Fonagy, 2001; DeRubeis & Crits-Christoph, 1998; Leichsenring & Leibing, 2003). And humanistic therapies may have the greatest benefits in helping individuals develop a more cohesive sense of self, connect with their innermost feelings, and mobilize their efforts toward self-actualization.

Recently, a task force of psychologists developed a list of psychological treatments whose effectiveness has been demonstrated in scientifically based studies. They identified a number of such treatments, called *empirically supported treatments* or ESTs, which they believe meet the grade (Chambless & Ollendick, 2001; Deegear & Lawson, 2003; Weisz et al., 2000; see Table 12.3). Since the process of identifying empirically supported treatments is an ongoing effort, other therapies may be added to the list as clear evidence supporting their effectiveness becomes available.

TABLE 12.3   Examples of Empirically Supported Treatments (ESTs)

Treatment	Effective in Treating
Cognitive therapy	Depression
Behavior therapy	Depression Persons with developmental disabilities Enuresis ("bed-wetting") Headache Agoraphobia and specific phobia Obsessive-compulsive disorder
Cognitive-behavioral therapy (CBT)	Panic disorder Generalized anxiety disorder Bulimia Smoking cessation
Interpersonal psychotherapy (a structured brief form of psychodynamic therapy)	Depression

Source: Adapted from Chambless et al., 1998.

What Accounts for the Benefits of Therapy?

Might the benefits of therapy have to do with the common characteristics shared by different therapies? These common characteristics are called **nonspecific factors** because they are not limited to any one therapy. They include aspects of the interpersonal relationship between the client and therapist such as the *therapeutic alliance*—that is, the attachment the client feels toward the therapist and the therapy. The quality of the therapeutic alliance is strongly linked to better outcomes in therapy (Brown & O'Leary, 2000; Martin, Garske, & Davis, 2000). Another nonspecific factor is the expectation of improvement (Perlman, 2001). Positive expectancies of change can become a type of self-fulfilling prophecy by motivating clients to mobilize their efforts to overcome their problems. Responses to positive expectancies are called **placebo effects** or *expectancy effects*. Investigators believe that the effectiveness of psychotherapy may be based on a combination of nonspecific factors and factors that are specific to particular forms of therapy (Ilardi & Craighead, 1994).

Nonspecific Factors   The effectiveness of psychotherapy is due in part to general or nonspecific factors, such as the therapeutic alliance and the engendering of positive expectations of change.

Multicultural Issues in Treatment

In our multicultural society, therapists treat people from diverse ethnic and racial groups. Members of ethnic and racial minorities may have different customs, beliefs, and philosophies than members of the dominant majority culture, and therapists must be aware of these differences to provide successful treatment. For example, with African American clients, therapists need to understand the long history of extreme racial discrimination and oppression to which African Americans have been exposed in our society. This history of negative treatment and cultural oppression may lead African Americans to develop a heightened sense of suspiciousness or reserve toward Whites, including White therapists, as a type of coping skill—a defense against exploitation. They may thus be hesitant to disclose personal information in therapy, especially during the early stages. Therapists should not press for disclosure or confuse culturally laden suspiciousness with paranoid thinking.

Asian cultures discourage public displays of emotion, which may conflict with the emphasis in Western models of psychotherapy on the open expression of emotions. Indeed, the failure of Asian Americans to keep their feelings to them-

CONCEPT 12.22
Therapists are trained to be sensitive to cultural differences among the different groups of people who seek their help.

nonspecific factors   General features of psychotherapy, such as attention from a therapist and mobilization of positive expectancies or hope.

placebo effects   Positive outcomes of a treatment resulting from positive expectations rather than from the effects of the treatment itself. Also called *expectancy effects*.

Culturally Sensitive Therapy Culturally sensitive therapy is structured to create a more receptive therapeutic environment for people from varied cultural backgrounds.

selves may be interpreted within the culture as reflecting poorly on their upbringing (Huang, 1994). Traditional Asian cultures also emphasize collective values, regarding the importance of the group as greater than that of the individual. By contrast, therapists in Western cultures often emphasize the importance of individuality and self-determination.

Value conflicts may also come into play in therapeutic situations involving Latinos from traditional Hispanic backgrounds. Traditional Hispanic cultures place a strong value on interdependency among family members—a value that may clash with the emphasis on independence and self-reliance in mainstream U.S. culture (De La Cancela & Guzman, 1991). Treatment providers need to be respectful of this difference and avoid imposing their own values on Latino clients. In working with Latinos as well as other ethnic groups, therapists must also be sensitive to the linguistic preferences of the people they serve.

At the same time, culturally sensitive therapists need to respect and understand the customs, cultures, and values of the people they treat (Stuart, 2004). In working with Native Americans, for example, they may find it helpful to bring elements of tribal culture into the therapy setting, such as healing ceremonies that are part of the client's cultural or religious traditions (Rabasca, 2000a). Native American clients may expect therapists to do most of the talking, consistent with the traditional healer role within their culture (Kahn, 1982).

TABLE 12.4   Disparities in Mental Health Care: Culture, Race, and Ethnicity

Disparities

As compared to other groups, racial or ethnic minorities have less access to mental health care and receive lower-quality care.

Causes

• Minority-group members are more likely to lack health insurance.

• Minority-group members lack access to treatment providers who are similar in ethnicity or who possess appropriate language skills.

• The lingering stigma about mental illness discourages help-seeking.

• There are few treatment providers in rural or isolated locations where minority-group members, especially Native Americans, may reside.

Vision for the Future

• Expand the scientific base to better understand relationships between mental health and sociocultural factors such as acculturation, stigma, and racism.

• Improve access to treatment, such as by improving language access and geographic availability of mental health services.

• Reduce barriers to mental health care, such as costs of services and societal stigma toward mental illness.

• Improve quality of care, such as by individualizing treatment to the person's age, gender, race, ethnicity, and culture.

• Increase minority representation among mental health treatment providers.

• Promote mental health by strengthening supportive families and working to eradicate contributors to mental health problems, such as poverty, community violence, racism, and discrimination.

Source: USDHHS, 2001.

In short, therapists need to adapt their treatment approaches to the cultural and social realities of clients from diverse backgrounds (Cardemil & Battle, 2003; Iwamasa, Sorocco, & Koonce, 2002; Wong et al., 2003). Therapists also need to be aware of their own cultural biases to avoid stereotyping clients from other cultural groups. When a therapist's own cultural biases are left unexamined, they can quickly become destructive of the therapeutic relationship.

The mental health system also needs to do a better job of providing quality care to all groups. A 2001 report by the U.S. Surgeon General concluded that minority group members typically receive lower-quality care and have less access to care than other Americans (USDHHS, 2001; see Table 12.4). Consequently, minority group members shoulder a greater mental health burden because of mental disorders that go undiagnosed and untreated (Stenson, 2001a).

Concept Chart 12.1 summarizes the differences among the types of psychotherapy discussed in this module.

CONCEPT CHART 12.1
Major Types of Psychotherapy: How They Differ

Type of Therapy	Focus	Length	Therapist's Role	Techniques
Classical psychoanalysis	Insight into unconscious causes of behavior	Long, at least several years	Passive, interpretive	Free association, dream analysis, interpretation
Modern psychodynamic approaches	Insight-oriented, but focuses more on ego functioning and current relationships than is the case in Freudian analysis	Briefer than traditional analysis	Probing, engaging client in back-and-forth discussion	More direct analysis of client's defenses and transference relationships; less use of free association
Humanistic, client-centered therapy	Promotes self-growth by helping clients become more aware of, and accepting of, their inner feelings, needs, and interests	Varies	Nondirective; allows client to lead, with therapist serving as an empathic listener	Demonstrating empathy, unconditional positive regard, and genuineness to create a warm and accepting therapeutic atmosphere
Humanistic, gestalt therapy	Helps clients develop a unified sense of self by bringing into present awareness their true feelings and conflicts with others	Brief, sometimes only a few sessions	Directive, engaging, even confrontational	Empty chair technique and other role-playing exercises
Behavior therapy	Changes problem behavior through use of learning-based techniques tailored to the specific problem	Brief, lasting perhaps 10 to 20 sessions	Direct, active problem solving	Systematic desensitization, exposure therapy, aversion therapy, operant conditioning techniques
Cognitive-behavioral therapy	Focuses on changing both maladaptive cognitions and overt behaviors	Brief, usually lasting 10 to 20 sessions	Direct, active problem solving	Combines cognitive and behavioral techniques
Rational-emotive behavior therapy	Helps clients replace irrational beliefs with more adaptive, logical alternatives	Brief, typically 10 to 20 sessions	Directive, challenging, sometimes confrontational	Identifying and disputing irrational beliefs, with behavioral homework assignments
Cognitive therapy	Helps clients identify and correct faulty styles of thinking	Brief, typically 10 to 20 sessions	Collaborative process of engaging client in an effort to logically examine beliefs and find evidence to support or refute them	Identifying and correcting distorted thoughts; specific homework assignments including thought recording and reality testing

MODULE 12.1 REVIEW

Types of Psychotherapy

CONCEPT CHECK

1. Match the following concepts from psychodynamic therapy with the appropriate descriptions: (a) free association; (b) insight; (c) resistance; (d) transference relationship.
   i. understanding the unconscious origins of a problem
   ii. responding to the analyst as a "father figure"
   iii. blocking that occurs when emotionally sensitive topics arise
   iv. saying whatever comes to mind

2. Name three important qualities shown by an effective client-centered therapist.

3. Jonathan's therapist trains him to use deep muscle relaxation and helps him construct a fear hierarchy. Which behavior therapy technique is this therapist likely to be using?

4. The form of therapy that holds that irrational beliefs underlie the development of psychological problems is _____.

5. List two advantages and two disadvantages of group therapy.

MODULE 12.2 Biomedical Therapies

- **What are the major types of psychotropic or psychiatric drugs?**
- **What are the advantages and disadvantages of psychiatric drugs?**
- **What is ECT, and how is it used?**
- **What are community-based mental health centers?**
- **How successful is the policy of deinstitutionalization?**

Remarkable gains have been made in treating a wide range of psychological disorders with biomedical forms of treatment, which most often involve the use of **psychotropic drugs** (also called *psychiatric* or *psychotherapeutic drugs*). Despite their success, psychiatric drugs have limitations, including unwelcome side effects and potential for abuse. Other forms of biomedical treatment, such as electroconvulsive therapy (ECT) and psychosurgery, are more controversial.

Drug Therapy

CONCEPT 12.23
Psychotropic drugs work on neurotransmitter systems in the brain to help regulate moods and thinking processes.

CONCEPT 12.24
Three major classes of psychotropic drugs are antianxiety drugs, antidepressants, and antipsychotics.

 **web.** Web Tutorials/Drug Therapy

psychotropic drugs Psychiatric drugs used in the treatment of psychological or mental disorders.
antianxiety drugs Drugs that combat anxiety.

Neurotransmitters ferry nerve impulses from one neuron to another. But irregularities in the workings of neurotransmitters in the brain are implicated in a wide range of psychological disorders, including anxiety disorders, mood disorders, eating disorders, and schizophrenia. Scientists have developed drugs that help regulate the functioning of neurotransmitters in the brain. These drugs—which, as noted above, are called *psychotropic drugs*—offer relief from symptoms of disorders ranging from panic disorder to depression to schizophrenia, but they are not cures. There are three major groupings of psychotropic drugs: antianxiety drugs, antidepressants, and antipsychotics.

Antianxiety Drugs

Antianxiety drugs (sometimes called *minor tranquilizers*) help quell anxiety, induce calmness, and reduce muscle tension. The most widely used antianxiety drugs are minor tranquilizers such as *diazepam* (Valium), *chlordiazepoxide* (Librium), and *alprazolam* (Xanax). They act on the neurotransmitter *gamma-aminobutyric acid—* or GABA for short (first discussed in Chapter 2). GABA is an inhibitory neurotransmitter, which means that it inhibits the flow of nerve impulses and thus prevents neurons in the brain from overly exciting their neighbors. The major types of antianxiety drugs, including Valium, Librium, and Xanax, make GABA receptors more sensitive, thereby enhancing the chemical's calming (inhibitory) effects.

Antidepressants

Antidepressants increase the availability in the brain of the neurotransmitters norepinephrine and serotonin. There are three major types of antidepressants: **tricyclics**, **monoamine oxidase (MAO) inhibitors**, and **selective serotonin-reuptake inhibitors (SSRIs)**. The tricyclics, such as *imipramine* (Tofranil), *amitriptyline* (Elavil), and *doxepin* (Sinequan), raise brain levels of norepinephrine and serotonin by interfering with the reuptake process by which these chemical messengers are reabsorbed by the transmitting cells. MAO inhibitors such as *phenelzine* (Nardil) and *tranylcypromine* (Parnate) inhibit the action of the enzyme *monoamine oxidase,* which normally breaks down (degrades) these neurotransmitters in the synapse. SSRIs, such as *fluoxetine* (Prozac) and *sertraline* (Zoloft), are a newer generation of drugs that have more specific effects on raising levels of serotonin in the brain by interfering with its reuptake (Jacobs, 2004). Though antidepressants are known to increase the availability of key neurotransmitters at the synaptic level in the brain, the precise mechanisms by which they help relieve depression remain unclear (Kupfer, 1999).

Use of antidepressant medication in outpatient treatment has risen sharply in recent years (Olfson et al., 2002). Antidepressants help relieve depression in perhaps 50 to 70 percent of cases (USDHHS, 1999). But even in these instances, depression is not necessarily eliminated; improvement is often modest at best (Kirsch et al., 2002). Though tricyclics and SSRIs are about equally effective, the SSRIs generally produce less severe side effects and are less dangerous in an overdose situation (Kupfer, 1999).

You may know that antidepressants are helpful in treating depression. But perhaps you didn't know that they also have therapeutic benefits in treating anxiety disorders such as panic disorder, social phobia, posttraumatic stress disorder (PTSD), generalized anxiety disorder, and obsessive-compulsive disorder, as well as bulimia (e.g., Brady et al., 2000; Glass, 2000; Hoehn-Saric et al., 2000; Hudson et al., 2003; Van Ameringen et al., 2001).

Why do antidepressants have such broad-ranging effects? One reason is that neurotransmitters, especially serotonin, are implicated in the regulation of emotional states, including anxiety and depression. Another, as noted in Chapter 8, is that serotonin plays a key role in controlling appetite, thus possibly accounting for the benefits of antidepressants that specifically target this neurotransmitter in reducing binges associated with bulimia (Walsh et al., 2004).

Antipsychotics

Antipsychotics (sometimes called *major tranquilizers*) are powerful drugs used to treat schizophrenia and other psychotic disorders. The first class of antipsychotic drugs to be developed were the *phenothiazines,* which includes the drugs Thorazine, Mellaril, and Prolixin. The introduction of these drugs in the 1950s revolutionized the treatment of schizophrenia, making it possible to control the more flagrant symptoms of the disorder, such as hallucinations and delusions (Essock et al., 2000; Kane, 1996). With their symptoms largely controlled on maintenance doses of these drugs, many schizophrenia patients were able to leave the confines of state hospitals and return to their families and communities.

Phenothiazines and newer types of antipsychotic drugs block the action of the neurotransmitter dopamine at receptor sites in the brain (Davis, Chen, &

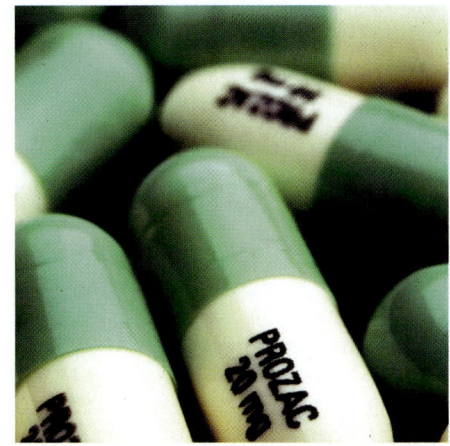

Psychotropic Drugs Though psychotropic drugs like Prozac are not a cure, they often help relieve symptoms associated with psychological disorders.

antidepressants   Drugs used to treat depression.

tricyclics   A class of antidepressant drugs that increase the availability of neurotransmitters in the brain by interfering with the reuptake of these chemicals by transmitting neurons.

monoamine oxidase (MAO) inhibitors A class of antidepressant drugs that increase the availability of neurotransmitters in the brain by inhibiting an enzyme, monoamine oxidase, that breaks down or degrades them in the synapse.

selective serotonin-reuptake inhibitors (SSRIs)   A class of antidepressant drugs that work specifically on increasing availability of the neurotransmitter serotonin by interfering with its reuptake.

antipsychotics   Drugs used in the treatment of psychotic disorders that help alleviate hallucinations and delusional thinking.

Glick, 2003). Though the underlying causes of schizophrenia remain unknown, researchers suspect that the disorder arises from disturbances in neural pathways that utilize dopamine (McGowan et al., 2004; see also Chapter 11).

Other Psychiatric Drugs

Mood-stabilizing drugs, such as the powdered form of the metallic element *lithium,* help stabilize mood swings in people with bipolar disorder and reduce the risks of recurrent manic episodes (Baldessarini & Tondo, 2003; Geddes et al., 2004). Other mood stabilizers include anticonvulsant drugs that are also used in the treatment of epilepsy (Ruvas-Vazquez et al., 2002).

Certain stimulant drugs, such as *methylphenidate* (Ritalin) and *pemoline* (Cylert), are widely used to improve attention spans and reduce disruptive behavior in hyperactive children (Biederman, 2003; Pelham et al., 2002). These drugs appear to work by increasing activity of the neurotransmitter dopamine in the frontal lobes of the cerebral cortex, the parts of the brain that regulate attention and control impulsive behavior (Faraone, 2003).

Evaluating Psychotropic Drugs

Though psychiatric drugs may reduce or control symptoms of many psychological disorders, they are not panaceas; none can produce a cure. Not all patients respond well to psychiatric drugs. Nor do drugs teach people how to resolve their problems or develop skills needed to relate more effectively with others or manage the challenges of daily life.

Psychiatric drugs also carry risks of adverse side effects, including drowsiness (from antianxiety drugs), dry mouth and problems with sexual response (from antidepressants), and muscular tremors, rigidity, and even severe movement disorders (from antipsychotic drugs). The drug lithium needs to be closely monitored because of potential toxic effects. It can also produce mild impairments in memory.

Clozapine (Clozaril), one of a newer generation of antipsychotics, appears to be at least as effective as conventional antipsychotics in controlling symptoms of schizophrenia—but with fewer troubling neurological side effects than the earlier antipsychotics (Kane et al., 2001). Still unclear, however, is whether these newer drugs, including *clozapine,* reduce the risk of the most serious side effect associated with the use of antipsychotic drugs, an often irreversible and potentially disabling movement disorder called **tardive dyskinesia (TD)** (Correll, Leucht, & Kane, 2004). The symptoms of TD include involuntary lip smacking, chewing, and facial grimacing.

Some drugs, such as the antianxiety drug Valium, can lead to psychological and physical dependence (addiction) if used regularly over time. Valium can also be very dangerous, even deadly, in overdoses or if mixed with alcohol or other drugs. Some people come to depend on antianxiety drugs to cope with life's travails rather than confronting the sources of their anxiety or relationship problems.

Relapses are common when people stop taking psychiatric drugs. Relapses also occur among 15 to 20 percent of schizophrenia patients who take their medications reliably (Kane, 1996).

CONCEPT 12.25
Psychotropic drugs help control symptoms of psychological disorders, but they do not cure the disorders.

THINK About It

Would You Take Psychotropic Drugs?

What are the advantages and disadvantages of psychotropic drugs? Would you consider using psychotropic drugs if you developed an anxiety disorder or a mood disorder? Why or why not?

tardive dyskinesia (TD) A potentially disabling motor disorder that may occur following regular use of antipsychotic drugs.

Critics claim that the large number of children on psychiatric drugs such as Ritalin and antidepressants suggests that mental health professionals may be too eager to find a "quick fix" for complex problems, rather than expending the effort needed to more fully explore the bases of problem behaviors or seek other treatment alternatives (Hancock, 1996). On the other hand, advocates of drug therapy point to benefits of using medication in treating children with serious psychological problems and to risks of leaving them untreated or undertreated (Kluger, 2003).

We shouldn't assume that psychiatric drugs are necessarily more effective than psychotherapy. Beck's cognitive therapy, for example, has proven to be at least as effective as antidepressants in treating mild to moderate depression (Clay, 2000; DeRubeis et al., 1999). More severe forms of depression may require biomedical therapies, such as antidepressants or electroconvulsive therapy (USDHHS, 1999). Even then, however, the inclusion of psychological treatment may be helpful.

Psychiatric drugs can be used to provide patients with temporary relief. But many health care providers use psychiatric drugs in tandem with psychotherapy or skills-building approaches, such as social skills training, which help individuals acquire more adaptive behaviors. Indeed, research evidence indicates that a combination of psychiatric drugs and psychotherapy may be more effective in some cases than either treatment alone in treating disorders such as major depression in adults and adolescents, panic disorder, and social phobia (e.g., Barlow et al., 2000; Feldman & Rivas-Vazquez, 2003; Harris, 2004; Kool et al., 2003).

Electroconvulsive Therapy

Electroconvulsive therapy (ECT) sounds barbaric. A jolt of electricity is passed through the head. It is strong enough to cause convulsions similar to those of a grand mal epileptic seizure. Yet it often produces dramatic relief from severe depression and can be a lifesaver for people who are suicidally depressed. When receiving ECT, the patient is first anesthetized to prevent any pain or discomfort. Muscle relaxants are used to prevent injuries that may result from the convulsive jerking that ensues. The person awakens shortly afterward, with no memory of the procedure. ECT typically involves a series of six to twelve treatments over several weeks.

ECT is used almost exclusively in the treatment of severe depression, especially in cases that are unresponsive to other forms of treatment. Though it can

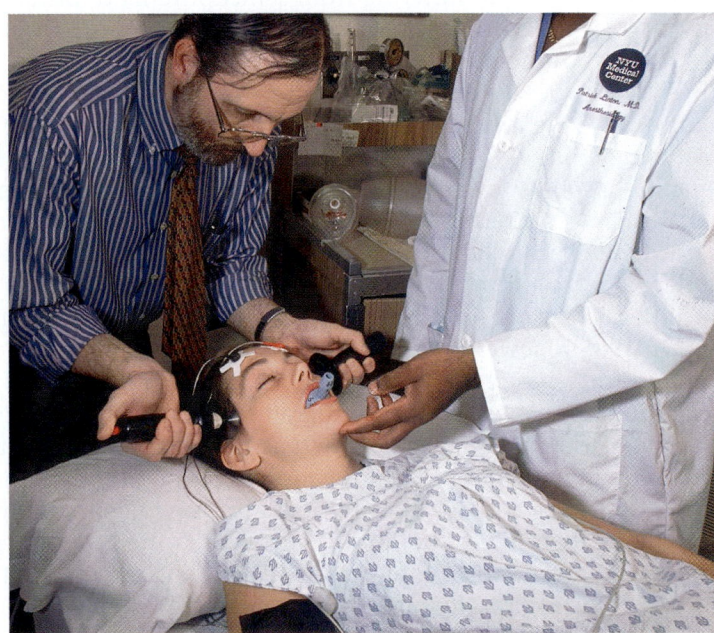

Electroconvulsive Therapy   In ECT, an electric current is passed through the head while the patient is anesthetized. It often produces dramatic relief from severe depression, but relapses are common.

electroconvulsive therapy (ECT)   A form of therapy for severe depression that involves the administration of an electrical shock to the head.

CONCEPT 12.26
Many mental health professionals view electroconvulsive therapy as a treatment of last resort for severe depression in cases where less invasive treatments have failed.

help relieve depression (Sanacora et al., 2003; UK ECT Review Group, 2003), no one knows for certain how it works. Most probably it serves to regulate levels of neurotransmitters in brain circuits that control moods.

However, investigators find a high rate of relapse in the weeks and months following a course of treatment (Prudic et al., 2004). ECT may also produce permanent memory losses for some events happening in the months preceding treatment and for several weeks afterward (Glass, 2001). In light of these concerns, it is not surprising that many health professionals view ECT as a treatment of last resort.

Psychosurgery

Psychosurgery is a procedure in which the brain is surgically altered to control deviant or violent behavior. The most widely practiced form of psychosurgery in the past was the **prefrontal lobotomy**, developed in the 1930s by Portuguese neurologist António Egas Moniz. In a prefrontal lobotomy, nerve pathways between the frontal lobe and lower brain centers are severed in order to control a patient's violent or aggressive behavior. More than one thousand patients underwent the procedure before it was eliminated because of serious complications, including death in some cases. Meanwhile, the introduction of psychiatric drugs offered a less radical alternative to controlling aberrant behavior. A sad footnote to this story was that one of Moniz's own patients (for whom the treatment failed) later shot him, leaving his legs paralyzed.

More sophisticated psychosurgery techniques have been introduced in recent years, involving surgical alterations that are limited to smaller areas of the brain. These procedures are used rarely—and, again, only as a treatment of last resort—in some cases of severe obsessive-compulsive behavior (Irle et al., 1998; Sachdev & Hay, 1996). Concerns remain about the potential long-term complications of such procedures.

The Movement Toward Community-Based Care

By the 1950s the public outcry over deplorable conditions in mental hospitals had led to a call for reform. The result was the community mental health system, which began to take shape in the 1960s. The hope was that community-based facilities would provide people suffering from schizophrenia or other severe and persistent psychological disorders with alternatives to long-term hospitalization. The advent of antipsychotic drugs, which helped control the flagrant symptoms of schizophrenia, was an additional impetus for the massive exodus of chronic mental patients from state institutions that began in earnest during the 1960s.

The social policy that redirected care of persons with severe mental disorders from state mental hospitals toward community-based treatment settings is called **deinstitutionalization**. As a result of this policy, the back wards of many mental hospitals were largely vacated. Many state mental hospitals were closed entirely and were replaced by community-based mental health centers and residential treatment facilities. The state hospital census in the United States dropped from about 550,000 in 1955 to fewer than 130,000 by the late 1980s.

Today, community-based mental health centers offer a variety of services, including outpatient care, day treatment programs, and crisis intervention. Many operate supervised residential facilities, such as halfway houses, that help formerly hospitalized patients make the transition to community life. The contemporary mental hospital now exists as a resource to provide patients with more structured treatment alternatives that may be needed during times of crisis and a protective living environment for long-term patients who are unable to manage the challenges of adjusting to life in the community. However, critics claim that

psychosurgery Brain surgery used to control violent or deviant behavior.

prefrontal lobotomy A surgical procedure in which neural pathways in the brain are severed in order to control violent or aggressive behavior.

deinstitutionalization A policy of reducing the population of mental hospitals by shifting care from inpatient facilities to community-based outpatient facilities.

TRY THIS OUT

"Hello, Can I Help You?"

Many campuses and local communities have telephone hotlines that people who are distressed or suicidal can call for immediate assistance, day or night. The volunteers who staff these call centers receive specialized training in crisis intervention services. The staffers field phone calls, provide emotional support to people in crisis, and make referrals to mental health agencies or counseling centers in the area. Serving as a volunteer for a hotline service can be a formative experience in helping you prepare for a career in the helping professions, including psychology, counseling, or social work. The work can be rewarding but also very challenging. Make sure the hotline is well supervised and provides the support and guidance you will need to handle the responsibilities of providing help to people in crisis. Keep a journal to document your experiences, noting how they shape your views of psychology and, more important, of yourself.

mental hospitals today are like revolving doors, repeatedly admitting patients and then rapidly discharging them once they become stabilized. Discharged patients are often returned to communities that are ill-prepared to provide them with adequate housing and other forms of support. Many wind up homeless (Lam & Rosenheck, 2000).

The objectives of deinstitutionalization are certainly laudable. But the question remains: Has it succeeded in its goal of reintegrating mental patients into their communities?

Deinstitutionalization receives at best a mixed grade. Though the community mental health movement has had some successes, far too many patients fail to receive the comprehensive range of psychological and support services they need to adapt successfully to community living (Jacobs, Newman, & Burns, 2001). Some simply fall through the cracks of the mental health system and are left to fend for themselves. Many of the homeless people seen wandering about or sleeping in bus terminals have unrecognized mental health and substance-abuse problems but are not receiving the help they need. Understaffed and underfunded, community-based mental health facilities continue to struggle to meet the demands of a generation of people with severe mental health problems who have come of age during the era of deinstitutionalization.

Not surprisingly, more intensive community-based programs that match services to the needs of people with severe and persistent mental health problems generally achieve better results (Rosenheck, 2000; Tolomiczenko, Sota, & Goering, 2000). Aggressive outreach efforts are especially important if we are to reach the large numbers of psychiatric homeless people who fail to seek out mental health services on their own. All in all, perhaps it is best to think of deinstitutionalization as a work in progress rather than a failed policy.

Concept Chart 12.2 summarizes the major types and uses of the psychotropic drugs discussed in this module.

> **CONCEPT 12.27**
> The community mental health movement offers the hope that mental patients can be reintegrated into society, but in far too many cases it remains a hope as yet unfulfilled.

Psychiatric Homelessness   Meeting the multifaceted needs of the psychiatric homeless population challenges the mental health system and the broader society.

CONCEPT CHART 12.2
Major Types and Uses of Psychotropic Drugs

	Generic Name	Brand Name	Clinical Uses	Possible Side Effects or Complications
Antianxiety Drugs	Diazepam Chlordiazepoxide Lorazepam Alprazolam	Valium Librium Ativan Xanax	Treatment of anxiety and insomnia	Drowsiness, fatigue, impaired coordination, nausea
Antidepressant Drugs	**Tricyclics** Imipramine Desipramine Amitriptyline Doxepin	 Tofranil Norpramin Elavil Sinequan	Depression, bulimia, panic disorder	Changes in blood pressure, heart irregularities, dry mouth, confusion, skin rash
	MAO Inhibitors Phenelzine Tranylcypromine	 Nardil Parnate	Depression	Dizziness, headache, sleep disturbance, agitation, anxiety, fatigue
	Selective Serotonin-Reuptake Inhibitors Fluoxetine Sertraline Paroxetine Citalopram	 Prozac Zoloft Paxil Celexa	Depression, bulimia, panic disorder, obsessive-compulsive disorder, post-traumatic stress disorder (Zoloft), social anxiety (Paxil)	Nausea, diarrhea, anxiety, insomnia, sweating, dry mouth, dizziness, drowsiness
	Other Antidepressant Drugs Bupropion Venlafaxine	 Wellbutrin, Zyban Effexor	Depression, nicotine dependence Depression	Dry mouth, insomnia, headaches, nausea, constipation, tremors Nausea, constipation, dry mouth, drowsiness, insomnia, dizziness, anxiety
Antipsychotic Drugs	**Phenothiazines** Chlorpromazine Thioridazine Trifluoperazine Fluphenazine	 Thorazine Mellaril Stelazine Prolixin	Schizophrenia and other psychotic disorders	Movement disorders (e.g., tardive dyskinesia), drowsiness, restlessness, dry mouth, blurred vision, muscle rigidity
	Other Antipsychotic Drugs Haloperidol Clozapine	 Haldol Clozaril	Schizophrenia and other psychotic disorders Schizophrenia and other psychotic disorders	Similar to phenothiazines Potentially lethal blood disorder, seizures, fast heart rate, drowsiness, dizziness, nausea
Antimanic Drugs	Lithium carbonate Divalproex sodium	Eskalith Depakote	Manic episodes and stabilization of mood swings associated with bipolar disorder	Tremors, thirst, diarrhea, drowsiness, weakness, lack of coordination Nausea, vomiting, dizziness, abdominal cramps, sleeplessness
Stimulant Drugs	Methylphenidate	Ritalin	Childhood hyperactivity	Nervousness, insomnia, nausea, dizziness, heart palpitations, headache; may temporarily retard growth

MODULE 12.2 REVIEW

Biomedical Therapies

CONCEPT CHECK

1. The most widely used biomedical form of therapy is
   a. psychosurgery.
   b. electroconvulsive therapy.
   c. drug therapy.
   d. psychiatric hospitalization.

2. The drugs Valium and Xanax are examples of which class of psychiatric drugs?

3. A widely used treatment for childhood hyperactivity involves the use of
   a. extensive psychotherapy.
   b. a stimulant drug.
   c. lithium.
   d. gamma-aminobutyric acid.

4. Psychiatric drugs are widely used because they
   a. teach people how to better solve their problems.
   b. correct nutritional deficiencies that give rise to psychological disorders.
   c. help reduce and control symptoms of psychological disorders.
   d. cure most types of psychological disorders.

5. Electroconvulsive therapy (ECT) is used
   a. only after successful treatment with antidepressant drugs.
   b. in treating severe cases of schizophrenia as well as depression.
   c. in treating mild to moderate cases of depression.
   d. in treating cases of severe depression, especially when other approaches have proved unsuccessful.

APPLICATION

MODULE 12.3   Getting Help

- **What steps can people take to find qualified mental health professionals?**

In most areas in the United States and Canada, there are pages upon pages of clinics and health professionals in the telephone directory. Many people have no idea whom to call for help. If you don't know where to go or whom to see, there are a number of steps you can take to ensure that you receive appropriate care:

1. *Seek recommendations from respected sources, such as your family physician, course instructor, clergyperson, or college health service.*

2. *Seek a referral from a local medical center or local community mental health center.* When making inquiries, ask about the services that are available or about opportunities for referral to qualified treatment providers in the area.

3. *Seek a consultation with your college counseling center or health services center.* Most colleges and universities offer psychological assistance to students, generally without charge.

4. *Contact professional organizations for recommendations.* Many local or national organizations maintain a referral list of qualified treatment providers in your area. If you would like to consult a psychologist, contact the American Psychological Association in Washington, DC (by telephone at 202-336-5650 or on the Web at www.apa.org), and ask for local referrals in your area. Alternatively, you can call your local or state psychology association in the United States or your provincial or territorial psychological association in Canada.

CONCEPT 12.28
Though consumers face a bewildering array of mental health services providers, there are a number of things they can do to ensure that they receive quality care.

5. *Let your fingers do the walking—but be careful!* Look under "Psychologists," "Physicians," "Social Workers," or "Social and Human Services" in your local Yellow Pages. However, be wary of professionals who take out large ads and claim to be experts in treating many different kinds of problems.

6. *Make sure the treatment provider is a licensed member of a recognized mental health profession, such as psychology, medicine, counseling, or social work.* In many states, anyone can set up practice as a "therapist," even as a "psychotherapist." These titles may not be limited by law to licensed practitioners. Licensed professionals clearly display their licenses and other credentials in their offices, usually in plain view. If you have any questions about the licensure status of a treatment provider, contact the licensing board in your state, province, or territory.

7. *Inquire about the type of therapy being provided (e.g., psychoanalysis, family therapy, behavior therapy).* Ask the treatment provider to explain how his or her particular type of therapy is appropriate to treating the problems you are having.

8. *Inquire about the treatment provider's professional background.* Ask about the person's educational background, supervised experience, and credentials. An ethical practitioner will not hesitate to provide this information.

9. *Inquire whether the treatment provider has had experience treating other people with similar problems.* Ask about their results and how they were measured.

10. *Once the treatment provider has had the opportunity to conduct a formal evaluation of your problem, discuss the diagnosis and treatment plan before making any commitments to undertake treatment.*

11. *Ask about costs and insurance coverage.* Ask about what types of insurance are accepted by the provider and whether co-payments are required on your part. Ask whether the provider will adjust his or her fees on a sliding scale that takes your income and family situation into account. If you are eligible for Medicaid or Medicare, inquire whether the treatment provider accepts these types of coverage. College students may also be covered by their parents' health insurance plans or by student plans offered by their colleges. Find out if the treatment provider participates in any health maintenance organization to which you may belong.

12. *Find out about the treatment provider's policies regarding charges for missed or canceled sessions.*

13. *If medication is to be prescribed, find out how long a delay is expected before it starts working.* Also inquire about possible side effects, and about which side effects should prompt you to call with questions. Don't be afraid to seek a second opinion before undergoing any course of medication.

14. *If the treatment recommendations don't sound quite right to you, discuss your concerns openly.* An ethical professional will be willing to address your concerns rather than feeling insulted.

15. *If you still have any doubts, request a second opinion.* An ethical professional will support your efforts to seek a second opinion. Ask the treatment provider to recommend other professionals—or select your own.

16. *Be wary of online therapy services.* The use of online counseling and therapy services is growing rapidly, even as psychologists and other mental health professionals raise the yellow flag of caution (Jacobs et al., 2001; Taylor & Luce, 2003). Concerns arise because unqualified practitioners may be taking advantage of unwary consumers, as we lack a system for ensuring that online therapists have the appropriate credentials and licensure to practice. We also lack evidence that therapy can be effective when people interact with a thera-

pist they never meet in person. Despite these concerns, many psychologists believe that online therapy services have potential value if proper safeguards are established (e.g., Glueckauf et al., 2003; Palmiter & Renjilian, 2003; Taylor & Luce, 2003).

TYING IT TOGETHER

A wide range of treatment methods are available to help people with mental health problems. Psychotherapy, or talk therapy, is a psychologically based form of treatment that helps individuals understand and resolve their problems. Each of the major theoretical models of abnormal behavior—the psychodynamic, behavioral, humanistic, and cognitive models—has spawned its own form of psychotherapy. Yet many therapists adopt an eclectic approach in which they draw from different therapeutic orientations or approaches (Module 12.1). Biomedical therapies are biologically based forms of treatment that derive from the medical model of abnormal behavior. The principal forms of biomedical therapy are drug therapy and electroconvulsive therapy (Module 12.2). By becoming informed consumers of psychological services, people in need of psychological help can ensure that they receive appropriate care (Module 12.3).

SUMMING UP: Q&A

Types of Psychotherapy (Module 12.1)

What is psychotherapy?

- Psychotherapy is a verbal form of therapy intended to help people overcome psychological or personal problems.

What are the major types of mental health professionals?

- The major types of professionals who provide mental health services are clinical and counseling psychologists, psychiatrists, clinical or psychiatric social workers, psychoanalysts, counselors, and nurses. They vary in their training backgrounds as well as in the services they provide.

What are the major forms of psychotherapy?

- Psychodynamic therapy is an insight-oriented approach to therapy based on the Freudian model. The psychodynamic therapist helps clients uncover and work through unconscious conflicts dating from childhood that are believed to be at the root of their problems.
- Humanistic therapists focus primarily on the client's subjective, conscious experience in the here-and-now.
- Behavior therapy is the systematic application of learning principles to help people unlearn maladaptive behaviors and acquire more adaptive behaviors.
- The techniques of behavior therapy include systematic desensitization, gradual exposure, modeling, aversive conditioning, and methods based on operant conditioning.
- Cognitive-behavioral therapy is a broader form of behavior therapy that incorporates both behavioral and cognitive techniques in treatment.

- Cognitive therapies, such as rational-emotive behavior therapy (REBT) and cognitive therapy, focus on modifying the individual's maladaptive thoughts and beliefs that are believed to underlie emotional problems such as anxiety and depression and self-defeating or maladaptive forms of behavior.
- In eclectic therapy, the therapist adopts principles or techniques from different schools of therapy.
- Group therapy is a form of psychotherapy in which several individuals receive treatment at the same time in a group format.
- Family therapy helps conflicted families learn to resolve their differences, clarify communications, resolve role conflicts, and avoid tendencies toward blaming individual family members.
- Couple therapy is used to help distressed couples improve their communication skills and resolve their differences.

Is psychotherapy effective?

- The answer is yes. Meta-analyses show that people who participate in psychotherapy are more likely to achieve a good outcome than those who remain untreated.
- There is a continuing debate about whether some forms of therapy are better than others.
- Evidence supports the effectiveness of particular forms of therapy for specific disorders.

What cultural factors do therapists need to consider when working with members of diverse groups?

- The cultural factors to be considered include differences in cultural beliefs, customs, values, and linguistic preferences, as well as the therapists' own cultural biases and stereotyping tendencies.

Biomedical Therapies (Module 12.2)

What are the major types of psychotropic or psychiatric drugs?

- The major classes of psychiatric drugs are antianxiety agents (e.g., Valium, Xanax), antidepressants (e.g., Elavil, Prozac), and antipsychotics (e.g., Thorazine, Clozaril).
- Other drugs, such as lithium and Ritalin, are used to treat specific disorders.

What are the advantages and disadvantages of psychiatric drugs?

- Psychiatric drugs can help relieve or control symptoms of many psychological disorders, including anxiety disorders, mood disorders, and schizophrenia.
- The major disadvantages of these drugs are the occurrence of troubling side effects, high relapse rates following discontinuance, and, in some cases, possible chemical dependence.

What is ECT, and how is it used?

- ECT (electroconvulsive therapy) involves the administration of brief pulses of electricity to the brain. It is used to treat severe depression, especially in cases that do not respond to other treatments.

What are community-based mental health centers?

- Community-based mental health centers are treatment facilities that provide a comprehensive range of mental health services and other supportive services to psychiatric patients in the communities in which they reside.

How successful is the policy of deinstitutionalization?

- The policy of deinstitutionalization remains a promise not yet fulfilled, as many patients fail to receive the services they need to adjust successfully to the community.

Application: Getting Help (Module 12.3)

What steps can people take to find qualified mental health professionals?

- People can seek recommendations and referrals from trusted sources, check the credentials and licensure status of mental health service providers, and inquire before making a commitment about the types of services offered, the practitioner's prior experience in treating people with similar problems, the costs and expected length of treatment, and the policies regarding insurance and canceled sessions.

Key Terms

psychotherapy (p. 418)
psychoanalysis (p. 418)
psychoanalysts (p. 418)
free association (p. 419)
dream analysis (p. 420)
interpretation (p. 420)
insight (p. 420)
resistance (p. 420)
transference relationship (p. 420)
countertransference (p. 420)
behavior therapy (p. 423)
systematic desensitization (p. 423)
fear hierarchy (p. 423)
gradual exposure (p. 424)
modeling (p. 425)

virtual therapy (p. 425)
aversive conditioning (p. 425)
cognitive-behavioral therapy (CBT) (p. 426)
rational-emotive behavior therapy (REBT) (p. 426)
cognitive therapy (p. 428)
eclectic therapy (p. 429)
group therapy (p. 430)
family therapy (p. 430)
couple therapy (p. 431)
meta-analysis (p. 431)
nonspecific factors (p. 433)
placebo effects (p. 433)

psychotropic drugs (p. 436)
antianxiety drugs (p. 436)
antidepressants (p. 437)
tricyclics (p. 437)
monoamine oxidase (MAO) inhibitors (p. 437)
selective serotonin-reuptake inhibitors (SSRIs) (p. 437)
antipsychotics (p. 437)
tardive dyskinesia (TD) (p. 438)
electroconvulsive therapy (ECT) (p. 439)
psychosurgery (p. 440)
prefrontal lobotomy (p. 440)
deinstitutionalization (p. 440)

Thinking Critically About Psychology

Based on your reading of this chapter, answer the following questions. Then, to evaluate your progress in developing critical thinking skills, compare your answers to the sample answers found in Appendix A.

Lauren has been depressed since the breakup of her relationship with her boyfriend two months ago. She is crying frequently, has difficulty getting out of bed in the morning, and has been losing weight. She claims she doesn't feel like eating. She tells the psychologist that she hasn't ever felt like hurting herself, but wavers when asked if she feels she might reach a point where she would consider ending her life. She says she feels like a failure and that no one will ever want her. Looking down at the floor, she tells the psychologist, "Everyone's always rejected me. Why should this be any different?"

Review the major approaches to therapy (psychodynamic, humanistic, behavioral, cognitive) and biomedical treatments discussed in this chapter. Then briefly describe how each might be used to help someone like Lauren.

Answers to Concept Check Questions

Module 12.1: 1. (a) iv, (b) i, (c) iii, (d) ii; 2. unconditional positive regard, empathy, genuineness; 3. systematic desensitization; 4. rational-emotive behavior therapy; 5. The advantages of group therapy include its lower cost and the fact that clients can gain experience relating to others and learn from others how to cope with problem situations; its disadvantages include a lower level of individual attention and clients' potential fear of revealing very personal matters to other members of the group. **Module 12.2:** 1. c; 2. antianxiety drugs; 3. b; 4. c; 5. d.

Key to Sample Rational Alternatives in Try This Out *(p. 429)*

1. We've got problems, but it's not a complete disaster. It's better to think of ways of making it better than thinking the worst.
2. I sometimes feel overwhelmed, but I've handled things like this before. I need to take things a step at a time to get through this.
3. Just because it feels that way doesn't make it so.
4. Focus on getting through this course, not on jumping to conclusions.
5. Stop taking the blame for other people's problems. There are many reasons why _____ has these problems that have nothing to do with me.
6. Stop dumping on yourself. Focus on what you need to do.
7. It doesn't help to compare myself to others. All I can expect of myself is to do the best I can.
8. It would be upsetting, but it wouldn't be the end of the world. It's awful only if I make it so.
9. What evidence do I have for believing that? People who get to know me like me more often than not.
10. Putting everything in context, it's really not so bad.

Psychology and Health

DID YOU KNOW THAT . . .

- Happy or joyous events can be a source of stress? (p. 451)

- The emotional stress of divorce or even college examinations may damage your health? (p. 453)

- Writing about traumatic experiences may boost the body's immune system? (p. 462)

- Optimistic people have fewer postoperative complications following coronary artery bypass surgery than pessimistic people? (p. 465)

- Chronic anger may be harmful to your heart? (p. 468)

- Two modifiable behaviors, smoking and diet, account for nearly two of three cancer deaths in the United States? (p. 470)

- Regular exercise increases resilience to stress? (p. 476)

The Paris morgue is a strange place for a famous philosopher to be rummaging about. But there among the corpses was the seventeenth-century French philosopher René Descartes (1596–1650) (Searle, 1996). You probably know Descartes for his famous statement "I think, therefore I am." Descartes believed that the mind and body are two fundamentally different entities. But if the mind and body are separate, there must be some connection between them. For example, if you decide to raise your arm and a fraction of a second later your arm moves up, the mind must have had an effect on the body. By examining corpses, Descartes hoped to find the part of the brain where the mind connected to the body. Modern science teaches that the mind and the body, the psychological and the physical, are more closely intertwined than Descartes would ever have imagined (Kendler, 2001; Lemonick, 2003a). The mind affects the body, and the body affects the mind. There is no single point in the brain where the mind and body intersect.

In previous chapters we focused on how the workings of the body, especially the brain, affect mental experiences such as sensations, perceptions, emotions, and thinking. Here we look at the other side of the coin by considering how the mind affects the body—how psychological factors, especially stress, affect our health and well-being.

In this chapter we examine how stress affects the body, the role that it plays in physical illness, and how psychological factors moderate the impact of stress. We then examine psychological factors that affect such major health problems as heart disease and cancer, the two leading killers of Americans. We will see that unhealthy behaviors and lifestyles, such as smoking and consumption of a high-fat diet, are linked to the risk of developing these life-threatening diseases. By better understanding the psychological links to physical illness, psychologists can develop health promotion programs to help people make healthful changes in their behaviors and lifestyles. Finally, we consider how each of us can apply psychological techniques and principles to better manage the stress we face in our daily lives. ■

| MODULE 13.1 | **Stress: What It Is and What It Does to the Body** |

- **What is health psychology?**
- **What is stress, and what are the major sources of stress?**
- **How does the body respond to stress?**
- **How does stress affect the immune system?**
- **What psychological factors buffer the effects of stress?**

The study of interrelationships between psychology and physical health is called **health psychology** (Revenson & Baum, 2001). Health psychologists work in universities, hospitals, and government agencies conducting research and using the knowledge they gain to develop health promotion and disease prevention programs (Schneiderman et al., 2001).

Health psychologists are especially concerned with the effects of stress on physical health. But what is stress, and how does it affect our health?

Psychologists use the term **stress** to describe pressures or demands placed upon an organism to adjust or adapt to its environment. Stress is a fact of life. We may even need a certain amount of stress to remain active, alert, and energized. But when the stress we face in our lives increases to a level that taxes our ability to cope, we may experience **distress**, which is an internal state of physical or mental pain or suffering. Distress may take the form of psychological problems, especially anxiety and depression, or physical health problems, including headaches, digestive problems, even heart conditions such as irregular heart rhythms (see Table 13.1). Though most people are remarkably resilient to stress, we all have our limits.

In this module, we discuss the sources of stress and examine how stress affects us. Some readers might be surprised to learn that not all sources of stress arise from negative life events or circumstances.

CONCEPT 13.1
When the level of stress in our lives taxes our ability to cope, we may experience states of distress in the form of psychological or physical health problems.

health psychology The specialty in psychology that focuses on the interrelationships between psychological factors and physical health.

stress Pressure or demand placed on an organism to adjust or adapt.

distress A state of emotional or physical suffering, discomfort, or pain.

stressors Sources of stress.

hassles Annoyances of daily life that impose a stressful burden.

chronic stress Continuing or lingering sources of stress.

TABLE 13.1 Examples of Stress-Related Health Problems

Biological Problems
Tension or migraine headaches
Allergic reactions
Back pain, especially low back pain
High blood pressure
Skin inflammations (such as hives and acne)
Rheumatoid arthritis (painful inflammation of the joints)
Regional enteritis (inflammation of the intestine, especially the small intestine)
Ulcerative colitis (inflammation and open sores of the colon, or large intestine)
Heart disease and cardiac irregularities such as arrhythmias (irregularities in the rhythm of the heart)

Sleep problems
Nausea and vomiting
Upset stomach or indigestion
Ulcers
Frequent urination or diarrhea
Skin rashes
Fatigue
Asthma

Psychological Problems
Depression
Anger
Irritability
Anxiety
Difficulty concentrating
Feeling overwhelmed
Alcohol or substance abuse

Source: Adapted from Nevid, Rathus, & Rubenstein, 1998.

What Are the Sources of Stress in Your Life?

Sources of Stress

If you had to identify the sources of stress in your life, what would you list? School or work demands, relationship problems, traffic jams, or such daily sources of stress as preparing meals, shopping, and doing household chores? Sources of stress are called **stressors**. We face many stressors in our lives. In this section we examine a number of stressors, including daily hassles, life events or life changes, frustration, conflict, trauma, Type A behavior pattern, and pressure to adjust to a new culture, which is a stressor faced by immigrant groups.

Positive as well as negative experiences can be sources of stress. Happy or joyous events, such as having a baby, getting married, or graduating from college, are stressors because they impose demands on us to adjust or adapt. Positive changes in our lives, like negative ones, can tax our ability to cope, as any new parent will attest. How well we are able to cope with the stress we experience in our daily lives plays a key part in determining our mental and physical well-being.

Hassles

Hassles are annoyances we commonly experience in our daily lives. Examples include traffic jams, household chores, coping with inclement weather, and balancing job demands and social relationships. Few, if any, of us are immune from daily hassles. Table 13.2 lists the ten most common hassles reported by a sample of college students.

We may experience some hassles on a daily basis, such as hunting for a parking spot in overcrowded parking lots. Others occur irregularly or unexpectedly, such as getting caught in a downpour without an umbrella. A single hassle may not amount to much in itself. But the accumulation of daily hassles can contribute to the general level of **chronic stress** in our lives. Chronic stress is a state of persistent tension or pressure that can lead us to feel exhausted, irritable, and depressed. Sources of chronic stress include ongoing financial problems, job-related problems, marital or relationship conflicts, and persistent or recurrent pain or other chronic medical conditions.

Life Events

Stress can also result from major changes in life circumstances, which psychologists call *life events*. These may be negative events, such as the loss of a loved one or a job termination, or positive events, such as getting married, receiving a

TABLE 13.2
The Ten Most Common Hassles Reported by College Students

Hassle	Students Reporting (%)
1. Troubling thoughts about the future	77
2. Not getting enough sleep	72.5
3. Wasting time	71
4. Inconsiderate smokers	71
5. Physical appearance	70
6. Too many things to do	69
7. Misplacing or losing things	67
8. Not enough time to do the things you need to do	66
9. Concerns about meeting high standards	64
10. Being lonely	61

Source: Kanner et al., 1981.

TRY THIS OUT

How Stressful Is Your Life?

The College Life Stress Inventory was designed to measure the amount of life stress experienced by college students. Circle the items in the inventory that you have experienced during the past year. Then compute your stress level by adding the stress ratings of the circled items. Use the scoring key to help you interpret your score.

Stress Rating	Event
100	Being raped
100	Finding out that you are HIV-positive
98	Being accused of rape
97	Death of a close friend
96	Death of a close family member
94	Contracting a sexually transmitted disease (other than AIDS)
91	Concerns about being pregnant
90	Finals week
90	Concerns about your partner being pregnant
89	Oversleeping for an exam
89	Flunking a class
85	Having a boyfriend or girlfriend cheat on you
85	Ending a steady dating relationship
85	Serious illness in a close friend or family member
84	Financial difficulties
83	Writing a major term paper
83	Being caught cheating on a test
82	Drunk driving
82	Sense of overload in school or work
80	Two exams in one day
77	Cheating on your boyfriend or girlfriend
76	Getting married
75	Negative consequences of drinking or drug use
73	Depression or crisis in your best friend
73	Difficulties with parents
72	Talking in front of a class
69	Lack of sleep
69	Change in housing situation (hassles, moves)
69	Competing or performing in public
66	Getting in a physical fight
66	Difficulties with a roommate
65	Job changes (applying, new job, work hassles)
65	Declaring a major or concerns about future plans
62	A class you hate
61	Drinking or use of drugs
60	Confrontations with professors
58	Starting a new semester
57	Going on a first date
55	Registration
55	Maintaining a steady dating relationship
54	Commuting to campus or work, or both
53	Peer pressures
53	Being away from home for the first time
52	Getting sick
52	Concerns about your appearance
51	Getting straight A's
48	A difficult class that you love
47	Making new friends; getting along with friends
47	Fraternity or sorority rush
40	Falling asleep in class
20	Attending an athletic event (e.g., football game)

Scoring Key: You can gauge your overall level of stress by comparing your total score with the scores obtained by the developers of the scale based on a sample of 257 introductory psychology students. The average (mean) score was 1,247, and approximately two out of three students obtained scores ranging from 806 to 1,688. Though your total score may give you insight into how high your level of stress is, it does not reveal how much stress may be affecting you. Some people thrive on higher levels of stress than others. They may possess the coping skills and social support that they need to handle stress more effectively. But anyone can become overstressed as pressures and life changes continue to pile up. If you are facing a high level of stress in your life, perhaps you can reduce some of these sources of stress. You might also benefit by learning effective ways of handling stressors you can't avoid. Module 13.3 at the end of the chapter offers some guidelines for managing stress that you may find helpful.

Source: Renner & Mackin, 1998.

promotion, or having a baby. In other words, changes for better or for worse can impose stressful burdens that require adjustment. Unlike daily hassles, life events occur irregularly and sometimes unexpectedly.

Data suggest that people who experience greater numbers of life changes are more likely to suffer from physical health problems (Smith, Smoll, & Ptacek, 1990; Stewart et al., 1994). We need to observe some cautions when interpreting these data, however. For one thing, relationships between life changes and later problems are typically small. For another, links between life events and health problems are correlational. As you may recall from Chapter 1, a correlation is a statistical association between two variables (in this case, level of stress and poor health) and, as such, does not necessarily reflect a causal linkage. It is possible that exposure to life events causes or aggravates physical or health problems. But it is also possible that health problems disrupt people's lives, leading them to encounter more life change events, such as job relocations or conflicts with family members. In the final analysis, relationships between life events and our physical health likely cut both ways.

Although everyone experiences hassles and life changes, some people are less vulnerable to these types of stressors than are others. They may have higher thresholds for coping with daily annoyances and are not as rattled by them. Others may lack skills needed to make adjustments brought about by changes in life circumstances, such as skills needed in making new friends when relocating to a new community. Then too, some hold more optimistic attitudes than others and believe they can control the future course of their lives. They may be better able to meet the challenges posed by various stressors.

The ways in which we appraise or evaluate a life event also have an important bearing on how stressful it becomes for us. The same event may hold different meanings for different people. A life event like a pregnancy is probably less stressful to people who welcome the pregnancy and believe they can cope with the changes that the birth of a child will bring. Similarly, whether or not you find work demands to be stressful may depend on whether or not you like your job and feel in control of how and when you do your work.

Frustration

Another major source of stress is **frustration**, the negative emotional state that occurs when our efforts to pursue our goals are blocked or thwarted. Adolescents may feel frustrated when they want to drive, date, or drink alcoholic beverages but are told they are too young. People desiring higher education may be frustrated when they lack the financial resources to attend the college of their choice. We may frustrate ourselves when we set unrealistically high goals that we are unable to achieve.

Conflict

Conflict is a state of tension resulting from the presence of two or more competing goals that demand resolution. People in conflict often vacillate, or shift back and forth, between competing goals. The longer they remain in conflict, the more stressed and frustrated they feel. Psychologists identify four major types of conflicts. Let us consider each in turn.

Approach-Approach Conflict In an approach-approach conflict (see Figure 13.1a), you feel drawn toward two positive but mutually exclusive goals at the same time. You may need to decide between taking a vacation in the mountains or at the beach, or dating Taylor or Alex this weekend, or choosing between two attractive job offers. Though you may initially vacillate between the two goals, an approach-approach conflict is generally resolved by deciding on one course of action or another. The approach-approach conflict is generally considered the least stressful type of conflict.

CONCEPT 13.4
People experiencing a greater number of life change events are at increased risk of physical health problems, but questions of cause and effect remain open to debate.

CONCEPT 13.5
In a state of psychological conflict a person may vacillate between two or more competing goals.

CONCEPT 13.6
The four major types of psychological conflict are approach-approach, avoidance-avoidance, approach-avoidance, and multiple approach-avoidance conflict.

frustration A negative emotional state experienced when one's efforts to pursue one's goals are thwarted.

conflict A state of tension brought about by opposing motives operating simultaneously.

Figure 13.1 Types of Conflicts
In an approach-approach conflict (a), the person (P) is motivated (M) to pursue two goals (G) but cannot pursue both of them at the same time. In an avoidance-avoidance conflict (b), the person is motivated to avoid each of two undesirable goals. In an approach-avoidance conflict (c), the same goal has both positive and negative qualities. And in a multiple approach-avoidance conflict (d), the person faces two or more goals, each with positive and negative features.

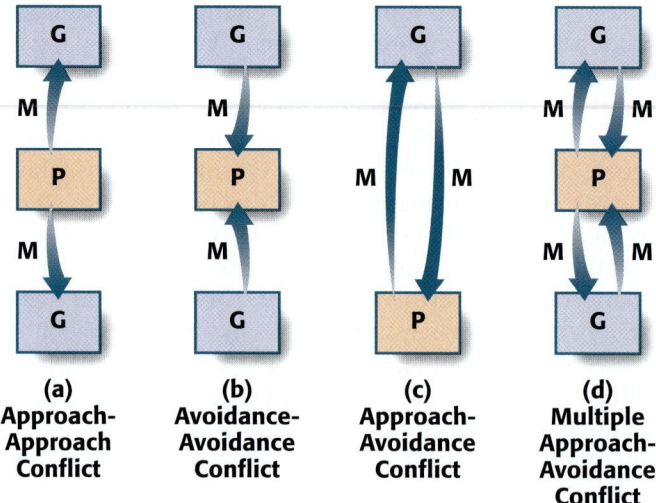

(a)
**Approach–
Approach
Conflict**

(b)
**Avoidance–
Avoidance
Conflict**

(c)
**Approach–
Avoidance
Conflict**

(d)
**Multiple
Approach–
Avoidance
Conflict**

Avoidance-Avoidance Conflict In avoidance-avoidance conflicts, you face two opposing goals, both of which are unpleasant (see Figure 13.1b). Moreover, avoiding one of these undesirable goals requires approaching the other. You may want to avoid a painful dental procedure, but also want to prevent tooth loss. You may avoid taking a less demanding major because of your strong tendency to avoid failure, but also want to avoid settling for a lesser job or career (Elliot & Sheldon, 1997). If there is no obvious resolution, you may put off dealing with the conflict, at least for a period of time. In cases where the conflict is highly stressful, you could become virtually immobilized and unable to attend to your usual responsibilities.

Approach-Avoidance Conflict In approach-avoidance conflicts, you face a goal that has both positive and negative qualities (see Figure 13.1c). You may want to ask someone for a date, but feel panic-stricken by fears of rejection. You may want to attend graduate school, but fear incurring heavy loans. Resolution of the conflict seems possible if you compare the relative pluses and minuses and then decide to commit yourself to either pursuing the goal or abandoning it. But like a piece of metal within proximity of a magnet's two opposing poles, you may at first feel pulled toward the goal by its desirable qualities, only to be repelled by its unattractive qualities as you get closer to it.

Multiple Approach-Avoidance Conflict The most complex type of conflict, this one involves two or more goals, each with compelling positive and negative characteristics (see Figure 13.1d). You may want to pursue further training after graduation because it will expand your career options, but are put off by the expense and additional time commitments involved. On the other hand, you may have a job opportunity waiting for you that will get you started in a career, but worry that you'll come to regret not having gone further with your education. Such conflicts can sometimes be resolved by combining both goals (getting started at the new job while taking night courses). At other times, the resolution comes from making a commitment to a course of action, even though it may entail nagging concerns about "the road not taken."

Conflicts are most easily resolved and least stressful when one goal is decidedly more attractive than another or when the positive qualities of a goal outweigh the negative. But when two goals pull you in opposite directions, or when the same goal both strongly attracts and repels you, you may experience high levels of stress and confusion about which course of action to pursue.

Traumatic Stressors

Traumatic stressors are potentially life-threatening events. Included in this category are natural or technological disasters (hurricanes, tornadoes, floods, nuclear accidents, etc.); combat experiences; serious accidents; physical or sexual assaults; a diagnosis of cancer, AIDS, or other life-threatening illness; and terrorist attacks, such as the devastating attack on September 11, 2001.

Exposure to traumatic stress may lead to the development of a psychological disorder called **posttraumatic stress disorder (PTSD)**. PTSD is characterized by a maladaptive reaction to traumatic events or stressors. People with PTSD encounter lingering problems in adjustment, such as those listed below, often for years after the traumatic event has passed.

web. **Netlab/When Trauma Causes Severe Stress**

- *Avoidance of cues associated with the trauma.* People with PTSD may avoid situations or cues that may be reminders of the traumatic experience. The rape survivor may avoid traveling in the same part of town in which she was attacked. The combat veteran may avoid viewing war movies or socializing with service buddies.

- *Reexperiencing the traumatic event.* Such people may experience intrusive memories, images, or dreams of the traumatic experience. They may even have flashbacks of the traumatic experience, as with combat veterans who momentarily have the feeling of being back on the battlefield.

CONCEPT 13.7
Traumatic events can be sources of intense stress that, in turn, can have profound, enduring effects on our psychological adjustment.

- *Impaired functioning.* They may experience depression or anxiety that interferes with the ability to meet ordinary responsibilities as workers, students, parents, or family members.

- *Heightened arousal.* They may be unusually tense or keyed-up, find it difficult to relax or fall asleep, or have a heightened heart rate (Bryant et al., 2000). They may also appear to be constantly on guard and show an exaggerated startle response to sudden noises.

- *Emotional numbing.* They may experience a numbing of emotional responses and find it difficult to feel love or other strong emotions.

Not everyone who experiences a traumatic event develops PTSD, but the disorder is quite common among trauma survivors. PTSD may not develop until months or years after exposure to a traumatic stressor (Zlotnick et al., 2001).

PTSD is not limited to Western cultures. Researchers have found high rates of PTSD among earthquake survivors in India and China, hurricane survivors in Nicaragua, Khmer refugees who survived the "killing fields" of the Pol Pot War in Cambodia from 1975 to 1979, and survivors of the Balkan conflicts of the 1990s (Goenjian et al., 2001; Mitka, 2000; Mollica et al., 2002; Wang et al., 2000). Culture plays a role in determining not only the ways in which people manage and cope with traumatic experiences but also the extent of their vulnerability to PTSD and other psychological disorders arising from stress (de Silva, 1993).

Type A Behavior Pattern

Are you the type of person whom others would describe as hard-driving, competitive, impatient, and ambitious? Do you seem to take life at a faster pace than others? Does the idea of waiting in line or being stuck in traffic make you want to pull out your hair or pound your fists? If these characteristics ring true, your personality style probably fits the **Type A behavior pattern (TABP)** (Friedman & Rosenman, 1974).

People with the Type A behavior pattern are impatient, competitive, and aggressive. They are constantly in a rush and have a strong sense of time urgency. They feel pressured to get the maximum amount done in the shortest possible amount of time. They tend to do everything fast; they talk fast, walk fast, even eat

posttraumatic stress disorder (PTSD) A psychological disorder involving a maladaptive reaction to traumatic stress.

Type A behavior pattern (TABP) A behavior pattern characterized by impatience, time urgency, competitiveness, and hostility.

fast. They quickly lose patience with others, especially those who move or work more slowly than they would like. They may become hostile and prone to anger when others fail to meet their expectations. They are intense even at play. While others are content to bat the ball around on the tennis court, people with the Type A behavior pattern play to win at all costs. By contrast, those with the opposite personality style, sometimes called the Type B behavior pattern, take a slower, more relaxed pace in life. The nearby Try This Out can help you determine whether you fit the Type A profile.

People with the Type A behavior pattern stand a modestly higher risk of coronary heart disease (CHD). Yet evidence points to hostility as the key element within the Type A profile that accounts for increased risk of CHD (Niaura et al., 2002; Smith & Gallo, 2001). Hostile people are angry much of the time, and strong negative emotions such as anger, anxiety, and depression are associated with an increased risk of cardiovascular problems and other health problems (Kiecolt-Glaser et al., 2002).

CONCEPT 13.8

The Type A behavior pattern is a source of stress that can pose a risk to one's health, perhaps even to one's life.

TRY THIS OUT

Are You Type A?

Check the appropriate column to indicate whether or not the item is generally true of you. Then consult the scoring key below to determine whether you fit the Type A profile.

YES NO Do you . . .

1. Walk briskly from place to place or from meeting to meeting?
2. Strongly emphasize important words in your ordinary speech?
3. Think that life is by nature dog-eat-dog?
4. Get fidgety when you see someone complete a job slowly?
5. Urge others to complete what they're trying to express?
6. Find it exceptionally annoying to get stuck in line?
7. Envision all the things you have to do even when someone is talking to you?
8. Eat while you're getting dressed, or jot down notes while you're driving?
9. Catch up on work during vacations?
10. Direct the conversation to things that interest you?
11. Feel as if things are going to pot because you're relaxing for a few minutes?
12. Get so wrapped up in your work that you fail to notice beautiful scenery passing by?

YES NO Do you . . .

13. Get so wrapped up in money, promotions, and awards that you neglect expressing your creativity?
14. Schedule appointments and meetings back to back?
15. Arrive early for appointments and meetings?
16. Make fists or clench your jaws to drive home your views?
17. Think that you've achieved what you have because of your ability to work fast?
18. Have the feeling that uncompleted work must be done *now* and fast?
19. Try to find more efficient ways to get things done?
20. Struggle always to win games instead of having fun?
21. Interrupt people who are talking?
22. Lose patience with people who are late for appointments and meetings?
23. Get back to work right after lunch?
24. Find that there's never enough time?
25. Believe that you're getting too little done, even when other people tell you that you're doing fine?

Scoring Key: "Yes" answers suggest a Type A behavior pattern—and the more items to which you answered "yes," the stronger your TABP. You should have little difficulty determining whether you are strongly or moderately inclined toward this behavior pattern—that is, if you are honest with yourself.

Source: Adapted from Nevid, Rathus, & Greene, 2003.

Type A Behavior Pattern Does your personality style contribute to the level of stress in your life?

Whether other features of the Type A behavior pattern, such as the hurried pace of life, directly contribute to health problems remains open to further study. Nonetheless, this behavior pattern is a modifiable source of stress. If you are seeking to reduce the level of stress in your life, a good place to start might be with modifying Type A behavior. Module 13.3 contains suggestions for reducing Type A behavior that you might find helpful.

Acculturative Stress

For immigrants, the demands of adjusting to a new culture can be a significant source of stress. Establishing a new life in one's adopted country can be a difficult adjustment, especially when there are differences in language and culture and few available job or training opportunities. One significant source of stress is pressure to become *acculturated*—to adapt to the values, linguistic preferences, and customs of the host or dominant culture. How does **acculturative stress**, which results from this pressure, affect psychological health and adjustment?

What we've learned is that relationships between acculturation and psychological adjustment are complex (Escobar & Vega, 2000). Some researchers find that acculturated Hispanic Americans are more likely to develop psychological disorders than their less acculturated counterparts (Ortega et al., 2000). Others find that Mexican Americans born in the United States tend to show higher rates of psychological problems than recent immigrants from Mexico (Escobar, Hoyos Nervi, & Gara, 2000). But still other researchers link *lower* acculturation status among Hispanic Americans to higher risks of depression and anxiety (e.g., Neff & Hoppe, 1993; Zamanian et al., 1992).

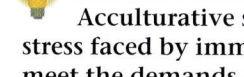 **CONCEPT 13.9**
Acculturative stress is a source of stress faced by immigrants struggling to meet the demands of adjusting to a new culture.

Adjusting to a New Culture Should immigrant groups adapt to their new culture or retain their identification with their traditional cultures? Or should they attempt both?

acculturative stress Demands faced by immigrants in adjusting to a host culture.

In attempting to understand these mixed findings, we should note that the process of adjusting successfully to a new society depends on a number of factors. For example, stress associated with economic hardship is a major contributor to adjustment problems in immigrant groups, as it is for members of the host culture. And difficulties faced by poorly acculturated immigrants in gaining an economic foothold in the host country may lead to anxiety and depression. Not surprisingly, a study of immigrant Chinese children in the United States showed more adjustment problems among those living in more economically stressful situations (Short & Johnston, 1997). Yet acculturation can lead to an erosion of traditional family networks, which in turn may increase vulnerability to psychological disorders in the face of stress (Ortega et al., 2000).

All in all, factors such as economic opportunity, language proficiency in the host language, connections to a social network of people with whom one can identify, and ethnic identity may all buffer the effects of acculturative stress faced by immigrant people (Kim et al., 2003; Ryder et al., 2000; Thompson, Anderson, & Bakeman, 2000). Studies of Asian Americans show that establishing contacts with the majority culture while maintaining one's ethnic identity generates less stress than withdrawal and separation (Huang, 1994). Withdrawal fails to prepare the individual to make the necessary adjustments to function effectively in a multicultural society. But we should not be surprised by evidence showing that Asian American adolescents with a stronger sense of ethnic identity tend to be better psychologically adjusted and to have higher self-esteem than their less affiliated counterparts (Phinney & Alipuria, 1990; Huang, 1994).

Before reading further you may wish to review the sources of stress outlined in Concept Chart 13.1.

CONCEPT CHART 13.1
Sources of Stress

Source	Description	Key Points
Hassles	Common annoyances of everyday life	The accumulation of a large number of daily hassles may contribute to chronic stress, which can impair psychological and physical well-being.
Life events	Changes in life circumstances, either positive or negative, that place demands on us to adjust	A greater number of life change events is associated with poorer psychological and physical health outcomes, but cause-and-effect relationships are difficult to tease out.
Frustration	A state of negative arousal brought about by the thwarting of one's efforts to attain personal goals	We feel frustrated when obstacles placed in our path prevent us from achieving our goals or when we set unattainable goals for ourselves.
Conflict	The state of tension that occurs when we feel torn between two opposing goals	Conflicts are most stressful when opposing goals are equally strong and no clear resolution appears in sight.
Traumatic stressors	Sudden, life-threatening events such as natural or technological disasters, combat experiences, accidents, or physical or sexual assault	Traumatic events can tax our coping abilities to the limit. Many survivors of trauma go on to develop a type of psychological disorder called post-traumatic stress disorder (PTSD).
Type A behavior pattern (TABP)	A behavior pattern characterized by impatience, competitiveness, aggressiveness, and time urgency	The TABP is linked to a higher risk of coronary heart disease. While Type A "hares" are not likely to become "tortoises," they can learn to reduce their Type A behavior.
Acculturative stress	Pressures imposed on immigrant people to adapt to the cultural and linguistic demands of the host country	Complex relationships exist between acculturation status and psychological adjustment. Adjustment depends on many factors, including economic opportunities, language proficiency, ethnic identification, and a supportive social network.

The Body's Response to Stress

Much of what we know about the body's response to stress is the result of pioneering research by Hans Selye (1907–1982), the famed stress researcher known affectionately as "Dr. Stress."

The General Adaptation Syndrome

Selye recognized that specific stressors, such as an invading virus, do elicit specific reactions in the body. But layered over these specific responses is a more general response to stress, which he called the **general adaptation syndrome (GAS)** (also called the *stress response*). The body responds in a similar manner to various stressors—cold, noise, infectious agents, pressures on the job, or mental stress in the form of worry or anxiety. Investigating this syndrome led him to believe that the way the body responds to persistent stress is much like an alarm clock that does not shut off until its energy becomes dangerously depleted. The general adaptation syndrome consists of three stages, each of which we consider below.

Alarm Stage The **alarm stage** is the body's first stage of response to a stressor, during which its defenses prepare for action. Suppose a car ahead of you on the road suddenly veers out of control. This is an immediate stressful event. Your heart starts pounding faster, speeding the flow of blood to your extremities and providing muscles with the oxygen and fuel they need to take swift action, such as performing an emergency maneuver to avoid a collision. The body's response during the alarm stage is called the **fight-or-flight response** because it is characterized by biological changes that prepare the body to deal with a threat by either fighting it off or fleeing from it.

The alarm stage is accompanied by strong physiological and psychological arousal. Our hearts pound, our breathing quickens, sweat pours down our foreheads, and we are flooded with strong emotions such as terror, fright, anxiety, rage, or anger.

Different stressful events may trigger the alarm stage of the GAS. The threat may be physical, as in an attack by an assailant, or psychological, as in an event that induces fear of failure (a professor handing out an examination, for example). In some people, the alarm is triggered whenever they meet a new person at a social gathering; they find themselves sweating heavily and feeling anxious, and they may become tongue-tied. In others, the body alarm system is activated whenever they visit the dentist. Whether the perceived threat is physical or psychological, the body's response is the same.

The alarm stage is like a "call to arms" that is prewired into the nervous system. This wiring is a legacy inherited from our earliest ancestors who faced many potential threats in their daily lives. A glimpse of a suspicious-looking object or a rustling sound in the bush might have cued them to the presence of a predator, triggering the fight-or-flight response, which helped prepare them to defend themselves against a threat. But the fight-or-flight response didn't last long. If they survived the immediate threat, their bodies returned to their normal state. If they failed, they simply perished.

Resistance Stage Death may occur within the first few hours or days of exposure to a stressor that is so damaging (such as extreme cold) that its persistence is incompatible with life. But if survival is possible and the stressor continues, the body attempts to adapt to it as best it can. Selye called this part of the GAS the **resistance stage** (also called *adaptation stage*). During this stage, the body attempts to return to a normal biological state by restoring spent energy and repairing damage. Yet arousal remains high, though not as high as during the alarm reaction. This prolonged bodily arousal may be accompanied by such emotional reactions as anger, fatigue, and irritability.

CONCEPT 13.10
The general adaptation syndrome (GAS) is a three-stage process by which the body responds to different types of stressors.

CONCEPT 13.11
The three stages in the general adaptation syndrome (GAS) are the alarm stage, the resistance stage, and the exhaustion stage.

CONCEPT 13.12
During the alarm stage of the GAS, the body mobilizes its resources in the face of stress, preparing to fend off a threat by either fighting or fleeing.

CONCEPT 13.13
During the resistance stage of the GAS, the body conserves its resources to adapt to the effects of enduring stress.

general adaptation syndrome (GAS) Selye's term for the three-stage response of the body to persistent or intense stress.
alarm stage The first stage of the general adaptation syndrome, involving mobilization of the body's resources to cope with an immediate stressor.
fight-or-flight response The body's built-in alarm system that allows it to quickly mobilize its resources to either fight or flee when faced with a threatening stressor.
resistance stage The second stage of the general adaptation syndrome, characterized by the body's attempt to adjust or adapt to persistent stress.

💡 **CONCEPT 13.14**

During the exhaustion stage of the GAS, continuing stress can lead to severe depletion of bodily resources and development of stress-related diseases.

Exhaustion Stage   If the stressor persists, the body may enter the final stage of the GAS—the **exhaustion stage**. Heart rate and respiration now *decrease* to conserve bodily resources. Yet with continued exposure to stress, the body's resources may become seriously depleted and the individual may develop what Selye called "diseases of adaptation"—stress-related disorders such as kidney disease, heart disease, allergic conditions, digestive disorders, and depression. Some people are hardier than others, but relentless, intense stress can eventually exhaust anyone. Figure 13.2 shows the changes that occur in the body's level of resistance across the three stages of the GAS.

A sensitive alarm system may have helped our ancient ancestors survive many of the physical threats they faced. Yet the alarm reaction was designed not to last very long. Our ancestors either escaped a predator or fought it off; within seconds, minutes perhaps, the threat was over and their bodies returned to their normal, prearoused state. The stresses of contemporary life are more persistent. Our ancestors didn't need to juggle school and jobs, fight daily traffic jams, or face the daily grind of working a double shift to make ends meet. The reality for many of us today is that the stressful demands of everyday life may repeatedly activate our alarm reaction day after day, year after year. Over time, persistent stress may tax our bodies' resources to the point where we become more susceptible to stress-related disorders (Kemeny, 2003).

Psychologists have found behavioral differences in how men and women respond to stress. Women tend to engage in more nurturing behaviors during times of stress than do men, such as by comforting and soothing infants and children, and befriending others who might help protect them and their children from threats. Women's stress-related behavior may be described as a "tend and befriend" pattern (Taylor et al., 2000). Among males, stressful experiences are more likely to

Figure 13.2   Level of Resistance During the Stages of the General Adaptation Syndrome
The body's resistance to stress first dips during the alarm stage, as the impact of the stressor takes a toll, but then increases as the body mobilizes its resources. Resistance remains steady through the resistance stage as the body attempts to cope with the stressor. But if the stressor persists, exhaustion eventually sets in as bodily reserves needed to resist stress become dangerously depleted.

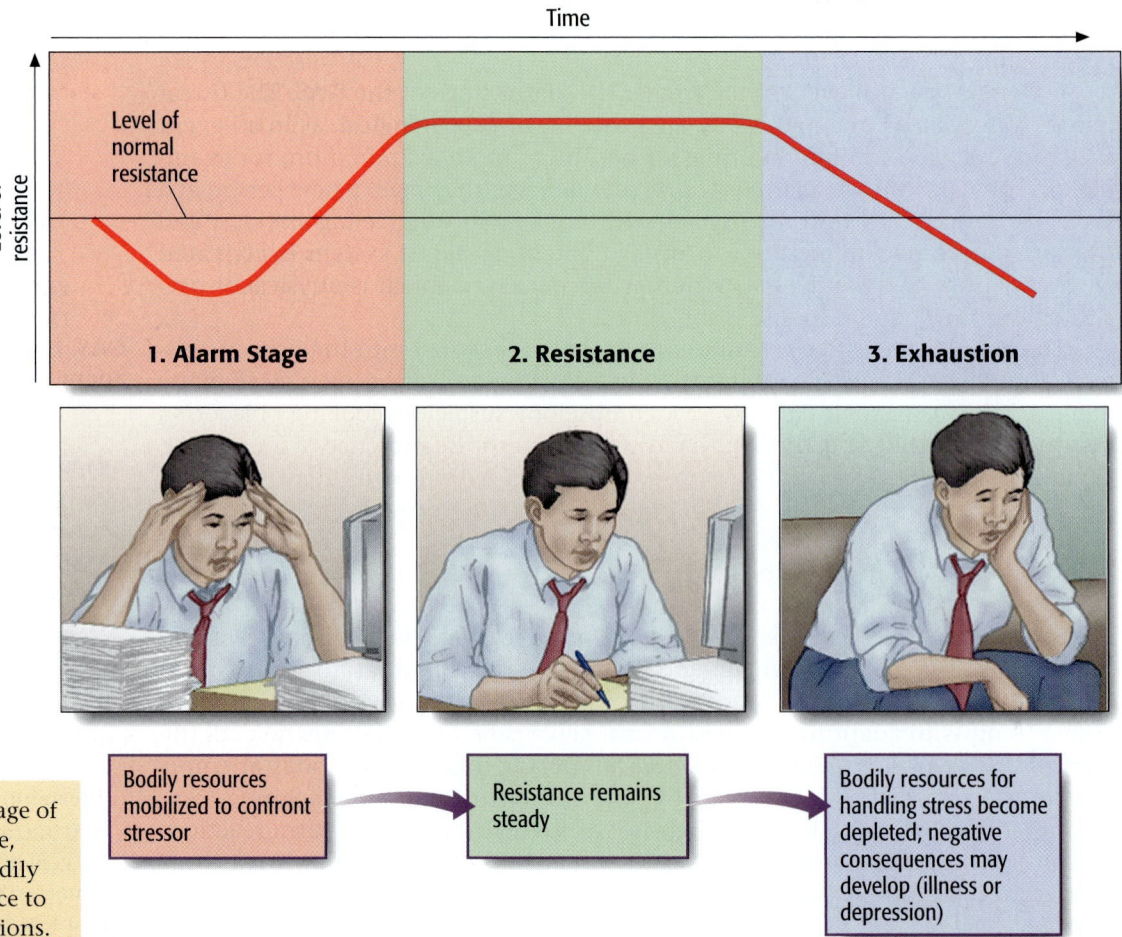

Time

Level of resistance

Level of normal resistance

1. Alarm Stage   2. Resistance   3. Exhaustion

Bodily resources mobilized to confront stressor → Resistance remains steady → Bodily resources for handling stress become depleted; negative consequences may develop (illness or depression)

exhaustion stage   The third stage of the general adaptation syndrome, characterized by depletion of bodily resources and a lowered resistance to stress-related disorders or conditions.

lead to aggressive responses in which the male sex hormone testosterone may play a pivotal role. For women, attachment and caregiving behaviors may be influenced by female reproductive and maternal hormones (Taylor et al., 2000).

Stress and the Endocrine System

The endocrine system is a system of ductless glands throughout the body that release secretions, called *hormones,* directly into the bloodstream (see Chapter 2). The hypothalamus, a small endocrine gland located in the midbrain, coordinates the endocrine system's response to stress. Like a series of falling dominoes, the chain reaction it sets off leads other glands to release their hormones.

Let's look closer at the falling dominoes. Under stress, the hypothalamus secretes **corticotrophin-releasing hormone (CRH)**, which in turn stimulates the pituitary gland to secrete **adrenocorticotrophic hormone (ACTH)**. ACTH travels through the bloodstream to the **adrenal glands**, the pair of small endocrine glands located just above the kidneys. ACTH stimulates the **adrenal cortex**, the outer layer of the adrenal glands, to release stress hormones called **corticosteroids** (or *cortical steroids*). These hormones help the body resist stress by making stored nutrients more available to meet the demands for energy that may be required to cope with stressful events.

The sympathetic branch of the autonomic nervous system triggers the **adrenal medulla**, the inner layer of each adrenal gland, to secrete the stress hormones *epinephrine* and *norepinephrine*. These hormones make the heart pump faster, allowing more oxygen and nutrient-rich blood to reach the muscles where it is needed to allow the organism to either flee from a threatening stressor or fight it. A "racing heart" during times of stress is explained by the surge of these stress hormones (Sternberg, 2000). The body's response to stress is depicted in Figure 13.3.

Figure 13.3   The Body's Response to Stress
Under stress, the body responds by releasing stress hormones (epinephrine and norepinephrine) from the adrenal medulla and corticosteroids from the adrenal cortex. These substances help the body prepare to cope with an immediate stressor. Stress hormones increase heart rate, respiration, and blood pressure, whereas secretion of corticosteroids leads to the release of stored reserves of energy.

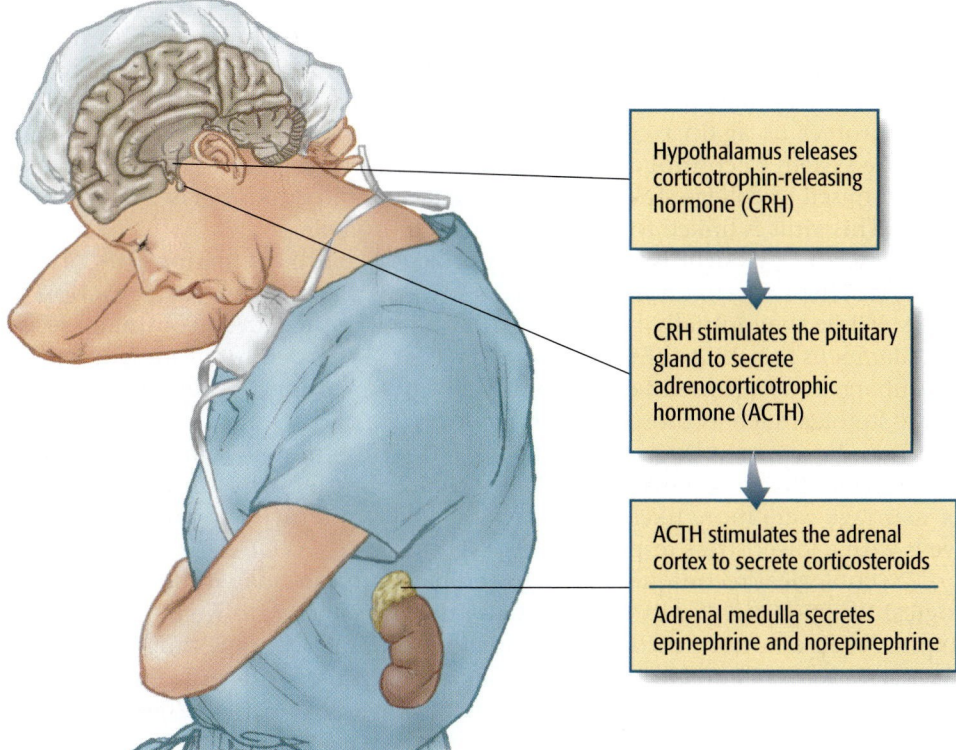

Hypothalamus releases corticotrophin-releasing hormone (CRH)

CRH stimulates the pituitary gland to secrete adrenocorticotrophic hormone (ACTH)

ACTH stimulates the adrenal cortex to secrete corticosteroids

Adrenal medulla secretes epinephrine and norepinephrine

CONCEPT 13.15
The endocrine system plays a key role in the body's response to stress.

corticotrophin-releasing hormone (CRH) A hormone released by the hypothalamus that induces the pituitary gland to release adrenocorticotrophic hormone.

adrenocorticotrophic hormone (ACTH) A pituitary hormone that activates the adrenal cortex to release corticosteroids (cortical steroids).

adrenal glands   A pair of endocrine glands that lie just above the kidneys and produce various stress-related hormones.

adrenal cortex   The outer layer of the adrenal glands that secretes corticosteroids (cortical steroids).

corticosteroids   Adrenal hormones that increase the body's resistance to stress by increasing the availability of stored nutrients to meet the increased energy demands of coping with stressful events. Also called *cortical steroids*.

adrenal medulla   The inner part of the adrenal glands that secretes the stress hormones epinephrine (adrenaline) and norepinephrine (noradrenaline).

Stress and the Immune System

The **immune system** is the body's primary system of defense against infectious diseases and worn-out or diseased cells (Delves & Roitt, 2000). The immune system fights disease in several ways. It dispatches billions of specialized white blood cells called **lymphocytes**. Lymphocytes constantly circulate throughout the body and remain on alert to the presence of foreign agents or **antigens** (literally *anti*body *gen*erators). An antigen is any substance recognized as foreign to the body, such as a bacterium, virus, foreign protein, or a body cell that has turned cancerous. As the term's literal meaning suggests, antigens activate the immune system to produce **antibodies**, which are specialized protein molecules that fit the invading antigen like a key fitting a lock. When antibodies lock into position on an antigen, they mark it for destruction by specialized "killer" lymphocytes.

Some lymphocytes hold a "memory" of specific antigens to which the body has been exposed, allowing the immune system to render a quick blow the next time the invader appears. Thus we may develop immunity or resistance to many disease-causing antigens—which is why we do not contract certain illnesses, such as chicken pox, more than once. We may also acquire immunity through **vaccination** (also called *immunization*). A vaccination involves the administration of dead or weakened infectious agents that will not cause an infection themselves but are capable of stimulating the body's natural production of antibodies to the particular antigen.

Occasional stress may not be harmful, but chronic stress can weaken the immune system, making us more vulnerable to disease (Dougall & Baum, 2001; Epstein, 2003; Kemeny, 2003). One way it may damage the immune system is by increasing levels of a chemical called *interleukin-6* (Kiecolt-Glaser et al., 2003a). This chemical is associated with several diseases, including potential killers such as heart disease, diabetes, and cancer.

The kinds of stressors most often linked to health problems include divorce; chronic illness; prolonged unemployment; persistent lack of sleep; loss of loved ones; exposure to trauma such as hurricanes, other natural or technological disasters, or acts of violence; and college examination periods (Ironson et al., 1997; Maier, Watkins, & Fleshner, 1994; Solomon et al., 1997). Chronic stress and worry can even increase the length of time it takes for wounds to heal (Kiecolt-Glaser et al., 1995).

Perhaps you've noticed that you become more vulnerable to "catching a cold" during times of stress, such as around final exams. The reason may be that exposure to stress is linked to lower production of *immunoglobulin A,* an antibody that helps protect us against cold viruses (Stone et al., 1994). The ability of the immune system to control another infectious virus, the Epstein-Barr virus, is also compromised in college students during examination periods (Glaser et al., 1991, 1993). This virus is linked to chronic fatigue syndrome.

Stress and physical illness are also linked through the actions of corticosteroids. These adrenal hormones are released as part of the body's reaction to stress. While they initially help the body cope with stress, their continued secretion dampens the ability of immune-system cells to respond to invading microbes (Sternberg, 2000). (Immune functioning also can be impaired by the use of synthetic steroids, such as those taken by some body builders and wrestlers.)

Stress hormones may even affect our relationship health. Evidence shows that newlyweds whose bodies pumped out more stress hormones during the first year of marriage were more likely to get divorced within ten years than were newlyweds with a lower stress response (Kiecolt-Glaser et al., 2003b).

Psychological techniques can help combat stress and may improve immunological functioning. For example, research participants who were instructed to express their emotions through writing about traumatic or stressful experiences showed fewer psychological and physical symptoms than did control participants (Smyth & Pennebaker, 2001; Sloan & Marx, 2004; Stone et al., 2000). In other

CONCEPT 13.16
Evidence suggests that stress can increase vulnerability to physical illness by impairing the functioning of the body's immune system.

immune system   The body system that protects the body from disease-causing organisms and rids the body of defective or diseased cells.

lymphocytes   White blood cells that protect the body against disease-causing organisms.

antigens   Substances, such as bacteria and viruses, that are recognized by the immune system as foreign to the body and that induce it to produce antibodies to defend against them.

antibodies   Protein molecules produced by the immune system that serve to mark antigens for destruction by specialized lymphocytes.

vaccination   A method of acquiring immunity by means of injecting a weakened or partial form of an infectious agent that can induce production of antibodies but does not produce a full-blown infection.

research, cancer patients who were instructed to write about their cancer in a journal reported sleeping better than those who wrote about neutral topics (de Moor et al., 2003).

Psychological Moderators of Stress

Here we examine psychological moderators that may lessen the impact of stress, including social support, self-efficacy, perceptions of control and predictability, psychological hardiness, and optimism (see Figure 13.4).

Buffers Against Stress

Social support is a major determinant of how well people cope with stress (Wills & Filer-Fegan, 2001). In some pioneering studies with medical students and dental students, two highly stressed groups, researchers showed that students with a wide range of friends had better immune-system functioning than those with fewer friends (Jemmott et al., 1983; Kiecolt-Glaser et al., 1984). And in other research, people with a wider social network were shown to be more resistant to infection when intentionally exposed to a common cold virus than were others with a more limited social network (Cohen et al., 1997). This same research group also showed that more sociable people were more resistant to developing the common cold after voluntarily receiving injections of a cold virus than were less sociable volunteers (Cohen et al., 2003). The mechanism through which social networks and sociability affect vulnerability to illness remains to be determined.

As you may recall from Chapter 10, *self-efficacy* is the belief that we are capable of accomplishing what we set out to do. High levels of self-efficacy are linked to an increased ability to withstand stress (Bandura, 1997). People with high levels of self-efficacy tend to view stressful situations more as challenges to be met than as obstacles to overcome. Self-confidence in their abilities leads them to tackle stressors head-on and persevere, even when they confront barriers in their path.

The impact of particular stressors also varies with how *predictable* and *controllable* they seem. Stressful events that seem more predictable and controllable, such as school assignments, have less impact on us than other events, such as hurricanes and fluctuations in the stock market, that seem to lie beyond our ability to predict or control them (Lazarus & Folkman, 1984). Interestingly, even stressful events that are not in fact

THINK About It

How Does Stress Affect You?

Have you experienced any physical or psychological effects of stress? How were you affected? What changes might you make to reduce stress or manage stress more effectively?

CONCEPT 13.17
Social support, self-efficacy, perceptions of control and predictability, psychological hardiness, and optimism are psychological factors that moderate or buffer the effects of stress.

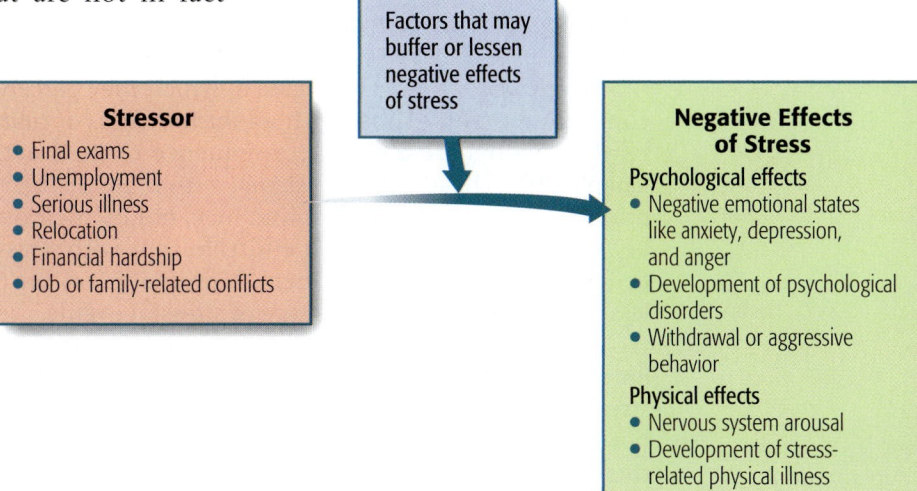

Figure 13.4   Psychological Moderators of Stress
Social support, self-efficacy, perceptions of control and predictability, psychological hardiness, and optimism are psychological moderators that help us better withstand the effects of stress.

Psychological Moderators
- Social support
- Self-efficacy
- Perceptions of control/predictability
- Psychological hardiness
- Optimism

Factors that may buffer or lessen negative effects of stress

Stressor
- Final exams
- Unemployment
- Serious illness
- Relocation
- Financial hardship
- Job or family-related conflicts

Negative Effects of Stress

Psychological effects
- Negative emotional states like anxiety, depression, and anger
- Development of psychological disorders
- Withdrawal or aggressive behavior

Physical effects
- Nervous system arousal
- Development of stress-related physical illness

TRY THIS OUT

Are You an Optimist or a Pessimist?

Do you tend to look on the bright side of things? Or do you usually expect the worst? The following scale, called the Life Orientation Test, can help raise your awareness about whether you are the type of person who tends to see the proverbial glass as half-full or half-empty (Scheier & Carver, 1985).

Directions: Using numbers from 0 to 4, indicate your responses to the following items in the spaces provided. Then check the scoring key.

    4 = strongly agree
    3 = agree
    2 = neutral
    1 = disagree
    0 = strongly disagree

_____ 1. In uncertain times, I usually expect the best.

_____ 2. It's easy for me to relax.

_____ 3. If something can go wrong for me, it will.

_____ 4. I always look on the bright side of things.

_____ 5. I'm always optimistic about my future.

_____ 6. I enjoy my friends a lot.

_____ 7. It's important for me to keep busy.

_____ 8. I hardly ever expect things to go my way.

_____ 9. Things never work out the way I want them to.

_____ 10. I don't get upset too easily.

_____ 11. I'm a believer in the idea that "every cloud has a silver lining."

_____ 12. I rarely count on good things happening to me.

Scoring Key: The first step is to reverse the scoring for items 3, 8, 9, and 12. In other words, change a 4 to 0, a 3 to a 1, a 1 to a 3, and a 0 to a 4. A 2 remains a 2. Next, add your scores for items 1, 3, 4, 5, 8, 9, 11, and 12. (Do not score items 2, 6, 7, and 10. These items are considered "fillers" and are not scored as part of the test.) Total scores can range from 0 to 32.

Now you can compare your score to those of a sample of 357 undergraduate men and 267 undergraduate women (Scheier & Carver, 1985). The average (mean) score for the men was 21.03 (standard deviation = 4.56), and for the women, 21.41 (standard deviation = 5.22). About two-thirds of the sample scored from 16 to 26. Scores above 26 reflect a generally optimistic attitude, while scores below 16 suggest a generally pessimistic attitude. Scores that range from 16 to 26 can be considered to fall within an average range. Yet higher scores within this range suggest relatively higher levels of optimism. Psychologists believe that people can change their attitudes—that optimism can be learned. If you scored high on pessimism, it might make sense to talk to a counselor or psychologist about your attitudes and ways of changing them.

Source: Scheier & Carver, 1985.

controllable tend to have this lesser impact when viewed as controllable (Thompson et al., 1993).

People also vary in the degree to which they perceive themselves as capable of controlling events. Those with an _internal locus of control_ believe that rewards or reinforcements are a direct consequence of their actions (Wallston, 2001; see Chapter 10). Those with an _external locus of control_ believe that their fate is determined by external factors or blind luck, not by their own efforts. "Internals" may be better able to marshal their efforts to cope with stressful events because of their belief that they can control them. "Externals," on the other hand, may feel helpless and overwhelmed in the face of stressful events.

An internal locus of control is also a defining characteristic of **psychological hardiness**, a cluster of personality traits associated with an increased resilience to stress. This term was introduced by psychologist Suzanne Kobasa (1979), based on her studies of business executives who maintained their physical health despite the high levels of stress they endured. She and her colleagues identified three key traits associated with psychological hardiness (Kobasa, Maddi, & Kahn, 1982):

psychological hardiness A cluster of traits (commitment, openness to challenge, internal locus of control) that may buffer the effects of stress.

- *Commitment.* The hardy executives had a strong commitment to their work and a belief that what they were doing was important.

- *Openness to challenge.* The hardy executives viewed the stressors they faced as challenges to be met, not as overwhelming obstacles. They believed that change is a normal part of life and not something to be dreaded.

- *Internal locus of control.* The hardy executives believed that they could control the future direction of their lives, for better or for worse.

web. Netlab/Coping with Stress

In short, people with psychological hardiness accept stress as a normal challenge of life. They feel in control of the stress they encounter and believe that the challenges they face make life more interesting. They seek to solve problems, not to avoid them. Psychologically hardy people tend to be better able than less hardy people to handle stress; they also report fewer physical symptoms and less depression in times of stress (Maddi & Khoshaba, 1994; Ouellette & DiPlacido, 2001; Pengilly & Dowd, 2000).

Another buffer is *optimism.* People with more optimistic attitudes tend to be more resilient to the effects of stress. For example, a study of college students showed that those who were higher in optimism reported fewer stress-related physical symptoms, such as fatigue, dizziness, and muscle soreness (Scheier & Carver, 1985). In separate studies, optimism measured at one point in time was associated with lower levels of depression at a later point in time among heart disease patients (Shnek et al., 2001) and breast cancer patients (Epping-Jordan et al., 1999). Optimism in pregnant women is associated with better birth outcomes, such as higher infant birth weights (Lobel et al., 2000). And coronary artery bypass surgery patients with more optimistic attitudes before the surgery experienced fewer postoperative complications requiring additional hospitalization or surgery (Scheier et al., 1999). Evidence tying optimism to better health outcomes is correlational, so we should be careful not to draw a causal link. Still, doesn't it make sense to take an optimistic approach toward the stressors you face, seeing the glass as half-full rather than half-empty?

Let's turn the discussion around to you. What about your own outlook on life? Do you tend to be an optimist or a pessimist? The nearby Try This Out allows you to evaluate your outlook on life.

MODULE 13.1 REVIEW

Stress: What It Is and What It Does to the Body

CONCEPT CHECK

1. (a) Give a psychological definition of stress.
   (b) At what point does stress lead to distress?

2. Match the following types of stressors with the appropriate descriptions: (a) hassles; (b) life events; (c) conflict; (d) traumatic stressors.
   i. two or more competing goals where a choice must be made
   ii. common annoyances such as traffic jams and balancing work and social demands
   iii. major changes in life circumstances
   iv. potentially life-threatening events

3. The stage of the GAS characterized by the fight-or-flight response is the _____ stage.

4. List some psychological moderators of stress.

5. Which of the following are characteristics of the Type A behavior pattern?
   a. impatient, competitive, hard-driving behavior
   b. experiencing flashbacks, heightened arousal, and emotional numbness
   c. approach-avoidance conflicts or multiple approach-avoidance conflicts
   d. experiencing chronic stress or frustration

6. Hans Selye's research on stress led him to propose the general adaptation syndrome (GAS) to describe
   a. how the body responds to specific types of stressors, such as extreme cold.
   b. the response of the body to exposure to toxic chemicals.
   c. how noise and infectious agents produce emotional consequences such as worry and anxiety.
   d. how the body responds in a similar manner to varying stressors.

MODULE 13.2 Psychological Factors in Physical Illness

- **How are psychological factors linked to the health of our heart and circulatory system?**
- **What roles do psychological factors play in the development of cancer?**
- **How can we protect ourselves from sexually transmitted diseases?**

Our health and our longevity are affected by what we eat, whether we use tobacco and alcohol, and whether we exercise regularly. The leading causes of death are not microbial agents like bacteria and viruses but, rather, unhealthy behaviors such as smoking, poor diet and inactivity (which contribute to obesity and heart disease), and use of alcohol (Holloway, 2004b; Mokdad, 2004) (see Table 13.3). Let us now examine the role of behavior and lifestyles in our physical health, starting with the nation's leading killer diseases: heart disease and cancer.

Coronary Heart Disease

The heart is composed of muscle tissue, which like other body tissue requires oxygen and nutrients carried through blood vessels called **arteries**. **Coronary heart disease (CHD)** is a disorder in which the flow of blood to the heart becomes insufficient to meet its needs. In most cases, the underlying cause is **atherosclerosis**, the narrowing of arteries that results from a buildup of fatty deposits called **plaque** along artery walls (Stoney, 2003). Atherosclerosis impairs circulation of blood to the heart. It is the major form of **arteriosclerosis**, or "hardening of the arteries," a condition in which artery walls become thicker, harder, and less elastic.

Blood clots are more likely to become lodged in arteries narrowed by atherosclerosis. If a blood clot forms in a coronary artery (an artery that brings oxygen

TABLE 13.3	Annual Causes of Death in the United States
Tobacco	435,000
Poor diet and physical inactivity	400,000
Alcohol	85,000
Microbial agents	75,000
Motor vehicle crashes	43,000
Adverse reactions to prescription drugs	32,000
Suicide	30,622
Incidents involving firearms	29,000
Homicide	20,308
Sexual behaviors	20,000
Illicit drug use	17,000
Non-steroidal anti-inflammatory drugs such as aspirin	7,600

Source: Drug War Facts, 2004, Common Sense for Drug Policy, Retrieved from http://www.drugwarfacts.org/causes.htm.
Note: Deaths due to alcohol-related motor vehicle accidents are represented under motor vehicle crashes.

arteries Blood vessels that carry oxygen-rich blood from the heart through the circulatory system.

coronary heart disease (CHD) The most common form of heart disease, caused by blockages in coronary arteries, the vessels that supply the heart with blood.

atherosclerosis A form of arteriosclerosis involving the narrowing of artery walls resulting from the buildup of fatty deposits or plaque.

plaque In the circulatory system, fatty deposits that accumulate along artery walls.

arteriosclerosis A condition in which artery walls become thicker and lose elasticity. Commonly called *hardening of the arteries*.

and nutrients to the heart), it may nearly or fully block the flow of blood to a part of the heart, causing a **heart attack** or *myocardial infarction (MI)*. During a heart attack, heart tissue literally dies from lack of oxygenated blood. Whether or not one survives a heart attack depends on the extent of damage to heart tissue and to the electrical system of the body that controls the heart rhythm.

CHD is the nation's leading killer of men and women, claiming more than 900,000 lives annually; most of these deaths result from heart attacks (Nabel, 2003). The disease accounts for more deaths in women than breast cancer. The good news, as we see next, is that people can take steps to greatly reduce their risk of developing CHD.

Risk Factors for CHD

Your personal risk of developing CHD varies with the number of risk factors you possess. The most prominent risk factors include age (CHD increases with age after about age forty), gender (men are at greater risk until about age sixty-five), family history (heredity), hypertension (high blood pressure), smoking, obesity, diabetes, lack of physical activity, and high cholesterol level (e.g., Chobanian et al., 2003; Hajjar & Kotchen, 2003; Tarkan, 2003).

Figure 13.5 shows that heart disease and cancer top the list of the nation's leading killers. Several of the leading risk factors for CHD are shown in Figure 13.6. Some of these factors cannot be controlled: You can't choose your parents or your gender; nor can you stop aging. Others, such as hypertension, smoking, obesity, diabetes, and cholesterol level, *can* be controlled through either behavioral changes (diet and exercise) or appropriate medical treatment. A study of more than 84,000 nurses showed that a combination of three risk factors associated with lifestyle—regular exercise, following a diet low in saturated fat and cholesterol, and not smoking—were associated with much lower risk of CHD (Stampfer et al., 2000).

Following a sedentary lifestyle also doubles the risk of heart disease (Manson et al., 2004). The good news is that regular exercise, even moderate exercise such as brisk walking, can reduce the risk of CHD (Pickering, 2003; "Writing Group,"

CONCEPT 13.18
Health-related behaviors, such as diet, exercise, and smoking, affect a person's risk of developing many physical disorders, including coronary heart disease.

CONCEPT 13.19
Risk factors for coronary heart disease include some factors you can't control, such as heredity, and some you can, such as hypertension, physical activity, and tobacco use.

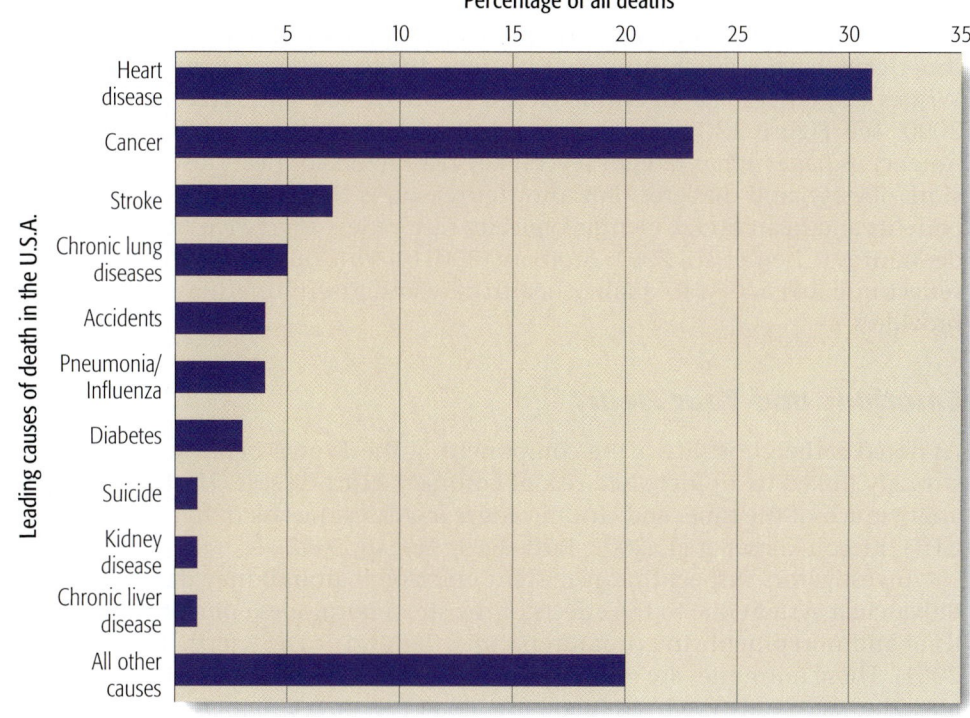

Figure 13.5   America's Leading Killers
Chronic diseases, including heart disease and cancer, are the leading causes of death in the United States.

heart attack   A potentially life-threatening event involving the death of heart tissue due to a lack of blood flow to the heart. Also called *myocardial infarction*.

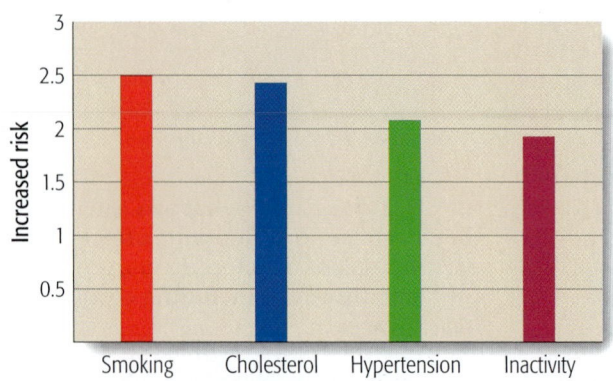

Figure 13.6 Risk Factors for Coronary Heart Disease
Shown here is the increased risk of CHD associated
with several leading risk factors: smoking, cholesterol,
hypertension, and inactivity. For example, people who
smoke are 2.5 times more likely to develop CHD than
are nonsmokers.

Source: Centers for Disease Control, 1987.

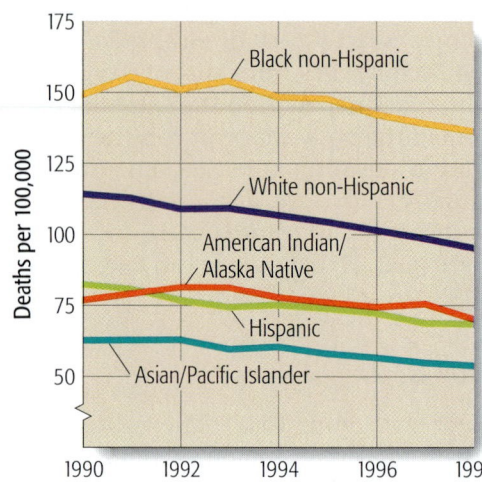

**Figure 13.7 Racial and Ethnic Differences in Death Rates
Due to Coronary Heart Disease in the United States**
Death rates from CHD are higher among Black (non-
Hispanic) Americans than among Whites or other ethnic or
racial groups in the United States. What factors might
account for these differences?

Source: Centers for Disease Control, 2001.

2003). Lifestyle modifications such as smoking cessation, regular exercise, and a
healthier diet also help reduce the risk of heart attacks in people with established
heart disease (Ades, 2001).

Smoking alone doubles the risk of heart attacks and is linked to more than
one in five deaths from CHD. Indeed, quitting smoking can reduce the risks of
premature death, as shown in Figure 13.6. (Some suggestions for quitting smoking
are provided in the Try This Out feature on the next page.) Many Americans have
heeded the health message and quit smoking. The percentages of Americans who
smoke have dropped from 42 percent in 1966 to about 25 percent today. Yet we
may be losing the battle against teenage smoking. During the 1990s, smoking
rates among high school students jumped by a third (Stolberg, 1998).

Heart disease is not an equal opportunity destroyer. Black (non-Hispanic)
Americans have a much higher death rate due to coronary heart disease than
Whites and other racial or ethnic groups in the United States (Freeman & Payne,
2000; see Figure 13.7). One explanation for this difference is that African
Americans have higher rates of several key risk factors for heart disease: hypertension, obesity, and diabetes. But another reason is that African American heart
patients and heart attack victims typically receive less aggressive treatments than
do Whites (Chen et al., 2001; Stolberg, 2001b). This dual standard of care may
reflect unequal access to quality health care and discrimination by health care
providers.

Emotions and Your Heart

CONCEPT 13.20
Negative emotions, such as anger,
anxiety, and depression, may have
damaging effects on the cardiovascular
system.

As noted earlier, hostility is the component of the Type A behavior profile most
strongly linked to an increased risk of coronary heart disease. Hostile people are
angry much of the time, and chronic anger increases the risk of hypertension and
CHD (Kiecolt-Glaser et al., 2002; Rutledge & Hogan, 2002).

Investigators suspect that persistent emotional arousal may damage the cardiovascular system due to the effects of the stress hormones epinephrine (adrenaline) and norepinephrine (noradrenaline) (Januzzi & DeSanctis, 1999; Melani,
2001). These hormones are released during the emotional states of anger and anxiety. They accelerate the heart rate, raise blood pressure, and increase the strength

TRY THIS OUT

Suggestions for Quitting Smoking

If you are a smoker, the first step toward becoming a nonsmoker is making the decision to quit. Many smokers quit on their own. But many others seek help from health professionals or organizations, like the American Lung Association, that offer smoking cessation programs either free of charge or at modest costs. If you decide to quit on your own, you may find the following suggestions to be of help:

- *Set a quit date.* Set a date several weeks ahead when you intend to quit smoking completely. Tell your friends and family of your commitment to quit smoking by that date. Publicly announcing your intentions will increase the likelihood that you'll stick to your plan of action.

- *Taper off.* Begin reducing the number of cigarettes you smoke daily in anticipation of your quitting date. A typical schedule to follow is cutting back the number of cigarettes you smoke daily by 25 percent each week for three weeks before quitting completely during the fourth week. Lengthen the interval between cigarettes to keep your smoking rate down to your daily limit.

- *Limit exposure to smoking environments.* Restrict the locations in which you smoke. Limit smoking to one particular room in your house, or outside on your porch, terrace, or deck. Break the habit of smoking while watching TV or conversing on the phone.

- *Increase exposure to nonsmoking environments.* Spend more time in settings where smoking isn't permitted or customary, such as the library. Also, socialize more with nonsmokers and, to the extent possible, avoid socializing with friends who smoke. What other smoke-free settings can you think of?

- *Limit the availability of cigarettes.* Carry only as many cigarettes as you need to meet your daily limit. Never buy more than a pack at a time.

- *Practice competing responses when tempted to smoke.* Preceding and following your quit date, substitute responses that are incompatible with smoking whenever you feel the urge to smoke. Delay reaching for a cigarette. Practice relaxation exercises. Exercise instead of smoking until the urge passes. Take a bath or a walk around the block (without your cigarettes). Use sugar-free mints or gum as substitutes whenever you feel the urge to smoke.

- *Mentally rehearse the benefits of not smoking.* Imagine yourself living a longer, healthier, noncoughing life.

- *Learn to cope, not smoke.* Learn healthier ways of coping with negative feelings, such as anxiety, sadness, and anger, than reaching for a cigarette.

Once you have quit smoking completely, remove all smoking-related paraphernalia from your house, including ashtrays and lighters. Remove as many cues as possible that were associated with your smoking habit. Establish a nonsmoking rule in your house, and request that friends and family members respect it. Ask others to be especially patient with you in the days and weeks following your quit date. Ask others not to smoke in your presence (explain that you have recently quit and would appreciate their cooperation). If you should lapse, don't despair. Make a commitment then and there not to have another cigarette. Many people succeed completely after a few near misses.

of heart contractions, resulting in a greater burden on the heart and circulatory system. These increased demands may eventually compromise the cardiovascular system, especially in vulnerable people. Stress hormones (primarily epinephrine) also increase the stickiness of blood clotting factors, which in turn may heighten the risk of potentially dangerous blood clots that can lead to heart attacks or strokes.

In addition, we need to consider that people who anger easily often stand a greater chance of developing high blood cholesterol levels and high blood pressure, which are two of the major risk factors for CHD and premature death (Iribarren et al., 2000;; Richards, Hof, & Alvarenga, 2000). Other forms of emotional distress, such as depression and marital distress, may also have damaging effects on the cardiovascular system (Ferketich et al., 2000; Orth-Gomér et al., 2000). Marital stress, for example, triples the risk of a subsequent heart attack in women who have had a prior attack. Persistent anxiety, another strong negative emotion, is also linked to an increased risk of heart disease (Smith & Gallo, 2001).

PsychAssist: The Relationship Between Chronic Hostility and Heart Disease

Psychologists are developing ways of helping chronically angry or anxious people learn to control their emotional responses. These programs have helped lower blood pressure and reduce the risks of recurrent heart attacks leading to death in coronary heart disease patients (Dusseldorp et al., 1999; Gidron, Davidson, & Bata, 1999). Whether there are more general benefits to people without established heart disease remains to be seen.

Cancer

The word *cancer* may strike more fear in people's hearts than any other word in the English language. The fear is understandable. Cancer causes more than one of every five deaths in the United States, making it the nation's second leading killer, after heart disease. By the time this book reaches your hands, cancer may have become our leading killer. Each year, more than 1.4 million Americans receive the dreaded diagnosis of cancer and about half a million die from it (Andersen, Golden-Kreutz, & DiLillo, 2001). The good news is that the cancer death rate has been inching downward in recent years ("Mixed Progress," 2003).

Cancer is a disease in which body cells exhibit uncontrolled growth. The body normally manufactures new cells only when they are needed. The genes in our cells direct them to replicate in orderly ways. But in cancer, cells lose the ability to regulate their growth. They multiply even when they are not needed, leading to the formation of masses of excess body tissue called **malignant tumors**. Malignant or cancerous tumors may spread to other parts of the body, where they invade healthy tissue. Cancerous tumors damage vital body organs and systems, leading to death in many cases. Cancers can form in any body tissue or organ.

There are many causes of cancer, including heredity, exposure to cancer-causing chemicals, and even exposure to some viruses (King et al., 2003; Lynch et al., 2004; Samuels et al., 2004). Yet two of three cancer deaths in this country are attributable to two modifiable behaviors: smoking and diet. Other modifiable behaviors, such as alcohol consumption and excess sun exposure, also contribute to the development of cancer. The good news is that these behaviors can be controlled.

CONCEPT 13.21
Two of three cancer deaths in the United States are accounted for by two modifiable behaviors: smoking and diet.

CONCEPT 13.22
If everyone practiced cancer-preventive behaviors, hundreds of thousands of lives would be saved each year.

Risk Factors for Cancer

Some risk factors, like family history and age (older people are at greater risk), are unavoidable. Others, including the factors we now review, can be controlled through lifestyle changes. If everyone practiced these cancer-preventive behaviors, hundreds of thousands of lives would be saved each year (see Table 13.4).

Smoking You probably know that smoking causes lung cancer, the leading cancer killer of men and women. Nearly 90 percent of lung cancer deaths are directly attributable to smoking. But smoking is also linked to many other cancers, including colorectal (colon or rectal) cancer. Overall, cigarette smoking accounts for

TABLE 13.4 Behaviors That Can Help Prevent Cancer
• Avoid tobacco use.
• If you use alcohol, limit consumption to one drink per day for women ot two drinks per day for men.
• Maintain a physically active lifestyle.
• Follow a healthy diet and limit intake of saturated fat.
• Maintain a healthy weight.
• Avoiding unprotected exposure to the sun.

malignant tumors Uncontrolled growths of body cells that invade surrounding tissue and spread to other parts of the body.

about one-third of all cancer deaths in the United States. Other means of using tobacco, such as pipe and cigar smoking, and smokeless tobacco, also can cause cancer.

Diet and Alcohol Consumption High levels of consumption of saturated fat, the type of fat found in meat and dairy products, is linked to two leading cancer killers: prostate cancer in men, and colorectal cancer (Whittemore et al., 1995). All told, dietary patterns may account for about 30 percent of cancer deaths. Obesity, which itself is linked to a high-fat diet, is also associated with an increased risk of some types of cancer (Calle et al., 2003; Hellmich, 2003).

Smoking and diet are not the only forms of behavior linked to cancer risk. Heavy alcohol consumption raises the risk of several cancers, including those of the mouth, pharynx, and esophagus.

Sun Exposure Prolonged sun exposure can lead to **basal cell carcinoma**, the most common type of skin cancer but also the least dangerous (Kalb, 2001b). This form of cancer, which accounts for 75 percent of skin cancers, typically appears on the head, neck, and hands—areas of the body frequently exposed to the sun. It is readily curable so long as it is detected at an early stage and removed surgically. Severe sunburns early in life increase the risk of developing the least common but most deadly form of skin cancer, **melanoma**, which accounts for about 5 percent of skin cancers and claims about 8,000 lives in the United States annually (Kalb, 2001b). To protect ourselves from skin cancer, we need to limit our exposure to the sun and use a sunscreen whenever this exposure exceeds a few minutes.

Stress The scientific verdict on the role of stress in cancer is yet to be determined (Delahanty & Baum, 2001; Dougall & Baum, 2001). It is possible that by weakening the immune system, persistent stress may diminish the body's ability to rid itself of cancerous cells. Some studies have found an increased rate of cancer among people who recently experienced stressful life events, such as the loss of loved ones (Levenson & Bemis, 1991; O'Leary, 1990). Others, however, have failed to show any significant links between stress and the development of cancer (e.g., McKenna et al., 1999). The best we can say at the present time is that connections between stress and cancer need further study.

Some psychologists counsel cancer patients and their families to help them cope with the devastating emotional effects of cancer, especially feelings of depression and hopelessness. Psychological interventions such as group support programs can help improve the psychological adjustment and well-being of cancer patients, but it remains unclear whether these interventions increase the length of survival (Goodwin et al., 2001; Spiegel, 2001; Taylor et al., 2003). We also lack solid evidence that use of particular coping styles, such as maintaining a "fighting spirit," improves the odds of surviving cancer (Petticrew, Bell & Hunter, 2002; Verghese, 2004).

Sexual Behavior and STDs: Are You at Risk?

AIDS (acquired immune deficiency syndrome) has become one of history's worst epidemics. More than 40 million people worldwide are living with HIV, the virus that causes AIDS, and more than 3 million lives annually are lost to the disease (United Nations, 2003). In total, HIV/AIDS has claimed more than 430,000 lives in the United States and more than 22 million lives worldwide. Most cases of HIV transmission worldwide (70 percent) result from heterosexual contact (Murphy, 2003).

HIV is transmitted by contact with infected bodily fluids, generally through intimate sexual contact or needle-sharing. HIV attacks and disables the body's immune system, making the person vulnerable to other infections the body is normally able to fend off.

THINK About It

Developing a Healthier Lifestyle

Based on your reading of the text, what lifestyle changes do you think might reduce your personal risk of developing chronic diseases such as coronary heart disease and cancer? What steps do you need to take to put these changes into effect?

basal cell carcinoma A form of skin cancer that is easily curable if detected and removed early.

melanoma The most deadly form of skin cancer.

HIV/AIDS is the most threatening **sexually transmitted disease (STD)**, but it is far from the most common. Whereas nearly 1 million Americans are infected with HIV, more than one in five adolescents and adults in the United States—an estimated 45 million people—are infected with HSV-2, the virus that causes genital herpes (Tuller, 2001). *Human papillomaviruses (HPVs)* are a group of viruses that cause warts to appear in different parts of the body, including the genitals. An estimated 20 million Americans are infected (CDCP, 2004). In addition, 3 million new cases of chlamydia, the most common bacterial type of STD, are reported each year in the United States (*Syphilis Down*, 2000). Altogether, some 15 million new cases of STDs occur annually in the United States.

Many STDs, not just HIV/AIDS, pose serious threats to our health. Several strains of HPV are known to cause cervical cancer in women, a potential killer (Muñoz et al., 2003). Untreated gonorrhea and chlamydia can lead to infertility in women, and untreated gonorrhea in men can lead to a serious infection of the internal reproductive system, which can cause fertility problems. Another bacterial disease, syphilis, can lead to serious damage to the heart and brain if left untreated. Genital herpes can cause serious complications, especially in women, including increased risks of miscarriage and cervical cancer (Nevid, 1998).

Treatment

Though antibiotics can cure bacterial forms of STD, they are of no use against viral STDs. Antiviral drugs may help control viral STDs, such as HIV/AIDS and genital herpes, but they cannot eliminate the infectious organisms from the body. The advent of a new generation of antiviral drugs does raise hopes that HIV infection may become a chronic but manageable disease (Reynolds et al., 2003). However, these hopes are tempered by the fact that many patients cannot obtain or do not benefit from antiviral drug combinations (Catz & Kelly, 2001). Physicians are also concerned that HIV shows the ability to mutate to drug-resistant strains (Lawrence et al., 2003; Lerner, 2003).

The lack of a cure for viral STDs, and awareness of the risks posed by untreated bacterial STDs, underscores the importance of prevention and early treatment. Arming yourself with information about the modes of transmission of these diseases, early signs of infection, and available treatments is an important step in protecting yourself from STDs (see Table 13.5). But information alone does not reduce the risks of transmitting STDs: It must be put into practice through changes in behavior. The section below lists suggestions for safer sexual practices and medical screening.

Prevention

The only sure way to prevent the sexual transmission of STDs is to practice lifelong abstinence, or to maintain a monogamous relationship with an uninfected partner who is also monogamous (Laino, 2002). Short of that, we can speak of reducing risk from sexual contact rather than eliminating it entirely, of practicing *safer* sex rather than *safe* sex. To lower our risk, we can avoid unsafe sexual and injection practices and take steps to ensure that we detect and treat any STDs we may have, even unknowingly. Here are some guidelines that can lower the risk of contracting an STD or suffering the consequences of an untreated STD (adapted from Nevid, Rathus, & Greene, 2003):

1. *Be careful in your choice of sex partners.* Get to know the person's sexual background before engaging in sexual activity. (Even so, getting to know someone is no guarantee that the person is not carrying HIV or some other infectious agent.)

2. *Avoid multiple partners, especially partners who themselves may have multiple partners.*

CONCEPT 13.23
Many STDs, not just HIV/AIDS, pose serious threats to our health.

CONCEPT 13.24
Modifiable behaviors such as unprotected sex and needle-sharing are major risk factors for transmission of sexually transmitted diseases, including HIV/AIDS.

THINK *About It*

Protecting Yourself from STDs

What are you doing to protect yourself from STDs? What—if anything—might you do differently?

sexually transmitted disease (STD) A disease caused by an infectious agent that is spread by sexual contact.

TABLE 13.5   Major Types of STDs

	Mode of Transmission	Symptoms	Treatment
Bacterial STDs			
Gonorrhea	Sexual contact (vaginal, oral, or anal intercourse); from mother to newborn during childbirth	Men may have a yellowish, thick penile discharge and burning urination; though most women do not show early symptoms, some have increased vaginal discharge, burning urination, and irregular menstrual bleeding.	Antibiotics
Syphilis	Sexual contact; by touching an infectious chancre (sore)	A round, painless but hard chancre develops at the site of infection within 2 to 4 weeks; symptoms progress through additional stages if left untreated.	Antibiotics
Chlamydia in women, or nongonococcal urethritis (NGU) in men	Sexual contact; touching an eye after contact with genitals of an infected partner; from infected mother to newborn during childbirth	Most women are symptom-free, but some have frequent and painful urination, lower abdominal pain and inflammation, and vaginal discharge. Men, too, are generally symptom-free but may have gonorrhea-like symptoms.	Antibiotics
Viral STDs			
HIV/AIDS	Sexual contact; injection-sharing; receiving contaminated blood; from mother to fetus during pregnancy or during childbirth or breast-feeding	Infected persons may be initially symptom-free or have mild flulike symptoms, but may progress to develop full-blown AIDS.	Antiviral drugs may help control the virus but do not cure the disease.
Genital herpes	Sexual contact	Painful, reddish bumps appear around the genitals, thighs, buttocks, or in the vagina or on the cervix in women. The bumps may develop into blisters or sores that fill with pus and break open before healing over.	Antiviral drugs can help control outbreaks but do not rid the body of the virus.
Viral hepatitis	Sexual contact, especially anal contact in the case of hepatitis A; contact with infected fecal matter; transfusion of contaminated blood (especially for hepatitis B and C)	Symptoms range from absence of symptoms to mild flulike symptoms to more severe symptoms, such as fever, abdominal pain, vomiting, and "jaundiced" (yellowish) skin and eyes.	Bed rest and possible use of the drug alpha interferon in cases of hepatitis C
Genital warts	Sexual contact; contact with infected towels or clothing	Painless warts resembling cauliflowers may develop on the genitals, the internal reproductive organs, around the anus, or in the rectum.	Warts may be removed, but the virus (HPV) remains in the body.

3. *Communicate your concerns.* Be assertive with your partner. Openly state your concerns about the risks of AIDS and other STDs and the need to practice safer sex.

4. *Avoid engaging in sexual contact with anyone with a sore or blister around the genitals.* Inspect your partner's sex organs before any sexual contact. Rashes, blisters, chancres, discharges, warts, disagreeable odors, and so on should be treated as warning signs of a possible infection. But be aware that some STDs, including HIV infection, do not have any obvious signs.

5. *Avoid unprotected sexual contact.* Latex condoms (not "natural" condoms, which are more porous) offer the most reliable protection against the spread of HIV during sexual contact. Spermicides should be used along with latex condoms,

not as a substitute for them. Condoms will not work if they are left in a drawer or coat pocket. The results of a recent study showed that carrying condoms was not significantly associated with using them (DiClemente et al., 2001).

6. *Obtain a medical evaluation if you suspect that you may have been exposed to a sexually transmitted disease.*

7. *Get regular medical checkups to detect and treat disorders you may not be aware you have.*

8. *When in doubt, don't.* Abstain from intimate sexual contact if you have any doubts about whether it is potentially harmful. Your safety and that of your partner should be your top priority.

In the following module we will examine ways of handling stress so that it does not lead to distress. But first you may want to review Concept Chart 13.2, which highlights some key points about psychological risk factors in physical disorders.

CONCEPT CHART 13.2
Psychological Risk Factors in Physical Disorders

Health Problem	Psychological or Behavioral Risk Factors	Healthier Habits
Coronary heart disease	Smoking, unhealthy diet, lack of physical activity, chronic anger or anxiety	Avoiding tobacco use, getting regular exercise, controlling anger and anxiety, limiting dietary fat, reducing excess weight, practicing stress-management techniques
Cancer	Smoking, high-fat diet, heavy alcohol consumption, unsafe sun exposure, inactivity, possible role of stress	Avoiding tobacco use and excessive alcohol consumption, regular exercise, using sunscreens, reducing excess weight, practicing stress-management techniques
Sexually transmitted diseases	Unsafe sexual and injection practices	Practicing abstinence, maintaining a monogamous relationship with an uninfected partner, practicing safer sex techniques, avoiding needle-sharing, having regular medical check-ups

MODULE 13.2 REVIEW

Psychological Factors in Physical Illness

CONCEPT CHECK

1. Match the following terms with the appropriate descriptions: (a) arteriosclerosis; (b) myocardial infarction (MI); (c) plaque; (d) atherosclerosis.
   i.   narrowing of vessels carrying blood to the heart
   ii. fatty deposits on artery walls
   iii. a heart attack (blood clot blocks blood flow in a coronary artery)
   iv. thicker, harder, and less elastic artery walls

2. (a) List some of the major risk factors for coronary heart disease. (b) Which of these are we able to control?

3. Smoking _____ the risk of suffering a heart attack.
   a. doubles
   b. triples
   c. quadruples
   d. has no effect on

4. _____ of cancer deaths are associated with two lifestyle factors: _____ and _____.

5. Bacterial forms of STDs include
   a. HIV/AIDS.
   b. HPV.
   c. genital herpes.
   d. chlamydia.

MODULE 13.3   Taking the Distress Out of Stress

• What are some ways of taking the distress out of stress?

We may not be able to eliminate all stress from our lives—indeed, a certain amount of stress might be good for us. But we can learn to cope more effectively with stress, so that stress doesn't lead to distress. Here let us summarize some of the basic skills needed to manage stress more effectively (adapted from Nevid, Rathus, & Rubenstein, 1998).

Maintain Stress at a Tolerable Level

Examine your daily life. Are you constantly running from place to place just to keep pace with all the demands on your time? Is it difficult to find time just to relax? Following are some suggestions for keeping stress within a manageable level:

- *Reduce daily hassles.* What can you do to reduce the stressful burdens of daily hassles? Might you rearrange your school or work schedule to avoid morning traffic jams? How about joining a car pool? You might still be stuck in traffic, but you can use that time to catch up on your reading rather than fighting traffic.

- *Know your limits.* Don't bite off more than you can chew. Avoid taking on more tasks than you can reasonably accomplish. Whenever possible, delegate responsibilities to others.

- *Follow a reasonable schedule.* Learn to schedule tasks so they don't pile up. In this way you break down stressful tasks into more manageable doses. If stressful demands become too taxing, try to extend some deadlines to give yourself added time to finish your work.

- *Take frequent breaks.* When working on an assignment, take frequent breaks to refresh your mind and body.

- *Develop more effective time-management skills.* Use a monthly calendar to organize your activities and tasks. Schedule as many of your activities as you can in advance to ensure that you have enough time to accomplish your goals. But don't overschedule yourself. Allow yourself some free, unstructured time.

- *Learn to prioritize.* Use a monthly calendar to list the tasks you must accomplish each day. Prioritize your daily goals. Assign the number 1 to tasks you must accomplish, the number 2 to those you'd like to accomplish but are less essential, and the number 3 to tasks you'd like to accomplish if time permits. Then arrange your daily schedule to progress downward in your list.

Develop Relaxation Skills

Tone down your body's response to stress by learning to relax. Some people find that listening to music helps them unwind at the end of the day. Some like to curl up with a book (not a textbook—not even this one). Others use more formal relaxation techniques, such as biofeedback training (see Chapter 2), meditation (see Chapter 4), and deep breathing exercises. To practice deep breathing, breathe only through your nose. Take about the same amount of time breathing in as breathing out, and pace yourself by silently repeating a resonant-sounding word like "relax" on each outbreath. Elongating the *x*-sound can help you lengthen

CONCEPT 13.25
Though stress may be an unavoidable part of life, how we cope with stress lies within our control.

each breath to ensure that you breathe deeply and evenly. Many colleges offer seminars or workshops in stress-management techniques where students can learn to develop relaxation skills. Why not check them out?

Take Care of Your Body

Prepare your body to cope more effectively with stress by getting enough sleep, following a nutritionally balanced diet, exercising regularly, obtaining regular medical check-ups, and avoiding harmful substances such as drugs. Evidence indicates that regular exercise increases resilience to stress and lessens the emotional consequences of stress, such as anxiety (Gaulin & McBurney, 2001; Salmon, 2001).

Gather Information

People facing a serious illness may cope more effectively if they obtain information about their underlying condition rather than keeping themselves in the dark. Whether you are facing an illness or the stress of adjusting to life in a new town or city, gather the information you need to adjust more effectively.

Expand Your Social Network

Social support helps people cope better during times of stress. You can expand your social network by forming relationships with others through participation in clubs and organizations sponsored at your college. The office of student life or counseling services at your college should be able to advise you about the availability of these resources.

Prevent Burnout

Burnout is a state of physical and emotional exhaustion resulting from excessive job demands, caregiving, and other stress-laden commitments (Maslach, 2003). You can take steps to prevent burnout, such as setting reasonable goals and limits for yourself. Establish personal goals that are attainable, and don't push yourself beyond your limits. Learn to say "no" when people make excessive demands on you. Start delegating responsibilities, and learn to cut back on low-priority tasks when commitments begin piling up.

Helping Hands Social support is an important buffer against the effects of stress associated with negative life circumstances or physical illness.

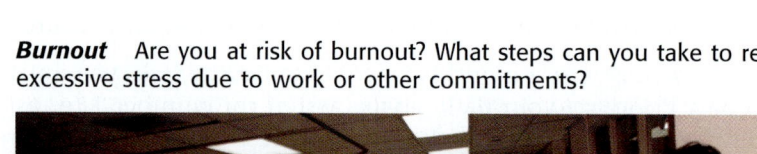

Burnout Are you at risk of burnout? What steps can you take to relieve excessive stress due to work or other commitments?

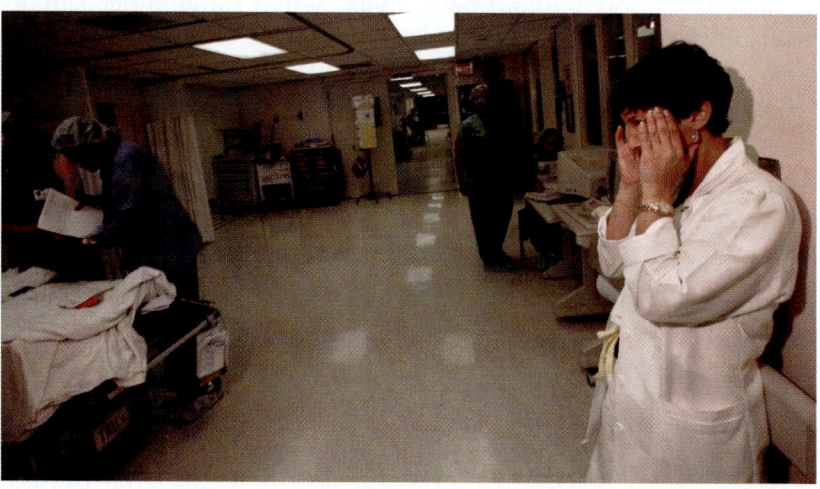

Replace Stress-Inducing Thoughts with Stress-Busting Thoughts

What you say to yourself under your breath about stressful events can influence your adjustment to them. Do you react to disappointing events by blowing them out of proportion—treating them as utter disasters rather than as mere setbacks? Do you see events only in all-or-nothing, black-and-white terms—as either total successes or total failures? Do you place unrealistic expectations on yourself and then hold yourself accountable for failing to measure up? If you have thought patterns like these, you may benefit from replacing them with rational alternatives. Examples include: "This is a problem, not a catastrophe. I am a good problem-solver. I can find a solution to this problem."

We are better able to withstand stressful demands when we believe we are capable of handling them. If your self-confidence has been shaky, try to boost it by setting achievable goals for yourself and taking steps to accomplish them. Remind yourself to respond to disappointments as opportunities to learn from your mistakes, not as signs of inevitable failure.

Don't Keep Upsetting Feelings Bottled Up

Keeping disturbing thoughts and feelings under wraps may place stressful demands on your autonomic nervous system, which in turn may weaken your immune system and make you more vulnerable to physical illness. Expressing your feelings about stressful or traumatic events may have positive effects on your emotional and physical health. In particular, consider writing down your feelings in a journal or sharing them with a trusted person or a helping professional.

Control Type A Behavior

People with the Type A behavior pattern place additional stressful demands on themselves by attempting to accomplish as much as possible in as little time as possible. Though it may not be feasible (or even desirable) to turn "hares" into "tortoises," researchers find that such people can learn to modify their Type A behavior, such as by reducing their sense of time urgency (Friedman & Ulmer, 1984). Here are some behavioral changes that may prove helpful, even to people who are not bona fide Type A's:

- *Take things slower.* Slow down your walking pace. Enjoy looking at your surroundings rather than rushing past them. Bear in mind that posted speed limits are the maximum speeds you are permitted to drive, not the minimum.

- *Read books for enjoyment.* Spend time reading enjoyable books—perhaps that latest techno-thriller or romance novel, but not one designed to help you climb the corporate ladder.

- *Leave your computer at home.* Don't bring a laptop or other work-related gadgets with you on vacation or when visiting friends.

- *Avoid rushing through your meals.* Don't wolf down your food. Take time to talk to your family members or dining companions.

- *Engage in enjoyable activities.* Go to the movies, visit art galleries and museums, or attend the theater or concerts. Give yourself a break from the stressful demands of daily life.

Reducing Type A Behavior What can you do to reduce Type A behavior?

- *Develop relaxing interests.* Daily stress is more manageable when you make it a practice to engage in some pleasant events every day. Choose activities you truly enjoy, not simply those that are preferred by others. Take up a hobby or pursue an interest that can help you unwind.

- *Set realistic daily goals.* Don't overschedule your activities or impose unrealistic demands on yourself. Lighten up.

Hostility, a component of the Type A behavior profile, is associated with quickness to anger. Suggestions for controlling anger are discussed in Chapter 8 (pp. 290–291).

In sum, stress is an inescapable part of life. But handling stress more effectively can help you keep it at a manageable level and tone down your body's alarm reaction. Stress may be a fact of life, but it is a fact you can learn to live with.

TYING IT TOGETHER

Health psychology is the study of interrelationships between psychology and physical health. Stress is a psychological factor that investigators link to a wide range of physical and mental health problems (Module 13.1). But stress is not the only psychosocial variable linked to physical health problems; connections have also been found between unhealthy behaviors or lifestyles (e.g., smoking, high-fat diets, excessive sun exposure, and lack of physical activity) and risks of serious, chronic diseases such as heart disease and cancer, as well as sexually transmitted diseases (Module 13.2). By learning stress-management skills, we can learn to keep stress at a manageable level and take the distress out of stress (Module 13.3).

SUMMING UP: Q&A

Stress: What It Is and What It Does to the Body (Module 13.1)

What is health psychology?

- Health psychology is the branch of psychology that studies interrelationships between psychological factors and health.

What is stress, and what are the major sources of stress?

- The term *stress* refers to pressures and demands to adjust or adapt.
- The major sources of stress include daily hassles, life changes, frustration, conflict, Type A behavior pattern, traumatic events, and pressures of acculturation faced by immigrant groups.

How does the body respond to stress?

- Stress activates a general pattern of physiological responses, described by Selye as the general adaptation syndrome, or GAS. GAS consists of three stages: the alarm stage, the resistance stage, and the exhaustion stage.

How does stress affect the immune system?

- Persistent or severe stress can impair the functioning of the immune system, leaving us more susceptible to many illnesses, including the common cold.

What psychological factors buffer the effects of stress?

- Psychological buffers against stress include social support, self-efficacy, perceptions of controllability and predictability, psychological hardiness, and optimism.

Psychological Factors in Physical Illness (Module 13.2)

How are psychological factors linked to the health of our heart and circulatory system?

- Behaviors such as smoking, inactivity, and adopting an unhealthy diet, and psychological traits such as hostility, are associated with an increased risk of heart disease.

What roles do psychological factors play in the development of cancer?

- Unhealthy behaviors, such as smoking and consumption of a high-fat diet, are linked to an increased risk of various forms of cancer.

How can we protect ourselves from sexually transmitted diseases?

- We can reduce our chances of contracting an STD by avoiding unsafe sexual and injection practices.

Application: Taking the Distress Out of Stress (Module 13.3)

What are some ways of taking the distress out of stress?

- Ways of taking the distress out of stress include maintaining stress at a tolerable level, developing relaxation skills, taking care of your body, gathering information, expanding your social network, preventing burnout, replacing stress-inducing thoughts and beliefs with rational alternatives, expressing negative feelings, controlling Type A behavior, and developing anger-management skills.

Key Terms

health psychology *(p. 450)*
stress *(p. 450)*
distress *(p. 450)*
stressors *(p. 451)*
hassles *(p. 451)*
chronic stress *(p. 451)*
frustration *(p. 453)*
conflict *(p. 453)*
posttraumatic stress disorder (PTSD) *(p. 455)*
Type A behavior pattern (TABP) *(p. 455)*
acculturative stress *(p. 457)*
general adaptation syndrome (GAS) *(p. 459)*
alarm stage *(p. 459)*

fight-or-flight response *(p. 459)*
resistance stage *(p. 459)*
exhaustion stage *(p. 460)*
corticotrophin-releasing hormone (CRH) *(p. 461)*
adrenocorticotrophic hormone (ACTH) *(p. 461)*
adrenal glands *(p. 461)*
adrenal cortex *(p. 461)*
corticosteroids *(p. 461)*
adrenal medulla *(p. 461)*
immune system *(p. 462)*
lymphocytes *(p. 462)*
antigens *(p. 462)*
antibodies *(p. 462)*

vaccination *(p. 462)*
psychological hardiness *(p. 464)*
arteries *(p. 466)*
coronary heart disease (CHD) *(p. 466)*
atherosclerosis *(p. 466)*
plaque *(p. 466)*
arteriosclerosis *(p. 466)*
heart attack *(p. 467)*
malignant tumors *(p. 470)*
basal cell carcinoma *(p. 471)*
melanoma *(p. 471)*
sexually transmitted disease (STD) *(p. 472)*

Thinking Critically About Psychology

Based on your reading of this chapter, answer the following questions. Then, to evaluate your progress in developing critical thinking skills, compare your answers to the sample answers found in Appendix A.

Every now and then we hear claims touting some miracle drug, vitamin, hormone, or alternative therapy that promises to enhance health and vitality, cure or prevent disease, or even reverse the effects of aging. Some of these claims are outright hoaxes. Others take promising scientific leads and exaggerate or distort the evidence. Still others tout psychological therapies as cures for medical conditions on the basis of unsupported testimonials. Although the federal watchdog agency, the Food and Drug Administration (FDA), regulates health claims for drugs and medications, many of the substances found in your health-food store or neighborhood supermarket purporting to have disease-preventive or anti-aging effects are classified as foods and are not regulated as drugs. It's basically a case of "buyer beware."

Critical thinkers do not take health claims at face value. They recognize that alternative therapies and health care products may not work as promised and could even be harmful. Another concern is that people advocating particular therapies may have a vested interest in getting consumers to try their services or use their products, and may play fast and loose with the truth.

Use your critical thinking skills to read between the lines in evaluating health claims. What do you think these claims for products found in your neighborhood health store actually mean?

- Designed to enhance vitality and well-being.
- Promotes muscle growth.
- Recommended by leading physicians.
- Backed by advanced research.
- Super-charge your metabolism!

Answers to Concept Check Questions

Module 13.1: 1. (a) pressures or demands placed upon an organism to adjust or adapt to its environment, (b) when stress reaches a level that taxes our ability to cope effectively; 2. (a) ii, (b) iii, (c) i, (d) iv; 3. alarm stage; 4. social support, self-efficacy, perceptions of control and predictability, psychological hardiness, and optimism; 5. a; 6. d.   **Module 13.2:** 1. (a) iv, (b) iii, (c) ii, (d) i; 2. (a) age, gender, heredity, lack of physical activity, obesity, high cholesterol, diabetes, high blood pressure, (b) all but the first three can potentially be controlled; 3. a; 4. Two-thirds, smoking and diet; 5. d.

Social Psychology

DID YOU KNOW THAT . . .

- Revealing too much about yourself when first meeting someone can convey a negative impression? (p. 482)

- The Japanese are more likely than Americans to attribute their successes to luck or fate than to themselves? (p. 485)

- People tend to believe that attractive people have more desirable personality traits than unattractive people? (p. 492)

- At least thirty-eight people in a quiet urban neighborhood heard the screams of a woman who was viciously attacked by a knife-wielding assailant but did nothing? (p. 494)

- The origins of prejudice may be traced back to ancestral times? (p. 498)

- Most people who participated in a famous but controversial study administered what they believed to be painful and dangerous electric shocks to other people when instructed to do so by the experimenter? (p. 507)

A stranger faints on a crowded street as you pass by. Several people gather about the fallen person. Do you offer assistance or continue on your way?

You participate in a psychology experiment in which you and other members of a group are asked to determine which of two lines is longer. One person after another chooses the line that looks shorter to you. Now comes your turn. Do you go along with the crowd or stand your ground and select the line you think is longer?

A man and a woman are standing on a street corner speaking privately in Italian. The man hands the woman an envelope, which she puts in her handbag. What do you make of this interaction? Do you suppose it was a lover's note that was passed between them? Or do you think it was an exchange related to Mafia business?

You volunteer for a psychology experiment on the effects of electric shock on learning. You are instructed to administer to another participant what you are told are painful shocks each time the other participant gives a wrong answer. At first you refuse. But the experimenter insists you continue and tells you the shocks will cause no serious harm to the other participant. You would still refuse such an unreasonable demand, wouldn't you?

These questions fall within the domain of *social psychology*, the branch of psychology that deals with how our thoughts, feelings, and behaviors are influenced by our social interactions with others and the culture in which we live. In this chapter we explore how we perceive others in our social environment, how we relate to them, and how we are influenced by them. We consider what social psychologists have learned about these social processes, beginning with how we perceive others and how our perceptions of others influence our behavior. ■

MODULE 14.1 Perceiving Others

- **What is social perception?**
- **What are the major influences on first impressions, and why do first impressions often become lasting impressions?**
- **What role do cognitive biases play in the judgments we make about the causes of behavior?**
- **What are attitudes, and how are they acquired?**
- **How are attitudes related to behavior?**
- **What is cognitive dissonance theory?**
- **How do persuasive appeals lead to attitude change?**

In Chapter 3 we explored the ways in which we perceive the physical world of objects and shapes. As we turn to the study of **social psychology**, we focus on the ways in which we perceive the social world, composed of the people whom we see and with whom we interact in our daily lives. **Social perception** is the process by which we come to form an understanding of our social environment based on observations of others, personal experiences, and information we receive. In this section we examine three major aspects of social perception: forming impressions of others, making sense of the causes of our own and other people's behaviors, and developing attitudes that incline us to respond to people, issues, and objects in positive or negative ways.

Impression Formation: Why First Impressions Count So Much

Impression formation is the process by which we form an opinion or impression of another person. We tend to form first impressions quickly. First impressions count so much because they tend to be long-lasting and difficult to change; they also affect how we relate to people who are the objects of these impressions. Suppose you meet a number of people at a party or social gathering. Within the first few minutes of talking to them—perhaps even the first few seconds—you begin forming impressions that will be hard to change. Even before you begin talking to someone, you have already started to size up their surface characteristics, such as how they look and how they dress. Let us examine some of the factors that influence impression formation, including personal disclosure, social schemas, stereotyping, and self-fulfilling prophecies.

Personal Disclosure: Going Beyond Name, Rank, and Serial Number

We generally form more favorable impressions of people who are willing to disclose personal information about themselves. But revealing too much too soon can lead to a negative impression. People who disclose too much about themselves in the first stages of a social relationship tend to be perceived as less secure, less mature, and more poorly adjusted than those who are more restrained regarding what they say about themselves. Cultural differences also come into play in determining how much disclosure is deemed acceptable. People in East Asian societies, such as China and Japan, tend to disclose less about themselves than do people in the West (Nevid & Sta. Maria, 1999).

Cultural Differences in Self-Disclosure People from East Asian cultures are typically more reserved about disclosing personal information when meeting new people.

 **CONCEPT 14.1**
Our preconceived ideas influence the impressions we form of people even before we meet them.

CONCEPT 14.2
The amount of personal information we disclose affects the impressions that other people form of us.

social psychology The subfield in psychology that deals with how our thoughts, feelings, and behaviors are influenced by our social interactions with others.

social perception The processes by which we form impressions, make judgments, and develop attitudes about the people and events that constitute our social world.

Impressions as Social Schemas: Why Early Impressions Are Hard to Budge

An impression is a type of **social schema**, a mental image or representation we use to understand our social environment. We filter information about others through these schemas. One reason that first impressions tend to be long-lasting is that we filter new information about people through the earlier impressions or social schemas we formed about them (Hamilton & Sherman, 1994). So if someone about whom we hold a favorable impression (schema) does something to upset us, we're more likely to look for extenuating factors that explain the person's behavior ("He must be having a bad day") than to alter our existing impression. On the other hand, when we hold a negative impression of someone, we're more likely to ignore or explain away any positive information we receive about that person.

Stereotyping: Judging Groups, Not Individuals

We all have preconceived ideas about groups of people, called **stereotypes**, that influence our first impressions (Aronson, Wilson, & Akert, 2004). Stereotypes are sets of beliefs about the characteristics, attributes, and behaviors of members of a particular group or category. For example, we might hold a stereotype that fraternity members are big drinkers or that people who wear glasses are intelligent.

Stereotypes influence first impressions. Recall the couple speaking in Italian on the street corner. Did you think they were engaged in a romantic exchange or in illegal, Mafia-related activities? Both interpretations are based on stereotypes of Italians as romantic or crooks (Lepore & Brown, 1997). As the example suggests, stereotypes may include positive attributes (romantic in this case) or negative attributes (criminal). However, stereotypes about members of other social or ethnic groups are usually more negative than those about members of one's own group.

Social psychologists believe that stereotyping is a normal cognitive tendency, a kind of cognitive shorthand that simplifies the process of making social judgments (Nelson, 2002). Upon meeting someone for the first time, we automatically classify the person as belonging to a particular group or category. Stereotypes allow us to more efficiently use stored information about other groups instead of expending cognitive resources to evaluate each individual member of the groups we encounter (Hilton & von Hippel, 1996). Efficient, perhaps—but not necessarily accurate.

Stereotyping on the basis of race, ethnicity, gender, age, disability, body weight, or sexual orientation leads us to make inferences about people that may prove to be unfounded as we get to know them as individuals. Yet there may be a "kernel of truth" in some commonly held stereotypes (e.g., that Mexicans enjoy spicy food) (Gordon, 2000; Judd & Park, 1993). Still, stereotypes are exaggerated and overgeneralized concepts that fail to take individual differences into account. Moreover, once stereotypes are formed, they are resistant to change in the face of new information.

Stereotyping can damage group relations and be used to justify social inequities. For example, beliefs that Blacks lack the ability to govern themselves were long used as a justification for colonial rule in Africa by European powers. And stereotypes of obese people as lazy and undisciplined may lead employers to pass them over for jobs or promotions.

Self-Fulfilling Prophecies: What Goes Around Comes Around

When you form an initial impression of someone, you may act toward the person in a way that mirrors your impression. Let's say you form an impression of someone as unfriendly. This belief can become a type of **self-fulfilling prophecy** if it leads you to be somewhat standoffish when interacting with the person and he or

CONCEPT 14.3
By filtering information through existing social schemas, first impressions become lasting impressions.

impression formation The process of developing an opinion or impression of another person.

social schema A mental image or representation that we use to understand our social environment.

stereotypes The tendency to characterize all members of a particular group as having certain characteristics in common.

self-fulfilling prophecy An expectation that helps bring about the outcome that is expected.

she responds in kind. Self-fulfilling prophecies may also lead to underperformance in school. Teachers who expect students to do poorly may convey their lower expectations to their students. Expecting less of themselves, the students may apply less than their best efforts, leading them to underperform (Jussim & Eccles, 1992).

Attributions: Why the Pizza Guy Is Late

The pizza guy delivers your pizza thirty minutes late. Do you believe the guy was loafing on the job or that some external influence (traffic, orders backing up) caused the delay? What about the times *you* arrive late? Are you likely to reach the same judgments about your own behavior as you do when explaining the behavior of others?

An **attribution** is a personal explanation of the causes of behavior or events we observe. When interpreting our social world, we act like personal scientists who seek to understand the underlying causes of events we observe. We tend to explain these events by attributing them to either dispositional causes or situational causes. **Dispositional causes** are internal factors, such as internal traits, needs, or personal choices of the person ("actor"). **Situational causes** are external or environmental factors, such as pressures or demands imposed upon the actor. Saying that the pizza guy is late because he is a loafer invokes a dispositional cause. Saying he is late because several other pies were in the oven at the time invokes a situational cause. Social psychologists have found that attributions can be affected by certain cognitive biases, such as the *fundamental attribution error,* the *actor-observer effect,* and the *self-serving bias.*

Fundamental Attribution Error

Social psychologist Fritz Heider (1958) proposed that people tend to focus more on the behavior of others than on the circumstances in which the behavior occurs. Consequently, they tend to overlook situational influences when explaining other people's behavior. The **fundamental attribution error** is a term that social psychologists use to describe the tendency to attribute behavior to internal causes, such as traits like intelligence or laziness, without regard to the situational influences that come to bear on people.

Note a cross-cultural difference. People in individualistic cultures like the United States and Canada are more likely to commit fundamental attribution errors than those in collectivist cultures like China and Japan (Kitayama et al., 2003). Tendencies to commit the fundamental attribution error are generally-weaker in collectivist cultures such as China and Japan than in individualistic cultures such as the United States in the West (Kitayama et al., 2003). Collectivist cultures tend to emphasize external causes of behavior that stem from the social environment, such as obligations imposed on people (Choi et al., 2003). Individualistic cultures, by contrast, emphasize individuality and autonomy of the self. People from these cultures are quicker to assume that behavior results from something inside us—our individual personalities, attitudes, or motives.

The Actor-Observer Effect

When people commit the fundamental attribution error, they ignore the external circumstances that influence the behavior of others. But do we commit the same error when explaining our own behavior? Apparently not. Social psychologists have identified another type of cognitive bias that comes into play, called the **actor-observer effect**. The actor-observer effect is the tendency to attribute the causes of one's own behavior to external factors, such as situational demands, while attributing other people's behavior to internal causes or dispositions (Jones, 1990; Jones & Nisbett, 1971). If you do poorly on an exam, you're likely to attribute your poor performance to external causes—the exam wasn't fair, you didn't

attribution An assumption about the causes of behavior or events.

dispositional causes Causes relating to the internal characteristics or traits of individuals.

situational causes Causes relating to external or environmental events.

fundamental attribution error The tendency to attribute behavior to internal causes without regard to situational influences.

actor-observer effect The tendency to attribute the causes of one's own behavior to situational factors while attributing the causes of other people's behavior to internal factors or dispositions.

have time to study, the material you studied wasn't on the exam, and so on. But when someone else does poorly, you're likely to think the person lacked the ability to do well or was too lazy to study.

Heider (1958) attributed the actor-observer effect to differences in perspective. As an actor, you look outward to the environment, so the situation engulfs your view. But your perspective as an observer is engulfed by your view of the actor within the situation.

Self-Serving Bias

A specific type of attributional bias occurring in performance situations is the **self-serving bias**—the tendency to attribute personal successes to internal or dispositional causes and personal failures to external or situational causes. In other words, people tend to take credit for their successes but to disclaim responsibility for their failures (Weiner, 1992). If you achieve a good grade on an exam, you are likely to attribute it to your ability or talent (an internal attribution). Yet you are likely to attribute a poor grade to an external cause beyond your control, such as too little time to study or unfair questions on the exam. Self-serving biases buttress our self-esteem (Kitayama et al., 1997).

The self-serving bias is widespread in Western cultures, such as the United States and Canada. But it occurs much less frequently in East Asian cultures, such as Japan, China, and Taiwan (DeAngelis, 2003; Heine et al., 2001). Unlike Americans, the Japanese tend to attribute their successes to luck and their failures to lack of ability or talent. The self-serving bias may be embedded within a cultural ethic in the United States and other individualistic Western cultures that value the protection of self-esteem (Markus & Kitayama, 1991). The opposite tendency (valuing self-criticism and humility) is found more often in collectivist cultures, such as China or Japan (Oyserman, Coon, & Kemmelmeier, 2002). In these cultures, people are more attuned to their responsibilities to the group than to their individuality or the need to enhance their individual self-esteem. Blaming oneself for personal failure affirms one's responsibility to the social group and the need to work harder to improve one's performance in the future (Fiske et al., 1998; Kitayama et al., 1997; Nisbett, 2003).

Attitudes: How Do You Feel About . . . ?

What are your attitudes toward gun control laws, sport utility vehicles (SUVs), and vegetarian diets? An **attitude** is an evaluation or judgment of either liking or disliking a person, object, or social issue. Social psychologists conceptualize attitudes as consisting of three components: (1) *cognitions* (sets of beliefs), (2) *emotions* (feelings of liking or disliking), and (3) *behaviors* (inclinations to act positively or negatively) (Crites, Fabrigar, & Petty, 1994). For example, you may hold favorable or unfavorable views about SUVs, feel positively or negatively toward them, and be either inclined or disinclined to purchase one if you were shopping for a vehicle (see Figure 14.1).

The importance we ascribe to attitudes is a function of their personal relevance. Our attitudes toward sport utility vehicles (love them, hate them) will be more important to us if we happen to be considering buying one. Yet it's also true that the more often we express a particular attitude, the more important it is likely to become to us (Roese & Olson, 1994).

Sources of Attitudes

Our attitudes are acquired from many sources in our social environment—our parents, teachers, peers, personal experiences, and media sources such as newspapers, television, and movies. Not surprisingly, people from similar backgrounds

CONCEPT 14.6
The actor-observer effect leads us to attribute the behavior of others to dispositional internal causes but to explain our own behavior in terms of the situational demands we face in the environment.

CONCEPT 14.7
Another type of cognitive bias, the self-serving bias, comes into play in accounting for the tendency of people to take credit for their successes but to explain away their failures.

CONCEPT 14.8
The self-serving bias is widespread in Western cultures but virtually absent in some Eastern cultures.

THINK *About It*

Learning from Mistakes

Do you have a tendency to take credit for your successes and explain away your failures? How might the self-serving bias prevent you from learning from your mistakes and taking appropriate steps to prevent them in the future?

CONCEPT 14.9
To social psychologists, attitudes are judgments of liking or disliking that can be conceptualized in terms of three components: cognitions, emotions, and behaviors.

self-serving bias   The tendency to take credit for our accomplishments and to explain away our failures or disappointments.

attitude   A positive or negative evaluation of persons, objects, or issues.

Figure 14.1   Attitudes
The attitudes we hold consist of cognitive, emotional, and behavioral components.

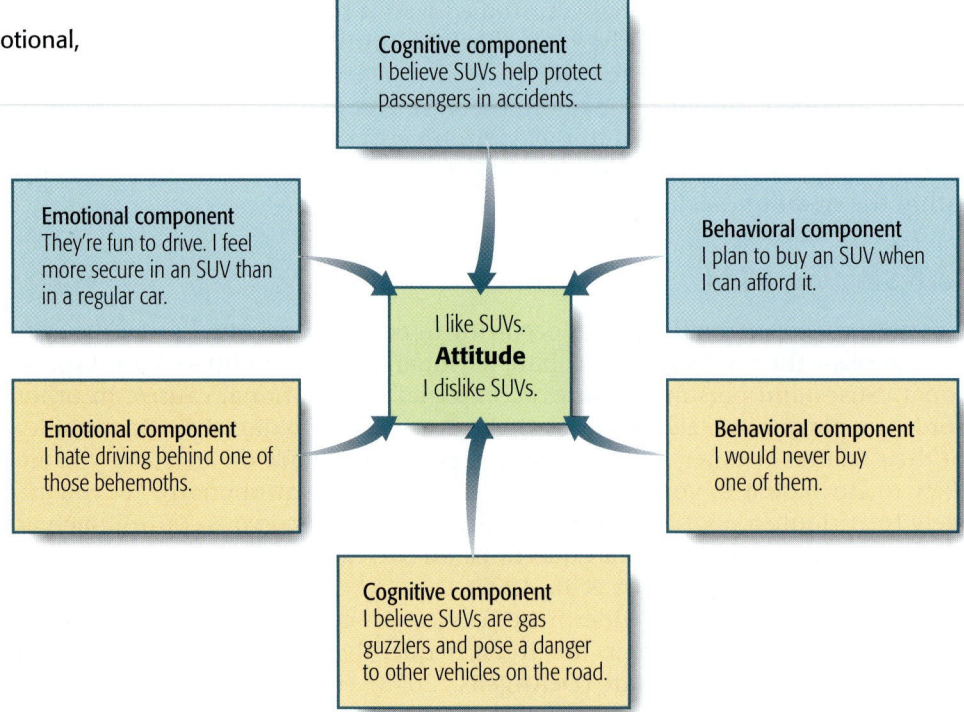

Cognitive component
I believe SUVs help protect passengers in accidents.

Emotional component
They're fun to drive. I feel more secure in an SUV than in a regular car.

Behavioral component
I plan to buy an SUV when I can afford it.

I like SUVs.
Attitude
I dislike SUVs.

Emotional component
I hate driving behind one of those behemoths.

Behavioral component
I would never buy one of them.

Cognitive component
I believe SUVs are gas guzzlers and pose a danger to other vehicles on the road.

CONCEPT 14.10
Our social environments shape the attitudes we develop, but research points to possible genetic influences as well.

tend to hold similar attitudes. Yet evidence also points to a possible genetic contribution (Abrahamson, Baker, & Caspi, 2002; Olson et al., 2001). Studies of twins reared apart show a surprising degree of shared attitudes on a range of issues that cannot be explained by a common environmental influence. People do not inherit a gene or genes for a particular attitude, such as liking or disliking SUVs. Rather, heredity works indirectly by influencing intelligence, temperaments, or personality traits that make people more or less likely to develop certain attitudes (Petty, Wegener, & Fabrigar, 1997). But evidence also suggests that genetic factors are less important determinants of attitudes than environmental influences (DeAngelis, 2004).

Attitudes and Behavior: Not as Strong a Link as You Might Expect

CONCEPT 14.11
Though attitudes predispose us to act in certain ways, they are not very strong predictors of behavior.

Attitudes may not carry over into behavior (Polinko & Popovich, 2001). You may hold favorable attitudes toward environmental issues but still purchase a high-performance car that guzzles gas. Or you may have a favorable attitude toward a particular product but purchase a competing product. Overall, attitudes are only modestly related to behavior (Eagly & Chaiken, 1998; Kraus, 1995). The lack of consistency reflects many factors, especially situational constraints. We may have an inclination to act in a certain way but be unable to carry out the action because of the particular demands we face in that particular situation. For example, you may hold a positive attitude toward a specific charity but be unable to make a contribution to the latest fund drive because you are running short of cash or need the money for another important purpose. Under other conditions, however, attitudes are more strongly linked to behavior—such as when the attitudes are more stable and held with a greater degree of confidence or certainty, when they relate specifically to the behavior at hand, when the person is free to perform or not perform the behavior, and when the attitude can be more readily recalled from memory (e.g., Kraus, 1995; Olson & Maio, 2003; Petty & Wegener, 1998).

Cognitive Dissonance: Maintaining Consistency Between Your Attitudes and Behavior

What happens when your actions deviate from your attitudes? Say you believe in protecting the environment but buy a gas-guzzling car. Are you likely to change your behavior (buy a different car)? Or would you change your beliefs, perceptions, or attitudes (*cognitions*) about the importance of protecting the environment or the risks posed by gas-guzzlers? In other words, how would you iron-out the kinks between your cognitions and your behavior? Or would you even bother?

According to **cognitive dissonance theory**, inconsistencies between attitudes and behavior lead to a state of dissonance, or emotional discomfort (Festinger, 1957). This uncomfortable state motivates people to change their attitudes or behavior to make them more compatible (Aronson, Wilson, & Akert, 2004). There are several ways people can reduce dissonance. They can change their behavior to fit their attitudes or beliefs, change their attitudes or beliefs to fit their behavior, attempt to explain away any inconsistencies between their behavior and their attitudes or beliefs, or simply ignore any discrepancies. For example, smokers who believe that smoking causes cancer but continue to smoke may reduce cognitive dissonance by altering their behavior (quitting smoking), altering their belief (adopting the belief that smoking isn't really all that harmful), or using a form of rationalization to explain away the inconsistency ("Cancer doesn't run in my family"). Yet perhaps the most common way of reducing dissonance is not to change either beliefs or behavior but simply to ignore inconsistencies until they fade away ("I'll worry about my smoking when I get older") (Newby-Clark, McGregor, & Zanna, 2002; Pittman, 1998). Figure 14.2 illustrates some ways of reducing cognitive dissonance. As we'll see in Module 14.4, salespersons, advertisers, fundraisers, and others who try to influence us often use strategies that seek to take advantage of our need for consistency in our behavior and attitudes.

CONCEPT 14.12
Cognitive dissonance theory holds that people are motivated to reconcile discrepancies between their behavior and their cognitions.

Figure 14.2   Ways of Reducing Cognitive Dissonance

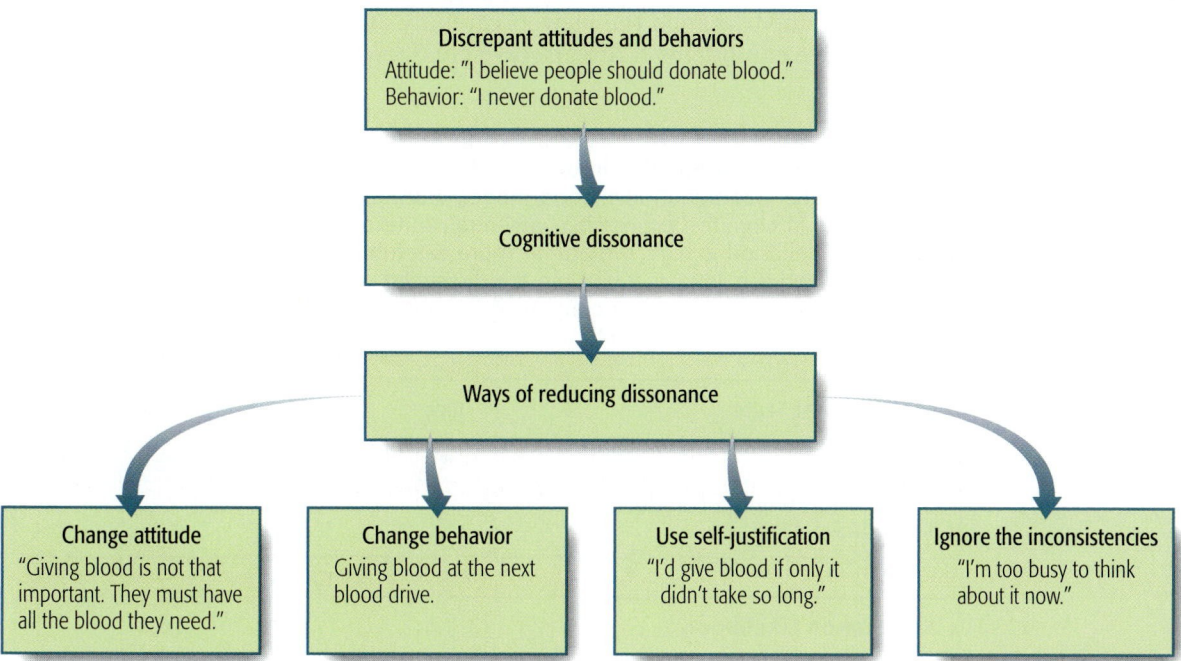

cognitive dissonance theory   The belief that people are motivated to resolve discrepancies between their behavior and their attitudes, beliefs, or perceptions.

Persuasion: The Fine Art of Changing People's Minds

We are constantly bombarded with messages attempting to persuade us to change our beliefs and attitudes. Commercials on radio and TV, and advertisements in newspapers and magazines, attempt to persuade us to adopt more favorable attitudes toward advertised products and to purchase them. Political candidates and political action groups seek to sway us to support their candidacies and causes. Doctors, religious leaders, teachers, friends, and family members regularly urge us to change our behaviors, beliefs, and attitudes in ways they believe would be beneficial to us.

Short of secluding ourselves in an isolated cabin in the woods, we can hardly avoid persuasive appeals. But how do such appeals lead to attitude change? And what factors are likely to increase their effectiveness?

The Elaboration Likelihood Model: Two Pathways to Persuasion

A leading model of attitude change is the **elaboration likelihood model (ELM)** (Petty & Wegener, 1998). According to this model, people are more likely to carefully evaluate ("elaborate") a persuasive message when their motivational state is high (i.e., when they are willing to exert the mental effort needed to evaluate the message) and when they possess the skills or knowledge needed to evaluate the information (see Figure 14.3).

When evaluation likelihood is high, attitude change occurs via a *central route* of processing information, whereby people carefully evaluate the content of the message. When elaboration likelihood is low, attitude change occurs through a *peripheral route* of cognitive processing, whereby people focus on cues not centrally related to the content of the message. Let us use the example of a televised political debate. Assume that viewers are alert, well informed about the issues, and interested in the views held by the candidates. Under these conditions, elaboration likelihood is high and attitude change is likely to occur through a central processing route by which the viewers carefully evaluate the arguments made by the respective candidates. Conversely, if the viewers are distracted, fatigued, or

CONCEPT 14.13

According to the elaboration likelihood model, attitude change occurs through either a central processing route or a peripheral processing route.

PsychAssist: Elaboration Likelihood Model of Attitude Change

elaboration likelihood model (ELM)
A theoretical model that posits two channels by which persuasive appeals lead to attitude change: a central route and a peripheral route.

Figure 14.3 Elaboration Likelihood Model
According to the elaboration likelihood model, attitude change occurs through one of two routes of cognitive processing—a central route or a peripheral route. When elaboration likelihood is high, we attend more carefully to the content of the message itself. When it is low, as when we are distracted or disinterested, we attend to peripheral cues unrelated to the content of the message.

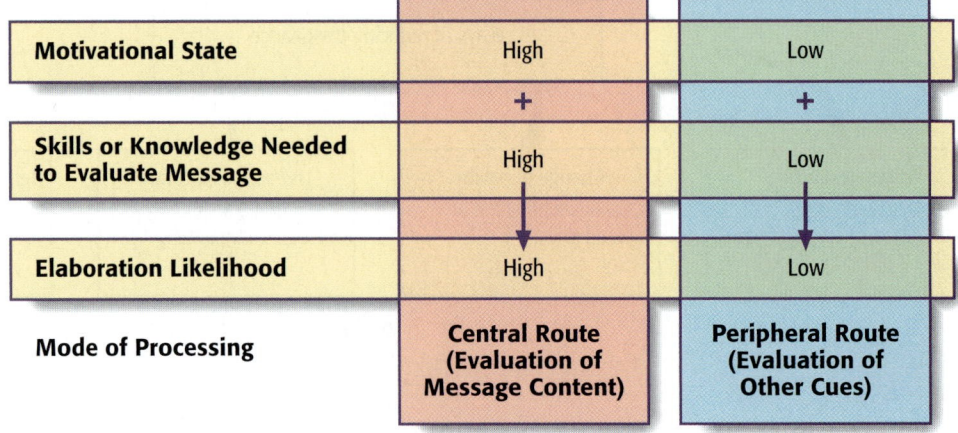

	High	Low
Motivational State	High	Low
	+	+
Skills or Knowledge Needed to Evaluate Message	High	Low
Elaboration Likelihood	High	Low
Mode of Processing	**Central Route** (Evaluation of Message Content)	**Peripheral Route** (Evaluation of Other Cues)

uninterested in the issues, they are not likely to carefully evaluate each candidate's message. Attitude change occurring under these conditions is likely to be based on peripheral cues that are not directly related to the content of the candidate's message, such as the physical attractiveness of the candidate. In other words, the viewers may be persuaded to endorse candidates on the basis of how they look in the debate rather than how they stand on the issues.

Advertisers often take advantage of the peripheral route of attitude change by using leading sports stars as commercial spokespersons. Celebrity endorsers needn't even mention the distinctive qualities of the product. Just using the product or wearing it may be sufficient to convey the message that the advertiser wants to get across.

Variables Influencing Persuasion

Some persuasive appeals are more effective than others. Persuasion is influenced by many variables, including those relating to the source, the message, and the recipient (see Figure 14.4).

- *Source variables.* Source variables are features of the communicator who presents the message. Communicators are generally more persuasive when they are perceived as *credible* (knowledgeable and trustworthy), *likable* (attractive and personable), and *similar* to the receiver in key respects (e.g., a former substance abuser may be more successful in persuading current substance abusers to accept treatment than a person who has never abused drugs) (e.g., Petty & Wegener, 1998; Wilder, 1990).

- *Message variables.* First, presenting both sides of an argument is generally more effective than presenting only one side, so long as the communicator refutes the other side. Second, messages that run counter to the perceived interests of the communicator tend to be perceived as more credible. Not surprisingly, people paid great attention a few years ago when a member of the R. J. Reynolds family of tobacco growers spoke out on the dangers of smoking. Third, the more often we are exposed to a message, the more favorably we are likely to evaluate it, but only up to a point (Petty, Wegener, & Fabrigar, 1997). When the message is repeated often enough, people may come to believe it, whether or not it is true. But with further repetition, irritation and tedium begin to set in and acceptance of the message begins to decline (Petty & Wegener, 1998).

- *Recipient variables.* Though nobody is immune to persuasive appeals, some people are easier to persuade than others. Those of low intelligence or low self-confidence are generally more susceptible to persuasive appeals (Petty & Wegener, 1998). People also tend to be more receptive to persuasive messages when they are in a positive mood rather than a negative one (Park & Banaji, 2000). A good mood may motivate people to see things in a more positive light.

The major influences on social perception are reviewed in Concept Chart 14.1.

CONCEPT 14.14
The effectiveness of persuasive appeals is influenced by variables relating to the source, the message itself, and the recipient.

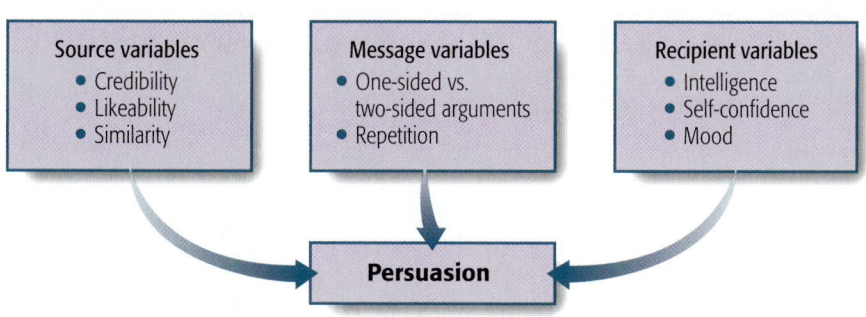

Source variables	Message variables	Recipient variables
• Credibility • Likeability • Similarity	• One-sided vs. two-sided arguments • Repetition	• Intelligence • Self-confidence • Mood

Persuasion

Figure 14.4   Getting Your Message Across: Factors in Persuasive Appeals
The effectiveness of persuasive appeals depends upon characteristics of the source of the message, the message itself, and the recipient of the message.

CONCEPT CHART 14.1
Perceiving Others

Topic	What It Is	Influences on Social Perception
Initial impressions	Initial evaluation (liking or disliking) of others	Initial impressions are influenced by physical appearance, attire, preexisting stereotypes, and degree of personal disclosure. They are difficult to dislodge because we tend to filter new information through them and because they may become self-fulfilling prophecies.
Attributions	Personal explanations of the causes of behavior	Attributional biases that affect social perception include the fundamental attribution error (the tendency to overemphasize internal or dispositional causes and to overlook external causes), the actor-observer effect (the tendency to explain other people's behavior in terms of their underlying personalities while explaining our own behavior in terms of situational demands), and the self-serving bias (the tendency to explain away our failures but take credit for our accomplishments).
Attitudes	Judgments of liking or disliking persons, objects, and issues	Attitudes are influenced by our social environment and possibly by genetic factors. They do not necessarily predict behavior. According to the elaboration likelihood model, attitude change occurs through either a central or peripheral route of processing, depending on the degree to which the message is elaborated. The effectiveness of persuasive appeals depends on source variables, recipient variables, and message variables.

MODULE 14.1 REVIEW

Perceiving Others

CONCEPT CHECK

1. Which of the following statements about first impressions is *incorrect*?
   a. First impressions are generally replaced by later in-depth, more accurate judgments.
   b. Preconceived ideas or stereotypes influence how we perceive others.
   c. Culture has an important bearing on how much information people disclose about themselves to others.
   d. Our behavior may elicit expected behaviors in others.

2. When we interpret a behavior or an event, we usually see it as due to either _____ or _____ causes.

3. The fundamental attribution error refers to
   a. underestimation of the influence of internal factors.
   b. underestimation of the influence of external factors.
   c. the tendency to attribute personal failure to external factors.
   d. the tendency to misinterpret the motives of others.

4. Give a social-psychological definition of the term *attitude*.

5. Discrepancies between behavior and attitudes may produce an unpleasant state of tension called _____.

6. Match the following terms with the appropriate descriptions: (a) peripheral processing route; (b) source variable(s); (c) message variable(s); (d) recipient variable(s).
   i.   the tendency of repetition to lead to more favorable evaluations
   ii. when people are not likely to carefully evaluate message contents
   iii. the relationship between low self-confidence and greater susceptibility to persuasion
   iv. credibility, likability, and similarity

MODULE 14.2   Relating to Others

- **What are the major determinants of attraction?**
- **What are the three components of love in Sternberg's model of love?**
- **What factors are linked to helping behavior?**
- **What is prejudice, and how does it develop?**
- **What can be done to reduce prejudice?**
- **What factors contribute to human aggression?**

Social psychologists are interested in how individuals relate to each other in their social environments. We may categorize ways of relating to others in terms of positive and negative interactions. Attraction, love, and helping are positive interactions. Negative ways of relating include prejudiced behavior and aggression. In this module we examine what psychologists have learned about these positive and negative ways of relating to others.

Attraction: Getting to Like (or Love) You

In nature, attraction is the tendency for two objects or bodies to be drawn toward each other, like the opposite poles of a magnet. In psychology, **attraction** describes feelings of liking others as well as having positive thoughts about them and inclinations to act positively toward them (Berscheid & Reis, 1998).

Attraction is not limited to romantic or erotic attraction (attraction toward a love interest). Social psychologists use the term more broadly to include other kinds of attraction as well, such as feelings of liking toward friends. Here we consider key determinants of attraction as well as that special type of attraction we associate with romantic love.

Determinants of Attraction

Psychologists have identified several key determinants of attraction, including similarity, physical attractiveness, proximity, and reciprocity.

Similarity   Like birds of a feather, we are generally attracted to people with whom we share similar values and attitudes (Angier, 2003b; Buston & Emlen, 2003). We also tend to like people who are similar to us in characteristics such as physical appearance, social class, race, height, musical tastes, and intelligence.

Why are people attracted to similar others? The mostly widely held view is that similarity is gratifying because each person in the relationship serves to validate, reinforce, and enhance the other's self-concept. If you echo my sentiments about movies, politics, and the like, I might feel better about myself.

Does this mean that relationships are doomed to fail if two people (roommates, friends, or lovers) differ in their attitudes, interests, or tastes? Not necessarily. For one thing, no two people are identical in all respects (fortunately so!). At least some common ground is necessary to anchor a relationship, but every successful relationship still requires compromise and accommodation to keep it afloat. Not surprisingly, the attitudes of dating partners tend to become more closely aligned over time (Davis & Rusbult, 2001).

Physical Attractiveness   We might think we are attracted romantically to people because of their inner qualities. However, evidence shows that it is the outer packaging, not the inner soul, that is the major determinant of initial

CONCEPT 14.15
Attraction is influenced by similarity, physical attractiveness, proximity, and reciprocity.

attraction   Feelings of liking for others, together with having positive thoughts about them and inclinations to act toward them in positive ways.

attraction (Berscheid & Reis, 1998). When investigators set up contrived dating situations in which male and female college students were randomly paired off and later asked to rate how attracted they were to their assigned partners, it turned out that partner physical attractiveness was the key reason for both attraction and interest in future dates (Hatfield & Sprecher, 1986).

Note some gender differences, however. Men typically place greater emphasis than women do on the physical attractiveness of potential partners (Buss, 1994; Feingold, 1991; Nevid, 1984). And in a study of Korean college students, the women were more interested in the education, jobs, and family of origin of prospective mates, whereas the men placed greater emphasis on the physical appearance of prospective partners (Brown, 1994).

Not only are people attracted to pretty packages, but they also tend to adopt the stereotype that "what is beautiful is also good" (Berscheid & Reis, 1998), judging attractive people more favorably on many personality traits such as sociability, popularity, intelligence, persuasiveness, and psychological health (Eagly & Wood, 1991; Feingold, 1992; Langlois et al., 2000). Yet there are exceptions to the "beautiful is good" stereotype: Attractive people are typically judged to be more vain and less modest than their less attractive peers (Feingold, 1992).

Beauty may be in the eye of the beholder, but beholders tend to view beauty in highly similar ways. We tend to agree on whom we find attractive or not attractive. Faces having symmetrical features and a clear complexion are universally perceived as more attractive (Fink & Penton-Voak, 2002).

Evidence suggests that the ideal female face varies little across cultures (Langlois et al., 2000). In one study, investigators asked groups of White, Euro-American students and recently arrived Asian and Hispanic students to judge the attractiveness of photographs of Asian, Hispanic, Black, and White women (Cunningham et al., 1995). Judgments of physical beauty were generally consistent for photographs of members of the different groups. Faces rated as more attractive typically had such features as high cheekbones and eyebrows, widely spaced eyes, a small nose, thin cheeks, a large smile, a full lower lip, a small chin, and a fuller hairstyle. Both male and female raters tended to judge the same faces as attractive; they also tended to agree that faces of women with more feminine features were more attractive than those with more masculine features (Angier, 1998b). Yet perhaps surprisingly, both male and female raters generally found male faces with *more feminine features* to be more attractive. The more refined and delicate features of a Leonardo DiCaprio, for example, are preferred over the more squared-jawed, masculinized features of an Arnold Schwarzenegger (Angier, 1998b).

Although some features of physical beauty appear to be universal, cultural differences certainly exist (Buss & Kenrick, 1998). In certain African cultures, for

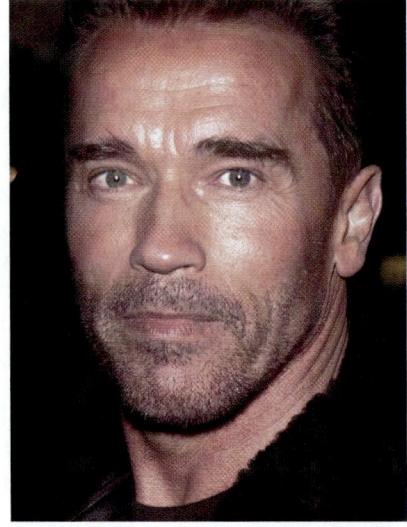

Sorry, Arnold When rating male faces, both men and women tend to rate those having more feminine features, such as the refined and delicate features of Leonardo DiCaprio, as more attractive than those with more masculinized, Arnold Schwarzenegger–type features.

example, feminine beauty is associated with such physical features as long necks and round, disk-like lips (Ford & Beach, 1951). Female plumpness is valued in some societies, while in others, including our own, the female ideal is associated with an unrealistic standard of thinness (see Chapter 8). Women themselves tend to associate curvaceousness with female attractiveness, but only so long as the curvaceous figure is lean and does not have large hips (Forestell, Humphrey, & Stewart, 2004). Slenderness in men is also valued in Western society, but social pressures to be thin are placed disproportionately on women (Franzoi & Herzog, 1987).

One explanation for why people who fall short of a physical ideal are likely to be saved from a lifetime of dinners-for-one is the **matching hypothesis**, the prediction that people will seek partners who are similar to themselves in physical attractiveness. Evidence generally supports the matching hypothesis and also shows that in mismatches, the less attractive partner usually compensates by having greater wealth or social position than the more attractive partner (Berscheid & Reis, 1998). The matching hypothesis applies to other characteristics as well. We tend to be attracted to mates who are similar to ourselves in personality, attitudes, and even body weight (Angier, 2003a; Buss, 1984; Schafer & Keith, 1990).

Proximity   Friendship patterns are strongly influenced by physical **proximity**. If you live in a college dormitory, your friends are more likely to live down the hall than across campus. Your earliest friends were probably children who lived next door or down the block from you.

Proximity increases the chances of interacting with others and getting to know them better, thus providing a basis for developing feelings of attraction toward them. Another explanation for the positive effects of proximity on attraction is the tendency for people to have more in common with people who live nearby or attend the same classes. Similarity in attitudes and background can increase feelings of liking.

Proximity can also increase negative attraction, or dislike. Repeated contact with someone you dislike may intensify negative feelings.

Reciprocity   **Reciprocity** is the tendency to like others who like us back. We typically respond in kind to people who compliment us, do us favors, or tell us how much they like us (Baron & Byrne, 2000; Berscheid & Reis, 1998). Reciprocal interactions build upon themselves, leading to feelings of liking. Yet we may be wary of people who compliment us too quickly or seem to like us too much before they get to know us. We may suspect that they want something from us or are not very discriminating.

Love: The Deepest Emotion

The subject of love has long intrigued and puzzled poets and philosophers. Only recently, however, have psychologists applied the scientific method to the study of love. Psychologists consider love to be both a motive (a need or want that drives us) and an emotion (or feeling state). According to a leading contemporary view of love, Robert Sternberg's (1988) triangular model, we can conceptualize love in terms of three basic components (see Figure 14.5):

1. *Intimacy,* the close bond and feeling of attachment between two people, including their desire to share their innermost thoughts and feelings

2. *Passion,* an intense sexual desire for the other person

3. *Decision/commitment,* the recognition that one loves the other person (decisional component) and is committed to maintaining the relationship through good times and bad (commitment component)

Decision and commitment need not go hand in hand. A person may acknowledge being in love but not be ready or willing to make a lasting commitment.

THINK
About It

Deconstructing Romantic Attraction

How might the factors determining attraction account for your choice of friends or romantic partners? To what extent is your attraction to others influenced by similarity of attitudes, backgrounds, physical attractiveness, proximity, and reciprocity?

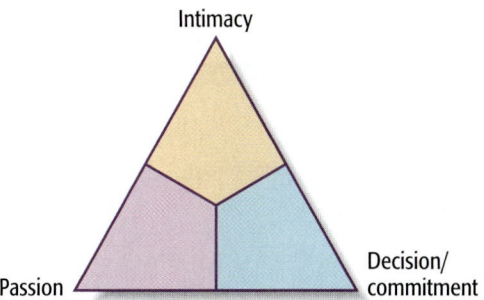

Figure 14.5   Sternberg's Triangular Model of Love
Sternberg conceptualizes love as a triangle with three components: intimacy, passion, and decision/commitment.

matching hypothesis   The belief that people tend to pair off with others who are similar to themselves in physical attractiveness and other characteristics.
proximity   Nearness or propinquity.
reciprocity   The principle that people tend to like others who like them back.

TABLE 14.1	Types of Love According to Sternberg's Triangular Model
Nonlove	A relationship in which all three components of love are absent. Most of our personal relationships are of this type—casual acquaintanceships that do not involve any elements of love.
Liking	A friendship in which intimacy is present but passion and decision/commitment are not.
Infatuation	A kind of "love at first sight," in which one experiences passionate desire for another person but in which there is neither intimacy nor decision/commitment.
Fatuous (foolish) love	The type of love associated with whirlwind romances and "quicky marriages," in which both passion and decision/commitment are present but intimacy is not.
Empty love	A kind of love characterized by the decision to love and a commitment to maintain the relationship but that lacks passion and intimacy. Stagnant relationships that no longer have the intimacy or physical attraction that once characterized them are of this type.
Romantic love	Love characterized by the combination of passion and intimacy but that lacks decision/commitment.
Consummate love	The complete measure of love, which combines passion, intimacy, and decision/commitment. Many of us strive to attain this type of love in our romantic relationships. Maintaining it is often harder than achieving it.
Companionate love	A kind of love that combines intimacy with decision/commitment. This kind of love often occurs in marriages in which passionate attraction between the partners has died down and been replaced by a kind of committed friendship.

Source: Adapted from Sternberg, 1988.

CONCEPT 14.16

Sternberg's triangular model of love proposes that different types of loving relationships can be characterized by different combinations of three basic components of love: intimacy, passion, and decision/commitment.

Consummate Love In Sternberg's model, consummate love combines intimacy, passion, and decision/commitment. Consummate love may not be as enduring as companionate love, which combines intimacy and decision/commitment but lacks passion. But even couples for whom the flames of passion have ebbed may occasionally stir the embers.

Sternberg believes that different combinations of these three basic components characterize different types of loving relationships (see Table 14.1). In his view, romantic love combines intimacy and passion but is lacking in decision/commitment. Romantic love may burn brightly but soon flicker out. On the other hand, it may develop into a more abiding form of love called consummate love, which combines all three components: intimacy, passion, and decision/commitment. Consummate love may be more of an ideal for many couples than an enduring reality. In companionate love, the type of love found in many long-term marriages, intimacy and commitment remain strong even though passion has ebbed.

Sternberg proposes that relationships are balanced when the love triangles of both partners are well matched or closely overlapping. But relationships may fizzle, rather than sizzle, when partners differ in these components. For example, one partner may want to make a lasting commitment to the relationship, while the other's idea of making a commitment is deciding to stay the night.

Next we turn to another positive way of relating to others—helping others in time of need. We begin with a tragic story of nonhelping in which a young woman was brutally attacked and people who heard her agonizing screams did nothing to help her.

Helping Behavior: Lending a Hand to Others in Need

Even now, some forty years after the 1964 murder of twenty-eight-year-old Kitty Genovese on a quiet street in Queens, New York, the shock remains. Kitty screamed for help as she was viciously attacked by an assailant who repeatedly stabbed her until she lay dying from her wounds. At least thirty-eight people living in the nearby apartment buildings heard her screams for help and did nothing. None came to her aid and only one person called the police some thirty minutes later, but too late to help her. Some witnesses looked out their windows in the direction of the commotion, but then went back to their dinners and television shows.

Why had no one helped? Is there something so callous in human nature that we would turn our backs on someone in desperate need of assistance? If so, how are we to explain the countless acts of simple kindness of people who selflessly help people in need, let alone the heroic acts of people who risk their lives in emergency situations to save others? Consider the heroic efforts of the firefighters and police officers who responded to the terrorist attack at the World Trade Center, many of whom lost their lives in a valiant attempt to save others. Many civilians at this site of tragedy also lost their lives as they stopped to help others escape the inferno. Clearly, the question is not whether people will help others in need but under what conditions they will help.

Helping is a form of **prosocial behavior**, or behavior that is beneficial to others. Psychologist C. Daniel Batson, a leading authority on helping, distinguishes between two types of motives that underlie helping behavior (Batson et al., 2002; Batson, & Powell, 2003). One type of helping arises from *altruistic* motives—the pure, unselfish desire to help others without expecting anything in return. But another type is based on self-centered motives, such as the desire to help someone in order to make oneself look good in the eyes of others or to avoid feeling guilty from failing to help. Batson believes that altruistic helping results from the helper's identification with the plight of the victim. By putting ourselves in the victim's position, we are able to empathize with the suffering of that person, which prompts us to take action. Batson's belief in pure altruism is not universally accepted by social psychologists (Shroeder et al., 1995). Some believe that all forms of helping benefit the helper to a certain extent.

Bystander Intervention: Deciding to Get Involved—Or Not

The decision-making model of helping behavior proposed by Bibb Latané & John Darley (1970) explains **bystander intervention** in terms of a decision-making process that can be broken down into a series of five decisions (see Figure 14.6). First, people must decide that a need for help exists. Second, they must decide that the situation is a clear emergency. Third, they must decide to assume personal responsibility for providing assistance. Fourth, they must decide what kind of help to give. Fifth, they must decide to implement this course of action.

Consider again the thirty-eight people who witnessed Kitty Genovese's murder but did nothing. Why didn't they help? The critical thinking exercise at the end of the chapter poses this question for you to answer. For now, however, let us examine what social psychologists have learned about the factors that affect helping behavior. Some of these factors may shed light on the inaction of those thirty-eight witnesses.

Influences on Helping

Many factors influence people's willingness to help, including the ambiguity of the situation, perceived cost, diffusion of responsibility, similarity, facial features, mood and gender, attributions of the cause of need, and social norms.

- *Situational ambiguity.* In ambiguous situations, as Latané and Darley would predict, people are much less likely to offer assistance than in situations involving a clear-cut emergency (Shotland & Heinold, 1985). They are also less likely to help in unfamiliar environments than in familiar ones (e.g., when they are in strange cities rather than in their hometowns).

- *Perceived cost.* The likelihood of helping increases as the perceived cost to ourselves declines (Simmons, 1991). We are more likely to lend our class notes to

CONCEPT 14.17
Helping may be motivated by both altruistic and self-centered motives.

CONCEPT 14.18
According to the decision-making model, bystander intervention depends on a series of decisions leading to intervention.

CONCEPT 14.19
Helping behavior is influenced by situational and individual factors and by social norms.

prosocial behavior   Behavior that benefits others.
bystander intervention   Helping a stranger in distress.

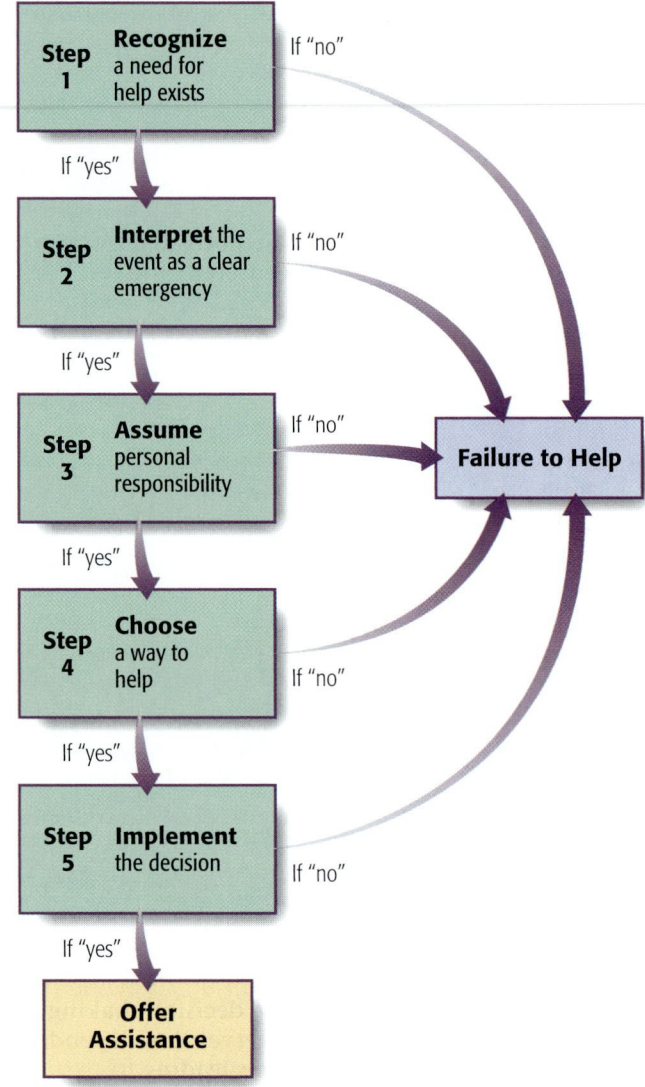

Figure 14.6 A Decision-Making Model of Bystander Intervention
The decision-making model of bystander intervention identifies five decision-making steps that precede either helping or failing to offer help.

Source: Latané & Darley, 1970.

someone whom we believe will return them than to a person who doesn't appear trustworthy.

- *Diffusion of responsibility.* The presence of others may *diffuse* the sense of individual responsibility. It follows that if you suddenly felt faint and were about to pass out on the street, you would be more likely to receive help if there are only a few passers-by present than if the street is crowded with pedestrians. With fewer people present, it becomes more difficult to point to the "other guy" as the one responsible for taking action. If everyone believes the other guy will act, then no one acts.

- *Similarity.* People are more willing to help others whom they perceive to be similar to themselves—people who share a common background and beliefs. They are even more likely to help others who dress the way they do than those in different attire (Cialdini & Trost, 1998). People also tend to be more willing to help their kin than to help nonkin (Gaulin & McBurney, 2001).

- *Facial features.* People with baby-faced features are more likely to elicit help than people with more mature facial features (Keating et al., 2003).

- *Mood and gender.* People are generally more willing to help others when they are in a good mood (Berkowitz, 1987). Despite changes in traditional gender roles, women in need are more likely than men in need to receive assistance from strangers (Benson, Karabenick, & Lerner, 1976).

- *Attributions of the cause of need.* People are much more likely to help others they judge to be innocent victims than those they believe have brought their problems on themselves (Batson, 1998). Thus, they may fail to lend assistance to homeless people and drug addicts whom they feel "deserve what they get."

- *Social norms.* **Social norms** prescribe behaviors that are expected of people in social situations (Batson, 1998). The social norm of "doing your part" in helping a worthy cause places a demand on people to help, especially in situations where their behavior is observed by others (Gaulin & McBurney, 2001). For example, people are more likely to make a charitable donation when they are asked to do so by a co-worker in full view of others than when they receive an appeal in the mail in the privacy of their own homes.

Let us now explore negative ways of relating to others, including prejudice and discrimination as well as human aggression.

Would You Help This Man? What influences the decision to help a person in need?

social norms Standards that define what is socially acceptable in a given situation.

Prejudice: Attitudes That Harm

Prejudice is a preconceived attitude, usually unfavorable, that is formed without critical thought or evaluation of the facts. Some prejudices reflect positive biases, such as when we prejudge members of our own ethnic or religious group more favorably than members of other groups. But most prejudices reflect negative biases against other groups or categories based on race, ethnicity, social class, gender, age, and occupational, disability, or social status.

Prejudice, like other attitudes, consists of cognitive, emotional, and behavioral components (Gaines & Reed, 1995). The cognitive component is the set of biased beliefs and stereotypes that a person holds about other groups. The emotional component consists of feelings of dislike that the person has toward members of these groups. And the behavioral component is the person's inclination to discriminate against them. **Discrimination** is unfair or biased treatment of people based on group membership. Examples of discrimination include denial of housing or job opportunities, exclusion from social clubs, and increased scrutiny by police officers or department-store security guards.

Social psychologists note a disparity between what people say about their racial attitudes and how they respond to racial cues (Banaji & Greenwald, 1995; Macrae, Stangor, & Milne, 1994). For instance, people who believe themselves to be unprejudiced might nonetheless clutch their pocketbooks or briefcases more tightly when a person from a negatively stereotyped group boards an elevator with them or sits down next to them on a train or bus.

Stereotypes and prejudices are generally resistant to change. Social psychologists find that Whites who hold stereotypical views of Blacks may perceive them as "lazy" even when they perform exactly the same as the Whites (Hilton & von Hippel, 1996).

Social scientists have long observed that prejudice and discrimination typically increase during times of social upheaval and increased competition among groups. Competition over jobs and scarce economic opportunities can strain intergroup relationships. It comes as no surprise, then, that acts of racial hatred tend to increase during economic downturns, when unemployment is high. Members of ethnic or racial minority groups may become convenient scapegoats when the economic security of the majority is threatened.

How Does Prejudice Develop?

Prejudice arises as an outgrowth of negative stereotypes of other groups as lazy, dishonest, violent, dumb, and so on (Hilton & von Hippel, 1996; Kleinpenning & Hagendoorn, 1993). These stereotypes are learned or acquired. Children may begin forming negative attitudes toward other groups by imitating the prejudiced attitudes they see modeled by parents, teachers, and peers. Prejudices may also be acquired through repeated exposure to negative, stereotypical depictions of other groups, especially racial minorities, in the media. We are repeatedly exposed to television and movie depictions of racial minorities in negative roles—as criminals, gang members, abusers, drug pushers, and so on.

Prejudices may also be acquired through direct experience. If a person has a few experiences with members of a particular group who are cold or nasty, he or she may overgeneralize and develop a stereotyped belief that all members of the particular group share these characteristics.

Though we may differ in the prejudices we acquire, we all harbor some prejudices. The universality of prejudice points to a basic cognitive tendency we have to parse our social environment into two general categories: people who belong to the same groups as we do and those who do not belong. Social psychologists describe these social categories as **in-groups** (one's own social, religious, ethnic, racial, and national groups) and **out-groups** (all other groups) (Hewstone, Rubin, & Willis, 2002).

CONCEPT 14.20
Social psychologists conceptualize prejudice, as they do other types of attitudes, as consisting of cognitive, emotional, and behavioral components.

CONCEPT 14.21
Prejudice develops as an outgrowth of negative stereotypes and is acquired in the same way that other attitudes are learned.

prejudice A preconceived opinion or attitude about an issue, person, or group.

discrimination Unfair or biased treatment of people based on their membership in a particular group or category.

in-groups Social, religious, ethnic, racial, or national groups with which one identifies.

out-groups Groups other than those with which one identifies.

CONCEPT 14.22

The cognitive bases of prejudice reflect tendencies to separate people into two basic categories, in-groups and out-groups, and to attribute more negative characteristics to out-group members and more positive characteristics to in-group members.

CONCEPT 14.23

Individual differences in prejudice may be explained by learning experiences, personality traits, and the tendency to emphasize either similarities or differences between people.

PsychAssist: Effects of Stereotypes and Prejudice on Stereotyped Groups

out-group negativism A cognitive bias involving the predisposition to attribute more negative characteristics to members of out-groups than to those of in-groups.

in-group favoritism A cognitive bias involving the predisposition to attribute more positive characteristics to members of in-groups than to those of out-groups.

out-group homogeneity A cognitive bias describing the tendency to perceive members of out-groups as more alike than members of in-groups.

authoritarian personality A personality type characterized by rigidity, prejudice, and excessive concerns with obedience and respect for authority.

racism Negative bias held toward members of other racial groups.

Prejudice develops when our thinking becomes biased in such a way that we attribute more negative characteristics to members of out-groups and more positive characteristics to members of in-groups. These two biased ways of thinking are called **out-group negativism** (also called *out-group prejudice*) and **in-group favoritism** (or *in-group bias*), respectively (Aboud, 2003; Hewstone, Rubin, & Willis, 2002). Negative stereotypes of out-groups—beliefs that "we" are better than "they"—bolster the self-esteem of in-group members. Labeling other groups as dumb, lazy, dishonest, and so on, makes us feel good in comparison.

Another type of biased thinking associated with prejudice is **out-group homogeneity**. This is the tendency to perceive members of out-groups as all alike or *homogeneous,* whereas people in our own groups are as "different as snowflakes" (Nelson, 2002). Whites are more likely to believe that Blacks are more similar to each other than are Whites, and vice versa. One prominent explanation of out-group homogeneity is based on the *exemplar model* (Linville & Fischer, 1993). It holds that people are likely to know more in-group members than out-group members and so can more easily recall differences among people within their own groups who are different from each other.

The cognitive bases of prejudice may have evolved over thousands of generations. As social psychologist Martin Fishbein (1996) argues, ancestral humans organized themselves into tribal groups that shared a common language and culture, and needed to keep their guard up against threats posed by outsiders— people from other groups who might harm them or kill them. Stereotyping other groups as "dangerous" or "evil" may have served an adaptive function to these early humans, who had good reason to fear outsiders. In the multicultural society of today, however, the adaptive demands we face are very different. We need to learn to get along with people of diverse backgrounds and to avoid branding people who are different from ourselves with unwarranted stereotypes.

Why Are Some People More Prejudiced Than Others?

Learning experiences play a key role in explaining individual differences in prejudice (Greenwald, McGhee, & Schwartz, 1998). Children exposed to the teachings of less prejudiced parents are likely to develop less prejudiced attitudes than are children of more intolerant parents. Low-prejudiced individuals also tend to differ in their cognitive style. They tend to look more at the similarities among people than at their differences, a cognitive framework that psychologists call a *universalist orientation* (Phillips & Ziller, 1997). By contrast, people with more prejudiced attitudes emphasize differences among people and use ethnicity as a basis for judging people.

The presence of an underlying personality type called the **authoritarian personality** may also contribute to the development of highly prejudiced attitudes. Theodore Adorno and his colleagues (1950) coined this term to describe a cluster of personality traits that include rigidity and excessive concern with obedience and respect for authority. Individuals with authoritarian personalities are prone to hate people who are different from themselves and those they perceive as weak or downtrodden.

How Do Stereotyping and Prejudice Affect Stereotyped Groups?

Racism is unfortunately a part of the everyday experience of many minority-group members in our society who are targets of stereotyping. Exposure to racism is a significant source of environmental stress for many African Americans and may have damaging effects on their psychological and physical health (Clark et al., 1999).

Stereotyping itself can have negative effects, including lowered expectations. Stereotypical beliefs that "girls can't do math" may discourage young women from pursuing promising career opportunities in engineering and the sciences. Negative stereotypes may also become internalized by members of stereotyped groups, leading them to perceive themselves as dumb or inferior. These negative beliefs may lead to underperformance in school, sap motivation to succeed, and lower self-esteem (e.g., Pungello et al., 1996). Underperformance of negatively stereotyped groups supports the existing stereotype, which thus may become a self-fulfilling prophecy (Pratto et al., 1997).

What can be done to counter stereotypes and prejudices more generally? Social psychologists suggest some possible remedies.

> **TRY THIS OUT**
>
> ### Examining Prejudice
>
> Interview two or three friends or acquaintances from different ethnic or religious backgrounds. Ask them to describe any experiences they may have had in which they encountered prejudice or discrimination. How did these experiences affect them? How did they affect their perceptions of their social environment? Of themselves? How did they cope with these experiences? Based on your reading of the text, how might you counter your own tendencies to think in stereotyped or prejudiced ways?

What Can We Do to Reduce Prejudice?

The most widely cited model for reducing prejudice, the **contact hypothesis**, was formulated in 1954 by psychologist Gordon Allport. Allport proposed that the best way to reduce prejudice and intergroup tension was to bring groups into closer contact with each other. But he recognized that intergroup contact alone was not sufficient. Under some conditions, intergroup contact may increase negative attitudes by making differences between groups more apparent. Allport outlined four conditions that must be met in order for intergroup contact to have a desirable effect on reducing prejudice and intergroup tension (Brewer & Brown, 1998):

CONCEPT 14.24
Stereotyping and prejudice negatively affect stereotyped groups in a number of ways, including lowered expectations and internalization of negative stereotypes.

- *Social and institutional support.* People in positions of authority must be clearly behind the effort to bring groups closer together. For example, school integration is more likely to facilitate race relations if it is fully supported by teachers, school administrators, and public officials.

- *Acquaintance potential.* Opportunities must exist for members of different groups to become better acquainted with each other. With opportunities for more face-to-face interaction, members of different groups have a better chance of finding common ground. They may also discover evidence that refutes negative stereotypes they hold about each other. Even knowing that a member of one's own group has a close relationship with a member of another group can promote more positive attitudes toward the other group (Wright et al., 1997).

CONCEPT 14.25
According to Allport, intergroup contact can help reduce prejudice, but only under conditions of social and institutional support, acquaintance potential, equal status, and intergroup cooperation.

- *Equal status.* Increased opportunities for contact with members of other groups who occupy subordinate roles may actually reinforce existing stereotypes and prejudices. When opportunities exist for members of different groups to meet on an equal footing, it becomes more difficult to maintain prejudiced beliefs.

- *Intergroup cooperation.* Working cooperatively to achieve a common goal can help reduce intergroup bias by bringing members of different groups closer together (Gaertner et al., 1999). Whether it involves a baseball team, a work team in the office, or citizens banding together to fight a common cause, cooperation can foster feelings of friendliness and mutual understanding.

Combating prejudice and discrimination begins with the lessons we teach our children in the home and at school (Sleek, 1997). Teaching empathy may be one way to reduce prejudice. Empathy is the ability to take the perspective of other people and understand their feelings. Popular movies that allow us to share emotional experiences of members of stigmatized groups—films such as *Rain Man, Schindler's List,* and *The Color Purple*—may be useful in promoting more accepting, prosocial attitudes. Enforcing laws against discrimination and strengthening a cultural climate that encourages tolerance are societal measures that help combat prejudice and discrimination.

contact hypothesis   Allport's belief that under certain conditions, increased intergroup contact helps reduce prejudice and intergroup tension.

Bringing People Together

Assume you have been asked to develop a proposal to improve intergroup relations among students of different racial and ethnic groups on campus by bringing them together. What are some factors that might determine whether your efforts are successful?

web Netlab/What's Aggression and What's Not?

web Web Tutorial/Aggression

CONCEPT 14.26
Like other forms of human behavior, aggression is too complex to be reduced to the level of instinct.

We as individuals can also take steps to counter prejudiced thinking. Simply telling ourselves not to think in stereotypical terms may actually strengthen these beliefs by bringing them more readily to mind (Sherman et al., 1997). Though stereotypical and biased attitudes may occur automatically or unconsciously, evidence suggests that it is possible to change these attitudes (Ashburn-Nardo, Voils, & Monteith, 2001; Dasgupta & Greenwald, 2001). Social psychologists offer a number of suggestions that may help reduce prejudiced and stereotypical thinking, including repeated practice in rejecting these thoughts when they occur, rehearsing more positive mental images of out-group members, taking part in cooperative works or projects in which we get to interact with people of different backgrounds, and participating in diversity education, such as workshops or seminars on prejudice and intergroup conflict (Blair, Ma, & Lenton, 2001; Kawakami et al., 2000; Nelson, 2002; Rudman, Ashmore, & Gary, 2001).

Human Aggression: Behavior That Harms

Far too often in human history these negative attitudes toward members of other groups have set the stage for violent behavior in the form of killing and warfare. Are human beings inherently aggressive? Or is aggression a form of learned behavior that can be modified by experience? There are many opinions among psychologists and other scientists about the nature of human aggression. Let us consider what the major perspectives in psychology might teach us about our capacity to harm one another.

Is Human Aggression Instinctual?

Some theorists believe that aggression in humans and other species is based on instinct. For example, the famed ethologist Konrad Lorenz (1966) believed that the fighting instinct is a basic survival mechanism in many animal species. Predators need to survive by instinctively attacking their prey. The more fortunate animals on which they prey survive by either instinctively fleeing from these attacks or fighting them off. In Lorenz's view, aggression can be an adaptive response that increases the chances of survival of predator and prey. But what of human aggression? Might it also be explained by instinct?

Contemporary theorists believe that human aggression is far too complex to be based on instinct. Human aggression takes many forms, from organized war-

Violence in America These empty shoes of gunshot victims in the United States provide a poignant reminder of the consequences of violent behavior.

fare and acts of terrorism to interpersonal forms of violent behavior such as muggings, spousal abuse, and sexual assaults. These different forms of aggression reflect a variety of political, cultural, and psychological motives. Moreover, instinct theories fail to account for the important roles that learning and culture play in shaping behavior, nor do they explain the diversity that exists in human aggression. Violence is unusual in some cultures but all too common in others, unfortunately including our own.

Theorists today believe that human aggression cannot be explained by any one cause. Accordingly, we next consider the multiple factors that contemporary theorists believe contribute to human aggression, including biological influences, learning influences, sociocultural influences, use of alcohol, emotional states and environmental influences (Anderson & Bushman, 2002, 2003; Geen, 1998).

Biological Influences

Though human aggression may not be explained by instinct, evidence points to other biological influences that appear to play a role. For example, investigators suspect that people with a history of violent behavior may have an abnormality in brain circuitry that regulates negative emotions, especially anger ("Brain Scans," 2000; Davidson, Putnam, & Larson, 2000). Researchers have also focused on the neurotransmitter serotonin, since this chemical is implicated in brain circuits that curb impulsive behavior. Serotonin has been likened to a "behavioral seat belt" because of its apparent role in holding back impulsive outbursts (Cowley & Underwood, 1998). Reduced availability of serotonin in the brains of aggressive men may create a predisposition that makes them more likely to respond aggressively to social provocation (Bjork et al., 2000). But researchers caution that it is far too early to form any definitive conclusions about the role of serotonin in human aggression (Berman, Tracy, & Coccaro, 1997).

The male sex hormone testosterone may also play a role in aggressive behavior, especially in men. Men have higher levels of testosterone than women, and cross-cultural evidence shows that men are generally more aggressive (Buss & Kenrick, 1998). In addition, there is more direct evidence of links between testosterone levels and aggressive behavior in males (Chance et al., 2000; Segell, 2000). However, not all aggressive or violent men have high testosterone levels, nor do all—or even most—men with high testosterone levels engage in violent behavior. Clearly the factors involved in aggression are more complex.

Evolutionary psychologists suggest that among ancestral humans, aggression may have benefited men in their primary role as hunters. Ancestral women, so far as we know, primarily engaged in food gathering and childcare roles in which aggressiveness may have been counterproductive. Perhaps the greater aggressiveness we find in males today is explained in part by inherited tendencies passed down through generations from ancestral times.

Learning Influences

The social-cognitive theorist Albert Bandura (1973, 1986) highlights the role of observational learning in the development of aggressive behavior. He notes that children learn to imitate aggressive behavior that they observe in the home, the schools, and the media, especially television (see Module 5.3 in Chapter 5). Young boys, for example, may learn by observing their peers or by watching male characters on television that conflicts are to be settled with fists or weapons, not with words.

Researchers find that aggressive or violent children often come from homes in which aggression was modeled by parents and other family members ("Risk Factors," 2000). Reinforcement also contributes to the learning of aggressive behavior. If children are rewarded for aggressive behavior, such as by receiving approval or respect from peers, or by getting their way, they are more likely to

CONCEPT 14.27
The biological underpinnings of aggression reflect genetic, hormonal, and neurotransmitter influences.

CONCEPT 14.28
Social-cognitive theorists view aggression as learned behavior that is acquired through observational learning and reinforcement.

repeat the same behavior. Indeed, people in general are more likely to resort to aggressive behavior if they have failed to learn alternative ways of resolving conflicts. Violent behavior may be perpetuated from generation to generation as children who are exposed to violence in the home learn that violent behavior is an acceptable way to settle disagreements.

Sociocultural Influences

Sociocultural theorists encourage us to consider the broader social contexts in which aggression takes place. Interpersonal violence often occurs against a backdrop of social stressors such as poverty, prolonged unemployment, lack of opportunity, child abuse and neglect, family breakdown, and exposure to violence in the family and community. Children who are abused by their parents may fail to develop the secure loving attachments to their parents that would otherwise provide the basis for acquiring empathy and concern for others. Not surprisingly, abused children often display violent behavior in childhood and adulthood (Davis & Boster, 1992).

Social psychologists recognize that violence may also be used as a social influence tactic—a means of coercion by which individuals seek to compel others to comply with their wishes. We need only consider such examples as the "mob-enforcer" who uses strong-arm tactics to obtain compliance or the abusive spouse who uses physical force or threat of force to get his wife to accede to his demands.

Alcohol Use

Investigators find strong links between alcohol use and violent behaviors, including domestic violence, homicide, and rape (Boles & Miottoa, 2003; Fals-Stewart, 2003; Marshal, 2003). Alcohol loosens inhibitions or restraints on impulsive behavior, including acts of impulsive violence. It also impairs our ability to weigh the consequences of our actions, reduces our sensitivity to cues that signal the threat of punishment, and leads us to misperceive other people's motives as malevolent (Giancola & Zeichner, 1997; Ito, Miller, & Pollock, 1996). Not everyone who drinks becomes aggressive, of course. Relationships between alcohol use and aggression may be influenced by the user's biological sensitivity to alcohol as well as by the social demands of the situation in which provocation occurs, such as a bar versus the family home.

Emotional States

Psychologists have long recognized that certain negative emotions, especially frustration and anger, may trigger aggression. As we learned in Chapter 13, **frustration** is a negative emotional state that is induced when our efforts to reach a goal are thwarted or blocked. Though frustration often leads to aggression, other outcomes are possible (Geen, 1998). You may feel frustrated when someone behind you in a movie theater talks throughout the picture, prompting a *state of readiness* to respond aggressively either verbally or physically (Berkowitz, 1993). But whether you actually respond aggressively may depend on your expectation that an aggressive response will yield a positive outcome and your history of aggressive behavior, among other factors. Questions remain about whether aggression is necessarily preceded by frustration. The cool, premeditated aggression of a mob "hit man" does not fit the pattern of frustration-induced aggression.

Anger is another negative emotion that can induce aggressive responses in some individuals. We might think of the husband who strikes out violently at his wife when she says something that angers him or the child abuser who lashes out angrily when a child is slow to comply with a demand. People who think angering thoughts ("I can't let him/her get away with this . . .") or who blow minor

frustration A negative emotional state experienced when one's efforts to pursue one's goals are thwarted.

provocations out of proportion are more likely to respond aggressively in conflict situations than others who think calmer thoughts.

Environmental Influences

People may get hot under the collar as the outdoor temperature rises, but are they more likely to become aggressive? Indeed they are. Environmental psychologists find that aggressive behavior increases with rising temperatures, although it may begin to decline at very high temperatures (Anderson & DeNeve, 1992; Sundstrom et al., 1996).

According to social-cognitive theorists, hot temperatures incite aggression by inducing angry, hostile thoughts and feelings, which in turn increase the readiness to respond aggressively to social provocations (Anderson, Bushman, & Groom, 1997; Geen, 1998). Links between rising temperature and aggression raise some interesting questions that might be pursued through more formal study: Might the use of air conditioning in prisons reduce the problems of inmate violence? Might air conditioning have a similar effect in reducing aggression in the workplace or in schools?

Before reading further, you may want to review the positive (helping) and negative ways of relating to others outlined in Concept Chart 14.2.

CONCEPT 14.32
High temperatures are linked to aggressive behavior, perhaps because they induce angry, hostile thoughts and feelings that become expressed in aggressive behavior.

CONCEPT CHART 14.2
Relating to Others

	Concept	Description	More About It
Determinants of Helping	Decision-making processes	The decision-making model proposed by Latané and Darley consists of the following steps: (1) recognizing that a need for help exists, (2) interpreting the situation as an emergency, (3) assuming personal responsibility for helping, (4) determining the type or kind of help needed, and (5) deciding to implement a course of action.	Helping is not an automatic response in situations of need but, rather, is based on a decision-making process in which one appraises the situation at hand as well as one's personal responsibility and resources to deal with it.
	Influences on helping	Influences include situational ambiguity, taking responsibility, similarity, mood and gender effects, attributions of the cause of need, and social norms.	Whether people help others in need depends on a combination of personal and situational factors.
Negative Ways of Relating	Prejudice	A cluster of (mostly) negative beliefs, feelings, and behavioral tendencies toward members of other social groups (e.g., racial or religious minorities) or categories (e.g., people with disabilities).	Efforts to reduce prejudice can be directed at increasing intergroup contacts under conditions of social and institutional support, acquaintanceship potential, equal status, and cooperativeness. Individuals can practice nonstereotyped ways of thinking and seek opportunities for contact with people of other social groups. And parents can help instill in their children nonprejudiced attitudes through what they teach them and by setting an example of tolerance.
	Discrimination	Unfair or biased treatment of people on the basis of their membership in particular social groups that reflects underlying prejudices.	Programs designed to reduce prejudice may also have the benefit of reducing discrimination. Moreover, laws against discrimination in housing, education, and employment need to be enforced.
	Aggression	Human aggression takes many forms, from organized warfare to interpersonal violence, such as assaults, rapes, and partner abuse.	Many factors are implicated in human aggression, including biological, learning, sociocultural, emotional, and environmental influences, as well as use of alcohol.

MODULE 14.2 REVIEW

Relating to Others

CONCEPT CHECK

1. Name several key factors that determine attraction.

2. Regarding physical attractiveness, which of the following statements is *incorrect*?
   a. Men tend to place greater emphasis on the physical attractiveness of their partners than do women.
   b. Standards for physical attractiveness cross cultural boundaries.
   c. Attractive people tend to be more favorably judged on many personality traits.
   d. People tend to rate male and female faces as more attractive when they have more masculine characteristics.

3. What is the proper order of the steps involved in determining whether bystanders will become involved in helping someone in need?
   a. Assume personal responsibility for helping.
   b. Determine that the situation is a true emergency.
   c. Implement the chosen course of action.
   d. Determine that a true need for help exists.
   e. Choose what kind of help to provide.

4. Prejudice, like other attitudes, consists of (a) cognitive, (b) emotional, and (c) behavioral components. Describe the major features of each component as they relate to prejudice.

5. What are the four conditions that Allport said must be met in order for intergroup contact to reduce prejudice?

MODULE 14.3 Group Influences on Individual Behavior

- **What is social identity?**
- **What was the significance of the Asch study on conformity?**
- **Why were Milgram's findings so disturbing , and why were his methods so controversial?**
- **How does the presence of others affect individual performance?**
- **What is groupthink?**

The view that humans are social creatures was expressed perhaps most clearly by the sixteenth-century English poet John Donne, who wrote "*no man is an island, sufficient unto himself.*" We influence others and are influenced in turn by them. In this module we consider ways in which others influence our behavior and even our self-concepts. We examine the tendency to conform our behavior to social pressure, even when we consider such demands unreasonable or immoral. We examine situations where the presence of others may enhance our performance and those where it may not. Finally, we explore the phenomenon of *groupthink* and see how group influences can sometimes lead to bad decisions. The last module (Module 14.4) examines the social influences underlying persuasive sales tactics and the steps people can take to avoid manipulative sales approaches.

Our Social Selves: "Who Are We?"

CONCEPT 14.33
Our social or group identity is an important part of our psychological identity or self-concept.

Many social psychologists separate psychological identity or self-concept into two parts: **personal identity** (individual identity) and **social identity** (group identity) (Brewer & Brown, 1998; Ellemers, Spears, & Doosje, 2002; Gaines et al., 1997). Your personal identity ("Who am I?") is the part of your psychological make-up

TRY THIS OUT

Sign on the Dotted Line

Sign your name on the line below:

_____

Sign your name again, but now imagine that you are signing as the president of the United States:

_____

Were your signatures the same size? Psychologist Richard Zweigenhaft (1970) found that students penned larger signatures when they were signing as president. Zweigenhaft also found that signatures of college professors were larger than those of blue-collar university employees. The social roles we play, as student, employee, husband or wife, or even president, are part of our social identity. Holding a high-status position bolsters our self-image, which may be reflected in the size of our signatures.

that distinguishes you as a unique individual. You might think of yourself as a caring, creative person who likes pepperoni pizza, jazz, and sci-fi movies. Your social identity ("Who are we?") refers to your sense of yourself as a member of the various family, kinship, religious, national, and social groups to which you belong. You might refer to this part of your identity by saying, "I am a Catholic . . . I am a software developer . . . I am a Mexican American . . . I am Jonathan's dad." Our social identity converts the "I" to the "we" (Brewer, 1991). Social psychologists believe that people have a fundamental need to be members of groups—to belong (Baumeister & Leary, 1995). Our social identity tends to rub off on our self-esteem (Blascovich et al., 1997). We are likely to feel better about ourselves when someone of the same ethnicity, religion, or even locality accomplishes something special.

Social identity is generally a more prominent part of one's psychological identity in collectivist cultures, such as those in the Far East, than it is in individualistic societies in the West (Fiske et al., 1998; Triandis & Gelfand, 1998). In collectivist cultures, individuals have a stronger desire to fulfill their social obligations to the group, whereas Western societies emphasize a more individualistic or autonomous sense of self. People in Western cultures tend to define themselves less by what they share in common with others and more in terms of their unique abilities, interests, and attributes. They expect to stand out from the crowd—being themselves means becoming unique individuals. Yet there are variations within Western cultures. Women tend to place a greater emphasis on an interdependent sense of self—defining themselves more in terms of their roles as mothers, wives, daughters, and so on, while men tend to have a more independent sense of self (Cross & Madson, 1997).

Conformity: Bending the "I" to Fit the "We"

You would not get arrested if you arrived at work in your pajamas, but you probably would hear some snickering comments or be asked to go home and change. Then again, perhaps pajama-wearing might become something of a new fashion statement. You might actually be thought of as a trendsetter. Well, perhaps not. In any event, we are expected to conform our behavior to prevailing social standards or norms. Though social norms don't carry the force of law, violation of these standards can incur social disapproval. If we deviate too far from social standards, we might even lose our friends or jobs or alienate our family members.

Conformity affects many aspects of our daily behavior, from the clothes we wear for specific occasions, to the custom of covering our mouths and saying

personal identity   The part of our psychological identity that involves our sense of ourselves as unique individuals.

social identity   The part of our psychological identity that involves our sense of ourselves as members of particular groups. Also called *group identity*.

conformity   The tendency to adjust one's behavior to actual or perceived social pressures.

CONCEPT 14.34
When we conform, we behave in ways that adhere to social norms.

CONCEPT 14.35
People are more likely to conform than they might think, even to the extent of claiming that something is true when they know it to be false.

web, **Netlab/Getting Assertive and Overcoming Pressures to Conform**

"excuse me" when we sneeze, to choosing a college to attend ("You're going to State, like your brother, right?"). Conformity pressures may also lead us to date or even marry the kinds of persons whom others deem acceptable.

We conform not only to general social norms but also to group or peer norms. Young people who color their hair purple may not be conforming to the standards of mainstream society, but they are conforming to those of their peer group—just as their parents are to their own.

We might consider ourselves to be free thinkers who can resist pressures to conform when we don't see eye-to-eye with others. But the results of a classic study by psychologist Solomon Asch (1956) lead us to recognize that we may conform more than we think. Asch set out to study independence, not conformity. He believed that if participants in the study were faced with a unanimous group judgment that was obviously false, they would stick to their guns, resist pressures to conform, and report the correct information. He was wrong.

Asch placed individuals in a group consisting of people who were actually in league with the experimenter. The group was presented with the task of choosing the one line among a group of three that was the same length as a test line (see Figure 14.7). But the twist was that the other group members—all confederates of the experimenter—unanimously made the wrong choice. Now it was the individual's turn. Would the person go along with the group and make an obviously incorrect choice? Asch was surprised by the results. Bowing under the pressure to conform, three out of four of the college students who participated in the study gave at least one incorrect answer in a series of trials.

Why were people so willing to conform in the Asch experiment, even to the extent of claiming that something was true when it was obviously false? Subsequent research has established at least three reasons: (1) People assume the majority must be correct; (2) they are so concerned about being accepted by the group that they don't care whether their judgments were correct; (3) they feel it is easier to go along with the group than to disagree (Cialdini & Trost, 1998; Jones, 1998). Even so, some groups of people are more susceptible to pressures to conform than others (Baron, Vandello, & Brunsman, 1996; Cialdini & Trost, 1998). Women, by a small margin, are more likely to conform than men. People from collectivist cultures such as China tend to conform more than people from indi-

Participant in Asch Experiment The person third from the right in the photograph is the actual participant. The others are confederates of the experimenter. The participant is asked to indicate which of three lines matches a standard line after the others in the room have unanimously given the wrong response.

Figure 14.7
Stimuli Similar to Those Used in the Asch Conformity Studies
Standard Line   **Comparison Lines**
1 2 3

vidualistic cultures such as the United States, Canada, and Great Britain. And conformity is greater among people with low self-esteem, social shyness, and a strong desire to be liked by the group. More generally, conformity tends to decline with age from childhood through older adulthood (Pasupathi, 1999).

Conformity is also influenced by situational factors. In the Asch paradigm, people were more likely to conform when they were required to disclose their responses publicly rather than privately, when the size of the group increased to about four or five people (beyond that number, conformity leveled off with increasing group size), and when more ambiguous stimuli were used (Bond & Smith, 1996; Cialdini & Trost, 1998). Yet just one dissenting voice in the group—one fellow traveler down the road of defection—can override group influence, regardless of the size of the group (Morris, Miller, & Spangenberg, 1977).

Asch believed that conformity can stifle individuality and independence. Yet some degree of conformity may help groups to function more smoothly. After all, sneezing on someone might be taken as a social affront; covering our noses and mouths and saying "excuse me" afterward shows respect for other people's rights.

Obedience to Authority: When Does It Go Too Far?

The study of **obedience** to authority has implications that go far beyond psychology. The atrocities of the Nazi regime in Germany preceding and during World War II raised disturbing questions about the tendency of soldiers and even ordinary citizens to obey authority figures in the commission of horrific acts. Many individuals, including civilians, participated in the Holocaust—the systematic genocide of the Jewish population of Europe. When later called to account for their deeds, many Nazis claimed they were "only following orders" (Elms, 1995). Years afterward, American soldiers who participated in a massacre of civilians in the village of My Lai during the Vietnam War would offer a similar defense.

Yale University psychologist Stanley Milgram developed a unique and controversial research program to find out whether ordinary Americans would perform clearly immoral actions if they were instructed to do so. Participants in these studies were residents of New Haven, Connecticut, and surrounding areas who answered newspaper ads requesting participants for studies on learning and memory. They ranged in age from twenty to fifty and included teachers, engineers, salespeople, and laborers. Some were college graduates; others had not even completed elementary school. When they arrived at the lab, they were told that they would be participating in a study designed to test the effects of punishment on learning. They would play the role of a "teacher." Another person to whom they were introduced would be the "learner."

The learner was seated in one room, the teacher in an adjoining room. The teacher was placed in front of a console that was described as a device for administering electric shocks to the learner. The console consisted of a series of levers with labels ranging from "Slight Shock" to "Danger: Severe Shock." The learner was presented with a list of word pairs to memorize. Then one word in each pair was presented and the learner's task was to respond with the correct word with which it had been paired in the list. The teacher was instructed that following each incorrect response from the learner, he was to deliver an electric shock. With each additional error, the voltage of the shock was to increase by 15 volts.

Unbeknown to the teachers, the learners were confederates of the experimenter. It was all part of an elaborate ruse. The experiment was not actually intended to study learning. What it tested was the teacher's willingness to inflict pain on another person when instructed to do so. No actual shocks were given. The learner's incorrect responses were all predetermined. But to the "teachers," it was all too real.

Each teacher was informed that while the shocks might be extremely painful they would cause "no permanent tissue damage" to the learner. To provide teach-

💡 **CONCEPT 14.36**
Many factors influence conformity, including personal and situational characteristics.

obedience Compliance with commands or orders issued by others, usually persons in a position of authority.

"Learner" in Milgram Experiment The participant is led to believe that the "learner," as shown here, receives actual electric shocks following each wrong answer. If you were a participant, would you have obeyed the experimenter even as the learner cried out for help?

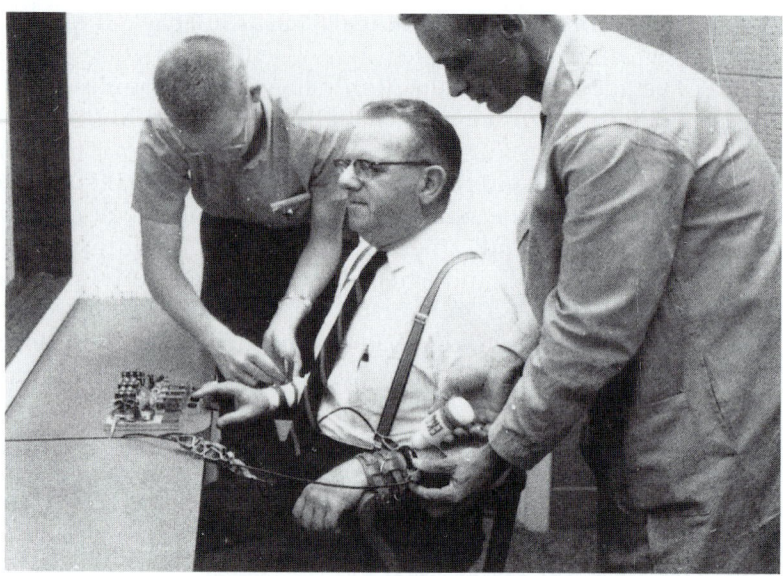

THINK *About It*

Obeying Authority

Agree or disagree with this statement, and support your answer: "Had I been a subject in the Milgram study, I would have refused to comply with the experimenter's demands."

CONCEPT 14.37
In the classic Milgram studies of obedience, ordinary people were willing to obey the dictates of an external authority even to the extent of inflicting what they believed were serious and even dangerous shocks to other supposed participants.

ers with a sense of what a mild shock felt like, they were administered an electric shock corresponding to 45 volts. As the number of errors mounted, the teacher was instructed to increase the voltage until it reached the "danger" level. Most teachers were visibly upset when given the order to raise the shock level to apparently hazardous levels. When they hesitated, the experimenter simply instructed them: "The experiment requires that you continue." If they still hesitated, the experimenter pressured them further, telling them: "It is absolutely essential that you continue. . . . You have no other choice. . . . You must go on." Now, would they comply and throw the switch? Would you?

The results were disturbing (Milgram, 1963, 1974). Although most participants (or "teachers") initially refused to obey, they eventually relented as the experimenter continued pressuring them to continue. Of the forty original participants, twenty-six (65 percent) obeyed every order, including the one to deliver the highest voltage shock. In another experimental condition, the teachers could hear the learner screaming to be let go and pounding on the wall. Even so, twenty-five of the forty participants administered the full series of shocks (Elms, 1995). In a variation in which participants themselves did not throw the switch activating the shock but instructed others (actually confederates) to do so, the rate of obedience rose to 92.5 percent (Meeus & Rajaijmakers, 1995). Placing the learner in the same room as the participant reduced obedience, but 40 percent still obeyed. Milgram later obtained similar results with female participants and groups of college undergraduates (Milgram, 1973).

Some commentators believe that Milgram's findings reveal something about the potential in ordinary people for a type of behavior akin to that of the Nazis, the soldiers who were "only following orders" when they committed the My Lai massacre, even the mass suicides at the behest of cult leaders like Jim Jones (Elms, 1995; Miller, Collins, & Brief, 1995). Perhaps Milgram's studies teach us how good people can commit bad deeds in situations where they are led to blindly follow authority. Yet critics claim there were unique features to Milgram's methods that prevent us from learning anything about the kind of destructive obedience found in Nazi Germany or other real-life atrocities. One related argument is that participants may not have believed that anything terrible was happening to the "learner"—after all, this was a respected university and someone would have stopped them if it were truly dangerous. (Wouldn't they?) In fact, a majority of Milgram's participants believed that the "learner" was receiving significant levels of pain (Meeus & Rajaijmakers, 1995). Even when Milgram moved his laboratory to a dingy storefront in a commercial district away from the hallowed halls of the university, nearly half of the participants (48 percent) complied (Milgram, 1974).

Milgram's studies provoked controversy on other grounds as well, much of it concerning the ethics of deceiving participants in research studies and the emotional aftereffects of raising people's awareness that they were capable of such behavior (Goode, 2000e; Jones, 1998). Ethical issues raised by the Milgram experiments played a large part in the American Psychological Association's adoption of a set of ethical guidelines to protect the welfare of participants in psychological research. (See Chapter 1 for a discussion of ethical principles.)

Why Do People Obey Immoral Commands?

The **legitimization of authority** is one explanation of the behavior of participants in Milgram's studies. We are taught from an early age to obey authority figures such as parents and teachers and not to question or second-guess them. This early socialization prepares us to comply when directed to do so by a legitimate authority figure, be it a police officer, government or military official, or a scientist. Another likely reason for obedience is **social validation** (also called social comparison). Participants in Milgram's studies may have lacked any basis for knowing what other people would do in a similar situation. The only basis for social comparison was the example set by the experimenter. For people in Nazi Germany, seeing respected others perform atrocities may have served to legitimize their activities not only as socially acceptable but, more disturbingly, as admirable. People are generally more willing to comply with more extreme requests once they have shown a willingness to comply with lesser requests. Once participants began to deliver shocks to "learners," they may have found it increasingly difficult to stop—just as soldiers who have been trained to respond unstintingly to commands may not hesitate to follow orders, even immoral ones.

Evaluating Milgram's Legacy

The scientific jury is still out regarding the ultimate significance of Milgram's findings. Ethical concerns about his procedure make it virtually impossible for similar research to be performed in any educational or research institution, at least in the United States (Elms, 1995). His findings stand etched in time as a reminder to us to look inward to our capacity for blind and destructive obedience. As some have observed, the Milgram studies may indicate that we do *too good* a job at socializing young people to be obedient to authority (Vecchio, 1997). Perhaps more emphasis should be placed on personal responsibility for one's actions, a teaching that might go a long way toward preventing destructive obedience.

Now we consider ways in which the presence of groups may influence individual performance—for better or worse.

Social Facilitation and Social Loafing: When Are You Most Likely to Do Your Best?

Do you perform better when you work in front of others? **Social facilitation** refers to the tendency for people to work better or harder when they work in the presence of others than when they work alone. The presence of others might be perceived as a threat or a challenge, which in turn may energize one to perform better (Blascovich et al., 1999). The social psychologist Robert Zajonc (1965) believes that mere exposure to others induces a state of arousal that can energize individual responses. But the presence of others does not necessarily *improve* performance. According to Zajonc, the presence of others increases performance of dominant responses. In the case of simple or well-learned tasks, the dominant response will usually be the correct response. However, for complex tasks in which the dominant response may be incorrect, the presence of others tends to impair performance. So, if you are a good typist, you may type faster when others

CONCEPT 14.38
The willingness to obey immoral commands may arise from the legitimization of authority.

CONCEPT 14.39
The presence of others may enhance individual performance on simple tasks but impair performance on more complex tasks.

legitimization of authority   The tendency to grant legitimacy to the orders or commands of persons in authority.

social validation   The tendency to use other people's behavior as a standard for judging the appropriateness of one's own behavior.

social facilitation   The tendency to work better or harder in the presence of others than when alone.

The Presence of Others: A Help or a Hindrance? The presence of others may impair performance of complex tasks but facilitate performance of simple or well-learned tasks.

CONCEPT 14.40

In social loafing, people fail to pull their own weight because they believe others will pick up the slack.

CONCEPT 14.41

When groups tackle a problem, they may become so focused on reaching a consensus that they fail to critically examine the issues before them.

social loafing The tendency to expend less effort when working as a member of a group than when working alone.

groupthink Janis's term for the tendency of members of a decision-making group to be more focused on reaching a consensus than on critically examining the issues at hand.

are present than when you are alone. But if you need to solve complex math problems, having an audience would likely slow your performance.

Social loafing is the tendency for people to apply less effort when they work as members of a group than when they work on their own. Perhaps you have observed social loafing in work that you did as part of a team effort. Did one or more members of the team fail to apply themselves as much as they could?

Underlying social loafing is the tendency for people to conserve individual effort when they expect that other team members will pick up the slack (Plaks & Higgins, 2000). But social loafing is not inevitable. It is more likely to occur when individual performance is not evaluated. But it can be reduced by making tasks more appealing, increasing the visibility of each individual's performance in the group, holding each member accountable for his or her own contributions, and giving public feedback of individual performance (Hoeksema van Orden, Gaillard, & Buunk, 1998; Levine & Moreland, 1998).

Groupthink: How Can Smart People Make Dumb Decisions?

This was the question President John Kennedy asked his advisers in the aftermath of the disastrous invasion of Cuba at the Bay of Pigs in 1961, when Cuban forces easily defeated a brigade of U.S.-backed Cuban exiles. Yale psychologist Irving Janis (1982, 1997) believed that stupidity wasn't the explanation. To Janis, the fault lay in a flawed approach to group decision making that he termed **groupthink**. Groupthink is the tendency for members of a group to become so concerned with reaching a consensus that they lose the ability to critically evaluate the problem before them. Groupthink can be likened to a kind of "tunnel vision" in which the group's perspective is limited to a single point of view (Nowak, Vallacher, & Miller, 2003).

In groupthink, the pressure to conform to majority opinion squelches any serious debate. Janis believed that groupthink is more likely to occur (1) when members are strongly attached to the group, (2) when an external threat is present, and (3) when there is a strong-minded leader directing the group. Group members may not want to "rock the boat" by expressing a dissenting opinion, or they may have a misplaced confidence that the leader and other group members must be right. Critics, however, point out that research evidence supporting the groupthink model is mixed (Kerr & Tindale, 2004). Others question whether the groupthink model can account for high-level foreign policy decisions (Tetlock, 1998). But Janis's recommendations for avoiding negative effects of groupthink are well worth considering at any level of decision making:

- Group members should be encouraged to consider all alternatives and carefully weigh the evidence on all sides of an issue.

- The group leader should avoid stating any preferences as the group begins its work.

- Outsiders should be called upon to offer their opinions and analyses.

- Group members or outsiders should be encouraged to play the role of "devil's advocate."

- The group should be subdivided into smaller groups to independently review the issues that are before the larger group.

- Several group meetings should be held to reassess the situation and evaluate any new information before final decisions are reached.

Concept Chart 14.3 summarizes the group influences on identity and behavior discussed in the text.

CONCEPT CHART 14.3
Group Influences on Identity and Behavior

Sources of Group Influence	Description
Conformity	Adherence to social standards or norms
Compliance	Acceding to demands or requests from others
Obedience	Adherence to the commands of external authority
Social facilitation	Improvement in performance occurring when we perform in front of others
Social loafing	Impaired performance occurring when our individual effort is obscured by a group effort
Groupthink	The tendency for groups to emphasize consensus-building rather than thoughtful consideration of the issues

MODULE 14.3 REVIEW

Group Influences on Individual Behavior

CONCEPT CHECK

1. One's social identity
   a. is that which distinguishes one as an individual.
   b. is a greater component of psychological identity in individualistic Western societies.
   c. is tied to one's unique abilities and attributes.
   d. reflects the fundamental need to be part of a group.

2. Which of the following statements is *not* correct with regard to characteristics associated with greater levels of conformity?
   a. Individuals who conform assume that the majority must be correct.
   b. Individuals who conform exhibit greater independence and self-esteem.
   c. Individuals who conform find it difficult to disagree with group opinion.
   d. Public disclosure leads to more conformity than disclosing responses in private.

3. In Milgram's classic study, what percentage of original participants administered the full series of electric shocks (i.e., to the highest level)?

4. Social facilitation is likely to lead to _____ performance on simpler, well-known tasks and _____ performance on less familiar or more difficult tasks.
   a. enhanced, impaired
   b. impaired, enhanced
   c. enhanced, enhanced
   d. impaired, impaired

5. The phenomenon of groupthink explains how
   a. groups often make better-informed decisions than individuals.
   b. groups often make bad decisions because of the desire to maintain harmony within the group.
   c. group members tend to think in similar ways because of their similar backgrounds.
   d. groups often make good decisions because of the desire to reach a consensus.

APPLICATION

MODULE 14.4

Compliance: Doing What Others Want You to Do

- **What psychological principles underlie manipulative sales techniques?**

Compliance is the process of acceding to the requests or demands of others (Cialdini & & Goldstein, 2004). One factor influencing compliance is authority. Appeals from a recognized authority figure are often extremely influential. You may be more willing to follow your doctor's advice about making changes in your diet than advice from your next-door neighbor. Another factor is *social validation*. We tend to use the actions of others as a standard or social norm for judging the appropriateness of our own behavior (Cialdini, 2001; Cialdini & & Goldstein, 2004). Thus, we are more likely to donate to a charity appeal if we find out that other people in the office are giving than if they are not.

The desire for consistency is yet another important determinant of compliance (Cialdini & & Goldstein, 2004). Salespeople, advertisers, fundraisers, and others try to get us to comply with their requests by using consistency to their advantage. Several market-honed techniques succeed because they first obtain a person's commitment to a particular course of action that is consistent with a later requested action. Here are three examples:

1. *Low-ball technique.* Say a car salesperson offers you an attractive price, only to pull the offer minutes later, claiming the sales manager couldn't approve it or the allowance offered for your trade-in came in lower than expected. You are then offered a higher price, which the salesperson swears is the best possible price. This is the **low-ball technique** at work. Committing yourself to the prior action of accepting a lower price may make you more likely to follow through on the subsequent, more costly action.

2. *Bait-and-switch technique.* In the **bait-and-switch technique**, a marketer advertises merchandise at an usually low price. When people come to buy the merchandise, they learn that it is actually of inferior quality or is sold out or back-ordered. Then comes the switch, as they are shown more expensive merchandise for sale. Here again the person making the pitch capitalizes on the desire for consistency. Prospective buyers who expressed an initial interest in the merchandise are often more receptive to buying more expensive merchandise than they would be otherwise.

3. *Foot-in-the-door technique.* In the **foot-in-the door technique**, the person making an appeal first asks for a small favor that will almost certainly be granted. After obtaining initial compliance, the person raises the ante by asking for a larger, related favor. Evidence shows that people who agree to smaller requests are more likely to comply with larger ones, apparently due to the desire for consistency (Cialdini & Trost, 1998). In an early example, Patricia Pliner and her colleagues (1974) showed that people who agreed to wear a lapel pin promoting a local charity were subsequently more willing to make a monetary donation to the charity. Yet investigators find that only those people with a strong preference for consistency show evidence of the foot-in-the-door effect (Cialdini, Trost, & Newsom, 1995).

Another sales strategy, the **door-in-the-face technique**, takes advantage of the psychological principle of *reciprocity* (Cialdini & Trost, 1998). First comes a large unreasonable request, which is rejected out of hand. Then the person making the request offers a lesser alternative in the form of a smaller request, which is actually what the person wanted in the first place. This smaller request is more likely to be

compliance The tendency to accede to the requests or demands of others.

low-ball technique A compliance technique based on obtaining a person's initial agreement to purchase an item at a lower price before revealing hidden costs that raise the ultimate price.

bait-and-switch technique A compliance technique based on "baiting" a person by making an unrealistically attractive offer and then replacing it with a less attractive offer.

foot-in-the-door technique A compliance technique based on securing compliance with a smaller request as a prelude to making a larger request.

door-in-the-face technique A compliance technique in which refusal of a large unreasonable request is followed by a smaller, more reasonable request.

accepted following rejection of the larger, unreasonable request than it would be had it been presented first. Why? Recall the concept of reciprocity. When requesters appear willing to compromise by withdrawing the original request in favor of a smaller one, people receiving the request may feel obliged to reciprocate by becoming more accommodating themselves.

Now let's turn the discussion around to you. The Try This Out feature below offers the opportunity to practice your skills at resisting persuasive sales tactics.

TYING IT TOGETHER

Social psychologists study how we relate to others in our social environment. They are concerned with how we perceive others and how our perceptions of others affects how we act toward them (Module 14.1). They are also concerned with positive forms of relating, such as attraction, love, and helping, and negative forms of relating, such as prejudice and aggression (Module 14.2). The study of social psychology also encompasses how people are influenced by the groups with which they interact (Module 14.3). We influence others and are influenced in turn by them. One form of social behavior that reflects how we are influenced by others is compliance. Understanding the psychological principles underlying compliance may help us avoid succumbing to unreasonable sales tactics (Module 14.4).

TRY THIS OUT

What Do You Say Now?

You are in the market for a new car. The salesperson shows you a model you like and after haggling for a while, you settle on a price that seems fair to you. The salesperson then says, "Let me get this approved by my manager and I'll be right back." What would you say to protect yourself against the types of influence tactics described in the text? For each of the following examples, write your response in the column provided below. Then compare your answers with some sample responses you'll find at the end of the chapter.

Type of Tactic	What the Salesperson Says	What Do You Say Now?
Low-ball technique	"I'm sorry. He says we can't let it go for this amount. It has nothing to do with you, but he's getting more pressure from the boss. Maybe if we went back to him with another two or three hundred dollars, he'd accept it."	
Bait-and-switch technique	"My manager tells me that we're having difficulty placing orders for that model. Something to do with a strike in Osaka. We can definitely get the LX version, however. It's got some great features."	
Foot-in-the-door technique	"Okay, we can get you the car." After completing some of the paperwork, the salesman slips in the following comment: "You know, you really should think about this factory-installed security system. You can never be too safe these days."	

Source: Adapted from Sternberg, 1988.

SUMMING UP: Q & A

Perceiving Others (Module 14.1)

What is social perception?

- Social perception is the process of forming impressions of others and attitudes about people, objects, and issues in our social environment.

What are the major influences on first impressions, and why do first impressions often become lasting impressions?

- First impressions are influenced by surface characteristics, such as physical appearance and attire, and by stereotypes and personal disclosures.
- A modest amount of self-disclosure is associated with a more favorable impression. However, self-disclosure is generally looked upon more favorably in Western cultures than in Eastern cultures.
- First impressions may become lasting impressions when people reconcile discrepant information with their existing impressions, or social schemas. Impressions may also become self-fulfilling prophecies.

What role do cognitive biases play in the judgments we make about the causes of behavior?

- The fundamental attribution error is an overemphasis on internal or dispositional causes of behavior to the exclusion of situational factors.
- The actor-observer effect is the tendency to explain our own behavior in terms of the demands of the situation while explaining the behavior of others in terms of internal or dispositional causes.
- The self-serving bias bolsters self-esteem in that it involves attributing personal success to one's talents or abilities while explaining personal failure in terms of external causes.

What are attitudes, and how are they acquired?

- Attitudes are evaluations or judgments of liking or disliking people, objects, or issues. Psychologists conceptualize attitudes as having three components: cognitions, emotions, and behaviors.
- The social environment, which encompasses our relationships and experiences with others as well as our exposure to mass media, is the learning ground for the acquisition of attitudes. Genetic factors may also play a role.

How are attitudes related to behavior?

- Attitudes are related to behavior only modestly at best. Our behavior is influenced by many factors, not just our attitudes.

What is cognitive dissonance theory?

- Cognitive dissonance theory holds that inconsistencies between our behavior and our attitudes, beliefs, or perceptions produce a state of psychological tension (dissonance) that motivates efforts to reconcile these inconsistencies.

How do persuasive appeals lead to attitude change?

- According to the elaboration likelihood model, attitudes may be altered by persuasive messages that are processed through either a central route (careful evaluation of the content of the message) or a peripheral route (focusing on cues that are peripheral to the content of the message).

Relating to Others (Module 14.2)

What are the major determinants of attraction?

- The major determinants of attraction include similarity, physical attractiveness, proximity, and reciprocity.

What are the three components of love in Sternberg's model of love?

- According to Sternberg's triangular model, the components of love are intimacy, passion, and decision/commitment.

What factors are linked to helping behavior?

- The decision-making model holds that bystander intervention is based on a series of decisions that must be made before helping occurs.
- Factors that influence helping behavior include the ambiguity of the situation, perceived cost, taking responsibility, social norms, similarity, mood, gender, and attributions of the cause of need.

What is prejudice, and how does it develop?

- Prejudice is a preconceived attitude or bias, usually unfavorable, that is formed without critical thought or evaluation.
- Prejudice derives from negative group stereotypes to which people are exposed in their social environment. The development of prejudice may also reflect basic cognitive processes that evolved over thousands of generations.
- Individual differences in prejudice may be explained by differences in learning experiences, authoritarian personality traits, and adoption of a universalist orientation.

What can be done to reduce prejudice?

- Prejudice may be reduced by creating opportunities for intergroup contact that have strong social and institutional support, are based on equal-status relationships, allow acquaintanceships to develop, and emphasize cooperation rather than competition.

What factors contribute to human aggression?

- Contemporary theorists attempt to explain human aggression on the basis of biological influences, learning influences, sociocultural influences, alcohol use, emotional states, and environmental influences.

Group Influences on Individual Behavior (Module 14.3)

What is social identity?

- Social identity (also called group identity) is our social self—that part of our self-concept that relates to our family and social roles and the collective identities we share with members of our own religious, ethnic, fraternal, or national groups.
- Social identities play a stronger role in collectivist cultures than in individualistic cultures.

What was the significance of the Asch study on conformity?

- Asch showed that people often conform to group judgments, even when those judgments are obviously false.
- Factors that influence conformity include gender, cultural background, self-esteem, social shyness, desire to be liked by the group, age, and situational features such as public disclosure, group size, and stimulus ambiguity.

Why were Milgram's findings so disturbing, and why were his methods so controversial?

- Milgram found that people from various walks of life could be induced to obey unreasonable or even immoral commands given by an authority figure.
- The use of deception, as well as the potential emotional aftereffects of raising awareness of participants' capabilities for such behavior, led to controversy over Milgram's methods.

How does the presence of others affect individual performance?

- The presence of others may improve performance in simple, well-learned tasks but impair performance in complex tasks.

- People may also exert less than their best effort in a group task when they know others will pick up the slack and their performance will not be individually evaluated.

What is groupthink?

- Groupthink is a type of group decision making that can lead to bad decisions. In groupthink, decisions derive from a desire for consensus rather than from a critical evaluation of the issues.

Application: Compliance: Doing What Others Want You to Do (Module 14.4)

What psychological principles underlie manipulative sales techniques?

- The foot-in-the-door technique, bait-and-switch technique, and low-ball technique are based on the desire for consistency. The door-in-the-face technique is based on the principle of reciprocity.

Key Terms

social psychology *(p. 482)*
social perception *(p. 482)*
impression formation *(p. 482)*
social schema *(p. 483)*
stereotypes *(p. 483)*
self-fulfilling prophecy *(p. 483)*
attribution *(p. 484)*
dispositional causes *(p. 484)*
situational causes *(p. 484)*
fundamental attribution error *(p. 484)*
actor-observer effect *(p. 484)*
self-serving bias *(p. 485)*
attitude *(p. 485)*
cognitive dissonance theory *(p. 487)*
elaboration likelihood model (ELM) *(p. 488)*

attraction *(p. 491)*
matching hypothesis *(p. 493)*
proximity *(p. 493)*
reciprocity *(p. 493)*
prosocial behavior *(p. 495)*
bystander intervention *(p. 495)*
social norms *(p. 496)*
prejudice *(p. 497)*
discrimination *(p. 497)*
in-groups *(p. 497)*
out-groups *(p. 497)*
out-group negativism *(p. 498)*
in-group favoritism *(p. 498)*
out-group homogeneity *(p. 498)*
authoritarian personality *(p. 498)*
racism *(p. 498)*

contact hypothesis *(p. 499)*
frustration *(p. 502)*
personal identity *(p. 504)*
social identity *(p. 504)*
conformity *(p. 505)*
obedience *(p. 507)*
legitimization of authority *(p. 509)*
social validation *(p. 509)*
social facilitation *(p. 509)*
social loafing *(p. 510)*
groupthink *(p. 510)*
compliance *(p. 512)*
low-ball technique *(p. 512)*
bait-and-switch technique *(p. 512)*
foot-in-the-door technique *(p. 512)*
door-in-the-face technique *(p. 512)*

Thinking Critically About Psychology

Based on your reading of this chapter, answer the following questions. Then, to evaluate your progress in developing critical thinking skills, compare your answers to the sample answers found in Appendix A.

Why didn't they help? Thirty-eight people reportedly witnessed Kitty Genovese being stabbed to death but did nothing. Based on your reading of the factors influencing helping behavior, speculate on the reasons why these bystanders failed to help.

Answers to Concept Check Questions

Module 14.1: 1. a; 2.dispositional, situational; 3. b; 4. an evaluation or judgment of liking or disliking a person, object, or social issue; 5. cognitive dissonance; 6. (a) ii, (b) iv, (c) i, (d) iii.
Module 14.2: 1. similarity, physical attractiveness, proximity, reciprocity; 2. d; 3. The correct order is (d), (b), (a), (e), (c); 4. (a) biased beliefs and stereotypes, (b) feelings of dislike toward target, (c) discrimination; 5. social and institutional support, acquaintance potential, equal status, intergroup cooperation.
Module 14.3: 1. d; 2. b; 3. 65 percent; 4. a; 5. b.

Sample Responses to Try This Out, "What Do You Say Now?" *(p. 513)*

- Low-ball technique: You might say, "Sorry, that's my best offer. We agreed on a price and I expect you to stick to it."
- Bait-and-switch technique: You might say, "If I wanted the LX version I would have asked for it. If you're having difficulty getting the car I want, then it's your problem. Now, what are you going to do for me?"
- Foot-in-the-door technique: You might say, "If you want to lower the price of the car, we can talk about it. But the price I gave you is all I can afford to spend."

APPENDIX A

Sample Answers to Thinking Critically About Psychology Questions

Chapter 1 Introduction to Psychology and Methods of Research

1. Unfortunately, a basic flaw in the research design casts serious doubt on the experimenter's conclusions. The experimenter did not use random assignment as the basis for assigning parateticipants to the experimental (sleep learning) or control (nonparticipating) groups. Rather, students who responded to the invitation to participate constituted the experimental group, and the control group was selected from nonparticipating students from the same class. Lacking random assignment, we have no way of knowing whether differences between the two groups were due to the independent variable (sleep learning) or to the characteristics of participants comprising these groups.

2. In the absence of random assignment, it is conceivable that the more motivated and committed students opted to participate and that these students would have achieved higher test grades than the nonparticipating students, whether they had participated in the sleep learning study or not.

3. To provide a fairer test of the sleep learning method, the experimenter should have randomly assigned students to experimental and control groups. Experimenters use random assignment to equates groups on differences that may exist among individuals in level of ability or other participant characteristics.

Chapter 2 Biological Foundations of Behavior

1. Fortunately for Gage, the rod that penetrated his skull did not damage structures in the brainstem that control basic bodily processes, such as breathing and heart rate. However, the rod did damage the prefrontal cortex, the part of the brain responsible for personality and other higher mental functions.

2. The prefrontal cortex, which was damaged in the accident, helps us weigh the consequences of our actions and inhibit impulsive behaviors, including aggressive behaviors.

Chapter 3 Sensation and Perception

1. The woman located an area on the map where the missing man might be found. But her success at locating the missing man could be explained in a number of ways other than ESP. It could have been a lucky guess. Or perhaps the woman used the process of elimination to systematically narrow the possible search areas by ruling out those in which the police had already focused their efforts. Or perhaps she arrived at a possible location by identifying areas where a person would be likely to have wandered off. What other explanations can you generate that do not rely on positing the existence of ESP?

2. To evaluate whether the woman's predictions were likely to have been mere chance events, we would need to know how often her predictions turn out to be right. In other words, we'd need to know whether her success rate significantly exceeds chance expectations. But even if she turned out to be right more often than you would expect by chance alone, we still couldn't conclude that her success was attributable to ESP rather than to more conventional explanations.

Chapter 4 Consciousness

1. No, the evidence does not directly demonstrate that ethnicity or race is the differentiating factor in rates of drug use. Statistics comparing rates of drug use in ethnic or racial groups may be misleading if they fail to take into account possible confounding factors, such as differences between groups in education and income levels or characteristics of the neighborhoods in which people of different ethnic or racial groups may live.

2. African Americans have disproportionately high rates of unemployment, and people who are unemployed tend to abuse drugs more often. Blacks and other ethnic minorities are also more likely than Whites to be poor and to live in socially distressed neighborhoods. People living under such conditions are more likely to use drugs than are more affluent people who live in more secure neighborhoods. Investigators who controlled for differences in types of neighborhoods found that African Americans are no more likely than (non-Hispanic) Whites to use crack cocaine (US-DHHS, 1999). Moreover, investigators who controlled for education and income level found that Black Americans are actually less likely than White Americans to develop alcohol or drug dependence problems (Anthony, Warner, & Kessler, 1994).

Chapter 5 Learning

1. the poison; 2. the sheep meat; 3. nausea; 4. taste aversion to sheep meat

Chapter 6 Memory

1. It is likely that the second man rehearsed the information by repeating the license plate number to himself a number of times. Acoustic rehearsal is generally a more efficient method of holding information in short-term memory and transferring it to long-term memory than trying to retain a visual image of the stimulus in mind.

2. The woman apparently had memorized the song phonologically (by sound) rather than semantically (by meaning).

Chapter 7 Thinking, Language, and Intelligence

1a. The shepherd led the sheep to reverse direction and move back behind the ambulance, thus freeing the ambulance to move ahead without obstruction.

1b. The medical technician relied on a mental set for making one's way past a crowd.

2a. The availability heuristic and the representativeness heuristic may help explain John's poor investment decisions. The availability heuristic applies when we base our decisions on whatever happens to come most readily to mind—in John's case, the news reports of the day or comments he hears from others. When using the representativeness heuristic, we treat small samples of occurrences as though they were representative of occurrences in general. An individual news report about a company may be a poor indication of the company's overall financial health or future prospects. Comments from others may be even less trustworthy as a basis for making sound investment decisions.

2b. As John's investment adviser, you should probably recommend that he adopt a sound investment strategy and stick to it rather than basing his investment decisions on daily news reports or comments from others.

Chapter 8 Motivation and Emotion

People commonly think of thoughts and feelings as opposites. You may have heard people say how they feel with their hearts, but think with their heads. Though poets take license with the view that the human heart can "feel," critical thinkers question underlying assumptions, including the assumption that thoughts and feelings are independent of each other (let alone the assumption that the heart has feelings). Psychologists conceptualize emotions as complex feeling states that have important cognitive (thinking) components. They believe that our emotions reflect our cognitions (beliefs, judgments, appraisals, etc.) about our experiences. For example, anger reflects a judgment we make that we have been treated unfairly, whereas fear reflects an appraisal of a situation or object as threatening. In this view, thoughts are bridges to our emotions. To better understand emotions, we need to better understand the interconnections between thoughts and feelings.

Chapter 9 Human Development

1. Three-year-old children like Trevor show a type of thinking pattern that Piaget called animistic thinking—the tendency to attribute human qualities to inanimate objects, such as the sun and the clouds. To Trevor, the sun has feelings ("gets sleepy") and engages in behaviors ("goes to sleep"), just as people do.

2a. To determine your identity status, you first need to decide whether you have achieved a commitment in each area (i.e., occupational choice, political and moral beliefs). A commitment represents either the adoption of a relatively firm set of beliefs or the pursuit of a course of action consistently over time. Critical thinkers weigh the validity of claims in terms of the evidence at hand—in this case, claims of achieving a commitment. What evidence would you seek to support these claims? Here are some examples of the types of criteria you may wish to apply:

  • Showing evidence in your actions and pronouncement to others of a relatively permanent or unswerving commitment to an occupational choice, political philosophy, or set of moral values.

  • Being able to describe your beliefs or actions in an organized and meaningful way.

  • Pursuing a course of action consistent with your career choice and your political and moral beliefs or values.

2b. Now you need to carefully evaluate whether you experienced an identity crisis to arrive at any of the commitments you have achieved. Bearing in mind, again, that critical thinkers weigh the evidence at hand, consider that evidence of an identity crisis might be based on meeting the following criteria:

  • Having undergone a serious examination of alternatives before arriving at a commitment (or are now undergoing this serious examination).

  • Having devoted a serious effort to arriving at a commitment (or are now devoting a serious effort).

  • Having gathered information (or are now gathering information) to seriously evaluate different points of view or courses of action.

Classify yourself in the *identity achievement* status in a given area (career choice, political and moral beliefs) if you have developed a commitment to a set of beliefs or a course of action and underwent an identity crisis to arrive at this commitment. Place yourself in the *moratorium* status if you are presently in a state of identity crisis and are making active efforts to arrive at a commitment. Place yourself in the *foreclosure* category if you arrived at a commitment without having experienced an identity crisis. Classify yourself in the *identity diffusion* category if you have neither achieved a commitment (i.e., currently lack a clear career course or a firmly held set of beliefs or values) nor are currently struggling to arrive at one.

Chapter 10 Personality

The confirmation bias leads us to give credence to information that confirms our preexisting beliefs and to ignore contrary evidence. Thus, for example, we are more likely to believe astrological readings when they conform to beliefs we already hold about ourselves than when they provide contrary information. Since astrological readings contain general personality descriptions that apply to a wide range of people, it's not surprising that many individuals believe these descriptions are true of themselves.

Chapter 11 Psychological Disorders

1. Ron's thought patterns illustrate several cognitive distortions or errors in thinking, including mistaken responsibility (assuming his girlfriend's bad moods were a response to him), catastrophizing (exaggerating the consequences of breaking off the relationship), and jumping to conclusions (assuming that when his girlfriend sat farther away from him in the car it meant she was trying to distance herself emotionally).

2. Lonnie's behavior appears to meet four of the six listed criteria: (a) unusualness (relatively few people are troubled by such obsessive concerns or compulsive rituals), (b) social deviance (repeated checking may be considered socially unacceptable behavior), (c) emotional distress (his compulsive behavior was a source of emotional distress), and (d) maladaptive behavior (his checking rituals were damaging his marital relationship). His behavior does not meet the criterion of dangerousness, since it does not appear to have posed any danger to himself or others. Nor does he exhibit faulty

perceptions or interpretations of reality, such as experiencing hallucinations or holding delusional beliefs.

Chapter 12 Methods of Therapy

A psychodynamic therapist might help Laura explore how her present relationships and feelings of rejection are connected with disappointments she may have experienced in other relationships, including her early relationships with her parents. A humanistic therapist might help Lauren learn to accept and value herself for who she is, regardless of how others respond to her, and not to judge herself by other people's expectations. A cognitive-behavioral therapist might help Lauren increase reinforcing or pleasurable activities in her life and identify and correct distorted thinking patterns ("Everyone's always rejected me. Why should this be any different?"). Biomedical treatment might involve antidepressant medication, or perhaps even electroconvulsive therapy if her depression deepens and fails to respond to other treatment approaches.

Chapter 13 Psychology and Health

The claims may mean the following:

- We may have designed our product to enhance vitality and well-being, but we can't claim that it actually accomplishes this purpose.

- Our product contains amino acids that the body uses to build muscle, but so do many other sources of protein, including meat and dairy products.

- We hired a few physicians with respectable credentials who said they would recommend our product, and we paid them for their endorsements.

- By *backed*, we mean that we conducted research on our product. We're not saying what our research actually found or whether the studies were well designed or carried out by impartial investigators. And when we say advanced, we're referring to research methods that went beyond just asking people if they liked our product.

- We're not really sure what we mean by super-charge, but it sounded good in the advertising copy.

Chapter 14 Social Psychology

Why didn't they help? Though we will never know for certain, several hypotheses can be offered based on factors that have been shown to influence bystander behavior:

- Situational ambiguity. It was dark, and observers may not have had a direct view of the situation. Perhaps they were confused or uncertain about what was happening and whether it was a true emergency.

- Diffusion of responsibility. Even if they recognized the situation as an emergency, perhaps they weren't willing to assume personal responsibility for getting involved. Or perhaps they thought others would act, so they didn't need to. Or perhaps they thought it was "none of their business."

- Perceived cost. Perhaps they believed the cost of helping would be too great—including possible injury or loss of their own lives. But what about the minimal cost involved in calling the police? Perhaps they didn't want to accept a personal role in the incident and become involved in a lengthy court case.

- Attributions of the cause of need. Perhaps they reasoned that the victim deserved what she got. Perhaps they figured the assailant was her boyfriend or husband and that she shouldn't have chosen such a partner.

What do you think is the likely explanation? What do you think *you* would do in a similar situation?

APPENDIX B
Statistics in Psychology

Dennis Hinkle Towson University   **Leping Liu** Towson University

The word *statistics* means different things to different people. Weatherpersons report daily weather statistics, such as high and low temperatures, amount of rainfall, and the average temperatures recorded for this day in history. Sportscasters flood us with statistics that include players' batting averages, fielding percentages, and ratios of home runs to times at bat. And in televised football games, commentators give half-time statistics that include total yards rushing and total yards passing.

Psychologists, too, use statistics. But to them, statistics are procedures for analyzing and understanding the results of research studies. For example, in Chapter 4 you read about studies showing that night-shift workers in sensitive positions tend to be sleepier and less alert than day-shift workers. Investigators in these studies used statistical techniques to determine whether the two groups of workers—night-shift and day-shift workers—differed from each other, *on the average*, on measures of sleepiness and alertness, among other variables. Psychologists also use statistics for describing the characteristics of particular groups of people, including themselves. In Chapter 1, for example, you learned about the characteristics of psychologists with respect to their ethnicities and places of employment.

Fundamental theories in modern psychology would not exist without the application of statistics in psychological research. Psychologists rely on statistics to explain the results of their research studies, as well as to provide empirical evidence to support or refute particular theories or beliefs. For example, investigators used statistical techniques to refute the original version of the *linguistic relativity hypothesis*, which was based on the theory that language determines how we think (see Chapter 7). In this case, statistical analysis of the research findings supported an alternative theory—that cultural factors influence how we think. We all need to understand statistics in order to become more knowledgeable consumers of psychological research. For example, we need to understand how the IQ scores of people in the general population are distributed in order to determine the relative standing of a particular score (again, see Chapter 7). And when seeking psychological assistance, we need to know which forms of therapy have been shown through methods of statistical analysis to be effective for which types of psychological problems (see the discussion in Chapter 12 about *empirically supported treatments*). Whatever the reason for using statistics, researchers and consumers alike should understand the information that statistics provide and the conclusions that can be drawn from them.

Populations and Samples

The terms *population* and *sample* are used frequently in psychological research involving statistical analysis. By definition, a *population* includes all members of a specified group, such as "all residents living in Washington, D.C.," "all patients in a psychiatric hospital at a specified time who are being treated for various psychological disorders," or "all students enrolled in an introductory psychology class in a particular university during the fall semester." In many research situations, however, it is not feasible to include all members of a given population. In such instances, a subset or segment of the population, called a *sample,* is selected to participate, and only the members of that sample are included in the research study.

Descriptive Statistics and Inferential Statistics

descriptive statistics Procedures used for classifying and summarizing information in numerical form—in short, for describing data.

The study of statistics can be divided into two broad categories: descriptive statistics and inferential statistics. Investigators use **descriptive statistics** to describe data (i.e., to classify and summarize information expressed in numerical form), and they use

TABLE 1 Final Examination Scores for Freshman Psychology Students

68	52	69	51	43	36	44	35	54	57	55	56
55	54	54	53	33	48	32	47	47	57	48	56
65	57	64	49	51	56	50	48	53	56	52	55
42	49	41	48	50	24	49	25	53	55	52	56
64	63	63	64	54	45	53	46	50	40	49	41
45	54	44	55	63	55	62	56	50	46	49	47
56	38	55	37	68	46	67	45	65	48	64	49
59	46	58	47	57	58	56	59	60	62	59	63
56	49	55	50	43	45	42	46	53	40	52	41
42	33	41	34	56	32	55	33	40	45	39	46
38	43	37	44	54	56	53	57	57	46	56	45
50	40	49	39	47	55	46	54	39	56	38	55
37	29	36	30	37	49	36	50	36	44	35	45
42	43	41	42	52	47	51	46	63	48	62	49
53	60	52	61	49	55	48	56	38	48	37	47

TABLE 2 Frequency Distribution of Final Examination Scores Using Class Intervals

Class Interval	f
65–69	6
60–64	15
55–59	37
50–54	30
45–49	42
40–44	22
35–39	18
30–34	7
25–29	2
20–24	1

inferential statistics Procedures for making generalizations about a population by studying the characteristics of samples drawn from the population.

frequency distribution A tabulation that indicates the number of times a given score or group of scores occurs.

histogram A graph that depicts the frequencies of individual scores or categories of scores, using bars of different lengths.

frequency polygon A graph on which the frequencies of class intervals are at their midpoints, which are then connected with straight lines.

central tendency A central point on a scale of measurement around which scores are distributed.

inferential statistics to make generalizations about a population by studying results based on a sample drawn from the population.

Descriptive and inferential statistics have three main purposes in scientific inquiry:

1. *To describe*
2. *To relate*
3. *To compare*

These approaches form a general framework for applying statistical procedures that allow researchers to interpret the results of a study, draw conclusions, make generalizations and inferences from samples to populations, and provide a focus for future studies. In the remainder of this appendix, we provide an overview of these three approaches to statistical analysis.

Using Statistics to Describe

The simplest application of statistics involves describing a distribution of scores collected from a group of individuals. Suppose, for example, that we have the final examination scores for 180 freshman psychology students, as shown in Table 1. In order to describe this distribution of scores, we must (1) identify the shape of the distribution, (2) compute the "average" score, and (3) determine the variability of the scores.

Frequency Distribution The first step in describing a distribution of scores is to develop a **frequency distribution** for individual scores or categories of scores.

Table 2 shows a frequency distribution constructed by combining our 180 scores into categories, called *class intervals*, beginning with the category of scores 20–24 and ending with the category of scores 65–69. Note that the categories with the most scores are 45 to 49, which contains 42 scores, and 55–59, which contains 37 scores. We can depict this frequency distribution using a type of bar graph, called a **histogram**. As shown in Figure 1, a histogram depicts the frequencies of class intervals of scores using bars of different lengths. Thus, for example, the class interval of 45–49 is represented by a bar with a value of 42.

Another way of graphing a frequency distribution is to use a **frequency polygon**, as shown in Figure 2. Here, the frequencies of class intervals are plotted at the intervals' midpoints, which are then connected with straight lines.

Measures of Central Tendency The second step in describing a distribution of scores is to compute the **central tendency** of the scores. Central tendency is an indicator of the average score in a distribution of scores. Three different statistical meas-

Figure 1   Histogram of Final Examination Scores

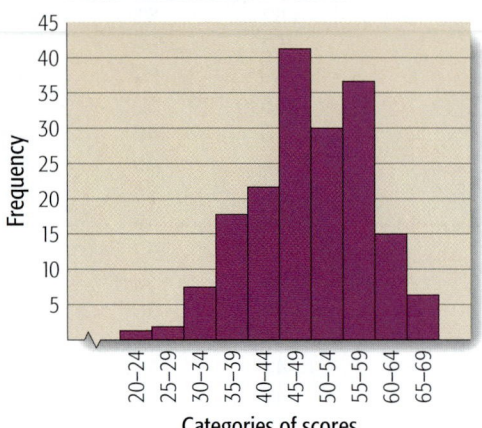

Figure 2   Frequency Polygon of Final Examination Scores

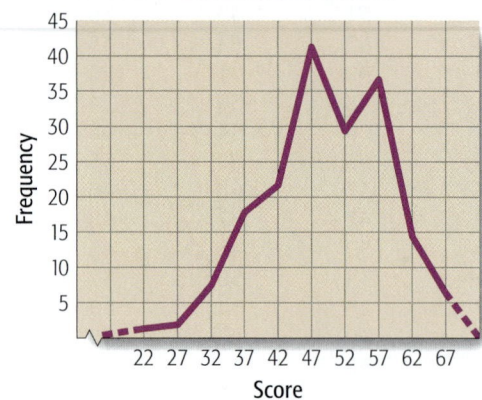

ures of central tendency are available. The researcher can determine the **mode** (most frequent score), the **median** (middle score), or the **mean** (arithmetic average).

As an example, consider the following distribution: 2, 5, 9, 10, 12, 13, 13. The mode is 13, which is the score that occurs most often. The median is the score that slices the distribution of scores in half (half of the scores fall above the median and half fall below). The median is 10, since three scores fall above this value and three fall below.

The mean is the most often used measure of central tendency. To find the mean $(\overline{X})$, sum all the scores (X) and then divide the sum by the number of scores. Symbolically,

$$\overline{X} = \Sigma X/n,$$

where ΣX is the sum of all the scores and n is the total number of scores. For the above distribution of scores, the mean would be computed as follows:

$$\overline{X} = 64/7 = 9.14$$

As you can see, the mode, median, and mean sometimes represent different values.

Similarly, for the final examination scores for the 180 freshman psychology students, the mean would be computed as follows:

$$\overline{X} = 8860/180 = 49.22$$

In other cases, such as the distribution shown in Figure 3(a), the mean, median, and mode are represented by the same value. But when the distribution is skewed ("tilted" to the right or left), as in Figure 3(b), the mean, median, and mode do not coincide.

What is the best measure of central tendency? The answer depends on what we want to know. If we're interested in finding out what score has been received most often on an examination, we would use the mode. But the most frequently occurring score may not be the best representation of how the class performed on the average. For that determination, we could use the median, which indicates the middle score

Figure 3   Comparisons of the Mode, Median, and Mean in Two Distributions

mode   The most frequent score in a distribution of scores.

median   The middle score in a distribution, above and below which half of the scores fall.

mean   The arithmetic average of the scores in a distribution.

Mean, median, mode
(a)

Mean   Mode
Median
(b)

in the distribution—that is, the score below which half of the scores fall and above which half of the scores fall. By knowing the median, we could specify which score separates the top half of the class from the bottom half.

We could also use the mean, which provides us with the arithmetic average of the whole class. But one limitation of the mean is that it is greatly influenced by extreme scores. Consider the following example of the distribution of salaries for employees in a small manufacturing company:

Position	Number of Employees	Salary	Measure of Central Tendency
President/CEO	1	$350,000	
Executive vice president	1	120,000	
Vice presidents	2	95,000	
Controller	1	60,000	
Senior salespeople	3	58,000	Mean
Junior salespeople	4	40,000	
Foreman	1	36,000	Median
Machinists	12	30,000	Mode

In this example, the mean is greatly influenced by one very high score—the salary of the president/CEO. If you were the chairperson of the local machinists' union, which measure of central tendency would you use to negotiate a new wage agreement? Alternatively, which would you use if you represented management's position in the negotiations?

Another consideration in choosing the best measure concerns how it is to be used. If we wish to generalize from samples to populations, the mean has a distinct advantage. It can be manipulated mathematically in ways that are inappropriate for the median or the mode. But if the purpose is primarily descriptive, then the measure that best characterizes the data should be used. In general, reporting all three measures of central tendency provides the most accurate description of a given distribution.

Measures of Variability The final step in describing a distribution of scores is to compute the **variability** of the scores. Variability is the spread of scores throughout the distribution of scores. One measure of variability is the **range** of scores, or the difference between the highest and lowest scores in the distribution. The final examination scores for the 180 freshman psychology students range from a low of 24 to a high of 69, so the range would be $69 - 24 = 45$.

Another, more commonly used measure of variability is the **standard deviation (SD)**, conceptually defined as the average difference between each individual score and the mean of all scores in the data set. A large standard deviation suggests considerable variability (spread) of scores around the mean, whereas a small standard deviation indicates little variability. Table 3 illustrates the computations involved in calculating the standard deviation based on a hypothetical data set. (The standard deviation of the 180 final examination scores is 8.98.)

TABLE 3 **Calculation of a Standard Deviation**

Score	Deviation from Mean (D)	Deviation Squared (D^2)
3	$3 - 9 = -6$	36
5	$5 - 9 = -4$	16
6	$6 - 9 = -3$	9
9	$9 - 9 = 0$	0
12	$12 - 9 = 3$	9
13	$13 - 9 = 4$	16
15	$15 - 9 = 6$	36
$\bar{X} = 63/7 = 9$		$\Sigma D^2 = 122$

Standard Deviation $= \sqrt{\Sigma D^2/n} = \sqrt{122/7} = \sqrt{17.43} = 4.17$

Figure 4 A Normal Distribution, Showing the Approximate Percentages of Cases Falling Within One and Two Standard Deviations from the Mean

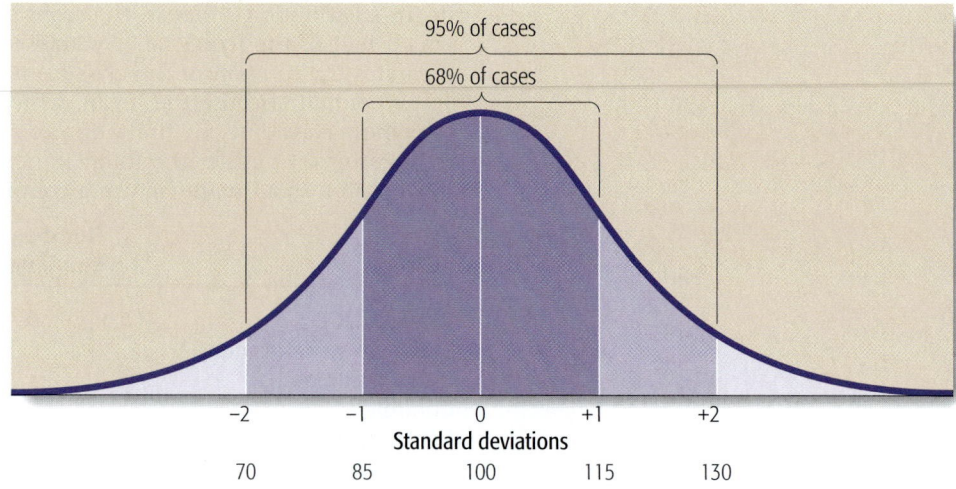

The Normal Distribution The histogram for the 180 final examination scores in Figure 1 illustrates a commonly observed phenomenon in psychological data—namely, that the majority of scores tend to fall in the middle of the distribution, with fewer scores in the extreme categories. For many measures used in psychological research, score distributions have this general shape and are said to resemble a "bell-shaped curve," which is otherwise known as a "normal curve" or "normal distribution." In statistics, the true normal distribution is a mathematical model. However, when the shape of a particular score distribution closely aligns with a normal distribution, we can use the general properties of the normal distribution to describe the distribution of actual scores under study. The normal distribution provides a good description of the distribution of many sets of data, such as measures of intelligence and achievement. Moreover, in a normal distribution, the mean, median, and mode all have the same value, so we can use the standard deviation to describe a particular score in the distribution relative to all scores in the distribution.

In a normal distribution, such as the one shown in Figure 4, half of all cases fall above the mean and half fall below. Based on the properties of the normal distribution, we can determine the percentages of cases that fall within each segment of the distribution. For example, approximately 68 percent of cases fall within one standard deviation above and below the mean (between −1.0 and +1.0), and approximately 95 percent of cases fall within two standard deviations above and below the mean (between −2.0 and +2.0).

The properties of the normal distribution can also be used to describe the distance between a score and the mean. Scores on most IQ tests, for example, are distributed with a mean of 100 and a standard deviation of 15. Thus, an IQ score of 115 would be about one standard deviation above the mean. We use the term **standard score** (also called a *z-score*) to refer to a transformed score that indicates how many standard deviations the actual (raw) score is above or below the mean. For example, the standard score corresponding to a raw score of 115, based on a mean of 100 and a standard deviation of 15, would be +1.0. Similarly, we could say that a score of 70 is two standard deviations below the mean; in this case, the standard score would be −2.0. These standard score properties of the normal distribution are critical in applying inferential statistical procedures in psychological research.

Using Statistics to Relate

A second application of statistics involves determining the relationship between two variables. As an example, let's say we want to determine the relationship between quantitative SAT scores and final examination scores, using the data for fifteen introductory psychology students shown in Table 4.

variability In statistics, the spread or dispersion of scores throughout the distribution.

range A measure of variability that is given by the difference in value between the highest and lowest scores in a distribution of scores.

standard deviation (SD) A measure of variability defined as the average difference between each individual score and the mean of all scores in the data set.

standard score A transformed score that indicates the number of standard deviations a corresponding raw score is above or below the mean. Also called a *z-score*.

TABLE 4   Quantitative SAT Scores and Final Examination Scores for Fifteen Introductory Psychology Students

Student	Quantitative SAT Score (X)	Final Examination Score (Y)
1	595	68
2	520	55
3	715	65
4	405	42
5	680	64
6	490	45
7	565	56
8	580	59
9	615	56
10	435	42
11	440	38
12	515	50
13	380	37
14	510	42
15	565	53
Σ	8,010	772

$\overline{X} = 534.00$ $\overline{Y} = 51.47$
$s_X = 96.53$ $s_Y = 10.11$

Figure 5
Scatterplot Illustrating the Relationship Between Final Examination Scores (Y) and Quantitative SAT Scores (X)

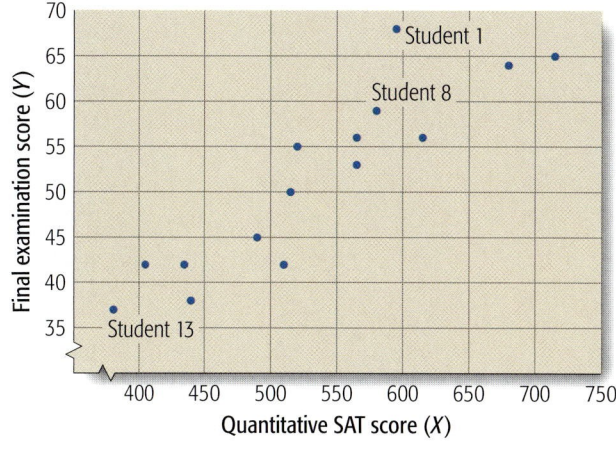

The Scatterplot: Plotting the Data   Our first step would be to enter these data in a **scatterplot**, a type of graph that represents the "scatter" of scores obtained by plotting each individual's scores on two variables. The two variables can be symbolized by the terms X and Y.

In Figure 5, each point represents the paired measurements for each of the fifteen students, three of whom—Students 1, 8, and 13—are labeled specifically. (For example, the point for Student 1 represents the paired scores "SAT = 595" and "Final Score = 68.") Notice that these points form a pattern that starts in the lower-left corner and ends in the upper-right corner of the scatterplot. This pattern occurs when there is a positive relationship, or *positive correlation*, between the two variables. A positive correlation between two variables means that higher scores on one variable are associated with higher scores on the other variable. The pattern shown in Figure 5 thus illustrates that students with higher SAT scores tend to have higher final examination scores, and vice versa.

Different scatterplot patterns emerge as a result of different types of relationships between two variables. Three of these patterns are illustrated in Figure 6. Pattern A depicts a positive correlation between two variables. Pattern B depicts a negative correlation—a relationship in which higher scores on one variable are associated with lower scores on the other variable. And Pattern C is a scatterplot in which the points have neither an upward nor a downward trend. This last pattern occurs in situations where there is a zero correlation (no relationship) between the two variables.

Figure 6
Scatterplots Illustrating Varying Degrees of Relationship Between X and Y

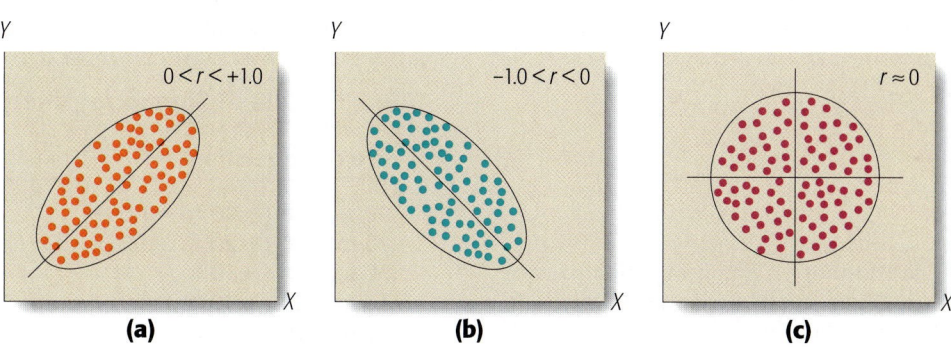

The Correlation Coefficient: Calculating the Relationship Between Two Variables The scatterplot gives us a visual representation of the relationship between two variables. But researchers also use a statistical measure that provides a more precise indication of both the magnitude (strength) and direction of the relationship (positive or negative). The statistical measure of the relationship between two variables is called the *correlation coefficient* (expressed by the letter *r*). The range of values for positive correlation coefficients is from 0 (minimum) to +1.0 (maximum); the range of values for negative correlation coefficients is from 0 (minimum) to −1.0 (maximum).

Table 5 shows a worked-out example of the computations involved in calculating a correlation coefficient based on the data presented in Table 4. The correlation coefficient is found to be +0.90, which represents a very high, positive relationship between SAT scores and final examination scores. In other words, as we saw earlier, freshmen with higher SAT scores tend to achieve higher scores in their psychology exams.

Table 6 provides some rules of thumb for interpreting the magnitude of a correlation coefficient.

TABLE 5 Calculation of Correlation Coefficient Between Quantitative SAT Scores and Final Examination Scores

Quantitative SAT Scores		Final Exam Scores		
X	X²	Y	Y²	XY
595	354,025	68	4,624	40,460
520	270,400	55	3,025	28,600
715	511,225	65	4,225	46,475
405	164,025	42	1,764	17,010
680	462,400	64	4,096	43,520
490	240,100	45	2,025	22,050
565	319,225	56	3,136	31,640
580	336,400	59	3,481	34,220
615	378,225	56	3,136	34,440
435	189,225	42	1,764	18,270
440	193,600	38	1,444	16,720
515	265,225	50	2,500	25,750
380	144,400	37	1,369	14,060
510	260,100	42	1,764	21,420
565	319,225	53	2,809	29,945
8,010	4,407,800	772	41,162	424,580

$$\text{Raw Score Formula} = \frac{n\Sigma XY - \Sigma X \Sigma Y}{\sqrt{n\Sigma X^2 - (\Sigma X)^2}\ \sqrt{n\Sigma Y^2 - (\Sigma Y)^2}}$$

$$= \frac{15(424,580) - (8,010)(772)}{\sqrt{15(4,407,800) - (8,010)^2}\ \sqrt{15(41,162) - (772)^2}}$$

$$= 0.90$$

TABLE 6 Rule of Thumb for Interpreting the Size of a Correlation Coefficient

Size of Correlation	Interpretation
.90 to 1.00 (−.90 to −1.00)	Very high positive (negative) correlation
.70 to .90 (−.70 to −.90)	High positive (negative) correlation
.50 to .70 (−.50 to −.70)	Moderate positive (negative) correlation
.30 to .50 (−.30 to −.50)	Low positive (negative) correlation
.00 to .30 (.00 to −.30)	Little if any correlation

scatterplot A graph in which pairs of scores are plotted for each research participant on two variables.

Using One Variable to Predict Another An important use of correlational statistics is prediction. If two variables are correlated, we can predict scores on one variable based upon scores on the other variable. For example, after determining the relationship between SAT scores and final examination scores for our fifteen introductory psychology students, let's suppose that we want to predict the final examination scores of similar students based upon our knowledge of their SAT scores. The process of prediction involves developing a mathematical equation that incorporates the paired sets of scores on the two variables obtained in the study. This equation can then be used to predict final examination scores based on SAT scores for comparable groups of students. The accuracy of the prediction reflects the magnitude of the correlation between the variables: The higher the correlation, the better the prediction. If a strong relationship exists between the two variables, knowing how students score on the SAT would allow us to make fairly accurate predictions about how they will perform in their psychology courses.

Using Statistics to Compare

A third application of statistics involves comparing two or more groups. Let's say, for example, that an educational psychologist is interested in examining the effects of computerized instruction on the mathematics achievement of fourth-grade students. The psychologist's first step would be to assign participants to either an experimental group or a control group based on the technique of *random assignment* (discussed in Chapter 1). The experimental group would use a computer program that allows them to acquire mathematical concepts through interactive on-screen exercises, whereas the control group would receive standard classroom instruction. Then, at the conclusion of the study, both groups would be tested on a mathematics achievement test.

Let's further suppose that the results of the initial descriptive data analysis are as follows:

	Control Group	Experimental Group
Mean ($\bar{X}$)	62.4	77.6
Standard Deviation (SD)	15.8	16.3

Using these data, the educational psychologist would be able to describe the performance of the two groups by examining their means and standard deviations. Note, however, that for drawing conclusions and making generalizations from these data, inferential statistical procedures would also be needed.

Beyond Description: Using Inferential Statistics Descriptive statistics allow us to summarize data, but the meaning of these statistical measures cannot be fully understood through descriptive statistics alone. In psychological research, it is important to determine whether the size of a correlation coefficient, or the difference between the means of two groups, is statistically significant. As discussed in Chapter 1 of the text, *statistical significance* indicates that the results obtained from a study are unlikely to have been due to chance or to the random fluctuations that would be expected to occur among scores in the general population.

Statistical significance can be determined only through the use of statistical techniques, called inferential statistics, that enable us to draw conclusions from our data and to make inferences and generalizations from samples to the populations from which they are drawn.

Stating the Null Hypothesis The first step in using inferential statistics is to state a **null hypothesis** for the study in question. Defined literally, the word *null* refers to something of no value or significance. By the same token, a null hypothesis is a prediction that a given finding has no value or significance. For the study of the relationship between SAT scores and final examination scores, we can state the following null hypothesis: "There is *no relationship* between the two variables." And for the study of the difference between experimental and control groups on the question of

null hypothesis A prediction of no difference between groups or no relationship between variables.

computerized versus standard instruction, we can offer this null hypothesis: "There is *no difference* between the two groups."

Testing the Null Hypothesis   The main purpose of inferential statistics is to test the null hypothesis. Using these techniques, scientific investigators can apply principles of probability to determine whether relationships between variables or differences between groups are large enough to be unlikely to be due to chance. In the process, they typically apply a criterion by which an outcome is judged to be significant when its likelihood of arising from chance is less than 5 percent. In other words, if the probability that an outcome would occur by chance alone is less than 5 percent, they would say that the finding is statistically significant. Depending on the nature of the research, researchers may set either more stringent or more liberal criteria for determining the threshold at which they would represent a given finding as statistically significant.

Let's return to our example of the fifteen introductory psychology students. First, if the correlation coefficient between their SAT scores and final examination scores is high enough to reach a level of statistical significance, we would reject the null hypothesis of "no relationship." In other words, we would conclude that the correlation is significantly different from zero (which in itself means "no relationship"). Second, in applying inferential statistics to the prediction of scores on one variable from scores on another, we would say that the null hypothesis is that SAT scores do not predict final examination scores. But since there *is* a statistically significant relationship between these two variables, our conclusion (based on probability theory) would be that SAT scores are a significant predictor of final examination scores.

Inferential statistics are used in a similar way when investigating differences between two or more groups. These statistical techniques involve mathematical constructs based on probability theory for determining whether differences between sample means are large enough to reject the null hypothesis of "no difference." If the difference between the means of the computer instruction group and the classroom instruction group are large enough to meet the threshold of statistical significance, we would reject the null hypothesis and conclude that the difference between the groups is statistically significant. The underlying rationale is that when group differences between samples of research participants on measures of interest meet the threshold for statistical significance, they are unlikely to reflect chanceful variations that would be expected to occur on these measures in the population in general.

Summing Up

In this brief introduction to statistics, we have provided some basic terminology, identified several approaches to using statistics in psychological research, and discussed descriptive and inferential statistics as well as their general application in research studies. We have also offered a convenient way of categorizing the main purposes of statistics: (1) to describe, (2) to relate, and (3) to compare. An understanding of all these aspects of statistics is necessary not only for researchers in psychology but also for consumers of research results.

GLOSSARY

absolute threshold The smallest amount of a given stimulus a person can sense. *(p. 84)*

accommodation (1) The process by which the lens changes its shape to focus images more clearly on the retina. (2) To Piaget, the process of creating new schemas or modifying existing ones to account for new objects or experiences. *(pp. 88 and 314)*

acculturative stress Demands faced by immigrants in adjusting to a host culture. *(p. 457)*

achievement motivation The motive or desire to achieve success. *(p. 262)*

acronym A word composed of the first letters of a series of words. *(p. 217)*

acrophobia Excessive fear of heights. *(p. 390)*

acrostic A verse or saying in which the first or last letter of each word stands for something else. *(p. 217)*

action potential An abrupt change from a negative to a positive charge of a nerve cell; also called a *neural impulse. (p. 43)*

activation-synthesis hypothesis The proposition that dreams represent the brain's attempt to make sense of the random discharges of electrical activity that occur during REM sleep. *(p. 132)*

actor-observer effect The tendency to attribute the causes of one's own behavior to situational factors while attributing the causes of other people's behavior to internal factors or dispositions. *(p. 484)*

acupuncture An ancient Chinese practice of inserting and rotating thin needles in various parts of the body in order to release natural healing energy. *(p. 103)*

adaptation To Piaget, the process of adjustment that enables people to function more effectively in meeting the demands they face in the environment. *(p. 314)*

adolescence The period of life beginning at puberty and ending with early adulthood. *(p. 319)*

adoptee studies Studies that examine whether adoptees are more similar to their biological or adoptive parents with respect to their psychological traits or to the disorders they develop. *(p. 75)*

adrenal cortex The outer layer of the adrenal glands that secretes corticosteroids (cortical steroids). *(p. 461)*

adrenal glands A pair of endocrine glands located just above the kidneys that produce various stress-related hormones. *(p. 70 and 461)*

adrenal medulla The inner part of the adrenal glands that secretes the stress hormones epinephrine (adrenaline) and norepinephrine (noradrenaline). *(p. 461)*

adrenocorticotrophic hormone (ACTH) A pituitary hormone that activates the adrenal cortex to release corticosteroids (cortical steroids). *(p. 461)*

afterimage The visual image of a stimulus that remains after the stimulus is removed. *(p. 91)*

agonists Drugs that either increase the availability or effectiveness of neurotransmitters or mimic their actions. *(p. 46)*

agoraphobia Excessive, irrational fear of being in public places. *(p. 390)*

alarm stage The first stage of the general adaptation syndrome, involving mobilization of the body's resources to cope with an immediate stressor. *(p. 459)*

alcoholism A chemical addiction characterized by impaired control over the use of alcohol and physiological dependence on it. *(p. 145)*

algorithm A step-by-step set of rules that will always lead to a correct solution to a problem. *(p. 227)*

all-or-none principle The principle by which neurons will fire only when a change in the level of excitation occurs that is sufficient to produce an action potential. *(p. 43)*

altered states of consciousness States of awareness that differ from one's usual waking state. *(p. 128)*

Alzheimer's disease An irreversible brain disease with a gradual onset and a slow but progressive course toward inevitable deterioration of mental functioning. *(p. 334)*

amnesia Loss of memory. *(p. 211)*

amniotic sac The uterine sac that contains the fetus. *(p. 297)*

amphetamines A class of synthetically derived stimulant drugs, such as methamphetamine or "speed." *(p. 46)*

amygdala A set of almond-shaped structures in the limbic system believed to play an important role in aggression, rage, and fear. *(p. 54)*

anal-expulsive personality In Freudian theory, a personality type characterized by messiness, lack of self-discipline, and carelessness. *(p. 350)*

anal-retentive personality In Freudian theory, a personality type characterized by perfectionism and excessive needs for self-control as expressed through extreme neatness and punctuality. *(p. 350)*

anal stage In Freudian theory, the second stage of psychosexual development, during which sexual gratification is centered on processes of elimination (retention and release of bowel contents). *(p. 350)*

animistic thinking To Piaget, the child's belief that inanimate objects have living qualities. *(p. 316)*

antagonists Drugs that block the actions of neurotransmitters by occupying the receptor sites in which the neurotransmitters dock. *(p. 45)*

anterograde amnesia Loss or impairment of the ability to form or store new memories. *(p. 212)*

antianxiety drugs Drugs that combat anxiety. *(p. 436)*

antibodies Protein molecules produced by the immune system that serve to mark antigens for destruction by specialized lymphocytes. *(p. 462)*

antidepressants Drugs that combat depression by affecting the levels or activity of neurotransmitters. *(pp. 46 and 437)*

antigens Substances, such as bacteria and viruses, that are recognized by the immune system as foreign to the body and that induce it to produce antibodies to defend against them. *(p. 462)*

antipsychotics Drugs used in the treatment of psychotic disorders that help alleviate hallucinations and delusional thinking. *(p. 437)*

antisocial personality disorder (APD) A type of personality disorder characterized by callous attitudes toward others and by antisocial and irresponsible behavior. *(p. 410)*

aphasia Loss or impairment of the ability to understand or express language. *(p. 63)*

applied research Research that attempts to find solutions to specific problems. *(p. 14)*

archetypes Jung's term for the primitive images contained in the collective unconscious that reflect ancestral or universal experiences of human beings. *(p. 352)*

arousal theory The belief that whenever the level of stimulation dips below an organism's optimal level, the organism seeks ways of increasing it. *(p. 260)*

arteries Blood vessels that carry oxygen-rich blood from the heart through the circulatory system. *(p. 466)*

arteriosclerosis A condition in which artery walls become thicker and lose elasticity. Commonly called *hardening of the arteries. (p. 466)*

assimilation To Piaget, the process of incorporating new objects or situations into existing schemas. *(p. 314)*

association areas Areas of the cerebral cortex that piece together sensory information to form meaningful perceptions of the world and perform higher mental functions. *(p. 57)*

atherosclerosis A form of arteriosclerosis involving the narrowing of artery walls resulting from the buildup of fatty deposits or plaque. *(p. 466)*

attachment The enduring emotional bond that infants and older children form with their caregivers. *(p. 306)*

attitude A positive or negative evaluation of persons, objects, or issues. *(p. 485)*

attraction Feelings of liking for others, together with having positive thoughts about them and inclinations to act toward them in positive ways. *(p. 491)*

attribution An assumption about the causes of behavior or events. *(p. 484)*

attributional style A person's characteristic way of explaining outcomes of events in his or her life. *(p. 402)*

audition The sense of hearing. *(p. 94)*

auditory nerve The nerve that carries electrical impulses from the ear to the brain, which gives rise to the experience of hearing. *(p. 96)*

authoritarian personality A personality type characterized by rigidity, prejudice, and excessive concerns with obedience and respect for authority. *(p. 498)*

autonomic nervous system The part of the peripheral nervous system that automatically regulates involuntary bodily processes, such as breathing, heart rate, and digestion. *(p. 50)*

availability heuristic The tendency to judge events as more likely to occur when information pertaining to them comes readily to mind. *(p. 229)*

aversive conditioning A form of behavior therapy in which stimuli associated with undesirable behavior are paired with aversive stimuli to create a negative response to these stimuli. *(p. 425)*

avoidance learning The learning of behaviors that allow an organism to avoid an aversive stimulus. *(p. 178)*

avoidance motivation The motive or desire to avoid failure. *(p. 262)*

axon The tubelike part of a neuron that carries messages away from the cell body toward other neurons. *(p. 40)*

Babinski reflex The reflexive fanning out and curling of the infant's toes and inward twisting of its foot upon stroking the sole of the foot. *(p. 301)*

bait-and-switch technique A compliance technique based on "baiting" an individual by making an unrealistically attractive offer and then replacing it with a less attractive offer. *(p. 512)*

basal cell carcinoma A form of skin cancer that is easily curable if detected and removed early. *(p. 471)*

basal ganglia An assemblage of neurons lying in the forebrain that is important in controlling movement and coordination. *(p. 54)*

basic anxiety In Horney's theory, a deep-seated form of anxiety in children that is associated with feelings of being isolated and helpless in a world perceived as potentially threatening and hostile. *(p. 352)*

basic hostility In Horney's theory, deep feelings of resentment that children may harbor toward their parents. *(p. 352)*

basic research Research focused on acquiring knowledge even if such knowledge has no direct practical application. *(p. 14)*

basilar membrane The membrane in the cochlea that is attached to the organ of Corti. *(p. 96)*

behavioral perspective An approach to the study of psychology that focuses on the role of learning in explaining observable behavior. *(p. 182)*

behaviorism The school of psychology that holds that psychology should limit itself to the study of overt, observable behavior. *(p. 6)*

behavior modification (B-mod) The systematic application of learning principles to strengthen adaptive behavior and weaken maladaptive behavior. *(p. 182)*

behavior therapy A form of therapy that involves the systematic application of the principles of learning. *(pp. 9, 167, and 423)*

binocular cues Cues for depth that involve both eyes, such as retinal disparity and convergence. *(p. 112)*

biofeedback training (BFT) A method of learning to control certain bodily responses by using information transmitted by physiological monitoring equipment. *(p. 77)*

biopsychosocial model An integrative model for explaining abnormal behavior patterns in terms of the interactions of biological, psychological, and sociocultural factors. *(p. 386)*

bipolar cells A layer of interconnecting cells in the eye that connect photoreceptors to ganglion cells. *(p. 89)*

bipolar disorder A type of mood disorder characterized by mood swings from extreme elation (mania) to severe depression. *(p. 400)*

blind spot The area in the retina where the optic nerve leaves the eye and that contains no photoreceptor cells. *(p. 89)*

borderline personality disorder A type of personality disorder characterized by unstable emotions and self-image. *(p. 410)*

bottom-up processing A mode of perceptual processing by which the brain recognizes meaningful patterns by piecing together bits and pieces of sensory information. *(p. 108)*

brain The mass of nerve tissue encased in the skull that controls virtually everything we are and everything we do. *(p. 40)*

brainstem The "stalk" in the lower part of the brain that connects the spinal cord to higher regions of the brain. *(p. 53)*

brainstorming A method of promoting divergent thinking by encouraging people to propose as many solutions to a problem as possible without fear of being judged negatively by others, no matter how far-fetched their proposals may be. *(p. 252)*

brightness constancy The tendency to perceive objects as retaining their brightness even when they are viewed in dim light. *(p. 112)*

Broca's area An area of the left frontal lobe involved in speech. *(p. 62)*

bystander intervention Helping a stranger in distress. *(p. 495)*

Cannon-Bard theory The belief that emotional and physiological reactions to triggering stimuli occur almost simultaneously. *(p. 284)*

cardinal traits Allport's term for the more pervasive dimensions that define an individual's general personality. *(p. 355)*

carpentered-world hypothesis An attempt to explain the Müller-Lyer illusion in terms of the cultural experience of living in a carpentered, right-angled world like our own. *(p. 116)*

case study method An in-depth study of one or more individuals. *(p. 23)*

castration anxiety In Freudian theory, unconscious fear of removal of the penis as punishment for having unacceptable sexual impulses. *(p. 350)*

catatonic type A subtype of schizophrenia characterized by bizarre movements, postures, or grimaces. *(p. 407)*

central executive The component of working memory responsible for coordinating the other subsystems, receiving and processing stored information, and filtering out distracting thoughts. *(p. 198)*

central nervous system The part of the nervous system that consists of the brain and spinal cord. *(p. 49)*

central tendency A central point on a scale of measurement around which scores are distributed. *(p. A-5)*

central traits Allport's term for personality characteristics that have a widespread influence on the individual's behavior across situations. *(p. 355)*

centration To Piaget, the tendency to focus on only one aspect of a situation at a time. *(p. 316)*

cerebellum A structure in the hindbrain involved in controlling coordination and balance. *(p. 53)*

cerebral cortex The wrinkled, outer layer of gray matter that covers the cerebral hemispheres; controls higher mental functions, such as thought and language. *(p. 54)*

cerebral hemispheres The right and left masses of the cerebrum, which are joined by the corpus callosum. *(p. 54)*

cerebrum The largest mass of the forebrain, consisting of two cerebral hemispheres. *(p. 54)*

chromosomes Rodlike structures in the cell nucleus that house the individual's genes. *(p. 72)*

chronic stress Continuing or lingering sources of stress. *(p. 451)*

chunking The process of enhancing retention of a large amount of information by breaking it down into smaller, more easily recalled chunks. *(p. 197)*

circadian rhythm The pattern of fluctuations in bodily processes that occur regularly each day. *(p. 129)*

clairvoyance The ability to perceive objects and events without using the known senses. *(p. 118)*

classical conditioning The process of learning by which a previously neutral stimulus comes to elicit a response identical or similar to one that was originally elicited by another stimulus as the result of the pairing or association of the two stimuli. *(p. 162)*

claustrophobia Excessive fear of enclosed spaces. *(p. 390)*

clinical psychologists Psychologists who use psychological techniques to evaluate and treat individuals with mental or psychological disorders. *(p. 15)*

closure The perceptual principle that people tend to piece together disconnected bits of information to perceive whole forms. *(p. 111)*

cochlea The snail-shaped organ in the inner ear that contains sensory receptors for hearing. *(p. 95)*

cognitive-behavioral therapy (CBT) A form of therapy that combines behavioral and cognitive treatment techniques. *(p. 426)*

cognitive dissonance theory The belief that people are motivated to resolve discrepancies between their behavior and their attitudes, beliefs, or perceptions. *(p. 487)*

cognitive learning Learning that occurs without the opportunity of first performing the learned response or being reinforced for it. *(p. 183)*

cognitive map A mental representation of an area that helps an organism navigate its way from one point to another. *(p. 184)*

cognitive perspective An approach to the study of psychology that focuses on the processes by which we acquire knowledge. *(p. 11)*

cognitive psychology The branch of psychology that focuses on such mental processes as thinking, problem solving, decision making, and use of language. *(p. 224)*

cognitive therapy Developed by Aaron Beck, a form of therapy based on a collaborative effort between clients and therapists that helps clients recognize and correct distorted patterns of thinking believed to underlie their emotional problems. *(p. 428)*

collective unconscious In Jung's theory, a part of the mind containing ideas and archetypal images shared among humankind that have been transmitted genetically from ancestral humans. *(p. 352)*

collectivistic culture A culture that emphasizes people's social roles and obligations. *(p. 366)*

color constancy The tendency to perceive an object as having the same color despite changes in lighting conditions. *(p. 112)*

comparative psychologists Psychologists who study behavioral similarities and differences among animal species. *(p. 15)*

compliance The tendency to accede to the requests or demands of others. *(p. 512)*

computer-assisted instruction A form of programmed instruction in which a computer is used to guide a student through a series of increasingly difficult questions. *(p. 182)*

concepts Mental categories for classifying events, objects, and ideas on the basis of their common features or properties. *(p. 225)*

conceptual combinations Combinations of two or more concepts into one concept, resulting in the creation of a novel idea or application. *(p. 231)*

conceptual expansion The expansion of familiar concepts into new uses. *(p. 231)*

concordance rates In twin studies, the percentages of cases in which both members of twin pairs share the same trait or disorder. *(p. 75)*

conditional positive regard Valuing a person only when the person's behavior meets certain expectations or standards. *(p. 365)*

conditioned emotional reaction (CER) An emotional response to a particular stimulus acquired through classical conditioning. *(p. 167)*

conditioned response (CR) An acquired or learned response to a conditioned stimulus. *(p. 162)*

conditioned stimulus (CS) A previously neutral stimulus that comes to elicit a conditioned response after it has been paired with an unconditioned stimulus. *(p. 162)*

conditioned taste aversions Aversions to particular tastes acquired through classical conditioning. *(p. 168)*

conduction deafness A form of deafness, usually involving damage to the middle ear, in which there is a loss of conduction of sound vibrations through the ear. *(p. 97)*

cones Photoreceptors that are sensitive to color. *(p. 88)*

confirmation bias The tendency to maintain allegiance to an initial hypothesis despite strong evidence to the contrary. *(p. 229)*

conflict A state of tension brought about by opposing motives operating simultaneously. *(p. 453)*

conformity The tendency to adjust one's behavior to actual or perceived social pressures. *(p. 505)*

connectedness The principle that objects positioned together or moving together will be perceived as belonging to the same group. *(p. 111)*

conscious To Freud, the part of the mind corresponding to the state of present awareness. *(p. 346)*

consciousness A state of awareness of ourselves and of the world around us. *(p. 126)*

conservation In Piaget's theory, the ability to recognize that the quantity or amount of an object remains constant despite superficial changes in its outward appearance. *(p. 316)*

consolidation The process of converting short-term memories into long-term memories. *(p. 198)*

constructionist theory A theory that holds that memory is not a replica of the past but a representation, or *reconstruction*, of the past. *(p. 202)*

consumer psychologists Psychologists who study why people purchase particular products and brands. *(p. 18)*

contact hypothesis Allport's belief that under certain conditions, increased intergroup contact helps reduce prejudice and intergroup tension. *(p. 499)*

continuity The principle that a series of stimuli will be perceived as representing a unified form. *(p. 111)*

control groups Groups of participants in a research experiment who do not receive the experimental treatment or intervention. *(p. 26)*

convergence A binocular cue for distance based on the degree of tension required to focus two eyes on the same object. *(p. 113)*

convergent thinking The attempt to narrow down a range of alternatives to converge on the one correct answer to a problem. *(p. 231)*

conversion disorder A type of somatoform disorder characterized by a change in or loss of a physical function that cannot be explained by medical causes. *(p. 396)*

cornea A transparent covering on the eye's surface through which light enters. *(p. 88)*

coronary heart disease (CHD) The most common form of heart disease, caused by blockages in coronary arteries, the vessels that supply the heart with blood. *(p. 466)*

corpus callosum The thick bundle of nerve fibers that connects the two cerebral hemispheres. *(p. 54)*

correlational method A research method that examines relationships between variables. *(p. 25)*

correlation coefficient A statistical measure of association between variables that can vary from -1.00 to +1.00. *(p. 25)*

corticosteroids Adrenal hormones that increase the body's resistance to stress by increasing the availability of stored nutrients to meet the increased energy demands of coping with stressful events. Also called *cortical steroids*. *(p. 461)*

corticotrophin-releasing hormone (CRH) A hormone released by the hypothalamus that induces the pituitary gland to release adrenocorticotrophic hormone. *(p. 461)*

counseling psychologists Psychologists who help people clarify their goals and make life decisions or find ways of overcoming problems in various areas of their lives. *(p. 17)*

countertransference The tendency for therapists to relate to clients in ways that mirror their relationships with important figures in their own lives. *(p. 420)*

couple therapy Therapy that focuses on helping distressed couples resolve their conflicts and develop more effective communication skills. *(p. 431)*

creative self In Adler's theory, the self-aware part of personality that organizes goal-seeking efforts. *(p. 352)*

creativity Originality of thought associated with the development of new, workable products or solutions to problems. *(p. 230)*

critical thinking The adoption of a skeptical, questioning attitude and careful scrutiny of claims or arguments. *(p. 32)*

crystallized intelligence A form of intelligence associated with the ability to use accumulated knowledge. *(p. 329)*

CT (computed tomography) scan A computer-enhanced imaging technique in which an X-ray beam is passed through the body at different angles to generate a three-dimensional image of bodily structures (also called a CAT scan, short for *computerized axial tomography*). *(p. 58)*

culture-fair tests Tests designed to eliminate cultural biases. *(p. 242)*

daydreaming A form of consciousness during a waking state in which one's mind wanders to dreamy thoughts or fantasies. *(p. 126)*

decay theory A theory of forgetting that posits that memories consist of traces laid down in the brain that gradually deteriorate and fade away over time (also called *trace theory*). *(p. 206)*

decision making A form of problem solving in which we must select a course of action from among the available alternatives. *(p. 228)*

declarative memory Memory of facts and personal information that requires a conscious effort to bring to mind (also called *explicit memory*). *(p. 199)*

defense mechanisms In Freudian theory, the reality-distorting strategies of the ego to prevent awareness of anxiety-evoking or troubling ideas or impulses. *(p. 348)*

deinstitutionalization A policy of reducing the population of mental hospitals by shifting care from inpatient facilities to community-based outpatient facilities. *(p. 440)*

delirium A mental state characterized by confusion, disorientation, difficulty in focusing attention, and excitable behavior. *(p. 151)*

delusions Fixed but patently false beliefs, such as believing that one is being hounded by demons. *(pp. 45 and 383)*

dementia A condition involving a major deterioration or loss of mental abilities involved in memory, reasoning, judgment, and ability to carry out purposeful behavior. *(p. 334)*

dendrites Rootlike structures at the end of axons that receive neural impulses from neighboring neurons. *(p. 40)*

denial In Freudian theory, a defense mechanism involving the failure to recognize a threatening impulse or urge. *(p. 348)*

deoxyribonucleic acid (DNA) The basic chemical material in chromosomes that carries the individual's genetic code. *(p. 72)*

dependent variables The effects or outcomes of an experiment that are believed to be dependent on the values of the independent variables. *(p. 26)*

depolarization A positive shift in the electrical charge in the neuron's resting potential, making it less negatively charged. *(p. 43)*

depressants Drugs, such as alcohol and barbiturates, that dampen central nervous system activity. *(p. 143)*

depressive attributional style A characteristic way of explaining negative events in terms of internal, stable, and global causes. *(p. 402)*

descriptive statistics Procedures used for classifying and summarizing information in numerical form—in short, for describing data. *(p. A-4)*

detoxification A process of clearing drugs or toxins from the body. *(p. 155)*

developmental psychologists Psychologists who focus on processes involving physical, cognitive, social, and personality development. *(p. 17)*

developmental psychology The branch of psychology that explores physical, emotional, cognitive, and social aspects of development. *(p. 296)*

diathesis A vulnerability or predisposition to developing a disorder. *(p. 386)*

diathesis-stress model A type of biopsychosocial model that relates the development of disorders to the combination of a diathesis, or predisposition, usually genetic in origin, and exposure to stressful events or life circumstances. *(p. 386)*

dichromats People who can see some colors but not others. *(p. 92)*

difference threshold The minimal difference in the magnitude of energy needed for people to detect a difference between two stimuli. *(p. 84)*

discrimination Unfair or biased treatment of people based on their membership in a particular group or category. *(p. 497)*

discriminative stimulus A cue that signals that reinforcement is available if the subject makes a particular response. *(p. 173)*

disinhibition effect The removal of normal restraints or inhibitions that serve to keep impulsive behavior in check. *(p. 405)*

disorganized type A subtype of schizophrenia characterized by confused behavior and disorganized delusions, among other features. *(p. 407)*

displacement In Freudian theory, a defense mechanism in which an unacceptable sexual or aggressive impulse is transferred to an object or person that is safer or less threatening than the original object of the impulse. *(p. 348)*

display rules Cultural customs and norms that govern the display of emotional expressions. *(p. 280)*

dispositional causes Causes relating to the internal characteristics or traits of individuals. *(p. 484)*

dissociative amnesia A psychologically based form of amnesia involving the "splitting off" from memory of traumatic or troubling experiences. *(p. 212)*

dissociative disorders A class of psychological disorders involving changes in consciousness, memory, or self-identity. *(p. 394)*

dissociative identity disorder (DID) A type of dissociative disorder characterized by the appearance of multiple personalities in the same individual. *(p. 394)*

distress A state of emotional or physical suffering, discomfort, or pain. *(p. 450)*

divergent thinking The ability to conceive of new ways of viewing situations and new uses for familiar objects. *(p. 231)*

divided consciousness A state of awareness characterized by divided attention to two or more tasks or activities performed at the same time. *(p. 127)*

door-in-the-face technique A compliance technique in which refusal of a large unreasonable request is followed by a smaller, more reasonable request. *(p. 512)*

double-blind studies In drug research, studies in which both subjects and experimenters are kept uninformed about which subjects are receiving the active drug and which are receiving the placebo. *(p. 27)*

dream analysis A technique in psychoanalysis in which the therapist attempts to analyze the underlying or symbolic meaning of the client's dreams. *(p. 420)*

drifting consciousness A state of awareness characterized by drifting thoughts or mental imagery. *(p. 126)*

drive A state of bodily tension, such as hunger or thirst, that arises from an unmet need. *(p. 259)*

drive for superiority Adler's term for the motivation to compensate for feelings of inferiority. Also called the *will-to-power*. *(p. 352)*

drive reduction Satisfaction of a drive. *(p. 259)*

drive theory The belief that behavior is motivated by drives that arise from biological needs that demand satisfaction. *(p. 259)*

drug abuse Maladaptive or dangerous use of a chemical substance. *(p. 142)*

drug addiction Drug dependence accompanied by signs of physiological dependence, such as the development of a withdrawal syndrome. (p. 143)

drug dependence A severe drug-related problem characterized by impaired control over the use of the drug. (p. 142)

dual-pathway model of fear LeDoux's theory that the brain uses two pathways (a "high road" and a "low road") to process fear messages. (p. 285)

Duchenne smile A genuine smile that involves contraction of a particular set of facial muscles. (p. 282)

dyslexia A learning disorder characterized by impaired ability to read. (p. 242)

eardrum A sheet of connective tissue separating the outer ear from the middle ear that vibrates in response to auditory stimuli and transmits sound waves to the middle ear. (p. 95)

echoic memory A sensory store for holding a mental representation of a sound for a few seconds after it registers in the ears. (p. 195)

eclectic therapy A therapeutic approach that draws upon principles and techniques representing different schools of therapy. (p. 429)

educational psychologists Psychologists who study issues relating to the measurement of intelligence and the processes involved in educational or academic achievement. (p. 17)

EEG (electroencephalograph) A device that records electrical activity in the brain. (p. 58)

efficacy expectations Bandura's term for the expectancies we have regarding our ability to perform behaviors we set out to accomplish. (p. 363)

ego Freud's term for the psychic structure that attempts to balance the instinctual demands of the id with social realities and expectations. (p. 347)

egocentrism To Piaget, the tendency to see the world only from one's own perspective. (p. 315)

ego identity In Erickson's theory, the attainment of a psychological sense of knowing oneself and one's direction in life. (p. 326)

eidetic imagery A lingering mental representation of a visual image (commonly called *photographic memory*). (p. 195)

elaboration likelihood model (ELM) A theoretical model that posits two channels by which persuasive appeals lead to attitude change: a central route and a peripheral route. (p. 488)

elaborative rehearsal The process of transferring information from short-term to long-term memory by consciously focusing on the meaning of the information. (p. 198)

Electra complex The term given by some psychodynamic theorists to the form of the Oedipus complex in young girls. (p. 350)

electrical recording As a method of investigating brain functioning, a process of recording the electrical changes that occur in a specific neuron or groups of neurons in the brain in relation to particular activities or behaviors. (p. 61)

electrical stimulation As a method of investigating brain functioning, a process of electrically stimulating particular parts of the brain to observe the effects on behavior. (p. 61)

electroconvulsive therapy (ECT) A form of therapy for severe depression that involves the administration of an electrical shock to the head. (p. 439)

electromyographic (EMG) biofeedback A form of BFT that involves feedback about changes in the level of muscle tension in the forehead or elsewhere in the body. (p. 77)

embryo The developing organism at an early stage of prenatal development. (p. 297)

embryonic stage The stage of prenatal development from implantation through about the eighth week of pregnancy during which the major organ systems begin to form. (p. 297)

emerging adulthood The period of psychosocial development, roughly spanning ages eighteen to twenty-five, during which the person makes the transition from adolescence to adulthood. (p. 330)

emotional intelligence The ability to recognize emotions in yourself and others and to manage your own emotions effectively. (p. 288)

emotions Feeling states that psychologists view as having physiological, cognitive, and behavioral components. (p. 278)

empirical approach A method of developing knowledge based on evaluating evidence gathered from experiments and careful observation. (p. 21)

endocrine system The body's system of glands that release their secretions, called hormones, directly into the bloodstream. (p. 68)

endorphins Natural chemicals released in the brain that have pain-killing and pleasure-inducing effects. (p. 46)

engram Lashley's term for the physical trace or etching of a memory in the brain. (p. 213)

environmental psychologists Psychologists who study relationships between the physical environment and behavior. (p. 17)

enzymes Organic substances that produce certain chemical changes in other organic substances through a catalytic action. (p. 45)

epilepsy A neurological disorder characterized by seizures that involve sudden, violent discharges of electrical activity in the brain. (p. 64)

episodic memory Memory of personal experiences. (p. 200)

erogenous zones Parts of the body that are especially sensitive to sexual or pleasurable stimulation. (p. 349)

escape learning The learning of behaviors that allow an organism to escape from an aversive stimulus. (p. 178)

ethics review committees Committees that evaluate whether proposed studies meet ethical guidelines. (p. 30)

evolutionary psychology A branch of psychology that focuses on the role of evolutionary processes in shaping behavior. (p. 10)

exhaustion stage The third stage of the general adaptation syndrome, characterized by depletion of bodily resources and a lowered resistance to stress-related disorders or conditions. (p. 460)

expectancies In social-cognitive theory, personal predictions about the outcomes of behavior. (p. 361)

experimental method A method of scientific investigation involving the manipulation of independent variables and observation or measurement of their effects on dependent variables under controlled conditions. (p. 26)

experimental psychologists Psychologists who apply experimental methods to the study of behavior. (p. 15)

explicit memory Memory accessed through conscious effort. (p. 202)

extinction The gradual weakening and eventual disappearance of a conditioned response. (p. 163)

extrasensory perception (ESP) Perception that occurs without benefit of the known senses. (p. 117)

extrinsic motivation Motivation reflecting a desire for external rewards, such as wealth or the respect of others. (p. 262)

eyeblink reflex The reflexive blinking of the eyes that protects the newborn from bright light and foreign objects. (p. 301)

facial-feedback hypothesis The belief that mimicking facial movements associated with a particular emotion will produce the corresponding emotional state. (p. 282)

familial association studies Studies that examine the degree to which disorders or characteristics are shared among family members. (p. 73)

family therapy Therapy for troubled families that focuses on changing disruptive patterns of communication and improving the ways in which family members relate to each other. (p. 430)

fear hierarchy An ordered series of increasingly fearful objects or situations. (p. 423)

feature detectors Specialized neurons in the visual cortex that respond only to particular features of visual stimuli, such as horizontal or vertical lines. (p. 90)

fertilization The union of sperm and ovum. (p. 297)

fetal alcohol syndrome (FAS) A syndrome caused by maternal use of alcohol during pregnancy in which the child shows developmental delays and facial deformities. (p. 300)

fetal stage The stage of prenatal development in which the fetus develops, beginning around the ninth week of pregnancy and lasting until the birth of the child. (*p. 298*)

fetus The developing organism in the later stages of prenatal development. (*p. 298*)

fight-or-flight response The body's built-in alarm system that allows it to quickly mobilize its resources to either fight or flee when faced with a threatening stressor. (*p. 459*)

five-factor model (FFM) The dominant contemporary trait model of personality, consisting of five broad personality factors: neuroticism, extraversion, openness, agreeableness, and conscientiousness. (*p. 358*)

fixations Constellations of personality traits characteristic of a particular stage of psychosexual development, resulting from either excessive or inadequate gratification at that stage. (*p. 349*)

flashbulb memories Enduring memories of emotionally charged events that seem permanently seared into the brain. (*p. 203*)

fluid intelligence A form of intelligence associated with the ability to think abstractly and flexibly in solving problems. (*p. 329*)

focused awareness A state of heightened alertness in which one is fully absorbed in the task at hand. (*p. 126*)

foot-in-the-door technique A compliance technique based on securing compliance with a smaller request as a prelude to making a larger request. (*p. 512*)

forebrain The largest and uppermost part of the brain; contains the thalamus, hypothalamus, limbic system, basal ganglia, and cerebral cortex. (*p. 53*)

forensic psychologists Psychologists involved in the application of psychology to the legal system. (*p. 18*)

formal operations The level of full cognitive maturity in Piaget's theory, characterized by the ability to think in abstract terms. (*p. 317*)

fovea The area near the center of the retina that contains only cones and that is the center of focus for clearest vision. (*p. 89*)

fraternal twins Twins who developed from separate zygotes and so have 50 percent of their genes in common (also called *dizygotic,* or *DZ,* twins). (*p. 75*)

free association A technique in psychoanalysis in which the client is encouraged to say anything that comes to mind. (*p. 419*)

free recall A type of recall task in which individuals are asked to recall as many stored items as possible in any order. (*p. 211*)

frequency distribution A tabulation that indicates the number of times a given score or group of scores occurs. (*p. A-5*)

frequency polygon A graph on which the frequencies of class intervals are at their midpoints, which are then connected with straight lines. (*p. A-5*)

frequency theory The belief that pitch depends on the frequency of vibration of the basilar membrane and the volley of neural impulses transmitted to the brain via the auditory nerve. (*p. 96*)

frontal lobes The parts of the cerebral cortex, located at the front of the cerebral hemispheres, that are considered the "executive center" of the brain because of their role in higher mental functions. (*p. 56*)

frustration A negative emotional state experienced when one's efforts to pursue one's goals are thwarted. (*pp. 453 and 502*)

functional fixedness The tendency to perceive objects as limited to the customary functions they serve. (*p. 228*)

functionalism The school of psychology that focuses on the adaptive functions of behavior. (*p. 6*)

fundamental attribution error The tendency to attribute behavior to internal causes without regard to situational influences. (*p. 484*)

ganglion cells Nerve cells in the back of the eye that transmit neural impulses in response to light stimulation, the axons of which make up the optic nerve. (*p. 89*)

gate-control theory of pain The belief that a neural gate in the spinal cord opens to allow pain messages to reach the brain and closes to shut them out. (*p. 103*)

gender identity The psychological sense of maleness or femaleness. (*p. 272*)

gender roles The cultural expectations imposed on men and women to behave in ways deemed appropriate for their gender. (*p. 272*)

general adaptation syndrome (GAS) Selye's term for the three-stage response of the body to persistent or intense stress. (*p. 459*)

generalized anxiety disorder (GAD) A type of anxiety disorder involving persistent and generalized anxiety and worry. (*p. 391*)

genes Basic units of heredity that contain the individual's genetic code. (*p. 72*)

genital stage In Freudian theory, the fifth and final stage of psychosexual development, which begins around puberty and corresponds to the development of mature sexuality and emphasis on procreation. (*p. 351*)

genotype An organism's genetic code. (*p. 72*)

germ cells Sperm and egg cells from which new life develops. (*p. 70*)

germinal stage The stage of prenatal development that spans the period from fertilization through implantation. (*p. 297*)

geropsychologists Psychologists who focus on psychological processes involved in aging. (*p. 18*)

gestalt A German word meaning "unitary form" or "pattern." (*p. 7*)

Gestalt psychology The school of psychology that holds that the brain structures our perceptions of the world in terms of meaningful patterns or wholes. (*p. 7*)

glands Body organs or structures that produce secretions. (*p. 41*)

glial cells Small but numerous cells in the nervous system that support neurons and that form the myelin sheath found on many axons. (*p. 42*)

gonads Sex glands (testes in men and ovaries in women) that produce sex hormones and germ cells (sperm in the male and egg cells in the female). (*p. 70*)

gradual exposure A behavior therapy technique for treating phobias based on direct exposure to a series of increasingly fearful stimuli. Also called *in-vivo ("real-life") exposure.* (*p. 424*)

grammar The set of rules governing how symbols in a given language are used to form meaningful expressions. (*p. 233*)

group therapy A form of therapy in which clients are treated within a group format. (*p. 430*)

groupthink Janis's term for the tendency of members of a decision-making group to be more focused on reaching a consensus than on critically examining the issues at hand. (*p. 510*)

habituation Reduction in the strength of a response to a repeated stimulus. (*p. 107*)

hair cells The auditory receptors that transform vibrations caused by sound waves into neural impulses that are then transmitted to the brain via the auditory nerve. (*p. 96*)

hallucinations Perceptions ("hearing voices" or seeing things) that are experienced in the absence of external stimuli. (*p. 45 and 383*)

hallucinogens Drugs that alter sensory experiences and produce hallucinations. (*p. 151*)

hassles Annoyances of daily life that impose a stressful burden. (*p. 451*)

health psychologists Psychologists who focus on the relationship between psychological factors and physical health. (*p. 18*)

health psychology The specialty in psychology that focuses on the interrelationships between psychological factors and physical health. (*p. 450*)

heart attack A potentially life-threatening event involving the death of heart tissue due to a lack of blood flow to the heart. Also called *myocardial infarction.* (*p. 467*)

heritability The degree to which heredity accounts for variations on a given trait within a population. (*p. 249*)

heuristic A rule of thumb for solving problems or making judgments or decisions. (*p. 227*)

hidden observer Hilgard's term for a part of consciousness that remains detached from the hypnotic experience but aware of everything that happens during it. (*p. 140*)

hierarchy of needs Maslow's concept that there is an order to human needs, which starts with basic biological needs and progresses to self-actualization. (p. 263)

hindbrain The lowest and, in evolutionary terms, oldest part of the brain; includes the medulla, pons, and cerebellum. (p. 52)

hippocampus A structure in the limbic system involved in memory formation. (p. 54)

histogram A graph that depicts the frequencies of individual scores or categories of scores, using bars of different lengths. (p. A-5)

homeostasis The tendency of systems to maintain a steady, internally balanced state. (p. 69)

hormones Secretions from endocrine glands that help regulate bodily processes. (p. 41)

humanistic perspective An approach to the study of psychology that applies the principles of humanistic psychology. (p. 10)

humanistic psychology The school of psychology that believes that free will and conscious choice are essential aspects of the human experience. (p. 10)

hypnosis An altered state of consciousness characterized by focused attention, deep relaxation, and heightened susceptibility to suggestion. (p. 139)

hypnotic age regression A hypnotically induced experience that involves reexperiencing past events in one's life. (p. 139)

hypnotic analgesia A loss of feeling or responsiveness to pain in certain parts of the body occurring during hypnosis. (p. 139)

hypochondriasis A somatoform disorder in which there is excessive concern that one's physical complaints are signs of underlying serious illness. (p. 396)

hypothalamus A small, pea-sized structure in the forebrain that helps regulate many vital bodily functions, including body temperature and reproduction, as well as emotional states, aggression, and responses to stress. (p. 54)

hypothesis A precise prediction about the outcomes of an experiment. (p. 21)

iconic memory A sensory store for holding a mental representation of a visual image for a fraction of a second. (p. 195)

id Freud's term for the psychic structure existing in the unconscious that contains our baser animal drives and instinctual impulses. (p. 347)

identical twins Twins who developed from the same zygote and so have identical genes (also called *monozygotic*, or *MZ*, twins). (p. 75)

identity crisis In Erikson's theory, a stressful period of serious soul-searching and self-examination of issues relating to personal values and one's direction in life. (p. 326)

imaginary audience The common belief among adolescents that they are the center of other people's attention. (p. 322)

immune system The body's system of defense against disease. (pp. 169 and 462)

implicit memory Memory accessed without conscious effort. (p. 202)

impression formation The process of developing an opinion or impression of another person. (p. 482)

imprinting The formation of a strong bond of the newborn animal to the first moving object seen after birth. (p. 307)

incentives Rewards or other stimuli that motivate us to act. (p. 261)

incentive theory The belief that our attraction to particular goals or objects motivates much of our behavior. (p. 261)

incentive value The strength of the "pull" of a goal or reward. (p. 262)

independent variables Factors that are manipulated in an experiment. (p. 26)

individual psychology Adler's theory of personality, which emphasizes the unique potential of each individual. (p. 352)

individualistic culture A culture that emphasizes individual identity and personal accomplishments. (p. 367)

industrial/organizational (I/O) psychologists Psychologists who study people's behavior at work. (p. 17)

inferential statistics Procedures for making generalizations about a population by studying the characteristics of samples drawn from the population. (p. A-5)

inferiority complex In Adler's theory, a concept involving the influence that feelings of inadequacy or inferiority in young children have on their developing personalities and desires to compensate. (p. 352)

informed consent Agreement to participate in a study following disclosure of information about the purposes and nature of the study and its potential risks and benefits. (p. 31)

in-group favoritism A cognitive bias involving the predisposition to attribute more positive characteristics to members of in-groups than to those of out-groups. (p. 498)

in-groups Social, religious, ethnic, racial, or national groups with which one identifies. (p. 497)

insight In Freud's theory, the awareness of underlying, unconscious wishes and conflicts. (p. 420)

insight learning The process of mentally working through a problem until the sudden realization of a solution occurs. (p. 184)

insomnia Difficulty falling asleep, remaining asleep, or returning to sleep after nighttime awakenings. (p. 136)

instinctive behaviors Genetically programmed, innate patterns of response that are specific to members of a particular species. (p. 258)

instinct theory The belief that behavior is motivated by instinct. (p. 258)

intelligence The capacity to think and reason clearly and to act purposefully and effectively in adapting to the environment and pursuing one's goals. (p. 238)

intelligence quotient (IQ) A measure of intelligence based on performance on tests of mental abilities, expressed as a ratio between one's mental age and chronological age or derived from the deviation of one's scores from the norms for those of one's age group. (p. 239)

interference theory The belief that forgetting is the result of the interference of memories with each other. (p. 207)

interneurons Nerve cells within the central nervous system that process information. (p. 41)

interpretation In psychoanalysis, the attempt by the therapist to explain the connections between the material the client discloses in therapy and his or her unconscious conflicts. (p. 420)

intoxicant A chemical substance that induces a state of drunkenness. (p. 143)

intrinsic motivation Motivation reflecting a desire for internal gratification, such as the self-satisfaction derived from accomplishing a particular goal. (p. 262)

introspection Inward focusing on mental experiences, such as sensations or feelings. (p. 5)

introversion-extraversion One of the three underlying dimensions of personality in Eysenck's model, referring to tendencies toward being solitary and reserved on the one end or outgoing and sociable on the other end. (p. 356)

ions Electrically charged chemical particles. (p. 42)

iris The pigmented, circular muscle in the eye that regulates the size of the pupil to adjust to changes in the level of illumination. (p. 88)

irreversibility To Piaget, the inability to reverse the direction of a sequence of events to their starting point. (p. 316)

James-Lange theory The belief that emotions occur after people become aware of their physiological responses to the triggering stimuli. (p. 428)

jet lag A disruption of sleep-wake cycles caused by the shifts in time zones that accompany long-distance air travel. (p. 129)

kinesthesis The sense that keeps us informed about movement of the parts of the body and their position in relation to each other. (p. 104)

language A system of communication composed of symbols (words, hand signs, etc.) that are arranged according to a set of rules (grammar) to form meaningful expressions. (p. 233)

language acquisition device Chomsky's concept of an innate, prewired mechanism in the brain that allows children to acquire language naturally. (p. 234)

latency stage In Freudian theory, the fourth stage of psychosexual development, during which sexual impulses remain latent or dormant. (p. 351)

latent learning Learning that occurs without apparent reinforcement and that is not displayed until reinforcement is provided. (p. 184)

lateral hypothalamus A part of the hypothalamus involved in initiating, or "turning on," eating. (p. 265)

lateralization The specialization of the right and left cerebral hemispheres for particular functions. (p. 62)

Law of Effect Thorndike's principle that responses that have satisfying effects are more likely to recur, while those that have unpleasant effects are less likely to recur. (p. 171)

laws of perceptual organization The principles identified by Gestalt psychologists that describe the ways in which the brain groups bits of sensory stimulation into meaningful wholes or patterns. (p. 109)

learned helplessness model The view that depression results from the perception of a lack of control over the reinforcements in one's life that may result from exposure to uncontrollable negative events. (p. 401)

learning A relatively permanent change in behavior acquired through experience. (p. 162)

legitimization of authority The tendency to grant legitimacy to the orders or commands of persons in authority. (p. 509)

lens The structure in the eye that focuses light rays on the retina. (p. 88)

lesioning In studies of brain functioning, the intentional destruction of brain tissue in order to observe the effects on behavior. (p. 60)

levels-of-processing theory The belief that how well or how long information is remembered depends on the depth of encoding or processing. (p. 199)

limbic system A formation of structures in the forebrain that includes the hippocampus, amygdala, and parts of the thalamus and hypothalamus. (p. 54)

linguistic relativity hypothesis The proposition that the language we use determines how we think and how we perceive the world (also called the *Whorfian hypothesis*). (p. 235)

locus of control In Rotter's theory, one's general expectancies about whether one's efforts can bring about desired outcomes or reinforcements. (p. 361)

logical concepts Concepts with clearly defined rules for membership. (p. 225)

long-term memory (LTM) The memory subsystem responsible for long-term storage of information. (p. 198)

long-term potentiation (LTP) The long-term strengthening of neural connections as the result of repeated stimulation. (p. 215)

low-ball technique A compliance technique based on obtaining a person's initial agreement to purchase an item at a lower price before revealing hidden costs that raise the ultimate price. (p. 512)

lucid dreams Dreams in which the dreamer is aware that he or she is dreaming. (p. 134)

lymphocytes White blood cells that protect the body against disease-causing organisms. (p. 462)

mainstreaming The practice of placing children with special needs in a regular classroom environment. (p. 243)

maintenance rehearsal The process of extending retention of information held in short-term memory by consciously repeating the information. (p. 197)

major depression The most common type of depressive disorder, characterized by periods of downcast mood, feelings of worthlessness, and loss of interest in pleasurable activities. (p. 398)

malignant tumors Uncontrolled growths of body cells that invade surrounding tissue and spread to other parts of the body. (p. 470)

manic episodes Periods of mania, or unusually elevated mood and extreme restlessness. (p. 400)

mantra A sound or phrase chanted repeatedly during transcendental meditation. (p. 138)

massed vs. spaced practice effect The tendency for retention of learned material to be greater with spaced practice than with massed practice. (p. 207)

matching hypothesis The belief that people tend to pair off with others who are similar to themselves in physical attractiveness and other characteristics. (p. 493)

maturation The biological unfolding of the organism according to the underlying genetic code. (p. 296)

mean The arithmetic average of the scores in a distribution. (p. A-6)

median The middle score in a distribution, above and below which half of the scores fall. (p. A-6)

medical model A framework for understanding abnormal behavior patterns as symptoms of underlying physical disorders or diseases. (p. 384)

meditation A process of focused attention that induces a relaxed, contemplative state. (p. 120)

medulla A structure in the hindbrain involved in regulating basic life functions, such as heartbeat and respiration. (p. 53)

melanoma The most deadly form of skin cancer. (p. 471)

memory The system that allows us to retain information and bring it to mind. (p. 194)

memory encoding The process of converting information into a form that can be stored in memory. (p. 194)

memory retrieval The process of accessing and bringing into consciousness information stored in memory. (p. 195)

memory storage The process of retaining information in memory. (p. 195)

menarche The first menstruation. (p. 320)

menopause The time of life when menstruation ends. (p. 330)

mental age A representation of a person's intelligence based on the age of people who are capable of performing at the same level of ability. (p. 238)

mental image A mental picture or representation of an object or event. (p. 224)

mental retardation A generalized deficit or impairment in intellectual and social skills. (p. 243)

mental set The tendency to rely on strategies that worked in similar situations in the past but that may not be appropriate to the present situation. (p. 228)

meta-analysis A statistical technique for averaging results across a large number of studies. (p. 431)

method of successive approximations The method used to shape behavior by reinforcing ever-closer approximations of the desired response. (p. 175)

midbrain The part of the brain that lies on top of the hindbrain and below the forebrain. (p. 53)

midlife crisis A state of psychological crisis, often occurring during middle adulthood, in which people grapple with the loss of their youth. (p. 331)

migraine headache A prolonged, intense headache brought on by changes in blood flow in the brain's blood vessels. (p. 77)

mindfulness meditation A form of meditation in which one adopts a state of nonjudgmental attention to the unfolding of experience on a moment-to-moment basis. (p. 138)

misinformation effect A form of memory distortion that affects eyewitness testimony and that is caused by misinformation provided during the retention interval. (p. 204)

mnemonic A device for improving memory. (p. 217)

mode The most frequent score in a distribution of scores. (p. A-6)

modeling A behavior therapy technique for overcoming phobias and acquiring more adaptive behaviors, based on observing and imitating models. (p. 425)

monoamine oxidase (MAO) inhibitors A class of antidepressant drugs that increase the availability of neurotransmitters in the brain by inhibiting an enzyme, monoamine oxidase, that breaks down or degrades them in the synapse. *(p. 437)*

monochromats People who have no color vision and can see only in black and white. *(p. 92)*

monocular cues Cues for depth that can be perceived by each eye alone, such as relative size and interposition. *(p. 113)*

mood disorders A class of psychological disorders involving disturbances in mood states, such as major depression and bipolar disorder. *(p. 398)*

Moro reflex An inborn reflex, elicited by a sudden noise or loss of support, in which the infant extends its arms, arches its back, and brings its arms toward each other as though attempting to grab hold of someone. *(p. 301)*

morphemes The smallest units of meaning in a language. *(p. 233)*

motivation Factors that activate, direct, and sustain goal-directed behavior. *(p. 258)*

motives Needs or wants that drive goal-directed behavior. *(p. 258)*

motor cortex A region of the frontal lobes involved in regulating body movement. *(p. 57)*

motor neurons Neurons that convey nerve impulses from the central nervous system to muscles and glands. *(p. 41)*

MRI (magnetic resonance imaging) A technique that uses a magnetic field to create a computerized image of internal bodily structures. *(p. 59)*

multiple intelligences Gardner's term for the distinct types of intelligence that characterize different forms of intelligent behavior. *(p. 245)*

myelin sheath A layer of protective insulation that covers the axons of certain neurons and helps speed transmission of nerve impulses. *(p. 42)*

narcissistic personality disorder A type of personality disorder characterized by a grandiose sense of self. *(p. 410)*

narcolepsy A disorder characterized by sudden unexplained "sleep attacks" during the day. *(p. 136)*

narcotics Addictive drugs that have pain-relieving and sleep-inducing properties. *(p. 147)*

natural concepts Concepts with poorly defined or fuzzy rules for membership. *(p. 226)*

naturalistic observation method A method of research based on careful observation of behavior in natural settings. *(p. 24)*

nature-nurture problem The debate in psychology about the relative influences of genetics (nature) and environment (nurture) in determining behavior. *(p. 72)*

need A state of deprivation or deficiency. *(p. 259)*

need for achievement The need to excel in one's endeavors. *(p. 262)*

negative reinforcement The strengthening of a response through the removal of a stimulus after the response occurs. *(p. 173)*

negative symptoms Behavioral deficits associated with schizophrenia, such as withdrawal and apathy. *(p. 407)*

neodissociation theory A theory of hypnosis based on the belief that hypnosis represents a state of dissociated (divided) consciousness. *(p. 140)*

nerve A bundle of axons from different neurons that transmit nerve impulses. *(p. 41)*

nerve deafness Deafness associated with nerve damage, usually involving damage to the hair cells or to the auditory nerve itself. *(p. 97)*

neural tube The area in the embryo from which the nervous system develops. *(p. 297)*

neuromodulators Chemicals released in the nervous system that influence the sensitivity of the receiving neuron to neurotransmitters. *(p. 45)*

neuronal networks Memory circuits in the brain that consist of complicated networks of nerve cells. *(p. 214)*

neurons Nerve cells. *(p. 40)*

neuropsychologists Psychologists who study relationships between the brain and behavior. *(p. 18)*

neuroticism One of the three underlying dimensions of personality in Eysenck's model, referring to tendencies toward emotional instability, anxiety, and worry. *(p. 356)*

neurotransmitters Chemical messengers that transport nerve impulses from one nerve cell to another. *(p. 40)*

neutral stimulus (NS) A stimulus that before conditioning does not produce a particular response. *(p. 162)*

nightmare disorder A sleep disorder involving a pattern of frequent, disturbing nightmares. *(p. 137)*

nodes of Ranvier Gaps in the myelin sheath that create noninsulated areas along the axon. *(p. 42)*

nonspecific factors General features of psychotherapy, such as attention from a therapist and mobilization of positive expectancies or hope. *(p. 433)*

norms The standards used to compare an individual's performance on a test with the performance of others. *(p. 239)*

null hypothesis A prediction of no difference between groups or no relationship between variables. *(p. A-11)*

obedience Compliance with commands or orders issued by others, usually persons in a position of authority. *(p. 507)*

objective tests Tests of personality that can be scored objectively and that are based on a research foundation. *(p. 369)*

object permanence The recognition that objects continue to exist even if they have disappeared from sight. *(p. 314)*

observational learning Learning by observing and imitating the behavior of others (also called *vicarious learning* or *modeling*). *(p. 185)*

obsessive-compulsive disorder (OCD) A type of anxiety disorder involving the repeated occurrence of obsessions and/or compulsions. *(p. 391)*

occipital lobes The parts of the cerebral cortex, located at the back of both cerebral hemispheres, that process visual stimuli. *(p. 55)*

Oedipus complex In Freudian theory, the psychological complex in which the young boy or girl develops incestuous feelings toward the parent of the opposite gender and perceives the parent of the same gender as a rival. *(p. 350)*

olfaction The sense of smell. *(p. 99)*

olfactory bulb The area in the front of the brain above the nostrils that receives sensory input from olfactory receptors in the nose. *(p. 100)*

olfactory nerve The nerve that carries impulses from olfactory receptors in the nose to the brain. *(p. 99)*

operant conditioning The process of learning in which the consequences of a response determine the probability that the response will be repeated. *(p. 172)*

operant response A response that operates on the environment to produce certain consequences. *(p. 172)*

opponent-process theory A theory of color vision that holds that the experience of color results from opposing processes involving two sets of color receptors, red-green receptors and blue-yellow receptors, and that another set of opposing receptors, black-white, is responsible for detecting differences in brightness. *(p. 92)*

optic nerve The nerve that carries neural impulses generated by light stimulation from the eye to the brain. *(p. 89)*

oral stage In Freudian theory, the first stage of psychosexual development during which the infant seeks sexual gratification through oral stimulation (sucking, mouthing, and biting). *(p. 349)*

organ of Corti A gelatinous structure in the cochlea containing the hair cells that serve as auditory receptors. *(p. 96)*

ossicles Three tiny bones in the middle ear (the hammer, anvil, and stirrup) that vibrate in response to vibrations of the eardrum. *(p. 95)*

osteoporosis A bone disease characterized by a loss of bone density in which the bones become porous, brittle, and more prone to fracture. *(p. 338)*

outcome expectations Bandura's term for our personal predictions about the outcomes of our behavior. *(p. 362)*

out-group homogeneity A cognitive bias describing the tendency to perceive members of out-groups as more alike than members of in-groups. *(p. 498)*

out-group negativism A cognitive bias involving the predisposition to attribute more negative characteristics to members of out-groups than to those of in-groups. *(p. 498)*

out-groups Groups other than those with which one identifies. *(p. 497)*

oval window The membrane-covered opening that separates the middle ear from the inner ear. *(p. 95)*

ovaries The female gonads, which secrete the female sex hormones estrogen and progesterone and produce mature egg cells. *(p. 70)*

overlearning Practice repeated beyond the point necessary to reproduce material without error. *(p. 208)*

palmar grasp reflex The reflexive curling of the infant's fingers around an object that touches its palm. *(p. 301)*

pancreas An endocrine gland located near the stomach that produces the hormone insulin. *(p. 69)*

panic disorder A type of anxiety disorder involving repeated episodes of sheer terror called panic attacks. *(p. 390)*

paranoid personality disorder A type of personality disorder characterized by extreme suspiciousness or mistrust of others. *(p. 410)*

paranoid type The most common subtype of schizophrenia, characterized by the appearance of delusional thinking accompanied by frequent auditory hallucinations. *(p. 408)*

parapsychology The study of paranormal phenomena. *(p. 118)*

parasympathetic nervous system The branch of the autonomic nervous system that regulates bodily processes, such as digestion, that replenish stores of energy. *(p. 51)*

parietal lobes The parts of the cerebral cortex, located on the side of each cerebral hemisphere, that process bodily sensations. *(p. 55)*

Parkinson's disease A progressive brain disease involving destruction of dopamine-producing brain cells and characterized by muscle tremors, shakiness, rigidity, and difficulty in walking and controlling fine body movements. *(p. 45)*

penis envy In Freudian theory, jealousy of boys for having a penis. *(p. 350)*

perception The process by which the brain integrates, organizes, and interprets sensory impressions to create representations of the world. *(p. 106)*

perceptual constancy The tendency to perceive the size, shape, color, and brightness of an object as remaining the same even when the image it casts on the retina changes. *(p. 111)*

perceptual set The tendency for perceptions to be influenced by one's expectations or preconceptions. *(p. 107)*

performance anxiety Anxiety experienced in performance situations stemming from a fear of negative evaluation of one's ability to perform. *(p. 276)*

peripheral nervous system The part of the nervous system that connects the spinal cord and brain with the sensory organs, muscles, and glands. *(p. 50)*

personal fable The common belief among adolescents that their feelings and experiences cannot possibly be understood by others and that they are personally invulnerable to harm. *(p. 322)*

personal identity The part of our psychological identity that involves our sense of ourselves as unique individuals. *(p. 504)*

personal unconscious Jung's term for an unconscious region of mind comprising a reservoir of the individual's repressed memories and impulses. *(p. 352)*

personality The relatively stable constellation of psychological characteristics and behavioral patterns that account for our individuality and consistency over time. *(p. 346)*

personality disorders A class of psychological disorders characterized by rigid personality traits that impair people's ability to adjust to the demands they face in the environment and that interfere with their relationships with others. *(p. 410)*

personality psychologists Psychologists who study the psychological characteristics and behaviors that distinguish us as individuals and lead us to act consistently over time. *(p. 17)*

personality tests Structured psychological tests that use formal methods of assessing personality. *(p. 369)*

person variables Mischel's term for internal personal factors that influence behavior, including competencies, expectancies, and subjective values. *(p. 363)*

PET (positron emission tomography) scan An imaging technique in which a radioactive sugar tracer is injected into the bloodstream and used to measure levels of activity of various parts of the brain. *(p. 59)*

phallic stage In Freudian theory, the third stage of psychosexual development, marked by erotic attention on the phallic region (penis in boys, clitoris in girls) and the development of the Oedipus complex. *(p. 350)*

phenotype The observable physical and behavioral characteristics of an organism, representing the influences of the genotype and environment. *(p. 73)*

pheromones Chemical substances that are emitted by many species and that have various functions, including sexual attraction. *(p. 100)*

phobias Excessive fears of particular objects or situations. *(p. 167 and 390)*

phonemes The basic units of sound in a language. *(p. 233)*

phonological loop The speech-based part of working memory that allows for the verbal rehearsal of sounds or words. *(p. 197)*

photoreceptors Light-sensitive cells (rods and cones) in the eye upon which light registers. *(p. 88)*

phrenology The now-discredited view that one can judge a person's character and mental abilities by measuring the bumps on his or her head. *(p. 369)*

physiological dependence A state of physical dependence on a drug caused by repeated usage that changes body chemistry. *(p. 142)*

physiological perspective An approach to the study of psychology that focuses on the relationships between biological processes and behavior. *(p. 10)*

physiological psychologists Psychologists who focus on the biological underpinnings of behavior. *(p. 15)*

pineal gland A small endocrine gland in the brain that produces the hormone melatonin, which is involved in regulating sleep-wake cycles. *(p. 70)*

pitch The highness or lowness of a sound that corresponds to the frequency of the sound wave. *(p. 95)*

pituitary gland An endocrine gland in the brain that produces various hormones involved in growth, regulation of the menstrual cycle, and childbirth. *(p. 70)*

placebo An inert substance or experimental condition that resembles the active treatment. *(p. 96)*

placebo effects Positive outcomes of a treatment resulting from positive expectations rather than from the effects of the treatment itself. Also called *expectancy effects*. *(pp. 26 and 433)*

placenta The organ that provides for the exchange of nutrients and waste materials between mother and fetus. *(p. 298)*

place theory The belief that pitch depends on the place along the basilar membrane that vibrates the most in response to a particular auditory stimulus. *(p. 96)*

plaque In the circulatory system, fatty deposits that accumulate along artery walls. *(p. 466)*

plasticity The ability of the brain to adapt itself after trauma or surgical alteration. *(p. 67)*

pleasure principle In Freudian theory, a governing principle of the id that is based on demand for instant gratification without regard to social rules or customs. *(p. 347)*

polyabusers People who abuse more than one drug at a time. *(p. 142)*

polygenic traits Traits that are influenced by multiple genes interacting in complex ways. *(p. 73)*

pons A structure in the hindbrain involved in regulating states of wakefulness and sleep. *(p. 53)*

population All the individuals or organisms that constitute particular groups. *(p. 23)*

positive psychology A contemporary movement within psychology that emphasizes the study of human virtues and assets, rather than weaknesses and deficits. *(p. 12)*

positive reinforcement The strengthening of a response through the introduction of a stimulus after the response occurs. *(p. 173)*

positive symptoms Symptoms of schizophrenia involving behavioral excesses, such as hallucinations and delusions. *(p. 407)*

posthypnotic amnesia An inability to recall what happened during hypnosis. *(p. 139)*

posthypnotic suggestion A hypnotist's suggestion that the subject will respond in a particular way following hypnosis. *(p. 139)*

posttraumatic stress disorder (PTSD) A psychological disorder involving a maladaptive reaction to traumatic stress. *(p. 455)*

precognition The ability to foretell the future. *(p. 118)*

preconscious To Freud, the part of the mind whose contents can be brought into awareness through focused attention. *(p. 346)*

prefrontal cortex The area of the frontal lobe that lies in front of the motor cortex and that is involved in higher mental functions, including thinking, planning, impulse control, and weighing the consequences of behavior. *(p. 66)*

prefrontal lobotomy A surgical procedure in which neural pathways in the brain are severed in order to control violent or aggressive behavior. *(p. 440)*

prejudice A preconceived opinion or attitude about an issue, person, or group. *(p. 497)*

premenstrual syndrome (PMS) A cluster of physical and psychological symptoms occurring in the few days preceding the menstrual flow. *(p. 71)*

primacy effect The tendency to recall items better when they are learned first. *(p. 208)*

primary drives Innate drives, such as hunger, thirst, and sexual desire, that arise from basic biological needs. *(p. 259)*

primary mental abilities Seven basic mental abilities that Thurstone believed constitute intelligence. *(p. 245)*

primary reinforcers Reinforcers, such as food or sexual stimulation, that are naturally rewarding because they satisfy basic biological needs or drives. *(p. 175)*

primary sex characteristics Physical characteristics, such as the gonads, that differentiate males and females and play a direct role in reproduction. *(p. 320)*

proactive interference A form of interference in which material learned earlier interferes with retention of newly acquired information. *(p. 207)*

problem solving A form of thinking focused on finding a solution to a particular problem. *(p. 227)*

procedural memory Memory of how to do things that require motor or performance skills. *(p. 201)*

programmed instruction A learning method in which complex material is broken down into a series of small steps that learners master at their own pace. *(p. 182)*

projection In Freudian theory, a defense mechanism involving the projection of one's own unacceptable impulses, wishes, or urges onto another person. *(p. 348)*

projective tests Personality tests in which ambiguous or vague test materials are used to elicit responses that are believed to reveal a person's unconscious needs, drives, and motives. *(p. 371)*

prosocial behavior Behavior that benefits others. *(p. 495)*

prospective memory Memory of things one plans to do in the future. *(p. 201)*

proximity (1) Nearness or propinquity. (2) The principle that objects that are near each other will be perceived as belonging to a common set. *(pp. 111 and 493)*

psychiatrists Medical doctors who specialize in the diagnosis and treatment of mental or psychological disorders. *(p. 16)*

psychoactive drugs Chemical substances that affect a person's mental or emotional state. *(p. 141)*

psychoanalysis The method of psychotherapy developed by Freud that focuses on uncovering and working through the unconscious conflicts that he believed were at the root of psychological problems. *(pp. 8 and 418)*

psychoanalysts Practitioners of psychoanalysis who are schooled in the Freudian tradition. *(p. 418)*

psychoanalytic theory Freud's theory of personality that holds that personality and behavior are shaped by unconscious forces and conflicts. *(p. 346)*

psychodynamic perspective The view that behavior is influenced by the struggle between unconscious sexual or aggressive impulses and opposing forces that try to keep this threatening material out of consciousness. *(p. 8)*

psychokinesis The ability to move objects by mental effort alone. *(p. 118)*

psychological dependence A pattern of compulsive or habitual use of a drug to satisfy a psychological need. *(p. 143)*

psychological disorders Abnormal behavior patterns characterized by disturbances in behavior, thinking, perceptions, or emotions that are associated with significant personal distress or impaired functioning. Also called *mental disorders* or *mental illnesses*. *(p. 386)*

psychological hardiness A cluster of traits (commitment, openness to challenge, internal locus of control) that may buffer the effects of stress. *(p. 464)*

psychology The science of behavior and mental processes. *(p. 4)*

psychophysics The study of the relationship between features of physical stimuli, such as the intensity of light and sound, and the sensation we experience in response to these stimuli. *(p. 84)*

psychosocial needs Needs that reflect interpersonal aspects of motivation, such as the need for friendship or achievement. *(p. 262)*

psychosurgery Brain surgery used to control violent or deviant behavior. *(p. 440)*

psychotherapy A verbal form of therapy derived from a psychological framework that consists of one or more treatment sessions with a therapist. *(p. 418)*

psychotic disorder A psychological disorder, such as schizophrenia, characterized by a "break" with reality. *(p. 407)*

psychoticism One of the three underlying dimensions of personality in Eysenck's model, referring to tendencies to be perceived as cold and antisocial. *(p. 356)*

psychotropic drugs Psychiatric drugs used in the treatment of psychological or mental disorders. *(p. 436)*

puberty The stage of development at which individuals become physiologically capable of reproducing. *(p. 320)*

punishment The introduction of an aversive stimulus or the removal of a reinforcing stimulus after a response occurs, which leads to the weakening or suppression of the response. *(p. 178)*

pupil The black opening inside the iris that allows light to enter the eye. *(p. 88)*

questionnaire A written set of questions or statements to which people reply by marking their responses on an answer form. *(p. 23)*

racism Negative bias held toward members of other racial groups. *(p. 498)*

radical behaviorism The philosophical position that free will is an illusion or myth and that human and animal behavior is completely determined by environmental and genetic influences. *(p. 172)*

random assignment A method of randomly assigning subjects to experimental or control groups. *(p. 26)*

random sampling A method of sampling in which each individual in the population has an equal chance of being selected. *(p. 23)*

range A measure of variability that is given by the difference in value between the highest and lowest scores in a distribution of scores. *(p. A-8)*

rapid-eye-movement (REM) sleep The stage of sleep that involves rapid eye movements and that is most closely associated with periods of dreaming. *(p. 131)*

rational-emotive behavior therapy (REBT) Developed by Albert Ellis, a form of therapy based on identifying and correcting irrational beliefs that are believed to underlie emotional and behavioral difficulties. (p. 426)

rationalization In Freudian theory, a defense mechanism involving the use of self-justification to explain away unacceptable behavior, impulses, or ideas. (p. 348)

reaction formation In Freudian theory, a defense mechanism involving behavior that stands in opposition to one's true motives and desires so as to prevent conscious awareness of them. (p. 348)

reality principle In Freudian theory, the governing principle of the ego that takes into account what is practical and acceptable in satisfying basic needs. (p. 348)

recency effect The tendency to recall items better when they are learned last. (p. 208)

receptor site A site on the receiving neuron in which neurotransmitters dock. (p. 44)

reciprocal determinism Bandura's model in which cognitions, behaviors, and environmental factors both influence and are influenced by each other. (p. 362)

reciprocity The principle that people tend to like others who like them back. (p. 493)

recognition task A method of measuring memory retention that assesses the ability to select the correct answer from among a range of alternative answers. (p. 211)

reconditioning The process of relearning a conditioned response following extinction. (p. 163)

reflex An automatic, unlearned response to particular stimuli. (p. 49)

refractory period A temporary state in which a neuron is unable to fire in response to continued stimulation. (p. 44)

regression In Freudian theory, a defense mechanism in which an individual, usually under high levels of stress, reverts to a behavior characteristic of an earlier stage of development. (p. 348)

reinforcer A stimulus or event that increases the probability that the response it follows will be repeated. (p. 172)

reliability The stability of test scores over time. (p. 241)

replication The attempt to duplicate findings. (p. 22)

representativeness heuristic A rule of thumb for making a judgment that assumes a given sample is representative of the larger population from which it is drawn. (p. 229)

repression In Freudian theory, a type of defense mechanism involving motivated forgetting of anxiety-evoking material. (pp. 210 and 348)

resistance In psychoanalysis, the blocking that occurs when therapy touches upon anxiety-evoking thoughts or feelings. (p. 420)

resistance stage The second stage of the general adaptation syndrome, characterized by the body's attempt to adjust or adapt to persistent stress. (p. 459)

resting potential The electrical potential across the cell membrane of a neuron in its resting state. (p. 42)

reticular formation A weblike formation of neurons involved in regulating states of attention, alertness, and arousal. (p. 53)

retina The light-sensitive layer of the inner surface of the eye that contains photoreceptor cells. (p. 88)

retinal disparity A binocular cue for distance based on the slight differences in the visual impressions formed in both eyes. (p. 112)

retrieval cues Cues associated with the original learning that facilitate the retrieval of memories. (p. 195)

retrieval theory The belief that forgetting is the result of a failure to access stored memories. (p. 209)

retroactive interference A form of interference in which newly acquired information interferes with retention of material learned earlier. (p. 207)

retrograde amnesia Loss of memory of past events. (p. 211)

retrospective memory Memory of past experiences or events and previously acquired information. (p. 201)

reuptake The process by which neurotransmitters are reabsorbed by the transmitting neuron. (p. 45)

rods Photoreceptors that are sensitive only to the intensity of light (light and dark). (p. 88)

role diffusion In Erikson's model, a lack of direction or aimlessness with respect to one's role in life or public identity. (p. 327)

rooting reflex The reflexive turning of the newborn's head in the direction of a touch on its cheek. (p. 301)

rubella A common childhood disease that can lead to serious birth defects if contracted by the mother during pregnancy (also called *German measles*). (p. 299)

samples Subsets of a population. (p. 23)

savings method A method of testing memory retention by comparing the numbers of trials needed to learn material with the number of trials needed to relearn the material at a later time. (p. 207)

scatterplot A graph in which pairs of scores are plotted for each research participant on two variables. (p. A-10)

schedule of continuous reinforcement A system of dispensing a reinforcement each time an operant response is produced. (p. 176)

schedule of partial reinforcement A system of reinforcement in which only a portion of responses is reinforced. (p. 176)

schedules of reinforcement Predetermined plans for timing the delivery of reinforcement. (p. 176)

schema To Piaget, a mental framework for understanding or acting on the environment. (p. 313)

schizoid personality disorder A type of personality disorder characterized by social aloofness and limited range of emotional expression. (p. 410)

schizophrenia A severe and chronic psychological disorder characterized by disturbances in thinking, perception, emotions, and behavior. (pp. 45 and 406)

school psychologists Psychologists who evaluate and assist children with learning problems or other special needs. (p. 17)

scientific method A method of inquiry involving careful observation and use of experimental methods. (p. 21)

secondary drives Drives that are learned or acquired through experience, such as the drive to achieve monetary wealth. (p. 259)

secondary gain Reward value of having a psychological or physical symptom, such as release from ordinary responsibilities. (p. 397)

secondary reinforcers Learned reinforcers, such as money, that develop their reinforcing properties because of their association with primary reinforcers. (p. 175)

secondary sex characteristics Physical characteristics that differentiate males and females but are not directly involved in reproduction. (p. 320)

secondary traits Allport's term for specific traits that influence behavior in relatively few situations. (p. 355)

selective attention The process by which we attend to meaningful stimuli and filter out irrelevant or extraneous stimuli. (p. 106)

selective serotonin-reuptake inhibitors (SSRIs) A class of antidepressant drugs that work specifically on increasing availability of the neurotransmitter serotonin by interfering with its reuptake. (p. 437)

self-actualization The motive that drives individuals to express their unique capabilities and fulfill their potentials. (p. 263)

self-fulfilling prophecy An expectation that helps bring about the outcome that is expected. (p. 483)

self-ideals Rogers's term for the idealized sense of how or what we should be. (p. 366)

self-report personality inventories Structured psychological tests in which individuals are given a limited range of response options to answer a set of questions about themselves. (p. 369)

self-serving bias The tendency to take credit for our accomplishments and to explain away our failures or disappointments. (p. 485)

self-theory Rogers's model of personality, which focuses on the importance of the self. *(p. 365)*

semantic memory Memory of facts. *(p. 200)*

semantic network model A representation of the organizational structure of long-term memory in terms of a network of associated concepts. *(p. 198)*

semantics The set of rules governing the meaning of words. *(p. 233)*

semicircular canals Three curved, tube-like canals in the inner ear that are involved in sensing changes in the direction and movement of the head. *(p. 104)*

sensation The process by which we receive, transform, and process stimuli from the outside world to create sensory experiences of vision, touch, hearing, taste, smell, and so on. *(p. 84)*

sensory adaptation The process by which sensory receptors adapt to constant stimuli by becoming less sensitive to them. *(p. 86)*

sensory memory The storage system that holds memory of sensory impressions for a very short time. *(p. 195)*

sensory neurons Neurons that transmit information from sensory organs, muscles, and inner organs to the spinal cord and brain. *(p. 40)*

sensory receptors Specialized cells that detect sensory stimuli and convert them into neural impulses. *(p. 84)*

sensory register A temporary storage device for holding sensory memories. *(p. 195)*

serial position effect The tendency to recall items at the start or end of a list better than items in the middle of a list. *(p. 208)*

set point theory The belief that brain mechanisms regulate body weight around a genetically predetermined "set point." *(p. 297)*

sexual dysfunctions Persistent or recurrent problems with sexual interest, arousal, or response. *(p. 276)*

sexual orientation The directionality of one's erotic interests. *(p. 272)*

sexual response cycle The term used by Masters and Johnson to refer to the characteristic stages of physiological response to sexual stimulation. *(p. 273)*

sexually transmitted disease (STD) A disease caused by an infectious agent that is spread by sexual contact. *(p. 472)*

shape constancy The tendency to perceive an object as having the same shape despite differences in the images it casts on the retina as the viewer's perspective changes. *(p. 111)*

shaping A process of learning that involves the reinforcement of increasingly closer approximations of the desired response. *(p. 175)*

short-term memory (STM) The memory subsystem that allows for retention and processing of newly acquired information for a maximum of about thirty seconds (also called *working memory*). *(p. 196)*

signal-detection theory The belief that the detection of a stimulus depends on factors involving the intensity of the stimulus, the level of background stimulation, and the biological and psychological characteristics of the perceiver. *(p. 85)*

similarity The principle that objects that are similar will be perceived as belonging to the same group. *(p. 111)*

single-blind studies In drug research, studies in which subjects are kept uninformed about whether they are receiving the experimental drug or a placebo. *(p. 27)*

situational causes Causes relating to external or environmental events. *(p. 484)*

situation variables Mischel's term for environmental influences on behavior, such as rewards and punishments. *(p. 363)*

size constancy The tendency to perceive an object as having the same size despite changes in the images it casts on the retina as the viewing distance changes. *(p. 111)*

skin senses The senses of touch, pressure, warmth, cold, and pain that involve stimulation of sensory receptors in the skin. *(p. 102)*

Skinner box An experimental apparatus developed by B. F. Skinner for studying relationships between reinforcement and behavior. *(p. 172)*

sleep apnea Temporary cessation of breathing during sleep. *(p. 136)*

sleep terror disorder A sleep disorder involving repeated episodes of intense fear during sleep, causing the person to awake abruptly in a terrified state. *(p. 137)*

sleepwalking disorder A sleep disorder characterized by repeated episodes of sleepwalking. *(p. 137)*

social-cognitive theory A learning-based model of personality that emphasizes both cognitive factors and environmental influences in determining behavior. *(pp. 9 and 361)*

social desirability bias The tendency to respond to questions in a socially desirable manner. *(p. 24)*

social facilitation The tendency to work better or harder in the presence of others than when alone. *(p. 509)*

social identity The part of our psychological identity that involves our sense of ourselves as members of particular groups. Also called *group identity. (p. 504)*

social loafing The tendency to expend less effort when working as a member of a group than when working alone. *(p. 510)*

social norms Standards that define what is socially acceptable in a given situation. *(p. 496)*

social perception The processes by which we form impressions, make judgments, and develop attitudes about the people and events that constitute our social world. *(p. 482)*

social phobia A type of anxiety disorder involving excessive fear of social situations. *(p. 390)*

social psychologists Psychologists who study group or social influences on behavior and attitudes. *(p. 17)*

social psychology The subfield in psychology that deals with how our thoughts, feelings, and behaviors are influenced by our social interactions with others. *(p. 482)*

social schema A mental image or representation that we use to understand our social environment. *(p. 483)*

social validation The tendency to use other people's behavior as a standard for judging the appropriateness of one's own behavior. *(p. 509)*

sociocultural perspective An approach to the study of psychology that emphasizes the role of social and cultural influences on behavior. *(p. 11)*

soma The cell body of a neuron that contains the nucleus of the cell and carries out the cell's metabolic functions. *(p. 40)*

somatic nervous system The part of the peripheral nervous system that transmits information between the central nervous system and the sensory organs and muscles; also controls voluntary movements. *(p. 50)*

somatoform disorders A class of psychological disorders involving physical ailments or complaints that cannot be explained by organic causes. *(p. 394)*

somatosensory cortex The part of the parietal lobe that processes information about touch and pressure on the skin, as well as the position of the parts of our bodies as we move about. *(p. 55)*

source traits Cattell's term for traits at a deep level of personality that are not apparent in observed behavior but must be inferred based on underlying relationships among surface traits. *(p. 356)*

specific phobia Phobic reactions involving specific situations or objects. *(p. 390)*

spina bifida A neural tube defect in which the child is born with a hole in the tube surrounding the spinal cord. *(p. 298)*

spinal cord The column of nerves that transmits information between the brain and the peripheral nervous system. *(p. 49)*

spinal reflex A reflex controlled at the level of the spinal cord that may involve as few as two neurons. *(p. 49)*

spine The protective bony column that houses the spinal cord. *(p. 49)*

split-brain patients Persons whose corpus callosum has been surgically severed. *(p. 64)*

spontaneous recovery The spontaneous return of a conditioned response following extinction. *(p. 163)*

sport psychologists Psychologists who apply psychology to understanding and improving athletic performance. *(p. 18)*

standard deviation (SD) A measure of variability defined as the average difference between each individual score and the mean of all scores in the data set. *(p. A-8)*

standardization The process of establishing norms for a test by administering the test to large numbers of people who constitute a standardization sample. *(p. 239)*

standard scores Scores that represent an individual's relative deviation from the mean of the standardization sample. *(pp. 371 and A-8)*

states of consciousness Levels of consciousness ranging from alert wakefulness to unconsciousness during deep sleep. *(p. 126)*

statistics The branch of mathematics involving the tabulation, analysis, and interpretation of numerical data. *(p. 22)*

stereotypes The tendency to characterize all members of a particular group as having certain characteristics in common. *(p. 483)*

stimulants Drugs that activate the central nervous system. *(pp. 46 and 147)*

stimulus discrimination The tendency to differentiate among stimuli so that stimuli that are related to the original conditioned stimulus, but not identical to it, fail to elicit a conditioned response. *(p. 164)*

stimulus generalization The tendency for stimuli that are similar to the conditioned stimulus to elicit a conditioned response. *(p. 164)*

stimulus motives Internal states that prompt inquisitive, stimulation-seeking, and exploratory behavior. *(p. 260)*

stress Pressure or demand placed on an organism to adjust or adapt. *(p. 450)*

stressors Sources of stress. *(p. 451)*

stroboscopic movement A type of apparent movement based on the rapid succession of still images, as in motion pictures. *(p. 116)*

structuralism The school of psychology that attempts to understand the structure of the mind by breaking it down into its component parts. *(p. 6)*

structured interview An interview in which a set of specific questions is asked in a particular order. *(p. 23)*

subjective value In social-cognitive theory, the importance that individuals place on desired outcomes. *(p. 361)*

sublimation In Freudian theory, a defense mechanism involving the channeling of unacceptable impulses into socially sanctioned behaviors or interests. *(p. 348)*

subliminal perception Perception of stimuli that are presented below the threshold of conscious awareness. *(p. 117)*

sucking reflex Rhythmic sucking in response to stimulation of the tongue or mouth. *(p. 301)*

sudden infant death syndrome (SIDS) The sudden and unexplained death of infants that usually occurs when they are asleep in their cribs. *(p. 300)*

superego Freud's term for the psychic structure that corresponds to an internal moral guardian or conscience. *(p. 347)*

superstitious behavior In Skinner's view, behavior acquired through coincidental association of a response and a reinforcement. *(p. 172)*

surface traits Cattell's term for personality traits at the surface level that can be gleaned from observations of behavior. *(p. 355)*

survey method A research method that uses structured interviews or questionnaires to gather information about groups of people. *(p. 23)*

symbolic representations A term referring to the use of words to represent (name) objects and describe experiences. *(p. 315)*

sympathetic nervous system The branch of the autonomic nervous system that accelerates bodily processes and releases stores of energy needed to meet increased physical demands. *(p. 51)*

synapse The small fluid-filled gap between neurons through which neurotransmitters carry neural impulses. *(p. 40)*

syntax The rules of grammar that determine how words are ordered within sentences or phrases to form meaningful expressions. *(p. 233)*

systematic desensitization A behavior therapy technique for treating phobias through the pairing of exposure in imagination to fear-inducing stimuli and states of deep relaxation. *(p. 423)*

tardive dyskinesia (TD) A potentially disabling motor disorder that may occur following regular use of antipsychotic drugs. *(p. 438)*

taste buds Pores or openings on the tongue containing taste cells. *(p. 101)*

taste cells Nerve cells that are sensitive to tastes. *(p. 101)*

telepathy Communication of thoughts from one mind to another that occurs without using the known senses. *(p. 118)*

temperament A characteristic style of behavior or disposition. *(p. 305)*

temporal lobes The parts of the cerebral cortex lying beneath and somewhat behind the frontal lobes that are involved in processing auditory stimuli. *(p. 57)*

teratogen An environmental influence or agent that may harm the developing embryo or fetus. *(p. 298)*

terminal buttons Swellings at the tips of axons from which neurotransmitters are dispatched into the synapse. *(p. 40)*

testes The male gonads, which produce sperm and secrete the male sex hormone testosterone. *(p. 70)*

thalamus A structure in the forebrain that serves as a relay station for sensory information and that plays a key role in regulating states of wakefulness and sleep. *(p. 54)*

theory A formulation that accounts for relationships among observed events or experimental findings in ways that make them more understandable and predictable. *(p. 21)*

thermal biofeedback A form of BFT that involves feedback about changes in temperature and blood flow in selected parts of the body; used in the treatment of migraine headaches. *(p. 77)*

thinking The process of mentally representing and manipulating information. *(p. 224)*

thought disorder A breakdown in the logical structure of thought and speech, revealed in the form of a loosening of associations. *(p. 407)*

three-stage model A model of memory that posits three distinct stages of memory: sensory memory, short-term memory, and long-term memory. *(p. 195)*

thyroid gland An endocrine gland in the neck that secretes the hormone thyroxin, which is involved in regulating metabolic functions and physical growth. *(p. 71)*

tip-of-the-tongue (TOT) phenomenon An experience in which people are sure they know something but can't seem to bring it to mind. *(p. 209)*

token economy program A form of behavior modification in which tokens earned for performing desired behaviors can be exchanged for positive reinforcers. *(p. 182)*

tolerance A form of physical habituation to a drug in which increased amounts are needed to achieve the same effect. *(p. 142)*

top-down processing A mode of perceptual processing by which the brain identifies patterns as meaningful wholes rather than as piecemeal constructions. *(p. 109)*

traits Relatively enduring personal characteristics. *(p. 355)*

transcendental meditation (TM) A form of meditation in which practitioners focus their attention by repeating a particular mantra. *(p. 138)*

transference relationship In therapy, the tendency of clients to reenact earlier conflicted relationships in the relationship they develop with their therapists. *(p. 420)*

triarchic theory of intelligence Sternberg's theory of intelligence that posits three aspects of intelligence: analytic, creative, and practical. *(p. 246)*

trichromatic theory A theory of color vision that posits that the ability to see different colors depends on the relative activity of three types of color receptors in the eye (red, green, and blue-violet). *(p. 91)*

trichromats People with normal color vision who can discern all the colors of the visual spectrum. *(p. 92)*

tricyclics A class of antidepressant drugs that increase the availability of neurotransmitters in the brain by interfering with the reuptake of these chemicals by transmitting neurons. *(p. 437)*

twin studies Studies that examine the degree to which concordance rates between twin pairs for particular disorders or characteristics vary in relation to whether the twins are identical or fraternal. *(p. 75)*

two-factor model The theory that emotions involve two factors: a state of general arousal and a cognitive interpretation (or labeling) of the causes of the arousal. *(p. 284)*

Type A behavior pattern (TABP) A behavior pattern characterized by impatience, time urgency, competitiveness, and hostility. *(p. 455)*

unconditional positive regard Valuing another person as having intrinsic worth, regardless of the person's behavior at the particular time. *(p. 365)*

unconditioned response (UR) An unlearned response to a stimulus. *(p. 162)*

unconditioned stimulus (US) A stimulus that elicits an unlearned response. *(p. 162)*

unconscious To Freud, the part of the mind that lies outside the range of ordinary awareness and that holds troubling or unacceptable urges, impulses, memories, and ideas. *(pp. 8 and 346)*

unconsciousness In ordinary use, a term referring to lack of awareness of one's surroundings or to loss of consciousness. *(p. 127)*

uterus The female reproductive organ in which the fertilized ovum becomes implanted and develops to term. *(p. 297)*

vaccination A method of acquiring immunity by means of injecting a weakened or partial form of an infectious agent that can induce production of antibodies but does not produce a full-blown infection. *(p. 462)*

validity The degree to which a test measures what it purports to measure. *(p. 241)*

variability In statistics, the spread or dispersion of scores throughout the distribution. *(p. A-8)*

variable A factor or measure that varies within an experiment or among individuals. *(p. 22)*

vasocongestion Swelling of tissues with blood, a process that accounts for penile erection and vaginal lubrication during sexual arousal. *(p. 273)*

ventromedial hypothalamus A part of the hypothalamus involved in regulating feelings of satiety. *(p. 266)*

vestibular sacs Organs in the inner ear that connect the semicircular canals. *(p. 104)*

vestibular sense The sense that keeps us informed about balance and the position of our body in space. *(p. 104)*

virtual therapy A form of exposure therapy in which virtual reality is used to simulate real-world environments. *(p. 425)*

visual illusions Misperceptions of visual stimuli. *(p. 114)*

visuospatial sketchpad The storage buffer for visual-spatial material held in short-term memory. *(p. 197)*

volley principle The principle that relates the experience of pitch to the alternating firing of groups of neurons along the basilar membrane. *(p. 96)*

volunteer bias The type of bias that arises when people who volunteer to participate in a survey or research study have characteristics that make them unrepresentative of the population from which they were drawn. *(p. 24)*

waxy flexibility A feature of catatonic schizophrenia in which people rigidly maintain the body position or posture in which they were placed by others. *(p. 408)*

Weber's law The principle that the amount of change in a stimulus needed to detect a difference is given by a constant ratio or fraction, called a constant, of the original stimulus. *(p. 85)*

Wernicke's area An area of the left temporal lobe involved in processing written and spoken language. *(p. 63)*

withdrawal syndrome A cluster of symptoms associated with abrupt withdrawal from a drug. *(p. 142)*

zone of proximal development (ZPD) In Vygotsky's theory, the range between children's present level of knowledge and their potential knowledge state if they receive proper guidance and instruction. *(p. 318)*

zygote A fertilized egg cell. *(pp. 75 and 297)*

REFERENCES

Aboud, F. E. (2003). The formation of in-group favoritism and out-group prejudice in young children: Are they distinct attitudes? *Developmental Psychology, 39,* 48–60.

Abraham, K. (1948). The first pregenital stage of the libido (1916). In D. Bryan & A. Strachey (Eds.), *Selected papers of Karl Abraham, M.D.* London: Hogarth Press.

Abrahamson, A. C., Baker, L. A., & Caspi, A. (2002). Rebellious teens? Genetic and environmental influences on the social attitudes of adolescents. *Journal of Personality and Social Psychology, 83,* 1392–1408.

Abramov, I., & Gordon, J. (1994). Color appearance: On seeing red or yellow, or green, or blue. *Annual Review of Psychology, 45,* 451–485.

Abrams, K. K., Allen, L., & Gray, J. J. (1993). Disordered eating attitudes and behaviors, psychological adjustment and ethnic identity: A comparison of Black and White female college students. *International Journal of Eating Disorders, 14,* 49–57.

Abramson, L. T., Seligman, M. E. P., & Teasdale, J. D. (1978). Learned helplessness in humans: Critique and reformulation. *Journal of Abnormal Psychology, 87,* 49–74.

Adelson, R. (2004, April). Stimulating the vagus nerve: Memories are made of this. *Monitor on Psychology,* pp. 36–38.

Ader, R., & Cohen, N. (1982). Behaviorally conditioned immunosuppression and murine systemic lupus erythematosus. *Science, 215,* 1534–1536.

Ades, P. A. (2001). Cardiac rehabilitation and secondary prevention of coronary heart disease. *New England Journal of Medicine, 345,* 892–902.

Adler, J. (1999, June 14). Stress. *Newsweek,* pp. 58–63.

Adler, J. (2003, October 20). In the grip of a deeper pain. *Newsweek,* pp. 48–49.

Adler, J., & Raymond, J. (2001, Fall/Winter). Fight back, with sweat. *Newsweek Special Issue,* pp. 35–41.

Adler, T. (1993, September). Sleep loss impairs attention. *APA Monitor, 24*(9), 22–23.

Adorno, T. W., Frenkel-Brunswik, E., Levinson, D., & Sanford, R. N. (1950). *The authoritarian personality.* New York: Harper.

Adult aggression, children's TV tied. (2003, March 10). *Associated Press Web Posting.* Retrieved March 29, 2003, from *http://www.msnbc.com/news/882914.asp.*

Aguiara, A., & Baillargeon, R. (2002). Developments in young infants' reasoning about occluded objects. *Cognitive Psychology, 45,* 267–336.

Ainsworth, M. D. S. (1979). Infant-mother attachment. *American Psychologist, 34,* 932–937.

Ainsworth, M. D. S., Blehar, M. C., Waters, E., & Wall, S. (1978). *Patterns of attachment: A psychological study of the Strange Situation.* Hillsdale, NJ: Erlbaum.

Aldrich, M. S. (1992). Narcolepsy. *Neurology, 42* (7, Suppl. 6), 34–43.

Aleman, A., Kahn, R. S., & Selten, J.-P. (2003). Sex differences in the risk of schizophrenia: Evidence from meta-analysis. *Archives of General Psychiatry, 60,* 565–571.

Alexander, C. N., Robinson, P., & Rainforth, M. (1995). "Treating and preventing alcohol, nicotine, and drug abuse through transcendental meditation: A review and statistical meta-analysis": Errata. *Alcoholism Treatment Quarterly, 13*(4), 97.

Alexander, C. N., Robinson, P., Orme-Johnson, D. W., & Schneider, R. H. (1995). "The effects of transcendental mediation compared to other methods of relaxation and meditation in reducing risk factors, morbidity, and mortality": Correction. *Homeostasis in Health and Disease, 36,* 240.

Alley, T. R., & Dillon, N. E. (2001). Sex-linked carrying styles and the attribution of homosexuality. *Journal of Social Psychology, 14,* 660–666.

Alloy, L. B., Abramson, L. Y., Hogan, M. E., Whitehouse, W. G., Rose, D. T., Robinson, M. S., et al. (2000). The Temple-Wisconsin cognitive vulnerability to depression project: Lifetime history of Axis I psychopathology in individuals at high and low cognitive risk for depression. *Journal of Abnormal Psychology, 109,* 403–418.

Allport, G. W. (1954). *The nature of prejudice.* Reading, MA: Addison-Wesley.

Allport, G. W. (1961). *Pattern and growth in personality.* New York: Holt, Rinehart & Winston.

Alpert, J. L., Brown, L. S., & Courtois, C. A. (1998). *Working group on investigation of memories of childhood abuse: Final report.* Washington, DC: American Psychological Association.

Altman, D. (2004, June). The dismal science measures the meaning of life. *Business 2.0.,* p. 56.

American Academy of Pediatrics, Committee on Psychosocial Aspects of Child and Family Health. (1998). Guidance for Effective Discipline. *Pediatrics, 101*(4), 723.

American Association for the Advancement of Sciences (1997, August 20). Sleep and the Monday Night Football effect. *InSCIght Web Posting.* Retrieved November 22, 2000, from *http://darwin.apnet.com/inscight/08191997/grapha.htm.*

American Cancer Society. (2001). *Cancer facts and figures 2001.* Atlanta, GA: Author.

American dream: Live long and prosper. (2001, June 13). Retrieved June 15, 2001, from http://www.cnn.com/2001/HEALTH/06/13/living.longer/index.html.

American Heart Association. (1995). *Risk factors for coronary heart disease.* Dallas, TX: Author.

American Psychiatric Association. (1994). *Diagnostic and statistical manual of mental disorders* (4th ed.). Washington, DC: Author.

American Psychiatric Association. (2000). *Diagnostic and statistical manual of mental disorders. DSMIVTR.* Washington, DC: Author.

American Psychiatric Association. (2000). *DSM-IV-TR: Diagnostic and statistical manual of mental disorders (Text Revision).* Washington, DC: Author.

American Psychiatric Association. (2000). *DSM-IV-TR: Diagnostic and statistical manual of mental disorders* (Text Revision). Washington, DC: Author.

American Psychological Association (1999). *1999 APA directory survey: Selected characteristics.* Washington, DC: APA Research Office.

American Psychological Association. (1992a). Ethical principles of psychologists and code of conduct. *American Psychologist, 47,* 1597–1611.

American Psychological Association. (1992b). *Guidelines for ethical conduct in the care and use of animals.* Washington, DC: Author.

American Psychological Association. (2003a, July). *Employment settings for PhD psychologists: 2001.* Washington, DC: APA Research Office.

American Psychological Association. (2003b, September). *Demographic shifts in psychology.* Washington, DC: APA Research Office.

American Psychological Association. (2004, April). *Current major fields of APA membership by membership status, 2002.* Washington, DC: APA Research Office.

Americans living longer. (2002, September 12). *CNN Web Posting.* Retrieved September 18, 2002, from http://www.cnn.com/2002/HEALTH/09/12/longer.life.expectancy.ap/index.html.

Anch, A. M., Browman, C. P., Mitler, M. M., & Walsh, J. K. (1988). *Sleep: A scientific perspective.* Upper Saddle River, NJ: Prentice-Hall.

Andersen, B. L., Golden-Kreutz, D. M., & DiLillo, V. (2001). Cancer. In A. Baum, T. A. Revenson, & J. E. Singer (Eds.), *Handbook of health psychology* (pp. 709–726). Mahwah, NJ: Lawrence Erlbaum Associates.

Anderson, C. A., & Bushman, B. J. (2003). Human aggression. *Annual Review of Psychology, 53,* 27–51.

Anderson, C. A., & DeNeve, K. M. (1992). Temperature, aggression, and the negative affect escape model. *Psychological Bulletin, 111,* 347–351.

Anderson, C. A., Bushman, B. J., & Groom, R. W. (1997). Hot years and serious and deadly assault: Empirical tests of the heat hypothesis. *Journal of Personality and Social Psychology, 73,* 1213–1223.

Anderson, D. E. (2003, August*). Longitudinal study of formal operations in college students.* Paper presented at the meeting of the American Psychological Association, Toronto, CA.

Anderson, E. M., & Lambert, M. J. (2001). A survival analysis of clincially significant change in outpatient psychotherapy. *Professional Psychology: Research and Practice, 57,* 875–888.

Anderson, M. B., Van Raalte, J. L, & Brewer, B. W. (2001). Sport psychology service delivery: Staying ethical while keeping loose. *Professional Psychology: Research and Practice, 32,* 12–18.

Anderson, S. E., Dallal, G. E., & Must, A. (2003). Relative weight and race influence average age at menarche: Results from two nationally representative surveys of US girls studied 25 years apart. *Pediatrics, 111,* 844–850.

Anderson, S. J., & Conway, M. A. (1997). Representations of autobiographic memories. In M. A. Conway (Ed.), *Cognitive models of memory* (pp. 217–246). Cambridge, MA: MIT Press.

Anderson, S. W., Bechara, A., Damasio, H., Tranel, D., & Damasio, A. R. (1999). Impairment of social and moral behavior related to early damage in human prefrontal cortex. *Nature Neuroscience, 2,* 1032–1037.

Andreasen, A. (2003). From molecule to mind: Genetics, genomics, and psychiatry [Editorial]. *American Journal of Psychiatry, 160,* 613.

Angier, N. (1998a, February 8). Separated by birth? *New York Times Book Review*, p. 9.

Angier, N. (1998b, September 1). Nothing becomes a man more than a woman's face. *New York Times*, p. F3.

Angier, N. (2000a, June 27). A pearl and a hodgepodge: Human DNA. *New York Times*, pp. A1, A21.

Angier, N. (2000b, July 21). Study finds region of brain may be key problem solver. *New York Times*, p. A13.

Angier, N. (2000c, November 7). Who is fat? It depends on culture. *New York Times*, pp. F1–F2.

Angier, N. (2003a, February 25). Not just genes: Moving beyond nature vs. nurture. *New York Times*, pp. F1, F10.

Angier, N. (2003b, July 8). Opposites attract? Not in real life. *New York Times*, pp. F1, F6.

Anniko, M., Arnold, W., & Stigbrand, T. (1993). Protein patterns in human vestibular ganglion cells and hair cells, with functional interpretations. *Acta Otolaryngologist Supplement, 503*, 136–142.

Anthony, J. C., Warner, L. A., & Kessler, R. C. (1994). Comparative epidemiology of dependence on tobacco, alcohol, controlled substances, and inhalants: Basic findings from the National Comorbidity Survey. *Experimental and Clinical Psychopharmacology, 2*, 244–268.

Applebome, P. (1997, May 7). Gender gap in testing narrower than believed, study finds. *New York Times*, p. A16.

Arbelle, S., Benjamin, J., Golin, M., Kremer, I., Belmaker, R. H., & Ebstein, R. P. (2003). Relation of shyness in grade school children to the genotype for the long form of the serotonin transporter promoter region polymorphism. *American Journal of Psychiatry, 160*, 671–676.

Arnett, J. (1992). Reckless behavior in adolescence: A developmental perspective. *Developmental Review, 12*, 339–373.

Arnett, J. J. (2000). Emerging adulthood: A theory of development from the late teens through the twenties. *American Psychologist, 55*, 469–480.

Arnett, J. J. (2004). *Adolescence and emerging adulthood: A cultural approach* (2nd ed.). Upper Saddle River, NJ: Pearson/Prentice Hall.

Arnett, P. A., Smith, S. S., & Newman, J. P. (1997). Approach and avoidance motivation in psychopathic criminal offenders during passive avoidance. *Journal of Personality and Social Psychology, 72*, 1413–1428.

Aronson, E., Wilson, T. D., & Akert, R. M. (2004). *Social psychology: Media and research update.* (5th ed.). Upper Saddle River, NJ: Prentice Hall.

Arrindell, W. A. (2003). Cultural abnormal psychology. *Behaviour Research and Therapy, 41*, 749–753.

Asch, S. E. (1956). Studies of independence and conformity: I. A minority of one against a unanimous majority. *Psychological Monographs, 70*, 70.

Aschwanden, C. (2000, September). Big fat fitness myths. *Health*, pp. 93–97.

Ashburn-Nardo, L., Voils, C. I., & Monteith, M. J. (2001). Implicit associations as the seeds of intergroup bias: How easily do they take root? *Journal of Personality and Social Psychology, 81*, 789–799.

A tasty gene may explain dietary choices. (2003, February 21). *Wall Street Journal*, p. B5.

Atkinson, R. C., & Shiffrin, R. M. (1971). The control of short-term memory. *Scientific American, 225*, 82–90.

Averhart, C. J., & Bigler, R. S. (1997). Shades of meaning: Skin tone, racial attitudes, and constructive memory in African American children. *Journal of Experimental Child Psychology, 67*, 363–388.

Axel, R. (1995, October). The molecular logic of smell. *Scientific American*, pp. 154–159.

Azar, B. (1995, May). Several genetic traits linked to alcoholism. *APA Monitor, 26*(5), 21–22.

Azar, B. (1996a, April). Musical studies provide clues to brain functions. *APA Monitor, 27*(4), 1, 24.

Azar, B. (1996b, August). Why men lose keys—and women find them. *APA Monitor, 27*(8), 32.

Azar, B. (1996c, October). Memory appears to dwell in various parts of the brain. *APA Monitor, 27*(10), 36.

Azar, B. (1998a, January). What predicts which foods we eat? *APA Monitor, 29*(1), 13.

Azar, B. (1998b, September). Of Zajonc's ever-changing focus, friends joke 'What about Bob?' *APA Monitor, 29*(9), 12.

Bachmann, G., Bancroft, J., Braunstein, G., Burger, H., Davis, S., Dennerstein, L., Goldstein, I., et al. (2002). Female androgen insufficiency: The Princeton consensus statement on definition, classification, and assessment. *Fertility and Sterility, 77*, 660–665.

Baddeley, A. D. (1996). *Human memory: Theory and practice* (2nd ed.). Hove, UK: Psychology Press.

Baddeley, A. D. (2001). Levels of working memory. In M. Naveh-Benjamin, M. Moscovitch, & H. L. Roediger (Eds.), *Perspectives on human memory and cognitive aging: Essays in honor of Fergus Craik*. Hove, England: Psychology Press.

Baddeley, A. D., & Hitch, G. J. (1974). Working memory. In G. Bower (Ed.), *The psychology of learning and motivation* (Vol. 8, pp. 47–90). New York: Academic Press.

Baddeley, A., Conway, M., & Aggleton, J. (Eds.). (2002). *Episodic memory: New directions in research*. Oxford, England: Oxford University Press.

Baer, R. A. (2003). Mindfulness training as a clinical intervention: A conceptual and empirical review. *Clinical Psychology: Science and Practice, 10*, 125–143.

Baeyens, F., Eelen, P., & Crombez, G. (1995). Pavlovian associations are forever: On classical conditioning and extinction. *Journal of Psychophysiology, 9*, 127–141.

Bagary, M. S., Symms, M. R., Barker, G. J., Mutsatsa, S. H., Joyce, E. M., & Ron, M. A. (2003). Gray and white matter brain abnormalities in first-episode schizophrenia inferred from magnetization transfer imaging. *Archives of General Psychiatry, 60*, 779–788.

Bagley, C., & D'Augelli, A. R. (2000). Suicidal behaviour in gay, lesbian, and bisexual youth. *British Medical Journal, 320*, 1617–1618.

Bailar, J. C., III. (2001). The powerful placebo and the wizard of Oz. *New England Journal of Medicine, 344*, 1630–1632.

Bailey, J. M., & Zucker, K. J. (1995). Childhood sex-typed behavior and sexual orientation: A conceptual analysis and quantitative review. *Developmental Psychology, 31*, 43–55.

Bailey, J. M., Bobrow, D., Wolfe, M., & Mikach, S. (1995). Sexual orientation of adult sons of gay fathers. *Developmental Psychology, 31*, 124–129.

Bailey, J. M., Dunne, M. P., & Martin, N. G. (2000). Genetic and environmental influences on sexual orientation and its correlates in an Australian twin sample. *Journal of Personality and Social Psychology, 78*, 524–536.

Baird, J. D., Wagner, M., & Fuld, K. (1990). A simple but powerful theory of the moon illusion. *Journal of Experimental Psychology: Human Perception and Performance, 16*, 675–677.

Baity, M. R., & Hilsenroth, M. J. (2002). Rorschach Aggressive Content (AgC) variable: A study of criterion validity. *Journal of Personality Assessment, 78*, 275–287.

Baldessarini, R. J., & Tondo, M. D. (2003). Suicide risk and treatments for patients with bipolar disorder. *Journal of the American Medical Association, 290*, 1517–1519.

Balkin, T. J., Braun, A. R., Wesensten, N. J., Jeffries, K., Varga, M., et al. (2002). The process of awakening: A PET study of regional brain activity patterns mediating the re-establishment of alertness and consciousness. *Brain, 125*, 2308–2319.

Ball, K., Berch, D. B., Helmers, K. F., Jobe, J. B., Leveck, M. D., Marsiske, M., et al. (2002). Effects of cognitive training interventions with older adults. A randomized controlled trial. *Journal of the American Medical Association, 288*, 2271–2281.

Balter, M. (2001, October 5). First gene linked to speech identified. *Science, 294*, p. 32.

Baltes, P. B. (1997). On the incomplete architecture of human ontogeny: Selection, optimization, and compensation as foundation of developmental theory. *American Psychologist, 52*, 366–380.

Baltimore, D. (2000, June 25). 50,000 genes, and we know them all (almost). *New York Times*, Section 4, p. 17.

Banaji, M. R., & Greenwald, A. G. (1995). Implicit gender stereotyping in judgments of fame. *Journal of Personality and Social Psychology, 68*, 181–198.

Bancroft, J., Loftus, J., & Long, J. S. (2003). Distress about sex: A national survey of women in heterosexual relationships. *Archives of Sexual Behavior, 32*(3), 193–208.

Bandura, A. (1973). *Aggression: A social learning analysis*. Englewood Cliffs, NJ: Prentice-Hall.

Bandura, A. (1986). *Social foundations of thought and action: A social-cognitive theory*. Englewood Cliffs, NJ: Prentice-Hall.

Bandura, A. (1991). Human agency: The rhetoric and the reality. *American Psychologist, 44*, 157–162.

Bandura, A. (1997). *Self-efficacy: The exercise of control*. New York: Freeman.

Bandura, A. (2001). Social cognitive theory: An agentic perspective. *Annual Review of Psychology, 52*, 1–26.

Bandura, A., Blanchard, E. B., & Ritter, B. (1969). The relative efficacy of desensitization and modeling approaches for inducing behavioral, affective, and cognitive changes. *Journal of Personality and Social Psychology, 13*, 173–199.

Bandura, A., Ross, S. A., & Ross, D. (1963). Imitation of film-mediated aggressive models. *Journal of Abnormal Psychology, 66*, 3–11.

Bandura, W. (1989). Social cognitive theory. In R. Vasta (Ed.), *Annals of child development: Theories of child development: Revised formulations and current issues*. Greenwich, CT: JAI Press.

Barber, T. X. (1999). A comprehensive three-dimensional theory of hypnosis. In I. Kirsch et al. (Eds.), *Clinical hypnosis and self-regulation: Cognitive-behavioral perspectives* (pp. 21–48). Washington, DC: American Psychological Association.

Barch, D. M. (2003). Cognition in schizophrenia: Does working memory work? *Current Directions in Psychological Science, 12,* 146–150.

Barch, D. M., Csernansky, J. G., Conturo, T., & Snyder, A. Z. (2002). Working and long-term memory deficits in schizophrenia: Is there a common prefrontal mechanism? *Journal of Abnormal Psychology, 111,* 478–494.

Bargh, J. A., & Chartrand, T. L. (1999). The unbearable automaticity of being. *American Psychologist, 54,* 462–279.

Barinaga, M. (2002). How the brain's clock gets daily enlightenment. *Science, 295,* 955–957.

Barlow, D. H., Gorman, J. M., Shear, M. K., & Woods, S. W. (2000). Cognitive-behavioral therapy, imipramine, or their combination for panic disorder: A randomized controlled trial. *Journal of the American Medical Association, 283,* 2529–2536.

Barnett, W. S., & Camilli, G. (2002). Compensatory preschool education, cognitive development, and "race". In J. M. Fish (Ed.), *Race and intelligence: Separating science from myth* (pp. 369–406). Mahwah, NJ: Lawrence Erlbaum Associates.

Baron, R. A., & Byrne, D. (2000). *Social psychology* (9th ed.). Boston: Allyn & Bacon.

Baron, R. S., Vandello, J. A., & Brunsman, B. (1996). The forgotten variable in conformity research: Impact of task importance on social influence. *Journal of Personality and Social Psychology, 71,* 915–927.

Barrett, D. (1996). Fantasizers and dissociaters: Two types of high hypnotizables, two different imagery styles. In R. G. Kunzeorf, N. P. Spanos, & B. Wallace (Eds.), *Hypnosis and imagination* (pp. 123–135). Amityville, NY: Baywood Publishing.

Barry, D. T., & Bullock, W. A. (2001). Culturally creative psychotherapy with a Latino couple by an Anglo therapist. *Journal of Family Psychotherapy, 12,* 15–30.

Barsky, A. J., & Ahern, D. K. (2004). Cognitive behavior therapy for hypochondriasis: A randomized controlled trial. *Journal of the American Medical Association, 291,* 1464–1470.

Bartoshuk, L. (1989). Taste: Robust across the age span? *Annals of the New York Academy of Sciences, 561,* 65–75.

Bartoshuk, L. M., & Beauchamp, G. K. (1994). Chemical senses. *Annual Review of Psychology, 45,* 419–449.

Basoglu, M., Marks, I., Livanou, M., & Swinson, R. (1997). Double-blindness procedures, rater blindness, and ratings of outcome: Observations from a controlled trial. *Archives of General Psychology, 54,* 744–748.

Bateman, A., & Fonagy, P. (2001). Treatment of borderline personality disorder with psychoanalytically oriented partial hospitalization: An 18-month follow-up. *American Journal of Psychiatry, 158,* 36–42.

Batson, C. D. (1991). *The altruism question: Toward a social-psychological answer.* Hillsdale, NJ: Erlbaum.

Batson, C. D. (1998). Altruism and prosocial behavior. In D. T. Gilbert, S. T. Fiske, & G. Lindzey (Eds.), *The handbook of social psychology* (4th ed., Vol. 2, pp. 282–316). Boston: McGraw-Hill.

Batson, C. D., Ahmad, N., Lishner, D. A., & Tsang, J. (2002). Empathy and altruism. In C. R. Snyder & S. J. Lopez (Eds.), *Handbook of positive psychology* (pp. 485–498). New York: Oxford University Press.

Batson, C. D., Batson, J. G., Slingsby, J. K., Harrell, K. L., et al. (1991). Empathic joy and the empathy-altruism hypothesis. *Journal of Personality and Social Psychology, 61,* 413–426.

Batson, C. D., Polycarpou, M. P., Harmon-Jones, E., Imhoff, H. J., Mitchener, E. C., Bednar, L., et al. (1997). Empathy and attitudes: Can feeling for a member of a stigmatized group improve feelings toward the group? *Journal of Personality and Social Psychology, 72,* 105–118.

Batson, C. Daniel, & Powell, A. A. (2003). Altruism and prosocial behavior. In T. Millon & M. J. Lerner (Eds.), *Handbook of psychology: Personality and social psychology, Vol. 5* (pp. 463–484). New York: John Wiley & Sons.

Batterham, R. L., Cohen, M. A., Ellis, S. M., Le Roux, C. W., Withers, D. J., et al. (2003). Inhibition of food intake in obese subjects by Peptide YY3–36. *New England Journal of Medicine, 349,* 941–948.

Baumeister, R. F., & Leary, M. R. (1995). The need to belong: Desire for interpersonal attachments as a fundamental human motivation. *Psychological Bulletin, 117,* 497–529.

Baumeister, R F., Campbell, J. D., Krueger, J. I., & Vohs, K. D. (2003). Does high self-esteem cause better performance, interpersonal success, happiness, or healthier lifestyle? *Psychological Science in the Public Interest, 4,* 1–44.

Baumrind, D. (1971). Current patterns of parental authority. *Developmental Psychology, 4*(1), Part 2, 1–103.

Baumrind, D. (1991). Parenting styles and adolescent development. In J. Brooks-Gunn, R. Lerner & A. C. Petersen (Eds.), *Encyclopedia of adolescence, II.* New York: Garland.

Baylis, G. C., & Cale, E. M. (2001). The figure has a shape, but the ground does not: Evidence from a priming paradigm. *Journal of Experimental Psychology: Human Perception and Performance, 27,* 633–643.

Bazell, R. (2000a, February 8). Is it forgetfulness or Alzheimer's? *MSNBC.* Retrieved February 10, 2000, from http://www.msnbc.com/health.

Bazell, R. (2000b, August 29). Cause of narcolepsy pinpointed. *MSNBC.* Retrieved September 2, 2000, from http://www.msnbc.com/news/452884.asp.

Bazell, R. (2000c, September 6). Patch boosts libido in some women. *MSNBC.* Retrieved September 7, 2000, from http://www.msnbc.com/news/456350.asp.

Bazell, R., The Associated Press, & Reuters. (2002, August 7). Hunger hormone may fight obesity: Natural chemical shown to make people feel full in buffet experiment. *MSNBC Web Posting.* Retrieved August 9, 2002, from *http://www.msnbc.com/news/791118.asp.*

Bean, J. L. (2002). Expressions of female sexuality. *Journal of Sex and Marital Therapy, 28*(Suppl.), 29–38.

Bechtoldt, H., Norcross, J. C., Wyckoff, L. A., Pokrywa, M. L., Campbell, L. F., et al. (2001, Winter). Theoretical orientations and employment settings of clinical and counseling psychologists: A comparative study. *Clinical Psychologist, 54,* 3–6.

Beck, A. T. (1976). *Cognitive therapy and the emotional disorders.* New York: International Universities Press.

Beck, A. T., & Young, J. E. (1985). Depression. In D. H. Barlow (Ed.), *Clinical handbook of psychological disorders* (pp. 206–244). New York: Guilford Press.

Beck, A. T., Rush, A. J., Shaw, B. F., & Emery, G. (1979). *Cognitive therapy of depression.* New York: Guilford Press.

Beekman, A. T. F., Geerlings, S. W., Deeg, D. J. H., Smit, J. H., Schoevers, R. S., de Beurs, E., et al. (2002). The natural history of late-life depression: A 6-year prospective study in the community. *Archives of General Psychiatry, 59,* 605–611.

Begley, S. (1998a, January 19). Aping language. *Newsweek,* pp. 56–58.

Begley, S. (1998b, January 26). Is everybody crazy? *Newsweek,* pp. 48–56.

Begley, S. (1998c, May 25). A gene for genius? *Newsweek,* p. 72.

Begley, S. (2000a, May 8). A world of their own. *Newsweek,* pp. 53–74.

Begley, S. (2000b, October 9). The science of laughs. *Newsweek,* pp. 75–76.

Begley, S. (2000c, July 3). What families should do. *Newsweek,* pp. 44–47.

Begley, S. (2000d, Fall/Winter). Tuning up the brain. *Newsweek Special Issue,* p. 28.

Begley, S. (2001a, April 23). Are we getting smarter? *Newsweek,* pp. 50–51.

Begley, S. (2001b, Fall/Winter). The brain in winter. *Newsweek Special Issue,* pp. 24–29.

Begley, S. (2001c). AIDS at 20. *Newsweek,* pp. 35–37.

Begley, S. (2001d, July 16). Memory's mind games. *Newsweek,* pp. 52–53.

Begley, S. (2001e, Fall/Winter). How it all starts inside your brain. *Newsweek,* pp. 40–42.

Being fat at 40 cuts years off life. (2003, January 6). *CNN Web Posting.* Retrieved January 8, 2003, from http://www.cnn.com/2003/HEALTH/diet.fitness/01/06/obesity.mortality/index.html.

Beitman, B. D. (1989). Why I am an integrationist (not an eclectic). *British Journal of Guidance and Counseling, 17*(3), 259–273.

Belkin, L. (2003, May 25). In tough times, graduates slink back home. *New York Times,* Section 10, p. 1.

Beller, M., & Gafni, N. (2000). Can item format (multiple choice vs. open-ended) account for gender differences in mathematics achievement? *Sex Roles, 42,* 1–21.

Bellis, M. (2001, April 14). *Your about.com guide to inventors.* Retrieved May 7, 2001, from *http://inventors.about.com/science/inventors/library/bl/bl12_2a_u.htm.*

Belluck, P. (2000, October 18). New advice for parents: Saying "That's great!" may not be. *New York Times,* p. A18.

Belluck, P. (2003, February 9). Methadone, once the way out, suddenly grows as a killer drug. *New York Times,* pp. A1, A30.

Belsky, J., & Cassidy, J. (1994). Attachment: Theory and evidence. In M. Rutter (Ed.), *Development through life: A handbook for clinicians* (pp. 373–402). Boston: Blackwell Scientific Publications.

Bem, D. J. (1996). Exotic becomes erotic: A developmental theory of sexual orientation. *Psychological Review, 103,* 320–335.

Benjamin, J., Ebstein, R. P., & Belmaker, R. H. (2002). Personality genetics, 2002. *Israel Journal of Psychiatry and Related Sciences, 39,* 271–279.

Benjamin, L. T. (1988). *A history of psychology: Original source and contemporary research.* New York: McGraw-Hill.

Benjamin, L. T. (1997). The origin of psychological species: History of the beginnings of American Psychological Association Divisions. *American Psychologist, 51,* 725–732.

Benjamin, L. T. (2000). The psychology laboratory at the turn of the 20th century. *American Psychologist, 55,* 318–321.

Benson, E. (2003a, February). Intelligence across cultures. *Monitor on Psychology,* pp. 56–58.

Benson, E. (2003b, February). Breaking new ground. *Monitor on Psychology,* pp. 52–54.

Benson, E. (2003c, February). Intelligent intelligence testing. *Monitor on Psychology,* pp. 48–51.

Benson, E. (2003d, March). Even hands-free cell phones may impair driving. *Monitor on Psychology,* p. 15.

Benson, E. (2003e, April). Both halves of brain process emotional speech. *Monitor on Psychology,* p. 12.

Benson, E. S. (2004a, April). Heritability: It's all relative. *Monitor on Psychology,* p. 44.

Benson, E. S. (2004b, April). Behavioral genetics: Meet molecular biology. *Monitor on Psychology,* pp. 42–45.

Benson, P. L., Karabenick, S. A., & Lerner, R. M. (1976). Pretty pleases: The effects of physical attractiveness, race, and sex on receiving help. *Journal of Experimental Social Psychology, 12,* 409–415.

Ben-Ya'acov, Y., & Amir, M. (2004). Posttraumatic symptoms and suicide risk. *Personality and Individual Differences, 36,* 1257–1264.

Berger, K. S. (1998). *The developing person through the life span* (4th ed.). New York: Worth Publishers.

Berger, K. S. (2001). *The developing person through the life span* (5th ed.). New York: Worth Publishers.

Berger, K. S., & Thompson, R. A. (1995). *The developing person through childhood and adolescence* (4th ed.). New York: Worth Publishers.

Berger, R. J., & Phillips, N. H. (1995). Energy conservation and sleep. *Behavioural Brain Research, 69,* 65–73.

Berk, L. E. (2000). *Child development* (5th ed.). Needham Heights, MA: Allyn and Bacon.

Berkowitz, L. (1987). Mood, self-awareness, and willingness to help. *Journal of Personality and Social Psychology 52,* 721–729.

Berkowitz, L. (1988). Frustrations, appraisals, and aversively stimulated aggression. *Aggressive Behavior, 14,* 3–11.

Berkowitz, L. (1993). *Aggression: Its causes, consequences, and control.* New York: McGraw-Hill.

Berland, G. K., Elliott, M. N., Morales, L. S., Algazy, J. I., Kravitz, R. L., Broder, M. S., et al. (2001). Information on the Internet: Accessibility, quality, and readability in English and Spanish. *Journal of the American Medical Association, 285,* 2612–2621.

Berman, J. R., Berman, L. A., Toler, S. M., Gill, J., Haughie, S., & Sildenafil Study Group. (2003). Safety and efficacy of sildenafil citrate for the treatment of female sexual arousal disorder: A double-blind, placebo controlled study. *Journal of Urology, 170,* 2333–2338.

Berman, M. E., Tracy, J. I., & Coccaro, E. F. (1997). The serotonin hypothesis of aggression revisited. *Clinical Psychology Review, 17,* 651–665.

Bernard, L. L. (1924). *Instinct.* New York: Holt, Rinehart & Winston.

Berscheid, E., & Reis, H. T. (1998). Attraction and close relationships. In D. T. Gilbert, S. T. Fiske, & G. Lindzey (Eds.), *The handbook of social psychology* (4th ed., Vol. 2, pp. 193–281). Boston: McGraw-Hill.

Berson, D. M., Dunn, F. A., & Takao, M. (2002). Phototransduction by retinal ganglion cells that set the circadian clock. *Science, 295,* 1070–1073.

Berthoz, S., Artiges, E., Van de Moortele, P.-F., Poline, J.-B., Rouquette, S., Consoli, S. M., et al. (2002). Effect of impaired recognition and expression of emotions on frontocingulate cortices: An fMRI study of men with alexithymia. *American Journal of Psychiatry, 159,* 961–967.

Beutler, L. E., Harwood, T. M., & Caldwell, R. (2001). Cognitive-behavioral therapy and psychotherapy integration. In K. S. Dobson (Ed.), *Handbook of cognitive-behavioral therapies* (2nd ed., pp. 138–170). New York: Guilford Press.

Biederman, J. (2003, August). Current concepts on the pharmacotherapy of ADHD. Paper presented at the meeting of the American Psychological Association, Toronto, CA.

Billy, J. O. G., Tanfer, K., Grady, W. R., & Klepinger, D. J. (1993). The sexual behavior of men in the United States. *Family Planning Perspectives, 25,* 52–60.

Binet, A. (1900). Reserches sur la technique de la mensuration de la tete vivante, plus other memoirs on cephalometry. *L'Année psychologique, 7,* 314–429.

Binge drinking no stranger on U.S. campuses. (2000, September 8). *Cable News Network,* Retrieved September 9, 2000, from http://www.cnn.com/2000/HEALTH/children/09/08/binge.drinking.reut/index.html.

Bingham, R. P., Porche-Burke, L., James, S., Sue, D. W., & Vasquez, M. J. T. (2002). Introduction : A report on the National Multicultural Conference and Summit II. *Cultural Diversity and Ethnic Minority Psychology, 8,* 75–87.

Bishop, E. G., Cherny, S. S., Corleya, R.., Plomin, R., DeFriesa, J. C., & Hewitt, J. K. (2003). Developmental genetic analysis of general cognitive ability from 1 to 12 years in a sample of adoptees, biological siblings, and twins. *Intelligence, 31,* 31–49.

Bivalacqua, T. J, Champion, H. C., Hellstrom, W. J. G., &. Kadowitz, P. J. (2000). Pharmacotherapy for erectile dysfunction. *Trends in Pharmacological Sciences, 21,* 484–489.

Bjork, J. M., Dougherty, D. M., Moeller, F. G., & Swann, A. C. (2000). Differential behavioral effects of plasma tryptophan depletion and loading in aggressive and nonaggressive men. *Neuropsychopharmacology, 22,* 357–359.

Bjorklund, D. F. (1995). *Children's thinking* (2nd ed.). Pacific Grove, CA: Brooks/Cole.

Blackman, M. R. (2000). Age-related alterations in sleep quality and neuroendocrine function: Interrelationships and implications [Editorial]. *Journal of the American Medical Association, 284,* 879–881.

Blair, I. V., Ma, J. E., & Lenton, A. P. (2001). Imagining stereotypes away: The moderation of implicit stereotypes through mental imagery. *Journal of Personality and Social Psychology, 81,* 828–841.

Blakeslee, S. (1996, November 26). Workings of split brain challenge notions of how language evolved. *New York Times,* p. C3.

Blakey, R. (2002, July). Advances in Alzheimer's research. *CNN.com.* Available online at *http://www.cnn.com/2002/HEALTH/conditions/07/18/blakey.alzheimers.otsc/index.html.*

Blanchard, E. B., & Diamond, S. (1996). Psychological treatment of benign headache disorders. *Professional Psychology, 27,* 541–547.

Blanchard, E. B., Appelbaum, K. A., Radnitz, C. L.Morrill, B., et al. (1990). A controlled evaluation of thermal biofeedback and thermal feedback combined with cognitive therapy in the treatment of vascular headache. *Journal of Consulting and Clinical Psychology, 58,* 216–224.

Blascovich, J., Mendes, W. B., Hunter, S. B., & Salomon, K. (1999). Social "facilitation" as challenge and threat. *Journal of Personality and Social Psychology, 77,* 68–77.

Blascovich, J., Spencer, S. J., Quinn, D., & Steele, C. (2002). African Americans and high blood pressure: The role of stereotype threat. *Psychological Science, 12,* 225–229.

Blascovich, J., Wyer, N. A., Swart, L. A., & Kibler, J. L. (1997). Racism and racial categorization. *Journal of Personality and Social Psychology, 72,* 1364–1372.

Blum, R. W., Beuhring, T. Shew, M. L., Bearinger, L. H., Sieving, R. E., & Resnick, M. D. (2000). The effects of race/ethnicity, income, and family structure on adolescent risk behaviors. *American Journal of Public Health, 90,* 1879–84.

Blumberg, H. P., Martin, A., Kaufman, J., Leung, H.-C., Skudlarski, P., Lacadie, C., et al. (2003). Frontostriatal abnormalities in adolescents with bipolar disorder: Preliminary observations from functional MRI. *American Journal of Psychiatry, 160,* 1345–1347.

Boles, S. M., & Miottoa, K. (2003). Substance abuse and violence: A review of the literature. *Aggression and Violent Behavior, 8,* 155–174.

Bond, M. H. (1993). Emotions and their expression in Chinese culture. *Journal of Nonverbal Behavior, 14,* 189–204.

Bond, R., & Smith, P. B. (1996). Culture and conformity: A meta-analysis of studies using Asch's (1952b, 1956) line judgment task. *Psychological Bulletin, 119,* 111–137.

Bonifati, V., Rizzu, P., van Baren, M. J., Schaap, O., Breedveld, G. J., Krieger, E., et al. (2003). Mutations in the DJ-1 Gene associated with autosomal recessive early-onset Parkinsonism. *Science, 299* (Issue 5604), 256–225.

Bonné, J. (2001, February 6). Meth's deadly buzz. *MSNBC.* Retrieved February 8, 2001, from http://www.MSNBC.com/news/510835.asp?bt=nm&btu=http://www.msnbc.com/tools/newstools/d/news_menu.asp&cp1=1.

Bornstein, R. F. (1989). Subliminal techniques as propaganda tools: Review and critique. *Journal of Mind and Behavior, 10,* 231–262.

Bornstein, R. F. (1999). Criterion validity of objective and projective dependency tests: A meta-analytic assessment of behavioral prediction. *Psychological Assessment, 11,* 48–57.

Boskind-White, M., & White, W. C. (1983). *Bulimarexia: The binge-purge cycle.* New York: W. W. Norton.

Botman, H. I., & Crovitz, H. F. (1989–1990). Dream reports and autobiographical memory. *Imagination, Cognition and Personality, 9,* 213–224.

Bouret, S. G., Draper, S. J., & Simerly, R. B. (2004) Trophic action of leptin on hypothalamic neurons that regulate feeding. *Science, 304,* 108–110.

Bouton, M. E., Mineka, S., & Barlow, D. H. (2001). A modern learning theory perspective on the etiology of panic disorder. *Psychological Review, 108,* 4–32.

Bowman, L. (2000, November 21). *Sleep on it for long-term memory.* Retrieved November 23, 2000, from http://www.psycport.com/news/2000/11/21/a/0000-0002-sleeplearn.html.

Boynton, R. S. (2004, January 11). In the Jung archives. *New York Times Book Review,* p. 8.

Bradley, R. G., & Follingstad, D. R. (2001). Utilizing disclosure in the treatment of the sequelae of childhood sexual abuse. A theoretical and empirical review. *Clinical Psychology Review, 21,* 1–32.

Brady, K. T., Pearlstein, T., Asnis, G. M., Baker, D., Rothbaum, B., Sikes, C. R., et al. (2000). "Efficacy and safety of sertraline treatment of posttraumatic stress disorder: A randomized controlled trial": Reply. *Journal of the American Medical Association, 283,* 1837–1844.

Brain scans suggest people feel emotions through effect on body. (2000, September 20). *Cable News Network.* Retrieved September 22, 2000, from http://www.cnn.com/2000/HEALTH/09/20/brain.emotions.ap/index.html.

Brainard, D. H., Wandell, B. A., & Chichilnisky, E. J. (1993). Color constancy: From physics to appearance. *Current Directions in Psychological Science, 12,* 165–170.

Brainteaser quizzes. (2001). *National Institute of Environment Health Sciences, National Institutes of Health.* Retrieved January 13, 2002, from http://www.niehs.nih.gov/kids/questionstx.htm.

Braswell, L., & Kendall, P. C. (2001). Cognitive-behavioral therapy with youth. In K. S. Dobson (Ed.), *Handbook of cognitive-behavioral therapies* (2nd ed., pp. 246–294). New York: Guilford Press.

Braun, B. G. (Ed.). (1986). *Treatment of multiple personality disorder.* Washington, DC: American Psychiatric Press.

Braun, S. (2001, Spring). Seeking insight by prescription. *Cerebrum,* 10–21.

Braver, T. S., Barch, D. M., Keys, B. A., Carter, C. S., Cohen, J. D., Kaye, J. A., et al. (2001). Context processing in older adults: Evidence for a theory relating cognitive control to neurobiology in healthy aging. *Journal of Experimental Psychology: General, 130,* 746–763.

Brazelton, T. B., & Greenspan, S. (2000, Fall/Winter). Our window to the future. *Newsweek Special Issue,* pp. 34–36.

Brebner, J. (2003). Gender and emotions. *Personality and Individual Differences, 34,* 387–394.

Breitenbecher, K. H. (2000). Sexual assault on college campuses: Is an ounce of prevention enough? *Applied and Preventive Psychology, 9,* 23–52.

Breitenbecher, K. H. (2001). Sexual revictimization among women. A review of the literature focusing on empirical investigations. *Aggression and Violent Behavior, 6,* 415–432.

Bremner, J. D., Vythilingam, M., Ng, C. K., Vermetten, E., Nazeer, A., Oren, D. A., et al. (2003). Regional brain metabolic correlates of methylparatyrosine-induced depressive symptoms implications for the neural circuitry of depression. *Journal of the American Medical Association, 289,* 3125–3134.

Brems, C., & Johnson, M. E. (1997). Clinical implications of the co-occurrence of substance use and other psychiatric disorders: *Professional Psychology: Research and Practice, 28,* 437–447.

Brener, N. D., Hassan, S. S., & Barrios, L. C. (1999). Suicidal ideation among college students in the United States. *Journal of Consulting and Clinical Psychology, 67,* 1004–1008.

Brewer, M. B. (1991). The social self: On being the same and different at the same time. *Personality and Social Psychology Bulletin, 17,* 475–482.

Brewer, M. B., & Brown, R. J. (1998). Intergroup relations. In D. T. Gilbert, S. T. Fiske, & G. Lindzey (Eds.), *The handbook of social psychology* (4th ed., Vol. 2, pp. 554–594). Boston: McGraw-Hill.

Brewer, W. F., & Treyens, J. C. (1981). Role of schemata in memory for places. *Cognitive Psychology, 13,* 207–230.

Brody, J. E. (1992, September 30). Myriad masks hide an epidemic of depression. *New York Times,* p. C12.

Brody, J. E. (1996, August 28). PMS need not be the worry it was just decades ago. *New York Times,* p. C9.

Brody, J. E. (1999, November 30). Yesterday's precocious puberty is norm today. *New York Times,* p. F8.

Brody, J. E. (2000a, January 18). Adding zest to the golden years, simply. *New York Times,* p. F8.

Brody, J. E. (2000b, October 17). One-two punch for losing pounds: Exercise and careful diet. *New York Times,* p. F6.

Brody, J. E. (2001a, January 23). Experts explore safer tests for Down syndrome. *New York Times,* p. F6.

Brody, J. E. (2001b, January 2). Sometimes, good health tastes bad. *New York Times,* p. F6.

Brody, J. E. (2002, September 10). High-fat diet: Count calories and think twice. *New York Times,* p. F6.

Brody, J. E. (2003, May 6). Another study finds a link between excess weight and cancer. *New York Times,* p. F7.

Brondolo, E., Baruch, C., Conway, E., & Marsh, L. (1994). Aggression among inner-city minority youth: A biopsychosocial model for school-based evaluation and treatment. *Journal of Social Distress and the Homeless, 3,* 53–80.

Brookmeyer, R., Corrada, M. M, Curriero, F. C., & Kawas, C. (2002). Survival following a diagnosis of Alzheimer's disease. *Archives of Neurology, 59,* 1764–1767.

Brown, G. M. (1994). Light, melatonin, and the sleep-wake cycle. *Journal of Psychiatry and Neuroscience, 19*(5), 345–353.

Brown, P. D., & O'Leary, K. D. (2000). Therapeutic alliance: Predicting continuance and success in group treatment for spouse abuse. *Journal of Consulting and Clinical Psychology, 268,* 340–345.

Brown, S. L., Nesse, R. M., Vinokur, A. D., & Smith, D. M. (2003). Providing social support may be more beneficial than receiving it: Results from a prospective study of mortality. *Psychological Science, 14,* 320–327.

Bruce, M. L., Ten Have, T. R., Reynolds, C. F., III, Katz, I. I., Schulberg, H. C., Mulsant, B. H., Brown, G. K., et al. (2004). Reducing suicidal ideation and depressive symptoms in depressed older primary care patients: A randomized controlled trial. *Journal of the American Medical Association, 291,* 1081–1091.

Bruer, J. T. (1999). *The myth of the first three years.* New York: Free Press.

Bruner, J. S., & Minturn, A. L. (1955). Perceptual identification and perceptual organization. *Journal of General Psychology, 53,* 21–28.

Bryant, R. A., Harvey, A. G., Guthrie, R. M., & Moulds, M. L. (2000). A prospective study of psychophysiological arousal, acute stress disorder, and posttraumatic stress disorder. *Journal of Abnormal Psychology, 109,* 341–344.

Bryant, R. A., & Mallard, D. (2002). Hypnotically induced emotional numbing: A real simulating analysis. *Journal of Abnormal Psychology, 111,* 203–207.

Bryant, R. A., Moulds, M. L., Guthrie, R. M., Dang, S. T., & Nixon , R. D. V. (2003). Imaginal exposure alone and imaginal exposure with cognitive restructuring in treatment of posttraumatic stress disorder. *Journal of Consulting and Clinical Psychology, 71,* 706–712.

Buchanan, C. M., Eccles, J. S., & Becker, J. B. (1992). Are adolescents the victims of raging hormones? Evidence for activational effects of hormones on moods and behavior at adolescence. *Psychological Bulletin, 111,* 62–107.

Buddhists are happier. (2003, May 22). *CNN Web Posting.* Retrieved May 23, 2003, from http://www.cnn.com/2003/HEALTH/05/22/buddhist.happiness.reut/index.html.

Bunney, W. E., Bunney, B. G., Vawter, M. P., Tomita, H., Li, J., Evans, S. J., et al. (2003). Microarray technology: A review of new strategies to discover candidate vulnerability genes in psychiatric disorders. *American Journal of Psychiatry, 160,* 657–666.

Burgio, K. L., Locher, J. L., Goode, P. S., Hardin, J. M., McDowell, B. J., Dombrowski, M., et al. (1998). Behavioral vs. drug treatment for urge urinary incontinence in older women: A randomized controlled trial. *Journal of the American Medical Association, 280,* 1995–2000.

Burke, D. M. (1992). Memory and aging. In M. Gruneberg & P. Morris (Eds.), *Aspects of memory: Vol. 1. The practical aspects* (2nd ed., pp. 124–146). London: Routledge.

Burke, D. M., & Shafto, M. A. (2004). Aging and language production. *Current Directions in Psychological Science, 13,* 21–24.

Burns, D. D. (1980). *Feeling good: The new mood therapy.* New York: Morris.

Burton, N., & Lane, R. C. (2001). The relational treatment of dissociative identity disorder. *Clinical Psychology Review, 21,* 301–320.

Buss, D. M. (1984). Marital assortment for personality dispositions: Assessment with three different data sources. *Behavior Genetics, 14,* 111–123.

Buss, D. M. (1994). *The evolution of desire.* New York: Basic Books.

Buss, D. M., & Kenrick, D. T. (1998). Evolutionary social psychology. In D. T. Gilbert, S. T. Fiske, & G. Lindzey (Eds.), *The handbook of social psychology* (4th ed., Vol. 2, pp. 982–1026). Boston: McGraw-Hill.

Buss, D. M., & Reeve, H. K. (2003). Evolutionary psychology and developmental dynamics: Comment on Lickliter and Honeycutt (2003). *Psychological Bulletin, 129,* 848–853.

Buston, P. M., & Emlen, S. T. (2003). Cognitive processes underlying human mate choice: The relationship between self-perception and mate preference in Western society. *Proceedings of the National Academy of Sciences, 100,* 8805–8810.

Butcher, J. N. (2000). Revising psychological tests: Lessons learned from the revision of the MMPI. *Psychological Assessment, 12,* 263–271.

Butterfield, F. (2001). Violence rises as club drug spreads out into the streets. *New York Times,* pp. A1, A14.

Byrne, M., Clafferty, B. A., Cosway, R., Grant, E., Hodges, A., Whalley, H. C., Lawrie, S. M., et al. (2003). Neuropsychology, genetic liability, and psychotic symptoms in those at high risk of schizophrenia. *Journal of Abnormal Psychology, 112,* 38–48.

Cabib, S., Orsini, C., LeMoal, M., & Piazza, P. V. (2000). Abolition and reversal of strain differences in behavioral responses to drugs of abuse after a brief experience. *Science, 289,* 463–465.

Cacioppo, J. T., Berntson, G. G., Sheridan, J. F., & McClintock, M. K. (2000). Multilevel integrative analyses of human behavior: Social neuroscience and the complementing nature of social and biological approaches. *Psychological Bulletin, 126,* 829–843.

Caetano, R. (1987). Acculturation and drinking patterns among U.S. Hispanics. *British Journal of Addiction, 82,* 789–799.

Cai, Z. J. (1995). An integrative analysis to sleep functions. *Behavioural Brain Research, 69,* 187–194.

Cale, E. M., & Lilienfeld, S. O. (2002). Sex differences in psychopathy and antisocial personality disorder: A review and integration. *Clinical Psychology Review, 22,* 1179–1207.

Calle, E. E., Rodriguez, C., Walker-Thurmond, K., & Thun, M. J. (2003). Overweight, obesity, and mortality from cancer in a prospectively studied cohort of U.S. adults. *New England Journal of Medicine, 348,* 1625–1638.

Callicott, J. H., Egan, M. F., Mattay, V. S., Bertolino, A., Bone, A. D, Verchinski, B., et al. (2003). Abnormal fMRI response of the dorsolateral prefrontal cortex in cognitively intact siblings of patients with schizophrenia. *American Journal of Psychiatry, 160,* 709–719.

Camara, W. J., Nathan, J. S., & Puente, A. E. (2000). Psychological test usage: Implications in professional psychology. *Professional Psychology: Research and Practice, 31,* 141–154.

Campfield, L. A., Smith, F. J., Guisez, Y., Devos, R., et al. (1995). Recombinant mouse OB protein: Evidence for a peripheral signal linking adiposity and central neural networks. *Science, 269,* 546–549.

Canfield, R. L., Henderson, C. R., Cory-Slechta, A. A., Cox, C., Jusko, T. A., & Lanphea, B. P. (2003). Intellectual impairment in children with blood lead concentrations below 10 µg per deciliter. *New England Journal of Medicine, 348,* 1517–1526.

Canli, T., Desmond , J. E., Zhao, Z., & Gabrieli, J. D. E. (2002). Sex differences in the neural basis of emotional memories. *Proceedings of the National Academy of Sciences, 99*(16), 10789–10794.

Cannon, W. (1927). The James-Lange theory of emotions: A critical examination as an alternative theory. *American Journal of Psychology, 39,* 106–112.

Caporael, L. R. (2001). Evolutionary psychology: Toward a unifying theory and a hybrid science. *Annual Review of Psychology, 52,* 607–628.

Caporael, L. R. (2001). Evolutionary psychology: Toward a unifying theory and a hybrid science. *Annual Review of Psychology, 52,* 607–628.

Cardemil, E. V., & Battle, C. L. (2003). Guess who's coming to therapy? Getting comfortable with conversations about race and ethnicity in psychotherapy. *Professional Psychology: Research and Practice, 34,* 278–286.

Carmichael, M. (2003a, January 20). Rx: Two martinis a day. *Newsweek,* p. 48.

Carmichael, M. (2003b, May 5). The fat factor. *Newsweek,* p. 69.

Carpenter, S. (2000a, September). Psychologists tackle neuoriimaging at APA-sponsored Advanced Training Institute. *Monitor on Psychology, 31*(9), 42–43.

Carpenter, S. (2000b, October). Biology and social environments jointly influence gender development. *Monitor on Psychology, 31*(10), 35.

Carpenter, S. (2000c, October). A taste expert sniffs out a long-standing measurement oversight. *Monitor on Psychology, 31*(10), 20–21.

Carpenter, S. (2000d, October). Research confirms the virtues of "sleeping on it." *Monitor on Psychology, 31,* pp. 49–50.

Carpenter, S. (2001a, February). Teens' risky behavior is about more than race and family resources. *Monitor on Psychology,* pp. 47–48.

Carpenter, S. (2001b, May). Stimulants boost achievement in ADHD teens. *Monitor on Psychology,* pp. 26–27.

Carroll, L. (2004, February 10). Parkinson's research focuses on links to genes and toxins. *New York Times,* p. F5.

Carstensen, L. (1997, August 17). *The evolution of social goals across the life span.* Paper presented at the meeting of the American Psychological Association, Chicago.

Carvajal, S. C., Parcel, G. S., Basen-Engquist, K., Banspach, S. W., Coyle, K. K., Kirby, D., et al. (1999). Psychosocial predictors of delay of first sexual intercourse by adolescents. *Health Psychology, 18,* 443–452.

Caspi, A., & Moffitt, T. E. (1991). Individual differences are accentuated during periods of social change: The sample case of girls at puberty. *Journal of Personality and Social Psychology, 61,* 157–168.

Caspi, A., et al. (2002). Role of genotype in the cycle of violence in maltreated children. *Science, 297,* 851–854.

Caspi, A., Sugden, K., Moffitt, T. E., Taylor, A., Craig, I. W., Harrington, H. L., McClay, J., et al. (2003). Influence of life stress on depression: Moderation by a polymorphism in the 5-HTT gene. *Science, 301,* 386–389.

Cassidy, J. (2003). Continuity and change in the measurement of infant attachment: Comment on Fraley and Spieker (2003). *Developmental Psychology, 39,* 409–412.

Cattell, R. B. (1941). Some theoretical issues in adult intelligence testing. *Psychological Bulletin, 38,* 592.

Cattell, R. B. (1950). *Personality: A systematic, theoretical, and factual study.* New York: McGraw-Hill.

Cattell, R. B. (1965). *The scientific analysis of personality.* Baltimore: Penguin.

Cattell, R. B., Eber, H. W., & Tatsuoka, M. M. (1970). *Handbook for the Sixteen Personality Factor Questionnaire (16PF).* Champaign, IL: Institute for Personality and Ability Testing.

Catz, S. L., & Kelly, J. A. (2001). Living with HIV disease. In A. Baum, T. A. Revenson, & J. E. Singer (Eds.), *Handbook of health psychology* (pp. 841–850). Mahwah, NJ: Lawrence Erlbaum Associates.

Ceci, S. J., Rosenblum, T. B., & Kumpf, M. (1998). The shrinking gap between high- and low-scoring groups: Current trends and possible causes. In U. Neisser (Ed.), *The rising curve: Long-term gains in IQ and related measures* (pp. 287–302). Washington, DC: American Psychological Association.

Cell phones and drivers don't mix. (2001, August 16). *MSNBC.* Retrieved August 18, 2001, from http://www.msnbc.com/news/614969.asp?0dm=h18qb.

Center for Mental Health Services (CMHS). (2001, May). National Strategy for Suicide Prevention: Goals and Objectives for Action: Summary. *A joint effort of SAMHSA, CDC, NIH, and HRSA.* Rockville, MD: Author.

Centers for Disease Control. (1987, July 10). Progress in chronic disease prevention: Protection effect of physical activity on coronary heart disease. *Morbidity and Mortality Weekly Report, 36/26,* 426–430.

Centers for Disease Control (CDC). (2001). Self-reported asthma prevalence among adults: United States, 2000. *Morbidity and Mortality Weekly Report, 50,* 682–686.

Centers for Disease Control and Prevention (CDCP) (2004, March). Report to Congress: Prevention of genital human papillomavirus infection. Retrieved March 25, 2004, from http://www.cdc.gov/std/HPV/2004HPV%20Report.pdf.

Centers for Disease Control. (2000a, June 9). National and state-specific pregnancy rates among adolescents—United States, 1995–1997. *Morbidity and Mortality Weekly Report, 49*(27).

Centers for Disease Control. (2000b, June 9). Youth risk behavior surveillance—United States, 1999. *Morbidity and Mortality Weekly Report, 49*(SS05), 1–96.

Chambless, D. L., & Ollendick, T. H. (2001). Empirically supported psychological interventions: Controversies and evidence. *Annual Review of Psychology, 52,* 685–716.

Chambless, D. L., et al. (1998, Winter). Update on empirically validated therapies, II. *Clinical Psychologist, 51,* 3–16.

Chance, S. E., Brown, R. T., Dabbs, J. M. Jr., & Casey, R. (2000). Testosterone, intelligence and behavior disorders in young boys. *Personality and Individual Differences, 28,* 437–445.

Chang, E. C., & Sanna, L. J. (2001). Optimism, pessimism, and positive and negative affectivity in middle-aged adults: A test of a cognitive-affective model of psychological adjustment. *Psychology and Aging, 16,* 524–531.

Charney, D. S., Nemeroff, C. B., Lewis, L., Laden, S. K., Gorman, J. M., & Laska, E. M. (2002). National depressive and manic-depressive association consensus statement on the use of placebo in clinical trials of mood disorders. *Archives of General Psychiatry, 59,* 262–270.

Charney, D. S., Reynolds, C. F., III, Lewis, L., Lebowitz, B. D., Sunderland, T., Alexopoulos, G. S., et al. (2003). *Archives of General Psychiatry, 60,* 664–672.

Chassin, L., Pitts, S. C., & Prost, J. (2002). Binge drinking trajectories from adolescence to emerging adulthood in a high-risk sample: Predictors and substance abuse outcomes. *Journal of Consulting and Clinical Psychology, 70,* 67–78.

Chassin, L., Presson, C. C., Sherman, S. J., & Kim, K. (2003). Historical changes in cigarette smoking and smoking-related beliefs after 2 decades in a Midwestern community. *Health Psychology, 22,* 347–353.

Chasteen, A. L., Park, D. C., & Schwarz, N. (2001). Implementation intentions and facilitation of prospective memory. *Psychological Science, 12,* 457–461.

Check, E. (2003). Battle of the mind. *Nature 422,* 370–372.

Chen, J., Rathore, S. S., Radford, M. J., Wang, Y., Krumholz, H. M., et al. (2001). Racial differences in the use of cardiac catheterization after acute myocardial infarction. *New England Journal of Medicine, 344,* 1443–1449.

Chen, S. J., Sweatt, J. D., & Klann, E. (1997). Enhanced phosphorylation of the postsynaptic protein kinase C substrate RC3/neurogranin during long-term potentiation. *Brain Research, 749,* 181–187.

Chess, S., & Thomas, A. (1996). *Temperament: Theory and practice.* New York: Brunner/Mazel.

Chevalier-Skolnikoff, S. (1973). Facial expression of emotion in nonhuman primates. In P. Ekman (Ed.), *Darwin and facial expression: A century of research in review* (pp. 11–82). New York: Academic Press.

Chobanian, A. V., Bakris, G. L., Black, H. R., Cushman, W. C., Green, L. A., Izzo, J. L., Jr., et al. (2003). The seventh report of the Joint National Committee on Prevention, Detection, Evaluation, and Treatment of High Blood Pressure: The JNC 7 report. *Journal of the American Medical Association, 289*, 2560–2572.

Choi, I., Dalal, R., Kim-Prieto, C., & Park, H. (2003). Culture and judgment of causal relevance. *Journal of Personality and Social Psychology, 84*, 46–59.

Chomsky, N. (1965). Aspects of the theory of syntax. Cambridge, MA: MIT Press.

Chomsky, N. (1972). *Language and mind.* New York: Harcourt Brace Jovanovich.

Chrisler, J. C., & Johnston-Robledo, I. (2002). Raging hormones? Feminist perspectives on premenstrual syndrome and postpartum depression. In M. Ballou & L. S. Brown (Eds.), *Rethinking mental health and disorder* (pp. 174–197). New York: Guilford.

Christensen, A., Atkins, D. C., Berns, S., Wheeler, J., Baucom, D. H., & Simpson, L. E. (2004). Traditional versus integrative behavioral couple therapy for significantly and chronically distressed married couples. *Journal of Consulting and Clinical Psychology, 72*, 176–191.

Cialdini, R. B. (1993). *Influence: Science and practice* (3rd ed.). New York: HarperCollins.

Cialdini, R. B. (2001). *Influence: Science and practice* (4th ed). Boston: Allyn & Bacon.

Cialdini, R. B., & Goldstein, N. J. (2004). Social influence: Compliance and conformity. *Annual Review of Psychology, 55*, 591–621.

Cialdini, R. B., & Trost, M. R. (1998). Social influence: Social norms, conformity, and compliance. In D. T. Gilbert, S. T. Fiske, & G. Lindzey (Eds.), *The handbook of social psychology* (4th ed., Vol. 2, pp. 151–192). Boston: McGraw-Hill.

Cialdini, R. B., Trost, M. R., & Newsom, J. T. (1995). Preference for consistency: The development of a valid measure and the discovery of surprising behavioral implications. *Journal of Personality and Social Psychology, 69*, 318–328.

Ciarrochi, J., Chan, A., Caputi, P., & Roberts, R. (2001). Measuring emotional intelligence. In J. Ciarrochi & J. P. Forgas et al. (Eds.), *Emotional intelligence in everyday life: A scientific inquiry.* (pp. 25–45). Philadelphia: Psychology Press.

Clancy, S. A., McNally, R. J., Schacter, D. L., Lenzenweger, M. F., & Pitman, R. K. (2002). Memory distortion in people reporting abduction by aliens. *Journal of Abnormal Psychology, 111*, 455–461.

Clark, D. A. (2004). *Cognitive-behavioral therapy for OCD.* New York: Guilford.

Clark, D. A., Cook, A., & Snow, D. (1998). Depressive symptom differences in hospitalized, medically ill, depressed psychiatric inpatients and nonmedical controls. *Journal of Abnormal Psychology, 107*, 38–48.

Clark, D. M. (1986). A cognitive approach to panic. *Behaviour Research and Therapy, 24*, 461–470.

Clark, K. B., & Clark, M. P. (1939). The development of self and the emergence of racial identification in Negro preschool children. *Journal of Social Psychology, 10*, 591–599.

Clark, R., Anderson, N. B., Clark, V. R., & Williams, D. R. (1999). Racism as a stressor for African Americans: A biopsychological model. *American Psychologist, 54*, 805–816.

Clarke, D., Gabriels, T., & Barnes, J. (1996). Astrological signs as determinants of extroversion and emotionality: An empirical study. *Journal of Psychology, 130*, 131–140.

Clay, R. A. (2000, January). Psychotherapy is cost-effective. *Monitor on Psychology, 31*(1), 38–39.

Clay, R. A. (2003a, April). An empty nest can promote freedom, improved relationships. *Monitor on Psychology*, pp. 40–41.

Clay, R. A. (2003b). Unraveling new media's effects on children. *Monitor on Psychology*, pp. 40–41.

Clements, J. (2003, March 5). Working late: Your friends won't retire at age 65, but here's how you can. *Wall Street Journal*, p. D1.

Clemetson, L. (2000a, May 7). Color my world. *Newsweek*, pp. 70–74.

Clemetson, L. (2000b, November 6). The new victims of hate. *Newsweek*, p. 61.

Cloitre, M. (2004). Aristotle revisited: The case of recovered memories. *Clinical Psychology: Science and Practice, 11*, 42–46.

Cocaine impairs brain's 'pleasure circuits' (2003, January 1). *CNN Web Posting.* Retrieved January 2, 2003, from http://www.cnn.com/2003/HEALTH/01/01/cocaine.brain.ap/index.html.

Cochran, S. V., & Rabinowitz, F. E. (2003). Gender-sensitive recommendations for assessment and treatment of depression in men. *Professional Psychology: Research and Practice, 34*, 132–140.

Cockell, S. J., Hewitt, P. L., Seal, B., Sherry, S., Goldner, E. M., Flett, G. L., et al. (2002). Trait and self-presentational dimensions of perfectionism among women with anorexia nervosa. *Cognitive Therapy and Research, 26*, 745–758.

Cohen, D. (1986). Psychopathological perspectives: Differential diagnosis of Alzheimer's disease and related disorders. In L. W. Poon (Ed.), *Handbook for clinical memory assessment of older adults* (pp. 81–88). Washington, DC: American Psychological Association.

Cohen, F. L., Ferrans, C. E., & Eshler, B. (1992). Reported accidents in narcolepsy. *Loss, Grief and Care, 5*, 71–80.

Cohen, L. J., Celnik, P., Pascual-Leone, A., Corwell, B., Faiz, L., & Dambrosia, J. (1997). Separate neural bases of two fundamental memory process in the human medial temporal lobe. *Science, 276*, 264–266.

Cohen, S., Doyle, W. J., Turner, R., Alper, C. M., & Skoner, D. P. (2003). Sociability and susceptibility to the common cold. *Psychological Science, 14*, 389–395.

Cohen, S., Frank, E., Doyle, W. J., Skoner, D. P., Rabin, B. S., & Gwaltney, J. M. Jr. (1998). Types of stressors that increase susceptibility to the common cold in healthy adults. *Health Psychology, 17*, 214–223.

Cohn, L. D., Macfarlane, S., Yanez, C., & Imai, W. K. (1995). Risk-perception: Differences between adolescents and adults. *Health Psychology, 14*, 217–222.

Cohn, L. D., Macfarlane, S., Yanez, C., Imai, W. K., et al. (1995). Risk-perception: Differences between adolescents and adults. *Health Psychology, 14*, 217–222.

Colcombe, S., & Kramer, A. F. (2003). Fitness effects on the cognitive function of older adults: A meta-analytic study. *Psychological Science, 14*, 125–130.

Cole, M. G., & Dendukuri, N. (2003). Risk factors for depression among elderly community subjects: A systematic review and meta-analysis. *American Journal of Psychiatry, 160*, 1163–1168.

College binge drinking tops parents' fears. (2001, August 29). *Cable News Network.* Retrieved September 4, 2001, from http://fyi.cnn.com/2001/fyi/teachers.ednews/08/29/binge.drinking.ap/index.html.

Collinge, W. (1999, August 25). *Sleep's healing properties.* Retrieved August 28, 1999, from http://www.cnn.com/HEALTH/alternative/9908/25/heal.sleep/

Collins, A. M., & Loftus, E. F. (1975). A spreading-activation theory of semantic processing. *Psychological Review, 82*, 407–428.

Collins, A. M., & Quillian, M. R. (1969). Retrieval times from semantic memory. *Journal of Verbal Learning and Verbal Behavior, 8*, 240–247.

Common Sense for Drug Policy. (2004). *Drug War Facts, 2004.* Available online at www.drugwarfacts.org/causes.htm.

Conrad, F. G., & Brown, N. R. (1996). Estimating frequency: A multiple-strategy perspective. In D. Herrmann, C. McEvoy, C. Hertzog, P. Hertel, & M. K. Johnson (Eds.), *Basic and applied memory research: Practical applications* (Vol. 2., pp. 166–178). Mahwah, NJ: Lawrence Erlbaum Associates.

Cooksey, E. C., & Fondell, M. M. (1996). Spending time with his kids: Effects of family structure on fathers' and children's lives. *Journal of Marriage and the Family, 58*, 693–707.

Cooper, M. L. (1992). Alcohol and increased behavioral risk for AIDS. *Alcohol World: Health and Research, 16*, 64–72. (National Institute on Alcohol Abuse and Alcoholism, NIH Publication No. 93–3466).

Cooper, M. L., Wood, P. K., Orcutt, H. K., & Albino, A. (2003). Personality and the predisposition to engage in risky or problem behaviors during adolescence. *Journal of Personality and Social Psychology, 84*, 390–410.

Corballis, M. C. (2001). Is the handedness gene on the X chromosome? Comment on Jones and Martin (2000). *Psychological Review, 108*, 805–810.

Coren, S. (1992). *The left-hander syndrome: The causes and consequences of left-handedness.* New York: Free Press.

Cordes, C. (1985, November). Common threads found in suicide. *APA Monitor, 16*(10), 11.

Corliss, R. (2003, January 20). Is there a formula for joy? *Time Magazine*, pp. 44–46.

Cororve, M. B., & Gleaves, D. H. (2001). Body dysmorphic disorder: A review of conceptualizations, assessment, and treatment strategies. *Clinical Psychology Review, 21*, 949–970.

Correll, C. U., Leucht, S., &. Kane, J. M. (2004). Lower risk for tardive dyskinesia associated with second-generation antipsychotics: A systematic review of 1-year studies. *American Journal of Psychiatry, 161*, 414–425.

Correll, J., Park, B., Judd, C. M., & Wittenbrink, B. (2002). The police officer's dilemma: Using ethnicity to disambiguate potentially threatening individuals. *Journal of Personality and Social Psychology, 83*, 1314–1329.

Costa, G. (1996). The impact of shift and night work on health. *Applied Ergonomics, 27*(1), 9–16.

Costa, P. T., & McCrae, R. R. (1992a). Four ways five factors are basic. *Personality and Individual Differences, 13*, 653–665.

Costa, P. T., & McCrae, R. R. (1992b). Normal personality assessment in clinical practice: The NEO Personality Inventory. *Psychological Assessment, 4*, 5–13.

Costello, F. J., & Keane, M. T. (2001). Testing two theories of conceptual combination: Alignment versus diagnosticity in the comprehension and production of combined concepts. *Journal of Experimental Psychology: Learning, Memory, and Cognition, 27,* 255–271.

Cowan, W. M., & Kandel, E. R. (2001). Prospects for neurology and psychiatry. *Journal of the American Medical Association, 285,* 594–600.

Cowley, G. (2000a, July 3). Generation XXL. *Newsweek,* pp. 40–44.

Cowley, G. (2000b, May 22). The new war on Parkinson's. *Newsweek,* pp. 52–58.

Cowley, G. (2000c, January 31). Alzheimer's: Unlocking the mystery. *Newsweek,* pp. 46–51.

Cowley, G., & Underwood, A. (2000). A revolution in medicine. *Newsweek,* pp. 58–62.

Coyle, J. T. (2003). Use it or lose it: Do effortful mental activities protect against dementia? *New England Journal of Medicine, 348,* 2489–2490.

Crabbe, J. C. (2002). Genetic contributions to addiction. *Annual Review of Psychology, 53,* 435–462.

Craik, F. I. M., & Lockhart, R. S. (1972). Levels of processing: A framework for memory research. *Journal of Verbal Learning and Verbal Behavior, 11,* 671–684.

Cramer, P. (2000). Defense mechanisms in psychology today: Further processes for adaptation. *American Psychologist, 55,* 637–646.

Crites, S. L., Jr., Fabrigar, L. R., & Petty, R. E. (1994). Measuring the affective and cognitive properties of attitudes: Conceptual and methodological issues. *Personality and Social Psychology Bulletin, 20,* 619–634.

Cross, S. E., & Madson, L. (1997). Models of the self: Self-construals and gender. *Psychological Bulletin, 122,* 89–103.

Crowe, R. A. (1990). Astrology and the scientific method. *Psychological Reports, 67,* 163–191.

Crowell, J. A., Treboux, D., & Waters, E. (2002). Stability of attachment representations: The transition to marriage. *Developmental Psychology, 38,* 467–479.

Csikszentmihalyi, M. (1996). Creativity: Flow and the psychology of discovery and invention. New York: Harper Perennial.

Cummings, D. E., et al. (2002). Plasma ghrelin levels after diet-induced weight loss or gastric bypass surgery. *New England Journal of Medicine, 346,* 1623–1630.

Cunningham, M. R., Roberts, A. R, Barbee, A. P., Druen, P. B., et al. (1995). "Their ideas of beauty are, on the whole, the same as ours": Consistency and variability in the cross-cultural perception of female physical attractiveness. *Journal of Personality and Social Psychology, 68,* 261–279.

Curran, P. J., Stice, E., & Chassin, L. (1997). The relation between adolescent alcohol use and peer alcohol use: A longitudinal random coefficients model. *Journal of Consulting and Clinical Psychology, 65,* 130–140.

Curran, R., & Schacter, D. L. (1996). Implicit memory and perceptual brain mechanisms. In D. Herrmann, C. McEvoy, C. Hertzog, P. Hertel, & M. K. Johnson (Eds.). *Basic and applied memory research: Theory in context* (Vol. 1, pp. 221–240). Mahwah, NJ: Lawrence Erlbaum Associates.

Curtin, J. J., Patrick, C. J., Lang, A. R, Cacioppo, J. T., & Birbaumer, N. (2001). Alcohol affects emotion through cognition. *Psychological Science, 12,* 527–531.

Cyranowski, J. M., Frank, E., Young, E., & Shear, K. (2000). Adolescent onset of the gender difference in lifetime rates of major depression: A theoretical model. *Archives of General Psychiatry, 57,* 21–27.

Daley, T. C., Whaley, S. E., Sigman, M. D., Espinosa, M. P., & Neumann, C. (2003). IQ on the rise: The Flynn Effect in rural Kenyan children. *Psychological Science, 14,* 215–219.

Damasio, A. R. (1994). *Descartes' error: Emotion, reason, and the human brain.* New York: Putnam.

Damasio, A. R. (2000). A neural basis for sociopathy. *Archives of General Psychiatry, 57,* 128–129.

Damasio, A. R., & Damasio, H. (1992, September). Brain and language. *Scientific American, 267,* 62–71.

Damasio, A. R., Grabowski,T. J., Bechara, A., Damasio, H., Ponto, L. L. B. Parvizi, J., et al. (2000). Subcortical and cortical brain activity during the feeling of self-generated emotions. *Nature Neuroscience, 3,* 1049–1056.

Dana, R. H. (Ed.). (2000). *Handbook of cross-cultural and multicultural personality assessment.* Mahwah, NJ: Lawrence Erlbaum Associates.

Darwin, C. A. (1872). *The expression of the emotions in man and animals.* London: J. Murray.

Dasen, P. R. (1994). Culture and cognitive development from a Piagetian perspective. In W. J. Lonner & R. Malpass (Eds.), *Psychology and culture.* Boston: Allyn & Bacon.

Dasgupta, N., & Greenwald, A. G. (2001). On the malleability of automatic attitudes: Combating automatic prejudice with images of admired and disliked individuals. *Journal of Personality and Social Psychology, 81,* 800–814.

Davidson, R. J. (2000). Affective style, psychopathology, and resilience: Brain mechanisms and plasticity. *American Psychologist, 55,* 1196–1214.

Davidson, R. J., Marshall, J. R., Tomarken, A. J., & Henriques, J. B. (2000). While a phobic waits: Regional brain electrical and autonomic activity in social phobics during anticipation of public speaking. *Biological Psychiatry, 47,* 85–95.

Davidson, R. J., Pizzagalli, D., Nitschke, J. B., & Putnam, K. (2002). Depression: Perspectives from affective neuroscience. *Annual Review of Psychology, 53,* 545–574.

Davidson, R. J., Putnam, K. M., & Larson, C. L. (2000). Dysfunction in the neural circuitry of emotion regulation—A possible prelude to violence. *Science, 289,* 591–594.

Davies, G., et al. (1996). Memory for cars and their drivers: A test of the interest hypothesis. In D. Herrmann, C. McEvoy, C. Hertzog, P. Hertel, & M. K. Johnson (Eds.), *Basic and applied memory research: Practical applications* (Vol. 2, pp. 37–50). Mahwah, NJ: Lawrence Erlbaum Associates.

Davis, D. L., & Boster, L. H. (1992). Cognitive-behavioral-expressive interventions with aggressive and resistant youths. *Child Welfare, 71,* 557–73.

Davis, J. L., & Rusbult, C. E. (2001). Attitude alignment in close relationships. *Journal of Personality and Social Psychology, 81,* 65–84.

Davis, J. M., Chen, N., & Glick, I. D. (2003). A meta-analysis of the efficacy of second-generation antipsychotics. *Archives of General Psychiatry, 60,* 553–564.

Dean, G., Mather, A., & Kelly, I. W. (1996). Astrology. In G. Stein (Ed.), *The encyclopedia of the paranormal.* Buffalo, NY: Prometheus.

DeAngelis, T. (1993). It's back: TV violence, concern for kid viewers. *APA Monitor, 24*(8), 16.

DeAngelis, T. (2000, September). School psychologists: In demand and expanding their reach. *Monitor on Psychology, 31*(9), 30–32.

DeAngelis, T. (2001, April). Our erotic personalities are as unique as our fingerprints. *Monitor on Psychology, 32,* 25.

DeAngelis, T. (2003, February). Why we overestimate our competence. *Monitor on Psychology,* pp. 60–62.

DeAngelis, T. (2004, April). Are beliefs inherited? *Monitor on Psychology, 35,* pp. 50–51.

de Bono, E. (1970). *Lateral thinking: Creativity step by step.* New York: Harper & Row.

DeCasper, A. J., & Prescott, P. A. (1984). Human newborns' perception of male voices. *Developmental Psychobiology, 17,* 481–491.

Deckel, A. W., Hesselbrock, V., & Bauer, L. (1996). Antisocial personality disorder, childhood delinquency, and frontal brain functioning: EEG and neuropsychological findings. *Journal of Clinical Psychology, 52,* 639–650.

Deegear, J., & Lawson, D. M. (2003). The utility of empirically supported treatments. *Professional Psychology: Research and Practice, 34,* 271–277.

Deegear, J., & Lawson, D. M. (2003). The utility of empirically supported treatments. *Professional Psychology: Research and Practice, 34,* 271–277.

De La Cancela, V., & Guzman, L. P. (1991). Latino mental health service needs: Implications for training psychologists. In H. F. Myers, L. P. Guzman, & R. J. Echemendia (Eds.), *Ethnic minority perspectives on clinical training and services in psychology* (pp. 59–64). Washington, DC: American Psychological Association.

Delahanty, D. L., & Baum, A. (2001). Stress and breast cancer. In A. Baum, T. A. Revenson, & J. E. Singer (Eds.), *Handbook of health psychology* (pp. 747–756). Mahwah, NJ: Lawrence Erlbaum Associates.

Delfino, R. J., Jamner, L. D., & Whalen, C. K. (2001). Temporal analysis of the relationship of smoking behavior and urges to mood states in men versus women. *Nicotine and Tobacco Research, 3,* 235–248.

Delves, P. J., & Roitt, I. M. (2000). Advances in immunology: The immune system. *New England Journal of Medicine, 343,* 37–39.

Democrats smell a rat. (2000, September 13). *ABC News Online,* Retrieved September 13, 2000, from http://abcnews.go.com/sections/politics/DailyNews/gopad0000912.html.

de Moor, C., Sterner, J., Hall, M., Warneke, C., Gilani, Z., Amato, R., et al. (2003). A pilot study of the effects of expressive writing on psychological and behavioral adjustment in patients enrolled in a Phase II trial of vaccine therapy for metastatic renal cell carcinoma. *Health Psychology, 21,* 615–619.

Dennerstein, L., Randolph, J., Taffe, J., Dudley, E., & Burger, H. (2002). Hormones, mood, sexuality, and the menopausal transition. *Fertility and Sterility, 77,* 42–48.

DePaulo, B. M., & Friedman, H. S. (1998). Nonverbal communication. In D. T. Gilbert, S. T. Fiske, & G. Lindzey (Eds.), *The handbook of social psychology* (4th ed., Vol. 2, pp. 3–40). Boston: McGraw-Hill, Inc.

Derlega, V., Winstead, B. A., & Jones, W. H. (Eds.). (1999). *Personality: Contemporary theory and research (2nd ed.). Nelson-Hall series in psychology* (pp. 3–26). Chicago: Nelson-Hall Publishers.

Derrington, A. M. (2004). Visual mechanisms of motion analysis and motion perception. *Annual Review of Psychology, 55,* 181–205.

DeRubeis, R. J., & Crits-Christoph, P. (1998). Empirically supported individual and group psychological treatments for adult mental disorders. *Journal of Consulting and Clinical Psychology, 66,* 37–52.

DeRubeis, R. J., Gelfand, L. A., Tang, T. Z., Simons, A. D., et al. (1999). Medications versus cognitive behavior therapy for severely depressed outpatients: Mega-analysis of four randomized comparisons. *American Journal of Psychiatry, 156,* 1007–1013.

DeRubeis, R. J., Tang, T. Z., & Beck, A. T. (2001). Cognitive therapy. In K. S. Dobson (Ed.), *Handbook of cognitive-behavioral therapies* (2nd ed., pp. 349–392). New York: Guilford Press.

de Silva, P. (1993). Post-traumatic stress disorder: Cross-cultural aspects. *International Review of Psychiatry, 5,* 217–229.

Deveny, K. (2003, June 30). We're not in the mood. Newsweel, pp. 41–46.

Devine, P. G., Plant, E. A., Amodio, D. M., Harmon-Jones, E., & Vance, S. L. (2002). The regulation of explicit and implicit race bias: The role of motivations to respond without prejudice. *Journal of Personality and Social Psychology, 82,* 835–848.

Dewsbury, D. A. (2000). Issues in comparative psychology at the dawn of the 20th century. *American Psychologist, 55,* 750–753.

Dick, D. M., Rose, R. J., Viken, R. J., Kaprio, J., & Koskenvuo, M. (2001). Exploring gene-environment interactions: Socioregional moderation of alcohol use. *Journal of Abnormal Psychology, 110,* 625–632.

Dickens, W. T., & Flynn, J. R. (2001). Heritability estimates versus large environmental effects: The IQ paradox resolved. *Psychological Review, 108,* 346–369.

DiClemente, R. J., Wingood, G. M., Crosby, R., Sionean, C., Cobb, B. K., Harrington, K., et al. (2001). Condom carrying is not associated with condom use and lower prevalence of sexually transmitted diseases among minority adolescent females. *Sexually Transmitted Diseases, 28,* 444–447.

Diehm, R., & Armatas, C. (2004). Surfing: An avenue for socially acceptable risk-taking, satisfying needs for sensation seeking and experience seeking. *Personality and Individual Differences, 36,* 663–677.

Diener, E., & Lucas, R. E. (1999). Personality and subjective well-being. In D. Kahneman et al. (Eds.), *Well-being: The foundations of hedonic psychology* (pp. 213–229). New York: Russell Sage Foundation.

Diener, E., Oishi, S., & Lucas, R. E. (2003). Personality, culture, and subjective well-being: Emotional and cognitive evaluations of life. *Annual Review of Psychology, 54,* 403–425.

Dietz, W. H. (2004). Overweight in childhood and adolescence. *New England Journal of Medicine, 350,* 855–857.

Dittmann, M. (2003, February). Psychology's first prescribers. *Monitor on Psychology,* pp. 36–37.

Dixon, W. E., Jr., & Smith, P.-H. (2000). Links between early temperament and language acquisition. *Merrill Palmer Quarterly, 46,* 417–440.

Dobson, K. S., & Dozois, D. J. A. (2001). Historical and philosophical bases of the cognitive-behavioral therapies. In K. S. Dobson (Ed.), *Handbook of cognitive-behavioral therapies* (2nd ed., pp. 3–40). New York: Guilford Press.

Docherty, N. M., Cohen, A. S., Nienow, T. M., Dinzeo, T. J., & Dangelmaier, R. E. (2003). Stability of formal thought disorder and referential communication disturbances in schizophrenia. *Journal of Abnormal Psychology, 112,* 469–475.

Does stress kill? (1995, July). *Consumer Reports on Health,* 75.

Dorahy, M. J. (2001). Dissociative identity disorder and memory dysfunction: The current state of experimental research and its future directions. *Clinical Psychology Review, 21,* 771–795.

Doty, R. L. (2001). Olfaction. *Annual Review of Psychology, 52,* 423–452.

Dougall, A. L., & Baum, A. (2001). Stress, health, and illness. In A. Baum, T. A. Revenson, & J. E. Singer (Eds.), *Handbook of health psychology* (pp. 339–348). Mahwah, NJ: Lawrence Erlbaum Associates.

Draguns, J. G., & Tanaka-Matsumi, J. (2003). Assessment of psychopathology across and within cultures: Issues and findings *Behaviour Research and Therapy, 41,* 755–776.

Driver study: Cell phones not major distraction. (2003, August 6). *CNN Web Posting.* Retrieved August 7, 2003, from http://www.cnn.com/2003/TRAVEL/08/06/distracted.driving.ap/index.html.

Droomers, M., Schrijvers, C. T. M., & Mackenbach, J. P. (2002). Why do lower-educated people continue smoking? Explanations from the longitudinal GLOBE study. *Health Psychology, 21,* 263–272.

Druckman, D., & Bjork, R. A. (Eds.). (1991). *In the mind's eye: Enhancing human performance.* Washington, DC: National Academy Press.

Drugs all stimulate brain in same way. (2003, February 19). *MSNBC Web Posting.* Retrieved February 21, 2003, from http://www.msnbc.com/news/874631.asp.

Drugs for aches and pains may also help slow the progress of Alzheimer's disease (2000, September). *Tufts University Health and Nutrition Letter, 18,* 1.

Druss, B. G., Rosenheck, R. A., & Sledge, W. H. (2000). Health and disability costs of depressive illness in a major U.S. corporation. *American Journal of Psychiatry, 157,* 1274–1278.

Dryden, W. (1984). *Rational-emotive therapy: Fundamentals and innovations.* London: Croom Helm.

Dryden, W., & Ellis, A. (2001). Rational emotive behavior therapy. In K. S. Dobson (Ed.), *Handbook of cognitive-behavioral therapies* (2nd ed., pp. 295–348). New York: Guilford Press.

Dudai, Y. (2004). The neurobiology of consolidations, or, How stable is the engram? *Annual Review of Psychology, 55,* 51–86.

Duenweld, M. (2003, June 18). More Americans seeking help for depression. *New York Times,* pp. A1, A22.

Dugas, M. L., Ladouceur, R., Léger, E., Freeston, M. H., Langlis, F., Provencher, M. D., et al. (2003). Group cognitive-behavioral therapy for generalized anxiety disorder: Treatment outcome and long-term follow-up. *Journal of Consulting and Clinical Psychology, 71,* 821–825.

Duman, R. S., Heninger, G. R., & Nestler, E. J. (1997). A molecular and cellular theory of depression. *Archives of General Psychiatry, 54,* 597–606.

Duncan, D. F., Donnelly, J. W., & Nicholson, T. (1992). Belief in the paranormal and religious belief among American college students. *Psychological Reports, 70,* 15–18.

Duncan, J., Seitz, R. J., Kolodny, J., Bor, D., Herzog, H., Ahmed, A., et al. (2000). A neural basis for general intelligence. *Science, 289,* 457–460.

Duncan, P. D., Ritter, P., Dornbush, S. K, Gross, P., & Carlsmith, J. (1985). The effects of pubertal timing on body image, school behavior, and deviance. *Journal of Youth and Adolescence, 14,* 227–235.

Duncker, K. (1945). On problem-solving. *Psychological Monographs, 58* (Whole No. 270).

Dunning, D., & Perretta, S. (2002). Automaticity and eyewitness accuracy: A 10- to 12-second rule for distinguishing accurate from inaccurate positive identifications. *Journal of Applied Psychology, 87,* 951–962.

Duryea, B. (2000, July 21). Illuminating the reasons for suicide. *St. Petersburg Times.* Retrieved July 21, 2000, from http://www.sptimes.com/News/072100/Floridian/Illuminating_the_reas.s.html.

Dusseldorp, E., van-Elderen, T., Maes, S., Meulman, J.& Kraaij, V. (1999). A meta-analysis of psychoeducational programs for coronary heart disease patients. *Health Psychology, 18,* 506–519.

Dweck, C. (1997, June). Cited in B. Murray, "Verbal praise may be the best motivator of all." *APA Monitor, 28,* 26.

Dwivedi, Y., Rizavi, H. S., Conley, R. R., Roberts, R. C., Tamminga, C. A., & Pandey, G. N. (2003). Altered gene expression of brain-derived neurotrophic factor and receptor tyrosine kinase b in postmortem brain of suicide subjects. *Archives of General Psychiatry, 60,* 804–815.

Eagly, A. H., & Chaiken, S. (1998). Structure and function. In D. T. Gilbert, S. T. Fiske, & G. Lindzey (Eds.), *The handbook of social psychology* (4th ed., Vol. 1, pp. 269–322). Boston: McGraw-Hill.

Eagly, A. H., & Wood, W. (1991). Explaining sex differences in social behavior: A meta-analytic perspective. *Personality and Social Psychology Bulletin, 17,* 306–315.

Ebbinghaus, H. (1885). *Über das Gedachtnis.* Leipzig: Duncker & Humblot.

Eberlein, T. (1997). *Child magazine's guide to whining.* New York: Pocket Books.

Ebrahim, S. H., Floyd, R. L., Merritt, R. K., II, Decoufle, P., &, Holtzman, D. (2000). Trends in pregnancy-related smoking rates in the U.S., 1987–1996. *Journal of the American Medical Association, 283,* 361–266.

Ecstasy use depletes brain chemical, study finds. (2000, July 25). *Cable News Network.* Retrieved July 26, 2000, from http://www.cnn.com/2000/HEALTH/07/25/ecstasy.brain.reut/index.html.

Edinger, J. D., Wohlgemuth, W. K., Radtke, R. A., Marsh, G. R.& Quillian, R. E. (2001). Cognitive behavioral therapy for treatment of chronic primary insomnia: A randomized controlled trial. *Journal of the American Medical Association, 285,* 1856–1864.

Edwards, J., Jackson, H. R., & Pattison, P. E. (2002). Emotion recognition via facial expression and affective prosody in schizophrenia: A methodological review. *Clinical Psychology Review, 22,* 789–832.

Egan,S., & Stelmack, R. M. (2003). A personality profile of Mount Everest climbers. *Personality and Individual Differences, 34,* 1491–1494.

Egeth, H. E. (1993). What do we not know about eyewitness identification? *American Psychologist, 48,* 577–580.

Egger, J. I. M., De Mey, H. R. A., Derksen, J. J. L., & van der Staak, C. P. F. (2003). Cross-cultural replication of the five-factor model and comparison of the NEO-PI-R and MMPI-2 PSY-5 scales in a Dutch psychiatric sample. *Psychological Assessment, 15,* 81–88.

Eichenbaum, H. (1997). How does the brain organize memories? *Science, 277,* 330–332.

Eichenbaum, H., & Fortin, N. (2003). Episodic memory and the hippocampus: It's about time. *Current Directions in Psychological Science, 12,* 53–57.

Einstein, G. O., & McDaniel, M. A. (1996). Remembering to do things: Remembering a forgotten topic. In D. Herrmann, C. McEvoy, C. Hertzog, P. Hertel, & M. K. Johnson (Eds.), *Basic and applied memory research: Practical applications* (Vol. 2, pp. 79–94). Mahwah, NJ: Lawrence Erlbaum Associates.

Ekman, P. (1980). Biological and cultural contributions to body and facial movement in the expression of emotions. In A. O. Rorty (Ed.), *Explaining emotions* (pp. 73–101). Berkeley: University of California Press.

Ekman, P. (2003). *Emotions revealed: Recognizing faces and feeling to improve communication and emotional life.* New York: Times Books.

El Nasser, H. (2004, March 18). Census projects growing diversity. *USA Today,* p. A1.

Elfenbein, H. A., & Ambady, N. (2002a). On the universality and cultural specificity of emotion recognition: A meta-analysis. *Psychological Bulletin, 128,* 203–235.

Elfenbein, H. A., & Ambady, N. (2002b). Is there an in-group advantage in emotion recognition? *Psychological Bulletin, 128,* 243–249.

Elkind, D. (1985). Egocentrism redux. *Developmental Review, 5,* 218–226.

Ellemers, N., Spears, R., & Doosje, B. (2002). Self and social identity. *Annual Review of Psychology, 53,* 161–186.

Elliot, A. J., & Sheldon, K. M. (1997). Avoidance achievement motivation: A personal goals analysis. *Journal of Personality and Social Psychology, 73,* 171–185.

Elliot, A. J., & Thrash, T. M. (2002). Approach-avoidance motivation in personality: Approach and avoidance temperaments and goals. *Journal of Personality and Social Psychology, 82,* 804–818.

Ellis, A. (1977). The basic clinical theory of rational-emotive therapy. In A. Ellis & R. Grieger (Eds.), *Handbook of rational-emotive therapy.* New York: Springer.

Ellis, A. (1991). *Reason and emotion in psychotherapy.* New York: Carol Publishing.

Ellis, A. (2001, January). "Intellectual" and "emotional" insight revisited. *NYS Psychologist, 13,* 2–6.

Ellis, A., & Dryden, W. (1987). *The practice of rational emotional therapy.* New York: Springer Publishing Company.

Ellis, H. D., & Shepherd, J. W. (1992). Face memory: Theory and practice. In M. Gruneberg & P. Morris (Eds.), *Aspects of memory: Second Edition, Volume 1: The practical aspects* (pp. 18–85). London: Routledge.

Ellis, L., & Bonin, S. L. (2003). Genetics and occupation-related preferences: Evidence from adoptive and non-adoptive families. *Personality and Individual Differences, 35,* 929–937.

Ellsworth, P. C. (1994). Sense, culture, and sensibility. In S. Kitayama & H. R. Markus (Eds.), *Emotion and culture: Empirical studies of mutual influence* (pp. 23–50). Washington, DC: American Psychological Association.

Elms, A. C. (1995). Obedience in retrospect. *Journal of Social Issues, 51,* 21–31.

Engel, J. (1996). Surgery for seizures. *New England Journal of Medicine, 334,* 647–652.

Engen, T. (1982). *The perception of odors.* New York: Academic Press.

Engle, R. W. (1996). Working memory and retrieval: An inhibition-resource approach. In J. T. E. Richardson, R. W. Engle, L. Hasher, R. H. Logie, et al. (Eds.), *Working memory and human cognition* (pp. 89–119). New York: Oxford University Press.

Epping-Jordan, J. E., Compas, B. E., Osowiecki, D. M., Oppedisano, G., Gerhardt, C., Primo, K., & Krag, D. N. (1999). Psychological adjustment in breast cancer: Processes of emotional distress. *Health Psychology, 18,* 315–326.

Epstein, H. (2003, October 12). Enough to make you sick? *New York Times Magazine,* pp. 75–81, 98, 102–108.

Epstein, R., Kirshnit, C. E., Lanza, R. P., & Rubin, L. C. (1984). "Insight" in the pigeon: Antecedents and determinants of an intelligent performance. *Nature, 308,* 61–62.

Epstein, S. (1996). Commentary: Recommendations for the future development of personality psychology. *Journal of Research in Personality, 30,* 435–446.

Erikson, E. H. (1963). *Childhood and society* (2nd ed.). New York: Norton.

Erikson, E. H. (1975). *Life history and the historical moment.* New York: Norton.

Erikson, E. H. (1980). *Identity and the life cycle.* New York: Norton.

Escobar, J. I., & Vega, W. A. (2000). Commentary: Mental health and immigration's AAAs: Where are we and where do we go from here? *Journal of Nervous and Mental Disease, 188,* 736–740.

Escobar, J. I., Hoyos-Nervi, C., & Gara, M. (2000). Immigration and mental health: Mexican-Americans in the United States. *Harvard Review of Psychiatry, 8,* 64–72.

Espenshade, T. (1993, April 25). Cited in F. Barringer, "Polling on sexual issues has its drawbacks." *New York Times,* p. A23.

Espie, C. A. (2002). Insomnia. *Annual Review of Psychology, 53,* 215–243.

Essock, S. M., Frisman, L. K., Covell, N. H., & Hargreaves, W. A. (2000). Cost-effectiveness of clozapine compared with conventional antipsychotic medication for patients in state hospitals. *Archives of General Psychiatry, 57,* 987–994.

Evans, R. B. (1999a, December). Controversy follows psychological testing. *APA Monitor, Online, 30*(11). Retrieved December 3, 2001, from http://www.apa.org/monitor/dec99/ss4.html.

Evans, R. B. (1999b, December). Behaviorism: the rise and fall of a discipline. *APA Monitor, 30*(11). Retrieved December 3, 2001, from http://www.apa.org/monitor/dec99/ss6.html.

Evans, R. B. (1999c, December). Once behind the scenes, now in the fore. *APA Monitor, 30*(11). Retrieved December 3, 2001, from http://www.apa.org/monitor/dec99/ss10.html.

Evans, R. B. (1999d, December). The long road to diversity. *APA Monitor, 30* (11). Retrieved December 3, 2001, from http://www.apa.org/monitor/dec99/ss11.html

Evans, W., & Rosenberg, I. H. (1991). *Biomarkers: The 10 determinants of aging you can control.* New York: Simon & Schuster.

Ewing, R., Schmid, T., Killingsworth, R., Zlot, A., & Raudenbush, S. (2003). Relationship between urban sprawl and physical activity, obesity and morbidity. *American Journal of Health Promotion, 18,* 47–57.

Exner, J. E. (1993). *The Rorschach: A comprehensive system: Vol. 1. Basic foundations* (3rd ed.). New York: Wiley.

Exner, J. E., Jr. (2002). Early development of the Rorschach test. *Academy of Clinical Psychology Bulletin, 8,* 9–24.

Eysenbach, G., Powell, J., Kuss, O., & Sa, E.-R. (2003) Empirical studies assessing the quality of health information for consumers on the World Wide Web: A systematic review. *Journal of the American Medical Association, 287,* 2691–2700.

Eysenck, H. J. (1952). *The scientific study of personality.* New York: Macmillan.

Eysenck, H. J. (1982). *Personality, genetics, and behavior.* New York: Praeger.

Eysenck, H. J. (Ed.). (1981). *A model for personality.* New York: Springer.

Fagan, J. F., & Holland, C. R. (2002). Equal opportunity and racial differences in IQ. *Intelligence, 30,* 361–387.

Fairburn, C. G., Stice, E., Cooper, Z., Doll, H. A., Norman, P. A., & O'Connor, E. E. (2003). Understanding persistence in bulimia nervosa: A 5-year naturalistic study. *Journal of Consulting and Clinical Psychology, 71,* 103–109.

Fals-Stewart, W. (2003). The occurrence of partner physical aggression on days of alcohol consumption: A longitudinal diary study. *Journal of Consulting and Clinical Psychology, 71,* 41–52.

Faraone, S. V. (2003, August). ADHD: Facts and fiction. Paper presented at the meeting of the American Psychological Association, Toronto, CA.

Farberman, R. K. (2003, April). Preparing for the "minority majority." *Monitor on Psychology,* pp. 42–43.

Farooqi, I. S., Keogh, J. M., Yeo, G. S. H., Lank, E. J., Cheetham, T., et al. (2003). Clinical spectrum of obesity and mutations in the melanocortin 4 receptor gene. *New England Journal of Medicine, 348,* 1085–1095.

Farrell, A. D., & White, K. S. (1998). Peer influences and drug use among urban adolescents: Family structure and parent/adolescent relationship as protective factors. *Journal of Consulting and Clinical Psychology, 66,* 248–258.

Feingold, A. (1991). Sex differences in the effects of similarity and physical attractiveness on opposite-sex attraction. *Basic and Applied Social Psychology, 12,* 357–367.

Feingold, A. (1992). Good-looking people are not what we think. *Psychological Bulletin, 111,* 304–341.

Feldman, L. B., & Rivas-Vazquez, R. A. (2003). Assessment and treatment of social anxiety disorder *Professional Psychology: Research and Practice, 34,* 396–405.

Ferketich, A. K., Schwartzbaum, J. A., Frid, D. J., & Moreschberger, M. L. (2000). Depression as an antecedent to heart disease among women and men in the NHANES I Study. *Archives of Internal Medicine, 160,* 1261–1268.

Festinger, L. (1957). *A theory of cognitive dissonance.* Palo Alto, CA: Stanford University Press.

Fingerman, K. L. (2002). *Mother and their adult daughter: Mixed emotions, enduring bonds.* New York: Prometheus Books.

Fink, B., & Penton-Voak, I. (2002). Evolutionary psychology of facial attractiveness. *Current Directions in Psychological Science, 11,* 154–158.

Finke, R. A., Ward, T. B., & Smith, S. M. (1992). *Creative cognition: Theory, research, and applications.* Cambridge, MA: MIT Press.

Fischer, A. H., Mosquera, P. M. R., van Vianen, A. E. M., & Manstead, A. S. R. (2004). Gender and culture differences in emotion. *Emotion, 4,* 87–94.

Fischer, H., Jesper, L. R., Furmark, T., Wik, G. , & Fredrikson, M. (2002). Right-sided human prefrontal brain activation during acquisition of conditioned fear. *Emotion, 2*, 233–241.

Fishbain, D. A., & Goldberg, M. (1991). The misdiagnosis of conversion disorder in a psychiatric emergency service. *General Hospital Psychiatry, 13*, 177–181.

Fishbein, M. D. (1996). *Peer prejudice and discrimination: Evolutionary, cultural, and developmental dynamics.* Boulder, CO: Westview Press.

Fisher, S., & Greenberg, R. (Eds.). (1978). *The scientific evaluation of Freud's theories and therapy: A book of readings.* New York: Basic Books.

Fiske, A. P., Kitayama, S., Markus, H. R., & Nisbett, R. E. (1998). The cultural matrix of social psychology. In D. T. Gilbert, S. T. Fiske, & G. Lindzey (Eds.), *The handbook of social psychology* (4th ed., Vol. 2, pp. 915–981). Boston: McGraw-Hill.

Fitness, J. (2001). Emotional intelligence and intimate relationships. In J. Ciarrochi & J. P. Forgas et al. (Eds.), *Emotional intelligence in everyday life: A scientific inquiry* (pp. 98–112). Philadelphia: Psychology Press.

Fitzpatrick, O. D., Jr., & Shook, S. L. (1994). Belief in the paranormal: Does identity development during the college years make a difference? An initial investigation. *Journal of Parapsychology, 58*, 315–329.

Flavell, J. H. (1992). Cognitive development: Past, present, and future. *Developmental Psychology, 28*, 998–1005.

Flavell, J. H., Miller, P. H., & Miller, S. A. (1993). *Cognitive development* (3rd ed.). Englewood Cliffs, NJ: Prentice-Hall.

Floyd, R. L., Rimer, B. K., Giovino, G. A., Mullen, P. D., & Sullivan, S. E. (1993). A review of smoking in pregnancy: Effects on pregnancy outcomes and cessation efforts. *Annual Review of Public Health, 14*, 379–411.

Flynn, J. R. (1999). Searching for justice: The discovery of IQ gains over time. *American Psychologist, 54*, 5–20.

Flynn, J. R. (2003). Movies about intelligence: The limitations of g. *Current Directions in Psychological Science, 12*, 95–98.

Fogelholm, M., Kukkonen-Harjual, K., Nenonen, A., & Pasenen, M. (2000). Effects of walking training on weight maintenance after a very-low-energy diet in premenopausal obese women: A randomized controlled trial. *Archives of Internal Medicine, 160*, 2177–2184.

Fontaine, K. R., Redden, D. T., Wang, C., Westfall, A. O, & Allison, D. B. (2003). Years of life lost due to obesity. *Journal of the American Medical Association, 289*, 187–193.

Foote, D. (2000, Fall/Winter). The war of the wills. *Newsweek Special Issue*, pp. 64–65.

Ford, C. S., & Beach, F. A. (1951). *Patterns of sexual behavior.* New York: Harper & Row.

Forestell, C. A., Humphrey, T. M., & Stewart, S. H. (2004). Is beauty in the eye of the beholder? Effects of weight and shape on attractiveness ratings of female line drawings by restrained and nonrestrained eaters. *Eating Behaviors, 5*, 89–101.

Fowler, R. D. (1992, June). Solid support needed for animal research. *APA Monitor, 23*(6), 2.

Foxhall, K. (2000a, January). Bringing law and psychology together. *Monitor on Psychology, 31*(1), 38–39.

Foxhall, K. (2000b, October). Dispatches from the prescription privileges fronts. *Monitor on Psychology, 31*(10), 30–31.

Foxhall, K. (2000c, October). Platform for a long-term push. *Monitor on Psychology, 31*(10), 30.

Frank, E., & Kupfer, D. J. (2000). Peeking through the door to the 21st century. *Archives of General Psychiatry, 57*, 83–85.

Frankenberger, K. D. (2000). Adolescent egocentrism: A comparison among adolescents and adults. *Journal of Adolescence, 23*, 343–354.

Franzoi, S. L., & Herzog, M. E. (1987). Judging physical attractiveness. *Personality and Social Psychology Bulletin, 13*, 19–33.

Frauenglass, S., Routh, D. K., Pantin, H. M., & Mason, C. A. (1997). Family support decreases influence of deviant peers on Hispanic adolescents' substance use. *Journal of Clinical Child Psychology, 26*, 15–23.

Freedman, R. (2003). Schizophrenia. *New England Journal of Medicine, 349*, 1738–1749.

Freeman, H. P., & Payne, R. (2000). Racial injustice in health care. *New England Journal of Medicine, 342*, 1045–1047.

Freeman, M. S., Spence, M. J., & Oliphant, C. M. (1993, June). *Newborns prefer their mothers' low-pass filtered voices over other female filtered voices.* Paper presented at the annual meeting of the American Psychological Society, Chicago.

Freemon, F. R. (1981). *Organic mental disease.* Jamaica, NY: Spectrum.

Freud, S. (1900). The interpretation of dreams. In J. Strachey (Ed.), *The standard edition of the complete psychological works of Sigmund Freud: Vol. 8.* London: Hogarth Press.

Freud, S. (1922/1959). Analysis of a phobia in a 5–year-old boy. In A. & J. Strachey (Ed. & Trans.), *Collected papers* (Vol. 3). New York: Basic Books. (Original work published 1909.)

Freud, S. (1938). *The psychopathology of everyday life.* Hammondsworth: Pelican Books.

Freud, S. (1957). Mourning and melancholia (1917). In J. Rickman (Ed.), *A general selection from the works of Sigmund Freud.* Garden City, NY: Doubleday.

Freud, S. (1964). New introductory lectures. In *Standard edition of the complete psychological works of Sigmund Freud* (Vol. 22). London: Hogarth. (Original work published 1933.)

Freund, A. M., & Baltes, P. B. (1999). Selection, optimization, and compensation as strategies of life management: Correction to Freund and Baltes (1998). *Psychology and Aging, 14*, 700–702.

Friedman, M., & Rosenman, R. H. (1974). *Type A behavior and your heart.* New York: Knopf.

Friedman, M., & Ulmer, D. (1984). *Treating Type A behavior and your heart.* New York: Fawcett Crest.

Friedman, R. A. (2002, December 31). Born to be happy, through a twist of human hard wire. *The New York Times*, p F5

Fruzzetti, A. E., Toland, K., Teller, S. A., & Loftus, E. F. (1992). Memory and eyewitness testimony. In M. M. Gruneberg & P. E. Morris (Eds.), *Aspects of memory: Vol. 1. The practical aspects* (2nd ed., pp. 18–50). Florence, KY: Taylor & Francis/Routledge.

Fuligni, A. J., Yip, T., & Tseng, V. (2002). The impact of family obligations on the daily activities and psychological well-being of Chinese American adolescents. *Child Development, 73*, 302–314.

Fulker, D. W., DeFries, J. C., & Plomin, R. (1988). Genetic influence on general mental ability increases between infancy and middle childhood. *Nature, 336*, 767–769.

Funder, D. C. (2001). Personality. *Annual Review of Psychology, 52*, 607–628.

Furmark, T., Tillfors, M., Marteinsdottir, I., Fischer, H., Pissiota, A., Langstrom, B., et al. (2002). Common changes in cerebral blood flow in patients with social phobia treated with citalopram or cognitive-behavioral therapy. *Archives of General Psychiatry, 59*, 425–433.

Furumoto, L. (1992). Joining separate spheres—Christine Ladd-Franklin, woman-scientist. *American Psychologist, 47*, 175–182.

Gabriel, T. (1995, June 12). A new generation seems ready to give bisexuality a place in the spectrum. *New York Times*, p. A12.

Gaertner, S. L., Dovidio, J. F., Rust, M. C., Nier, J. A., Banker, B. S., Ward, C. M., et al. (1999). Reducing intergroup bias: Elements of intergroup cooperation. *Journal of Personality and Social Psychology, 76*, 388–402.

Gaines, S. O., & Reed, E. S. (1995). Prejudice: From Allport to DuBois. *American Psychologist, 50*, 96–103.

Gaines, S. O., Jr., Marelich, W. D., Bledsoe, K. L., Steers, W. N., et al. (1997). Links between race/ethnicity and cultural values as mediated by racial/ethnic identity and moderated by gender. *Journal of Personality and Social Psychology, 72*, 1460–1476.

Gelman, D. (1994, April 18). The mystery of suicide. *Newsweek*, pp. 44–49.

Ganellen, R. J. (2001). Weighing evidence for the Rorschach's validity: A response to Wood et al. (1999). *Journal of Personality Assessment, 77*, 1–15.

Garcia, J., & Koelling, R. A. (1966). Relation of cue to consequence in avoidance learning. *Psychonomic Science, 4*, 123–124.

Garcia, J., & Koelling, R. A. (1971). The use of ionizing rays as a mammalian olfactory stimulus. In H. Autrum et al. (Eds.), *Handbook of sensory physiology: Vol. 4. Chemical senses* (Part 1). New York: Springer-Verlag.

Gardner, F. L. (2001). Applied sport psychology in professional sports: The team psychologist. *Professional Psychology: Research and Practice, 32*, 34–39.

Gardner, H. (1983). *Frames of mind.* New York: Basic Books.

Gardner, H. (1993). Intelligence in seven phases. In H. Gardner (Ed.), *Multiple intelligences: The theory in practice* (pp. 213–230). New York: Basic Books.

Gardner, H. (1998). Are there additional intelligences? The case for naturalist, spiritual, and existential intelligences. In J. Kane (Ed.), *Education information, and transformation.* Upper Saddle River, NJ: Prentice-Hall.

Gardner, H., & Hatch, T. (1989). Multiple intelligences go to school: Educational implications of the theory of multiple intelligences. *Educational Research, 18*, 4–10.

Gardner, H., & Traub, J. (1999, Fall). Debate on "multiple intelligences." *Cerebrum, 1*, 2.

Gardner, R. A., & Gardner, B. T. (1969). Teaching sign language to a chimpanzee. *Science, 165*, 664–672.

Gardner, R. A., & Gardner, B. T. (1978). Comparative psychology and language acquisition. *Annals of the New York Academy of Sciences, 309*, 37–76.

Garnets, L. D. (2002). Sexual orientations in perspective. *Cultural Diversity and Ethnic Minority Psychology, 8*, 115–129.

Garwood, S. G., et al. (1980). Beauty is only "name deep": The effect of first name in ratings of physical attraction. *Journal of Applied Social Psychology, 10,* 431–435.

Gaser, C., Nenadic, I., Buchsbaum, B. R., Hazlett, E. A., & Buchsbaum, M. S. (2004). Ventricular enlargement in schizophrenia related to volume reduction of the thalamus, striatum, and superior temporal cortex. *American Journal of Psychiatry, 161,* 154–156.

Gatchel, R. J. (2001). Biofeedback and self-regulation of physiological activity: A major adjunctive treatment modality in health psychology. In A. Baum, T. A. Revenson, & J. E. Singer (Eds.), *Handbook of health psychology* (pp. 95–104). Mahwah, NJ: Lawrence Erlbaum Associates.

Gaulin, S. J. C., & McBurney, D. H. (2001). *Psychology: An evolutionary approach.* Upper Saddle River, NJ: Prentice-Hall.

Gauthier, J. G., Ivers, H., & Carrier, S. (1996). Nonpharmacological approaches in the management of recurrent headache disorders and their comparison and combination with pharmacotherapy. *Clinical Psychology Review, 16,* 543–571.

Gauthier, J., Coté, G., & French, D. (1994). The role of home practice in the thermal biofeedback treatment of migraine headache. *Journal of Consulting and Clinical Psychology, 62,* 180–184.

Gawin, F. H., & Ellinwood, E. H. (1988). Cocaine and other stimulants: Actions, abuse, and treatment. *New England Journal of Medicine, 318,* 1173–1182.

Gazzaniga, M. (1999). The interpreter within: The glue of conscious experience. *Cerebrum, 1*(1), 68–78.

Gazzaniga, M. S. (1992). *Nature's mind.* New York: Basic Books.

Gazzaniga, M. S. (1995). Consciousness and the cerebral hemispheres. In M. S. Gazzaniga (Ed.), *The cognitive neurosciences* (pp. 1391–1400). Cambridge, MA: MIT Press.

Gazzaniga, M. S. (1997). Why can't I control my brain? Aspects of conscious experience. In M. Ito, Y. Miyashita, et al. (Eds.), *Cognition, computation, and consciousness.* (pp. 69–79). New York: Oxford University Press

Ge, X., Kim, I J, Brody, G. H., Conger, R. D., Simons, R. L., Gibbons, F. X., & Cutrona, C. E. (2003). It's about timing and change: Pubertal transition effects on symptoms of major depression among African American youths. *Developmental Psychology, 39,* 430–439.

Geddes, J. R., Burgess, S., Hawton, K., Jamison, K., & Goodwin, G. M. (2004). Long-term lithium therapy for bipolar disorder: Systematic review and meta-analysis of randomized controlled trials. *American Journal of Psychiatry, 161,* 217–222.

Geen, R. G. (1998). Aggression and antisocial behavior. In D. T. Gilbert, S. T. Fiske, & G. Lindzey (Eds.), *The handbook of social psychology* (4th ed., Vol. 2, pp. 317–356). Boston: McGraw-Hill.

Geller, B., Craney, J. L., Bolhofner, K., Nickelsburg, M. J., Williams, M., & Zimerman, B. (2002). Two-year prospective follow-up of children with a prepubertal and early adolescent bipolar disorder phenotype. *American Journal of Psychiatry, 159,* 927–933.

Gershoff, E. T. (2002a). Corporal punishment by parents and associated child behaviors and experiences: A meta-analytic and theoretical review. *Psychological Bulletin, 128,* 539–579.

Gershoff , E. T. (2002b). Corporal punishment, physical abuse, and the burden of proof: Reply to Baumrind, Larzelere, and Cowan (2002), Holden (2002), and Parke (2002). *Psychological Bulletin, 128,* 602–611.

Giancola, P. R., & Zeichner, A. (1997). The biphasic effects of alcohol on human physical aggression. *Journal of Abnormal Psychology, 106,* 598–607.

Gibbons, A. (1991). Deja vu all over again: Chimp-language wars. *Science, 251,* 1561–1562.

Gibbs, N. (1995, October 2). EQ factor. *Time,* pp. 61–65.

Gibson, E. J., & Walk, R. D. (1960, April). The visual cliff. *Scientific American,* pp. 64–71.

Gidron, Y., Davidson, K., & Bata, I. (1999). The short-term effects of a hostility-reduction intervention on male coronary heart disease patients. *Health Psychology, 18,* 416–420.

Gil, K. M., Williams, D. A., Keefe, F. J., & Beckham, J. C. (1990). The relationship of negative thoughts to pain and psychological distress. *Behavior Therapy, 21,* 349–362.

Gilbert, S. (2004, March 16). New clues to women veiled in black. *New York Times, Science Times,* pp. F1, F7.

Gilbert, S. C. (2003). Eating disorders in women of color. *Clinical Psychology: Science and Practice, 10,* 444–455.

Gilligan, C. (1982). *In a different voice: Psychological theory and women's development.* Cambridge, MA: Harvard University Press.

Glaser, R., Pearson, G. R., Bonneau, R. H., Esterling, B. A., et al. (1993). Stress and the memory T-cell response to the Epstein-Barr Virus in healthy medical students. *Health Psychology, 12,* 435–442.

Glaser, R., Pearson, G. R., Jones, J. F., Hillhouse, J., et al. (1991). Stress-related activation of Epstein-Barr virus. *Brain, Behavior, and Immunity, 5,* 219–232.

Glass, R. M. (2000). Panic disorder: It's real and it's treatable [Editorial]. *Journal of the American Medical Association, 283,* 2573–2574.

Glass, R. M. (2001). Electroconvulsive therapy: Time to bring it out of the shadows [Editorial]. *Journal of the American Medical Association, 285,* 1346–1348.

Gleaves, D. H. (1996). The sociocognitive model of dissociative identity disorder: A reexamination of the evidence. *Psychological Bulletin, 120,* 42–59.

Gleaves, D. H., Smith, S. M., Butler, L. D., & Spiegel, D. (2004). False and recovered memories in the laboratory and clinic: A review of experimental and clinical evidence. *Clinical Psychology: Science and Practice, 11,* 3–28.

Glueckauf, R. L., Pickett, T. C., Ketterson, T. U., Loomis, J. S., & Rozensky, R. H. (2003). Preparation for the delivery of telehealth services: A self-study framework for expansion of practice. *Professional Psychology: Research and Practice, 34,* 159–163.

Goddard, A. W., Mason, G. F., Almai, A., Rothman, D. L., Behar, K. L., Petroff, O. A., et al. (2001). Reductions in occipital cortex GABA levels in panic disorder detected with sup-1H-magnetic resonance spectroscopy. *Archives of General Psychiatry, 58,* 556–561.

Goenjian, A. K., Molina, L., Steinberg, A. M., Fairbanks, L. A., Alvarez, M. L., Goenjian, H. A., et al. (2001). Posttraumatic stress and depressive reactions among Nicaraguan adolescents after Hurricane Mitch. *American Journal of Psychiatry, 158,* 788–794.

Goff, D. C., & Coyle, J. T. (2001). The emerging role of glutamate in the pathophysiology and treatment of schizophrenia. *American Journal of Psychiatry, 158,* 1367–1377.

Goldberg, I. J., Mosca, L., Piano, M. R., & Fisher, E. A. (2001). AHA Science Advisory: Wine and your heart. *Circulation, 103,* 472–475.

Goldberg, J. H., Halpern-Felsher, B. L., & Millstein, S. G. (2002). Beyond invulnerability: The importance of benefits in adolescents' decision to drink alcohol. *Health Psychology, 21,* 477–484.

Goldberg, L. R. (1993). The structure of phenotypic personality traits. *American Psychologist, 48,* 26–34.

Goldstat, R., Briganti, E., Tran, J., Wolfe, R., & Davis, S. R. (2003). Transdermal testosterone therapy improves well-being, mood, and sexual function in premenopausal women. *Menopause, 10,* 390–398.

Goldstein, A. (1994). *Addiction: From biology to drug policy.* New York: W. H. Freeman and Company.

Goldstein, J. M., Seidman, L. J., O'Brien, L. M., Horton, N. J., Kennedy, D. N., Makris, N., et al. (2002). Impact of normal sexual dimorphisms on sex differences in brain abnormalities in schizophrenia assessed by magnetic resonance imaging. *Archives of General Psychiatry, 59,* 154–164.

Goleman, D. (1995a, March 8). 75 years later, study still tracking geniuses. *New York Times,* pp. C1, C9.

Goleman, D. (1995b, March 28). The brain manages happiness and sadness in different centers. *New York Times,* pp. C1, C9.

Goleman, D. (1995c) *Emotional Intelligence.* New York: Bantam Books.

Goleman, D. (1995d, June 21). Virtual reality conquers fear of heights. *New York Times,* p. C11.

Goleman, D. (1995e, October 4). Eating disorder rates surprise experts. *New York Times,* p. C11.

Goleman, D. (1996, July 21). A set point for happiness. *New York Times,* p. E2.

Goleman, D. (2003, February 4). Finding happiness: Cajole your brain to lean to the left. *New York Times,* p. F5.

Gone, J. (2004). Mental health services for Native Americans in the 21st century United States. *Professional Psychology: Research and Practice, 35,* 10–18.

Goode, E. (1998, October 27). Happiness may grow with aging, study finds. *New York Times,* p. F7.

Goode, E. (1999a, February 16). New study finds middle age is prime of life. *New York Times,* p. F6.

Goode, E. (1999b, November 23). New clues to why we dream. *New York Times,* pp. F1, F4.

Goode, E. (2000a, January 1). Rx for brain makeovers. *New York Times, The Millennium,* p. E27.

Goode, E. (2000b, May 18). Chronic-depression study backs the pairing of therapy and drugs. *New York Times,* p. A23.

Goode, E. (2000c, March 14). Human nature: Born or made? *New York Times,* pp. F1, F9.

Goode, E. (2000d, October 24). Watching volunteers, experts seek clues to eating disorders. *New York Times,* pp. F1, F6.

Goode, E. (2000e, August 27). Hey, what if contestants give each other shocks? *New York Times Week in Review,* p. 2.

Goode, E. (2001a, January 2). Researcher challenges a host of psychological studies. *New York Times,* pp. F1, F7.

Goode, E. (2001b, January 25). Rats may dream, it seems, of their days at the mazes. *New York Times*, pp. A1, A16.

Goode, E. (2001c, April 3). Scientist at work: Robert Sternberg. His goal: Making intelligence tests smarter. *New York Times*, pp. F1, F7.

Goode, E. (2001d, May 22). For users of heroin, decades of despair. *New York Times*, p. F5.

Goode, E. (2001e, August 1). Study says 20% of girls reported abuse by a date. *New York Times*, p. A10.

Goode, E. (2001f, August 27). Disparities seen in mental care for minorities. *New York Times*, pp. A1, A12.

Goode, E. (2001g, February 20). What's in an inkblot? Some say, not much. *New York Times*, pp. F1, F4.

Goode, E. (2002, December 17). The heavy cost of chronic stress. *New York Times*, pp. F1, F4.

Goode, E. (2003, February 6). New method aids evaluation of Alzheimer's drugs. *New York Times*, p. A30.

Goodman, G. S., Ghetti, S., Quas, J. A., Edelstein, R. S., Alexander, K. W., & Redlich, A. D. (2003). A prospective study of memory for child sexual abuse: New findings relevant to the repressed-memory controversy. *Psychological Science, 14*, 113–118.

Goodwin, I. (2003). The relevance of attachment theory to the philosophy, organization, and practice of adult mental health care. *Clinical Psychology Review, 23*, 35–56.

Goodwin, P. J., Leszcz, M., Ennis, M., Koopmans, J., Vincent, L., Guther, H., et al. (2001). The effect of group psychosocial support on survival in metastatic breast cancer. *New England Journal of Medicine, 345*, 1719–1726.

Gooren, L. J. G., & Kruijver, P. M. (2002). Androgens and male behavior. *Molecular and Cellular Endocrinology, 198*, 31–40.

Gopnik, A. (2000, December 24). Children need childhood, not vocational training. *New York Times Week in Review*, p. 6.

Gordon, R. A. (2000). Stereotype measurement and the 'kernel of truth' hypothesis. In M. E. Ware & D. E. Johnson (Eds.), *Handbook of demonstrations and activities in the teaching of psychology, Vol. III: Personality, abnormal, clinical-counseling, and social* (2nd ed.). Mahwah, NJ: Lawrence Erlbaum Associates.

Gorman, C. (2003, October 20). How to eat smarter. *Time*, pp. 48–59.

Gorman, J. M., Kent, J. M., Sullivan, G. M., & Coplan, J. D. (2000). Neuroanatomical hypothesis of panic disorder, revised. *American Journal of Psychiatry, 157*, 493–505.

Gosling, S. D., Rentfrow, P. J., & Swann, W. B., Jr. (2003). A very brief measure of the Big-Five personality domains. *Journal of Research in Personality, 37*, 504–528.

Gottesman, I. I. (1991). *Schizophrenia genetics: The origins of madness*. New York: Freeman.

Gottesman, I. I. (1997). Twins: En route to QTLs for cognition. *Science, 276*, 1522–1523.

Gottesman, I. I., & Gould, T. D. (2003). The endophenotype concept in psychiatry: Etymology and strategic intentions. *American Journal of Psychiatry, 160*, 636–645.

Gottesman, I. I., McGuffin, P., & Farmer, A. E. (1987). Clinical genetics as clues to the "real" genetics of schizophrenia. Schizophrenia Bulletin, 13, 23–47.

Gottesman, I. J. (2001). Psychopathology through a life span–genetic prism. *American Psychologist, 56*, 867–878.

Gottfredson, L. S. (2003a). Dissecting practical intelligence theory: Its claims and evidence. *Intelligence, 31*, 343–397.

Gottfredson, L. S. (2003b). Discussion on Sternberg's "Reply to Gottfredson." *Intelligence, 31*, 415–424.

Gottfredson, L. S. (2004). Intelligence: Is it the epidemiologists' elusive "fundamental cause" of social class inequalities in health? *Journal of Personality and Social Psychology, 86*, 174–199.

Gottfredson, L. S., & Deary, I. J. (2004). Intelligence predicts health and longevity, but why? *Current Directions in Psychological Science, 13*, 1–4.

Gouzoulis-Mayfrank, E., Daumann, J., Tuchtenhagen, F., Pelz, S., Becker, S., Kunert, H. J., et al. (2000). Impaired cognitive performance in drug free users of recreational ecstasy (MDMA). *Journal of Neurology, Neurosurgery, and Psychiatry, 68*, 719–725.

Grady, D. (1997, May 21). Exercise may not curb depression. *New York Times*, p. C11.

Grady, D. (2002, November 26). Why we eat (and eat and eat). *New York Times*, pp. F1, F4.

Grady, D. (2003, April 15). Quest for weight-loss drug takes an unusual turn. *New York Times*, p. F5.

Graham, J. R. (2000). *MMPI-2: Assessing personality and psychopathology* (3rd ed.). New York: Oxford University Press.

Grant, R. M., et al. (2002). Time trends in primary HIV-1 drug resistance among recently infected persons. *Journal of the American Medical Association, 288*, 181–188.

Gray-Little, B., & Hafdahl, A. R. (2000). Factors influencing racial comparisons of self-esteem: A quantitative review. *Psychological Bulletin, 126*, 26–54.

Greenberg, L. S., & Malcolm, W. (2002). Resolving unfinished business: Relating process to outcome. *Journal of Consulting and Clinical Psychology, 70*, 406–416.

Greenberg, S. H., & Springen, K. (2000, October 16). Back to day care. *Newsweek*, pp. 61–62.

Greenberg, S. H., & Springen, K. (2001, Fall/Winter). Keeping hope alive. *Newsweek Special Issue*, pp. 60–63.

Greenwald, A. G., & Draine, S. G. (1997). Do subliminal stimuli enter the mind unnoticed? Tests with a new method. In J. D. Cohen & J. W. Schooler (Eds.), *Scientific approaches to consciousness* (pp. 83–108). Mahwah, NJ: Lawrence Erlbaum Associates.

Greenwald, A. G., McGhee, D. E., & Schwartz, J. L. K. (1998). Measuring individual differences in implicit cognition: The Implicit Association Test. *Journal of Personality and Social Psychology, 74*, 1464–1480.

Greer, M. (2004, May). Interventions help reduce HIV risk. *Monitor on Psychology*, p. 23.

Gregg, E. W., Cauley, J. A., Stone, K., Thompson, T. J., Bauer, D. C., Cummings, S. R., et al. (2003). Relationship of changes in physical activity and mortality among older women. *Journal of the American Medical Association, 289*, 2379–2386.

Grigorenko, E. L. (2002). Other than g: The value of persistence. In R. J. Sternberg & E. L. Grigorenko (Eds.), *The general factor of intelligence: How general is it?* (pp. 299–327). Mahwah, NJ: Lawrence Erlbaum Associates.

Grigoriadis, V. (2003, July 20). Smiling through the 30th, a birthday once apocalyptic. *New York Times*, Section 9, pp. 1, 8.

Grochowicz, P. M., Schedlowski, M., Husband, A. J., & King, M. G., Hibberd, A. D., & Bowen, K. M. (1991). Behavioral conditioning prolongs heart allograft survival in rats. *Brain, Behavior, and Immunity, 5*, 349–356.

Grossman, L. (2003, January 20). Can Freud get his job back? *Time*, pp. 48–51.

Gründer, G., Carlsson, A., & Wong, D. F. (2003). Mechanism of new antipsychotic medications: Occupancy is not just antagonism. *Archives of General Psychiatry, 60*, 974–977.

Gruneberg, M. M. (1992). The practical application of memory aids. In M. Gruneberg & P. Morris (Eds.), *Aspects of memory: 2nd ed., Vol. 1. The practical aspects* (pp. 168–195). London: Routledge.

Guenther, R. K. (1998). *Human cognition*. Englewood Cliffs, NJ: Prentice-Hall.

Guilford, J. P., Christensen, P. R., Merrifield, P. R., & Wilson, R. C. (1978). *Alternate uses: Form B, Form C*. Orange, CA: Sheridan Psychological Services.

Gupta, S. (2003, January 20). If everyone were on Prozac. *Time*, p. 49.

Gustafsson, J. E., & Undheim, J. O. (1996). Individual differences in cognitive functions. In D. C. Berliner & R. C. Calfee (Eds.), *Handbook of educational psychology* (pp. 186–242). New York: Macmillan Library Reference.

Gustavson, C. R., & Garcia, J. (1974). Aversive conditioning: Pulling a gag on the wily coyote. *Psychology Today, 8*, 68–72.

Gustavson, C. R., Garcia, J., Hawkins, W. G., & Rusiniak, K. W. (1974). Coyote predation control by aversive conditioning. *Science, 184*, 581–583.

Haber, R. N. (1979). Twenty years of haunting eidetic imagery: Where's the ghost? *Behavioral and Brain Sciences 2*, 583–629.

Hacker, C. M. (2002). United States Women's National Soccer Team: Psychological skills training program and history. *Exercise and Sport Psychology Newsletter, 16*, pp. 4–6.

Hackett, G., Betz, N. E., Casas, J. M., & Rocha Singh, I. A. (1992). Gender, ethnicity, and social cognitive factors predicting the academic achievements of students in engineering. *Journal of Counseling Psychology, 39*, 527–538.

Hafdahl, A. R., & Gray-Little, B. (2002). Explicating methods in reviews of race and self-esteem: Reply to Twenge and Crocker (2002). *Psychological Bulletin, 128*, 409–416.

Haith, M. M., & Benson, J. B. (1997). Infant cognition. In W. Damon (Editor-in-Chief), D. Kuhn & R. Siegler (Vol. Eds.), *Handbook of child psychology, 5th ed.: Vol. 2. Cognition, perception and language* (pp. 199–254). New York: John Wiley & Sons.

Hajjar, I., & Kotchen, T. A. (2003). Trends in prevalence, awareness, treatment, and control of hypertension in the United States, 1988–2000. *Journal of the American Medical Association, 290*, 199–206.

Hall, S. S. (1998, February 15). Our memories, our selves. *New York Times Magazine*, 26–33, 49, 56–57.

Halmi, K. A., Sunday, S. R., Strober, M., Kaplan, A., Woodside, D. B., Fichter, M., et al. (2000). Perfectionism in anorexia nervosa: Variation by clinical subtype, obsessionality, and pathological eating behavior. *American Journal of Psychiatry, 157,* 1799–1805.

Halmi, K., Agras, W. S., Mitchell, J., Wilson, G. T., Crow, S., Bryson, S. W., & Kraemer, H. (2003). Relapse predictors of patients with bulimia nervosa who achieved abstinence through cognitive behavioral therapy. *American Journal of Psychiatry, 59,* 1105–1109.

Halpern, D. F., & LaMay, M. L. (2000). The smarter sex: A critical review of sex differences in intelligence. *Educational Psychology Review, 12*(2), 229–246.

Hamann, S. B., Ely, T. D., Hoffman, J. M., & Kilts, C. D. (2003). Ecstasy and agony: Activation of the human amygdala in positive and negative emotion. *Psychological Science, 13,* 135–141.

Hamilton, D. L., & Sherman, J. W. (1994). Stereotypes. In R. S. Wyer, Jr., & T. K. Srull (Eds.), *Handbook of social cognition* (2nd ed., Vol. 2, pp. 1–68). Hillsdale, NJ: Lawrence Erlbaum Associates.

Hamilton, K. E., & Dobson, K. S. (2002). Cognitive therapy of depression: Pretreatment patient predictors of outcome. *Clinical Psychology Review, 22,* 875–893.

Hancock, L. (1996, March 18). Mother's little helper. *Newsweek,* pp. 51–56.

Haney, M., Castanon, N., Cador, M., Le-Moal, M., et al. (1994). Cocaine sensitivity in Roman high- and low-avoidance rats is modulated by sex and gonadal hormone status. *Brain Research, 645,* 179–185.

Harackiewicz, J. M., & Elliot, A. J. (1993). Achievement goals and intrinsic motivation. *Journal of Personality and Social Psychology, 65,* 904–915.

Hardy, S. A., & Raffaelli, M. (2003). Adolescent religiosity and sexuality: An investigation of reciprocal influences. *Journal of Adolescence, 26,* 731–739.

Hariri, A. R., Mattay, V. S., Tessitore, A., Kolachana, B., Fera, F., Goldman, D., & Egan, M. F. (2002). Serotonin transporter genetic variation and the response of the human amydgala. *Science 297,* 400–403.

Harlow, H. F., & Harlow, M. K. (1966). Learning to love. *American Scientist, 54,* 244–272.

Harlow, H. F., & Zimmermann, R. R. (1959). Affectional responses in the infant monkey. *Science, 130,* 421–432.

Harlow, H. F., Harlow, M. K., & Meyer, D. R. (1950). Learning motivated by a manipulation drive. *Journal of Experimental Psychology, 40,* 228–234.

Harmon-Jones, E., & Sigelman, J. (2001). State anger and prefrontal brain activity: Evidence that insult-related relative left-prefrontal activation is associated with experienced anger and aggression. *Journal of Personality and Social Psychology, 80,* 797–803.

Harris, G. (2004, June 2) . Antidepressants seen as effective for adolescents. *New York Times,* pp. A1, A16.

Harris, M. B., & Knight-Bohnhoff, B. K. (1996). Gender and aggression: II. Personal aggressiveness. *Sex-Roles, 35,* 27–42.

Harrison, Y., & Horne, J. A. (2000). The impact of sleep deprivation on decision making: A review. *Journal of Experimental Psychology: Applied, 6,* 236–249.

Harrop, C., & Trower, P. (2001). Why does schizophrenia develop at late adolescence? *Clinical Psychology Review, 20,* 823–851, 241–266.

Harshman, R. A., & Paivio, A. (1987). Paradoxical sex differences in self-reported imagery. *Canadian Journal of Psychology, 41,* 287–302.

Hartshorn, K., & Rovee-Collier, C. (1997). Infant learning and long-term memory at 6 months: A confirming analysis. *Developmental Psychobiology, 30,* 71–85.

Hassert, D. L., Miyashita, T., & Williams, C. L. (2004). The effects of peripheral vagal nerve stimulation at a memory-modulating intensity on norepinephrine output in the basolateral amygdala. *Behavioral Neuroscience, 118,* 79–88.

Hasty, P., Campisi, J., Hoeijmakers, J., van Steeg, H., & Vijg, J. (2003). Aging and genome maintenance: Lessons from the mouse? *Science, 299,* 1355–1359.

Hatfield, E., & Sprecher, S. (1986). Measuring passionate love in intimate relationships. *Journal of Adolescence, 9,* 383–410.

Häusser, M., Spruston, N., & Stuart, G. J. (2000). Diversity and dynamics of dendritic signaling. *Science, 290,* 739–744.

Häusser, M., Spruston, N., & Stuart, G. J. (2000). Diversity and dynamics of dendritic signaling. *Science, 290,* 739–744.

Haydel, M. J., Preston, C. A., Mills, T. J., Luber, S., Blaudeau, E., & Deblieux, P. M. (2000). Indications for computed tomography in patients with minor head injury. *New England Journal of Medicine, 343,* 100–105.

Hays, K. F. (2002, Fall). Giving sport psychology away. *Exercise and Sport Psychology Newsletter, 16,* pp. 1, 2.

Headache coping strategies depend on the cause. (2000, August 14). *Cable News Network.* Retrieved August 20, 2000, from http://www.cnn.com/2000/HEALTH/08/14/headache.redux/index.html.

Health groups directly link media to child violence. (2000, July 26). *Cable News Network.* Retrieved July 27, 2000, from http://www. cnn.com/2000.

Healthy habits: Why bother? (1995, May). *Consumer Reports on Health, 7*(5), 49–51.

Hebb, D. O. (1955). Drive and the CNS (central nervous system). *Psychological Review, 62,* 243–254.

Hedges, L. V., & Nowell, A. (1995, July). Sex differences in mental test scores, variability, and numbers of high-scoring individuals. *Science, 269,* 41–45.

Heider, E. (1958). *The psychology of interpersonal relations.* New York: Wiley.

Heider, E., Rosch, E., & Olivier, D. C. (1972). The structure of the color space in naming and memory for two languages. *Cognitive Psychology, 3,* 337–354.

Heimberg, R. G., Turk, C. L., & Mennin, D. S. (Eds.). (2004). *Generalized anxiety disorde*r. New York: Guilford.

Heine, S. J., Kitayama, S., Lehman, D. R., Takata, T., Ide, E., Leung, C., & Matsumoto, H. (2001). Divergent consequences of success and failure in Japan and North America: An investigation of self-improving motivations and malleable selves. *Journal of Personality and Social Psychology, 81,* 599–615.

Hekimi, S., & Guarente, L. (2003). Genetics and the specificity of the aging process. *Science, 299,* 1351–1354.

Hellige, J. B. (1993). *Hemispheric asymmetry: What's right and what's left.* Cambridge, MA: Harvard University Press.

Hellmich, N. (2003, April 24). Being overweight linked to dying of cancer. *USA Today,* p. 1A.

Helms, J. E. (1992). Why is there no study of culture equivalence in standardized cognitive ability testing? *American Psychologist, 47,* 1083–1101.

Helmuth, L. (2001, January 26). Glia tell neurons to build synapses. *Science, 291,* 569–570.

Henderlong, J., & Lepper, M. R. (2002). The effects of praise on children's intrinsic motivation: A review and synthesis. *Psychological Bulletin, 128,* 774–795.

Hepper, P. G., Shahidullah, S., & White, R. (1990). Origins of fetal handedness. *Nature, 347,* 431.

Hergenhahn, B. R. (1997). *An introduction to the history of psychology* (3rd ed.). Pacific Grover, CA: Brooks/Cole Publishing Co.

Hergovich, A. (2004). The effect of pseudo-psychic demonstrations as dependent on belief in paranormal phenomena and suggestibility. *Personality and Individual Differences, 36,* 365–380.

Herrmann, D. J., & Palmisano, M. (1992). The facilitation of memory performance. In M. Gruneberg & P. Morris (Eds.), *Aspects of memory: 2nd ed.: Vol. 1. The practical aspects* (pp. 147–167). London: Routledge.

Hertel, P. T. (1996). Practical aspects of emotion and memory. In D. Herrmann, C. McEvoy, C. Hertzog, P. Hertel, & M. K. Johnson (Eds.), *Basic and applied memory research: Theory in context* (Vol. 1, pp. 317–336). Mahwah, NJ: Lawrence Erlbaum Associates.

Hertzog, C., & Dunlosky, J. (1996). The aging of practical memory: An overview. In D. Herrmann et al. (Eds.), *Basic and applied memory research: Theory in context* (Vol. 1., pp. 337–358). Mahwah, NJ: Lawrence Erlbaum Associates.

Herzog, A. R., Franks, M. M., Markus, H. R., & Holmberg, D. (1998). Activities and well-being in older age: Effects of self-concept and educational attainment. *Psychology and Aging, 13,* 179–185.

Hestick, H., Perrino, S. C., Rhodes, W. A., & Sydnor, K. D. (2001). Trial and lifetime smoking risks among African American college students. *Journal of American College Health, 49,* 213–219.

Hewstone, M., Rubin, M., & Willis, H. (2002). Intergroup bias. *Annual Review of Psychology, 53,* 575–604.

Hilgard, E. R. (1977). *Divided consciousness: Multiple controls in human thought and action.* New York: Wiley.

Hilgard, E. R. (1994). Neodissociation theory. In S. Lynn & J. W. Rhue (Eds.), *Dissociation: Clinical and theoretical perspectives.* New York: Guilford Press.

Hill, C. E., & Nakayama, E. Y. (2000). Client-centered therapy: Where has it been and where is it going? A comment on Hathaway (1948). *Journal of Clinical Psychology, 56,* 861–873.

Hill, J. O., Wyatt, H. R., Reed, G. W., & Peters, J. C. (2003). Obesity and the environment: Where do we go from here? [Editorial]. *Science, 299,* 853–855.

Hill, K. G., White, H. R., Chung, I. J., Hawkins, J. D., & Catalano, R. F. (2000). Early adult outcomes of adolescent binge drinking: Person-and variable-centered analyses of binge drinking trajectories. *Alcohol: Clinical and Experimental Research, 24,* 892–901.

Hilton, J. L., & von Hippel, W. (1996). Stereotypes. In J. T. Spence, J. M. Darley, & D. J. Foss (Eds.), *Annual Review of Psychology* (Vol. 47, pp. 237–271). Palo Alto, CA: Annual Reviews.

Hilts, P. J. (2001, May 23). Web sites inconsistent on health, study finds. *New York Times,* p. A19.

Hirosumi, J., Tuncman, G., Chang, L., Görgün, C. Z., Uysal, T., Maeda,K., et al. (2002). A central role for JNK in obesity and insulin resistance. *Nature, 420,* 333–336.

Hobson, J. A. (1988). *The dreaming brain.* New York: Basic Books.

Hobson, J. A., & McCarley, R. W. (1977). The brain as a dream state generator: An activation-synthesis hypothesis of the dream process. *American Journal of Psychiatry, 134,* 1335–1348.

Hoehn-Saric, R., Ninan, P., Black, D. W., Stahl, S., Greist, J. H., Lydiard, B., et al. (2000). Multicenter double-blind comparison of sertraline and desipramine for concurrent obsessive-compulsive and major depressive disorders. *Archives of General Psychiatry, 57,* 76–82.

Hoeksema van Orden, C. Y. D., Gaillard, A. W. K., & Buunk, B. P. (1998). Social loafing under fatigue. *Journal of Personality and Social Psychology, 75,* 1179–1190.

Hoelscher, C. (Ed.). (2001). *Neuronal mechanisms of memory formation: Concepts of long-term potentiation and beyond.* New York: Cambridge University Press.

Hoffman, D. D. (1999). *Visual intelligence.* New York: Norton.

Hoffman, R. R., Sherrick, M. F., & Warm, J. S. (Eds.). (1998). *Viewing psychology as a whole: The integrative science of William N. Dember.* Washington, DC: American Psychological Association.

Hoffman, S. G. (2000a). Self-focused attention before and after treatment of social phobia. *Behavior Research and Therapy, 38,* 717–725.

Hoffman, S. G. (2000b). Treatment of social phobia: Potential mediators and moderators. *Clinical Psychology: Science and Practice, 7*(1), 3–16.

Hollis, K. L. (1997). Contemporary research on Pavlovian conditioning: A "new" functional analysis. *American Psychologist, 52,* 956–965.

Holloway, J. D. (2004a, June). Gaining prescriptive knowledge. *Monitor on Psychology,* pp. 22–24.

Holloway, J. D. (2004b, May). Unhealthy behaviors cause approximately half of U.S. deaths. *Monitor on Psychology, 35,* p. 15.

Holt, C. L., Clark, E. M., & Kreuter, M. W. (2001). Weight locus of control and weight-related attitudes and behaviors in an overweight population. *Addictive Behaviors, 26,* 329–340.

Horn, J. (2001). Raymond Bernard Cattell (1905–1998). *American Psychologist, 56,* 71–72.

Horn, J. L., & Noll, J. (1997). Human cognitive capabilities: Gf-Gc theory. In D. P. Flanagan, J. L. Genshaft, P. L., & Harrison (Eds.), *Contemporary intellectual assessment: Theories, tests, and issues* (pp. 53–91). New York: Guilford Press.

Hothersall, D. (1995). *History of psychology* (3rd ed.) New York: McGraw-Hill.

House, R. (1977). A 1976 theory of charismatic leadership. In J. G. Hunt & L. L. Larson (Eds.), *Leadership: The cutting edge* (pp. 194–205). Carbondale, IL: Southern Illinois University Press.

Houston, D. M., & Jusczyk, P. W. (2003). Infants' long-term memory for the sound patterns of words and voices. *Journal of Experimental Psychology: Human Perception and Performance, 29,* 1143–1154.

How to protect your memory as you age. (2001, October). *Tufts University Health and Nutrition Letter, 19*(8), pp. 1, 4–5.

Hrobjartsson, A., & Gotzsche, P. C. (2001). Is the placebo powerless? An analysis of clinical trials comparing placebo with no treatment. *New England Journal of Medicine, 344,* 1594–602.

Hu, F. B., Stampfer, M. J., Manson, J. E., Grodstein, F., Colditz, G. A., Speizer, F. E., et al. (2000). Trends in the incidence of coronary heart disease and changes in diet and lifestyle in women. *New England Journal of Medicine, 343,* 530–537.

Huang, L. H. (1994). An integrative approach to clinical assessment and intervention with Asian-American adolescents. *Journal of Clinical Child Psychology, 23,* 21–31.

Hubel, D. H. (1988). *Eye, brain, and vision.* New York: Scientific American Library.

Hubel, D. H., & Wiesel, T. N. (1979). Brain mechanisms of vision. *Scientific American, 241,* 130–144.

Hudson, J. I., Mangweth, B., Pope, Jr., H. G., De Col, C., Hausmann, A., Gutweniger, S., et al. (2003). Family study of affective spectrum disorder. *Archives of General Psychiatry, 60,* 170–177.

Huesmann, L. R., Moise-Titus, J., Podolski, C.-L., & Eron, L. D. (2003). Longitudinal relations between children's exposure to TV violence and their aggressive and violent behavior in young adulthood: 1977–1992. *Developmental Psychology, 39,* 201–221.

Hull, C. L. (1943). *Principles of behavior.* New York: Appleton-Century-Crofts.

Hull, C. L. (1952). *A behavior system.* New Haven: Yale University Press.

Hull, J. G., Slone, L. B., Meteyer, K. B., & Matthews, A. R. (2002). The nonconsciousness of self-consciousness. *Journal of Personality and Social Psychology, 83,* 406–424.

Hulme, C., Newton, P., Cowan, N., Stuart, G., & Brown, G. (1999). Think before you speak: Pauses, memory search, and trace redisintegration processes in verbal memory span. *Journal of Experimental Psychology: Learning, Memory and Cognition, 25,* 447–463.

Human genome sequence completed. (2003, April 14). Scientists release final version of genetic blueprint. *MSNBC.* Retrieved April 15, 2003, from *http://www.msnbc.com/news/899806.asp.*

Hunsley, J., & Bailey, J. M. (2001). Whither the Rorschach? An analysis of the evidence. *Psychological Assessment, 13,* 472–485.

Hunt, M. (1993). *The story of psychology.* New York: Anchor Books.

Hyde, J. S., & Linn, M. C. (1988). Gender differences in verbal ability: A meta-analysis. *Psychological Bulletin, 104,* 53–69.

Iacono, W. G., & Lykken, D. T. (1997). The validity of the lie detector: Two surveys of scientific opinion. *Journal of Applied Psychology, 82,* 426–433.

Ilardi, S. S., & Craighead, W. E. (1994). The role of nonspecific factors in cognitive-behavior therapy for depression. *Clinical Psychology: Science and Practice, 1,* 138–156.

Inglehart, R., & Klingemann, H.-D. (2000). Genes, culture, democracy, and happiness. In E. Diener & E. M. Suh (Eds.), *Culture and subjective well-being* (pp. 165–183). Cambridge, MA: MIT Press.

Ingram, R. E., & Siegle, G. J. (2001). Cognition and clinical science: From revolution to evolution. In K. S. Dobson (Ed.), *Handbook of cognitive-behavioral therapies* (2nd ed., pp. 111–137). New York: Guilford Press.

Instant recall. (2000, February 14). *Newsweek,* p. 8.

Ioannidis, J. P. A., Haidich, A. B., Pappa, M., Pantazis, N., Kokori, S. I., Tektonidou, M. G., et al. (2001). Comparison of evidence of treatment effects in randomized and nonrandomized studies. *Journal of the American Medical Association, 286,* 821–830.

Iribarren, C., Sidney, S., Bild, D. E., Liu, K. Markovitz, J. H., Roseman, J. M., & Matthews, K. (2000). Association of hostility with coronary artery calcification in young adults: The CARDIA study. Coronary Artery Risk Development in Young Adults. *Journal of the American Medical Association, 283,* 2546–2551.

Irle, E., Exner, C., Thielen, K., Weniger, G., & Ruether, E. (1998). Obsessive-compulsive disorder and ventromedial frontal lesions: Clinical and neuropsychological findings. *American Journal of Psychiatry, 155,* 255–263.

Ironson, G., Wynings, C., Schneiderman, N., Baum, A., Rodriguez, M., Greenwood, D., et al. (1997). Posttraumatic stress symptoms, intrusive thoughts, loss, and immune function after Hurricane Andrew. *Psychosomatic Medicine, 59,* 128–141.

Irwin, C. E., Jr., Burg, S. J., & Cart, C. U. (2002). America's adolescents: Where have we been, where are we going? *Journal of Adolescent Health, 31,* 91–121

Isay, R. A. (1990). Psychoanalytic theory and the therapy of gay men. In D. P. McWhirter, S. A. Saers, & J. M. Reinisch (Eds.), *Homosexuality/Heterosexuality: Concepts of sexual orientation* (pp. 283–303). New York: Oxford University Press.

Ito, T. A., Miller, N., & Pollock, V. E. (1996). Alcohol and aggression: A meta-analysis on the moderating effects of inhibitory cues, triggering events, and self-focused attention. *Psychological Bulletin, 120,* 60–82.

Iversen, L. L. (2000). The science of marijuana. New York: Oxford University Press.

Iwamasa, G. Y., Sorocco, K. H., & Koonce, D. A. (2002). Ethnicity and clinical psychology: A content analysis of the literature. *Clinical Psychology Review, 22,* 931–944.

Izard, C. E. (1990a). Facial expression and the regulation of emotions. *Journal of Personality and Social Psychology, 58,* 487–498.

Izard, C. E. (1990b). The substrates and functions of emotion feelings: William James and current emotion theory. *Personality and Social Psychology Bulletin, 16,* 626–635.

Jablensky, A., Sartorius, N., Ernberg, G., & Anker, M. (1992). Schizophrenia: Manifestations, incidence and course in different cultures: A World Health Organization ten-country study [Monograph Suppl.]. *Psychological Medicine, 20,* 1–97.

Jackson, L A., Ervin, K. S., Gardner, P. D., & Schmitt, N. (2001). The racial digital divide: Motivational, affective and cognitive correlates of Internet use. *Journal of Applied Social Psychology, 31,* 2019–2046.

Jackson, L. A., Ervin, K. S., Gardner, P. D., & Schmitt, N. (2001). Gender and the Internet: Women communicating and men searching. *Sex Roles, 44,* 363–379.

Jacobi, C., Hayward, C., de Zwaan, M., Kraemer, H. C., & Agras, W. S. (2004). Coming to terms with risk factors for eating disorders: Application of risk terminology and suggestions for a general taxonomy. *Psychological Bulletin, 130,* 19–65.

Jacobs, B. L. (2004). Depression: The brain finally gets into the act. *Current Directions in Psychological Science, 13,* 103–106.

Jacobs, L .F., & Schenk, F. (2003). Unpacking the cognitive map: The parallel map theory of hippocampal function. *Psychological Review, 110*, 285–315.

Jacobs, M. K., Christensen, A., Snibbe, J. R., Dolezal-Wood, S., Huber, A., & Polterok, A. (2001). A comparison of computer-based versus traditional individual psychotherapy. *Professional Psychology: Research and Practice, 32*, 92–96.

Jacobs, W., Newman, G. H., & Burns, J. C. (2001). The Homeless Assessment Program: A service-training model for providing disability evaluations for homeless, mentally ill individuals. *Professional Psychology: Research and Practice, 32*, 319–323.

Jaffee, S., & Hyde, J. S. (2000). Gender differences in moral orientation: A meta-analysis. *Psychological Bulletin, 126*, 703–726.

Jahnke, C. J., Nowaczyk, R. H. (1998). *Cognition.* Upper Saddle River, NJ: Prentice-Hall.

James, L. E., & MacKay, D. G. (2001). H.M., word knowledge and aging: Support for a new theory of long-term retrograde amnesia. *Psychological Science, 12*, 485–492.

James, W. (1890/1970). *The principles of psychology* (Vol. 1). New York: Holt.

Janis, I. L. (1982). *Groupthink* (2nd ed.). Boston: Houghton Mifflin.

Janis, I. L. (1997). Groupthink. In R. P. Vecchio (Ed.), *Leadership: Understanding the dynamics of power and influence in organizations* (pp. 163–176). Notre Dame: University of Notre Dame Press.

Januzzi, J., & DeSanctis, R. (1999). Looking to the brain to save the heart. *Cerebrum, 1*, 31–43.

Jemmott, J. B., III, Borysenko, J. Z., Borysenko, M., McClelland, D. C., Chapman, R., et al. (1983, June 25). Academic stress, power motivation, and decrease in secretion rate of salivary secretory immunoglobulin A. *Lancet*, 1400–1402.

Jenkins, L., Myerson, J., Joerding, J. A., & Hale, S. (2000). Converging evidence that visuospatial cognition is more age-sensitive than verbal cognition. *Psychology and Aging, 15*, 157–175.

Jennings, C. (1999, October 19). The neurobiology of morals. *Nature News Service.* Retrieved December 23, 1999, from http://www.nature.com/nsu/991021/991021-6.html.

Jensen, A. R. (2002). Psychometric g: Definition and substantiation. In R. J. Sternberg & E. L. Grigorenko (Eds.), *The general factor of intelligence: How general is it?* (pp. 39–53). Mahwah, NJ: Lawrence Erlbaum Associates.

Jevning, R., Wallace, R. K., & Beidebach, M. (1992). The physiology of meditation: A review: A wakeful hypometabolic integrated response. *Neuroscience and Biobehavioral Reviews, 16*, 415–424.

Johnson, D. F. (2000). Cultivating the field of psychology: Psychological journals at the turn of the century and beyond. *American Psychologist, 55*, 1144–1147.

Johnson, G. (1994, October 23). Learning just how little is known about the brain. *New York Times*, p. E5.

Johnson, G. (1999, October 24). How much give can the brain take? *New York Times Week in Review*, pp. 1, 6.

Johnson, G. (2000, October 15). The Nobels: Dazzled by the digital light. *New York Times Week in Review*, p. 4.

Johnson, I. M. (1993). Complementary medicine: Acupuncture has weak scientific foundations. *British Medical Journal, 307*, 624–627.

Johnson, M. H. (1997). The neural basis of cognitive development. In W. Damon (Editor-in-Chief), D. Kuhn & R. Siegler (Vol. Eds.), *Handbook of child psychology, 5th ed.: Vol. 2. Cognition, perception, and language* (pp. 1–50). New York: John Wiley & Sons.

Johnson, R. E., Chutuape, M. A., Strain, E. C., Walsh, S. L., Stitzer, M. L., & Bigelow, G. E. (2000). A comparison of levomethadyl acetate, buprenorphine, and methadone for opioid dependence. *New England Journal of Medicine, 343*, 1290–1297.

Johnson, W., McGue, M., Krueger, R. J., & Bouchard, T. J., Jr. (2004). Marriage and personality: A genetic analysis. *Journal of Personality and Social Psychology, 86*, 285–294.

Johnston-Brooks, C. H., Lewis, M. A., & Garg, S. (2002). Self-efficacy impacts self-care and HbA1c in young adults with Type I diabetes. *Psychosomatic Medicine, 64*, 43–51.

Johnston, L. D., O'Malley, P. M., & Bachman, J. G. (1996). *National survey results on drug use from The Monitoring the Future Study, 1975–1995: Vol. I. Secondary School Students.* Washington, DC: U. S. Department of Health and Human Services, Public Health Service, National Institutes of Health: National Institute on Drug Abuse.

Jones, E. E. (1990). *Interpersonal perception.* New York: W. H. Freeman.

Jones, E. E. (1998). Major developments in five decades of social psychology. In D. T. Gilbert, S. T. Fiske, & G. Lindzey (Eds.), *The handbook of social psychology* (4th ed., Vol. 1, pp. 1–57). Boston: McGraw-Hill.

Jones, E. E., & Nisbett, R. E. (1971). The actor and the observer: Divergent perceptions of the causes of behavior. In E. E. Jones, D. E. Kanouse, H. H. Kelley, R. E. Nisbett, S. Valins, & B. Weiner (Eds.), *Attribution: Perceiving the causes of behavior.* Morristown, NJ: General Learning Press.

Jones, G. (2003). Testing two cognitive theories of insight. *Journal of Experimental Psychology: Learning, Memory, and Cognition, 29*, 1017–1027.

Jones, G. V., & Martin, M. (2001). Confirming the X-linked handedness gene as recessive, not additive: Reply to Corballis (2001). *Psychological Review, 108*, 811–813.

Jones, S. L., & Yarhouse, M. A. (2001). *Homosexuality: The use of scientific research in the Church's moral debate.* Downers Grove, IL: InterVarsity Press.

Josefsson, A. M., Magnusson, P. K., Ylitalo, N., Sorensen, P., Qwarforth-Tubbin, P., Andersen, P. K., et al. (2000). Viral load of human papilloma virus 16 as a determinant for development of cervical carcinoma in situ: A nested case-control study. *The Lancet, 355*, 2189–2193.

Joule, R. V., Gouilloux, F., Weber, F. (1989). The lure: A new compliance procedure. *Journal of Social Psychology, 129*, 741–749.

Judd, C. M., & Park, B. (1993). Definition and assessment of accuracy in social stereotypes. *Psychological Review, 100*, 109–128.

Jussim, L., & Eccles, J. S. (1992). Teacher expectations II: Construction and reflection of student achievement. *Journal of Personality and Social Psychology, 63*, 947–961.

Just, N., Abramson, L. Y., & Alloy, L. B. (2001). Remitted depression studies as tests of the cognitive vulnerability hypotheses of depression onset. A critique and conceptual analysis. *Clinical Psychology Review, 21*, 63–83.

Kabat-Zinn, J. (1993). Mindfulness meditation: Health benefits of an ancient Buddhist practice. In D. Goleman & J. Gurin (Eds.), *Mind/body medicine: How to use your mind for better health.* Yonkers, NY: Consumer Reports Books.

Kabat-Zinn, J. (2003). Mindfulness-based interventions in context: Past, present, and future. *Clinical Psychology: Science and Practice, 10*, 144–156.

Kagan, J. (1997). Biology and the child. In W. Damon (Editor-in-Chief) & N. Eisenberg (Vol. Ed.), *Handbook of child psychology: 5th ed., Vol. 3. Social, emotional, and personality development* (pp. 177–236). New York: John Wiley & Sons.

Kagan, J. (2003). Biology, context, and developmental inquiry. *Annual Review of Psychology 54*, 1–23.

Kahler, C. W., Read, J. P., Wood, M. D., & Palfai, T. P. (2003). Social environmental selection as a mediator of gender, ethnic, and personality effects on college student drinking. *Psychology of Addictive Behaviors, 17*, 226–234.

Kahn, M. W. (1982). Cultural clash and psychopathology in three aboriginal cultures. *Academic Psychology Bulletin, 4*, 553–561.

Kahneman, D. (1991). Judgment and decision making: A personal view. *Psychological Science, 2*, 142–145.

Kahneman, D., & Tversky, A. (1973). On the psychology of prediction. *Psychological Review, 80*, 237–251.

Kalb, C. (1999, November 8). What dreams are made of. *Newsweek*, p. 77.

Kalb, C. (2001a, February 12). Can this pill stop you from hitting the bottle? *Newsweek*, pp. 48–51.

Kalb, C. (2001b, August 20). Overexposed. *Newsweek*, pp. 34–38.

Kalb, C. (2001c, January 22). Seeing a virtual shrink. *Newsweek*, pp. 54–56.

Kalechstein, A. D., & Nowicki, S., Jr. (1997). A meta-analytic examination of the relationship between control expectancies and academic achievement: An 11-year follow-up. *Genetic, Social, and General Psychology Monographs, 123*, 27–56.

Kamei, Y., Ishizuka, Y., Usui, A., Okado, T., et al. (1994). Bright light improves self-evaluation for day-time sleep in nurses after night work. *Journal of Mental Health, 40*, 49–54.

Kamphuis, J. H., Emmelkamp, P. M. G., & Krijn, M. U. (2002). Specific phobia. In M. Hersen (Ed.), *Clinical behavior therapy: Adults and children* (pp. 75–89). New York: John Wiley & Sons.

Kandel, D. B. (2003). Does marijuana use cause the use of other drugs? *Journal of the American Medical Association, 289*, 482–483.

Kandel, D. B. (Ed.). (2002). *Stages and pathways of drug involvement: Examining the gateway hypothesis.* Cambridge, England: Cambridge University Press.

Kandel, E. R. (1995). Cellular mechanisms of learning and memory: Synaptic integration. In E. R. Kandel, J. H., Schwartz, & T. M. Jessel (Eds.), *Essentials of neural science and behavior.* Norwalk, CT: Appleton & Lange.

Kandel, E. R., & Hawkins, R. D. (1993). The biological basis of learning and individuality. In *Mind and brain: Readings from Scientific American Magazine* (pp. 40–53). New York: W. H. Freeman & Co.

Kane, J. M. (1996). Drug therapy: Schizophrenia. *New England Journal of Medicine, 334*, 34–41.

Kane, J. M., Marder, S. R., Schooler, N. R., Wirshing, W. C., Umbricht, D., Baker, R. W., et al. (2001). Clozapine and haloperidol in moderately refractory schizophrenia: A 6-month randomized and double-blind comparison. *Archives of General Psychiatry, 58,* 965–972.

Kanner, A. D., Coyne, J. C., Schaefer, C., & Lazarus, R. S. (1981). Comparison of two modes of stress measurement: Daily hassles and uplifts versus major life events. *Journal of Behavioral Medicine, 4,* 1–39.

Kantor, M. (1998). *Homophobia: Description, development and dynamics of gay bashing.* Westport, CT: Praeger.

Kantrowitz, B., & Springen, K. (2003, September 22). Why sleep matters. *Newsweek,* pp. 75–77.

Kantrowitz, B., & Wingert, P. (1999, October 18). The truth about teens. *Newsweek,* pp. 62–72.

Kaplan, R. M. (2000). Two pathways to prevention. *American Psychologist, 55,* 382–396.

Kaptchuk, R., Eisenberg, D., & Komaroff, A. (2002, December 2). Finding out what works. *Newsweek,* p. 73.

Kareev, Y. (2000). Seven (indeed, plus or minus two) and the detection of correlations. *Psychological Review, 107,* 397–402.

Karoly, P., & Ruehlman, L. S. (1996). Motivational implications of pain. *Health Psychology, 15,* 383–390.

Kasai, K., et al. (2003). Gray matter volume in patients with first-episode schizophrenia. *American Journal of Psychiatry, 160,* 156–164.

Kasai, K., Shenton, M. E., Salisbury, D. F., Hirayasu, Y., Lee, C.-U., Ciszewski, A. A., et al. (2003). Gray matter volume in patients with first-episode schizophrenia. *American Journal of Psychiatry, 160,* 156–164.

Kaslow, N. J., Thompson, M. P., Okun, A., Price, A., Young, S., Bender, M., et al. (2002). Risk and protective factors for suicidal behavior in abused African American women. *Journal of Consulting and Clinical Psychology, 70,* 311–319.

Kauer, J. A. (2003). Addictive drugs and stress trigger a common change at VTA synapses. *Neuron, 37,* 549–550.

Kawakami, K., Dovidio, J. F., Moll, J., Hermsen, S., & Russin, A. (2000). Just say no (to stereotyping): Effects of training in the negation of stereotypic associations on stereotype activation. *Journal of Personality and Social Psychology, 78,* 871–888.

Kawas, C. H., & Brookmeyer, R. (2001). Aging and the public health effects of dementia [Editorial]. *New England Journal of Medicine, 344,* 1160–1161.

Kazdin, A. E. (1993). Adolescent mental health. *American Psychologist, 48,* 127–141.

Kazdin, A. E. (1997). Parent management training: Evidence, outcomes, and issues. *Journal of the American Academy of Child and Adolescent Psychiatry, 36,* 1349–1356.

Keating, C. F., Randall, D., Kendrick, T., & Gutshall, K. (2003). Do babyfaced adults receive more help? The (cross-cultural) case of the lost resume. *Journal of Nonverbal Behavior, 27,* 89–109.

Keesey R. E., & Powley, T. L. (1986). The regulation of body weight. *Annual Review of Psychology, 37,* 109–133.

Keith, J. B., McCreary, C., Collins, K., Smith, C. P., et al. (1991). Sexual activity and contraceptive use among low-income urban Black adolescent females. *Adolescence, 26,* 769–785.

Keller, S. N., & Brown, J. D. (2002). Media interventions to promote responsible sexual behavior. *Journal of Sex Research, 39,* 1–6.

Kelley, B. B. (1997, May/June). Running on empty. *Health,* pp. 64–68.

Kellman, P. J., & Banks, M. S. (1997). Infant visual perception. In W. Damon (Editor-in-Chief), D. Kuhn & R. Siegler (Vol. Eds.), *Handbook of child psychology: 5th ed., Vol. 2. Cognition, perception and language* (pp. 103–146). New York: John Wiley & Sons.

Kemeny, M. E. (2003). The psychobiology of stress. *Current Directions in Psychological Science, 12,* 124–129.

Kendell, R., & Jablensky, A. (2003). Distinguishing between the validity and utility of psychiatric diagnoses. *American Journal of Psychiatry, 160,* 4–12.

Kendler, K. S. (2001). A psychiatric dialogue on the mind-body problem. *American Journal of Psychiatry, 158,* 989–1000.

Kendler, K. S., Bulik, C. M., Silberg, J., Hettema, J. M., Myers, J., & Prescott, C. A. (2000b). Childhood sexual abuse and adult psychiatric and substance use disorders in women: An epidemiological and cotwin control analysis. *Archives of General Psychiatry, 57,* 953–959.

Kendler, K. S., Jacobson, K. C., Prescott, C. A., & Neale, M. C. (2003). Specificity of genetic and environmental risk factors for use and abuse/ dependence of cannabis, cocaine, hallucinogens, sedatives, stimulants, and opiates in male twins. *American Journal of Psychiatry, 160,* 687–695.

Kendler, K. S., Kuhn, J., & Prescott, C. A. (2004). The interrelationship of neuroticism, sex, and stressful life events in the prediction of episodes of major depression. *American Journal of Psychiatry, 161,* 631–636.

Kendler, K. S., Myers, J. M., & Neale, M. C. (2000). A multidimensional twin study of mental health in women. *American Journal of Psychiatry, 157,* 506–513.

Kendler, K. S., Myers, J., Prescott, C. A., & Neale, M. C. (2001). The genetic epidemiology of irrational fears and phobias in men. *Archives of General Psychiatry, 58,* 257–265.

Kendler, K. S., Thornton, L. M., Gilman, S. E., & Kessler, R. C. (2000a). Sexual orientation in a U.S. national sample of twin and nontwin sibling pairs. *American Journal of Psychiatry, 157,* 1843–1846.

Kennedy, M. B. (2000). Signal-processing machines at the postsynaptic density. *Science, 290,* 750–754.

Kenrick, D. T., Li, N. P., & Butner, J. (2003). Dynamical evolutionary psychology: Individual decision rules and emergent social norms. *Psychological Review, 110,* 3–28.

Kerr, N. L., & Tindale, R. S. (2004). Group performance and decision making. *Annual Review of Psychology, 55,* 623–655.

Kessler, D. A., Natanblut, S. L., Wikenfeld, J. P., Lorraine, C. C., Mayl, S. L., Bernstein, I. B., et al. (1997). Nicotine addiction: A pediatric disease. *Journal of Pediatrics, 130,* 518–524.

Kessler, R. C. (1994). The National Comorbidity Survey: Preliminary results and future directions. *International Journal of Methods in Psychiatric Research, 4,* 114.1–114.13.

Kessler, R. C., Berglund, P., Demler, O., Jin, R., Koretz, D., Merikangas, K. R., et al. (2003). The epidemiology of major depressive disorder: Results from the national Comorbidity Survey Replication (NCS-R). *Journal of the American Medical Association, 289,* 3095–3105.

Kessler, R. C., Borges, G., & Walters, E. E. (1999). Prevalence of and risk factors for lifetime suicide attempts in the National Comorbidity Survey. *Archives of General Psychiatry, 56,* 617–626.

Kessler, R. C., McGonagle, K. A., Zhao, S., & Nelson, C. B. (1994). Lifetime and 12–month prevalence of DSM-III-R psychiatric disorders in the United States: Results from the National Comorbidity Survey. *Archives of General Psychiatry, 51,* 8–19.

Kessler, R., & Dane, J. R. (1996). Psychological and hypnotic preparation for anesthesia and surgery: An individual differences perspective. *International Journal of Clinical and Experimental Hypnosis, 44*(3), 189–207.

Kiecolt-Glaser, J. K., Bane, C., Glaser, R., & Malarkey, W. B. (2003b). Love, marriage, and divorce: Newlyweds' stress hormones foreshadow relationship changes. *Journal of Consulting and Clinical Psychology, 71,* 176–188.

Kiecolt-Glaser, J. K., Marucha, P. T., Atkinson, C., & Glaser, R. (2001). Hypnosis as a modulator of cellular immune dysregulation during acute stress. *Journal of Consulting and Clinical Psychology, 69,* 674–682.

Kiecolt-Glaser, J. K., Marucha, P. T., Malarkey, W. B., Mercado, A. M., & Glaser, R. (1995). Slowing of wound healing by psychological stress. *Lancet, 346,* 1194–1196.

Kiecolt-Glaser, J. K., McGuire, L., Robles, T. F., & Glaser, R. (2002). Emotions, morbidity, and mortality: New perspectives from psychoneuroimmunology. *Annual Review of Psychology, 53,* 83–107.

Kiecolt-Glaser, J. K., Preacher, K. J., MacCallum, R. C., Atkinson, C., Malarkey, W. B., & Glaser, R. (2003a). Chronic stress and age-related increases in the proinflammatory cytokine IL-6. *Proceedings of the National Academy of Sciences, 100*(15), 9090–9095.

Kiecolt-Glaser, J. K., Speicher, C. E., Holliday, J. E., & Glaser, R. (1984). Stress and the transformation of lymphocytes in Epstein-Barr virus. *Journal of Behavioral Medicine, 7,* 1–12.

Kiefer, F., Jahn, H., Tarnaske, T., Helwig, H., Briken, P., Holzbach, R., et al. (2003). Comparing and combining naltrexone and acamprosate in relapse prevention of alcoholism: A double-blind, placebo-controlled study. *Archives of General Psychiatry, 60,* 92–99.

Kiesler, D. J. (1999). *Beyond the disease model of mental disorders.* Westport, CT: Praeger.

Kihlstrom, J. F. (2004). An unbalanced balancing act: Blocked, recovered, and false memories in the laboratory and clinic. *Clinical Psychology: Science and Practice, 11,* 34–39.

Kilgore, K., Snyder, J., & Lentz, C. (2000). The contribution of parental discipline, parental monitoring, and school risk to early-onset conduct problems in African American boys and girls. *Developmental Psychology, 36,* 835–845.

Kim, B. S. K., Brenner, B. R., Liang, C. T. H., & Asay, P. A. (2003). A qualitative study of adaptation experiences of 1.5-generation Asian Americans. *Cultural Diversity and Ethnic Minority Psychology, 9,* 156–170.

Kim, U., Jorgenson, E., Coon, H., Leppert, M., Risch, N., & Drayna1, D. (2003). Positional cloning of the human quantitative trait locus underlying taste sensitivity to phenylthiocarbamide. *Science, 299,* 1221–1225.

Kimura, D. (1992). Sex differences in the brain. *Scientific American, 267*(3), 118–125.

King, M.-C., Marks, J. H., Mandell, J. B., & the New York Breast Cancer Study Group. (2003). Breast and ovarian cancer risks due to inherited mutations in BRCA1 and BRCA2. *Science, 302,* 643–646.

Kirsch, I. (1994). Clinical hypnosis as a nondeceptive placebo: Empirically derived techniques. *American Journal of Clinical Hypnosis, 37,* 95–106.

Kirsch, I. (2004). Conditioning, expectancy, and the placebo effect: Comment on Stewart-Williams and Podd (2004). *Psychological Bulletin, 130,* 341–343.

Kirsch, I., & Lynn, S. J. (1995). Altered state of hypnosis: Changes in the theoretical landscape. *American Psychologist, 50*(10), 846–858.

Kirsch, I., Montgomery, G., & Sapirstein, G. (1995). Hypnosis as an adjunct to cognitive-behavioral psychotherapy: A meta-analysis. *Journal of Consulting and Clinical Psychology, 63,* 214–220.

Kirsch, I., Moore, T. J., Scoboria, A., & Nicholls, S. S. (2002, July 15). The emperor's new drugs: An analysis of antidepressant medication data submitted to the U.S. Food and Drug Administration. *Prevention and Treatment, 5.* Retrieved July 16, 2003, from http://journals.apa.org/preveniton/volume5/pre0050023a.html.

Kirsch, J. F., & Lynn, S. J. (1998). Dissociation theories of hypnosis. *Psychological Bulletin, 123,* 100–115.

Kirsch, J. F., Silva, C. E., Comey, G., & Reed, S. (1995). A spectral analysis of cognitive and personality variables in hypnosis: Empirical disconfirmation of the two-factor model of hypnotic responding. *Journal of Personality and Social Psychology, 69,* 167–175.

Kirsch, T. B. (1996). A brief history of analytical psychology. *Psychoanalytic Review, 83,* 569–577.

Kisilevsky, B. S., Hains, S. M. J., Lee, K., Xie, X., Huang, H., Ye, H.-H., et al. (2003). Effects of experience on fetal voice recognition. *Psychological Science, 14,* 220–224.

Kitayama, S., Duffy, S., Kawamura, T., & Larsen, J. T. (2003). Perceiving an object and its context in different cultures: A cultural look at new look. *Psychological Science, 14,* 201–206.

Kitayama, S., Markus, H. R., Matsumoto, H., & Norasakkunkit, V. (1997). Individual and collective processes in the construction of the self: Self-enhancement in the United States and self-criticism in Japan. *Journal of Personality and Social Psychology, 72,* 1245–1267.

Klein, D. F. (1993). False suffocation alarms, spontaneous panics, and related conditions: An integrative hypothesis. *Archives of General Psychiatry, 50,* 306–317.

Klein, P. D. (1997). Multiplying the problems of intelligence by eight: A critique of Gardner's theory. *Canadian Journal of Education, 22,* 377–394.

Kleinfield, N. R., & Connelly, M. (2003, September 8). 9/11 still strains New York psyche. *New York Times,* pp. A1, A22.

Kleinman, A. (1987). Anthropology and psychiatry: The role of culture in cross-cultural research on illness. *British Journal of Psychiatry, 151,* 447–454.

Kleinpenning, G., & Hagendoorn, L. (1993). Forms of racism and the cumulative dimension of ethnic attitudes. *Social Psychology Quarterly, 56,* 21–36.

Kleinplatz, P. J. (2003). What's new in sex therapy? From stagnation to fragmentation. *Sexual and Relationship Therapy, 18*(1), 95–106.

Klinger, E. (1987, October). The power of daydreams. *Psychology Today,* pp. 37–44.

Kluger, J. (2001, June 18). How to manage teen drinking (the smart way). *Time,* pp. 42–44.

Kluger, J. (2003, October 26). Medicating young minds. *Time Magazine Online.* Retrieved October 27, 2003, from http://www.time.com/time/magazine/article/0,9171,1101031103-526331,00.html.

Knoedler, A. J., Hellwig, K. A., & Neath, I. (1999). The shift from recency to primacy with increasing delay. *Journal of Experimental Psychology: Learning, Memory, and Cognition, 25,* 474–487.

Kobasa, S. C. (1979). Stressful life events, personality, and health: An inquiry into hardiness. *Journal of Personality and Social Psychology, 37,* 1–11.

Kobasa, S. C., Maddi, S. R., & Kahn, S. (1982). Hardiness and health: A prospective study. *Journal of Personality and Social Psychology, 42,* 168–177.

Kodl, M. M., & Mermelstein, R. (2004). Beyond modeling: Parenting practices, parental smoking history, and adolescent cigarette smoking. *Addictive Behaviors, 29,* 17–32.

Kogan, M. (2001, January). Where happiness lies. *Monitor on Psychology, 32*(1), 74–76.

Kohlberg, L. (1969). *Stages in the development of moral thought and action.* New York: Holt, Rinehart and Winston.

Kohlberg, L. (1981). *The philosophy of moral development.* San Francisco: Harper & Row.

Köhler, W. (1927). *The mentality of apes.* New York: Harcourt Brace.

Kohout, J. (2001, February). Who's earning those psychology degrees? *Monitor on Psychology,* 42.

Kolata, G. (2000a, October 17). How the body knows when to gain or lose. *New York Times,* pp. F1, F8.

Kolata, G. (2000b, October 18). Days off are not allowed, experts argue. *New York Times,* pp. A1, A20.

Kolata, G. (2001a, March 3). 2 endocrinology groups raise doubt on earlier onset of girls' puberty. *New York Times,* p. A10.

Kolata, G. (2001b, November 22). Hints of an Alzheimer's aid in anti-inflammatory drugs. *New York Times,* p. A24.

Kolata, G. (2003, September 4). Study finds appetites reduced by hormone. *New York Times,* p. A16.

Kolko, D. J., & Rickard-Figueroa, J. L. (1985). Effects of video games on the adverse corollaries of chemotherapy in pediatric oncology patients: A single-case analysis. *Journal of Consulting and Clinical Psychology, 53,* 223–228.

Komaroff, A. L. (2004, March 25). Sleep improves insight. *Journal Watch Psychiatry.* Retrieved March 25, 2004, from http://psychiatry.jwatch.org/cgi/content/full/2004/325/10?q=etoc.

Konradi, C., Eaton, M., MacDonald, M. L., Walsh, J., Benes, F. M., & Heckers, S. (2004). Molecular evidence for mitochondrial dysfunction in bipolar disorder. *Archives of General Psychiatry, 61,* 300–308.

Kool, S., Dekker, J., Duijsens, I. J., de Jonghe, F., & Puite, B. (2003). Changes in personality pathology after pharmacotherapy and combined therapy for depressed patients. *Journal of Personality Disorders, 17,* 60–72.

Koriat, A. (1993). How do we know that we know? The accessible model of the feeling of knowing. *Psychological Review, 100,* 609–639.

Koriat, A., & Goldsmith, M. (1996). Memory as something that can be counted versus memory as something that can be counted on. In D. Herrmann, C. McEvoy, C. Hertzog, P. Hertel, & M. K. Johnson (Eds.), *Basic and applied memory research: Practical applications* (Vol. 2, pp. 3–18). Mahwah, NJ: Lawrence Erlbaum Associates.

Korner, J., & Leibel, R. L. (2003). To eat or not to eat—how the gut talks to the brain. *New England Journal of Medicine, 349,* 926–928.

Kosslyn, S. M. (1994). *Image and brain: The resolution of the imagery debate.* Cambridge, MA: MIT Press.

Kosslyn, S. M., Thompson, W. L., Costantini-Ferrando, M. F., Alpert, N. M., & Spiegel, D. (2000). Hypnotic visual illusion alters color processing in the brain. *American Journal of Psychiatry, 157,* 1279–1284.

Kramer, A. F., & Willis, S. L. (2002). Enhancing the cognitive vitality of older adults. *Current Directions in Psychological Science, 11,* 173–177.

Kraus, S. J. (1995). Attitudes and the prediction of behavior: A meta-analysis of the empirical literature. *Personality and Social Psychology Bulletin, 21,* 58–75.

Krauss, R. M., Curran, N. M., & Ferleger, N. (1983). Expressive conventions and the cross-cultural perception of emotion. *Basic and Applied Social Psychology, 4,* 295–305.

Kray, J., & Frensch, P. A. (2002). A view from cognitive psychology: g—(G)host in the correlation matrix? In R. J. Sternberg & E. L. Grigorenko (Eds.), *The general factor of intelligence: How general is it?* (pp. 183–220). Mahwah, NJ: Lawrence Erlbaum Associates.

Kroll, L., & Goldman, L. (Eds.). (2004, March 15). Rising tide. *Forbes,* p. 91.

Krueger, R. F., Hicks, B. M., Patrick, C. J., Carlson, S. R., Iacono, W. G., & McGue, M. (2002). Etiologic connections among substance dependence, antisocial behavior, and personality: Modeling the externalizing spectrum. *Journal of Abnormal Psychology, 111,* 411–424.

Kruger, T. E., & Jerrells, T. R. (1992). Potential role of alcohol in human immunodeficiency virus infection. *Alcohol World: Health and Research, 16* (NIH Publication No. 93-3466, pp. 57–63). Washington, DC: National Institute on Alcohol Abuse and Alcoholism.

Kryger, M. H., Roth, T., & Dement, W. C. (Eds.). (2000). *Principles and practice of sleep medicine.* (3rd ed.). Philadelphia: W. B. Saunders.

Kubey, R. W., Lavin, M. J., & Barrows, J. R. (2001). Internet use and collegiate academic performance decrements: Early findings. *Journal of Communication, 51,* 366–382.

Kubiszyn, T. W., Meyer, G. J., Finn, S. E., Eyde, L. D., Kay, G. G., Moreland, K. L., et al. (2000). Empirical support for psychological assessment in clinical health care settings. *Professional Psychology: Research and Practice, 31,* 119–130.

Kübler-Ross, E. (1969). *On death and dying.* New York: Macmillan.

Kuhn, C. M., & Wilson, W. A. (2001, Spring). Our dangerous love affair with ecstasy. *Cerebrum,* 22–33.

Kuncel, N. R., Hezlett, A. A., & Ones, D. S. (2004). Academic performance, career potential, creativity, and job performance: Can one construct predict them all? *Journal of Personality and Social Psychology, 86,* 148–161.

Kuperberg, G. R., Broome, M. R., McGuire, P. K., David, A. S., Eddy, M., Ozawa, F., et al. (2003). Regionally localized thinning of the cerebral cortex in schizophrenia. *Archives of General Psychiatry, 60,* 878–888.

Kupfer, D. J. (1999). Research in affective disorders comes of age [Editorial]. *American Journal of Psychiatry, 156,* 165–167.

Kupfersmid, J. (1995). Does the Oedipus complex exist? *Psychotherapy, 32,* 535–547.

Kurth, T., Gaziano, J. M., Berger, K., Kase, C. S., Rexrode, K. M., Cook, N. R., et al. (2002). Body mass index and the risk of stroke in men. *Archives of Internal Medicine, 162,* 2557–2562.

Kusnecov, A. W. (2001). Behavioral conditioning of the immune system. In A. Baum, T. A. Revenson, & J. E. Singer (Eds.), *Handbook of health psychology* (pp. 105–116). Mahwah, NJ: Lawrence Erlbaum Associates.

Kyle, T. (2000, February). Minorities and women in undergraduate psychology: Where are we? *Monitor on Psychology, 31*(2), 15.

LaBerge S., & Gackenbach, J. (2000). Lucid dreaming. In E. Cardena, S. J. Lynn, et al. (Eds.), *Varieties of anomalous experience: Examining the scientific evidence* (pp. 151–182). Washington, DC: American Psychological Association.

Lachman, M. E. (2004). Development in midlife. *Annual Review of Psychology, 55,* 305–331.

Lachman, M. E., & Weaver, S. L. (1998). Sociodemographic variations in the sense of control by domain: Findings from the MacArthur Studies of Midlife. *Psychology and Aging, 13,* 553–562.

LaFrance, M., Hecht, M. A., & Paluck, E. L. (2003). The contingent smile: A meta-analysis of sex differences in smiling. *Psychological Bulletin, 129,* 305–334.

LaGory, M., & Fitzpatrick, K. (1992). The effects of environmental context on elderly depression. *Journal of Aging and Health, 4,* 459–479.

Lahn, B. T., & Page, D. C. (1999). Four evolutionary strata on the human X chromosome.

Lai, C. S. L., Fisher, S. E., Hurst, J. A., Vargha-Khadem, F., & Monaco, A. P. (2001). A forkhead-domain gene is mutated in a severe speech and language disorder. *Nature, 413,* 519–523.

Laino, C. (2002, April 25) Gender gap in longevity narrowing. MSNBC. Retrieved May 5, 2002, from http://www.msnbc.com/news/743069.asp.

Lam, J. A., & Rosenheck, R A. (2000). Correlates of improvement in quality of life among homeless persons with serious mental illness. *Psychiatric Services, 51,* 116–118.

Lam, L. S., & Hope, D. A. (2003). College students and problematic drinking: A review of the literature. *Clinical Psychology Review, 23,* 719–759.

Lamberg, L. (2000). Sleep disorders, often unrecognized, complicate many physical illnesses. *Journal of the American Medical Association, 284,* 2173–2175.

Lamberg, L. (2003). Advances in eating disorders offer food for thought. *Journal of the American Medical Association, 290,* 1437–1442.

Lambert, M. J., Hansen, N. B., & Finch, A. E. (2001). Patient-focused research: Using patient outcome data to enhance treatment effects. *Journal of Consulting and Clinical Psychology, 69,* 159–172.

Langenbucher, J. W., & Chung, T. (1995). Onset and staging of DSM-IV alcohol dependence. *Journal of Abnormal Psychology, 104,* 346–354.

Langlois, J. H., Kalakanis, L., Rubenstein, A. J., Larson, A., Hallam, M., & Smoot, M. (2000). Maxims or myths of beauty? A meta-analytic and theoretical review. *Psychological Bulletin, 126,* 390–423.

Latané, B., & Darley, J. M. (1970). *The unresponsive bystander: Why doesn't he help?* New York: Appleton-Century-Crofts.

Laumann, E. O., Gagnon, J. H., Michael, R. T., & Michaels, S. (1994). *The social organization of sexuality: Sexual practices in the United States.* Chicago: University of Chicago Press.

Lavie, P. (2001). Sleep-wake as a biological rhythm. *Annual Review of Psychology, 52,* 607–628.

Lawrence, J., Mayers, D. L, Hullsiek, K. H., Collins, G., Abrams, D. I., Reisler, R. B., et al. (2003). Structured treatment interruption in patients with multidrug-resistant Human Immunodeficiency Virus. *New England Journal of Medicine, 349,* 837–846.

Lawton, M. P., Moss, M. S., Winter, L., & Hoffman, C. (2002). Motivation in later life: Personal projects and well-being. *Psychology and Aging, 17,* 539–547.

Lazarus, R. S. (1995). Vexing research problems inherent in cognitive-mediational theories of emotion and some solutions. *Psychological Inquiry, 6,* 183–197.

Lazarus, R. S., & Folkman, S. (1984). *Stress, appraisal, and coping.* New York: Springer.

Lear, J. (2000, February 27). Freud's second thoughts. *New York Times Book Review,* p. 39.

Leary, W. E. (1995, July 18). Clues on faltering memory in aging. *New York Times,* p. C10.

Leber, P. (2000). Placebo controls: No news is good news. *Archives of General Psychiatry, 57,* 319–320.

LeDoux, J. E. (1994, June). Emotion, memory, and the brain. *Scientific American, 270,* 32–39.

LeDoux, J. E. (1995). Emotion: Clues from the brain. *Annual Review of Psychology, 46,* 209–235.

LeDoux, J. E. (1996). *The emotional brain.* New York: Touchstone.

LeDoux, J. E. (2000) Emotion circuits in the brain. *Annual Review of Neuroscience, 23,* 155–184.

Leibowitz, H. W. (1971). Sensory, learned, and cognitive mechansims of size perception. *Annals of the New York Academy of Sciences, 1988,* 47–62.

Leichsenring, F., & Leibing, E. (2003). The effectiveness of psychodynamic therapy and cognitive behavior therapy in the treatment of personality disorders: A meta-analysis. *American Journal of Psychiatry, 160,* 1223–1232.

Lemonde, S., Turecki, G., Bakish, D., Du, L., Hrdina, P. D., Bown, C. D., Sequeira, A., et al. (2003). Impaired repression at a 5-hydroxytryptamine 1A receptor gene polymorphism associated with major depression and suicide. *Journal of Neuroscience, 23,* 8788–8799.

Lemonick, M. D. (2003a, January 20). Your mind your body. *Time,* p. 35.

Lemonick, M. D. (2003b, January 20). The power of mood. *Time,* pp. 36–41.

Lemonick, M. D., & Park, A. (2001, May 14). Alzheimer's: The Nun study. *Time,* pp. 54–64.

Lemons, J. A., Baur, C. R., Oh, W., Korones, S. B., Stoll, B. J., Verter, J., et al. (2001). Very low birth weight outcomes of the National Institute of Child Health and Human Development neonatal research network, January 1995 through December 1996. *Pediatrics, 107,* 1.

Leon, A. C. (2000). Placebo protects subjects from nonresponse: A paradox of power. *Archives of General Psychiatry, 57,* 329–330.

Lepore, L., & Brown, R. (1997). Category and stereotype activation: Is prejudice inevitable? *Journal of Personality and Social Psychology, 72,* 275–287.

Lerner, S. (2003, July 22). A desperate global scavenger hunt to keep AIDS patients alive. *New York Times,* p. F5.

Leshner, A. I. (1999). Science-based views of drug addiction and its treatment. *Journal of the American Medical Association, 282,* 1314–1316.

LeVay, S. (2003). *The biology of sexual orientation.* Retrieved December 19, 2003, from http://members.aol.com/slevay/page22.html.

Levenson, J. L., & Bemis, C. (1991). The role of psychological factors in cancer onset and progression. *Psychosomatics, 32,* 124–132.

Levenson, R. W. (1994). The search for autonomic specificity. In P. Ekman & R. J. Davidson (Eds.), *The nature of emotion: Fundamental questions* (pp. 252–257). New York: Oxford University Press.

Levine, J. M., & Moreland, R. L. (1998). Small groups. In D. T. Gilbert, S. T. Fiske, & G. Lindzey (Eds.), *The handbook of social psychology* (4th ed., Vol. 2, pp. 415–469). Boston: McGraw-Hill.

Levine, M. (1994). *Effective problem solving* (2nd ed.). Englewood Cliffs, NJ: Prentice-Hall.

Levinson, D. J., with Darrow, C. N., Klein, E. R., Levinson, M. H., & McKee, B. (1978). *The seasons of a man's life.* New York: Knopf.

Levy, B. R, Slade, M. D., Kunkel, S. R., & Kasl, S. V. (2002). Longevity increased by positive self-perceptions of aging. *Journal of Personality and Social Psychology, 83,* 261–270.

Levy-Lahad, E., & Plon, S. E. (2003). A risky business—assessing breast cancer risk. *Science, 302,* 574–575.

Lewin, T. (2001, September 10). Study finds little change in working mothers debate. *New York Times,* p. A26.

Lewinsohn, P. M, Joiner, T. E., & Rohde, P. (2001). Evaluation of cognitive diathesis-stress models in predicting major depressive disorder in adolescents. *Journal of Abnormal Psychology, 110,* 203–215.

Lewinsohn, P. M. (1974). A behavioral approach to depression. In R. J. Friedman & M. M. Katz (Eds.), *The psychology of depression: Contemporary theory and research.* Washington, DC: Winston-Wiley.

Lewis, C. (1995). Improving attendance-reducing truancy: A school-based approach. *AEP (Association of Educational Psychologists) Journal, 11,* 36–40.

Leyton, M., Boileau, I., Benkelfat, C., Diksic, M., Baker, G., & Dagher, A. (2002). Amphetamine-induced increases in extracellular dopamine, drug wanting, and novelty seeking: A PET/[11C]raclopride study in healthy men. *Neuropsychopharmacology, 27,* 1027–1035.

Li, S.-C. (2003). Biocultural orchestration of developmental plasticity across levels: The interplay of biology and culture in shaping the mind and behavior across the life span. *Psychological Bulletin, 129,* 171–194.

Liben, L. W., Susman, E. J., Finkelstein, J. W., Chinchilli, V. M., Susan Kunselman, Schwab, J., et al. (2002). The effects of sex steroids on spatial performance: A review and an experimental clinical investigation. *Developmental Psychology, 38,* 236–253.

Libkuman, T. M., Love, K. G., & Donn, P. D. (1998). An empirically based selection and evaluation system for collegiate football. *Journal of Sport Management, 12,* 220–241.

Lieberman, P. (1998). *Eve spoke: Human language and human evolution.* New York: Norton.

Lilienfeld, S. O., Kirsch, I., Sarbin, T. R., Lynn, S. J., Chaves, J. F., Ganaway, G. K., et al. (1999). Dissociative identity disorder and the sociocognitive model: Recalling the lessons of the past. *Psychological Bulletin, 125,* 507–523.

Lilienfeld, S. O., Wood, J. M., & Garb, H. N. (2000). The scientific status of projective techniques. *Psychological Science in the Public Interest, 1,* 27–66.

Limebeer, C. L., &. Parker, L. A. (2000). The antiemetic drug ondansetron interferes with lithium-induced conditioned rejection reactions, but not lithium-induced taste avoidance in rats. *Journal of Experimental Psychology-Animal Behavior Processes, 26,* 371–384.

Lindeman, B., Libkuman, T., King, D., & Kruse, B. (2000). Development of an instrument to assess jump-shooting form in basketball. *Journal of Sport Behavior, 23,* 336–348.

Lingenfelser, T., Kaschel, R., Weber, A., Zaiser-Kaschel, H., Jakober, B., & Kuper, J. (1994). Young hospital doctors after night duty: Their task-specific cognitive status and emotional condition. *Medical Education, 28,* 566–572.

Linville, P. W., & Fischer, G. W. (1993). Exemplar and abstraction models of perceived group variability and stereotypicality. *Social Cognition, 11,* 92–125.

Lippa, R. A. (2003). Are 2D:4D finger-length ratios related to sexual orientation? Yes for men, no for women. *Journal of Personality and Social Psychology, 85,* 179–188.

Litt, M. D., Kadden, R. M., Cooney, N. L, & Kabela, E. (2003). Coping skills and treatment outcomes in cognitive-behavioral and interactional group therapy for alcoholism. *Journal of Consulting and Clinical Psychology, 71,* 118–128.

Little, S. J., Holte, S., Routy, J.-P., Daar, E. S., Markowitz, M., Collier, A. C., et al. (2002). Antiretroviral-drug resistance among patients recently infected with HIV. *New England Journal of Medicine, 347,* 385–394.

Lobel, M., DeVincent, C. J., Kaminer, A., & Meyer, B. A. (2000). The impact of prenatal maternal stress and optimistic disposition on birth outcomes in medically high-risk women. *Health Psychology, 19,* 544–553.

Loeb, S., Fuller. B., Kagan, S. L., & Carrol, B. (2004). Child care in poor communities: Early learning effects of type, quality, and stability. *Child Development, 75,* 47–65.

Loftus, E. F. (1993a). The reality of repressed memories. *American Psychologist, 48,* 518–537.

Loftus, E. F. (1993b). Psychologists in the eyewitness world. *American Psychologist, 48,* 550–552.

Loftus, E. F. (1997, September). Creating false memories. *Scientific American,* pp. 71–75.

Loftus, E. F. (2003). Make-believe memories. *American Psychologist, 58,* 867–873.

Loftus, E. F., Miller, D. G., & Burns, H. J. (1978). Semantic integration of verbal information into a visual memory. *Journal of Experimental Psychology: Human Learning and Memory, 4,* 19–31.

Logan, G. D. (2003). Executive control of thought and action: In search of the wild homunculus. *Current Directions in Psychological Science, 12,* 45–48.

Logie, R. H. (1996). The seven ages of working memory. In J. T. E. Richardson et al. (Eds.), *Working memory and human cognition* (pp. 31–65). New York: Oxford University Press.

Logsdon-Conradsen, S. (2002). Using mindfulness meditation to promote holistic health in individuals with HIV/AIDS. *Cognitive and Behavioral Practice, 9,* 67–72.

Lorayne, H. (2002). *The complete guide to memory mastery.* Hollywood, FL: Fell Publishers.

Lorenz, K. (1966). *On aggression.* New York: Harcourt Brace Jovanovich.

Love, J. M., as cited in Gilbert, S. (2003, July 22). Turning a mass of data on child care into advice for parents: Four views. *New York Times,* p. F5.

Luborsky, L., Rosenthal, R., Digue, L., Andrusyna, T. P., Berman, J. S., Levitt, J. T., et al. (2002). The Dodo bird verdict is alive and well—mostly. *Clinical Psychology: Science and Practice, 9,* 2–12.

Luna, T. D., French, J., & Mindtcha, J. L. (1997). A study of USAF air traffic controller shiftwork: Sleep, fatigue, activity, and mood analyses. *Aviation, Space, and Environmental Medicine, 68,* 18–23.

Luntz, B. K., & Widom, C. S. (1994). Antisocial personality disorder in abused and neglected children grown up. *American Journal of Psychiatry, 151,* 670–674.

Luoma, J. B., Martin, C. E., & Pearson, J. L. (2002). Contact with mental health and primary care providers before suicide: A review of the evidence. *American Journal of Psychiatry, 159,* 909–916.

Luria, A. R. (1968). *The mind of a mnemonist.* New York: Basic Books.

Lykken, D. (1999). *Happiness: What studies on twins show us about nature, nurture, and the happiness set-point.* New York: Golden Books.

Lykken, D., & Csikszentmihalyi, M. (2001). Happiness–stuck with what you've got? *Psychologist, 14,* 470–472.

Lynch, H. T., Coronel, S. M., Okimoto, R., Hampel, H., Sweet, K., Lynch, J. F., et al. (2004). A founder mutation of the MSH2 gene and hereditary non-polyposis colorectal cancer in the United States. *Journal of the American Medical Association, 291,* 718–724.

Lynn, S. J., & Rhue, J. W. (1991). Preface: Theories of hypnosis: An introduction. In S. J. Lynn & J. W. Rhue (Eds.), *Theories of hypnosis: Current models and perspectives* (pp. ix–x, 1–15). New York: Guilford Press.

MacAndrew, D. K., Katzky, R. J., Fiez, J. A., McClelland, J. L., & Becker, J. T. (2002). The phonological-similarity effect differentiates between two working memory tasks. *Psychological Science, 13,* 465–467.

MacDonald, T. K., MacDonald, G., Zanna, M. P., & Fong, G. (2000). Alcohol, sexual arousal, and intentions to use condoms in young men: Applying alcohol myopia theory to risky sexual behavior. *Health Psychology, 19,* 290–298.

MacGregor, J. N., Ormerod, T. C., & Chronicle, E. P. (2001). Information processing and insight: A process model of performance on the nine-dot and related problems. *Journal of Experimental Psychology: Learning, Memory, and Cognition, 27,* 176–201.

MacPherson, S. E., Phillips, L. H., & Della Sala, S. (2002). Age, executive function, and social decision making: A dorsolateral prefrontal theory of cognitive aging. *Psychology and Aging, 17,* 598–609.

Macrae, C. N., Stangor, C., & Milne, A. B. (1994). Activating social stereotypes: A functional analysis. *Journal of Experimental Social Psychology, 30,* 370–389.

Maddi, S. R., & Khoshaba, D. M. (1994). Hardiness and mental health. *Journal of Personality Assessment, 63,* 265–274.

Magee, W. J., Eaton, W. W., Wittchen, H. U., McGonagle, K. A., & Kessler, R. C. (1996). Agoraphobia, simple phobia, and social phobia in the National Comorbidity Survey. *Archives of General Psychiatry, 53,* 159–168.

Maier, N. R. F. (1931). Reasoning in humans: II. The solution of a problem and its appearance in consciousness. *Journal of Comparative Psychology, 12,* 181–194.

Maier, S. F., Watkins, L. R., & Fleshner, M. (1994). Psychoneuroimmunology: The interface between behavior, brain, and immunity. *American Psychologist, 49,* 1004–1017.

Main, M. (1996). Introduction to the special section on attachment and psychopathology: 2. Overview of the field of attachment. *Journal of Consulting and Clinical Psychology, 64,* 237–243.

Main, M., & Solomon, J. (1990). Procedures for identifying infants as disorganized/disoriented during the Ainsworth Strange Situation. In M. T. Greenberg, D. Cicchetti, & E. M. Cummings (Eds.), *Attachment in the preschool years: Theory, research, and intervention* (pp. 121–160). Chicago: University of Chicago Press.

Maldonado, J. R., Butler, L. D., & Spiegel, D. (1998). Treatments for dissociative disorders. In P. E. Nathan & J. M. Gorman (Eds.), *A guide to treatments that work* (pp. 423–446). New York: Oxford University Press.

Malloy, T. E., Albright, L., Kenny, D A., Agatstein, F., & Winquist, L. (1997). Interpersonal perception and metaperception in nonoverlapping social groups. *Journal of Personality and Social Psychology, 72,* 390–398.

Manson, J. E., & Bassuk, S. S. (2003). Obesity in the United States: A fresh look at its high toll. *Journal of the American Medical Association, 289,* 229–230.

Manson, J. E., Greenland, P., LaCroix, A. Z., Stefanick, M. L., Mouton, C. P., et al. (2002). Walking compared with vigorous exercise for the prevention of cardiovascular events in women. *New England Journal of Medicine, 347,* 716–725.

Manson, J. E., Skerrett, P. J., Greenland, P., & VanItallie, T. B. (2004). The escalating pandemics of obesity and sedentary lifestyle: A call to action for clinicians. *Archives of Internal Medicine, 164,* 249–258.

Manson, J. E., Skerrett, P. J., Greenland, P., & VanItallie, T. B. (2004). The escalating pandemics of obesity and sedentary lifestyle: A call to action for clinicians. *Archives of Internal Medicine, 164,* 249–258

Maquet, P. (2001). The role of sleep in learning and memory. *Science, 294,* 1048–1052.

Marcia, J. E. (1966). Development and validation of ego-identity status. *Journal of Personality and Social Psychology, 3,* 551–558.

Marcia, J. E. (1980). Identity in adolescence. In J. Adelson (Ed.), *Handbook of adolescent psychology* (pp. 159–187). New York: Wiley.

Marcia, J. E., Waterman, A. S., Matteson, D. R., Archer, S. L., & Orlofsky, J. L. (Eds.). (1993). *Ego identity: A handbook for psychosocial research.* New York: Springer-Verlag.

Marcus, R., Hardy, R., Kuh, D., & Wadsworth, M. E. J. (2001). Birth weight and cognitive function in the British 1946 birth cohort: Longitudinal population-based study. *British Medical Journal, 322,* 199–203.

Margoshes, P. (1995, May). For many, old age is the prime of life. *APA Monitor, 26*, 36–37.

Marijuana leads to hard drugs. (2002, January 21). *MSNBC Web Posting.* Retrieved January 22, 2002, from http://www.msnbc.com/news/862289.asp.

Marijuana linked to greater risk of lung cancer. (2000, June 22). *Albuquerque Tribune.* Retrieved June 30, 2000, from http://www.mapinc.org/drugnews/v00.n860.a06.html.

Markel, H. (2002, October 27). For addicts, relief may be an office visit away. *New York Times Week in Review*, pp. 14.

Markel, H. (2003, September 3). Lack of sleep takes it toll on student psyches. *New York Times, Science Times*, p. F6.

Markus, H. R., & Kitayama, S. (1991). Culture and the self: Implications for cognition, emotion, and motivation. *Psychological Review, 98*, 224–253.

Marsh, A. A., Elfenbein, H. A., & Ambady, N. A. (2003). Nonverbal "accents": Cultural differences in facial expressions of emotion. *Psychological Science, 14*, 373–376.

Marsh, R. L., Hicks, J. L., & Watson, V. (2002). The dynamics of intention retrieval and coordination of action in event-based prospective memory. *Journal of Experimental Psychology: Learning, Memory, and Cognition, 28*, 652–659.

Marshal, M. P. (2003). For better or for worse? The effects of alcohol use on marital functioning. *Clinical Psychology Review, 23*, 959–997.

Martin, D. J., Garske, J. P., & Davis, M. K. (2000). Relation of the therapeutic alliance with outcome and other variables: A meta-analytic review. *Journal of Consulting and Clinical Psychology, 68*, 438–450.

Martindale, C. (2001). Oscillations and analogies: Thomas Young, MD, RFS, genius. *American Psychologist, 56*, 342–345.

Maslach, C. (2003). Job burnout: New directions in research and intervention. *Current Directions in Psychological Science, 12*, 189–192.

Maslow, A. H. (1970). *Motivation and personality* (2nd ed.). New York: Harper & Row.

Maslow, A. H. (1971). *Farther reaches of human nature.* New York: Viking Penguin.

Masters, W. H., & Johnson, V. E. (1966). *Human sexual response.* Boston: Little, Brown.

Masters, W. H., & Johnson, V. E. (1970). *Human sexual inadequacy.* Boston: Little, Brown.

Matsumoto, K., Suzuki, W., & Tanaka, K. (2003). Neuronal correlates of goal-based motor selection in the prefrontal cortex. *Science, 301*, 229–232.

Matsumoto, K., Suzuki, W., & Tanaka, K. (2003). Neuronal correlates of goal-based motor selection in the prefrontal cortex. *Science, 301*, 229–232.

Mattson, M. P. (2003). Neurobiology: Ballads of a protein quartet. *Nature, 422*, 385–387.

Mayou, R. A., Bryant, B. M., Sanders, D., Bass, C., Klimes, I., & Forfar, C. (1997). A controlled trial of cognitive behavioural therapy for non-cardiac chest pain. *Psychological Medicine, 27*, 1021–1031.

Mayr, U., & Kliegl, R. (2000). Complex semantic processing in old age: Does it stay or does it go? *Psychology and Aging, 15*, 29–43.

Mazzoni, G., & Memom, A. (2003). Imagination can create false autobiographical memories. *Psychological Science, 14*, 186–188.

McAdams, D. P. (1992). The five-factor model in personality. *Journal of Personality, 60*, 329–361.

McBride, C. K., Paikoff, R. L., & Holmbeck, G. N. (2003). Individual and familial influences on the onset of sexual intercourse among urban African American adolescents. *Journal of Consulting and Clinical Psychology, 71*, 159–167.

McClearn, G. E., Johansson, B., Berg, S., Pedersen, N. L., et al. (1997). Substantial genetic influence on cognitive abilities in twins 80 or more years old. *Science, 276*, 1560–1563.

McClelland, D. C. (1958). Risk-taking in children with high and low need for achievement. In J. W. Atkinson (Ed.), *Motives in fantasy, action, and society*. Princeton, NJ: Van Nostrand.

McClelland, D. C. (1965). Achievement and entrepreneurship: A longitudinal study. *Journal of Personality and Social Psychology, 1*, 389–392.

McClelland, D. C. (1985). *Human motivation.* Glenview, IL: Scott, Foresman.

McCrae, R. R. (2004). Human nature and culture: A trait perspective. *Journal of Research in Personality, 38*, 3–14.

McCrae, R. R., & Costa, P. T., Jr. (1986). Clinical assessment can benefit from recent advances in personality psychology. *American Psychologist, 41*, 1001–1003.

McCrae, R. R., & Costa, P. T., Jr. (1996). Toward a new generation of personality theories: Theoretical contexts for the five-factor model. In J. S. Wiggins (Ed.), *The five-factor model of personality: Theoretical perspectives.* New York: Guilford Press.

McCrae, R. R., Costa, P. T., Jr. Martin, T. A., Oryol, V. E., Rukavishnikov, A. A., Senin, I.G., et al. (2004). Consensual validation of personality traits across cultures. *Journal of Research in Personality, 38*, 179–201.

McCrae, R. R., Costa, P. T. Jr., Ostendorf, F., Angleitner, A., Hrebickova, M., Avia, M., et al. (2000). Nature over nurture temperament, personality, and life span development. *Journal of Personality and Social Psychology, 78*, 173–186.

McDermut, J. F., Haaga, D. A. F., & Bilek, L. A. (1997). Cognitive bias and irrational beliefs in major depression and dysphoria. *Cognitive Therapy and Research, 21*, 459–476.

McDermut, W., Miller, I W., & Brown, R. A. (2001). The efficacy of group psychotherapy for depression: A meta-analysis and review of the empirical research. *Clinical Psychology: Science and Practice, 8*, 98–116.

McDougall, W. (1908). *An introduction to social psychology.* New York: Methuen.

McGinn, L. K., & Sanderson, W. C. (2001). What allows cognitive behavioral therapy to be brief: Overview, efficacy, and crucial factors facilitating brief treatment. *Clinical Psychology: Science and Practice, 8*, 23–37.

McGovern, F. J., & Nevid, J. S. (1986). Evaluation apprehension on psychological inventories in a prison-based setting. *Journal of Consulting and Clinical Psychology, 54*, 576–578.

McGowan, S., Lawrence, A. D., Sales, T., Quested, D., & Grasby, P. (2004). Presynaptic dopaminergic dysfunction in schizophrenia: A positron emission tomographic [18f]fluorodopa study. *Archives of General Psychiatry, 61*, 134–142.

McGrath, R. E, Pogge, D. L., & Stokes, J. M. (2002). Incremental validity of selected MMPI-A content scales in an inpatient setting. *Psychological Assessment, 14*, 401–409.

McGrath, R. E., Wiggins, J. G., Sammons, M. T., Levant, R. F., Brown, A., & Stock, W. (2004). Professional issues in pharmacotherapy for psychologists. *Professional Psychology: Research and Practice, 35*, 158–163,

McGreal, D., & Evans, B. J. (1994). Recall during hypnosis. *Australian Journal of Clinical and Experimental Hypnosis, 22*, 177–180.

McGue, M., & Christensen, K. (2001). The heritability of cognitive functioning in very old adults: Evidence from Danish twins aged 75 years and older. *Psychology and Aging, 16*, 272–280.

McGuffin, P., & Scourfield, J. (1997). A father's imprint on his daughter's thinking. *Nature, 387*, 652–653.

McGuffin, P., Rijsdijk, F., Andrew, M., Sham, P., Katz, R., & Cardno, A. (2003). The heritability of bipolar affective disorder and the genetic relationship to unipolar depression. *Archives of General Psychiatry, 60*, 497–502.

McGuire, P. A. (1998, July). Wanted: Workers with flexibility for 21st century jobs. *APA Monitor, 29*(7), 7.

McGuire, P. A. (2000, February). New hope for people with schizophrenia. *Monitor on Psychology, 31*(2), 24–28.

McKee, B. (2003, September 4). As suburbs grow, so do waistlines. *New York Times*, pp. F1, F 13.

McKellar, J., Stewart, E., & Humphreys, K. (2003). Alcoholics Anonymous involvement and positive alcohol-related outcomes: Cause, consequence, or just a correlate? A prospective 2-year study of 2,319 alcohol-dependent men. *Journal of Consulting and Clinical Psychology, 71*, 302–308.

McKenna, M. C., Zevon, M. A., Corn, B., & Rounds, J. (1999). Psychosocial factors and the development of breast cancer: A meta-analysis. *Health Psychology, 18*, 520–531.

McKinley, J. C., Jr. (2001, July 1). Landmark cell phone ban. *New York Times Week in Review*, p. 2.

McKnight Investigators. (2003). Risk factors for the onset of eating disorders in adolescent girls: Results of the McKnight Longitudinal Risk Factor Study. *American Journal of Psychiatry, 160*, 248–254.

McLean, C. R. K., Walton, K. G., Wenneberg, S. R., Levitsky, D. K., et al. (1997). Effects of the Transcendental Meditation program on adaptive mechanisms: Changes in hormone levels and responses to stress after 4 months of practice. *Psychoneuroendocrinology, 22*, 277–295.

McLellan, A. T., Lewis, D. C., O'Brien, C. P., & Kleber, H. D. (2000). Peer and parent influences on smoking and drinking among early adolescents. *Journal of the American Medical Association, 284*, 1689–1695.

McNally, R J. (2003). Recovering memories of trauma: A view from the laboratory. *Current Directions in Psychological Science, 12*, 32–35.

McNamar, M. P. (2004, February 10). Research on day care finds few timeouts. *New York Times*, p. F7.

Means, B., & Loftus, E. (1991). When personal history repeats itself: Decomposing memories for recurring events. *Applied Cognitive Psychology, 5*, 297–318.

Meeus, W. H. J., & Raaijmakers, Q. A. W. (1995). Obedience in modern society: The Utrecht studies. *Journal of Social Issues, 51*, 155–175.

Melani, D. (2001, January 17). Emotions can pull trigger on heart attack.

Evansville Courier and Press, Scripps Howard News Service. Retrieved February 20, 2001, from http://www.psycport.com/news/2001/01/17/eng-courierpress_features/eng-courierpress_features_134435_74_9803814571351.html.

Melding, P. S. (1995). How do older people respond to chronic pain? A review of coping with pain and illness in elders. *Pain Reviews, 2,* 65–75.

Meltzoff, A. N., & Gopnik, A. (1997). *Words, thoughts, and theories.* Cambridge, MA: MIT Press.

Melzack, R., & Wall, P. D. (1965). Pain mechanisms: A new theory. *Science, 150,* 971–979.

Melzack, R., & Wall, P. D. (1983). *The challenge of pain.* New York: Basic Books.

Memory capacity. *Journal of Experimental Psychology: General, 126,* 178–203.

Memory loss. (2000, May). *Harvard Health Letter, 25,* p. 1–3.

Merckelbach, H., Arntz, A., & de Jong, P. (1991). Conditioning experiences in spider phobics. *Behaviour Research and Therapy, 29,* 301–304.

Merckelbach, H., de Jong, P. J., Muris, P., & van den Hout, M. A. (1996). The etiology of specific phobias: A review. *Clinical Psychology Review, 16,* 337–361.

Merikangas, K. R., & Risch, N. (2003). Will the genomics revolution revolutionize psychiatry? *American Journal of Psychiatry, 160,* 625–635.

Messer, S. B. (2001). What makes brief psychodynamic therapy time efficient? *Clinical Psychology: Science and Practice, 8,* 5–22.

Metcalfe, J. (1986). Feelings of knowing in memory and problem solving. *Journal of Experimental Psychology: Learning, Memory, and Cognition, 12,* 288–294.

Meyer, G. J. (2000). Incremental validity of the Rorschach Prognostic Rating Scale over the MMPI Ego Strength Scale and IQ. *Journal of Personality Assessment, 74,* 365–370.

Meyer, G. J., Finn, S. E., Eyde, L. D., Kay, G. G., Dies, R. R., Eisman, E. J., et al. Amplifying issues related to psychological testing and assessment [Letter]. *American Psychologist, 57,* 140–141.

Meyer, I. H. (2003). Prejudice, social stress, and mental health in lesbian, gay, and bisexual populations: Conceptual issues and research evidence. *Psychological Bulletin, 129,* 674–697.

Meyer, J. H., McMain, S., Kennedy, S. H., Korman, L., Brown, G. M., DaSilva, J., et al. (2003). Dysfunctional attitudes and 5-HT2 receptors during depression and self-harm. *American Journal of Psychiatry, 160,* 90–99.

Meyers, A. W., Coleman, J. K., Whelan, J. P., Mehlenbeck, R. S. (2001). Examining careers in sport psychology: Who is working and who is making money? *Professional Psychology: Research and Practice, 32,* 5–11.

Mignot, E., & Thorsby, E. (2001). Narcolepsy and the HLA System. *New England Journal of Medicine, 344,* 692.

Milgram, S. (1963). Behavioral study of obedience. *Journal of Abnormal and Social Psychology, 67,* 371–378.

Milgram, S. (1974). *Obedience to authority.* New York: Harper & Row.

Milgram, S. (1974). *Obedience to authority.* New York: Harper & Row.

Miller, A. (2000, Fall/Winter). Growing up in the new family. *Newsweek Special Issue,* pp. 80–84.

Miller, A. G., Collins, B. E., & Brief, D. E. (1995). Perspectives on obedience to authority: The legacy of the Milgram experiments. *Journal of Social Issues, 51,* 1–19.

Miller, E. (1987). Hysteria: Its nature and explanation. *British Journal of Clinical Psychology, 26,* 163–173.

Miller, J. G., & Bersoff, D. M. (1992). Culture and moral judgment: How are conflicts between justice and interpersonal responsibilities resolved? *Journal of Personality and Social Psychology, 62,* 541–554.

Miller, J. J., Fletcher, K., & Kabat, A. J. (1995). Three-year follow-up and clinical implications of a mindfulness meditation-based stress reduction intervention in the treatment of anxiety disorders. *General Hospital Psychiatry, 17*(3), 192–200.

Miller, L. S., & Lachman, M. E. (2000). Cognitive performance and the role of health and control beliefs in midlife. *Aging, Neuropsychology, and Cognition, 7,* 69–85.

Miller, R. R., Barnet, R. C., & Grahame, N. J. (1995). Assessment of the Rescorla-Wagner model. *Psychological Bulletin, 117,* 363–386.

Miller, S. D., Blackburn, R., Scholes, G., White, G. L., & Mamalis, N. (1991). Optical differences in multiple personality disorder: A second look. *Journal of Nervous and Mental Disease, 179,* 132–135.

Miller, W. R., & Brown, S. A. (1997). Why psychologists should treat alcohol and drug problems. *American Psychologist, 52,* 1269–1279.

Miller-Jones, D. (1989). Culture and testing. *American Psychologist, 44,* 36–366.

Mills, J. L. (2000). Fortification of foods with folic acid—How much is enough? *New England Journal of Medicine, 342,* 1442–1445.

Mind over matter: Meditation helps ease pain for some patients. (2000, September 4). Retrieved September 6, 2000, from http://www.cnn.com/2000/HEALTH/alternative/09/04/meditation.pain.wmd/index.html.

Minda, J. P., & Smith, J. D. (2001). Prototypes in category learning: The effects of category size, category structure, and stimulus complexity. *Journal of Experimental Psychology: Learning, Memory, and Cognition, 27,* 775–799.

Minsky, S., Vega, W., Miskimen, T., Gara, M., & Escobar, J. (2003). Diagnostic patterns in Latino, African American, and European American psychiatric patients. *Archives of General Psychiatry, 60,* 637–644.

Mischel, W. (1973). Toward a cognitive social learning reconceptualization of personality. *Psychological Review, 80,* 252–283.

Mischel, W. (2004). Toward an integrative science of the person. *Annual Review of Psychology, 55,* 1–22.

Mischel, W., & Shoda, Y. (1995). Cognitive-affective system theory of personality: Reconceptualizing situations, dispositions, dynamics, and invariance in personality structure. *Psychological Review, 102,* 246–268.

Mischel, W., & Shoda, Y. (1999). Integrating dispositions and processing dynamics within a unified theory of personality: The cognitive-affective personality system. In L. A. Pervin, & O. P. John (Eds.), *Handbook of personality: Theory and research* (2nd ed.) (pp. 197–218). New York: Guilford Press.

Mitka, M. (2000). Psychiatrists help survivors in the Balkans. *Journal of the American Medical Association, 283,* 1277–1278.

Mitka, M. (2003). Economist takes aim at "big fat" US lifestyle. *Journal of the American Medical Association, 289,* 33–34.

Mixed progress on cancer front. (2003, September 3). *MSNBC Web Posting.* Retrieved September 4, 2003, from http://www.msnbc.com/news/960534.asp.

Mohr, C. D., Armeli, S., Tennen, H., Carney, M. A., Affleck, G., & Hromi, A. (2001). Daily interpersonal experiences, context, and alcohol consumption: Crying in your beer and toasting good times. *Journal of Personality and Social Psychology, 80,* 489–500.

Mokdad, A. H., Ford, E. S., Bowman, B. A., Dietz, W. H., Vinicor, F., Bales, V. S., et al. (2003). Prevalence of obesity, diabetes, and obesity-related health risk factors. *Journal of the American Medical Association, 289,* 76–79.

Mokdad, A. H., Ford, E. S., Bowman, B. A., Dietz, W. H., Vinicor, F., Bales, V. S., et al. (2003). Prevalence of obesity, diabetes, and obesity-related health risk factors. *Journal of the American Medical Association, 289,* 76–79.

Mollica, R. F., Henderson, D. C., & Tor, S. (2002). Psychiatric effects of traumatic brain injury events in Cambodian survivors of mass violence. *British Journal of Psychiatry, 181,* 339–347.

Monroe, S. M., Rohde, P., Seeley, J. R., & Lewinsohn, P. M. (1999). Life events and depression in adolescence: Relationship loss as a prospective risk factor for first onset of major depressive disorder. *Journal of Consulting and Clinical Psychology, 108,* 606–614.

Montes, R., Bedmar, M., & Martin, M. S. (1993). EMG biofeedback of the abductor pollicis brevis in piano performance. *Biofeedback and Self Regulation, 18,* 67–77.

Monti, P. M., Binkoff, J. A., Abrams, D. B., & Zwick, W. R. (1987). Reactivity of alcoholics and nonalcoholics to drinking cues. *Journal of Abnormal Psychology, 96,* 122–126.

Moon, C., Cooper, R. P., & Fifer, W. P. (1993). Two-day-olds prefer their native language. *Infant Behavior and Development, 16,* 495–500.

Mooney, M., White, T., & Hatsukami, D. (2004). The blind spot in the nicotine replacement therapy literature: Assessment of the double-blind in clinical trials. *Addictive Behaviors, 29,* 673–684.

Moos, R. H., & Moos, B. S. (2004). Long-term influence of duration and frequency of participation in alcoholics anonymous on individuals with alcohol use disorders. *Journal of Consulting and Clinical Psychology, 72,* 81–90.

Morgenstern, J., Bux, D., Labouvie, E., Blanchard, K. A., & Morgan, T. I. (2002). Examining mechanisms of action in 12-step treatment: The role of 12-step cognitions. *Journal of Studies on Alcohol, 63,* 665–672.

Morin, C. M. (2000). The nature of insomnia and the need to refine our diagnostic criteria. *Psychosomatic Medicine, 62,* 483–485.

Morin, C. M., & Wooten, V. (1996). Psychological and pharmacological approaches to treating insomnia: Critical issues in assessing their separate and combined effects. *Clinical Psychology Review, 16,* 521–542.

Morris, P. E., & Gruneberg, M. M. (1996). Practical aspects of memory: The first 2500 years. In D. Herrmann et al. (Eds.), *Basic and applied memory research: Theory in context* (Vol. 1, pp. 27–50). Mahwah, NJ: Lawrence Erlbaum Associates.

Morris, W. N., Miller, R. S., & Spangenberg, S. (1977). The effects of dissenter position and task difficulty on conformity and response conflict. *Journal of Personality, 45,* 251–256.

Motl, R. W., Dishman, R. K., Saunders, R. P., Dowda, M., Felton, G., Ward, D. S., et al. (2002). Examining social-cognitive determinants of intention and physical activity among Black and White adolescent girls using structural equation modeling. *Health Psychology, 21,* 459–467.

Mueser, K. T., & Liberman, R. P. (1995). Behavior therapy in practice. In B. Bongar & L. E. Beutler (Eds.), *Comprehensive textbook of psychotherapy: Theory and practice* (pp. 84–110). New York: Oxford.

Mukamal, K. J., Conigrave, K. M., Mittleman, M. A., Camargo, Jr., C. A., Stampfer, M. J., Willett, W. C., et al. (2003). Roles of drinking pattern and type of alcohol consumed in coronary heart disease in men. *New England Journal of Medicine, 348*, 109–118.

Munakata, Y., McClelland, J. L., Johnson, M. H., & Siegler, R. S. (1997). Rethinking infant knowledge: Toward an adaptive process account of successes and failures in object permanence tasks. *Psychological Review, 104*, 686–713.

Muñoz, N., Bosch, X., de Sanjosé, S., Herrero, R., Castellsagué, X., Shah, K. V., Snijders, P. J. F., et al. (2003). Epidemiologic classification of human papillomavirus types associated with cervical cancer. *New England Journal of Medicine, 348*, 518–527.

Murphy, E. M. (2003). Being born female is dangerous for your health. *American Psychologist, 58*, 205–210.

Murphy, S. T., & Zajonc, R. B. (1993). Affect, cognition, and awareness: Affective priming with optimal and suboptimal stimulus exposures. *Journal of Personality and Social Psychology, 64*, 723–739.

Murray, B. (1995, November). Gender gap in math scores is closing. *APA Monitor, 26*(11), 43.

Murray, D. J., Kilgour, A. R., & Wasylkiw, L. (2000). Conflicts and missed signals in psychoanalysis, behaviorism, and Gestalt psychology. *American Psychologist, 55*, 422–426.

Murray, H. A. (1938). *Explorations in personality*. New York: Oxford University Press.

Murray, J. B. (1995). Evidence of acupuncture's analgesic effectiveness and proposals for the physiological mechanisms involved. *Journal of Psychology, 129*, 443–461.

Murstein, B. I., & Mathes, S. (1996). Projection on projective techniques pathology: The problem that is not being addressed. *Journal of Personality Assessment, 66*, 337–349.

Murtagh, D. R. R., & Greenwood, K. M. (1995). Identifying effective psychological treatments for insomnia: A meta-analysis. *Journal of Consulting and Clinical Psychology, 63*, 79–89.

Myers, D. G., & Diener, E. (1997). The pursuit of happiness. *Scientific American Mysteries of the Mind, Special Issue 7*(1), 18–26.

Nabel, E. G. (2003). Cardiovascular disease. *New England Journal of Medicine, 349*, 60–72.

Nadol, J. B., Jr. (1993). Hearing loss. *New England Journal of Medicine, 329*, 1092–1102.

Nagourney, E. (2001, January 23). Curbing aggression with the off switch. *New York Times*, p. F7.

Nagourney, E. (2003). Cellphone peril, hands on or off. *New York Times*, p. F6.

Naimi, T. S., Brewer, R. D., Mokdad, A., Denny, C., Serdula, M. K., & Marks, J. S. (2003). Binge drinking among US adults. *Journal of the American Medical Association, 289*, 70–75.

Nash, M. (1987). What, if anything, is regressed about hypnotic age regression? A review of the empirical literature. *Psychological Bulletin, 102*, 42–52.

Näslund, J., Haroutunian, V., Mohs, R., Davis, K. L. Davies, P., Greengard, P., et al. (2000). Correlation between elevated levels of amyloid-peptide in the brain and cognitive decline. *Journal of the American Medical Association, 283*, 1571–1577.

Nathan, P. E., Stuart, S. P., & Dolan, S. L. (2000). Research on psychotherapy efficacy and effectiveness: Between Scylla and Charybdis? *Psychological Bulletin, 126*, 964–981.

National Cancer Institute, National Institutes of Health. (1996, April). *Cancer facts, sites and types: Questions and answers about metastatic cancer*. Bethesda, MD: Author.

National Institute on Drug Abuse (NIDA). (1995). *NIDA capsule: LSD (Lysergic Acid Diethylamindde; C-92-01)*. Bethesda, MD: Author.

National Institute on Alcohol Abuse and Alcoholism. (1996). *Epidemiologic data reference manuals, 1979–92*. Bethesda, MD: Author.

National Science Foundation, Division of Science Resources Statistics. (2004, April). *Science and engineering degrees, by race/ethnicity of recipients: 1992–2001*, NSF 04-318, Project Officers Susan T. Hill and Jean M. Johnson (Arlington, VA).

Naughton, K. (2004, February 2). The soft sell. *Newsweek*, pp. 46–47.

Neff, J. A., & Hoppe, S. K. (1993). Race/ethnicity, acculturation, and psychological distress: Fatalism and religiosity as cultural resources. *Journal of Community Psychology, 21*, 3–20.

Neher, A. (1996). Jung's theory of archetypes: A critique. *Journal of Humanistic Psychology, 36*(2), 61–91.

Neisser, U., Boodoo, G., Bouchard, T. J., Jr., Boykin, A. W., Brody, N., Ceci, S. J., et al. (1996). Intelligence: Knowns and unknowns. *American Psychologist, 51*, 77–101.

Neitz, M., & Neitz, J. (1995). Numbers and ratios of visual pigment genes for normal red-green color vision. *Science, 267*, 1013–1016.

Nelson, D. L., McEvoy, C. L., & Pointer, L. (2003). Spreading activation or spooky action at a distance? *Journal of Experimental Psychology: Learning, Memory, and Cognition, 29*, 42–52.

Nelson, T. D. (2002). *The psychology of prejudice*. Needham Heights, MA: Allyn and Bacon.

Nemiah, J. C. (1978). Psychoneurotic disorders. In A. M. Nicholi, Jr. (Ed.), *The new Harvard guide to psychiatry* (pp. 234–258). Cambridge, MA: Belknap Press.

Nevid, J. S. (1984). Sex differences in factors of romantic attraction. *Sex Roles, 11*, 401–411.

Nevid, J. S. (1998). *Choices: Sex in the age of STDs* (2nd ed.). Needham Heights, MA: Allyn & Bacon.

Nevid, J. S., & Greene, B. (2003). *Abnormal psychology in a changing world* (5th ed.). Upper Saddle River, NJ: Prentice-Hall.

Nevid, J. S., & Sta. Maria, N. (1999). Multicultural issues in qualitative research. *Psychology and Marketing, 16*, 305–325.

Nevid, J. S., Rathus, S. A., & Fichner-Rathus, L. (1995). *Human sexuality in a world of diversity* (2nd ed.). Boston: Allyn & Bacon.

Nevid, J. S., Rathus, S. A., & Greene, B. (2006). Abnormal psychology in a changing world (6th ed.). Upper Saddle River, NJ: Prentice-Hall.

Nevid, J. S., Rathus, S. A., & Greene, B. A. (1997). *Abnormal psychology in a changing world* (3rd ed.). Upper Saddle River, NJ: Prentice-Hall.

Nevid, J. S., Rathus, S. A., & Greene, B. A. (2000). *Abnormal psychology in a changing world* (4th ed.). Upper Saddle River, NJ: Prentice-Hall.

Nevid, J. S., Rathus, S. A., & Greene, B. A. (2003). *Abnormal psychology in a changing world* (5th ed.) Upper Saddle River, NJ: Prentice-Hall.

Nevid, J. S., Rathus, S. A., & Rubenstein, H. R. (1998). *Health in the new millennium*. New York: Worth.

New studies define cell-phone hazards. (2003, May). *Consumer Reports*, p. 8.

Newby-Clark, I. R., McGregor, I., & Zanna, M. P. (2002). Thinking and caring about cognitive inconsistency: When and for whom does attitudinal ambivalence feel uncomfortable? *Journal of Personality and Social Psychology, 82*, 157–166.

Newton, J., Toby, O., Spence, S. H., & Schotte, D. (1995). Cognitive-behavioral therapy versus EMG biofeedback in the treatment of chronic low back pain. *Behaviour Research and Therapy, 33*, 691–697.

Niaura, R., Todaro, J. F., Stroud, L., Spiro, A., III, Ward, K. D., & Weiss, S. (2002). Hostility, the metabolic syndrome, and incident coronary heart disease. *Health Psychology, 21*, 588–593.

NICHD Early Child Care Research Network. (1997). The effects of infant child care on infant-mother attachment security: Results of the NICHD study of early child care. *Child Development, 68*, 860–879.

Nicholson, R. A., Mouton, G. J., Bagby, R. M., Buis, T., Peterson, S. A., Buigas, R. A. (1997). Utility of MMPI-2 indicators of response distortion: Receiver operating characteristic analysis. *Psychological Assessment, 9*, 471–479.

Nickerson, R. A., & Adams, M. J. (1979). Long-term memory for a common object. *Cognitive Psychology, 11*, 287–307.

Nieto, F. J., Young, T. B., Lind, B. K., Shahar, E., Samet, J. M., Redline S., et al. (2000). Association of sleep-disordered breathing, sleep apnea, and hypertension in a large community-based study. *Journal of the American Medical Association, 283*, 1829–1836.

NIH Consensus Development Panel on Osteoporosis Prevention, Diagnosis, and Therapy. (2001). Osteoporosis prevention, diagnosis, and therapy. *Journal of the American Medical Association, 285*, 785–795.

NIMH (National Institute of Mental Health). (2001). *Seeing our feelings: Imaging emotion in the brain* (NIH Publication No. 01-460). Bethesda, MD: Author.

Nisbett, R. E. (2003). *The geography of thought: How Asians and Westerners think differently. . . and why*. New York: Free Press.

Nolen-Hoeksema, S., & Girgus, J. S. (1994). The emergence of gender differences in depression during adolescence. *Psychological Bulletin, 115*, 424–443.

Nolen-Hoeksema, S., Morrow, J., & Fredrickson, B. L. (1993). Response styles and the duration of episodes of depressed mood. *Journal of Abnormal Psychology, 102*, 20–28.

Nosek, B. A., Banaji, M. R., & Greenwald, A. G. (2003). Math = male, me = female, therefore math (me. *Journal of Personality and Social Psychology, 83*, 44–59.

Nowak, A., Vallacher, R. R., & Miller, M. E. (2003). Social influence and group dynamics. In T. Millon & M. J. Lerner (Eds.), *Handbook of psychology: Personality and social psychology, Vol. 5* (pp. 383–418). New York: John Wiley & Sons.

NSAID use may help prevent Parkinson's. (2003, August 19). *USA Today*, p. 7D.

Nurnberger, J. I. Jr., Foroud, T., Flury, L., Su, J., Meyer, E. T., Hu, K., et al. (2001). Evidence for a locus on chromosome 1 that influences vulnerability to alcoholism and affective disorder. *American Journal of Psychiatry, 158*, 718–724.

Nussbaum, R. L., & Ellis, C. E. (2003). Alzheimer's disease and Parkinson's disease. *New England Journal of Medicine, 348*, 1356–1364.

Nyberg, L., Maitland, S. B., Rönnlund, M., Bäckman, L., Dixon, R., et al. (2003). Selective adult age differences in an age-invariant multifactor model of declarative memory. *Psychology and Aging, 18*, No. 1, 149–160.

O'Brien, C. P., Childress, A. R., Mclellan, A. T., & Ehrman, R. (1992). Classical conditioning in drug-dependent humans. *Annals of the New York Academy of Sciences, 654*, 400–415.

O'Connor, E. (2001a, January). Law sanctions new treatment for heroin addiction—and recommends psychological counseling. *Monitor on Psychology, 32*(1), 18.

O'Connor, E. (2001b, February). Researchers pinpoint potential cause of autism. *Monitor on Psychology*, p. 13.

O'Connor, P. G. (2000). Treating opioid dependence—New data and new opportunities [Editorial]. *New England Journal of Medicine, 343*, 1332–1334.

O'Connor, T. G., Caspi, A., DeFries, J. C., & Plomin, R. (2000). Are associations between parental divorce and children's adjustment genetically mediated? An adoption study. *Developmental Psychology, 36*, 429–437.

O'Donnell, J. (2003, April 24). Traffic deaths rise to 12-year high. *USA Today*, p. 1D.

Öhman, A., & Mineka, S. (2001). Fears, phobias, and preparedness: Toward an evolved module of fear and fear learning. *Psychological Review, 108*, 483–522.

O'Leary, A. (1990). Stress, emotion, and human immune functions. *Psychological Bulletin, 108*, 383–382.

Olfson, M. Marcus, S. C, Druss, B., Elinson, L., Tanielian, T., & Pincus, A. (2002). National trends in the outpatient treatment of depression. *Journal of the American Medical Association, 287*, 203–209.

Olfson, M., Marcus, S. C., Druss, B., Elinson, L., Tanielian, T., & Pincus, H. A. (2002). National trends in the outpatient treatment of depression. *Journal of the American Medical Association, 287*, 203–209.

Olkin, R. (2002). Could you hold the door for me? Including disability in diversity. *Cultural Diversity and Ethnic Minority Psychology, 8*, 130–137.

Olson, E. (2001, October 7). Countries lag in treating mental illness, W. H. O. says. *New York Times*, p. A24.

Olson, G. A., Olson, R. D., & Kastin, A. J. (1992). Endogenous opiates: 1991. *Peptides, 13*, 1247–1287.

Olson, J. M., & Maio, G. R. (2003). Attitudes in social behavior. In T. Millon & M. J. Lerner (Eds.), *Handbook of psychology: Personality and social psychology, Vol. 5* (pp. 299–326). New York: John Wiley & Sons.

O'Neil, J. (2003, February 4). Jog your memory? At the gym? *New York Times*, p. F6.

Onion, A. (2000, September 12). Mind games: Subliminal ads mostly ineffective, but Americans think otherwise. *ABC News.com*. Retrieved September 19, 2000, from http://abcnews.go.com/sections/science/DailyNews/subliminal000912.html.

Oquendo, M. A., Friend, J. M., Halberstam, B., Brodsky, B. S., Burke, A. K., Grunebaum, M. F., Malone, K. M., & Mann, J. J. (2003). Association of comorbid posttraumatic stress disorder and major depression with greater risk for suicidal behavior. *American Journal of Psychiatry, 160*, 580–582.

Ormel, J., Oldehinkel, A. J., & Brilman, E. I. (2001). The interplay and etiological continuity of neuroticism, difficulties, and life events in the etiology of major and subsyndromal, first and recurrent depressive episodes in later life. *American Journal of Psychiatry, 158*, 885–891.

Ormerod, T. C., MacGregor, J. N., & Chronicle, E. P. (2002). Dynamics and constraints in insight problem solving. *Journal of Experimental Psychology: Learning, MEMORY, AND COGNITION, 28*, 791–799.

Ortega, A. N., Rosenheck, R., Alegria, M., Desai, R. A. (2000). Acculturation and the lifetime risk of psychiatric and substance use disorders among Hispanics. *Journal of Nervous and Mental Disease, 188*, 728–735.

Orth-Gomer, K., Wamala, S. P., Horsten, M., Schenck-Gustafsson, K., Schneiderman, N., & Mittleman, M. A. (2000). Marital stress worsens prognosis in women with coronary heart disease: The Stockholm Female Coronary Risk Study. *Journal of the American Medical Association, 284*, 3008–3014.

Osborne, A. F. (1963). *Applied imagination: Principles and procedures of creative problem solving*. New York: Scribners.

Ostler, K., Thompson, C., Kinmonth, A. L. K., Peveler, R. C., Stevens, L., &

Stevens, A. (2001). Influence of socio-economic deprivation on the prevalence and outcome of depression in primary care: The Hampshire Depression Project. *British Journal of Psychiatry, 178*, 12–17.

Otto, R. K., & Heilbrun, K. (2002). The practice of forensic psychology: A look toward the future in light of the past. *American Psychologist, 57*, 5–18.

Ouellette, S. C., & DiPlacido, J. (2001). Personality's role in the protection and enhancements of health: Where the research has been, where it is stuck, how it might move. In A. Baum, T. A. Revenson, & J. E. Singer (Eds.), *Handbook of health psychology* (pp. 175–194). Mahwah, NJ: Lawrence Erlbaum Associates.

Oyserman, D., Coon, H. M., & Kemmelmeier, M. (2002). Rethinking individualism and collectivism: Evaluation of theoretical assumptions and meta-analyses. *Psychological Bulletin, 128*, 3–72.

Ozegovic, J. J., Bikos, L H., & Szymanski, D. M. (2001). Trends and predictors of alcohol use among undergraduate female students. *Journal of College Student Development, 42*, 1–9.

Özgen, E. (2004). Language, learning, and color perception. *Current Directions in Psychological Science, 13*, 95–102.

Özgen, E., & Davies, I. R. L. (2002). Acquisition of categorical color perception: A perceptual learning approach to the linguistic relativity hypothesis. *Journal of Experimental Psychology: General, 131*, 477–493.

Pallesen, S., Hilde, I. N., Havik, O. E., & Nielsen, G. H. (2001). Clinical assessment and treatment of insomnia. *Professional Psychology: Research and Practice, 32*, 115–124.

Palmiter, D. Jr., & Renjilian, D. (2003). Clinical Web pages: Do they meet expectations? *Professional Psychology: Research and Practice, 34*, 164–169.

Pankratz, N., Nichols, W. C., Uniacke, S. K., Halter, C., Rudolph, A., Shults, C., et al. (2002). Genome screen to identify susceptibility genes for Parkinson disease in a sample without Parkinson mutations. *American Journal of Human Genetics, 71*, 124–135.

Park, D. C., Lautenschlager, G., Hedden, T., Davidson, N. S., Smith, A. D., & Smith, P. K. (2002). Models of visuospatial and verbal memory across the adult life span. *Psychology and Aging, 17*, 299–320.

Park, J., & Banaji, M. R. (2000). Mood and heuristics: The influence of happy and sad states on sensitivity and bias in stereotyping. *Journal of Personality and Social Psychology, 78*, 1005–1023.

Parke, R. D. (2004). Development in the family. *Annual Review of Psychology, 55*, 365–399.

Parke, R. D., & Buriel, R. (1997). Socialization in the family: Ethnic and ecological perspectives. In W. Damon (Editor-in-Chief) & N. Eisenberg (Vol. Ed.), *Handbook of child psychology: 5th ed., Vol. 3. Social, emotional, and personality development* (pp. 463–552). New York: John Wiley & Sons.

Parker, G., Gladstone, G., & Chee, K. T. (2001). Depression in the planet's largest ethnic group: the Chinese. *American Journal of Psychiatry, 158*, 857–864.

Parkes, J. D., Clift, S. J., Dahlitz, M. J., Chen, S. Y., & Dunn, G. (1995). The narcoleptic syndrome. *Journal of Neurology, Neurosurgery and Psychiatry, 59*, 221–224.

Parloff, R. (2003, February 3). Is fat the next tobacco? *Fortune*, pp. 51–54.

Partinen, M., & Telakivi, T. (1992). Epidemiology of obstructive sleep apnea syndrome. *Sleep, 15*(6), S1–S4.

Pascalis, O., de Haan, M., & Nelson, C. A. (2002). Is face processing species-specific during the first year of life? *Neuroscience, 296*, 1321–1323.

Pascalis, O., deHaan, M., Nelson, C. A., & de Schonen, S. (1998). Long-term recognition memory for faces assessed by visual paired comparison in 3- and 6-month-old infants. *Journal of Experimental Psychology: Learning, Memory, and Cognition, 24*, 249–260.

Pasupathi, M. (1999). Age differences in response to conformity pressure for emotional and nonemotional material. *Psychology and Aging, 14*, 170–174.

Pate, J. L. (2000). Psychological organizations in the United States. *American Psychologist, 55*, 1139–1143.

Pate, R. R., Pratt, M. Blair, S. N., Haskell, W. L., Macera, C. A., Bouchard, C., et al. (1995). Physical activity and public health: A recommendation from the Centers for Disease Control and Prevention and the American College of Sports Medicine. *Journal of the American Medical Association, 273*, 402–407.

Patterson, D. R., & Jensen, M. P. (2003) Hypnosis and clinical pain. *Psychological Bulletin, 129*, 495–521.

Patton, G. C., Coffey, C., Carlin, J. B., Degenhardt, L., Lynskey, M., & Hall, W. (2002). Cannabis use and mental health in young people: Cohort study. *British Medical Journal, 325*, 1195–1198.

Paunonen, S. V. (1998). Hierarchical organization of personality and prediction of behavior. *Journal of Personality and Social Psychology, 74*, 538–556.

Paunonen, S. V. (2003). Big Five factors of personality and replicated predictions of behavior. *Jouurnal of Personality and Social Psychology, 84*, 411–424.

Payne, D. G., & Wenger, M. J. (1996). Practice effects in memory: Data, theory, and unanswered questions. In D. Herrmann, C. McEvoy, C. Hertzog, P. Hertel, & M. K. Johnson (Eds.), *Basic and applied memory research: Practical applications* (Vol. 2, pp. 123–138). Mahwah, NJ: Lawrence Erlbaum Associates.

Pearson, J. L., & Brown, G. K. (2000). Suicide prevention in late life: Direction for science and practice. *Clinical Psychology Review, 20*, 685–705.

Pedersen, D. M., & Wheeler, J. (1983). The Mueller-Lyer illusion among Navajos. *Journal of Social Psychology, 121*, 3–6.

Pelham, W. E., Hoza, B., Pillow, D. R., Gnagy, E. M., Kipp, H. L., Greiner, A. R., et al. (2002). Effects of methylphenidate and expectancy on children with ADHD: Behavior, academic performance, and attributions in a summer treatment program and regular classroom settings. *Journal of Consulting and Clinical Psychology, 70*, 320–335

Pengilly, J. W., & Dowd, E. T. (2000). Hardiness and social support as moderators of stress. *Journal of Clinical Psychology, 56*, 813–820.

Perlman, L. M. (2001). Nonspecific, unintended, and serendipitous effects in psychotherapy. *Professional Psychology: Research and Practice, 32*, 283–288.

Petkova, K. G., Ajzen, I., & Driver, B. L. (1995). Salience of anti-abortion beliefs and commitment to an attitudinal position: On the strength, structure, and predictive validity of anti-abortion attitudes. *Journal of Applied Social Psychology, 25*, 463–483.

Petticrew, M., Bell, R., & Hunter, D. (2002). Influence of psychological coping on survival and recurrence in people with cancer: Systematic review. *British Medical Journal, 325*, 1066–1069.

Petty, R. E., & Cacioppo, J. T. (1986). The elaboration-likelihood model of persuasion. In L. Berkowitz (Ed.), *Advances in experimental social psychology* (Vol. 19). New York: Academic Press.

Petty, R. E., & Wegener, D. T. (1998). Multiple roles for persuasion. In D. T. Gilbert, S. T. Fiske, & G. Lindzey (Eds.), *The handbook of social psychology* (4th ed., Vol. 1, pp. 323–390). Boston: McGraw-Hill.

Petty, R. E., Wegener, D. T., & Fabrigar, L. R. (1997). Attitudes and attitude change. *Annual Review of Psychology, 48*, 609–647.

Phillips, S. T., & Ziller, R. C. (1997). Toward a theory and measure of the nature of nonprejudice. *Journal of Personality and Social Psychology, 72*, 420–434.

Phillips, T. J., Belknap, J. K., Hitzemann, R. J., Buck, K. J., Cunningham, C. L., & Crabbe, J. C. (2002). Harnessing the mouse to unravel the genetics of human disease. *Genes, Brain and Behavior, 1*, 14–26.

Phinney, J., & Alipuria, L. (1990). Ethnic identity in older adolescents from four ethnic groups. *Journal of Adolescence, 13*, 171–183.

Piaget, J. (1952). *The origins of intelligence in children*. New York: International Universities Press.

Pickering, T. G. (2003). Lifestyle modification and blood pressure control: Is the glass half full or half empty? *Journal of the American Medical Association, 289*, 2131–2132.

Pihl, R. O., Peterson, J., & Finn, P. (1990). Inherited predisposition to alcoholism: Characteristics of sons of male alcoholics. *Journal of Abnormal Psychology, 99*, 291–301.

Pilcher, H. R. (2003, May 28). Men's underarms may hold clue to new fertility drug. *Nature Science Update*. Retrieved June 10, 2003, from http://www.nature.com/nsu/030527/030527-2.html.

Pinel, J. P. J., Assanand, S., & Lehman, D. R. (2000). Hunger, eating, and ill health. *American Psychologist, 55*, 1105–1116.

Pink, D. (2003, December 14). Gratitude visits. *New York Times Magazine*, p. 73.

Pinker, S. (1994). *The language instinct*. New York: William Morrow.

Pinker, S. (2003). Language as an adaptation to the cognitive niche. In M. H. Christiansen & S. Kirby (Eds.), *Language evolution* (pp. 16–37). New York: Oxford University Press.

Pinquart, M., & Sörensen, S. (2000). Influences of socioeconomic status, social network, and competence on subjective well-being in later life: A meta-analysis.

Pi-Sunyer, X. (2003). A clinical view of the obesity problem [Editorial]. *Science, 299*, 859–860.

Pittman, T. S. (1998). Motivation. In D. T. Gilbert, S. T. Fiske, & G. Lindzey (Eds.), *The handbook of social psychology* (4th ed., Vol. 1, pp. 549–590). Boston: McGraw-Hill.

Plaks, J. E., & Higgins, E. T. (2000). Pragmatic use of stereotyping in teamwork: Social loafing and compensation as a function of inferred partner-situation fit. *Journal of Personality and Social Psychology, 79*, 962–974.

Playboy Enterprises Inc. (1994). *The Bill Gates Interview*. Retrieved December 8, 1994, from http://ei.cs.vt.edu/~history/Bill.Gates.html.

Pliner, P. H., Hart, H., Kohl, J., & Saari, D. (1974). Compliance without pressure: Some further data on the foot-in-the door technique. *Journal of Experimental Social Psychology, 10*, 17–22.

Plomin, R. (2003, April). 65 years of DNA. *APS Observer, 16*(4), pp. 7–8.

Plomin, R., & Crabbe, J. C. (2001). DNA. *Psychological Bulletin, 126*, 806–828.

Plomin, R., & McGuffin, P. (2003). Psychopathology in the postgenomic era. *Annual Review of Psychology, 54*, 205–228.

Plomin, R., & Petrill, S. A. (1997). Genetics and intelligence: What's new. *Intelligence, 24*, 53–57.

Plomin, R., DeFries, J. C., Craig, I. W., & McGuffin, P. (Eds.). (2003). *Behavioral genetics in the postgenomic era*. Washington, DC: APA Books.

Plomin, R., DeFries, J., & McClearn, G. E., & Rutter, M. (1997). *Behavioral genetics* (3rd ed.). New York: Freeman.

Plomin, R., Owen, M. J., & McGuffin, P. (1994). The genetic basis of complex human behaviors. *Science, 264*, 1733–1739.

Plous, S. (1996). Attitudes toward the use of animals in psychological research and education. *American Psychologist, 51*, 1167–1180.

Podolsky, D. (1996, May 13). No to an ancient art. *U.S. News and World Report*, pp. 78–80.

Polinko, N. K., & Popovich, P. M. (2001). Evil thoughts but angelic actions: Responses to overweight job applicants. *Journal of Applied Social Psychology, 31*, 905–924.

Pollack, A. (2004a, January 13). Sleep experts debate root of insomnia: Body, mind or a little of each. *The New York Times*, p. F8.

Pollack, A. (2004b, January 13). Putting a price on a good night's sleep. *New York Times*, pp. F1, F8.

Pollan, M. (2003, October 12). The (Agri)cultural contradictions of obesity. *NEW YORK TIMES MAGAZINE*, PP. 41, 48.

Pollock, V. E. (1992). Meta-analysis of subjective sensitivity to alcohol in sons of alcoholics. *American Journal of Psychiatry, 149*, 1534–1538.

Pope, H., & Katz, D. (1990). Homicide and near-homicide by anabolic steroid users. *Journal of Clinical Psychiatry, 51*, 28–31.

Pope, H.G., Kouri, E. M., & Hudson, J. I. (2000). Effects of supraphysiologic doses of testosterone on mood and aggression in normal men: a randomized controlled trial. *Archives of General Psychiatry, 57,* 133–140.

Potkin, S. G., Alva, G., Fleming, K., Anand, R., Keator, D., Carreon, D., et al. (2002). A PET study of the pathophysiology of negative symptoms in schizophrenia. *American Journal of Psychiatry, 159*, 227–237.

Pratto, F., Stallworth, L. M., Sidanius, J., Siers, B., et al. (1997). The gender gap in occupational role attainment: A social dominance approach. *Journal of Personality and Social Psychology, 72*, 37–53.

Premack, D. (1971). Language in chimpanzees. *Science, 172*, 808–822.

Preti, G., Wysocki, C. J., Barnhart, K. T., Sondheimer, S. J., & Leyden, J. J. (2003). Male axillary extracts contain pheromones that affect pulsatile secretion of luteinizing hormone and mood in women recipients. *Biology of Reproduction, 68*, 2107–2113.

Preuss, U. W., Schuckit, M. A, Smith, T. L., Danko, G. P., Bucholz, K. K., & Hesselbrock, M. N., et al. (2003). Predictors and correlates of suicide attempts over 5 years in 1,237 alcohol-dependent men and women. *American Journal of Psychiatry, 160*, 56–63.

Probst, T., Katterbach, T., & Wist, E. R. (1995). Vestibularly evoked potentials (VESTEPs) of the horizontal semicircular canals under different body positions in space. *Journal of Vestibular Research: Equilibrium and Orientation, 5*, 253–263.

Prudic, J., Olfson, M., Marcus, S. C., Fuller, R. B., & Sackeim, H. A. (2004). Effectiveness of electroconvulsive therapy in community settings. *Biological Psychiatry, 55*, 301–312.

Pungello, E. P., Kupersmidt, J. B., Burchinal, M. R., & Patterson, C. J. (1996). Environmental risk factors and children's achievement from middle childhood to early adolescence. *Developmental Psychology, 32*, 755–767.

Pushkar, D., Etezadi, J., Andres, D., Arbuckle, T., Schwartzman, A. E., & Chaikelson, J. (1999). Models of intelligence in late life: Comment on Hultsch et al. (1999). *Psychology and Aging, 14*, 520–527.

Qin, P., Agerbo, E., & Mortensen, P. B. (2003). Suicide risk in relation to socioeconomic, demographic, psychiatric, and familial factors: A national register–based study of all suicides in Denmark, 1981–1997. *American Journal of Psychiatry, 160*, 765–772.

Quesnel, C., Savard, J., Simard, S., Ivers, H., & Morin, C. M. (2003). Efficacy of cognitive-behavioral therapy for insomnia in women treated for nonmetastatic breast cancer. *Journal of Consulting and Clinical Psychology, 71*, 189–200.

Quinn, K. P., & McDougal, J. L. (1998). A mile wide and a mile deep: Comprehensive interventions for children and youth with emotional an behavioral disorders and their families. *School Psychology Review, 27*, 191–203.

Quinn, S. (1987). *A mind of her own: The life of Karen Horney*. New York: Summit Books.

Rabasca, L. (2000a, March). Listening instead of preaching. *Monitor on Psychology, 31*(3), pp. 50–51.

Rabasca, L. (2000b, July/August). Therapy that starts online but aims to continue in the psychologist's office. *Monitor on Psychology*, p. 15.

Rahman, Q., & Wilson, G. D. (2002). Born gay? The psychobiology of human sexual orientation. *Personality and Individual Differences, 34*, 1337–1382.

Raine, A., Lencz, T., Bihrle, S., LaCasse, L., & Colletti, P. (2000). Reduced prefrontal gray matter volume and reduced autonomic activity in antisocial personality disorder. *Archives of General Psychiatry, 57*, 119–127.

Ravert, A. A., & Martin, J. (1997). Family stress, perception of pregnancy, and age of first menarche among pregnant adolescents. *Adolescence, 32*(126), 261–270.

Ray, O., & Ksir, C. (1990). *Drugs, society, and human behavior* (5th ed.). St. Louis: Times Mirror/Mosby.

Raymond, J. (2000a, Fall/Winter). Kids, start your engines. *Newsweek Special Issue*, pp. 8–11.

Raymond, J. (2000b, Fall/Winter). The world of the senses. *Newsweek Special Issue*, pp. 16–18.

Read, J. P., Wood, M. D., Kahlera, C. W., Maddock, J. E., & Palfaid, T. P. (2003). Examining the role of drinking motives in college student alcohol use and problems. *Psychology of Addictive Behaviors, 17*, 13–23.

Recarte, M. A., & Nunes, L. M. (2003). Mental workload while driving: Effects on visual search, discrimination, and decision making. *Journal of Experimental Psychology—Applied, 9*, 119–137.

Rector, N. A., & Beck, A. T. (2001). Cognitive behavioral therapy for schizophrenia: An empirical review. *Journal of Nervous and Mental Disease, 189*, 278–287.

Redd, W. H. (1995). Behavioral research in cancer as a model for health psychology. *Health Psychology, 14*, 99–100.

Redelmeier, D. A., & Tibshirani, R. J. (1997). Association between cellular-telephone calls and motor vehicle collisions. *New England Journal of Medicine, 336*, 453–458.

Reese-Weber, M., (2000). Middle and late adolescents' conflict resolution skills with siblings: Associations with interparental and parent-adolescent conflict resolution. *Journal of Youth and Adolescence, 29, 697–711.*

Reese-Weber, M., & Marchand, J. E. (2002). Family and individual predictors of late adolescents' romantic relationships. *Journal of Youth and dolescence, 31, 197–206.*

Refinetti, R. (2000). *Circadian physiology*. Boca Raton, FL: CRC Press.

Reid, P. T. (2002). Multicultural psychology: Bringing together gender and ethnicity. *Cultural Diversity and Ethnic Minority Psychology, 8*, 103–114.

Reisberg, B., Doody, R., Stoffler, A., Schmitt, F., Ferris, S., Mobius, H. J., & Memantine Study Group. (2003). Memantine in moderate-to-severe Alzheimer's disease. *New England Journal of Medicine, 348*, 1333–1341.

Reiss, D., Neiderhiser, J. M., Hetherington, E. M., & Plomin, R. (2000). *The relationship code: Deciphering genetic and social influences on adolescent development*. Cambridge, MA: Harvard University Press.

Reneman, L., Lavalaye, J., Schmand, B., de Wolff, F. A., van den Brink, W., et al. (2001). Cortical serotonin transporter density and verbal memory in individuals who stopped using 3,4-methylenedioxymethamphetamine (MDMA or "Ecstasy"): Preliminary findings. *Archives of General Psychiatry, 58*, 901–906.

Renner, M. J., & Mackin, R. S. (1998). A life stress instrument for classroom use. *Teaching of Psychology, 25*, 46–48.

Report: Americans living longer. (2002, September 12). *CNN Web Posting*. Retrieved September 18, 2002, from http://www.cnn.com/2002/HEALTH/09/12/longer.life.expectancy.ap/index.html.

Rescorla, R. A. (1967). Pavlovian conditioning and its proper control procedures. *Psychological Review, 74*, 71–80.

Rescorla, R. A. (1988). Pavlovian conditioning: It's not what you think it is. *American Psychologist, 43*, 151–160.

Rescorla, R. A. (1999). Partial reinforcement reduces the associative change produced by nonreinforcement. *Journal of Experimental Psychology: Animal Behavior Processes, 25*, 403–414.

Resnick, M. D., Bearman, P. S., Blum, R. W., Bauman, K. E., Harris, K. M., Jones, J., et al. (1997). Protecting adolescents from harm: Findings from the National Longitudinal Study on Adolescent Health. *Journal of the American Medical Association, 278*, 823–832.

Restle, F. (1970). Moon illusion explained on the basis of relative size. *Science, 167*, 1092–1096.

Reuters. (2002, May 16). Infants learn early to spot faces. *MSNBC Web Posting*. Retrieved May 18, 2002, from http://www.msnbc.com/news/753093.asp.

Revenson, T. A., & Baum, A. (2001). Introduction. In A. Baum, T. A. Revenson, & J. E. Singer (Eds.), *Handbook of health psychology* (pp. xv–xx). Mahwah, NJ: Lawrence Erlbaum Associates.

Rey, J. M., & Tennant, C. C. (2002). Cannabis and mental health: More evidence establishes clear link between use of cannabis and psychiatric illness. *British Medical Journal, 325*, 1183–1184.

Reynolds, S. J., Bartlett, J. G., Quinn, T. C., Beyrer, C., & Bollinger, R. C. (2003). Antiretroviral therapy where resources are limited. *New England Journal of Medicine, 348*, 1806–1809.

Rhee, S. H., & Waldman, I. D. (2002). Genetic and environmental influences on antisocial behavior: A meta-analysis of twin and adoption studies. *Psychological Bulletin, 128*, 490–529.

Riccio, D. C., Millin, P. M., & Gisquet-Verrier, P. (2003). Retrograde amnesia: Forgetting back. *Current Directions in Psychological Science, 12*, 41–44.

Richards, J. C., & Hof, A., & Alvarenga, M. (2000). Serum lipids and their relationships with hostility and angry affect and behaviors in men. *Health Psychology, 19*, 393–398.

Ridley, M. (2003). *Nature via nurture genes, experience, and what makes us human*. New York: HarperCollins.

Rilling, J. K., Gutman, D. A., Zeh, T. R., Pagnoni, G., Berns, G. S., & Kilts, C. D. (2002). CD: A neural basis for social cooperation. *Neuron, 35*, 395–405.

Rilling, M. (2000). John Watson's paradoxical struggle to explain Freud. *American Psychologist, 55*, 301–312.

Risk factors help ID violence-prone youths, psychiatrists say. (2000, May 16). *Risk Factors for Heart Disease*. A Publication of the American Heart Association.

Robbins, J. (2000, September 26). Some see hope in biofeedback for attention disorder. *New York Times*, p. F7.

Roberti, J. W. (2004). A review of behavioral and biological correlates of sensation seeking. *Journal of Research in Personality, 38*, 256–279.

Roberts, W. A. (2002). Are animals stuck in time? *Psychological Bulletin, 128*, 473–489.

Robins, R. W., Trzesniewski, K. H., Tracy, J. L., Gosling, S. D., & Potter, J. (2002). Global self-esteem across the life span. *Psychology and Aging, 17*, 423–434.

Robinson, M. D., Johnson, J. T., & Herndon, F. (1997). Reaction time and assessments of cognitive effort as predictors of eyewitness memory accuracy and confidence. *Journal of Applied Psychology, 82*, 416–425.

Robinson, N. M., Zigler, E., & Gallagher, J. J. (2001). Two tails of the normal curve: Similarities and differences in the study of mental retardation and giftedness. *American Psychologist, 55*, 1413–1424.

Rochat, P. (1993). Hand-mouth coordination in the newborn: Morphology, determinants, and early development of a basic act. In G. J. P. Savelsbergh (Ed.), *The development of coordination in infancy* (pp. 265–288). Amsterdam, Netherlands: North-Holland.

Rodriguez, I. Greer, C. A., Mok, M. Y., & Mombaerst, P. (2000). A putative pheromone receptor gene expressed in human olfactory mucosa. *Nature and Genetics, 26*, 18–19.

Rodriguez, N., Myers, H. F., Mira, C. B., Flores, T., & Garcia-Hernandez, L. (2002). Development of the Multidimensional Acculturative Stress Inventory for adults of Mexican origin. *Psychological Assessment, 14*, 451–461.

Roemer, L., & Orsillo, S. M. (2003). Mindfulness: A promising intervention strategy in need of further study. *Clinical Psychology: Science and Practice, 10*, 172–178.

Roese, N. J., & Olson, J. M. (1994). Attitude importance as a function of repeated attitude expression. *Journal of Experimental Social Psychology, 30*, 39–51.

Rogers, C. R. (1951). *Client-centered therapy: Its current practice, implications, and theory*. Boston: Houghton Mifflin.

Rogers, C. R. (1961). *On becoming a person*. Boston: Houghton Mifflin.

Rogers, C. R. (1980). *A way of being*. Boston: Houghton Mifflin.

Romaine, S. (1994). *Language in society: An introduction to sociolinguistics*. Oxford, England: Oxford University Press.

Rosch, E. (1975).Cognitive representation of semantic categories. *Journal of Experimental Psychology: General, 105*, 192–223.

Rosenbaum, D. E. (2000, May 16). On left-handedness, its causes and costs. *New York Times*, pp. E1, E8.

Rosenberg, D. R., Averbach, D. H., O'Hearn K. M., Seymour, A. B., Birmaher, B., & Sweeney, J. A. (1997). Oculomotor response inhibition abnormalities in pediatric obsessive-compulsive disorder. *Archives of General Psychiatry, 54*, 831–838.

Rosenheck, R. (2000). Cost-effectiveness of services for mentally ill homeless people: The application of research to policy and practice. *American Journal of Psychiatry, 157,* 1563–1570.

Rosenthal, D., Wender, P. H., Kety, S. S., Schulsinger, F., Welner, J., & Rieder, R. O. (1975). Parent-child relationships and psychopathological disorder in the child. *Archives of General Psychiatry, 32,* 466–476.

Rosenthal, D., Wender, P. H., Keyt, S. S., Schulsinger, F., Welner, J., & Ostergaard, L. (1968). Schizophrenics' offspring reared in adoptive homes. In D. Rosenthal & S. S. Kety (Eds.), *The transmission of schizophrenia.* Oxford, England: Pergamon Press.

Roth, R. M., Flashman, L. A., Saykin, A. J., McAllister, T. W., & Vidaver, R. (2004). Apathy in schizophrenia: Reduced frontal lobe volume and neuropsychological deficits. *American Journal of Psychiatry, 161,* 157–159.

Rothbart, M. K., & Bates, J. E. (1997). Temperament. In W. Damon (Editor-in-Chief) & N. Eisenberg (Vol. Ed.), *Handbook of child psychology: 5th ed., Vol. 3. Social, emotional, and personality development* (pp. 105–176). New York: John Wiley & Sons.

Rothbart, M. K., Ahadi, S. A., & Evans, D. E. (2000). Temperament and personality. Origins and outcomes. *Journal of Personality and Social Psychology, 78,* 122–135.

Rothbaum, B. A., Hodges, L., Smith, S., Lee, J. H., & Price, L. (2000). A controlled study of virtual reality exposure therapy for the fear of flying. *Journal of Consulting and Clinical Psychology, 68,* 1020–1026.

Rothbaum, B. O., Hodges, L., Anderson, P. L., Price, L., & Smith, S. (2002). Twelve-month follow-up of virtual reality and standard exposure therapies for the fear of flying. *Journal of Consulting and Clinical Psychology, 70,* 428–432.

Rotter, J. B. (1990). Internal versus external control of reinforcement: A case history of a variable. *American Psychologist, 45,* 489–493.

Rovee-Collier, C. (1996). Measuring infant memory: A critical commentary. *Developmental Review, 16,* 301–310.

Rovee-Collier, C., & Fagen, J. W. (1981). The retrieval of memory in early infancy. *Advances in Infancy Research, 1,* 225–254.

Rowe, D. C. (2001). Do people make environments or do environments make people? In A. Damasio and A. Harrington et al. (Eds.), *Unity of knowledge: The convergence of natural and human science.* New York: New York Academy of Sciences.

Roy, A. (2003). Characteristics of HIV patients who attempt suicide. *ACTA Psychiatrica Scandinavica, 107,* 41–44.

Rozin, P., Bauer, R., & Catanese, D. (2003). Food and life, pleasure and worry, among American college students: Gender differences and regional similarities. *Journal of Personality and Social Psychology, 85,* 132–141.

Rubin, D. C., & Wenzel, A. E. (1996). One hundred years of forgetting: A quantitative description of retention. *Psychological Review, 103,* 734–760.

Rubin, K. H., Burgess, K. B., & Dwyer, K. M. (2003). Predicting preschoolers' externalizing behaviors from toddler temperament, conflict, and maternal negativity. *Developmental Psychology, 39,* 164–176.

Rubin, L. J. (1996). Childhood sexual abuse: False accusations of "false memory"? *Professional Psychology: Research and Practice, 27,* 447–451.

Rubinow, D. R., & Schmidt, P. J. (1995). The treatment of premenstral syndrome—Forward into the past. *New England Journal of Medicine, 332,* 1574–1575.

Rubinow, D. R., & Schmidt, P. J. (1996). Androgens, brain, and behavior. *American Journal of Psychiatry, 153,* 974–984.

Rubinow, D. R., Schmidt, P. J., & Roca, C. A. (1998). Estrogen-serotonin interactions: Implications for affective regulation. *Biological Psychiatry, 44,* 839–850.

Rubinstein, J. S., Meyer, D. E., & Evans, J. E. (2001). Executive control of cognitive processes in task switching. *Journal of Experimental Psychology: Human Perception and Performance, 27,* 763–797.

Rubinstein, S., & Caballero, B. (2000). Is Miss America an undernourished role model? *Journal of the American Medical Association, 283,* 1569.

Rudd, M. D., Joiner, T. E. Jr., Jobes, D. A., & King, C. A. (1999). The outpatient treatment of suicidality: An integration of science and recognition of its limitations. *Professional Psychology: Research and Practice, 30,* 437–446.

Rudman, L. A., Ashmore, R. D., & Gary, M. L. (2001). "Unlearning" automatic biases: The malleability of implicit prejudice and stereotypes. *Journal of Personality and Social Psychology, 81,* 856–868.

Ruggiero, K. M., & Taylor, D. M. (1997). Why minority group members perceive or do not perceive the discrimination that confronts them: The role of self-esteem and perceived control. *Journal of Personality and Social Psychology, 72,* 373–389.

Runco, M. A. (2004). Creativity. *Annual Review of Psychology, 55,* 657–687.

Rupp, R. (1998). *Committed to memory: How we remember and why we forget.* New York: Crown.

Ruscio, A. M., Borkovec, T. D., & Ruscio, J. (2001). A taxometric investigation of the latent structure of worry. *Journal of Abnormal Psychology, 110,* 413–422.

Russell, J. A., Bachorowski, J. A., & Fernández-Dol, J.-M. (2003). Facial and vocal expressions of emotion. *Annual Review of Psychology, 54,* 329–349.

Rutledge, T., & Hogan, B. E. (2002). A quantitative review of prospective evidence linking psychological factors with hypertension development. *Psychosomatic Medicine, 64,* 758–766.

Ruvas-Vazquez, R. A., Johnson, S. L., Rey, G. J., Blais, M. A., & Rivas-Vazquez, A. (2002). Current treatments for bipolar disorder: A review and update for psychologists. *Professional Psychology: Research and Practice, 33,* 212–223.

Ryan, R. M., & Deci, E. L. (2000). Self-determination theory and the facilitation of intrinsic motivation, social development, and well-being. *American Psychologist, 55,* 68–78.

Rybarczyk, B., Lopez, M., Benson, R., Alsten, C., & Stepanski, E. (2002). Efficacy of two behavioral treatment programs for comorbid geriatric insomnia. *Psychology and Aging, 17,* 288–298.

Ryder, A. G., Alden, L. E., & Paulhus, D. L. (2000). Is acculturation unidimensional or bidimensional? A head-to-head comparison in the prediction of personality, self-identity, and adjustment. *Journal of Personality and Social Psychology, 79,* No. 1, 49–65.

Rypma, B., Prabhakaran, V., Desmond, J. E., & Gabrieli, J. D. E. (2001). Age differences in prefrontal cortical activity in working memory. *Psychology and Aging, 16,* 371–384.

Saal, D., Dong, Y., Bonci, A., & Malenka, R. (2003) Drugs of abuse and stress trigger a common synaptic adaptation in dopamine neurons. *Neuron, 37,* 577–582.

Sachdev, P., & Hay, P. (1996). Site and size of lesion and psychosurgical outcome in obsessive-compulsive disorder: A magnetic resonance imaging study. *Biological Psychiatry, 39,* 739–742.

Sacks, O. (1985). *The man who mistook his wife for a hat and other clinical tales.* New York: Summit.

Salkovskis, P. M., & Clark, D. M. (1993). Panic disorder and hypochondriasis. *Advances in Behaviour Research and Therapy, 15,* 23–48.

Salkovskis, P. M., Thorpe, S. J., Wahl, K., Wroe, A. L., & Forrester, E. (2003). Neutralizing increases discomfort associated with obsessional thoughts: An experimental study with obsessional patients. *Journal of Abnormal Psychology, 112,* 709–715.

Salmon, P. (2001). Effects of physical exercise on anxiety, depression, and sensitivity to stress. A unifying theory. *Clinical Psychology Review, 21,* 33–61.

Samalin, N., & Whitney, C. (1997, December). When to praise. *Parents Magazine,* pp. 51–55.

Samuels, Y., Wang, Z., Bardelli, A., Silliman, N., Ptak, J., Szabo, S., et al. (2004). High frequency of mutations of the PIK3CA gene in human cancers. *Science, 23,* 554.

Sanacora, G., Mason, G. F., Rothman, D. L., Hyder, F., Ciarcia, J. J., Ostroff, R. B., et al. (2003). Increased cortical GABA concentrations in depressed patients receiving ECT. *American Journal of Psychiatry, 160,* 577–579.

Sandlin-Sniffen, C. (2000, November 2). How are we raising our children? *St. Petersburg Times.* Retrieved November 5, 2000, from http://www.psycport.com/news/2000/11/02/eng-sptimes_floridian/eng-sptimes_floridian_071015_110_905256867409.html.

Sapolsky, R. (2000, April 10). It's not "all in the genes." *Newsweek,* pp. 43–44.

Sapolsky, R. M. (2003). Gene therapy for psychiatric disorders. *American Journal of Psychiatry, 160,* 208–220.

Savage-Rumbaugh, E. S., McDonald, K., Sevcik, R. A., Hopkins, W. D., & Rubert, E. (1986). Spontaneous symbol acquisition and communicative use by pygmy chimpanzees (Pan paniscus). *Journal of Experimental Psychology: General, 115,* 211–235.

Savage-Rumbaugh, E. S., Murphy, J., Sevcik, R. A., Brakke, K. E., Williams, S. L., & Rumbaugh, D. M. (1993). Language comprehension in ape and child. *Monographs of the Society for Research in Child Development, 58,* 3–4.

Saxe, R., Carey, S., & Kanwisher, N. (2004). Understanding other minds: Linking developmental psychology and functional neuroimaging. *Annual Review of Psychology, 55,* 87–124.

Say it ain't so. (2003). *Tufts University Health and Nutrition Letter, 20*(9), p. 8.

Scarr, S., & Eisenberg, M. (1993). Child care research: Issues, perspectives, and results. *Annual Review of Psychology, 44,* 613–644.

Schachter, S. (1971). *Emotion, obesity, and crime.* New York: Academic Press.

Schachter, S., & Singer, J. E. (1962). Cognitive, social, and physiological determinants of emotional state. *Psychological Review, 69,* 377–399.

Schafer, R. B., & Keith, P. M. (1990) Matching by weight in married couples: A life cycle perspective. *Journal of Social Psychology, 130,* 657–664.

Schaie, K. W. (1996). *Intellectual development in adulthood: The Seattle Longitudinal Study*. Cambridge, England: Cambridge University Press.

Scheier, M. F., & Carver, C. S. (1985). Optimism, coping, and health: Assessment and implications of generalized outcome expectancies. *Health Psychology, 4*, 219–247.

Scheier, M. F., Matthews, K. A., Owens, J. F., Schulz, R., Bridges, M. W., Magovern, G. J., et al. (1999). Optimism and rehospitalization after coronary artery bypass graft surgery. *Archives of Internal Medicine, 159*, 829–935.

Schneider, B. H., Atkinson, L., & Tardif, C. (2001). Child-parent attachment and children's peer relations: A quantitative review. *Developmental Psychology, 37*, 86–100.

Schneiderman, N., Antoni, M. H., Saab, P. G., & Ironson, G. (2001). Health psychology: Psychosocial and biobehavioral aspects of chronic disease management. *Annual Review of Psychology, 52*, 555–580.

Schneidman, E. S. (1983). On abolishing "death": An etymological note. *Suicide and Life Threatening Behavior, 13*, 176–178.

Schwartz, B. L., & Smith, S. M. (1997). The retrieval of related information influences tip-of-the-tongue states. *Journal of Memory and Language, 36*, 68–86.

Schwartz, C. E., Wright, C. I., Shin, L. M., Kagan, J., & Rauch, S. L. (2003). Inhibited and uninhibited infants "grown up": Adult amygdalar response to novelty. *Science, 300*, 1952–1953.

Schwartz, M. S. (Ed.). (1995). *Biofeedback: A practitioner's guide* (2nd ed., pp. 763–767). New York: Guilford Press.

Scientists answer ticklish question. (2000, September 11). *Cable News Network*. Retrieved from http://www.cnn.com/2000/HEALTH/09/11/tickle.mechanism. reut/index.html.

Scientists learn why stress can kill. (2003, June 30). *MSNBC Web Posting*. Retrieved July 1, 2003 from http://www.msnbc.com/news/933118.asp?cp1=1.

Scott, A. J. (1994). Chronobiological considerations in shiftworker sleep, performance and shiftwork scheduling. *Human Performance, 7*, 207–233.

Searle, J. R. (1996). *Dualism: Descartes' legacy. The philosophy of mind: The Superstar Teachers Series* [Audiotape]. Springfield, VA: The Teaching Company.

Segall, M. H. (1994). A cross-cultural research contribution to unraveling the nativist/empiricist controversy. In J. Lonner & R. Malpass (Eds.), *Psychology and culture* (pp. 135–138). Boston: Allyn & Bacon.

Segall, M. H., Campbell, D. T., & Herskovits, M. J. (1963). Culture differences in the perception of geometric illusions. *Science, 139*, 769–771.

Segall, M. H., Campbell, D. T., & Herskovits, M. J. (1966). *The influence of culture on visual perception*. Indianapolis: Bobbs-Merrill.

Segell, M. (2000, October 24). Testosterone's not so bad after all. *MSNBC*. Retrieved October 24, 2000, from http://www.msnbc.com/news/480175.asp.

Segraves, R. T., & Althof, S. (1998). Psychotherapy and pharmacotherapy of sexual dysfunction. In P. E. Nathan & J. M. Gorman (Eds.), *A guide to treatments that work* (pp. 447–471). New York: Oxford University Press.

Seifert, K. L, & Hoffnung, R. J. (2000). *Child and adolescent development*. Boston: Houghton Mifflin.

Seifert, K. L., Hoffnung, R. J., & Hoffnung, M. (2000). *Lifespan development* (2nd ed.). Boston: Houghton Mifflin.

Sekuler, A. B., & Bennett, P. J. (2001). Generalized common fate: Grouping by common luminance changes. *Psychological Science, 12*, 437–444.

Seligman, M. E. P. (1973). Fall into helplessness. *Psychology Today, 7*, 43–48.

Seligman, M. E. P. (1975). *Helplessness: On depression, development, and death*. San Francisco: Freeman.

Seligman, M. E. P. (1991). *Learned optimism*. New York: Knopf.

Seligman, M. E. P. (2002). *Authentic happiness*. New York: Free Press.

Seligman, M. E. P. (2003, August). Positive psychology: Applications to work, love, and sports. Paper presented at the meeting of the American Psychological Association, Toronto, CA.

Seligman, M. E. P., & Csikszentmihalyi, M. (2000). Positive psychology: An introduction. *American Psychologist, 55*, 5–14.

Seligman, M. E. P., & Csikszentmihalyi, M. (2001). Reply to comments. *American Psychologist, 56*, 89–90.

Selye, H. (1976). *The stress of life* (rev. ed.). New York: McGraw-Hill.

Sen, S., Nesse, R. M., Stoltenberg, S. F., Li, S., Gleiberman, L., Chakravarti, A., et al. (2003). A BDNF coding variant associated with the NEO personality inventory domain neuroticism. A risk factor for depression. *Neuropsychopharmacology, 28*, 397–401.

Senécal, C., Nouwen, A., & White, D. (2000). Motivation and dietary self-care in adults with diabetes: Are self-efficacy and autonomous self-regulation complementary or competing constructs? *Health Psychology, 19*, 452–457.

Seyfarth, R. M., & Cheney, D. L. (2003). Signalers and receivers in animal communication *Annual Review of Psychology 54*, 145–173.

Shadish, W. R., Matt, G. E., Navarro, A. M., & Phillips, G. (2000). The effects of psychological therapies under clinically representative conditions: A meta-analysis. *Psychological Bulletin, 126*, 512–529.

Shadish, W. R., Montgomery, L. M., Wilson, P., & Wilson, M. R. (1993). Effects of family and marital psychotherapies: A meta-analysis. *Journal of Consulting and Clinical Psychology, 61*, 992–1002.

Shapiro, A. P. (2001). Nonpharmacological treatment of hypertension. In A. Baum, T. A. Revenson, & J. E. Singer (Eds.), *Handbook of health psychology* (pp. 697–708). Mahwah, NJ: Lawrence Erlbaum Associates.

Shebilske, W. L., & Peters, A. L. (1995). Perceptual constancies: Analysis and synthesis. In W. Prinz & B. Bridgeman (Eds.), *Handbook of perception and action, Vol. 1: Perception* (pp. 227–251). San Diego: Academic Press.

Shellenbarger, S. (2003a, February 27). Multitasking makes you stupid: Studies show pitfalls of doing too much at once. *Wall Street Journal*, p. D1.

Shellenbarger, S. (2003b, March 20). Female rats are better multitaskers; with humans, the debate rages on. *Wall Street Journal*, p. D1.

Sherman, J. W., Stroessner, S. J., Loftus, S. T., & Deguzman, G. (1997). Stereotype suppression and recognition memory for stereotypical and non-stereotypical information. *Social Cognition, 15*, 205–215.

Shiffman, H. R. (2000). *Sensation and perception: An integrated approach* (5th ed.). New York: John Wiley & Sons.

Shiffman, S., Balabanis, M. H., Paty, J. A., Engberg, J., Gwaltney, C. J., Liu, K. S., et al. (2000). Dynamic effects of self-efficacy on smoking lapse and relapse. *Health Psychology, 19*, 315–323.

Shifren, J. L., Braunstein, G. D., Simon, J. A., Casson, P. R., Buster, J. E., Redmond, G. P., et al. (2000). Transdermal testosterone treatment in women with impaired sexual function after oophorectomy. *New England Journal of Medicine, 343*, 682–688.

Shiner, R. L., Masten, A. S., & Tellegen, A. (2002). A developmental perspective on personality in emerging adulthood: Childhood antecedents and concurrent adaptation. *Journal of Personality and Social Psychology, 83*, 1165–1177.

Shneidman, E. S. (1987). A psychological approach to suicide. In G. R. Vanderbos & B. K. Bryant (Eds.), *Cataclysms, cries, and catastrophes: Psychology in action* (Master Lecture Series, Vol. 6, pp. 151–183). Washington, DC: American Psychological Association.

Shnek, Z. M., Irvine, J., Stewart, D., & Abbey, S. (2001). Psychological factors and depressive symptoms in ischemic heart disease. *Health Psychology*, 141–145.

Short, K. H., & Johnston, C. (1997). Stress, maternal distress, and children's adjustment following immigration: The buffering role of social support. *Journal of Consulting and Clinical Psychology, 65*, 494–503.

Shotland, R. L., & Heinold, W. D. (1985). Bystander response to arterial bleeding: Helping skills, the decision-making process, and differentiating the helping response. *Journal of Personality and Social Psychology, 49*, 347–356.

Shroeder, D. A., Penner, L. A., Dovidio, J. F., & Piliavin, J. A. (1995). *The psychology of helping and altruism: Problem and puzzles*. New York: McGraw-Hill.

Shumaker, S. A., & Hill, D. R. (1991). Gender differences in social support and physical health. *Health Psychology, 10*, 102–111.

Shweder, R. A. (1994). Liberalism as destiny. In B. Puka (Ed.), *The great justice debate: Kohlberg criticism. Moral development: A compendium, Vol. 4* (pp. 71–74). New York: Garland Publishing.

Siegal, M., Varley, R., & Want, S. C. (2001). Mind over grammar: Reasoning in aphasia and development. *Trends in Cognitive Sciences, 5*, 296–301.

Siegel, J. M. (2001). The REM sleep–memory consolidation hypothesis. *Science, 294*, 1058–1063.

Siegel, J. M. (2004). Hypocretin (orexin): Role in normal behavior and neuropathology. *Annual Review of Psychology, 55*, 125–148.

Siegel, J. M. (2004). Hypocretin (orexin): Role in normal behavior and neuropathology. *Annual Review of Psychology, 55*, 125–148.

Silver, H., Feldman, P., Bilker, W., & Gur, R. C. (2003). Working memory deficit as a core neuropsychological dysfunction in schizophrenia. *American Journal of Psychiatry, 160*, 1809–1816.

Silverman, L. H. (1984). Beyond insight: An additional necessary step in redressing intrapsychic conflict. *Psychoanalytic Psychology, 1*, 215–234.

Simeon, D., Greenberg, J., Knutelska, M., Schmeidler, J., & Hollander, E. (2003). Peritraumatic reactions associated with the World Trade Center disaster. *American Journal of Psychiatry, 160*, 1702–1705.

Simmons, R. G. (1991). Presidential address on altruism and sociology. *Sociological Quarterly, 46*, 36–46.

Simons-Morton, B., Haynie, D. L., Crump, A. D., Eitel, S. P., & Saylor, K. E. (2001). Peer and parent influences on smoking and drinking among early adolescents. *Health Education and Behavior, 28*, 95–107.

Simonton, D. K. (2000). Creativity: Cognitive, personal, developmental, and social aspects. *American Psychologist, 55*, 151–158.

Singer, R. N. (2003). Creating an identity for sport psychology. *APS Observer, 16*(5), pp. 14, 19.

Singer, T., Verhaeghen, P., Ghisletta, P., Lindenberger, U., & Baltes, P. B. (2003). The fate of cognition in very old age: Six-year longitudinal findings in the Berlin Aging Study (BASE). *Psychology and Aging, 18,* 318–331.

Sleek, S. (1997, October). People's racist attitudes can be unlearned. *APA Monitor, 28*(10), 38.

Sloan, D. M., & Marx, B. P. (2004). A closer examination of the structured written disclosure procedure. *Journal of Consulting and Clinical Psychology, 72,* 165–175.

Slutske, W. S., Heath, A. C., Madden, P. A. F., Bucholz, K. K., Statham, D. J., & Martin, N. G. (2002). Personality and the genetic risk for alcohol dependence. *Journal of Abnormal Psychology, 111,* 124–133.

Smith, D. (2001a, October). Sleep psychologists in demand. *Monitor on Psychology,* pp. 36–38.

Smith, D. (2001b, September). Harassment in the hallways. *Monitor on Psychology,* pp. 38–40.

Smith, E. R. (1998). Mental representation and memory. In D. T. Gilbert, S. T. Fiske, & G. Lindzey (Eds.), *The handbook of social psychology* (4th ed., Vol. 1, pp. 391–445). Boston: McGraw-Hill.

Smith, G. T., Goldman, M. S., Greenbaum, P. E., & Christiansen, B. A. (1995). Expectancy for social facilitation from drinking: The divergent paths of high-expectancy and low-expectancy adolescents. *Journal of Abnormal Psychology, 104,* 32–40.

Smith, K. H., & Rogers, M. (1994). Effectiveness of subliminal messages in television commercials: Two experiments. *Journal of Applied Psychology, 79,* 866–874.

Smith, L., Totterdell, P., & Folkard, S. (1995). Shiftwork effects in nuclear power workers: A field study using portable computers. *Work and Stress, 9*(2–3), 235–244.

Smith, M. L., Glass, G. V., & Miller, T. I. (1980). *The benefits of psychotherapy.* Baltimore: Johns Hopkins University Press.

Smith, R. E., Smoll, F. L., & Ptacek, J. T. (1990). Conjunctive moderator variables in vulnerability and resiliency research: Life stress, social support and coping skills, and adolescent sport injuries. *Journal of Personality and Social Psychology, 58,* 360–370.

Smith, T. K. (2003, February). We've got to stop eating like this. *Fortune,* pp. 58–70.

Smith, T. W., & Gallo, L. C. (2001). Personality traits as risk factors for physical illness. In A. Baum, T. A. Revenson, & J. E. Singer (Eds.), *Handbook of health psychology* (pp. 139–174). Mahwah, NJ: Lawrence Erlbaum Associates.

Smyth, J. M., & Pennebaker, J. W. (2001). What are the health effects of disclosure? In A. Baum, T. A. Revenson, & J. E. Singer (Eds.), *Handbook of health psychology* (pp. 339–348). Mahwah, NJ: Lawrence Erlbaum Associates.

Snarey, J. R. (1985). Cross-cultural universality of social-moral development: A critical review of Kohlbergian research. *Psychological Bulletin, 97,* 202–232.

Solomon, G. F., Segerstrom, S. C.,Grohr, P., Kemeny, M.& Fahey, J. (1997, March/April). Shaking up immunity: Psychological and immunologic changes after a natural disaster. *Psychosomatic Medicine, 59,* 114–127.

Solomon, P. R., Adams, F., Silver, A., Zimmer, J., & DeVeaux, R. (2002). Ginkgo for memory enhancement: A randomized controlled trial. *Journal of the American Medical Association, 288,* 835–840.

Some shyness may be inherited. (2003, June 19). *CNN Web Posting.* Retrieved July 2, 2003, from http://www.cnn.com/2003/HEALTH/parenting/06/19/shy.kids.ap/index.html.

Sommer, R. (1999). Psychology applied to the environment. In A. Stec & D. A. Bernstein (Eds.), *Psychology: Fields of application* (pp. 148–164). Boston: Houghton Mifflin.

Sommerfeld, J. (2002, August 25). Simple test may predict Alzheimer's. *MSNBC Web Posting.* Retrieved August 26, 2002, from http://www.msnbc.com/news/797904.asp.

Soussignan, R. (2002). Duchenne smile, emotional experience, and autonomic reactivity: A test of the facial feedback hypothesis. *Emotion, 2,* 52–74.

Spanos, N. P. (1994). Multiple identity enactments and multiple personality disorder: A sociocognitive perspective. *Psychological Bulletin, 116,* 143–165.

Spearman, C. (1927). *The abilities of man.* New York: Macmillan.

Sperry, R. W. (1982). Some effects of disconnecting the cerebral hemispheres. *Science, 217,* 1223–1226.

Spiegel, D. (2001). Mind matters—Group therapy and survival in breast cancer. *New England Journal of Medicine, 345,* 1767–1768.

Springer, S. P., & Deutsch, G. (1993). *Left brain, right brain* (4th ed.). New York: Freeman.

Squier, L. H., & Domhoff, G. W. (1998). The presentation of dreaming and dreams in introductory psychology textbooks: A critical examination with suggestions for textbook authors and course instructors. *Dreaming, 8,* 149–168.

Sroufe, L. A., Cooper, R. G., & DeHart, G. B. (1992). *Child development: Its nature and course* (2nd ed.). New York: McGraw-Hill.

Staddon, J. E. R., & Cerutti, D. T. (2003). Operant conditioning. *Annual Review of Psychology, 54,* 115–144.

Stamler, J., Stamler, R., Neaton, J. D., Wentworth, D., Daviglus, M. L., Garside, D., et al. (1999). Low risk-factor profile and long-term cardiovascular and noncardiovascular mortality and life expectancy: Findings for 5 large cohorts of young adult and middle-aged men and women. *Journal of the American Medical Association, 282,* 2012–2018.

Stampfer, M. J., Hu, F. B., Manson, J. E., Rimm, E. B., & Willett, W. C. (2000). Primary prevention of coronary heart disease in women through diet and lifestyle. *New England Journal of Medicine, 343,* 16–22.

Stattin, H., & Magnusson, D. (1990). *Pubertal maturation in female development.* Hillsdale, NJ: Lawrence Erlbaum Associates.

Stein, D., Asherov, J., Lublinksy, E., Sobol-Havia, D., et al. (2002). Sociodemographic factors associated with attempted suicide in two Israeli cities between 1990 and 1998. *Journal of Nervous and Mental Disease, 190,* 115–118.

Steiner, M., Steinberg, S., Stewart, D., Certer, D., Berger, C., Reid, R., et al. (1995). Fluoxetine in the treatment of premenstrual dysphoria. *New England Journal of Medicine, 332,* 1529–1534.

Steinhausen, H.-C. (2002). The outcome of anorexia nervosa in the 20th century. *American Journal of Psychiatry, 159,* 1284–1293.

Stenson, J. (2001a, August 26). Burden of mental illness in America falls on minorities. *MSNBC.* Retrieved August 26, 2001, from http://www.msnbc.com/news/619545.asp.

Stenson, J. (2001b, August 27). Breaking down a male myth: Men not "emotional mummies," suggests new research. *MSNBC.* Retrieved August 28, 2001, from http://www.msnbc.com/news/620211.asp.

Stenson, J. (2001c, August 26). Many teens abused by dating partners. *MSNBC.* Retrieved August 27, 2001, from http://www.msnbc.com/news/619696.asp.

Sternberg, E. M. (2000). *The balance within: The science connecting health and emotions.* New York: W. H. Freeman & Co.

Sternberg, R. J. (1988). Triangulating love. In R. J. Sternberg & M. J. Barnes (Eds.), *The psychology of love.* New Haven: Yale University Press.

Sternberg, R. J. (1997). The triarchic theory of intelligence. In D. P. Flanagan, J. L. Genshaft, P. L., & Harrison (Eds.), *Contemporary intellectual assessment: Theories, tests, and issues* (pp. 92–104). New York: Guilford Press.

Sternberg, R. J. (2001). What is the common thread of creativity? Its dialectical relation to intelligence and wisdom. *American Psychologist, 56,* 360–362.

Stewart, A. J., & McDermott, C. (2004). Gender in psychology. *Annual Review of Psychology, 55,* 519–544.

Stewart, M. W., et al. (1994). Differential relationships between stress and disease activity for immunologically distinct subgroups of people with rheumatoid arthritis. *Journal of Abnormal Psychology, 1103,* 251–258.

Stickgold, R., LaTanya, J., & Hobson, J. A. (2000). Visual discrimination learning requires sleep after training. *Nature Neuroscience, 3,* 1237–1238.

Stipp, D. (2003, February). The quest for the antifat pill. *Fortune,* pp. 66–67.

Stolberg, S. G. (1998). Rise in smoking by young Blacks erodes a success story. *New York Times,* p. A24.

Stolberg, S. G. (2001a, April 22). Science, studies and motherhood. *New York Times Week in Review,* p. 3.

Stolberg, S. G. (2001b, May 10). Blacks found on short end of heart attack procedure. *New York Times,* p. A20.

Stolberg, S. G. (2001c, June 2). In AIDS war, new weapons and new victims. *New York Times,* pp. A1, A24.

Stone, A. A., Neale, J., Cox, D. S., & Napoli, A., et al. (1994). Daily events are associated with a secretory immune response to an oral antigen in men. *Health Psychology, 13,* 440–446.

Stone, A. A., Smyth, J. M., Kaell, A., & Hurewitz, A. (2000). Structured writing about stressful events: Exploring potential psychological mediators of positive health effects. *Health Psychology, 19,* 619–624.

Stoney, C. M. (2003). Gender and cardiovascular disease: A psychobiological and integrative approach. *Current Directions in Psychological Science, 12,* 129–133.

Storandt, M., Kaskie, B., & Von Dras, D. D. (1998). Temporal memory for remote events in healthy aging and dementia. *Psychology and Aging, 13,* 4–7.

Strayer, D. L., & Johnston, W. A. (2001). Driven to distraction: Dual-task studies of simulated driving and conversing on a cellular telelphone. *Psychological Science, 12,* 462–466.

Stricker, G., & Gold, J. R. (1999). The Rorschach: Toward a nomothetically based, idiographically applicable configurational model. *Psychological Assessment, 11*, 240–250.

Stricker, G., & Gold, J. R. (2001, January). An introduction to psychotherapy integration. *NYS Psychologist, 13*, 7–12.

Strickland, B. R. (2000). Misassumptions, misadventures, and the misuse of psychology. *American Psychologist, 55*, 331–338.

Striegel-Moore, R. H., Dohm, F. A., Kraemer, H. C., Taylor, C. B., Daniels, S. D., Crawford, P. B., et al. (2003). Eating disorders in white and black women. *American Journal of Psychiatry, 160*, 1326–1331.

Strober, M., Freeman, R., Lampert, C., Diamond, J., & Kaye, W. (2000). Controlled family study of anorexia nervosa and bulimia nervosa: Evidence of shared liability and transmission of partial syndromes. *American Journal of Psychiatry, 157*, 393–401.

Strote, J. L., Lee, J. E., & Wechsler, H. (2002). Increasing MDMA use among college students: Results of a national survey. *Journal of the American Academy of Child and Adolescent Psychiatry, 41*, 1215.

Stuart, R. B. (2004). Twelve practical suggestions for achieving multicultural competence. *Professional Psychology: Research and Practice, 35*, 3–9.

Sullivan, M. P. (2000). Preventing the downward spiral. *American Journal of Nursing, 100*, 26–32.

Sullivan, P. F., Neale, M. C., & Kendler, K. S. (2000). Genetic epidemiology of major depression: Review and meta-analysis. *American Journal of Psychiatry, 157*, 1552–1562.

Sullivan, R. (1998, February). Like you, I haven't been sleeping well. *Life*, pp. 56–66.

Sundstrom, E., Bell, P. A., Busby, P. L., & Asmus, C. (1996). Environmental psychology: 1989–1994. *Annual Review of Psychology, 47*, 485–512.

Suzuki, K. (1991). Moon illusion simulated in complete darkness: Planetarium experiment reexamined. *Perception and Psychophysics, 49*, 349–354.

Swendsen, J. D. Tennen, H., Carney, M. A., Affleck, G., Willard, A., & Hromi, A. (2000). Mood and alcohol consumption: An experience sampling test of the self-medication hypothesis. *Journal of Abnormal Psychology, 109*, 198–204.

Syphilis down, gonorrhea up in U.S., study finds. (2000, December 5). Retrieved December 10, 2000, from http://www.cnn.com/2000/HEALTH/12/05/health.stds.reut/index.html.

Szanto, K., Mulsant, B. H., Houck, P., Dew, M. A., & Reynolds, C. F. (2003). Occurrence and course of suicidality during short-term treatment of late-life depression. *Archives of General Psychiatry, 60*, 610–617.

Takahashi, Y. (1990). Separation distress of Japanese infants in the Strange Situation. *Research and Clinical Center for Child Development, 12*, 141–150.

Talan, J. (1998, February 3). The power of dreams: It's all in understanding them. *Newsday*, pp. B15, B16.

Talarico, J. M., & Rubin, D. C. (2003). Confidence, not consistency, characterizes flashbulb memories. *Psychological Science, 14*, 455–461.

Tarkan, L. (2003, April 22). New test for hearts at risk: What it can and can't do. *New York Times*, p. F5.

Taylor, C. B., & Luce, K. H. (2003). Computer- and Internet-based psychotherapy interventions. *Current Directions in Psychological Science, 12*, 18–22.

Taylor, E. (2000). Psychotherapeutics and the problematic origins of clinical psychology in America. *American Psychologist, 55*, 1029–1033.

Taylor, K. L., Lamdan, R. M., Siegel, J. E., Shelby, R., Moran-Klimi, K., & Hrywna, M. (2003). Psychological adjustment among African American breast cancer patients: One-year follow-up results of a randomized psychoeducational group intervention. *Health Psychology, 22*, 316–323.

Taylor, S. E., Klein, L. C., Lewis, B. P, Gruenewald, T. L., Gurung, R. A., & Updegraff, J. A. (2000). Biobehavioral responses to stress in females: Tend-and-befriend, not fight-or-flight. *Psychological Review, 7*, 411–429.

Tecott, L. H. (2003). The genes and brains of mice and men. *American Journal of Psychiatry, 160*, 646–656.

Teen drug use, smoking up slightly. (2003, September 4). *CNN Web Posting.* Retrieved September 6, 1003, from http://www.cnn.com/2003/HEALTH/parenting/09/04/drug.survey.ap/index.html.

Teens not waiting to have sex. (2003, May 20). *MSNBC Web Posting.* Retrieved May 22, 2003, from http://stacks.msnbc.com/news/915814.asp.

Teens say they get along with parents. (2003, August 5). *Associated Press, MSNBC Web Posting.* Retrieved August 8, 2003, from http://www.msnbc.com/news/948480.asp.

Teens see little risk in ecstasy. (2003, February 11). *CNN Web Posting.* Retrieved February 15, 2003, from http://www.cnn.com/2003/HEALTH/parenting/02/11/drug.survey/index.html.

Tekcan, A. I., & Peynircioglu, Z. F. (2002). Effects of age on flashbulb memories. *Psychology and Aging, 17*, 416–422.

Tellegen, A., Lykken, D. T., Bouchard, T. J., & Wilcox, K. J. (1988). Personality similarity in twins reared apart and together. *Journal of Personality and Social Psychology, 54*, 1031–1039.

Terrace, H. S. (1980). *Nim*. New York: Knopf.

Tetlock, P. E. (1998). Social psychology and world politics. In D. T. Gilbert, S. T. Fiske, & G. Lindzey (Eds.), *The handbook of social psychology* (4th ed., Vol. 2, pp. 868–914). Boston: McGraw-Hill.

Tett, R. P., & Burnett, D. D. (2003). A personality trait–based interactionist model of job performance. *Journal of Applied Psychology, 88*, 500–517.

Thaker, G. V. (2002). Current progress in schizophrenia research: Search for genes of schizophrenia. *Journal of Nervous and Mental Disease, 190*, 411–312.

Thapar, A., Gottesman, I. I., Owen, M. J., O'Donovan, M. C., & McGuffin, P. (1994). The genetics of mental retardation. *British Journal of Psychiatry, 164*, 747–758.

Think positive, live longer. (2002, July 28). *MSNBC Web Posting.* Retrieved July 30, 2002, from http://www.msnbc.com/news/786749.asp.

Thompson, C. P., Anderson, L. P. & Bakeman, R. A. (2000). Effects of racial socialization and racial identity on acculturative stress in African American college students. *Cultural Diversity and Ethnic Minority Psychology, 6*, 196–210.

Thompson, P. M., Hayashi, K. M., de Zubicaray, G., Janke, A. L., Rose, S. E., Semple, J., et al. (2003). Dynamics of gray matter loss in Alzheimer's disease. *Journal of Neuroscience, 23*, 994.

Thompson, R. A. (1997). Early sociopersonality development. In W. Damon (Editor-in-Chief) & N. Eisenberg (Vol. Ed.), *Handbook of child psychology: 5th ed. Vol. 3: Social, emotional, and personality development* (pp. 25–104). New York: John Wiley & Sons.

Thompson, R. A., & Nelson, C. A. (2001). Developmental science and the media: Early brain development. *American Psychologist, 56*, 5–15.

Thompson, S. (1995). *Going all the way*. New York: Hill and Wang.

Thompson, S. C., Sobolew-Shubin, A., Galbraith, M. E., & Schwankovsky, L., et al. (1993). Maintaining perceptions of control: Finding perceived control in low control circumstances. *Journal of Personality and Social Psychology, 64*, 293–304.

Thompson-Brenner, H., Glass, S., & Westen, D. (2003). A multidimensional meta-analysis of psychotherapy for bulimia nervosa. *Clinical Psychology: Science and Practice, 10*, 269–287.

Thomsen, D. K., Mehlsen, M. Y., Christensen, S., & Zachariae, R. (2003). Rumination—relationship with negative mood and sleep quality. *Personality and Individual Differences, 34*, 1293–1301.

Thomson, E., Hanson, T. L., & McLanahan, S. S. (1994). Family structure and child well-being: Economic resources vs. parental behaviors. *Social Forces, 73*, 221–242.

Thorndike, E. L. (1905). *The elements of psychology*. New York: Seiler.

Thorndike, R. M. (1997). The early history of intelligence testing. In D. P. Flanagan, J. L. Genshaft, & P. L. Harrison (Eds.), *Contemporary intellectual assessment: Theories, tests, and issues* (pp. 92–104). New York: Guilford Press.

Thornhill, R., & Palmer, C. T. (2000). *A natural history of rape*. Cambridge, MA: MIT Press.

Thurstone, L. L., & Thurstone, T. G. (1941). Factorial studies of intelligence. *Psychometric Monographs, 94*(2).

Tienari, P., Wynne, L. C., Läksy, K., Moring, J., Nieminen, P., Sorri, A., et al. (2003). Genetic boundaries of the schizophrenia spectrum: Evidence from the Finnish adoptive family study of schizophrenia. *American Journal of Psychiatry, 160*, 1587–1594.

Time Capsule. (2000, November). *Monitor on Psychology, 31*(11), 10.

Tohen, M., Baker, R. W., Altshuler, L. L., Zarate, C. A., Suppes, T., Ketter, T. A., et al. (2002). Olanzapine versus divalproex in the treatment of acute mania. *American Journal of Psychiatry, 159*, 1011–1017.

Tohen, M., Ketter, T. A., Zarate, C. A., Suppes, T., Frye, M., Altshuler, L., Zajecka, J., et al. (2003). Olanzapine versus divalproex sodium for the treatment of acute mania and maintenance of remission: A 47-week study. *American Journal of Psychiatry, 160*, 1263–1271.

Tolman, E. C., & Honzik, C. H. (1930). Introduction and removal of reward, and maze performance in rats. *University of California Publications in Psychology, 4*, 257–275.

Tolomiczenko, G. S., Sota, T., & Goering, P. N. (2000). Personality assessment of homeless adults as a tool for service planning. *Journal of Personality Disorders, 14*, 152–161.

Toomey, R., Lyons, M. J., Eisen, S. A., Xian, H., Chantarujikapong, S., Seidman, L. J., et al. (2003). A twin study of the neuropsychological consequences of stimulant abuse. *Archives of General Psychiatry, 60*, 303–310.

Tracy, R. J., Fricano, G., & Greco, N. (2000–2001). Images can be more powerful than memories. *Imagination, Cognition and Personality, 20*, 3–19.

Trevarthen, C. (1995). Mother and baby—Seeing artfully eye to eye. In R. L. Gregory et al. (Eds.), *The artful eye* (pp. 157–200). New York: Oxford University Press.

Triandis, H. C., & Gelfand, M. J. (1998). Converging measurement of horizontal and vertical individualism and collectivism. *Journal of Personality and Social Psychology, 74*, 118–128.

Triandis, H. C., & Suh, E. M. (2002). Cultural influences on personality. *Annual Review of Psychology, 53*, 133–160.

Tries, J., & Brubaker, L. (1996). Application of biofeedback in the treatment of urinary incontinence. *Professional Psychology: Research and Practice, 27*, 554–560.

Trinh, N. H., Hoblyn, J., Mohanty, S., & Yaffe, K. (2003). Efficacy of cholinesterase inhibitors in the treatment of neuropsychiatric symptoms and functional impairment in Alzheimer's disease: A meta-analysis. *Journal of the American Medical Association, 289*, 210–216.

Tuller, D. (2001, May 8). Experts voice new alarm on herpes. *New York Times*, p. F1, F6.

Tulving, E. (2002). Episodic memory: From mind to brain. *Annual Review of Psychology, 53*, 1–25.

Tune, L. (1998). Treatments for dementia. In P. E. Nathan & J. M. Gorman (Eds.), *A guide to treatments that work* (pp. 90–126). New York: Oxford University Press

Turati, C. (2004). Why faces are not special to newborns: An alternative account of the face preference. *Current Directions in Psychological Science, 13*, 5–8.

Turkington, C. (1996). *12 steps to a better memory*. New York: MacMillan.

Turnbull, C. (1961). *The forest people*. New York: Simon & Schuster.

Tweney, R. D., & Budzynski, C. A. (2000). The scientific status of American psychology in 1900. *American Psychologist, 55*, 1014–1017.

Twenge, J. M., & Crocker, J. (2002). Race and self-esteem revisited: Reply to Hfdahl and Gray-Little (2002). *Psychological Bulletin, 128*, 417–420.

Uhl, G. R., & Grow, R. W. (2004). The burden of complex genetics in brain disorders. *Archives of General Psychiatry, 61*, 223–229.

UK ECT Review Group. (2003). Efficacy and safety of electroconvulsive therapy in depressive disorders: A systematic review and meta-analysis. *Lancet, 361*, 799–808.

Umaña-Taylor, A. J. (2004). Ethnic identity and self-esteem: Examining the role of social context. *Journal of Adolescence, 27*, 139–146.

Underwood, A., & Watson, R. (2001, Fall/Winter). Keeping hope alive. *Newsweek Special Issue*, pp. 55–58.

United Nations. (2003, November 25). AIDS deaths, infections at new highs. *CNN Web Posting*. Retrieved January 14, 2004, from http://www.cnn.com/2003/HEALTH/conditions/11/25/aids.reut.

USA: The way we'll live then. *Newsweek*, January 1, 2000, p. 35.

U.S. Bureau of the Census (U.S. Census Bureau). (2001). *Resident population of the United States: Middle series projections, 1996–2000, by sex, race, and Hispanic origin, with median age*. Washington, DC: Author.

U.S. Bureau of the Census (U.S. Census Bureau). (2001). *Resident population of the United States: Middle series projections, 2035–2050, by sex, race, and Hispanic origin, with median age*. Washington, DC: Author.

U.S. Bureau of the Census. (1995). *Statistical abstract of the United States* (115th ed.). Washington, DC: U.S. Government Printing Office.

U.S. Bureau of the Census. (2000). *Statistical abstract of the United States* (120th ed.). Washington, DC: U.S. Government Printing Office.

U.S. Census Bureau. (1994, March). *Current Population Reports, Series, Household and Family Characteristics*.

U.S. Department of Agriculture (USDA), Health Nutrition Information Services (1991). *Nutritive value of foods* (Pub. No. G-72). Washington, DC: U.S. Government Printing Office.

U.S. Department of Health and Human Services (USDHSS). (1991a). *Healthy people 2000: National health promotion and disease prevention objectives* (DHHS Pub. No. PHS 91–50212). Washington, DC: Public Health Service.

U.S. Department of Health and Human Services (USDHSS). (1991b). *NIDA capsules: Summary of findings from the 1991 National Household Survey on Drug Abuse* (No. 20). Public Health Service, Alcohol Drug Abuse and Mental Health Administration, National Institute on Drug Abuse. Rockville, MD: National Institute on Drug Abuse.

U.S. Department of Health and Human Services (USDHSS). (1992a). *Healthy People 2000*. Boston: Jones and Bartlett.

U.S. Department of Health and Human Services (USDHSS). (1992b). *NIDA capsules: Highlight of an attitudes and knowledge survey about illegal drug use* (No. 19). Public Health Service, Alcohol Drug Abuse and Mental Health Administration, National Institute on Drug Abuse. Rockville, MD: National Institute on Drug Abuse.

U.S. Department of Health and Human Services (USDHSS). (1992c). *NIDA capsules: LSD (Lysergic Acid Diethylamindde)* (No. 39). Public Health Service, Alcohol Drug Abuse and Mental Health Administration, National Institute on Drug Abuse. Rockville, MD: National Institute on Drug Abuse.

U.S. Department of Health and Human Services, Substance Abuse and Mental Health Services Administration. (USDHSS) (1993, October). *National Household Survey on Drug Abuse: Population estimates 1992* (DHHS Publication No. SMA 93–2053). Washington, DC: U.S. Government Printing Office.

U.S. Department of Health and Human Services, Substance Abuse and Mental Health Services Administration. (USDHSS) (1999). *Mental Health: A Report of the Surgeon General*. Rockville, MD: U.S. Department of Health and Human Services, Substance Abuse and Mental Health Services Administration, Center for Mental Health Services, National Institutes of Health, National Institute of Mental Health.

U.S. Department of Health and Human Services, Substance Abuse and Mental Health Services Administration, Center for Mental Health Services, National Institutes of Health, National Institute of Mental Health. (USD-HHS) (2001). *Mental health: Culture, race, and ethnicity: A supplement to mental health: A report of the Surgeon General—Executive summary*. Rockville, MD: Author.

Uttl, B., Graf, P., Miller, J., & Tuokko, H. (2001). Pro- and retrospective memory in late adulthood. *Consciousness and Cognition: An International Journal, 10*, 451–472.

Van Ameringen, M. A., Lane, R. M., Walker, J. R., Bowen, R. C., Chokka, P. R., Goldner, E. M., et al. (2001). Sertraline treatment of generalized social phobia: A 20-week, double-blind, placebo-controlled study. *American Journal of Psychiatry, 158*, 275–281.

Van Cauter, E., Leproult, R., & Plat, L. (2000). Age-related changes in slow-wave sleep and REM sleep and relationship with growth hormone and cortisol levels in healthy men. *Journal of the American Medical Association, 284*, 861–868.

Van Raalte, J. L., & Brewer, B. W. (2002). *Exploring sport and exercise psychology*. Washington, DC: American Psychological Association.

Van-Ree, J. M. (1996). Endorphins: An experimental addiction. *Alcohol, 13*, 25–30.

Vastag, B. (2004). Obesity is now on everyone's plate. *Journal of the American Medical Association, 291*, 1186–1188.

Vecchio, R. P. (1997). *Leadership: Understanding the dynamics of power and influence in organizations*. Notre Dame: University of Notre Dame Press.

Verghese, A. (2004, February 22). Hope and clarity: Is optimism a cure? *New York Times Magazine*, pp. 11–12.

Verhaeghen, P. (2003). Aging and vocabulary scores: A meta-analysis. *Psychology and Aging, 18*, 332–339.

Verhovek, S. H. (2000). What is the matter with Mary Jane? *New York Times Week in Review*, p. 3.

Virkkunen, M., & Linnoila, M. (1993). Brain serotonin, Type II alcoholism and impulsive violence. *Journal of Studies on Alcohol* (Suppl. 11), 163–169.

Volkow, N. D., Wang, G. J., Firsch, J. S., Logan, J., et al. (1997). Decreased striatal dopaminergic responsiveness in detoxified cocaine-dependent subjects. *Nature, 386*, 830–833.

Volpe, K. (2003, May). Geography of thought. *APS Observer, 16*(5), p. 33.

Von Békésy, G. (1957, August). The ear. *Scientific American*, pp. 66–78.

Von-Hofsten, C., & Rosander, K. (1996). The development of gaze control and predictive tracking in young infants. *Vision Research, 36*, 81–96.

Vygotsky, L. S. (1978). *Mind in society: The development of higher psychological processes*. Cambridge, MA: Harvard University Press.

Vygotsky, L. S. (1986). *Thought and language*. Cambridge, MA: MIT Press. (Original work published 1934.)

Wadden, T A., Brownell, K. D., & Foster, G. D. (2002). Obesity: Responding to the global epidemic. *Journal of Consulting and Clinical Psychology, 70*, 510–525.

Wade, N. (1997, May 24). Doctors record signals of brain cells linked to memory. *New York Times*, p. A9.

Wade, N. (2003a, April 15). Once again, scientists say human genome is complete. *New York Times*, p. F1.

Wade, N. (2003b, June 3). Gene sweepstakes ends, but winner may well be wrong. *New York Times*, pp. F1, F. 2.

Wadsworth, S. J., DeFries, J. C., Fulker, D. W., & Plomin, R. (1995). Cognitive ability and academic achievement in the Colorado Adoption Project: A multivariate genetic analysis of parent/offspring and sibling data. *Behavior Genetics, 25*, 1–15.

Wagner, U., Gais, S., Haider, H., Verleger, R., & Born, J. (2004). Sleep inspires insight. *Nature, 427*, 352–355.

Wagstaff, G. F., & Frost, R. (1996). Reversing and breaching posthypnotic amnesia and hypnotically created pseudomemories. *Contemporary Hypnosis, 13*(3), 191–197.

Waldman, I. D., Weinberg, R. A., & Scarr, S. (1994). Racial-group differences in IQ in the Minnesota Transracial Adoption Study: A reply to Levin and Lynn. *Intelligence, 19*, 29–44.

Walker, E., Kestler, L., Bollini, A., & Hochman, K. M. (2004). Schizophrenia: Etiology and course. *Annual Review of Psychology, 55*, 401–430.

Walker, L. (1989). A longitudinal study of moral reasoning. *Child Development, 60*, 157–166.

Walker, L. J. (1997). Is morality gendered in early parent-child relationships? A commentary on the Lollis, Ross, and Leroux study. *Merrill-Palmer Quarterly, 43*, 148–159.

Walker, R. (2004, February 8). Cialis. *New York Times Magazine*, p. 26.

Wall, T. L., Carr, L. G, & Ehlers, C. L. (2003). Protective association of genetic variation in alcohol dehydrogenase with alcohol dependence in Native American Mission Indians. *American Journal of Psychiatry, 160*, 41–46.

Wall, T. L., Shea, S. H., Chan, K. K., & Carr, L. G. (2001). A genetic association with the development of alcohol and other substance use behavior in Asian Americans. *Journal of Abnormal Psychology, 110*, 173–178.

Wallach, C., & Callahan, S. (1994). The 1st grade plant museum. *Educational Leadership, 52*, 32–34.

Wallston, K. A. (2001). Conceptualization and operationalization of perceived control. In A. Baum, T. A. Revenson, & J. E. Singer (Eds.), *Handbook of health psychology* (pp. 49–58). Mahwah, NJ: Lawrence Erlbaum Associates.

Walsh, B. T., Fairburn, C. G., Mickley, D., Sysko, R., & Parides, M. K. (2004). Treatment of bulimia nervosa in a primary care setting. *American Journal of Psychiatry, 161*, 556–561.

Walsh, J. M., Wheat, M. E., & Freund, K. (2000). Detection, evaluation, and treatment of eating disorders: The role of the primary care physician. *Journal of General Internal Medicine, 15*, 577–579.

Wampold, B. E., Mondin, G. W., Moody, M., Stich, F., Benson, K., & Ahn, H. (1997). A meta-analysis of outcome studies comparing bona fide psychotherapies: Empirically, "All must have prizes." *Psychological Bulletin, 122*, 203–215.

Wang, X., Gao, L., Shinfuku, N., Zhang, H., Zhao, C., & Shen, Y. (2000). Longitudinal study of earthquake-related PTSD in a randomly selected community sample in North China. *American Journal of Psychiatry, 157*, 1260–1266.

Ward, T. B., Smith, S. M., & Vaid, J. (1997). Conceptual structures and processes in creative thought. In T. B. Ward, S. M. Smith, & J. Vaid (Eds.), *Creative thought: An investigation of conceptual structures and processes* (pp. 1–30). Washington, DC: American Psychological Association.

Waterworth, D. M., Bassett, A. S., & Brzustowicz, L. M. (2002). Recent advances in the genetics of schizophrenia. *Cellular and Molecular Life Sciences, 59*, 331–348.

Watson, J. B. (1913). Psychology as the behaviorist views it. *Psychological Bulletin, 20*, 158–177.

Watson, J. B. (1924). *Behaviorism*. New York: W. W. Norton.

Watson, J. B., & Rayner, R. (1920). Conditioned emotional reactions. *Journal of Experimental Psychology, 3*, 1–14.

Webster, A., & Beveridge, M. (1997). The role of educational psychologists in educational research: Some implications for professional training. *Educational Psychology in Practice, 13*, 155–164.

Wechsler, D. (1975). Intelligence defined and undefined: A relativistic appraisal. *American Psychologist, 34*, 135–139.

Weems, C. F. (1998). The evaluation of heart rate biofeedback using a multielement design. *Journal of Behavior Therapy and Experimental Psychiatry, 29*, 157–162.

Weiner, B. (1992). *Human motivation: Metaphors, theories, and research*. Thousand Oaks, CA: Sage Publications.

Weiss, R. D., & Mirin, S. M. (1987). *Cocaine*. Washington, DC: American Psychiatric Press.

Weisz, J. R., Pilkonis, P. A., Woody, S. R., & Follette, W. C. (2000). Stressing the (other) three Rs in the search for empirically supported treatments: Review procedures, research quality, relevance to practice and the public interest. *Clinical Psychology: Science and Practice, 7*, 243–258.

Weisz, J. R., Weiss, B., Han, S. S., Granger, D. A., & Morton, T. (1995). Effects of psychotherapy with children and adolescents revisited: A meta-analysis of treatment outcome studies. *Psychological Bulletin, 117*, 450–468.

Wells, G. L., & Olson, E. A. (2003). Eyewitness testimony. *Annual Review of Psychology, 54*, 277–295.

Welsh, R. S. (2003). Prescription privileges: Pro or con [Letter]. *Clinical Psychology: Science and Practice, 10*, 371–372.

Westen, D., & Gabbard, G. O. (2002). Developments in cognitive neuroscience: 1. Conflict, compromise, and connectionism. *Journal of the American Psychoanalytic Association, 50*, 53–98.

Westman, J., Hasselström, J., Johansson, S.-E., & Sundquist, J. (2003). The influences of place of birth and socioeconomic factors on attempted suicide in a defined population of 4.5 million people. *Archives of General Psychiatry, 60*, 409–411.

Wheeler, M. A., Stuss, D. T., & Tulving, E. (1997). Toward a theory of episodic memory: The frontal lobes and autonoetic consciousness. *Psychological Bulletin, 121*, 331–354.

Wheeler, M. E., Petersen, S. E., & Buckner, R. L. (2000, September 26). Memory's echo: Vivid remembering reactivates sensory-specific cortex. *Proceedings of the National Academy of Sciences*.

Whittemore, A. S., Kolonel, L. N., Wu, A. H., John, E. M., Gallagher, R. P., Howe, G. R., et al. (1995). Prostate cancer in relation to diet, physical activity, and body size in blacks, whites, and Asians in the United States and Canada. *Journal of the National Cancer Institute, 87*, 652–661.

Whooley, M. A., Kiefe, C. I., Chesney, M. A., Markovitz, J. H., Matthews, K., & Hulley, S. B., et al. (2002). Depressive symptoms, unemployment, and loss of income: The CARDIA Study. *Archives of Internal Medicine, 162*, 2614–2620.

Whorf, B. L. (1956). Science and linguistics. In J. B. Carrroll (Ed.), *Language, thought, and reality: Selected writings of Benjamin Lee Whorf*. Cambridge, MA: MIT press.

Widiger, T. A., & Clark, L. A. (2000). Toward DSM-V and the classification of psychopathology. *Psychological Bulletin, 126*, 946–963.

Wiers, R. W., & Kummeling, R. H. C. (2004). An experimental test of an alcohol expectancy challenge in mixed-gender groups of young heavy drinkers. *Addictive Behaviors, 29*, 215–220.

Wiersma, D., Jenner, J. A., van de Willige, G., Spakman, M., & Nienhuis, F. J. (2001). Cognitive behaviour therapy with coping training for persistent auditory hallucinations in schizophrenia: A naturalistic follow-up study of the durability of effects. *Acta Psychiatrica Scandinavica, 103*, 393–399.

Wilcox, L. M., & Duke, P. A. (2003). Stereoscopic surface interpolation supports lightness constancy. *Psychological Science, 14*, 525–530.

Wilder, D. A. (1990). Some determinants of the persuasive power of in-groups and out-groups: Organization of information and attribution of independence. *Journal of Personality and Social Psychology, 59*, 1202–1213.

Wilding, J., & Valentine, E. (1996). Memory expertise. In D. Herrmann et al. (Eds.), *Basic and applied memory research: Theory in context* (Vol. 1, pp. 399–420). Mahwah, NJ: Lawrence Erlbaum Associates.

Williams, T. J., Pepitone, M. E., Christensen, S. E., Cooke, B. M., Huberman, A. D., Breedlove, N. J., et al. (2000, April). Finger length patterns and human sexual orientation. *Nature, 404*, 455–456.

Williams, W. M. (1998). Are we raising smarter children today? School- and home-related influences on IQ. In U. Neisser (Ed.), *The rising curve: Long-term gains in IQ and related measures* (pp. 125–154). Washington, DC: American Psychological Association.

Willingham, D. B. (2001). *Cognition: The thinking animal*. Upper Saddle River, NJ: Prentice-Hall.

Willis, D. J. (2003, Fall). The case for prescription privileges. *The Clinical Psychologist, 56*, 1–4.

Willis, S. L., & Schaie, K. W. (1999). Intellectual functioning in midlife. In S. L. Willis & J. D. Reid (Eds.), *Life in the middle: Psychological and social development in middle age* (pp. 233–247). San Diego: Academic Press.

Wills, T. A., & Cleary, S. D. (1999). Peer and adolescent substance use among 6th–9th graders: Latent growth analyses of influence versus selection mechanisms. *Health Psychology, 18*, 453–463.

Wills, T. A., & Filer-Fegan, M. (2001). Social networks and social support. In A. Baum, T. A. Revenson, & J. E. Singer (Eds.), *Handbook of health psychology* (pp. 209–234). Mahwah, NJ: Lawrence Erlbaum Associates.

Wilson, G. T., Fairburn, C. C., Agras, W. S., Walsh, B. T., & Kraemer, H. (2002). Cognitive behavioral therapy for bulimia nervosa: Time course and mechanisms of change. *Journal of Consulting and Clinical Psychology, 70*, 267–274.

Wilson, R. S., Bennett, D. A., Bienias, J. L., Aggarwal, N. T., Mendes de Leon, C. F., Morris, M. C., et al. (2002). Cognitive activity and incident AD in a population-based sample of older persons. *Neurology, 59*, 1910–1914.

Wilson, R., S., Bennett, D. A, Bienia, J. L., Mendes de Leon, C. F., Morris, M. C., &, Evans, D. A. (2003). Cognitive activity and cognitive decline in a biracial community population. *Neurology, 61*, 812–816.

Windholz, G., & Lamal, P. A. (1985). Koehler's insight revisited. *Teaching of Psychology, 12*, 165–167.

Winerman, L. (2004, April). A second look at twin studies. *Monitor on Psychology*, pp. 46–47.

Winner, E. (2000). The origins and ends of giftedness. *American Psychologist, 55*, 159–169.

Winterer, G., Coppola, R., Goldberg, T. E., Egan, M. F., Jones, D. W., et al. (2004). Prefrontal broadband noise, working memory, and genetic risk for schizophrenia. *American Journal of Psychiatry, 161*, 490–500.

Wixted, J. T. (2004). The psychology and neuroscience of forgetting. *Annual Review of Psychology, 55*, 235–269.

Wolchik, S. A., Sandler, I. N., Millsap, R. E., Plummer, B. A., Greene, S. M., Anderson, E. R., et al. (2002). Six-year follow-up of preventive interventions for children of divorce: A randomized controlled trial. *Journal of the American Medical Association, 288*, 1874–1881.

Wong, E. C., Kim, B. S. K., Zane, N. W. S., Kim, I. J., & Huang, J. S. (2003). Examining culturally based variables associated with ethnicity: Influences on credibility perceptions of empirically supported interventions. *Cultural Diversity and Ethnic Minority Psychology, 9*, 88–96.

Wood, J. M, Lilienfeld, S. O., Nezworski, M. T., & Garb, H. N. (2001). Coming to grips with negative evidence for the comprehensive system for the Rorschach: A comment on Gacono, Loving, and Bodholdt; Ganellen; and Bornstein. *Journal of Personality Assessment, 77*, 48–70.

Wood, M. D., Vinson, D. C., & Sher, K. J. (2001). Alcohol use and misuse. In A. Baum, T. A. Revenson, & J. E. Singer (Eds.), *Handbook of health psychology* (pp. 280–320). Mahwah, NJ: Lawrence Erlbaum Associates.

Wright, S. C., Aron, A., McLaughlin-Volpe, R., & Ropp, S. A. (1997). The extended contact effect: Knowledge of cross-group friendships and prejudice. *Journal of Personality and Social Psychology, 73*, 73–90.

Writing Group of the PREMIER Collaborative Research Group. (2003). Effects of comprehensive lifestyle modification on blood pressure control: Main results of the PREMIER Clinical Trial. *Journal of the American Medical Association, 289*, 2083–2093.

Wu, K. D., & Clark, L. A. (2003). Relations between personality traits and self-reports of daily behavior. *Journal of Research in Personality, 37*, 231–256.

Yankelovich Partners. (1995, May/June). Growing old. *American Enterprise,* p. 108.

Yasuno, F., Suhara, T., Nakayama, T., Ichimiya, T., Okubo, Y., Takano, A., et al. (2003). Inhibitory effect of hippocampal 5-HT1A receptors on human explicit memory. *American Journal of Psychiatry, 160*, 334–340.

Young, E. A., McFatter, R., & Clopton, J. R. (2001). Family functioning, peer influence, and media influence as predictors of bulimic behavior. *Eating Behaviors, 2*, 323–337.

Younger, J. D. (2001, October). When drivers' attention takes a detour. *Car and Travel,* pp. 20–21.

Zajonc, R. (1965). Social facilitation. *Science, 149*, 269–274.

Zajonc, R. B. (1980). Feeling and thinking: Preferences need no inferences. *American Psychologist, 35*, 151–175.

Zajonc, R. B. (1984). On the primacy of affect. *American Psychologist, 39*, 117–123.

Zamanian, K., Thackrey, M., Starrett, R. A., & Brown, L.G. et al. (1992). Acculturation and depression in Mexican-American elderly. *Gerontologist, 11*, 109–121.

Zane, N., & Sue, S. (1991). Culturally responsive mental health services for Asian Americans: Treatment and training issues. In H. F. Myers, P. Wohlford, L. P. Guzaman, & R. J. Echemendia (Eds.), *Ethnic minority perspectives on clinical training and services in psychology* (pp. 49–58). Washington, DC: American Psychological Association.

Zatzick, D. F., Kang, S.-M., Müller, H.-G., Russo, J. E., Rivera, F. P., Katon, W., et al. (2002). Predicting posttraumatic distress in hospitalized trauma survivors with acute injuries. *American Journal of Psychiatry, 159*, 941–946.

Zigler, E., & Styfco, S. J. (1994). Head Start: Criticisms in a constructive context. *American Psychologist, 49*, 127–132.

Zimprich, D., & Martin, M. (2002). Can longitudinal changes in processing speed explain longitudinal age changes in fluid intelligence? *Psychology and Aging, 17*, 690–695.

Zinser, O., Freeman, J. E., & Ginnings, D. K. (1999). A comparison of memory for and attitudes about alcohol, cigarette, and other product advertisements in college students. *Journal of Drug Education, 29*, 175–185.

Zlotnick, C., Bruce, S. E., Shea, M. T., & Keller, M. B. (2001). Delayed posttraumatic stress disorder (PTSD) and predictors of first onset of PTSD in patients with anxiety disorders. *Journal of Nervous and Mental Disease, 189*, 404–406.

Zoellner, L. A., Craske, M. G., & Rapee, R. M. (1996). Stability of catastrophic cognitions in panic disorder. *Behaviour Research and Therapy, 34*, 399–402.

Zoellner, L. A., Foa, E. B., Brigidi, B. D., & Przeworski, A. (2000). Are trauma victims susceptible to "false memories"? *Journal of Abnormal Psychology, 109*, 517–524.

Zubin, J., & Spring, B. (1977). Vulnerability—A new view of schizophrenia. *Journal of Abnormal Psychology, 86*, 103–126.

Zucker, A. N., Ostrove, J. M., & Stewart, A. J. (2002). College-educated women's personality development in adulthood: Perceptions and age differences. *Psychology and Aging, 2*, 236–244.

Zuckerman, M. (1980). Sensation seeking. In H. London & J. Exner (Eds.), *Dimensions of personality.* New York: John Wiley & Sons.

Zuckerman, M. (1995). Good and bad humors: Biochemical bases of personality and its disorders. *Psychological Science, 6*, 325–332.

Zuckerman, M. (1996). The psychobiological model for impulsive unsocialized sensation seeking: A comparative approach. *Neuropsychobiology, 34*, 125–129.

Zuckerman, M. (2004). The shaping of personality: Genes, environments, and chance encounters. *Journal of Personality Assessment, 82*, 11–22.

Zuger, A. (1997 August 19). Removing half of brain improves young epileptics' lives. *The New York Times,* p. C4.

Zukow-Goldring, P. (1997). A social ecological realist approach to the emergence of the lexicon: Educating attention to amodal invariants in gesture and speech. In C. Dent-Read & P. Zukow-Goldring (Eds.), *Evolving explanations of development: Ecological approaches to organism-environment systems* (pp. 199–250). Washington, DC: American Psychological Association.

Zweigenhaft, R. L. (1970). Signature size: A key to status awareness. *Journal of Social Psychology, 81*, 49–54.

CREDITS

Photo Credits

Chapter opener photos: Ch. 1, p. 2: © Jim West/The Image Bank; Ch. 2, p. 38: © David Parker/SPL/Photo Researchers; Ch. 3, p. 82: © LWA-Dann Tardif/CORBIS; Ch. 4, p. 124: © Chris Lowe/Index Stock Imagery/PictureQuest; Ch. 5, p. 160: © Bob Daemmrich/Stock Boston; Ch. 6, p. 192: © Michael Newman/PhotoEdit; Ch. 7, p. 222: © Gary Conner/PhotoEdit; Ch. 8, p. 256: © Ezra Shaw/Getty; Ch. 9, p. 294: © Walter Hodges/CORBIS; Ch. 10, p. 344: © David Young-Wolff/PhotoEdit; Ch. 11, p. 380: © IT Stock Int'l/Index Stock Imagery; Ch. 12, p. 416: © Michael Newman/PhotoEdit; Ch. 13, p. 448: © Paul Barton/CORBIS; Ch. 14, p. 480: © Beryl Goldberg.

Chapter 1: p. 4: © Jeff Greenberg/Photo Researchers; p. 5: Archives of the History of American Psychology; p. 7: J.P. Laffont/Sygmas/CORBIS; p. 11: © Ellen Senisi/The Image Works; p. 19: (left) Wellesley College Archives, photo by Partridge; (center) Archives of the History of American Psychology; (right) Courtesy of Wilberforce University, Archives and Special Collections; p. 22: Brand X Pictures/Getty; p. 24: © Penelope Breese/Getty Images; p. 25: © David Young-Wolff/PhotoEdit; p. 39: © Bob Daemmrich/The Image Works.

Chapter 2: p. 46: © AFP/Getty Images; p. 49: © Alex Wong/Newsmakers/Getty Images; p. 57: © The Natural History Museum; p. 58: © Richard Nowitz/Photo Researchers; p. 59: © SIU/Photo Researchers; p. 60: (left) © Pascal Goetgheluck/Science Photo Library/Photo Researchers; (right) © Scott Grafton MD/Visuals Unlimited; p. 61: © Raoul Minsart/CORBIS; p. 62: © David Young-Wolff/PhotoEdit; p. 63: © Neil Bromhall/Science Photo Library/Photo Researchers; p. 78: © Will & Deni McInyre/Photo Researchers.

Chapter 3: p. 88: © Ralph C. Eagle/Photo Researchers; p. 93: Used with permission of Richmond Products; p. 100: © Rolf Bruderer/CORBIS; p. 103: © Spencer Grant/PhotoEdit; p. 104: © Richard Francis; p. 109: © John Chiasson/Getty Images; p. 113: © Susan Van Etten/PhotoEdit; p. 114: (top left) © William Johnson/Stock Boston; (top center) © David Stoecklein/CORBIS Stock Market; (top right) © Art Wolfe/Stone/Getty Images; (bottom left) © DeRichemond/The Image Works; (bottom center) © Bob Daemmrich/The Image Works; p. 116: (top) © Phyllis Picardi; (bottom) © Abe Rezny/The Image Works; p. 117: © Peter Menzel/Stock Boston; p. 118: © AFP/Getty Images.

Chapter 4: p. 127: © Bob Daemmrich/Stock Boston; p. 133: © Albert Rocarols; p. 136: © Tony Anderson/FPG International/Getty Images; p. 138: © Gary Conner/PhotoEdit; p. 143: (left) Bill Bachmann/Photo Edit; (right) © Karen Moskowitz/Stone/Getty Images; p. 144: Frank Driggs Collection/Hulton Archive/Getty Images; p. 145: © Victoria Yee/Stone/Getty Images; p. 149: © Mark Richards/PhotoEdit; p. 150: © Michael Newman/PhotoEdit; p. 151: © R. Flynt/The Image Works; p. 154: © David Young-Wolff/PhotoEdit; p. 156: © T. Petillot/Explorer/Photo Researchers.

Chapter 5: p. 167: Archives of the History of American Psychology; p. 168: © Adam Tanner/The Image Works; p. 169: (top) © Tom Stack & Associates; (bottom) Courtesy of Dr. John Garcia; p. 173: © L. Clarke/CORBIS; p. 174: © Bob Daemmrich/The Image Works; p. 186: (left) Courtesy of Albert Bandura; (upper right) Courtesy of Albert Bandura; (lower right) Courtesy of Albert Bandura; p. 188: © Steve Skjold/PhotoEdit.

Chapter 6: p. 201: © Steve Starr/Stock Boston; p. 203: (top) Courtesy of W. F. Brewer, from Brewer, W. F. and Treyens, J.C. (1981), "Role of Schemata in Memory of Places," Cognitive Psychology, 13, 207-230; (bottom) AP/Wide World Photos; p. 204: Courtesy of Elizabeth Loftus; p. 209: © Dana White/PhotoEdit; p. 211: © Jeff Persons/Stock Boston; p. 215: Courtesy of Eric Kandel.

Chapter 7: p. 224: © Laura Dwight/CORBIS; p. 226: © T. Brakefield/The Image Works; p. 234: Donna Coveney/MIT; p. 235: © Art Wolfe/Stone/Getty Images; p. 236: © A. Ramey/Stock Boston; p. 237: Language Research Center, Georgia State University; p. 245: (left) © David Young-Wolff/PhotoEdit; (top) © Jonathan Nourok/PhotoEdit; (right) © Owen Franken/Stock Boston; (bottom) © David Young-Wolff/PhotoEdit; p. 247: (left) © Stephen Collins/Photo Researchers; (top) © Michael Newman/PhotoEdit; (right) © Mike Greenlar/The Image Works; p. 250: © Mark Wexler/Woodfin Camp.

Chapter 8: p. 258: © Philippe Wojazer/Reuters/CORBIS; p. 260: AP/Wide World Photos; p. 263: © Fabian Falcon/Stock Boston; p. 266: Courtesy of Neal E. Miller, Dept. of Psychology, Yale University; p. 267: © Joel Gordon Photography; p. 269: © Tony Freeman/PhotoEdit; p. 277: © Esbin-Anderson/The Image Works; p. 280: Paul Ekman, from *The face of man: Expression of universal emotions in a New Guinea Village*, 1980; p. 282: Paul Ekman, from *Telling Lies*, 1975; p. 283: National Institute of Mental Health; p. 288: © Willie L. Hill, Jr./Stock Boston.

Chapter 9: p. 297: (top) © D.W. Fawcett/SS/Photo Researchers; (lower right) © Petit Format/Nestle/Photo Researchers; (lower left) © Petit Format/Nestle/Photo Researchers; p. 301 (top) © J.daCunha/Petit Format/Photo Researchers; (left) © Charles Gupton/Stock Boston; (right) © Elizabeth Crews; p. 302: © 2003 PhotoDisc; p. 302: (bottom) © Robert Birnbach; p. 306: © Jonathan Nourok/PhotoEdit; p. 307: (left) Thomas McAvoy/Time & Life Pictures/Getty Images; (right) Harlow Primate Laboratory, University of Wisconsin; p. 310: © Mahaux Photography/The Image Bank/Getty Images; p. 315: (left) © Doug Goodman/Photo Researchers; (right) © Doug Goodman/Photo Researchers; p. 316: © Lew Merrim/Science Source/Photo Researchers; p. 322: © Elizabeth Crews; p. 326: © Tony Freeman/PhotoEdit; p. 333: © Gary Conner/PhotoEdit; p. 334: © Laura Dwight/PhotoEdit; p. 335: © Joseph Nettis/Stock Boston; p. 338: © Barbara Stitzer/PhotoEdit.

Chapter 10: p. 346: Leo Baeck Institute/Hulton Archive/Getty Images; p. 350: © Royalty-Free/CORBIS; p. 352: CORBIS; p. 358: © Ed Bock/CORBIS; p. 362: © Davis Barber/PhotoEdit; p. 365: © Myrleen F. Cate/PhotoEdit.

Chapter 11: p. 382: © G.D.T./Stone/Getty Images; p. 384: The Granger Collection, New York; p. 390: © Jim Whitmer; p. 399: © Michael Newman/PhotoEdit; p. 402: © Najlah Feanny/Stock Boston; p. 404: © Mary Kate Denny/PhotoEdit; p. 408: © Grunnitus/Photo Researchers; p. 409: Photofest.

Chapter 12: p. 421: © Zigy Kaluzny/Stone/Getty Images; p. 424: (left) © Jim Whitmer; (right) Georgia Tech Photo – Stanley Leary; p. 431: © Bob Daemmrich/Stock Boston; p. 433: © Vision/Photo Researchers; p. 434: © Michael Newman/PhotoEdit; p. 437: © Paul S. Howell/Getty Images; p. 439: © Najlah Feanny/Stock Boston; p. 441: © David Young-Wolff/PhotoEdit.

Chapter 13: p. 451: (left) © Phil Martin/PhotoEdit; (right) Robert Brenner/PhotoEdit; p. 457: (top) © Rob Van Petten/Getty Images; (left) © Tony Freeman/PhotoEdit; p. 476 (left) © Amy Etra/PhotoEdit; (right) © Tony Savino/The Image Works; p. 477: © Felicia Martinez/PhotoEdit.

Chapter 14: p. 482: © Tomas del Amo/Index Stock; p. 491: (left) © Vince Bucci/Liaison/Getty Images; (right) © Frank Trapper/Sygma/CORBIS; p. 494: © Bruce Ayres/Stone/Getty Images; p. 496: © Phyllis Picardi/Stock, Boston Inc./PictureQuest; p. 500: © Wally McNamee/CORBIS Sygma; p. 506: William Vandivert/Courtesy Susan Vandivert; p. 508: From the film Obedience ©1965 by Stanley Milgram.

Text Credits

Chapter 4: p. 144: *Table 4.1:* From O. Ray and C. Kasir, *Drugs, Society and Human Behavior*, Fifth Edition, 1990. Copyright © 1990 by The McGraw-Hill Companies, Inc. Reprinted with permission.

Chapter 6: p. 210: *Try This Out:* Adapted and reprinted from *Cognitive Psychology*, Vol. 11, Nickerson and Adams, "What Does a Penny Look Like? Long-Term Memory for a Common Object," pp. 287–307. Copyright © 1979, with permission from Elsevier.

Name Index

Subject Index

NOTE: Boldfaced numbers indicate pages where key terms are defined in the text.

Abnormal behavior, 8, 348
  criteria for, 382–384, 415
  cultural bases of, 383
  models of, 384–386, 388(chart)
  See also Psychological disorder(s)
Absolute threshold(s), **84**, 85(table),
  86(chart)
Abstinence syndrome, 142
Abstract thinking, 318(chart), 321–322
Abuse, child. *See* Child abuse
Accommodation
  in cognitive development, **314**, 317,
    318(chart)
  in eye structure, **88**
Acculturation, 153–154, 434(table)
Acculturative stress, **457**, 457–458, 458(chart)
Achievement, need for, 261, **262**, 264(chart)
Achievement motivation, **262**
Acoustic coding, 194, 195, 196
Acquired immune deficiency syndrome
  (AIDS), 299, 388, 471, 472, 473(table)
Acronyms and acrostics, as mnemonics, **217**
Acrophobia, **390**
ACTH (adrenocorticotrophic hormone),
  69(chart), 70, **461**(illus.)
Action potential, **43**(illus.), 45
Activation-synthesis hypothesis, **132**, 132–
  133, 133(illus.)
Active sleep, 131
Actor-observer effect, 379, 484–485, **485**,
  490(chart)
Acupuncture, **103**
AD. *See* Alzheimer's disease
ADA. *See* Americans with Disabilities Act
Adaptation, in cognitive development, **314**,
  318(chart)
Adaptation stage, of general adaptation syndrome, 459
Addiction, drug, 147, 148–149, 155, 168, 438
ADHD. *See* Attention-deficit hyperactivity
  disorder
Adolescence, 308, 311, **319**, 319–328, 330
  cognitive development in, 321–325
  eating disorders in, 269, 270
  moral reasoning in, 322–324, 324(chart)
  peer relationships in, 327
  physical development in, 320–321
  psychosocial development in, 325–328,
    335(chart)
  sexual activity in, 327–328
  suicide in, 322, 328, 404, 405
  Adoptee studies, 74(chart), **75**, 75–76
  anxiety disorders and, 391
  intelligence and, 248, 249(illus.), 250
  schizophrenia and, 408
Adrenal cortex, 70, **461**(illus.)
Adrenal glands, 68(illus.), 69(chart), **70**, 276,
  282, 330, **461**(illus.)
Adrenaline, 46, 69(chart), 468. *See also*
  Epinephrine
Adrenal medulla, 70, **461**(illus.)
Adrenocorticotrophic hormone (ACTH),
  69(chart), 70, **461**(illus.)
Adulthood
  cognitive changes in, 329(illus.), 329–330

emerging, **330**
  moral reasoning in, 323
  physical changes in, 330
  sleep patterns in, 135
  social changes in, 330–331, 325–328,
    335(chart)
  See also Late adulthood
Affection, 280
Afferent neurons, 40
Affiliation, need for, 262
Afterimage(s), **91**(illus.)
Age of viability, 298
Age regression, hypnotic, **139**, 140
Aggression, 54, 346, 347, 491, 500–503,
  503(chart)
  alcohol and, 144, 502
  anger and, 180, 279, 290, 501, 502–503
  biological influences on, 501
  day care and, 308–309
  emotional influences on, 502–503
  environmental influences on, 11, 503
  genetic factors in, 10–11, 359
  instinct theories of, 500–501
  learning influences on, 185, 186(illus.),
    501–502
  sociocultural influences on, 502
  television and, 185
  testosterone and, 70–71, 461, 501
Aggressive instinct, in psychodynamic
  theory, 346
Aging, successful, 12, 335–336
Agonists, at receptor sites, **46**, 47
Agoraphobia, **390**, 393(chart), 432,
  433(table)
Agreeableness, 358(table), 359(chart)
AIDS (acquired immune deficiency syndrome), 299, 388, 471, 472, 473(table)
Alarm stage, of general adaptation syndrome, **459**, 460(illus.)
Alcohol, 46, 128, 141, 142, 143–146,
  153(chart), 154, 155, 178, 219, 276, 339,
  383
  aggression and, 144, 502
  barbiturates and, 144, 147
  binge drinking and, 145–146
  illness and, 466(table), 470(table), 471,
    474(chart)
  prenatal development and, 300
  suicide and, 404, 405
Alcoholics Anonymous (AA), 155
Alcoholism, 33, 73, **145**, 146, 152–153, 154,
  168, 212, 425
Alcohol overdose, signs of, 146(table)
Alertness, 70
Algorithm(s), **227**
All-or-none principle, **43**
All-or-nothing thinking, 401(table)
Alpha waves, 130(illus.), 132(chart)
Alprazolam, 436, 442(chart)
Altered states of consciousness, **128**(chart),
  139. *See also* Hypnosis; Meditation;
  Psychoactive drugs
Alternate-forms method, 241
Alternate personalities, 395, 396
Alternate Uses Test, 231

Altruism, 11, 12, 495
Alzheimer's disease (AD), 206, 212, 216, **334**,
  336(chart), 339
Ambiguity, situational, 495, A-3
American Psychological Association, found-
  ing of, 6, 18
American Sign Language (ASL), 233, 236
Americans with Disabilities Act (ADA),
  419(table)
Amitriptyline, 437, 442(chart)
Amnesia, 206, **211**, 214, 394, 395
  causes of, 212
  types of, 211–212, 212(chart)
Amniocentesis, 295
Amniotic fluid, 297, 298(illus.)
Amniotic sac, **297**, 298(illus.)
Amobarbital, 146
Amphetamine(s), **46**, 136, 147–148,
  153(chart), 154
Amphetamine psychosis, 148
Amphetamine sulfate, 148
Amplitude, 94(illus.)
Amygdala, **54**
  emotions and, 282–283, 283(illus.),
    286(illus.), 289(chart)
  memory and, 214(illus.)
Anabolic steroids, 70–71
Anal-expulsive personality, **350**
Analgesia, hypnotic, **139**
Analogies, 231, 252
Anal-retentive personality, **350**
Anal sex, 272
Anal stage, in personality development, **350**,
  351(table)
Analysts, 418
Analytical psychology, 351–352, 354(chart)
Analytic intelligence, 246, 247(illus.),
  248(chart)
Androgens, 330
Anesthesia, 396
Angel dust, 151
Anger, 51, 214, 257, 268, 276, 280, 281, 282,
  284, 285, 286, 287, 337, 459
  aggression and, 180, 279, 290, 501, 502–
    503
  depression and, 400
  illness and, 290, 456, 468, 469, 470,
    474(chart)
  management of, 290–291, 291(table), 478
Animal Mind, The (Washburn), 19
Animals, in psychological research, 31
Animistic thinking (thought), **316**,
  318(chart)
Anorexia nervosa, 268, 269, 270, 271(chart)
ANS. *See* Autonomic nervous system
Antagonists, at receptor sites, **45**
Anterograde amnesia, **212**(chart), 214
Antianxiety drugs, 46, **436**, 436–437, 438,
  442(chart)
Antibodies, **462**
Anticonvulsant drugs, 438
Antidepressants, **46**, 277, 436, **437**, 438,
  439, 442(chart), A-3
Antigens, **462**
Antimanic drugs, 442(chart)